YES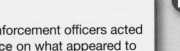

Was the warrant EITHER:
A. actually valid because it:
  1. was supported by **probable cause**;
  2. was stated with **particularity**, both:
     (a) the places and/or people to be searched; and
     (b) the items to be seized; and
  3. was issued by a **neutral, detached judicial officer**?
OR
B. facially valid such that law enforcement officers acted reasonably in **good faith reliance** on what appeared to be a valid warrant?

YES

Was the warrant executed:

A. in a **timely manner** (i.e., without unnecessary delay);

B. after being **announced** (if required); and

C. within the authorized **scope**?

NO

YES   **NO**

Was the behavior of law enforcement during the search and seizure **reasonable** (e.g., free from excessive force)?

YES

The search or seizure is **valid** under the Fourth Amendment and the evidence is **admissible**.

NO

The search or seizure is **invalid** under the Fourth Amendment.

Evidence is **inadmissible**.

If the constitutional violation led police to the discovery of secondary/derivative evidence, the "**fruit of the poisonous tree**" doctrine must be applied to determine the admissibility of evidence that is "tainted fruit."

Can either the independent source, inevitable discovery, or attenuation doctrines (which applies to "knock-and-announce" violations) be applied to the fruit/derivative evidence

YES

Derivative evidence/"fruit" may be **admissible** in spite of initial Fourth Amendment violation.

NO

Derivative evidence/"fruit" is also **inadmissible**.

CRIMINAL
PROCEDURE
FOR THE CRIMINAL JUSTICE PROFESSIONAL

Twelfth Edition

JOHN N. FERDICO, J.D.

Member of the Maine Bar, Former Assistant Attorney General, and
Director of Law Enforcement Education for the State of Maine

HENRY F. FRADELLA, J.D., Ph.D.

Arizona State University
Member of the State Bar of Arizona

CHRISTOPHER D. TOTTEN, J.D., LL.M.

Kennesaw State University
Member of the State Bar of Maryland

CENGAGE
Learning

Australia • Brazil • Japan • Korea • Mexico • Singapore • Spain • United Kingdom • United States

CENGAGE
Learning®

***Criminal Procedure for the Criminal Justice Professional,* Twelfth Edition**
John N. Ferdico, Henry F. Fradella, and Christopher D. Totten

Product Director: Marta Lee-Perriard

Senior Product Manager:
Carolyn Henderson-Meier

Content Developer: Wendy Langerud,
S4Carlisle Publishing Services

Product Assistant: Stephen Lagos

Media Developer: Ting Jian Yap

Senior Marketing Manager: Kara Kindstrom

Senior Content Project Manager:
Christy Frame

Managing Art Director: Andrei Pasternak

Senior Manufacturing Planner: Judy Inouye

Production Service: Jill Traut, MPS Limited

Photo Researcher: Saranya Sarada, Lumina
Datamatics

Text Researcher: Dharanivel Baskar, Lumina
Datamatics

Copy Editor: Laura Larson

Text and Cover Designer: Brenda Carmichael,
Lumina Datamatics

Cover Images: crime scene investigation:
© iStock.com/adamkaz; fingerprint: © David
Alary/Shutterstock; conference between
judge and attorneys: © iStock.com/Alina555

Composition: MPS Limited

Unless otherwise noted, all content is © 2016 Cengage Learning

Library of Congress Control Number: 2014953379

ISBN: 978-1-305-26148-8

Cengage Learning
20 Channel Center Street
Boston, MA 02210
USA

Cengage Learning is a leading provider of customized learning solutions with office locations around the globe, including Singapore, the United Kingdom, Australia, Mexico, Brazil, and Japan. Locate your local office at **www.cengage.com/global**.

Cengage Learning products are represented in Canada by Nelson Education, Ltd.

To learn more about Cengage Learning Solutions, visit **www.cengage.com**.

Purchase any of our products at your local college store or at our preferred online store **www.cengagebrain.com.**

Printed in the United States of America
Print Number: 02   Print Year: 2015

DEDICATION

For Cassia C. Spohn, Ph.D.,
for her support and friendship—H.F.F.

For Sebastian Christopher Totten, may he grow swift and strong—C.D.T.

About the Authors

John N. Ferdico holds a J.D. from Northwestern University School of Law and a B.A. in sociology from Dartmouth College. He is a former assistant attorney general and director of law enforcement education for the State of Maine. Other books he has published are *Ferdico's Criminal Law and Justice Dictionary* and the *Maine Law Enforcement Officer's Manual*. Mr. Ferdico currently writes and runs a legal publishing company in Bowdoinham, Maine.

Henry F. Fradella is a professor in and associate director of the School of Criminology and Criminal Justice at Arizona State University. He earned a B.A. in psychology from Clark University, both a master's in forensic science and J.D. from The George Washington University, and a Ph.D. in interdisciplinary justice studies from Arizona State University. In addition to having published more than seventy-five scholarly articles, comments, and reviews, Dr. Fradella is also the author of eight other books, including three published by Wadsworth: *America's Courts and the Criminal Justice System*; *Key Cases, Comments, and Questions on Substantive Criminal Law*; and *Forensic Psychology: The Use of Behavioral Science in Civil and Criminal Justice*. Dr. Fradella has twice served as a guest editor of the *Journal of Contemporary Criminal Justice* and as the Legal Literature editor of West's *Criminal Law Bulletin* for four terms (Volumes 41–44). A fellow of the Western Society of Criminology, he currently serves as the editor of the society's journal, *Criminology, Criminal Justice, Law & Society*. He teaches a variety of courses, including criminal law, criminal procedure, courts and judicial processes, and forensic psychology.

Christopher D. Totten has an A.B. from Princeton University and a J.D. and LL.M. (Master's in Law) from Georgetown University Law Center. He is a member of the State Bar of Maryland and has worked as an attorney and client advocate at a number of law firms. He is an associate professor of criminal justice (law) at Kennesaw State University, where he teaches numerous law and criminal justice courses to both undergraduate and graduate students. His scholarship spans criminal law and procedure, international crime (focus on adjudication), and interdisciplinary law and social science research (focus on courts/ jurisprudence and police attitudes). He has published in key journals such as the *Journal of Criminal Law and Criminology*, the *Criminal Law Bulletin*, the *New Criminal Law Review*, the *Berkeley Journal of International Law*, and the *Georgetown Journal of International Law*. Finally, he is the criminal law commentator for the *Criminal Law Bulletin* (Volumes 46–51).

Brief Contents

Contents

Chapter 3 Basic Underlying Concepts: Property, Privacy, Probable Cause, and Reasonableness   90

Chapter 7   Arrests, Searches Incident to Arrest, and Protective Sweeps   238

Chapter 8 | Stops and Frisks 306

PART III | **Exceptions to the Search Warrant Requirement**

Chapter 9 | Consent Searches   366

Chapter 15 Criminal Trials, Appeals, and Postconviction Remedies   610

Criminal Procedure for the Criminal Justice Professional was originally published in 1975 as *Criminal Procedure for the Law Enforcement Officer*. Its primary emphasis was on providing practical guidelines for law enforcement officers with respect to the legal aspects of their daily duties. Although the main emphasis remains on the policing aspects of criminal procedure, additional materials have been added since then that are relevant to professionals who work in other areas of the justice system.

Because we believe that criminal justice professionals should not have to read and interpret lengthy and complicated court opinions in order to determine the powers, duties, limitations, and liabilities associated with performing their jobs, this book is written in a clear, concise, and coherent narrative to make it accessible and understandable. Sufficient detail is provided to enable the reader to operate competently and effectively within the criminal justice system. Actual case excerpts are used to provide authoritative statements of legal principles, explanations of the "reasons behind the rules," and examples of the application of the law to real-life scenarios.

As appellate courts continue to deal with significant numbers of complex criminal procedure cases, the design and approach of this book provide an enduring vehicle for imparting the knowledge necessary to properly comply with this ever-changing area of the law.

Criminal Procedure for the Criminal Justice Professional is intended for courses in criminal procedure or administration at both two- and four-year colleges for students preparing for careers in criminal justice, especially in law enforcement and corrections. Titles of courses that have used this book include "Criminal Procedure," "Constitutional Law in Criminal Justice," "Law of Arrest, Search, and Seizure," "Legal Aspects of Law Enforcement," "Constitutional Criminal Procedure," and "Court Systems and Practices." Because it is written in plain English rather than in technical legal jargon, this book is also suitable as a criminal procedure textbook at law enforcement training academies and for high school courses dealing with constitutional law or law enforcement. Over the years, in response to suggestions and comments from professors and students who have used it, many changes have been made to enhance the book's suitability for use as a classroom text.

What's New in the Twelfth Edition

The twelfth edition of the book has been revised such that most chapters have thirty or fewer key terms (a dramatic reduction for some chapters). All chapters in the book have also been updated with citations to (and often discussions of) the latest case law on each and every topic in the book. Textual changes have also been made to increase readability and students' mastery of the material (e.g., more tables and more bulleted and numbered lists). Key changes to individual chapters are as follows:

- **Chapter 1**, "Individual Rights Under the United States Constitution," has been revised to focus more on constitutional rights relevant to criminal procedure; the discussion of other constitutional rights and constitutional history has been shortened significantly, especially those pertaining to the First Amendment. The following recent U.S. Supreme Court decisions have been added to the chapter: *Hall v. Florida*, *Hinton v. Alabama*, *Missouri v. Frye*, *Lafler v. Cooper*, and *Peugh v. United States*.

- **Chapter 2**, "Criminal Courts, Pretrial Processes, and the Exclusionary Rule," has been divided into two chapters. Chapter 2 contains expanded coverage of plea bargaining (including *Missouri v. Frye* and *Lafler v. Cooper*). A new Criminal Procedure in Action box on the movie theater shootings in Aurora, Colorado has been added.

- **Chapter 3**, "Basic Underlying Concepts: Property, Privacy, Probable Cause, and Reasonableness," has undergone a major restructuring to incorporate the dual property and privacy approaches to the Fourth Amendment in light of the U.S. Supreme Court's decision in *United States v. Jones*. In addition, a major "follow-up" case to *Jones* by the U.S. Supreme Court, *Florida v. Jardines*, has been added to this chapter.

- **Chapter 4**, "Criminal Investigatory Search Warrants," contains significant updates to state and lower federal court rulings on search warrants. A new section on the variable times it takes to obtain a search warrant has been added. The section on the use of force has been updated to better differentiate between force against premises and force against persons.

  Chapter 5, "Searches for Electronically Stored Information and Electronic Surveillance," has been significantly restructured with regard to how the materials on electronically stored information searches are presented. The U.S. Supreme Court decisions in *United States v. Jones* and *Riley v. California* have been integrated. New scholarship and case law has been infused throughout the chapter.

- **Chapter 6**, "Administrative and Special Needs Searches," now begins with an introductory section outlining the basic requirements of special needs searches. The following U.S. Supreme Court cases have been added: *City of Ontario v. Quon*, *Florence v. Board of Chosen Freeholders of County of Burlington*, and *Maryland v. King*.

- **Chapter 7**, "Arrests, Searches Incident to Arrest, and Protective Sweeps," has been updated to include the most recent U.S. Supreme Court cases, including *Florence v. Burlington*, *Maryland v. King*, *Missouri v. McNeely*, *Plumhoff v. Rickard*, *Stanton v. Sims*, and *Riley v. California*. The sections on hot pursuits and conducted energy devices (Tasers) have also been expanded with recent case law and scholarship.

- **Chapter 8**," Stops and Frisks," now includes *Navarette v. California* along with a Discussion Point addressing this recent U.S. Supreme Court case. The material dealing with racial profiling has been expanded to include recent scholarship as well as the U.S. Supreme Court decision of *Arizona v. United States* addressing the "show me your papers" laws. The section on detentions, the USA PATRIOT Act, and the war on terror has been updated with the latest case law, legislation, and executive orders, including coverage of the National Defense Authorization Act (NDAA). Finally, a new Criminal Procedure in Action feature has been added concerning a recent lower court decision interpreting *United States v. Arvizu*.

- **Part III**, "Exceptions to the Search Warrant Requirement," has been significantly updated with recent lower federal and state case law, including **Chapter 9**, "Consent Searches"; **Chapter 10**, "The Plain View Doctrine"; **Chapter 11**, "Search and Seizure of Vehicles and Containers"; and **Chapter 12**, "Open Fields and Abandoned Property." Key leading cases decided since the eleventh edition have been added, including *Fernandez v. California*, *Florida v. Jardines*, *Florida v. Harris*, and *United States v. Jones*. Finally, new or revised Criminal Procedure in Action features have been integrated into each of the chapters in Part III.

- **Chapter 13**, "Interrogations, Admissions, and Confessions," now incorporates key leading cases decided since the eleventh edition, including *Salinas v. Texas* and *Howes v. Fields*. In addition, we have expanded coverage of purposeful attempts to avoid *Miranda* by exploiting *Elstad* in the wake of *Missouri v. Seibert*.

- **Chapter 14**, "Pretrial Visual Identification Procedures," has been updated to include more recent information on wrongful convictions. A new section has been added on the latest approaches to suggestive identifications, comparing new state law approaches with the latest Supreme Court pronouncement on the matter in *Perry v. New Hampshire*.

- **Chapter 15**, "Criminal Trials, Appeals, and Postconviction Remedies," has been updated to include *Melendez-Diaz v. Massachusetts*, *Bullcoming v. New Mexico*, *Williams v. Illinois*, and *McQuiggin v. Perkins*. A new table has been included that summarizes some of the major shortcomings of various forensic scientific evidence. The section on sentencing has been expanded to include more material on discrimination and sentencing disparities.

Learning Tools

In recent years, several learning tools and pedagogical devices have been added to the book to enhance understanding of the law of criminal procedure.

Learning Objectives (LO)—Student learning goals appear at the beginning of each chapter and are designed to provide purpose and context. All learning objectives have been revised to use the measurable verbs associated with Bloom's Taxonomy. Corresponding end-of-chapter summaries have been revised so that they provide concise statements that are responsive to the learning objectives at the start of each chapter. Learning Objectives are also indicated in the Key Points sections to assist students in finding the sections where each objective is discussed.

Key Points—Concise, clear statements of the essential principles of criminal procedure appear at the end of major sections of chapters and serve as mini-summaries of those sections. Their purpose is to aid the student in "separating the wheat from the chaff" and to expedite review by boiling down complexities into simple statements of fundamentals. These Key Point sections also correlate to the Learning Objectives.

"Supreme Court Nuggets"—Essential quotations from U.S. Supreme Court opinions appear in **boldface** throughout the text. Their purpose is to familiarize students with judicial language as well as to highlight authoritative definitions of terms, clear statements of important legal principles, and the rationales behind those principles.

Discussion Points—Fact patterns and holdings from recent controversial opinions are summarized in a concise manner in these boxed features so that students can see how the "black letter law" was applied in a case related to the main points in a chapter. These summaries are then followed by discussion questions that instructors can use to stimulate class discussion on the law and related public policy issues.

Criminal Procedure in Action—A feature found in every chapter helps students relate what they are learning to the real world by providing in-depth coverage of a case illustrating an important or controversial area of criminal procedure law, as well as probing critical thinking questions designed to engage student debate and reflection.

Review and Discussion Questions—New review and discussion questions have been included to stimulate discussion and to expand students' understanding beyond the principles and examples used in the text.

Glossary—Definitions of major terms used in criminal procedure law have been streamlined for easier use by students.

References—Citations to statutes and case law appear in the actual text. This twelfth edition also adds a formal bibliography to reflect the many new interdisciplinary sources that have been integrated into the textual pedagogy.

Supplements

A number of supplements are provided by Cengage Learning to help instructors use *Criminal Procedure for the Criminal Justice Professional* in their courses and to aid students in preparing for exams. Supplements are available to qualified adopters. Please consult your local sales representative for details.

To access additional course materials, please visit **www.cengagebrain.com.** At the CengageBrain.com home page, search for the ISBN of your title (from the back cover of your book), using the search box at the top of the page. This will take you to the product page where these resources can be found.

CENGAGE **brain**.com

Instructor's Resource Manual with Lesson Plans and Test Bank includes learning objectives, key terms, a detailed chapter outline, a chapter summary, lesson plans, discussion topics, student activities, "What If" scenarios, media tools, a sample syllabus, and an expanded test bank with 30 percent more questions than the prior edition. The learning objectives are correlated with the discussion topics, student activities, and media tools.

Each chapter of the test bank contains questions in multiple-choice, true/false, completion, essay, and new critical thinking formats, with a full answer key. The test bank is coded to the learning objectives that appear in the main text, and includes the section in the main text where the answers can be found. Finally, each question in the test bank has been carefully reviewed by experienced criminal justice instructors for quality, accuracy, and content coverage so instructors can be sure they are working with an assessment and grading resource of the highest caliber.

Cengage Learning Testing Powered by Cognero This assessment software is a flexible, online system that allows you to import, edit, and manipulate test bank content from the *Corrections Today* test bank or elsewhere, including your own favorite test questions; create multiple test versions in an instant; and deliver tests from your LMS, your classroom, or wherever you want.

Online PowerPoint® Lectures Helping you make your lectures more engaging while effectively reaching your visually oriented students, these handy Microsoft PowerPoint® slides outline the chapters of the main text in a classroom-ready presentation. The PowerPoint slides are updated to reflect the content and organization of the new edition of the text, are tagged by chapter learning objective, and feature some additional examples and real-world cases for application and discussion.

Acknowledgments

We are grateful to the following criminal justice instructors for their time and effort in reviewing this edition of the book and their helpful comments and suggestions for its improvement: Mark Brown, University of South Carolina; Joel Weinstein, George Mason University; Nancy Dempsey, Cape Cod Community College; Cheryl Furdge, North Central Texas College; Andrew Kozal, Northwest State Community College; Tosha Wilson-Davis, Bainbridge College.

We also wish to thank again the following professors for their reviews of previous editions of this text: Kenneth Agran, Jack E. Call, Joseph Robert Caton, Alan W. Clarke, Nigel Cohen, Nancy Dempsey, Charles Dreveskracht, Jack Elrod, Jacinta Gau, John W. Grimes, David V. Guccione, James Hague, Judy Hails, Craig Hemmens, Gerald W. Hildebrand, G. G. Hunt, William Hyatt, Susan Jacobs, Richard Janikowski, David Kramer, Richard Kuiters, Elizabeth Lewis, Michael J. McCrystle, Milo Miller, Eric Moore, Kenneth Novak, Thomas O'Connor, Philip Reichel, Ray Reynolds, Joseph G. Sandoval, Caryl Lynn Segal, Kurt Siedschlaw, Mark Stelter, Gene Straughan, Susette M. Talarico, G. Anthony Wolusky, John Worrall, John Wyant, and Alvin J. T. Zumbrun.

Our appreciation also extends to the staff at Cengage Learning and those who worked with them at all stages of the production of the twelfth edition. We are particularly grateful to Jill Traut and the staff at MPS Limited, as well as our content developer, Wendy Langerud. Special thanks to our lead editorial and creative design team for all of their help and patience throughout the publication process: Christy

Frame, Stephen Lagos, Sarah Shainwald, and Carolyn Henderson-Meier. And Chris and Hank remain deeply indebted to Julie Martinez, who assisted us with reconceptualizing the book for its eleventh edition three years ago. Her influence remains evident in the twelfth edition. Finally, we owe a special debt to John Ferdico, who first created this book in the mid-1970s and then shepherded its evolution over eight more editions spanning thirty years.

Finally, we thank our families—most especially our spouses—for their support and understanding while we went "MIA" from daily life during the preparation of this edition.

Henry F. Fradella
Christopher D. Totten

LO1 EXPLAIN how criminal law and criminal procedure are often in conflict as courts try to balance the need for crime control with constitutional guarantees of due process.

LO2 SUMMARIZE the historical context that gave birth to the concern for the individual rights embodied in the United States Constitution.

LO3 EXPLAIN how the legislative, judicial, and executive branches of government are involved in the protection of the constitutional rights of citizens.

LO4 DEFINE the individual rights protected by the original Constitution of 1788, and the terms *habeas corpus*, *bill of attainder*, *ex post facto law*, and *treason*.

LO5 EXPLAIN the general nature and limits of the rights embodied in the Bill of Rights, especially the First Amendment freedoms of religion, speech, press, assembly, and petition; the Fourth Amendment prohibition against unreasonable searches and seizures; the Fifth Amendment protections against double jeopardy and self-incrimination; the Sixth Amendment rights to a speedy and public trial, notice of charges, confrontation with adverse witnesses, compulsory process for favorable witnesses, and assistance of counsel; and the Eighth Amendment rights against excessive bail and fines and against cruel and unusual punishment.

LO6 DIFFERENTIATE the concepts of due process and equal protection as guaranteed by the Fifth and Fourteenth Amendments.

Defining law is no easy task. One of the most influential definitions comes from sociologist Max Weber. Weber (1954: 5) viewed **law** as a rule of conduct that is "externally guaranteed by the probability that coercion (physical or psychological), to bring about conformity or avenge violation, will be applied by a staff of people holding themselves specially ready for that purpose." Weber's definition of law has been modified into three distinct elements:

- Explicit rules of conduct
- Planned use of sanctions to support the rules
- Designated officials to interpret and enforce the rules, and often to make them

Law can be categorized in many ways. One of the most common ways to categorize it is to use the distinction between civil and criminal law. *Criminal law*, also referred to as *penal law*, is that body of law that defines conduct that is criminally punishable by the government as a wrong committed against the people in society as a whole. In contrast, wrongs committed against an individual, such as defamation, are the realm of torts, a branch of *civil law*. Civil law also encompasses business law (e.g., corporate and contract law), family law (e.g., marriage, divorce, and child custody), and property law (e.g., the law of real estate; wills, trusts, estates, and inheritance; and landlord–tenant relations).

Criminal law is often studied from two perspectives: substantive and procedural.

Substantive criminal law sets forth legal prescriptions and proscriptions—the "rules" of what one must do, may do, and may not do. **Procedural criminal law** sets forth the mechanisms through which substantive criminal laws are administered. Homicide statutes are examples of a substantive law. The rules regulating how police investigate a homicide, such as searching for and seizing evidence and interrogating suspects, are examples of criminal procedure. Table 1.1 summarizes the major sources of procedural criminal law in the United States.

TABLE 1.1	Sources of Criminal Procedure	
The United States Constitution	As the supreme law of the land, the U.S. Constitution is the ultimate authority for regulating criminal procedure.
State Constitutions	Each state constitution contains provisions that govern criminal procedure within that state. These constitutions may provide greater protections than those found in the U.S. Constitution, but they may not reduce the protections contained in the federal Constitution as interpreted by the U.S. Supreme Court.
Decisions of the Federal Courts of the United States	These decisions interpret and apply the U.S. Constitution and various federal laws.
Decisions of the various state courts within the United States	These decisions also interpret and apply the U.S. Constitution and various federal laws.
Rules of Criminal Procedure	Both the federal and state court systems have promulgated rules that govern the nonconstitutional aspects of criminal procedure.

© Cengage Learning®

Criminal Procedure as the Balance Between Due Process and Crime Control

The law of criminal procedure can be described as rules designed to balance the important governmental functions of maintaining law and order and protecting the rights of citizens. These functions are common to every government that is not totally authoritarian or anarchistic, yet they conflict because an increased emphasis on maintaining law and order will necessarily involve greater intrusions on individual rights. Conversely, an increased emphasis on protecting individual rights will impede the efficient maintenance of law and order. The justice system in the United States, like those in most constitutional democracies, continually experiences a tension between the need to respect individual rights, on one hand, and the need to maintain public order, on the other. Herbert L. Packer summarized this tension in his classic text, *The Limits of the Criminal Sanction* (1968). As Table 1.2 illustrates, Packer

TABLE 1.2 | Herbert Packer's Crime Control Versus Due Process Models

Crime Control Model	Due Process Model
Primary goal: Apprehension, conviction, and punishment of offenders	Primary goal: Protection of the innocent; limiting governmental power
Focus: Crime control; repression of criminal conduct	Focus: Due process; respect for individual rights
Mood: Certainty	Mood: Skepticism
"Assembly-line justice": Processes cases quickly and efficiently to promote finality of convictions	"Obstacle-course justice": Presents numerous obstacles to prevent errors and wrongful convictions
Concerned with factual guilt: Assumes that someone arrested and charged is probably guilty. Relies on informal, nonadjudicative fact finding—primarily by police and prosecutors	Concerned with legal guilt: Assumes that someone is innocent until proven guilty beyond a reasonable doubt; relies on formal, adjudicative, adversary fact-finding processes
Expeditious processing of offenders to achieve justice for victims and society as a whole	Dignity and autonomy of both the accused and the system are to be preserved

© Cengage Learning®

viewed this tension as being embodied in two competing value systems: the crime control model and the due process model.

Shifting the Balance over Time

In practice, we do not choose between one model and the other. Rather, we strive to control crime while simultaneously honoring the constitutional rights of the accused. At different stages in our nation's history, we have clearly focused more on the underlying values of one model over the other—put simply, the criminal justice system has had different emphases at different times. Consider the following examples of how the pendulum can swing from a societal emphasis on crime control to due process and then back to crime control.

In the first half of the twentieth century, increased urbanization, immigration, and industrialization "transformed America from a rural agrarian, Anglo-Protestant society" into a more racially, ethnically, and religiously diverse one (Feld 2003: 1453). These changes produced great uncertainty in the minds of those whose more traditional ways of life were being challenged by the changes that accompanied this more diverse and industrial society. One of the by-products of these changes was an increase in criminal activity, probably partly because of an ever-increasing population density. The increase in crime combined with fears of people from different races and cultures led to great increases in police power (Walker 1980) with a focus on "law and order" crime control (Monkkonen 1981).

In the civil rights era, social consciousness began to focus on social equality and equal justice under law. Part of this new consciousness brought to light abuses of police power, which disproportionately affected poor and uneducated minorities (Kamisar 1965; Neely 1996). Led by Chief Justice Earl Warren, a former public defender, the Supreme Court began to "constitutionalize" criminal procedure with a focus on the individual rights and liberties. "Tired of the steady stream of abuses that continued to filter up from the states, the Supreme Court of the 1960s made policing the police, as well as state courts, a distinctly federal concern" (Barrett-Lain 2004: 1372). Today, we refer to this shift in policy as the due process revolution of the 1960s.

Many critics felt as if the due process revolution went too far, allowing criminals to escape punishment due to the technicalities of constitutional criminal procedures (e.g., Bradley 1993; Friendly 1968). During the Nixon administration, such feelings led to a renewed focus on "law and order." As part of his "tough on crime" agenda, Nixon appointed conservative jurist Warren Burger as Chief Justice Earl Warren's successor on the U.S. Supreme Court. In the last twenty-five years of the twentieth century, the "war on drugs" led to an even greater shift away from many of the Warren Court's due process protections toward a renewed emphasis on crime control. In the early twenty-first century, as the United States fights the "war on terror," the nation once again finds itself seeking to balance the need for social order and security with due process rights.

A Brief History of the U.S. Constitution

The Law of England

Early procedural protections for the criminally accused can be traced back to the English common law tradition to the thirteenth century. In 1215, the Magna Carta was formally adopted in England. Clause 30 of the original text (later numbered Chapter 29 of the statutory version of the Magna Carta) provided:

> No free man shall be taken, imprisoned, or disseised of his free hold, or liberties or free customs, or outlawed, exiled or in any way destroyed, nor will we proceed against him, save by the lawful judgment of his peers or by the law of the land. We shall not sell, deny or delay to any man right or justice.

For centuries, these provisions were interpreted as guaranteeing certain pillars of criminal procedure, including the right to have adequate notice of what is prohibited by law before being punished for violating law, the right to a fair trial, and the protection of property or possessions (Baker 2004). Yet these guarantees were not always honored. For example, a number of procedural safeguards were commonly disregarded by the Star Chamber, a royal court whose abuses became so infamous that the very term *star chamber* is still synonymous with injustices perpetuated by a court (Riebli 2002). Although the Star Chamber was abolished by the Long Parliament in 1641, the English crown still wielded considerable influence over courts. This influence often led courts to issue decisions favorable to the crown as well as to those of the British aristocracy (Berman 2000).

Ultimately, dissatisfaction with a life that favored a select few in England was partially responsible for both the founding of the American colonies and the Glorious Revolution in Great Britain (Berman 2000). The latter event forever changed English common law, granting a new level of judicial independence to judges and focusing trials on proof, the independent decisions of juries, and rules of evidence.

Drafting a New Constitution

In light of their experience with governmental tyranny, when the United States was born as a nation, the Founders had a strong commitment to the protection of individual rights from governmental abuse. This commitment was embodied in the original Constitution of 1788 and in the Bill of Rights that was adopted shortly thereafter.

On September 17, 1787, a convention of delegates representing twelve of the original thirteen states (Rhode Island was not represented) proposed a new constitution to the Continental Congress and the states for ratification. The rights expressed and protected by this constitution, and by the amendments adopted four years later, were not new. Some had roots in the societies of ancient Rome and Greece, and all were nurtured during the almost six hundred years of English history since the signing of the Magna Carta.

As colonists under English rule, Americans before the Revolution were familiar with the ideas that government should be limited in power and that the law was superior to any government, even the king. As the Declaration of Independence shows, the colonists rebelled because the English king and Parliament refused to allow them their historic rights as free English citizens. In September 1774, delegates from twelve colonies met in the First Continental Congress to petition England for their rights "to life, liberty, and property" and to trial by jury; "for a right peaceably to assemble, consideration of their grievances, and petition the King"; and for other rights they had been denied. The petition was ignored, and soon afterward fighting broke out at Lexington and Concord, Massachusetts.

Meanwhile, citizens in Mecklenburg County, North Carolina, declared the laws of Parliament to be null and void and instituted their own form of local government with the adoption of the Mecklenburg Resolves in May 1775. In June 1776, a resolution was introduced in the Continental Congress. Just one month later, on July 4, 1776, the thirteen united colonies declared themselves free and independent. Their announcement was truly revolutionary. They listed a large number of abuses they had suffered and justified their independence in these historic words: "We hold these truths to be self-evident, that all men are created equal, that they are endowed by their Creator with certain Inalienable Rights, that among these are Life, Liberty and the pursuit of Happiness."

Two years later, in July 1778, the newly independent states joined in a united government under the Articles of Confederation, which was our nation's first constitution. It soon became evident, however, that the Articles of Confederation did not adequately provide for a workable, efficient government. Among other weaknesses, the articles gave Congress no authority to levy taxes or regulate foreign or interstate commerce. In May 1787, a convention of delegates, meeting in Philadelphia with Congress's approval, began to consider amendments to the Articles. Soon, however, they realized that a new system of government was necessary. After much debate and several heated arguments, a compromise constitution was negotiated.

Although we now honor their wisdom, the delegates had a different opinion of their work. Many were dissatisfied, and a few even thought an even newer constitution should be written. No delegate from Rhode Island attended the convention or signed the document on September 17, 1787, when the proposed constitution was announced. Delaware was the first state to accept the Constitution, ratifying it on December 7, 1787, by a unanimous vote. Not all states were as enthusiastic as Delaware, and in some states the vote was extremely close. For a while, it was uncertain whether a sufficient number of states would ratify. A major argument against ratification was the absence of a Bill of Rights. Many feared that a failure to limit the federal government's power would diminish individual rights. Only after a general agreement that the first order of business of the new government would be to propose amendments for a Bill of Rights did a sufficient number of states accept the Constitution. On June 21, 1788, New Hampshire became the ninth state to sign on, and ratification of the new Constitution was completed. By the end of July 1788, the important states of Virginia and New York had also ratified the Constitution.

On September 25, 1789, Congress proposed the first ten amendments to the new Constitution—the **Bill of Rights**. With this proposal, North Carolina and Rhode Island, the last of the thirteen original colonies, ratified the Constitution. Ratification of the Bill of Rights was completed on December 15, 1791. Since that date, the Bill of Rights has served as our nation's testimony to its belief in the basic and inalienable rights of the people and in limitations on the power of government. Together with provisions of the original Constitution, it protects the great body of liberties that belongs to every citizen.

For ease of discussion, the remainder of this chapter treats the original Constitution separately from the Bill of Rights and later amendments.

The Original Constitution

The Constitution of 1789 has served as the fundamental instrument of our government for almost all of our country's history as an independent nation. Drawn at a time when there were only thirteen states, each dotted with small towns, small farms, and small industry, the Constitution has provided a durable and viable instrument of government—despite enormous changes in technology and in the political, social, and economic environments.

The Constitution was originally designed to serve a weak country on the Atlantic sea-board. Today, it serves a continental nation of fifty states, a federal district, and numerous territorial possessions, with more than 311 million people producing goods and services at a rate thousands of times faster than in 1789. Nevertheless, the framework for democratic government set out in the Constitution has remained workable and progressive. Similarly, the rights of individuals listed in the Constitution and its twenty-seven amendments have retained an extraordinary vitality despite being tested in situations that could not have been envisioned by the Framers. Freedom of the press, for example, was originally under-stood only in the context of the small, primitive printing presses of the late eighteenth century. Today, that freedom applies not only to modern presses but also to radio, televi-sion, motion pictures, and computers—all products of the twentieth century.

Structure of the Original Constitution

The original Constitution of the United States is divided into seven parts: a preamble and six articles. Although the preamble is technically not a part of the Constitution, it sets forth important principles. The articles that follow it each address a different topic relevant to the structure and operations of government.

- The preamble states both the purpose of the Constitution and specifies that it is the people who are the source of the document's authority:

   > We the People of the United States, in Order to form a more perfect Union, establish Justice, insure domestic Tranquility, provide for the common defence, promote the general Welfare, and secure the Blessings of Liberty to ourselves and our Posterity, do ordain and establish this Constitution for the United States of America.

- **Article I** establishes the U.S. Congress as the legislative branch of the United States and sets forth both the structure of Congress and its major powers.
- **Article II** establishes the president as the head of the executive branch of gov-ernment and sets forth some of the major powers of the presidency.
- **Article III** establishes the U.S. Supreme Court as the highest judicial body in the United States and specifies the Court's original and appellate jurisdiction.
- **Article IV** defines the relationship between the states.
- **Article V** prescribes the method for amending the Constitution.
- **Article VI** declares that the Constitution and treaties made by the U.S. government under its authority are "the supreme Law of the Land." Given the supremacy of the Constitution, this article requires that all state and federal judges and elected of-ficials must swear an oath to support, uphold, and defend the Constitution.

The Constitution governs the government. This means that constitutional law establishes the structure of government and limits the power of government. Although the Constitution does not govern the day-to-day lives of the people, as statutory and administrative law does, people within the jurisdictional boundaries of the country possess rights that the Constitution grants to them. It is important to understand that these rights exist because the drafters of the Constitution wanted to limit the power of the government in ways that would maximize liberty for the citizens of the country.

The Impact of Article VI on the Courts: The Power of Judicial Review

Article VI, Section 2 of the U.S. Constitution is known as the *Supremacy Clause.* As previously stated, it declares that the Constitution is the "supreme law of the land." As the highest form of law in the nation, *constitutional law* trumps all other forms of law, including *statutory law* (laws enacted by a legislative body), *common law* (the law as set forth by judges in published judicial decisions), and *administrative law* (rules and regulations promulgated by a governmental agency that is empowered through statutory law to make such rules).

Each branch of the government—legislative, judicial, and executive—is charged by the Constitution with the protection of individual liberties. Within this framework, the judicial branch has assumed perhaps the largest and arguably most important role. Chief Justice John Marshall, speaking for the Supreme Court in the early case of *Marbury v. Madison*, 5 U.S. (1 Cranch) 137 (1803), declared that it was the duty of the judiciary to say what the law is and that this duty included expounding and interpreting the law. Marshall stated that the law contained in the Constitution was paramount and that other laws that were repugnant to its provisions must fall. It was the province of the courts, he concluded, to decide when other laws were in violation of the basic law of the Constitution and, where this was found to occur, to declare those laws null and void and thus unconstitutional. This doctrine, known as judicial review, became the basis for the application of constitutional guarantees by courts in cases brought before them:

> *Judicial review is the exercise by courts of their responsibility to determine whether acts of the other two branches are illegal and void because those acts violate the constitution. The doctrine authorizes courts to determine whether a law is constitutional, not whether it is necessary or useful. In other words, judicial review is the power to say what the constitution means and not whether such a law reflects a wise policy.* Adherence to the doctrine of judicial review is essential to achieving balance in our government. . . . Judicial review, coupled with the specified constitutional provisions which keep the judicial branch separate and independent of the other branches of government and with those articles of the constitution that protect the impartiality of the judiciary from public and political pressure, enables the courts to ensure that the constitutional rights of each citizen will not be encroached upon by either the legislative or the executive branch of the government. *State v. LaFrance*, 471 A.2d 340, 343–44 (N.H. 1983) (italics added).

The judicial branch is not the only protector of constitutional rights. Congress has played an important role in the protection of constitutional rights by enacting legislation designed to guarantee and apply those rights in specific contexts. Laws that guarantee the rights of Native Americans, afford due process to military service personnel, and give effective right to counsel to poor defendants are examples of this legislative role.

Finally, the executive branch, which is charged with implementing the laws Congress enacts, contributes to the protection of individual rights by devising its own regulations and procedures for administering the law without intruding on constitutional guarantees.

To properly understand the scope of constitutional rights, one must recognize that our government is a *federal republic*, which means that an American lives under two governments: the federal government and the government of the state in which the person lives. The Constitution limits the authority of the federal government to the powers specified in the Constitution; all remaining governmental power is reserved to the states. The federal government is authorized, for example, to settle disputes among states, to conduct relations with foreign governments, and to act in certain matters of common national concern. The states hold the remainder of governmental power, which is to be exercised within their respective boundaries.

The Bill of Rights

Only a few individual rights were specified in the Constitution when it was adopted in 1788. The principal design of the original Constitution was not to specify individual rights, but to state the division of power between the new central federal government and the states. Shortly after its adoption, however, ten amendments—the Bill of Rights—were added to the Constitution to guarantee basic individual liberties, including freedom of speech, freedom of the press, freedom of religion, and freedom to assemble and petition the government.

Originally, the guarantees of the Bill of Rights applied only to acts of the federal government and did not prevent state and local governments from taking action that might threaten civil liberty. States had their own constitutions, some containing their own bills of rights that guaranteed the same or similar rights as those guaranteed by the Bill of Rights against federal intrusion. Not all states guaranteed these rights, however; the rights that did exist were subject to varying interpretations. In short, citizens were protected only to the extent that the states themselves recognized their basic rights.

In 1868, the Fourteenth Amendment, which provides in part that no state shall "deprive any person of life, liberty, or property without due process of law," was added to the U.S. Constitution. Although the Fourteenth Amendment was enacted as part of the post–Civil War Reconstruction process in the wake of the end of slavery and persistent problems in Southern states with the proper treatment and protection of African Americans, it was not until 1925, in *Gitlow v. New York*, 268 U.S. 652, that the Supreme Court interpreted the phrase "due process of law" to mean, in effect, "without abridgement of certain of the rights guaranteed by the Bill of Rights." Since *Gitlow*, the Supreme Court has ruled that a denial by a state of certain rights contained in the Bill of Rights represents a denial of due process of law. The members of the Court, however, have long argued about which provisions of the Bill of Rights are applicable to the states and to what extent. The approach that has dominated constitutional law since the early 1960s is commonly referred to as the selective incorporation approach. It posits that the Fourteenth Amendment's Due Process Clause limits the ability of states to infringe on rights specified in the Bill of Rights that are "fundamental," but it recognizes that not every right in the Bill of Rights may qualify. As the Court said in *Duncan v. Louisiana*, "Because we believe that trial by jury in criminal cases is fundamental to the American scheme of justice, we hold that the Fourteenth Amendment guarantees a right of jury trial in all criminal cases which—*were they to be tried in a federal court*—would come within the Sixth Amendment's guarantee" 391 U.S. 145, 149 (1968) (italics added).

What rights are fundamental to the concept of ordered liberty or to the American scheme of justice? Table 1.3 shows which rights set forth in the Bill of Rights have been deemed "fundamental" to our American sense of justice and therefore have been selectively incorporated by the Fourteenth Amendment. Most of these are incorporated by the Fourteenth Amendment's Due Process Clause. The only guarantees in the Bill of Rights specifically concerning criminal procedure that do not apply to the states are (1) the right to indictment by grand jury in the Fifth Amendment, (2) the prohibition against excessive bail in the Eighth Amendment, and (3) any guarantee that convictions be obtained only from unanimous twelve-member juries that may be implicit in the Sixth Amendment's right to a jury trial. However, in *Burch v. Louisiana*, 441 U.S. 130 (1979), the Supreme Court held that when as few as six jurors are impaneled, their verdict must be unanimous. And finally, although not relevant to criminal procedure, note that the Seventh Amendment's guarantee to the right to a jury trial in civil cases has not been incorporated by the Fourteenth Amendment. See *Curtis v. Loether*, 415 U.S. 189 (1974).

To place these rights in a broader perspective, note that they make up only the core of what are considered to be *civil rights*—the privileges and freedoms that are accorded all Americans by virtue of their citizenship. Many other civil rights that are not specifically mentioned in the Constitution but nonetheless are recognized by the courts have often been guaranteed by statute and are embedded in our democratic traditions. The

TABLE 1.3 | Provisions of the Bill of Rights Incorporated by the Fourteenth Amendment Relevant to Criminal Law and Constitutional Criminal Procedure

Amendment	Right	Landmark Cases and Year
First	Freedom of speech	*Gitlow v. New York*, 268 U.S. 652 (1925).
	Freedom of peaceable assembly	*DeJonge v. Oregon*, 299 U.S. 353 (1937).
	Freedom of the press	*Near v. Minnesota*, 283 U.S. 697 (1931).
	Free exercise of religion	*Cantwell v. Connecticut*, 310 U.S. 296 (1940).
	Freedom from governmental establishment of religion	*Everson v. Board of Education*, 330 U.S. 1 (1947).
Second	Right to bear arms	*McDonald v. City of Chicago, Ill.*, 561 U.S. 3025 (2010).
Fourth	Unreasonable search and seizure	*Wolf v. Colorado*, 338 U.S. 25 (1949).
	Warrant requirement	*Ker v. California*, 374 U.S. 23 (1963); *Aguilar v. Texas*, 378 U.S. 108 (1964).
	Exclusionary rule	*Mapp v. Ohio*, 367 U.S. 643 (1961).
Fifth	Double jeopardy	*Benton v. Maryland*, 395 U.S. 784 (1969).
	Self-incrimination	*Brown v. Mississippi*, 297 U.S. 278 (1936). *Malloy v. Hogan*, 367 U.S. 643 (1964).
	Taking of private property	*Chicago, Burlington & Quincy Railway Co. v. Chicago*, 166 U.S. 226 (1897).
Sixth	Right to counsel (capital cases)	*Powell v. Alabama*, 287 U.S. 45 (1932).
	Right to counsel (felony cases)	*Gideon v. Wainright*, 372 U.S. 335 (1963).
	Right to counsel (misdemeanors)	*Argersinger v. Hamlin*, 407 U.S. 25 (1972).
	Right to counsel (plea bargaining)	*Missouri v. Frye*, 132 S. Ct. 1399 (2012). *Lafler v. Cooper*, 132 S. Ct. 1376 (2012).
	Confrontation of adverse witnesses	*Pointer v. Texas*, 380 U.S. 400 (1965).
	Compulsory process to obtain witness testimony	*Washington v. Texas*, 388 U.S. 14 (1967).
	Notice of accusation	*Rabe v. Washington*, 405 U.S. 313 (1972).
	Public trial	*In re Oliver*, 333 U.S. 257 (1948).
	Trial by impartial jury in "non-petty" criminal cases	*Parker v. Gladden*, 385 U.S. 363 (1966). *Duncan v. Louisiana*, 391 U.S. 145 (1968).
	Speedy trial	*Klopfer v. North Carolina*, 386 U.S. 213 (1967).
Eighth	Cruel and unusual punishment	*Robinson v. California*, 370 U.S. 66 (1962).
	Excessive fines	*Cooper Industries v. Leatherman Tool Group, Inc.*, 532 U.S. 424 (2001).

© Cengage Learning®

right to buy, sell, own, and bequeath property; the right to enter into contracts; the right to marry and have children; the right to live and work where one desires; and the right to participate in the political, social, and cultural processes of our society are a few of the rights that must be considered just as fundamental to a democratic society as those specified by the Constitution.

Despite the premise that the rights of American citizenship are incontrovertible, the rights guaranteed by the Constitution or otherwise are not absolute rights in the sense that they entitle citizens to act in any way they please. Rather, to be protected by the law, people must exercise their rights so that the rights of others are not denied. As Justice Oliver Wendell Holmes observed, "Protection of free speech would not protect a man falsely shouting 'Fire' in a theater and causing a panic." Nor does freedom of speech and press sanction the publication of libel and obscenity. Similarly, the rights of free speech and free assembly prohibit knowingly engaging in conspiracies to overthrow by force the government of the United States. Civil liberties demand of all Americans an obligation to exercise their rights within a framework of law and mutual respect for the rights of others.

This obligation implies not only a restraint on the part of those exercising these rights but also a tolerance on the part of those who are affected by that exercise. Citizens may on occasion be subjected to annoying political tirades, disagreeable entertainment, or noisy protest demonstrations. They may feel aggravated when a defendant refuses to testify or when they see a seemingly guilty defendant go free because certain evidence was ruled inadmissible in court. But these frustrations or inconveniences are a small price to pay for the freedom American citizens enjoy. If one person's rights are suppressed, everyone's freedom is jeopardized. Ultimately, a free society is a dynamic society in which thoughts and ideas are forever challenging and being challenged. In such a society, people may listen to the wrong voice or follow the wrong plan. But a free society is one that learns by its mistakes and freely pursues the happiness of its citizens.

Individual Rights in the Original Constitution

Habeas Corpus

Article I, Section 9, Clause 2

> The Privilege of the Writ of Habeas Corpus shall not be suspended, unless when in Cases of Rebellion or Invasion the public Safety may require it.

This guarantee enables a person whose freedom has been restrained in some way to petition a federal court for a writ of *habeas corpus* to test whether the restraint violates the Constitution or laws of the United States. A petition for a writ of *habeas corpus* asks a federal court to examine an alleged illegal detention and order authorities to release an illegally confined petitioner. *Habeas corpus* can be suspended only when the president, with congressional authorization, declares that a national emergency requires its suspension and probably only when the courts are physically unable to function because of war, invasion, or rebellion. (President Lincoln suspended the writ during the U.S. Civil War, but he did so without valid congressional authorization.) *Habeas corpus* is an important safeguard to prevent unlawful imprisonment and is discussed in further detail in Chapter 15.

Bills of Attainder

Article I, Section 9, Clause 3

> No Bill of Attainder . . . shall be passed [by the federal government].

Article I, Section 10, Clause 1

No State shall . . . pass any Bill of Attainder.

Historically, a bill of attainder is a special act of a legislature declaring that a person or group of persons has committed a crime and imposing punishment without a court trial. Under our system of separation of powers, only courts may try a person for a crime or impose punishment for violation of the law. Section 9 restrains Congress from passing bills of attainder, and Section 10 restrains the states.

Ex Post Facto Laws

Article I, Section 9, Clause 3

No . . . ex post facto Law shall be passed [by the federal government].

Article I, Section 10, Clause 1

No state shall . . . pass any . . . ex post facto Law.

These two clauses prohibit the states and the federal government from enacting any *ex post facto* law—literally, a law passed "after the fact." "[A]ny statute which punishes as a crime an act previously committed, which was innocent when done, which makes more burdensome the punishment for a crime, after its commission, or which deprives one charged with crime of any defense available according to law at the time when the act was committed, is prohibited as *ex post facto.*" *Beazell v. Ohio*, 269 U.S. 167, 169–70 (1925). For example, in *Peugh v. United States*, 133 S. Ct. 2072 (2012), the Court ruled that the bar against *ex post facto* laws prohibited federal courts from sentencing a defendant under harsher sentencing guidelines that were themselves put into effect after the defendant committed his crime.

However, laws that retroactively determine how a person is to be tried for a crime may be changed so long as substantial rights of the accused are not curtailed. Laws that make punishment less severe than it was when the crime was committed are not *ex post facto*. An example of a statutory change that is not prohibited as *ex post facto* is the elimination of statutes of limitations—the time period in which a state must commence a criminal action. State legislatures are increasingly removing such limitations on sexual crimes that involve young victims.

Trial Rights

Article III, Sections 1 and 2

Article III, Sections 1 and 2, of the Constitution deal with the judicial system of the United States and are too long to be reproduced here.

Article III, Section 1 of the Constitution outlines the structure and power of our federal court system and establishes a federal judiciary that helps maintain the rights of American citizens. Article III, Section 2 also contains a guarantee that the trial of all federal crimes, except impeachment, shall be by jury. The Supreme Court carved out exceptions to this guarantee for "trials of petty offenses," trials before a court martial or other military tribunal, and some trials in which the defendant has voluntarily waived the right to a jury. The right to a jury trial is discussed further in Chapter 15.

Section 2 also requires that federal criminal trials be held in a federal court sitting in the state in which the crime was committed. This protects a person from being tried in a part of the United States far distant from the place where the alleged violation of federal law occurred.

Conviction for Treason

Article III, Section 3

Treason against the United States, shall consist only in levying War against them, or in adhering to their Enemies, giving them Aid and Comfort. No Person shall be convicted of Treason unless on the Testimony of two Witnesses to the same overt Act, or on Confession in open Court. The Congress shall have power to declare the Punishment of Treason, but no Attainder of Treason shall work Corruption of Blood, or Forfeiture except during the Life of the Person attainted.

Treason is the only crime defined by the Constitution. The precise description of this offense reflects awareness by the Framers of the Constitution of the danger that unpopular views might be branded as traitorous. Recent experience in other countries with politically based prosecutions for conduct loosely labeled treason confirms the wisdom of the Constitution's authors in expressly stating what constitutes this crime and how it shall be proved.

KEY POINTS

LO2
LO4

■ The original provisions of the U.S. Constitution contain a number of provisions regulating criminal procedure, including the right to petition for a writ of *habeas corpus*, bars on bills of attainder, a prohibition on *ex post facto* laws and punishments, and special procedures for treason convictions.

Select Individual Rights in the Bill of Rights

Amendment I

Congress shall make no law respecting an establishment of religion, or prohibiting the free exercise thereof; or abridging the freedom of speech, or of the press; or the right of the people peaceably to assemble, and to petition the Government for a redress of grievances.

Freedom of Speech, Expression, and Peaceable Assembly As a general rule, citizens may speak out freely on any subject they choose. They may do so alone or in concert with others. Thus, whether meeting for political activity, religious services, or other purposes, the First Amendment guarantees not only the right to speak one's mind but also the right to assemble peaceably to share one's thoughts with others. Like other constitutional rights, however, the First Amendment rights to free speech and assembly are not absolute. Public authorities may impose limitations reasonably designed to prevent fire, health hazards, obstruction and occupation of public buildings, or traffic obstruction.

Symbolic Speech A long string of judicial decisions have made it clear that "speech" goes beyond oral communication. "Free speech" includes nonverbal communication that includes both artistic expression and symbolic speech—conduct that expresses an idea or opinion. Wearing buttons or clothing with political slogans, displaying a sign or a flag, or burning a flag as a mode of expression are examples of symbolic speech.

Time, Place, and Manner Restrictions on the First Amendment Although state, local, and federal governments may not constitutionally ban the content of speech they may find objectionable, governmental entities are entitled to regulate the time, place, and manner of speech—including picketing and symbolic speech—in a content-neutral way for the good of society. In *United States v. O'Brien*, 391 U.S. 367 (1968), the Supreme Court established a four-part test to determine if a law is a valid governmental *time, place, and manner regulation of speech*. The case held that a governmental regulation on the time, place, and manner of speech is permissible if

1. the regulation furthers an important or substantial governmental interest;
2. the governmental interest served by the regulation is unrelated to the suppression of free expression;
3. the regulation is narrowly tailored to serve the government's interest such that the restriction on free speech is not greater than is necessary to achieve the governmental interest; and
4. the regulation still leaves open ample, alternative means for people to communicate their message.

An example of a valid restriction on the time of speech would be restrictions on political protesters. Organizers of a protest may want to hold a demonstration in a large city to gain national media attention to their cause. Clearly, such protestors have a First Amendment right to hold their demonstration, but not whenever they choose. For example, no one has the right to "insist upon a street meeting in the middle of Times Square at the rush hour as a form of freedom of speech." *Cox v. Louisiana*, 379 U.S. 536 (1965). Thus, the time of the demonstration can be prescribed, but its content may not. Even groups espousing distasteful, unpopular, or offensive messages still have the right to speak their minds. A group of neo-Nazis, for example, had the right to parade down the streets in a predominantly Jewish neighborhood. *National Socialist Party of America v. Village of Skokie*, 432 U.S. 43 (1977). However, they had to obtain valid permits and conduct their demonstration at a time when authorities could maintain order.

Speech That Lies Beyond the Realm of First Amendment Protection The protections afforded by the First Amendment do not extend to all forms of expression. The Supreme Court has specifically identified a number of categories of speech as being of such little value to the core principles underlying the First Amendment that they receive no constitutional protection. This includes defamation (false, public statements of fact, not opinion, that injure or damage a person's reputation); words that incite immanent lawlessness, such as inciting a riot; and obscenity. Under *Miller v. California*, 413 U.S. 15 (1973), material is obscene if three criteria are met:

1. The work, taken as a whole by an average person applying contemporary community standards, appeals to the prurient interest (a shameful or morbid interest, in nudity, sex, or excretion).
2. The work depicts sexual conduct in a patently offensive way (meaning the work goes substantially beyond customary limits of candor in describing or representing such matters).
3. The work, when taken as a whole, lacks serious literary, artistic, political, or scientific value.

As laws against a range of *inchoate* (preparatory) crimes—such as solicitation, facilitation, aiding and abetting, and conspiracy—illustrate, speech that induces or encourages someone to commit a crime lies beyond the protection of the First Amendment. Some criminal restraints on speech, however, are constitutionally questionable. For example, the crime of *sedition* is defined as inciting a revolt against the government. Given the broad protection the First Amendment offers to criticize the government, prosecutions for sedition are rare. However, when someone advocates the violent overthrow of the government in a manner that creates a clear and present danger to governmental operations or workers, such seditious speech may be punished. *Schenck v. United States*, 249 U.S. 47 (1919).

Freedom of the Press Freedom of the press is a further guarantee of the right to express oneself, in this case by writing or publishing one's views on a particular subject. The Framers recognized the importance of a free interplay of ideas in a democratic society and sought to secure the right of all citizens to speak or publish their views, even if those views were contrary to those of the government or society as a whole. Accordingly, the First Amendment generally forbids censorship or other restraints on speech or the printed word, so long as the material is not defamatory or obscene.

Freedom of Religion The First Amendment contains two different types of freedoms having to do with religion. The first restricts the establishment of any government-sponsored religion. This means that no legislature may enact a law that establishes an official church that all Americans must accept and support, or to whose tenets all must subscribe, or that favors one church over another. The second preserves people's rights to practice their religious beliefs without undue interference from the government in most circumstances. Note, however, that the free exercise of religion by inmates may be limited by correctional institutions if the restrictions are narrowly tailored to achieve a compelling penological interest, such as maintaining institutional order and security (see Gaubatz 2005).

Amendment II

A well regulated Militia, being necessary to the security of a free State, the right of the people to keep and bear Arms, shall not be infringed.

The Second Amendment's "right of the people to keep and bear arms" has engendered some of the most spirited public debate since the adoption of the Bill of Rights. Two distinct interpretations emerged. One theory holds that the amendment was primarily meant to convey individual rights, like other parts of the Bill of Rights. A contrasting theory contends that the Second Amendment was spelling out the right of the states, independent of a central federal government, to establish and maintain state militias such as state police forces and the National Guard. This debate was settled, in large part, by the Supreme Court's decisions in *District of Columbia v. Heller*, 554 U.S. 570 (2008), and *McDonald v. City of Chicago, Ill.*, 561 U.S. 3025 (2010). These cases make clear that the right to bear arms is held by individuals regardless of whether they are acting as part of a militia or in a military capacity. In other words, as understood back in the era of the Framers in which the right of citizens to protect themselves against both disorder in the community and attack from foreign enemies was deemed paramount, individuals possess a basic right to armed self-defense under the Second Amendment. That being said, Second Amendment rights, like all other constitutional rights, are limited, not absolute. For example, *United States v. Skoien*, 614 F.3d 638 (7th Cir. 2010) (*en banc*), upheld a federal statute that prohibits possession of a firearm by those who have been convicted of a misdemeanor of domestic violence offense. In the coming years, the courts will undoubtedly clarify the contours of the Second Amendment as they review the constitutionality of a wide range of gun control laws in the wake of *Heller* and *McDonald*, such as those prohibiting the carrying of concealed weapons, requiring the registration of firearms, and limiting the sale of certain types of firearms for other than military uses.

Amendment III

No Soldier shall, in time of peace be quartered in any house, without the consent of the Owner, nor in time of war, but in a manner to be prescribed by law.

Before the American Revolution, colonists were frequently required, against their will, to provide lodging and food for British soldiers. The Third Amendment prohibited the continuation of this onerous practice.

Amendment IV

The right of the people to be secure in their persons, houses, papers, and effects, against unreasonable searches and seizures, shall not be violated, and no Warrants shall issue, but upon probable cause, supported by Oath or affirmation and particularly describing the place to be searched, and the persons or things to be seized.

In some countries, police officers may, at their whim or the whim of political leaders, invade citizens' homes, seize citizens' property, or arrest or detain citizens without fear of punishment or reprisal. In the United States, the Fourth Amendment protects people and their property from unreasonable searches and seizures by governmental officers. In general, although there are exceptions to the rule, a police officer may not search the home of a private citizen, seize any of the citizen's property, or arrest the citizen without first obtaining a court order called a *warrant*. Before a warrant is issued, the police officer must convince an impartial judicial officer that there is *probable cause*—defined by the U.S. Supreme Court as a fair probability—either that the person involved has committed a crime or that contraband or evidence, fruits, or implements of a crime are in a particularly described place.

Because most of this book deals with the topics of arrest, search and seizure, and probable cause, further discussion of the Fourth Amendment appears in the chapters dealing with those topics.

Amendment V

No person shall be held to answer for a capital, or otherwise infamous crime, unless on a presentment or indictment of a Grand Jury, except in cases arising in the land or naval forces, or in the Militia, when in actual service in time of War or public danger; nor shall any person be subject for the same offense to be twice put in jeopardy of life or limb; nor shall be compelled in any criminal case to be a witness against himself, nor be deprived of life, liberty, or property, without due process of law; nor shall private property be taken for public use, without just compensation.

Indictment by Grand Jury The Fifth Amendment requires that before a person is tried in federal court for an infamous crime, he or she must first be indicted by a grand jury. The grand jury's duty is to make sure that there is probable cause to believe that the accused person is guilty. This provision prevents a person from being subjected to a trial when there is not sufficient proof that he or she has committed a crime.

Generally, an infamous crime is a *felony* (a crime for which a sentence of more than one year's imprisonment may be imposed) or a lesser offense that is punishable by confinement in a penitentiary or at hard labor. An indictment is not required for a trial by court martial. Furthermore, the constitutional requirement of grand jury indictment does not apply to trials in state courts because the Supreme Court's decision in *Hurtado v. California*, 110 U.S. 516 (1884), refused to incorporate the Fifth Amendment's guarantee of a grand jury indictment through the Fourteenth Amendment's Due Process Clause. However, the Supreme Court has ruled that when states do use grand juries in their criminal proceedings, they must be free of racial bias. The grand jury is discussed in further detail in Chapter 2.

Freedom from Double Jeopardy The clause "nor shall any person be subject for the same offense to be twice put in jeopardy of life or limb" is often referred to as the *Double Jeopardy Clause*. The U.S. Supreme Court has recognized three separate guarantees embodied in the Double Jeopardy Clause: "It protects against a second prosecution for the same offense after acquittal, against a second prosecution for the same offense after conviction, and against multiple punishments for the same offense." *Justices of Boston Municipal Court v. Lydon*, 466 U.S. 294, 306–07 (1984). Note that the Double Jeopardy Clause "protects only against the imposition of multiple criminal punishments for the same offense." *Hudson v. United States*, 522 U.S. 93, 99 (1997). It does not protect against criminal prosecution of a person after the person has been penalized in a civil proceeding.

Jeopardy attaches in a jury trial when the jury is impaneled and sworn. In *Martinez v. Illinois*, 134 S. Ct. 2070 (2014), the trial of the defendant was set to begin on a date certain. He and his counsel were present and ready to proceed; the prosecution was not because two key witnesses could not be located. The prosecution asked for a continuance (a delay to another date) to locate the witnesses. The judge denied the request because the court had previously granted the prosecution numerous continuances to find the witnesses and prepare its case. After the court swore in the jury, the judge asked the prosecution to present its opening statement. The prosecution declined to do so. The defense then moved for a judgment of acquittal since the state had not presented any evidence of the defendant's guilt. The court granted the motion. The state appealed the judge-entered acquittal, arguing that the trial judge should have granted the prosecution a continuance to beings to present its case. The Illinois Supreme Court granted the appeal, but the U.S. Supreme Court reversed, holding that the Double Jeopardy Clause barred the defendant's retrial. "There are few if any rules of criminal procedure clearer than the rule that "jeopardy attaches when the jury is empaneled and sworn." 134 S. Ct. at 2074.

> [C]ritically, the court told the State on the day of trial that it could "move to dismiss [its] case" before the jury was sworn. Had the State accepted that invitation, the Double Jeopardy Clause would not have barred it from recharging Martinez. Instead, the State participated in the selection of jurors and did not ask for dismissal before the jury was sworn. When the State declined to dismiss its case, it took a chance, entering upon the trial of the case without sufficient evidence to convict. Here, the State knew, or should have known, that an acquittal forever bars the retrial of the defendant when it occurs after jeopardy has attached. 134 S. Ct. at 2076–77 (internal citations omitted).

In a nonjury trial (i.e., a *bench trial*), jeopardy attaches when the judge begins to hear evidence. Jeopardy attaches to all criminal proceedings, whether felony or misdemeanor, and to juvenile adjudicatory proceedings, even though they are civil in nature.

There are exceptions to the general rules protecting a person from double jeopardy. First, a second trial for the same offense may occur when the first trial results in a mistrial declared on account of a deadlocked jury (i.e., the jury could not reach a verdict). *Blueford v. Arkansas*, 132 S. Ct. 2044 (2012).

Second, the Double Jeopardy Clause does not usually bar reprosecution of a defendant whose conviction is overturned on appeal. "It would be a high price indeed for society to pay were every accused granted immunity from punishment because of any defect sufficient to constitute reversible error in the proceedings leading to conviction." *United States v. Tateo*, 377 U.S. 463, 466 (1964). If, however, the reason for the reversal of the conviction was insufficiency of the evidence to support the conviction, the government may not reprosecute the defendant. *Burks v. United States*, 437 U.S. 1 (1978).

Third, double jeopardy does not arise when a single act violates both federal and state laws and the defendant is exposed to prosecution in both federal and state courts. This is called the *dual sovereignty doctrine*, and it also applies to prosecutions by two different states. In *Heath v. Alabama*, 474 U.S. 82 (1985), the U.S. Supreme Court held that the key question under this doctrine was whether the two entities seeking to prosecute the defendant for the same criminal act are separate sovereigns that derive their power to prosecute from independent sources. Because local governments are not sovereigns for double jeopardy purposes, the Double Jeopardy Clause prohibits successive prosecutions by a state and a municipality in that state or by two municipalities in the same state. A criminal prosecution in either a state court or a federal court does not exempt the defendant from being sued for damages by anyone who is harmed by his or her criminal act. Finally, a defendant may be prosecuted more than once for the same conduct if that conduct involves the commission of more than one crime. For instance, a person who kills three victims at the same time and place can be tried separately for each killing.

It should be noted that the Double Jeopardy Clause embodies the **collateral estoppel doctrine**. The U.S. Supreme Court explained that collateral estoppel "means simply that when an issue of ultimate fact has once been determined by a valid and final judgment, that issue cannot again be litigated between the same parties in any future lawsuit." *Ashe v. Swenson*, 397 U.S. 436 (1970). The collateral estoppel doctrine is often applied in civil suits brought by a citizen against a police officer where (1) the citizen has been previously convicted of a crime associated with the same event providing the basis for the lawsuit, and (2) as part of the conviction, the court determined that the citizen had acted with a particular state of mind. To the extent that the plaintiff's state of mind becomes significant in the civil litigation, the plaintiff is estopped (precluded) from litigating that issue because of the collateral estoppel doctrine. In other words, because the issue of state of mind has previously been determined "by a valid and final judgment" (the criminal conviction), it cannot be relitigated.

Privilege Against Self-Incrimination The Fifth Amendment protects a person against being incriminated by his or her own *compelled testimonial communications*. This protection is applicable to the states through the Due Process Clause of the Fourteenth Amendment. *Malloy v. Hogan*, 378 U.S. 1 (1964). To be testimonial, a "communication must itself, explicitly or implicitly, relate a factual assertion or disclose information" that is "the expression of the contents of an individual's mind." *Doe v. United States*, 487 U.S. 201, 210 n.9 (1988). Therefore, the privilege against self-incrimination is not violated by compelling a person to appear in a lineup, produce voice exemplars, furnish handwriting samples, be fingerprinted, shave a beard or mustache, or take a blood alcohol or Breathalyzer test. With respect to the requirement that the communication be incriminating, the U.S. Supreme Court said:

> The privilege afforded not only extends to answers that would in themselves support a conviction under a . . . criminal statute but likewise embraces those which would furnish a link in the chain of evidence needed to prosecute the claimant for a . . . crime. . . . But this protection must be confined to instances where the witness has reasonable cause to apprehend danger from a direct answer. . . . To sustain the privilege, it need only be evident from the implications of the question, in the setting in which it is asked, that a responsive answer to the question or an explanation of why it cannot be answered might be dangerous because injurious disclosure could result. The trial judge in appraising the claim must be governed as much by his personal perception of the peculiarities of the case as by the facts actually in evidence. *Hoffman v. United States*, 341 U.S. 479, 486–87 (1951).

In other words, the Fifth Amendment protects not only the compelled confession to the commission of a crime but also incriminating admissions that, although not sufficient in and of themselves to support a conviction, would provide "a link in the chain of evidence needed to prosecute" the person. An example of the latter is a suspect's statements that he or she was at or near the scene of a crime.

The protection against self-incrimination enables a person to refuse to testify against himself or herself at a criminal trial in which the person is a defendant and also "privileges him not to answer official questions put to him in any other proceeding, civil or criminal, formal or informal, where the answers might incriminate him in future criminal proceedings." *Minnesota v. Murphy*, 465 U.S. 420, 426 (1984). The privilege also applies to the compelled preparation or offering of incriminating documents. *United States v. Doe*, 465 U.S. 605 (1984). When a defendant chooses not to testify at trial, neither the prosecutor nor the trial judge may make any adverse comment about the defendant's failure to testify. *Griffin v. California*, 380 U.S. 609 (1965). Moreover, the defendant is entitled to have the jury instructed that no inference of guilt may be drawn from his or her failure to testify. The *Miranda* safeguards to secure the privilege against self-incrimination when a defendant is subjected to custodial interrogation are discussed in detail in Chapter 13.

The Fifth Amendment privilege protects a witness at a civil or criminal proceeding from answering questions when the answers might be incriminating in some future criminal prosecution. If authorized by statute, however, the prosecution may compel the witness to testify by granting *immunity* from prosecution. The type of immunity usually granted is use immunity, which prevents the prosecution from using the compelled testimony and any evidence derived from it in a subsequent prosecution. A witness who has been granted immunity and still refuses to testify may be held in contempt of court.

The Right to Due Process The phrase due process of law expresses the fundamental ideals of American justice. Due process is violated if a practice or rule "offends some principle of justice so rooted in the traditions and conscience of our people as to be ranked as fundamental." *Snyder v. Massachusetts*, 291 U.S. 97, 105 (1934). A Due Process Clause is found in both the Fifth and Fourteenth Amendments. Although originally construed as a restraint only on the federal government, later interpretations by the U.S. Supreme Court have established that the restraint is similarly applicable to the states. "The Due Process Clause of the Constitution prohibits deprivations of life, liberty, or property without 'fundamental fairness' through governmental conduct that offends the community's sense of justice, decency and fair play." *Roberts v. Maine*, 48 F.3d 1287, 1291 (1st Cir. 1995).

The following rights are recognized as within the protection of the Due Process Clause:

- the right to timely notice of a hearing or trial that adequately informs the accused of the charges against him or her,
- the right to present evidence in one's own behalf before an impartial judge or jury,
- the right to be presumed innocent until proven guilty by legally obtained evidence, and
- the right to have the verdict supported by the evidence presented at trial.

These types of rights are sometimes referred to as procedural due process. Note that "due process of law" also applies to noncriminal matters and does not necessarily require a proceeding in a court or a trial by jury in every case involving personal or property rights.

The Due Process Clauses of the Fifth and Fourteenth Amendments also provide other basic protections against the enactment by states or the federal government of arbitrary and unreasonable legislation or other measures that would violate peoples' rights. This is sometimes referred to as substantive due process:

> It is manifest that it was not left to the legislative power to enact any process which might be devised. The article is a restraint on the legislative as well as on the executive and judicial powers of the government, and cannot be so construed as to leave congress free to make any process "due process of law" by its mere will. *Murray's Lessee v. Hoboken Land and Improvement Co.*, 59 U.S. (18 How.) 272, 276 (1856).

Due process imposes limits on governmental interference with important individual liberties—such as the freedom to enter into contracts, engage in a lawful occupation, marry, move without unnecessary restraints, and make intimately private decisions about sexual activity between consenting adults, including decisions regarding procreation. To be valid, governmental restrictions placed on these liberties must be reasonable and consistent with justice and fair play. Courts have applied this type of due process analysis to subjects as varied as regulation of railroads and public utilities, collective bargaining, interstate commerce, taxation, and bankruptcy.

The Due Process Clause of the Fifth Amendment has been interpreted as also guaranteeing the equal protection of law—the notion that similarly situated people should be treated in a similar manner. *Plyler v. Doe*, 457 U.S. 202 (1982). The Fifth Amendment does not mention equal protection per se; it is specified in the Equal Protection Clause of the Fourteenth Amendment. These two concepts are associated with each other and sometimes overlap. "[Due process] tends to secure equality of law in the sense that it makes a required minimum of protection for every one's right of life, liberty and property, which the Congress or the legislature may not withhold. Our whole system of law is predicated on the general, fundamental principle of equality of application of the law." *Truax v. Corrigan*, 257 U.S. 312, 331 (1921). For example, in *Bolling v. Sharpe*, 347 U.S. 497, 499 (1954), the Court held that segregation of pupils in the public schools of the District of Columbia violated the Due Process Clause:

> The Fifth Amendment, which is applicable in the District of Columbia, does not contain an equal protection clause as does the Fourteenth Amendment which applies only to the states. But the concepts of equal protection and due process, both stemming from our American ideal of fairness, are not mutually exclusive. The "equal protection of the laws" is a more explicit safeguard of prohibited unfairness than "due process of law," and, therefore, we do not imply that the two are always interchangeable phrases. But, as this Court has recognized, discrimination may be so unjustifiable as to be violative of due process.

The Right to Just Compensation The power of the government to acquire private property is called *eminent domain*. The Fifth Amendment limits the government to taking a person's property for "public use" and requires that the full value of the property be paid to the owner. Thus, governmental entities cannot simply take property from one person and give it to another. However, what constitutes "public use" is a matter of some debate. In *Kelo v. City of New London*, 545 U.S. 469 (2005), the Supreme Court upheld the use of eminent domain to transfer land from one private owner to another to further economic development under a comprehensive redevelopment plan for an economically depressed city. The Court reasoned that the economic benefits that such redevelopment would bring to the community as a whole qualified the taking as a permissible "public use."

Amendment VI

> In all criminal prosecutions, the accused shall enjoy the right to a speedy and public trial, by an impartial jury of the State and district wherein the crime shall have been committed, which district shall have been previously ascertained by law, and to be informed of the nature and cause of the accusation; to be confronted with the witnesses against him; to have compulsory process for obtaining witnesses in his favor, and to have the Assistance of Counsel for his defence.

As your reading of the Sixth Amendment should make clear, it forms the basis of many important criminal procedural rights.

- The right to have one's case heard in the district where the crime is alleged to have taken place concerns questions of jurisdiction and venue. These concepts are explored in detail in Chapter 2, along with the right to be given notice of the charges against the accused.
- The following rights concern trial processes and, as such, are covered in Chapter 15:
    - The right to a speedy and public trial
    - The right to trial by an impartial jury
    - The right to confront witnesses
    - The right to compel witnesses to testify on one's behalf

One of the rights contained in the Sixth Amendment permeates all aspects of a criminal case: the right to counsel. Accordingly, that right is covered here, at the outset of this text.

The Right to Representation by Counsel Finally, the Sixth Amendment provides a right to be represented by counsel in all criminal prosecutions that may result in imprisonment. "[A]bsent a knowing and intelligent waiver, no person may be imprisoned for any offense, whether classified as petty, misdemeanor, or felony unless he was represented by counsel at his trial." *Argersinger v. Hamlin*, 407 U.S. 25, 37 (1972). As the quotation implies, by knowingly and intelligently waiving the right to counsel, defendants have the right to conduct their own defense in a criminal case. This is known as a *pro se* defense. "[I]t is one thing to hold that every defendant, rich or poor, has the right to the assistance of counsel, and quite another to say that a state may compel a defendant to accept a lawyer he does not want." *Faretta v. California*, 422 U.S. 806, 832–33 (1975).

The right to counsel attaches at the initiation of adversary judicial criminal proceedings "whether by way of formal charge, preliminary hearing, indictment, information or arraignment." *Kirby v. Illinois*, 406 U.S. 682, 689 (1972). A person is entitled to the assistance of counsel, however, only at a "critical stage" of the prosecution "where substantial rights of a criminal accused may be affected." *Mempa v. Rhay*, 389 U.S. 128, 134 (1967). The U.S. Supreme Court has accorded this right at the following stages of criminal cases:

- Preindictment preliminary hearings and bail hearings, *Coleman v. Alabama*, 399 U.S. 1 (1970).
- Initial appearances at which a defendant's liberty is subject to restriction, *Rothgery v. Gillespie Country, Texas*, 554 U.S. 191 (2008).
- Postindictment pretrial lineups, *United States v. Wade*, 388 U.S. 218 (1967).
- Postindictment interrogations, *Massiah v. United States*, 377 U.S. 201 (1964).
- Arraignments, *Hamilton v. Alabama*, 368 U.S. 52 (1961).
- Interrogations after arraignment, *Brewer v. Williams*, 430 U.S. 387 (1977).
- Plea bargaining, *Missouri v. Frye*, 132 S. Ct. 1399 (2012); *Lafler v. Cooper*, 132 S. Ct. 1376 (2012).
- Felony trials, *Gideon v. Wainwright*, 372 U.S. 335 (1963).
- Misdemeanor trials involving a potential jail sentence, *Argersinger v. Hamlin*, 407 U.S. 25 (1972).
- First appeals as a matter of right, *Douglas v. California*, 372 U.S. 353 (1963).
- Juvenile delinquency proceedings involving potential confinement, *In re Gault*, 387 U.S. 1 (1967).
- Sentencing hearings, *Mempa v. Rhay*, 389 U.S. 128 (1967).
- Hearings regarding psychiatric examinations, *Estelle v. Smith*, 451 U.S. 454 (1981).

Separate and apart from the Sixth Amendment right to counsel, prior to the initiation of adversary judicial criminal proceedings, a person has a Fifth Amendment right to counsel during custodial interrogation under *Miranda v. Arizona*, 384 U.S. 436 (1966) (see Chapter 13).

For many years, courts interpreted the guarantee of representation by counsel to mean only that defendants had a right to be represented by a lawyer if they could afford to hire one. In the 1930s, however, the U.S. Supreme Court began to vastly expand the class of persons entitled to the right to counsel in preparing and presenting a defense. *Powell v. Alabama*, 287 U.S. 45 (1932), held that the right to counsel was so fundamental that the Due Process Clause of the Fourteenth Amendment required states to provide all defendants charged with capital crimes with the effective aid of counsel. Six years later, *Johnson v. Zerbst*, 304 U.S. 458 (1938), held that the Sixth Amendment required all federal defendants to be provided legal counsel for their defense unless the right to counsel was properly waived. That decision raised the question of whether the constraint on the federal courts expressed a rule so fundamental and essential to a fair trial—and thus to due process of law—that it was made obligatory on the states by the Fourteenth Amendment. The Supreme Court said no in *Betts v. Brady*, 316 U.S. 455 (1942), holding that "while want of counsel in a particular case may result in a conviction lacking in such fundamental fairness, we cannot say that the amendment embodies an inexorable command that no trial for any offense, or in any court, can be fairly conducted and justice accorded a defendant who is not represented by counsel." 316 U.S. at 473.

Twenty-one years after deciding *Betts,* the Court changed its mind, recognizing that "lawyers in criminal courts are necessities, not luxuries." In *Gideon v. Wainwright*, 372 U.S. 335 (1963), the Supreme Court overruled *Betts*. The Court now held that the Sixth Amendment imposed an affirmative obligation on the part of the federal and state governments to provide at public expense legal counsel for those who could not afford it in order to have all defendants' cases adequately presented in courts of law. In addition, indigent persons were given the right to a free copy of their trial transcripts for pur-poses of appealing their convictions. *Griffin v. Illinois*, 351 U.S. 12 (1956).

The Sixth Amendment right to counsel is a right to the effective assistance of counsel. "The very premise of our adversary system of criminal justice is that par-tisan advocacy on both sides of a case will promote the ultimate objective that the guilty be convicted and the innocent go free." *Herring v. New York*, 422 U.S. 853, 862 (1975). The absence of effective counsel undermines faith in the proper functioning of the adversarial process. In *Strickland v. Washington*, 466 U.S. 668 (1984), the Court held that to establish a claim of ineffective assistance of counsel, a defendant must show that

- counsel's representation fell below an objective standard of reasonableness, and
- there is a reasonable probability that, but for counsel's unprofessional errors, the result of the proceeding would have been different. A reasonable probability is one sufficient to undermine confidence in the trial's outcome.

In *Lockhart v. Fretwell*, 506 U.S. 364 (1993), the Court refined the *Strickland* test to require that not only would a different trial result be probable because of attorney per-formance but also that the actual trial result was fundamentally unfair or unreliable. For example, in *Hinton v. Alabama*, 134 S. Ct. 1081 (2014), the defendant faced two counts of capital murder for homicides committed during armed robberies. The state's case rested entirely on a single piece of scientific evidence presented by the state's forensic scientific experts—namely, that six bullets found at the scenes of the crimes were all fired from a gun found at the defendant's house. There was no other physical evidence in the case. The Court held that Hinton's defense counsel's performance was constitution-ally deficient because his lawyer failed to obtain a skilled, competent forensic expert to challenge the state's experts. The Court remanded the case to a lower court to determine if the deficient performance was prejudicial to the outcome of Hinton's case.

Amendment VII

In suits at common law, where the value in controversy shall exceed twenty dollars, the right of trial by jury shall be preserved, and no fact tried by a jury, shall be otherwise re-examined in any Court of the United States, than according to the rules of the common law.

The Seventh Amendment applies only to federal civil trials and not to civil suits in state courts. Except as provided by local federal court rules, if a case is brought in a federal court and a money judgment is sought that exceeds $20, then the party bringing the suit and the defendant are entitled to have the controversy decided by the unanimous verdict of a jury of twelve people.

Amendment VIII

Excessive bail shall not be required, nor excessive fines imposed, nor cruel and unusual punishments inflicted.

The Right to Bail Bail has traditionally meant the money or property pledged to the court or actually deposited for the release from custody of an arrested or imprisoned person as a guarantee of that person's appearance in court at a specified date and time. Accused persons who are released from custody and subsequently fail to appear for trial forfeit their bail to the court.

The Eighth Amendment does not specifically provide that all citizens have a right to bail but only that bail may not be excessive. A right to bail has, however, been recognized in common law and in statute since 1789. Excessive bail was defined in *Stack v. Boyle*, 342 U.S. 1, 4–5 (1951):

> From the passage of the Judiciary Act of 1789 . . . to the present . . . federal law has unequivocally provided that a person arrested for a noncapital offense shall be admitted to bail. This traditional right to freedom before conviction permits the unhampered preparation of a defense, and serves to prevent the infliction of punishment prior to conviction. . . . Unless this right to bail before trial is preserved, the presumption of innocence, secured only after centuries of struggle, would lose its meaning.
>
> The right to release before trial is conditioned upon the accused's giving adequate assurance that he will stand trial and submit to sentence if found guilty. . . . Like the ancient practice of securing the oaths of responsible persons to stand as sureties for the accused, the modern practice of requiring a bail bond or the deposit of a sum of money subject to forfeiture serves as additional assurance of the presence of an accused. *Bail set at a figure higher than an amount reasonably calculated to fulfill this purpose is "excessive" under the Eighth Amendment.* (italics added)

The excessive bail clause "has been assumed" to be applicable to the states through the Fourteenth Amendment. *Schilb v. Kuebel*, 404 U.S. 357 (1971). Under many state constitutions, when a capital offense such as murder is charged, bail may be denied altogether if "the proof is evident or the presumption great."

In 1966, Congress enacted the Bail Reform Act to provide for pretrial release of persons accused of noncapital federal crimes. Congress sought to end pretrial imprisonment of indigent defendants who could not afford to post money bail and who were, in effect, confined only because of their poverty. The act also discouraged the traditional use of money bail by requiring the judge to seek other means as likely to ensure that the defendant would appear when the trial was held.

The Bail Reform Act of 1984 substantially changed the 1966 act to allow an authorized judicial officer to impose conditions of release to ensure community safety. This change marked a significant departure from the basic philosophy of the 1966 act: namely, that the only purpose of bail laws was to ensure the defendant's appearance at judicial proceedings. The 1984 act also expanded appellate review and eliminated the presumption in favor of bail pending appeal. Most significant, however, the 1984 act allowed an authorized judicial officer to detain an arrested person pending trial if the government could demonstrate by clear and convincing evidence after an adversary hearing that no release conditions "will reasonably assure . . . the safety of any other person and the community." In *United States v. Salerno*, 481 U.S. 739 (1987), the U.S. Supreme Court held that pretrial detention under the act, based solely on risk of danger to the community, did not violate due process or the Eighth Amendment.

Freedom from Cruel and Unusual Punishment The prohibition against the infliction of cruel and unusual punishment is concerned with punishments imposed after a formal adjudication of guilt. The prohibition is applicable to the states through the Due Process Clause of the Fourteenth Amendment. *Robinson v. California*, 370 U.S. 660 (1962). The Cruel and Unusual Punishment Clause of the Eighth Amendment limits the punishment that may be imposed on conviction of a crime in two ways.

First, the clause "imposes substantive limits on what can be made criminal and punished as such." *Ingraham v. Wright*, 430 U.S. 651, 667 (1977). For example, a statute making the condition or status of narcotics addiction a crime was held unconstitutional because it imposed punishment of personal characteristics rather than illegal acts. *Robinson v. California*, 370 U.S. 660 (1962). Similarly, a person may not be punished in retaliation for exercising a constitutional right. *United States v. Heubel*, 864 F.2d 1104 (3d Cir. 1988).

Second, the Cruel and Unusual Punishment Clause proscribes certain kinds of punishment, such as torture and divestiture of citizenship. It does not, however, prohibit capital punishment in and of itself. *Gregg v. Georgia*, 428 U.S. 153 (1976). However, particular modes of capital punishment may be unconstitutional if they violate "evolving standards of decency that mark the progress of a maturing society." *Trop v. Dulles*, 356 U.S. 86, 101 (1958). Under such a standard, the Court has invalidated the death penalty under the following circumstances:

- Statutes that give the juries complete sentencing discretion that may result in the arbitrary or capricious imposition of death sentences are cruel and unusual, *Furman v. Georgia*, 408 U.S. 238 (1972).

- Mandatory death statutes that leave the jury or trial judge no discretion to consider individual defendants and their crime are cruel and unusual, *Woodson v. North Carolina*, 428 U.S. 280 (1976).

- Execution of someone who is incompetent or insane at the time of his execution is cruel and unusual, *Ford v. Wainwright*, 477 U.S. 399 (1986).

- The execution of people who suffer from significant intellectually disabilities constitutes cruel and unusual punishment, *Atkins v. Virginia*, 536 U.S. 304 (2002). States may not rigidly rely on the results of IQ tests as conclusive evidence of intellectual incapacity, but rather must consider other evidence in light of the imprecise measurement of IQ tests alone. *Hall v. Florida*, 134 S. Ct. 1986 (2014).

- The execution of offenders who were under the age of eighteen when their crimes were committed is cruel and unusual, *Roper v. Simmons*, 543 U.S. 551 (2005).

- Death sentences for crime against the person in which the victim's life was not taken is unconstitutionally disproportionate to the offense, even if imposed for the rape of child, *Kennedy v. Louisiana*, 554 U.S. 407 (2008).

Under certain circumstances, the Cruel and Unusual Punishment Clause limits the criminal sanction by prohibiting punishment that is excessive in relation to the crime committed. This limitation is referred to as the principle of proportionality. In short, this is the embodiment of the notion that the punishment should "fit the crime."[1]

In *Weems v. United States*, 217 U.S. 349 (1910), the U.S. Supreme Court first signaled that the principle of proportionality was a part of Eighth Amendment jurisprudence. In this case, the defendant was convicted of falsifying a cash book for a small amount of money. He was sentenced to a fine and fifteen years of punishment called a *cadena temporal*—imprisonment in shackles at the ankles and hands while being forced to perform hard labor. The Supreme Court sided with Mr. Weems, finding his sentence was disproportionately lengthy in light of the offense he committed—and, further, that it was "cruel and unusual because of its harsh and oppressive nature." Decades later, however, in *Rummel v. Estelle*, 445 U.S. 263 (1980), the Court explained that it was not the length of Weems's incarceration that rendered his sentence violative of the Eighth Amendment but rather the "unique nature" of the cadena punishment that was cruel and unusual.

In *Gregg v. Georgia*, 428 U.S. 153 (1976), the Supreme Court made it clear "that excessiveness alone, without regard to the barbaric nature of the punishment, was sufficient to invalidate a sentence" (Grossman 1995: 113). In the year after the *Gregg* decision, the Court decided *Coker v. Georgia*. It held that the death penalty for the crime of rape was unconstitutionally cruel and unusual punishment in light of the

---

[1] Fradella, H. F. (2006). "Mixed Signals and Muddied Waters: Making Sense of the Proportionality Principle and the Eighth Amendment." *Criminal Law Bulletin, 42*(4), 498–503. Used by the gracious permission of Thomson/ West and the *Criminal Law Bulletin*.

disproportionate nature of the offense to the punishment, again signaling that the excessiveness of a sentence was in and of itself a sufficient basis to render a criminal sanction unconstitutional. The *Rummel* Court, however, dismissed both of these decisions as being "'of limited assistance' in deciding the constitutionality of terms of imprisonment" because they involved sentences of death, not imprisonment (Grossman 1995: 113).

The dismissive approach the Supreme Court took in *Rummel* toward the principle of proportionality was further solidified in *Hutto v. Davis*. In Virginia, the defendant was sentenced to forty years in prison and a fine of $20,000 for possession with intent to distribute nine ounces of marijuana. In upholding the sentence, the Supreme Court reiterated its pronouncement in *Rummel* that the cases requiring an Eighth Amendment proportionality analysis were limited to death penalty cases; any "assessment of the excessiveness of a prison term was inherently subjective and therefore 'purely a matter of legislative prerogative'" (Grossman 1995: 122, citing *Hutto*, 454 U.S. at 373, and quoting *Rummel*, 445 U.S. at 274).

Surprisingly, the Supreme Court breathed new life into the principle of proportionality just six years after deciding *Hutto* when it rendered its decision in *Solem v. Helm*, 463 U.S. 277 (1983). The defendant had been convicted of offering a forged check, a felony under applicable state law that carried a maximum penalty of incarceration up to five years and a $5,000 fine. But the defendant already had three prior felony convictions, so he was sentenced under a recidivist statute ("three strikes") to life in prison without the possibility of parole. The Court vacated the defendant's sentence as being excessive and, therefore, unconstitutional under the Eighth Amendment's Cruel and Unusual Punishment Clause. In doing so, it set forth three factors to guide courts when wrestling with questions of proportionality:

- the proportionality between the severity of the crime and the severity of the sentence,
- the proportionality of sentence imposed in other jurisdictions for the crime at issue in a case, and
- the proportionality of the sentence imposed in the jurisdiction at issue in the given case on other criminals who commit similar or more serious crimes. 463 U.S. at 291–92.

When weighing these factors, the *Solem* Court noted that "there are generally accepted criteria for comparing the severity of different crimes." 463 U.S. at 294. These criteria reflect back to utilitarian ideals such as the "harm caused or threatened to the victim or society" and the relative culpability of the defendant in terms of his or her level of *mens rea* (i.e., criminal intent). 463 U.S. at 292–94. Decisions of the Supreme Court after *Solem*, however, have cast serious doubt on the validity of these factors in proportionality challenges, even though *Solem* has not yet been expressly overruled.

The decisions of the Supreme Court just discussed sent "a mixed and confusing message with respect to . . . the requirement of proportional sentencing" (Grossman 1995: 141). This confusion led the Court to issue another pronouncement on the role of the proportionality principle in Eighth Amendment jurisprudence in *Harmelin v. Michigan*, 501 U.S. 957 (1991). The defendant in *Harmelin* was convicted of possession of 672 grams of cocaine. Under Michigan law, anyone possessing more than 650 grams of cocaine received a mandatory sentence of life in prison without the possibility of parole. The highly fractured Court appeared to agree on very little. A majority of five justices agreed the sentence was not disproportionate to the offense, so they affirmed his sentence. But two justices—Chief Justice Rehnquist and Justice Scalia—wrote a concurring opinion to emphasize their view that the Cruel and Unusual Punishment Clause contains no guarantee of proportional punishment. Justice Thomas later echoed their views when he wrote in *Ewing v. California*, 539 U.S. 11, 32 (2003), "that the proportionality test announced in *Solem v. Helm* . . .

is incapable of judicial application" and that "the Cruel and Unusual Punishments Clause of the Eighth Amendment contains no proportionality principle."

Since the Court's decision in *Harmelin*, most proportionality-based appeals have failed. It appears the lower courts have embraced Justice Kennedy's conclusion regarding the proportionality principle in his concurring opinion in *Harmelin*: "The Eighth Amendment does not require strict proportionality between crime and sentence. Rather, it forbids only extreme sentences that are 'grossly disproportionate' to the crime." 501 U.S. at 1001. The Supreme Court cited Justice Kennedy's concurrence in *Harmelin* favorably in its two most recent pronouncements on proportionality. In *Ewing v. California*, 539 U.S. 11, 32 (2003), the Court upheld California's "three strikes and you're out" sentencing scheme. The defendant in that case had been sentenced to life in prison for having shoplifted three golf clubs valued at approximately $1,200. He had several prior misdemeanor and felony convictions, including one for robbery and three for residential burglary, which served as the triggering crimes for application of the three-strikes rule. In affirming his sentence, the Court found Ewing's life sentence was not unconstitutionally disproportionate to the theft, but rather that it reflected "a rational legislative judgment, entitled to deference, that offenders who have committed serious or violent felonies and who continue to commit felonies must be incapacitated." Using the same logic, the Court reached an identical result in *Lockyer v. Andrade*, 538 U.S. 63, 72 (2003), upholding two consecutive life sentences under California's three-strikes law for a defendant who had stolen approximately $150 worth of videotapes. Thus, it appears that the principle of proportionality has little relevance today to Eighth Amendment jurisprudence other than in death penalty cases.

Amendment IX

> The enumeration in the Constitution, of certain rights, shall not be construed
> to deny or disparage others retained by the people.

The Ninth Amendment emphasizes the Framers' view that powers of government are limited by the rights of the people. The Constitution did not intend, by expressly guaranteeing certain rights of the people, to grant the government unlimited power to invade other rights of the people.

The Supreme Court has on at least one occasion suggested that this amendment is a justification for recognizing certain rights not specifically mentioned in the Constitution or for broadly interpreting those that are. The case involving the Ninth Amendment was *Griswold v. Connecticut*, 381 U.S. 479 (1965), in which a statute prohibiting the use of contraceptives was voided as an infringement of the right of marital privacy. At issue was whether the right to privacy was a constitutional right and, if so, whether the right was one reserved to the people under the Ninth Amendment or only derived from other rights specifically mentioned in the Constitution.

Courts have long recognized particular rights to privacy that are part of the First and Fourth Amendments. As the Court in *Griswold* said, the "specific guarantees in the Bill of Rights have penumbras, formed by emanations from those guarantees that help give them life and substance." 381 U.S. at 484. Thus, freedom of expression guarantees freedom of association and the related right to be silent and free from official inquiry into such associations. It also includes the right not to be intimidated by government for the expression of one's views. The Fourth Amendment's guarantee against unreasonable search and seizure confers a right to privacy because its safeguards prohibit unauthorized entry onto one's property and tampering with one's person, property, or possessions.

The Court in *Griswold* ruled that the Third and Fifth Amendments, in addition to the First and Fourth, created "zones of privacy" safe from governmental intrusion and, without resting its decision on any one of these or on the Ninth Amendment itself, simply held that the right of privacy was guaranteed by the Constitution.

Amendment X

The powers not delegated to the United States by the Constitution, nor prohibited by it to the States, are reserved to the States respectively, or to the people.

The Tenth Amendment embodies the principle of federalism, which reserves for the states the remainder of powers not granted to the federal government or expressly withheld from the states. For example, in *United States v. Lopez*, 514 U.S. 549 (1995), the Supreme Court invalidated Congress' enactment of the Gun-Free School Zones Act, reasoning that the regulation of gun possession near schools was a matter for the states, not the federal government, to regulate.

Amendment XIV

Section 1. All persons born or naturalized in the United States, and subject to the jurisdiction thereof, are citizens of the United States and of the State wherein they reside. No State shall make or enforce any law which shall abridge the privileges or immunities of citizens of the United States; nor shall any State deprive any person of life, liberty, or property, without due process of law; nor deny to any person within its jurisdiction the equal protection of the laws. . . .

   Section 5. The Congress shall have power to enforce, by appropriate legislation, the provisions of this article.

The Right to Due Process As previously discussed, the Fifth Amendment contains a Due Process Clause that applies to actions of the federal government. The Fourteenth Amendment's Due Process Clause limits the states from infringing on the rights of individuals. Through judicial interpretation of the phrase *due process of law* in the Fourteenth Amendment, many of the Bill of Rights guarantees have been made applicable to actions by state governments and their subdivisions, such as counties, municipalities, and cities (see Table 1.2).

The Right to Equal Protection of the Laws In addition to guaranteeing due process, the Fourteenth Amendment also prohibits the denial of the *equal protection of the laws*. This requirement prevents any state from making unreasonable, arbitrary distinctions between different persons as to their rights and privileges. If a law does not discriminate in any way but applies evenly to all people, then the mandates of equal protection are satisfied. However, if a law treats different classifications of people differently even though the people are similarly situated (e.g., they are in similar circumstances under similar conditions), then the law might run afoul of the Constitution's guarantee of equal protection. Because so many laws have historically denied women and minorities the same rights and privileges that were guaranteed or extended to others, Section 5 of the Fourteenth Amendment provided the authority for Congress to address this history of inequality by enacting much of the civil rights legislation passed by Congress in the 1960s. Section 5 remains the source of constitutional authority for antidiscrimination legislation enacted today.

   Analyzing a classification in the law that treats different classes of people differently is a multistep process. First, a court must determine if the distinctions made in the law are "similarly situated" with respect to their circumstances and conditions under the law. If the groups are not similarly situated, then the constitutional line of inquiry ends because groups that are not similarly situated do not have to be treated in a similar manner. Only if the groups are found to be similarly situated do courts have to analyze the classifications at issue in the law under the relevant standard of review—the level of scrutiny to be applied to judicial review of the law in question. Three standards of review are generally used in the equal protection litigation.

Strict scrutiny is the most exacting level of judicial review. The formal test for strict scrutiny is whether a law is narrowly tailored to achieve a compelling governmental interest. If the government does not have a "compelling" reason for justifying a law's failure to treat similarly situated people in a similar manner, then the law will be declared unconstitutional under this test. Even if the government has such a "compelling" governmental interest, if there were other ways of achieving its goals without burdening the right to equal protection, then the law will also fail strict scrutiny review.

Strict scrutiny under the Equal Protection Clause applies only to laws that make classifications based on suspect classifications or those that burden fundamental rights. Race, religion, and national origin have all been held to be **suspect classifications**. Courts will presume that laws that treat suspect classes differently than the way other people are treated are unconstitutional unless the government can prove that the differential treatment under the law is narrowly tailored to achieve a compelling governmental interest. Using such strict scrutiny, courts have struck down racial segregation in public schools and other public places, *Brown v. Bd. of Educ.*, 347 U.S. 483 (1954), and laws that prohibit the sale or use of property to certain races or minority groups. *E.g., Reitman v. Mulkey*, 387 U.S. 369 (1967). Furthermore, the Supreme Court has held that purely private acts of discrimination can be in violation of the equal protection clause if they are customarily enforced throughout the state, whether or not there is a specific law or other explicit manifestation of action by the state. *Shelley v. Kraemer*, 334 U.S. 1 (1948).

Strict scrutiny is also used when a law makes distinctions among people with regard to a fundamental right. **Fundamental rights** are those rights that are "implicit in the concept of ordered liberty," *Palko v. Connecticut*, 302 U.S. 319, 325 (1937)—that is, fundamental to American notions of liberty and justice. These include the freedom of speech, the freedom of religion, the freedom to travel, the right to access the courts, and the right to vote. In fact, courts have interpreted the Equal Protection Clause to mean that a citizen may not arbitrarily be deprived of the right to vote and that every citizen's vote must be given equal weight to the extent possible. Thus, the Supreme Court held that state legislatures and local governments must be strictly apportioned in terms of their populations in such a way as to accord one person one vote. *E.g., Reynolds v. Sims*, 377 U.S. 533 (1964). There are also a select group of fundamental rights that are not explicitly provided for in the text of the Constitution, but are strongly implied therein, and thus are considered "fundamental." These include the right to marry, *Loving v. Virginia*, 388 U.S. 1 (1967), and the right to privacy, *Griswold v. Connecticut*, 381 U.S. 479 (1965).

Intermediate scrutiny asks whether the governmental classifications at issue in a case are substantially related to achieving an important governmental interest. This intermediate level of judicial scrutiny is used only when a law makes a distinction using what the Supreme Court has held to be **quasi-suspect classifications**. Gender and illegitimacy are the only classifications that the Supreme Court has determined to be quasi-suspect classifications. For an example of a case applying intermediate scrutiny, see the Discussion Point on statutory rape laws, on page 31.

Finally, most equal protection challenges to laws are reviewed under the **rational basis test.** This deferential standard of review asks if the governmental classification at issue is rationally related to a legitimate governmental interest. If so, then the law is constitutional. Laws reviewed

KEY POINTS

LO5
LO6

■ The Bill of Rights sets for a number of important substantive rights relevant to criminal law, including the rights to free speech, expression, and peaceable assembly; the guarantee of a free press; a prohibition on the establishment of a state religion; the right to freely practice one's religion; and the right to bear arms.

■ The Fourth Amendment protects people in the United States against unreasonable searches and seizures.

■ The Fifth Amendment protects people from being forced to incriminate themselves and from facing double jeopardy.

■ The Sixth Amendment provides those who are accused of crimes with a host of pretrial and trial rights to jurisdiction and venue rights, speedy and public trial rights, the right to trial by impartial jury, the right to confront adverse witnesses, the right to compel witnesses to testify, and the right to effective assistance of counsel.

■ The Eighth Amendment prohibits excessive bail, fines, and cruel and unusual punishments.

■ The Fifth and Fourteenth Amendments guarantee due process of law and the equal protection of the laws.

DISCUSSION POINT

Do Gender-Specific Statutory Rape Laws Violate the Equal Protection Clause?

Michael M. v. Superior Ct. of Sonoma County, Cal., 450 U.S. 464 (1981). In the early 1980s, California's statutory rape law mirrored the centuries-old common law definition of the crime, defining statutory rape as "an act of sexual intercourse accomplished with a female not the wife of the perpetrator, where the female is under the age of 18 years."

450 U.S. at 466. Thus, the statute only criminalized the statutory rape of an underage female by a male; it did not criminalize the statutory rape of an underage male by a female.

Michael M. was seventeen and a half years old when he had sexual intercourse with a sixteen-and-a-half-year-old girl. He was charged with statutory rape and sought to have the case dismissed on equal protection grounds. Specifically, Michael M. claimed that the law unconstitutionally discriminated on the basis of sex because only males were punished under the statutory rape law. The Supreme Court disagreed, determining that the sexes were not similarly situated with respect to the underlying purpose of the law: to prevent illegitimate teenage pregnancies. The Court accepted this purpose as being an important governmental interest. It reasoned that is **"hardly unreasonable for a legislature acting to protect minor females to exclude them from punishment"** because **"young men and young women are not similarly situated with respect to the problems and the risks of sexual intercourse. Only women may become pregnant, and they suffer disproportionately the profound physical, emotional, and psychological consequences of sexual activity."** 450 U.S. at 471. Because no **"similar natural sanctions deter males,"** the Court concluded that a **"criminal sanction imposed solely on males thus**

serves to roughly 'equalize' the deterrents on the sexes." 450 U.S. at 473.

■ Do you agree with the outcome of the *Michael M.* case? Why or why not?

■ What do you think most feminists would say about the Supreme Court's reasoning? Why?

Today, many states have abandoned this gender-specific approach to statutory rape. They impose criminal liability to males and females alike. Indeed, several notable cases have highlighted situations in which female high school teachers have taken sexual advantage of their underage male students (Levine 2006). When these women are convicted of statutory rape, however, they tend to receive significantly more lenient sentences than when a male statutorily rapes a female. Many researchers in psychology have documented what these light sentences seem to intuitively tell us—namely, that we appear to have a double standard for what is acceptable intergenerationally (Broussard et al. 1991; Dollar et al. 2004; Quas et al. 2002). One of these researchers concluded that people see "sexual interaction between a fifteen-year-old male and a thirty-five-year-old female [as] an acceptable means of providing sex education for boys" (Broussard et al. 1991: 275).

■ What do you make of these findings? What, if anything, does this say about societal notions regarding statutory rape and sex between teenagers and people who are significantly older than they are?

under the rational basis test will only be declared unconstitutional if they bear no reasonable relationship to any legitimate governmental interest.

For example, in 1982, Alaska experimented with legalizing marijuana by allowing adults over the age of nineteen to possess less than four ounces of the drug. Possession of marijuana remained illegal for minors who could be charged through the juvenile justice system for violating the law. The law, however, criminalized possession of marijuana by eighteen-year-olds, even though they were no longer minors. In *Allam v. State*, 830 P.2d 435 (Alaska App. 1992), the validity of a state's possession law was challenged by an eighteen-year-old who was caught in possession of a small amount of the substance. He argued that the law illegally discriminated on the basis of age because all adults in the state could possess small quantities of the drug except for those who were eighteen years of age. Because age is neither a suspect classification nor a quasi-suspect classification, and because possession of marijuana is not a fundamental right, the court applied the rational basis test to review the constitutionality of the law. Applying that test, the court upheld the age-based classification, finding that the state had two rational bases to discriminate against eighteen-year-olds. First, many eighteen-year-olds are in high school, where they would be able to share marijuana with underage minors. Second, eighteen-year-olds are still relatively inexperienced drivers; giving them an extra year to mature before allowing them access to a drug was a "rational" legislative judgment.

SUMMARY

Criminal procedure attempts to balance the rights of the criminally accused with the need to maintain public order in the name of crime control. Many of the constitutional protections afforded to criminal defendants stem from judicial process abuses at early English Common Law. For example, the constitutional prohibition on bills of attainder prohibits legislatures from enacting laws declaring someone guilty of crime without a trial. Similarly, the ban on *ex post facto* laws prevents people from being prosecuted and criminal detention in violation of their constitutional rights may petition the U.S. courts for a writ of *habeas corpus* ordering their release.

The Bill of Rights limits both substantive and procedural criminal law by protecting people in the United States from government establishment of religion or prohibitions on the free exercise of religion; governmental suppression of free speech, press, assembly, and petition rights; unreasonable searches and seizures; and both double jeopardy and self-incrimination. The Sixth Amendment guarantees rights to a speedy and public trial, notice of charges, confrontation with adverse witnesses, compulsory process for favorable witnesses, and the effective assistance of counsel. And the Eighth Amendment protects against excessive bail, fines, and against cruel and unusual punishments.

In addition to the specific constitutional rights outlined in this chapter, certain safeguards for the individual are inherent in the structure of American government. The separation of powers among legislative, executive, and judicial branches of government is the basis for a system of checks and balances—which prevents excessive concentration of power, with its inevitable threat to individual liberties. With respect to legislative power itself, the existence of two houses of Congress—each chosen by a different process—is itself a protection against ill-advised laws that might threaten constitutional rights. Similarly, our federal system, which divides authority between the national government and the various state governments, has provided a fertile soil for the nourishment of constitutional rights.

No matter how well a constitution may be written, the rights it guarantees have little meaning unless there is popular support for those rights and that constitution. Fortunately, that support has historically existed in the United States. Indeed, in this country the most fundamental protection of personal liberty rests in the well-established American traditions of constitutional government, obedience to the rule of law, and respect for the individual. These traditions provide the groundwork for the entire body of law dealing with criminal procedure and should be foremost in the minds of students of and participants in the American criminal justice system. The remainder of this book shows how the criminal justice system operates to achieve a balance between the protection of individual rights guaranteed by the Constitution and the maintenance of the rule of law and public order in our society.

KEY TERMS

bail 24	Double Jeopardy Clause 18	*ex post facto* 13
bill of attainder 13	due process model 5	fundamental rights 30
Bill of Rights 7	due process of law 20	*habeas corpus* 12
collateral estoppel doctrine 19	due process revolution 5	intermediate scrutiny 30
crime control model 5	effective assistance of counsel 24	judicial review 9
cruel and unusual punishment 25	equal protection of law 21	law 3

REVIEW AND DISCUSSION QUESTIONS

1. How has the Constitution been able to remain a durable and viable instrument of government despite the enormous changes that have occurred in our society since its adoption? Discuss this issue in terms of specific changes.

2. Discuss generally the most important roles and functions under the Constitution of each of the following: the three branches of the federal government, the state governments, the average citizen, and the law enforcement officer. Explain the interrelationships among some of those roles and functions.

3. The Constitution speaks predominantly in terms of the protection of individual rights from governmental abuse or abridgment. What corresponding obligations and burdens must each citizen undertake or bear to ensure that everyone remains free to exercise these rights to their full extent?

4. Discuss the nature of First Amendment liberties and the restraints on them that are constitutionally permissible to the public at large.

5. Name three constitutional sources for the protection of the right to privacy, and explain how they differ.

6. A state legislature passes a law requiring all bookstores that have, in the last six months, sold or advertised for sale pictures of the pope to be closed down and their owners immediately arrested and jailed. What provisions of the Constitution might be violated by this law?

7. Because of religious beliefs, a terminally ill cancer patient wishes to refuse medical treatment and die a "natural" death. Can that person be required under state law to undergo treatment? What if the wish to die is not based on a religious belief, but the person is a minor or is mentally incompetent? What if the cancer was caused by exposure to radiation and the person wishes his or her death to be a political statement on the dangers of nuclear power and nuclear war?

8. A journalist is being compelled to reveal a confidential source of information, but the source would be useful to the government in a criminal investigation or helpful to a criminal defendant at trial. What constitutional issues are involved? Should the government be able to obtain a search warrant to look into files, audit tapes, or view films that are in the possession of the news media to find evidence of crime?

9. Should members of the news media have greater access than the general public to court proceedings and court records? What about greater access to prisons to interview prisoners? What about greater access to police investigative files?

10. Would the Fifth Amendment privilege against self-incrimination prohibit the government from any of the following: requiring all participants in a lineup to speak certain words; requiring a person to produce income tax records; threatening a person with a reduction in pay in his government job if he does not make incriminating testimonial admissions about a matter not related to his job?

11. What are the similarities and differences between due process of law and equal protection of the laws?

12. What are the three standards of review in equal protection litigation? When are they used?

2

Criminal Courts, Pretrial Processes, and the Exclusionary Rule

LO1 DESCRIBE the dual court structure of the United States.

LO2 TRACE the progress of a criminal case through its various pretrial stages from arrest through pretrial motions.

LO3 EXPLAIN the characteristics and functions of a complaint, an affidavit, a summons, a warrant, an indictment, an information, a motion, a subpoena, and a deposition.

LO4 DIFFERENTIATE preliminary hearings, grand jury proceedings, and arraignments.

LO5 ANALYZE the nature of prosecutorial discretion, including how it can manifest in selective or vindictive prosecution.

LO6 ASSESS why plea bargaining and discovery are essential to the administration of criminal justice.

LO7 CONTRAST the difference between venue and jurisdiction.

LO8 EVALUATE the reasons underpinning the exclusionary rule, its exceptions, and its significance to criminal procedure.

The law enforcement officer's daily duties include enforcing laws, investigating and preventing crime, keeping the public peace, and community caretaking. To perform these duties properly, police officers must be sensitive to the constitutional rights of all persons (discussed in Chapter 1) and be familiar with the criminal laws of their jurisdictions. Just as important, officers must understand the laws dealing with arrest, search and seizure, confessions, and pretrial identifications. The remainder of this book is concerned with these legal topics.

Most police officers are not as familiar with the rules and procedures that govern the course of a prosecution after the investigatory or arrest stage; nevertheless, police play an important role in this process, often as important witnesses for the prosecution. Moreover, law enforcement officers' early actions in a case vitally affect its outcome at nearly all stages of the prosecution, so they should have a basic understanding of what happens to the case—and why—when it reaches the prosecutor and the courts.

Criminal court procedure is governed primarily by law and rules designed to ensure the just and efficient processing of criminal offenders. This chapter highlights pertinent court procedures and legal terms to provide a comprehensive, chronological view of a criminal prosecution up until the point of a trial for serious offenses; this chapter does not cover procedures for traffic violations and other less serious misdemeanors.

Trials, appeals, and postconviction remedies are covered in Chapter 15. In addition, when any other chapter covers certain aspects of criminal court procedure, reference is made to that chapter. Because the information about judicial processes in this book is general, and because criminal court procedures differ by state, readers should consult their own state's pertinent statutes and rules for authoritative information.

The Dual Court Systems in the United States

At the time of the Constitutional Convention in 1787, there was great debate as to how to divide power between the state and federal governments. The resulting Constitution of the United States set forth the unique compromises of the Framers. In sum, the states formed a union and granted power to the federal government over national matters while maintaining their separate existence and power over local matters. This unique interrelationship between the states and the federal government is known as *federalism*. As a result of federalism, each state, as well as the District of Columbia and the federal government, has its own separate court system, each with its own limited jurisdictional authority. Figure 2.1 illustrates the interrelated structure of the dual U.S. court systems.

Jurisdiction

Jurisdiction is defined as "the authority given by law to a court to try cases and rule on legal matters within a particular geographic area and/or over certain types of legal cases" (Law.Com Dictionary 2014). More simply, jurisdiction refers to the power of a court to hear and decide a case.

Geographical Jurisdiction and Venue Courts do not have the power to adjudicate any and all disputes. The cases that courts are empowered to adjudicate are limited to disputes that occur within specified territorial boundaries. The lands within these territorial boundaries are referred to as being within a court's *geographical jurisdiction*. For example, if a violation of Wyoming state criminal law were committed in Wyoming, then the Wyoming courts would have proper geographical jurisdiction over that criminal case. Courts in other states would lack geographical jurisdiction. But which courts within the state of Wyoming would hear the case? That is a matter of venue.

"*Venue* is defined as the particular county or geographical area in which a court with jurisdiction may hear and determine a case" (Norwood 1995: 270). Proper venue is based on geographical subdivisions within a given geographical jurisdiction. These subdivisions are often determined by city or county boundaries, but other geographical boundaries can be set that are unrelated to county lines. Divisions in the federal system are a good example of this. The state of Washington is a large and populous state. Instead of having one federal district coterminous with the boundaries of the state, Washington has two federal districts: the eastern district and the western district. Larger states are subdivided even further; California, for example, has northern, eastern, central, and southern districts. A federal case that arises from an act in Sacramento is properly tried in the northern district of California; the other districts in California would lack proper venue.

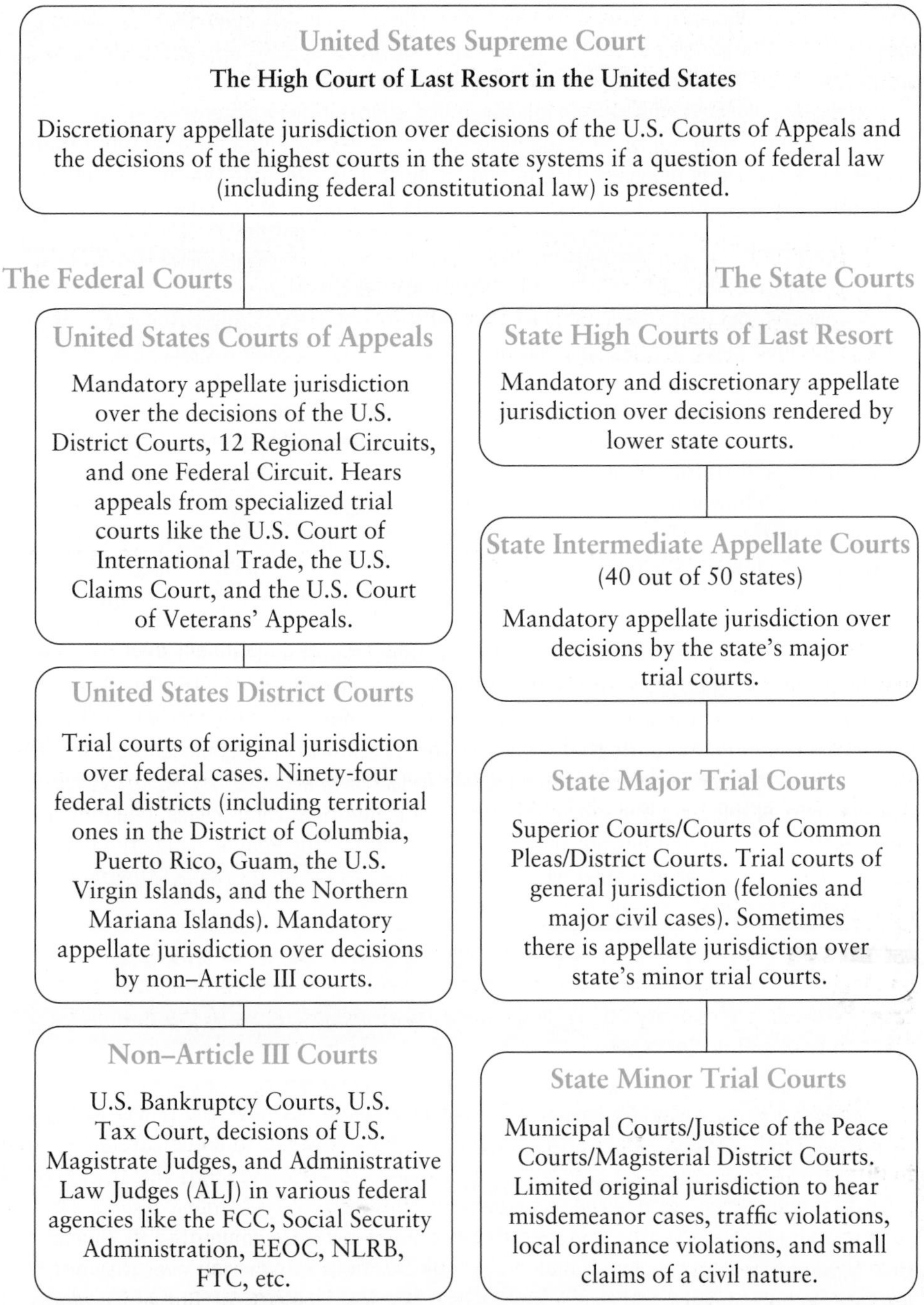

United States Supreme Court
The High Court of Last Resort in the United States

Discretionary appellate jurisdiction over decisions of the U.S. Courts of Appeals and the decisions of the highest courts in the state systems if a question of federal law (including federal constitutional law) is presented.

The Federal Courts

The State Courts

United States Courts of Appeals

Mandatory appellate jurisdiction over the decisions of the U.S. District Courts, 12 Regional Circuits, and one Federal Circuit. Hears appeals from specialized trial courts like the U.S. Court of International Trade, the U.S. Claims Court, and the U.S. Court of Veterans' Appeals.

State High Courts of Last Resort

Mandatory and discretionary appellate jurisdiction over decisions rendered by lower state courts.

State Intermediate Appellate Courts
(40 out of 50 states)

Mandatory appellate jurisdiction over decisions by the state's major trial courts.

United States District Courts

Trial courts of original jurisdiction over federal cases. Ninety-four federal districts (including territorial ones in the District of Columbia, Puerto Rico, Guam, the U.S. Virgin Islands, and the Northern Mariana Islands). Mandatory appellate jurisdiction over decisions by non–Article III courts.

State Major Trial Courts

Superior Courts/Courts of Common Pleas/District Courts. Trial courts of general jurisdiction (felonies and major civil cases). Sometimes there is appellate jurisdiction over state's minor trial courts.

Non–Article III Courts

U.S. Bankruptcy Courts, U.S. Tax Court, decisions of U.S. Magistrate Judges, and Administrative Law Judges (ALJ) in various federal agencies like the FCC, Social Security Administration, EEOC, NLRB, FTC, etc.

State Minor Trial Courts

Municipal Courts/Justice of the Peace Courts/Magisterial District Courts. Limited original jurisdiction to hear misdemeanor cases, traffic violations, local ordinance violations, and small claims of a civil nature.

© Cengage Learning®

FIGURE 2.1 | Structure of the U.S. Court Systems

The federal constitution guarantees (in both Article III, Section 2, and the Sixth Amendment) that a criminal trial will be held in the state in which the crime was committed. A typical state statute or rule requires that the trial of certain types of cases be held in the geographical division of the court in which the offense was committed. Most jurisdictions also have special rules relating to the proper venue for an offense that is committed on a boundary of two counties and for offenses partly committed in one county and partly in another. (These technicalities are not discussed here.) Because of the Fourteenth Amendment's guarantee of due process, however, both the federal government and all states have provisions that allow a criminal defendant to waive these rights and have venue transferred to another forum so that a case can be tried in a different place than the one authorized by statute.

To accomplish this, the defendant may make a motion for a change of venue. The motion is usually required to be made before the jury is impaneled or, in nonjury trials, before any evidence is received. The defendant must give adequate reasons in support of the motion. Typical grounds for granting a motion for change of venue are

- such prejudice prevails in the county where the case is to be tried that the defendant cannot obtain a fair and impartial trial there, or
- another location is much more convenient for the parties and witnesses than the intended place of trial, and the interests of justice require a transfer of location.

Hierarchical Jurisdiction and Court Structure Although the states and the federal government have separate court systems that were established by their own constitutions and statutes, some basic similarities exist in American court systems. Most court systems follow a hierarchical structure beginning at the lowest level with *courts of limited jurisdiction* and followed by major trial courts of *general jurisdiction*, intermediate courts of appeal, and courts of last resort. The following general characteristics of the trial and appellate systems are applicable to both the state and federal courts.

Trial Courts and Original Jurisdiction *Original jurisdiction* means that a court has the power to hear a case for the first time. In other words, the court will act as a trial court. In popular culture, most of our exposure to the court system is to trial level courts. It is in the trial level of courts that witnesses testify and evidence is presented. The *litigants* at the trial court are the parties involved in the specific case. In criminal cases, the *prosecution* files the case. The prosecution may be called by several names, depending on the jurisdiction, including but not limited to "the State," "the People," and "the Commonwealth." Finally, the party against whom the criminal case is filed is called the *defendant*.

CRIMINAL PROCEDURE IN ACTION

The Trial of James Holmes

James Holmes graduated from college with highest honors in 2010, earning a degree in neuroscience. The following year, he entered a doctoral program in neuroscience at the Anschutz Medical Campus of the University of Colorado, located in Aurora—a suburb of Denver. His academic performance declined, presumably as a function of Holmes's deteriorating mental health. In June 2012, Holmes failed a key comprehensive examination and dropped out of graduate school. Before doing so, however, he had sought psychiatric services from the university's health service. One of the psychiatrists who treated him reported to campus police that Holmes had made homicidal threats and she considered him to be a danger to the public. The following month, in July 2012, Holmes entered a local movie theater in Aurora dressed in a gas mask and Kevlar suit, armed with an assault rifle, a shotgun, and two handguns. He entered a theater in which *The Dark Knight Rises* was playing and opened fire, killing twelve people and injuring seventy others.

Holmes entered a plea of not guilty by reason of insanity. At the time of this writing, his trial was scheduled to take place in December 2014. Where that trial should take place, however, was disputed by the parties. Holmes's lawyers attempted to get the trial moved out of the county in which the shooting occurred so that jury selection would not involve screening so many potential jurors who are directly affected by the shooting. But the court denied the motion for a change of venue and instead opted to summon more than 3,500 prospective jurors in the hopes of seating a fair and impartial jury.

- Do you think the decision to keep Holmes's trial in the county in which the shooting took place was a good one or a bad one? Explain your reasoning.
- What do you think of the insanity defense? Why?

Trial courts are presided over by one judge, sitting with or without a jury. A trial court hears evidence, applies the law, and decides which side should prevail. To arrive at a final determination, usually two types of decisions need to be made during the course of a trial: legal decisions and factual decisions. The judge makes all of the legal decisions, ruling on all matters of law. Factual decisions, however, are made by the *trier-of-fact*. In a *jury trial*, the jury is the trier-of-fact responsible for making factual findings such as whether the defendant is guilty of a crime. In a *bench trial*, a trial is conducted without a jury. The judge acts as the trier-of-fact in addition to ruling on matters of law.

Both the state and federal trial courts of the United States are empowered to hear certain types of cases. *Subject matter jurisdiction* is concerned with the type of case a court hears. It is an absolute prerequisite to a court hearing a case. Courts are either courts of limited subject matter jurisdiction or courts of general subject matter jurisdiction. A court of *special or limited subject matter jurisdiction* will only hear specialized cases. Small claims courts are not the proper forum to adjudicate multimillion-dollar disputes because their subject matter jurisdiction is limited to a specific, small amount. Similarly, traffic courts do not adjudicate murder cases because their subject matter jurisdiction is limited to determining whether quasi-criminal violations of motor vehicle laws have occurred. Tax cases are adjudicated in tax court, bankruptcy cases are heard in bankruptcy court, and violations of ordinances are determined in municipal courts. Collectively, the trials courts of limited subject matter jurisdiction in the state system are typically referred to as *minor trial courts*. These minor trial courts have jurisdiction over misdemeanor or traffic cases, the initial setting of bail, preliminary hearings in felony cases, and occasionally felony trials in which the penalty prescribed for the offense is below a statutorily specified limit.

Courts of *general subject matter jurisdiction* are the courts of original jurisdiction having the power to adjudicate all types of disputes not specifically delegated to a court of limited jurisdiction. These courts are typically referred to as *major trial courts*. States' major trial courts are typically arranged by county and are empowered to hear all types of criminal and civil cases. The federal system, in contrast, has no such courts of general jurisdiction because the federal courts of the United States are all courts of limited subject matter jurisdiction. As such, federal courts only adjudicate criminal cases that involve violations of federal laws.

Appellate Courts and Appellate Jurisdiction

Appellate jurisdiction refers to the power to review decisions originally made by a court that exercised original jurisdiction over a given case. Although appellate courts and their processes are discussed in detail in Chapter 15, some basic appellate terminology is presented here to assist the reader in understanding the nature of the appellate cases discussed in Chapters 3 through 14.

In appellate cases, the party bringing an appeal is known as the *petitioner* or the *appellant*, depending on the jurisdiction. The party responding to the appeal is called the *respondent* or *appellee*. The petitioner or appellant is arguing that an error was made by the court below. Not every error, however, is grounds for appeal. For an appeal to be successful, there must have been some kind of *prejudicial error*. In other words, the error must have been such that it could have affected the outcome of the case. Errors that were not prejudicial (i.e., mistakes that were not likely to have had an effect on the outcome of the case) are called *harmless errors*. In order to prevail on an appeal, the appellant is usually required to show harmful or prejudicial error. Harmless errors are rarely, if ever, grounds for a successful appeal.

In forty states, appellate jurisdiction is first exercised by *intermediate courts of appeals*. In terms of the hierarchical structure of the courts, the intermediate courts of appeals rank higher than trial courts of original jurisdiction and below the court of last resort. They typically comprise an uneven number of judges who hear and decide an appeal as a panel. These judges review the record of the lower court and the merits of the case as set forth in both written and oral arguments of the attorneys. If the appellate court agrees with the decision of the lower court, it affirms the lower court decision; if it disagrees, it reverses. The appellate court may also modify the decision of the lower court, or *remand* (send back) the case, so that the lower court may retry all or part of the case in accordance with the rulings of the appellate court.

Ten states—Delaware, Maine, Montana, Nevada, New Hampshire, Rhode Island, South Dakota, Vermont, West Virginia, and Wyoming—do not have intermediate courts of appeal. Instead, appellate jurisdiction in these states is exercised by the *state court of last resort*. Courts of last resort are the highest courts in a court system's hierarchical structure, and every state and the federal system has one. These courts are referred to as the *Supreme Court* by forty-six states. The court of last resort in New York and Maryland is called the *Court of Appeals*. In Maine and Massachusetts, the court of last resort is called the *Supreme Judicial Court*. Courts of last resort exercise appellate jurisdiction as a second level of review in the federal court system and in the forty states that have intermediate courts of appeals; they are the first and only courts exercising appellate jurisdiction in the ten states that do not have intermediate courts of appeals. As with the intermediate court of appeals, a panel of judges or justices on courts of last resort hears and decides cases based on a review of the record from the lower courts, as well as the arguments of attorneys.

In addition to exercising appellate jurisdiction, courts of last resort have original jurisdiction over a limited range of cases. This is quite rare, however; original jurisdiction usually lies in the major trial courts, and courts of last resort almost always exercise their appellate jurisdiction.

Nature of Mandatory and Discretionary Appellate Jurisdiction If an appellate court is required by law to hear an appeal of a certain type of case, it is called an *appeal of right*. When such a right exists, the appellate court is said to have *mandatory appellate jurisdiction*. Appeals of right exist to the courts of last resort in the ten states without intermediate courts of appeals. In the forty jurisdictions that have intermediate courts of appeals, though, the appeal of right from a decision made by a court of original jurisdiction generally exists only to the intermediate court of appeals. (The one major exception to this rule is in death penalty cases; capital crimes are always reviewed by a state's highest court.) Any appeal of right must be exercised by the appealing party within a statutorily prescribed period of time, typically ten or thirty days, depending on the laws of the particular state.

There are also appeals of right that exist to courts of last resort even when an intermediate court of appeals has heard a case, although they are uncommon. For example, if a federal court of appeals invalidates a state statute, a party relying on that statute has a right to appeal the decision to the United States Supreme Court, which has mandatory appellate jurisdiction over the case under 28 U.S.C. Section 1253. Barring one of these rare appeals of right to a court of last resort, courts of last resort exercise *discretionary appellate jurisdiction*. The party seeking review of a lower court's decision asks the appellate court to exercise its discretionary appellate jurisdiction by filing a petition for a writ of *certiorari* along with a formal brief that sets forth the reasons why the court should accept jurisdiction. If the high court decides to accept discretionary appellate jurisdiction and thereby review a decision of a lower court, it grants the petition and issues a **writ of *certiorari***. This writ is an order compelling the lower court to produce the record from the proceedings below. If the court decides not to hear the case, *certiorari* is denied, and the decision of the lower court stands. Denial of a petition for *certiorari* is not, however, an approval of the lower court decision; it is merely the conclusion of the high court that its limited resources should not be discretionarily used to review the lower court decision.

Concurrent and Exclusive Jurisdiction *Concurrent jurisdiction* exists when both the state and federal courts have jurisdiction over a particular case. (Concurrent jurisdiction can also exist when two courts within the same court system have original jurisdiction over the same matter.) In most general federal questions and civil rights cases, federal jurisdiction is concurrent with the state courts. In these cases, parties bringing the action must decide whether they should file suit in state or federal court. In some cases, such as bankruptcy, patent, or copyright actions, the federal courts have *exclusive jurisdiction*, meaning that these actions must be brought in federal court.

Federal Courts

Article III, Section 1 of the United States Constitution provides:

> The judicial power of the United States shall be vested in one supreme Court, and in such inferior Courts as the Congress may from time to time ordain and establish. The Judges, both of the supreme and inferior Courts, shall hold their Offices during good Behaviour, and shall, at stated Times, receive for their Services, a Compensation, which shall not be diminished during their Continuance in Office.

With the Judiciary Act of 1789, Congress established the lower federal courts. Although the Judiciary Act of 1789 has been amended several times since its inception, the basic structure of the federal courts remains the same, with specialized courts, trial-level courts, intermediate courts of appeal, and the court of last resort remaining the United States Supreme Court. *See* 28 U.S.C. § 1 *et seq.*; *see also* www.uscourts.gov.

Federal District Courts

The trial-level court for the federal court system is the United States District Court (see Figure 2.1). Each state has at least one district court, although some of the larger states have as many as four. As Figure 2.2 illustrates, there are a total of ninety-four district courts in the fifty states, the District of Columbia, the Commonwealth of Puerto Rico, and the territories of Guam, the U.S. Virgin Islands, and the Northern Mariana Islands. District courts may have divisions (e.g., Eastern and Western Divisions of North Dakota), usually in districts covering a large geographical area, and they may have several locations where the court hears cases.

With the exception of the territorial courts, all district court judges are appointed for life by the president, with the advice and consent of the Senate. Congress authorizes judgeships for each district based in large part on the district's caseload. At this writing, there are more than 677 district court judges. Usually, only one judge is required to hear and decide a case in a district court. The district courts have original jurisdiction over criminal cases, and the great majority of federal criminal cases begin in the district courts. Cases from the district courts are reviewable on appeal by the applicable court of appeals. Each district court has one or more bankruptcy judges, a clerk, a U.S. attorney, a U.S. marshal, probation officers, court reporters, and a support staff.

Each district court also has one or more U.S. magistrate judges. Magistrate judges are appointed for eight-year terms by district court judges and are required to be members of the bar. A magistrate judge, at the designation of the district court judge, may issue search warrants, hear and determine certain kinds of pretrial matters, conduct preliminary and other hearings, and submit proposed findings and recommendations on motions for the court's approval. Perhaps the most important power magistrate judges

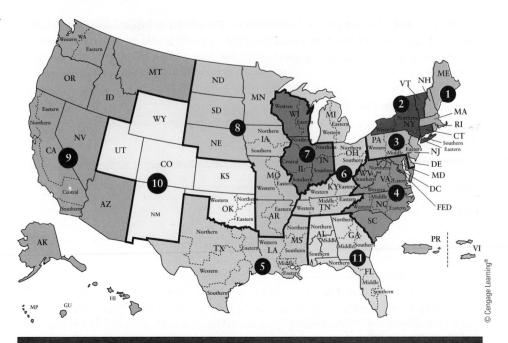

FIGURE 2.2 | Geographical Boundaries of Federal District and Circuit Courts

possess is the authority to conduct misdemeanor trials with the defendant's consent and to conduct trials in civil cases with the consent of the parties involved. Since the enactment of the Federal Magistrates Act in 1968, Congress has expanded the services magistrate judges may perform. As a result, magistrate judges are playing an increasingly significant role in the administration of justice in the federal system.

Federal Circuit Courts of Appeals

The U.S. Circuit Courts of Appeals are intermediate appellate courts created by Congress to relieve the U.S. Supreme Court from considering all appeals in cases originally decided by the federal trial courts. The courts of appeal are empowered to review all final decisions and certain interlocutory decisions of district courts. They also have the power to review and enforce orders of many federal administrative bodies. The decisions of the courts of appeals are final, except that they are subject to discretionary review or appeal in the U.S. Supreme Court. The Circuit Courts of Appeals are divided into circuits, each circuit hearing appeals from specific district courts. Presently, there are thirteen circuits in the United States Courts of Appeals; eleven numbered circuits (each containing at least three states); a Circuit Court of Appeals for the District of Columbia; and the Court of Appeals for the Federal Circuit, which was created by act of Congress in 1982 to have nationwide jurisdiction to hear specialized appeals, primarily in patent and copyright cases. The geographical locations of the thirteen federal judicial circuits and the ninety-four federal districts are presented in Figure 2.2.

Appeals court judges are appointed for life by the president of the United States, with the advice and consent of the Senate. Each court of appeals has from six to twenty-eight permanent circuit judgeships, depending on the amount of judicial work in the circuit. At this writing, there are 179 judges in the thirteen judicial circuits. One of the justices of the U.S. Supreme Court is assigned as a circuit justice for each of the thirteen judicial circuits. Each court of appeals normally hears cases in panels consisting of three judges but may sit *en banc*—a session of a court in which all the judges of the court participate, as opposed to a session presided over by a single judge or a mere quorum of judges. The judge who has served on the court the longest and who is less than sixty-five years of age is designated as the chief judge and performs administrative duties in addition to hearing cases. The chief judge serves for a maximum term of seven years.

U.S. Supreme Court

The U.S. Supreme Court is the court of last resort in the federal court system, meaning that it is a court from which no appeal is possible. The Supreme Court has one chief justice and such number of associate justices as may be fixed by Congress. By act of Congress in 1948, the number of associate justices is eight. Power to nominate the justices is vested in the president of the United States, and appointments are made with the advice and consent of the Senate. Once confirmed to the Supreme Court, there is no mandatory retirement age for Supreme Court justices; as long as they maintain "good behavior," the justices may remain on the court until their death or until they voluntarily choose to retire. Article III, Section 1, of the Constitution further provides that "[t]he Judges, both of the supreme and inferior Courts, shall hold their Offices during good Behaviour, and shall, at stated Times, receive for their Services, a Compensation, which shall not be diminished during their Continuance in Office." The term of the United States Supreme Court commences on the first Monday in October and usually ends nine months later.

The Constitution grants the Supreme Court original jurisdiction in a limited number of cases. In other words, the Supreme Court acts as a trial court in certain types of cases, such as controversies between the United States and a state, between two states, or those involving foreign ministers or ambassadors. Such cases are quite rare; so in the overwhelming majority of cases, the Supreme Court exercises its appellate jurisdiction, reviewing the decisions of the lower federal courts and the highest state courts.

The Supreme Court exercises its appellate jurisdiction through the granting of a *writ of certiorari*, which means that the Court, on petition of a party, agrees to review a case decided by one of the circuit courts of appeals or the highest court of a state. A vote of four Supreme Court justices is required to grant *certiorari* to review a case (sometimes referred to as the "rule of four"). *Certiorari* is granted at the Court's discretion when a case presents questions the resolution of which will have some general "importance beyond the facts and parties involved." *Boag v. MacDougall*, 454 U.S. 364, 368 (1982) (Rehnquist, J., dissenting). For example, the Court may grant *certiorari* in cases involving important and unsettled questions of federal law, or in situations involving a conflict among state high courts or the federal circuits concerning the interpretation of federal law, most especially one ruling on a question of interpretation of the U.S. Constitution. Note that failure to grant *certiorari* is not an affirmation in disguise of the lower court's decision. It simply means that the petitioner failed to persuade four of the nine justices to hear the appeal.

Federal Courts Not Included in Article III

In addition to the courts already described, the federal court system also includes a number of specialized courts of limited subject matter jurisdiction established to hear particular classes of cases. Examples are the U.S. Court of International Trade, the U.S. Court of Federal Claims, the U.S. Tax Court, and the U.S. Court of Military Appeals. There are also quasi-judicial boards or commissions that have special and limited jurisdiction under specific federal statutes.

State Courts

The constitution and statutes of each state dictate the structure of their individual court systems. A typical state court system has the same basic structure as the federal system. Courts of original jurisdiction are usually divided into (1) courts of limited jurisdiction with

L07
L01

- *Jurisdiction* refers to the power of a court to hear and decide a case based on considerations of geography, hierarchical structure, subject matter, and power of persons.

- Federal courts are courts of limited subject matter jurisdiction. Federal trials usually take place in federal district courts, whereas appeals as a right are adjudicated in federal circuit courts of appeals. The highest federal court is the U.S. Supreme Court; it exercises original jurisdiction over a handful of rare cases, and its docket consists primarily of appeals it elects to adjudicate through the *certiorari* process.

- State courts of original jurisdiction are usually divided into (1) courts of limited jurisdiction with trial jurisdictions that either include no felonies or are limited to less than all felonies, and (2) higher courts of general jurisdiction with trial jurisdiction over all criminal offenses, including all felonies. Appeals as a right are adjudicated in state intermediate courts of appeals, whereas state high courts of last resort primarily exercise discretionary appellate jurisdiction.

trial jurisdictions that either include no felonies or are limited to less than all felonies, and (2) higher courts of general jurisdiction with trial jurisdiction over all criminal offenses, including all felonies. The courts of limited jurisdiction are usually established on a local level and may be called *municipal courts, police courts, magistrate courts, district courts,* or something similar. These courts have jurisdiction over misdemeanor cases, traffic cases, initial setting of bail and preliminary hearings in felony cases, and, occasionally, felony trials in which the penalty prescribed for the offense is below a statutorily specified limit. The courts of general jurisdiction have original jurisdiction over all criminal offenses and are usually established on a county or regional level. They may be called *circuit courts, district courts, superior courts,* or something similar. Generally, the most serious criminal cases are tried in these courts.

In some states, courts of general jurisdiction may also exercise a limited appellate jurisdiction over certain cases appealed from courts of limited jurisdiction. Such appeals result in a *trial de novo* in the court of general jurisdiction. A trial de novo is a new trial or retrial in which the whole case is examined again as if no trial had ever been held in the court of limited jurisdiction. In a trial de novo, matters of fact as well as law may be considered, witnesses may be heard, and new evidence may be presented, regardless of what happened at the first trial. Some states also have lower-level specialized courts—such as juvenile courts, traffic courts, or family courts—that may have criminal jurisdiction or partial criminal jurisdiction.

From a court of general jurisdiction, a case may usually be appealed as a right to an intermediate appellate court. Some of the less populous states, however, do not have an intermediate court of appeals; therefore, in those states, appeals from the trial courts go straight to the courts of last resort as a matter of right. In the majority of states that have intermediate appellate courts, however, most appeals are resolved at that level. Few cases, other than death penalty cases, are heard by the highest court of a state. This state court of last resort, usually called a *state supreme court,* typically exercises discretionary appellate jurisdiction over cases from the intermediate appellate courts using a process much like the U.S. Supreme Court's *certiorari* process.

If a case decided by a state high court involves important federal constitutional issues or questions of federal law, it may finally reach the U.S. Supreme Court for review. Generally, the state high court of last resort also has the power to prescribe rules of pleading, practice, and procedure for itself and the other lower courts of the state.

Preliminary Pretrial Criminal Proceedings

The remainder of this chapter focuses on the progress of a *felony* case through the criminal court system. A brief note about misdemeanor cases is useful at the outset to emphasize the differences between the two types of cases. Generally, *misdemeanors* are crimes for which the maximum possible sentence is less than one year's imprisonment. Misdemeanors are tried in courts of limited jurisdiction. Although misdemeanor proceedings are similar to felony proceedings, they are usually less formal and more abbreviated. For example, jury trials are available but unusual in misdemeanor cases, and six-person juries are common. Also, in some jurisdictions, if the defendant pleads guilty, misdemeanor charges may be disposed of at the initial appearance before the magistrate. Because misdemeanor proceedings differ greatly from jurisdiction to jurisdiction, and because they are similar in many ways to felony proceedings, the remainder of this chapter focuses primarily on felony proceedings. Figure 2.3 gives a general view of the progress of a case through the criminal justice system.

Charging

Prosecutorial Discretion Police investigate crimes, but they do not officially charge people as criminal defendants; prosecutors do. Prosecutors have great *discretion* with regard to their charging function, both in terms of "the initial screening determination as to whether or not to charge (the 'screening function'); and, if the answer is yes, the subsequent decisions as to choice and number of charges (the 'selection function')" (Krug 2002: 645). "[S]o long as the prosecutor has probable cause to believe that the accused committed an offense defined by statute, the decision whether or not to prosecute, and what charge to file or bring before a grand jury, generally rests entirely in his discretion." *Wayte v. United States*, 470 U.S. 598, 607 (1985). A prosecutor also has broad discretion in determining when to bring charges, whether to investigate, whether to grant immunity, whether to plea bargain, and, if so, the type of plea that will ultimately be acceptable.

Why might a prosecutor decline to file charges against someone? The most common reason for releasing someone without prosecution is insufficient evidence. "Witness availability, credibility, and memory also influence the results of prosecutions, as well as the existence of alternative remedies, such as restitution to the victim." *McCleskey v. Kemp*, 481 U.S. 279, 307 n. 28 (1987). The American Bar Association's Standards for Criminal Justice set forth the main factors prosecutors are supposed to consider when exercising their charging discretion in Standard 3-3.9 (b) (3d ed. 1993):

> The prosecutor is not obliged to present all charges which the evidence might support. The prosecutor may in some circumstances and for good cause consistent with the public interest decline to prosecute, notwithstanding that sufficient evidence may exist which would support a conviction. Illustrative of the factors which the prosecutor may properly consider in exercising his or her discretion are:
>
> **(i)** the prosecutor's reasonable doubt that the accused is in fact guilty;
> **(ii)** the extent of the harm caused by the offense;
> **(iii)** the disproportion of the authorized punishment in relation to the particular offense or the offender;
> **(iv)** possible improper motives of a complainant;
> **(v)** reluctance of the victim to testify;
> **(vi)** cooperation of the accused in the apprehension or conviction of others; and
> **(vii)** availability and likelihood of prosecution by another jurisdiction.

The discretion exercised by prosecutors in both the screening and selection is broad but not absolute; it is constrained by the Constitution. Accordingly, prosecutorial discretion is subject to limited judicial review in cases in which selective prosecution or vindictive prosecution is alleged.

Selective prosecution is a violation of the Constitution's guarantee of equal protection of the law. To establish selective prosecution, a defendant bears a heavy burden to show that others similarly situated were not prosecuted and that the defendant's prosecution was "deliberately based upon an unjustifiable standard such as race, religion, or other arbitrary classification." *Bordenkircher v. Hayes*, 434 U.S. 357, 364 (1978).

Vindictive prosecution violates due process. Vindictive prosecution occurs when a prosecutor increases the number or severity of charges to penalize a defendant who exercises constitutional or statutory rights. In *Blackledge v. Perry*, 417 U.S. 21 (1974), a case involving a felony charge brought against a defendant who exercised a statutory

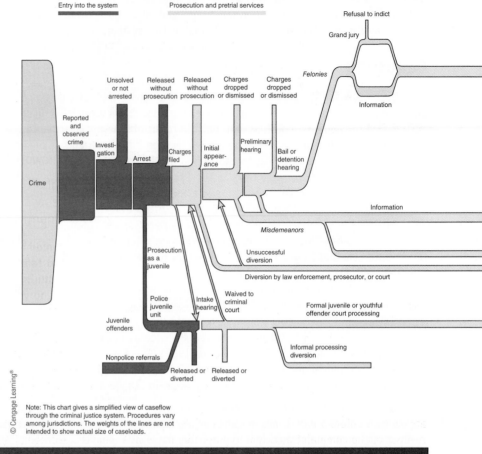

What is the sequence of events in the criminal justice system?

Note: This chart gives a simplified view of caseflow through the criminal justice system. Procedures vary among jurisdictions. The weights of the lines are not intended to show actual size of caseloads.

© Cengage Learning®

FIGURE 2.3 | The Sequence of Events in the Criminal Justice System

right to appeal from a misdemeanor conviction for the same offense, the Court said the real basis of the vindictiveness rule is that "the fear of such vindictiveness may unconstitutionally deter a defendant's exercise of the right to appeal or collaterally attack his first conviction." 417 U.S. at 28.

Once a prosecutor has decided to move forward with a criminal prosecution, criminal charges may be filed against someone in one of three ways: by a complaint, an information, or an indictment.

The Complaint A criminal process against a felony defendant formally begins with a **complaint**. The word *formally* is used here because a person can be arrested for an offense before a complaint is filed or a warrant is issued. However, because an arrest without a warrant is viewed as an exception to the basic warrant requirement, the complaint is still considered the formal beginning of proceedings. Also, a person may be arrested based on a report of, or a law enforcement officer's observation of, the commission of a crime, but for various reasons the prosecutor may decide not to charge the defendant.

According to Federal Rule of Criminal Procedure 3, a complaint is "a written statement of the essential facts constituting the offense charged." The complaint serves a dual purpose in a criminal proceeding. If the defendant has been arrested without a warrant, the complaint serves as the charging document at the defendant's initial

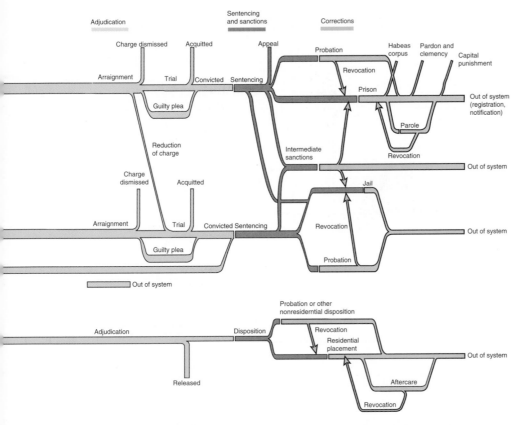

appearance before a *magistrate,* a *justice of the peace,* or a municipal court judge. The reading of the complaint at this initial appearance is what converts someone from being a suspect to a formal criminal defendant. If the defendant has not been arrested and is not before the court, then the complaint serves as the basis for determining whether an arrest warrant should be issued.

The complaint must be made on oath or affirmation, must state the essential facts of the offense being charged, must be in writing, and must be made before a judicial officer authorized to issue process in criminal cases. This officer is usually a magistrate or a justice of the peace, although a judge may also authorize a complaint. The data in the complaint may come from a law enforcement officer's personal observation or experience, or it may come from victims, witnesses, or informants. Nevertheless, the evidence put forth in the complaint must be strong enough to convince the magistrate that there is **probable cause** that an offense has been committed and that the defendant committed it. Probable cause is explored in much greater detail in Chapter 3. For now, think of probable cause as being a fair probability, under all of the reliable facts and circumstances known at the time, to believe that a crime has been or is being committed. *Draper v. United States,* 358 U.S. 307 (1959). A typical complaint appears in Figure 2.4.

Affidavits Facts not contained in the body of the complaint, or that come from witnesses other than the complainant, may be brought to the court's attention in the form of an **affidavit**. An affidavit is a sworn written statement of the facts relied on in seeking the issuance of a warrant. An affidavit need not be prepared with any particular formality. It is filed with the complaint, and together the complaint and affidavit provide a written record for a reviewing court to examine in determining whether probable cause existed for the issuance of a warrant.

AO91 (Rev. 12/03) Criminal Complaint

UNITED STATES DISTRICT COURT

_____ DISTRICT OF _____

UNITED STATES OF AMERICA
V.

CRIMINAL COMPLAINT

Case Number:

(Name and Address of Defendant)

I, the undersigned complainant, state that the following is true and correct to the best of my

knowledge and belief. On or about _____ in _____ County, in
(Date)

the _____ District of _____ defendant(s) did,

(Track Statutory Language of Offense)

in violation of Title _____ United States Code, Section(s) _____ .

I further state that I am a(n) _____ and that this complaint is based on the
Official Title

following facts:

Continued on the attached sheet and made a part of this complaint: ☐ Yes   ☐ No

_____
Signature of Complainant

_____
Printed Name of Complainant

Sworn to before me and signed in my presence,

_____ at _____
Date   City   State

_____
Name of Judge   Title of Judge   Signature of Judge

United States District Court

FIGURE 2.4 | A Sample Criminal Complaint

Warrant or Summons Issued on the Complaint Once the magistrate has determined from the complaint and accompanying affidavits that there is probable cause to believe that an offense has been committed and that the defendant committed it, the magistrate issues either a summons or an arrest warrant for the defendant's appearance in court. A _summons_, pictured in Figure 2.5, is a court order that commands someone to appear before a court to respond to charges filed against them. An _arrest warrant_ authorizes police to take someone into custody and bring that person before the court to respond to the charges against him or her. As you can see in Figure 2.5, an arrest warrant looks very much like a summons, but it is directed at law enforcement personnel rather than the defendant. If the defendant is already before the court, then neither a summons nor an arrest warrant is necessary.

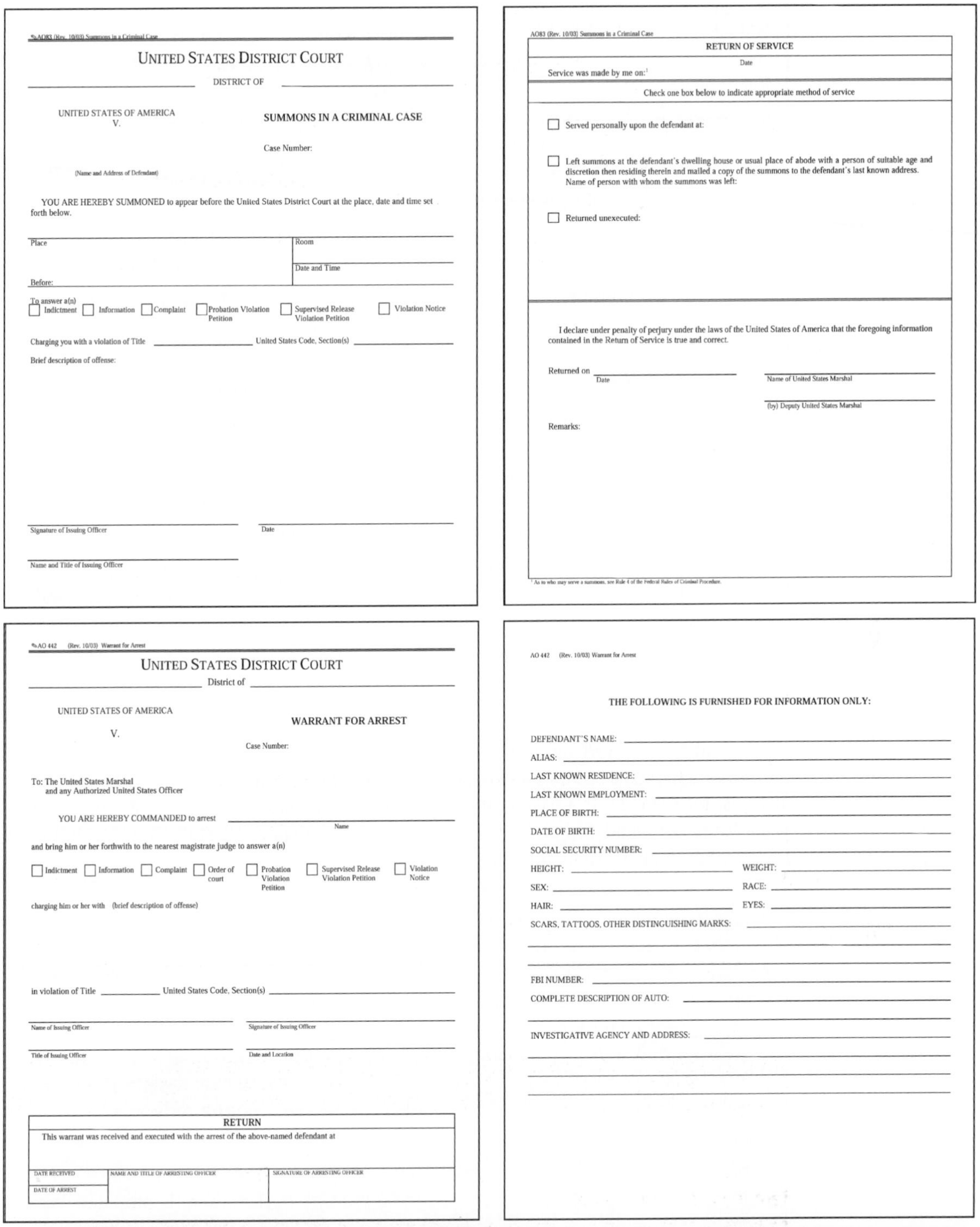

AO83 (Rev. 10/03) Summons in a Criminal Case

UNITED STATES DISTRICT COURT

DISTRICT OF

UNITED STATES OF AMERICA
V.

SUMMONS IN A CRIMINAL CASE

Case Number:

(Name and Address of Defendant)

YOU ARE HEREBY SUMMONED to appear before the United States District Court at the place, date and time set forth below.

Place	Room
Before:	Date and Time

To answer a(n)
☐ Indictment ☐ Information ☐ Complaint ☐ Probation Violation Petition ☐ Supervised Release Violation Petition ☐ Violation Notice

Charging you with a violation of Title ______ United States Code, Section(s) ______

Brief description of offense:

Signature of Issuing Officer — Date

Name and Title of Issuing Officer

AO83 (Rev. 10/03) Summons in a Criminal Case

RETURN OF SERVICE

Service was made by me on:[1] — Date

Check one box below to indicate appropriate method of service

☐ Served personally upon the defendant at:

☐ Left summons at the defendant's dwelling house or usual place of abode with a person of suitable age and discretion then residing therein and mailed a copy of the summons to the defendant's last known address.
Name of person with whom the summons was left:

☐ Returned unexecuted:

I declare under penalty of perjury under the laws of the United States of America that the foregoing information contained in the Return of Service is true and correct.

Returned on ______ Date — Name of United States Marshal

(by) Deputy United States Marshal

Remarks:

[1] As to who may serve a summons, see Rule 4 of the Federal Rules of Criminal Procedure.

AO 442 (Rev. 10/03) Warrant for Arrest

UNITED STATES DISTRICT COURT

District of

UNITED STATES OF AMERICA
V.

WARRANT FOR ARREST

Case Number:

To: The United States Marshal
and any Authorized United States Officer

YOU ARE HEREBY COMMANDED to arrest ______ Name

and bring him or her forthwith to the nearest magistrate judge to answer a(n)

☐ Indictment ☐ Information ☐ Complaint ☐ Order of court ☐ Probation Violation Petition ☐ Supervised Release Violation Petition ☐ Violation Notice

charging him or her with (brief description of offense)

in violation of Title ______ United States Code, Section(s) ______

Name of Issuing Officer — Signature of Issuing Officer

Title of Issuing Officer — Date and Location

RETURN

This warrant was received and executed with the arrest of the above-named defendant at

DATE RECEIVED	NAME AND TITLE OF ARRESTING OFFICER	SIGNATURE OF ARRESTING OFFICER
DATE OF ARREST		

AO 442 (Rev. 10/03) Warrant for Arrest

THE FOLLOWING IS FURNISHED FOR INFORMATION ONLY:

DEFENDANT'S NAME:
ALIAS:
LAST KNOWN RESIDENCE:
LAST KNOWN EMPLOYMENT:
PLACE OF BIRTH:
DATE OF BIRTH:
SOCIAL SECURITY NUMBER:
HEIGHT: WEIGHT:
SEX: RACE:
HAIR: EYES:
SCARS, TATTOOS, OTHER DISTINGUISHING MARKS:

FBI NUMBER:
COMPLETE DESCRIPTION OF AUTO:

INVESTIGATIVE AGENCY AND ADDRESS:

United States District Court

FIGURE 2.5 | Samples of a Typical Summons and an Arrest Warrant

Once a summons or warrant is issued, a law enforcement officer to whom it is directed must serve the summons or execute the warrant by arresting the defendant and bringing the defendant before a judicial officer as commanded in the warrant. A detailed discussion of summons and arrest warrant procedures appears in Chapter 7.

Initial Appearance

A person who has been arrested without a warrant is required by statute to be brought before a magistrate "without unnecessary delay," or "forthwith," or some similar statutory language for an initial appearance. The initial appearance is also called a *Gerstein* hearing, so called after the case *Gerstein v. Pugh,* 420 U.S. 103 (1975), which held a prompt judicial determination of probable cause is required when someone is arrested without an arrest warrant in order to

- verify that the person arrested is the person named in the complaint;
- advise arrested persons of the charges so they may prepare a defense;
- advise arrested persons of their rights—such as the right to a preliminary hearing, the right to counsel, and the right to remain silent;
- protect arrested persons from being abandoned in jail and forgotten by, or otherwise cut off from contact with, people who can help them;
- prevent secret and extended interrogation of arrested persons by law enforcement officers;
- give arrested persons an early opportunity to secure release on bail while awaiting the final outcome of the proceedings or, alternatively, have a judicial officer review a prior bail determination (see the later section on bail);
- give arrested persons an opportunity to speedily conclude proceedings on charges of minor offenses by pleading guilty to the charges, paying fines, and carrying on with their lives; and
- obtain a prompt, neutral "judicial determination of probable cause as a prerequisite to extended restraint of liberty following arrest." 420 U.S. at 114.

Not all states, however, provide for a judicial determination of probable cause at the initial appearance before a magistrate or justice of the peace. In indictment jurisdictions, for example, if a grand jury has already returned an indictment, an initial appearance is not mandated under *Gerstein v. Pugh,* although some states require an initial appearance on all arrests. Moreover,

> [t]here is no single preferred pretrial procedure, and the nature of the probable cause determination usually will be shaped to accord with a State's pretrial procedure viewed as a whole. . . . It may be found desirable, for example, to make the probable cause determination at the suspect's first appearance before a judicial officer, . . . or the determination may be incorporated into the procedure for setting bail or fixing other conditions of pretrial release. In some States, existing procedures may satisfy the requirement of the Fourth Amendment. Others may require only minor adjustment, such as acceleration of existing preliminary hearings. Current proposals for criminal procedure reform suggest other ways of testing probable cause for detention. Whatever procedure a State may adopt, it must provide a fair and reliable determination of probable cause as a condition for any significant pretrial restraint of liberty, and this determination must be made by a judicial officer either before or promptly after arrest. 420 U.S. at 123–25.

County of Riverside v. McLaughlin, 500 U.S. 44 (1991), held that, to satisfy the "promptness" requirement of *Gerstein*, a jurisdiction that chooses to combine probable cause determinations with other pretrial proceedings must do so as soon as reasonably feasible, but not later than forty-eight hours after arrest. As a general rule, defendants possess a Sixth Amendment right to counsel at these hearings. In *Rothgery v. Gillespie*

Country, Texas, 554 U.S. 191, 213 (2008), the U.S. Supreme Court held that "a criminal defendant's initial appearance before a judicial officer, where he learns the charge against him and his liberty is subject to restriction, marks the start of adversary judicial proceedings that trigger attachment of the Sixth Amendment right to counsel."

Even if a probable cause hearing is provided within forty-eight hours, the hearing might not pass constitutional muster if it is unreasonably delayed. As the Court said:

> Such a hearing may nonetheless violate *Gerstein* if the arrested individual can prove that his or her probable cause determination was delayed unreasonably. Examples of unreasonable delay are delays for the purpose of gathering additional evidence to justify the arrest, a delay motivated by ill will against the arrested individual, or delay for delay's sake. In evaluating whether the delay in a particular case is unreasonable, however, courts must allow a substantial degree of flexibility. Courts cannot ignore the often unavoidable delays in transporting arrested persons from one facility to another, handling late-night bookings where no magistrate is readily available, obtaining the presence of an arresting officer who may be busy processing other suspects or securing the premises of an arrest, and other practical realities. 500 U.S. at 56–57.

When an arrested person does not receive a probable cause determination within forty-eight hours, the burden shifts to the government to demonstrate the existence of a bona fide emergency or other extraordinary circumstance. The Court specifically stated that neither intervening weekends nor delays related to consolidating pretrial proceedings qualify as extraordinary circumstances.

Bail

In many states, a preliminary determination about bail is also made at an initial appearance; in other states, a formal bail hearing is scheduled shortly after the initial appearance. Regardless of when a bail decision is made, bail serves as a form of security designed to guarantee that the accused promises to return to court as needed in exchange for being released from custody pending the disposition of criminal charges. If the defendant appears in court when requested, the security is returned. If he or she fails to appear, the security can be forfeited.

The practice of allowing defendants to be released from jail pending trial originated in England, largely as a convenience to local sheriffs. The colonists brought the concept of bail with them across the Atlantic. It eventually became embedded in the Eighth Amendment to the U.S. Constitution. The Eighth Amendment, however, does not create a right to bail; rather, it mandates that if bail is granted, it must not be "excessive." A statutory right to bail, though, has been recognized since 1789 for all those accused of committing noncapital crimes. *Stack v. Boyle,* 342 U.S. 1 (1951).

In many states, formal bail schedules determine the amount of bail for many minor crimes. For more serious crimes, however, judicial officers possess a great deal of discretion when deciding if bail is warranted in a particular case. Their discretion is typically guided by a number of factors, including the seriousness of the offense(s) charges; the prior criminal history of the defendant, if any; and whether it is likely that the defendant will show up for future court appearances or flee. This final factor, sometimes referred to as *flight risk,* typically involves an assessment of defendants' ties to the community, including their employment status, whether they have family within the community, whether they own property within the community, and how long they have lived in the area. If there is a serious risk that defendants will flee or if the defendants' crimes or background make it likely that their release on bail would pose a risk to members of the community, then the defendants may be denied bail and held in custody pending the disposition of the case.

Judges may release a defendant on *recognizance* (without any formal bail) if they believe the defendant is unlikely to flee and poses little risk to the community. If, however, the judge believes some bail should be posted to ensure appearance at future court dates, a defendant can post bail in one of three ways. Defendants who have access to a sufficient amount of money to cover their bail expenses can post their bail in cash. A second alternative available in most states is a *property bond*, which allows a defendant (or friends or relatives) to pledge a piece of property as collateral. If the defendant fails to appear in court, the property is forfeited. The most common form of bail, however, is a *surety bond* secured from a bail agent (often called a "bail bondsman" or "bail bondsperson") who posts the amount required and charges a fee for services rendered, usually 10 percent of the amount of the bond. Thus, a bail agent would normally collect $1,000 for writing a $10,000 bond. None of that money is refundable.

The higher the amount of bail set, the less likely it is that the accused will be able to post the required bond. Thus, the bail system of the United States favors those whose socioeconomic status allows them to buy their freedom pending trial; the poor, however, await trial in jail. In addition to financial resources, it should also be noted that judges consider specific characteristics of the defendant when making bail decision such as the defendant's appearance and demeanor while in court. Such considerations, in turn, potentially permit judges, either unconsciously or purposefully, to consider stereotypes and assumptions that may be attributable to certain defendants based on demographic characteristics. It should not be surprising, then, that racial, ethnic, gender, and sexual orientation disparities routinely manifest themselves in bail decisions (e.g., Katz & Spohn 1995; Spohn 2008).

Preliminary Hearing

The initial appearance before the magistrate may or may not include a preliminary hearing. At the **preliminary hearing** (also called the *preliminary examination*), the magistrate must determine whether there is probable cause to believe that a felony was committed and that the defendant committed it. The purpose of the preliminary hearing is to provide another judicial determination of probable cause and to protect the defendant from a totally baseless felony prosecution. Rule 5 of the Federal Rules of Criminal Procedure provides that, when the preliminary hearing is required, "[t]he magistrate judge must hold the preliminary hearing within a reasonable time, but no later than 10 days after the initial appearance if the defendant is in custody and no later than 20 days if not in custody." A preliminary hearing is not required if the defendant is charged with a petty offense or misdemeanor or if the defendant waives the hearing. Moreover, a defendant is not entitled to a preliminary hearing if the defendant has been indicted by a grand jury because that body has already established probable cause exists for the defendant to stand felony trial.

The preliminary hearing is a formal adversarial proceeding conducted in open court with a transcript made of the proceedings. The U.S. Supreme Court held that the preliminary hearing is a "critical stage" of a criminal prosecution, entitling the defendant to have an attorney present at the hearing. *Coleman v. Alabama*, 399 U.S. 1 (1970). Indigent defendants who cannot afford an attorney must be provided one at the government's expense. The preliminary hearing consists mainly of the presentation of evidence against the defendant by the prosecuting attorney. The Court in *Coleman v. Alabama* described the defense attorney's function:

> First, the lawyer's skilled examination and cross-examination of witnesses may expose fatal weaknesses in the State's case that may lead the magistrate to refuse to bind the accused over. Second, in any event, the skilled interrogation of witnesses by an experienced lawyer can fashion a vital impeachment tool for use in cross-examination of the State's witnesses at the trial, or preserve

testimony favorable to the accused of a witness who does not appear at the trial. Third, retained counsel can more effectively discover the case the State has against his client and make possible the preparation of a proper defense to meet that case at the trial. Fourth, counsel can also be influential at the preliminary hearing in making effective arguments for the accused on such matters as the necessity for early psychiatric examination or bail. 399 U.S. at 9.

If the magistrate finds probable cause to believe that the defendant committed the offense, then the magistrate *binds over* the defendant to the trial court for adjudication of the felony charges. The magistrate may admit the defendant to bail at the preliminary hearing or may continue, increase, or decrease the original bail. If the magistrate does not find probable cause, then the magistrate dismisses the complaint and releases the defendant. A dismissal at this stage does not invoke the constitutional safeguard against double jeopardy. This means that the prosecution may recharge the defendant and submit new evidence at a later preliminary hearing. Nor does a dismissal prevent the prosecution from going to the grand jury and obtaining an indictment in states that have both grand jury and preliminary hearing procedures. Table 2.1 compares the preliminary hearing with grand jury proceedings.

TABLE 2.1 | Differences in Pretrial Procedures to Determine Whether Probable Cause Exists to Make a Defendant Stand Trial in Felony Cases

Grand Jury Proceedings	Preliminary Hearing
Primary function is to determine whether there is probable cause to believe that the defendant committed the crime or crimes charged.	Primary function is to determine whether there is probable cause to believe that the defendant committed the crime or crimes charged.
If probable cause is found, the grand jury returns an indictment or true bill against the defendant that is signed both by the prosecutor and by the foreperson of the grand jury.	If probable cause is found, the judge binds over the defendant for the trial court for adjudication by signing an information.
Held in the grand jury room in a closed session (i.e., secret proceedings not open to the public)	Held in open court (i.e., open to the public)
Informal proceeding in which no judicial officer presides	Formal judicial proceeding presided over by a judge or magistrate
Nonadversarial proceeding in which the grand jury only hears evidence presented by the prosecution	Adversarial proceeding in which both the prosecution and the defense may present evidence to the presiding judicial officer
Defendant has no right to be present or to offer evidence.	Defendant has the right to be present, to offer evidence, and to cross-examine adverse witnesses.
Defendant has no Sixth Amendment right to counsel.	Defendant has a right to the effective assistance of counsel under the Sixth Amendment.
Grand jury has the power to investigate crimes on its own initiative.	No power to investigate crime
Grand jury has the power to subpoena witnesses and evidence.	No subpoena power
Grand jury has the power to grant immunity.	No power to grant immunity

© Cengage Learning®

Indictments and Informations

In felony cases in jurisdictions that have a grand jury system, an **indictment** replaces the complaint as the document that charges the defendant with an offense and on which the defendant is brought to trial. Under Rule 7 of the Federal Rules of Criminal Procedure, an indictment "must be a plain, concise, and definite written statement of the essential facts constituting the offense charged and must be signed by an attorney for the government" as well as by the foreperson of the grand jury.

In some jurisdictions, grand jury indictments are not required to move forward with felony trials. Instead, felony trials may proceed using an **information**—a charging document that is signed and sworn to only by the prosecuting attorney and without the approval or intervention of the grand jury. Laws governing when the indictment or the information is used vary from state to state.

An example of a typical indictment appears in Figure 2.6. Note the language "a true bill" in the example. This means that the grand jury found probable cause to justify the

---

UNITED STATES DISTRICT COURT
DISTRICT OF MAINE

UNITED STATES OF AMERICA   )

)   Criminal Case Number: CR-2007-0142

                      v.   )   For Violations of: 21 U.S.C §§ 841(a)(1),

)   841(b)(1)(B), 853(a); and 18 U.S.C § 2.

ROY L. PAINE   )

_____   )

INDICTMENT

The Grand Jury Charges:

Count One

On or about February 15, 2007, in the District of Maine, ROY L. PAINE, defendant herein, did unlawfully, knowingly and intentionally manufacture and aid and abet in the manufacture of in excess of one hundred (100) marijuana plants, a Schedule I controlled substance listed in Title 21, United States Code, Section 812, in violation of Title 21, United States Code, Sections 841(a)(1), 841(b)(1)(B), and Title 18, United States Code Section 2.

Count Two

On or about February 15, 2007, in the District of Maine, ROY L. PAINE, defendant herein, did unlawfully, knowingly and intentionally possess with intent to distribute and aid and abet the possession with intent to distribute in excess of one hundred (100) marijuana plants, a Schedule I controlled substance listed in Title 21, United States Code, Section 812, in violation of Title 21, United States Code, Sections 841(a)(1) and 841(b)(1)(B) and Title 18, United States Code, Section 2.

Count Three

In committing violations of Title 21, United States Code, Section 841(a)(1) which are punishable by imprisonment for more than one year, to wit: the offenses charged by Counts One and Two of this indictment, ROY L. PAINE, defendant herein, used and intended to use real property located off the John Tarr Road in the Town of Bowdoin, County of Sagadahoc and State of Maine which is better described in a deed from Guy Dwyer to the said ROY L. PAINE, defendant herein, dated November 9, 2000 and recorded in the Sagadahoc County Registry of Deeds at Book 733 and Page 231, including any buildings and structures located thereon, to commit and facilitate the commission of said offenses, and by virtue of the commission of said felony offenses, ROY L. PAINE, defendant herein, is forfeit of any and all interest in the said real property and such interest is vested in the United States of America and is forfeitable thereto pursuant to Title 21, United States Code, Section 853.

A TRUE BILL.

_____

Grand Jury Foreperson

_____   A TRUE COPY
Assistant U.S. Attorney

Dated: _____   ATTEST: Ray Van Rant, Clerk

                                             By: _____

United States District Court

FIGURE 2.6 | A Sample Indictment—A "True Bill"

prosecution of the defendant. If the grand jury had rejected the prosecutor's evidence and found no grounds for prosecution (which is rare), it would have endorsed on the indictment form "no true bill," "not a true bill," "no bill," or some similar language. A variety of technical statutes and rules deal with drafting, amending, and dismissing indictments and informations. These provisions are of direct concern only to judges and attorneys and are not discussed here.

Grand Jury The Fifth Amendment provides that "[n]o person shall be held to answer for a capital, or otherwise infamous crime, unless on a presentment or indictment of a Grand Jury." As explained in Chapter 1, this requirement applies only to the federal government, although states have developed their own laws and rules regarding the use of the grand jury. The primary duty of the grand jury is to receive complaints in criminal cases, hear the evidence put forth by the state, and return an indictment when a majority of the grand jury is satisfied that there is probable cause that the defendant has committed an offense.

The grand jury usually consists of sixteen to twenty-three jurors selected from their communities according to law to serve during the criminal term of the appropriate court. Either the prosecution or the defendant, on the grounds of improper selection or legal disqualification, may challenge the composition of a grand jury. In *Rose v. Mitchell*, the U.S. Supreme Court said, "selection of members of a grand jury because they are of one race and not another destroys the appearance of justice and thereby casts doubt on the integrity of the judicial process." 443 U.S. 545, 555 (1979). If such bias in grand jury selection is proven, the indictment may be dismissed.

Grand jury proceedings are nonadversarial and are traditionally conducted in secrecy. During deliberations or voting, no one other than the jurors is allowed to be present. When the grand jury is taking evidence, however, the attorneys for the state, the witnesses under examination, and, when ordered by the court, an interpreter and an official court reporter may be present. Matters occurring before the grand jury, other than the deliberations or the votes of any juror, may be disclosed to the prosecuting attorney for use in performing his or her duties. Otherwise, these matters are to be kept secret, unless the court orders that they be disclosed.

The reasons for keeping grand jury proceedings secret were summarized in *United States v. Procter & Gamble Co.*, 356 U.S. 677, 681 n.6 (1958):

> (1) to prevent the escape of those whose indictment may be contemplated; (2) to insure the utmost freedom to the grand jury in its deliberations, and to prevent persons subject to indictment or their friends from importuning the grand jurors; (3) to prevent subornation of perjury or tampering with the witnesses who may testify before grand jury and later appear at the trial of those indicted by it; (4) to encourage free and untrammeled disclosures by persons who have information with respect to the commission of crimes; (5) to protect innocent accused who is exonerated from disclosure of the fact that he has been under investigation, and from the expense of standing trial where there was no probability of guilt.

The grand jury also has broad investigative powers, including the power to subpoena people or documents as illustrated by the grand jury subpoena contained in Figure 2.7.

Traditionally, the grand jury has been accorded wide latitude to inquire into violations of criminal law. No judge presides to monitor its proceedings. It deliberates in secret and may alone determine the course of its inquiry. The grand jury may compel the production of evidence or the testimony of witnesses as it considers appropriate, and its operation generally is unrestrained by the technical procedural and evidentiary rules governing the conduct of criminal trials. *United States v. Calandra,* 414 U.S. 338 (1974).

✎AO110 (Rev. 12/89) Subpoena to Testify Before Grand Jury

UNITED STATES DISTRICT COURT

DISTRICT OF _____

TO:

**SUBPOENA TO TESTIFY
BEFORE GRAND JURY**

SUBPOENA FOR:
☐ PERSON   ☐ DOCUMENT(S) OR OBJECT(S)

YOU ARE HEREBY COMMANDED to appear and testify before the Grand Jury of the United States District Court at the place, date, and time specified below.

PLACE	COURTROOM
	DATE AND TIME

YOU ARE ALSO COMMANDED to bring with you the following document(s) or object(s):*

☐ *Please see additional information on reverse.*

This subpoena shall remain in effect until you are granted leave to depart by the court or by an officer acting on behalf of the court.

CLERK	DATE
(By) Deputy Clerk	

This subpoena is issued on application of the United States of America	NAME, ADDRESS AND PHONE NUMBER OF ASSISTANT U.S. ATTORNEY

* If not applicable, enter "none".

United States District Court

FIGURE 2.7 | Subpoena to Testify Before the Grand Jury

The Fourth Amendment prohibits unreasonably vague or overbroad subpoenas for documents, and some courts hold that the evidence sought must be relevant to the investigation. Failure to obey a subpoena is punishable as contempt of court.

A grand jury may also grant *immunity* to compel testimony from witnesses who exercise their Fifth Amendment privilege against self-incrimination and refuse to testify. There are two different types of immunity: use immunity and transactional immunity. *Transactional immunity* is the broader type of protection because it immunizes the witness from prosecution for the offense(s) concerning the witness's testimony, as well as from future prosecutions for crimes uncovered as a result of evidence derived from the immunized testimony. *Use immunity* proves much less protection; it prohibits the government from using the immunized testimony in any subsequent prosecution of the witness (except in a subsequent prosecution for perjury or giving a false statement).

Waiver of Right to Grand Jury Indictment In some jurisdictions, a defendant who does not wish to be prosecuted by indictment may waive the indictment and be prosecuted by information. The waiver of indictment procedure is of great advantage to a defendant who wishes to plead guilty or *nolo contendere*. (These pleas are discussed in further detail later in this chapter.) In effect, the waiver of indictment procedure enables a defendant to begin serving a sentence sooner instead of having to wait for a grand jury, which sits only during the criminal term of court. The defendant can thereby secure release from custody at an earlier date than by going through the indictment procedure.

Warrant or Summons Issued on the Indictment An indictment may sometimes be handed down against a defendant by a grand jury before the defendant has been taken into custody and brought before the court. In these cases, at the request of the prosecuting attorney or by direction of the court, a summons or arrest warrant is issued for each defendant named in the indictment. This process indicates no change of procedure for law enforcement officers, who are required to execute the warrant or serve the summons in the same way as they would any other warrant or summons. Procedures for executing an arrest warrant appear in Chapter 7.

Arraignment and Pleas

After the issuance of a true bill on the indictment or a bind over order in the preliminary hearing, the next step is the arraignment. The term *arraignment* is sometimes confused with the term *initial appearance* because the two procedures are often combined in misdemeanor proceedings in courts of limited jurisdiction. In most felony prosecutions, though, an arraignment is a separate proceeding in which the defendant is called on to plead formally to the charge after the magistrate reads the substance of the charge. In misdemeanor proceedings, if there is no requirement of prosecution by indictment or information, then the complaint is read to the defendant and the plea is made to the complaint. However, in courts that require prosecution by grand jury indictment or a bind over at a preliminary hearing, either the indictment or the information must be read to the defendant at an arraignment and the defendant must then enter a formal plea on each charge.

Pleas Although the pleas available to defendants vary by jurisdiction, a defendant may always plead guilty or not guilty. In some jurisdictions, a defendant may also plead *nolo contendere* (no contest), although these pleas are rare. And, in most jurisdictions, a fourth plea of not guilty by reason of insanity is also available. A plea of *not guilty* puts in issue all the material facts alleged in the indictment, information, or complaint. Unless a not guilty plea is subsequently changed to a plea of guilty as part of the plea-bargaining process (more on plea bargaining follows), then the factual question of the defendant's guilt will be resolved at trial. A defendant may refuse to plead at all, in which case the court must enter a plea of not guilty on the defendant's behalf. Refusing to plead (sometimes called *standing mute*) may occur for various reasons such as obstinacy, dumbness, insanity, mental illness or intellectual disability, or ignorance of the language used in the proceedings.

Requirements of Guilty Pleas and *Nolo Contendere* Pleas To plead guilty or *nolo contendere*, the defendant must obtain the court's consent. Both these pleas simply mean that the defendant does not wish to contest the charge and will submit to the judgment of the court. A *guilty plea* may constitute an admission of guilt by the defendant and may be used against him or her in a civil action based on the same facts. A plea of *nolo contendere,* however, is not an admission of guilt and cannot be used against the defendant in a civil action. Therefore, the court may not accept a plea of guilty or *nolo contendere* in a felony proceeding unless the court is satisfied, after inquiry, (1) that the defendant committed the crime charged; (2) that the plea is made knowingly, intelligently, and voluntarily; and (3) that the defendant is mentally competent to enter the plea and thereby waive several important constitutional rights. This inquiry by the court is often referred to as a "Rule 11 proceeding" because Rule 11 of the Federal Rules of Criminal Procedure and similar state provisions establish guidelines for courts in making these and other determinations.

Rule 11 requires that the judge "address the defendant personally in open court and determine that the plea is voluntary and did not result from force, threats, or promises (other than promises [contained] in the plea agreement)." In addition to finding that a plea is voluntary, the court must also be sure that a plea is a knowing and intelligent waiver of the defendant's constitutional rights. A plea of guilty is more than an admission of conduct; under *Boykin v. Alabama*, 395 U.S. 238 (1969), it is a conviction that also involves a defendant's waiver of many constitutional rights, including

- the right to a trial by jury,
- the right to confront and cross-examine adverse witnesses,
- the right to compel the attendance and testimony of witnesses,
- the right to testify on one's own behalf,
- the right to be free from being forced to incriminate oneself,
- the right to be presumed innocent until proven guilty beyond a reasonable doubt, and
- the right to appeal one's conviction.

Courts often use a *Boykin* form to ensure that defendants have been informed of the rights they are waiving. *Boykin* forms, a sample of which appears in Figure 2.8, also provide the added benefit of evidencing the defendant's knowing waiver of these rights.

To satisfy Rule 11's requirement that the court be satisfied that the defendant actually committed the crime charged in order for the court to accept a plea, the defendant must *allocute* to each charge. (In some jurisdictions, the Rule 11 hearing is therefore called an *allocution hearing*.) To allocute, a defendant must provide a "factual basis" for the plea; in other words, the defendant must admit in open court to the conduct central to the criminality of crimes charged.

Rule 11 does not specifically state that a court must ensure a criminal defendant is competent to waive any constitutional rights. But the Supreme Court has held that because pleading guilty involves waiving the numerous rights discussed later, a court may not accept a guilty or *nolo contendere* plea from a defendant who is not mentally competent. *Godinez v. Moran*, 509 U.S. 389 (1993). This determination involves the same considerations as the determination of competency to stand trial, discussed later in this chapter.

Normally, a defendant's lawyer plays a key role in negotiating a plea. But what if a defendant wishes to waive the right to counsel and serve as his or her own attorney? In *Indiana v. Edwards*, 554 U.S. 164 (2008), the Supreme Court held that the U.S. Constitution permits states to insist on representation by counsel for those who are competent enough to stand trial but who still suffer from severe mental illness to the point where they are not competent to conduct trial proceedings by themselves. If, however, the defendant is found competent to waive counsel, the court need not inform the defendant that waiving counsel's assistance in deciding whether to plead guilty risks overlooking

	For Official Use

State of Wisconsin, Plaintiff,
    -vs-

**Plea Questionnaire/
Waiver of Rights**

_____, Defendant   Case No. _____ ☐

Name

I am the defendant and intend to plea as follows:

Charge/Statute	Plea	Charge/Statute	Plea
	☐ Guilty ☐ No Contest		☐ Guilty ☐ No Contest
	☐ Guilty ☐ No Contest		☐ Guilty ☐ No Contest

☐ See attached sheet for additional charges.

I am _____ years old. I have completed _____ years of schooling.

I	☐ do	☐ do not	have a high school diploma, GED, or HSED.
I	☐ do	☐ do not	understand the English language.
I	☐ do	☐ do not	understand the charge(s) to which I am pleading.
I	☐ am not	☐ am	currently receiving treatment for a mental illness or disorder.
I	☐ have not	☐ have	had any alcohol, medications, or drugs within the last 24 hours.

Constitutional Rights

I understand that by entering this plea, I give up the following constitutional rights:

☐ I give up my right to a trial.

☐ I give up my right to remain silent and I understand that my silence could not be used against me at trial.

☐ I give up my right to testify and present evidence at trial.

☐ I give up my right to use subpoenas to require witnesses to come to court and testify for me at trial.

☐ I give up my right to a jury trial, where all 12 jurors would have to agree that I am either guilty or not guilty.

☐ I give up my right to confront in court the people who testify against me and cross-examine them.

☐ I give up my right to make the State prove me guilty beyond a reasonable doubt.

I understand the rights that have been checked and give them up of my own free will.

Understandings

- I understand that the crime(s) to which I am pleading has/have elements that the State would have to prove beyond a reasonable doubt if I had a trial. These elements have been explained to me by my attorney or are as follows: ☐ See Attached sheet.

  _____
  _____

- I understand that the judge is not bound by any plea agreement or recommendations and may impose the maximum penalty. The maximum penalty I face upon conviction is: _____
  _____

- I understand that the judge must impose the mandatory minimum penalty, if any. The mandatory minimum penalty I face upon conviction is: _____
  _____

- I understand that the presumptive minimum penalty, if any, I face upon conviction is: _____
  _____

  The judge can impose a lesser sentence if the judge states appropriate reasons.

This form shall not be modified. It may be supplemented with additional material.

United States District Court

FIGURE 2.8 | Sample *Boykin* Form

Understandings

- I understand that if I am placed on probation and my probation is revoked:
  - if sentence is withheld, the judge could sentence me to the maximum penalty, or
  - if sentence is imposed and stayed, I will be required to serve that sentence.

- I understand that if I am not a citizen of the United States, my plea could result in deportation, the exclusion of admission to this country, or the denial of naturalization under federal law.

- I understand that if I am convicted of any felony, I may not vote in any election until my civil rights are restored.

- I understand that if I am convicted of any felony, it is unlawful for me to possess a firearm.

- I understand that if I am convicted of any violent felony, it is unlawful for me to possess body armor.

- I understand that if I am convicted of a serious child sex offense, I cannot engage in an occupation or participate in a volunteer position that requires me to work or interact primarily and directly with children under the age of 16.

- I understand that if any charges are read-in as part of a plea agreement they have the following effects:
  - Sentencing – although the judge may consider read-in charges when imposing sentence, the maximum penalty will not be increased.
  - Restitution – I may be required to pay restitution on any read-in charges.
  - Future prosecution – the State may not prosecute me for any read-in charges.

- I understand that if the judge accepts my plea, the judge will find me guilty of the crime(s) to which I am pleading based upon the facts in the criminal complaint and/or the preliminary examination and/or as stated in court.

Voluntary Plea

I have decided to enter this plea of my own free will. I have not been threatened or forced to enter this plea. No promises have been made to me other than those contained in the plea agreement. The plea agreement will be stated in court or is as follows: ☐ See Attached.

_____

_____

Defendant's Statement

I have reviewed and understand this entire document and any attachments. I have reviewed it with my attorney (if represented). I have answered all questions truthfully and either I or my attorney have checked the boxes. I am asking the court to accept my plea and find me guilty.

_____   _____
Signature of Defendant   Date

Attorney's Statement

I am the attorney for the defendant. I have discussed this document and any attachments with the defendant. I believe the defendant understands it and the plea agreement. The defendant is making this plea freely, voluntarily, and intelligently. I saw the defendant sign and date this document.

_____   _____
Signature of Attorney   Date

CR-227, 05/04 Plea Questionnaire/Waiver of Rights   Wis. Stats. §971.08
This form shall not be modified. It may be supplemented with additional material.

FIGURE 2.8 | (Continued)

a viable defense and foregoes the opportunity to obtain an independent opinion on the wisdom of pleading guilty. *Iowa v. Tovar*, 541 U.S. 77 (2004). In other words, the defendant who acts as his own counsel proceeds at his own peril and is stuck with the consequences of that decision.

Judicial Approval of Guilty Pleas and *Nolo Contendere* Pleas   Although there are minor variations by jurisdiction, most states follow the same procedures used in the federal system concerning judicial approval of plea agreements. Rule 11(c) gives the trial court judge the discretion to accept or reject a plea agreement. Thus, even though the prosecutor, defense counsel, and the defendant may all agree on a plea, ultimately the court must approve the agreement. If the court finds that the plea agreement is not in the interest of justice, the court may reject it—a rare occurrence.

Pleading Insane   In most but not all U.S. jurisdictions, another plea that a defendant may enter at an arraignment is a plea of *not guilty by reason of insanity* or some variation on it such as "guilty except insane." Such a plea is required if the defendant intends to raise the defense of insanity at trial. A defendant may plead not guilty and not guilty by reason of insanity to the same charge. When a plea of not guilty by reason of insanity is entered, a court usually orders the defendant committed to an appropriate institution for the mentally ill for a comprehensive examination, the results of which are critical to the issue of legal insanity at trial. The specific tests for insanity vary by jurisdiction. Most states and the federal government define insanity using a variation of the test set forth in an English case decided in 1843. *M'Naghten*, 8 Eng. Rep. 718 (H.L. 1843). Under the modified version of the *M'Naghten* test of insanity used today, a person is not responsible for criminal conduct if, at the time of acts constituting the offense, the defendant suffered from a severe mental disease or defect that caused the defendant to be unable to appreciate either the nature and quality of his or her acts or the wrongfulness of his or her acts (Fradella 2007).

The insanity plea is rarely raised. It is almost never pled in a misdemeanor proceeding, and it is only raised in approximately 1 percent of all felony cases. Moreover, when invoked in this small percentage of cases, the insanity defense is successful less than 25 percent of the time (Perlin 1997). Defendants found not guilty by reason of insanity usually face a lengthy postacquittal period of confinement in a secure mental institution. In fact, most states automatically commit someone found not guilty by reason of insanity to a mental hospital for at least a sixty-day period and then place the burden on the person committed to show when he or she is no longer mentally ill and dangerous. This typically results in insanity acquittees spending many more years incarcerated in a mental institution than what they would have served in prison had they been criminally convicted (Morris 1997).

Plea Bargaining

The disposition of criminal charges by agreement between the prosecutor and the accused, sometimes loosely called "plea bargaining," is an essential component of the administration of justice. In fact, between 90 and 95 percent of most criminal cases are resolved through the plea bargaining process (Neubauer & Fradella 2014). Properly administered, it is to be encouraged. If every criminal charge were subjected to a full-scale trial, the states and the federal government would need to multiply by many times the number of judges and court facilities.

Disposition of charges after plea discussions is an essential part of the process and a highly desirable part for many reasons. It leads to prompt and largely final disposition of most criminal cases; it avoids much of the corrosive impact of enforced idleness during pretrial confinement for those who are denied release pending trial; it protects the public from those accused persons who are prone to continue criminal conduct even while on pretrial release; and, by shortening the time between charge and disposition, it enhances whatever may be the rehabilitative prospects of the guilty when they are ultimately imprisoned.

This phase of the process of criminal justice, and the adjudicative element inherent in accepting a plea of guilty, must include safeguards to ensure the defendant what is reasonably due in the circumstances. Thus, defendants have a Sixth Amendment right to the effective assistance of counsel during plea bargaining. *Missouri v. Frye*, 132 S. Ct. 1399 (2012); *Lafler v. Cooper*, 132 S. Ct. 1376 (2012). And when a plea rests in any significant degree on a promise or agreement of the prosecutor such that it can be said to be part of the inducement or consideration, such promise must be fulfilled. *Santobello v. New York*, 404 U.S. 257, 260–62 (1971).

Most states have developed statutes or rules governing the plea bargaining process, just as the federal government has done in Rule 11(c) of the Federal Rules of Criminal Procedure.

In general, plea agreements are treated as contracts. If the defendant breaches the agreement, the prosecution may not only reprosecute the defendant but also bring more serious charges. For example, in *Bordenkircher v. Hayes*, 434 U.S. 357 (1978), the U.S. Supreme Court found no due process violation when the prosecutor carried out a threat made during plea negotiations to reindict the defendant on more serious charges if the defendant did not plead guilty to the original charge. In *Ricketts v. Adamson*, 483 U.S. 1 (1987), the defendant was permitted to plead guilty to second-degree murder in exchange for agreeing to testify against another defendant. When he later refused to do so, the prosecutor was permitted to vacate the plea agreement and prosecute the defendant on first-degree murder charges. The defendant was not protected by double jeopardy because he breached the plea agreement.

Prosecutors must also live up to their ends of a plea bargain. When "a plea rests in any significant degree on a promise or agreement of the prosecutor, so that it can be said to be a part of the inducement or consideration, such promise must be fulfilled." *Santobello v. New York*, 404 U.S. 257 (1971). If the defendant alleges that the prosecution breached a plea agreement and the allegations are not "palpably incredible" or "patently frivolous or false," the defendant is entitled to an evidentiary hearing. *Blackledge v. Allison*, 431 U.S. 63 (1977). If the defendant establishes such a breach, the court may allow the defendant to withdraw the plea, alter the sentence, or require the prosecution to honor the agreement.

Preparing for Trial

Motions A *motion* is an oral or written request asking a court to make a specified finding, decision, or order. Many standard motions are available, but an attorney may also fashion unique motions in response to particular circumstances requiring court action. Some of the most common standard pretrial motions are motion to be admitted to bail, motion to quash a grand jury indictment, motion to inspect grand jury minutes, motion to challenge the sufficiency of the indictment, motion for a competency hearing, motion for discovery, motion for a continuance, motion for change of venue, motion to dismiss an indictment, and motion to withdraw a guilty plea. Most of these motions are discussed elsewhere in this chapter or are primarily of concern to judges and attorneys and, therefore, beyond the scope of this book. Pretrial motions to suppress evidence or a confession are central to criminal procedure law and are discussed in detail later in this chapter.

Depositions A court may order the *deposition* of a witness who is unable to attend a criminal trial and whose testimony is material to a just determination of the case to be taken at any time after the filing of an indictment or information. A deposition involves taking the out-of-court testimony of a witness and preserving that testimony in writing for later use in court. A deposition is used only in exceptional circumstances in criminal cases and not for the mere convenience of a witness or party. Either the prosecution or the defendant may request a deposition, and the opposing party may attend the taking of the deposition. A deposition, or a part of a deposition, may be used at a trial or hearing if it appears that

- the witness who gave the deposition is dead,
- the witness is out of the jurisdiction (unless the party offering the deposition caused the witness's absence),
- the witness is unable to attend or testify because of sickness or infirmity, or
- the party offering the deposition is unable to procure the attendance of the witness by subpoena.

Furthermore, depositions may be used even if the witness does testify at the trial, but only for the purposes of contradicting the witness's testimony. This is known as *impeaching* the witness.

Discovery Discovery is a procedure whereby the defendant and the prosecution are each allowed to inspect, examine, copy, or photograph items in the possession of the other party. The general purpose of discovery is to make the criminal trial "less a game of blindman's bluff and more a fair contest with the basic issues and facts disclosed to the fullest practical extent." *United States v. Procter & Gamble Co.*, 356 U.S. 677, 682 (1958).

Although there is "no general constitutional right to discovery in a criminal case," *Weatherford v. Bursey,* 429 U.S. 545, 559 (1977), a series of court decisions, statutes, and court rules provides the framework for the criminal discovery process. Discovery is governed primarily by the Federal Rules of Criminal Procedure and their state counterparts. Collectively, these rules provide a defendant, upon motion, rights to discovery concerning tangible objects—tape recordings, books, papers, and documents (including written or recorded statements made by the defendants or witnesses) that are relevant to the case; the defendant's prior criminal record, if any; the results or reports of physical examinations, scientific tests, experiments, and forensic comparisons; and summaries of any expert testimony that the government intends to offer in its *case in chief*. The rules often afford the government similar reciprocal discovery on its compliance with the request of the defendant.

Ordinarily, to obtain discoverable evidence, a party must make a timely motion before the court and show that the specific items sought are material to the preparation of its case and that its request is reasonable. Nevertheless, jurisdictions differ considerably with respect to both the conditions under which discovery is allowed and the items subject to discovery. A recent development is automatic informal discovery for certain types of evidence without the necessity for motions and court orders. The state of the law governing discovery is constantly changing, but the trend appears to be in favor of broadening the right of discovery for both the defense and the prosecution.

There is no general constitutional right to discovery in criminal cases. Nonetheless, in order to protect defendants' due process rights, courts have created rules requiring disclosure of evidence in certain situations.

KEY POINTS

LO6
LO7

- Formal pleas to criminal charges are entered at an arraignment. Initial pleas of "not guilty" are changed to "guilty" pleas in upward of 90 percent of all felony prosecutions after a plea bargain is negotiated.

- Discovery is a procedure whereby the defendant and prosecution are both allowed to inspect, examine, copy, or photograph items in the possession of the other party. Although there is no general constitutional right to discovery in criminal cases, due process requires that all exculpatory and impeachment evidence be turned over to the defense.

- Criminal defendants must be competent to stand trial, meaning they must understand the proceedings against them and be able to assist their attorney with their own defense.

- Evidence, which may directly or circumstantially prove a fact in issue, may be testimonial, physical, scientific, or demonstrative. Evidence is introduced to overcome presumptions and allow for inferences to be drawn that might satisfy the burden of persuasion at different stages of a case. Ultimately, it is the prosecution's burden to prove the existence of each and every element of a crime beyond a reasonable doubt.

Exculpatory Evidence Exculpatory evidence is any evidence that may be favorable to the defendant at trial either by tending to cast doubt on the defendant's guilt or by tending to mitigate the defendant's culpability, thereby potentially reducing the defendant's sentence. In *Brady v. Maryland*, 373 U.S. 83, 87 (1963), the U.S. Supreme Court held that "the suppression by the prosecution of evidence favorable to an accused upon request violates due process where the evidence is material either to guilt or punishment, *irrespective of the good faith or bad faith of the prosecution*" (italics added). This is commonly referred to as the *Brady rule*. Exculpatory evidence is material "only if there is a 'reasonable probability' that, had the evidence been disclosed to the defense, the result of the proceeding would have been different. A 'reasonable probability' is a probability sufficient to undermine confidence in the outcome." *United States v. Bagley*, 473 U.S. 667, 682 (1985).

As the Court explained in *Kyles v. Whitley*, 514 U.S. 419, 434 (1995), "[t]he question is not whether the defendant would more likely than not have received a different verdict with the evidence, but whether in its absence he received a fair trial, understood as a trial resulting in a verdict worthy of confidence." *Kyles v. Whitley* required disclosure of exculpatory evidence to the defense even if the police had not revealed the evidence to the prosecutor. According to the Court, prosecutors are responsible for ensuring that police communicate relevant evidence to the prosecutor's office.

The *Brady* rule is limited to admissible evidence. Thus, the prosecution has no obligation to provide the defense potentially exculpatory information that would not be admissible in court. For example, in *Wood v. Bartholomew*, 516 U.S. 1 (1995), the U.S. Supreme Court held that there is no requirement to turn over the results of a polygraph examination of a witness because polygraph results are inadmissible.

Brady does not require the prosecution to make its files available to the defendant for an open-ended "fishing expedition." Nor does *Brady* require the disclosure of inculpatory, neutral, or speculative evidence. However, prosecutors' obligations under *Brady* are not limited to situations in which the defendant specifically requests the evidence. As the "attorney for the sovereign," the prosecutor "must always be faithful to his client's overriding interest that 'justice shall be done.'" *United States v. Agurs*, 427 U.S. 97, 110–11 (1976).

Impeachment Material In *Jencks v. United States*, 353 U.S. 657 (1957), the Supreme Court ruled that the government must disclose any prior inconsistent statements of prosecutorial witnesses so that the defense could conduct a meaningful cross-examination of such witnesses. Congress both expanded and limited the holding in *Jencks* when it enacted the Jencks Act, 18 U.S.C. § 3500. That act requires the prosecutor to disclose, after direct examination of a government witness and on the defendant's motion, any statement of a witness in the government's possession that relates to the subject matter of the witness's testimony. Thus, the Jencks Act requires disclosure of all prior statements of witnesses, even if the prior statements are not inconsistent with any subsequent statement by the witnesses, expanding the holding of *Jencks*. Yet Congress placed the burden on defense counsel to ask for the information (unlike *Brady* material that the prosecutor has an ethical obligation to disclose even if not asked). Congress also limited the time frame for such disclosure such that it need not take place until after the direct examination of a governmental witness by the prosecution.

In *Giglio v. United States*, 405 U.S. 150 (1972), the Supreme Court clarified that all impeachment evidence, even if not a prior statement by a witness, also falls within the *Brady* rule. Thus, *Giglio* mandated that the prosecution disclose any and all information that may be used to impeach the credibility of prosecution witnesses, including law enforcement officers. Impeachment information under *Giglio* includes information such as the prior criminal records or other acts of misconduct of prosecution witnesses, or such information as promises of leniency or immunity offered to prosecution witnesses. *United States v. Henthorn,* 931 F.2d 29 (9th Cir. 1991), held that the government has a duty to examine the personnel files of testifying law enforcement officers for *Brady* or *Giglio* material; for example, information that could compromise the officers' credibility, including past accusations of misconduct.

As with *Brady* material, the mandates of *Jencks* and *Giglio* do not require the prosecution to make its files available to the defendant for an open-ended "fishing expedition."

Subpoenas A *subpoena* is a court order used to secure the attendance of witnesses at a criminal proceeding. A *subpoena duces tecum* production of books, papers, documents, or other objects is the primary vehicle by which a defendant exercises the Sixth Amendment right to "compulsory process for obtaining witnesses in his favor" (see Chapter 1). The subpoena is usually issued by a judicial officer, and it commands the person to whom it is directed to attend a trial, hearing, or deposition for the purpose of testifying at the proceeding or bringing a named document or object. As discussed earlier, the grand jury also has broad subpoena powers. A law enforcement officer or any other adult person who is not a party to the proceedings may serve a subpoena. A typical form for a subpoena in a criminal case appears in Figure 2.9.

Competency to Stand Trial The U.S. system of criminal justice requires that one be competent or "fit" to stand trial before one's guilt or innocence is assessed at a criminal trial. Accordingly, when the fitness of a particular criminal defendant to stand

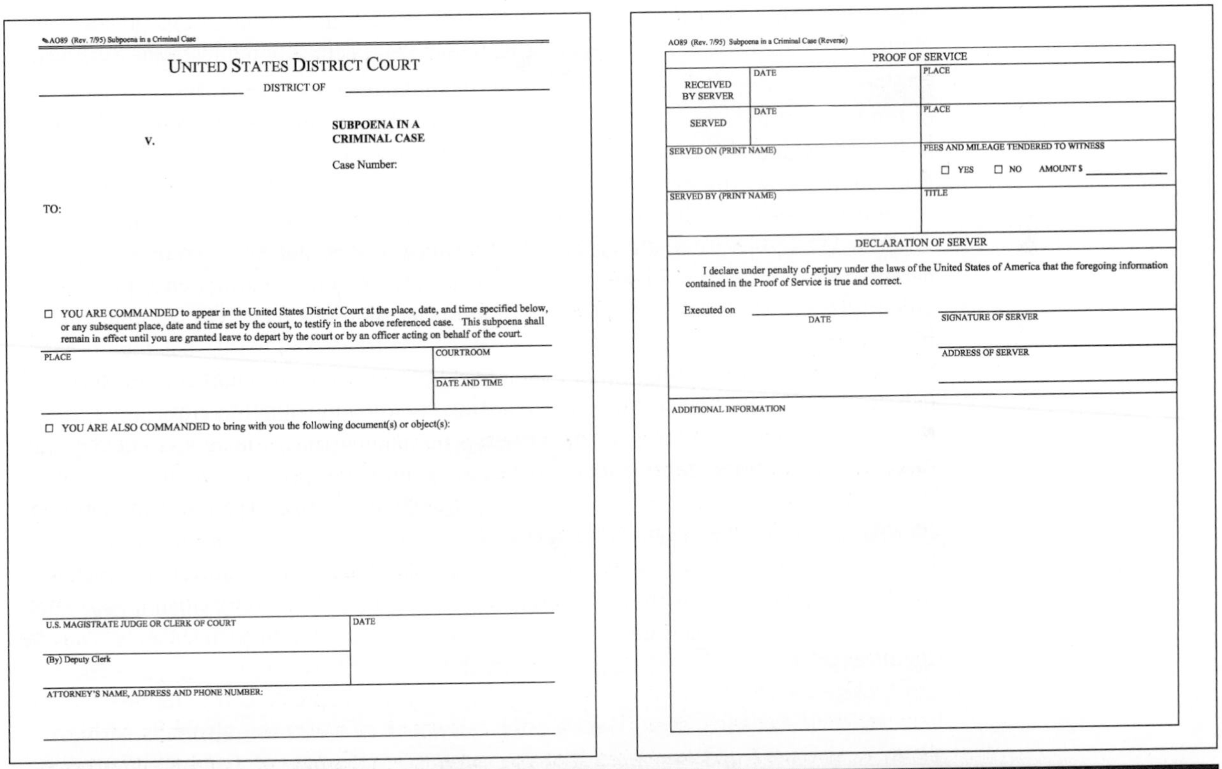

AO89 (Rev. 7/95) Subpoena in a Criminal Case

UNITED STATES DISTRICT COURT

DISTRICT OF

v.

SUBPOENA IN A CRIMINAL CASE

Case Number:

TO:

☐ YOU ARE COMMANDED to appear in the United States District Court at the place, date, and time specified below, or any subsequent place, date and time set by the court, to testify in the above referenced case. This subpoena shall remain in effect until you are granted leave to depart by the court or by an officer acting on behalf of the court.

PLACE	COURTROOM
	DATE AND TIME

☐ YOU ARE ALSO COMMANDED to bring with you the following document(s) or object(s):

U.S. MAGISTRATE JUDGE OR CLERK OF COURT	DATE
(By) Deputy Clerk	

ATTORNEY'S NAME, ADDRESS AND PHONE NUMBER:

AO89 (Rev. 7/95) Subpoena in a Criminal Case (Reverse)

PROOF OF SERVICE

	DATE	PLACE
RECEIVED BY SERVER		
SERVED	DATE	PLACE
SERVED ON (PRINT NAME)		FEES AND MILEAGE TENDERED TO WITNESS ☐ YES ☐ NO AMOUNT $
SERVED BY (PRINT NAME)		TITLE

DECLARATION OF SERVER

I declare under penalty of perjury under the laws of the United States of America that the foregoing information contained in the Proof of Service is true and correct.

Executed on ______ DATE

SIGNATURE OF SERVER

ADDRESS OF SERVER

ADDITIONAL INFORMATION

United States District Court

FIGURE 2.9 | A Sample Subpoena

trial becomes an issue in a case, his or her *competency to stand trial* must be determined before a trial can proceed. Competency to stand trial, however, may be raised at any time in the criminal process, even after conviction. While the issue of competency to stand trial is usually raised by the defense, the prosecution can raise the issue, as can the court on its own.

Due process requires a court to hold a competency hearing if there is bona fide doubt regarding a defendant's competency. "[E]vidence of a defendant's irrational behavior, his demeanor at trial, and any prior medical opinion on competence to stand trial are all relevant in determining whether further inquiry is required." *Drope v. Missouri*, 420 U.S. 162, 180 (1975). Most requests for a clinical determination of competency go unopposed by opposing counsel and are routinely granted by judges. Once granted the opportunity to have such a determination made, the process of determining competency to stand trial involves forensic psychological evaluations followed by an evidentiary hearing on the issue of competency.

At the competency hearing, the prosecution must usually prove that, by a preponderance of the evidence, the defendant is competent to proceed with the criminal trial. *E.g.*, 18 U.S.C. § 4241(d). However, some states have shifted the burden of persuasion to the defense, which must show the incompetency of the defendant by a preponderance of the evidence. The Supreme Court specifically approved of this allocation of the burden of persuasion over a due process challenge in *Medina v. California*, 505 U.S. 437 (1992). The Court, however, struck down laws requiring the defendant to show his or her competence by clear and convincing evidence, finding it to violate the guarantee of due process. *Cooper v. Oklahoma*, 517 U.S. 348, 369 (1996).

The test for determining competency to stand trial was set forth by the Supreme Court in *Dusky v. United States*, 362 U.S. 402, 402 (1960). *Dusky* held that to be competent to stand trial, a defendant must have (1) "a rational as well as factual understanding of the proceedings against him" and (2) "sufficient present ability to consult with his lawyer with a reasonable degree of rational understanding." The first question—can the defendant understand the proceedings against him or her—is not directed at whether the defendant understands the intricacies of the criminal process. Rather, it is concerned with whether the defendant has a basic understanding of the circumstances in which he or she finds him- or herself. More simply, does the defendant understand that he or she has been charged with a crime and faces government-imposed punishment if convicted? The second criterion is whether the defendant is capable of assisting in his or her own defense. If the defendant cannot communicate with his or her attorney in a manner that permits the defense lawyer the ability to formulate a defense, the defendant will likely not be found competent.

Although the determination of competency to stand trial is purely a legal determination—not a clinical one—the importance of the role of evaluating clinicians cannot be overstated. First and foremost, the overwhelming number of competency determinations are based on the clinical assessment of a single clinician. Second, although courts are supposed to hold competency hearings, defendants are frequently determined to be incompetent by a court without an actual hearing. In this case, the prosecution and the defense stipulate that the defendant is not competent if the evaluating clinician's psychological report finds that the defendant is not competent. Even when a hearing is held, judges almost always defer to the findings of mental health professionals. Thus, if a psychologist or psychiatrist determines that a defendant is incompetent, the court is likely to agree.

When a court finds that a defendant is incompetent to stand trial, criminal proceedings against the defendant are suspended until the defendant is found competent. If future competency is highly probable, the defendant may be committed to a mental institution for a reasonable period of time to determine future competency. During this period, the court may order periodic examinations of the defendant to determine whether competency has been regained. After a reasonable period of time, the government must either institute civil commitment proceedings or release the defendant. *Jackson v. Indiana*, 406 U.S. 715 (1972).

A claim that a defendant is incompetent to stand trial is different from a claim that a defendant is not guilty by reason of insanity. The former concerns only the defendant's mental fitness at the time of trial and is unrelated to any determination of guilt. The latter is a defense to prosecution on the ground that the defendant was mentally impaired at the time that an alleged crime was committed.

Evidence and Burdens of Proof

Both at pretrial hearings and at trials (see Chapter 15), the parties—most often the prosecution—need to introduce evidence in order to allow the trier-of-fact to draw inferences that might overcome presumptions established by applicable burden of proof. Several of the terms in the previous sentence require explanation.

- **Evidence** is information or items offered to prove or disprove the existence of a fact either directly or circumstantially, a distinction explored in Table 2.2.

  - *Testimonial evidence* is oral testimony given under oath. Anyone called to give testimony is subject to the requirements of the Sixth Amendment's Confrontation Clause.

  - *Real evidence* (also referred to as *physical evidence*) consists of tangible objects such as contracts, bank statements, or other documentary evidence; firearms; drug paraphernalia; clothing; and traces of objects that may be found at a crime or accident scene, such as fingerprints or trace amounts of drugs.

  - The scientific examination of real evidence, in a laboratory, for example, yields *scientific evidence*—the formal results of forensic investigatory techniques (often in documentary form) such as autopsy reports, firearm matches, and DNA analyses.

TABLE 2.2 | Direct Versus Circumstantial Evidence

Type of Evidence	Definition	Example
Direct evidence	Firsthand evidence that does not require presumptions or inferences in order to establish a proposition of fact.	Eyewitness testimony. One need not draw any inference from a witness's testimony that she saw something. She either saw it or she did not. Thus, direct evidence does not necessarily establish truth; witnesses can be mistaken or misleading. In fact, some commentators consider faulty eyewitness testimony to be the leading cause of wrongful convictions in the United States (see Chapter 13).
Circumstantial evidence	Indirect evidence that requires the trier-of-fact to reason through the circumstantial evidence and infer the existence of some fact in dispute. If circumstantial evidence is believed, it requires additional inferences or presumptions, and it may require the fact finder to examine a chain of evidence in order to accept the fact at issue.	The defendant's behavior around the time of the offense can be powerful circumstantial evidence. For example, if the accused earns little money but bought an expensive car, then that might be circumstantial evidence of the defendant's guilt of a theft-related offense.

- Prosecutors possess great discretion in deciding whether to charge someone and, if so, with what specific crimes so long as they do not exercise this discretion selectively (which would violate equal protection) or vindictively (which would violate due process).

- In federal court and in several states, grand juries review the preliminary evidence in felony cases. They issue an indictment if there is probable cause to require a defendant to stand trial on felony charges. In some states, the defendant may waive grand jury review and opt to have a judge determine probable cause to stand trial on felony charges at a preliminary hearing. For most misdemeanors and for felony prosecutions in select states, a defendant may be formally charged either by the filing of a complaint or an information.

- A person who has been arrested without a warrant is required by statute to be brought before a magistrate for an initial appearance, which typically must occur within forty-eight hours of a warrantless arrest so that a judicial officer may evaluate the legality of the arrest.

- Bail serves as a form of security designed to guarantee that in exchange for being released from custody pending the disposition of criminal charges, the accused promises to return to court as needed. If the defendant appears in court when requested, the security is returned. Although the Eighth Amendment does not guarantee bail, it does mandate that bail not be excessive.

- *Demonstrative evidence* has no evidential value by itself. Rather, it serves as a visual or auditory aid to assist the fact finder in understanding the evidence. Charts, maps, videos, and courtroom demonstrations are forms of demonstrative evidence.

- *Judicial notice* does not involve evidence per se but rather is a process that excuses a party from having to introduce evidence in order to prove something. It is a shortcut that excuses a party from the burden of having to prove certain commonly known facts. For example, a court would take judicial notice of the fact that Halloween falls on October 31 or that Christmas falls on December 25 without the requirement of having a calendar introduced into evidence. This would be appropriate because the dates of these holidays are within the common knowledge of the jury and the community at large. The meaning of certain words and phrases might be another example of something that a court might take judicial notice such as "turning a trick" or "getting a fix."

- A *presumption* is a conclusion or deduction that the law *requires* the trier-of-fact to make in the absence of evidence to the contrary.

- *Inferences* are permissive; they are conclusions or deductions that the trier-of-fact may reasonably make based on the facts that have been established by the evidence, although the trier-of-fact is not required to do so.

- The *burden of proof* is a concept that actually encompasses two separate burdens: the burden of production and the burden of persuasion.

  - If a party has the *burden of production* (often referred to as the *burden of going forward*), it must produce *prima facie* evidence to put facts in issue.

  - The *burden of persuasion* is the obligation of a party to prove a fact to one of the levels presented in Table 2.3 by the time all of the evidence has been produced in court and it is time for the judge or jury to decide the matter at issue. In pretrial hearings, probable cause and preponderance of the evidence are the most common burdens of persuasion, although clear and convincing evidence may be required in select proceedings. At trial, the prosecution always bears the burden in persuading the trier-of-fact that the defendant committed each and every element of all crimes charged. In some circumstances, however, the defendant in a criminal trial bears the burden of persuasion to prove certain defense, such as insanity. When the defendant bears the burden of persuasion to prove a defense, it is called an *affirmative defense*.

At the low end of the scale, there is no proof. Just above that, there is what the law calls *mere suspicion*—a hunch or the feeling of intuition. Although intuitively knowing something is undoubtedly a skill that serves law enforcement officers well, mere suspicion is insufficient proof of any fact in a court of law.

The next level up from mere suspicion is reasonable, articulable suspicion. It differs from mere suspicion only slightly but in an important way. Instead of just having a hunch or an intuitive feeling, a person can articulate the reasons *why* he or she is suspicious. Moreover, the explanations offered as the bases for the suspicion are objectively

TABLE 2.3 | Levels of Proof

0%--50%--100%

No Proof	Mere Suspicion	Articulable Reasonable Suspicion	Probable Cause	Preponderance of the Evidence	Clear and Convincing Evidence	Beyond a Reasonable Doubt	Beyond All Doubt
	A "hunch" that serves law enforcement officers well but is insufficient proof in any stage in the judicial process	Standard established in *Terry v. Ohio* for a "stop and frisk"—a limited investigative detention	Necessary to arrest a person, conduct a search, or seize evidence	Plaintiff's burden in most civil cases; burden for establishing "knowing, intelligent, and voluntary" waivers of most constitutional rights; burden for establishing exceptions to exclusionary rule	Plaintiff's burden in some civil cases; defendant's burden for proving insanity; government's burden to civilly commit a dangerous person	Prosecution's burden to prove each element of a criminal offense	Proof to an absolute certainty not required in any phase of the judicial process in the United States

© 2016 Cengage Learning®

reasonable—clearly understandable to another person who hears the explanations. This level of proof is necessary for law enforcement personnel to conduct a "stop and frisk." These brief, limited, investigative detentions are also known as "*Terry* stops" as a result of the U.S. Supreme Court's landmark decision in *Terry v. Ohio,* 392 U.S. 1 (1968). Details of these types of brief detentions are covered in Chapter 7.

The next highest level of proof is called *probable cause.* Defining probable cause is no easy task. It is differentiated from reasonable, articulable suspicion by the existence of *facts*—independently verifiable factual information that supports the conclusion that there is a "fair probability" that a crime occurred or that a particular person was involved in a crime. Probable cause is covered in greater detail in Chapter 3 and revisited in particular criminal procedural contexts throughout the text.

In most civil cases, the standard of proof is a preponderance of the evidence. It is commonly understood as proof that something is more likely than not. Thus, if the plaintiff is able to show the probability is more than 50 percent that the defendant did what is claimed, the judgment will be for the plaintiff. It is also the standard of proof used to establish the validity of waivers of constitutional rights, as well as the burden for proving that exceptions to the exclusionary rule apply (see Chapter 3).

Clear and convincing evidence is a higher level of proof than the preponderance of the evidence standard, yet it falls short of proof beyond a reasonable doubt. It is the standard of proof in some civil cases. It is also the level of proof to which a defendant in some criminal cases must establish an affirmative defense. If there is clear and convincing evidence, the trier-of-fact should be reasonably satisfied as to the existence of the fact, yet he or she may have some doubts.

Because the accused is presumed innocent, the prosecution has the burden to prove all the elements of the crime(s) charged in its case beyond a reasonable doubt. If the prosecution fails to meet this burden of proof on any element, the defendant must be acquitted. *In re Winship,* 397 U.S. 358 (1970). *Reasonable doubt* is a term requiring little interpretation, although various courts have attempted to formulate somewhat involved definitions that add little beyond its plain meaning. A specific definition for the "beyond a reasonable doubt" standard has not been adopted by the U.S. Supreme Court, leading to some confusion among jurists and jurors alike. In fact, jury instructions explaining reasonable doubt are often the basis for appeal. It is sufficient to say that proof beyond a reasonable doubt requires that the guilt of the defendant be established to a reasonable, but not absolute or mathematical, certainty. Probability of guilt is not enough. In other words, to satisfy the beyond a reasonable doubt standard, the jury must be satisfied that the charges against the defendant are almost certainly true. A challenged definition of beyond a reasonable doubt that was upheld by the U.S. Supreme Court reads as follows: *"A reasonable doubt is an actual and substantial doubt arising from the evidence, from the facts or circumstances shown by the evidence, or from the lack of evidence."* *Victor v. Nebraska,* 511 U.S. 1 (1994). Keep in mind that reasonable doubt is an inherently qualitative concept; it cannot be quantified, and any attempt to do so for a jury is likely to result in reversible error. *McCullough v. State,* 657 P.2d 1157 (Nev. 1983).

Motions to Suppress Evidence and the Exclusionary Rule

A **motion to suppress** is made by defendants who believe they are aggrieved by either an unlawful search and seizure or an unlawfully obtained admission or confession. The purpose of a motion to suppress is twofold:

- To enable the defendant to invoke the exclusionary rule and prevent the use of illegally obtained evidence at trial
- To enable the court to resolve the issue of the legality of a search and seizure or confession without interrupting the trial

The hearing on a motion to suppress is often the point in the proceedings at which the court carefully scrutinizes a law enforcement officer's performance in a case. If a defendant is able to prove that an officer illegally obtained evidence, and if the evidence is essential to the prosecution's case, then suppression of the evidence may result in a dismissal of charges or the granting of a motion for judgment of acquittal. Therefore, law enforcement officers must know the law not only when they conduct a search and seizure or obtain a confession but also when they are called on to justify their actions at a hearing on a motion to suppress.

The **exclusionary rule** requires that any evidence obtained by police using methods that violate a person's Fourth, Fifth, or Sixth Amendment rights must be excluded from use in a criminal prosecution against that person. This rule is judicially imposed and arose relatively recently in the development of the U.S. legal system. Under the common law, the seizure of evidence by illegal means did not affect its admissibility in court. The exclusionary rule changed that. It was first developed in 1914 in the case of *Weeks v. United States,* 232 U.S. 383, and was limited to a prohibition on the use of evidence illegally obtained by *federal* law enforcement officers. Not until the case of *Wolf v. Colorado,* 38 U.S. 25 (1949), did the U.S. Supreme Court take the first step toward applying the exclusionary rule to the states by ruling that the Fourth Amendment was applicable to the states through the due process clause of the Fourteenth Amendment.

Wolf, however, left enforcement of Fourth Amendment rights to the discretion of the individual states and did not specifically require application of the exclusionary rule. That mandate did not come until the landmark decision of *Mapp v. Ohio,* 367 U.S. 643 (1961). With *Mapp,* the exclusionary rule became the principal method to deter Fourth Amendment violations. Other methods do exist, however, as explained later in this chapter.

The U.S. Supreme Court has invoked the exclusionary rule to protect certain "due process of law" rights that are not specifically contained in the Constitution. For example, a confession that has been coerced and is therefore involuntary is excluded from evidence because it is a violation of due process of law (see Chapter 13). Similarly, pretrial identification procedures that are not administered fairly, such as an unnecessarily suggestive police lineup, may be violations of due process of law and therefore excludable from evidence at trial (see Chapter 14).

The Exclusionary Rule Requires State Action

The exclusionary rule was designed to deter police misconduct. Generally speaking, it does not apply to evidence obtained by private citizens because it would usually have no deterrent effect. Most private citizens are unfamiliar with constitutional rules such as those governing search and seizure, have no reason to learn them, and would not be disciplined for violating them. *Burdeau v. McDowell,* 256 U.S. 465 (1921). If, however, police encourage, order, or join in an illegal search by a private citizen, then the private citizen is considered an agent of the government and any evidence obtained by the citizen would be subject to exclusion. *Corngold v. United States,* 367 F.2d 1 (9th Cir. 1966); *Machlan v. State,* 225 N.E.2d 762 (1967). Evidence gathered by a private citizen acting in conjunction with or on the orders of a government official is subject to the exclusionary rule, just as if it had been gathered by a governmental official. In such a case, the private citizen is considered to be an agent or instrument of the government. *Coolidge v. New Hampshire,* 403 U.S. 443 (1971); *United States v. Lambert,* 771 F.2d 83, 89 (6th Cir. 1985). Also, evidence gathered by governmental actors who are not police officers, which includes many types of government inspectors and even public school teachers, may also be subject to the exclusionary rule. *See, e.g., New Jersey v. T.L.O.,* 469 U.S. 325 (1985).

Federal–State Conflicts on the Exclusionary Rule

Individual states do not need to follow all interpretations of the U.S. Supreme Court in the area of criminal procedure. Rather, the states must only abide by what the Supreme Court sets as minimum thresholds for constitutional guarantees.

> The States are not . . . precluded from developing workable rules governing arrests, searches and seizures to meet "the practical demands of effective criminal investigation and law enforcement" in the States, *provided that those rules do not violate the [federal] constitutional proscription of unreasonable searches and seizures and the concomitant command that evidence so seized is inadmissible against one who has standing to complain.* Ker v. California, 374 U.S. 23, 34 (1963) (italics added).

Thus, when a state court is faced with a decision of whether or not a particular search or seizure is constitutional, it must apply standards *at least equal* to those on the federal level in determining whether the search or seizure is constitutional. However, if the state's own constitutional or statutory standards are more demanding than those in the federal system, then the state may apply its own standards, affording the accused greater protections than required by the U.S. Constitution. This practice is sometimes referred to as the "new federalism." It is derived from the well-established rule that state court decisions based on "adequate and independent state grounds" are immune from federal review. *Murdock v. Memphis,* 87 U.S. (20 Wall.) 590 (1874); *Herb v. Pitcairn,* 324 U.S. 117 (1945). Under this rule, state courts are free (as a matter of state constitutional, statutory, or case law) to expand individual rights by imposing greater restrictions on police than those imposed under federal constitutional law. State courts may not, however, decrease individual rights below the level established by the U.S. Constitution. Nor may state courts impose greater restrictions on police activity as a matter of federal constitutional law when the U.S. Supreme Court specifically refrains from imposing such restrictions. *Oregon v. Hass,* 420 U.S. 714 (1975).

A state court may respond in various ways to a U.S. Supreme Court decision that raises issues of federal constitutional law. For example, it may choose to do the following:

- Apply the ruling as it thinks the Supreme Court would. This might include adopting the ruling, or holding of the Court, as a matter of state law.

- Avoid applying the holding of the Supreme Court by factually distinguishing the case before it from the Supreme Court case. Such a decision, however, may be subject to reversal by the Supreme Court.

- Reject the Supreme Court ruling on adequate and independent state grounds by interpreting the state constitution or state statutes to provide additional rights unavailable under the U.S. Constitution as interpreted by the Supreme Court. This approach clearly expresses disapproval of the Supreme Court ruling and insulates the state court decision from Supreme Court review. When a state court opinion is ambiguous as to whether it is based on an adequate and independent ground, the Supreme Court applies the so-called plain statement rule:

> [W]hen . . . a state court decision fairly appears to rest primarily on federal law, or to be interwoven with the federal law, and when the adequacy and independence of any possible state law ground is not clear from the face of the opinion, we will accept as the most reasonable explanation that the state court decided the case the way it did because it believed that federal law required it to do so. If a state court chooses merely to rely on federal precedents as it would on the precedents of all other jurisdictions, then it need only make clear by a plain statement in its judgment or opinion that the federal cases are being used only for the purpose of guidance, and do not themselves compel the result that the court has reached. If the state court decision indicates clearly and expressly that it is alternatively based on bona fide separate, adequate, and independent grounds, we, of course, will not undertake to review the decision. *Michigan v. Long,* 463 U.S. 1032, 1040–41 (1983).

In recent years, several state courts have reacted to the U.S. Supreme Court's reluctant approach to protecting the rights of the accused by resorting to this option to keep alive the due process revolution (Chapter 1) and its commitment to the protection and expansion of individual rights.

Criticism of the Exclusionary Rule

The exclusionary rule has, throughout its existence, been the target of criticism and attempted reform. One such criticism is that individual police officers are not personally impacted by the exclusion of evidence they obtained unconstitutionally. In fact, Warren Burger, the former chief justice of the U.S. Supreme Court, offered this criticism in his dissent opinion in the case of *Bivens v. Six Unknown Named Agents of the Federal Bureau of Narcotics,* 403 U.S. 388 (1971):

The rule does not apply any direct sanction to the individual official whose illegal conduct results in the exclusion of evidence in a criminal trial. With rare exceptions law enforcement agencies do not impose direct sanctions on the individual officer responsible for a particular judicial application of the suppression doctrine. . . . Thus there is virtually nothing done to bring about a change in his practices. The immediate sanction triggered by application of the rule is visited upon the prosecutor whose case against a criminal is either weakened or destroyed. The doctrine deprives the police in no real sense. 403 U.S. at 416.

Burger went on to explain that prosecutors, though most directly affected by the exclusionary rule, cannot themselves exact any punishment on individual police officers whose behavior directly leads to the exclusion of evidence. Specifically, Burger argued the following:

The suppression doctrine vaguely assumes that law enforcement is a monolithic governmental enterprise. . . . But the prosecutor who loses his case because of police misconduct is not an official in the police department; he can rarely set in motion any corrective action or administrative penalties. Moreover, he does not have control or direction over police procedures or police actions that lead to the exclusion of evidence. 403 U.S. at 416–17.

In addition, Burger argued that any educational effect the exclusionary rule might offer for police officers is substantially lessened by both the everyday practicalities of police work and the passage of time between a particular police action and a legal case:

Whatever educational effect the rule conceivably might have in theory is greatly diminished in fact by the realities of law enforcement work. Policemen do not have the time, inclination, or training to read and grasp the nuances of the appellate opinions that ultimately define the standards of conduct they are to follow. The issues that these decisions resolve often admit of neither easy nor obvious answers, as sharply divided courts on what is or is not "reasonable" demonstrate. Nor can judges, in all candor, forget that opinions sometimes lack helpful clarity. The presumed educational effect of judicial opinions is also reduced by the long time lapse—often several years—between the original police action and its final judicial evaluation. Given a policeman's pressing responsibilities, it would be surprising if he ever becomes aware of the final result after such a delay. 403 U.S. at 417.

Finally, on a related note, Burger questioned the overall ability of the exclusionary rule to deter police misconduct given the fact that criminal prosecutions do not necessarily arise after a particular instance of misconduct. In particular, Burger pointed out that "there are large areas of police activity that do not result in criminal prosecutions—hence the rule has virtually no applicability and no effect in such situations." 403 U.S. at 418.

Another significant criticism of the exclusionary rule is that it allows factually guilty individuals to be set free. Note, however, that the exclusionary rule does not necessarily bar or stop a prosecution. At most, it renders inadmissible evidence obtained as the result of a constitutional violation. If that evidence is essential to the prosecution's case against a defendant, however, the prosecution may decide that it is futile to continue the prosecution. On the other hand, if the prosecution has sufficient other legally obtained evidence, the prosecution may go forward despite the illegal police conduct.

Criticism and attempts at reform of the exclusionary rule have resulted in numerous limitations on the application of the rule and refusals to further extend the rule beyond the criminal trial context. Consider the following examples:

- *United States v. Calandra,* 414 U.S. 338 (1974), held that the Fourth Amendment did not prevent the use of illegally obtained evidence by a grand jury. In other words, illegally obtained evidence may serve as the basis for a grand jury's determination that probable cause exists to make someone stand trial for a felony offense even if that evidence cannot be introduced at the trial.

- *United States v. Janis,* 428 U.S. 433 (1976), held that illegally obtained evidence need not be excluded at certain civil trials brought by the United States. The Court reasoned that excluding evidence in the particular civil trial at issue in *Janis*— a federal tax proceeding—would not advance the deterrence purpose of the exclusionary rule. According to the Court, police officers would not be deterred from conducting an illegal search or seizure by applying the exclusionary rule to federal tax proceedings because these proceedings do not fall within the primary interest or focus of a typical police officer's work.

- *Immigration and Naturalization Service v. Lopez-Mendoza,* 468 U.S. 1032 (1984), refused to apply the exclusionary rule in a civil deportation hearing after immigration officers had obtained incriminating statements following an apparently illegal arrest.

- *Pennsylvania Board of Probation and Parole v. Scott,* 524 U.S. 357, 364 (1998), held that "the federal exclusionary rule does not bar the introduction at parole revocation hearings of evidence seized in violation of parolees' Fourth Amendment rights."

- *Harris v. New York,* 401 U.S. 222 (1971), allowed the use of evidence obtained in violation of the *Miranda* warnings to impeach the defendant's testimony at trial. Thus, after *Harris,* confessions and other incriminating statements obtained in violation of Miranda will not be excluded at trial if the prosecutor uses those statements to impeach the defendant's credibility or trustworthiness. Those statements, however, will still be excluded if the prosecutor attempts to use them to prove the defendant's guilt. *Kansas v. Ventris,* 556 U.S. 586 (2009), extended *Harris* to allow statements by the defendant obtained in violation of the Sixth Amendment right to counsel to be used to impeach a defendant's testimony. (See Chapter 13 for more information on interrogations.)

- *Stone v. Powell,* 428 U.S. 465 (1976), held that the exclusionary rule did not apply to a *habeas corpus* proceeding in which the prisoner attempts to prove the illegality of his or her detention. *Stone v. Powell* essentially eliminated federal review through *habeas corpus* claims of state court decisions concerning the Fourth Amendment. In particular, the Court held that "where the State has provided an opportunity for full and fair litigation of a Fourth Amendment claim, a state prisoner may not be granted federal *habeas corpus* relief on the ground that evidence obtained in an unconstitutional search or seizure was introduced at his trial." 428 U.S. at 494. *Stone v. Powell* is noteworthy not only because it limited the application of the exclusionary rule but also because it strengthened the authority of state courts in interpreting the Fourth Amendment.

- *Hudson v. Michigan,* 547 U.S. 586 (2006), held that the exclusionary rule does not apply to evidence seized in a home after police officers fail to knock on the owner's door and announce their presence as required under the Fourth Amendment. Furthermore, the *Hudson* case is significant because Justice Scalia's majority opinion casts doubt more generally on the overall efficacy of the exclusionary rule. Scalia explains that because of certain changes since the Court's decision in *Mapp v. Ohio*, other remedies for Fourth Amendment violations by police may be able to replace the exclusionary rule. Scalia mentions civil rights lawsuits and internal police discipline as examples of other potential remedies. (See Chapter 4 for more information on the knock-and-announce rule.)

■ Several decisions of U.S. Circuit Courts of Appeal have held that sentencing decisions may be based on consideration of illegally obtained evidenced that was suppressed from admission at trial. *United States v. Stark,* 499 F.3d 72 (1st Cir. 2007); *United States v. Skilling,* 554 F.3d 529 (5th Cir. 2009).

■ *Herring v. United States,* 555 U.S. 135 (2009), held that the exclusionary rule does not apply to errors stemming from police negligence in maintaining warrant databases absent a showing of systemic errors that lead to reckless disregard of constitutional requirements. (See the Discussion Point on page 76.)

Despite the limitations on the application of the exclusionary rule by Supreme Court decisions, the Court's basic holding in *Mapp v. Ohio* remains good law, and the basic tenets of the exclusionary rule remain valid legal doctrine. Further limitations or expansions on the exclusionary rule will depend largely on the makeup of the Supreme Court and the opportunities presented to the Court in the cases brought before it.

Alternatives to the Exclusionary Rule

Theoretically, there are several alternatives to the exclusionary rule. Might these alternatives deter police misconduct without resulting in the prosecution's inability to use illegally obtained evidence in their case-in-chief at trial?

Criminalize Certain Conduct Conducting an illegal search and seizure could be designated as a crime. Under such an approach, an officer performing an illegal search or seizure could be criminally prosecuted. However, examples of officers being prosecuted in state courts for overzealous law enforcement are extremely rare due to strict state requirements regarding legal proof and broad legal defenses. An officer may also be liable criminally under 18 U.S.C. § 242, a federal statute making an officer who, under color of state law, willfully deprives a person of his federal constitutional rights, subject to fines and imprisonment. This statute, however, has not often been applied against officers by state prosecutors. In addition, on the federal level, though a law enforcement officer may also be sued criminally under various statutes, few prosecutions against officers have actually occurred.

Job-Related Discipline An officer who makes an illegal search and seizure may also be subject to internal departmental disciplinary procedures resulting from a formal complaint brought by a citizen. Examples of meaningful and effective disciplinary actions against officers stemming from citizen complaints, however, are exceedingly rare. Internal police disciplinary procedures are sometimes reinforced through the findings of independent police review boards, which consist of citizens who hear complaints against officers and who can recommend disciplinary action against them. Findings of police misconduct by these review boards have not generally led to the successful discipline of police officers (Whitebread & Slobogin 2000: 64–65).

Civil Lawsuits Victims of unconstitutional actions by police officers may also bring civil lawsuits against offending officers for monetary damages. For example, persons who have been illegally arrested or have had their privacy invaded in an illegal search by a state or local law enforcement officer (e.g., officers employed by a municipality or county) may sue the offending officer in a tort action available under state statute or common law. Moreover, state or local law enforcement officers acting under color of state law who violate Fourth Amendment or other federal constitutional rights are subject to a suit for damages and other remedies in federal courts under a federal civil rights statute: 42 U.S.C. § 1983. Officers sued under Section 1983, however, may claim qualified immunity if they acted reasonably under existing law. This immunity may prevent a Section 1983 action against many local law enforcement officers. Also, under Section 1983, individuals deprived of their federal constitutional rights by local officers may, in certain circumstances, sue the corresponding local government entity (e.g., the municipality or county). *See Monell v. Dept. of Soc. Servs. of N.Y.*, 436 U.S. 658 (1978).

Lawsuits under Section 1983 have become much more prevalent in recent times, because the Supreme Court has clarified provisions of that section and provided a mechanism by which plaintiffs can recover significant legal costs if they prevail. Moreover, there are no limits on money damages in Section 1983 suits, making these actions more popular than tort actions under state laws, which usually place limits on liability and can also be subject to claims of immunity. However, Congress placed limits on inmates' ability to file Section 1983 lawsuits when it enacted the Prison Litigation Reform Act of 1996. And, as explored in the next Discussion Point, the Supreme Court's decision in *Connick v. Thompson*, 131 S. Ct. 1350 (2011), also placed limits on the ability to use Section 1983 lawsuits as a means of deterring misconduct by justice professionals.

DISCUSSION POINT

Should Money Be Paid for Official Misconduct?
Connick v. Thompson, 131 S. Ct. 1350 (2011).

John Thompson was prosecuted by the Orleans Parish, Louisiana District Attorney's Office for attempted armed robbery in 1985. Prosecutors failed to disclose exculpatory evidence that should have been turned over to the defense under *Brady v. Maryland*. Specifically, they withheld the results of crime lab tests performed on a swatch from one of the victim's pants that

had been stained with the robber's blood. Thompson was convicted. A few weeks later, he was tried for murder. He chose not to testify because of his armed robbery conviction. He was convicted and sentenced to death. In 1999, Thompson's private investigator discovered the crime lab report from the armed robbery investigation in the files of the New Orleans Police Crime Laboratory. Thompson was tested and found to have blood type O, proving that the blood on the swatch was not his. His execution was stayed, and his conviction for the robbery was vacated. His murder conviction was then reversed on the ground that the robbery conviction unconstitutionally deprived Thompson of his right to testify in his own defense at the murder trial.

Thompson sued the district attorney and several members of his office alleging that their *Brady* violation caused him to be wrongfully convicted, incarcerated for 18 years, and nearly executed. A jury awarded Thompson $14 million in damages, finding the district attorney's office liable for failing to train its prosecutors properly to comply with *Brady*. The Supreme Court ultimately ruled that Thompson was not entitled to any compensation because, without a pattern of evidence of *Brady* violations, Thompson had not proved that the district attorney's office had

been deliberately indifferent to the need to train the prosecutors about their *Brady* disclosure obligations.

■ Do you agree with the outcome in the case? Why or why not?

■ *Connick v. Thompson* is unusual in that prosecutors are normally immune from Section 1983 lawsuits for their actions in prosecuting criminal cases. This case, however, was premised on *Monell*'s holding that local governments and their entities may be held liable when they have an official municipal policy that violates constitutional rights or when municipalities fail to properly train certain employees about their legal duty to avoid violating citizens' rights. The specifics of the case aside, though, do you think that civil suits resulting in money damages are a good method to punish misbehaving police officers for constitutional violations? How about to punish municipalities that fail to train their officers and prosecutors correctly?

■ What about using criminal lawsuits against misbehaving officers that may result in possible jail time? If so, do you think the same standard should apply to prosecutors? Why or why not?

Federal officers and others acting under color of federal law are not subject to Section 1983, though they may be liable for constitutional violations in other types of civil actions known as "Bivens" actions. *Bivens v. Six Unknown Named Agents of the Federal Bureau of Narcotics*, 403 U.S. 388, 397 (1971), held that a plaintiff who sued federal narcotics agents "is entitled to recover money damages for any injuries he has suffered as a result of the agents' violation of the [Fourth] Amendment." In a *Bivens* action, which is essentially a civil action for monetary damages against federal officers for constitutional violations, absolute or qualified immunity may apply. For example, federal law enforcement officers are entitled to qualified immunity if, measured objectively, they acted reasonably, or in "good faith," under existing law. In the Fourth Amendment context, officers may be entitled to qualified immunity if they can establish that a reasonable officer could have believed that his or her conduct comported with the Fourth Amendment, even though it actually did not. As stated in *Anderson v. Creighton*, 483 U.S. 635, 639 (1987), "whether an official protected by qualified immunity may be held personally liable for an allegedly unlawful official action generally turns on the 'objective legal reasonableness' of the action assessed in light of the legal rules that were 'clearly established' at the time it was taken." Besides the legal problem of immunity, other practical problems stand in the way of a truly effective civil damage remedy. For example, potential plaintiffs are often disreputable people toward whom juries are unsympathetic, or they are indigent or imprisoned and cannot afford to bring suit.

Individuals who suffer a Fourth Amendment or other constitutional violation at the hands of federal law enforcement officers may also be able to sue the U.S. government in a Federal Torts Claim Act (FTCA) action under 28 U.S.C. Section 1346(b) and 28 U.S.C. Section 2680(h). This avenue can be especially helpful to plaintiffs given the vast financial resources (or "deep pockets") of the federal government.

Though civil lawsuits and other remedies for constitutional violations may provide some relief to potential plaintiffs, many scholars believe the exclusionary rule should still remain the principal deterrent against police misconduct. This is because successful civil lawsuits against officers as well as meaningful internal police discipline are both rare occurrences. In particular, officers may be immune from civil suits or damages associated with these suits may be too small for a suit to be brought by an attorney in the first place. In the case of police discipline, police officers will obviously be reluctant to impose punishment on a fellow officer. Even when they do, the punishment may not be significant enough to have an effect on the misbehaving officer.

Fruit of the Poisonous Tree Doctrine

The exclusionary rule is not limited to evidence that is the direct product of illegal police behavior, such as a coerced confession or items seized during an illegal search. The rule also requires exclusion of evidence *indirectly* obtained as a result of a constitutional violation. This type of evidence is sometimes called derivative evidence or *secondary evidence*. In *Silverthorne Lumber Co. v. United States*, 251 U.S. 385 (1920), the U.S. Supreme Court invalidated a subpoena issued on the basis of information obtained through an illegal search and, in the process, overturned the contempt conviction for failure to obey this subpoena. The Court reasoned as follows:

> The essence of a provision forbidding the acquisition of evidence in a certain way is that not merely evidence so acquired shall not be used before the Court but that it shall not be used at all [e.g., to support a subpoena]. Of course this does not mean that the facts thus obtained [through an illegality] become sacred and inaccessible. If knowledge of them is gained from an independent source they may be proved like any others, but the knowledge gained by the Government's own wrong cannot be used by it in the way proposed. 251 U.S. at 392.

Thus, the prosecution may not use in court evidence obtained directly *or indirectly* from a constitutional violation, such as the illegal search in *Silverthorne*. The prohibition against using this derivative, or secondary, evidence is often called the **fruit of the poisonous tree doctrine**, the "tree" being the initial constitutional violation and the "fruit" being the evidence obtained as a direct or indirect result of that violation.

Although the fruit of the poisonous tree doctrine was originally developed in applying the exclusionary rule to unconstitutional searches, it has been applied equally to evidence obtained as the indirect result of other constitutional violations. Thus, evidence is inadmissible if it is acquired directly or indirectly as a result of an illegal stop, illegal arrest, illegal identification procedure, or involuntary confession. In this way, the fruit of the poisonous tree doctrine may lead to the exclusion of additional evidence beyond the evidence obtained during the initial constitutional violation.

The fruit of the poisonous tree doctrine applies only when a person's *constitutional* rights have been violated. Nevertheless, the doctrine may apply in different ways, depending on the type and severity of the underlying constitutional violation. As the U.S. Supreme Court stated, "unreasonable searches under the Fourth Amendment are different from unwarned interrogation under the Fifth Amendment." *Dickerson v. United States*, 530 U.S. 428, 441 (2000). Indeed, a failure to give *Miranda* warnings before a suspect's confession may not trigger fruit of the poisonous tree analysis as to future incriminating statements by that same suspect. (See the discussion of *Oregon v. Elstad* in Chapter 13.)

Exceptions to the Fruit of the Poisonous Tree Doctrine

Courts loathe excluding derivative evidence under the fruit of the poisonous tree doctrine. Accordingly, the courts have developed several doctrines, summarized in Table 2.4, that mitigate the harsh effects of preventing the use of both illegally obtained evidence and the fruits derived from the illegality.

Independent Source The **independent source doctrine** allows the admission of tainted evidence if that evidence was also obtained through a source wholly independent of the primary constitutional violation (e.g., when evidence was obtained by a source other than the police). In other words, when there is a legal, independent source for the evidence the prosecutor seeks to use at trial, little or no deterrent value is gained by applying the exclusionary rule to that evidence. *Nix v. Williams,* 467 U.S. 431 (1984).

Segura v. United States, 468 U.S. 796 (1984), summarized in Table 2.4, provides an example of how the independent source doctrine applies. *Segura* was extended *in Murray v. United States,* 487 U.S. 533 (1988). Federal agents made an unlawful search of a warehouse they suspected contained marijuana and discovered the drug. They then obtained a warrant to search the warehouse without revealing the unlawful search to the issuing magistrate. In executing this warrant, the police unsurprisingly found the marijuana again. The Supreme Court found that if the police and prosecutor could prove that there was an independent source for the warrant apart from the initial unlawful search, then the same marijuana discovered during the second search would be admissible at trial. As a result of the *Murray* decision, evidence initially found during an illegal, warrantless entry by police may now be admissible if the prosecutor can show that the officers' subsequent discovery with a warrant of this very same evidence is based on a source independent of the illegal entry.

Attenuation Under the **attenuation doctrine**, evidence obtained as the result of a constitutional violation is admissible if the means of obtaining the evidence is sufficiently remote from and distinguishable from the primary illegality. The key question

TABLE 2.4 | Exceptions to the Fruit of the Poisonous Tree Doctrine

Exception	Key Cases	Effect	Example
Independent source	*Nix v. Williams* (1984); *Segura v. United States* (1984).	Evidence that is tainted by a Fourth Amendment violation is admissible if it is also obtained from an independent source—a source that had nothing to do with the underlying constitutional violation.	In *Segura,* police illegally entered an apartment and remained inside for nearly nineteen hours until a search warrant arrived. Even though the entry was illegal, the evidence collected during the search was admissible because the warrant was supported by probable cause established by information independent from the illegal entry.
Attenuation	*Nardone v. United States* (1939); *Won Sun v. United States* (1963); *United States v. Ceccolini* (1978).	If evidence is obtained in a manner that is so far removed from a constitutional violation such that the initial illegality is sufficiently attenuated (meaning weakened), then the evidence is admissible.	In *Ceccolini,* police conducted an illegal search that led them to discover a key witness. That witness was allowed to testify at trial in spite of the illegal entry because the witness's voluntary cooperation with the police sufficiently attenuated the original violation from the testimonial evidence.
Inevitable discovery	*Murray v. United States* (1988); *State v. Miller* (Or. 1984).	Allows illegally obtained evidence to be admitted if it would have inevitably been discovered by lawful means.	In *Miller,* police violated a defendant's *Miranda* rights and got him to confess that he had "hurt someone" in his hotel room. During a warrantless search of the room, a dead body was found. The court ruled that the body would have inevitably been discovered by a hotel maid, so evidence from the room (including the body) was admissible in spite of the *Miranda* violation and the warrantless search of the room.
Good faith	*United States v. Leon* (1984); *Arizona v. Evans* (1995); *Herring v. United States* (2009).	If a police officer acts in good-faith reliance on a warrant that she or he reasonably believes to be valid but later is determined to be invalid, the officer's good faith should allow the evidence to be admissible. There is no police misconduct to be deterred when an officer does not know that she or he is doing anything wrong.	In *Evans,* police lawfully stopped a motor vehicle and found that there was an outstanding arrest warrant for the driver. The officer therefore arrested the driver and searched the vehicle, finding marijuana. The warrant, however, had been dismissed. Thus, the arrest was invalid. However, because the officer acted in good-faith reliance on a warrant believed to be valid, the search of the vehicle was upheld.

© Cengage Learning®

is "whether granting establishment of the primary illegality, the evidence to which instant objection is made has been come at by exploitation of that illegality or instead by means sufficiently distinguishable to be purged of the primary taint." *Wong Sun v. United States*, 371 U.S. 471, 488 (1963). If evidence is obtained in a way that is not sufficiently connected to the primary illegality, then the causal connection between the primary illegality and the evidence is said to be *attenuated* (or weakened), and the evidence is admissible. The rationale behind this exception to the exclusionary rule is this: the deterrent purpose of the rule is not served when officers could not have been aware of the possible benefit to be derived from their illegal actions at the time they took those actions.

In *Wong Sun*, narcotics agents illegally broke into Toy's laundry and followed Toy into his living quarters, where they arrested and handcuffed him. Almost immediately after that, Toy told the agents that Yee had been selling narcotics and that he (Toy) used the drug at Yee's home. The agents then seized heroin from Yee, who told them that it had been brought to him by Toy and Wong Sun. Wong Sun was illegally arrested, arraigned, and released on his own recognizance. Several days later, Wong Sun returned voluntarily and confessed to a narcotics agent. Toy claimed that his statement and the heroin later seized from Yee were fruit of the illegal entry into his dwelling and his illegal arrest. The Court agreed and held both inadmissible against Toy. In particular, as to the statement, the Court said that it was not "sufficiently an act of free will to purge the primary taint of the unlawful invasion." 371 U.S. at 416, 417. Wong Sun claimed that his statement was the fruit of his illegal arrest. The Court disagreed:

> We have no occasion to disagree with the finding of the Court of Appeals that his arrest, also, was without probable cause or reasonable grounds. At all events no evidentiary consequences turn upon that question. For Wong Sun's unsigned confession was not the fruit of that arrest, and was therefore properly admitted at trial. On the evidence that Wong Sun had been released on his own recognizance after a lawful arraignment, and had returned voluntarily several days later to make the statement, we hold that the connection between the arrest and the statement has "become so attenuated as to dissipate the taint." 371 U.S. at 491.

Thus, the Court in *Wong Sun* reasoned that though the police illegally arrested Wong Sun, the causal connection between this illegality and Wong Sun's subsequent confession was sufficiently weakened due to both the passage of time and the voluntary nature of the confession. Thus, it may be said that Wong Sun's confession was "sufficiently an act of free will" that "purged the primary taint" of the unlawful arrest.

The U.S. Supreme Court set out three factors to consider in determining whether the connection between the primary illegality and the resulting evidence derived from it has been sufficiently weakened:

1. the time elapsed between the illegality and the acquisition of the evidence,
2. the presence of intervening circumstances, and
3. the purpose and flagrancy of the official misconduct.

In the particular case of confessions as the resulting evidence (or fruit) derived from an illegality, another "attenuation" factor is whether *Miranda* warnings were given before the confession. *Brown v. Illinois,* 422 U.S. 590 (1975). Since *Brown,* Supreme Court cases analyzing the fruit of poisonous tree doctrine and possible attenuation have placed special emphasis on intervening circumstances and the flagrancy of police behavior (the preceding factors 2 and 3). In the process, the Court has tended to place less importance on the time factor, as well as whether or not *Miranda* warnings were given before a confession.

Courts applying the attenuation doctrine may make a distinction between physical evidence (such as live witnesses and lineup identifications) and verbal evidence (like a suspect's confession). As summarized in Table 2.4, *United States v. Ceccolini,* 435 U.S. 268 (1978), held that, because of the cost to the truth-finding process of disqualifying knowledgeable witnesses, the exclusionary rule should be invoked with much greater reluctance when the fruit of the poisonous tree is a live witness rather than a confession. Therefore, courts do not exclude the testimony of a witness discovered as the result of a constitutional violation unless the court finds a more direct link between the discovery and the violation than is required to exclude physical evidence.

Inevitable Discovery The inevitable discovery doctrine allows admission of tainted evidence if the evidence would ultimately or inevitably have been discovered by lawful means—for example, as the result of the predictable and routine behavior of a law enforcement agency, some other agency, or a private person. Thus, it is really an extension of the independent source doctrine. *Murray v. United States*, 487 U.S. 533, 539 (1988).

The U.S. Supreme Court specifically adopted the inevitable discovery doctrine in *Nix v. Williams*, 467 U.S. 431 (1984), in which police initiated a search for a ten-year-old girl who had disappeared. While the search was going on, the defendant was arrested and arraigned. In response to illegal questioning without his attorney present, Williams led police to the girl's body. The search had been called off, but the girl's body was found in a place that was essentially within the area to be searched. Although the defendant's illegally obtained statements led directly to the discovery of the body, the Court found the evidence of the girl's body admissible under the inevitable discovery doctrine. The Court reasoned that volunteer search parties were approaching the actual location of the body, these parties would have resumed the search had the defendant not led the police to the body, and the body would inevitably have been found.

The Court dismissed arguments that the inevitable discovery doctrine would promote police misconduct. A police officer faced with an opportunity to obtain evidence illegally will rarely, if ever, be able to determine whether that evidence would inevitably be discovered by other lawful means and hence be found admissible by a court despite the illegality. Departmental discipline and potential civil liability are other disincentives to obtaining evidence illegally.

The timing of conduct is highly relevant to any claim of inevitable discovery. Courts carefully scrutinize claims of inevitable discovery to make sure that law enforcement personnel were actively seeking lawful means to get at the evidence *before* they engaged in any illegal conduct. The case of *United States v. Satterfield*, 743 F.2d 827 (11th Cir. 1984), illustrates this point. In *Satterfield*, police entered a private home without an arrest or search warrant to look for a man a neighbor claimed to have witnessed committing a murder using a shotgun. After arresting the suspect and putting him in custody, police reentered the house to search for the shotgun, which they eventually found. The defense moved to suppress the shotgun on the grounds that neither the initial entry into the defendant's home nor the subsequent search for the shotgun had been supported by a valid warrant. The trial court ruled that the inevitable discovery doctrine applied because (1) the police, based on the neighbor's statement, would have been granted a valid warrant to search the house; and (2) during such an authorized search, they would have inevitably discovered the shotgun. An appellate court disagreed, stating:

> To qualify for admissibility, there must be a reasonable probability that the evidence in question would have been discovered by lawful means, and the prosecution must demonstrate that the lawful means which made discovery inevitable were possessed by the police and were being actively pursued *prior* to the occurrence of the illegal conduct. 743 F.2d 846 (italics in original).

Thus, because the police had not sought a warrant before they entered and searched the defendant's home, the inevitable discovery doctrine was deemed inapplicable.

United States v. Rullo, 748 F. Supp. 36 (D. Mass. 1990), is another good example of how the timing of police conduct is critical to claims of inevitable discovery. The defendant in *Rullo* was arrested and forced to make incriminating statements by police, who used physical force to beat a confession out of him that included the location of a gun that he had disposed of shortly before his encounter with the police. As a result of his coerced statements, the police located the gun. The trial court ruled that the statements were illegally obtained and therefore subject to suppression under the exclusionary rule. The trial court also suppressed the gun as fruit of the poisonous tree. The prosecution contended, however, that the gun should have been admitted under the inevitable discovery doctrine: The police would have conducted a thorough search of the area in which they found the suspect, and that search would have led in turn to the inevitable discovery of the weapon. The court agreed that such a search would have taken place and that the gun would have been found during such a search. But the court found the fact that a lawful search of the area had not been previously undertaken by law enforcement officers who did not participate in any police misconduct to be critical:

> [F]or a legal search to have been "truly independent" of the coerced admissions, it would have had to be conducted by officers who were unaware and uninformed of the content of defendant's statements. The participation or intervention in the lawful search of officers who were not involved in the police misconduct is a constant theme in decisions upholding the application of the inevitable discovery rule. . . . Yet in this case, the agents who would have participated in and directed the "inevitable" search of the area include the same officers who participated in the beating of the defendant and who heard him disclose the location of the weapon, or were told of his statements. It was apparently with precisely such situations in mind that [courts have required] active pursuit of the legal means *at the time* of the misconduct. 748 F. Supp. at 44 (emphasis added).

Occasionally, courts find inevitable discovery based on the behavior not of law enforcement officers but of ordinary civilians. *State v. Miller,* 680 P.2d 676 (Or. 1984), summarized in Table 2.4, illustrates this point.

Good Faith In *United States v. Leon,* 468 U.S. 897 (1984), the U.S. Supreme Court adopted the good-faith exception to the exclusionary rule. Unlike the fruit of the poisonous tree doctrine (which can lead to the exclusion of additional evidence), the good-faith exception, if applicable, will work to admit evidence otherwise excludable. Under this exception, if a law enforcement officer acting with objective good faith obtains a warrant from a neutral and detached magistrate and acts within the scope of the warrant, evidence seized pursuant to the warrant will be admissible even if the warrant is later determined to be invalid. The Court reasoned that excluding such evidence would not further the purposes of the exclusionary rule—deterrence of police misconduct—because officers who act in reliance on a warrant they believe in good faith to be valid are doing exactly what they should be doing under such circumstances. In determining what good faith is, the Court said:

> [O]ur good-faith inquiry is confined to the objectively ascertainable question whether a reasonably well-trained officer would have known that the search was illegal despite the magistrate's authorization. In making this determination, all of the circumstances—including whether the warrant application has previously been rejected by a different magistrate—may be considered. 468 U.S. at 922–23 n.23.

The Court described several circumstances under which an officer would not have reasonable grounds to believe that a warrant was properly issued (and hence the good-faith exception would not be found to apply):

- The issuing magistrate was misled by information in an affidavit that the affiant knew was false or would have known was false except for a reckless disregard of the truth (see Chapter 4).

- The issuing magistrate wholly abandoned a neutral and detached judicial role and acted as an arm of the prosecution (see Chapter 4 for further discussion of this topic).
- The warrant was based on an affidavit so lacking in indicia of probable cause as to render official belief in its existence entirely unreasonable. This type of warrant, issued by a "rubber stamp" magistrate, cannot be relied on in good faith by a police officer. (See the section on probable cause in Chapter 3.)
- The warrant was so facially deficient—failing to particularize the place to be searched or the things to be seized—that the executing officers could not reasonably presume it to be valid (see Chapter 4).

Under such circumstances, the warrant would be declared invalid and any evidence seized under the warrant would be ruled inadmissible.

Massachusetts v. Sheppard, 468 U.S. 981 (1984), gives an example of reasonable, good-faith behavior in the context of a facially defective warrant that failed to mention, or "particularize," all of the items eventually seized. The U.S. Supreme Court explained:

> The officers in this case took every step that could reasonably be expected of them. Detective O'Malley prepared an affidavit which was reviewed and approved by the District Attorney. He presented that affidavit to a neutral judge. The judge concluded that the affidavit established probable cause to search Sheppard's residence . . . and informed O'Malley that he would authorize the search as requested. O'Malley then produced the warrant form and informed the judge that it might need to be changed. He was told by the judge that the necessary changes would be made. He then observed the judge make some changes and received the warrant and the affidavit. At this point, a reasonable police officer would have concluded, as O'Malley did, that the warrant authorized a search for the materials outlined in the affidavit. 468 U.S. at 989.

Thus, even though the warrant in *Sheppard* failed to mention relevant evidentiary items outlined in the attached affidavit, the Court found these items admissible at trial because Detective O'Malley had an objective, good-faith belief that the warrant authorized a search for these items. This belief stemmed from the fact that the detective had included these items in the affidavit he prepared, and the judge informed him that the warrant would contain these items.

Arizona v. Evans, 514 U.S. 1 (1995), summarized in Table 2.4, provides another example of good-faith behavior by police officers. Evans was applied in *Herring v. United States*, 555 U.S. 135 (2009), as explained in the following Discussion Point.

Some courts, like the one in *Sheppard* (previously discussed), proceed directly to the good-faith issue when reviewing suppression rulings and bypass fundamental Fourth Amendment questions such as whether probable cause supported the warrant or whether the warrant was sufficiently particularized. For example, in *United States v. McLaughlin*, 851 F.2d 283, 284–85 (9th Cir. 1988), the court said:

> We need not decide whether the warrant was based on probable cause, because we find that even if the warrant lacked probable cause, the evidence was properly admitted under the exception to the exclusionary rule announced in *United States v. Leon*. . . . The officers in this case [reasonably] relied on the determination of a neutral magistrate that they had probable cause to search.

Illinois v. Krull, 480 U.S. 340 (1987), extended the good-faith exception to the exclusionary rule to evidence obtained by police acting in objectively reasonable reliance on a *statute* that had authorized warrantless administrative searches but was later held

DISCUSSION POINT

How Bad Does Official Record Keeping Need to Be Before Police Reliance on a Defective Warrant Becomes Reckless?

Officers in Coffee County, Alabama, arrested Herring based on a warrant listed in neighboring Dale County's database. When Herring was searched incident to that arrest, police found drugs and a gun. After Herring was charged with illegally possessing the gun and drugs, he moved to suppress the evidence against him on the grounds that his arrest had been illegal

because the warrant had been recalled months earlier, though that information had never been entered into the database. Assuming, for the sake of argument, that the arrest had been illegal under the Fourth Amendment, the district court concluded that the exclusionary rule did not apply and denied the motion to suppress. The Eleventh Circuit affirmed, finding that the arresting officers were innocent of any wrongdoing and that Dale County's failure to update the records was merely negligent. The court therefore concluded that the benefit of suppression would be marginal or nonexistent and that the evidence was admissible under the good-faith rule of *United States v. Leon*, 468 U.S. 897 (1984). The U.S. Supreme Court affirmed the lower courts' decisions, reasoning that when police mistakes lead to an unlawful search as a result of isolated negligence attenuated from the search, the exclusionary rule does not apply. The Court stated, however, that if systemic errors or reckless disregard of constitutional requirements occur, then the application of the exclusionary rule would be appropriate.

The dissent in *Herring* argued that the majority opinion underestimated "the need for a forceful exclusionary rule and the gravity of recordkeeping errors in law enforcement." 555 U.S. at 150. Justice Ginsburg reasoned that "the risk of exclusion of evidence encourages policymakers and systems managers to monitor the performance of the systems they install and the personnel employed to operate those systems." 555 U.S. at 154. She emphasized that in

the Information Age, electronic databases "form the nervous system of contemporary criminal justice operations. 555 U.S. at 155.

- Do you agree with the Court that an error arising from attenuated negligence is far removed from the core concerns that led to the exclusionary rule's adoption? Explain.

- *Herring* made clear that the exclusionary rule should be applied only when police conduct is sufficiently deliberate that exclusion of evidence can meaningfully deter sufficiently culpable conduct. In *Herring*, the error was an isolated incident. What if, as a result of budgetary cutbacks, a state or county falls significantly behind in updating its warrant databases and, as a result, "systemic errors" lead to many illegal searches? Would a police officer relying on the information in the database still be without any culpability? Should the exclusionary rule be applied then? Why or why not?

- In examining an officer's conduct, the *Herring* court said that the "pertinent analysis is objective, not an inquiry into the subjective awareness of arresting officers." 555 U.S. at 703. Do you think that an officer's subject intent should matter? Why or why not?

- Unlike the judicial recordkeeping error in *Arizona v. Evans*, *Herring* involved negligence in police record keeping. Do you think that police recordkeeping errors should be treated differently than judicial ones? Why or why not?

to violate the Fourth Amendment. Following the approach used in *Leon,* the Court explained that applying the exclusionary rule to an officer's objectively reasonable reliance on a statute would have little deterrent effect:

Unless a statute is clearly unconstitutional, an officer cannot be expected to question the judgment of the legislature that passed the law. If the statute is subsequently declared unconstitutional, excluding evidence obtained pursuant to it prior to such judicial declaration will not deter future Fourth Amendment violations by an officer who has simply fulfilled his responsibility to enforce the statute as written. 480 U.S. at 349–50.

Thus, after *Krull,* unless an officer unreasonably relies on a clearly unconstitutional statute, evidence discovered during a search by an officer pursuant to a statute will not be excluded at trial, even if the statute is later found unconstitutional by a court.

Similarly, in *Davis v. United States*, 131 S. Ct. 2419 (2011), the U.S. Supreme Court further extended the good-faith exception to cover reliance on valid court precedent applicable at the time even if that court case is subsequently overturned. In *Davis,* a police officer conducted a search in full accordance with the law as it existed on the date of the search. The law subsequently changed, however, when the Supreme Court decided a case that rendered the search unconstitutional. Because the officer relied in good faith on then-applicable valid precedent, however, the Court ruled that the absence of any police culpability in the case rendered the application of the exclusionary rule unnecessary.

Interestingly, several states do not recognize the good-faith exception. For example, the Georgia Supreme Court "declined to adopt the 'good faith' exception to the exclusionary rule . . . holding that because the Georgia legislature has statutorily protected the right to be free from unreasonable search and seizure . . . 'the State of Georgia has chosen to impose greater requirements upon its law enforcement officers than that required by the U.S. Supreme Court.'" *Davis v. State,* 422 S.E.2d 546, 549 n.1 (Ga. 1992) (citing *Gary v. State,* 422 S.E.2d 426 Ga. 1992).

Standing to Assert an Exclusionary Rule Claim

To challenge the admissibility of evidence and potentially have evidence excluded at trial, a defendant must first have standing—the ability to raise a legal claim. A defendant has standing when his or her own constitutional rights have been allegedly violated.

In *Rakas v. Illinois*, 439 U.S. 128 (1978), a police search of a car yielded a box of rifle shells in the glove compartment and a sawed-off rifle under the passenger seat. The U.S. Supreme Court held that the defendants—passengers in the car who had no ownership interest in the car, the rifle shells, or the sawed-off rifle—had no legitimate expectation of privacy in the areas searched. Therefore, according to the Court, the passengers suffered no invasion of their Fourth Amendment rights and, therefore, had no standing to object to the intrusion:

> "Fourth Amendment rights are personal rights which, like some other constitutional rights, may not be vicariously asserted." . . . A person who is aggrieved by an illegal search and seizure only through the introduction of damaging evidence secured by a search of a third person's premises or property has not had any of his Fourth Amendment rights infringed. . . . And since the exclusionary rule is an attempt to effectuate the guarantees of the Fourth Amendment, . . . it is proper to permit only defendants whose Fourth Amendment rights have been violated to benefit from the rule's protections. 439 U.S. at 133–34 (1978).

Rakas went on to say that "capacity to claim the protection of the Fourth Amendment depends not upon a property right in the invaded place but upon whether the person who claims the protection of the Amendment has a legitimate expectation of privacy in the invaded place." 439 U.S. at 143. A subjective expectation of privacy is legitimate if it is "one that society is prepared to recognize as 'reasonable.'" *Katz v. United States*, 389 U.S. 347, 361 (1967). For example, the Supreme Court held that a person's status as an overnight guest in a home is alone enough to show that the person had an expectation of privacy that society is prepared to recognize as reasonable. *Minnesota v. Olson*, 495 U.S. 91 (1990). Notably, the defendant in

- To deter police misconduct, the exclusionary rule requires that any evidence obtained by police using methods that violate a person's constitutional rights must be excluded from use in a criminal prosecution against that person.

- The exclusionary rule does not apply to evidence obtained illegally by a private citizen unless the private citizen acts as an agent of the police. This may happen if police order the private citizen to conduct a search or seizure.

- The exclusionary rule does not apply to evidence used in certain civil trials, deportation hearings, grand jury proceedings, parole revocation hearings, or *habeas corpus* proceedings or to evidence used to impeach a defendant's testimony at trial. It also does not apply to violations of the knock-and-announce rule.

- Under the fruit of the poisonous tree doctrine, evidence is inadmissible in court if it was directly or indirectly obtained by exploitation of some prior unconstitutional police activity (such as an illegal arrest or search). Evidence directly or indirectly obtained in this manner is called *tainted evidence*.

- The fruit of the poisonous tree doctrine does not require suppression of the tainted evidence if (1) the evidence was also obtained through a source wholly independent of the primary constitutional violation, (2) the evidence inevitably would have been discovered by some other lawful means already in process, or (3) the means of obtaining the tainted evidence were sufficiently remote from and distinguishable from the primary illegality.

- Under the good-faith exception to the exclusionary rule, evidence obtained by police who

Continued on next page

Olson had standing even though he stayed only one night, possessed no key to the apartment, and was never left alone there. Standing has also been found within a hotel room, even when other individuals who are not the defendant are staying there, provided that the defendant was provided a key and consent to stay in the room. *United States v. Jeffers,* 342 U.S. 48 (1951).

In contrast, the U.S. Supreme Court has held that a temporary, commercial visitor has no reasonable expectation of privacy in a home he or she is visiting. In *Minnesota v. Carter*, 525 U.S. 83 (1998), while the defendants bagged cocaine in the apartment, a law enforcement officer investigating a tip observed them by looking through a drawn window blind. The defendants did not live in the apartment, they had never visited that apartment before, their visit only lasted a matter of hours, and they did not possess a key to the apartment. Their only purpose there was to package cocaine. After they were arrested, they moved to suppress evidence obtained from the apartment and their car, arguing that the officer's initial observation was an unreasonable search in violation of the Fourth Amendment. The U.S. Supreme Court ruled they could not invoke the Fourth Amendment because they were in the apartment for such a short time for what amounted to no more than an illegal business transaction.

"An expectation of privacy in commercial premises . . . is different from, and indeed less than, a similar expectation in an individual's home." *New York v. Burger*, 482 U.S. 691 (1987). Importantly, however, an individual will generally be found to have a legitimate expectation of privacy in his or her own commercial office space, even if that space is shared with others. *Mancusi v. DeForte,* 392 U.S. 364 (1968). This means that an individual will be found to have standing to challenge a search of his or her business office, and consequently to have excluded any evidence illegally seized there by police.

In addition to the temporary business visitor, other individuals may be found to lack standing. For instance, a co-defendant in a crime (like a co-conspirator or an accessory) has no standing to object to a search, unless he or she has a reasonable expectation of privacy in the place to be searched. *United States v. Padilla,* 508 U.S. 77 (1993). Likewise, one who carelessly places contraband belonging to him into another's purse may not have standing to object to a search of the purse. *Rawlings v. Kentucky,* 448 U.S. 98 (1980). Also, if an individual voluntarily hands over records to a bank and the government later subpoenas these records, that individual will not have standing under the Fourth Amendment to challenge the government's action. *United States v. Miller,* 425 U.S. 435 (1976).

Standing also applies in the context of the privilege against self-incrimination under the Fifth Amendment. For example, only the person who is forced by the government to speak incriminating information may raise a Fifth Amendment claim. This means that if the government forces (through threats or otherwise) *another* person to speak incriminating information about you, the concept of "standing" will prevent you from challenging and excluding that information under the Fifth Amendment. In this example, because another person's Fifth Amendment rights were violated and not yours, standing will not be found to exist.

SUMMARY

This chapter is designed to help criminal justice students and professionals understand the dual federal and state court structure in the United States and some of the most common pretrial processes used by the criminal courts. Although a review of the chapter should make clear that each jurisdiction's court system has its own unique characteristics, the criminal pretrial process presented in this chapter should serve as a framework for the further study of one or more of these systems.

After a warrantless arrest, the judicial process in criminal cases usually begins with an initial appearance and then a bail hearing. Initial appearances are generally unnecessary when an arrest is made pursuant to a warrant.

Prosecutors possess great discretion in deciding whether to charge someone and, if so, with what specific crimes so long as they do not exercise this discretion selectively (which would violate equal protection) or vindictively (which would violate due process).

If a grand jury has issued an indictment, the defendant enters a formal plea at an arraignment. If, however, the defendant has been charged using a process other than a grand jury indictment, then a preliminary hearing typically occurs. If a judge binds over a defendant for trial, a formal plea to the charges must be entered at an arraignment. After an arraignment, discovery may occur and pretrial motions, including the motion to suppress evidence, may be adjudicated, although the latter occurs in less than 10 percent of felony cases. Most frequently, the parties enter into plea negotiations that result in the defendant pleading guilty at an allocution hearing.

When researching a specific court system, one should seek guidance from the applicable constitution, statutes, rules of court, and rules of evidence for that jurisdiction. The information contained in this chapter can enhance the justice professional's perception of his or her role in the entire criminal justice system and the importance of properly performing that role to the effective and just operation of the system.

This chapter also introduced the exclusionary rule, a concept that will resurface throughout this book. Law enforcement officers who know both the effect and scope of the exclusionary rule will surely understand why it is so important to abide by the commands of the Fourth, Fifth, Sixth, and Fourteenth Amendments as explained in the remainder of this book. Such knowledge should enable criminal justice professionals to function effectively within our criminal justice system.

acted in good faith in objectively reasonable reliance on a warrant or statute is admissible, even if the warrant or statute is subsequently determined to be invalid.

■ To have standing to invoke the exclusionary rule challenging the admissibility of evidence, a defendant's own constitutional rights must have been allegedly violated in obtaining the evidence.

KEY TERMS

REVIEW AND DISCUSSION QUESTIONS

1. Draw a diagram of the hierarchy of federal and state courts with criminal jurisdiction in your state. Indicate whether each court has original or appellate criminal jurisdiction. Further explain the specifics of each court's subject matter jurisdiction (e.g., if it hears only misdemeanors or whether it has a limited appellate jurisdiction).

2. What is the difference between jurisdiction and venue?

3. What is a writ of *certiorari*? Under what circumstances might a court of last resort such as the U.S. Supreme Court grant *certiorari*?

4. Discuss the similarities and differences among the three types of charging documents (i.e., a complaint, an indictment, and an information).

5. Explain the purposes of an initial appearance and how it differs from an arraignment.

6. What is an affidavit? What documents in the pretrial criminal justice process are usually supported by affidavits?

7. What is a grand jury and what are its functions? Compare and contrast the similarities and the differences between preliminary hearings and grand jury proceedings.

8. What are the four types of pleas that defendants in most U.S. jurisdictions might enter at an arraignment?

9. Describe the things that are supposed to happen at a Rule 11 or similar state law proceeding at which a defendant enters a plea of guilty or *nolo contendere*. Be sure to include a discussion of the rights that a defendant waives when entering one of these pleas.

10. Describe the types of information that must be disclosed by a prosecutor to the defense as part of the mandatory criminal discovery process.

11. What is a motion to suppress evidence? Why is it particularly important to constitutional criminal procedure and, therefore, criminal justice professionals—especially law enforcement officers?

12. Explain why the application of the exclusionary rule does not necessarily mean that the prosecution is ended and that the defendant goes free.

13. Discuss the probable effectiveness in deterring illegal police conduct of the following suggested alternatives to the exclusionary rule: criminal prosecution of law enforcement officers, administrative discipline of officers, and bringing civil actions for damages against officers.

14. Explain why a state court may refuse to follow certain holdings of the U.S. Supreme Court.

15. Discuss four theories under which evidence may be admissible in court even though it is fruit of the poisonous tree.

3

Basic Underlying Concepts: Property, Privacy, Probable Cause, and Reasonableness

Before examining the law of criminal procedure in detail—arrest, search and seizure, admissions and confessions, and pretrial identifications—it's important to understand four concepts fundamental to criminal procedure: **property, privacy, probable cause**, and **reasonableness**. They are developed in greater detail throughout the book and clarified by examples. Because these concepts are so pervasive and so essential to an understanding of criminal procedure, discussing them at the outset should make the following chapters more meaningful and easier to understand.

Property and privacy rights play a critical role in shaping the overall Fourth Amendment inquiry. In the context of criminal procedure, an individual's property is protected from certain intrusions by police. An individual's reasonable expectations of privacy are similarly protected from governmental intrusion. Accordingly, a "search" occurs under the Fourth Amendment when police physically intrude, or "trespass," onto an individual's property to obtain information or discover something, or when police violate a reasonable expectation of privacy. In addition, police officers must generally have probable cause to arrest and search with or without a warrant, and this chapter explores particular contexts when officers have (or do not have) probable cause to arrest or search.

Finally, for searches and seizures to be valid under the Fourth Amendment, they must be reasonable. Normally, this means that searches and seizures must be based on a warrant supported by probable cause, and that describes with particularity the items police intend to search or seize. Without such a warrant, a search or seizure may still be found reasonable if a valid exception to the normal warrant requirement has been met.

Property and Privacy Inquiries for Criminal Searches and Seizures

For the Fourth Amendment to be applicable to a particular fact situation in a criminal case, there must be a search or seizure accompanied by an attempt by the prosecution to introduce what was searched or seized as evidence in court. Whether there was a search or seizure within the meaning of the Fourth Amendment—and, if so, whether the search or seizure violated someone's constitutional rights—depends on the nature of the interest that the Fourth Amendment protects.

The Property Rights Approach

Under the common law, it was clear that the security of one's property was a sacred right and that protection of that right was a primary purpose of government. In an early English case, the court said:

> The great end for which men entered into society was to secure their property. That right is preserved sacred and incommunicable in all instances where it has not been taken away or abridged by some public law for the good of the whole. . . . By the laws of England, every invasion of private property, be it ever so minute, is a trespass. No man can set foot upon my ground without my license but he is liable to an action though the damage be nothing. . . . *Entick v. Carrington*, 19 Howell's State Trials 1029, 1035, 95 Eng. Rep. 807, 817–18 (1765).

The U.S. Supreme Court first adopted this common-law approach to protection of property interests as the basis for the interests protected by the Fourth Amendment. Under this approach, analysis of Fourth Amendment issues centers on whether a physical intrusion into a "constitutionally protected area" had occurred. Several cases involving electronic surveillance illustrate this approach.

In *Olmstead v. United States,* 277 U.S. 438 (1928), the Court held that wiretapping was not covered by the Fourth Amendment in part because there had been no physical invasion of the defendant's premises—the wiretap had not been installed *on* the defendant's property. Because the wiretap did not physically intrude into the defendant's home, the Court rejected the Fourth Amendment as a basis for any alleged invasion of privacy. Similarly, in *Goldman v. United States*, 316 U.S. 129 (1942), the Court found no search or seizure under the Fourth Amendment because police placed a listening device against a wall in an office that adjoined the defendant's office. Thus, yet again, the lack of a physical intrusion into the area in which a defendant expected privacy was key to the Court's reasoning.

In contrast to *Olmstead* and *Goldman,* in *Silverman v. United States,* 365 U.S. 505 (1961), a "spike mike" was pushed through a common wall until it hit a heating duct in defendant Silverman's home. The Court held that the electronic surveillance was an illegal search and seizure. And in *Clinton v. Virginia*, 377 U.S. 158 (1964), the Court ruled inadmissible evidence obtained by means of a mechanical listening device stuck into the wall of an apartment adjoining the defendant's residence. The rationale for the *Silverman* and *Clinton* cases was that the listening devices had actually physically invaded the target premises, even though the invasion was slight.

Moreover, the Court in *On Lee v. United States*, 343 U.S. 747 (1952), found no invasion onto defendant's property—and hence no search for Fourth Amendment purposes—when the defendant freely allowed an undercover agent, secretly bugged with a recording device, onto his property and began speaking with him. In this sense, *On Lee* is typical of "property" cases finding "no search" under the Fourth Amendment when the defendant consents to the intrusion onto his or her property.

Though the emphasis on property concepts in interpreting the Fourth Amendment began to decline in the 1960s, these concepts experienced a resurgence with the U.S. Supreme Court case of *United States v. Jones*, 132 S. Ct. 945 (2012). In *Jones*, the FBI and Washington, D.C., police investigated Antoine Jones, a nightclub owner, because they suspected his involvement in drug trafficking. This investigation initially included the following techniques: visual surveillance of the club, the use of a video camera, and a pen register and wiretap on Jones's cell phone. Using the information obtained from these techniques, the police obtained a warrant to place an electronic monitoring device on a vehicle registered to Jones's wife. The warrant authorized the installation of the device in the District of Columbia and gave police ten days to install it. On the eleventh day and while in Maryland, not D.C., police installed a global positioning satellite (GPS) device on the vehicle. The police then monitor Jones's movements for twenty-eight days.

The prosecutor charged Jones and his accomplices in a conspiracy for illegal drug distribution. Jones responded in court with a motion to exclude the evidence obtained by police from the GPS device. This evidence, which included information on Jones's location, linked Jones to a "stash house" that contained cash and cocaine. 132 S. Ct. at 948–49.

The Supreme Court held that "the Government's installation of a GPS device on [Jones'] vehicle, and its use of that device to monitor the vehicle's movements, constitutes a 'search'" under the Fourth Amendment. 132 S. Ct. at 949. The Court reached this conclusion because the police had intruded on Jones's property rights when they secretly installed the GPS device on his vehicle:

> It is important to be clear about what occurred in this case: The Government physically occupied private property for the purpose of obtaining information. We have no doubt that such a physical intrusion would have been considered a "search" within the meaning of the Fourth Amendment when it was adopted. . . .
>
> [W]e must assure preservation of that degree of privacy against government that existed when the Fourth Amendment was adopted. . . . [F]or most of our history the Fourth Amendment was understood to embody a particular concern for government trespass upon the areas ("persons, houses, papers, and effects") it enumerates. . . . [W]hen the Government does engage in physical intrusion of a constitutionally protected area in order to obtain information, that intrusion may constitute a violation of the Fourth Amendment. We have embodied that preservation of past rights in our very definition of "reasonable expectation of privacy" which we have said to be an expectation "that has a source outside of the Fourth Amendment, either by reference to concepts of real or personal property law or to understandings that are recognized and permitted by society." 132 S. Ct. at 948–949, 950–951.

The Court explained in a footnote in *Jones* that a "technical" trespass by police is not sufficient by itself to constitute a Fourth Amendment search. Rather, a trespass must be accompanied by police obtaining information (or discovering something). 132 S. Ct. at 951 n.5. In addition, note that for a trespass by police to constitute a search under the Fourth Amendment, the trespass must be of an item that is explicitly mentioned within that Amendment—a paper, effect, house, or person. 132 S. Ct. at 953 n.8.

For a Supreme Court case applying the *Jones* "property" test to determine if a Fourth Amendment search has occurred, see the Discussion Point below.

DISCUSSION POINT

Florida v. Jardines—Dog Sniffs at Your Home: Are They Fourth Amendment Searches by Police?

The facts of *Jardines* are as follows:

In 2006, Detective William Pedraja of the Miami-Dade Police Department received an unverified tip that marijuana was being grown in the home of respondent Joelis Jardines. One month later, the Department and the Drug Enforcement Administration sent a joint

surveillance team to Jardines's home. Detective Pedraja was part of that team. He watched the home for fifteen minutes and saw no vehicles in the driveway or activity around the home, and he could not see inside because the blinds were drawn. Detective Pedraja then approached Jardines's home accompanied by Detective Douglas Bartelt, a trained canine handler who had just arrived at the scene with his drug-sniffing dog. The dog was trained to detect the scent of marijuana, cocaine, heroin, and several other drugs, indicating the presence of any of these substances through particular behavioral changes recognizable by his handler.

Detective Bartelt had the dog on a six-foot leash, owing in part to the dog's "wild" nature and tendency to dart around erratically while searching. As the dog approached Jardines's front porch, he apparently sensed one of the odors he had been trained to detect and began energetically exploring the area for the strongest point source of that odor. As Detective Bartelt explained, the dog "began tracking that airborne odor by . . . tracking back and forth," engaging in what is called "bracketing, back and forth, back and forth." Detective Bartelt gave the dog "the full six feet of the leash plus whatever safe distance [he could] give him" to do this—he testified that he needs to give the dog "as much distance as I can." And Detective Pedraja stood back while this was occurring, so that he would not "get knocked over" when the dog was "spinning around trying to find" the source.

After sniffing the base of the front door, the dog sat, which is the trained behavior upon discovering the odor's strongest point. Detective Bartelt then pulled the dog away from the door and returned to his vehicle. He left the scene after informing Detective Pedraja that there had been a positive alert for narcotics.

On the basis of what he had learned at the home, Detective Pedraja applied for and received a warrant to search the residence. When the warrant was executed later that day, Jardines attempted to flee and was arrested; the search revealed marijuana plants, and he was charged with trafficking in cannabis. At trial, Jardines moved to suppress the marijuana plants on the ground that the canine investigation was an unreasonable search. *Florida v. Jardines*, 133 S. Ct. 1409, 1413 (2013).

Ultimately, the Court in *Jardines* found that a Fourth Amendment search had occurred because the detectives physically intruded onto the front porch of Jardines's home without justification or permission: "The government's use of trained police dogs to investigate the home and its immediate surroundings is a 'search' within the meaning of the Fourth Amendment." 133 S. Ct. at 1417–18. In particular, the Court indicated that the detectives "were gathering information in an area belonging to Jardines and immediately surrounding his house [i.e., the front porch]. . . , which we have held enjoys protection as part of the home itself. And [the detectives] gathered that information by physically entering and occupying the area to engage in conduct not explicitly or implicitly permitted by the homeowner." 133 S. Ct. at 1414.

Continued on next page

- Do you agree with the Court's decision in *Jardines* that a Fourth Amendment search had occurred? Fully explain your answer.

- Assume for purposes of this question that police detectives had instead approached the front porch of Jardines's home in the hopes of knocking on his front door and asking him several questions related to their suspicions that Jardines was growing marijuana at his home. Do you believe these police actions would constitute a "search" under the Fourth Amendment? Why or why not?

- What if police approached Jardines's home with a metal detector and used this device in the area immediately surrounding the home to attempt to find objects related to a crime for which they suspected Jardines to be involved? Does this activity constitute a police "search"? Why or why not? Fully explain your answer.

- You will learn later in this book that canine inspections for drugs in other locations have been held not to constitute Fourth Amendment searches. Consider, for example, *Illinois v. Caballes*, 543 U.S. 405 (2005), which found that police use of a canine during a traffic stop in the area immediately surrounding a vehicle in order to detect drugs inside that vehicle does not constitute a Fourth Amendment search. The Court in *Caballes* had essentially determined that canine inspections around vehicles are not Fourth Amendment searches because they do not violate a person's reasonable expectation of privacy: "A dog sniff conducted during a concededly lawful traffic stop that reveals no information other than the location of [an illegal drug substance] does not violate the Fourth Amendment." 543 U.S. at 409–10. Do you think that *Jones* and *Jardines* have affected the continued validity of *Caballes* as good law? Why or why not? What if the dog "trespasses" the vehicle by sticking its nose inside?

- Separate from the issue of trespass to property, do you believe that a canine inspection by police of the area around a home (e.g., on the front porch or in bushes around the home) violate a homeowner's reasonable expectations of privacy? How do you reconcile your perspective with the Court's conclusion in *Caballes* that police dog sniffs by vehicles do not violate an individual's privacy?

The "Reasonable Expectation of Privacy" Approach

The U.S. Supreme Court's opinion in *Jones* made it clear that Fourth Amendment privacy would also be evaluated using the reasonable expectation of privacy approach, an approach that began in the 1960s with the landmark case of *Katz v. United States*, 389 U.S. 347 (1967). In *Katz*, FBI agents had attached an electronic listening and recording device to the *outside* of a public telephone booth to overhear telephone conversations. They used this device to record the defendant Katz obtaining gambling-related information and placing illegal bets. These conversations were then transcribed and used against Katz at trial. In a major reversal of its prior physical invasion of property rights line of analysis, the *Katz* Court held that the FBI's actions violated the Fourth Amendment. The Court said:

> [T]his effort to decide whether or not a given "area," viewed in the abstract, is "constitutionally protected" deflects attention from the problem presented by this case. For the Fourth Amendment protects people, not places. What a person knowingly exposes to the public, even in his own home or office, is not a subject of Fourth Amendment protection. . . . But what he seeks to preserve as private, even in an area accessible to the public, may be constitutionally protected. 389 U.S. at 351–52.

The Court held that the government's electronically listening to and recording the defendant's words violated the privacy on which the defendant justifiably relied when using the telephone booth. Thus, it constituted a search and seizure within the meaning of the Fourth Amendment. The Court added, "The fact that the electronic device employed to achieve that end did not happen to penetrate the wall of the booth can have no constitutional significance." 389 U.S. at 353.

As *Jones* makes clear, "the *Katz* reasonable-expectation-of-privacy test . . . *added to*, not *substituted for*, the common-law trespassory test" (italics in original).

Thus, *Katz* significantly expanded Fourth Amendment protections beyond a property-rights approach to privacy. When analyzing cases under *Katz*'s privacy approach to the Fourth Amendment "search" question, most courts borrow from the approach to privacy suggested by Justice Harlan in his concurring opinion in the *Katz* case. He said that "there is a twofold requirement, first that a person has exhibited an actual (subjective) expectation of privacy and, second, that the expectation be one that society is prepared to recognize as [objectively] 'reasonable.'" 389 U.S. at 361. If these requirements are satisfied, any governmental intrusion on the expectation of privacy is a search for purposes of the Fourth Amendment.

Reflecting Justice Harlan's thoughts under the privacy approach, the U.S. Supreme Court defined the terms search and seizure as follows:

> A "search" occurs when an expectation of privacy that society is prepared to consider reasonable is infringed. A "seizure" of property occurs when there is some meaningful interference with an individual's possessory interests in that property. *United States v. Jacobsen*, 466 U.S. 109, 113 (1984).

Maryland v. Macon, 472 U.S. 463 (1985), illustrates the application of these definitions. A plainclothes county police detective entered an adult bookstore. After browsing for several minutes, he purchased two magazines from a salesclerk and paid for them with a marked $50 bill. He then left the store and showed the magazines to his fellow officers, who were waiting nearby. The officers concluded that the magazines were obscene, reentered the store, and arrested the salesclerk. In determining that there had been no Fourth Amendment search under these facts, the Court said:

> [R]espondent did not have any reasonable expectation of privacy in areas of the store where the public was invited to enter and to transact business. . . . The mere expectation that the possibly illegal nature of a product will not come to the attention of the authorities, whether because a customer will not complain or because undercover officers will not transact business with the store, is not one that society is prepared to recognize as reasonable. The officer's action in entering the bookstore and examining the wares that were intentionally exposed to all who frequent the place of business did not infringe a legitimate expectation of privacy and hence did not constitute a search within the meaning of the Fourth Amendment. 472 U.S. at 469.

Thus, because the plainclothes police officers acted in a manner consistent with a paying member of the public, no search occurred under the Fourth Amendment.

Also, in determining whether there had been a seizure, the Court said:

> [R]espondent voluntarily transferred any possessory interest he may have had in the magazines to the purchaser upon the receipt of the funds. . . . Thereafter, whatever possessory interest the seller had was in the funds, not the magazines. At the time of the sale the officer did not "interfere" with any interest of the seller; he took only that which was intended as a necessary part of the exchange. 472 U.S. at 469.

Therefore, no seizure occurred for the purposes of the Fourth Amendment.

However, if government officials search an adult bookstore and seize material thereby removing its packaging without paying for it, a search and seizure will be found. *Lo-Ji Sales, Inc. v. New York*, 442 U.S. 319 (1979). Here, the officials are going beyond what a member of the public could see and do. 442 U.S. at 329. One might say that the owner of the bookstore in *Lo-Ji Sales* did not knowingly expose his material to the public in the way the officers chose to access the material. Therefore, a search and seizure occurred.

Using this same rationale originally developed from *Katz* that what one knowingly exposes to the public is not protected by the Fourth Amendment, the Court has also held that physical characteristics such as one's facial profile, the sound of one's voice, or the characteristics of one's handwriting do not implicate the Fourth Amendment. *See United States v. Dionisio*, 410 U.S. 1 (1973). This is because these characteristics are frequently exposed to members of the public. 410 U.S. at 14. Therefore, no seizure occurs for Fourth Amendment purposes when the police obtain an example of a person's handwriting or a recording of one's voice, provided these items will be used for identification purposes only and have been requested by a grand jury (as in *Dionisio*).

In sum, a search occurs under the Fourth Amendment when law enforcement either:

1. physically intrude, or trespass, onto an individual's property to obtain information or discover something; or

2. violate an individual's reasonable expectation of privacy.

It's important to note that even when no search occurs via one of these two ways, the Fourth Amendment still protects against unreasonable seizures of property. Recall that a "seizure" of property occurs when there is some meaningful interference with an individual's possessory interests in that property. *Jacobsen*, 466 U.S. at 113. *Soldal v. Cook County, Ill.*, 506 U.S. 56 (1992), involved the forcible repossession of a mobile home by deputy sheriffs and the owner of a mobile home park. In holding that the repossession of the mobile home constituted a seizure under the Fourth Amendment, the Court said that its past cases "unmistakably hold that the [Fourth] Amendment protects property as well as privacy." 506 U.S. at 62.

Probable Cause

The text of the Fourth Amendment introduces the concept of probable cause:

> The right of the people to be secure in their persons, houses, papers, and effects, against unreasonable searches and seizures, shall not be violated, and no Warrants shall issue, but upon probable cause, supported by Oath or affirmation, and particularly describing the place to be searched, and the persons or things to be seized.

From this language, it is apparent that probable cause is necessary for the issuance of an arrest or search warrant. It is not so apparent that the other clause of the Fourth Amendment declaring the right of the people to be secure against "unreasonable searches and seizures" is also founded on probable cause. In general, that clause governs the various situations in which police are permitted to make warrantless arrests, searches, and seizures. These warrantless police actions are usually held to be unreasonable unless based on probable cause. As the U.S. Supreme Court explained, if the requirements for warrantless arrests, searches, and seizures were less stringent than those for warrants, "a principal incentive now existing for the procurement of . . . warrants would be destroyed." *Wong Sun v. United States*, 371 U.S. 471, 479–80 (1963).

Defining Probable Cause

Two different but similar definitions of probable cause are presented here—one for search and one for arrest—because different types of information are required to

KEY POINTS

LO1

■ The principal objects of the Fourth Amendment are the protection of property and privacy.

■ Wherever an individual may harbor a reasonable expectation of privacy, he or she is entitled to be free from unreasonable governmental intrusion under the Fourth Amendment.

■ An individual's property is also protected under the Fourth Amendment from certain physical intrusions by police when they seek to obtain information or discover something.

■ A search occurs under the Fourth Amendment when an expectation of privacy that society is prepared to consider reasonable is violated, or when police physically intrude ("trespass") onto an individual's property to obtain information or discover something. A seizure of property occurs when there is some meaningful interference with an individual's possessory interests in that property.

■ In determining whether a person has a reasonable expectation of privacy, there is a twofold requirement: (1) that a person has exhibited an actual expectation of privacy and (2) that the expectation is one that society is prepared to recognize as objectively reasonable.

establish probable cause in each instance. In *Carroll v. United States*, 267 U.S. 132, 162 (1925), the Court said that probable cause to search exists when "the facts and circumstances within their [the officers'] knowledge and of which they had reasonably trustworthy information [are] sufficient in themselves to warrant a man of reasonable caution in the belief that [seizable property would be found in a particular place or on a particular person]." 267 U.S. at 162. Paraphrasing *Carroll*, *Brinegar v. United States*, 338 U.S. 160, 175–76 (1949), defined probable cause to arrest:

> Probable cause exists where the "facts and circumstances within [the officers'] knowledge and of which they had reasonably trustworthy information [are] sufficient in themselves to warrant a man of reasonable caution in the belief that" an offense has been or is being committed [by the person to be arrested].

These definitions differ only in that the facts and circumstances that would justify an arrest may be different from those that would justify a search. This chapter is primarily concerned with the part of the definition of probable cause that is common to both arrests and searches—namely, the nature, quality, and amount of information (e.g., "facts and circumstances") necessary to establish probable cause. The definition of probable cause in *Illinois v. Gates*, 462 U.S. 213, 235 (1983), is helpful in this regard:

> "[T]he term 'probable cause,' according to its usual acceptation, means less than evidence which would justify condemnation. . . ." Finely tuned standards such as proof beyond a reasonable doubt or by a preponderance of the evidence, useful in formal trials, have no place in the magistrate's decision. While an effort to fix some general, numerically precise degree of certainty corresponding to "probable cause" may not be helpful, it is clear that "only the probability, and not a prima facie showing, of criminal activity is the standard of probable cause."

The *Gates* opinion also said:

> Perhaps the central teaching of our decisions bearing on the probable cause standard is that it is a "practical, non-technical conception." . . . In dealing with probable cause, . . . as the very name implies, we deal with probabilities. These are not technical; they are the factual and practical considerations of everyday life on which reasonable and prudent men, not legal technicians, act. 462 U.S. at 231.

Stated simply, probable cause to search is "a fair probability that contraband or evidence of a crime will be found in a particular place." *Illinois v. Gates*, 462 U.S. 213, 238 (1983). Probable cause to arrest is a fair probability that a particular person has committed or is committing a crime.

Preference for Warrants

As later chapters will show, many arrests and searches are conducted without a warrant. The amount of evidence required to establish probable cause for a warrantless arrest or search is somewhat greater than that required if a warrant is sought. The reason for the more stringent requirement in the warrantless situation is that the Supreme Court has a strong preference for both arrest warrants, *Beck v. Ohio*, 379 U.S. 89 (1964), and search warrants, *United States v. Ventresca*, 380 U.S. 102 (1965). This preference is so strong that less persuasive evidence will justify the issuance of a warrant than would justify a warrantless search or arrest. In *Aguilar v. Texas*, the Supreme Court said that "when a search is based upon a magistrate's, rather than a police officer's, determination of probable cause, the reviewing courts will accept evidence of a less 'judicially competent or persuasive character than would have justified an officer in acting on his own without a warrant,' . . . and will sustain the judicial determination so long as 'there was a substantial basis for [the magistrate] to conclude that [seizable evidence was] probably present.'" 378 U.S. 108, 111 (1964).

The warrant procedure is preferred because it places responsibility for deciding the delicate question of probable cause with a neutral and detached judicial officer, who usually has more formal legal training than a police officer. Warrants enable law enforcement officers to search certain places and seize certain persons or things when they can show a fair probability that those persons, places, or things are significantly connected with criminal activity. Warrants also protect the Fourth Amendment rights of citizens because the decision to allow a search and seizure is removed from the sometimes hurried and overzealous judgment of law enforcement officers engaged in the competitive enterprise of investigating crime.

Methods of Establishing Probable Cause

Police officers and magistrates may at times interpret the legal standard of probable cause differently. This section is designed to clarify this standard by giving specific examples of information that law enforcement officers must have before they may arrest or search, with or without a warrant.

Collective Knowledge of Police Probable cause is evaluated by examining the collective information in the possession of the police at the time of the arrest or search, not merely the personal knowledge of the arresting or searching officer. Therefore, if the police knowledge is sufficient in its totality to establish probable cause, an individual officer's actions in making a warrantless arrest or search on orders to do so is justified—even though that officer does not personally have all the information on which probable cause is based. *United States v. Nafzger* explained:

> [L]aw enforcement officers in diverse jurisdictions must be allowed to rely on information relayed from officers and/or law enforcement agencies in different localities in order that they might coordinate their investigations, pool information, and apprehend fleeing suspects in today's mobile society. In an era when criminal suspects are increasingly mobile and increasingly likely to flee across jurisdictional boundaries, this rule is a matter of common sense: it minimizes the volume of information concerning suspects that must be transmitted to other jurisdictions and enables police in one jurisdiction to act promptly in reliance on information from another jurisdiction. *United States v. Nafzger*, 974 F.2d 906, 910–11 (7th Cir. 1992).

Like information from fellow officers, "information received from the NCIC (National Crime Information Center) computer bank has been routinely accepted in establishing probable cause for a valid arrest." *United States v. Hines*, 564 F.2d 925 (10th Cir. 1977). Of course, if the collective knowledge of the police is later determined insufficient to establish probable cause, then the actual arrest would be constitutionally invalid due to the absence of probable cause. *Whiteley v. Warden*, 401 U.S. 560 (1971). However, even though such an arrest would be invalid because it was not supported by probable cause, so long as an officer making such an arrest acts in good faith on the basis of the collective information from other officers, the arresting officer would be protected from civil and criminal liability. *Henry v. United States*, 361 U.S. 98 (1959). If, on the other hand, an officer who makes an arrest without a good-faith basis for the arrest's legality may be liable in a civil lawsuit for violation of the Fourth Amendment rights of the arrestee. *Albright v. Oliver*, 510 U.S. 266 (1994).

KEY POINTS

L02
- Probable cause exists where the facts and circumstances within a law enforcement officer's knowledge, and of which the officer has reasonably trustworthy information, are sufficient in themselves to warrant a person of reasonable caution in the belief that (1) a crime has been or is being committed by a particular person or (2) seizable property will be found in a particular place or on a particular person.
- The fair probability of criminal activity is the standard for probable cause.
- Probable cause is evaluated by examining the collective information in the possession of the police at the time of the arrest or search, not merely the personal knowledge of the arresting or searching officer.

Individual Officer Knowledge Individual law enforcement officers applying for an arrest or search warrant are usually required to state *in writing* in the complaint or affidavit the underlying facts on which probable cause for the issuance of the warrant is based. All warrantless arrests and most warrantless searches must also be based on probable cause. Although no written document is required, officers must be prepared to justify a warrantless arrest or search with underlying facts if its validity is later challenged. Therefore, whether or not a warrant is sought, officers must have sufficient information supporting probable cause *before* conducting a search, arrest, or other seizure. Information on which probable cause may be based may come to the attention of a law enforcement officer in two ways: (1) the officer may personally perceive or gather the information using his or her own senses, or (2) other persons (e.g., victims, witnesses, reporters, informants, or other police agencies) may perceive or gather the information and provide it to the officer. These information sources are treated differently by the courts and are discussed separately here.

Information Obtained Through the Officer's Own Senses One type of information used to support probable cause is information from the officer's own senses: sight, hearing, smell, touch, and taste. Furthermore, an officer's experience or expertise in a particular area gives his or her perceptions additional credence:

> [I]n some situations a police officer may have particular training or experience that would enable him to infer criminal activity in circumstances where an ordinary observer would not. . . . In such situations, when an officer's experience and expertise is relevant to the probable cause determination, the officer must be able to explain sufficiently the basis of that opinion so that it "can be understood by the average reasonably prudent person." *State v. Demeter*, 590 A.2d 1179, 1183–84 (N.J. 1991).

A law enforcement officer's perceptions that a crime is being committed in his or her presence clearly provide probable cause to arrest the person committing the crime. Crimes are seldom committed in an officer's presence, however. Usually, an officer must develop probable cause over time from perceptions of a variety of facts and circumstances. The following discussion focuses on specific facts and circumstances that indicate criminal activity, together with court cases explaining their relative importance in the probable cause equation. It is important to remember that in all cases, the facts and circumstances establishing probable cause to arrest must come to the attention of the officer *before* the actual arrest and a search incident to that arrest.

In particular, this section will explore the following facts and circumstances an officer may use to establish probable cause:

- flight,
- furtive conduct,
- real or physical evidence,
- admissions,
- false or implausible answers,
- presence at a crime scene or in a high-crime area,
- association with other known criminals, and
- past criminal conduct.

Flight "[D]eliberately furtive actions and flight at the approach of strangers or law officers are strong indicia of *mens rea* [guilty mind], and when coupled with specific knowledge on the part of the officer relating the suspect to the evidence of crime, they are proper factors to be considered in the decision to make an arrest." *Sibron v. New York*, 392 U.S. 40, 66–67 (1968). Accordingly, flight should be thought of as a factor in the overall probable cause determination but not as an action that automatically justifies arrest. *United States v. Bell*, 892 F.2d 959 (10th Cir. 1989), which first held that the following facts gave a narcotics officer reasonable suspicion to detain a suspect for investigation of transporting illegal drugs, illustrates this principle: The suspect disembarked from a flight originating in Hawaii and repeatedly went to a group of phones but did not appear to be talking; he had no luggage except his shoulder bag and appeared visibly nervous; he met another person, who was carrying a package, and walked with him around the airport. After citing the additional fact that when the officer detained and questioned the suspect, he dropped his bag and ran down the concourse, the court then held that this flight *plus* the other indications of criminal activity provided probable cause to arrest.

By itself, however, flight does not support a finding of probable cause. In *Wong Sun v. United States*, 371 U.S. 471 (1963), federal officers arrested a man named Hom Way at 2 A.M. and found narcotics in his possession. Hom Way told the officers that he had purchased an ounce of heroin from a person named Blackie Toy. Four hours later, at 6 A.M., the officers went to a laundry operated by James Wah Toy. When Toy answered the door and an officer identified himself, Toy slammed the door and ran to his living quarters at the rear of the building. The officers broke in and followed Toy to his bedroom, where they arrested him. The U.S. Supreme Court held that the officers did not have probable cause to arrest Toy. First, the officers had no basis for confidence in the reliability of Hom Way's information. (The reliability of informants is discussed later.) Second, the Court explained that the mere fact of Toy's flight did not provide a probable cause justification for a warrantless arrest, at least without any further information. The Court said:

> Toy's refusal to admit the officers and his flight down the hallway thus signified a guilty knowledge no more clearly than it did a natural desire to repel an apparently unauthorized intrusion. . . . A contrary holding here would mean that a vague suspicion could be transformed into probable cause for arrest by reason of ambiguous conduct [e.g., flight] which the arresting officers themselves have provoked. 371 U.S. at 483–84.

However, when flight is combined with other factors, such as secretive or furtive conduct (discussed more fully later), lower courts are more willing to find the probable cause standard met as illustrated by the following quotation from *United States v. Hayes*, 236 F.3d 891, 894 (7th Cir. 2001):

> At the time that Hayes was arrested, the officers had been presented with facts sufficient to indicate that Hayes was committing the offense of carrying a concealed weapon. At that time, the officers had already heard from Webb who told them that he observed Hayes with the gun, and that Hayes attempted to place the gun in the couch cushions but then ran off with it. That eyewitness account was consistent with the officer's own observation of Hayes attempting to place something in the couch. Moreover, the officers had recovered a magazine for a nine-millimeter firearm that another witness identified as having been dropped by Hayes. In conjunction with Hayes' flight upon seeing the officers approaching him, the facts certainly warranted a person of reasonable caution to believe that Hayes had committed the offense of carrying a concealed weapon. [The] evidence established probable cause for the arrest.

Furtive Conduct Law enforcement officers frequently observe persons acting secretively or furtively. Such conduct usually at least justifies an officer's further investigation to determine whether a crime is being or is about to be committed. (See Chapter 7 on stops and frisks.) By itself, however, furtive conduct is insufficient to establish probable cause to arrest.

The person may be making a totally innocent gesture, exhibiting a physical or mental problem, or reacting in fear to an officer's presence. A person's nervousness in the presence of a law enforcement officer does not alone amount to probable cause. As the Supreme Court of Colorado stated, "It is normal for law-abiding persons, as well as persons guilty of criminal activity, to be nervous when stopped by a policeman for a traffic offense." *People v. Goessl*, 526 P.2d 664, 665 (Colo. 1974). A person should not be subject to arrest or search on the basis of a mistaken interpretation of an innocent action.

United States v. McCarty, 862 F.2d 143 (7th Cir. 1988), highlights the idea that furtive conduct should be accompanied by other facts and circumstances before probable cause will be found to exist. Officers in *McCarty* had corroborated information from informants that the defendant was a convicted felon, that he was driving a tan compact car with Michigan license plates bearing the number 278, and that he was likely to be carrying a gun. Officers on routine patrol saw the described car and followed it. The car attempted to evade the officers, and, when stopped, the driver was observed leaning to the right as if to hide something under the passenger seat. The officers arrested the defendant and seized a handgun found in his car. The court found probable cause to arrest the defendant for possession of a firearm by a convicted felon. "The fact that McCarty tried to evade [the officers] while they were following him, and his furtive gesture when he was stopped, reinforced the reasonableness of the officers' belief that McCarty had committed or was committing a crime." 862 F.2d at 147. Furtive conduct, therefore, is relevant to probable cause but must be evaluated in light of all the facts and circumstances, including time of day, setting, weather conditions, persons present, and nature of the crime.

United States v. Burhoe, 409 F.3d 5, 10 (1st Cir. 2005), found probable cause to arrest a suspect named Burhoe based on a combination of facts observed by the officer, one of which was furtive conduct (number 6 in the list created by the court):

> There was ample evidence of probable cause for [the suspect's arrest]. When Detective Fahey saw Burhoe on St. James Road, he knew: (1) a bank robbery had just taken place minutes earlier by two white males; (2) the suspects' getaway car had been abandoned on Fourth Street, the next street north of St. James Road; (3) the suspects were escaping on foot in the immediate vicinity; (4) Burhoe, a white male, emerged from a private yard, consistent with the route of a fugitive escaping from the abandoned car on Fourth Street one block to the north; (5) Burhoe did not look like he belonged there—at 10:30 on a workday morning, Burhoe was disheveled, dirty, and possibly intoxicated, not the usual sight in a residential neighborhood; (6) Burhoe behaved strangely: his furtive, "hide-and-seek" movements, quick dash across the road, and his attempt to remain hidden; (7) Fahey noticed an abnormal bulge in Burhoe's waist; and (8) to boot, Burhoe attempted to run away from Fahey. A "reasonably prudent person" would believe [Burhoe] had committed or was committing a crime.

Although furtive behavior by itself does not justify a search, furtive behavior may be considered a factor, and, as in this case, in combination with other factors, it may help establish probable cause.

Real or Physical Evidence Officers may establish probable cause by the observation and evaluation of real or physical evidence. For example, in *United States v. Harrell*, 268 F.3d 141 (2d Cir. 2001), the observation by the officer of tinted car windows, a violation of local traffic law, provided the probable cause to stop the vehicle.

In *State v. Heald*, 314 A.2d 820 (Me. 1973), officers were summoned at 2:00 A.M. to a store that had recently been burglarized. The officers discovered two sets of footprints in freshly fallen snow that led from the store to the tire tracks of an automobile. Because the tire tracks were identifiable by a distinctive tread, the officers followed them. After a short distance, the officers met another officer. He had found a checkbook belonging to the storeowner in the road. Farther down the road, the officers found a bag containing electrical parts. Then the officers came upon a car parked in the middle of the road with its lights off—the only other vehicle the officers had seen since leaving the scene of the crime. As the patrol car approached the parked car, its lights came on and the car was driven away. The officers stopped the car and arrested its two occupants for breaking and entering. The court held that the items of real evidence found and the reasonable inferences drawn from the evidence, together with the highly suspicious circumstances, provided probable cause to arrest the defendants. The court added that "although the possibility of mistake existed, as it invariably does in a probable cause situation, they would have been remiss in their duty if they had not arrested the defendants promptly." 314 A.2d at 825.

Admissions A person's admission of criminal conduct to a law enforcement officer provides probable cause to arrest. In *Rawlings v. Kentucky*, 448 U.S. 98 (1980), a law enforcement officer with a search warrant ordered the defendant's female companion (Cox) to empty the contents of her purse. When she poured out a large quantity and variety of controlled substances, she told the defendant to take what was his. The defendant immediately claimed ownership of some of the controlled substances. The Court held that "[o]nce petitioner admitted ownership of the sizable quantity of drugs found in Cox's purse, the police clearly had probable cause to place the petitioner under arrest." 448 U.S. at 111.

Some "admissions," however, may not give rise to probable cause to arrest. For example, in *Kent v. Katz*, 312 F.3d 568 (2d Cir. 2002), the court found that redness of the eyes and the arrestee's statement "not too much" in response to an officer's question regarding whether the arrestee had been drinking, did not provide probable cause to arrest for driving while intoxicated:

> [T]he existence of probable cause is to be determined on the basis of the totality of the circumstances, and we cannot conclude that it would have been objectively reasonable as a matter of law for [the officer] to infer intoxication solely from the redness of [the arrestee's] eyes, while ignoring as a possible cause of discoloration the fact that [the arrestee] had been burning brush for the past 18 days, and from [the arrestee's] statement that he had not been drinking very much, while ignoring all other comportment that might reflect on the state of [the arrestee's] sobriety. 312 F.3d at 576.

The court explained that the officer's interpretation of the arrestee's "admission" of intoxication was misguided:

> And while [the officer] contends that [the arrestee's] "[n]ot very much" statement, regardless of the intention that lay behind those words, constituted an admission of alcohol consumption, even taken at face value the words "[n]ot very much" would not ordinarily seem to imply "enough to be intoxicated." 312 F.3d at 576.

False or Implausible Answers False or implausible answers to routine questions may be considered in determining probable cause, but standing alone they do not provide probable cause. For example, *United States v. Velasquez*, 885 F.2d 1076 (3d Cir. 1989), held that the following facts provided probable cause to arrest the defendant for interstate smuggling of contraband: (1) the defendant and her companion were on a long-distance trip from Miami, a major drug importation point, to the New York area; (2) they had given a law enforcement officer conflicting stories about the purpose of their trip and their relationship; (3) they appeared nervous when answering the officer's questions; (4) the defendant told the officer that the automobile she was driving belonged to her "cousin" but could not give her cousin's name; and (5) the automobile had a false floor in its trunk and appeared specially modified to carry contraband in a secret compartment. Facts 2 and 4 appeared to contain false or implausible answers. It is important to note, however, that the Court only found probable cause to arrest in light of other existing, "suspicious" facts, including ones related to physical evidence.

In *United States v. Reed*, 443 F.3d 600, 605 (7th Cir. 2006), the court found probable cause to arrest the defendant, a passenger in a vehicle, based, in part, on implausible and inconsistent answers to routine questions:

> [The defendant's] own conduct furthered that inference of a common enterprise [to conceal the proceeds of illegal activity], in that his response to the purpose of the [road] trip was also contradictory. His explanation that the purpose of the trip was so that [his companion] could finalize his divorce was inconsistent with [the companion's] explanation [which was that defendant and he were traveling to purchase horses], and [the defendant] too provided no explanation as to the origin of the horses [in a trailer attached to the vehicle]. The evidence was sufficient to support a finding of probable cause in this case.

Presence at a Crime Scene or in a High-Crime Area Mere presence at a crime scene or in a high-crime area does not by itself constitute probable cause to arrest. For instance, in *Johnson v. United States*, 333 U.S. 10 (1948), the Court found an absence of probable cause to arrest when police officers placed a woman under arrest for suspicion of drug activity while she was inside a hotel room. They then searched the hotel room. The officers' suspicions regarding the room stemmed from a tip they had received that unknown persons were smoking in a hotel as well as the smell of drugs emanating from the room. The Court acknowledged that the room was essentially a crime scene (drugs and drug paraphernalia were found there during a subsequent search). But *before* entering without a warrant, the officers lacked evidence that established probable cause to *arrest* a *specific* individual for drug use within the room (e.g., perhaps not everyone or perhaps no one was engaging in drug use within the room). The Court did acknowledge that had the police sought a *search* warrant before entering the room, probable cause may have existed to issue such a warrant. Of course, had the police had a search warrant for the room and then discovered drugs upon entering the room, probable cause may have also existed to arrest the sole female occupant.

On more specific and numerous facts linking particular individuals to a crime, another case found probable cause to arrest the defendant at an automobile crime scene. *Maryland v. Pringle*, 540 U.S. 366 (2003), held that an officer who found drugs in the backseat of a car had probable cause to arrest the driver and the front-seat and backseat passengers. The officer had stopped the car for speeding and, when the driver opened the glove compartment to obtain his registration, the officer observed "a large amount of rolled-up money." After obtaining consent to search the car, the officer found five baggies containing cocaine placed between the back armrest and the backseat of the car. Although the Court did not announce a bright-line rule that the discovery of drugs or contraband in the passenger compartment of a vehicle provides probable cause to arrest all the occupants, the Court found probable cause to arrest the defendant in the totality of the circumstances of this case:

- The defendant was one of three men riding in a car at 3:16 A.M.
- The glove compartment in front of the defendant contained $763 of rolled-up cash.
- Five baggies of cocaine were found behind the backseat armrest.
- The cocaine was accessible to all three occupants.
- All three occupants denied any knowledge about the money and cocaine.
- The amount of drugs and money found indicated that one or more of the occupants were selling drugs.

- It was reasonable for the officer to believe that all the occupants knew about the cocaine because drug dealing is "an enterprise to which a dealer would be unlikely to admit an innocent person with the potential to furnish evidence against him." 540 U.S. at 373.

Because these circumstances made it reasonable for the officer to believe "that any or all three of the occupants had knowledge of, and exercised dominion and control over, the cocaine," the arrest of the defendant was lawful.

Even when no crime has been reported, suspicious activity in a high-crime area may contribute to probable cause. Simply being present in a high-crime area, however, is not enough for probable cause. *United States v. Green*, 670 F.2d 1148 (D.C. Cir. 1981), identified four factors to be evaluated in determining whether the "totality of the circumstances" provides probable cause to arrest for drug trafficking:

- the suspect's presence in a neighborhood notorious for drug trafficking or other crimes,
- the suspect's engaging with others in a sequence of events typical of a drug transaction,
- a suspect's flight after being confronted by police, and
- a suspect's attempt to conceal the subject of his business.

Association with Other Known Criminals A suspect's association with other known criminals does not by itself provide probable cause to arrest, but it may be considered in the probable cause equation. *United States v. Di Re*, 332 U.S. 581 (1948), held that a defendant's presence in a car with others who illegally possessed counterfeit ration coupons did not provide probable cause to arrest because no other information linked him to the crime.

> The argument that one who "accompanies a criminal to a crime rendezvous" cannot be assumed to be a bystander, forceful enough in some circumstances, is farfetched when the meeting is not secretive or in a suspicious hideout but in broad daylight, in plain sight of passersby, in a public street of a large city, and where the alleged substantive crime is one which does not necessarily involve any act visibly criminal. If Di Re had witnessed the passing of papers from hand to hand, it would not follow that he knew they were ration coupons, and if he saw that they were ration coupons, it would not follow that he would know them to be counterfeit. . . . Presumptions of guilt are not lightly to be indulged from mere meetings. 332 U.S. at 593.

In contrast to *Di Re*, the Court in *Ker v. California*, 374 U.S. 23 (1963), found probable cause to arrest the wife of a drug suspect based on her presence in an apartment she shared with her husband that police knew was being used as the base for his narcotics operation. Besides this particular knowledge, police also found the wife in a room of the apartment where drugs were located, yet another distinction from the earlier *Di Re* case (where the suspect was found near less obvious illegal evidence). The Court explained:

> Probable cause for the arrest of petitioner Diane Ker, while not present at the time the officers entered the apartment to arrest her husband, was nevertheless present at the time of her arrest. Upon their entry and announcement of their identity, the officers were met not only by George Ker but also by Diane Ker, who was emerging from the kitchen. Officer Berman immediately walked to the doorway from which she emerged and, without entering, observed the brickshaped package of marijuana in plain view. Even assuming that her presence in a small room with the

contraband in a prominent position on the kitchen sink would not alone establish a reasonable ground for the officers' belief that she was in joint possession with her husband, that fact was accompanied by the officers' information that Ker had been using his apartment as a base of operations for his narcotics activities. Therefore, we cannot say that at the time of her arrest there were not sufficient grounds for a reasonable belief that Diane Ker, as well as her husband, was committing the offense of possession of marijuana in the presence of the officers. 374 U.S. at 36–37.

In *United States v. Lima*, 819 F.2d 687 (7th Cir. 1987), the Court also found probable cause to arrest a suspect clearly associated with other criminal actors. Here the suspect arrived at the scene of a drug transaction shortly after the other participants, parked directly behind another participant's car, and conversed with another participant who walked over to the suspect's car while the transaction was taking place. The court added that "any innocent interpretation is further undermined by the fact that neither [of the other principals] called off or postponed the delivery of the drugs despite [the suspect's] presence." 819 F.2d at 690.

Past Criminal Conduct A suspect's criminal record does not by itself give an officer probable cause to arrest the suspect:

> We do not hold that the officer's knowledge of the petitioner's physical appearance and previous record was either inadmissible or entirely irrelevant upon the issue of probable cause. . . . But to hold that knowledge of either or both of these facts constituted probable cause would be to hold that anyone with a previous criminal record could be arrested at will. *Beck v. Ohio*, 379 U.S. 89, 97 (1964).

A suspect's prior criminal activity may, however, be considered with other indications of criminal activity in establishing probable cause. In *United States v. Harris*, 403 U.S. 573 (1971), an affidavit for a search warrant stated that the defendant had a reputation for four years as a trafficker in illegal whiskey, that during this period a large cache of illegal whiskey had been found in an abandoned house under the defendant's control, and that an informant said that he had purchased illicit whiskey inside the house for two years and within the past two weeks. The U.S. Supreme Court found that this information provided probable cause for issuance of the search warrant. And in *United States v. Reed*, discussed earlier, the Seventh Circuit found probable cause to arrest defendant based, in part, on his prior record:

> In addition, the officers knew that two of the travelers in the vehicle [which included defendant] had prior drug arrests, which further supports the reasonableness of the belief that the currency [found in the vehicle] was the proceeds of illegal activity. [Defendant's] prior drug arrests did nothing to dispel the suspicion that he was involved in a common enterprise to conceal the proceeds of illegal activity [i.e., the currency]. 443 F.3d at 604–605.

Officer Training, Knowledge, and Experience Officers may use their experience, training, and knowledge in determining probable cause to connect a defendant with criminal activity. *See Texas v. Brown*, 460 U.S. 730 (1983); *see also Terry v. Ohio*, 392 U.S. 1 (1968). Note, however, that officers must be ready and able to explain to others how their

KEY POINTS

LO2 ■ Information perceived by a law enforcement officer through any of the five senses may support probable cause.

■ An officer's perceptions used in establishing probable cause may be given additional credence because of the officer's personal training, knowledge, or experience in a particular area. Officers should be prepared to explain how their training, knowledge, or experience, along with other perceived factors, led them to develop probable cause.

LO3 ■ The following facts and circumstances may be considered in determining probable cause: flight, furtive conduct, real or physical evidence connecting a person with criminal activity, admission of criminal conduct, false or implausible answers to routine questions, presence at a crime scene or in a high-crime area, association with other known criminals, and past criminal conduct.

experience, training, and knowledge led them to develop probable cause. *United States v. Munoz*, 738 F. Supp. 800 (S.D.N.Y. 1990), held that an FBI agent's observations, knowledge, and assumptions that a kidnapper would take several people along for security when he went to pick up ransom money were enough to establish probable cause to arrest an accomplice who was "observed doing nothing but sitting as a passenger in the Jeep." 738 F. Supp. at 802. But *Ybarra v. Illinois*, 444 U.S. 85 (1979), a Supreme Court case, held that the search of a patron in a bar violated the Fourth Amendment because the patron was not named in the warrant and the searching officer, though possessing a warrant to search the bar premises and bartender, did not have probable cause connecting the patron to the criminal activity under investigation.

Information Obtained by an Officer Through Informants

Few crimes are committed in the presence of law enforcement officers. Therefore, officers must usually rely on information from sources other than their own perceptions to establish probable cause to arrest or search. This information may come from ordinary citizen informants or criminal informants who have themselves personally perceived indications of criminal activity. (The term **informant** means any person from whom a law enforcement officer obtains information on criminal activity.) The method of establishing probable cause through the use of an informant's information is sometimes referred to as the *hearsay method*, as opposed to the direct observation method discussed earlier. The problem with using information from informants is ensuring that the information is trustworthy and credible enough to be acted on. Courts have developed elaborate rules and procedures to ensure the trustworthiness of information from informants used to support probable cause. The various approaches used by courts to evaluate whether informant testimony can serve as a basis for probable cause are discussed later (beginning with the two-part *Aguilar-Spinelli* approach and ending with the *Gates* totality-of-circumstances approach).

As an important side note, the ensuing discussion on probable cause and informant testimony focuses on a law enforcement officer applying for a search warrant based on information from informants. This approach helps to emphasize that an officer should *write down* in the affidavit or complaint, which serves as the basis for the search warrant, all the information on which probable cause is based, including information from informants. The same probable cause considerations in the informant context are involved in arrest warrants and warrantless arrests and searches, except that the information is not written down in the warrantless situation. Officers should, however, keep careful written records of the circumstances surrounding warrantless arrests and searches.

The Dual-Pronged Approach of *Aguilar-Spinelli* In *Illinois v. Gates*, 462 U.S. 213 (1983), the U.S. Supreme Court abandoned a particular approach to determining probable cause through the use of informants established by two previous decisions: *Aguilar v. Texas*, 378 U.S. 108 (1964), and *Spinelli v. United States*, 393 U.S. 410 (1969). *Aguilar* and *Spinelli* had established a two-pronged test for law enforcement officers to follow in determining probable cause using information from informants. The *Gates* decision abandoned rigid adherence to this test in favor of a "totality of the circumstances" approach to determining probable cause.

Despite *Gates*, there are good reasons for discussing *Aguilar* and *Spinelli* in detail. First, the underlying rationales of these decisions retain their vitality in analyzing the totality of the circumstances under *Gates*. Second, several states have rejected *Gates* on the basis of state constitutions or statutes. They still require affidavits based on informant testimony to be prepared according to the *Aguilar* and *Spinelli* requirements. For example, *People v. Griminger*, 524 N.E.2d 409 (N.Y. 1988), held that, as a matter of New York law, the *Aguilar-Spinelli* two-pronged test should be employed in determining the sufficiency of an affidavit submitted in support of a search warrant application. The court specifically

CRIMINAL PROCEDURE **IN ACTION**

Can Matching a Criminal Profile Establish Probable Cause?

If a suspect's actions, demeanor, or appearance matches the components of a predetermined criminal profile, can this fact alone give rise to probable cause to arrest? To understand the answer to this question, consider *Florida v. Royer*, 460 U.S. 491 (1983), a major U.S. Supreme Court decision in the area of criminal profiling. In that case, the police detained an

individual at an airport because he fit the following components of the "drug courier" profile: (1) he carried a certain brand of luggage that appeared heavy in weight; (2) he was young and dressed casually; (3) he appeared nervous; (4) he bought his ticket with cash; (5) he failed to identify himself fully on his luggage tags; (6) he traveled from a drug import city (Miami); and (7) he possessed a different name from the one appearing on his airline ticket (i.e., it appeared that he used an alias while traveling). On these facts, the U.S. Supreme Court determined there was no probable cause to arrest the suspect but that there was reasonable suspicion to briefly detain and question him. 460 U.S. at 506. (See Chapter 8 for a detailed description of two other cases—*Reid v. Georgia* and *United States v. Sokolow*—where the Court analyzed whether reasonable

suspicion for a detention, or "stop," by police existed in so-called drug courier profile cases.)

1. Do you agree or disagree with the Court's opinion in Royer that police should not be able to use criminal profiles to establish probable cause for an arrest? Defend and explain your position.

2. In your mind, what is the concern, if any, with police using criminal profiles to establish probable cause for an arrest? In other words, are these types of profiles a legitimate law enforcement technique?

3. What if the police were required to create and make known the profile before being allowed to arrest individuals based on it? Does this change your thinking in any way?

found that the *Gates* test did not offer a suitable alternative to the *Aguilar-Spinelli* approach of determining credibility and reliability in the informant context.

Before *Gates*, *Aguilar v. Texas*, 378 U.S. 108 (1964), was the leading case on establishing probable cause either partially or entirely from informant testimony. *Aguilar* set out a *two-pronged test*, both of which prongs had to be satisfied to establish probable cause:

1. The affidavit must describe underlying circumstances from which a neutral and detached magistrate may determine that the informant had a *sufficient basis* for his or her knowledge and that the information was not the result of mere rumor or suspicion.

2. The affidavit must describe underlying circumstances from which the magistrate may determine that the informant was *credible* or that the informant's information was *reliable*.

Prong 1: Informant's Basis of Knowledge A law enforcement officer must demonstrate underlying circumstances to enable a magistrate to independently evaluate the accuracy of an informant's conclusion. The affidavit must show how the informant knows his or her information (e.g., the basis of the informant's information) by demonstrating that

- the informant personally perceived the information given to the officer (e.g., the informant's information is firsthand), or
- the informant's information came from another source, but there is good reason to believe it (e.g., the informant's information is secondhand).

Informant's Information Is Firsthand If the informant obtained the information by personal perception, the officer merely has to state in the affidavit *how*, *when*, and *where* the informant obtained the information furnished to the officer. In *State v. Daniels*, 200 N.W.2d 403 (Minn. 1972), the affidavit stated:

> For approximately the past two months I have received information from an informant whose information has recently resulted in narcotic arrests and convictions that a Gregory Daniels who resides at 929 Logan N (down) has been selling marijuana, hashish and heroin. My informant further states that he has seen Daniels sell drugs, namely: heroin and further that he has seen Daniels with heroin on his person. The informant has seen heroin on the premises of 929 Logan N (down) within the past 48 hours. 200 N.W.2d at 404.

The court said, "There seems to be no dispute that such personal observation satisfies that part of the *Aguilar* test which requires that the affidavit contain facts to enable the magistrate to judge whether the informant obtained his knowledge in a reliable manner." 200 N.W.2d at 406. Similarly, in *Jones v. United States*, 362 U.S. 257, 271 (1960), the U.S. Supreme Court found a sufficient basis of knowledge when the informant explained that he personally purchased drugs from the suspects at their apartment.

Stating the *time* when the informant obtained the information is very important, especially in applications for search warrants, because probable cause to search can become stale with time. In *United States v. Huggins*, 733 F. Supp. 445 (D.D.C. 1990), the court said, "[T]here is nothing in the affidavit from which the date of the controlled purchase can be determined and accordingly there was no way for the judicial officer to determine whether the information was stale. The controlled purchase could have occurred 'a day, a week, or months before the affidavit.'" 733 F. Supp. at 447. Also, in *United States v. Kennedy*, 427 F.3d 1136, 1141–43 (8th Cir. 2005), the Court found no probable cause to search the trunk of a vehicle because the informant's tip failed to include the time when she had apparently observed drugs in that location.

Informant's Information Is Secondhand (Hearsay) If the informant's information comes from a third person, the third person and his or her information must also satisfy both prongs of the *Aguilar* test. The affidavit must show how the third person knows the information furnished to the informant. For example, if the third person saw criminal activity taking place at a particular time, a statement to that effect would be sufficient to satisfy *Aguilar*'s first prong. The officer must, however, also satisfy *Aguilar*'s second prong with respect to both the informant *and* the third person. (*Aguilar*'s second prong, dealing with whether the informant is trustworthy or credible, will be discussed later in this chapter.)

Detailing Informant's Information Courts recognize another method of satisfying *Aguilar*'s first prong besides stating how, when, and where the informant obtained his or her information. In *Spinelli v. United States*, 393 U.S. 410 (1969), the Court said:

> In the absence of a statement detailing the manner in which the information was gathered, it is especially important that the tip describe the accused's criminal activity in sufficient detail that the magistrate may know that he is relying on something more substantial than a casual rumor circulating in the underworld or an accusation based merely on an individual's general reputation. 393 U.S. at 416.

In *Spinelli* itself, the Court concluded that sufficient detail was not provided by the informant to satisfy *Aguilar*'s first prong because the informant only mentioned that the defendant was using two particular telephones for his illegal gambling operations. *Spinelli* cited *Draper v. United States*, 358 U.S. 307 (1959), as an example of sufficient use of detail to satisfy *Aguilar*'s first prong. Although the informant in *Draper* did not state the manner in which he obtained his information, he did report that the defendant had gone to Chicago the day before by train and that he would return to Denver by train with three ounces of heroin on one of two specified mornings. The informant went on to describe, with minute particularity, the clothes the defendant would be wearing and the bag he would be carrying on his arrival in Denver. The Supreme Court said that "[a] magistrate, when confronted with such detail, could reasonably infer that the informant had gained his information in a reliable way." 393 U.S. at 417; *see also United States v. Nieman*, 520 F.3d 834, 840 (8th Cir. 2008) (probable cause to issue search warrant because five separate, trustworthy informants gave police detailed and consistent information concerning the defendant).

In summary, if a law enforcement officer does not know how, when, or where an informant obtained information, the officer can still satisfy *Aguilar*'s first prong by obtaining as much detail as possible from the informant and stating all of it in the affidavit.

Prong 2: Informant's Veracity or Truthfulness *Aguilar*'s second prong requires the officer to demonstrate in the affidavit underlying circumstances to convince the magistrate of the informant's veracity—that is, that the informant is trustworthy or credible. The vast majority of cases have dealt with the credibility aspect of the informant's veracity rather than with the reliability of the informant's actual information. The amount and type of information required to establish credibility depends on whether the informant is an ordinary citizen informant or a criminal informant.

Ordinary Citizen Informants Ordinary citizen informants, such as victims and eyewitnesses, are usually presumed credible, and no further evidence of credibility need be stated in the affidavit beyond their name and address and their status as a victim of, or witness to, a crime.

> [A]n ordinary citizen who reports a crime which has been committed in his presence, or that a crime is being or will be committed, stands on much different ground than a police informer. He is a witness to criminal activity who acts with an intent to aid the police in law enforcement because of his concern for society or for his own safety. He does not expect any gain or concession for his information. An informer of this type usually would not have more than one opportunity to supply information to the police, thereby precluding proof of his reliability by pointing to previous accurate information which he has supplied. *State v. Paszek*, 184 N.W.2d 836, 843 (Wis. 1971).

Another reason for accepting the credibility of an ordinary citizen is the average person's fear of potential criminal or civil action for deliberately or negligently providing false information. *People v. Hicks*, 341 N.E.2d 227 (N.Y. 1975). Indeed, the U.S. Supreme Court, in *Chambers v. Maroney*, 399 U.S. 42 (1970), did not require a special credibility showing for ordinary teenage citizens who were eyewitnesses to a robbery.

Nevertheless, some courts require additional information to establish the credibility of an ordinary citizen informant if the citizen merely provides an anonymous tip. For example, in *State v. White*, 396 S.E.2d 601, 603 (Ga. App. 1990), the court said:

> This court has always given the concerned citizen informer a preferred status insofar as testing the credibility of his information. . . . However, before an anonymous tipster can be elevated to the status of "concerned citizen," thereby gaining entitlement to the preferred status regarding credibility concomitant with that title, there must be placed before the magistrate facts from which it can be concluded that the anonymous tipster is, in fact, a "concerned citizen." . . . The affidavit in the case at bar contained no information from which it could be gleaned that the tipster was, in fact, a "concerned citizen." The magistrate was given nothing other than the affiant's conclusory statement that the tipster was a concerned citizen. That will not suffice.

Brown v. Commonwealth, 187 S.E.2d 160 (Va. 1972), found an ordinary citizen informant credible when the affidavit stated that, although the informant had not previously furnished information to the police concerning violations of the narcotics laws, he was steadily employed, was a registered voter, enjoyed a good reputation in his neighborhood, and had expressed concern for young people involved with narcotics.

In general, the cases discussed in this area show that regardless of whether the ordinary citizen informant is an anonymous or known informant, the more information provided in the affidavit about an ordinary citizen informant, the more likely this type of informant will be found to be credible. If, however, the informant appears in person before the magistrate and testifies under oath, subject to a charge of perjury if the information provided is false, no further evidence of credibility is needed. Personally testifying "provides powerful indicia of veracity and reliability." *United States v. Elliott*, 893 F.2d 220, 223 (9th Cir. 1990).

Also, as previously explained in the context of probable cause and the collective knowledge of police, generally no special credibility showing is needed when a police officer provides probable cause information to another officer. In this sense, police officers are treated similarly to "ordinary citizen informants."

For certain crimes, the law enforcement officer must show not only that the informant is credible but also that the informant has some expertise in recognizing that a crime has been committed. In *United States v. Hernandez*, 825 F.2d 846 (5th Cir. 1987), the informant (Marone) told the police that the defendant (Hernandez) had attempted to pass counterfeit money. The Court determined that Marone had sufficient expertise and experience with recognizing counterfeit bills because he dealt frequently with currency in his profession and was able to confidently ascertain the counterfeit nature of the bill Hernandez gave him. 825 F.2d at 849–50.

Criminal Informants Unlike an ordinary citizen's credibility or truthfulness, which may sometimes be presumed, the criminal informant's credibility must always be established by a statement of underlying facts and circumstances. Criminal informants may be professional police informants, persons with a criminal record, accomplices in a crime, or persons seeking immunity for themselves. Usually, criminal informants do not want their identities disclosed in an affidavit. The U.S. Supreme Court held that an informant's identity need not be disclosed if his or her credibility is otherwise satisfactorily established. *McCray v. Illinois,* 386 U.S. 300, 306–07 (1967), stated the reasons for this rule:

> If a defendant may insist upon disclosure of the informant in order to test the truth of the officer's statement . . . , we can be sure that every defendant will demand disclosure. He has nothing to lose and the prize may be the suppression of damaging evidence if the State cannot afford to reveal its source, as is so often the case. . . . The result would be that the State could use the informant's information only as a lead and could search only if it could gather adequate evidence of probable cause apart from the informant's data. . . . [W]e doubt that there would be enough talent and time to cope with crime upon that basis. Rather we accept the premise that the informer is a vital part of society's defensive arsenal. The basic rule protecting his identity rests upon that belief.

Furthermore, although statements made by the police officer in the affidavit can be challenged by a defendant, statements by informants are much more difficult to challenge. *See Franks v. Delaware*, 438 U.S. 154, 171 (1978). (*Franks* is discussed in more detail in Chapter 4.) Whether or not the criminal informant's identity is disclosed, the affidavit must contain a statement of underlying facts and circumstances supporting credibility. The following facts and circumstances are relevant.

1. Informant has given accurate information in the past. The usual method of establishing the credibility of a criminal informant is by showing that the informant has in the past given accurate information that has led to arrests, convictions, recovery of stolen property, or the like. The affidavit may not state simply that an informant is credible because of proven credibility. Stating facts demonstrating that the informant has given accurate information in the past is sometimes referred to as establishing the informant's "track record." Magistrates are required to evaluate affidavits attempting to establish the credibility of informants in a commonsense manner and not with undue technicality. *United States v. Ventresca,* 380 U.S. 102 (1965). The main concern of the magistrate is the *accuracy* of the information supplied by the informant in the past.

For example, *People v. Lawrence,* 273 N.E.2d 637 (Ill. App. 1971), found an informant credible even though none of his prior tips had resulted in convictions. The Court stated that "[c]onvictions, while corroborative of an informer's reliability, are not essential in establishing his reliability. Arrests, standing alone, do not establish reliability. . . . The true test of his reliability is the accuracy of his information." 273 N.E.2d at 639. Another case, *United States v. Dunnings,* 425 F.2d 836, 839 (2d Cir. 1969), found sufficient a statement that the informant had "furnished reliable and accurate information on approximately 20 occasions over the past four years." *State v. Daniels,* 200 N.W.2d 403, 406–07 (Minn. 1972), held that the credibility of the informant was sufficiently shown when the affidavit stated that the informant's information "has recently resulted in narcotic arrests and convictions." In addition, in *McCray v. Illinois,* 386 U.S. 300 (1967), informant credibility was found when the informant gave police accurate information at least fifteen different times, many of these instances leading to arrest and conviction. *See also United States v. Nieman,* 520 F.3d at 840 (informants found to be trustworthy because "many of the informants [had] previously provided reliable information later used to convict other drug traffickers and money launderers").

Generally, the more information provided about an informant's track record, the more likely the magistrate will find the informant credible. Types of information considered relevant in determining informant credibility are

- the time when the informant furnished previous information;
- specific examples of verification of the accuracy of the informant's information;
- a description of how the informant's information helped in bringing about an arrest, conviction, or other result;
- documentation of the informant's consistency in providing accurate information; and
- details of the informant's "general background, employment, personal attributes that enable him to observe and relate accurately, position in the community, reputation with others, personal connection with the suspect, any circumstances which suggest the probable absence of any motivation to falsify, the apparent motivation for supplying the information, the presence or absence of a criminal record or association with known criminals, and the like." *United States v. Harris,* 403 U.S. 573 (1971) (dissenting opinion).

If an officer has no *personal* knowledge of an informant's credibility, the officer may state in the affidavit information about the informant's credibility received from other law enforcement officers. *State v. Lambert,* 363 A.2d 707 (Me. 1976). The officer should state the names of other law enforcement officers and describe in detail how those officers acquired personal knowledge of the informant's credibility.

2. Informant made a criminal admission or turned over evidence against the informant's own penal interest. *United States v. Harris*, 403 U.S. 573 (1971), held that an admission made by an informant against the informant's own penal interest is sufficient to establish the credibility of the informant. The Court reasoned:

> People do not lightly admit a crime and place critical evidence in the hands of the police in the form of their own admissions. Admissions of crime, like admissions against proprietary interests, carry their own indicia of credibility—sufficient at least to support a finding of probable cause to search. That the informant may be paid or promised a "break" does not eliminate the residual risk and opprobrium of having admitted criminal conduct. 403 U.S. at 583–84.

State v. Appleton, 297 A.2d 363 (Me. 1972), held that an informant's turning over to police recently purchased drugs against his own penal interest was also strongly convincing evidence of credibility. "An informant is not likely to turn over to the police such criminal evidence unless he is certain in his own mind that his story implicating the persons occupying the premises where the sale took place will withstand police scrutiny." 297 A.2d at 369.

Corroboration An officer may use corroboration to bolster information that is insufficient to satisfy either or both *Aguilar* prongs. Corroboration means strengthening or confirming the information supplied by the informant with supporting information obtained by law enforcement officers. For example, assume an officer receives a tip from a reliable informant about criminal activity. Through surveillance or independent investigation, the officer personally perceives further indications of that criminal activity. By including this corroborating information in the affidavit with the informant's information, the officer enables a magistrate to consider all facts that support probable cause, no matter what the source of the information.

The corroborative information provided by the law enforcement officer in the affidavit may work in three possible ways:

1. The information obtained by the officer may *in itself* provide probable cause independent of the informant's information. (See "Information Obtained Through the Officer's Own Senses" earlier in this chapter.) Corroborating information of this degree provides probable cause to search even if neither *Aguilar* prong is satisfied.

2. The officer's information may confirm or verify the information provided by the informant. In this case, the corroborating information may largely be of an innocent nature and not itself provide probable cause. For example, if significant yet innocent details of the informant's information are shown to be true by the independent observation of a law enforcement officer, the magistrate is more likely to be convinced of the trustworthiness of all the information provided by the informant. This occurred in the *Draper* case previously mentioned when officers, through observation, were able to corroborate the intricate yet innocent details provided by the tip.

3. The officer's information may be added to an informant's information that meets *Aguilar* standards. Although neither standing alone is sufficient to establish probable cause, a combination of all the information may be sufficient.

Therefore, to ensure that a magistrate is presented with sufficient information on which to base a determination of probable cause, the affidavit should include

- all information directed toward satisfying *Aguilar*'s two-pronged test for informant information,

- all information perceived by law enforcement officers that corroborates the informant's information, and

- all additional corroborating information perceived by officers relating to the criminal activity for which a search warrant is being sought.

To illustrate how courts deal with corroboration, let's look in detail at *Spinelli* and *Dawson*, two cases with similar fact situations but different results.

Spinelli v. United States, 393 U.S. 410 (1969) *Spinelli* is the leading case on corroboration. The defendant (Spinelli) was convicted of traveling to St. Louis, Missouri, from a nearby Illinois suburb with the intention of conducting gambling activities prohibited by Missouri law. On appeal, he challenged the validity of a search warrant used to obtain incriminating evidence against him. The affidavit in support of the search warrant contained the following allegations:

1. The FBI had tracked the defendant's movements during five days in August 1965. On four of those days, the defendant was seen crossing a bridge from Illinois to St. Louis between 11 A.M. and 12:15 P.M. and parking his car in a lot used by residents of a certain apartment house between 3:30 P.M. and 4:45 P.M. On one day, the defendant was followed and was observed entering a particular apartment.

2. An FBI check with the telephone company revealed that this apartment contained two telephones with different numbers listed in the name Grace Hagen.

3. The defendant was known to the officer preparing the affidavit (the affiant) and to federal and local law enforcement agents as a "bookmaker, an associate of bookmakers, a gambler, and an associate of gamblers." 393 U.S. at 414.

4. The FBI had been informed by a confidential reliable informant that the defendant was operating a handbook, accepting wagers, and disseminating wagering information using Grace Hagen's telephone numbers.

The Court first discussed in detail allegation 4, the information obtained from the informant. The Court said:

> The informer's report must first be measured against Aguilar's standards so that its probative value can be assessed. If the tip is found inadequate under Aguilar, the other allegations which corroborate the information contained in the [informant's] report should then be considered. 393 U.S. at 415.

The Court found that *Aguilar*'s second prong, addressing informant veracity, was not satisfied because the affiant merely stated that he had been informed by a "confidential reliable informant." This was insufficient because no *underlying circumstances* were stated to show the magistrate that the informant was credible, such as examples from the informant's past track record.

Nor was *Aguilar*'s first prong satisfied. The officer's affidavit failed to state sufficient underlying circumstances (e.g., a "basis") for the informant's conclusion that the defendant was running a bookmaking operation. It said nothing about how, when, or where the informant received his information—whether he personally observed the defendant "at work" or whether he ever placed a bet with him. If the informant obtained his information from third persons, the affidavit did not explain why these sources were credible or how they obtained their information.

Finally, as previously mentioned, the informant's information did not describe the defendant's alleged criminal activity in sufficient detail to convince a magistrate that the information was more than mere rumor or suspicion.

The Court then considered allegations 1 and 2 of the affidavit tracking defendant's movements to the apartment to see if they provided sufficient corroboration of the informant's information or probable cause in and of themselves. The Court found no suggestion of criminal conduct. The defendant's travels to and from an apartment building and his entering a particular apartment did not necessarily indicate gambling activity. And certainly nothing was unusual about an apartment containing two separate telephones. The Court concluded:

> At most, these allegations indicated that Spinelli could have used the telephones specified by the informant for some purpose. This [corroborating information] cannot by itself be said to support both the inference that the informer was generally trustworthy and that he had made his charge against Spinelli on the basis of information obtained in a reliable way. 393 U.S. at 417.

Lastly, the Court considered allegation 3—that the defendant was "known" to the FBI and others as a gambler. The Court called this a bald and unilluminating assertion of police suspicion because it contained no facts indicating the defendant's past gambling activities to support it. Although criminal reputation may be considered in determining probable cause, without factual statements in support, such an allegation would not be useful in evaluating the affidavit.

The *Spinelli* case is instructive because it evaluates the *Aguilar* tests for establishing probable cause based on informant information and gives reasons why the affidavit failed those tests. It then evaluates other information in the affidavit in corroboration of the informant's information and shows why the corroborative information was inadequate to credit the informant's information or itself support a probable cause finding.

Dawson v. State, 276 A.2d 680 (Md. Spec. App. 1971) *Dawson* is similar to *Spinelli* except that the search warrant in *Dawson* was found to be valid. This discussion focuses on the differences between the two cases that caused the court in *Dawson* to reach a different conclusion.

The defendant (Dawson) was convicted of unlawfully maintaining premises for the purpose of selling lottery tickets and unlawfully betting, wagering, or gambling on the results of horse races. He appealed, claiming among other things that the search warrant of his home was illegal because probable cause was lacking.

The affidavit for the warrant contained nine paragraphs. The first paragraph listed the investigative experience of the affiant and ended with his conclusion that gambling activities were at that time being conducted at the defendant's premises. The third through ninth paragraphs contained the direct observations of the affiant officer. (These paragraphs are considered later.) The second paragraph dealt with an informant's information and is quoted here:

> That on Thursday April 17, 1969 your affiant interviewed a confidential source of information who has given reliable information in the past relating to illegal gambling activities which has resulted in the arrest and conviction of persons arrested for illegal gambling activities and that the source is personally known to your affiant. That this source related that there was illegal gambling activities taking place at 8103 Legation Road, Hyattsville Prince George's County, Maryland by one Donald Lee Dawson. That the source further related that the source would call [telephone number] and place horse and number bets with Donald Lee Dawson. 276 A.2d at 685.

The court analyzed this paragraph under *Aguilar*'s two-pronged test. By stating that the informant personally called the phone number and placed horse and number bets with the defendant, the affidavit established the informant's basis of knowledge.

In contrast, in *Spinelli*, nothing was said about how the informant obtained his information. The information supplied about the credibility of the informant was found barely sufficient, however. Because the affidavit stated that both arrests and convictions had resulted from the informant's information in the past, it was more than a mere conclusion or opinion of the affiant. It also went further than the affidavit in *Spinelli*, in which the informant was merely described as a "confidential reliable informant." Although more specific information on credibility would have been desirable, the court said:

> It may well be that the facts here recited are enough to establish the credibility of the informant. In view of the strong independent verification hereinafter to be discussed, however, it is unnecessary for the State to rely exclusively on such recitation. 276 A.2d at 686.

The court assumed that the credibility of the informant had *not* been adequately established and proceeded to discuss corroboration, carefully comparing the affidavit with that in *Spinelli*.

Paragraphs 3 through 9 of the *Dawson* affidavit stated that surveillance by the officer of the defendant's activities conducted during a six-day period in April 1969 revealed the following information:

- The defendant was observed to be engaged in no apparent legitimate employment during the period.

- The defendant had two telephones in his residence with two separate lines, both of which had silent listings. One of the defendant's silent listings had been picked up in the course of a raid on a lottery operation three years earlier in another town. In *Spinelli*, neither Spinelli's nor Grace Hagen's phone number had been previously picked up in a raided gambling headquarters.

- On each day of observation, the defendant was observed purchasing an *Armstrong scratch sheet*, which gives information about horses running at various tracks that day. In *Spinelli*, there was no daily purchase of an Armstrong scratch sheet or the like to evidence some daily interest in horse races.

- On each morning of observation, the defendant was observed to leave his house between 9:02 and 10:20 A.M., to return to his house between 11:20 A.M. and 12:06 P.M., and to remain in his house until after 6:00 P.M. The affiant, an expert, experienced gambling investigator, stated that during the hours between noon and 6:00 P.M., horse and number bets can be placed and betting results become available.

- On each day of observation, the defendant was observed during his morning rounds stopping at a number of places, including liquor stores and restaurants, for very short periods. He never purchased anything from any of the stores, nor did he eat or drink at the restaurants. The affiant stated that such brief regular stops are classic characteristics of the pickup-man phase of a gambling operation: "He picks up the 'action' (money and/or list of bets) from the previous day or evening from prearranged locations—'drops.' At the same time, he delivers cash to the appropriate locations for the payoff of yesterday's successful players." 276 A.2d at 689. In *Spinelli*, there were no observations of the pickup-man type of activity.

- On one of the days, the defendant was observed in close association all day with a person who had been arrested for alleged gambling violations three years earlier. In *Spinelli*, there was no observed association with a previously arrested gambler.

- Finally, the defendant had been arrested and convicted of gambling violations about three years earlier. In *Spinelli*, Spinelli was not a convicted gambler.

The court evaluated these allegations in their totality:

> [P]robable cause emerges not from any single constituent activity but, rather, from the overall pattern of activities. Each fragment of conduct may communicate nothing of significance, but the broad mosaic portrays a great deal. The whole may, indeed, be greater than the sum of its parts. 276 A.2d at 687.

Thus, any doubt as to the credibility of the informant in *Dawson* was effectively removed by the officer's investigative efforts in corroborating the informant's information. Indeed, the court gave great weight to the officer's experience in investigating gambling activities and his interpretations of the defendant's conduct. The court concluded by noting how the direct observations of the officer and the informant information reinforced each other, and that the entire pattern of activity observed by the officer "weaves[s] a strong web of guilt." 276 A.2d at 689, 690. The court's emphasis on analyzing the overall pattern of activities and the totality of facts and circumstances in *Dawson* was an early harbinger of the approach to probable cause taken in the landmark decision of the U.S. Supreme Court in *Illinois v. Gates*.

Totality-of-the-Circumstances Test Under *Illinois v. Gates* As discussed earlier, *Illinois v. Gates*, 462 U.S. 213 (1983), abandoned rigid adherence to the *Aguilar-Spinelli* two-pronged test for determining probable cause through the use of informants for a totality-of-the-circumstances test. Nevertheless, the elements of the *Aguilar-Spinelli* test remain important considerations under the *Gates* test.

The* Gates *Case On May 3, 1978, the Bloomingdale, Illinois, police department received an anonymous letter that included statements that the defendants, Mr. and Mrs. Gates, made their living selling drugs; that the wife would drive their car to Florida on May 3 and leave it to be loaded up with drugs; that the husband would fly down in a few days to drive the car back loaded with more than $100,000 worth of drugs; and that the defendants had more than $100,000 worth of drugs in the basement of their home. Acting on the tip, a police officer obtained the defendants' address and learned that the husband had made a reservation for a May 5 flight to Florida. The officer then made arrangements with a Drug Enforcement Administration (DEA) agent for surveillance of the May 5 flight. The surveillance revealed that the husband took the flight and stayed overnight in a motel room registered to his wife. The next morning he headed north with an unidentified woman toward Bloomingdale in a car bearing Illinois license plates issued to the husband. A search warrant for the defendants' residence and automobile was obtained, based on these facts observed by police and the anonymous informant letter. When the defendants arrived home, the police searched the car and the residence and found marijuana.

At the state level, the Illinois Supreme Court found that the *Aguilar-Spinelli* two-pronged test had not been satisfied. First, the veracity prong was not satisfied because there was no basis for concluding that the anonymous person who wrote the letter to the police department was credible. Second, the basis-of-knowledge prong was not satisfied because the letter gave no information about how its writer knew of the defendants' activities. The Court therefore concluded that no showing of probable cause had been made.

In reversing the Illinois Supreme Court's decision, the U.S. Supreme Court first said:

> We agree with the Illinois Supreme Court that an informant's "veracity," "reliability" and "basis of knowledge" are all highly relevant in determining the value of his report. We do not agree, however, that these elements should be understood as entirely separate and independent

KEY POINTS

L05 ■ Corroboration means strengthening the information supplied by the informant in the affidavit by stating supporting or confirming information obtained by the independent investigation of law enforcement officers.

L06 ■ Corroboration is a two-way street. Direct observation of law enforcement officers may reinforce the information provided by the informant, and vice versa.

requirements to be rigidly exacted in every case, which the opinion of the Supreme Court of Illinois would imply. Rather . . . they should be understood simply as closely intertwined issues that may usefully illuminate the commonsense, practical question whether there is "probable cause" to believe that contraband or evidence is located in a particular place. 462 U.S. at 230.

In effect, the Court said that the elements of the *Aguilar-Spinelli* two-pronged test are important considerations in determining the existence of probable cause, but they should be evaluated only as part of the ultimate commonsense determination and not as independent, inflexible requirements or mechanistic rules. The Court believed that this totality-of-the-circumstances approach was more in keeping with the nature of probable cause as a fluid concept. According to the Court, the two prongs of *Aguilar-Spinelli* should be understood as "relevant considerations in the totality of circumstances that traditionally has guided probable cause determinations: a deficiency in one may be compensated for, in determining the overall reliability of a tip, by a strong showing as to the other, or by some other indicia of reliability." *Illinois v. Gates*, 462 U.S. at 233. For example, if an informant has a very long and successful track record of providing accurate information leading to arrests and convictions, this fact may compensate for a relatively weak showing on how the informant obtained his information in a particular case (e.g., his or her basis of knowledge). The entire process of determining probable cause can be stated simply as follows:

The task of the issuing magistrate is simply to make a practical, commonsense decision whether, given all the circumstances set forth in the affidavit before him, including the "veracity" and "basis of knowledge" of persons supplying hearsay information, there is a fair probability that contraband or evidence of a crime will be found in a particular place. 462 U.S. at 238–39.

With respect to the anonymous letter in *Gates*, the Supreme Court said that police corroboration of the letter's predictions that the defendants' car would be in Florida, that the husband would fly to Florida in a few days, and that the husband would drive the car back to Illinois indicated that the informant's other assertions regarding illegal activity were also true. In particular, the letter's accurate predictions of the defendants' future *innocent* actions made it more likely that the informant also had access to reliable information of the defendants' alleged illegal activities. Although the tip was corroborated only as to the defendants' seemingly innocent behavior, and although it by no means indicated with certainty that illegal drugs would be found in defendants' home, the Court believed that it provided details only "insiders" could know. "It is enough, for purposes of assessing probable cause, that 'corroboration through other sources of information reduced the chances of a reckless or prevaricating tale,' thus providing 'a substantial basis for crediting the hearsay.'" 462 U.S. at 244.

The *Gates* totality-of-the-circumstances test does not radically change the procedure for law enforcement officers applying for search warrants. Affidavits prepared to satisfy the *Aguilar-Spinelli* test will very likely satisfy the *Gates* test. The *Gates* emphasis on the value of law enforcement officials corroborating detailed but facially innocent information from an informant should also make it easier to obtain a search warrant based on information from an anonymous informant. As the *Gates* opinion indicated, overly rigid application of the two-pronged test tended to reject anonymous tips, because ordinary citizens generally do not provide extensive recitations of the basis of their everyday observations, and because the veracity, or truthfulness, of anonymous informants is largely unknown and unknowable. The Court said:

[A]nonymous tips seldom could survive a rigorous application of either of the . . . prongs. Yet, such tips, particularly when supplemented by independent police investigation, frequently contribute to the solution of otherwise "perfect crimes." While a conscientious assessment of the basis for crediting such tips is required by the Fourth Amendment, a standard that leaves virtually no place for anonymous citizen informants is not. 462 U.S. at 237–38.

Application of the Totality-of-the-Circumstances Test Under **Gates.** As a result of the Supreme Court's decision in *Gates*, some lower courts construct a list of factors that they will consider in ascertaining the overall reliability of informant information. For example, *United States v. Morales*, 171 F.3d 978, 981–82 (5th Cir. 1999), held that the totality-of-the-circumstances test includes four factors, one of which includes the *Aguilar* two-pronged test:

- the nature of the information,
- whether there has been an opportunity for the police to see or hear the matter reported,
- the veracity and the basis of the knowledge of the informant, and
- whether there has been any independent verification of the matters through police investigation.

In *United States v. De Los Santos*, 810 F.2d 1326 (5th Cir. 1987), the court essentially applied these four factors and determined that the informant's testimony could serve as a reliable basis for probable cause:

[O]fficers had probable cause to believe that contraband would be found, and therefore they properly stopped and arrested De Los Santos. First, [DEA Special Agent] Castro knew that De Los Santos had dealt in heroin on previous occasions. He then received a tip from an informant whom Castro knew and who had provided reliable information in the past. The informant told Castro that De Los Santos would travel to a certain area to store drugs and would pick them up the next day at a certain time. As predicted by the informant, the next morning De Los Santos arrived in the neighborhood in the same vehicle he had been in before. The agents observed him go to a residence and stay there for only two to four minutes. This surveillance, therefore, corroborated information provided by the informant.

Moreover, Castro testified in [the judge's chambers] as to other information that the informant supplied. This information also is supportive of probable cause. . . . The officer[s] in this case described with specificity "what the informer actually said, and why the officer thought the information was credible." . . . The testimony of each of the officers informed the court of the "underlying circumstances from which the informant concluded that the narcotics were where he claimed they were, and some of the underlying circumstances from which the officer concluded that the informant . . . was 'credible' or his information 'reliable.'" . . . Thus, under the totality of the circumstances test, "[t]here can be no doubt upon the basis of the circumstances related by [Castro], that there was probable cause to sustain the arrest." 810 F.2d at 1336.

The *De Los Santos* case illustrates the continuing validity of the *Aguilar-Spinelli* two-pronged test in determining probable cause using information supplied by an informant.

In contrast to *De Los Santos*, the *Gates* test was not satisfied in *United States v. Campbell*, 920 F.2d 793 (11th Cir. 1990), because law enforcement officials did not sufficiently corroborate information provided by the informant:

The totality of the circumstances do not suggest that the Montgomery police had probable cause to arrest the defendants, much less search the vehicle when they first encountered it at the truck stop. The district court found that the confidential informant was not reliable, but still found that the officers had probable cause to arrest the occupants of the pickup based on reliability of the information provided by the informant. The key to the district court's conclusion was that the informant provided the police with the approximate time of the vehicle's arrival and the location where it would stop. In [another Supreme Court case], the police kept the suspect under surveillance in order to corroborate the information. [Here], there was not the type of corroboration of criminal activity . . . to elevate it to the level of probable cause. 920 F.2d at 796–97.

In *United States v. Danhauer*, 229 F.3d 1002 (10th Cir. 2000), the Court found a confidential informant's information insufficient to establish probable cause for the original issuance of the warrant because the confidential informant's basis of knowledge and trustworthiness were not established by the officer, and the officer failed to adequately corroborate the informant's information:

The affidavit in this case failed to allege facts sufficient to establish probable cause. The affidavit contains repetitive statements regarding the physical description of the Danhauer residence and the identity of the occupants. Further, the affidavit contains statements about the criminal histories of both Dennis and Robbi Danhauer. The affidavit does not reveal, however, the informant's basis of knowledge [for this information] or adequately verify the informant's most serious allegation, that the Danhauers were manufacturing methamphetamine. An affidavit replete with repetitive and tenuous facts does not provide a magistrate with a sufficient basis for drawing a reasonable inference that a search would uncover evidence of criminal activity.

When there is sufficient independent corroboration of an informant's information, there is no need to establish the veracity of the informant. . . . In this case, however, the affiant neither established the veracity of the informant, nor obtained sufficient independent corroboration of the informant's information. The only police corroboration of the informant's information was the affiant's verification of the Danhauer residence's physical description, a records check to confirm that the Danhauers resided at the premises in question, an observation of Robbi Danhauer coming and going from the house to the garage, and a search of the Danhauers' criminal histories, which brought to light Robbi Danhauer's latest urinalysis revealing the presence of methamphetamine. The detective made little attempt to link methamphetamine to the Danhauer residence. . . . The only possible nexus between Danhauer's residence and the alleged criminal activity [of manufacturing methamphetamine] was his wife's urinalysis result. This is not the type of [corroborating] evidence that enables the state magistrate to draw a reasonable inference that the items subject to the search warrant would be located at Danhauer's residence. Such a nebulous connection does not give a magistrate a substantial basis for concluding that probable cause existed. 229 F.3d at 1006.

However, in *United States v. Datcu*, 627 F.3d 1074 (8th Cir. 2010), the judge determined that probable cause to search the suspects' vehicle existed when police corroborated detailed information provided by a citizen informant over the phone indicating that the suspects were burglarizing a nearby bank.

KEY POINTS

LO6

- Under the *Gates* totality-of-the-circumstances test for whether informant testimony can serve as a basis for probable cause, the task of the issuing magistrate is to make a practical, common-sense decision whether, given all the circumstances set forth in the affidavit, there is a fair probability that contraband or evidence of crime will be found in a particular place.

- The elements of the *Aguilar-Spinelli* two-pronged test are important considerations in determining the existence of probable cause based on informant testimony. Nonetheless, they should be evaluated only as part of the commonsense determination under the totality of the circumstances—not as rigid rules to be applied mechanically.

- Corroboration of the details of an informant's tip by independent police investigation reduces the chances of a reckless or prevaricating tale and strengthens the reliability of the tip. It is a valuable means of satisfying the *Gates* totality-of-the-circumstances test for determining probable cause based on informant information.

We agree with the district court, however, that at the time the officers searched the SUV a reasonable person could believe there was a fair probability that contraband would be found in it. A concerned citizen had reported his suspicion that two men were burglarizing the night deposit boxes at the Bremer and TCF banks located near Maplewood Mall. Officer Bartz responded just two minutes after the call and observed two men matching the descriptions the caller had provided. [One of the male suspects named] Cipu was dressed in blue jeans and [another male suspect named] Datcu was dressed in all black. Bartz also observed an SUV matching the caller's description and parked in a concealed fashion beside a dumpster near the closed banks. Bartz also observed that the SUV had California license plates. When Bartz pulled up in his fully marked police car, Cipu got out of the SUV and started to walk in the other direction. Datcu appeared from between the banks but changed direction when he saw the police car. Bartz ordered Datcu to stop, but he initially continued walking in the direction of the mall. We conclude that the totality of these circumstances would lead a reasonable person to believe that there was a fair probability that burglary and theft tools would be found in the vehicle.

Not only was the concerned citizen's tip about suspected illegal activity specific and detailed, but most of it was corroborated by Officer Bartz's observations when he arrived at the scene. The only individuals present matched the race and attire the caller had described, and the only vehicle in the vicinity matched the caller's description and was parked in a concealed fashion. 627 F.3d at 1078.

DISCUSSION POINT

How Much Corroboration Is Needed to Support the Information of a Cooperating Criminal Informant?

United States v. Button, 1999 WL 2463 (10th Cir. 1999), a federal magistrate judge issued a search warrant for the defendant's residence based on an affidavit submitted by a DEA agent. The affidavit described an ongoing drug trafficking conspiracy dating from 1989, with three drug seizures linked to Stephen Michael Pollack and those working with him. In a drug raid related to Pollack's alleged conspiracy, the police found defendant Button's phone number next to Pollack's in a confiscated notebook. The affidavit also indicated that a cooperating source had told agents that Button was a drug courier for Pollack. Among other details, the source stated that Pollack's conspiracy involved drug trafficking in Alamogordo, New Mexico, and Durango, Colorado.

The affidavit showed that the police had corroborated the information provided by the cooperating source through (1) telephone records showing calls between Pollack and Button; (2) agent surveillance of Button's car in Pollack's driveway; (3) information showing that Button lived in Alamogordo, New Mexico, and that Pollack lived in Durango, Colorado; and (4) information provided by New Mexico state police that they had an informant who also said Button was a courier for Pollack. When agents executed the search warrant at Button's residence, they seized a semiautomatic pistol and a rifle. Button filed a motion to suppress the weapons, asserting the underlying affidavit to the warrant was defective.

■ Applying the totality-of-the-circumstances test of *Illinois v. Gates*, do you think the motion to suppress should have been granted or denied? The trial court denied the motion and Button was convicted of being a convicted felon in possession of a firearm. The appellate court affirmed, saying "the affidavit provided a range of sensibly connected evidence beyond bare conclusions and that the totality of the evidence supports a 'substantial basis' for a search warrant."

■ Do you agree that the *Gates* test was satisfied? Why or why not?

Reasonableness

The Fourth Amendment requires searches and seizures to be "reasonable." One way a search or seizure will be found reasonable is if there exists a valid warrant, supported by probable cause. Without such a warrant, a search or seizure may still be found reasonable if a valid exception to the normal warrant requirement has been met. At this time, please review the figure shown inside the front cover of this book, which illustrates the overall Fourth Amendment inquiry. (Note that future chapters will comprehensively address the warrant requirement and exceptions to that requirement, such as plain view and consent searches.)

Generally, the Fourth Amendment prohibits searches and seizures that are unreasonable. *Reasonableness* has therefore, at times, been called the "touchstone" of the Fourth Amendment.

The fundamental command of the Fourth Amendment is that searches and seizures be reasonable, and although "both the concept of probable cause and the requirement of a warrant bear on the reasonableness of a search, . . . in certain limited circumstances neither is required." . . . Thus, we have in a number of cases recognized the legality of searches and seizures based on suspicions that, although "reasonable," do not rise to the level of probable cause. . . . Determining the reasonableness of any search involves a twofold inquiry: first, one must consider "whether the . . . action was justified at its inception," . . . second, one must determine whether the search as actually conducted "was reasonably related in scope to the circumstances which justified the interference in the first place." *New Jersey v. T.L.O.*, 469 U.S. 325, 340–41 (1985).

Other Fourth Amendment considerations, such as warrants, probable cause, exigency, and good faith, while necessary, depending on the particular circumstances, are factors subservient to reasonableness. In *Terry v. Ohio*, 392 U.S. 1, 19 (1968), the Supreme Court said that "the central inquiry under the Fourth Amendment [is] the reasonableness in all the circumstances of the particular governmental invasion of a citizen's personal security." Also, the Court pointed out that reasonableness does not necessarily mean correctness:

It is apparent that in order to satisfy the "reasonableness" requirement of the Fourth Amendment, what is generally demanded of the many factual determinations that must regularly be made by agents of the government—whether the magistrate issuing a warrant, the police officer executing a warrant, or the police officer conducting a search or seizure under one of the exceptions to the warrant requirement—is not that they always be correct, but that they always be reasonable. *Illinois v. Rodriguez*, 497 U.S. 177, 185–86 (1990).

Finally, the Court has said that "[t]here is no formula for the determination of reasonableness. Each case is to be decided on its own facts and circumstances." *Go-Bart Importing Co. v. United States*, 282 U.S. 344, 357 (1931).

KEY POINTS

LO7

- The fundamental command of the Fourth Amendment is that searches and seizures be reasonable. This generally means that a valid warrant exists supported by probable cause, or in the absence of such a warrant, a valid exception to the warrant requirement applies.

- Probable cause and the warrant requirement as primary indicators of reasonableness under the Fourth Amendment are very important. Nonetheless, searches and seizures based on suspicions that are "reasonable"—but do not rise to the level of probable cause—are nevertheless legal, where a careful balancing of governmental and private interests suggests that the public interest is best served by a Fourth Amendment standard of reasonableness that stops short of probable cause. For example, stops and frisks and certain administrative searches may be found reasonable under the Fourth Amendment in the absence of both probable cause and a warrant.

Continued on next page

The outcomes of cases in which the U.S. Supreme Court has applied a reasonableness balancing test have varied with the particularities of the cases and the philosophies of individual justices. Examples can be found in the discussions of administrative searches in Chapter 6 and elsewhere in this book. Consider that a "stop" of a person by police under the Fourth Amendment can be justified on reasonable suspicion, which is lower than the standard of probable cause (see Chapter 8 on "stops and frisks" for detailed discussion of this topic).

Essential to an understanding of the concept of reasonableness is an appreciation that it is a flexible standard to be liberally construed for the protection of individual freedom.

> Implicit in the Fourth Amendment's protection from unreasonable searches and seizures is its recognition of individual freedom. That safeguard has been declared to be "as of the very essence of constitutional liberty," the guaranty of which "is as important and as imperative as are the guaranties of the other fundamental rights of the individual citizen. . . ." While the language of the Amendment is "general," it "forbids every search that is unreasonable; it protects all, those suspected or known as to be offenders as well as the innocent, and unquestionably extends to the premises where the search was made." *Ker v. California*, 374 U.S. 23, 32-34 (1963)(citing *Go-Bart Importing Co. v. United States*, 282 U.S. 344, 357 (1931)(other citations omitted).

It is fitting in these times to conclude this chapter with a quotation from former U.S. Supreme Court Justice Brennan that succinctly summarizes the essence of the Fourth Amendment and neatly ties together the concepts of privacy, probable cause, and reasonableness:

> The Fourth Amendment was designed not merely to protect against official intrusions whose social utility was less as measured by some "balancing test" than its intrusion on individual privacy; it was designed in addition to grant the individual a zone of privacy whose protections could be breached only where the "reasonableness" requirements of the probable cause standard were met. Moved by whatever momentary evil has aroused their fears, officials—perhaps even supported by a majority of citizens—may be tempted to conduct searches that sacrifice the liberty of each citizen to assuage the perceived evil. But the Fourth Amendment rests on the principle that a true balance between the individual and society depends on the recognition of "the right to be let alone—the most comprehensive of rights and the right most valued by civilized men." *New Jersey v. T.L.O.*, 469 U.S. 325, 361–62 (1985).

SUMMARY

This chapter rounds out preparation for the detailed study of the law of criminal procedure. Chapter 1 introduced the Constitution, the wellspring from which flow all the rules and principles that follow. Emphasis was placed on the constitutional sources of individual rights and the inevitable conflict between the protection of individual rights and the maintenance of law and order. Future chapters deal with specific examples of this conflict and show how the delicate balance among these competing interests is maintained.

Chapter 2 presented an overview of the criminal courts and the pretrial process, including the application of the exclusionary rule. These are the arenas in which the balancing takes place and in which the reasonableness, appropriateness, and thoroughness of the law enforcement officer's activities are ultimately tested. Chapter 2 gave an overall picture of the criminal justice system as a backdrop for a more integrated understanding of the law of criminal procedure.

This chapter introduced the basic concepts of property, privacy, probable cause, and reasonableness, all of which will resurface throughout this book. The law enforcement officer or other criminal justice professional who is sensitive to the constitutional rights of all citizens, especially their property and privacy interests; who understands the meaning and importance of probable cause; and who embraces the concept of reasonableness as a guide is well on the way to appreciating the fundamental constitutional standards and restraints that characterize the operation of our criminal justice system.

In particular, privacy is understood through one of two approaches—a physical intrusion or trespass onto an individual's property to obtain information or discover something, or an infringement of a reasonable expectations of privacy. Therefore, a "search" occurs under the Fourth Amendment when either of these approaches to privacy is violated. A seizure of property occurs when there is some meaningful interference with an individual's possessory interests in that property. In addition, officers must generally have probable cause to arrest and search with or without a warrant. Probable cause exists where the facts and circumstances within a law enforcement officer's knowledge, and of which the officer has reasonably trustworthy information, are sufficient in themselves to warrant a person of reasonable caution in the belief that (1) a crime has been or is being committed by a particular person or (2) seizable property will be found in a particular place or on a particular person. Probable cause is evaluated by examining (1) the collective information in the possession of the police at the time of the arrest or search; (2) the information possessed by individual officers relying upon their senses, knowledge, training, and experience; and (3) the information police obtain from informants. Regarding whether information obtained from informants can serve as a basis for probable cause, police must examine the totality of the circumstances, including the informant's basis of knowledge and truthfulness and any information police obtain through corroboration.

Finally, for searches and seizures to be valid under the Fourth Amendment, they must be reasonable.

KEY TERMS

admission 103
corroboration 113
informant 107

privacy 91
probable cause 91
property 91

reasonableness 91
search 96
seizure 96

REVIEW AND DISCUSSION QUESTIONS

1. What are the two principal interests protected by the Fourth Amendment? What interest did the *Jones* case focus on? Why?

2. Should a person in a telephone booth be given the same degree of Fourth Amendment privacy protection as a person in his or her bedroom? As a person in his or her garage? As a person in his or her car?

3. Why did the Supreme Court in *Jardines* find that a canine inspection by police of a residential front porch is a "search" under the Fourth Amendment? Why, according to the Court, is such a canine inspection not a search when conducted by police outside a vehicle during a traffic stop?

4. Compare the standard of probable cause against the following statements of degree of certainty: absolutely positive; pretty sure; good possibility; beyond a reasonable doubt; reasonable suspicion; preponderance of the evidence; reasonable probability; strong belief; convinced.

5. Why is it important for a law enforcement officer to write down in a complaint or affidavit the facts and circumstances on which probable cause is based?

6. Give an example of a strong indication of probable cause to arrest that is arrived at through each of the five senses: sight, hearing, smell, taste, and touch.

7. List three possible strong indications of probable cause to arrest for each of the following crimes: (a) theft, (b) assault, (c) arson, (d) breaking and entering, (e) rape, and (f) driving to endanger.

8. Discuss the significance in the probable cause context of the phrase "conduct innocent in the eyes of the untrained may carry entirely different 'messages' to the experienced or trained . . . observer." *Davis v. United States*, 409 F.2d 458, 460 (D.C. Cir. 1969). Discuss this point specifically in terms of drug offenses and gambling offenses.

9. Must law enforcement officers know exactly the elements and name of the specific crime for which they are arresting or searching to have probable cause? *See People v. Georgev*, 230 N.E.2d 851 (Ill. 1967).

10. What does *corroboration* mean, and why is it important to a law enforcement officer in establishing probable cause through the use of informants?

11. How did the U.S. Supreme Court case of *Illinois v. Gates* change the requirements for establishing probable cause through the use of informants? Does the *Gates* decision make the law enforcement officer's task easier or harder?

12. Mr. A walks into a police station, drops three wristwatches on a table, and tells an officer that Mr. B robbed a local jewelry store two weeks ago. Mr. A will not say anything else in response to police questioning. A quick investigation reveals that the three watches were among a number of items stolen in the jewelry store robbery. Do the police have probable cause to do any or all of the following?

   a. Arrest Mr. A.

   b. Arrest Mr. B.

   c. Search Mr. A's home.

   d. Search Mr. B's home.

13. If you answered no to any of the items in question 12, explain why in detail. If you answered yes to any of them, draft the complaint or affidavit for a warrant or explain why a warrant is not needed.

14. Why do reviewing courts accept evidence of a "less judicially competent or persuasive character" to justify the issuance of a warrant than they would to justify officers acting on their own without a warrant?

4

Criminal Investigatory Search Warrants

LO1 DESCRIBE the general history of the development of the Fourth Amendment.

LO2 EXPLAIN how to obtain a search warrant, including the following: who issues search warrants, the grounds for issuance, what may be seized, and how to describe the person or place to be searched and the things to be seized.

LO3 DISCUSS how triggering conditions affect the validity and execution of an anticipatory search warrant.

LO4 ANALYZE how to execute a search warrant, including the following: who may execute a search warrant; when a search warrant may be executed, allowable delays, and how long the search may last; gaining entry to premises; authority to search persons not named in the warrant; allowable scope of the search and seizure; and duties after the search is completed.

LO5 IDENTIFY the consequences of having acted with reckless disregard for the truth when applying for search warrants.

LO6 EXPLAIN the Rule 41 notice and inventory requirements and how those requirements might be altered by the rules covering covert entry and delayed notification.

LO7 APPLY the constitutional limits on the seizure of items found in a search.

LO8 ANALYZE the permissible scope of searching third parties and their belongings during the execution of a valid search.

The law governing search warrants is based on guarantees in the Fourth Amendment to the U.S. Constitution:

The right of the people to be secure in their persons, houses, papers and effects, against unreasonable searches and seizures, shall not be violated, and no Warrants shall issue, but upon probable cause, supported by Oath or affirmation, and particularly describing the place to be searched and the persons or things to be seized.

The Fourth Amendment to the Constitution was adopted in response to abuses of governmental search and seizure authority originating in England in the seventeenth and eighteenth centuries. The early development of legally authorized searches and seizures under English common law is somewhat obscure. It appears that search warrants were first used in cases involving stolen property. The use of warrants to recapture stolen goods became widespread and increasingly violated citizens' privacy.

Eventually, the use of warrants was extended to the enforcement of other laws. For example, in the eighteenth century, the government issued general warrants to enforce strict libel laws. A **general warrant** is one that fails to specify the person or place to be searched or the person or item to be seized and leaves the time and manner of the search to the discretion of the searching officer. Law enforcement officers abused these general warrants, and soon no person or property was free from unlimited search conducted at the whim of an officer on the mere suspicion that the person possessed literature critical of the king or others in high places. Despite their unpopularity with the citizenry, these abusive practices were transplanted to the American colonies. In the mid-eighteenth century, Parliament enacted legislation authorizing general searches, called *writs of assistance*, to be conducted against the colonists to enforce the Trade Acts. Writs of assistance authorized royal customs officers to search houses and ships at will to discover and seize smuggled goods or goods on which the required duties had not been paid. The colonists' strong reaction against the writs of assistance was one of the major causes of the American Revolution.

The experiences of the Founders with general warrants and writs of assistance caused them to insist on including suitable guarantees against unreasonable searches and seizures in the basic charters of the states and nation. A prohibition against searches conducted at the whim of a law enforcement officer without any restrictions on the person or place to be searched or the person or item to be seized was first embodied in the Virginia Bill of Rights, adopted in 1776. By the close of the Revolutionary War, most of the states had adopted similar provisions. The present Fourth Amendment to the Constitution, with its emphasis on the protection of warrants issued on probable cause, was included in the Bill of Rights in 1791. Today, every state's constitution contains a similar provision.

Pursuant to the mandates of the plain text of the Fourth Amendment, the Supreme Court held in *Katz v. United States*, 389 U.S. 347, 357 (1967), that warrantless searches "are per se unreasonable under the Fourth Amendment subject only to a few specifically established and well-delineated exceptions." Accordingly, warrants play a very important role in criminal procedure. This chapter examines a broad array of matters concerning warrants for conducting searches of persons and places, as well as warrants authorizing the seizure of evidence.

Recall from Chapter 3 that a **search** is generally defined as an examination or inspection of a location, vehicle, or person by a law enforcement officer for the purpose of locating objects or substances relating to or believed to relate to criminal activity. And a **seizure** of property occurs when there is some meaningful interference with an individual's possessory interests in that property. *United States v. Jacobsen*, 466 U.S. 109, 113 (1984). As the Fourth Amendment specifically states, searches and seizures by law enforcement officials require **probable cause**—a concept explored in great detail in Chapter 3.

Applying for Search Warrants

The point of the Fourth Amendment, which often is not grasped by zealous officers, is not that it denies law enforcement the support of the usual inferences which reasonable men draw from evidence. Its protection consists in requiring that those inferences be drawn by a neutral and detached magistrate instead of being judged by the officer engaged in the often competitive enterprise of ferreting out crime. Any assumption that evidence sufficient to support a magistrate's disinterested determination to issue a search warrant will justify the officers in making a search without a warrant would reduce the Amendment to a nullity and leave the people's homes secure only in the discretion of police officers. . . . When the right of privacy must reasonably yield to the right of search is, as a rule, to be decided by a judicial officer, not by a policeman or Government enforcement agent. *Johnson v. United States,* 333 U.S. 10, 13–14 (1948).

As the preceding quotation should make clear, search warrants issued by a neutral judicial officer are the preferred mechanism for authorizing and conducting searches and seizures, although several exceptions to the warrant requirement have been carved out over the years (see Part 3 of this book). A **search warrant** is

1. an order in writing,
2. issued by a proper judicial authority,
3. in the name of the people,
4. directed to a law enforcement officer,
5. commanding the officer to search for certain personal property, and
6. commanding the officer to bring that property before the judicial authority named in the warrant.

Law enforcement officers applying for search warrants must follow established laws and procedures. Otherwise, a magistrate will deny the application or a court will invalidate an illegally issued warrant. In either instance, valuable evidence may be lost to the prosecution. Search warrant procedures are set out in statutes, rules, and court decisions and vary among different jurisdictions. This chapter summarizes and discusses the procedures common to most jurisdictions.

Who May Issue Search Warrants

Only judicial officers who have been specifically authorized to do so may issue search warrants. Most jurisdictions give this authority to judicial officers, such as clerks of court, magistrates, complaint justices, justices of the peace, and judges. The vesting of warrant-issuing power in a neutral and detached judicial officer stems from the Supreme Court's mandate that warrants can only be issued by people who are not involved in the "activities of law enforcement." *Shadwick v. City of Tampa*, 407 U.S. 345, 350 (1972).

Law enforcement officers need to know which judicial officers are authorized to issue search warrants in their jurisdictions. They may be different from the judicial officers authorized to issue arrest warrants. A search warrant issued by a person without authority has no legal effect, and a search made under such a warrant is illegal. For convenience, the term **magistrate** is used in this chapter to designate an official authorized to issue search warrants.

In *Shadwick v. City of Tampa*, 407 U.S. 345 (1972), the U.S. Supreme Court rejected the notion that all warrant authority must reside exclusively in a lawyer or judge and upheld a city charter provision authorizing municipal court clerks to issue arrest warrants for municipal ordinance violations. The Court held that "an issuing magistrate must meet two tests. He must be neutral and detached, and he must be capable of determining whether probable cause exists for the requested arrest or search." 407 U.S. at 350. The clerk in *Shadwick* met these two tests because the clerk worked in the judicial branch of government as an employee assigned to a municipal court judge, and the process of determining probable cause for municipal violations was not very complicated. *See also United States v. Malveaux*, 350 F.3d 555 (6th Cir. 2003).

In contrast, *Coolidge v. New Hampshire*, 403 U.S. 443 (1971), held that a state attorney general—who, by his office, was also the state's chief investigator and was later to be the chief prosecutor at trial—was not a neutral and detached judicial officer. The same holding would apply to any law enforcement officer or any other officials of the executive branch of government. *See United States v. U.S. Dist. Court*, 407 U.S. 297 (1972).

Shadwick, however, should not be read as permitting nonjudicial officers from authorizing the issuance of search warrants. For example, *United States v. Scott*, 260 F.3d 512, 515 (6th Cir. 2001), invalidated the issuance of a search warrant by a retired judge because he no longer held a judicial office and an active judge was available. But mere employment as a judicial official does not necessarily mean that a person is "neutral and detached." Consider that the U.S. Supreme Court and a federal appellate court have held that the following persons were not sufficiently "neutral and detached" to issue warrants in spite of the fact that they held magistrate positions:

- An unsalaried magistrate who received a fee each time he issued a search warrant, but received nothing for denying a warrant application. *Connally v. Georgia*, 429 U.S. 245 (1977).

- A magistrate who participated in a search, helping officers determine what should be seized. *Lo-Ji Sales, Inc. v. New York*, 442 U.S. 319 (1979).

- A magistrate who also worked as a deputy jailer at a county jail who "stood to gain financially" when bookings and arrests were processed through her jail. *United States v. Parker*, 373 F.3d 770, 773–74 (6th Cir. 2004).

- A magistrate who merely acted as a "rubber stamp" by signing a warrant without reading it or any of the supporting documentation submitted with it. *United States v. Decker*, 956 F.2d 773, 776 (8th Cir. 1992).

Grounds for Issuing Search Warrants

Before issuing a search warrant, a magistrate must have probable cause to believe that items subject to seizure are in a particular place or on a particular person at the time the warrant is issued. *See Warden v. Hayden*, 387 U.S. 294 (1967).

Establishing Probable Cause

A law enforcement officer applying for a search warrant must supply the magistrate with the grounds for issuance of the warrant. This is usually accomplished by means of an affidavit, a written declaration or statement of facts sworn to before the magistrate. *See* FED. R. CRIM. P. 41(d). The person swearing out an affidavit is referred to as the affiant. Figure 4.1 is a typical form for an affidavit for a search warrant. Several jurisdictions permit issuance of search warrants over the telephone or by e-mail or facsimile (fax), but they still require that

United States District Court

DISTRICT OF _____

In the Matter of the Search of

(Name, address or brief description of person, property or premises to be searched)

APPLICATION AND AFFIDAVIT
FOR SEARCH WARRANT

CASE NUMBER: _____

I _____ being duly sworn depose and say:

I am a(n) _____ and have reason to believe
                      Official Title

that ☐ on the person of or ☐ on the property or premises known as (name, description and/or location)

in the _____ District of _____
there is now concealed a certain person or property, namely (describe the person or property to be seized)

which is (state one or more bases for search and seizure set forth under Rule 41(b) of the Federal Rules of Criminal Procedure)

concerning a violation of Title _____ United States code, Section(s)_____ .
The facts to support a finding of Probable Cause are as follows:

Continued on the attached sheet and made a part hereof. ☐ Yes ☐ No

_____
Signature of Affiant

Sworn to before me, and subscribed in my presence

_____ at _____
Date   City and State

_____   _____
Name and Title of Judicial Officer   Signature of Judicial Officer

United States District Court

FIGURE 4.1 | A Typical Affidavit for a Search Warrant

the information provided by the affiant to the magistrate be taken under oath and recorded. Given, however, the strong preference for affidavits—and, indeed, the requirement of them in many jurisdictions—this chapter examines the probable cause inquiry as if a written affidavit were the exclusive vehicle for applying for a search warrant. Figures 4.2 and 4.3 illustrate the typical forms for search warrants, the first based on a traditional application supported by an affidavit, and the second based on oral testimony.

Completeness of Affidavits

All the information on which probable cause is based should be written in the affidavit. In *Whiteley v. Warden*, 401 U.S. 560 (1971), overruled on other grounds by

UNITED STATES DISTRICT COURT

_____ District of _____

In the Matter of the Search of
(Name, address or brief description of person or property to be searched)

SEARCH WARRANT

Case Number:

TO: _____ and any Authorized Officer of the United States

Affidavit(s) having been made before me by _____ who has reason to believe
Affiant

that ☐ on the person of, or ☐ on the premises known as (name, description and/or location)

in the _____ District of _____ there is now
concealed a certain person or property, namely (describe the person or property)

I am satisfied that the affidavit(s) and any record testimony establish probable cause to believe that the person or property so described
is now concealed on the person or premises above-described and establish grounds for the issuance of this warrant.

YOU ARE HEREBY COMMANDED to search on or before _____
Date

(not to exceed 10 days) the person or place named above for the person or property specified, serving this warrant and making the
search ☐ in the daytime — 6:00 AM to 10:00 P.M. ☐ at anytime in the day or night as I find reasonable cause has been
established and if the person or property be found there to seize same, leaving a copy of this warrant and receipt for the person
or property taken, and prepare a written inventory of the person or property seized and promptly return this warrant to
_____ as required by law.
U.S. Judge or Magistrate

_____ at _____
Date and Time Issued   City and State

_____
Name and Title of Judicial Officer   Signature of Judicial Officer

United States District Court

FIGURE 4.2a | A Typical Search Warrant Form

Arizona v. Evans, 514 U.S. 1 (1995), the Supreme Court made it clear that "an otherwise insufficient affidavit cannot be rehabilitated by testimony concerning information possessed by the affiant when he sought the warrant but not disclosed to the issuing magistrate." A majority of U.S. jurisdictions are in accord with _Whiteley_, insofar as they require that an affidavit contain _all_ the information on which a magistrate is to base a finding of probable cause to issue a search warrant. This requirement forces law enforcement officers to think carefully about cases before applying for a warrant, and it provides a complete record for reviewing courts to evaluate the magistrate's decision if the warrant is challenged. A minority of U.S. jurisdictions allow supplementation of a defective or incomplete affidavit by sworn oral testimony given before the magistrate. _E.g._, _State v. Hendricks_, 328 N.E.2d 822 (Ohio 1974).

RETURN	Case Number:	
DATE WARRANT RECEIVED	DATE AND TIME WARRANT EXECUTED	COPY OF WARRANT AND RECEIPT FOR ITEMS LEFT WITH
INVENTORY MADE IN THE PRESENCE OF		
INVENTORY OF PERSON OR PROPERTY TAKEN PURSUANT TO THE WARRANT		

CERTIFICATION

I swear that this inventory is a true and detailed account of the person or property taken by me on the warrant.

_____

Subscribed, sworn to, and returned before me this date.

_____   _____
U.S. Judge or Magistrate   Date

United States District Court

FIGURE 4.2b | _(Continued)_

Contents of Affidavits

An affidavit for a search warrant should inform a magistrate of three things:

- that a criminal offense has been or is being committed,
- that seizable evidence relating to that offense is in a particular place at a particular time, and
- the method(s) law enforcement officers will use to identify the appropriate premises or persons.

Law enforcement officers do not need to use legalese or police jargon in affidavits submitted in support of a search warrant application. Magistrates are supposed to

UNITED STATES DISTRICT COURT

District of _____

In the Matter of the Search of
(Name, address or brief description of person or property to be searched)

SEARCH WARRANT UPON ORAL TESTIMONY

Case Number: _____

TO: _____ and any Authorized Officer of the United States

Sworn oral testimony has been communicated to me by _____
                                                        Affiant

that ☐ on the person of, or ☐ on the premises known as (name, description and/or location)

in the _____ District of _____ there is now
concealed a certain person or property, namely (describe the person or property)

I am satisfied that the circumstances are such as to make it reasonable to dispense with a written affidavit and that there is probable cause to believe that the property or person so described is concealed on the person or premises above described and that grounds for application for issuance of the search warrant exist as communicated orally to me in a sworn statement which has been recorded electronically, stenographically, or in long-hand and upon the return of the warrant, will be transcribed, certified as accurate and attached hereto.

YOU ARE HEREBY COMMANDED to search on or before _____
                                                                        Date

the person or place named above for the person or property specified, serving this warrant and making the search ☐ in the day-time — 6:00 AM to 10:00 PM ☐ at anytime in the day or night as I find reasonable cause has been established and if the person or property be found there to seize same, leaving a copy of this warrant and receipt for the person or property taken, and prepare a written inventory of the person or property seized and promptly return this warrant to _____
                                                                        U.S. Judge or Magistrate Judge

as required by law.

_____ at _____
Date and Time Issued   City and State

_____   _____
Name and Title of Judicial Officer   Signature of Judicial Officer

I certify that on _____ at _____
                        Date   Time

_____ orally authorized the
U.S. Judge or Magistrate Judge

issuance and execution of a search warrant conforming to all the foregoing terms.

_____ _____ _____
Name of affiant   Signature of affiant   Exact time warrant

FIGURE 4.3 | Page 1 of a Typical Search Warrant Form Based on Oral Testimony

review these documents for the three factors specified above in a "practical, common sense" manner in light of the particular criminal conduct alleged. *Illinois v. Gates*, 462 U.S. 213, 238 (1983); *United States v. Hicks*, 575 F.3d 130, 137 (1st Cir. 2009).

Number of Affidavits

Only one sworn affidavit is necessary to obtain a search warrant. However, if multiple affidavits are submitted from several law enforcement officers, the judicial officer may review all of them and make a determination of probable cause based on the aggregate information contained in all affidavits submitted. *See United States v. Smith*, 499 F.2d 251 (7th Cir. 1974); *Blankenship v. State*, 527 S.W.2d 636 (Ark. 1975). If multiple affidavits are to be submitted, it is essential that they all be satisfactorily incorporated into the application for a warrant in a sequential manner. The following procedure should ensure proper incorporation:

- Entitle the first or primary affidavit "Affidavit and Request for Search Warrant."
- Entitle all additional affidavits "Supplemental Affidavit 1," "Supplemental Affidavit 2," and so forth.
- Include the following statement in the first or primary affidavit: "This request is also based on the information in the sworn statements in Supplemental Affidavit 1, Supplemental Affidavit 2, . . . which are attached." (The law requires that clear reference be made to all supplemental affidavits.)
- Securely attach all supplemental affidavits to the primary affidavit. Use a stapler or other semipermanent method of binding. A paper clip is unsatisfactory because it can easily slip off.

By following these simple steps, the officer ensures that the magistrate will be simultaneously presented with all the information on which probable cause is to be based and that the appellate court will be able to effectively review the magistrate's decision.

Affidavits Must Be Sworn by Oath or Affirmation

An affiant must swear or affirm that the information contained in the affidavit is true. Although no particular ceremony or form of swearing is mandated, it normally takes place face to face between the affiant and the judicial officer. But face-to-face contact is not necessarily required (especially, for example, for telephonic warrants in which the affiant swears to tell the truth under penalty of perjury over the phone). However the swearing takes place, the procedures followed must be sufficient to allow criminal perjury charges to be filed against the affiant if any material allegation in the affidavit turns out to be false.

Sufficiency of Factual Allegations in Affidavits to Establish Probable Cause

The factual allegations in an affidavit must persuade the magistrate that there is probable cause to issue the search warrant. The affiant must state the underlying facts and circumstances that, under the totality of the facts and circumstances, demonstrate "a fair probability that contraband or evidence of a crime will be found in a particular place." *Gates*, 462 U.S. at 238.

Recall from the discussion in Chapter 3 that the facts and circumstances known to a law enforcement officer can establish probable cause in many ways. The knowledge of these facts and circumstances can come both from the affiant officer's own senses and from what the affiant officer learned from other police officers, informants, and witnesses who had personal knowledge based on what they perceived using their own senses. This knowledge typically includes one or more of the following:

- what officers viewed as a crime took place;
- what officers viewed as they examined a crime scene after the fact;
- what officers learned from interviewing victims and witnesses;
- what officers learned from credible or reliable informants (reread the part of Chapter 3 devoted to the *Aguilar–Spinelli–Gates* line of cases);
- what officers learned from the observation and evaluation of real or physical evidence, including the results of forensic tests performed on such evidence; and
- what officers learned from observing or talking with a suspect, including
    - a suspect's flight,
    - a suspect's furtive conduct,

- admissions made by a suspect,

- statements made by a suspect that contain false or implausible information,

- a suspect's presence at a crime scene,

- a suspect's presence in a high-crime area,

- a suspect's association with other known criminals, and

- a suspect's past criminal record.

Staleness Concerns Time is a very important factor in determining probable cause to search. The passage of time can render a search warrant void on the grounds of staleness. If the information on which probable cause was initially based becomes stale, there may no longer be good reason to believe that property is still at the same location:

> Staleness is not measured merely on the basis of the maturity of the information[, but also] in relation to (1) the nature of the suspected criminal activity (discrete crime or "regenerating conspiracy"), (2) the habits of the suspected criminal ("nomadic" or "entrenched"), (3) the character of the items to be seized ("perishable" or "of enduring utility"), and (4) the nature and function of the premises to be searched ("mere criminal forum" or "secure operational base"). *United States v. Bucuvalas*, 970 F.2d 937, 940 (1st Cir. 1992).

The length of time that an item of property is likely to remain at a given location depends on the nature of the property, the nature of the criminal activity, the duration of the criminal activity, the criminal suspects, and many other factors. *United States v. Laury*, 985 F.2d 1293 (5th Cir. 1993), found probable cause to search a suspected bank robber's home for instrumentalities and evidence of the crime was not stale, even though nearly two months had passed since the date of the robbery. The affiant, an expert in bank robbery investigation, stated that bank robbers tend to keep evidence of the crime in their homes for as long as several years.

In contrast, in *United States v. Wagner*, 989 F.2d 69 (2d Cir. 1993), the information supporting probable cause to search the suspect's home was (1) a single small purchase of marijuana from the suspect in her home more than six weeks before the search, (2) a recorded statement of the suspect identifying her source for the marijuana, and (3) an unsubstantiated assertion that the suspect's home was owned by the source. These facts were insufficient for the court to find that the suspect engaged in continuing criminal activity in her home as a member of the source's drug distribution network. Because marijuana is the type of property that is likely to disappear or be moved, probable cause was found to be stale at the time the warrant was issued and the search was conducted. A similar finding of staleness occurred in *United States v. Helton*, 314 F.3d 812, 822 (6th Cir. 2003), in which allegations in an affidavit for a search warrant seeking stored drug money were based on a two-month-old report. The staleness finding resulted because "stacks of money" were unlikely to still be present after the passage of that much time.

Evidence of continuing crimes, especially white-collar crimes such as fraud, is also likely to stay in one place for a long time. In *Andreson v. Maryland*, 427 U.S. 463, 478 n.9 (1976), the U.S. Supreme Court upheld a three-month delay between the application for a search warrant and the dates of allegedly fraudulent real estate transactions, reasoning that it was "eminently reasonable to expect that such records would be maintained . . . for a period of time" after the real estate transactions had occurred.

Other examples of continuing crimes are the cultivation and distribution of illegal drugs, *e.g., United States v. Leasure*, 319 F.3d 1092 (9th Cir. 2003); gun control violations, *e.g., United States v. Maxim*, 55 F.3d 394 (8th Cir. 1995); counterfeiting, *e.g., United States v. Farmer*, 370 F.3d 435 (4th Cir. 2004); and the downloading of child pornography. For instance, *United States v. Allen*, 625 F.3d 830, 843 (5th Cir. 2010), upheld an eighteen-month delay between the time the defendant accessed online images and the time a search warrant was issued not only because people interested in child pornography "often maintain their collection on a computer and maintain these collections for several years," but also because "computer files or remnants of such files can be recovered months or even years after they have been downloaded onto a hard drive, deleted, or viewed via the internet."

Truthfulness of Affidavit The information that a law enforcement officer swears to in an affidavit (or in live testimony) to establish probable cause for a warrant must be "truthful in the sense that the information put forth is believed or appropriately accepted by the affiant as true." *Franks v. Delaware,* 438 U.S. 154, 165 (1978). A law enforcement officer who intentionally or knowingly makes false statements in an application for a warrant clearly violates this requirement. But the rule on truthfulness is also violated if an officer swears to information with reckless disregard for the truth (i.e., disregarding a known risk that information may not be true even if the officer does not actually know the truth or falsity of the information). This rule is also violated if a law enforcement officer knowingly or recklessly omits material information from a warrant application. *United States v. Pace,* 898 F.2d 1218 (7th Cir. 1990). Any such violation of the truthfulness requirement resulting from a knowing or reckless misrepresentation or omission can serve as grounds for invalidating the warrant and for the evidence being deemed inadmissible under the exclusionary rule (see "Constitutionally Defective Warrants" later in this chapter).

CRIMINAL PROCEDURE **IN ACTION**

Evaluating an Application for a Search Warrant

You are a U.S. magistrate judge who receives an application from an FBI agent for a warrant to search for and seize evidence of child pornography at a defendant's home. The affidavit submitted in support of the warrant application explains the following points:

- Individuals who exploit children, including collectors of child pornography, commonly use computers to communicate with like-minded individuals, store their child pornography collections, and locate, view, download, collect, and organize images of child pornography found on the Internet.

- Forensic behavioral science has found that a "majority of individuals who collect child pornography are persons who have a sexual attraction to children."

- The FBI had obtained the Internet protocol address of a website that contained approximately eleven images of child pornography and advertised additional child pornography at an Internet address that was hidden until a membership was purchased.

- An undercover FBI agent paid $99 for a one-month membership and then received an e-mail that provided the Internet address, log-in number, and password for its membership website.

- Forensic examination of the website revealed "several possible subscribers along with e-mail addresses and other information."

- The FBI subpoenaed subscriber information for these e-mail addresses, which included the defendant's Yahoo e-mail address.

- The residential address associated with the defendant's Yahoo account had active Internet service during the period immediately preceding the warrant request.

- "It appeared [that the defendant] either gained access or attempted to gain access to the nonmember portion of the Web site."

- Eighteen years earlier, the defendant pled guilty to endangering the welfare of a child stemming from having inappropriately touched a seven-year old girl.

1. What facts in the affidavit support the issuance of a search warrant?

2. What reasons can you explain for denying the search warrant based on the insufficiency of the search warrant?

See United States v. Falso, 544 F.3d 110 (2d Cir. 2008).

Items Subject to Seizure

Rule 41(c) of the Federal Rules of Criminal Procedure illustrates the types of property (and people) authorized to be seized under a search warrant:

(c) Persons or Property Subject to Search or Seizure—A warrant may be issued for any of the following:

1. evidence of a crime;

2. contraband, fruits of crime, or other items illegally possessed;

3. property designed for use, intended for use, or used in committing a crime; or

4. a person to be arrested or a person who is unlawfully restrained.

For each item of property sought in the search warrant, the affidavit should indicate the type of seizable property under which the item is classified according to the law of the jurisdiction. This informs the magistrate that the items sought are connected with criminal activity. The remainder of this chapter refers to items of property allowed to be seized under state or federal law as "items subject to seizure" or "seizable items" under Rule 41(c)(1)–(3); Chapter 7 deals with the search for and seizure of persons under Rule 41(c)(4).

Seizure Limited to Nontestimonial Evidence Examples of items that may be seized under Rule 41(c) include clothing, blood, hair, fingerprints, money, weapons, drugs, computers, personal papers, and business records. Note that all of these examples are tangible items, not "testimonial evidence." Testimonial evidence may not be seized because the Fifth Amendment prevents witnesses from being compelled to testify against themselves. Nontestimonial evidence may be lawfully seized. Some physical items are clearly nontestimonial, but the legal status of some written items requires further explanation.

Personal Papers and Business Records *Andresen v. Maryland*, 427 U.S. 463 (1976), held that a seizure of personal papers or business records from persons under a search warrant does not necessarily compel those persons to be witnesses against themselves in violation of the Fifth Amendment. The defendant in *Andresen* was not compelled to be a witness against himself because he was not required to say or to do anything during the search. If, however, law enforcement authorities had attempted to subpoena the records instead of searching for and seizing the records for themselves, then the defendant could have refused to give up the records by exercising his Fifth Amendment rights. The Court said:

> [A]lthough the Fifth Amendment may protect an individual from complying with a subpoena for the production of his personal records in his possession because the very act of production may constitute a compulsory authentication of incriminating information, . . . a seizure of the same materials by law enforcement officers differs in a crucial respect—the individual against whom the search is directed is not required to aid in the discovery, production, or authentication of incriminating evidence. 427 U.S. at 473–74.

Bank Records Bank records have even less protection. *United States v. Miller*, 425 U.S. 435 (1976), held that a person's bank records are not private papers of the kind protected against compulsory production by the Fifth Amendment. By choosing to deal with a bank, people lose their expectation of Fourth Amendment protection against government investigation. "The checks are not confidential communications but negotiable instruments to be used in commercial transactions. All of the documents obtained, including financial statements and deposit slips, contain only information voluntarily conveyed to the banks and exposed to their employees in the ordinary course of business." 425 U.S. at 442. The *Miller* case concerned a subpoena, but either a search warrant or subpoena could be used to obtain a person's bank records without violating the Fifth Amendment right against compulsory self-incrimination. Note, however, that *Miller* does not automatically grant unrestricted access to bank records. Access may be restricted by state or federal statute.

Both *Andresen* and *Miller* highlight a basic principle regarding searches and seizures of papers: "There is no special sanctity in papers, as distinguished from other forms of property, to render them immune from search and seizure, if only they fall within the scope of the principles of the cases in which other property may be seized, and if they be adequately described in the affidavit and warrant." *Gouled v. United States*, 255 U.S. 298, 309 (1921). *How* the items are seized, however, is key to the legality of any seizure of personal papers or business records. Officers may *request* a suspect's assistance in seizing personal papers or business records, but they may not *compel* the suspect's assistance in any way. Any compulsion would violate the defendant's Fifth Amendment rights and render the evidence inadmissible.

Seizure Must Aid in Particular Apprehension or Conviction Another limitation on the seizure of "evidence of a crime" is that it must aid in a particular apprehension or conviction. *Warden v. Hayden*, 387 U.S. 294, 306–07 (1967), stated the reason for this requirement:

> The requirements of the Fourth Amendment can secure the same protection of privacy whether the search is for "mere evidence" or for fruits, instrumentalities, or contraband. There must, of course, be a nexus—automatically provided in the case of fruits, instrumentalities, or contraband—between the item to be seized and criminal behavior. Thus, in the case of "mere evidence," probable cause must be examined in terms of cause to believe that the evidence sought will aid in a particular apprehension or conviction. In doing so, consideration of police purposes will be required.

Applying this logic, *Warden v. Hayden* upheld the seizure of clothing from a washing machine because the clothes matched the description of what a robber had been wearing. The police seizing the clothes reasonably believed that the clothes could help them identify the robber.

■ Particularity Requirement

As the text of the Fourth Amendment makes clear, warrants must describe with particularity "the place to be searched and the persons or things to be seized." The particularity requirement prohibits "general, exploratory rummaging in a person's belongings." *Coolidge v. New Hampshire*, 403 U.S. 443, 467 (1971). It is designed to protect people's property and privacy rights against "the wide-ranging exploratory searches the Framers [of the Constitution] intended to prohibit." *Maryland v. Garrison*, 480 U.S. 79, 84 (1987).

Particular Description of the Place to Be Searched

The affidavit supporting a request for a search warrant for a place must contain a description that points directly to a definitely ascertainable place to the exclusion of all others. *Steele v. United States*, 267 U.S. 498, 503 (1925), stated that "[i]t is enough if the description is such that the officer with a search warrant can with reasonable effort ascertain and identify the place intended."

The place to be searched need not be owned, occupied, or used by a particular suspect. A warrant may be issued for the search of the premises of a party who is not suspected of any crime. In *Zurcher v. The Stanford Daily*, 436 U.S. 547, 556 (1978), involving the search of newspaper offices, the U.S. Supreme Court said, "The critical element in a reasonable search is not that the owner of the property is suspected of crime but that there is reasonable cause to believe that the specific 'things' to be searched for and seized are located on the property to which entry is sought." *Zurcher* involved a warrant to search for photographs of demonstrators who had injured several police officers. (Note that the Privacy Protection Act of 1980, 42 U.S.C. § 2000aa, provides extensive protection against searches and seizures of the communications media, unless there is probable cause to believe that the party in possession of the items is involved in the crime being investigated.)

Specific Addresses A *correct* street address, especially in urban and suburban areas, is sufficient to identify the place to be searched because it allows the officers who will be executing the warrant to "locate the premises with reasonable effort, and (2) to be sure that the wrong premises are not mistakenly searched." *United States v. Dancy*, 947 F.2d 1232, 1234 (5th Cir. 1991); *United States v. Johnson*, 944 F.2d 396 (8th Cir.1991). But because mistakes can be made with regard to street address numbers (e.g., numbers may be inadvertently omitted or transposed), affidavits should include detailed descriptions of the place to be searched to help ensure that the particularity requirement is satisfied. *See, e.g., United States v. Palega*, 556 F.3d 709 (8th Cir. 2009). For example, in *United States v. Turner*, 770 F.2d 1508, 1509–10 (9th Cir. 1985), the affidavit for search warrant and the search warrant itself described the house as follows:

> 2762 Mountain View, Escondido, California, and further described as a beige two-story stucco and adobe house with an attached two-car garage. The garage has entry doors on either side of a large garage door. The entry door located on the south side of the garage door has a brass-plated deadbolt lock installed. On the south side of this door are two windows covered by tinfoil. The doors and trim of the house are painted brown. The entry to the residence is located on the south side of the residence and the garage entry faces west. The driveway to the residence off of Mountain View Drive leads north from Mountain View Drive and is marked by three mailboxes numbered 2800, 2810 and 2756. This driveway leads past these three residences, the last identified by a residence marker of 2756, D.A. Mieir. The driveway then turns to concrete and dead ends at the 2762 Mountain View Drive residence. There is a farm road leading past 2762 Mountain View Drive and into an avocado grove. The driveway leads north from Mountain View Drive. Entry to the 2762 Mountain View Drive residence is located on the south side.

The description of the house was correct except for the street number. The house that the agents had under surveillance, intended to search, and actually did search was 2800 Mountain View Drive. Number 2762 Mountain View Drive was located approximately two-tenths of a mile away in a location that the agents did not know existed, and it did not resemble the description of the suspect house. The court held that the description in the search warrant was sufficiently particular despite the wrong street address:

> The verbal description contained in the warrant described the house to be searched with great particularity; no nearby house met the warrant's detailed description; the address in the warrant was reasonable for the location intended; the house had been under surveillance before the warrant was sought; the warrant was executed

by an officer who had participated in applying for the warrant and who personally knew which premises were intended to be searched; and the premises that were intended to be searched were those actually searched. Under these circumstances, there was virtually no chance that the executing officer would have any trouble locating and identifying the premises to be searched, or that he would mistakenly search another house. When additional, particularized information like that provided in *Lora-Solano* is not included in an affidavit, then a mistaken address can serve as the basis for invalidating a warrant. *See United States v. Thomas*, 263 F.3d 805 (8th Cir. 2001).

Descriptions Without Addresses When a specific address is unknown, affidavits must be particularly detailed in describing the location of premises to be searched. Merely using some general description of the location of property may not be sufficient to meet the particularly requirement of the Fourth Amendment. For example, in *United States v. Ellis*, 971 F.2d 701 (11th Cir. 1992), the warrant described the place to be searched as the "third mobile home on the north side" without any further description of its physical characteristics or mention of its occupant's name. The court found the description insufficiently particular.

The location of rural property is sometimes more difficult to describe, but may be easier to locate. Therefore, a description of a farm or other rural property by the owner's name, the dwelling's color and style, the rural route and box number, and general directions will usually suffice. *Gatlin v. State*, 559 S.W.2d 12 (Ark. 1977); *Cooper v. State*, 441 S.E.2d 448 (Ga. App. 1994).

Descriptions of Multiple-Occupancy Dwellings When the place to be searched is a multiple-occupancy dwelling, such as an apartment house, hotel, or rooming house, the affidavit must go beyond merely stating the location of the premises. In *Manley v. Commonwealth*, 176 S.E.2d 309 (Va. 1970), the affidavit on which the warrant was based described the place to be searched as "313 West 27th Street, a dwelling. The apartment of Melvin Lloyd Manley." The court held that the defendant's apartment was sufficiently described for the searching officers to locate it with very little effort because the warrant adequately specified the name of the apartment's occupant and provided "the searching officers with sufficient information to identify, without confusion or excessive effort, such apartment unit." 176 S.E.2d at 314.

Similarly, *United States v. Strother*, 318 F.3d 64, 69–70 (1st Cir. 2003), held that a warrant was sufficiently particular even though it did not specify an apartment number because a reliable informant had identified the suspect's residence as the apartment on the first floor and the U.S. Postal Service confirmed that the suspect lived in the building described.

In contrast to *Manley* and *Strother,* when affidavits contain errors without additional supporting information that helps particularize the place to be searched, courts may invalidate a search warrant. *Jacobs v. City of Chicago*, 215 F.3d 758, 767–77 (7th Cir. 2000), for example, invalidated a warrant as insufficiently particular because the affidavit incorrectly described an apartment building as being a single-family residence. Therefore, *whenever possible, an affidavit in support of a warrant to search premises located in multiple-occupancy dwellings should always include information such as room number, apartment number, building, and floor.* If necessary, a diagram showing the location should be attached to the affidavit. Doing so should allow a reviewing court to come to the same conclusion that was reached in *United States v. Darensbourg*, 520 F.2d 985, 987 (5th Cir. 1975), another case involving a multiple-occupancy dwelling. In *Darensbourg,* the description in the warrant of the place to be searched (a four-building apartment complex) gave an incorrect street address but correctly stated the apartment number. Because there was only one apartment with that number in the entire complex, the court held that the description was sufficient.

To obtain sufficiently descriptive information, officers may need to view the premises, examine floor plans, or make inquiries of landlords, tenants, or others to determine the correct limits of the place to be searched. *Maryland v. Garrison*, 480 U.S. 79, 85 (1987), held that "[t]he validity of the warrant must be assessed on the basis of the information that the officers disclosed, or had a duty to discover and to disclose, to the issuing magistrate." If an officer is diligent in gathering the descriptive information of the place to be searched, the warrant will be valid even though hindsight reveals that honest mistakes were made.

Descriptions of Motor Vehicles Unless one or more of the established warrant exceptions for the search of a motor vehicle apply (see Chapter 11), a warrant is required to search a motor vehicle. Because vehicles are considered "places" for search and seizure purposes, an affidavit must describe the vehicle to be searched with sufficient particularity that it can be located with reasonable certainty. Some courts hold that only the license plate number is necessary to sufficiently describe a motor vehicle for purposes of issuance of a warrant. *E.g., United States v. Vaughn*, 830 F.2d 1185 (D.C. Cir. 1987). To avoid any problems with the particularity requirement, though, a detailed description of a motor vehicle to be searched should include information such as the make, body style, color, year, location, and owner or operator of the vehicle.

Descriptions of Domestic Mail In *United States v. Ramsey*, 431 U.S. 606 (1977), the U.S. Supreme Court held that international mail can be searched without a warrant under the border exception to the Fourth Amendment (see border searches in Chapter 6). Domestic mail, on the other hand, is considered a "place" for search and seizure purposes. Domestic mail is considered to be any letter or package traveling wholly within the United States. For more than a century, courts have ruled that first-class domestic mail may not be lawfully opened without a warrant. *See Ex Parte Jackson*, 96 U.S. 727 (1878). The affidavit for a warrant to search first-class domestic mail must describe the mail with particularity, just as for places, persons, and vehicles.

Descriptions of E-Mail E-mail has become a common form of communication. Like first-class domestic mail, e-mail is protected by the Fourth Amendment because senders of electronic communications have a reasonable expectation that their messages will remain private "until the transmissions are received." *United States v. Maxwell*, 45 M.J. 406, 418 (C.A.A.F. 1996). Thus, Internet service providers, although conduits for e-mail transmissions, may not disclose e-mails to law enforcement personnel without a warrant that describes, with particularity, the specific e-mails that are the targets of the criminal investigation. When an affidavit does so and therefore complies with the particularity requirement, federal law allows for nationwide searches of both opened and unopened e-mail that may be stored on the servers of Internet service providers. *See* 18 U.S.C. § 2703. See Chapter 5 for more in-depth coverage of searches for electronically stored information.

Particular Description of a Person to Be Searched

A magistrate may issue a search warrant to search a particular person for particular items of evidence, although such warrants are much rarer than warrants authorizing the search of particular places. If a warrant to search a person is desired, the affidavit in support of that warrant must describe the person to be searched with sufficient particularity to enable identification with reasonable certainty.

Physical Descriptions Law enforcement officers should always describe the physical characteristics of any person they seek authority to search. When known, such information should include the suspect's name, race, gender, age (even if an approximation), aliases, address, and as many details about the person's physical appearance as possible, such as height, weight, eye color, hair color, tattoos, piercings, and any other identifying characteristics that would enable the searching officer(s) to locate and identify the person with reasonable effort. *State v. Hamilton*, 840 P.2d 1061 (Ariz. App. 1992). Indeed, accurate physical descriptions can even help cure mistakes in the names of persons to be searched. *State v. Tramantano*, 260 A.2d 128 (Conn. Super. 1969); *United States v. Sirmans*, 278 Fed. Appx. 171 (3d Cir. 2008).

"All Persons" Courts frown upon warrants authorizing the search of "all persons" present at a particular location. In *Ybarra v. Illinois*, 444 U.S. 85 (1980), the U.S. Supreme Court held that a warrant authorizing the search of a public tavern did not authorize police to search individuals not mentioned within the warrant. But if affidavits establish probable cause that everyone found on particular premises is likely to be in possession of evidence relevant to the crime being investigated, then such warrants may be constitutionally permissible. In *State v. Kinney*, 698 N.E.2d 49 (Ohio 1998), for instance, the court upheld a warrant authorizing the search of everyone located in a particular apartment based upon an affidavit from a specially-trained narcotics detective that established probable cause to believe that cocaine was being sold out of the apartment. In fact, the court described the premises as a "crack house."

> Individuals who are present in a drug-trafficking residence raise special concerns for law enforcement. A drug-trafficking residence often has more than one person on the premises. Individuals may be present for the preparation and packaging of the drugs. Some are present to collect cash, others to protect drug dealers. Some have come to purchase drugs. Most occupants are armed and dangerous. Combined, these concerns involve the safety of all individuals on the premises, since drugs and concealed weapons are involved. This is far different from a general exploratory search. 698 N.E.2d at 53.

Particular Description of Items to Be Seized

The affidavit supporting a request for a search warrant must contain a particular description of the items to be seized:

> The requirement that warrants shall particularly describe the things to be seized makes general searches under them impossible and prevents the seizure of one thing under a warrant describing another. As to what is to be taken, nothing is left to the discretion of the officer executing the warrant. *Marron v. United States,* 275 U.S. 192, 196 (1927).

In general, the items to be seized must be described with sufficient particularity so that the officer executing the warrant

- can identify the items with reasonable certainty and
- is left with no discretion as to which property is to be taken.

The primary concern of courts evaluating descriptions of things to be seized in search warrants is to ensure that a person will not be deprived of lawfully possessed property by a seizure made under an imprecise warrant. A description of items merely as "stolen goods," "obscene materials," or "other articles of merchandise too numerous to mention" is inadequate because it is imprecise. *Marcus v. Search Warrant*, 367 U.S. 717 (1961).

Particular Descriptions of Items When an item can be described in detail, all available information about it should be included in the affidavit. For example, number, size, color, weight, condition, brand name, serial number, and other distinguishing features of an item to be seized should be a part of the description where applicable. The affidavit should also indicate how the item is connected with criminal activity by stating the category of items subject to seizure within which the item falls.

When Specificity Cannot Be Achieved A more general description is allowed when specificity is impossible or very difficult. For example, in a case involving the robbery of a post office, the court found sufficiently specific a warrant directing the seizure of "a variety of items, including 'currency' and 'United States postage stock (stamps; envelopes; checks)." The court said:

> At the time of the application and issuance of the warrant in the instant case, a more precise description of the stamps and currency taken during the robbery was unascertainable. Although the postal inspectors knew that stamps and currency had been stolen, no further information was available to more particularly describe the items in the warrant. We find that the description of the stamps and currency by generic classes was reasonably specific under the circumstances of this case. *United States v. Porter*, 831 F.2d 760, 764 (8th Cir. 1987).

Large Numbers of Indistinguishable Common Items A more general description may also be allowed when a large number of items to be seized are of a common nature and not readily distinguishable. In a case involving a stolen shipment of women's clothing, a search warrant authorized the seizure of "[c]artons of women's clothing, the contents of those cartons, lists identifying the contents of the cartons, and control slips identifying the stores intended to receive these cartons." *United States v. Fuccillo*, 808 F.2d 173, 176 (1st Cir. 1987). Because government agents could have but did not obtain specific information that would have enabled the agents executing the search to differentiate contraband cartons of women's clothing from legitimate ones, the warrants were invalidated for failure to specify as nearly as possible the distinguishing characteristics of the goods to be seized.

Fraudulent Business Records Courts also allow a relaxation of the particularity requirement for search warrants seeking business records of businesses "permeated with fraud":

> [W]here there is probable cause to believe that a business is "permeated with fraud," either explicitly stated in the supporting affidavit or implicit from the evidence therein set forth, a warrant may authorize the seizure of all documents relating to the suspected criminal area but may not authorize the seizure of any severable portion of such documents relating to legitimate activities. *United States v. Oloyede*, 982 F.2d 133, 141 (4th Cir. 1992).

Note, however, that the "permeated with fraud doctrine" does not authorize "all records" search warrants whenever businesses allegedly commit acts of fraud. "If the fraudulent conduct infects only one part of the business, the warrant must be limited to documents related to that particular aspect of the business operation. But when the whole business is permeated with fraud, a warrant authorizing the seizure of all the business records of a corporation is permissible." *State v. Norris*, 48 P.3d 872, 879 (Utah 2001).

Contraband Courts generally allow greater leeway in descriptions of contraband material. For example, in *United States v. Spears*, 965 F.2d 262 (7th Cir. 1992), the warrant authorized a search for and seizure of "controlled substances and other drug-related paraphernalia, and materials for packaging controlled substances." The court held:

> The terms "controlled substances" and "materials for packaging controlled substances" are sufficiently specific on their face. The catch-all term "other drug-related paraphernalia" also passes constitutional muster in that such items are

easily identifiable and quickly found by drug law enforcement officers. A search warrant delineating those items generally, in combination with named contraband, sufficiently limits an officer's discretion to execute the warrant. 965 F.2d at 277.

United States v. Appoloney, 761 F.2d 520, 524 (9th Cir. 1985), similarly upheld a warrant that used the following description: "'wagering paraphernalia' such as betting slips, bottom sheets and owe sheets, and journals and schedules of sporting events." *Andresen v. Maryland*, 427 U.S. 463 (1976), permitted the use of the "catch-all" phrase: "together with other fruits, instrumentalities and evidence of crime at this [time] unknown." The warrant's validity was upheld because the underlying crime, a complex fraud case, depended on evidence that police had diligently described in the warrant that they thought they would find on the premises, as well as other evidence about which they could not know until the search was completed.

In contrast, however, a general description is usually not allowed if a more specific description is possible. In *United States v. Townsend*, 394 F. Supp. 736, 739 (E.D. Mich. 1975), a search warrant commanded the seizure of "stolen firearms, [approximately 10], which are stored in the basement of the above location, and in bedrooms, and any and all other stolen items, contraband." The court held that the phrase "any and all other stolen items" was impermissibly vague. The court also found the phrase "10 firearms" to be constitutionally deficient because firearms may be easily characterized by color, length, type, and other defining attributes. Thus, whenever specific descriptions are possible, applicants for search warrants should take care not to provide generic descriptions.

General descriptions are also not allowed if the contraband to be searched for and seized is books, films, recordings, or other materials that have not yet been adjudged obscene. Because these materials are presumed protected by the First Amendment, a very high degree of particularity is required in both the affidavit and the warrant. In *Lo-Ji Sales, Inc. v. New York*, 442 U.S. 319 (1979), a magistrate viewed two films from the defendant's adult bookstore, concluded they were obscene, and issued a warrant authorizing the seizure of all other obscene materials. The U.S. Supreme Court invalidated the warrant for being too general.

> [T]he warrant left it entirely to the discretion of the officials conducting the search to decide what items were likely obscene and to accomplish their seizure. The Fourth Amendment does not permit such action. . . . Nor does the Fourth Amendment countenance open-ended warrants, to be completed while a seizure is being conducted and items seized or after the seizure has been carried out. 442 U.S. at 325.

On the other hand, the First Amendment does not protect materials depicting child pornography. *Osborne v. Ohio*, 495 U.S. 103 (1990). In child pornography investigations, search warrants should be phrased to allow the seizure of "pornographic or erotic materials to include, but not limited to, books, magazines, articles, photographs, slides, movies, albums, letters, diaries, sexual aids or toys or other items relating to sexual acts or sexual acts with children, [and] photographs of the alleged crime scene." *State v. Kirsch*, 662 A.2d 937, 939 (N.H. 1995). Care should be taken to ensure that such warrants are limited to seizure of materials depicting sexually explicit conduct involving either an actual minor or someone who appears to be a minor since *Ashcroft v. Free Speech Coalition*, 535 U.S. 234 (2002), held that computer-generated images that do not depict an actual minor are protected by the First Amendment (see Chapter 1).

Anticipatory Search Warrants

An **anticipatory search warrant**, also called a *prospective search warrant*, is a "search warrant based on an affidavit showing probable cause that evidence of a certain crime (such as illegal drugs) will be located at a specific place in the future" (*Black's Law Dictionary*, 2004: 1379). In *United States v. Grubbs*, 547 U.S. 90 (2006), the U.S. Supreme Court upheld the constitutionality of anticipatory search warrants under the Fourth Amendment. The Court found that anticipatory warrants are, at least in principle, no different from regular search warrants. The only real difference between anticipatory search warrants and regular warrants is that anticipatory warrants are dependent on some triggering condition. The warrant application must demonstrate that it is *now* probable that contraband, evidence of a crime, or a fugitive *will be* on the described premises when the warrant is executed. So long as there is reliable evidence that the triggering event will take place, and assuming that the other requirements of valid warrants are met (i.e., the warrant is particularized and not otherwise defective), then the fact that "contraband has not yet reached the premises to be searched at the time the warrant issues is not, in constitutional terms, an insuperable obstacle." *United States v. Ricciardelli*, 998 F.2d 8, 11 (1st Cir. 1993).

To ensure that a magistrate is provided with sufficient information to justify the issuance of an anticipatory search warrant, the affidavit should present strong evidence that the continuation of a process already initiated will result in seizable items arriving at a particular place at a particular time. To guard against premature execution of the warrant, the affidavit should carefully specify the time when the item to be seized will arrive at the place to be searched and the time when the execution of the warrant is planned. This information should satisfy the magistrate that the warrant will not be executed prematurely.

Content of Search Warrants

Although search warrants vary among jurisdictions, most search warrants contain the following information:

- the caption of the court or division of the court from which the warrant issues;
- a particular description of the place or person to be searched;
- a particular description of the property to be seized;
- the names of persons whose affidavits have been taken in support of the warrant;
- a statement of grounds for issuance of the warrant;
- the name of the officer or class of officers to whom the warrant is directed, together with a command to search the person or place named for the property specified;
- a specification of the time during the day when the search may be conducted;
- the name of the judicial officer to whom the warrant is to be returned;
- the date of issuance; and
- the signature of the issuing magistrate, together with a statement of the magistrate's official title.

Recall that Figures 4.2 and 4.3 are typical search warrant forms, the former based exclusively on an affidavit, the latter based on oral testimony (including testimony given telephonically).

KEY POINTS

LO2

- An issuing magistrate for a search warrant must be neutral, detached, and capable of determining whether probable cause exists for the requested search.

- Before issuing a search warrant, the magistrate must have probable cause to believe that items subject to seizure are in a particular place or on a particular person at the time of the issuance of the warrant.

- Time is a very important factor in determining probable cause to search. If the information on which probable cause was initially based becomes stale, there may no longer be good reason to believe that property is still at the same location.

- Generally, the types of property allowed to be seized under a search warrant are evidence of a crime, contraband, fruits of crime, other items illegally possessed, and instrumentalities of crime. A search warrant may also be issued to search for a person to be arrested or a person who is unlawfully restrained.

- The affidavit supporting a request for a search warrant for a place must contain a description of the premises to be searched that points directly to a definitely ascertainable place to the exclusion of all others.

- The affidavit supporting a request for a search warrant must contain a particular description of the items to be seized.

Continued on next page

Time Frame for Obtaining a Search Warrant

Although the formal requirements for obtaining search warrants are fairly standard across the United States, the time it takes to obtain any particular warrant ranges from being quick and easy (i.e., within 15 minutes) to protracted and cumbersome (i.e., days or even weeks). The variance depends on both the structure of a particular jurisdiction's criminal justice system and on the type of case being investigated.

In some jurisdictions, an on-call "duty judge" or magistrate is available to issue warrants twenty-four hours a day, seven days per week. In other jurisdictions, finding a neutral judicial officer during off-hours can be challenging. Similarly, in some jurisdictions, police officers can obtain a warrant by phone, fax, email, iPad, iPhones, or even using Skype (see Swingle & Thomasson 2013). In other jurisdictions, search warrant applications and affidavits not only need to be in writing but also need to be reviewed by command-level police staff (e.g., a lieutenant or captain) or even a prosecutor.

The type of case also matters. In Phoenix, Arizona, for example, police can obtain a search warrant in less than ten minutes in cases involving suspected driving under the influence (DUI) using an "eSearch Warrant Application" they can send electronically from their patrol cars (Chan 2013). In other jurisdictions, it might take a skilled police officer two to three hours to prepare an affidavit summarizing his or her personal observations during a stop of a driver suspected of DUI (e.g., detailing erratic driving, bloodshot eyes, slurred speech, the smell of alcohol on the suspect's breath, etc.) and then have a judge approve the warrant. In contrast, given the requirements of particularly describing the place or person to be searched, the items to be seized, and the details necessary to establish probable cause when informants and other nonfirsthand sources of information are involved, it should come as no surprise that it can take many hours—even days—to prepare search warrant applications and supporting affidavits in complex cases.

Constitutionally Defective Warrants

Warrants containing errors, misrepresentations, and material omissions may be constitutionally defective and, therefore, invalid. Unless the offending parts of the warrant can be severed and the remaining parts still constitute a valid warrant, then the exclusionary rule may result in the suppression of the evidence garnered from the search, depending on whether one of the exceptions to the exclusionary rule discussed in Chapter 2 applies.

Material Misrepresentations and Omissions

If a law enforcement officer knowingly and intentionally, or with reckless disregard for the truth, makes false statements or material omissions in an affidavit supporting a request for a search warrant, the warrant may not be lawfully issued. If the warrant does issue, evidence seized under the warrant may be suppressed by application of the exclusionary rule in a procedure known as a *Franks* hearing. *Franks* hearings are named after the case *Franks v. Delaware*, 438 U.S. 154 (1978), in which the U.S. Supreme Court held that a defendant may challenge the veracity of an affidavit used by the police to obtain a search warrant.

Necessary Preliminary Showing to Obtain a *Franks* Hearing A mere allegation of falsity or material omission or both is insufficient to trigger a *Franks* hearing. "A mere allegation standing alone, without an offer of proof in a sworn affidavit of a witness or some other reliable corroboration, is insufficient. . . . When no proof is offered

147

that an affiant deliberately lied or recklessly disregarded the truth, a *Franks* hearing is not required." *United States v. Mathison*, 157 F.3d 541, 548 (8th Cir. 1998). Thus, for a defendant to qualify for a *Franks* hearing, he or she must first make a *prima facie* showing that the affiant's statement was deliberately false or demonstrated reckless disregard for the truth by coming forward with some evidence that makes a "substantial preliminary showing" to support an allegation of police misconduct in establishing probable cause for the issuance of a warrant. *Franks*, 438 U.S. at 155. If the defendant does so, then the trial court is obliged to hold a *Franks* hearing. For example, in *United States v. Tate*, 524 F.3d 449, 457 (4th Cir. 2008), a police officer obtained a warrant to search the defendant's home for drugs because of items the officer had discovered in the defendant's trash. (As explained more fully in Chapter 12, the search of trash that is placed outside for collection does not ordinarily implicate the Fourth Amendment because it is usually considered to be abandoned property.) The defendant submitted affidavits establishing that the officer had omitted an important fact in his search warrant application. The affidavit "was constructed intentionally to mislead the state judge into assuming that the trash investigation had been conducted legally, even though, . . . the trash bags had been taken by means of a trespass into [the defendant's] fenced backyard, resulting in an unconstitutional search" since the "trash bags had not been abandoned for trash pick-up, as required for a trash search to be constitutional." 524 F.3d at 452. Hence, Tate was entitled to a *Franks* hearing to determine if the warrant should be invalidated and the fruits of the search suppressed via the exclusionary rule.

In contrast, if a defendant cannot demonstrate a *prima facie* case of deliberate or reckless falsity or material omission in the establishment of probable cause, then the defendant is not entitled to a *Franks* hearing. In other words, even if a defendant makes a preliminary showing of an affiant's deliberate or reckless disregard for the truth, a defendant is not entitled to a *Franks* hearing without a corresponding showing that the offending statement or omission was essential to establishing probable cause. For example, in *United States v. Blauvelt*, 638 F.3d 281 (4th Cir. 2011), officers received a tip from the defendant's ex-girlfriend that he possessed child pornography. He argued that the affidavit should have disclosed, but did not disclose, that he and his ex-girlfriend "were engaged in child support and custody litigation at or near the time of this incident; . . . and that [she] had a criminal record, allegedly having been convicted for driving under the influence. This information, Blauvelt claims, would have caused a reasonable reviewing magistrate to question [her] credibility and motives." 638 F.3d at 289. The court ruled that the omission of such information shedding light on the ex-girlfriend's reputation and motives was not central to the probable cause determination since she had shown police pictures that the defendant had taken and emailed to himself—pictures she was able to access since she knew the password to her ex-boyfriend's email account.

Burden of Proof at a *Franks* Hearing A *Franks* hearing involves a two-step process. Initially, the defendant bears the burden of proving, by a preponderance of the evidence, that an application for a warrant contained false statements that were knowingly or recklessly made or, alternatively, that material information was knowingly or recklessly omitted from the warrant application. If the defendant fails to meet this burden of proof:

> [T]he inquiry is at an end and the fruits of the search should not be suppressed. However, should the defendant meet his burden . . . , the court must expand its inquiry and determine whether the affidavit, when stricken of its falsity, is nonetheless sufficient to establish probable cause for issuance of the search warrant. *United States v. Whitley*, 249 F.3d 614, 620 (7th Cir. 2001).

After the offending material is stricken from the application, if the remaining information still establishes probable cause, the warrant will be upheld. If, however, the remaining information contained in the affidavit after the offending data is set aside fails to establish probable cause, then "the search warrant must be voided and the fruits of the search excluded to the same extent as if probable cause was lacking on the face of the affidavit." *Franks*, 438 U.S. at 155–56. Moreover, the officer may be subject to criminal prosecution for perjury or a related offense, as well as to damages liability in a civil lawsuit. *See Malley v. Briggs*, 475 U.S. 335 (1986).

In *United States v. Reinholz*, 245 F.3d 765, 774 (8th Cir. 2001), an officer implied in his affidavit that his "confidential and reliable" informant had personal knowledge of the defendant's alleged drug use and dealings. However, the informant had no such knowledge and came forward to acknowledge his lack of personal knowledge. The court ruled that the defendant was entitled to a *Franks* hearing after which the court excised all of the information in the affidavit concerning the informant after concluding the statements were made with reckless disregard for the truth. Yet the search and subsequent seizure were both upheld because the court determined that the remaining information in the affidavit was sufficient to establish probable cause based on the defendant's drug conviction record and drug paraphernalia that had been collected lawfully from the defendant's trash.

In contrast, the officer's misrepresentations about the steps he had taken to verify the accuracy of an informant's tip was fatal to the prosecution's case in *United States v. Hammond*, 351 F.3d 765 (6th Cir. 2003). In *Hammond*, an officer admitted that he made false statements in his affidavit regarding the steps he had allegedly taken to verify the reliability of an informant's tip when in fact he had not taken such steps. Not only did this justify a *Franks* hearing, but also the court ultimately concluded that the violation warranted application of the exclusionary rule because probable cause could not be established on the basis of an unverified tip by an informant whose reliability was otherwise not known or demonstrated. Because there was insufficient information in the affidavit to establish probable cause once the tip was excised, the search was invalidated by the court.

Severability of Search Warrants

Search warrants may inadvertently contain some clauses that are constitutionally sufficient and other clauses that are not, due to human error—either a lack of probable cause or a lack of particularity. Should courts apply the exclusionary rule to suppress all evidence under these warrants, or only the evidence seized under the constitutionally insufficient clauses? To avoid the severe remedy of total suppression of all evidence seized under these warrants, courts have adopted the theory of redaction or severability, also called *partial suppression*.

The Doctrine of Severability Severability invalidates and redacts clauses in a warrant that are constitutionally insufficient for lack of probable cause or particularity and preserves clauses that satisfy the Fourth Amendment. *See United States v. Ninety-Two Thousand Four Hundred Twenty-Two Dollars and Fifty-Seven Cents*, 307 F.3d 137 (3rd Cir. 2002).

> By redaction, we mean striking from a warrant those severable phrases and clauses that are invalid for lack of probable cause or generality and preserving those severable phrases and clauses that satisfy the Fourth Amendment. Each part of the search authorized by the warrant is examined separately to determine whether it is impermissibly general or unsupported by probable cause. Materials seized under the authority of those parts of the warrant struck for invalidity must be suppressed, but the court need not suppress materials seized pursuant to the valid portions of the warrant. *United States v. Yusuf*, 461 F.3d 374, 389 (3d Cir. 2006).

L05

KEY POINTS

- If a law enforcement officer knowingly and intentionally or with reckless disregard for the truth makes false statements or material omissions in an affidavit supporting a request for a search warrant, the warrant may not be lawfully issued. If, however, a warrant based on an affidavit containing false statements or material omissions was issued, and a defendant can make a strong preliminary showing of this fact, the defendant is entitled to challenge the legality of the warrant and the ensuing search at a *Franks* hearing.

- At a *Franks* hearing, the defendant bears the burden of proving, by a preponderance of the evidence, either that an application for a warrant contained false statements that were knowingly or recklessly made or, alternatively, that material information was knowingly or recklessly omitted from the warrant application. If the defendant fails to meet this burden of proof, the warrant will be upheld and the evidence gathered as a result of the search will be admissible. If, however, the defendant meets his or her burden, then the court must determine whether the affidavit, when stricken of its false or misleading statement, is nonetheless sufficient to establish probable cause for issuance of the search warrant. If the remaining information establishes probable cause, then the warrant will be upheld. If, however, the remaining information contained in the affidavit after the offending data are set aside fails to establish probable

Continued on next page

Determining Severability The severance of the unparticular descriptions is not allowed if the entire warrant "is facially general in nature" because that would render the entire warrant constitutionally deficient. *United States v. Giresi,* 488 F. Supp. 445, 459 (D.N.J. 1980). Similarly, the severance doctrine does not apply if the entire warrant is unsupported by probable cause. But, assuming that at least some portions of a warrant are sufficiently particular and supported by probable cause, courts subscribing to the doctrine of severability then engage in a complicated process to determine (1) whether the doctrine of severability is applicable to a particular warrant and, (2) if so, to which parts of the warrant. This process was described in detail by the Tenth Circuit Court of Appeals in *United States v. Sells,* 463 F.3d 1148 (10th Cir. 2006). The process described by the court is presented in Figure 4.4. Although all courts do not rigidly adhere to particulars of the four-step process set forth in *Sells,* they all apply a test that is qualitatively similar.

Step 1: The warrant must be divided "in a commonsense, practical manner into individual clauses, portions, paragraphs, or categories." 463 F.3d at 1151.

Step 2: The constitutionality of each individual part must be examined "to determine whether some portion of the warrant satisfies the probable cause and particularity requirements of the Fourth Amendment." 463 F.3d at 1151.
   A. "If no part of the warrant particularly describes items to be seized for which there is probable cause, then severance does not apply, and all items seized by such a warrant should be suppressed." 463 F.3d at 1151. This ends the inquiry.
   B. "If, however, at least a part of the warrant is sufficiently particularized and supported by probable cause," courts then proceed to step 3. 463 F.3d at 1151.

Step 3: Courts must then "determine whether the valid portions are distinguishable from the invalid portions." 463 F.3d at 1151.
   A. If the parts are not distinguishable, then severance is inapplicable and the items seized must be suppressed.
   B. "If, however, parts of the warrant may be meaningfully severed," then courts proceed to step 4. 463 F.3d at 1151.

Step 4: The warrant as a whole must be examined both quantitatively and qualitatively, "to determine whether the valid portions make up 'the greater part of the warrant,'" in comparison to the invalid portion(s). "This analysis ensures that severance does not render the Fourth Amendment's warrant requirement meaningless." 463 F.3d at 1151.
   A. If the valid portions fail to comprise "the greater part of the warrant" (i.e., there are more invalid parts than there are valid sections), then severance is inapplicable and all of the evidence seized will be suppressed. 463 F.3d at 1151; *see also United States v. Naugle,* 997 F.2d 819, 822 (10th Cir. 1993).
   B. If, however, the valid portions make up "the greater part of the warrant" then those portions may be severed and evidence seized pursuant to these valid, severed portions is admissible. The evidence seized pursuant to the invalid portions will be suppressed.

© Cengage Learning®

FIGURE 4.4 | Steps in the Severability Decision Process

Executing Search Warrants

The execution (also called *service*) of a search warrant is essentially the carrying out of the commands in the warrant. "The Fourth Amendment confines an officer executing a search warrant strictly within the bounds set by the warrant." *Bivens v. Six Unknown Named Agents*, 403 U.S. 388, 394 n.7 (1971). Furthermore, "a search which is reasonable at its inception may violate the Fourth Amendment by virtue of its intolerable intensity and scope. . . . The scope of the search must be 'strictly tied to and justified by' the circumstances which rendered its initiation permissible." *Terry v. Ohio*, 392 U.S. 1, 18 (1968). Although officers can determine many of their duties from simply reading the warrant, several aspects of the execution of search warrants need further explanation.

Who May Execute a Search Warrant

A search warrant is directed to a particular officer or class of officers. Usually, only the named officer or a member of the named class of officers may execute or serve the warrant. Normally, the officer to whom the warrant is directed must be personally present at the search. But if a warrant is directed to a sheriff, a deputy may execute the warrant without the sheriff present. However, a narrow set of circumstances may exist in which a search warrant may be executed by a civilian even outside the presence of a police officer. *United States v. Bach*, 310 F.3d 1063 (8th Cir. 2002), upheld the execution of a search warrant that allowed for the retrieval of certain e-mails from an Internet service provider. The court ruled that is was permissible for the warrant to have included a provision allowing for it to be faxed to an Internet service provider and executed by technicians there. Key to the court's rationale was that the actual physical presence of an officer would not have aided the search.

Police behavior during the execution of a search warrant must be related to the objectives specified in the warrant. Therefore, officers are limited with regard to whom they may bring with them during the execution of a search warrant. Officers may enlist private persons to help in the execution of a warrant so long as they serve a purpose within the authorized scope of the intrusion. Thus, for example, it would be permissible for police to bring civilian evidence technicians or forensic experts to the execution of a search warrant, but it would not be constitutional for them to bring members of the media or other third-party observers with them who are of no assistance to actually executing the warrant. *See Wilson v. Layne*, 526 U.S. 603 (1999); *Hanlon v. Berger*, 526 U.S. 808 (1999).

Time Considerations

Three different aspects of time affect law enforcement officers in the execution of search warrants:

- how long after the issuance of a search warrant it is executed,
- the time of day the warrant is executed, and
- how long it takes to fully execute the search.

Delay and Staleness Concerns How much time may pass between the issuance of a warrant and its execution? Courts are concerned with delays in the execution of warrants because probable cause might become stale if not acted upon promptly. But there are many valid reasons for delaying the execution of a search warrant. Weather conditions, long travel distances, traffic problems, and similar obstacles may prevent the prompt execution of the warrant. Delays may be necessary to gather sufficient human resources for the search, to protect the safety of the searching officers, to prevent the destruction of evidence, and to prevent the flight of a suspect. When the warrant is for the search of both a person and premises, the search may be delayed until the person is present on the premises. *People v. Stansberry*, 268 N.E.2d 431 (Ill. 1971). Regardless of the justification for a delay, however, warrants must be executed before probable cause dissipates, a process commonly referred to as going "stale."

Fixed Time Limits To combat staleness problems, most U.S. jurisdictions set such a time limit by statute, court rule, or judicial decision. If a warrant is not executed within the prescribed time limit, then the warrant is usually deemed void and any subsequent execution of the warrant will be invalid. *E.g.*, *Spera v. State*, 467 So. 2d 329 (Fla. App. 1985). A minority of jurisdictions, however, merely consider the expiration of the prescribed time for warrant execution to give rise to grounds for applying the exclusionary rule on a showing of prejudice to the defendant. *E.g.*, *State v. Weaver*, 602 S.E.2d 786 (S.C. App. 2004).

"Forthwith" Requirements Other U.S. jurisdictions do not have any fixed time limits for the execution of search warrants and simply require that warrants be executed "forthwith." But even in such states, warrants must still be executed within a reasonable time after issuance. Reasonableness, of course, depends on the facts and circumstances of each case. *See, e.g.*, *Turner v. Comm.*, 420 S.E.2d 235 (Va. 1992) (upholding a delay of eleven days because there were good reasons for the delay and probable cause had not gone stale).

Combination Requirements Just because a warrant is executed within the prescribed time limit does not necessarily mean that the search was constitutionally valid; a warrant can still go stale within the prescribed time period. Thus, many jurisdictions have dual requirements that warrants not only be executed within the relevant prescribed time period but also be executed "forthwith" or "without unnecessary delay" that would cause legal prejudice to the defendant. For example, Texas law provides:

> A peace officer to whom a search warrant is delivered shall execute it without delay and forthwith return it to the proper magistrate. It must be executed within three days from the time of its issuance, and shall be executed within a shorter period if so directed in the warrant by the magistrate. Vernon's Ann. Texas C.C.P. Art. 18.06(a).

In the federal system, Federal Rule of Criminal Procedure 41 specifies that search warrants must be executed within ten days if the issuing authority has not specified a shorter limit, *so long as probable cause continues to exist*. Unnecessary delay is determined by evaluating all the facts and circumstances surrounding the execution of the warrant. In states with dual rules, a search can be invalidated because it occurred too long after the issuance of the warrant (i.e., not "forthwith") even though the warrant was executed within the relevant time frame. For example, in *Huffines v. State*, 739 N.E.2d 1093 (Ind. Ct. App. 2000), *cert. denied*, 753 N.E.2d 9 (Ind. 2001), a court invalidated a search that occurred eight days after a warrant had been issued even though state statute required warrants to be executed within ten days. The court reasoned that probable cause had gone stale in the case because the warrant had been issued based on the defendant's purchase of a small amount of cocaine. With no evidence of any additional drug purchases, the court concluded that the evidence was no longer likely to have been found so many days later.

Time-of-Day Concerns In general, search warrants should be executed in the daytime. Courts have always frowned on nighttime searches. In *Jones v. United States*, 357 U.S. 493, 498 (1958), the U.S. Supreme Court said that "it is difficult to imagine a more severe invasion of privacy than the nighttime intrusion into a private home"; *see also* *State v. Richardson*, 904 P.2d 886 (Haw. 1995). Furthermore, nighttime searches are more likely to be met with armed resistance. *State v. Brock*, 633 P.2d 805 (Or. App. 1981). Therefore, many states have either statutes or court-mandated rules akin to Rule 41 of the Federal Rules of Criminal Procedure that require warrants to be executed during daytime. *E.g.*, CAL. PENAL CODE § 1533.

Defining Daytime Daytime is expansively defined as the hours between 6:00 A.M. and 10:00 P.M. FED. R. CRIM. P. 41(h). But the terms *daytime* and *nighttime* are defined differently in different jurisdictions by statute, court rule, or court decision. If these terms are not defined in a particular jurisdiction, a good rule of thumb is that it is daytime when there is sufficient natural light to recognize a person's features; otherwise, it is nighttime.

Nighttime Searches In spite of the normal rules that require warrants to be executed during the daytime, courts may authorize a nighttime search if the affidavit in support of the warrant sets forth specific facts showing some need to execute the warrant at night. For example, Delaware's statute permits the issuance of warrants that authorize a nighttime search when "necessary in order to prevent the escape or removal of the person or thing to be searched." DEL. CODE ANN. tit. 11, § 2308 (2000). Justification for a nighttime search has been found when a nighttime delivery of contraband was expected, when the property to be seized was likely to be removed promptly, and when part of a criminal transaction was to take place at night. Such circumstances most frequently exist when there is probable cause to suspect that a nighttime drug transaction will take place. *E.g.*, *United States v. Diehl*, 276 F.3d 32, 44 (1st Cir. 2002). In fact, Congress enacted a law specifically providing for nighttime searches in drug cases:

> A search warrant relating to offenses involving controlled substances may be served at any time of the day or night if the judge or United States magistrate judge issuing the warrant is satisfied that there is probable cause to believe that grounds exist for the warrant and for its service at such time. 21 U.S.C. § 879.

In interpreting this statutory provision, the Supreme Court ruled in *Gooding v. United States*, 416 U.S. 430 (1970), that the probable cause showing it requires is targeted at the existence of illicit drugs on premises only. Accordingly, no special showing needs to be made to justify a nighttime search other than that there is probable cause to believe that controlled substances are likely to be on the property or person to be searched at the time the warrant is executed. Thus, Congress created what has become known as the "narcotics exception" to the rule that a special showing must be made to justify the nighttime execution of a search warrant.

Even if a nighttime search is not authorized, the execution of a search warrant that was begun in the daytime may be continued into the nighttime if it is a reasonable continuation of the daytime search. An officer is not required to cut short the reasonable execution of a daytime search warrant just because it becomes dark outside. *United States v. Squillacote*, 221 F.3d 542 (4th Cir. 2000).

Duration of Search In light of the Fourth Amendment's command of reasonableness, courts are also concerned with the amount of time it takes law enforcement personnel to perform a search once it is initiated pursuant to a valid warrant. *Segura v. United States*, 468 U.S. 796 (1984). *State v. Chaisson*, 486 A.2d 297, 303 (N.H. 1984), stated the general rule: "The police, in executing a search warrant for a dwelling, may remain on the premises only so long as it is reasonably necessary to conduct the search." Therefore, after all the objects described in a warrant have been found and seized, "the authority under the warrant expires and further governmental intrusion must cease." *United States v. Gagnon*, 635 F.2d 766, 769 (10th Cir. 1980). If, however, only some of the described items have been found, the search may lawfully continue.

Simply examining how long a search lasted is insufficient to determine the reasonableness of the duration of a search because the number of hours is only one factor in the totality of the circumstances. For example, *State v. Swain*, 269 N.W.2d 707 (Minn. 1978), upheld a search of a home that lasted for three days because chemical tests needed to be run in order to analyze bloodstains that were discovered on the first and second days of the search. And *United States v. Squillacote*, 221 F.3d 542 (4th Cir. 2000), upheld a search that lasted six days, during which time FBI agents stayed in the defendant's house overnight for five nights to guard against the possible destruction of evidence. Even though the "extensive and exhaustive" search lasted so long, the court determined the search was reasonable in light of the following circumstances that, when examined together, established the reasonableness of the search:

> A search for evidence of espionage requires extreme thoroughness in order to discover the covert instruments, communications, and records of the illegal activity. In addition, the search was complicated by the condition of the home. . . . The house was extremely cluttered, and the [appellants'] personal possessions and documents were of such quantity and in such a state of disarray as to create a great obstacle to the execution of the warrant. The search was further complicated because the house was undergoing renovations, which increased the clutter and made it difficult to search certain areas of the house. . . . The agents were unable to search the basement, where many items were located, for long stretches of time due to the irritation caused by an immense amount of dust and the odor of cat urine. Therefore, notwithstanding the large number of agents involved in the search, it is apparent that the search could not have been completed in a single day. 221 F.3d at 557 (internal quotations and citations omitted).

Securing People and Places While a Search Warrant Is Being Sought

When officers have probable cause to believe that evidence of criminal activity is in a dwelling, temporarily securing the dwelling to prevent removal or destruction of evidence while a search warrant is being sought is not an unreasonable seizure of either the dwelling or its contents:

> [T]he home is sacred in Fourth Amendment terms not primarily because of the occupants' possessory interests in the premises, but because of their privacy interests in the activities that take place within. . . . [A] seizure affects only possessory interests, not privacy interests. Therefore, the heightened protection we accord privacy interests is simply not implicated where a seizure of premises, not a search, is at issue. *Segura v. United States*, 468 U.S. 796, 810 (1984).

Segura held that, insofar as the seizure of the premises is concerned, it made no difference whether the premises were secured by stationing officers within the premises or by establishing a perimeter stakeout after a security check of the premises revealed that no one was inside. Under either method, officers control the premises pending arrival of the warrant. Both an internal securing and a perimeter stakeout interfere to the same extent with the possessory interests of the owners.

In *Illinois v. McArthur*, 531 U.S. 326 (2001), police officers, with probable cause to believe that the defendant had hidden marijuana in his home, prevented him from entering the home for about two hours while they obtained a warrant. The U.S. Supreme Court balanced the privacy-related and law enforcement–related concerns and found the warrantless intrusion reasonable. First, the police had probable cause to believe that the defendant's home contained evidence of a crime and contraband—namely, unlawful drugs. Second, the police had good reason to fear that, unless restrained, the defendant would destroy the drugs before they could return with a warrant. Third, the police neither searched the home nor arrested the defendant but imposed the significantly less restrictive restraint of preventing him from entering the home unaccompanied. Finally, the police imposed the restraint for a limited period of time—namely, two hours, or the time reasonably necessary to obtain a warrant. "Given the nature of the intrusion and the law enforcement interest at stake, this brief seizure of the premises was permissible." 531 U.S. at 333.

The Knock-and-Announce Requirement

Law enforcement officers are generally required to "knock and announce" their presence, authority, and purpose before entering premises to execute a search warrant. In 1603, an English court explained the logic of the rule that some historians believe had been a common law requirement since the late thirteenth century:

> But before he breaks it, he ought to signify the cause of his coming, and to make request to open doors . . ., for the law without a default in the owner abhors the destruction or breaking of any house (which is for the habitation and safety of man) by which great damage and inconvenience might ensue to the party, when no default is in him; for perhaps he did not know of the process, of which, if he had notice, it is to be presumed that he would obey it. *Semayne's Case*, 5 Co. Rep. 91a, 91b 77 Eng. Rep. 194, 195 (K.B. 1603).

The U.S. Supreme Court quoted this language in its decision in *Wilson v. Arkansas*, 514 U.S. 927 (1995), in which it held that the knock-and-announce principle was part of the Fourth Amendment's reasonableness requirement. The purposes of the knock-and-announce requirement are

- to prevent violence to the police or other persons on the premises,
- to protect the privacy of the occupants of the premises from unexpected intrusions,
- to prevent property damage, and
- to give the occupant an opportunity to examine the warrant and point out a possible mistaken address or other errors.

An announcement of identity as a law enforcement officer accompanied by a statement that the officer has a search warrant is usually sufficient. But failure to comply with this requirement, absent some exigent circumstance, can render a search constitutionally unreasonable. For example, in *State v. Maldonado*, 121 P.3d 901 (Haw. 2005), police opened a closed screen door and entered a home before they announced their presence and purpose. The court ruled that the knock-and-announce requirement had been violated.

Under 18 U.S.C. Section 3109 (2000), a person who refuses entry to an officer executing a warrant risks forcible entry:

> The officer may break open any outer or inner door or window of a house, or any part of a house, or anything therein, to execute a search warrant, if, after notice of his authority and purpose, he is refused admittance or when necessary to liberate himself or a person aiding him in the execution of the warrant.

To comply with this statute, courts usually require police officers to wait at least ten to twenty, if not thirty, seconds after the knock and announce. *United States v. Valdez,*

KEY POINTS

LO4

- Only the named officer or a member of the named class of officers may execute or serve a search warrant. Normally, the officer to whom the warrant is directed must be personally present at the search. Officers may enlist private persons to help in the execution of a warrant so long as they serve a purpose within the authorized scope of the intrusion.

- In general, a search warrant should be executed in the daytime within a reasonable time after its issuance unless a warrant specifically provides for nighttime execution or nighttime execution is specifically statutorily authorized.

- Officers should remain on the searched premises only so long as is reasonably necessary to conduct the search.

- When officers have probable cause to believe that evidence of criminal activity is in a dwelling, temporarily securing the dwelling to prevent removal or destruction of evidence while a search warrant is being sought is not an unreasonable seizure of either the dwelling or its contents.

302 F.3d 320 (5th Cir. 2002). But if officers knock and announce their authority and purpose and are refused entry, then they may forcibly enter the premises. Refusal does not have to be explicit, but most commonly it is implied by an occupant's failure to admit officers within a reasonable time after they have knocked and announced. *United States v. Banks*, 540 U.S. 31 (2003), addressed the issue of what is a reasonable time for an occupant to respond. In *Banks*, officers arrived at Banks's two-bedroom apartment at 2:00 P.M. on a weekday afternoon to execute a warrant to search for cocaine and evidence of cocaine sales. An officer knocked loudly on the front door and shouted, "Police—search warrant." Receiving no response from inside, the officers waited fifteen to twenty seconds and then broke open the door and entered. The search produced weapons, crack cocaine, and evidence of drug sales. Banks testified that he was in the shower when the officers entered and did not hear the knock or announcement.

The Court held that the totality of the circumstances known to the officers at the time of entry is what counts in judging reasonable waiting time. Absent emergency circumstances, relevant factors include the size and nature of the structure, the time of day, valid reasons for delay known to the officers, and other reasons affecting the speed with which the occupant could reach the door. In this case, however, the crucial fact in examining their actions was not the time to reach the door but the nature of the exigent circumstances claimed by the police:

> [W]hat matters is the opportunity to get rid of cocaine, which a prudent dealer will keep near a commode or kitchen sink. The significant circumstances include the arrival of the police during the day, when anyone inside would probably have been up and around, and the sufficiency of 15 to 20 seconds for getting to the bathroom or the kitchen to start flushing cocaine down the drain. That is, when circumstances are exigent because a pusher may be near the point of putting his drugs beyond reach, it is imminent disposal, not travel time to the entrance, that governs when the police may reasonably enter; since the bathroom and kitchen are usually in the interior of a dwelling, not the front hall, there is no reason generally to peg the travel time to the location of the door, and no reliable basis for giving the proprietor of a mansion a longer wait than the resident of a bungalow, or an apartment like Banks's. And 15 to 20 seconds does not seem an unrealistic guess about the time someone would need to get in a position to rid his quarters of cocaine. 540 U.S. at 40.

The Court therefore ruled the entry lawful. Applying similar logic, *United States v. Gay*, 240 F.3d 1222 (10th Cir. 2001) upheld police entry into the home of a drug dealer whom they believed to be armed and dangerous after only two to three seconds.

It should be noted that if police must use force to gain entry, the means they use to do so must be reasonable and necessary. In *Dalia v. United States* 441 U.S. 238 (1979), the U.S. Supreme Court said that officers executing a search warrant may use whatever method is reasonably necessary to gain access to premises to be searched, even to the extent of damaging property, if no reasonable alternative is available.

Exceptions to the Knock-and-Announce Requirement

Exigent Circumstances The Supreme Court has made it clear that it is not necessary for police to knock and announce their presence and purpose if exigent circumstances exist for dispensing with the rule:

It is not necessary when circumstances present a threat of physical violence, or if there is reason to believe that evidence would likely be destroyed if advance notice were given, or if knocking and announcing would be futile. We require only that police have a reasonable suspicion under the particular circumstances that one of these grounds for failing to knock and announce exists, and we have acknowledged that this showing is not high. *Hudson v. Michigan*, 547 U.S. 586, 589–90 (2006).

What types of circumstances justify reasonable suspicion to ignore the knock-and-announce rule? There is no blanket exception to the knock-and-announce requirement in drug cases—*see Richards v. Wisconsin*, 520 U.S. 385 (1997). Yet the destruction of evidence, especially drug evidence, as in *Banks* and *Hudson*, is clearly the common reason for dispensing with the knock-and-announce requirement under a totality of the circumstances approach. *E.g., United States v. Johnson*, 267 F.3d 498 (6th Cir. 2001). But courts have also upheld entries without a prior knock and announce under such exigent circumstances, including the following:

- The sound of footsteps, whispers, or flushing toilets that indicate possible escape or destruction of evidence may create exigent circumstances justifying an immediate forcible entry. *United States v. Stiver*, 9 F.3d 298 (3d Cir. 1993); *United States v. Mitchell*, 783 F.2d 971 (10th Cir. 1986).

- The suspect had a criminal record of violence and was armed, and police suspected that he was aware of the fact that police were investigating him. *United States v. Hawkins*, 139 F.3d 29, 32 (1st Cir. 1998).

- Police saw smoke and smelled what they believed to be explosives. *United States v. Combs*, 394 F.3d 739 (9th Cir. 2005).

- Police anticipated that the suspect had a rocket launcher inside the premises to be searched. *United States v. Crippen*, 371 F.3d 842, 846 (D.C. Cir. 2004).

- Police observed the suspect exiting his apartment through a back door. *United States v. McGee*, 280 F.3d 803 (7th Cir. 2002).

Of course, even when the knock-and-announce requirement is excused, the police must still act reasonably or risk exclusion of the evidence. For example, in *State v. Fanelle*, 960 A.2d 825 (N.J. Super. 2008), the court held from the particular circumstances of the case that it was unreasonable for police to use two or more flash-bang devices when executing a no-knock search warrant for the defendant's home under commando-raid–like conditions, and thus evidence seized during the search was suppressed.

Entry by Ruse or Deception Some courts also allow an exception to the knock-and-announce requirement for entries accomplished by ruse or deception. For example, in *United States v. Contreras-Ceballos*, 999 F.2d 432 (9th Cir. 1993), an officer executing a search warrant for drugs knocked on the defendant's door and replied "Federal Express" when asked who was there. When the door was opened, the officer pushed his way in and announced his authority and purpose. The court held that the use of force to keep the door open and to enter did not violate the knock-and-announce requirement because there was no "breaking." "To rule otherwise would dictate a nonsensical procedure in which the officers, after having employed a permissible ruse to cause the door to be opened, must permit it to be shut by the occupants so that the officers could then knock, re-announce, and open the door forcibly if refused admittance." 999 F.2d at 435.

If Police Presence and Purpose Is Already Known Finally, knocking and announcing "is excused when the officers are justifiably and virtually certain that the occupants already know their purpose." *United States v. Eddy*, 660 F.2d 381, 385 (8th Cir. 1981); *see also United States v. Dunnock*, 295 F.3d 431 (4th Cir. 2002).

No-Knock Warrants Some states have enacted no-knock warrant laws that permit magistrates to issue search warrants specifically authorizing officers to enter premises without knocking and announcing their authority and purpose. An officer applying for such a warrant needs only to articulate reasonable suspicion for believing that compliance with the knock-and-announce rule would result in the destruction of evidence or in some harm to the executing officer or others. If such grounds exist, it is wise for an officer to seek a no-knock warrant for two reasons. First, it would insulate the officer from potential civil liability for having misjudged exigent circumstances for him- or herself at the time of the execution of the warrant. Second, if the warrant issues and is later determined to have been invalid (i.e., if the reviewing judge were to determine that a no-knock entry was not appropriate after the fact), the good-faith exception under *Leon* would clearly apply.

Remedy for Knock-and-Announce Violations

Prior to the U.S. Supreme Court's decision in *Hudson v. Michigan,* the exclusionary rule was used as a remedy for knock-and-announce violations. Thus, if police failed to comply with the requirement of the knock-and-announce rule, the evidence seized as a result of the ensuing search would be suppressed. *See, e.g., United States v. Valdez*, 302 F.3d 320 (5th Cir. 2002). However, in *Hudson v. Michigan*, 547 U.S. 586 (2006), the U.S. Supreme Court reversed this long-standing application of the exclusionary rule by holding that the exclusionary rule was not an appropriate remedy for knock-and-announce violations. The Court's rationale in *Hudson* is discussed in the following Discussion Point.

DISCUSSION POINT

Are "Knock-and-Announce" Violations Sufficiently Attenuated to Avoid Application of the Exclusionary Rule?

Police officers entered a home with a warrant authorizing a search for drugs and guns. They discovered both items of contraband. Even though the police announced their presence and authority prior to entering the home, they failed to wait a reasonable time before "breaking" into the home and thereby violated the knock-and-announce rule of the Fourth Amendment.

The U.S. Supreme Court determined that even though the rule had been violated, the contraband should not be excluded.

In his opinion for the Court's majority, Justice Scalia attacked the use of the exclusionary rule for knock-and-announce violations by arguing that insufficient causation exists between an illegal, no-knock entry and subsequently discovered evidence. The required causal link is absent, according to Scalia, because "whether that preliminary misstep [of violating the knock-and-announce rule] had occurred *or not,* the police would have executed the warrant they had obtained and would have discovered the [the evidence] inside the house." 547 U.S. at 592.

In addition, Scalia identified a different reason why the causal connection in *Hudson* was too

weakened or attenuated: The interests protected by applying the knock-and-announce rule—preventing harm to police and others while protecting property from unnecessary damage and occupants from unnecessary privacy intrusions—would not be served by excluding the evidence of the guns and drugs found in this case pursuant to the warrant.

Finally, Scalia argued that the social costs associated with applying the exclusionary rule to knock-and-announce violations outweigh any benefits the rule may have in this context. For example, Scalia mentioned that criminals will go free and needless litigation will occur as a result of applying the exclusionary rule. Any deterrence benefits gained by applying the rule would be minimal because officers do not have any significant incentive not to knock-and-announce.

Continued on next page

- Do you agree with Justice Scalia's principal arguments for not applying the exclusionary rule to the knock-and-announce violations ("attenuation" of causal connection argument and costs-exceed-benefits argument)? Why or why not?
- In light of the holding in *Hudson v. Michigan*, if you were a police officer, would you bother

complying with the knock-and-announce rule? Explain your reasoning.
- If you were a police chief and an officer in your department routinely violated the knock-and-announce requirement while executing search warrants, would you discipline that officer? If so, why? And how would you discipline to the officer? If not, explain why not.

Since *Hudson* was decided, its logic has been squarely applied by lower courts to both generalized (i.e., common law) and statutory knock-and-announce violations. *See United States v. Bruno*, 487 F.3d 304 (5th Cir. 2007); *United States v. Southerland*, 466 F.3d 1083 (D.C. Cir. 2006), *cert. denied*, 549 U.S. 1241 (2007). And *Hudson* has also been extended to the execution of arrest warrants. *United States v. Pelletier*, 469 F.3d 194 (1st Cir. 2006). So what, then, is the status of the knock-and-announce rule?

The Supreme Court's decision in *Hudson* did not abandon the knock-and-announce rule in its entirety. Rather, it changed the remedy for a knock-and-announce violation from the application of the exclusionary rule to a civil enforcement mechanism. Thus, police may be held civilly liable for damages for violating the knock-and-announce. However, given issues of proof, litigation costs, and a variety of defenses to civil rights actions, some commentators, like Supreme Court Justice Breyer, view the decision in *Hudson* as having destroyed "much of the practical value of the Constitution's knock-and-announce protection." *Hudson*, 547 U.S. at 605 (Breyer, J., dissenting).

Even if that is the case, compliance with the knock-and-announce requirement is simple and effortless. Recall that one of the main reasons for the knock-and-announce rule is to prevent violence to the police or other persons on the premises. A failure to knock and announce is likely to lead to the unnecessary destruction of property and increased violence stemming from the surprise and fright of an unexpected entry. Thus, unless circumstances give police reasonable suspicion that knocking and announcing would put them in more danger than they would face by announcing their presence and purpose, it is in law enforcement officers' own best interest to comply with the knock-and-announce rule both for their own safety and to avoid the possibility of civil liability. Law enforcement officers also should keep abreast of case law developments in their own jurisdictions because any state is free to disregard *Hudson* and apply the exclusionary rule to knock-and-announce violations on state constitutional law grounds as Alaska has done. *Berumen v. State*, 182 P.3d 635 (Alaska App. 2008).

Other Notice Requirements

Unless one of the special exceptions discussed below applies, law enforcement generally must provide notice to the owner or occupant that they have executed a search warrant.

Notice When Premises Are Searched Without Owner or Occupant Present

The Federal Rules of Criminal Procedure Rule 41(f) provides:

> The officer executing the warrant must give a copy of the warrant and a receipt for the property taken to the person from whom, or from whose premises, the property was taken or leave a copy of the warrant and receipt at the place where the officer took the property.

The mandate of this rule is that people are entitled to have notice that their premises have been searched and, if items were seized during a search, that those items have been taken. This is not a problem when the person whose premises have been searched was present during the execution of a search warrant, even if authorities did not knock and announce their presence and purpose. But if a search warrant is executed when premises are unoccupied, Rule 41 requires that timely notice be given to the lawful occupant of the searched property not only that a search warrant was executed but also what was taken. It should be noted, however, that states differ on their approaches to warrant notice. Several states have much more strict notice requirements than those imposed under Rule 41(f). For example, North Carolina law states:

> Before undertaking any search or seizure pursuant to the warrant, the officer must read the warrant and give a copy of the warrant application and affidavit to the person to be searched, or the person in apparent control of the premises or vehicle to be searched. If no one in apparent and responsible control is occupying the premises or vehicle, the officer must leave a copy of the warrant affixed to the premises or vehicle. N.C. Gen. Stat. § 15A-252.

Other states have similar laws. But federal law and the laws of many states have created a major exception to the usual notice requirements: covert entry warrants.

Covert Entry Under Sneak-and-Peek Warrants In some circumstances, law enforcement officers may need to execute a search warrant in complete secrecy. Complete secrecy means that officers enter the target premises when the occupants are absent, conduct the search, and leave without seizing anything and leaving no indication that a search has been conducted. Complete secrecy may be necessary if (1) officers need to determine whether certain evidence is on the target premises and (2) officers reasonably believe that suspects would disrupt the investigation by destroying evidence, threatening or killing witnesses, or fleeing if they knew that a search had occurred.

A covert entry warrant, also known as a sneak-and-peek warrant, is a search warrant that specifically authorizes officers to enter unoccupied premises, search for specified evidence, and then leave—without seizing the evidence they find and without leaving a trace that an entry has been made. In conducting such a search, officers usually photograph or videotape the evidence or otherwise document exactly what they saw and its exact location.

The U.S. Supreme Court upheld a covert entry to place wiretapping equipment in a suspect's home in *Dalia v. United States*, 441 U.S. 238 (1979). Relying on *Dalia*, cases examining sneak-and-peek warrants upheld the covert entry, but they ruled nonetheless that searches conducted pursuant to these warrants were invalid if they did not subsequently provide the notice that the version of Rule 41 required at the time since such notice requirement enables the person whose property was to be searched to assert their Fourth Amendment rights, such as pointing out errors, irregularities, and limitations in the warrant. *E.g., United States v. Villegas*, 899 F.2d 1324, 1336-67 (2d Cir. 1990). Few courts, however, applied the exclusionary rule to violations of the notice requirements unless the defendant could show how he or she was prejudiced by the delay. Their reasoning was basically that notice is a requirement of Rule 41, not of the Fourth Amendment itself. *E.g., United States v. Simons*, 206 F.3d 392, 403 (4th Cir. 2000).

The USA PATRIOT Act, first enacted less than two months after the terrorist attacks of September 11, 2001, statutorily authorizes covert entry warrants. Subsequent amendments to the law required two forms of notice. First, the owner or occupant of property must be notified of a covert entry search within thirty days of its execution, unless the particular facts of a case justify a longer period of delay. Second, judges must report to Congress each time such a warrant is applied for and the results of the application.

PATRIOT Act Sneak-and-Steal Warrants Prior to the adoption of the USA PATRIOT Act, if law enforcement officers discovered contraband or other evidence of criminal activity during a surreptitious search, they were supposed to go back to court and seek a regular search warrant that specifically detailed the items to be seized. But the USA PATRIOT Act specifically authorized the seizure of items discovered during the execution of a covert entry warrant if there is a "reasonable necessity for the seizure." The practice has come to be known as a sneak-and-steal search. As of the time of this writing, no court has explicitly ruled on the constitutionality of these searches. However, at least one court has recognized that Section 213 of the USA PATRIOT Act specifically authorized these new types of searches and that this statutory provision trumps the notice requirements of Rule 41 of the Federal Rules of Criminal Procedure. *See ACLU v. U.S. Dep't of Justice*, 265 F. Supp. 2d 20, 24 (D.C. Cir. 2003). The court, however, commented in a footnote that although a sneak-and-steal warrant must specifically authorize the seizure of evidence on the basis of "reasonable necessity," there is some doubt as to whether such a warrant would comply with the requirements of due process. 265 F. Supp. 2d at 24 n.5. Only time will tell whether such warrants will remain a part of the U.S. criminal procedure process.

Search and Seizure of Third Parties and Their Property

When a search warrant is issued for the search of a named person or a named person and premises, officers executing the warrant clearly may simultaneously detain and search the person named. May officers detain and search a person on the premises who is not named in the warrant? What rules apply?

Searches of Third Parties During Warrant Executions The general rule is that a search warrant for premises gives a law enforcement officer no authority to search a person not named in the warrant who merely happens to be on the premises. In *Ybarra v. Illinois*, 444 U.S. 85 (1979), police had a warrant to search a bar and a bartender who worked there. The defendant in the case was a patron in the bar who was not named in the warrant. The U.S. Supreme Court held that a search of the defendant was illegal because the police did not have probable cause particularized with respect to the defendant:

> [A] person's mere propinquity to others independently suspected of criminal activity does not, without more, give rise to probable cause to search that person. . . . Where the standard is probable cause, a search or seizure of a person must be supported by probable cause particularized with respect to that person. This requirement cannot be undercut or avoided by simply pointing to the fact that coincidentally there exists probable cause to search or seize another or to search the premises where the person may happen to be. 444 U.S. at 91.

The Court said that a warrant to search a place cannot normally be construed to authorize a search of each person in that place. Therefore, if an officer wishes to search a place and also specific persons expected to be at that place, then the officer should obtain a search warrant to search the place and each specific person. To obtain such a warrant, the officer must establish in the affidavit probable cause to search the place and each specific individual.

Detentions and Pat-Downs of Third Parties During Warrant Executions A search warrant may authorize detention of persons present on premises to be searched in certain circumstances, however. *Michigan v. Summers*, 452 U.S. 692 (1981), held that officers executing a valid search warrant for contraband may detain the occupants of the premises while the search is being conducted. The Court said that "[i]f the evidence that a citizen's residence is harboring contraband is sufficient to persuade a judicial officer that an invasion of the citizen's privacy is justified, it is constitutionally reasonable to require that citizen to remain while officers of the law execute a valid warrant to search his home." 452 U.S. at 704–05. In explaining the justification for the detention, the Court emphasized the limited additional intrusion represented by the detention once a search of the home had been authorized by a warrant:

> In assessing the justification for the detention of an occupant of premises being searched for contraband pursuant to a valid warrant, both the law enforcement interest and the nature of the "articulable facts" supporting the detention are relevant. Most obvious is the legitimate law enforcement interest in preventing flight in the event that incriminating evidence is found. Less obvious, but sometimes of greater importance, is the interest in minimizing the risk of harm to the officers. Although no special danger to the police is suggested by the evidence in this record, the execution of a warrant to search for narcotics is the kind of transaction that may give rise to sudden violence or frantic efforts to conceal or destroy evidence. The risk of harm to both the police and the occupants is minimized if the officers routinely exercise unquestioned command of the situation. . . . Finally, the orderly completion of the search may be facilitated if the occupants of the premises are present. Their self-interest may induce them to open locked doors or locked containers to avoid the use of force that is not only damaging to property but may also delay the completion of the task at hand. 452 U.S. at 702–03.

Courts have interpreted *Summers* as holding that "police have limited authority to detain the occupant of a house without probable cause while the premises are searched, when the detention is neither prolonged nor unduly intrusive, and when police are executing a validly executed search warrant for contraband." *Heitschmidt v. City of Houston*, 161 F.3d 834, 838 (5th Cir. 1998); *Leveto v. Lapina*, 258 F.3d 156, 170 n.6 (3d Cir. 2001). Thus, in *Heitschmidt*, the court ruled that the defendant had been illegally detained in light of *Summers* because he was handcuffed on the street, pushed into the trunk of a car, and then detained for more than four hours without a bathroom break. Moreover, the search warrant in that case was targeted at finding evidence that the defendant's roommate was running a prostitution ring, not any type of contraband.

In *Williams v. Kaufman County*, 352 F.3d 994 (5th Cir. 2003), a group of people filed a civil suit under Section 1983 for various civil rights deprivations that occurred during the execution of a search warrant at a nightclub connected to a crack cocaine distribution ring. During the three-hour search, approximately one hundred people were detained. During that time, the occupants of the club were strip-searched and some were handcuffed. Even though the warrant authorized a search for contraband, the court still held that the search was unreasonable. First and foremost, the strip searches were invalid because the police had no reasonable, articulable suspicion that any one of the club's patrons, other than the few people specifically named in the warrant, would be carrying contraband. But the issue of the strip searches aside, the court still held the mass detention of club patrons unreasonable in light of the length of the detention and because the club "was a public establishment and not a private residence"; therefore, the detainees "had no reason to remain at the club during the search." 352 F.3d at 1010.

In contrast to the detentions and searches at issue in *Heitschmidt* and *Williams*, officers are permitted to conduct a limited pat-down search or frisk for weapons of any person at the search scene whom the officer reasonably suspects is armed and dangerous. The officer must be able to justify the frisk with specific facts and circumstances to support the belief that a particular person is armed and dangerous; a mere suspicion or hunch or an unsupported assertion of "officer safety" does not justify a protective frisk. (See Chapters 7 and 8 for details on conducting frisks.)

Of course, if an officer at a search scene obtains information constituting probable cause to make a felony arrest, or if a crime is being committed in the officer's presence, then the officer may arrest the offender and search him or her incident to the arrest. (See Chapter 6 for details on searches incident to arrest.)

Searches and Seizures of Third Parties' Property During Warrant Execution Similar rules apply to the search and seizure of the property of third persons on the premises described in a warrant. For purposes of this discussion, a third person is a person who is not the target of the warrant and is not a resident of the target premises. Courts are split on which of two tests to apply to such searches and seizures.

The Actual or Constructive Knowledge Test Under this approach, when a law enforcement officer executing a search warrant knows or reasonably should know that personal property located within the described premises belongs to a third person, the officer may not search or seize the property under authority of the warrant. However, when officers have no reason to believe that property belongs to a third person, they may search or seize the property. *E.g.*, *Waters v. State*, 924 P.2d 437, 439 (Alaska App. 1996). A comparison of the following two cases nicely illustrates the difference.

In *State v. Lambert*, 710 P.2d 693 (Kan. 1985), a police officer executing a warrant for an apartment and its male occupant discovered three women in the kitchen of the apartment. The officers searched a purse lying on the kitchen table and found drugs. The court invalidated the search, finding that the officer had no reason to believe that the purse either belonged to the occupant of the premises or was part of the premises described in the search warrant. In contrast, *Carman v. State*, 602 P.2d 1255 (Alaska 1979), upheld the search of a purse because the court found that the police neither knew nor did they have any objective reason to know whether the purse belonged to a permanent resident of the apartment or a visitor.

The Physical Possession Test "Under the 'physical possession' test, officers executing a warrant may search all items that could contain articles identified in the warrant except those that are in the actual physical possession of a person not subject to the warrant." *State v. Reid*, 77 P.3d 1134, 1140 (Or. App. 2003). This test allows police to search any container that could conceal an item listed in the warrant "unless the container is being worn by, or is in the actual possession of, a person not named in the warrant." *State v. Leiper*, 761 A.2d 458, 461 (N.H. 2000). In *Leiper*, police executed a search warrant in an apartment looking for "marijuana and/or hallucinogenic mushrooms" during a time when they knew that the apartment's tenant would be hosting a party. The defendant was one of approximately a dozen people at the party when the police arrived. He was seated on the couch and his knapsack was "near him on the couch." When he was removed from the premises during the search "because he was acting in a disruptive manner," the police searched his knapsack and found hallucinogenic mushrooms in it. 761 A.2d at 460. Because the knapsack was on the premises being searched, could contain the items named in the warrant, and was not in the defendant's physical possession at the time it was searched, the court upheld the search of the knapsack and the seizure of the contraband found in it.

The Automobile Exception As the material in Chapter 11 makes clear, given the inherently movable nature of motor vehicles, neither the constructive knowledge test nor the physical possession test provides a workable framework for searching vehicles and their contents. In *Wyoming v. Houghton*, 526 U.S. 295 (1999), a highway patrol officer stopped a car for speeding and driving with a faulty break light. In addition to the male driver, his girlfriend and other female passenger were both in the front seat. The officer noticed a hypodermic syringe in the driver's shirt pocket, which the driver admitted possessing for the purpose of taking drugs. Because of this admission, the officer then searched the car for contraband. The officer removed a purse located on the back seat. Houghton, one of the female passengers in the car, admitted it was hers. When the officer searched the purse, he found a syringe containing methamphetamine. Houghton admitted the syringe was hers after the officer saw needle-track marks on the Houghton's arms. Houghton challenged the legality of the search on the basis that the officer knew or should have known that the purse did not belong to the male driver, but to one of the female passengers for whom no probable cause existed based on the driver's possession of a syringe and his corresponding admission of drug use. In upholding the search and the admissibility of the evidence found in the purse, the Court reasoned that the officer had probable cause to believe there were illegal drugs in the car.

> If probable cause justifies the search of a lawfully-stopped vehicle, it justifies the search of *every part of the vehicle and its contents* that may conceal the object of the search. . . . The critical element in a reasonable search is not that the owner of the property is suspected of crime, but that there is reasonable cause to believe that the specific things to be searched for and seized are located on the property to which entry is sought. 526 U.S. at 301–02 (italics in original).

Thus, police officers with probable cause to search a car may inspect passengers' belongings found in the car that are capable of concealing the object of the search.

Scope of the Search

The scope of law enforcement activities during the execution of the warrant must be strictly limited to achieving the objectives that are set forth with particularity in the warrant. If officers exceed the scope of the authorized invasion under the terms of the warrant, then the exclusionary rule may render the evidence seized inadmissible. *E.g., United States v. Fuccillo*, 808 F.2d 173, 177–78 (1st Cir. 1987).

The Physical Boundaries to Be Searched A search may not extend beyond the items or premises particularly identified in the warrant. For example, in *State v. Matsunaga*, 920 P.2d 376 (Haw. Ct. App. 1996), *cert. denied*, 922 P.2d 973 (Haw. 1996), a search warrant authorized police to search the office of a particular business located in an office building. When the police extended their search of the building to an office of an adjacent business, the court held that they had exceeded the scope of the warrant even though the other office was in the same building. The same rule holds true for smaller places to be searched. *People v. McPhee*, 628 N.E.2d 523 (Ill. App. 1993), for instance, invalidated the search of a residence where a Federal Express parcel had been delivered because the warrant only authorized the search of the parcel itself, not the home to which it was being delivered.

Expansive Scope of Searches of Specific Premises *United States v. Ross*, 456 U.S. 798, 820–21 (1982), stated the general rule: "A lawful search of fixed premises generally extends to the entire area in which the object of the search may be found and is not limited by the possibility that separate acts of entry or opening may be required to complete the search." The Court provided examples of the application of the rule:

KEY POINTS

LO4
- Before law enforcement officers may lawfully force their way into a dwelling to execute a search warrant, they must knock on the door, announce their authority and purpose, demand admittance, and have their demand for admittance either be refused or go unacknowledged for a reasonable period of time, usually at least twenty to thirty seconds. To justify an exception to this requirement, officers must either have a previously authorized no-knock warrant or have a reasonable suspicion that knocking and announcing, under the particular circumstances, would be dangerous or futile or that it would inhibit the investigation of the crime by risking the destruction of evidence or the escape of a suspect.

- Unless specifically authorized to do otherwise by a valid covert entry warrant, officers executing a search warrant must give a copy of the warrant and a receipt for the property taken to the person from whom, or from whose premises, the property was taken or leave a copy of the warrant and receipt at the place where the officer took the property.

[A]warrant that authorizes an officer to search a home for illegal weapons also provides authority to open closets, chests, drawers, and containers in which the weapon might be found. A warrant to open a footlocker to search for marijuana would also authorize the opening of packages found inside. A warrant to search a vehicle would support a search of every part of the vehicle that might contain the object of the search. When a legitimate search is under way, and when its purpose and its limits have been precisely defined, nice distinctions between closets, drawers, and containers, in the case of a home, or between glove compartments, upholstered seats, trunks and wrapped packages, in the case of a vehicle, must give way to the interest in the prompt and efficient completion of the task at hand. 456 U.S. at 821–22.

Curtilage and Areas "Appurtenant" to Specified Premises A search warrant authorizing the search of particularly described premises justifies a search not only of the described premises but also of the areas within the *curtilage* of the premises. Curtilage was defined by the U.S. Supreme Court in *Oliver v. United States*, 466 U.S. 170, 180 (1984), as the "land immediately surrounding and associated with the home" in which the owner or resident has taken steps to protect from observation by people passing by, such as a screened-in porch, a gated courtyard, or fenced-in backyard. (For more details on curtilage, see Chapter 12.)

A search warrant authorizing the search of particularly described premises also justifies a search of all things appurtenant—incident to, belonging to, or going with—the principal property, such as buildings on the land (e.g., sheds) and other things attached to or annexed to the land. For example, a detached garage, even if not named in a warrant, can be searched as an appurtenant building to a house. *See United States v. Bonner*, 808 F.2d 864 (1st Cir. 1986). *United States v. Ferreras*, 192 F.3d 5, 10 (1st Cir. 1999), upheld the search of an attic that was not named in a search warrant as being appurtenant to a second-floor apartment that has exclusive access to the attic.

The rule on the searchability of appurtenant areas extends to structures that are not single-family dwellings. For example, in *United States v. Principe*, 499 F.2d 1135 (1st Cir. 1974), a search of a cabinet in a hallway several feet away from the apartment described in the search warrant was justified when the owner testified that the cabinet "went with the apartment." The same result occurred in *State v. Llamas-Villa*, 836 P.2d 239 (Wash. App. 1992), with regard to a padlocked locker located in a storage room next to defendant's apartment.

Of course, officers executing a search warrant may look only where the items described in the warrant might be concealed. Thus, searches of an appurtenant area that could not contain specific items to be seized would not be authorized under this doctrine.

Motor Vehicles on Property A warrant generally authorizes the search of all items on the premises in which the objects of a search might be found, including motor vehicles. *United States v. Ross*, 456 U.S. 798, 820–21 (1982) ("the scope of a warrant authorizing the search of a particularly described residence includes any automobiles, owned or controlled by the owner of such residence, which are located within the curtilage of the premises at the time the warrant is executed"). *Commonwealth v. McCarthy*,

---

KEY POINTS

- A covert entry, or sneak-and-peek warrant, may authorize a search without contemporaneous notice of the search upon a showing of reasonable cause to believe that providing immediate notification of the execution of the warrant may endanger the life or physical safety of an individual, prompt flight from prosecution, destruction or tampering with evidence, intimidation of potential witness, or otherwise seriously jeopardize an investigation or unduly delay a trial. If such a covert entry warrant is issued, notice must be given to the person whose premises were searched within a reasonable period not to exceed thirty days after the date of the execution of the warrant unless the facts of the case justify a longer period of delay.

- A search warrant for premises gives a law enforcement officer no authority to search a person not named in the warrant who merely happens to be on the premises. Officers are permitted, however, to conduct a limited pat-down for weapons of any person at the search scene who the officer reasonably suspects is armed and dangerous.

- Police have limited authority to detain the occupants of premises being searched without probable cause so long as the detention is neither prolonged nor unduly intrusive and when police are executing a validly executed search warrant for contraband.

705 N.E.2d 1110 (Mass. 1999). *State v. Brown*, 820 P.2d 878 (1991), *rev. denied*, 830 P.2d 596 (1992), upheld a search of the defendant's trailer even though it was not located within the legal boundary of the street address specified in the warrant. The court reasoned:

> Although the trailer was not within the property line . . . , it was located only 40 to 50 feet from the residence at the address and reasonably appeared associated with the premises and is specifically and accurately described in the warrant. No fence or other obvious demarcation separated the two properties, and the officers executing the warrant had no reason to believe that the trailer was not within the boundary specified in the warrant. The warrant authorized the invasion of defendant's privacy and, [therefore,] his protected property interest in the trailer. Under the circumstances, we hold that the legal boundary or property line did not circumscribe the officers' authority under the warrant to search the trailer. The search of the trailer was within the . . . Oregon Constitution or the Fourth Amendment. 820 P.2d at 883.

If, however, a motor vehicle is not on the property or seemingly within its reasonable curtilage, then most courts hold that a warrant to search the premises will not justify a search of such a vehicle unless the vehicle was specifically named in the warrant. Thus, for example, a car not named in the warrant, and which was parked in the street along the curb, could not be lawfully searched pursuant to a warrant to search premises. *See, e.g., Henderson v. State*, 685 So. 2d 970, 971 (Fla. App. 1996).

Neighboring or Adjacent Property Searches of areas neighboring or adjacent to the particularly described premises are usually not allowed. *E.g., United States v. Schroeder*, 129 F.3d 439 (8th Cir. 1997). If neighboring or adjacent areas are only nominally separate, however, and are actually used as a single living or commercial area, courts may allow the search of the entire area despite a limited warrant description. *United States v. Elliott*, 893 F.2d 220 (9th Cir. 1990), held that the search of a storeroom behind an apartment did not exceed the scope of the warrant authorizing the search of the apartment. The storeroom was accessible through a hole cut in the wall of the suspect's bathroom and was covered by a burlap bag. The court found that the unconventional means of access did not sever the room from the rest of the apartment.

Common Areas on Shared Property As the court noted in *United States v. King*, 227 F.3d 732 (6th Cir. 2000), courts appear to draw a "distinction between a dwelling occupied by a limited number of tenants, such as a small two-family house, and a large multi-unit apartment building for purposes of [the] Fourth Amendment." Courts usually hold that searches of common areas in the latter type of property do not give rise to Fourth Amendment concerns because people do not have a reasonable expectation of privacy in foyers, garages, backyards, lounges, and other common areas of large multiunit apartment buildings. *E.g., United States v. McGrane*, 746 F.2d 632 (8th Cir. 1984).

In contrast, courts are divided as to whether occupants of smaller, shared dwellings have a reasonable expectation of privacy in the common areas. In *United States v. McGrane*, the Eighth Circuit held that tenants of a two-story building that contained four apartment units (two on each floor) and a basement did not enjoy a reasonable expectation of privacy in the basement area. Fifteen years after *McGrane*, the Eighth Circuit extended its holding when it ruled that a defendant did not have a reasonable expectation of privacy in a hallway closet that was located in the common area of a duplex. *United States v. McCaster*, 193 F.3d 930, 933 (8th Cir. 1999). The court reasoned that the defendant had not taken any steps to evidence any subjective expectation of privacy in the contents of the closet since the landlord and two other tenants had access to the closet.

Other courts disagree with the Eighth Circuit's approach and hold that the residents of smaller shared dwellings, like duplexes, have a reasonable expectation of privacy in the common areas of those buildings. *United States v. Fluker*, 543 F.2d 709 (9th Cir. 1976), ruled that a corridor separating the door of the defendant's apartment from the outer doorway of the apartment building was protected by the Fourth Amendment. Critical to the court's ruling was the fact that there were only two other tenants in the building and no one else could enter that hallway. The same conclusion was reached with regard to a backyard shared by the tenants of a four-unit apartment building in *Fixel v. Wainwright*, 492 F.2d 480 (5th Cir. 1974) and a common hallway shared by only two apartment units in *People v. Killebrew*, 256 N.W.2d 581 (1977).

More recently, some courts have recognized a legitimate expectation of privacy in the common basement shared by the dwellers of a two-family home. *See Connecticut v. Reddick*, 541 A.2d 1209 (Conn. 1988). In *United States v. King*, 227 F.3d 732, 753 (6th Cir. 2000), the warrant authorized the search of "the premises, curtilage, containers, and persons therein" at a location described as "1437 East 116th Street, Cleveland, Cuyahoga County, Ohio, and being more fully described as the downstairs unit in a two-family, two and one half story, white wood-sided dwelling with green trim." 227 F.3d at 737. Because this warrant only authorized the unit on the first floor of the duplex, the court ruled that police had exceeded the scope of a search warrant when they searched the basement and seized evidence in it.

Inaccurate Descriptions of Property An inaccurate description of premises to be searched may cause officers to exceed the scope of a warrant, especially with respect to multiple-occupancy dwellings. In *Maryland v. Garrison*, 480 U.S. 79 (1987), officers obtained and executed a warrant to search the person of Lawrence McWebb and "the premises known as 2036 Park Avenue third floor apartment." The officers reasonably believed, on the basis of the information available, that only one apartment was located on the third floor. In fact, the third floor was divided into two apartments, one occupied by McWebb and one by the defendant. Before the officers discovered that they were in the wrong person's apartment, they had discovered contraband that led to the defendant's conviction.

The Court held that the officers had made a reasonable effort to ascertain and identify the place intended to be searched and that their failure to realize the overbreadth of the warrant was objectively understandable and reasonable. Nevertheless, the Court said:

> If the officers had known, or should have known, that the third floor contained two apartments before they entered the living quarters on the third floor, and thus had been aware of the error in the warrant, they would have been obligated to limit their search to McWebb's apartment. Moreover . . . they were required to discontinue the search of respondent's apartment as soon as they discovered that there were two separate units on the third floor and therefore were put on notice of the risk that they might be in a unit erroneously included within the terms of the warrant. 480 U.S. at 86–87.

Therefore, although some latitude is allowed for honest mistakes in executing search warrants, officers may not rely blindly on the descriptions in a warrant but must make a reasonable effort to determine that the place they are searching is the place intended to be searched. *See also United States v. Lora-Solano*, 330 F.3d 1288, 1294–95 (10th Cir. 2003) (evidence admissible even though a warrant misstated the address by a single digit because officers did not deliberately misstate the address, and a controlled delivery to the proper premises had been precisely described in the warrant).

Seizure of Unauthorized Items In *Coolidge v. New Hampshire*, 403 U.S. 443, 465 (1971), the Court said that "[a]n example of the applicability of the 'plain view' doctrine is the situation in which the police have a warrant to search a given area for specific objects, and in the course of the search come across some other article of incriminating character." In *Cady v. Dombrowski*, 413 U.S. 433 (1973), police investigating a possible homicide were told by the defendant that he believed there was a body lying near his brother's farm. The police found the body and the defendant's car at the farm. Police observed through the car window a pillowcase, a backseat, and a briefcase covered with blood. They then obtained a warrant to search the car for those items. While executing the warrant, they discovered in "plain view" a blood-covered sock and floor mat, which they seized. The defendant claimed that the sock and the floor mat taken from his car were seized illegally because they were not specifically listed in the warrant. The Court held that the seizure of the items was constitutional. The warrant was validly issued, and the car was the item designated to be searched; therefore, the police were authorized to search the car. Although the sock and floor mat were not listed in the warrant, the officers discovered these items in plain view in the car while executing the warrant and therefore could constitutionally seize them without a warrant. Decisions of many courts since the *Dombrowski* decision have established the rule that a law enforcement officer lawfully executing a valid search warrant may seize items of evidence not particularly described in the warrant that are found at the searched premises if the seizure satisfies all the requirements of the plain view doctrine. (See Chapter 10 for a complete discussion of the plain view doctrine.)

If, however, the plain view doctrine does not apply, unless one of the other warrant exceptions discussed in Part III of this text applies such as open fields (see Chapter 12) or some exigent circumstance justifies the warrantless seizure of an item that is beyond the scope authorized for seizure in the warrant, then items beyond the scope of a search may not be seized. Rather, police must apply for a separate warrant that authorizes the seizure of the suspect material. *E.g., United States v. Robinson*, 275 F.3d 371, 382 (4th Cir. 2001) (holding seized evidence admissible because officers suspended search and obtained second warrant before seizing items not described with particularity within the original warrant). If officers fail to do so, then the items seized that were not authorized for seizure by the warrant will be inadmissible in court. Moreover, if officers act in flagrant disregard of the terms of a search warrant and treat a search as a general one, they risk the suppression of all evidence seized during the search—even the evidence that would have otherwise been lawfully seizable under the warrant. Which of these outcomes will occur depends not only on the degree of impropriety of the officer's conduct but also on the law of the governing jurisdiction.

The Total Suppression Approach for Any Flagrant Disregard Some courts hold that when "law enforcement officers grossly exceed the scope of a search warrant in seizing property, the particularity requirement is undermined and a valid warrant is transformed into a general warrant thereby requiring suppression of all evidence seized under that warrant." *United States v. Medlin*, 842 F.2d 1194, 1199 (10th Cir. 1988). *Medlin* involved a search warrant that had authorized the entry into the defendant's home to search for and seize firearms illegally possessed by the defendant. While the search was being conducted, a deputy sheriff searched the premise for stolen property that he believed may have been on the defendant's property based on a tip he had received from an informant. The deputy seized more than 660 items. The court ruled that the deputy sheriff's actions transformed the search from one that was particularized and authorized by the warrant into an unconstitutional "general search." The Tenth Circuit reaffirmed this approach more recently in *United States v. Foster*, 100 F.3d 846 (10th Cir. 1996), and several other circuits have also adopted the flagrant disregard approach. *See United States v. Shi Yan Liu*,

239 F.3d 138 (2d Cir. 2000); *United States v. Squillacote*, 221 F.3d 542 (4th Cir. 2000), *cert. denied*, 532 U.S. 971 (2001); *United States v. Rettig*, 589 F.2d 418 (9th Cir. 1978).

The Partial Suppression Approach Not all jurisdictions follow the "flagrant disregard" approach of suppressing all evidence seized during an overbroad search. Some jurisdictions exclude from evidence only those items that the warrant did not authorize and were not otherwise seizable under the plain view doctrine (see Chapter 10) while admitting all items for which there was probable cause to support their seizure under the particular terms of the warrant. *E.g., United States v. Photogrammetric Data Services, Inc.*, 259 F.3d 229 (4th Cir. 2001), *cert. denied*, 535 U.S. 926 (2002); *Klingenstein v. State*, 624 A.2d 532 (Md. 1993); *State v. Johnson*, 605 So.2d 545 (Fla. App. 1992). And although the U.S. Supreme Court has not ruled squarely on the issue, its language in *Waller v. Georgia*, 467 U.S. 39, 43–44, n. 3 (1984), strongly suggests that the Court would reject the "flagrant disregard/total suppression" approach.

> Petitioners' second Fourth Amendment challenge is that police so "flagrant[ly] disregard[ed]" the scope of the warrants in conducting the seizures at issue here that they turned the warrants into impermissible general warrants. Petitioners rely on lower court cases . . . for the proposition that in such circumstances the entire fruits of the search, and not just those items as to which there was no probable cause to support seizure, must be suppressed. Petitioners do not assert that the officers exceeded the scope of the warrant in the places searched. Rather, they say only that the police unlawfully seized and took away items unconnected to the prosecution. The Georgia Supreme Court found that all items that were unlawfully seized were suppressed. In these circumstances, there is certainly no requirement that lawfully seized evidence be suppressed as well.

Use of Force Officers executing a search warrant may use reasonable force in conducting the search. An otherwise reasonable search may be invalidated if excessive force is used.

Use of Force to Search Property A search warrant gives officers authority to break into a house or other objects of the search and to damage property if reasonably necessary to properly execute the warrant. *United States v. Becker*, 929 F.2d 442 (9th Cir. 1991), held that the jackhammering of a concrete slab to execute a search warrant for drugs was reasonable, based on an examination of all the facts and circumstances: (1) officers had found evidence of the manufacture of methamphetamine in the shop next to the slab, (2) the concrete slab had been poured within the preceding forty-five days, and (3) the shop appeared to have been recently and hastily repainted and repaired. In *United States v. Ross*, 456 U.S. 798, 823 (1982), involving a search of a vehicle for contraband, the Court said:

> An individual undoubtedly has a significant interest that the upholstery of his automobile will not be ripped or a hidden compartment within it opened. These interests must yield to the authority of a search, however.

KEY POINTS

L02

■ A search warrant authorizing the search of particularly described premises justifies a search of the described land, all of the buildings on the land, and other things attached or annexed to the land.

■ A warrant authorizing a search for a particular object allows a search of the entire area in which the object may be found and allows the opening of closets, chests, drawers, and containers in which the object might be found.

■ A law enforcement officer lawfully executing a valid search warrant may seize items not particularly described in the warrant that are found at the searched premises if the seizure satisfies all the requirements of the plain view doctrine (see Chapter 11) or some other valid exception for

Continued on next page

KEY POINTS

warrantless seizures (see Part III). If the plain view doctrine does not apply, then items beyond the scope of what a warrant authorized to be seized may not be taken. Rather, police must apply for a separate warrant that authorizes the seizure of the suspect material. A violation of this rule may result in the suppression of evidence.

■ Officers executing a search warrant may use reasonable force in conducting the search. An otherwise reasonable search may be invalidated if excessive force is used.

LO7 ■ Once the items specified in a warrant have been found during a search and seized, the legal justification for law enforcement officers' intrusion onto premises comes to an end. They must therefore leave the premises in a timely manner. However, before departing, unless a sneak-and-peak or sneak-and-steal warrant provides otherwise, searching officers must inventory all the property seized and leave a copy of the warrant and inventory with the occupants or on the premises if no occupant is present.

■ After leaving the searched premises (regardless of whether the warrant is a traditional search warrant or one of the covert entry–type warrants), officers must return the warrant itself, together with a copy of the inventory, to the judicial officer designated in the warrant.

Nevertheless, officers must exercise great care to avoid unnecessary damage to premises or objects. They must conduct a search in a manner designed to do the least damage possible while still making a thorough examination of the premises. They should carefully replace objects that were necessarily moved or rearranged during the search. Generally, "[i]n executing a search warrant, to the extent possible, due respect should be given to the property of the occupants of the premises searched." *State v. Sierra*, 338 So.2d 609, 616 (La. 1976). Finally, common decency and fair play mandate that officers executing a search warrant avoid any unnecessary injury to the feelings of persons present at the premises searched.

Use of Force to Search People The U.S. Constitution places substantive limits on how far a search of a person can go before the search becomes "unreasonable" for Fourth Amendment purposes or violates due process under the Fifth or Fourteenth Amendments. Some searches and seizures on a person are clearly permissible in light of their minimal invasiveness so long as they are supported by probable cause, such as

■ seizing a hair sample by plucking it, *In re Will County Grand Jury*, 604 N.E.2d 929, 936 (Ill. 1992);

■ swabbing someone's mouth for a DNA sample, *Rise v. Oregon*, 59 F.3d 1556 (9th Cir. 1995); and

■ scraping under someone's fingernail for biological evidence, *Cupp v. Murphy*, 412 U.S. 291 (1973).

The permissibility of other searches and seizures that are more invasive of the human body depend largely on the context. See "Intrusive Searches Within the Body" in Chapter 7 for details about the constitutional issues surrounding drawing blood from a suspect, pumping a suspect's stomach, and other invasive procedures.

After a Search Warrant Is Executed

Once the items specified in a warrant have been found during a search and seized, the legal justification for law enforcement officers' intrusion onto premises comes to an end. They must therefore leave the premises in a timely manner. *E.g., Taylor v. State*, 7 P.3d 15 (Wyo. 2000); *United States v. Menon*, 24 F.3d 550 (3d Cir. 1994). However, before departing, Federal Rule of Criminal Procedure 41 and its state-law counterparts say that proper execution of a search warrant entails several duties after the actual search is completed. Unless a sneak-and-peak or sneak-and-steal warrant provides otherwise, searching officers must inventory all the property seized and leave a copy of the warrant and inventory with the occupants or on the premises if no occupant is present.

After leaving the searched premises—regardless of whether the warrant is a traditional search warrant or one of the covert entry–type warrants—the warrant itself, together with a copy of the inventory, must be returned to the judicial officer designated in the warrant. A typical form for the return and inventory (which is usually on the back of the search warrant) appears in Figure 4.2b (on page 133).

Courts generally hold that these postsearch duties are ministerial acts. Thus, failure to perform them will not result in the suppression of evidence via the exclusionary rule unless the defendant demonstrates legal prejudice or shows that the failure was intentional or in bad faith. *United States v. Simons*, 206 F.3d 392 (4th Cir. 2000).

DISCUSSION POINT

What About Excessive Force When Executing a Warrant?
Turner v. Fallen, 1993 WL 15647 (N.D. Ill. 1993).

The court explained the facts of the case as follows:

The present action arises out of the police officers' execution of a search warrant in Ms. Turner's establishment, a consignment clothing store known as Dynasty II located at 5222-24 West North Avenue in Chicago, Illinois. A search warrant set forth the following articles to be seized:

three pairs of silk pants "Index" brand, two silk jackets "Index" brand, two silk shirts "Index" brand, one beige jacket "Index" brand, and one double breasted jacket "Index" brand. The warrant states that the above listed items to be seized constitute evidence of the offense of possession of stolen property and that there is probable cause to believe that these items are located upon the person and premises of Dynasty II. Ms. Turner alleges that the actions of the police officers, in executing this search warrant of her consignment shop, were unreasonable. She claims that the officers were not searching for drugs, which could be concealed in crevices and small places. Despite this fact, Ms. Turner alleges that the police officers took the following unreasonable actions in executing their search for the clothing items identified in the warrant: broke the front door, broke several ceiling tiles, broke open the cash register without asking for the key despite the key's ready availability, broke open the file cabinet, and smashed the glass display cases.

Ms. Turner further alleges that the police officers confiscated a number of items, totally unrelated to the search warrant, including the following: all licenses from the consignment shop and the hair salon; approximately 300 skirts, blouses, dresses, slacks, and other clothing items; all business records and consignment receipts for clothing, which were in a six-drawer file cabinet; dress racks; checks payable to Ms. Turner; diamond earrings; several hundred dollars of U.S. currency; and numerous other clothing items. Allegedly, Ms. Turner's establishments were emptied in truckloads despite the police officers' having no evidence that this merchandise was stolen. Ms. Turner claims that the actions of the police officers put her out of business.

Ms. Turner's complaint also states that she had another establishment, the Dynasty II Hair Salon, located next door to the Dynasty II consignment shop. She alleges that, despite the fact that the hair salon did not sell clothes and, thus, had nothing to do with the search warrant, the police officers searched throughout the hair salon, committing damage, disrupting business, and harassing salon customers.

In reviewing and upholding Ms. Turner's complaint for damages, the court wrote:

In the present case, the damage alleged by Ms. Turner surpasses the mere breaking down of her shop's door. Rather, Ms. Turner alleges specific facts to support her claim that the police officers' search was unreasonable. For example, she alleges that the police officers intentionally smashed the glass display cases in her shop in order to confiscate certain items found within the cases. Yet, the officers did not first notify her of their need to enter the cases, nor did they try to find another way into the display cases that could have avoided the unnecessary property damage. Likewise, Ms. Turner alleges that the police officers broke her cash register and file cabinet, when they could have avoided this property damage merely by asking her to unlock these items. As such, Ms. Turner alleges that the police officers destroyed and damaged property not reasonably necessary to effectively execute their search warrant. 1993 WL 15647 at *1–*4.

- Do you think excessive force was used during the execution of the search warrant? Explain your answer.

- What do you make of the seizure of the items not named in the warrant? Do you think these seizures violate the Fourth Amendment? Why or why not?

SUMMARY

The general rule is that all searches and seizures conducted without a warrant are unreasonable and violate the Fourth Amendment to the U.S. Constitution. Although there are many well-defined exceptions to this rule, searches made under the authority of a warrant not only are greatly preferred by the courts but also give law enforcement officers greater protection from liability.

A search warrant is a written order issued by a proper neutral judicial officer commanding a law enforcement officer to search for certain personal property and bring it before the judicial authority named in the warrant. An officer may obtain a search warrant by submitting a written application in the form of a sworn affidavit to a magistrate. The affidavit must state underlying facts and circumstances supporting probable cause to believe that particularly described items are located in a particularly described place or on a particularly described person. A search warrant may authorize seizure only of items connected with criminal activity, such as contraband, fruits, and instrumentalities of crime; illegally possessed items; and evidence of crime.

A magistrate who finds probable cause to search issues a search warrant directing an officer or class of officers to execute the warrant. Officers must conduct the search within a reasonable time after the warrant's issuance and within any time period specified by law or court rule. Before entering premises by force to execute the warrant, officers must knock and announce their authority and purpose and be refused admittance after waiting about thirty seconds unless the officer reasonably suspects that this notice will result in the loss or destruction of evidence, the escape of a suspect, or danger to an officer or others. Persons on the premises may not be searched unless the search warrant authorizes the search of a particular person. Property of persons who are not the target of the warrant and not residents of the target premises may not be seized. If officers are executing a warrant to search for contraband, then persons on the premises may be detained during the course of the search. Any person on the premises whom officers reasonably believe to be armed and dangerous may be frisked for weapons.

A search under authority of a search warrant may extend to the entire premises described in the warrant but only to those parts of the premises where the items to be seized might be concealed. The search must be conducted in a manner to avoid unnecessary damage to the premises or objects. Items not named in the warrant may be seized if all elements of the plain view doctrine are satisfied. After the search is completed, the officer must leave at the searched premises a copy of the warrant and an inventory of and receipt for property taken. The officer must return the warrant, along with a written inventory of property seized, to the judicial officer designated in the warrant.

KEY TERMS

affiant 130
affidavit 130
anticipatory search warrants 145
appurtenant 165
covert entry warrant 160
curtilage 165
Franks hearing 147

general warrant 127
knock and announce 155
magistrate 129
no-knock warrant 158
particularity 139
probable cause 128
redaction (severability) 149

search 128
search warrant 129
seizure 128
sneak-and-peak warrant 160
sneak-and-steal search 160
staleness 136
triggering condition 146

REVIEW AND DISCUSSION QUESTIONS

1. Why is time a more important factor in determining probable cause to search than it is in determining probable cause to arrest?

2. Formulate a set of circumstances in which there is probable cause to search but not probable cause to arrest; in which there is probable cause to arrest but not probable cause to search; in which there is probable cause both to arrest and to search.

3. Name three kinds of property that are unlikely to remain in a particular place for longer than a week. Name three kinds of property that are likely to remain in a particular place for longer than a week.

4. Why should law enforcement officers executing a search warrant refrain from asking the person against whom the search is directed to assist them in any way?

5. Assume that you are a law enforcement officer attempting to obtain a search warrant for urban premises, rural premises, a multiple-unit dwelling, and a motor vehicle. Describe, as you would in the affidavit, one of each of these places that is familiar to you. (For example, describe for purposes of a search warrant application a friend's farm in the country.)

6. Law enforcement officers have a search warrant to search a house for heroin and to search the person of the house owners' eighteen-year-old daughter. When the officers arrive at the house to execute the warrant, the following persons are present:
   a. the owners;
   b. their eighteen-year-old daughter;
   c. their fifteen-year-old son, who appears extremely nervous;
   d. the daughter's boyfriend, whom the officers recognize as a local gang member who is known to carry a knife; and
   e. an unidentified elderly couple.

   To what extent may the officers search or detain each person present?

7. A law enforcement officer has a search warrant to search the defendant's house for cameras stolen from a particular department store. May the officer
   a. look in desk drawers?
   b. search the defendant's body?
   c. seize a brown paper bag containing a white powder resembling heroin that is found in a desk drawer?
   d. search the defendant's garage?
   e. look in the defendant's wife's jewelry box?
   f. break open a locked wall safe?
   g. seize a portable radio found on a table with a tag from the department store attached to it?

8. Is each of the following descriptions in a search warrant of items to be seized sufficiently particular?
   a. A .38-caliber, blue steel, wood-gripped revolver of unknown make. *See United States v. Wolfenbarger*, 696 F.2d 750 (10th Cir. 1982).
   b. Videotape and equipment used in a copyright infringement. *See United States v. Smith*, 686 F.2d 234 (5th Cir. 1982).
   c. All doctor's files concerning an accident patient. *See United States v. Hershenow*, 680 F.2d 847 (1st Cir. 1982).
   d. Plaques, mirrors, and other items. *See United States v. Apker*, 705 F.2d 293 (8th Cir. 1983).
   e. Items related to the smuggling, packing, distribution, and use of controlled substances. *See United States v. Ladd*, 704 F.2d 134 (4th Cir. 1983).
   f. Business papers that are evidence and instrumentalities of a violation of a general tax fraud statute. *See United States v. Cardwell*, 680 F.2d 75 (9th Cir. 1982).

9. Does a warrant to search a house authorize a search of a tent set up on the premises near the house? Does a warrant authorizing the seizure of stolen computers authorize the seizure of nonstolen computers commingled with them? Is the seizure of an entire book of accounts permissible when only two or three pages of the book are relevant to the specifications of the search warrant?

5

Searches for Electronically Stored Information and Electronic Surveillance

Technology has significantly altered the ways in which we communicate and store information. Like traditional searches for physical evidence, searches of electronically stored information (ESI) are governed by the Fourth Amendment. Thus, ESI searches normally require a duly authorized warrant supported by probable cause. However, as this chapter should make clear, some courts have imposed additional requirements on both the application for and execution of search warrants for ESI. It is, therefore, essential that law enforcement officers stay abreast of both new technologies and the evolving law governing the search and seizure of data.

In addition to ESI searches, law enforcement personnel often need to use technology to monitor telephone conversations on both landlines and cell phones, e-mail communications, pager and text messages, and Internet-based communications. Such electronic surveillance is especially important for fighting terrorism and organized crime. Although the law lags behind technological advances, a series of judicially created and statutory rules governing high-tech searches and surveillance have slowly emerged in an attempt to balance privacy concerns against the needs of law enforcement and public safety in the Information Age.

Searches of Electronically Stored Information

ESI is "information created, manipulated, communicated, stored, and best utilized in digital form, requiring the use of computer hardware and software" (Withers 2006: 173). Computer files and programs are the most obvious sources of ESI, but ESI can also be found on servers (including those in "the cloud"), tablets, thumb/jump drives, CDs and DVDs, floppy disks, memory cards and sticks, tape media, external hard drives, cell phones, and other electronic devices with data storage capacity such as digital cameras, iPods, e-mail servers, voicemail systems, fax machines, copy machines, and even cars. These devices contain ESI in a variety of forms, ranging from images and text files to databases and video files. Conducting searches of ESI in this wide variety of formats increasingly requires the skills of computer forensic experts.

As with searches for physical evidence, most searches for ESI require a search warrant, the basic requirements of which are explained in Chapter 4. But searches of ESI generally occur in a two-phase process.

1. Law enforcement officers need to enter the place(s) housing the devices on which data are stored. They then search the premises and seize the devices on which data may be stored.

2. These devices are subsequently examined by forensic computer specialists for data described in a warrant.

Federal Rule of Criminal Procedure 41(e) requires that a search warrant be executed to accomplish the first phase—the physical search of premises and seizure of data storage devices (or just data, if practicable)—within ten to fourteen days. The rule specifically provides that the second phase—the off-site analyses of the information—may be conducted later. Many magistrates specify the time-frame in which this latter step is to be completed in the warrants they issue (say 60, 90, or 120 days), although Rule 41 does not require them to do so, largely because it is often unpredictable how long it will take for a complete computer forensic analysis to occur.

Computer Forensics and Anti-forensics

Computer forensics concerns "[t]he use of scientifically derived and proven methods toward the preservation, collection, validation, identification, analysis, interpretation, documentation and presentation of digital evidence derived from digital sources for the purpose of facilitating or furthering the reconstruction of events found to be criminal" (Carroll, Brannon, & Song 2008: 1).

Forensic examination of digitally stored information is an exacting process. For example, even starting a computer by pressing the power button and allowing the normal boot process to load the operating system can taint a forensic examination (Mohay et al. 2003). Thus, computers need to be started in a specially controlled manner and write-protected (to preserve the contents of both system files and data files on the hard drive), and then the hard drive needs to be imaged. *Imaging* "duplicates every bit and byte on the target drive including all files, the slack space, Master File Table, and metadata in exactly the order they appear on the original." (U.S. Department of Justice 2009: 86; see also Mohay et al. 2003). After imagining is complete, an examiner then analyzes the copy, leaving the original intact. Such analyses typically involve the use of specialized computer forensic software that has been developed to assist investigators in conducting searches of ESI in a manner that comports with the scope of a warrant.

Most computer forensic software programs organize the data on an imaged hard drive into a format that allows the examiner to

- perform searches for names, e-mail addresses, keywords, phrases, or particular file types (regardless of named extensions);
- sort by file size;
- search by dates of creation, modification, or last access;
- identify altered files;
- recover deleted material by reassembling files and file fragments; and
- analyze files using sophisticated mathematical algorithms—a process known as *hashing*.

177

CHAPTER 5
SEARCHES FOR
ELECTRONICALLY STORED
INFORMATION AND
ELECTRONIC SURVEILLANCE

Hashing creates a numerical value that can serve as type of unique identifier for files. Using file signature recognition software, the hash values of files on a particular digital storage medium (like a hard drive) can be compared to the hash values of known contraband files, allowing for rapid identification of pirated music, videos, or child pornography images (Nelson, Phillips, & Steuart 2010).

It should be noted, however, that there is a growing industry in antiforensics—tools for "hiding, destroying, or counterfeiting the information on which digital forensics experts rely and by extension, undermining the evidentiary reliability of that information" (Behr 2008: 10). This, in turn, may lead to forensic computing evidence being declared inadmissible when offered by *either* the prosecution or defense. Alternatively,

[c]omputer anti-forensics gives non-expert computer users the ability (1) to eliminate or obfuscate computer-generated evidence or (2) to make the process of investigating a computer crime so complex, time-consuming and expensive that the inquiry may not proceed. It essentially automates the process of obstructing justice by destroying, altering hiding and/or creating evidence. (Brenner 2011: 94–95)

Plain View and ESI Searches

As explained more fully in Chapter 10, the *plain view doctrine* allows law enforcement officers to seize an object in "plain view" without first obtaining a warrant if two criteria are met. First, the officer cannot "violate the Fourth Amendment in arriving at the place from which the object could be plainly viewed." *Horton v. California*, 496 U.S. 128, 136 (1990). In other words, police must have a prior valid justification for intrusion into a zone of privacy. Second, there must be probable cause to believe that the observed object in plain view is incriminating in nature; put differently, "the object's incriminating character must . . . be 'immediately apparent.'" 496 U.S. at 136. For instance, if officers entered a residence to execute a valid search warrant to locate evidence of a homicide (such as bloody clothes and the murder weapon), but saw marijuana plants in plain view when they searched the house, the plants would be admissible in prosecution for a drug offense.

The plain view doctrine was developed within the context of searches for physical evidence. But the volume and nature of information that is stored electronically makes the application of the plain view doctrine controversial in the context of ESI searches since many of the tools computer forensics employ have the potential to reveal far more information than is relevant to the object of the search, effectively transforming ESI searches into the very type of general search against which the Fourth Amendment was designed to protect (see Chapter 3). To date, courts have generally taken one of three approaches to the applicability of the plain view doctrine in the context of ESI searches.

The Undifferentiated Approach In *United States v. Williams*, 592 F.3d 511 (4th Cir. 2010), a church had been receiving harassing e-mail messages. The FBI agents obtained a warrant to search the sender's computers and digital storage media for evidence of the crime of harassment by computer. During the search, agents found child pornography. The court refused to apply the exclusionary rule and suppress the images because they were in "plain view" during the search. In other words, the plain view doctrine rendered irrelevant the fact that the evidence of child pornography possession was beyond the scope of the evidence for which the warrant authorized agents to search.

At least two other federal circuit courts are in accord with the holding in *Williams* that the plain view doctrine applies the same way in ESI searches as it does in physical searches. *See United States v. Farlow*, 681 F.3d 15 (1st Cir. 2012); *United States v. Stabile*, 633 F.3d 219, 240–41 (3d Cir. 2011).

The Middle-Ground Approach In an attempt to limit the sweeping scope of the plain view doctrine in ESI searches, at least two federal circuit courts have added an inadvertence requirement to the requirements of the plain view doctrine outlined earlier from *Horton v. California*. Specifically, the investigator must have inadvertently discovered any evidence in plain view that falls outside the scope of the search warrant.

United States v. Carey, 172 F.3d 1268, 1270 (10th Cir. 1999), concerned a warrant authorizing a search of files on computers "for names, telephone numbers, ledger receipts, addresses, and other documentary evidence pertaining to the sale and distribution of controlled substances." When no evidence was found by searching the computers' hard drives using certain keywords such as "money, accounts, [and] people," the investigating officer began looking through the file directories on the computer when he came across image files in .jpg format with sexually suggestive names, some of which, once opened, contained child pornography. The officer then searched more than two hundred additional images for evidence of child pornography before returning to his initial task of searching for evidence of involvement in the illicit drug business. The defendant's motion to suppress the images was granted because the search went beyond the scope of what the search warrant had authorized. Moreover, the court rejected the application of the plain view doctrine to the search to all but the very first picture that was inadvertently opened by the investigating officer because each time the officer opened a .jpg file after the first one, he expected to find child pornography and not material related to drugs. See the Discussion Point on the inadvertence requirement for information on the other case adopting this approach, *United States v. Mann*, 592 F.3d 779 (7th Cir. 2010).

The Inapplicability Approach A controversial 2009 case reasoned that digital evidence was so different from physical evidence that the plain view doctrine should not apply to ESI searches. Hence, the court mandated that all U.S. magistrate judges in the Ninth Circuit require the government to waive reliance on the plain view doctrine in digital evidence cases as a precondition to issuing a search warrant, thereby providing the government with no incentive to conduct data searches in a broad manner. *United States v. Comprehensive Drug Testing, Inc.*, 579 F.3d 989 (9th Cir. 2009). A year later, the Ninth Circuit, sitting *en banc*, issued a revised opinion in the *Comprehensive Drug Testing* case in which it abandoned this mandate but still endorsed it as a guideline. *United States v. Comprehensive Drug Testing, Inc.*, 621 F.3d 1162 (9th Cir. 2010).

DISCUSSION POINT

How Practical Is the Inadvertence Approach to the Plain View Doctrine as Applied to ESI Searches?

In *United States v. Mann*, 592 F.3d 779 (7th Cir. 2010), the defendant worked as a lifeguard as a pool. After a camera was discovered and traced to the defendant, police obtained a warrant to search his home for "video tapes, CDs or other digital media, computers, and the contents of said computers, tapes, or other electronic media, to search for images of women in locker rooms or

other private areas." 592 F.3d 780–781. The detective conducting the search of his computer hard drive used computer forensic software that indexed all image, video, and document files on the computer. But using hashing technology, the software the investigator used also flagged several files as containing child pornography after comparing their contents against a known database of offending files. The investigator then opened the files to confirm their contents, searched another computer on which he found more child pornography, and, two months later, searched an external hard drive belonging to the defendant that the same computer forensic software identified as containing approximately 680 flagged files.

The defendant moved to suppress all of the digital evidence, arguing that the search of his digital media exceeded the scope of the warrant's authorization. The trial court denied his motion, reasoning that "'with limited exceptions' the search was within the scope of the warrant, and that any images uncovered outside the scope of the warrant were discovered in plain view." 592 F.3d at 782. On appeal, however, the Seventh Circuit agreed with the defendant, reasoning that once the hashing software flagged files as containing child pornography, the detective "knew (or should have known) that files in a database of known child pornography images would be outside the scope of the warrant." 592 F.3d at 785. Thus, the proper course of action would have been to secure a second warrant to search for evidence of child pornography, using the hashing software's flagging of files as the basis for probable cause. Nonetheless, the appellate court upheld the defendant's conviction because some of the images that were within the scope of the warrant depicted underage girls. Thus, the Seventh Circuit merely severed the offending images from the case and found that even without those images, "the government still possessed ample evidence of child pornography to sustain both [the defendant's] conviction and sentence." 592 F.3d at 785.

The court concluded its opinion by saying, "[W]e simply counsel officers and others involved in searches of digital media to exercise caution to ensure that warrants describe with particularity the things to be seized and that searches are narrowly tailored to uncover only those things described." 592 F.3d at 786.

■ Do you think that the court's admonition to law enforcement officers is helpful? Does it provide them with adequate guidance regarding how to ensure that they comply with the "inadvertence" prong of the plain view doctrine in jurisdictions adopting this approach to ESI searches? Explain your reasoning.

■ The defendant in *Mann* unsuccessfully asserted that the investigator should not have used hashing software with a filter for tagging images of child pornography since the warrant in the case did not authorize a search for such materials. What do you think of this argument? If the search had occurred within the Ninth Circuit, might this argument have been successful in light of the decision in the *Comprehensive Drug Testing case?*

■ One critic of the "inadvertence" approach argued that it really only applies

in the rare situations in which (1) the investigator admits that he was deliberately searching for evidence of a crime not within the warrant, or (2) the circumstances of the search directly demonstrate that the investigator was no longer searching for evidence of the crime within the warrant. Although one can envision cases in which either of these scenarios might unfold, the cases in which the inadvertence requirement will make a difference in nullifying the plain view doctrine are likely to be rare. (Yeager 2013: 710)

Do you agree? Why or why not?

■ Which approach to the plain view doctrine in ESI searches do you think is the best? Why?

Limitations on Searches for ESI

Courts vary in the degree of specificity required in applications for warrants to conduct searches for ESI with respect to how both phases of the search will be conducted.

In 2002, the federal government commenced an investigation into the Bay Area Lab Cooperative (Balco), which it suspected of providing steroids to professional baseball players. That year, Major League Baseball (MLB) began suspicionless drug testing of all players. The players were assured that the results would remain anonymous and confidential. During the Balco investigation, federal authorities learned of ten players who had tested positive in the program. The government obtained a search warrant authorizing computer forensic specialists, rather federal agents, to search the office of the drug testing company for the results of ten specific players for whom the government had probable cause. When the warrant was executed, however, the government seized and reviewed the drug testing records for hundreds of baseball players. MLB then filed civil actions forcing the government to return all of the information outside the scope of the warrant and preventing the government from using any of the information discovered with regard to any player other than the ten named in the warrant. The Ninth Circuit sided with the baseball players and barred the government from using any evidence found in violation of the search protocols. Notably, the court then encouraged magistrates to limit warrants for ESI in several distinct ways. In addition to requiring the government to waive reliance upon the plain view doctrine in digital evidence cases as previously discussed, the court stated magistrates should also

1. craft search protocols which forbid the use of computer forensic tools that would discover evidence of crimes outside the scope of the warrant;

2. mandate that only governmental computer specialists who are not investigators in the case or nongovernment third parties hired to conduct digital forensic analyses, conduct the search and that they will not disclose to the case investigators any information other than that which is the target of the warrant;

3. require that computers and related equipment be returned to their owners within a reasonable, specific time frame; and

4. order that all copies of data obtained during the digital forensic investigation be destroyed unless a judicial officer specifically authorizes the retention of such copies. *Comprehensive Drug Testing*, 579 F.3d 989 (9th Cir. 2009).

The U.S. government successfully petitioned the Ninth Circuit to reconsider its decision in the *Comprehensive Drug Testing* case by arguing that it was having a "calamitous effect" on computer searches within the region—and not just for issues concerning the plain view doctrine. The requirement of specifying search protocols was significantly interfering with investigators' abilities to adapt their computer forensics to changes in criminal methodologies—an argument with which other federal circuit courts subsequently agreed. *E.g., United States v. Burgess*, 576 F.3d 1078, 1093 (10th Cir. 2009) ("It is unrealistic to expect a warrant to prospectively restrict the scope of a search by directory, filename, or extension or to attempt to structure search methods—that process must remain dynamic"). A year later, the Ninth Circuit, sitting *en banc*, issued a revised opinion in the *Comprehensive Drug Testing* case in which it removed all of the factors listed earlier as binding, but endorsed them as

KEY POINTS

LO1 ■ A warrant to search for the devices on which ESI may be stored must be executed within the usual time frame for any search warrant. However, analyses of the data contained on any media or devices seized may occur later.

LO2 ■ Investigators specially trained in computer forensics must image and then analyze ESI, often using specialized software that indexes and organizes files, recovers deleted data, and compares files to databases of known contraband.

LO3 ■ To ensure compliance with the Fourth Amendment's particularity requirement, officers should specify the following in their applications for search warrants of ESI:

■ the crimes for which evidence is being sought,

■ the reasons why there is probable cause to believe the computer will contain such evidence,

Continued on next page

guidelines. 621 F.3d 1162 (9th Cir. 2010). It should be noted, however, that subsequent amendments to Federal Rule of Criminal Procedure Rule 41 conflict with the guideline that officers must return or destroy all copies of seized data. Rather, the rule permits the officer to retain a copy of the ESI that was seized or copied.

U.S. Department of Justice Recommendations for ESI Search Warrant Applications

In 2009, the U.S. Department of Justice (DOJ) updated its guidelines for ESI searches. Suggestions for investigators include the following highlights:

1. Both search warrant applications and the warrants themselves should differentiate whether hardware or merely information may be seized. This distinction depends, in part, on the crime being investigated. The entire computer is likely seizable when it contains contraband or when it was used as the instrumentality of crime, such as in hacking offenses. In contrast, hardware should not be seized if electronic storage media needs to be searched for evidence of a crime, such as when electronic business records are relevant to a white-collar crime prosecution. (DOJ 2009: 72). In the latter situation, the warrant should authorize law enforcement to image a hard drive and examine it later.

2. Warrant applications need to specify the types of data that are the objects of the authorized search by using limiting language that "identify records that relate to a particular crime and to include specific categories of the types of records likely to be found" (DOJ 2009: 73).

3. Agents should obtain multiple warrants if they have probable cause to believe that a network search will retrieve data stored in multiple locations (DOJ 2009: 84).

4. If the computer forensic search reveals evidence of a crime not identified in the warrant, then it is best to suspend the search and obtain a second warrant to search for evidence of the second crime. *See United States v. Walser*, 275 F.3d 981, 986–87 (10th Cir. 2001).

Notably, the Department of Justice cautions that "limitations on search methodologies have the potential to seriously impair the government's ability to uncover electronic evidence" (DOJ 2009: 79). Several courts agree that a "computer search may be as extensive as reasonably required to locate the items described in the warrant." *United States v. Grimmett*, 439 F.3d 1263, 1270 (10th Cir. 2006); *see also United States v. Long*, 425 F.3d 482 (7th Cir. 2005).

In summary, the Fourth Amendment is playing catch-up with ever-evolving technologies when it comes to searches of ESI. The law will likely remain in a state of flux until Congress acts to set clearer statutory privacy protections for searches of ESI, or until the U.S. Supreme Court resolves the inconsistent approaches taken by lower courts in this regard.

Electronic Surveillance

Electronic surveillance—searches conducted using wiretaps, bugs, or other devices to overhear conversations or obtain other kinds of information—poses unique challenges for balancing privacy interests against the need for effective law enforcement in the area of electronic surveillance. On the one hand, electronic listening, tracking, and recording devices provide a very powerful tool for law enforcement officials in investigating and prosecuting crime. On the other hand, the potential for the abuse of individual rights can be far greater with electronic surveillance than with any ordinary search or seizure. The task of resolving these competing interests has fallen on state legislatures, the U.S. Congress, and ultimately the courts.

Early Developments in Electronic Interceptions Law

Although wiretapping has been used as an information-gathering technique since the mid-1800s, the U.S. Supreme Court did not decide its first electronic eavesdropping case until 1928. In *Olmstead v. United States*, 277 U.S. 438 (1928), the Court held that wiretapping of telephone conversations was not covered by the Fourth Amendment for two reasons. First, because there had been no physical trespass into the defendant's premises, there was no search. Second, because the evidence had been obtained by hearing only, rather than the seizure of tangible items, the interception of a conversation could not qualify as a seizure. *Berger v. New York*, 388 U.S. 41 (1967), disposed of the second rationale of *Olmstead* by holding that conversations were protected by the Fourth Amendment and that the use of electronic devices to capture conversations was a seizure within the meaning of the Fourth Amendment. But *Olmstead*'s first prong concerning property rights retains some traction. For example, in *Goldstein v. United States*, 316 U.S. 114 (1942), the Court found no search or seizure under the Fourth Amendment when police placed a listening device against a wall in an office that adjoined the defendant's office, again relying on the lack of a physical intrusion. And, as discussed in Chapter 3, physical trespass to one's property interests remains one way of examining whether a search or seizure occurred for Fourth Amendment purposes. *See United States v. Jones*, 132 S. Ct. 945 (2012). But also recall from Chapter 3 that *Katz v. United States*, 389 U.S. 347 (1967), significantly broadened the focus of Fourth Amendment analysis beyond examination of property interests to include a "privacy" approach.

The U.S. Supreme Court first explicitly considered the constitutionality of electronic surveillance conducted under authority of a warrant in *Osborn v. United States*, 385 U.S. 323 (1966). In that case, federal law enforcement officials had information that an attorney was trying to bribe a prospective juror. The officials obtained a warrant authorizing an undercover agent with a concealed tape recorder to record a specific conversation with the attorney. The tape of the conversation was admitted at trial, and the attorney was convicted of attempting to bribe a juror. The Court upheld the conviction, emphasizing that "[t]he issue here is . . . the permissibility of using such a device under the most precise and discriminate circumstances." 385 U.S. at 329.

The Supreme Court's limited grant of constitutional permissibility for electronic surveillance was tested again the next year in *Berger v. New York*, 388 U.S. 41 (1967). In *Berger*, the issue was the constitutionality of a New York statute that authorized electronic surveillance pursuant to a judicial warrant. Ultimately, the Court invalidated the law because it failed to properly limit the nature, scope, or duration of the electronic surveillance.

Despite the U.S. Supreme Court's invalidation of the statute in *Berger*, the possibility that a properly circumscribed warrant procedure for electronic surveillance could be created was left open. This possibility was given further credence by *Katz v. United States*, 389 U.S. 347, 354 (1967), in which FBI agents attached an electronic listening device to a public telephone booth and recorded the defendant's calls. The Court held that the interception was unlawful because there was no warrant, but strongly indicated that a proper warrant could have been issued, paving the way for congressional action.

Omnibus Crime Control and Safe Streets Act of 1968

The year following the *Berger* and *Katz* opinions, Congress enacted the Omnibus Crime Control and Safe Streets Act of 1968. Title III of that act superseded earlier statutory prohibitions against intercepted communications and provided authorization for electronic surveillance pursuant to warrant.

Terminology Before discussing the details of applications for and judicial supervision of electronic surveillance, it is necessary to define some important terms, which appear in Table 5.1.

Title III Predicate Offenses Interception orders may only be issued for specified crimes, including

- espionage,
- treason,
- labor racketeering,
- murder,
- kidnapping,
- robbery,
- extortion,
- bribery of public officials,
- gambling,
- drug trafficking, and
- escape.

183

CHAPTER 5
SEARCHES FOR
ELECTRONICALLY STORED
INFORMATION AND
ELECTRONIC SURVEILLANCE

TABLE 5.1 | Electronic Surveillance Terminology

Aural transfer	"A transfer containing the human voice at any point between and including the point of origin and the point of reception." 18 U.S.C. § 2510(18).
Electronic communication	"[A]ny transfer of signs, signals, writing, images, sounds, data, or intelligence of any nature transmitted in whole or in part by a wire, radio, electromagnetic, photo-electronic or photo-optical system that affects interstate or foreign commerce but does not include (A) any wire or oral communication; (B) any communication made through a tone-only paging device; (C) any communication from a tracking device . . .; or (D) electronic funds transfer information stored by a financial institution in a communications system used for the electronic storage and transfer of funds." 18 U.S.C. § 2510(12).
Intercept	[T]he aural or other acquisition of the contents of any wire, electronic, or oral communication through the use of any electronic, mechanical, or other device." 18 U.S.C. § 2510(4).
Oral communication	"Any oral communication uttered by a person exhibiting an expectation that such communication is not subject to interception under circumstances justifying such expectation, but such term does not include any electronic communication." 18 U.S.C. § 2510(2).
Wire communication	"[A]ny aural transfer made in whole or in part through the use of facilities for the transmission of communications by the aid of wire, cable, or other like connection between the point of origin and the point of reception (including the use of such connection in a switching station) furnished or operated by any person engaged in providing or operating such facilities for the transmission of interstate or foreign communications or communications affecting interstate or foreign commerce and such term includes any electronic storage of such communication." 18 U.S.C. § 2510(1).

The USA PATRIOT Act added

- crimes "relating to terrorism,"

- crimes "relating to chemical weapons," and

- violations of 18 U.S.C. Section 1030 dealing with computer fraud and abuse. (Before the enactment of the USA PATRIOT Act, interception orders for wire communications in computer hacking investigations were not permitted.)

Application, Authorization, and Issuance of Interception Orders Only federal or state law enforcement officers or attorneys may apply for an interception order. Most courts include prison officials within the meaning of "law enforcement officers," although they are often exempted from Title III warrant application procedures under one of two theories:

1. So long as the monitoring of prisoners' phone calls occurs "in the ordinary course" of their duties, correctional official are statutorily exempt from needing a warrant under Section 2510(5)(a)(ii) of Title III. *E.g., United States v. Lewis*, 406 F.3d 11 (1st Cir. 2005).

2. A prison's recording of inmate's calls is not an "intercept" for Title III purposes because inmates implicitly consent to monitoring when they use a prison phone after receiving warnings that calls are subject to monitoring. *E.g., United States v. Verdin-Garcia*, 516 F.3d 884, 895 (10th Cir. 2008).

Before going to court for a warrant, law enforcement officials must first receive administrative authorization to apply for an interception order. Only the U.S. attorney general or a select group of his or her deputies in the U.S. Department of Justice may authorize an application for a wire or oral interception order. In contrast, any government lawyer authorized to prosecute Title III offenses may authorize an application for an electronic communication interception order. If administrative authorization is granted, the approved application must then be submitted to a court for judicial review.

For jurisdictional purposes, an interception involving a wiretap takes place at both the location of the tapped telephone and the original listening post. *United States v. Denman*, 100 F.3d 399 (5th Cir. 1996). Therefore, judges in either jurisdiction have authority under Title III to issue interception orders. Before issuing an interception order, the court must find the following:

1. Probable cause to believe that the person whose communication is to be intercepted is committing, has committed, or is about to commit one of the specified crimes. "The probable cause showing required . . . for electronic surveillance does not differ from that required by the Fourth Amendment for a search warrant." *United States v. Macklin*, 902 F.2d 1320, 1324 (8th Cir. 1990), *cert. denied*, 498 U.S. 1031 (1991).

2. Probable cause to believe that particular communications concerning that offense will be obtained through the interception

3. That normal investigative procedures have been tried and have failed, or reasonably appear to be unlikely to succeed if tried, or reasonably appear to be too dangerous. This condition—often referred to as the "necessity requirement"—is intended to ensure that electronic surveillance is not used unless normal investigative procedures are inadequate. For example, in *United States v. Wagner*, 989 F.2d 69 (2d Cir. 1993), the necessity for a wiretap was established because (a) the rural location of the house and the presence of dogs made surveillance difficult; (b) the confidential informant was unable to determine the source of supply and method of delivery of marijuana; and (c) the government did not think it could infiltrate the marijuana distribution network with undercover agents.

4. Probable cause to believe that the facilities from which, or the place where, the wire, oral, or electronic communications are to be intercepted are being used

(or are about to be used) in connection with the commission of the specified offense; or are leased to, listed in the name of, or commonly used by the suspect

In making these four findings, courts must consider all of the following factors:

■ The identity of the investigative or law enforcement officer making the application and the officer authorizing the application

■ A full and complete statement of the facts and circumstances relied upon by the applicant, to justify his belief that an order should be issued, including the details as to the particular predicate offense that has been, is being, or is about to be committed

■ A particular description of the nature and location of the facilities from which or the place where the communication is to be intercepted, unless a roving wiretap is sought, which allows for interception of a particular suspect's communications wherever they are made, thereby dispensing with the normal requirement that interceptions be limited to a fixed location. Roving taps on either landline or cellular phones do not violate the particularity requirement of the Fourth Amendment if the surveillance is limited to communications involving an identified speaker and relates to crimes in which the speaker is a suspected participant. *See United States v. Wilson*, 237 F.3d 827, 831 (7th Cir. 2001); *United States v. Petti*, 973 F.2d 1441 (9th Cir. 1991).

■ A particular description of the type of communications sought to be intercepted, including the identity of the person (if known) committing the offense and whose communications are to be intercepted

■ A full and complete statement as to whether or not other investigative procedures have been tried and failed or why they reasonably appear to be unlikely to succeed if tried or to be too dangerous

■ A statement of the period of time for which the interception is required to be maintained. If the nature of the investigation is such that the authorization for interception should not automatically terminate when the described type of communication has been first obtained, a particular description of facts establishing probable cause to believe that additional communications of the same type will occur thereafter.

■ A full and complete statement of the facts concerning all previous applications known to the individual authorizing and making the application, made to any judge for authorization to intercept, or for approval of interceptions of, wire, oral, or electronic communications involving any of the same persons, facilities, or places specified in the application, and the action taken by the judge on each such application

■ When the application is for the extension of an order, a statement setting forth the results thus far obtained from the interception, or a reasonable explanation of the failure to obtain such results

Other aspects of judicial supervision of electronic surveillance are the court's power to require, at any time, reports on the progress of the interception toward the achievement of authorized objectives; the requirement of court approval for any extension of the surveillance; and the requirement that the recordings of any communications be sealed under directions of the court immediately on the order's expiration.

As with any other type of search warrant, the contents of an application for an interception order and the affidavits in support thereof must be true. If the contents of these documents contain material falsehoods, material omissions, or were made with reckless disregard for the truth, the warrants may be challenged in a *Franks* hearing. See Chapter 4; *United States v. Shryock*, 342 F.3d 948 (9th Cir. 2003).

If, on the basis of the application, the judge makes the required findings, the judge may issue an interception order. Pursuant to 18 U.S.C. Section 2518(4), the order must specify

185

CHAPTER 5
SEARCHES FOR
ELECTRONICALLY STORED
INFORMATION AND
ELECTRONIC SURVEILLANCE

- the identity of the person, if known, whose communications are to be intercepted;

- the nature and location of the communications facilities as to which, or the place where, authority to intercept is granted;

- a particular description of the type of communication sought to be intercepted, and a statement of the particular offense to which it relates;

- the identity of the agency authorized to intercept the communications, and of the person authorizing the application; and

- the period of time during which such interception is authorized, including a statement as to whether or not the interception shall automatically terminate when the described communication has been first obtained.

Execution of Interception Orders

Orders Must Be Executed as Soon as Practicable Every intercept order must be executed "as soon as practicable." Delay in the execution of an interception order, however, does not require the suppression of evidence obtained if the delay was not willful and if the information on which probable cause was initially based had not become stale. *United States v. Martino*, 664 F.2d 860 (2d Cir. 1981). For example, suppression was not required after a five-month delay in installing the interception devices, when the government adequately explained that the installation was extremely difficult and the crime was one of continuing conduct, in which probable cause was "freshened" by visual surveillance. *United States v. Gallo*, 863 F.2d 185 (2d Cir. 1988).

Separate Order for Covert Entry Not Necessary Neither Title III nor the Fourth Amendment requires law enforcement officers to obtain judicial authorization to covertly enter premises to install a listening device after an inception order has been issued. In *Dalia v. United States*, 441 U.S. 238 (1979), a federal court authorized the interception of all oral communications concerning an interstate stolen-goods conspiracy at the defendant's office. Although the order did not explicitly authorize entry into the defendant's office, FBI agents secretly entered the office and installed a listening device in the ceiling. Six weeks later, after the surveillance had terminated, the agents reentered the office and removed the device. The defendant was convicted, partly on the basis of intercepted conversations. The Supreme Court considered the legislative history of Title III and concluded that Congress, "by authorizing electronic interception of oral communications in addition to wire communications, . . . necessarily authoriz[ed] surreptitious entries." 441 U.S. at 252. Moreover, with respect to the Fourth Amendment, the Court found that nothing in the language of that Amendment or the Court's decisions suggested that search warrants must include a specification of the precise manner in which those warrants must be executed. "[I]t is generally left to the discretion of the executing officers to determine the details of how best to proceed with the performance of a search authorized by warrant—subject of course to the general Fourth Amendment protection 'against unreasonable searches and seizures.'" 441 U.S. at 257.

Minimization Requirements Title III requires that authorized interceptions be conducted so as to minimize the interception of communications not subject to the interception order. This minimization effort must be objectively reasonable under the circumstances. *E.g.*, *United States v. McGuire*, 307 F.3d 1192 (9th Cir. 2002). *Scott v. United States*, 436 U.S. 128 (1978), held an interception reasonable although only 40 percent of the intercepted conversations related to crimes specified in the order, because the remaining conversations were ambiguous and brief. *United States v. Smith*, 909 F.2d 1164 (8th Cir. 1990), held that minimization efforts were reasonable despite failure to minimize interceptions of the defendant's sister's phone conversations with his ex-girlfriend, because the officers suspected the defendant's family of aiding in drug activities but did not know which family members were doing so.

Interceptions Beyond Scope of Order When law enforcement officers intercept communications that relate to offenses other than those specified in the interception order, the government may use the evidence of these other crimes only if another application is made to a court "as soon as practicable" for a determination that the interception complied with Title III requirements. *See United States v. Angiulo*, 847 F.2d 956 (1st Cir. 1988).

Termination upon Achieving Objective Authorized interceptions must terminate on attainment of the authorized objective or, in any event, in thirty days. *United States v. Carneiro*, 861 F.2d 1171 (9th Cir. 1988), held that suppression of communications intercepted after the discovery of a drug source was not required, because the objective of the wiretap was to investigate the entire drug operation, not merely to discover a drug source. Extensions of an interception order may be granted, but only on reapplication in accordance with the same procedures as for an original application.

Confidentiality Requirements Law enforcement officers who learn information by listening to intercepted communications have an obligation to keep the contents of what they hear confidential. They are only permitted to disclose the contents of what they learned from hearing an intercepted communication under limited circumstances:

- Information may be disclosed to another law enforcement officer "to the extent such disclosure is appropriate." 18 U.S.C. § 2517(1). For example, when state authorities, pursuant to a valid wiretap order, discovered evidence of illegal gambling in *United States v. Williams*, 124 F.3d 411 (3d Cir. 1997), the court upheld their disclosure of their lawfully obtained recordings to Criminal Investigation Division agents of the Internal Revenue Service for potential prosecution of tax-related charges stemming from the gambling operation.

- Information learned may be used by a law enforcement officer in the performance of his or her official duties. For example, a law enforcement officer may briefly quote or paraphrase an intercepted communication to establish probable cause for defendant's arrest. *United States v. VanMeter*, 278 F.3d 1156 (10th Cir. 2002). Such information may also be disclosed in state or federal court while giving testimony related to the intercepted communication.

- Information may be disclosed to any federal "law enforcement, intelligence, protective, immigration, national defense, or national security official" if it assists them with a matter of foreign intelligence or counterterrorism. 18 U.S.C. § 2517(6).

- Information may be disclosed to law enforcement in foreign countries if necessary to assist the foreign officer in the performance of his or her official duties. 18 U.S.C. § 2517(7).

- If the information learned concerns a threat of attack or other hostile act by terrorists or a foreign power, it may be disclosed to any appropriate governmental official of the United States or a foreign country in order to allow the government to prevent or help respond to such an attack. 18 U.S.C. § 2517(8).

187

CHAPTER 5
SEARCHES FOR
ELECTRONICALLY STORED
INFORMATION AND
ELECTRONIC SURVEILLANCE

Seal upon Expiration of Order Immediately upon the expiration of an interception order (meaning without unnecessary or unreasonable delay), both the interception order and all recordings made pursuant to it are required to be delivered to the judge who issued the order to be sealed under the judge's directions. Putting material under seal means it is not accessible to anyone without a special court order. The purposes of the sealing requirement are to prevent tampering, aid in establishing the chain of custody, protect confidentiality, and establish judicial control over the surveillance. A failure to comply with the sealing requirement renders intercepted communications inadmissible. *United States v. Ojeda Rios*, 495 U.S. 257 (1990). Before ordering such suppression, however, courts will examine "not only why a delay occurred, but also why it is excusable," 495 U.S. at 265, "the length of any delay before sealing, the care taken in handling the recordings, prejudice to the defendants, any tactical advantage accruing to the government, and whether deliberate or gross dereliction of duty or honest mistake caused the failure to file." *United States v. Suarez*, 906 F.2d 977, 982 (4th Cir. 1990).

Inventory and Notice Requirements Within a reasonable time, but not later than ninety days after the termination of the period of an order, an inventory must be served on the persons named in the order and on such other parties to intercepted communications as the judge determines in the interest of justice. An inventory must also be served after emergency interceptions are carried out. It must include a notice of the fact of the order, the date of approval of the application, the period of the authorized interception, and a statement of whether or not wire, oral, or electronic communications were intercepted during the period. Failure to serve the inventory is not grounds for suppression unless the failure causes actual, incurable prejudice. *United States v. Donovan*, 429 U.S. 413 (1977).

The USA PATRIOT Act amended 18 U.S.C. Section 3103a to permit law enforcement officers to delay notice of the execution of a search warrant or interception order in certain circumstances. Specifically, that section now permits delaying notice when "the court finds reasonable cause to believe that providing immediate notification of the execution of the warrant may have an adverse result," such as

- endangering the life or physical safety of an individual,
- flight from prosecution,
- destruction of or tampering with evidence,
- intimidation of potential witnesses, or
- otherwise seriously jeopardizing an investigation or unduly delaying a trial.

Exigent Circumstances Exception Title III provides authority for designated officials to intercept wire, oral, or electronic communications without a prior interception order if

- an emergency situation exists that involves immediate danger of death or serious physical injury to any person, conspiratorial activities threatening the national security interest, or conspiratorial activities characteristic of organized crime; and
- an interception order cannot be obtained in sufficient time.

The determination of emergency must be made by the U.S. attorney general or one of the other few governmental officials specified in Title III. The law enforcement officer carrying out the emergency surveillance must apply for an interception order under Section 2518 within forty-eight hours after the interception has occurred or begins to occur. If an order is not obtained, the interception must immediately terminate when the sought-after communication is obtained or when the application is denied, whichever is earlier.

Title III and Its Applicability to the States

189

CHAPTER 5
SEARCHES FOR
ELECTRONICALLY STORED
INFORMATION AND
ELECTRONIC SURVEILLANCE

Title III specifically authorizes state law enforcement officials to apply for, obtain, and execute interception orders using procedures similar to those governing federal officials. The primary difference is that the state procedure must be authorized by a separate state statute. If a state statute so authorizes, the principal prosecuting attorney of the state, or of a political subdivision of the state, may apply to a state court judge of competent jurisdiction for an interception order. In granting the order, the judge must comply with both the applicable state statute and Title III. The interception order may be granted only when the interception may provide or has provided

> evidence of the commission of the offense of murder, kidnapping, gambling, robbery, bribery, extortion, or dealing in narcotic drugs, marihuana or other dangerous drugs, or other crime dangerous to life, limb, or property, and punishable by imprisonment for more than one year, designated in any applicable State statute authorizing such interception, or any conspiracy to commit any of the foregoing offenses. 18 U.S.C. § 2516(2).

"Generally speaking, insofar as wiretapping is concerned, states are free to superimpose more rigorous requirements upon those mandated by the Congress . . . but not to water down federally devised safeguards." *United States v. Mora*, 821 F.2d 860, 863 n.3 (1st Cir. 1987). Federal courts are not obliged to adhere to more restrictive state laws, however, and generally admit evidence that violates such a law, as long as the evidence was not obtained in violation of Title III. *E.g.*, *United States v. Charles*, 213 F.3d 10 (1st Cir. 2000). For example, even if a consensual interception of a conversation without a search warrant violated state law, the evidence might still be admissible in federal court because Title III does not require a warrant when one of the parties to the intercepted conversation consents to the interception. *United States v. Goodapple*, 958 F.2d 1402 (7th Cir. 1992).

Standing to Challenge Title III Intercepts

Any "aggrieved person" may move to suppress the contents of or evidence derived from oral or wire intercepts that were obtained in violation of Title III in either a state or federal proceeding. An **aggrieved person** means "a person who was a party to any intercepted" wire or oral communication or "a person against whom the interception was directed." 18 U.S.C. § 2510(11). The Supreme Court held that the term aggrieved person should be construed in accordance with existing standing rules. Therefore:

> [A]ny petitioner would be entitled to the suppression of government evidence originating in electronic surveillance violative of his own Fourth Amendment right to be free of unreasonable searches and seizures. Such violation would occur if the United States unlawfully overheard conversations of a petitioner himself or conversations occurring on his premises, whether or not he was present or participated in those conversations. *Alderman v. United States*, 394 U.S. 165, 176 (1969).

Thus, to challenge the legality of an intercept, one must either have been

- a party to the illegally intercepted conversation (a reasonable expectation of privacy approach) or
- a person with a possessory interest in the premises where the illegal interception occurred, even if such person did not participate in any intercepted conversations (a property rights approach). *United States v. Gonzalez, Inc.*, 412 F.3d 1102 (9th Cir. 2005), *amended on denial of reh'g* 437 F.3d 854 (9th Cir. 2006).

Remedies for Title III Violations

Title III is broader in both scope and remedies than the Fourth Amendment. Notably, Title III applies to private searches and seizures of wire, oral, or electronic communications, not just those involving governmental actors. When its mandates are violated, Title III provides its own statutory remedies.

Civil and Criminal Penalties Title III provides for both criminal and civil penalties for violations of its commands aimed at protecting privacy. For example, *United States v. Councilman*, 418 F.3d 67 (1st Cir. 2005) upheld criminal charges against an Internet service provider for the illegal interception and copying of e-mail messages. Similarly, *DIRECTV, Inc. v. Rawlins*, 523 F.3d 318 (4th Cir. 2008), ordered damages for a satellite TV provider against a customer who used illegal devices to access programming beyond the terms of his subscription.

Statutory Exclusionary Rule Title III contains its own statutory exclusionary rule for intercepts that were illegally obtained by either government actors or private persons. The reach of this exclusionary rule is much broader under 18 U.S.C. Section 2515 than the judicially created exclusionary rule applicable to Fourth Amendment violations:

> [N]o part of the contents of such communication and no evidence derived therefrom may be received in evidence in any trial, hearing, or other proceeding in or before any court, grand jury, department, officer, agency, regulatory body, legislative committee, or other authority of the United States, a State, or a political subdivision thereof if the disclosure of that information would be in violation of this chapter. *See also Gelbard v. United States*, 408 U.S. 41 (1972).

It should be noted, however, that this statutory exclusionary rule only applies to wire or oral communications. It does not apply to illegally intercepted electronic communications, the remedies for which include only criminal penalties and civil suits, not suppression of evidence.

In spite of the broad language of the statutory exclusionary rule in Title III, suppression is seldom imposed for inadvertent, unavoidable, or unintentional violations. A violation of Title III does not require suppression of evidence if the provision violated is not central to the statute's underlying purpose of guarding against unwarranted use of wiretapping or electronic surveillance. *United States v. Chavez*, 416 U.S. 562 (1974). For example, *United States v. Callum*, 410 F.3d 571, 576 (9th Cir. 2005), held that a failure to properly meet identification requirements in Title III did not require suppression of an otherwise properly executed interception order since it otherwise complied with all statutory requirements. On the other hand, a major violation of Title III, such as failing to obtain proper authorization from the Attorney General's designee, warrants suppression. *United States v. Reyna*, 218 F.3d 1108 (9th Cir. 2000).

Title III Exemptions

Many types of interceptions of wire, oral, or electronic communications are either not covered by provisions of Title III or are specifically exempted from coverage. Some of the most important exemptions are discussed here.

Willful and Voluntary Disclosure A party to an oral communication who has no reasonable expectation of privacy with respect to the communication is not protected by either Title III or the Fourth Amendment. Other than certain privileged communications (e.g., between attorney and client, psychotherapist and patient, or clergy and penitent), people generally have no reasonable expectation of privacy that what they tell another person in conversation will not, in turn, be disclosed by the person to whom they were talking.

191

CHAPTER 5
SEARCHES FOR
ELECTRONICALLY STORED
INFORMATION AND
ELECTRONIC SURVEILLANCE

> In the course of conversing with others, persons assume certain risks that may bear on the viability of any Fourth Amendment rights they subsequently assert. Inescapably, one contemplating illegal activities must realize and risk that his companions may be reporting to the police. If he sufficiently doubts their trustworthiness, the association will very probably end or never materialize. But if he has no doubts, or allays them, or risks what doubt he has, the risk is his. *In re Askin*, 47 F.3d 100, 105 (4th Cir. 1995).

In other words, no matter how confidential one may think a discussion is, the person to whom one reveals information may elect not to keep such information confidential. If that person then voluntarily discloses information to others, including law enforcement or other governmental authorities, the Fourth Amendment will not serve as a basis to prevent such third-party disclosure. The same principle applies to Title III for electronic communications. Thus, one has no reasonable expectation of privacy that the recipient of an e-mail, instant or text message, or chat room communication will not voluntarily disclose its contents to authorities. *E.g.*, *United States v. Meek*, 366 F.3d 705 (9th Cir. 2004).

Eavesdropping If a conversation takes place in public where other parties can overhear the conversation, there is no reasonable expectation of privacy, because the participants exposed their conversation to the ears of others. Thus, any recording of such a conversation would not violate Title III. For example, in *Kee v. City of Rowlett*, 247 F.3d 206 (5th Cir. 2001), the court upheld the use of recordings of conversations and prayers made at a graveside burial service. The public nature of the outdoor conversations rendered them outside of the definition of an "oral communication" for Title III purposes because there was no reasonable expectation of privacy in such a setting.

Similarly, if a conversation takes place in an area where the participants ought not expect any privacy, such as in a correctional facility or in the back of a police car, then neither the Fourth Amendment nor Title III would serve to stop any recording of such a conversation from being used as evidence in court. *E.g.*, *United States v. Harrelson*, 754 F.2d 1153 (5th Cir. 1985); *United States v. McKinnon*, 985 F.2d 525 (11th Cir. 1993).

Under 18 U.S.C. Section 2510(5)(a), neither telephones nor extensions are considered intercepting devices when they are used in the ordinary course of business. *O'Sullivan v. NYNEX Corp.*, 687 N.E.2d 1241 (Mass. 1997). Thus, what an employer overhears while monitoring phone conversations over extensions for legitimate business reasons will not implicate Title III. Courts have extended this exception to cover what family members overhear while eavesdropping on the conversations of other family members using an extension telephone. *E.g.*, *Commonwealth v. Vieux*, 671 N.E.2d 989 (Mass. App. 1996), *cert. denied*, 520 U.S. 1245 (1997).

Consent Title III excludes **consent surveillance** from its regulatory scheme. Therefore, when one party to a communication consents to the interception of the communication, neither Title III nor the Fourth Amendment prevents the use of the communication in court against another party to the communication. Thus, a law enforcement officer or a private citizen who is a party to a communication may intercept the communication or permit a law enforcement official to intercept the communication without violating Title III or the Fourth Amendment. *United States v. Caceres*, 440 U.S. 741 (1979). This exception allows a law enforcement officer or agent, an informant, an accomplice or co-conspirator, or a victim to wear a body microphone; act as an undercover agent without being wired; or eavesdrop or record a telephone conversation with the permission of the person receiving the call even though the person making the call has no knowledge of this activity. A private citizen, however, may not intercept a communication "for the purpose of committing any criminal or tortious act in violation of the Constitution or laws of the United States or of any State." 18 U.S.C. § 2511(2)(d).

Provider Exception Under the provider exception, an employee or agent of a communications service provider may intercept and disclose communications to protect the rights or property of the provider as part of the ordinary course of business. 18 U.S.C. Section 2511(2)(a)(i). Thus, a system administrator of a computer network may monitor a hacker intruding into the network and then disclose the evidence obtained to law enforcement officials without violating Title III. A college or university could monitor e-mail communications of students to ensure compliance with student access agreements, such as not using the school's Internet service to run a business. *Hall v. EarthLink Network, Inc.*, 396 F.3d 500 (2d Cir. 2005), held that an Internet service provider's interception and storage of a suspected spammer's e-mails were permissible under this exception because it occurred as part of the provider's ordinary course of business. If, however, such interception of communications is not a part of the provider's ordinary course of business, then the surveillance would not be authorized under this exception.

Computer Trespasser Exception Under the computer trespasser exception, victims of computer attacks by hackers may authorize law enforcement officials to intercept wire or electronic communications of a computer trespasser, if specific statutory requirements are satisfied. 18 U.S.C. § 2511(2)(i).

Public Access Exception Under the accessible to the public exception, 18 U.S.C. Section 2511(2)(g)(i), any person may intercept an electronic communication made through a system "that is configured so that . . . [the] communication is readily accessible to the general public." This section allows for access to public Web sites, but prohibits access to Web sites protected from public access via usernames and passwords. *E.g., Konop v. Hawaiian Airlines, Inc.*, 302 F.3d 868 (9th Cir. 2002), *cert. denied*, 537 U.S. 1193 (2003). Similarly, it allows for public access to publicly broadcast radio and television programs. But 18 U.S.C. Section 2510 (16) specifically defines "readily accessible to the general public" as meaning radio communications that are not scrambled, encrypted, specially modulated, or transmitted on special frequencies to preserve the privacy of the communications.

Trap-and-Trace Devices and Pen Registers A trap-and-trace device records incoming addressing information (e.g., caller ID information). A pen register records outgoing addressing information (e.g., numbers dialed from a particular, monitored telephone). Neither device "intercepts" communications, because it does not record or otherwise allow someone to listen to the contents of a wire, oral, or electronic communication. Title III, therefore, does not apply to the use of these devices. The Electronic Communications Privacy Act of 1986 (ECPA), however, regulates these devices.

Smith v. Maryland, 442 U.S. 735 (1979), held that the installation and use of a pen register is not a search and is therefore not subject to the Fourth Amendment. The Court reasoned that the defendant had no reasonable expectation of privacy in the destination of his outgoing phone calls because the telephone company routinely monitors these calls to check billing, detect fraud, and prevent other violations of law.

Since the *Smith* decision, Congress enacted the Pen Registers and Trap and Trace Devices chapter of Title 18 (18 U.S.C. §§ 3121–27), prohibiting the installation or use of a pen register or a trap-and-trace device except by court order. Quite unlike wiretaps under Title III, use of pen registers and trap-and-trace devices only requires certification from a government attorney that "the information likely to be obtained by such installation and use is relevant to an ongoing criminal investigation." *See* 18 U.S.C. § 3123(a). Upon such a showing, a court may issue an *ex parte* order for the use of either or both types of devices. This order must specify, if known,

- the owner and location of the phone to which the device will be attached and the identity of the person who is the subject of the criminal investigation, and

- a statement of the offense to which it relates.

Before the enactment of the USA PATRIOT Act, the statutory definitions of pen registers and trap-and-trace devices did not explicitly allow them to be used to capture Internet communications (such as the "To" and "From" information in an e-mail). The USA PATRIOT Act broadened the definitions, allowing them to be used on Internet and other electronic communications.

Video Surveillance Title III does not cover video surveillance—the use of video cameras that record only images and not aural communications. Thus, surreptitious video surveillance without any audio component is analyzed under state invasion of privacy laws and under the Fourth Amendment. Legal analysis under the latter, of course, depends on whether the video surveillance violated an aggrieved person's reasonable expectation of privacy:

> [T]he Fourth Amendment forbids warrantless videotaping of a private office and hotel rooms. However, video surveillance does not in itself violate a reasonable expectation of privacy. Indeed, videotaping of suspects in public places, such as banks, does not violate the Fourth Amendment; the police may record what they normally may view with the naked eye. We have not defined the precise contours of Fourth Amendment protection in the video context. However, in this case, given the public nature of the mailroom in a community hospital where individuals— even DEA agents—strolled nearby without impediment during the transaction, we conclude the defendant had no objectively reasonable expectation of privacy that would preclude video surveillance of activities already visible to the public." *United States v. Gonzalez*, 328 F.3d 543 (9th Cir. 2003).

In *United States v. Corona-Chavez*, 328 F.3d 974 (8th Cir. 2003), police officers conducted silent video surveillance of an informant with suspected drug dealers in a hotel room. The video surveillance was upheld because the participants in the hotel-room drug transaction had no reasonable expectation of privacy when meeting with others who could have been and, in fact, were government informants. Had covert video surveillance caught someone alone in the privacy of a hotel room, however, a reasonable expectation of privacy may have been violated.

If surveillance contains *both* audio and video components, then the video sections are controlled by the Fourth Amendment (and state privacy laws) and audio portions are reviewed under Title III and the Fourth Amendment. *See United States v. Shryock*, 342 F.3d 948, 977–79 (9th Cir. 2003).

Library Surveillance Under Section 505 of the of the USA PATRIOT Act, the FBI may issue *National Security Letters* that require records of electronic communications from any library or library consortium that is deemed to be a "wire or electronic communications service provider." Nearly all modern libraries qualify as such if they have the ability to send or receive wire or electronic communications, such as via the internet. Not only is this process outside the scope of Title III, but also, it is not subject to any judicial oversight. No warrant is required; the FBI simply needs to send such a letter and explain that the "records sought are relevant to an authorized investigation to protect against international terrorism or clandestine intelligence activities." 18 U.S.C. § 2709.

193

CHAPTER 5
SEARCHES FOR
ELECTRONICALLY STORED
INFORMATION AND
ELECTRONIC SURVEILLANCE

Tracking Devices Falling Outside the Scope of Title III

Title III does not apply to the use of electronic devices emitting signals that enable law enforcement officials to track the location of objects and persons. These devices are incapable of transmitting speech and therefore do not intercept any communications. They are, however, regulated by the ECPA and the Fourth Amendment.

Tracking Beepers In *United States v. Knotts*, 460 U.S. 276 (1983), the U.S. Supreme Court held that the warrantless monitoring of a **tracking beeper** placed inside a container of chemicals did not violate the Fourth Amendment when it revealed no information that could not have been obtained through visual surveillance. The *Knotts* Court did not, however, reach the question regarding the constitutionality of the installation of a tracking beeper on the containing with regard to the presence or absence of a physical intrusion that may have interfered with any property rights. That was a function of the defendant in *Knotts* having failed to contest the installation of the beeper, but rather having chosen to focus on the act of surveillance using the radio-transmitting tracking beeper. Thus, the Court focused its inquiry solely on the privacy rights at issue.

In keeping with the privacy approach, the Court held that

> [m]onitoring the beeper signals did not invade any legitimate expectation of privacy on respondent's part, and thus there was neither a "search" nor a "seizure" within the contemplation of the Fourth Amendment. The beeper surveillance amounted principally to following an automobile on public streets and highways. A person traveling in an automobile on public thoroughfares has no reasonable expectation of privacy in his movements. While respondent had the traditional expectation of privacy within a dwelling place insofar as his cabin was concerned, such expectation of privacy would not have extended to the visual observation from public places of the automobile arriving on his premises after leaving a public highway, or to movements of objects such as the chloroform container outside the cabin. The fact that the officers relied not only on visual surveillance, but on the use of the beeper, does not alter the situation. 460 U.S. at 285.

The *Knotts* Court did not consider the constitutionality of monitoring such a device in areas that could not have been achieved by visual surveillance alone. But the Court squarely addressed this question the following year in *United States v. Karo*, 468 U.S. 705 (1984).

As with *Knotts*, *Karo* involved a defendant suspected of involvement in a drug conspiracy. And, like in *Knotts*, DEA agents placed a tracking beeper inside a container of chemicals that was to be purchased by the defendant. But the surveillance in *Karo* far exceeded the tracking of the container in *Knotts*. Over the course of five months, agents tracked the defendant's movement of the container not just on open roads but also into two storage facilities and six private homes. This activity, in turn, allowed the government to determine the location of a home in which drugs were being stored and obtain a search warrant for the home based on the tracking beeper data.

The Court stated that the installation of a tracking beeper *may* implicate the Fourth Amendment, depending on where it was installed. On the one hand, if it was installed in a place in which a person has a reasonable expectation of privacy, then probable cause and a warrant are required before a tracking device may be installed in such a location. On the other hand, if a tracking device is to be installed in some object or container in which a person has no reasonable expectation of privacy, then, consistent with *Knotts*, the Fourth Amendment is not implicated. Because the installation of the beeper at issue in *Karo* occurred in a location in which the defendant did not have a reasonable expectation of privacy, the Court ruled that the installation of the beeper did not violate the Fourth Amendment. In contrast, the subsequent monitoring of the beeper did violate the Fourth Amendment.

195

CHAPTER 5
SEARCHES FOR
ELECTRONICALLY STORED
INFORMATION AND
ELECTRONIC SURVEILLANCE

> At the risk of belaboring the obvious, private residences are places in which the individual normally expects privacy free of governmental intrusion not authorized by a warrant, and that expectation is plainly one that society is prepared to recognize as justifiable. Our cases have not deviated from this basic Fourth Amendment principle. Searches and seizures inside a home without a warrant are presumptively unreasonable absent exigent circumstances. In this case, had a DEA agent thought it useful to enter the Taos residence to verify that the ether was actually in the house and had he done so surreptitiously and without a warrant, there is little doubt that he would have engaged in an unreasonable search within the meaning of the Fourth Amendment. For purposes of the Amendment, the result is the same where, without a warrant, the Government surreptitiously employs an electronic device to obtain information that it could not have obtained by observation from outside the curtilage of the house. The beeper tells the agent that a particular article is actually located at a particular time in the private residence and is in the possession of the person or persons whose residence is being watched. Even if visual surveillance has revealed that the article to which the beeper is attached has entered the house, the later monitoring not only verifies the officers' observations but also establishes that the article remains on the premises. Here, for example, the beeper was monitored for a significant period after the arrival of the ether in Taos and before the application for a warrant to search. 468 U.S. at 714–15.

Karo is generally understood to stand for the proposition that if the monitoring of a tracking device merely assists law enforcement in "seeing" where they could if they used visual surveillance, then the Fourth Amendment is not implicated (presuming no constitutional issues with the installation of the tracking device). But if the monitoring of a device allows law enforcement to "see" where they could not without the device (such as inside a private residence, as was the case in *Karo* itself), then the Fourth Amendment prohibits the use of such a device without probable cause and a warrant.

The *Karo* case is notable in terms of its effect on statutory law. A particular provision in the ECPA was enacted in response to the *Karo* decision. The act specifically authorized the monitoring of tracking devices that may move across district lines:

> If a court is empowered to issue a warrant or other order for the installation of a mobile tracking device, such order may authorize the use of that device within the jurisdiction of the court, and outside that jurisdiction if the device is installed in that jurisdiction. 18 U.S.C. § 3117(a).

Thus—using the usual search warrant procedure in Federal Rule of Criminal Procedure 41 (or an equivalent state rule)—upon a showing of probable cause, courts may authorize the installation of tracking devices within their jurisdiction and the subsequent monitoring of those devices wherever they may roam. *United States v. Gbemisola*, 225 F.3d 753 (D.C. Cir. 2000).

Pagers Title III specifically exempts tone-only pagers from its requirements. 18 U.S.C. § 2510(12)(B). Therefore, law enforcement officials do not need a warrant to activate a suspect's pager to confirm an identity or location. *E.g.*, *United States v. Diaz-Lizaraza*, 981 F.2d 1216 (11th Cir. 1993). In contrast, if the pager alphanumerically displays callback numbers or text messages (as opposed to being a tone-only pager), then Title III applies. *Brown v. Waddell*, 50 F.3d 285 (4th Cir. 1995).

Cell Phones and GPS When the government seeks to intercept conversations in which a party is using a cellular telephone, the usual requirements of Title III must be followed. But separate from the interception of calls made via cell phone, a cell phone's ground positioning satellite (GPS) capabilities can be used to track a person's location in much the same way that a free-standing GPS device may be used. **GPS** is a satellite-based navigation system. A GPS receiver compares the time a signal was transmitted by several satellites with the time those signals were received, allowing the GPS unit to determine the user's position and display it on an electronic map with great accuracy—typically within two meters (a little more than six feet). Regardless of whether law enforcement use utilize a cell phone's GPS system or a different GPS-enabled device, GPS tracking raises Fourth Amendment privacy concerns that lie beyond the scope of Title III.

The early decisions addressing the use of GPS tracking "hesitated to distinguish GPS technology from the beeper in *Knotts*, analogizing GPS surveillance to following a vehicle on public roads" (Plourde-Cole 2010: 590). Thus, relying on *Knotts*, most courts held that GPS tracking did not implicate the Fourth Amendment and therefore did not require a warrant. *United States v. Garcia*, 474 F.3d 994 (7th Cir. 2007); *United States v. Pineda-Moreno*, 591 F.3d 1212 (9th Cir. 2010). In 2009, however, two state courts held that the placement and monitoring of a GPS device constituted a "search" under the state constitutions, reasoning that the GPS was a "vastly different and exponentially more sophisticated and powerful" technology than a beeper. *People v. Weaver*, 909 N.E.2d 1195, 1199 (N.Y. 2009). The Supreme Judicial Court of Massachusetts went even further when it held that the installation of a GPS tracking device on a car amounted to both a search and a seizure, reasoning that the defendant's right "to exclude others from his vehicle" and the right to the "use and enjoyment of his vehicle" had been violated. *Commonwealth v. Connolly*, 913 N.E.2d 356, 370 (Mass. 2009).

The following year in *United States v. Maynard*, 615 F.3d 544, 563 (D.C. Cir.), *cert. denied*, 131 S. Ct. 671 (2010), the First Circuit held that the installation and monitoring of a GPS device constitutes a search for Fourth Amendment purposes and therefore requires a warrant supported by probable cause. Key to the court's rationale was that because a GPS allows for twenty-four-hour surveillance over extended periods of time, it can violate a person's reasonable expectation of privacy under *Katz* by presenting a composite of a person's life. The *Maynard* court referred to this as the **mosaic theory** because the "detailed patchwork of information reveals the so-called 'mosaic' of an individual's life—a profile not simply of where he goes, but also of his associations—the implications of which conjure the protections of the First Amendment as well as the Fourth" (Plourde-Cole 2010: 620).

> First, unlike one's movements during a single journey, the whole of one's movements over the course of a month is not actually exposed to the public because the likelihood anyone will observe all those movements is effectively nil. Second, the whole of one's movements is not exposed constructively even though each individual movement is exposed, because that whole reveals more—sometimes a great deal more—than does the sum of its parts. . . . Repeated visits to a church, a gym, a bar, or a bookie tell a story not told by any single visit. . . . The sequence of a person's movements can reveal still more; a single trip to a gynecologist's office tells little about a woman, but that trip followed a few weeks later by a visit to a baby supply store tells a different story. A person who knows all of another's travels can deduce whether he is a weekly churchgoer, a heavy drinker, a regular at the gym, an unfaithful husband, an outpatient receiving medical treatment, an associate of particular individuals or political groups—and not just one such fact about a person, but all such facts. 615 F.3d at 558, 562.

As of the publication of this book, the only U.S. Supreme Court decision in this area is *United States v. Jones*, 132 S. Ct. 945 (2012). Recall from Chapter 3, though, that *Jones* was premised on the police having trespassed Jones's property to install the GPS tracking device on his wife's car. Thus, the Court did not analyze the privacy concerns raised by tracking a suspect using GPS in the absence of a trespass to property. But at least five justices in the *Jones* case hinted that whether electronic surveillance interferes with a reasonable expectation of privacy may depend on the length of the monitoring and the corresponding amounts of data collected (see Kerr 2012). A future case will need to resolve how the Fourth Amendment's protection of privacy applies to monitoring people's whereabouts using GPS or similar technologies.

Cell Phones and Cell Site Tracking A cellular phone may be used to track the location of a person using real-time, cell-site data searching—a practice that, like tracking using GPS, raises Fourth Amendment concerns beyond the scope of Title III. The process of real-time, cell-site data searching was described by one court as follows:

> When a cell phone is powered up, it acts as a scanning radio, searching through a list of control channels for the strongest signal. The cell phone re-scans every seven seconds or when the signal strength weakens, regardless of whether a call is placed. The cell phone searches for a five-digit number known as the System Identification Code assigned to service providers. After selecting a channel, the cell phone identifies itself by sending its programmed codes which identify the phone, the phone's owner, and the service provider. These codes include an Electronic Serial Number (a unique 32-bit number programmed into the phone by the manufacturer), and a Mobile Identification Number, a 10-digit number derived from the phone's number. . . . The cell site relays these codes to the mobile telecommunications switching office in a process known as registration. . . . [Thus], a cell phone is (among other things) a radio transmitter that automatically announces its presence to a cell tower via a radio signal over a control channel which does not itself carry the human voice. By a process of triangulation from various cell towers, law enforcement is able to track the movements of the target phone, and hence locate a suspect using that phone. *In re Application for Pen Register and Trap/Trace Device with Cell Site*, 396 F. Supp.2d 747, 750 (S.D. Tex. 2005).

The majority of courts that have addressed the constitutionality of using real-time, cell-site data to track the user's physical location have held that such information qualifies as tracking device information under the ECPA. The government must therefore demonstrate probable cause to obtain a search warrant that authorizes obtaining such information. *In re U.S. Order Authorizing the Release of Historical Cell-Site Info.*, No. 10-MJ-0550, 2010 U.S. Dist. LEXIS 88781, at *1, *3 (E.D.N.Y. Aug. 27, 2010); *In re Application for Pen Register and Trap/Trace Device with Cell Site*, 396 F. Supp. 2d 747 (S.D. Tex. 2005). In *United States v. Davis*, 2014 WL 2599917, *10 (11th Cir. 2014), the Eleventh Circuit embraced the mosaic theory and squarely held that "cell site location information is within the subscriber's reasonable expectation of privacy. The obtaining of that data without a warrant is a Fourth Amendment violation." Other courts, however, have disagreed. They have held that a court may issue an order authorizing the disclosure of a cell phone user's location without a probable cause showing or a warrant, so long as the government does not seek triangulation information or location information other than that transmitted at the beginning and end of particular calls. *See In re Application of U.S. for an Order for Prospective Cell Site Location Information on a Certain Cellular Telephone*, 460 F. Supp. 2d 448 (S.D.N.Y. Oct 23, 2006); *In re Application of U.S. for Historical Cell Site Data*, 724 F.3d 600, 612 (5th Cir. 2013) (allowing time tracking information based on "specific and articulable facts"); *In re Application of U.S.*, 415 F. Supp.2d 663 (S.D. W. Va. 2006) (same). Either an act of Congress or consistent rulings of higher courts will be necessary to resolve these conflicts.

197

CHAPTER 5
SEARCHES FOR
ELECTRONICALLY STORED
INFORMATION AND
ELECTRONIC SURVEILLANCE

Electronic Surveillance of Stored Communications

E-Mail Although e-mail is ubiquitous and has replaced telephone communication in many spheres, it is not considered a wire communication for Title III purposes. Under a portion of the ECPA referred to as the **Stored Communications Act (SCA)**, e-mail, like other forms of stored electronic communications, may be obtained by law enforcement authorities during the first 180 days of storage using normal search warrant procedures; after 180 days, the government may access stored communications using either a search warrant or, after giving notice to the subscriber, a subpoena. 18 U.S.C. § 2703(a).

The explicit provisions of the SCA notwithstanding, there are significant questions concerning the constitutionality of the SCA insofar as it dispenses with the need for a warrant after a communication has been stored for six months. In *United States v. Forrester*, 512 F.3d 500, 511 (9th Cir. 2007), the court held that e-mail communications fall outside the scope of the third-party doctrine. Although the U.S. Supreme Court has not yet ruled on this provision in the SCA, three years after *Forrester* was decided, the Court stated in another context that "a search of [an individual's] personal e-mail account" would be just as intrusive as "a wiretap on his home phone line," thereby implying more protection of e-mail under the Fourth Amendment than exists under the SCA. *City of Ontario v. Quon*, 130 S. Ct. 2619, 2631, (2010). Relying on that language, the Sixth Circuit extended Fourth Amendment protection to e-mail correspondence stored with a third-party Internet service provider (ISP), holding that the SCA's subpoena provision (applicable 180 days after a communication is stored) is unconstitutional.

If we accept that an email is analogous to a letter or a phone call, it is manifest that agents of the government cannot compel a commercial ISP to turn over the contents of an email without triggering the Fourth Amendment. An ISP is the intermediary that makes email communication possible. Emails must pass through an ISP's servers to reach their intended recipient. Thus, the ISP is the functional equivalent of a post office or a telephone company. As we have discussed above, the police may not storm the post office and intercept a letter, and they are likewise forbidden from using the phone system to make a clandestine recording of a telephone call—unless they get a warrant, that is. . . . The mere *ability* of a third-party intermediary to access the contents of a communication cannot be sufficient to extinguish a reasonable expectation of privacy. *United States v. Warshak*, 631 F.3d 266, 286 (6th Cir. 2010).

Various bills have been introduced in Congress to strengthen privacy protections for e-mail and other stored communications. As of this writing, however, none have been enacted into law. Displeased with congressional inaction, in June 2013, Texas became the first state to enact a law requiring that law enforcement officers obtain a search warrant based on probable cause before they access any electronic communications and customer data stored by a third-party service provider. TEXAS CODE OF CRIM. PRO. ART. 18.02.

Voicemail Prior to the enactment of the USA PATRIOT Act, voicemail was considered to be a stored wire communication. As such, in order to retrieve a stored voicemail message, law enforcement authorities had to comply with the requirements of Title III to access stored voicemail messages. But Section 209 of the USA PATRIOT Act changed that by deleting the phrase "electronic storage" of wire communications from the definition of "wire communication." As a result, voicemail is no longer

Continued on next page

covered by Title III. Voicemail, like e-mail, is now accessible under SCA using a standard search warrant subject to various date and time limitations. 18 U.S.C. § 2703(a). As with e-mail, it remains to be seen whether the SCA's removal of the warrant requirement after 180 days violates the Fourth Amendment.

Text Messaging The ECPA also applies to law enforcement efforts to obtain text messages from cellular service providers. But the ECPA does not apply when it comes to reading texts—or any content, including e-mail—on a person's phone (rather than obtaining them from the carrier). The Fourth Amendment governs such searches of phones.

The sender of a text message has no reasonable expectation of privacy in that message. *E.g.*, *United States v. Meriwether*, 917 F.2d 955 (6th Cir. 1990). In contrast, the owner of a cell phone or similar wireless personal communications device reasonably expects privacy in its contents. Thus, a warrant is normally required for law enforcement to search such a device, even one taken from an arrestee (meaning that, as explained in Chapter 7, a valid search incident to arrest does not give police the legal right to search the contents of cell phone). *Riley v. California*, 134 S. Ct. 2473 (2014). Note, however, that a range of other warrant exceptions and exclusionary rule exceptions also affect the applicability of this general proposition in any particular case, including doctrines such as exigent circumstances, inevitable discovery, and independent source. *E.g.*, *United States v. Brooks*, 715 F.3d 1069 (8th Cir. 2013); *United States v. Morales-Ortiz*, 376 F. Supp. 2d 1131 (D.N.M. 2004); *State v. Carroll*, 778 N.W.2d 1 (Wis. 2010). Consider the U.S. Supreme Court's decision in *City of Ontario v. Quon*, 130 S. Ct. 2619 (2010).

In *Quon*, a municipality had provided alphanumeric pagers to the members of its SWAT team. After a SWAT officer exceeded his usage limit, the city obtained transcripts from the pager provider and discovered that the officer had used the pager for personal purposes, including sending some sexually explicit text messages. He was disciplined and subsequently sued the city, claiming that their search violated the Fourth Amendment. The U.S. Supreme Court sided with the city without ever having reached the issue of whether the officer's reasonable expectation of privacy had been violated. Rather, the Court determined that the city's actions were reasonable, and therefore did not violate the Fourth Amendment, because the search was motivated by a legitimate, work-related purpose and it was not excessive in scope.

Social Media Some social media publications or postings are meant for the world to see. Thus, it should come as no surprise that there is no reasonable expectation of privacy concerning postings on publically accessible websites, blogs, or even hard drives that are left open for anyone to access using a peer-to-peer connection. *United States v. Ganoe*, 538 F.3d 1117 (9th Cir. 2008). The same would be true for text, photo, and video postings open to the public on Facebook, YouTube, Twitter, and other social networking sites. But what if the user of a social media account has taken some steps to preserve the privacy of his or her postings?

An empirical study of 2,500 social media users in Canada and the United States reported a "theory of network privacy" that users of social media "have developed a new and arguably legitimate notion of privacy online" as a function of 72 percent manually enabling various privacy settings

KEY POINTS

LO5
LO6

■ Title III balances the need to use electronic surveillance for effective law enforcement against the need to protect the privacy rights by providing for judicial supervision of all aspects of electronic surveillance and establishing warrant procedures based on probable cause. Special exigent circumstances provisions, however, allow for emergency interceptions that must be judicially supervised within forty-eight hours after the interception has occurred or begins to occur.

LO7

■ Although a judicially issued interception order is required to lawfully intercept wire, oral, or electronic communications, separate judicial approval is not required to covertly enter premises to install a listening device.

■ Judicially authorized interceptions must terminate on attainment of the authorized objective, or on the expiration of the intercept order.

■ Information gained through the lawful execution of a judicially authorized intercept order must be kept confidential unless one of the specific provisions of Title III authorizes disclosure.

■ Immediately upon the expiration of an interception order (meaning without unnecessary or unreasonable delay), both the interception order and all recordings made pursuant to it are required to be delivered to the judge who issued the order to be sealed under the judge's directions. Failure to comply with the sealing requirement may render intercepted communications inadmissible.

■ Within a reasonable time, but not later than ninety days after the termination of the period of an order, an inventory must be served

Continued on next page

Continued on next page

200

on their accounts (Levin & Abril 2009: 1002). A few courts have agreed, at least in principle, that social network users maintain a reasonable expectation of privacy in at least some types of online communications, such as private chats/instant messaging. *E.g.*, *R.S. v. Minnewaska Area Sch. Dist. No. 2149*, 2012 WL 3870868 (D. Minn. Sept. 6, 2012); *Crispin v. Christian Audigier, Inc.*, 717 F. Supp. 2d 965 (C.D. Cal. 2010). But other types of online communications, even if intended to be private, are clearly not. For instance, "[w]here Facebook privacy settings allow viewership of postings by 'friends,' the Government may access them through a cooperating witness who is a 'friend' without violating the Fourth Amendment." *United States v. Meregildo*, 2012 WL 3264501, at *2 (S.D.N.Y. Aug. 10, 2012).

No matter what steps social media users take to keep their information private, law enforcement can obtain data stored on social media servers using a variety of tools. Because social media services like Facebook, Foursquare, Twitter, and Google+ are "public network service providers," Section 2703(d) of the SCA permits the government to subpoena their basic subscriber records. In other words, no search warrant is needed to obtain a subscriber's name, length of service, credit card information, e-mail address(es), IP address(es), and logs of the dates, time, and durations that the user logged into their networks. All law enforcement need do is aver "specific and articulable facts showing that there are reasonable grounds to believe" that such basic subscriber data are "relevant and material to an ongoing criminal investigation"—a low standard compared to probable cause.

Additionally, government investigators and prosecutors can compel social networking sites to turn over the content of a user's account through a search warrant under Section 2703(a) if they are able to demonstrate probable cause that evidence of a crime will be found on the site. This includes tweets, wall postings, e-mail messages, instant messages, chat logs, photos, videos, and other online communications. *United States v. Anderson*, 664 F.3d 758 (8th Cir. 2012).

Documents Stored in the Cloud At the time the SCA was adopted in 1986, it was more science fiction than foreseeable fact that people would digitally store their "papers and effects" with a *remote computing service* (RCS), like iCloud, Drive, Dropbox, SkyDrive, or SugarSync. Thus, the files one stores in "the cloud" with an RCS receive even less protection than e-mails, voicemails, text messages, and social networking data. In fact, the SCA authorizes the government to obtain data sent to an RCS for storage or processing with only a subpoena or court order, regardless of how old it is. 18 U.S.C. § 2703(b)(1)(B)(i)–(ii).

As cloud-based computing grows, it seems that Congress will need to take action to protect the "papers and effects" stored in the cloud.

> The many types of documents that are subject to [transfer to the cloud] include: photographs, records, books, magazines, multimedia, personal planners, and more. These types of documents are inherently like those that people normally keep in their homes or businesses. People have bookshelves, photo albums, filing cabinets, drawers, and safes primarily to store these types of documents. . . . If society begins to store these documents primarily on the Internet . . . and if the third-party doctrine precludes Fourth Amendment protection for these documents, the results will be absurd: The types of objects that are generally less likely to be evidence in

a crime, and more likely to be personal and sensitive, will become easier for the government to search and seize. At the same time, physical evidence, generally more likely to be relevant to a criminal investigation, will continue to be subject to the Fourth Amendment requirement of a warrant, authorized by a neutral magistrate and supported by probable cause. (Small 2013: 274–275)

Other Electronic Surveillance Technologies Not Implicating Title III

As technology evolves, law enforcement continues to increase its ability to conduct surveillance in ways that were unimaginable only a generation ago (Weaver 2011). Some of these technologies fall within the scope of Title III regulation, while others fall within the legal ambit of the ECPA or other statutory laws. Still others have yet to be addressed by Congress or any state legislatures. But the use of all sophisticated technologies to conduct electronic surveillance implicates the Fourth Amendment, often in one or both of two distinct, albeit related, ways.

First, when technology allows law enforcement to see, hear, or otherwise sense that which would not be discoverable through less intrusive means, it has the potential to transform the nature of the surveillance (say, from mere visual surveillance that traditionally could be achieved without a warrant) into a "search" for Fourth Amendment purposes, which, of course, generally requires a warrant supported by probable cause. Second, even if a valid warrant is obtained, some technologies are so sophisticated that their use in a particular manner may be "unreasonable" under the Fourth Amendment.

Common Technologies Police may use ordinary binoculars and flashlights to assist them in seeing over distances or in the dark. In *Texas v. Brown*, 460 U.S. 730, 740 (1983), a unanimous U.S. Supreme Court concluded that "the use of artificial means to illuminate a darkened area simply does not constitute a search, and thus triggers no Fourth Amendment protection." Similarly, the use of telephoto lens cameras does not elevate traditional visual surveillance into a search for Fourth Amendment purposes, even when such cameras are used to conduct aerial photography from a plane or helicopter flying at a reasonable altitude in navigable airspace. *California v. Ciraolo*, 476 U.S. 207 (1986) (1,000 feet); *Florida v. Riley*, 488 U.S. 445 (1989) (400 feet); *Dow Chemical Company v. United States*, 476 U.S. 227 (1986).

Forward-Looking Infrared Technology (FLIT) In *Kyllo v. United States*, 533 U.S. 27 (2001), police used an infrared thermal imaging detector to determine the amount of heat coming from inside a home in which they believed the defendant was growing marijuana using "grow lights." When the device demonstrated that there were excessive levels of heat coming from the house, police used that information to establish probable cause to obtain a search warrant. Two lower courts denied Kyllo's attempt to suppress the evidence found during the subsequent search, reasoning that he did not attempt to conceal the heat radiating from his home, and because the thermal imaging device "did not expose any intimate details of [his] life, only amorphous hot spots on his home's exterior." 533 U.S. at 31. In reversing and invalidating the defendant's conviction, the Supreme Court relied heavily on *Katz*

Continued on next page

KEY POINTS

least during the first six months after the message was stored. Thereafter, the materials might be able to be accessed by subpoena, but since the constitutionality of doing so is dubious, it is advisable for law enforcement officers to seek a warrant to obtain such data.

■ The SCA permits law enforcement to access documents stored in the cloud to be accessed with only a subpoena or court order, regardless of how old the documents are.

when it reasoned the high-tech device allowed police to obtain information about the interior of the defendant's home—a space given the highest levels of Fourth Amendment protection. "Where, as here, the Government uses a device that is not in general public use to explore details of the home that would previously have been unknowable without physical intrusion, the surveillance is a 'search' and is presumptively unreasonable without a warrant." 533 U.S. at 40.

As the quote from *Kyllo* makes clear, the Court supported its holding by relying on the fact that FLIT devices were not "in general public use." But as Justice Stevens noted in his dissent, this language suggests that Fourth Amendment's protection "dissipates as soon as the relevant technology is in general public use." 533 U.S. at 47. We do not yet know whether this was dicta or whether widespread public use (or at least availability) will, in fact, be the dividing line between technology that law enforcement may use to conduct electronic surveillance and technology that implicates the Fourth Amendment.

CRIMINAL PROCEDURE IN ACTION

Driving Data in Your Car's Black Box

At 12:30 A.M., a white SUV struck and killed a 6'7", 260-pound teenager wearing dark clothing as he was crossing a street. A witness testified that she thought the SUV was traveling near or just over the 45-mile-per-hour (mph) speed limit. Another witness stated that he was driving at "roughly 50, 55 miles an hour" and believed the SUV was traveling at about

the same speed. He also said that he saw the pedestrian's legs in stride lit up by the SUV's headlights and "then almost simultaneously thereafter [he saw] brake lights and then the collision," that a pedestrian wearing dark clothing would have been difficult to see against the dark background, and that he had not anticipated anybody stepping out into the pedestrian walkway against a red light. When he saw the SUV drive away, he followed the vehicle, called 911, and gave the license plate number.

When a police officer spoke with driver of the SUV, he admitted to having had "a little" to drink that night. The officer surmised the driver was intoxicated from his "red bloodshot watery eyes, slurred speech, and a stagger in his gait." The driver refused to take a breath alcohol test in the field. The driver was then arrested and, at 2:35 A.M., his blood alcohol concentration (BAC) was 0.18.

After investigating the accident scene, officers determined that the SUV was likely traveling at 55 mph. The lead investigating officer found that an unimpaired driver, traveling at 45 to 55 mph, would have about 1.5 seconds to respond to an unexpected danger in the roadway. Thus, even if the SUV had been traveling at the speed limit, a reasonable driver would not have been able to react quickly enough

to avoid hitting a pedestrian stepping out unexpectedly against a red light at night. Accordingly, police concluded that neither the vehicle's speed nor the driver's BAC was the primary cause of the accident.

A year later, while the SUV was in storage, police downloaded information from the car's "black box"—a data recorder designed to monitor sensors that help regulate airbag deployment and monitor speed, breaking, seat belt use, and changes from front-to-back and side-to-side velocity. The black box data recorded speeds of 69 to 76 mph immediately before the SUV hit the pedestrian. Data also revealed that the driver had begun breaking 1.3 to 2.1 seconds before impact. An accident reconstruction expert used this information to determine that the SUV hit the teenager at 60 to 61 mph and that the driver had sufficient time to swerve and miss the pedestrian.

The driver was charged with vehicular manslaughter. He moved to suppress the evidence against him gathered from the search and seizure of data from the SUV's black box because it was conducted without a warrant. The trial court denied the motion on the basis that the driver had no reasonable expectation of privacy in the black box data. On appeal, however, the court ruled in favor of the defendant.

Continued on next page

- The appellate court reasoned that black box data is distinguishable from cases in which technology is used to allow law enforcement to capture information that a person knowingly exposes to the public. Unlike tracking beepers, for example, the defendant's own vehicle was internally producing data for its safe operation that was not being exposed to the public or beyond conveyed to any other person. Thus, the defendant had a reasonable expectation of privacy with regard to the black box data. Do you agree? Why or why not?

- The appellate court also found that there was no probable cause to download the black box data because, at the time the data was retrieved, investigators had already concluded that the driver was not guilty of any crimes other than DUI and leaving the scene offenses, and the defendant had already pled guilty to these offenses and was awaiting sentencing. The police had not downloaded the data sooner because the airbags had not deployed in the accident and they erroneously believed that no data would have been recorded as a result. They only did so a year after the accident at the request of the district attorney's office, which informed them that black boxes may record data even when airbags are not deployed. Because the police did not know this critical fact, the court concluded that under the facts known at time they were investigating a fatal collision, there was no probable cause to download the black box data for evidence of a crime. If this case were appealed to the state high court of last resort and you were a justice on that court, how would you rule? Why? *See People v. Xinos,* 121 Cal. Rptr. 3d 496 (Cal. App. 2011).

Intelligence Surveillance

For more than forty years prior to the enactment of Title III, the U.S. government conducted warrantless electronic surveillance of foreign powers and their agents for intelligence purposes under a broad and amorphous "national security exception" to the warrant requirement of the Fourth Amendment. That changed in the 1970s, when the Watergate scandal illustrated governmental abuses of that power. Congress responded by passing the Foreign Intelligence Surveillance Act (FISA) in 1978.

FISA authorizes and regulates the electronic surveillance of foreign powers and their agents within the United States where a "significant purpose" of the surveillance is to gather foreign intelligence information that cannot reasonably be obtained through normal investigative techniques. FISA therefore allows for surveillance of domestic communications between persons located within the United States (who are agents of foreign powers), as well as surveillance of international communications between persons located within the United States and persons located outside the United States (when one or both are agents of foreign powers).

Additionally, pursuant to amendments made to the law in 2004 and 2008, FISA authorizes surveillance of so-called lone wolves—any individual or group that is not linked to a foreign government but who "engages in international terrorism or activities in preparation therefore," 50 U.S.C. § 1801(b)(1)(C), or "engages in the international proliferation of weapons of mass destruction, or activities in preparation therefor." 50 U.S.C. § 1801(d).

Finally, pursuant to 2008 amendments to FISA, the U.S. attorney general and the U.S. director of national intelligence may jointly authorize, for a period of up to one year, the surveillance of "persons reasonably believed to be located outside the United States to acquire foreign intelligence information." 50 U.S.C. § 1881a(a). In 2009, a group of attorneys and human rights, labor, legal, and media organizations challenged this provision in FISA. They argued it failed to "protect the privacy interest of Americans in the content of their telephone calls and emails" as mandated by the Fourth Amendment and, furthermore, that it violated the First Amendment by chilling "the constitutionally protected speech of Americans who fear that their telephone calls and emails will be subject to surveillance." *Amnesty Intern. USA v. McConnell,*

646 F. Supp. 2d 633 (S.D.N.Y. 2009). But the court did not decide the case on the merits, finding that the plaintiffs lacked standing to challenge this provision in FISA. Ultimately, the U.S. Supreme Court agreed that the plaintiffs lacked standing because they failed to offer any evidence that their communications had been monitored, and any arguments about potential future surveillance were "too speculative." *Clapper v. Amnesty International USA*, 133 S. Ct. 1138, 1147 (2013).

FISA does not regulate U.S. governmental intelligence operations wholly outside the United States, such as operations conducted by the Central Intelligence Agency (CIA). The Fourth Amendment is inapplicable to persons who are searched outside of the country if they are not U.S. citizens and have no voluntary connections to the United States. *See United States v. Verdugo-Urquidez*, 494 U.S. 259 (1990). Moreover, extraterritorial investigations (i.e., those conducted by U.S. agents outside the United States) remain within the scope of the national security exemption to the warrant requirement of the Fourth Amendment. *In re Terrorist Bombings of U.S. Embassies in East Africa*, 552 F.3d 157 (2d Cir. 2008).

FISA Applications

FISA permits federal agents to conduct electronic surveillance and physical searches for national defense purposes. Technically, any federal agent may apply for such a warrant, although according to the Federal Judicial Center, most FISA applications "are drafted by attorneys in the General Counsel's Office at the National Security Agency at the request of an officer of one of the federal intelligence agencies." Each FISA warrant application must first be approved by the U.S. attorney general. Additionally, 50 U.S.C. Section 1804(a) requires that the application contain information similar to what Title III requires for other electronic surveillance warrants, such as

- the identity of the officer making the application;
- the identity or a description of the target of the surveillance;
- a statement demonstrating that the target of the electronic surveillance is a foreign power or an agent of a foreign power;
- a description of the facilities or places at which the electronic surveillance will occur and the correspondingly proposed time periods; a description of the nature of the information sought, type of communications or activities to be subjected to the surveillance, and the means that will be used to obtain this intelligence (including if physical entry will be required); and
- the proposed minimization procedures.

In addition, FISA applications must contain a certification by the assistant to the president for National Security Affairs or the deputy director of the Federal Bureau of Investigation that a significant purpose of the surveillance is to obtain foreign intelligence information that cannot reasonably be obtained by normal investigative techniques.

Notably, FISA does not require a showing of probable cause to believe that a crime has been or is being committed. Rather, FISA only requires probable cause that the surveillance is of an authorized person or group for purposes relating to the gathering of foreign intelligence or preventing terrorism. Additional findings, however, are required if the targets of the investigation are U.S. citizens or lawful resident aliens.

In addition to electronic surveillance, FISA authorizes physical searches of "premises, information, material, or property used exclusively by, or under the open and exclusive control of, a foreign power or powers." 50 U.S.C. § 1822(a)(1)(A)(i). Unlike either regular search warrants or covert entry warrants, the fact that such physical searches take place need not be disclosed unless and until the U.S. attorney general "determines there is no national security interest in continuing to maintain the secrecy of the search." 50 U.S.C. § 1825(b).

Approval by the Foreign Intelligence Surveillance Court Congress created a special Article III court to review FISA applications called the **Foreign Intelligence Surveillance Court (FISC)**. 50 U.S.C. § 1803(a). The composition of the court is determined by the chief justice of the U.S. Supreme Court, who selects eleven district court judges from seven judicial circuits, at least three of whom reside within twenty miles of Washington, D.C.

Prior to the enactment of the USA PATRIOT Act, the FISC was authorized to issue a FISA warrant only if the court determined that the "primary purpose" of the warrant was to engage in the collection of foreign intelligence collection and not criminal prosecution. But the USA PATRIOT Act amended FISA so that the intelligence gathering need only be a "significant purpose" of such surveillance, thereby expanding the government's ability to use FISA warrants for investigative purposes. If the "significant purpose" test is met, then any information gathered during the execution of a duly authorized FISA warrant may be used in subsequent criminal prosecutions, including those involving domestic crimes, even if the defendants were not named in the FISA warrant. *E.g.*, *United States v. Stewart*, 590 F.3d 93 (2d Cir. 2009); *United States v. Ning Wen*, 477 F.3d 896 (7th Cir. 2007); *United States v. Duggan*, 743 F.2d 59 (2d Cir. 1984).

If the FISC denies an application, that denial may be appealed by the Department of Justice to the Foreign Intelligence Surveillance Court of Review. The Court of Review is a three-judge panel. 50 U.S.C. § 1803(b). This court comes into session infrequently. As of this writing, it has issued only two published decisions:

- *In re Sealed Case*, 310 F.3d 717 (FISA Ct. Rev. 2002), upheld the USA PATRIOT Act's change from the "primary purpose" of an application being intelligence gathering to needing only a "significant purpose" for such surveillance. The court found the law constitutionally balanced the government's need to gather information for national security purposes and an individual's privacy rights.

- *In re Directives Pursuant to Section 105B of the Foreign Intelligence Surveillance Act*, 551 F.3d 1004 (FISA Ct. Rev. 2008), upheld certain provisions of the Protect America Act of 2007 that permitted the executive to conduct warrantless foreign intelligence surveillance. The court held that telecommunications companies had to cooperate with the U.S. government to intercept international phone calls and e-mail messages of U.S. citizens suspected of being spies or terrorists. These provisions were subsequently repealed by Congress.

Section 215 of the USA PATRIOT Act also permits the FISC to issue *ex parte* (from one party) orders "requiring the production of any tangible things (including books, records, papers, documents, and other items) for an investigation to protect against international terrorism or clandestine intelligence activities," provided that such investigation of a U.S. citizen or resident alien "is not conducted solely upon the basis of activities protected by the First Amendment to the U.S. Constitution." 50 U.S.C. § 1861. If a library received such an order, it may be required to produce not only documents relating to a patron's library records, but also any ESI relating to the patron's use of databases and other electronic sources accessed on a library computer.

Alternate Executive Approval Procedures FISA does not require compliance with the procedures previously detailed under all circumstances. The president, through the U.S. attorney general, is authorized under 50 U.S.C. Section 1802(a) to approve an application for FISA surveillance for periods up to one year without FISC approval if the following conditions are met:

- the electronic surveillance is solely directed at
  - the acquisition of the contents of communications transmitted by means of communications used exclusively between or among foreign powers; or

205

CHAPTER 5
SEARCHES FOR
ELECTRONICALLY STORED
INFORMATION AND
ELECTRONIC SURVEILLANCE

■ the acquisition of technical intelligence, other than the spoken communications of individuals, from property or premises under the open and exclusive control of a foreign power;

■ there is no substantial likelihood that the surveillance will acquire the contents of any communication to which a U.S. person is a party; and

■ proper minimization procedures are used.

If this executive authorization procedure is used, the U.S. attorney general must certify that he or she has made the requisite statutory findings and has followed all procedures mandated by FISA. This certification must be provided to the intelligence committees of both the U.S. House of Representatives and the U.S. Senate, as well as filed under seal with the FISC.

Notably, the executive authorization provisions in Section 1802(a)(1)(A) of FISA are limited exclusively to intelligence information targeting foreign powers or their agents. Thus, executive authorization to monitor individuals or groups that may be engaged in sabotage or international terrorism is not authorized under FISA. Approval of the surveillance of such individuals or groups is supposed to be the exclusive province of the FISC. But as the following Discussion Point explores, the U.S. government has not always obeyed FISA's commands.

DISCUSSION POINT

Does the NSA's Surveillance Program Go Too Far?

In the wake of the terrorist attacks on September 11, 2001, the USA PATRIOT Act gave the U.S. president broad powers to combat terrorism. Using these powers and those he claimed were inherent presidential powers under Article II of the U.S. Constitution as the commander-in-chief, President George W. Bush issued an executive order authorizing the National Security

Agency (NSA) to launch a program it called the Terrorist Surveillance Program (TSP) in an attempt to prevent more terrorist attacks on the United States. Although the complete details of the executive order are not known, it authorized the NSA to engage in secret intelligence gathering by intercepting electronic communications (including phone calls, e-mails, text messages, and web-browsing activities), without a warrant, from people whom the agency believed were linked, either directly or indirectly, to suspected terrorists.

The NSA had historically been permitted to intercept electronic communications originating from foreign counties, even if the recipients of calls or messages were in the United States. Under FISA, the government is required to obtain a warrant before engaging in electronic surveillance of Americans. Yet, the NSA was not only provided warrantless, unsupervised access to the networks of major U.S. communications companies, but also used this access to eavesdrop on wholly domestic communications. More than forty civil lawsuits seeking hundreds of billions of dollars were filed against numerous telecommunications for their role in the TSP. In July of 2008, Congress amended

FISA to provide retroactive immunity for these companies. *See In re Nat'l Sec. Agency Telecomms. Records Litig.*, 671 F.3d 881, 891–93 (9th Cir. 2011). This effectively ended all lawsuits against electronic service providers alleged to have provided assistance "in connection with an intelligence activity involving communications that was . . . designed to detect or prevent a terrorist attack . . . against the United States." FISA Amendments Act of 2008 § 201.

In the wake of great controversy over the legality of the TSP, the Bush administration voluntarily ceased the program. But, of course, different NSA surveillance activities continued, albeit these were arguably within the scope of FISA. Consider that in 2013, former NSA contractor Edward Snowden revealed that the NSA had been conducting a massive dragnet of phone calls and online activity. Snowden revealed the FISC had ordered Verizon "to produce all metadata—information about who is calling whom, when, and for how long, though not the contents of any call—for calls within or with one end in the United States" (Chesney & Wittes 2013: para. 3). It was subsequently revealed that the U.S. government

Continued on next page

had reportedly asked the FISA court every 90 days since 2006 to renew an order that compels the nation's telecommunication providers to surrender telephony metadata pertaining to millions of U.S. citizens (Donohue 2013). The *Washington Post* then broke a story about a massive NSA computer system—the "Planning Tool for Resource Integration, Synchronization, and Management" (PRISM). "It reportedly involves agreements between the government and an array of U.S.-based internet companies (like Google and Facebook) that enable the NSA to monitor the online communications of non-U.S. persons believed to be physically located outside the United States" (Chesney & Wittes 2013: para. 3).

According to the NSA, PRISM is designed to collect and process foreign intelligence that passes through American servers under the supervision of FISC. It creates giant datasets of metadata that might later be queried on a case-by-case basis. The Obama administration asserts that Section 702 of FISA grants the government the authority to conduct programs like PRISM, so long as U.S. citizens are not intentionally targeted. 50 U.S.C. § 1881a. According to the NSA, PRISM and its telephony metadata programs are designed to intentionally target the communications of non-U.S. citizens in ways authorized by FISA; the data gathered on U.S. citizens is incidental to their primary surveillance targets. But there can be no doubt that, even if incidental, the NSA has amassed vast quantities of data "concerning individuals who are neither the target of any investigation nor an agent of a foreign power" (Donahue 2013: para. 11).

Unlike the Bush administration's use of TSP that was conducted in violation of the law, the Obama administration's use of PRISM is arguably authorized under the express provisions of FISA and the USA PATRIOT Act, and the telephony metadata program was specifically authorized by orders of the FISC and, therefore, complied with mandates of FISA. But critics counter that even though no laws appear to have been broken, the ways in which FISA and the USA PATRIOT Act have been interpreted and put into practice are flawed since they run contrary to the principles of a democratic society (see, e.g., Feldman 2013).

> [FISA] allows the government to seek and receive an order from the FISC requiring third parties (like Verizon) to produce "tangible things" like business records, so long as the government can certify that the information sought is "relevant" to a national security investigation. It is the analog in the context of national security investigations to the grand jury subpoena in a criminal probe—the instrument by which the government can compel people to turn over material germane to the investigation. Most people assumed, prior to the [Snowden leaks], that this provision was being used on discrete occasions to obtain individual collections of records about known counterintelligence or terrorist suspects—for records showing, say, that a certain person made certain purchases from a certain vendor or used a particular telephone to make specific calls. . . . [But the actual NSA surveillance program] is simply different and grander in scope and scale from anything we had thought the law meant. (Chesney & Wittes 2013: paras. 18, 21)

Other critics go further by arguing that even though the NSA surveillance programs revealed by Snowden are legal under various statutory laws, these laws are unconstitutional under the Fourth Amendment (e.g., Donohue 2013). On the other hand, the NSA maintains that these programs have prevented dozens of terrorist attacks.

- Do you think that Article II gives the U.S. president the inherent constitutional authority to wiretap in the name of national security that FISA cannot abrogate? Or do you feel that FISA reflects Congress's view that it has the authority to regulate the president's use of any inherent constitutional authority to conduct warrantless surveillance. Explain your reasoning.

- Separate and apart from FISA concerns, do you think that evidence gathered by the U.S. government under a program like PRISM would be admissible in a criminal prosecution for terrorism activities, or would the Fourth Amendment bar the use of such evidence? Why?

- What if, instead of evidence of terrorism, the U.S. government uncovered evidence using PRISM of interstate criminal activity involving drug smuggling, human trafficking, child pornography, or a similar major crime? Do you think that the Fourth Amendment should prevent the use of such evidence in a criminal prosecution for such crimes?

- In the wake of the most recent disclosures about the NSA surveillance program, legal scholars and civil libertarians have called for a reexamination of intelligence surveillance laws. On the other hand, both Democrats and Republicans in Congress explain that NSA surveillance programs are essential counter-terrorism tools. Where do you stand on this matter? Explain your reasoning.

Continued on next page

KEY POINTS

L10
- Title III does not regulate foreign intelligence surveillance. Rather, FISA authorizes and regulates the electronic surveillance and physical searches of foreign powers and their agents as well as any individual or group that is not linked to a foreign government but who "engages in international terrorism or activities in preparation therefor."

- FISA does not regulate U.S. governmental intelligence operations outside of the United States. Extraterritorial investigations remain within the scope of the national security exemption to the warrant requirement of the Fourth Amendment.

- Although any federal agent may apply for a FISA warrant, each application must first be approved by the U.S. attorney general. Moreover, such an application must contain information similar to what Title III requires for other electronic surveillance warrants with one notable exception. Unlike normal search warrants or Title III intercept orders, FISA warrants may be issued without any showing of probable cause to believe that a crime has been or is being committed. Rather, FISA only requires probable cause that the surveillance is of an authorized person or group and that a "significant purpose" of the surveillance relates to the gathering of foreign intelligence or preventing terrorism.

L11
- Normally, applications for FISA warrants are reviewed by a special Article III court called the Foreign Intelligence Surveillance Court (FISC). If the FISC denies an application, that denial may be appealed by the U.S. Department of Justice to the Foreign Intelligence Surveillance Court of Review. However, the president, through the U.S. attorney

In the wake of the NSA's wiretapping during the administration of President George W. Bush, Congress amended FISA such that the attorney general may not bypass the FISC if the target of the surveillance is a U.S. citizen or registered resident alien. Intelligence surveillance of such people may only occur if the FISC issues a warrant based on a finding that there is probable cause that the target is a member of a foreign terrorist group or an agent of a foreign power. Moreover, no U.S. citizen or registered resident alien may be deemed an agent of a foreign power just because they exercise their First Amendment rights expressing support for a foreign power.

FISA permits the attorney general to authorize domestic surveillance in an emergency situation in which seeking FISC approval would unnecessarily delay the gathering of necessary evidence. 50 U.S.C. § 1805(e). If this emergency provision is used, however, the attorney general must (1) notify the FISC at the time of his or her authorization to conduct an emergency search; and (2) within seven days, have the FISC approve his or her actions after the fact and authorize any continued surveillance, if necessary.

Challenging FISA Surveillance Warrants A defendant may challenge the admissibility of such evidence on the grounds that "the information was unlawfully acquired" or that "the surveillance was not made in conformity with an order of authorization or approval." 50 U.S.C. § 1806(e). However, given the sensitive nature of information that may be at stake in an espionage or terrorism case, these motions are not decided in open court *Franks* hearings. Rather, FISA authorizes courts to conduct *ex parte, in camera reviews* of surveillance materials if the U.S. attorney general certifies under oath that "disclosure or an adversary hearing would harm the national security of the United States." 50 U.S.C. § 1806(f). This means that a judge may review the relevant information on his or her own, without all of the information being disclosed to defense counsel or being revealed in open court. Defendants have challenged *ex parte, in camera* reviews on the grounds that the process violates due process, equal protection, separation of powers, the Sixth Amendment Confrontation Clause, and the Sixth Amendment right to counsel, but courts have routinely rejected these challenges and have uniformly upheld closed review procedures by FISC judges. *See, e.g., United States v. Nicholson*, 955 F. Supp. 588 (E.D. Va. 1997); *United States v. Benkahla*, 437 F. Supp. 2d 541 (E.D. Va. 2006).

SUMMARY

Electronic surveillance was originally considered beyond the coverage of the Fourth Amendment because it involved no trespass into the defendant's premises and no seizure of tangible items. In a series of U.S. Supreme Court decisions in the mid-1960s, the Court reversed this approach and held that electronic surveillance by agents of the government is a search and seizure governed by the Fourth Amendment. The leading case adopting this new approach was *Katz v. United States*, which expanded the focus of the Fourth Amendment beyond property right to privacy interests. In addition, the Court held that electronic surveillance is permissible only if conducted pursuant to a warrant that carefully limits the surveillance in nature, scope, and duration.

In 1968, Congress enacted Title III of the Omnibus Crime Control and Safe Streets Act, which attempts to balance the need to use electronic surveillance for effective law enforcement against the need to protect individuals' privacy rights. Title III provides for judicial supervision of all aspects of electronic surveillance and establishes warrant procedures similar to those required for the search and seizure of tangible objects. These procedures are designed to limit who can authorize an application for an interception order, who can apply for an order, the duration of electronic surveillance allowed, and various aspects of the execution of an interception order.

The coverage of Title III has many exceptions. Title III does not protect a party to a conversation who has no reasonable expectation of privacy with respect to that conversation. If one party to a conversation consents to the interception of that conversation, the conversation may be used against the other party. Title III does not apply to the use of electronic devices such as beepers, trap-and-trace devices, and pen registers, although the installation and use of these devises is regulated by other federal laws. Title III covers intercepts from cell phone conversations, but does not cover real-time, cell-site tracking or tracking by GPS.

Although an interception order is required to intercept wire, oral, or electronic communications, judicial approval is not required to covertly enter premises to install a listening device. Neither is an interception order required to intercept wire, oral, or electronic communications in emergencies involving immediate danger of death or serious physical injury, or conspiracies threatening national security or involving organized crime, although an interception order must be applied for within forty-eight hours of the emergency interception.

An illegal search and seizure by either a private or state actor under Title III, whether caused by a failure to comply with warrant procedures or by a failure to satisfy one of the exceptions to the warrant requirement, results in application of the exclusionary rule to illegally intercepted wire or oral communications. Thus, evidence obtained from an illegal interception of a wire or oral communication is inadmissible in court, often resulting in termination of the prosecution and release of the person charged. And even though the exclusionary rule does not apply to illegally intercepted electronic communications, people, including law enforcement officers, who conduct an illegal search or seizure of a wire, oral, or electronic communication may be civilly or criminally liable for their actions.

Searches and seizures concerning foreign intelligence and antiterrorism efforts are authorized and regulated by the Foreign Intelligence Surveillance Act. FISA applies to domestic electronic surveillance and physical searches of foreign powers and their agents, as well as any individual or group that is not linked to a foreign government but who "engages in international terrorism or activities in preparation therefor." FISA warrants do not need to be supported by probable cause in the traditional sense; rather, they may be issued upon certification from the U.S. attorney general that the surveillance is of an authorized person or group and that a "significant purpose" of the surveillance relates to the gathering of foreign intelligence or preventing terrorism. Although FISA warrant applications are normally reviewed by a special Article III court called the Foreign Intelligence Surveillance Court, the president, through the U.S. attorney general, is authorized to approve an application for FISA surveillance for periods up to one year without FISC approval under certain circumstances so long as FISA procedures are followed and such surveillance is reported to Congress and filed under seal with the FISC.

KEY TERMS

accessible to the public
  exception 192
aggrieved person 189
antiforensics 177
aural transfer 183
computer forensics 176
computer trespasser exception 192
consent surveillance 191
electronic communication 183
Electronic Communications Privacy
  Act (ECPA) of 1986 192
electronic surveillance 181

ex parte, in camera review 208
Foreign Intelligence Surveillance Act
  (FISA) 203
Foreign Intelligence Surveillance
  Court (FISC) 205
GPS 196
intercept 183
minimization requirements 186
mosaic theory 196
Omnibus Crime Control and Safe
  Streets Act of 1968 182
oral communication 183

pen register 192
provider exception 192
real-time, cell-site data searching 197
roving wiretap 185
Stored Communications Act (SCA) 198
tone-only pagers 195
tracking beeper 194
trap-and-trace device 192
under seal 188
video surveillance 193
wire communication 183

REVIEW AND DISCUSSION QUESTIONS

1. How are warrants for searches of ESI like warrants for traditional physical searches? How do they differ?

2. How does the plain view doctrine affect ESI searches? What steps can investigators conducting computer forensics take to make sure that any evidence beyond the scope of a warrant authorizing an ESI search that is found in plain view will subsequently be admissible in a prosecution on the unrelated crime?

3. How is a Title III interception order different from a standard search warrant?

4. Name and discuss four types of electronic surveillance that either are not covered by or are specifically exempted from coverage of Title III of the Omnibus Crime Control and Safe Streets Act of 1968.

5. How did the Communications Privacy Act of 1986 and the Stored Wire and Electronic Communications

and Transactional Records Access Act alter the use of pen registers, trap-and-trace devices, and tracking beepers?

6. Explain some of the current privacy concerns regarding searches of e-mail, voicemail, text messages, and social media.

7. Explain the controversy in the courts concerning the use of real-time, cell-site data searching in order to track the location of a cell phone's user.

8. Compare and contrast the standards for issuance of a Title III interception order and a FISA warrant that authorizes electronic surveillance.

9. Under what circumstances must applications for FISA warrants be reviewed and issued by the FISC as opposed to ones that may be initially authorized by the executive branch of the federal government?

6 Administrative and Special Needs Searches

LO1 DIFFERENTIATE an administrative search warrant from a criminal search warrant.

LO2 EXPLAIN the meaning of and rationale justifying *special needs* searches.

LO3 COMPARE and contrast the special needs searches allowing for warrantless searches and seizures based on reasonable suspicion and those permitting warrantless searches and seizures without any particularized suspicion.

Protecting public safety is among the highest of governmental priorities. Certain governmental activities aimed at protecting the public health, safety, and welfare have a long history of regulatory enforcement that is quite different—in both practice and intent—from criminal investigation. As a result, the usual strictures of the Fourth Amendment have been modified to allow for more flexible enforcement of laws that keep us safer.

Enforcement of administrative or regulatory law is therefore governed not by normal criminal investigatory search warrants, but instead by administrative search warrants. Similarly, other searches and seizures that serve a special public safety need other than the enforcement of criminal law have given rise to the *special needs doctrine*: a theoretical framework for examining governmental searches and seizures that need not comply with the usual Fourth Amendment requirements of a warrant based on probable cause.

Administrative Search Warrants

An administrative search is a routine inspection of a home or business by governmental authorities responsible for determining compliance with various statutes and regulations. An administrative search seeks to enforce fire, health, safety, and housing codes; licensing provisions; and the like. Whereas a criminal search is directed toward gathering evidence to convict a person of a crime, an administrative search ordinarily does not result in a criminal prosecution.

Special Warrant Requirements for Administrative Searches

In 1967, in *Camara v. Municipal Court*, 387 U.S. 523 (involving the safety inspection of a dwelling) and *See v. City of Seattle*, 387 U.S. 541 (involving inspection of business premises for fire safety reasons), the U.S. Supreme Court reversed earlier decisions and held that administrative inspections were subject to the warrant requirement of the Fourth Amendment. The basis for both decisions was the Court's belief that a person's right of privacy should not be determined by the nature of the search. In *Camara*, the Court said, "It is surely anomalous to say that the individual and his private property are fully protected by the Fourth Amendment only when the individual is suspected of criminal behavior." 387 U.S. at 530. In *See*, the Court said that "a businessman, like the occupant of a residence, has a constitutional right to go about his business free from unreasonable official entries upon his private commercial property." 387 U.S. at 543. Nevertheless, because administrative searches differ in nature and purpose from criminal searches, the Court held that the probable cause standard for administrative searches differs in nature and is less stringent than the standard for criminal searches. *Marshall v. Barlow's, Inc.*, 436 U.S. 307, 320–21 (1978), involving a search of a business for occupational safety reasons, explained the less stringent probable cause standard:

> Probable cause in the criminal law sense is not required. For purposes of an administrative search such as this, probable cause justifying the issuance of a warrant may be based not only on specific evidence of an existing violation but also on a showing that "reasonable legislative or administrative standards for conducting an . . . inspection are satisfied with respect to a particular [establishment]" [citing *Camara*]. A warrant showing that a specific business has been chosen for an [Occupational Safety and Health Agency] search on the basis of a general administrative plan for the enforcement of the Act derived from neutral sources such as, for example, dispersion of employees in various types of industries across a given area, and the desired frequency of searches in any of the lesser divisions of the area, would protect an employer's Fourth Amendment rights.

Exceptions to Administrative Warrant Requirements

In spite of the commands of *Camara* and *See* and their less stringent probable cause standard, the Supreme Court began to reshape the landscape for administrative searches in *Collonade Catering Corp. v. United States*, 397 U.S. 72 (1970). In that case, the Court refused to apply *See* to inspections performed under the federal liquor law. Finding that there was a long history of pervasive regulation in the liquor industry, the Court upheld a provision of federal law that allowed for a warrantless inspection of places in which liquor was sold. In doing so, the Court began to pave the way for a warrant exception for certain types of administrative searches.

Two years after deciding *Collonade Catering*, the Supreme Court recognized another exception allowing warrantless inspection of certain licensed and closely regulated enterprises in *United States v. Biswell*, 406 U.S. 311 (1972). *Biswell* upheld a warrantless search of a gun dealer's storeroom licensed under the Gun Control Act of 1968. The Court said:

> [I]f inspection is to be effective and serve as a credible deterrent, unannounced, even frequent, inspections are essential. In this context, the prerequisite of a warrant could easily frustrate inspection; and if the necessary flexibility as to time, scope, and frequency is to be preserved, the protections afforded by a warrant would be negligible. It is also plain that inspections for compliance with the Gun Control Act pose only limited threats to the dealer's justifiable expectations of privacy. When a dealer chooses to engage in this pervasively regulated business and to accept a federal license, he does so with the knowledge that his business records, firearms, and ammunition will be subject to effective inspection. 406 U.S. at 316.

A few years later, in *Donovan v. Dewey*, 452 U.S. 594 (1981), the Court upheld warrantless inspections of mines, again finding the mining industry to be so comprehensively regulated that the statutory and regulatory scheme provided adequate notice to the owners of businesses that they could be inspected at any time without additional, prior notice. And a few years after that, the Supreme Court clarified its administrative search jurisprudence by holding, in *New York v. Burger*, 482 U.S. 691 (1987), that warrantless inspections of licensed and closely regulated enterprises are reasonable if they satisfy three criteria:

1. a "substantial" government interest must support the regulatory scheme under which the inspection is made;
2. warrantless inspections must be necessary to further the regulatory scheme; and
3. the regulatory statute must provide a constitutionally adequate substitute for a warrant by advising the owner of commercial premises that the search is being made pursuant to the law, has a properly defined scope, and limits the discretion of the inspecting officers.

In *Burger*, the Court found that a New York statute allowing warrantless inspection of automobile junkyards satisfied these criteria. The state had a substantial interest in regulating the automobile junkyard industry because motor vehicle theft had increased in the state and was associated with this industry. Warrantless inspections were necessary because frequent and unannounced inspections provide an element of surprise crucial to regulating the market in stolen cars and parts. Finally, the statute gave adequate notice to automobile junkyard operators and authorized inspections only during business hours and within a narrowly defined scope.

Distinguishing Between Administrative and Criminal Searches

The line between an administrative and a criminal search sometimes blurs. In distinguishing between them, it is important to look at the search's purpose and competing privacy expectations.

When an administrative search begins to take on the characteristics of a criminal search, the stricter standards applicable to criminal searches apply. If these standards are not satisfied, any evidence obtained is inadmissible in a criminal prosecution.

Fire investigations often require both administrative and criminal searches because they serve several different purposes and present varying degrees of emergency. In addition, reasonable privacy expectations may remain in fire-damaged premises, necessitating compliance with the Fourth Amendment:

> Privacy expectations will vary with the type of property, the amount of fire damage, the prior and continued use of the premises, and in some cases the owner's efforts to secure it against intruders. Some fires may be so devastating that no reasonable privacy interests remain in the ash and ruins, regardless of the owner's subjective expectations. The test essentially is an objective one: whether "the expectation [is] one that society is prepared to recognize as 'reasonable.'" . . . If reasonable privacy interests remain in the fire-damaged property, the warrant requirement applies, and any official entry must be made pursuant to a warrant in the absence of consent or exigent circumstances. *Michigan v. Clifford*, 464 U.S. 287, 292–93 (1984).

If a warrant is necessary because a reasonable expectation of privacy remains in the premise and no exception to the warrant requirement applies, the purpose of the search determines the type of warrant required. If the primary purpose is to determine the cause and origin of a recent fire, only an administrative warrant is needed. To obtain an administrative warrant, "fire officials need show only that a fire of undetermined origin has occurred on the premises, that the scope of the proposed search is reasonable and will not intrude unnecessarily on the fire victim's privacy, and that the search will be executed at a reasonable and convenient time." 464 U.S. at 294. If the primary purpose of the search is to gather evidence of criminal activity, a criminal search warrant may be obtained only on a showing of probable cause to believe that particularly described seizable property will be found in the place to be searched.

Criminal Evidence Discovered in Administrative Search

Evidence of criminal activity discovered during the course of a valid administrative search may be seized under the plain view doctrine. Chapter 5 introduced the plain view doctrine in the context of searches for electronically stored information (ESI). Although plain view is covered in more detail in Chapter 10, it is important to understand the doctrine's relevance to administrative searches. As the U.S. Supreme Court explained in *Minnesota v. Dickerson*, 508 U.S. 366, 375 (1993), an administrative search is permissible if

- police are lawfully in a position from which they view an object (i.e., police must have a prior valid justification for intrusion into a zone of privacy); and
- there is probable cause to believe that the observed object in plain view is incriminating in nature (i.e., the object's incriminating character must be immediately apparent).

The plain view doctrine allows evidence of criminal activity discovered during the course of a valid administrative search to be used to establish probable cause to obtain a criminal search warrant. Fire officials may not, however, rely on such evidence to expand the scope of their administrative search without first satisfying an independent judicial officer that probable cause exists for a criminal search. The purpose of the search is important even if exigent circumstances exist:

> Circumstances that justify a warrantless search for the cause of a fire may not justify a search to gather evidence of criminal activity once that cause

has been determined. If, for example, the administrative search is justified by the immediate need to ensure against rekindling, the scope of the search may be no broader than reasonably necessary to achieve its end. A search to gather evidence of criminal activity not in plain view must be made pursuant to a criminal warrant upon a traditional showing of probable cause. *Michigan v. Clifford*, 464 at 294–95.

An administrative search took on the characteristics of a criminal search in *Michigan v. Tyler*, 436 U.S. 499 (1978), involving a late-night fire in a furniture store leased by the defendant. When the fire was reduced to smoldering embers, the fire chief, while investigating the cause of the fire, discovered two plastic containers of flammable liquid. He summoned a police detective who took several pictures but because visibility was hindered by darkness, steam, and smoke, departed the scene at 4:00 A.M. and returned shortly after daybreak to continue the investigation. More evidence of arson was found and seized at that time. About a month later, a state police arson investigator made several visits to the fire scene and obtained evidence that was used at trial in convicting the defendant. At no time was any warrant or consent to search obtained. The Court held that the investigative activity on the date of the fire was legal but that the evidence-gathering activity a month after the fire was an illegal search and seizure:

> [W]e hold that an entry to fight a fire requires no warrant, and that once in the building, officials may remain there for a reasonable time to investigate the cause of the blaze. Thereafter, additional entries to investigate the cause of the fire must be made pursuant to the warrant procedures governing administrative searches. . . . Evidence of arson discovered in the course of such investigations is admissible at trial, but if the investigating officials find probable cause to believe that arson has occurred and require further access to gather evidence for a possible prosecution, they may obtain a warrant only upon a traditional showing of probable cause applicable to searches for evidence of crime. 436 U.S. at 511–12.

To summarize, once an administrative search focuses on gathering evidence for a criminal prosecution, a criminal search warrant must be obtained or the search must satisfy an exception to the warrant requirement.

Special Needs Searches

In much the same way that the plain view doctrine recognizes that enforcing the warrant requirement is impracticable under certain circumstances, certain types of searches, when conducted for a special governmental need other than the investigation of criminal activity, not only excuse the usual requirement of a warrant but also can occur without probable cause. Under the **special needs doctrine**, such searches are evaluated under the *reasonableness* standard of the Fourth Amendment. The key to such searches is that they are directed at people in general, for some special need, rather than being directed at any specific individual for criminal investigatory purposes. If, however, the search yields evidence of a crime, then the evidence may be used in a criminal prosecution so long as the search was executed in a reasonable manner.

217

Courts analyzing special needs searches generally employ the following approach:

1. Is there a special need that involves a real and significant problem—"beyond the normal need for law enforcement" to detect crime—that is "sufficiently vital" to justify dispensing with the usual Fourth Amendment requirements, such as combatting employee misconduct in the public sector or promoting safety in transportation, schools, and correctional institutions? *Chandler v. Miller*, 520 U.S. 305, 313 (1997).

2. If so, would allowing searches (without probable cause and a warrant) meet these special needs?

3. If both of the previous questions are answered in the affirmative, then the reasonableness of the search must be assessed in "a context-specific inquiry" that balances the nature and quality of the intrusion on the individual's Fourth Amendment interests against the importance of the governmental special needs alleged to justify the intrusion.

Searches of Government Employees

In *O'Connor v. Ortega*, 480 U.S. 709 (1987), a psychiatrist who worked at a state hospital had his desk and files searched by a hospital administrator for evidence of misconduct that was eventually used against him at an administrative hearing that resulted in the termination of his employment. The physician subsequently sued his employer for this invasion of privacy. Although the Supreme Court found that the search did implicate the Fourth Amendment, it nonetheless sided with the employer, holding that *special needs* may justify a warrantless search of a public employee's office by the employee's supervisor. For searches conducted by a public employer, the invasion of the employee's legitimate expectations of privacy must be balanced against the government's need for supervision, control, and the efficient operation of the workplace.

> [R]equiring an employer to obtain a warrant whenever the employer wished to enter an employee's office, desk, or file cabinets for a work-related purpose would seriously disrupt the routine conduct of business and would be unduly burdensome. Imposing unwieldy warrant procedures in such cases upon supervisors, who would otherwise have no reason to be familiar with such procedures, is simply unreasonable. 480 U.S. at 722.

The Court applied a reasonableness standard rather than a probable cause standard for legitimate work-related, noninvestigatory intrusions, as well as investigations of work-related misconduct. This determination is to be made on a case-by-case basis by balancing these factors:

- whether the work area in question was given over to an employee's exclusive use,
- the extent to which others had access to the work space,
- the nature of the employment, and
- whether office regulations placed the employee on notice that certain areas were subject to employer intrusions.

For example, in *City of Ontario v. Quon*, 130 S. Ct. 2619 (2010), the U.S. Supreme Court upheld the search of a pager a municipality had issued to a SWAT team member after he exceeded his usage limit. He was disciplined for using his work pager to send sexually explicit messages. The Court sided with the city without ever having reached the issue of whether the officer's reasonable expectation of privacy had been violated.

The search was justified at its inception because there were "reasonable grounds for suspecting that the search [was] necessary for a noninvestigatory work-related purpose." The City . . . had a legitimate interest in ensuring that employees were not being forced to pay out of their own pockets for work-related expenses, or on the other hand that the City was not paying for extensive personal communications. Furthermore, . . . [e]ven if he could assume some level of privacy would inhere in his messages, it would not have been reasonable for Quon to conclude that his messages were in all circumstances immune from scrutiny. Quon was told that his messages were subject to auditing. . . . Under the circumstances, a reasonable employee would be aware that sound management principles might require the audit of messages to determine whether the pager was being appropriately used. 130 S. Ct. at 2631.

Similarly, *Gossmeyer v. McDonald*, 128 F.3d 481 (7th Cir. 1997), upheld the search of a public employee's desk and file cabinet at work. The employee in *Gossmeyer* was a child protective services investigator. A co-worker "made serious and specific allegations of misconduct—that [she] had pornographic pictures of children; and stated where those pictures could be found—in [her] file cabinets and desk." 128 F.3d at 491. Given her state-sanctioned access to and authority over children, the court found the search satisfied *Ortega's* mandates insofar as it was reasonable at the inception of the search and reasonable in terms of the scope of execution.

In contrast to *Quon* and *Gossmeyer,* the court in *Sabin v. Miller,* 423 F. Supp. 2d 943 (S.D. Iowa 2006), refused to extend *Ortega* to a situation in which state investigators entered the home of a state correctional worker to seize her computer and search for evidence that she had violated a number of the conditions of her employment in various interactions with inmates. Key to the court's decision was that the investigators entered her home to search her computer, where she had intermingled both personal and work-related files. Because the investigators intruded into Sabin's home rather than her office space at the correctional institution, any state employer's "interest in 'the efficient and proper operation of the workplace' was not as great as was the interest of the government employers under the circumstances considered in *O'Connor.*" 423 F. Supp. 2d at 950.

In *Ortega*, *Sabin*, and *Gossmeyer,* the courts all concluded that the public employee had a reasonable expectation of privacy in the area that was searched. But if a public employee does not have a reasonable expectation of privacy in the area searched, then *Ortega's* balancing test is inapplicable because the Fourth Amendment is not implicated. For example, *Shaul v. Cherry Valley–Springfield Cent. School Dist.*, 363 F.3d 177 (2d Cir. 2004), upheld the search of a teacher's classroom, including his private desk, after the teacher had been suspended. The court reasoned:

Whatever reasonable expectation of privacy [the teacher] may have had in his classroom while he was a teacher in good standing, . . . he had no such expectation on January 30, 1999, by which date [he] had (1) been suspended from teaching and barred from his classroom, (2) surrendered the key to the classroom's locked file cabinet at the same time that he declined to retrieve his personal property from the classroom, and (3) been afforded a second opportunity to spend an hour and a half removing personal items from the classroom. 363 F.3d at 182–83.

Law enforcement personnel must understand the limited nature of *Ortega's* holding as applying to searches conducted by public employers looking for evidence of job malfeasance. "Warrantless work-related searches conducted by police should not be upheld under the *Ortega* exception because a less intrusive warrantless search by the employee's supervisor will fully realize the concern for workplace efficiency." *Rossi v. Town of Pelham*, 35 F. Supp. 2d 58, 67 (D.N.H. 1997).

Governmental Drug Testing

To protect public safety, governmental entities have sometimes required their employees to submit to drug testing. The Supreme Court has allowed these practices under circumstances that satisfy the requirements of the special needs doctrine.

In *Skinner v. Railway Labor Executives' Ass'n.*, 489 U.S. 602 (1989), the U.S. Supreme Court upheld governmental regulations requiring railroad companies to test the blood and urine of employees involved in major train accidents and employees who violate particular safety rules. The Court found that the tests were not significant intrusions and that railroad workers have a diminished expectation of privacy because they work in a heavily regulated industry. The searches were held to be reasonable, despite the absence of individualized suspicion, because the government's significant special need to ensure public safety outweighed the employee's diminished privacy interest.

National Treasury Employees Union v. Von Raab, 489 U.S. 656 (1989), upheld Customs Service regulations requiring employees seeking transfers or promotions to certain sensitive positions within the Service to submit to urinalysis. The Court found that the government's special need to deter drug use outweighed the diminished privacy interests of the employees. Specifically, the Court emphasized the public interest in "ensuring that front-line interdiction personnel are physically fit, and have unimpeachable integrity and judgment" [and in] "prevent[ing] the promotion of drug users to positions that require the incumbent to carry a firearm, even if the incumbent is not engaged directly in the interdiction of drugs." 489 U.S. at 670.

Relying on *Von Raab, National Treasury Employees Union v. Yeutter*, 918 F.2d 968 (D.C. Cir. 1990), upheld random urinalysis drug testing of state motor vehicle operators, but this case invalidated the mandatory drug testing of employees who did not hold safety or security-sensitive jobs without reasonable suspicion of on-duty drug use or drug-impaired work performance.

The decision in *Yeutter* illustrates how a random, suspicionless search must be justified by some special need that goes beyond general law enforcement. Not all cases, however, prevent strong enough justifications to qualify as a bona fide special need. For example, *Chandler v. Miller*, 520 U.S. 305 (1997), struck down as unconstitutional a Georgia statute requiring candidates for designated state offices to certify that they have taken a drug test within thirty days prior to qualifying for nomination or election and that the test result was negative. The Court found that the alleged incompatibility of unlawful drug use with holding high state office was not sufficiently important to qualify as a special need for drug testing of candidates for state office: "[T]he proffered special need for drug testing must be substantial—important enough to override the individual's acknowledged privacy interest, sufficiently vital to suppress the Fourth Amendment's normal requirement of individualized suspicion." 520 U.S. at 318. The need to deter unlawful drug users from attaining high state office was not considered a concrete danger giving rise to a special need to depart from the Fourth Amendment's usual requirements, especially because there was no evidence of a drug problem among the state's elected officials; those officials did not perform high-risk, safety-sensitive tasks; and the required certification of nondrug use did not immediately aid any drug interdiction effort.

The court in *Robinson v. City of Seattle*, 10 P.3d 452 (Wash. App. 2000), similarly refused to uphold a policy requiring a drug test for a broad array of government employment applicants. The court ruled that such a policy would only be permissible with regard to "applicants whose duties will genuinely implicate public safety... [such as] sworn police officers and firefighters, and positions requiring an employee to carry a firearm." 10 P.3d at 470.

Distinguishing Special Needs Drug Testing from Law Enforcement Goals In *Michigan Dep't of State Police v. Sitz*, 496 U.S. 444, 447 (1990), the Supreme

Court upheld a program that established roadside sobriety checkpoints without a warrant or particularized suspicion:

> All vehicles passing through a checkpoint would be stopped and their drivers briefly examined for signs of intoxication. In cases where a checkpoint officer detected signs of intoxication, the motorist would be directed to a location out of the traffic flow where an officer would check the motorist's driver's license and car registration and, if warranted, conduct further sobriety tests. Should the field tests and the officer's observations suggest that the driver was intoxicated, an arrest would be made. All other drivers would be permitted to resume their journey immediately.

Although the stops were determined to be "seizures" within the meaning of the Fourth Amendment, the Court upheld them even though they occurred without a warrant or individual suspicion. Key to the Court's reasoning was the fact that a significant public safety need met by these motor vehicle stops outweighed the minimal intrusions such stops caused to drivers' privacy rights.

In contrast, the U.S. Supreme Court invalidated a program in which a warrantless highway checkpoint had been established to discover and interdict illegal drugs in *City of Indianapolis v. Edmond*, 531 U.S. 32 (2000). Unlike the special need in *Sitz* for which the sobriety checkpoint had been designed—namely, public safety reasons—the primary purpose of the program at issue in *Edmund* was related to crime control. Thus, the Court refused to allow warrantless, suspicionless searches.

Ferguson v. Charleston, 532 U.S. 67 (2001), held unconstitutional a state hospital's policy involving warrantless, suspicionless, and nonconsensual testing of pregnant women for cocaine to obtain evidence for criminal prosecution. The policy, in which law enforcement authorities were extensively involved, used the threat of prosecution to coerce the patients into substance abuse treatment. Comparing this case to *Skinner*, *Von Raab*, and *Chandler*, the Court found the invasion of privacy here far more substantial than in the previous cases because the special needs in the prior cases were divorced from the State's general interest in law enforcement. In *Ferguson*, however, "the central and indispensable feature of the policy from its inception was the use of law enforcement to coerce the patients into substance abuse treatment." 532 U.S. at 80.

Searches in Correctional Facilities

Jails and prisons are "unique place[s] fraught with serious security dangers. Smuggling of money, drugs, weapons, and other contraband is all too common an occurrence." *Bell v. Wolfish*, 441 U.S. 520, 559 (1979). Keeping correctional institutions as safe as possible is a bona fide special need that justifies warrantless and suspicionless searches of inmates, visitors, and others.

Searches of Cells "The recognition of privacy rights for prisoners in their individual cells simply cannot be reconciled with the concept of incarceration and the needs and objectives of penal institutions." *Hudson v. Palmer*, 468 U.S. 517, 526 (1984). Accordingly, prisoners have no reasonable expectation of privacy in their cells, and the Fourth Amendment thus does not apply to searches conducted in an inmate's cell or to seizure of items found inside it. In fact, even searches that occur out of a malicious motivation are beyond the scope of Fourth Amendment protections. 468 U.S. at 519–20.

Searches of Persons Given a correctional institution's compelling interest in preventing contraband from entering its facility, strip searches—even those including body cavity searches—are constitutionally permissible, so long as they are not done in an abusive manner. *Bull v. City & Cnty. of San Francisco*, 595 F.3d 964 (9th Cir. 2010). In *Florence v. Board of Chosen Freeholders of County of Burlington*, 132 S. Ct. 1510 (2012), the U.S. Supreme Court upheld a local jail's policy of strip searching every person being booked into the jail, even those arrested on minor offenses. The Court reasoned that such policies allow officials to reduce "danger of introducing lice or contagious infections," to identify "wounds or other injuries requiring immediate medical attention," to identify certain tattoos and other signs of gang affiliation, and to detect contraband:

> Lighters and matches are fire and arson risks or potential weapons. Cell phones are used to orchestrate violence and criminality both within and without jailhouse walls. Pills and medications enhance suicide risks. Chewing gum can block locking devices; hairpins can open handcuffs; wigs can conceal drugs and weapons. Something as simple as an overlooked pen can pose a significant danger. Inmates commit more than 10,000 assaults on correctional staff every year and many more among themselves. Contraband creates additional problems because scarce items, including currency, have value in a jail's culture and underground economy. 132 S. Ct. at 1519.

Correctional officers must take care, however, to make sure that the manner in which they conduct strip searches are reasonable, and therefore, constitutional. In *Vaughn v. Ricketts*, 859 F.2d 736 (9th Cir. 1988), *cert. denied*, 490 U.S. 1012 (1989), digital rectal cavity searches performed on inmates were found to be so brutal and offensive to human dignity that it shocked the conscience of the court. The searches had been performed in an open hallway on an unsanitary table. The medical assistants who performed the searches did not wash their hands between searches, nor did they inspect medical records to ensure that individual inmates did not have medical conditions that made the searches dangerous.

DISCUSSION POINT

Should the State Review Patient Prescriptions? *Murphy v. State*, 62 P.3d 533 (Wash. 2003).

A Washington state statute provides:

> Every proprietor or manager of a pharmacy shall keep readily available a suitable record of prescriptions which shall preserve for a period of not less than two years the record of every prescription dispensed at such pharmacy which shall be numbered, dated, and filed, and shall produce the same in court or before any grand jury whenever lawfully required to do so.

The record shall be maintained either separately from all other records of the pharmacy or in such form that the information required is readily retrievable from ordinary business records of the pharmacy. All record-keeping requirements for controlled substances must be complied with. Such record of prescriptions shall be for confidential use in the pharmacy, only. *The record of prescriptions shall be open for inspection by the board of pharmacy or any officer of the law, who is authorized to enforce* [relevant drug and pharmacy laws].

A review by the state pharmacy board of the defendant's prescription resulted in his being prosecuted for having obtained prescription narcotic drugs by deceit. He argued that the purpose of the pharmacy statute was to require recordkeeping and allow inspection for the purpose of regulating pharmacies, but not to allow a warrantless examination of a patient's prescription records to gather criminal evidence against the patient. The court rejected this contention and ruled that by indicating pharmacy records shall be "open for inspection . . . by any officer of the law," the legislature clearly contemplated unrestricted access by the appropriate law enforcement personnel.

In upholding the constitutionality of the statute and a search performed pursuant to it, the court found that the regulation of the warrantless review of patients' prescription information was a part of a valid special

Continued on next page

needs search. The court focused on the fact that the governmental interest in monitoring the flow of drugs from pharmacies to patients outweighed a patient's limited expectation of privacy. The court wrote:

> When a patient brings a prescription to a pharmacist, the patient has a right to expect that his or her use of a particular drug will not be disclosed arbitrarily or randomly. But a reasonable patient buying narcotic prescription drugs knows or should know that the State, which outlaws the distribution and use of such drugs without a prescription, will keep careful watch over the flow of such drugs from pharmacies to patients. 62 P.3d at 541.

After concluding that the warrantless search of the defendant's prescription records by the state pharmacy board was a lawful special needs search, the court upheld the board's disclosure of the improprieties it had discovered to law enforcement personnel.

- Do you agree with the court that such a law and the actions taken pursuant to it (i.e., the review of a patient's prescription information) fall within the realm of a special needs search? Why or why not?

- Of what consequence, if any, is the statutory inclusion of permission for law enforcement officers to review pharmacy records? Does this not transform the nature of the warrantless searches authorized under the statute into ones that have a criminal investigatory purpose, rather than ones primarily aimed at generalized public safety? Explain your position.

Searches of Probationers and Parolees

Griffin v. Wisconsin, 483 U.S. 868 (1987), upheld a warrantless search of a probationer's home by probation officers under the authority of Wisconsin's probation regulation, which permitted such searches on reasonable grounds to believe that contraband was present. When two probation officers searched Griffin's home due to suspected gun possession in violation of his probation conditions, officers indeed found such a weapon. In upholding the admissibility of the weapons seized, the Supreme Court found that the probation system's necessity for nonadversarial supervision of probationers is a special need justifying lessened Fourth Amendment protection for the probationer. This special need makes the warrant requirement impracticable and justifies replacement of the probable cause standard by a reasonable grounds standard. The Court said:

> A warrant requirement would interfere to an appreciable degree with the probation system, setting up a magistrate rather than the probation officer as the judge of how close a [level of] supervision the probationer requires. Moreover, the delay inherent in obtaining a warrant would make it more difficult for probation officials to respond quickly to evidence of misconduct . . . and would reduce the deterrent effect that the possibility of expeditious searches would otherwise create. 483 U.S. at 876.

The logic of *Griffin* applies to parolees as well. *E.g.*, *Motley v. Parks*, 432 F.3d 1072 (9th Cir. 2005); *United States v. Trujillo*, 404 F.3d 1238 (10th Cir. 2005). A probation or parole search, however, should not serve as a subterfuge or ruse for a criminal investigation. Probation and parole officers may work together with police, provided that the correctional personnel are pursuing probation- or parole-related objectives and are not acting as "a stalking horse for the police." *United States v. McFarland*, 116 F.3d 316, 318 (8th Cir. 1997).

United States v. Knights, 534 U.S. 112 (2001), reaffirmed the reasonable suspicion approach to searches of probationer and parolees. In *Knights*, a warrantless search was conducted based on a document that the defendant had signed as a condition of probation. The agreement provided for police access to his "person, property, place of residence, vehicle, personal effects, to search at anytime, with or without a search warrant, warrant of arrest or reasonable cause by any probation officer or law enforcement officer." 534 U.S. at 114. The defendant challenged the constitutionality of the document because there was no special need beyond normal law enforcement to support a warrantless search. The Supreme Court did not address the issue of defendant's consent for the search, evidenced by him signing the document, because it found that the search was reasonable under the Fourth Amendment, regardless of consent as a result of the police having reasonable suspicion to conduct the search. Thus, *Knights* stands for the proposition that law enforcement authorities need only reasonable suspicion to conduct a warrantless search of probationers or parolees, their homes, and their belongings. Key to the Court's rationale was that probationers and parolees have a diminished expectation of privacy that is outweighed when balanced against the government's concern that the defendant "will be more likely to engage in criminal conduct than an ordinary member of the community." 534 U.S. at 121.

The Court did not consider the question, however, if a condition of release could "so diminish or eliminate a released prisoner's reasonable expectation of privacy" such that a suspicionless search by a law enforcement officer would be permissible under the Fourth Amendment. *Samson v. California*, 547 U.S. 843, 847 (2006). But the Court answered that question in the affirmative in *Samson*, when it upheld the suspicionless search of a parolee. Under California law, all parolees are required to sign an agreement as a condition of their release that consents to warrantless, suspicionless searches for the duration of their parole. The Supreme Court did not apply a special needs analysis, but rather upheld the law under the "general Fourth Amendment principle" of reasonableness. 547 U.S. at 848.

Thus, warrantless searches of probationers and parolees will depend on the law of the particular jurisdiction. If state law permits warrantless, suspicionless searches as a condition of release, then such searches would be valid under *Samson*. If, however, state law does not authorize warrantless, suspicionless searches as a condition of release, then a warrantless search would be constitutionally permissible only if there were reasonable suspicion that the probationer or parolee were involved in criminal activity.

Searches of Elementary and High School Students

Our school systems are another example of places that require special measures to be taken in order to protect the health, safety, and well-being of the students. To help achieve this goal, the courts have established a specialized set of criteria governing searches of elementary and high school students.[1]

The Fourth Amendment Applies, but the Warrant Requirement Does Not In *New Jersey v. T.L.O.*, 469 U.S. 325 (1985), a fourteen-year-old girl was suspected of smoking cigarettes in a high school lavatory in violation of school policy. The school's vice principal questioned the girl about her smoking; and when she denied smoking, the vice principal demanded to see her purse. Upon looking in the girl's purse, the vice principal not only saw a pack of cigarettes but also some rolling papers typically used for smoking marijuana. This prompted the vice principal to search the purse more thoroughly. That search yielded a "small amount of marijuana, a pipe, a number of empty plastic bags, a substantial quantity of money in one dollar bills, an index card that appeared to be a list of students who owed T.L.O. money, and two letters that implicated T.L.O. in marijuana dealing." 469 U.S. at 328. The school turned over the evidence to the police who, in turn, used the evidence in juvenile delinquency proceedings against the girl. The Supreme Court upheld the actions of the vice principal.

First, the Court affirmed that the Fourth Amendment was clearly applicable to the search in question because "public school officials do not merely exercise authority voluntarily conferred on them by individual parents; rather, they act in furtherance of publicly mandated educational and disciplinary policies." 469 U.S. at 336. The Court went on to reject the state's argument that students in public schools have

---

[1] Fradella, H. F., and J. Connelly. (2007). "The 'Incredible Shrinking Amendment' Redux: Continued Erosion of the Fourth Amendment Rights of Students." *Criminal Law Bulletin*, 42(2), 246–251. Reprinted with the gracious permission of Thomson/West and the *Criminal Law Bulletin*.

no reasonable expectation of privacy in their personal effects while at school. However, given the substantial state interest in maintaining security, order, and an appropriate educational environment in public schools, the Court concluded that the full protection of the Fourth Amendment was not applicable in the public school setting.

> It is evident that the school setting requires some easing of the restrictions to which searches by public authorities are ordinarily subject. The warrant requirement, in particular, is unsuited to the school environment; requiring a teacher to obtain a warrant before searching a child suspected of an infraction of school rules (or of the criminal law) would unduly interfere with the maintenance of the swift and informal disciplinary procedures needed in the schools. Just as we have in other cases dispensed with the warrant requirement when "the burden of obtaining a warrant is likely to frustrate the governmental purpose behind the search," . . . we hold today that school officials need not obtain a warrant before searching a student who is under their authority.
>
> The school setting also requires some modification of the level of suspicion of illicit activity needed to justify a search. Ordinarily, a search, even one that may permissibly be carried out without a warrant, must be based upon "probable cause" to believe that a violation of the law has occurred. However, "probable cause" is not an irreducible requirement of a valid search. . . . [W]e have in a number of cases recognized the legality of searches and seizures based on suspicions that, although "reasonable," do not rise to the level of probable cause. 469 U.S. at 340–41 (internal citations omitted).

Applying these principles to the vice principal's actions, the Court determined his initial search of the girl's purse was reasonable because a teacher had reported that the girl had been smoking in a lavatory. Given the teacher's report of her smoking, coupled with her denial, the Court concluded it was reasonable for the vice principal to check the girl's purse because "if she did have cigarettes, her purse was the obvious place in which to find them." 469 U.S. at 346. And, once the vice principal saw the rolling papers, the Court determined he had reason to suspect the purse contained further contraband, making his continued search of the purse reasonable.

The Diminution of Suspicion for Drug and Alcohol Testing With the knowledge that warrantless searches of students were constitutionally permissible with less suspicion than probable cause, a number of school districts adopted policies permitting random, suspicionless searches of students to screen for drug use. At first blush, such policies appeared to violate the constitutional requirements of the Fourth Amendment as interpreted in *T.L.O.* because they permitted students to be searched without the type of individual, particularized suspicion that had existed against the girl suspected of smoking in *T.L.O.* Such policies, however, were upheld by the Supreme Court in *Vernonia School District 47J v. Acton*, 515 U.S. 646 (1995), at least as they applied to a drug testing program for student athletes.

The Court began its analysis of the issue by recognizing that high school student drug use is a matter of great concern, as it has "deleterious effects . . . on motivation, memory, judgment, reaction, coordination, and performance." 515 U.S. at 649. The Court then reiterated its line of Fourth Amendment inquiry in the student setting as set forth in *T.L.O.*, focusing on the requirement of reasonableness. Although the Court acknowledged the search at issue in *T.L.O.* was based on reasonable suspicion, it emphasized that "the Fourth Amendment imposes no irreducible requirement of such suspicion." 515 U.S. at 653. "We have upheld suspicionless searches and seizures to conduct drug testing of railroad personnel involved in train accidents;

to conduct random drug testing of federal customs officers who carry arms or are involved in drug interdiction; to maintain automobile checkpoints looking for illegal immigrants and contraband; and drunk drivers." 515 U.S. at 653–54. The Court then extended this line of reasoning to cover random, suspicionless searches of student athletes for drug and alcohol violations.

Key to the reasoning in *Vernonia* was that the already diminished expectation of privacy in the school setting was even lower for student athletes. "School sports are not for the bashful. They require 'suiting up' before each practice or event, and showering and changing afterwards. Public school locker rooms, the usual sites for these activities, are not notable for the privacy they afford." 515 U.S. at 657. Moreover, the Court reasoned that by the very nature of voluntarily "go[ing] out for the team," students "subject themselves to a degree of regulation even higher than that imposed on students generally." 515 U.S. at 657.

> In Vernonia's public schools, they must submit to a preseason physical exam . . . includ[ing] the giving of a urine sample . . . , they must acquire adequate insurance coverage or sign an insurance waiver, maintain a minimum grade point average, and comply with any "rules of conduct, dress, training hours and related matters as may be established for each sport by the head coach and athletic director with the principal's approval." 515 U.S. at 657.

Accordingly, the Court reasoned that much like adults who enter into a closely regulated industry, students who participate in school athletic programs should expect to have fewer privacy rights than might otherwise exist. Moreover, according to the majority opinion in *Vernonia*, this diminished level of privacy is what needed to be balanced against the state interest at issue in the case—namely, reducing and preventing teenage drug and alcohol use. The Court called such a need "important enough"—perhaps even 'compelling'" to justify the intrusion into student athlete's diminished privacy rights. 515 U.S. at 661. However, the Court cautioned against the assumption that suspicionless drug testing would readily pass constitutional muster in other contexts.

The Supreme Court expanded *Vernonia* when it upheld the random, suspicionless drug testing of students participating in extracurricular activities in *Board of Education of Ind. School District 92 of Pottawatomie County v. Earls*, 536 U.S. 822 (2002). As it did in *Vernonia*, the Court started with the premise that public school students have a diminished expectation of privacy while at school, and that drug testing via urinalysis posed only a minimal or "negligible" intrusion into students' privacy rights. But over a strong dissent that focused on the unique diminished expectation of privacy for student athletes in light of the factors elaborated upon in *Vernonia*, the *Earls* majority similarly asserted that "students who participate in competitive extracurricular activities voluntarily subject themselves to many of the same intrusions on their privacy as do athletes." 536 U.S. at 831. To support this proposition, the Court wrote:

> Some of these clubs and activities require occasional off-campus travel and communal undress. All of them have their own rules and requirements for participating students that do not apply to the student body as a whole. For example, each of the competitive extracurricular activities governed by the Policy must abide by the rules of the Oklahoma Secondary Schools Activities Association, and a faculty sponsor monitors the students for compliance with the various rules dictated by the clubs and activities. This regulation of extracurricular activities further diminishes the expectation of privacy among schoolchildren. 536 U.S. at 832.

Yet, as Justice Ginsburg's dissent pointed out, although athletics "require close safety and health regulation, a school's choir, band, and academic team do not." 536 U.S. at 846. The rationale offered in *Vernonia* relied on medical literature that addressed the particular dangers of drug use and physical exertion that, when combined, "pose substantial physical risks to athletes." *Vernonia*, 515 U.S. at 662. Moreover, the record in *Vernonia* demonstrated a severe drug problem in the district in which student athletes "were the leaders of the drug culture." 515 U.S. at 649. In contrast, there was no evidence that students engaging in extracurricular activities were involved with drugs. Quite the contrary, as Justice Ginsburg's dissent in *Earls* stated: "nationwide, students who participate in extracurricular activities are significantly less likely to develop substance abuse problems than are their less involved peers." 536 U.S. at 853. Thus, the policy upheld by the *Earls* Court had the ironic effect of testing students who needed drug deterrence least while risking "steering students at greatest risk for substance abuse away from extracurricular involvement that potentially may palliate drug problems." 536 U.S. at 853.

A year after *Earls* was decided, the New Jersey Supreme Court upheld an extension of a random, suspicionless drug testing program to all students who drive to school. *Joye v. Hunterdon Central Bd. of Educ.*, 826 A.2d 624 (N.J. 2003). A similar policy was also upheld by the Indiana Supreme Court. *Linke v. Northwestern School Corp.*, 763 N.E.2d 972 (Ind. 2002).

When school officials conduct a search, they must do so in a reasonable manner because even if a search by a school official is justified at its inception, it can be executed in an excessively intrusive manner, thereby rendering the search unconstitutional, such as the case explored in the next section.

Strip Searches in Schools In *Safford Unified School Dist. v. Redding*, 557 U.S. 364 (2009), a middle school student told the school principal and assistant principal that "certain students were bringing drugs and weapons on campus" and that he had been sick after taking some pills that "he got from a classmate." The boy provided assistant principal Kerry Wilson a white pill that he claimed he had received from another student, Marissa Glines. The boy also told Wilson that students were planning to take the pills at lunch.

Wilson learned from Peggy Schwallier, the school nurse, that the pill was a 400-milligram tablet of ibuprofen, available only by prescription. Wilson then called Marissa out of class. Outside the classroom, Marissa's teacher handed Wilson the day planner, found within Marissa's reach, containing various contraband items. Wilson escorted Marissa back to his office.

In the presence of Helen Romero, his administrative assistant, Wilson requested Marissa to turn out her pockets and open her wallet. Marissa produced a blue pill, several white ones, and a razor blade. Wilson asked where the blue pill came from, and Marissa answered, "I guess it slipped in when she gave me the IBU 400s." When Wilson asked whom she meant, Marissa replied, "Savana Redding." Wilson then inquired about the day planner and its contents; Marissa denied knowing anything about them. Wilson did not ask Marissa any follow-up questions to determine whether there was any likelihood that Savana presently had pills, asking neither when Marissa received the pills from Savana nor where Savana might be hiding them.

Wilson then entered a math classroom and asked thirteen-year-old Savana Redding to go to his office. Once there, Wilson showed her the day planner in which there were several knives, lighters, a permanent marker, and a cigarette. Wilson asked Savana whether the planner was hers. Savana said it was, but that a few days earlier, she had lent it to her friend, Marissa Glines. She stated that none of the items in the planner belonged to her.

Wilson then showed Savana four white prescription-strength ibuprofen 400-mg pills, and one over-the-counter blue naproxen 200-mg pill, all used for pain and inflammation but banned under school rules without advance permission. He asked Savana if she knew anything about the pills. Savana answered that she did not. Wilson then told Savana that he had received a report that she was giving these pills to fellow students; Savana denied it and agreed to let Wilson search her belongings. Helen Romero came into the office, and together with Wilson they searched Savana's backpack, finding nothing.

At that point, Wilson instructed Romero to take Savana to the school nurse's office to search her clothes for pills. Romero and Schwallier, the nurse, asked Savana to remove her jacket, socks, and shoes, leaving her in stretch pants and a T-shirt (both without pockets), which she was then asked to remove. Finally, Savana was told to pull her bra out and to the side and shake it, and to pull out the elastic on her underpants, thus exposing her breasts and pelvic area to some degree. No pills were found. The Supreme Court ultimately ruled that school officials went too far by exceeding the scope of a reasonable search.

> The exact label for this final step in the intrusion is not important, though strip search is a fair way to speak of it. [She was directed] to remove her clothes down to her underwear, and then "pull out" her bra and the elastic band on her underpants. Although Romero and Schwallier stated that they did not see anything when Savana followed their instructions, we would not define strip search and its Fourth Amendment consequences in a way that would guarantee litigation about who was looking and how much was seen. The very fact of Savana's pulling her underwear away from her body in the presence of the two officials who were able to see her necessarily exposed her breasts and pelvic area to some degree, and both subjective and reasonable societal expectations of personal privacy support the treatment of such a search as categorically distinct, requiring distinct elements of justification on the part of school authorities for going beyond a search of outer clothing and belongings.
>
> Savana's subjective expectation of privacy against such a search is inherent in her account of it as embarrassing, frightening, and humiliating. The reasonableness of her expectation (required by the Fourth Amendment standard) is indicated by the consistent experiences of other young people similarly searched, whose adolescent vulnerability intensifies the patent intrusiveness of the exposure. The common reaction of these adolescents simply registers the obviously different meaning of a search exposing the body from the experience of nakedness or near undress in other school circumstances. Changing for gym is getting ready for play; exposing for a search is responding to an accusation reserved for suspected wrongdoers and fairly understood as so degrading that a number of communities have decided that strip searches in schools are never reasonable and have banned them no matter what the facts may be. 557 U.S. at 374–375 (internal citations omitted).

In light of these cases, the following propositions summarize the status of the law concerning school-initiated searches of elementary and high school students:

- Physical searches of students and their possessions may be conducted by school officials without a warrant based merely on reasonable suspicion of a crime or violation of a school rule.

- Warrantless, random, suspicionless testing of students by school officials for controlled substances based on any seemingly logical reason appear to be constitutionally valid tools to combat teenage drug and alcohol use.

- A search ordered by a school official, even if justified at its inception, crosses the boundary of constitutional reasonableness if it becomes excessively intrusive, as in the case of certain strip searches, in light of the age and sex of the student and the nature of the infraction. In order to conduct a strip search of a public elementary or high school student, school officials must develop reasonable suspicion to believe contraband is present beneath the clothing/undergarments of the student. Before conducting such searches, school officials must also have reason to believe that the contraband underneath the clothing poses a danger to students in terms of its power and quantity, and that some known practice or pattern exists among students at the school of hiding the contraband underneath their clothing/undergarments. Finally, school officials must consider the age and sex of the student whom they intend to strip search. *Safford*, 557 U.S. at 375.

Searches of College Students

The law of search and seizure in the college and university setting is downright inconsistent. A comprehensive review of the case law in this area is beyond the scope of this text. Moreover, such a review would be unnecessarily confusing because there are a multitude of contradictions in cases across time and across jurisdictional lines. That being said, however, we can make a few generalizations.

Police-Initiated Investigations If law enforcement officials initiate an investigation that involves a college or university campus (whether private or public), and they gain entry to a student's room without a warrant through cooperation with school officials, such a search would be invalid and all evidence seized would be inadmissible under the Fourth Amendment. *E.g., Piazzola v. Watkins*, 316 F. Supp. 624 (M.D. Ala. 1970), *aff'd* 442 F.2d 284 (5th Cir. 1971). Similarly, if police enlist school officials to participate in a criminal investigation and get them to act on their behalf, then the school officials will be deemed state actors for Fourth Amendment purposes. Thus, police are well advised that there are no "college student exceptions" to the normal requirements of the Fourth Amendment. The materials in this subsection are concerned with searches and seizures that take place as a result of actions initially taken by college or university officials.

Actions by Private College or University Officials Courts are generally consistent in holding that the Fourth Amendment does not protect students at private colleges and universities from searches conducted by school officials. For example, in *Duarte v. Commonwealth*, 407 S.E.2d 41 (Va. App. 1991), a college official at a private university, acting at the direction of the dean of students, conducted a search of a student's room. The dean of students had been advised by police that the student was suspected of having participated in a burglary and that stolen property might be found in the student's dormitory room. Even though the police specifically asked the dean to refrain from taking any action, including searching the student's room, until the police had completed their investigation, the dean instructed two college officials to search the student's dormitory room "and to confiscate any contraband or stolen items, pursuant to the guidelines for searches and seizures set forth in the [college's] Student Handbook." 407 S.E.2d at 42. The search yielded several bags of marijuana and drug paraphernalia that the college turned over to police, which, in turn, resulted in the student being charged with possession of a controlled substance with intent to distribute. The court upheld the search and seizure finding that the Fourth Amendment was "wholly inapplicable 'to a search or seizure, even an unreasonable one, effected by a private individual not acting as an agent of the Government or with the participation or knowledge of any governmental official.'" 407 S.E.2d at 42.

State v. Burroughs, 926 S.W.2d 243 (Tenn. 1996), similarly upheld a search of a student's room at a private college by a residence director (RD) who acted pursuant to school policy that allowed unannounced, unscheduled entries into student rooms for the purpose of ensuring compliance with school policies. The RD had been told that a particular student was engaged in selling cocaine from his dorm room, so the RD went to the student's room and knocked. Receiving no response, the RD "used a master key to gain entry. He searched and discovered a set of electronic scales and a cigar box containing a quantity of 'white powdery substance.'" 926 S.W.2d at 245. The residence director contacted a dean, who, in turn, contacted the college's liaison at the local police department. The officer arrived on the scene, identified the substance as cocaine, and seized the evidence, which was then used in the student's criminal prosecution. The court held the search and seizure valid because it had been conducted by the RD "not as an agent of the state, but as a college official whose purpose and actions were in furtherance of college policy, not state policy." 926 S.W.2d at 246.

Actions by Public College or University Officials The Fourth Amendment clearly applies to searches and seizures conducted on the campuses of public colleges and universities. Although school officials have some latitude to enforce campus disciplinary regulations, they may not act as instruments of law enforcement. The purpose and intent of their search-related activities is key to the legality of their actions.

Smyth v. Lubbers, 398 F. Supp. 777 (D. Mich. 1975), involved the search of several students' dormitory rooms by officials at a public college. The college had a written policy that allowed students' rooms to be entered and searched if school officials had "reasonable cause to believe that students" were violating federal, state, or local laws. Pursuant to that policy, two campus police officers and several residential life staff members searched several students' rooms and discovered marijuana. In reviewing the college's actions, the court began by stating that students' interest in the privacy of their rooms was "not at the 'outer limits,' . . . but on the contrary . . . , at the very core of the Fourth Amendment's protections." 398 F. Supp. at 786. The court then went on to reject the college's contention that the search qualified as a special needs search:

> This case clearly involves a full search which focused upon the room of a specific individual who was suspected of criminal activity, and which aimed at discovering specific evidence. The search was not 'administrative' in the sense of a generalized or routine inspection for violations of housing, health, or other regulatory code. Since the College authorities were looking for marijuana in Smith's room, the search was specifically for instrumentalities of crime, defining 'instrumentalities' here as contraband. 398 F. Supp. at 786–87.

Notably, the court refused to rely on the consent search doctrine (see Chapter 9) because the students had agreed to abide by certain residence life policies as a precondition to living on campus. The court found such consent was ineffective because it was contained in a contract of adhesion to which students were forced to agree; and, therefore, any alleged waiver of their privacy rights was not truly voluntary. The court therefore concluded that the college needed a search warrant, duly supported by probable cause, to search the student's rooms. The court specifically stated that the fact that campus police officers were involved in the search was of no consequence, as the same result would have occurred if the search had been solely conducted by college residence life staff. *See, e.g., Morale v. Grigel*, 422 F. Supp. 988 (D.N.H. 1976) (finding that repeated searches of a student's dormitory room by a student resident advisor searching for evidence of criminal drug use constituted state action for Fourth Amendment purposes).

In *State v. Kappes*, 550 P.2d 121, 122 (Ariz. App. 1976), a state university had a housing regulation that provided university officials could enter dormitory rooms and "inspect for cleanliness, safety, or the need for repairs and maintenance." Once per month, students who were employed by the university as resident advisors (RAs) inspected all rooms at a time announced by a posting one day in advance of the inspections. During one such inspection, two RAs found marijuana in the defendant's dormitory room. They called campus police to the room and admitted the officers into the room. The court upheld the validity of the search because the purpose of the room inspection was "not to collect evidence for criminal proceedings against the student, but to insure that the rooms are used and maintained in accordance with the university regulations." 550 P.2d 124. Moreover, the court held that the subsequent seizure of the drugs by police did not violate the Fourth Amendment because they were in plain view (see Chapter 10). Although the logic of *Kappes* with respect to the search is still good law, its holding with respect to the subsequent warrantless seizure under the plain view doctrine is suspect in light of more recent case law.

In *Washington v. Chrisman*, 455 U.S. 1 (1982), a campus police officer observed what he believed to be an underage student in possession of alcohol. When the student was asked for identification, he could not produce it and therefore asked the officer if they could go back to his dormitory room to retrieve it. When the student opened the door and admitted the officer with him, the police officer saw the student's roommate in possession of drugs and drug paraphernalia. The U.S. Supreme Court upheld the warrantless seizure of the drugs that were in plain view because the police officer was lawfully admitted to the dormitory room. But the plain view doctrine does not apply to a police seizure when officers are not lawfully present in the dormitory room at the time they make a plain view observation. *Commonwealth v. Lewin*, 555 N.E.2d 551 (1990).

In *Commonwealth v. Neilson*, 666 N.E.2d 984 (Mass. 1996), college officials lawfully entered and searched a room looking for a cat, which residence hall rules forbade. Once inside the dorm room, however, they discovered marijuana. They notified police, who then entered the room and seized the contraband. The court ruled that even though it was perfectly appropriate for university officials to have notified law enforcement, police should not have entered the room and seized the contraband without a warrant. Of course, a warrant could easily have been issued in *Neilson* based on the university officials' statements. But the police had failed to obtain such a warrant before entering a dormitory room and seizing evidence contained inside. This violated the Fourth Amendment because no other warrant exception, such as exigent circumstances, was deemed to have been applicable in the case. Notably, the state argued that the student had given consent for such a warrantless entry by police because he had signed a residence hall contract authorizing university officials to enter his room. The court rejected this argument:

> [T]here was no consent to the police entry and search of the room. The defendant's consent was given, not to police officials, but to the University and the latter cannot fragmentize, share, or delegate it. While the college officials were entitled to conduct a health and safety inspection, they clearly ... had no authority to consent to or join in a police search for evidence of crime. 666 N.E.2d at 987 (internal quotations and citations omitted).

In *Smyth*, the search was clearly motivated by criminal investigatory purposes. *Kappes* and *Neilson*, in contrast, concerned searches motivated by a desire to enforce campus disciplinary and safety regulations. That distinction is clearly what differentiated the legality of the searches. But not all cases are so clear-cut, as illustrated by *State v. Hunter*, 831 P.2d 1033 (Utah App. 1992). A wave of vandalism in a particular residence hall prompted university officials to call meetings of the residents and inform them that room-to-room inspections would be conducted as a way of combating the vandalism. During one such inspection, college officials found both a sign and a banner that had been stolen from the university. The court upheld the search because it was "a reasonable exercise of the university's authority to maintain an educational environment"—a responsibility "incumbent upon the university to ... provide a clean, safe, well-disciplined environment in its dormitories." 831 P.2d at 1036. Although the court found the enforcement of disciplinary rules to have been the motivation for the searches, the fact that the searches had been instituted in response to criminal actions could have led a court to conclude that university officials were searching for criminal evidence connected to the acts of vandalism.

Border Searches

Border searches are arguably the ultimate special needs search. Accordingly, there is no reasonable expectation of privacy at any of the U.S. borders or their functional equivalents, such as international airline terminals, cruise ship terminals, or some other place where someone may be stopped for the first time upon entering the country. Border searches not only are a part of maintaining the sovereignty of the country by controlling the flow of both people and articles into or out of the country but also play a vital role in maintaining national security. *United States v. Montoya de Hernandez*, 473 U.S. 531, 538 (1985). As a result, "routine searches of the persons and effects of entrants are not subject to any requirement of reasonable suspicion, probable cause, or warrant." *United States v. Flores-Montano*, 541 U.S. 149 (2004). Border patrol or U.S. customs officials may "search carry-on bags and checked luggage, conduct canine sniffs or pat-downs, photograph and fingerprint travelers, and even disassemble the gas tank on a vehicle without an independent trigger for the search" (Gilmore, 2007: 767); *see also, e.g., Bradley v. United States*, 299 F.3d 197 (3d Cir. 2002) (pat-downs); *United States v. Hernandez*, 424 F.3d 1056, 1057 (9th Cir. 2005). They may also X-ray luggage and people. *United States v. Okafor*, 285 F.3d 842 (9th Cir. 2002). Given the scope of permissible searches at borders, the only substantive restraint on the searches of objects is that they be conducted in a reasonable manner. Thus, for example, searches conducted in a "particularly offensive manner," such as one that is unnecessarily destructive, may violate the Fourth Amendment. *Flores-Montano*, 541 U.S. at 154 n.2 & 156.

In contrast to routine border searches, more invasive searches of people—such as strip searches, body cavity searches, or extended periods of detention—do require reasonable suspicion, although they do not require a warrant. *Montoya de Hernandez*, 473 U.S. at 541. However, these invasive searches still need to be executed in a reasonable manner. (For detailed information on physically invasive searches, see the section on "Searches on or in the Body" in Chapter 7.)

Airport and Courthouse Searches

Airports, courthouses, and select other public places present special public safety concerns. Courts, therefore, allow warrantless, suspicionless searches in these areas under both the special needs doctrine and the theory of consent, since people seeking to enter a place with special security needs (e.g., a courthouse or the boarding areas of an airport) voluntarily place themselves in a position where they know they will be subject to a search. In doing so, they give implied consent to be subjected to routine screening procedures. *See United States v. Hartwell*, 296 F. Supp. 2d 596 (E.D. Pa. 2003). Moreover, once this implied consent is given, it cannot be revoked. Thus, for example, a person who attempts to pass through an airport security checkpoint cannot then decline secondary screening procedures by revoking consent. *United States v. Aukai*, 440 F.3d 1168 (9th Cir. 2006).

Scope of Search and Requirement of Reasonability An airport screening search is reasonable if (1) it is no more extensive or intensive than necessary, in light of current technology, to detect weapons or explosives; (2) it is confined in good faith to that purpose; and (3) passengers may avoid the search by electing not to fly. *Torbet v. United Airlines, Inc.*, 298 F.3d 1087, 1089 (9th Cir. 2002).

Requesting Identification Requesting identification is not a "seizure" within the meaning of the Fourth Amendment, especially because passengers are normally able to leave the airport if they cannot or elect not to comply with the request. *See Gilmore v. Gonzales*, 435 F.3d 1125 (9th Cir. 2006), *cert. denied*, 549 U.S. 1110 (2007).

Routine Initial Screening Processes Under the test as set forth in *Torbet*, the usual screening process of having would-be passengers pass through magnetometers as their carry-on luggage passes through X-ray machines easily passes constitutional muster:

> The scan and subsequent search involves only a slight privacy intrusion as long as the scope of the search is limited to the detection of weapons, explosives, or any other dangerous devices, and is conducted in a manner which produces negligible social stigma. Given these circumstances, a visual inspection and limited hand search of luggage which is used for the purpose of detecting weapons or explosives, and not in order to uncover other types of contraband, is a privacy intrusion we believe free society is willing to tolerate. *United States v. Figueroa Cruz*, 822 F. Supp. 853 (D.P.R. 1993).

Random Manual Searches of "Selectees" Random manual searches of a would-be passenger and his or her belongings for weapons or explosives does not violate the Fourth Amendment. *Torbet*, 298 F.3d at 1090; *United States v. Marquez*, 410 F.3d 612 (9th Cir. 2005).

Advance Routine Screening Processes If magnetic or X-ray scans yield inconclusive results, further searches are warranted so long as they are reasonably conducted. But at that point, because of the inconclusive results, security personnel have reasonable suspicion to conduct a pat-down of a person or more extensively search a person's carry-on luggage. And, depending on what is found, probable cause to do an even more extensive search may then exist. For example, in *United States v. Hartwell*, 436 F.3d 174 (3rd Cir. 2006), the defendant set off an alarm when he passed through a metal detector. Transportation Security Administration (TSA) agents then used a magnetic wand to pinpoint any metal on his person. When they detected something in Hartwell's pocket, they asked to see it. When he refused, a TSA agent reached into the defendant's pocket and pulled out a package that contained crack cocaine. In upholding the search as reasonable under the Fourth Amendment, the court concluded the intrusions of privacy were minimal when compared to the gravity of the public interests that are served by warrantless, administrative searches.

The Limits of a Search Some courts have found that by agreeing to be searched at an airport or courthouse, people grant a limited form of consent to be searched for weapons, explosives, or other items that pose a danger to public safety. *E.g., United States v. $124,570 U.S. Currency*, 873 F.2d 1240 (9th Cir. 1989). When, as in *Hartwell*, routine screening yields contraband such as drugs, there is no Fourth Amendment violation. However, when preliminary screening fails to identify the presence of something that is the legitimate target of a special needs search—namely, weapons or explosives—then a further search of the person and/or the person's belongings may not be constitutionally permissible. For example, if an initial screening yields the presence of large amounts of money, that does not permit screeners to conduct a full search of the person's belongings for contraband. *United States v. Doe*, 61 F.3d 107 (1st Cir. 1995); *United States v. Williams*, 267 F. Supp. 2d 1130 (M.D. Ala. 2003).

Public Transit System Searches

In response to the terrorist attacks on September 11, 2001, cities across the United States took steps to increase security. Of particular concern to New York City was the vulnerability of its subway system to attack. This concern was due, in large part, to terrorist attacks on a number of urban subway systems around the world, including one using nerve gas that had killed 12 people and injured 6,000 more on a Tokyo subway in 1995 and two others in 2004 that had killed approximately 230 and injured more than 1,500 in Moscow and Madrid. Since that time, an attack on the London Underground was thwarted, but one in Mumbai in 2006 killed more than 200 and wounded another

800 people (Martin, 2007: 1286) and one in Moscow in 2010 killed 38. To help prevent such attacks on the New York subway system, the city implemented a checkpoint system in which police would randomly stop every fifth or tenth person as they attempted to enter the transit system and ask for permission to conduct a visual search of any bags or packages the would-be subway riders were carrying. The inspection program the city designed was upheld as a valid special needs search in *MacWade v. Kelly*, 460 F.3d 260 (2d Cir. 2006).

According to the City of New York, its goal in establishing the subway screening checkpoints was "to deter terrorists from carrying concealed explosives onto the subway system and, to a lesser extent, to uncover any such attempt." 460 F.3d at 264. The scope of the inspections was limited as follows:

> As to scope, officers search only those containers large enough to carry an explosive device, which means, for example, that they may not inspect wallets and small purses. Further, once they identify a container of eligible size, they must limit their inspection "to what is minimally necessary to ensure that the . . . item does not contain an explosive device," which they have been trained to recognize in various forms. They may not intentionally look for other contraband, although if officers incidentally discover such contraband, they may arrest the individual carrying it. Officers may not attempt to read any written or printed material. Nor may they request or record a passenger's personal information, such as his name, address, or demographic data. Anyone who refused to grant consent to have the containers they were carrying searched by police were denied access to the transit system, but they were allowed to leave the subway without any further questioning.

Both a federal district court and the U.S. Court of Appeals for the Second Circuit upheld the city's subway checkpoint scheme under the special needs doctrine. Considering the subway checkpoints analogous to the checkpoints in airports, the courts found that the searches were designed to advance public safety—a need "distinct from ordinary post-hoc criminal investigation." 460 F.3d at 271. Moreover, the courts found that the city's need to prevent attacks on its subway system was enormous and compelling; that even though the searches infringe on a full privacy interest, the nature of the intrusion into that privacy was minimal; and that the program was reasonably effective as a deterrent.

A few months after the decision, *MacWade* was applied to a similar screening process that had been implemented on a commuter ferry system serving the Lake Champlain area of Vermont. Pursuant to the authority granted by the Maritime Transportation Security Act of 2002 (MTSA), *see* 46 U.S.C. §§ 70101–119 (2006), the U.S. Coast Guard conducted random, warrantless searches of ferry commuters' carry-on baggage and motor vehicles. Coming to the same conclusions about the specific requirement of special needs searches that were reached in *MacWade*, the court upheld the search program. *Cassidy v. Chertoff*, 471 F.3d 67 (2d Cir. 2006). The court emphasized that although such screening programs may not be the perfect way to stop a terrorist attack, they are a reasonable, minimally intrusive method that "may well stymie an attack, disrupt the synchronicity of multiple bombings, or at least reduce casualties." 471 F.3d at 87.

If *MacWade* and *Cassidy* are applied consistently on a nationwide basis, it is clear that random, warrantless, suspicionless searches may become commonplace as part of law enforcement efforts to protect buses, trains, ferries, and other forms of public transportation from terrorist attack.

DNA Searches

Federal law and the law of all fifty states now provide for collection of DNA samples from offenders convicted of felonies. Some states also collect DNA samples from

CRIMINAL PROCEDURE **IN ACTION**

Are TSA "Virtual Strip Searches" Constitutional?

The Transportation Safety Administration began using advanced imaging technology (AIT), which utilizes either backscatter X-rays or millimeter wave machines, to screen people at U.S. airports in December 2006. These devices produce a digital image of an airline passenger in a nude form, leading some to call them "virtual strip searches". There is no question that

AIT assists in protecting public safety. Some critics, however, question the extent to which they might meaningfully improve public safety. For example, the nonpartisan Government Accountability Office (GAO) released a report in March 2010 stating that it remained unclear whether AIT would have detected the weapon used by a Nigerian national when he attempted to blow up a U.S.-bound Northwest Airlines flight on Christmas Day in 2009. And although AIT can see beneath clothing, it cannot reveal what is beneath the skin; thus, they cannot detect materials hidden inside a person whether ingested, surgically implanted (e.g., the "bosom bomber"), or hidden in someone's rectum (e.g., the "Trojan bomber"). As a result, the GAO concluded that AIT only performed as well as physical pat-downs in operational tests.

There is also a question about the degree of intrusion AIT poses. When AIT was first adopted, the TSA assured that scanned images could not be stored or recorded. Yet, in August 2010, the government admitted that it had saved tens of thousands of images that had been recorded with an AIT system at the security checkpoint of a single Florida courthouse. The TSA responded that although the U.S. Marshall Service had activated the storing capability at that courthouse, it had never activated the storage feature on the AIT systems it uses at airports. Still, there is no doubt that airport AIT reveals intimate details about one's body. Consider, for example, the TSA worker at the Miami International Airport who snapped and used his baton to beat a co-worker after being subjected to jokes about the size of

his genitalia on a daily basis after his supervisor observed his body image during a training exercise.

At first, the government responded to criticisms about AIT by pointing out that people were not required to be screened by such technology. They were free to refuse a full-body scan and opt to submit to an invasive physical search of their person. But because these searches involve TSA agents touching intimate parts of the body, including running of agents' hands across breasts, buttocks, inner thighs, and even the genital area, they, too, have given rise to privacy complaints. As a result of privacy concerns, the TSA stopped using AIT with backscatter technology in 2013. AIT machines that use the less-intrusive millimeter wave technology remain in use because they have been retrofitted with privacy software that displays a generic outline of the human body, rather than a naked image of the person being scanned.

- If AITs that employ backscatter x-rays were still in use at airports, do you think such technology would be "reasonable" within the meaning of the Fourth Amendment? Explain your answer by balancing three factors: (1) the necessity to promote public safety; (2) the efficacy of the search procedures; and (3) privacy concerns about degree of intrusion.

- As an airline passenger, are you willing to pass through AIT, or do you think such screening goes too far? If you elect to opt out of AIT screening, do you think the pat-down searches are more or less invasive? Explain your reasoning.

---

misdemeanants. And a few states allow DNA samples to be collected from people arrested for certain crimes even though they have not yet been convicted. The purpose of doing so is to allow police to run **DNA searches** comparing unknown DNA samples collected from a crime scene against a known database of DNA profiles.

In *Maryland v. King*, 133 S. Ct. 1958 (2012), the U.S. Supreme Court upheld the constitutionality of a Maryland law requiring DNA samples to be taken from suspects arrested for certain offenses. The Court reasoned that the collection of DNA is a legitimate police booking procedure, much like fingerprinting and photographing. Thus, the majority concluded the focus of the collection was on the identification of an arrestee, not the investigation of crime. *See also State v. O'Hagen*, 914 A.2d 267 (N.J. 2007). Moreover, given the minimally invasive nature

Continued on next page

KEY POINTS

L02
- An exception to the warrant and probable cause requirements of the Fourth Amendment exists where special needs of the government, beyond the normal need for law enforcement gathering evidence for crime investigation, make the warrant and probable cause requirements impracticable.

L03 ■ Special needs exceptions are evaluated under the reasonableness standard of the Fourth Amendment, by balancing (1) the weight and immediacy of the government interest; (2) the nature of the privacy interest allegedly compromised by the search; (3) the character of the intrusion imposed by the search; and (4) the efficacy of the search in advancing the government interest. Applying this balancing test allows for warrantless searches based on reasonable suspicion in some circumstances, while in other circumstances warrantless, suspicionless searches may be appropriate.

oral DNA swabs engender, the Court concluded the procedure is "reasonable" and therefore complies with the requirements of the Fourth Amendment. The dissent, however, disputed that DNA searches are really concerned with identification, but rather are undertaken for the purpose of aiding a criminal investigation—a purpose specifically prohibited by the special needs doctrine.

> The most regrettable aspect of the suspicionless search that occurred here is that it proved to be quite unnecessary. All parties concede that it would have been entirely permissible, as far as the Fourth Amendment is concerned, for Maryland to take a sample of King's DNA as a consequence of his conviction for second-degree assault. So the ironic result of the Court's error is this: The only arrestees to whom the outcome here will ever make a difference are those who have been acquitted of the crime of arrest (so that their DNA could not have been taken upon conviction). In other words, this Act manages to burden uniquely the sole group for whom the Fourth Amendment's protections ought to be most jealously guarded: people who are innocent of the State's accusations. 133 S. Ct. at 1989.

SUMMARY

An administrative search is a routine inspection of a home or business to determine compliance with codes and licensing provisions dealing with fire, health, safety, housing, and so on. Although administrative searches are not directed toward convicting a person of a crime, they are still subject to the warrant requirement of the Fourth Amendment. However, the probable cause standard for administrative search warrants is less stringent than the standard for criminal searches. However, if an administrative search takes on the characteristics of a criminal search, the traditional probable cause standard applies. Exceptions to the administrative search warrant requirement are similar to the exceptions for a criminal search warrant with less stringent standards. Also, warrantless searches are allowed for certain licensed and closely regulated enterprises.

An exception to the warrant and probable cause requirements of the Fourth Amendment exists where special needs of the government, beyond the normal need for law enforcement, make the warrant and probable cause requirements impracticable. Special needs searches are evaluated under the reasonableness standard of the Fourth Amendment. Some special needs searches may be lawfully conducted without a warrant upon a showing of reasonable suspicion. Other special needs searches justify warrantless, suspicionless searches in light of the important governmental needs at stake when balanced against the intrusiveness of the search upon a person's reasonable expectation of privacy.

KEY TERMS

administrative search 214
border searches 232

DNA searches 235
plain view doctrine 216

special needs doctrine 217

1. What are the differences among conventional search warrants (directed toward gathering evidence for a criminal prosecution), administrative search warrants, and special needs searches?

2. What is the justification for requiring an administrative search warrant to conduct certain administrative searches, but allowing for other types of administrative searches to be conducted without a warrant?

3. Under what circumstances are random, warrantless, and suspicionless searches of high school students permitted? What is the underlying rationale of these searches? Critique this rationale.

4. What are the differences between the limitations on searches that may be conducted of passengers arriving by plane at an international airport and those that may be conducted of boarding passengers on a domestic flight? Explain and critique the rationale for the differences you identify.

5. What are the special needs that justify the warrantless seizure of DNA samples from people arrested or convicted of certain crimes? Compare and contrast the arguments that these justifications fit within the usual scope of the special needs doctrine with the arguments that these justifications fail to conform to the usual requirements of special needs searches.

The authority to arrest is the most important power a law enforcement officer possesses. An officer who arrests a person deprives that person of the freedom to carry out daily personal and business affairs. Also, an arrest initiates against that person the process of criminal justice, which may ultimately result in that person being fined or imprisoned. Because of the potential extremely detrimental effect on a person's life, liberty, and privacy, the law governing arrest provides many protections to ensure that persons are arrested only when it is reasonable and necessary. These protections take the form of severe limitations and restrictions on the law enforcement officer's exercise of the power of arrest. The law governing arrest is based on guarantees in the Fourth Amendment to the U.S. Constitution:

> The right of the people to be secure in their *persons*, houses, papers and effects, against unreasonable searches and *seizures*, shall not be violated and no Warrants shall issue, but upon probable cause, supported by Oath or affirmation, and particularly describing the place to be searched and the *persons* or things to be *seized*. U.S. Constitution, Fourth Amendment (italics added).

Because the Fourth Amendment does not specifically mention arrest, some believe that it applies only to searches and seizures of material things and not to people. The word

LO1 DEFINE the elements of a formal arrest.

LO2 EXPLAIN the distinctions among a seizure, a stop, and a seizure tantamount to arrest (de facto arrest).

LO3 EVALUATE the difference between arrest warrant and a summons; explain why arrests made pursuant to a warrant are preferred.

LO4 DIFFERENTIATE between the warrantless arrest authority for misdemeanors and for felonies.

LO5 IDENTIFY and examine the procedures for making a formal arrest. Explain the law relating to citizen's arrest, arrest in "hot pursuit," arrest in "fresh pursuit," and other arrests made in emergency circumstances.

LO6 IDENTIFY and examine the limitations on the use of force in making arrests, self-defense, defense of others, and entry of dwellings.

LO7 ANALYZE the legal requirements and procedures for dealing with an arrested person after the arrest is made.

LO8 IDENTIFY and evaluate the consequences of an illegal arrest.

LO9 EVALUATE the law's preference for search warrants and why exceptions to the warrant requirement are allowed.

LO10 IDENTIFY and examine the allowable purposes of a search incident to arrest as set forth in *Chimel v. California*.

LO11 DESCRIBE the limits on the allowable scope of a search incident to arrest with respect to the search of other areas of premises for accomplices and destructible evidence (e.g., the "protective sweep").

LO12 ANALYZE the principal requirements of a valid search incident to arrest, including (1) lawful custodial arrest and (2) contemporaneous nature of arrest and search.

persons is italicized in the preceding passage to indicate clearly that the Fourth Amendment protects individuals from illegal seizures of their persons. *An arrest is a type of seizure.* It clearly is governed by the Fourth Amendment. This chapter explores law enforcement officers' powers and duties concerning both arrests made pursuant to warrants and warrantless arrests. Before doing so, it bears emphasizing that courts prefer arrests made under the authority of an arrest warrant because the determination of probable cause for arrest is made by a neutral and detached judge with training and experience in the legal aspects of issuing warrants.

Arrests

Arrest is difficult to define because it is used in different ways. In its narrow sense, sometimes called a *formal* or *technical arrest*, arrest is defined as "the taking of a person into custody for the commission of an offense as the prelude to prosecuting him for it." *State v. Murphy*, 465 P.2d 900, 902 (Or. App. 1970). In its broader sense, sometimes called a *seizure tantamount to arrest*, a *de facto arrest*, the *functional equivalent of arrest*, or *an arrest for constitutional purposes*, arrest means any seizure of a person significant enough to resemble a formal arrest in important respects.

Formal Arrest

Four basic elements are necessary for a formal arrest:

1. a law enforcement officer's purpose or intention to take a person into the custody of the law,
2. the officer's exercise of real or pretended authority,
3. that the arrestee be taken into custody either by physical force or by submission to assertion of authority, and
4. understanding by the person to be arrested of the officer's intention to arrest.

Intention to Arrest To satisfy the first element of formal arrest, a law enforcement officer must intend to take a person into the custody of the law. This element distinguishes a formal arrest from lesser forms of detention, such as restraining a person who is acting dangerously; stopping a person to seek information or to render assistance; serving a subpoena or summons; asking a suspect or witness to appear at the stationhouse for questioning; or stopping a vehicle to inspect license, equipment, or load. Thus, if a law enforcement officer does not intend to take a person into custody, there is no formal arrest.

The brief seizure of a person for investigation based on an officer's reasonable suspicion of criminal activity—commonly referred to as a **stop**—is another detention that does not involve an intention to arrest. Because a separate body of law governs stops, they are discussed separately in Chapter 8.

Real or Pretended Authority to Arrest A law enforcement officer's seizure of a person must be under real or pretended authority. *Real authority* means the officer has the legal right to make a formal arrest with or without a warrant. *Pretended authority* means the officer has no legal right to make a formal arrest, but erroneously assumes that right. The arrest is still technically a formal arrest despite the officer's error. The authority requirement distinguishes arrests from seizures for which no authority is claimed, such as a kidnapping.

Custody Through Detention or Restraint According to the U.S. Supreme Court, a formal arrest requires that a person be taken into custody either through the actual use of physical force, "or, where that is absent, submission to the assertion of authority." *California v. Hodari D.*, 499 U.S. 621, 626 (1991).

Physical Force "To constitute an arrest, . . . the quintessential 'seizure of the person' under our Fourth Amendment jurisprudence—the mere grasping or application of physical force with lawful authority, whether or not it succeeded in subduing the arrestee, [is] sufficient." *Hodari D.*, 499 U.S. at 624. Thus, the slightest application of physical force results in an arrest even if the force was unsuccessful in ultimately taking a person into custody. Therefore, a person who escapes immediately after an officer's intentional application of the slightest force has still been arrested, because a seizure is a single act and not a continuous fact.

Constructive Seizures Through a Show of Authority An arrest may occur without any physical touching if the officer makes a **show of authority** and the person to be arrested submits to this authority. Words alone (e.g., "Stop, in the name of the law!") do not constitute an arrest by a show of authority. In contrast, if an officer's words and actions convey to a reasonable person that his freedom of movement is being restricted such that the person is not free to leave, and the person then submits to the officer's authority, an arrest has been made. For example, an officer yelling "Stop or I'll shoot" while drawing a weapon and pointing it at a suspect has, by a combination of words and actions, demonstrated a show of authority designed to get a suspect to comply with the officer's orders. If the suspect submits to the show of authority, an arrest has been made. If, however, the suspect does not submit to the officer's show of authority and attempts to flee, then no arrest occurs.

Understanding of Arrestee The final element of formal arrest is the arrested person's understanding that an arrest is being made. Usually, the officer's notifying the person of the arrest conveys this understanding. However, handcuffing or other physical restraint or confinement may satisfy the understanding requirement, even though the officer never says a word. If the arrested person is unconscious, under the influence of drugs or alcohol, or mentally impaired, the understanding requirement may be delayed or eliminated.

The understanding requirement presents problems when an encounter between the police and a person does not quite fit the description of a formal arrest, but the intrusion on the person's freedom of action is significantly greater than an ordinary, brief investigative detention or minimal street encounter. The next section discusses such seizures. Although not formal arrests, they may be tantamount to arrests for the purposes of Fourth Amendment protection.

Seizures Tantamount to Arrest

Law enforcement officers have varying degrees of contact with members of the public. These contacts range in intensity from a brief observation or questioning to a formal arrest accompanied by force. With respect to the most minimal of these police contacts, the U.S. Supreme Court said:

> [L]aw enforcement officers do not violate the Fourth Amendment by merely approaching an individual on the street or in another public place, by asking him if he is willing to answer some questions, by putting questions to him if the person is willing to listen, or by offering in evidence in a criminal prosecution his voluntary answers to such questions. . . . Nor would the fact that the officer identifies himself as a police officer, without more, convert the encounter into a seizure requiring some level of objective justifications. . . . The person approached, however, need not answer any question put to him; indeed, he may decline to listen to the questions at all and may go on his way. . . . He may not be detained even momentarily without reasonable, objective grounds for doing so; and his refusal to listen or answer does not, without more, furnish those grounds. . . . If there is no detention—no seizure within the meaning of the Fourth Amendment—then no constitutional rights have been infringed. *Florida v. Royer*, 460 U.S. 491, 497–98 (1983).

Furthermore:

> Even when law enforcement officers have no basis for suspecting a particular individual, they may pose questions, ask for identification, and request consent to search luggage—provided they do not induce cooperation by coercive means. . . . If a reasonable person would feel free to terminate the encounter, then he or she has not been seized. *United States v. Drayton*, 536 U.S. 194, 201 (2002).

Other encounters between the police and members of the public are more intrusive than those previously described and involve greater encroachments on freedom of movement and privacy. An example is a stop (mentioned earlier), which is sometimes accompanied by a limited search for weapons called a **frisk**. (See Chapter 8.)

At a still higher level of intrusiveness are police contacts that restrain a person's freedom of action more than a stop but do not satisfy the four elements of a formal arrest. The missing element is usually the officer's intention to arrest. In these instances, courts hold that the seizure is so similar to a formal arrest in important respects that it should be allowed only if supported by probable cause to believe a crime has been or is being committed. These seizures are called *seizures tantamount to arrest*, *de facto arrests*, or the *functional equivalents of arrest*. Regardless of terminology, each and every seizure of a person that has "the essential attributes of a formal arrest, is unreasonable unless it is supported by probable cause." *Michigan v. Summers*, 452 U.S. 692, 700 (1981).

In *Dunaway v. New York*, 442 U.S. 200 (1979), the defendant was picked up at his neighbor's home by the police and taken to the police station for questioning about an attempted robbery and homicide. Although the defendant was not told that he was under arrest, he would have been physically restrained had he attempted to leave. The police did not have probable cause to arrest the defendant. The police gave him *Miranda* warnings, and he waived his right to counsel. The police then questioned him, and he eventually made statements and drew sketches incriminating himself. His motions to suppress the statements and sketches were denied.

The Supreme Court held that the police violated Dunaway's constitutional rights under the Fourth and Fourteenth Amendments. The seizure was much more intrusive than a traditional stop and frisk (see Chapter 8) and could not be justified on the mere grounds of "reasonable suspicion" of criminal activity. Whether or not technically characterized as a formal arrest, the seizure was, in important respects, indistinguishable from a formal arrest. Instead of being questioned briefly where he was found, the defendant was taken from a neighbor's home to a police car, transported to a police station, and placed in an interrogation room. He was never informed that he was free to go and would have been physically restrained had he refused to accompany the officers or tried to escape their custody. That he was not formally arrested, was not booked, and would not have had an arrest record if the interrogation had proven fruitless did not make his seizure something less than an arrest for purposes of Fourth Amendment protections. Because it was unsupported by probable cause, Dunaway's seizure was illegal. Therefore, even though an officer does not intend to formally arrest a person, a seizure or detention of the person that is indistinguishable from a formal arrest in important respects is illegal unless supported by probable cause.

In *Hayes v. Florida*, 470 U.S. 811, 816 (1985), police took a burglary–rape suspect against his will from his home to the police station for fingerprinting. The Court reiterated the principles set out in *Dunaway*:

> [W]hen the police, without probable cause or a warrant, forcibly remove a person from his home or other place in which he is entitled to be and transport him to the police station, where he is detained, although briefly, for investigative purposes . . . such seizures, at least where not under judicial supervision, are sufficiently like arrests to invoke the traditional rule that arrests may constitutionally be made only on probable cause.
> 470 U.S. at 816.

The Court did not, however, rule out the possibility that an investigative seizure on less than probable cause might be permissible if judicially authorized:

> [U]nder circumscribed procedures, the Fourth Amendment might permit the judiciary to authorize the seizure of a person on less than probable cause and his removal to the police station for the purpose of fingerprinting. . . . [S]ome States . . . have enacted procedures for judicially authorized seizures for the purpose of fingerprinting. The state courts are not in accord on the validity of these efforts to insulate investigative seizures from Fourth Amendment invalidation.
> 470 U.S. at 817.

Many issues involving seizures tantamount to arrest arise as a result of detentions of suspected drug law violators at airports. In *Florida v. Royer*, 460 U.S. 491 (1983), narcotics agents had adequate grounds to suspect the defendant of carrying drugs: he was traveling under an assumed name and his appearance and conduct fit the "drug courier profile." Therefore, the agents

KEY POINTS

L01
- The requirements for a formal arrest are a law enforcement officer's intention to take a person into the custody of the law to answer for an alleged crime, under real or pretended authority, accompanied by detention or restraint of the person and an understanding by the person that an arrest is being made.

- The custody by detention or restraint requirement of a formal arrest may be satisfied either by actually touching the person to be arrested or by the person's submitting to an officer's show of authority.

- A seizure of a person that is substantially indistinguishable from a formal arrest is illegal unless it is supported by probable cause to believe that the person has committed or is committing a crime.

had the right to temporarily detain the defendant to confirm or dispel their suspicions. The agents, however, went beyond requesting identification and asking the defendant to accompany them to another room. They told him they were narcotics agents and had reason to believe he was carrying illegal drugs, and they kept his identification and airline ticket. They then took him to a small room, where he found himself alone with two police officers. They also retrieved his checked luggage from the airline without his consent. They never informed him he was free to board his plane if he so chose, and they would not have allowed him to leave the interrogation room even if he had asked to do so.

Under these circumstances, the Court found the officers' conduct much more intrusive than a stop, which might have been justified on the basis of reasonable suspicion. The detention was instead a seizure tantamount to an arrest; and because the officers did not have probable cause to arrest, it was an illegal seizure. The defendant's consent to search his luggage in the interrogation room was tainted by the illegal seizure and was also ruled illegal as a "fruit of the poisonous tree" (see Chapter 2).

Authority to Arrest

Although law enforcement officers have long been authorized to make warrantless arrests, arrests made under the authority of a warrant have always been preferred. This section discusses the details involved with arrests pursuant to a warrant, warrantless arrests, and citizens' arrests by police officers.

Arrests Pursuant to a Warrant

The U.S. Supreme Court said that "the informed and deliberate determinations of magistrates empowered to issue warrants . . . are to be preferred over the hurried action of officers . . . who may happen to make arrests." *Aguilar v. Texas*, 378 U.S. 108, 110–11 (1964). In other words, impartial judicial authorities are better suited to determining probable cause than law enforcement officers who, in their eagerness to enforce the law and investigate crime, may violate constitutional rights.

Although law enforcement officers often consider warrants a hindrance, arrest warrants protect officers in an important way. If a warrant is proper on its face and officers do not abuse their authority in obtaining or executing the warrant, they have qualified immunity against civil liability for damages, even though the warrant is later determined to be invalid. In *Malley v. Briggs*, 475 U.S. 335 (1986), a state trooper applied for a warrant to arrest the defendants for marijuana possession, the judge issued the warrant, and the defendants were arrested. The charges were subsequently dropped, however, when the grand jury failed to find probable cause to indict. The defendants then brought a civil action for damages under 42 U.S.C. Section 1983, alleging that the officer violated their rights under the Fourth and Fourteenth Amendments when he applied for the warrant. The U.S. Supreme Court held that a law enforcement officer applying for a warrant has qualified immunity from liability for damages if the officer's actions were "objectively reasonable." Under that standard, "[o]nly where the warrant application is so lacking in indicia of probable cause as to render official belief in its existence unreasonable . . . will the shield of immunity be lost." 475 U.S. at 344–45. In short, the question is

> whether a reasonably well-trained officer in petitioner's position would have known that his affidavit failed to establish probable cause and that he should not have applied for the warrant. If such was the case, the officer's application for a warrant was not objectively reasonable, because it created the unnecessary danger of an unlawful arrest. 475 U.S. at 345.

Issuance of Arrest Warrants

Complaints   As explained in Chapter 2, the criminal process against a defendant usually begins with the filing of a complaint. (Recall from Chapter 2 that a complaint may also function as the charging instrument in misdemeanor cases.) According to Federal Rule of Criminal Procedure 3, a complaint is "a written statement of the essential facts constituting the offense charged." A complaint serves as the basis for determining whether an arrest warrant should be issued. The complaint must be made on oath or affirmation, must state the essential facts of the offense being charged, must be in writing, and must be made before a neutral judicial officer authorized to issue process in criminal cases. This judicial officer is usually a magistrate or a justice of the peace, although a judge may also authorize a complaint. The information in the complaint may come from a law enforcement officer's personal observation or experience or it may come from victims, witnesses, or informants. Nevertheless, the evidence put forth in the complaint must be strong enough to convince the magistrate that there is probable cause that an offense has been committed and that the defendant committed it. (See Figure 2.4 in Chapter 2 for a typical form of a criminal complaint.)

Information not contained in the body of the complaint or that comes from witnesses other than the complainant may be brought to the court's attention in the form of an affidavit: a sworn written statement of the facts relied on in seeking the issuance of a warrant. An affidavit need not be prepared with any particular formality. It is filed with the complaint. Together, the complaint and affidavit provide a written record for a reviewing court to examine in determining whether probable cause existed for the issuance of a warrant.

Warrants or Summons Issued on a Complaint   Once the magistrate has determined from a sworn complaint (and accompanying affidavits, if any) that there is probable cause to believe that an offense has been committed and that the defendant committed it, the magistrate may issue a summons or an arrest warrant.

Summons   A summons is a court order that commands someone to appear before a court to respond to charges. (See Figure 2.5 in Chapter 2.) Court rules and statutes usually provide that, if a defendant fails to appear in response to a summons, then a warrant will issue for his or her arrest.

When Used   A summons is typically issued when the offense charged in a complaint is a misdemeanor, a violation of a municipal ordinance, or some other petty offense. If the alleged offender is a citizen with "roots firmly established in the soil of the community" and can be easily found if the summons is ignored, the summons procedure is more efficient and less intrusive than formal arrest as a means of inducing the defendant to appear in court.

Required Contents   The requirements for a summons are generally the same as those for an arrest warrant (described next), except that a summons directs the defendant to appear before a court at a stated time and place rather than ordering the defendant's arrest.

Different from Citations   The term *summons* may be confusing because it is often used to describe a citation, ticket, or notice to appear issued by a law enforcement officer, especially in traffic cases. Such a notice is not a summons in the legal sense, because it is not issued by a magistrate on the basis of a complaint. A citation, ticket, or notice to appear merely gives notice to offenders that they may be arrested if they do not voluntarily appear in court to answer the charges against them.

Service and Return of Process   A summons is served by personally delivering a copy to the defendant, or by leaving it at the defendant's home or usual place of abode with a person of suitable age and discretion who resides there. Depending on the rules of a particular jurisdiction, mailing a summons to the defendant's last known address with a return receipt may be permitted as service. As with an arrest warrant, most states provide that a summons for a violation of state law may be served at any place within the state. In addition, the officer serving the summons must return it to the proper judicial authority before the return date on the summons.

Arrest Warrant An arrest warrant is a written order directing the arrest of a particular person or persons. Figure 2.5 in Chapter 2 contains a typical form for an arrest warrant. (In some jurisdictions, a form is used that combines a complaint, a summons, an arrest warrant, and an order of detention.) An arrest warrant may only be issued on a sworn complaint. If an arrest warrant is issued on an unsworn complaint, it is void; an arrest made under such a warrant is illegal. An arrest warrant must conform to additional requirements, which vary by jurisdiction. In general, an arrest warrant must contain the following information:

- The caption of the court or division of the court from which the warrant issues
- The name of the person to be arrested, if known; if not known, any name or description by which the person can be identified with reasonable certainty. The warrant must show on its face that it is directed toward a particular, identifiable person to satisfy the Fourth Amendment requirement that a warrant particularly describe the person to be seized.
- A description of the offense charged in the complaint. The description should be in the language of the appropriate statute or ordinance. More important, the description must be specific enough for the defendant to readily understand the charge. Charging the defendant merely with a "felony" or a "misdemeanor," for example, is insufficient and will invalidate the warrant.
- The date of issuance
- The officer or officers to whom the warrant is directed, together with a command that the defendant be brought before the proper judicial official
- The signature of the issuing magistrate, together with a statement of the magistrate's official title

An officer to whom an arrest warrant is directed should read the warrant carefully. If the warrant satisfies the preceding requirements, the officer may execute the warrant without fear of civil liability.

Warrantless Arrests

Law enforcement officers are often faced with the decision of whether to apply for an arrest warrant or to arrest without a warrant. *United States v. Watson*, 423 U.S. 411 (1976), held that the Fourth Amendment permits warrantless arrests in a public place under certain circumstances. Generally, authority to arrest without a warrant depends on the difference between a felony and a misdemeanor.

In most jurisdictions, a felony is defined as any crime that may be punished by death or imprisonment in a state prison. This means that a crime is probably not a felony unless the penalty is at least one year of incarceration. Note that the punishment that *may* be imposed under the statute defining the crime determines whether a crime is a felony or misdemeanor, not the penalty that *actually* is imposed. Therefore, a felony can be defined as any crime for which the punishment could possibly be imprisonment for a term of one year or more.

All crimes that do not amount to a felony are classified as misdemeanors. Jurisdictions differ greatly as to which crimes are classified as felonies and misdemeanors. Thus, law enforcement officers must familiarize themselves with the classifications of crimes in their respective jurisdictions.

Felonies As a matter of federal constitutional law, a law enforcement officer may make a warrantless public arrest for a felony if, at the time of arrest, the officer has probable cause to believe that a felony has been committed and that the person to be arrested is committing or has committed the felony. The U.S. Supreme Court said:

> Law enforcement officers may find it wise to seek arrest warrants where practicable to do so, and their judgments about probable cause may be more readily accepted where backed by a warrant issued by a magistrate. . . . But we decline to transform this judicial preference into a constitutional rule when the judgment of the Nation and Congress has for so long been to authorize warrantless public arrests on probable cause rather than to encumber criminal prosecutions with endless litigation with respect to the existence of exigent circumstances, whether it was practicable to get a warrant, whether the suspect was about to flee, and the like. *United States v. Watson*, 423 U.S. 411, 423–24 (1976).

Requirement of Probable Cause to Arrest

Majority Approach Before making a warrantless felony arrest, nearly all U.S. jurisdictions require that a law enforcement officer have probable cause to make such an arrest. That is to say, the arresting officer must have specific facts or circumstances that the person to be arrested has committed, or is committing, a particular felony. *E.g., Qualls v. State*, 947 So.2d 365 (Miss. App. 2007). An officer who is unable to justify an arrest by articulating the facts and circumstances supporting probable cause risks having the arrest declared illegal. An arrest without a warrant is valid if the arresting officer has probable cause to believe a felony has been committed and probable cause to believe the suspect to be arrested committed the felony.

If an officer has probable cause to believe that a felony has been committed and that the defendant committed it, it makes no difference whether the officer turns out to be wrong or whether the defendant is later acquitted. Probable cause justifies the arrest and makes it legal. On the other hand, if an officer makes a warrantless felony arrest on mere suspicion or chance, the arrest is illegal whether the defendant is guilty or not. Therefore, probable cause is the main consideration in determining the validity of a warrantless felony arrest.

Minority Approach A minority of U.S. jurisdictions require that law enforcement officers obtain an arrest warrant before making an arrest for any felony that did not occur in the officer's presence, unless exigent circumstances make it impracticable to obtain an arrest warrant first. *E.g., Akins v. State*, 202 S.W.3d 879 (Tex. App. 2006) (citing Vernon's Ann. Texas C.C.P. art. 14.04); *People v. Casias*, 563 P.2d 926 (Colo. 1977); *Payne v. State*, 343 N.E.2d 325 (Ind. App. 1976). Exigent circumstances include situations when the suspect would be able to destroy evidence, flee or otherwise avoid capture; or when the suspect might, during the time necessary to procure a warrant, endanger the safety or property of others. *State v. Canby*, 252 S.E.2d 164 (W. Va. 1979).

Timing of Arrest Unlike warrantless arrests for misdemeanors, warrantless arrests for a felony may be delayed, whether or not it was committed in the officer's presence. *United States v. Drake*, 655 F.2d 1025 (10th Cir. 1981). Delay may be justified for a variety of reasons, as long as the delay is not designed to prejudice a person's constitutional rights. Reasons justifying delay include inability to locate the defendant, the need to complete additional undercover investigation, the desire to avoid alerting other potential offenders, and the need to protect the identity of undercover agents or informants:

> The police are not required to guess at their peril the precise moment at which they have probable cause to arrest a suspect, risking a violation of the Fourth Amendment if they act too soon, and a violation of the Sixth Amendment if they wait too long. Law enforcement officers are under no constitutional duty to call a halt to a criminal investigation the moment they have the minimum evidence to establish probable cause, a quantum of evidence which may fall far short of the amount necessary to support a criminal prosecution. *Hoffa v. United States*, 385 U.S. 293, 310 (1966).

The safest procedure for the law enforcement officer is to arrest soon after a crime is committed unless there are good reasons for delay.

Misdemeanors

Requirement of Probable Cause to Arrest

Minority Approach Some states follow the same rules for warrantless misdemeanor arrests as for warrantless felony ones. Thus, in a handful of states, warrantless misdemeanor arrests may be made if supported by probable cause; in a few others, a warrant is required to make a misdemeanor arrest unless exigent circumstances are present. *Compare*, e.g., *State v. Martin*, 268 S.E.2d 105 (S.C. 1980) (applying probable cause approach), *with State v. Remy*, 711 A.2d 665 (Vt. 1998) (requiring exigent circumstances for warrantless misdemeanor arrests).

Majority Approach The overwhelming number of U.S. jurisdictions follow a variation of the common-law rule that a law enforcement officer may make a warrantless arrest on a misdemeanor charge only when the misdemeanor is committed *in the officer's presence*. (Note: The common law is a body of unwritten law developed in England and based on court decisions. It receives its binding force from traditional usage, custom, and universal acceptance.) At common law, the misdemeanor had to be one that caused a "breach of the peace." A handful of jurisdictions still follow that rule precisely. *Commonwealth v. Lockridge*, 810 A.2d 1191 (Pa. 2002). But in *Atwater v. City of Lago Vista*, 532 U.S. 318 (2001), the U.S. Supreme Court held that the Fourth Amendment does not forbid a warrantless arrest for a minor criminal offense that does not involve a "breach of the peace," such as a misdemeanor seatbelt violation punishable only by a fine. Thus, unless otherwise provided by statute, most states permit law enforcement officers to make an arrest without a warrant for *any* misdemeanor so long as the misdemeanor was committed in the officer's presence. *Virginia v. Moore*, 553 U.S. 164 (2008), emphasized this point when it upheld an arrest for driving on a suspended license over a Fourth Amendment challenge, even though state law directed officers to issue a summons for that misdemeanor.

The requirement that a misdemeanor occur "in the officer's presence" ordinarily means that the officer must personally perceive the misdemeanor being committed before making an arrest. Sight, of course, is the primary sense used to perceive the commission of a crime, but it is not the only one. For example, *People v. Nitz*, 863 N.E.2d 817 (Ill. App. 2007), upheld the warrantless arrest of a defendant when a police officer smelled marijuana coming from the driver's vehicle. *See also Harding v. State*, 641 S.E.2d 285 (Ga. App. 2007). And *Sharp v. State*, 621 S.E.2d 508 (Ga. App. 2005), upheld a warrantless arrest for hunting without a license and obstruction of law enforcement officers when park rangers heard shots being fired, followed by the defendant's flight from the rangers as soon as he observed them.

The presence requirement may even be satisfied by the defendant's admission of guilt. *Jaegly v. Couch*, 439 F.3d 149 (2d Cir. 2006). But information from victims, witnesses, or informants may not be used to satisfy the presence requirement. The officer must present such evidence to a magistrate and seek an arrest warrant. Moreover, officers may enhance their senses in various ways to satisfy the presence requirement:

> Permissible techniques of surveillance include more than just the five senses of officers and their unaided physical abilities. Binoculars, dogs that track and sniff out contraband, search lights, fluorescent powders, automobiles and airplanes, burglar alarms, radar devices, and bait money contribute to surveillance without violation of the Fourth Amendment in the usual case. *United States v. Dubrofsky*, 581 F.2d 208, 211 (9th Cir. 1978).

However, law enforcement officers may not use devices that allow them to sense things in areas that would otherwise be unobservable. Thus, although using binoculars, telescopic lenses on cameras, and radar guns do not violate the Fourth Amendment, the same cannot be said for devices that actual invade the privacy of the home. For example, in *Kyllo v. United States*, 533 U.S. 27, 34 (2001), the Supreme Court invalidated a search of a private residence using a thermal imaging device that revealed the presence of marijuana plants. **"We think that obtaining by sense-enhancing technology any information regarding the interior of the home that could not otherwise have been obtained without physical 'intrusion into a constitutionally protected area' constitutes a search—at least where . . . the technology in question is not in general public use."** *Kyllo* clearly implies that advances in technology that allow the previously unknowable to be known—such as ultrasound and infrared radiation sensors, laser listening devices, and handheld sniffing devices that use gas chromatography and mass spectrometry, just to name a few—will certainly be subject to Fourth Amendment scrutiny. Thus, it is highly doubtful that the use of advanced technologies not in widespread, "general public use" (as opposed to being available to military, law enforcement, and scientific personnel) can be used to satisfy the "in the officer's presence" requirement for warrantless arrests.

Timing of Arrest Unlike warrantless arrests for felonies, an arrest without a warrant for a misdemeanor committed in an officer's presence must be made promptly and without unnecessary delay. For example, *State v. Warren*, 709 P2d 194 (N.M. App. 1985), held that a delay of two and a half hours before making an arrest for drinking in public was untimely. Accordingly, the officer must set out to make the arrest at the time the offense is perceived and must continue until the arrest is accomplished or abandoned. Any delay in making the arrest must be due to some reason concerning the arrest itself. Thus, if there is a delay in making a warrantless misdemeanor arrest because the offender fled, or because the officer thought it reasonably necessary to seek assistance before making the arrest, then such delays would be constitutionally permissible. If, however, the delay is unrelated to the process of making the arrest, then any subsequent warrantless arrest would be unlawful. Instead, other types of delay require the officer to obtain a warrant and to arrest in accordance with the warrant. *See, e.g.*, *Torres v. State*, 807 A.2d 780 (Md. App. 2002).

Citizen's Arrests

Unless altered by the statutory law of a particular jurisdiction, private citizens, which would normally include private security guards and law enforcement officers outside their legal jurisdiction, may make lawful arrests under certain circumstances. When such an arrest is made, it is referred to as a **citizen's arrest**.

L04

KEY POINTS

- In most jurisdictions, a law enforcement officer may make a warrantless public arrest for a felony if, at the time of arrest, the officer has probable cause to believe that a felony has been committed and that the person to be arrested is committing or has committed the felony.

- A law enforcement officer may arrest without a warrant for a misdemeanor only when the misdemeanor is committed in the officer's presence, unless otherwise provided by statute or state constitution. All five senses may be used to satisfy the "in the officer's presence" requirement. Devices that enhance the senses may also be used to meet this requirement if they are in general public use and do not allow officers to sense things that would otherwise be unknowable without the use of technology.

- An arrest without a warrant for a misdemeanor committed in a law enforcement officer's presence must be made as quickly after commission of the offense as circumstances permit. An arrest without a warrant for a felony on probable cause, however, may be delayed for various reasons, as long as the delay is not designed to prejudice a person's constitutional rights.

Arrests by Private Persons

Felonies Under the common-law rule in force in most states, a private citizen may arrest a person if the citizen has probable cause to believe that the person has committed a felony. *Tekle ex rel. Tekle v. United States*, 457 F.3d 1088 (9th Cir. 2006) (citing Cal. Penal Code § 834). This includes, of course, felonies committed in the presence of the private citizen. *Miles v. State*, 194 S.W.3d 523 (Tex. App. 2006) (citing Vernon's Ann. Texas Code Crim Pro. art. 14.01).

Misdemeanors A law enforcement officer may arrest a person without a warrant when he or she has probable cause to believe that the arrestee committed a misdemeanor in his presence. A private person, however, may only arrest someone for a misdemeanor when the offense actually has been committed or attempted in his or her presence. *Hamburg v. Wal-Mart Stores, Inc.*, 10 Cal. Rptr.3d 568, 580 (Cal. App. 2004). Reasonable cause to believe that a misdemeanor has been committed is not sufficient. Many states, however, limit the power to conduct a citizen's arrest for misdemeanor offenses to those committed in the citizen's presence that constitute a "breach of the peace"—crimes that present "an imminent threat to the public security or morals to justify a citizen taking immediate action." *Johnson v. Barnes & Noble Booksellers, Inc.*, 437 F.3d 1112, 1116 (11th Cir. 2006).

Use of Force A private citizen may use the same degree of force as a law enforcement officer in making an arrest. As with law enforcement, only force that is reasonable under the circumstances may be used to restrain the individual arrested. *Patel v. State*, 620 S.E.2d 343 (Ga. 2005). (See the discussion of use of force later in this chapter.)

Effect of Mistake If the private citizen arresting for a felony is mistaken and no felony was actually committed, the citizen may be civilly liable for damages. In contrast, law enforcement officers who arrest in their jurisdiction for a felony based on probable cause are protected from civil liability, even if they are mistaken.

Citizen's Arrests by Police Outside Jurisdictional Power Law enforcement officers generally have no official authority to arrest without a warrant outside the jurisdiction in which they were elected or appointed unless they do so while in fresh and continuous pursuit of a suspect who has fled their jurisdiction (fresh pursuit is discussed in more detail later in this chapter). Nevertheless, officers outside their territorial jurisdiction generally have the same authority as private citizens to arrest without a warrant. *United States v. Atwell*, 470 F. Supp. 2d 554 (D. Md. 2007). Thus (unless neighboring states have modified the common-law rule regarding citizen's arrests by statute), when law enforcement officers are beyond the territorial limits of their jurisdiction, they may make a warrantless felony arrest if they have probable cause to believe that a felony has occurred; and they may make a warrantless misdemeanor arrest if a misdemeanor was committed or attempted in their presence (and, in some jurisdictions, the misdemeanor must be one that constitutes a breach of the peace). Like private citizens, however, officers making an arrest as private citizens risk civil liability if they cannot prove that a felony was actually committed or that a misdemeanor constituting a breach of the peace was committed or attempted in their presence.

KEY POINTS

L05

- A private person may make a valid citizen's arrest if he or she has probable cause to believe that the person to be arrested (1) has committed a felony or (2) actually committed or attempted to commit a misdemeanor that constitutes a breach of the peace in the presence of the person seeking to make the citizen's arrest. A private citizen may use the same degree of force as a law enforcement officer in making an arrest. Unlike law enforcement officers, who are protected by qualified immunity from civil liability for good-faith mistakes made while arresting someone in their jurisdiction, private citizens who are mistaken when they make a citizen's arrest may be civilly liable for damages.

- Law enforcement officers outside their jurisdiction generally have the same authority as private citizens to arrest without a warrant so long as they do not use the powers of their office that are unavailable to private citizens when making a citizen's arrest. Law enforcement officers making arrests outside their jurisdiction are subject to civil liability for their mistakes in the same way a private citizen would be.

DISCUSSION POINT

Should Police Conduct a Citizen's Arrest? *People v. Williams*, 829 N.E.2d 1203 (N.Y. 2005).

While patrolling a housing project, two peace officers employed by the Buffalo Municipal Housing Authority observed the defendant driving an automobile on a public street adjacent to the project. The officers stopped the defendant because he allegedly was not wearing a seat belt. After the defendant informed the officers that he did not have a valid

driver's license, the officers ordered him to step out of his vehicle. In response to questioning by an officer, the defendant replied in a manner that led the officer to suspect that the defendant had an object in his mouth. The defendant opened his mouth, revealing what appeared to be a plastic bag protruding from underneath his tongue. When asked to lift his tongue, the defendant shoved the officer and fled. Upon being apprehended after a brief chase, the defendant spit the bag onto the ground. The bag, which was recovered by the officers, appeared to contain crack cocaine.

As a result of this incident, the defendant was indicted for criminal possession of a controlled substance in the fifth degree and several violations of the Vehicle and Traffic Law. Before trial, the defendant moved to dismiss the charges, arguing that the initial seizure for a traffic infraction was unlawful because the Housing Authority peace officers lacked jurisdiction outside the boundaries of the housing project and the officers were not acting pursuant to their special duties as Housing Authority peace officers when they stopped him for a seat belt violation. The People countered that the seizure was lawful because the peace officers were within their geographical jurisdiction and, even if they were not, the stop was justified as a "citizen's arrest."

The trial court agreed with the defendant and dismissed the charges. The court concluded that

there was no statutory authority for the peace officers to apprehend the defendant for an offense committed outside their geographical area of employment, and the People had failed to demonstrate that the officers were acting pursuant to their special duties when they stopped the defendant for a seat belt violation. The court further rejected the People's contention that the traffic stop was a valid citizen's arrest.

An appeals court affirmed. The highest court in the State of New York accepted discretionary appellate jurisdiction and affirmed, reasoning that the alleged traffic infractions and the seizure of the defendant occurred outside the geographical jurisdiction of the Buffalo Municipal Housing Authority peace officers. The court also rejected the assertion that the apprehension of the defendant was the equivalent of a citizen's arrest because the Housing Authority peace officers were not "acting other than as a police officer or a peace officer" at the time of the stop and subsequent arrest.

■ Do you think that the officers in this case were acting "under color of law and with all the accoutrements of official authority"? Why or why not?

■ Assume, for the sake of argument, the officers were acting under color of law. Do you think that should deprive them of the authority to have made the arrest in this case? Explain your answer and your underlying reasoning.

Making an Arrest

To make a formal arrest, a law enforcement officer must satisfy the basic requirements of a formal arrest. To summarize, these requirements are a law enforcement officer's intention to take a person into the custody of the law to answer for an alleged crime, under real or pretended authority, accompanied by detention or restraint of the person and an understanding by the person that an arrest is being made.

Provisions for All Arrests

In addition to the requirements already noted, there are other aspects of making an arrest. These include notice, time of day, assistance, and discretion. Additional considerations are involved in executing an arrest warrant.

Notice As a matter of constitutional law, someone being arrested does not have to be informed that he or she is under arrest. *Kladis v. Brezek*, 823 F.2d 1014 (7th Cir. 1987). *See also Spencer v. Nat'l R.R. Pass. Corp.*, 141 F. Supp. 2d 1147, 1150 (N.D. Ill. 2001) (finding no constitutional violation even though "[male police officer] did not inform [the female suspect] of the nature and basis of the accusation against her when he handcuffed her and detained her on the platform of the [train] station"). However, a law enforcement officer may be required to give notice when making an arrest under the statutory law of a particular jurisdiction. *E.g.*, N.Y. CRIM. PRO. L. § 140.15 (McKinney 1970). But regardless of whether notice is legally required, it is a good idea that an officer tell a suspect that he or she is under arrest so that the person being taken into custody is aware that the detention is legal, and therefore the suspect is unlikely to resist arrest. *See Pullins v. State*, 256 N.E.2d 553, 556 (Ind. 1970). This point becomes especially important if the arresting officer's authority is not already known to the arrestee due to an obvious display of a badge, uniform, or other indicia of authority. *See State v. Erdman*, 292 N.W.2d 97 (S.D. 1980).

Time of Day An arrest, with or without a warrant, may be made on any day of the week and at any time of the day or night, unless otherwise provided in the warrant or by statute. *See, e.g.*, *Robinette v. Jones*, 476 F.3d 585 (8th Cir. 2007) (citing Mo. Rev. Stat. § 544.210). Unlike the execution of a search warrant, generally no specific provision in an arrest warrant is required to authorize a nighttime arrest. Note, however, that some states limit the time during which a misdemeanor warrant may be served, unless another time period is specifically authorized in the warrant. *See, e.g.*, *People v. Dinneen*, 119 Cal. Rptr. 186 (Cal. App. Super. 1974) (citing West's Ann. CAL. PENAL CODE § 840); *State v. McCoy*, 131 N.E.2d 679 (Ohio App. 1955).

Entry in Dwellings *Payton v. New York*, 445 U.S. 573 (1980), held that, absent exigent circumstances or consent, a law enforcement officer may not make a warrantless entry into a suspect's home to make a routine felony arrest. *See* also *Kyllo v. United States*, 533 U.S. 27, 40 (2001) ("We have said that the Fourth Amendment draws a 'firm line at the entrance to the house.' That line, we think, must be not only firm, but also bright.") The Supreme Court said that physical entry of the home is the chief evil against which the Fourth Amendment is directed and that the warrant procedure minimizes the danger of needless intrusions into a person's home. The Court went on to say that an arrest warrant requirement, although providing less protection than a search warrant requirement, was sufficient to interpose the magistrate's determination of probable cause between a zealous officer and a citizen. The Court concluded that "an arrest warrant founded on probable cause implicitly carries with it the limited authority to enter a dwelling in which the suspect lives when there is reason to believe the suspect is within." 445 U.S. at 603. Thus, entry into a home to make an arrest usually requires a warrant executed in accordance with the special procedures discussed later in the section dealing with the "Place of Execution" of an arrest warrant.

Discretion Even though a law enforcement officer clearly has the ability and authority to arrest, good police practice may call for the arrest to be delayed or not to be made at all. It is beyond the scope of this book to give detailed guidelines in this area, but a brief discussion is necessary to set out general principles.

A law enforcement officer's primary duty is to protect the public at large. Therefore, when an arrest would create a great risk of public harm or would cause embarrassment to a person who poses no real threat to the community, proper police practice may call for delay or restraint in exercising the power of arrest. For example, when a crowd is present, it is often unwise to arrest a person who is creating a minor disturbance. An arrest may aggravate the disturbance and possibly precipitate a riot or civil disorder.

Additional Procedures for Executing an Arrest Warrant

Executing an arrest warrant involves additional considerations in addition to those applicable to making a warrantless arrest. First, when officers are directed to execute an arrest warrant, their belief in the guilt of the defendant or their personal knowledge of facts pertaining to the offense is immaterial. The offense does not need to be committed in their presence and they do not need to have probable cause to believe that the defendant committed the offense. Officers are simply required to carry out the command of the warrant in a constitutionally reasonable manner if the warrant is valid on its face.

Determining the Facial Validity of a Warrant When the accused is identified in the warrant by name or description, a law enforcement officer is required to exercise reasonable diligence to make sure only the person designated in the warrant is arrested. If the person being arrested claims not to be the person identified in the warrant, the arresting officer should make a reasonable effort to verify the claim or the officer risks civil liability for damages.

A warrant that is invalid on its face gives the officer executing it no protection and no authority to arrest. An officer must examine the warrant if it is available and risks civil liability for damages for executing a warrant obviously invalid on its face. An arrest warrant is invalid on its face if one or more of the following are true:

- The court issuing the warrant clearly has no jurisdiction.
- The warrant fails to adequately indicate the crime charged.
- The warrant fails to name or describe any identifiable person.
- The warrant is not signed by the issuing magistrate.
- The warrant is not directed to the officer who is about to execute it. (If a warrant is directed to all law enforcement officers in a jurisdiction, any officer may execute it. If, however, the warrant is directed only to the sheriff of a particular county, only that sheriff or a deputy sheriff may execute it.)

Once an officer determines that a warrant is valid on its face, the officer must carry out the warrant's commands and arrest the person identified in the warrant. The officer no longer has any personal discretion and is merely carrying out an order of the court.

Place of Execution

Territorial Limits Most states allow arrest warrants for violations of state law to be executed at any place within the boundaries of the state. However, a law enforcement officer of one state may not go into another state to arrest under a warrant except in fresh pursuit (discussed later in this chapter).

Entry into a Suspect's Home Under *United States v. Watson*, 423 U.S. 411 (1976), police may make a warrantless arrest in a public place based on probable cause. *See also McClish v. Nugent*, 483 F.3d 1231 (11th Cir. 2007). But, as stated earlier, *Payton v. New York* held that absent consent or exigent circumstances, law enforcement officers must have at least an arrest warrant to lawfully enter a suspect's home to arrest the suspect. Moreover, at the time of the execution of such an arrest warrant, an officer must have "reason to believe the suspect is within" the dwelling that officers seek to enter. 445 U.S. at 603.

The Supreme Court has repeatedly reinforced *Payton*'s holding that, absent consent or exigent circumstances, "the firm line at the entrance to the house may not reasonably be crossed without a warrant." *Kirk v. Louisiana*, 536 U.S. 635, 636 (2002);

cf. United States v. Santana, 427 U.S. 38 (1976) (arrest without a warrant in the doorway of a dwelling upheld because no Fourth Amendment expectation of privacy existed in such a location).

Entry into a Third Party's Home *Steagald v. United States*, 451 U.S. 204 (1981), held that an arrest warrant does not authorize law enforcement officers to enter the home of a third person to search for the person to be arrested, in the absence of consent or exigent circumstances. To protect the Fourth Amendment privacy interests of persons not named in an arrest warrant, a search warrant must be obtained to justify the entry into the home of any person other than the person to be arrested. The Court reasoned:

> A contrary conclusion—that the police, acting alone and in the absence of exigent circumstances, may decide when there is sufficient justification for searching the home of a third party for the subject of an arrest warrant—would create a significant potential for abuse. Armed solely with an arrest warrant for a single person, the police could search all the homes of that individual's friends and acquaintances. . . . Moreover, an arrest warrant may serve as the pretext for entering a home in which the police have suspicion, but not probable cause to believe, that illegal activity is taking place. 451 U.S. at 215.

If police have probable cause to believe that someone for whom they have an arrest warrant is located in the home of a third person, *Steagald* requires that law enforcement seek a search warrant to enter the third party's home. The Supreme Court suggested that in most instances the police may avoid altogether the need to obtain a search warrant simply by waiting for a suspect to leave the third person's home before attempting to arrest the suspect. When the suspect leaves either the home of a third person or his or her own home and is in a public place, officers may arrest on probable cause alone. Neither an arrest warrant nor a search warrant is required to support an arrest made in a public place.

Exigent Circumstances Justifying Warrantless Arrest in a Home In neither *Payton* nor *Steagald* did the Supreme Court specify the nature of the exigent circumstances that would justify a warrantless entry of a home to make an arrest. *Welsh v. Wisconsin*, 466 U.S. 740, 753 (1984), however, held:

> [A]n important factor to be considered when determining whether any exigency exists is the gravity of the underlying offense for which the arrest is being made. Moreover, although no exigency is created simply because there is probable cause to believe that a serious crime has been committed . . . application of the exigent circumstances exception in the context of a home entry should rarely be sanctioned when there is probable cause to believe that only a minor offense . . . has been committed.

Thus, *Welsh* appears to have held that for an exigent circumstance exception to apply, thereby allowing a warrantless home arrest, the underlying crime for which the arrest will be made needs to be a serious one. As a result, even when emergency circumstances exist, such as the threat of removal or destruction of evidence from a home, warrantless home arrests for misdemeanors are highly suspect under *Welsh*.

In the wake of *Welsh*, courts have established several categories of exigent circumstances that have been held to authorize a law enforcement officer's warrantless entry into a home:

- a risk that evidence will be destroyed,
- hot pursuit of a fleeing felon,
- a threat to the safety of a suspect or others, and
- a likelihood that the suspect will flee and thereby escape.

Let's look at these types of exigencies in more detail, keeping in mind that officers may not deliberately create exigent circumstances to subvert the warrant requirements of the Fourth Amendment. *State v. Carter*, 160 S.W.3d 526 (Tenn. 2005), *cert. denied*, 547 U.S. 1081 (2006).

Destruction of Evidence A warrantless entry into a dwelling may be made if there is a strong likelihood that evidence or contraband will be lost, destroyed, or removed from premises if police fail to take immediate action. *E.g., United States v. Martins*, 413 F.3d 139 (1st Cir.), *cert. denied*, 546 U.S. 1011 (2005).

In *Welsh v. Wisconsin*, the warrantless arrest of the defendant in his home for a "nonjailable" traffic offense (fleeing the scene of an accident) was held illegal. The driver in *Welsh* had lost control of his car and ended up in a field, causing no injury or damage. But a witness told police that the man who walked away from the car was either intoxicated or sick. They went to his home (not in hot pursuit) and made a warrantless arrest on the theory that they needed to quickly obtain a blood sample from him for blood-alcohol testing. When he refused to give the sample, his license was suspended for violating the state's implied consent law. He challenged the license suspension on the grounds that the police violated *Payton* in entering his home to arrest him without a warrant. The Supreme Court sided with the driver and held that there was no exigency that justified violating *Payton*'s command that a warrant is necessary to enter a home to make an arrest. Key to the Court's rationale, however, was the nature of the underlying offense—one that under relevant state law was merely a civil forfeiture traffic violation, not a criminal offense for which any imprisonment was possible. *See also United States v. Mikell*, 102 F.3d 470 (11th Cir. 1996).

In the wake of *Welsh*, some states upheld warrantless entries when the underlying crime was a serious one. For example, *State v. Lamont*, 631 N.W.2d 603 (S.D. 2001), upheld a warrantless entry into a suspect's home to obtain a blood alcohol sample from him after a felony hit-and-run accident caused a vehicular homicide. And in *Illinois v. McArthur*, 531 U.S. 326 (2001), the Court held that the need to preserve evidence of "jailable offenses" (possession of marijuana and drug paraphernalia in *McArthur*) was sufficiently urgent or pressing to justify the police in keeping the defendant from entering his home. The Court noted, however, that "[t]emporarily keeping a person from entering his home, a consequence whenever police stop a person on the street, is considerably less intrusive than police entry into the home itself in order to make a warrantless arrest or conduct a search." 531 U.S. at 336. Note that the Court did not decide whether the need to preserve evidence would have justified a greater allowance for a "jailable offense" than a "nonjailable" offense (although *Welsh* clearly implies that more latitude will be given for warrantless home entries to preserve evidence for jailable offenses). A more definite resolution of these issues awaits a case that presents them.

In *Minnesota v. Olson*, 495 U.S. 91 (1990), the U.S. Supreme Court approved the Minnesota Supreme Court's standard for determining whether exigent circumstances exist. The Minnesota court held that "a warrantless intrusion may be justified by hot pursuit of a fleeing felon, or imminent destruction of evidence . . . or the need to prevent a suspect's escape, or the risk of danger to the police or to other persons inside or outside the dwelling." 436 N.W.2d at 97. Furthermore, "in the absence of hot pursuit there must be at least probable cause to believe that one or more of the other factors justifying the entry were present and that in assessing the risk of danger, the gravity of the crime and likelihood that the suspect is armed should be considered." 495 U.S. at 100.

Applying this standard, exigent circumstances justifying the warrantless entry into a home to make an arrest were determined not to exist in the *Olson* case, in which

- although a grave crime was involved, the defendant was known not to be the murderer;
- the police had already recovered the murder weapon;
- there was no suggestion of danger to the two women with whom the defendant was staying;
- several police squads surrounded the house;
- the time was 3 p.m. on a Sunday;
- it was evident the suspect was not going anywhere; and
- if he came out of the house, he would have been promptly apprehended.

Hot Pursuit *Warden v. Hayden*, 387 U.S. 294 (1967), held that hot pursuit of the perpetrator of a serious crime constituted exigent circumstances that justified a warrantless entry by police into a house. In that case, police officers had reliable information that an armed robbery had taken place and that the perpetrator had entered a certain house five minutes earlier. The Court held that the officers:

> [a]cted reasonably when they entered the house and began to search for a man of the description they had been given and for weapons which he had used in the robbery or might use against them. The Fourth Amendment does not require police officers to delay in the course of an investigation if to do so would gravely endanger their lives or the lives of others. Speed here was essential, and only a thorough search of the house for persons and weapons could have insured that Hayden was the only man present and that the police had control of all weapons which could be used against them or to effect an escape. 387 U.S. at 298–99; *see also Brigham City, Utah v. Stewart,* 547 U.S. 398, 403 (2006); *United States v. Santana,* 427 U.S. 38, 42-43 (1976) ("This case [*Santana*], involving a true hot pursuit, is clearly governed by *Warden* [discussed above]; the need to act quickly here [to prevent the destruction of drug evidence] is even greater than in [*Warden*] while the intrusion [consisting of police pursuing Santana from the doorway of her house to the foyer/vestibule area] is much less [distance]. The District Court was correct in concluding that hot pursuit means some sort of a chase, but it need not be an extended hue and cry in and about (the) public streets. The fact that the pursuit here ended almost as soon as it began did not render it any the less a hot pursuit sufficient to justify the warrantless entry into Santana's house.").

It should be noted that "federal and state courts nationwide are sharply divided on the question whether an officer with probable cause to arrest a suspect for a misdemeanor may enter a home without a warrant while in hot pursuit of that suspect." *Stanton v. Sims*, 134 S. Ct. 3 (2013). The *Stanton* Court declined to resolve the question since the case could be resolved without addressing the constitutional matter. Accordingly, the Supreme Court will need to address this question in the future.

Threats to Safety A real and imminent threat to the safety of a suspect, to officers, or to others justifies an entry into a dwelling to make an arrest without a warrant. *United States v. Martins*, 413 F.3d 139 (1st Cir.), *cert. denied*, 546 U.S. 1011 (2005). The primary motive for such a warrantless entry must be to render emergency aid and assistance, not to find evidence. *E.g.*, *State v. Frankel*, 847 A.2d 561 (N.J.), *cert. denied*, 543 U.S. 876 (2004). Courts have upheld such warrantless entries in a number of situations, including

- to extinguish a fire in a burning building, *see Michigan v. Tyler*, 436 U.S. 499 (1978);

- to break up a violent fight, *see Brigham City v. Stuart*, 547 U.S. 398 (2006);

- to stop acts of domestic violence, *see United States v. Martinez*, 406 F.3d 1160 (9th Cir. 2005);

- to rescue a kidnapped infant, *see United States v. Laboy*, 909 F.2d 581, 586 (1st Cir.1990);

- to attend to a shooting or stabbing victim, *see United States v. Gillenwaters*, 890 F.2d 679, 682 (4th Cir. 1989); *United States v. Russell*, 436 F.3d 1086, 1090 (9th Cir. 2006); and

- to prevent the imminent escape of the person during the time it would take to obtain a warrant authorizing entry and arrest. *E.g.*, *United States v. Amburn*, 412 F.3d 909 (8th Cir. 2005). However, if police surround a home to make escape impossible, then they must wait for a warrant to enter and seize people and evidence inside the dwelling unless other exigent circumstances justify entry. *State v. Bowe*, 557 N.E.2d 139 (Ohio App. 1988).

Manner of Execution

Notice Officers executing an arrest warrant should give the same notice, discussed earlier, they would give in making any arrest. In addition, officers should have the warrant in their possession at the time of arrest and should show the warrant to the person arrested. Failure to have the warrant in the arresting officer's possession does not affect the legality of the arrest. Officers must, however, inform the defendant of the offense charged and the existence of the warrant. If the defendant requests, officers must produce the warrant as soon as possible.

Timing Like a warrantless felony arrest, an arrest made under a warrant (for a felony or misdemeanor) need not be made immediately. Officers have considerable discretion in deciding the time to make an arrest under a warrant. They may have lawful strategic reasons for delay, or they may wish to select a time when the arrest can be accomplished with the least difficulty. "[T]he general rule is that, while execution should not be unreasonably delayed, law enforcement officers have a reasonable time in which to execute a warrant and need not arrest at the first opportunity." *United States v. Drake*, 655 F.2d 1025, 1027 (10th Cir. 1981).

Forced Entry As with the execution of search warrants, before making a forcible entry to execute an arrest warrant at a dwelling, officers must knock and announce their presence and authority; demand entry into the home; and be actually or constructively denied entry. *Wilson v. Arkansas*, 514 U.S. 927 (1995). As with search warrants, there are a number of exceptions to the knock-and-announce rule. The

KEY POINTS

L05

- Unless there are extenuating circumstances, an officer arresting a person should give notice that the person is under arrest as well as notice of the officer's authority and the cause of arrest.

- Warrantless arrests are discretionary and should always be justified by the circumstances.

- If an arrest warrant is valid on its face, a law enforcement officer must execute the warrant within a reasonable time according to its terms, and the officer has no personal discretion in this matter.

- In general, law enforcement officers have no authority to make warrantless arrests beyond that of an ordinary citizen outside the geographical limits of the jurisdiction for which they have been elected or appointed.

- Law enforcement officers may arrest outside their jurisdiction in "fresh pursuit." Fresh pursuit means an officer's immediate and continuously maintained pursuit of a criminal suspect into another jurisdiction after the officer has attempted to arrest the person in the officer's own jurisdiction.

- Absent exigent circumstances or consent, law enforcement officers may not make a warrantless entry into a suspect's home to make a routine felony arrest. Officers must have at least an arrest warrant to lawfully enter a suspect's home to arrest the suspect.

- Absent exigent circumstances or consent, an arrest warrant does not authorize law enforcement

Continued on next page

KEY POINTS

officers to enter the home of a third person to search for the person to be arrested. In addition, a search warrant must be obtained to justify the entry into the home of any person other than the person to be arrested.

- Exigent circumstances that would justify a warrantless entry of a dwelling to arrest are (1) hot pursuit of a fleeing felon, (2) imminent destruction of evidence, (3) the need to prevent a suspect's escape, and (4) and the risk of danger to the police or to other persons. In assessing the risk of danger, the gravity of the crime and the likelihood that the suspect is armed should be considered.

- If an arrest is begun in a public place, officers in hot pursuit may enter a dwelling without a warrant to complete the arrest.

- Before law enforcement officers may lawfully force their way into a dwelling to arrest someone inside (absent extenuating circumstances), they should first knock on the door, announce their authority and purpose, and then demand admittance and be refused admittance.

- An officer executing an arrest warrant must make a return of the warrant. The return is made by (1) entering on the warrant the date of the arrest, (2) signing the warrant, and (3) filing the warrant with the court. Failure to return an arrest warrant may invalidate the arrest and subject the officer to civil liability for damages.

issues regarding the knock-and-announce rule, its exceptions, and the rules regarding forced entry are discussed in great detail in Chapter 4.

Return of the Warrant An officer executing an arrest warrant must make a return of the warrant. The return is made by entering on the warrant the date of the arrest, signing the warrant, and filing the warrant with the court. (See the arrest warrant forms in Figure 2.6.) Failure to return an arrest warrant may invalidate the arrest and subject the officer to civil liability for damages.

Place of Arrest

Territorial jurisdiction limits where someone may actually be arrested. However, a widely recognized exception to this rule allows law enforcement officers to arrest someone they began to pursue while within their territorial jurisdiction.

Territorial Limits In most states, law enforcement officers acting under authority of a warrant may make an arrest at any place within the state where the defendant may be found. Similarly, officers may serve a summons at any place within the state.

With respect to warrantless arrests, however, law enforcement officers acting outside the jurisdiction for which they were elected or appointed do not have any official power to arrest. *People v. Williams*, 829 N.E.2d 1203 (N.Y. 2005). Thus, sheriffs may not arrest without a warrant beyond the counties in which they have been elected, nor may municipal police officers arrest without a warrant beyond the limits of the cities in which they have been appointed. On the other hand, the authority of state law enforcement officers is statewide, and their power to arrest without a warrant runs throughout the state. Generally, a law enforcement officer of one state has no authority to arrest in another state.

There are two exceptions to the rule that officers may not arrest without a warrant outside their jurisdiction. The first, explored earlier, is when police make a citizen's arrest outside their jurisdiction as private persons. The other exception is when an extraterritorial arrest is made in fresh pursuit, a concept similar to hot pursuit, but used to describe the pursuit of a suspect across jurisdictional lines.

Fresh Pursuit Exception Under the common law and most statutes, law enforcement officers may make a lawful arrest without a warrant beyond the borders of their jurisdiction in **fresh pursuit**. Fresh pursuit means an officer's immediate pursuit of a criminal suspect into another jurisdiction after the officer has attempted to arrest the suspect in the officer's jurisdiction. The common law allowed a warrantless arrest in fresh pursuit only in felony cases; but today most state statutes allow warrantless arrests for both felonies and misdemeanors (subject to *Welsh*'s limitation on warrantless misdemeanor arrests at a suspect's home as described earlier). For a warrantless arrest in fresh pursuit to be legal, all of the following conditions must be met:

- The officer must have authority to arrest for the crime in the first place.
- The pursuit must be of a fleeing criminal attempting to avoid immediate capture.
- The pursuit must begin promptly and be maintained continuously.

The main requirement is that the pursuit be fresh. The pursuit must flow out of the act of attempting to make an arrest and must be a part of the continuous process of apprehension. The pursuit need not be instantaneous, but it must be made without unreasonable delay or interruption, and there should be no side trips or diversions, even for other police business. The continuity of pursuit is not legally broken by unavoidable interruptions connected with the act of apprehension, such as eating, sleeping, summoning assistance, or obtaining further information.

Fresh pursuit may lead a law enforcement officer outside the boundaries of his or her state. Ordinarily, an officer has no authority beyond that of a private citizen to make arrests in another state. Most states, however, have adopted the Uniform Act on Fresh Pursuit or similar legislation, which permits law enforcement officers from other states, entering in fresh pursuit, to make an arrest.

> Any member of a duly organized state, county, or municipal law enforcing unit of another state of the United States who enters this state in fresh pursuit, and continues within this state in such fresh pursuit, of a person in order to arrest the person on the ground that the person is believed to have committed a felony in such other state, shall have the same authority to arrest and hold such person in custody, as has any member of any duly organized state, county, or municipal law enforcing unit of this state, to arrest and hold in custody a person on the ground that the person is believed to have committed a felony in this state. IOWA CODE ANN. § 806.1.

Because some states extend the privilege to make an arrest in fresh pursuit to out-of-state officers only on a reciprocal basis, law enforcement officers must be familiar with not only the fresh pursuit statutes in their own state but also those of all neighboring states.

A law enforcement officer who makes an arrest in fresh pursuit under such a statute in a neighboring state must take the arrested person before an appropriate judicial officer in that state without unreasonable delay. Some states, however, allow an arresting officer from another state to take a person arrested in fresh pursuit back to the officer's home state after the arrested person is brought before an appropriate judicial officer. Other states allow this only by means of extradition or waiver of extradition. Extradition is a procedure whereby authorities in one state (the demanding state) demand from another state (the asylum state) that a fugitive from justice in the demanding state, who is present in the asylum state, be delivered to the demanding state. Federal law requires extradition of a "fugitive from justice." *See* 18 U.S.C. § 3182. Additionally, forty-eight states have adopted the Uniform Criminal Extradition Act, which provides uniform extradition procedures among the states, including the extradition of persons who commit criminal acts in states where they were never physically present.

Use of Force

A law enforcement officer's right to use force to arrest depends on the degree of force used and the context in which it is used. The basic rule covering the use of force while making an arrest is that law enforcement personnel may use whatever force is necessary and reasonable to make the arrest, but may not use excessive force. *E.g., Papineau v. Parmley*, 465 F.3d 46 (2d Cir. 2006); *Smith v. District of Columbia*, 882 A.2d 778 (D.C. 2005). This section is devoted to exploring the limitations the Fourth Amendment places on the use of force in contextually differentiating reasonable force under the totality of the circumstances from that which is "excessive."

Resisting Arrest When a suspect submits to the authority of law enforcement and offers no resistance, officers may not use any force to make such an arrest other than the minor levels of physical force needed to apply handcuffs and escort the arrestee to a police vehicle or station. *See, e.g., Couden v. Duffy*, 446 F.3d 483 (3d Cir. 2006). It is only when a suspect is not cooperative that the use of force will be deemed reasonable under the Fourth Amendment. But there is a difference between a suspect who is merely not cooperative and one who is truly resisting arrest. *See Sheehan v. State*, 201 S.W.3d 820 (Tex. App. 2006).

Defining the Crime The crime of resisting arrest consists of interfering with a law enforcement officer's lawful ability to take the person into custody. The following statute is a typical one defining the crime of resisting arrest:

A person commits the crime of resisting arrest if he knowingly prevents or attempts to prevent a police officer, acting under color of his official authority, from effecting an arrest of the actor or another, by:

(1) using or threatening to use physical force or violence against the police officer or another; or

(2) using any other means which creates a substantial risk of causing bodily injury to such police officer or another. Mass. Gen. Laws ch. 268, § 32B(a).

As the language of the quoted statutes implies, active opposition such as shooting, striking, pushing, or some other form of actively resisting the officer is usually required. *Commonwealth v. Grandison*, 741 N.E.2d 25 (Mass. 2001). Struggling to prevent being handcuffed, for example, is sufficient active resistance to justify a resisting arrest charge. *State v. Briggs*, 894 A.2d 1008 (2006). Actual injury to the officer, however, is not an element of the crime. *Sampson v. State*, 640 S.E.2d 673 (Ga. Ct. App. 2006).

In contrast, mere flight, concealment, or other avoidance or evasion of arrest may not constitute the crime of resisting arrest because state laws differ on the issue of flight. Some states consider flight to constitute resisting arrest if the defendant fled with the knowledge that the officer had intended to lawfully arrest him or her. *See, e.g., Jean-Marie v. State*, 947 So.2d 484 (Fla. Dist. Ct. App. 2006); *Whaley v. State*, 843 N.E.2d 1 (Ind. App. 2006). Other states make flight a separate offense if the evasion is done in a manner that creates a risk of death or injury. *See State v. Turner*, 193 S.W.3d 522 (Tenn. 2006) (applying Tenn. Code Ann. § 39-16-603(b)(3)). And still other states would consider flight as satisfying the elements of some other crime like eluding or reckless endangerment. *See, e.g., State v. Ferebee*, 630 S.E.2d 460 (N.C. App. 2006).

Similarly, verbal objections—even loud protests that use curse words—or threats unaccompanied by force usually do not constitute the crime of resisting arrest. *See, e.g., Woodward v. Gray*, 527 S.E.2d 595 (2000). However, a minority of states do allow strictly verbal conduct to constitute the crime of resisting arrest. *See, e.g., People v. Christopher*, 40 Cal. Rptr. 3d 615 (Cal. App. 2006); *People v. Vasquez*, 612 N.W.2d 162 (Mich. App. 2000). However, even in states that follow the majority approach that mere words, without more, are insufficient, a serious, imminent threat that prevents an officer from acting because of reasonable fear of serious bodily injury may constitute the crime of resisting arrest. *See State v. Wozniak*, 486 P.2d 1025 (1971); *Wise v. Commonwealth*, 641 S.E.2d 134 (Va. App. 2007).

Common-Law Approach to Resisting Arrest Under the common-law rule, the crime of resisting arrest required that the arrest be lawful. Thus, if the arrest was unlawful, a person had the right to resist the unlawful arrest using what amount of force was reasonably necessary for self-defense and prevention of impending injury. *See, e.g., Bad Elk v. United States*, 177 U.S. 529 (1900). As a result of these rules, it was always important for arresting officers to: establish their identity, if not already known or obvious; and to explain their purpose and authority.

The right to resist an unlawful arrest extended to arrests that were being executed in an unlawful manner, such as when police used excessive force to effectuate what would have otherwise been a legal seizure of a person.

Two qualifications on the citizen's right to defend against and to repel an officer's excessive force must be noticed. He cannot use greater force in protecting himself against the officer's unlawful force than reasonably appears to be necessary. If he employs such greater force, then he becomes the aggressor and forfeits the right to claim self-defense to a charge of assault and battery on the officer. . . .

Furthermore, if he knows that if he desists from his physically defensive measures and submits to arrest the officer's unlawfully excessive force would cease, the arrestee must desist or lose his privilege of self-defense. *State v. Mulvihill*, 270 A.2d 277, 280 (N.J. 1970).

Modern Approach to Resisting Arrest Although some states continue to use the common-law rule allowing resistance to an illegal arrest, an increasing number of states have adopted a trend that began in the 1960s. Modern law rejects the common-law rule in light of the dangers inherent in its approach, and because the consequences of an illegal arrest are at most a brief period of detention during which arrested persons can resort to nonviolent legal remedies for regaining their liberty. However, even in those states that hold an arrestee has no right to resist an unlawful arrest, all states adhere to the common law's approach on the right to use force in self-defense against an arresting officer's excessive force. Thus, for example, the court in *Shoultz v. State*, 735 N.E.2d 818 (Ind. Ct. App. 2000), held that because an officer had used excessive force in making a misdemeanor arrest, the defendant was privileged to offer reasonable resistance to the excessive force without running afoul of the state's resistance statute. Key to the court's reasoning was that the defendant never threatened the officer with any force or violence, nor had anyone touched the officer before he used pepper spray and a flashlight to subdue the defendant. Moreover, the officer neither informed the defendant that he was under arrest nor attempted to handcuff him before using force. *See also Sapen v. State*, 869 N.E. 2d 1273, 1280 (Ind. App. 2007) (finding no crime of resisting arrest when suspect applies reasonable force in response to officer's excessive force).

The Common-Law Approach to Using Force to Make an Arrest If a suspect resisted arrest, the common law differentiated the permissible levels of force that an officer could use in making an arrest based upon the underlying crime. Thus, there was one rule governing the use of force for misdemeanor arrests and another rule for felony arrests.

Misdemeanors At common law, law enforcement officers were permitted to use any reasonably necessary *nondeadly* force to arrest for a misdemeanor. However, an officer was not justified in using *deadly* force to arrest for a misdemeanor. *E.g., State v. Wall*, 286 S.E.2d 68 (N.C. 1982). The rationale underlying the common-law rule was that it would be better for a misdemeanant to escape than for a human life to be taken in the pursuit of a minor lawbreaker. Thus, the common law held that the use of deadly force on a misdemeanant was excessive force constituting an assault or battery. Moreover, an officer who killed a suspected misdemeanant could be held criminally liable for murder or manslaughter, as well as civilly liable for damages.

Felonies Under the common-law rule, a law enforcement officer could use any reasonably necessary *nondeadly* force to arrest for a felony. But unlike with misdemeanor arrests, deadly force could be used to make a felony arrest if the suspect fled. Under this approach, an officer was not required to retreat from making an arrest to avoid extreme measures, but he or she was required to press on and use all necessary force to bring the offender into custody. The use of deadly force was therefore permitted as a last resort if the only alternative was to abandon the attempt to arrest.

Self-Defense and Defense of Others It should be noted that the common law's felony and misdemeanor distinction to the use of force applied only to an officer making an arrest when the would-be arrestee fled or resisted arrest; it did not apply when the arrestee used or attempted to use unlawful force against the police officer or a third party. If such unlawful force was being used against the officer or a third party, then the rules of self-defense or defense of others came into play, and the arresting officer was not bound by the usual rules for the use of force in making arrests.

Self-Defense A law enforcement officer may use a reasonable amount of nondeadly force to defend him- or herself against the imminent, unlawful application of nondeadly force to the officer. If, however, the officer is faced with imminent, unlawful deadly force, then the officer is privileged to use deadly force to defend him- or herself against such unlawful deadly force.

Defense of Others A law enforcement officer may use a reasonable amount of nondeadly force to defend a third party against an imminent, unlawful attack involving nondeadly force. If, however, the third party is faced with imminent, unlawful deadly force, then an officer is privileged to use deadly force to defend the third party against such unlawful deadly force.

> When making an arrest, if someone begins to assault or batter a law enforcement officer, then the arrestee has transformed the situation into a self-defense one, thereby making it lawful for the officer to use any force reasonably necessary under the circumstances, including deadly force, if the officer reasonably believes that the person to be arrested is about to commit an assault and that the officer is in danger of death or serious bodily injury. For example, an officer faced with the choice of abandoning an arrest or using deadly force in self-defense has the right to use deadly force in response to an immediate threat of death or serious bodily injury. *See, e.g., Salim v. Proulx*, 93 F.3d 86 (2d Cir. 1996).

The Modern Approach The common law's approach to a law enforcement officer's privilege to use force, even deadly force, in self-defense or in defense of others remains the law today in nearly all U.S. jurisdictions. However, the common law's distinction between felonies and misdemeanors in the lawful use of force to make an arrest over a suspect's flight or resistance has become "untenable" in modern times. *Tennessee v. Garner*, 471 U.S. 1, 14 (1985).

Compared to earlier times, most felonies today are not punishable by death, fewer felons are convicted or executed, and police are organized, trained, equipped with sophisticated weapons and are capable of killing accurately at a distance and under circumstances posing little danger to officers or others, especially if the felon is unarmed. Operation of the earlier common-law rule under these circumstances would allow police to kill fleeing persons merely suspected of offenses that, on conviction, would very likely result in only brief imprisonment or even probation. Thus, today, the misdemeanor and felony distinction has been replaced by a balancing test that analyzes the use of force for its reasonableness under the Fourth Amendment, applying a totality-of-the-circumstances approach. *Graham v. Connor*, 490 U.S. 386 (1989).

In *Graham*, the U.S. Supreme Court set forth the following factors as the three primary ones to be examined when making a reasonableness inquiry about the use of force:

- the severity of the crime at issue,
- whether the suspect poses an immediate threat to the safety of the officers or others, and
- whether he is actively resisting arrest or attempting to evade arrest by flight.

The application of this balancing test has produced rules that are similar, but not identical, to the common law's approach.

Nondeadly Force A law enforcement officer making an arrest—whether for a felony or a misdemeanor—has the right to use a reasonable amount of nondeadly force to make the arrest.

The officer has discretion to determine the degree of force required under the circumstances as they appear to the officer at the time. The reasonableness of the force used is a question for the trier of facts. The test to determine the actual amount of force necessary is not one of hindsight. The degree of force used may be reasonable even though it is more than is actually required. The officer may not, however, use an unreasonable amount of force or wantonly or maliciously injure a suspect. *Clark v. Thomas*, 505 F. Supp. 2d 884 (D. Kan. 2007).

Under this approach, only minimal force, such as that necessary to apply handcuffs, would be necessary to make an arrest of a cooperative suspect. However, the more a suspect resists, the more nondeadly force could be lawfully used to make the arrest.

Deadly Force The modern parameters for the use of deadly force were established by the U.S. Supreme Court in *Tennessee v. Garner*, 471 U.S. 1 (1985). In *Garner*, a woman called the police to report that a "prowler" was attempting to break in to her neighbor's home. When police arrived on the scene, the woman gestured toward an adjacent property and told police that she had heard glass breaking. When officers went to investigate, they heard a door slam and saw someone, later identified as Edward Garner, running across the backyard until he came to a stop at a six-foot-high chain link fence.

> With the aid of a flashlight, [the officer] was able to see Garner's face and hands. He saw no sign of a weapon, and, though not certain, was "reasonably sure" and "figured" that Garner was unarmed. He thought Garner was 17 or 18 years old and about 5'5" or 5'7" tall. While Garner was crouched at the base of the fence, [the officer] called out "police, halt" and took a few steps toward him. Garner then began to climb over the fence. Convinced that if Garner made it over the fence he would elude capture, [the officer] shot him. The bullet hit Garner in the back of the head. Garner was taken by ambulance to a hospital, where he died on the operating table. Ten dollars and a purse taken from the house were found on his body. 471 U.S. at 3–4.

The officer's use of deadly force to seize Garner would have been permissible under the common law because burglary is a felony and therefore Garner was a fleeing felon. And, at the time, both the laws of the state of Tennessee and the relevant police regulations governing the use of deadly force were in accord with the common law. Thus, according to the law in effect at the time of the shooting, the use of deadly force to stop Garner was justified.

Garner's father filed a suit under 42 U.S.C. Section 1983 asserting that his son was unconstitutionally seized in violation of the Fourth Amendment because the use of deadly force against him was unreasonable under the facts and circumstances of the case. The Supreme Court ultimately agreed with Garner's father and declared that the "use of deadly force to prevent the escape of all felony suspects, whatever the circumstances, is constitutionally unreasonable." 471 U.S. at 11. In so ruling, the Court overruled the centuries-old common-law approach governing the use of deadly force in making arrests and, accordingly, the Tennessee statute based on the common-law rule.

In its place, the Court reasoned that the reasonableness command of the Fourth Amendment required the following approach:

> It is not better that all felony suspects die than that they escape. Where the suspect poses no immediate threat to the officer and no threat to others, the harm resulting from failing to apprehend him does not justify the use of deadly force to do so. It is no doubt unfortunate when a suspect who is in sight escapes, but the fact that the police arrive a little late or are a little slower afoot does not always justify killing the suspect. A police officer may not seize an unarmed, nondangerous suspect by shooting him dead. . . .
>
> Where the officer has probable cause to believe that the suspect poses a threat of serious physical harm, either to the officer or to others, it is not constitutionally unreasonable to prevent escape by using deadly force. *Thus, if the suspect threatens the officer with a weapon or there is probable cause to believe that he has committed a crime involving the infliction or threatened infliction of serious physical harm, deadly force may be used if necessary to prevent escape, and if, where feasible, some warning has been given.* 471 U.S. at 11–12 (italics added).

In effect, the *Garner* decision constitutionalized the common-law approach to misdemeanants, as even violent misdemeanors rarely involve the inflection of *serious* bodily harm. Thus, just as it was under the common law, police are not justified in using deadly force to arrest for a misdemeanor. But *Garner* altered the common-law rule regarding fleeing felons. Today, deadly force may only be used by law enforcement officers

- in defense of their own lives (i.e., to prevent an imminent, unlawful attack that poses a risk of death or serious bodily harm to the officer);
- in defense of the lives of others (i.e., again to prevent an imminent, unlawful attack that poses a risk of death or serious bodily harm to a third party);
- to stop the escape of a fleeing suspect if there is probable cause to believe that the suspect has committed a crime involving the infliction or threatened infliction of serious physical harm.

DISCUSSION POINT

Does Reckless Driving During an Attempt to Flee Justify the Use of Potentially Deadly Force Under Garner? *Scott v. Harris*, 550 U.S. 372 (2007) and *Plumhoff v. Rickard*, 134 S. Ct. 2012 (2014)

On the night of March 29, 2001, a Coweta County, Georgia, deputy clocked Victor Harris's car at 73 mph in a 55 mph zone. The deputy activated his blue flashing lights, but the 19-year-old driver sped away. The deputy radioed his dispatch to report that he was pursuing a fleeing radio communication and joined the pursuit along with other officers. In the midst of the chase,

Harris pulled into the parking lot of a shopping center and was nearly boxed in by the various police vehicles. He evaded the trap by making a sharp turn, colliding with Scott's police car, exiting the parking lot, and speeding off once again down a two-lane highway. At times, Harris traveled at speeds between 85 and 90 miles per hour.

Six minutes and nearly 10 miles after the chase had begun, Scott decided to attempt to terminate the episode by employing a precision intervention technique (PIT) maneuver, "which causes the fleeing vehicle to spin to a stop." Having radioed his supervisor for permission, Scott was told to "[g]o ahead and take him out." Instead, Scott applied his push bumper to the rear of Harris's car. This caused Harris to lose control of his vehicle. The car left the roadway, ran down an embankment, overturned, and crashed. Harris was badly injured and was rendered a quadriplegic. He filed a 42 U.S.C. Section 1983 lawsuit alleging that Scott

Continued on next page

had used excessive force, constituting an unreasonable seizure under the Fourth Amendment.

Harris argued that Scott violated the law as set forth in *Tennessee v. Garner* because "there was little, if any, actual threat to pedestrians or other motorists, as the roads were mostly empty and [respondent] remained in control of his vehicle." 550 U.S. at 378. A videotape of the chase, however, convinced a majority of the U.S. Supreme Court that the reality of the story differed from Harris's version.

> There we see respondent's vehicle racing down narrow, two-lane roads in the dead of night at speeds that are shockingly fast. We see it swerve around more than a dozen other cars, cross the double-yellow line, and force cars traveling in both directions to their respective shoulders to avoid being hit. We see it run multiple red lights and travel for considerable periods of time in the occasional center left-turn-only lane, chased by numerous police cars forced to engage in the same hazardous maneuvers just to keep up. Far from being the cautious and controlled driver the lower court depicts, what we see on the video more closely resembles a Hollywood-style car chase of the most frightening sort, placing police officers and innocent bystanders alike at great risk of serious injury. 550 U.S. at 379–80.

The Court reasoned that these facts presented a qualitatively different type of situation than *Garner* did.

> *Garner* did not establish a magical on/off switch that triggers rigid preconditions whenever an officer's actions constitute "deadly force." *Garner* was simply an application of the Fourth Amendment's "reasonableness" test . . . to the use of a particular type of force in a particular situation. *Garner* held that it was unreasonable to kill a "young, slight, and unarmed" burglary suspect . . . by shooting him "in the back of the head" while he was running away on foot . . . and when the officer "could not reasonably have believed that [the suspect] posed any threat," and "never attempted to justify his actions on any basis other than the need to prevent an escape." . . . Whatever Garner said about the factors that might have justified shooting the suspect in that case, such "preconditions" have scant applicability to this case, which has vastly different facts . . . [because] the threat posed by the flight on foot of an unarmed suspect [is not] even remotely comparable to the extreme danger to human life posed by respondent in this case. . . . Whether or not Scott's actions constituted application of "deadly force," all that matters is whether Scott's actions were reasonable. 550 U.S. at 382–83.

- Initially, Harris was speeding—an offense that is not an inherently dangerous felony or one that provides probable cause to believe that Harris himself is a dangerous person. Why, then, do you think the case was not disposed of under the modern rules prohibiting the use of deadly force against fleeing misdemeanants?

- Do you agree that Scott's actions were reasonable under the circumstances? Why or why not?

- Given the dangers associated with high-speed pursuits to suspects, police officers, and the general public, many police departments have enacted policies barring officers from engaging in high-speed chases. Do you think it would have been more reasonable, from a constitutional perspective, for the police to have ceased pursuit? Would your answer differ if the county had a formal policy barring high-speed chases? Explain your reasoning.

Recently, the Court decided *Plumhoff v. Rickard*, in which the Court essentially maintained the earlier precedents it had set in the *Garner* and *Scott* cases. *Plumhoff* found that officers who fired fifteen shots at a motorist's vehicle to attempt to stop that vehicle from continuing to flee police, did not use excessive or unreasonable force under the circumstances, and did not violate the Fourth Amendment. The facts of *Plumhoff* are as follows:

> Near midnight on July 18, 2004, Lieutenant Joseph Forthman of the West Memphis, Arkansas, Police Department pulled over a white Honda Accord because the car had only one operating headlight. Donald Rickard was the driver of the Accord, and Kelly Allen was in the passenger seat. Forthman noticed an indentation, roughly the size of a head or a basketball in the windshield of the car. He asked Rickard if he had been drinking, and Rickard responded that he had not. Because Rickard failed to produce his driver's license upon request and appeared nervous, Forthman asked him to step out of the car. Rather than comply with Forthman's request, Rickard sped away.
>
> Forthman gave chase and was soon joined by five other police cruisers driven by Sergeant Vance Plumhoff and Officers Jimmy Evans, Lance Ellis, Troy Galtelli, and John Gardner. The

Continued on next page

officers pursued Rickard east on Interstate 40 toward Memphis, Tennessee. While on I-40, they attempted to stop Rickard using a rolling road-block, but they were unsuccessful. The District Court described the vehicles as swerving through traffic at high speeds, and respondent does not dispute that the cars attained speeds over 100 miles per hour. During the chase, Rickard and the officers passed more than two dozen vehicles.

It is also undisputed that Forthman [originally] saw glass shavings on the dashboard of Rickard's car, a sign that the windshield had been broken recently; that another officer testified that the windshield indentation and glass shavings would have justified a suspicion that someone had possibly been struck by that vehicle, like a pedestrian; and that Forthman saw beer in Rickard's car.

Rickard eventually exited I-40 in Memphis, and shortly afterward he made a quick right turn, causing contact to occur between his car and Evans' cruiser. As a result of that contact, Rickard's car spun out into a parking lot and collided with Plumhoff 's cruiser. Now in danger of being cornered, Rickard put his car into reverse in an attempt to escape. As he did so, Evans and Plumhoff got out of their cruisers and approached Rickard's car, and Evans, gun in hand, pounded on the passenger-side window. At that point, Rickard's car made contact with yet another police cruiser. Rickard's tires started spinning, and his car was rocking back and forth, indicating that Rickard was using the accelerator even though his bumper was flush against a police cruiser. At that point, Plumhoff fired three shots into Rickard's car. Rickard then reversed in a 180 degree arc and maneuvered onto another street, forcing Ellis to step to his right to avoid the vehicle. As Rickard continued fleeing down that street, Gardner and Galtelli fired 12 shots toward Rickard's car, bringing the total number of shots fired during this incident to 15. Rickard then lost control of the car and crashed into a building. Rickard and Allen both died from some combination of gunshot wounds and injuries suffered in the crash that ended the chase. 134 S. Ct. at 2017–18.

Mentioning the *Scott* case described earlier in this Discussion Point, the Court in *Plumhoff* found that under the circumstances, the officers acted reasonably in firing multiple shots at Rickard's vehicle in an attempt to stop it from fleeing, and were entitled to qualified immunity against a civil lawsuit for their conduct:

> [A]t the moment when the shots were fired, all that a reasonable police officer could have concluded was that Rickard was intent on resuming his flight and that, if he was allowed to do so, he would once again pose a deadly threat for others on the road. Rickard's conduct even after the shots were fired—as noted, he managed to drive away despite the efforts of the police to block his path—underscores the point.
>
> In light of the circumstances we have discussed, it is beyond serious dispute that Rickard's flight posed a grave public safety risk, and here, as in Scott, the police acted reasonably in using deadly force to end that risk.

* * *

Under the circumstances present in this case, we hold that the Fourth Amendment did not prohibit petitioners from using the deadly force that they employed to terminate the dangerous car chase that Rickard precipitated. In the alternative, we note that petitioners are entitled to qualified immunity for the conduct at issue because they violated no clearly established law. 134 S. Ct. at 2022, 2024.

■ Do you agree with the Court's finding in *Plumhoff* that the officers' actions under the circumstances constituted reasonable force (i.e., in light of the threat Rickard's actions posed at the time of the firing of the shots by police and possibly later, if he was able or permitted to flee)?

■ How easy is it to predict how much of a risk Rickard posed to others in the future, if he was able or permitted to flee (i.e., without police following him closely)?

■ Recalling the *Scott* case discussed earlier, do you believe there were any alternative, safer methods for the officers in *Plumhoff* to monitor and/or stop Rickard's vehicle under the circumstances? In other words, could the officers have reasonably prevented Rickard from escaping in his vehicle through any other means besides shooting him and his passenger, which directly contributed to the crash of the vehicle and their deaths? Or is it better to defer to officers' actions in situations like these involving "split second" decisions under stressful conditions, rather than try to "second guess" these actions "after-the-fact"? Fully explain your answers.

Excessive Force Under the Fourth Amendment Using unnecessary force against a cooperative suspect is nearly always unreasonable. For example, in *Couden v. Duffy*, 446 F.3d 483 (3d Cir. 2006), police set up a surveillance team outside a home based on a tip that a fugitive wanted on drug and weapons-related charges might be staying at that address. At approximately 8:30 P.M., the occupant of the home pulled up in a car in front of the house and let her fourteen-year-old son, carrying a skateboard, out of the vehicle. The boy was supposed to put his skateboard in the garage and then get his sister from the house so the family could then all go out to dinner together. But the boy then "saw a man charging towards him with a gun. Frightened, he slammed the garage door shut, remaining inside." 446 F.3d at 490. Mistakenly believing the boy was the fugitive they wanted, four police officers pursued the boy into the house. They jumped on him to subdue him; one officer put his knee into the boy's back; other officers pointed guns at the boy's head, handcuffed him, and sprayed him with mace. Because the boy was cooperative and police had no reason to believe that the boy was armed or dangerous, or that any accomplice was present, the court held that police officers used **excessive force** to seize the boy in violation of the Fourth Amendment.

When police use unnecessary force against a cooperative suspect, they expose themselves to liability. In refusing to apply the doctrine of qualified immunity to the facts of one such case, *Payne v. Pauley*, 337 F.3d 767, 780 (7th Cir. 2003), held that it was "well established" that applying handcuffs unusually tightly and then violently yanking the arms of arrestees "who were not resisting arrest, did not disobey the orders of a police officer, did not pose a threat to the safety of the officer or others" constituted excessive force prohibited by the Fourth Amendment.

On the other hand, when police have reason to believe someone is armed and dangerous, then their use of even deadly force is justified. In *Boyd v. Baeppler*, 215 F.3d 594 (6th Cir. 2000), for example, police officers used deadly force against a suspect who had a gun in his hand and who pointed it at officers and others. This rule applies even when the police are mistaken, so long as their mistake is both honest and reasonable. For example, in *Bell v. City of East Cleveland*, 125 F.3d 855 (6th Cir. 1997), the court upheld the actions of a police officer who shot a young boy who was carrying only a toy gun. The officer thought the gun was real. When the boy did not follow the officer's command to put the gun down, and the boy pointed the gun at the officer, the officer shot the boy.

Countless situations, however, lie in between a cooperative suspect who submits to the authority of an arresting officer and one who resists using actual or perceived deadly force. These are the "tough cases" that need to be judged under the totality of the circumstances under *Graham*'s balancing test. Although a comprehensive review of the use of force by law enforcement is beyond the scope of this book, several scenarios in the "gray area" receive much attention in the courts and are therefore summarized in a general manner here.

Nondeadly Force and Special Medical Circumstances If the use of nondeadly force by law enforcement while making an arrest inadvertently causes the death of a suspect or bodily injury to a suspect, courts usually find in favor of the police unless the officer either knew or had objective reasons to know of a suspect's particular susceptibility to the tactic used. For example, in *Hendon v. City of Piedmont*, 163 F. Supp. 2d 1316 (N.D. Ala. 2001), police arrested a seventy-four-year-old woman in connection with her behavior while driving. The woman had disregarded a police roadblock for a funeral procession and was pulled over accordingly. However, she drove away from the scene before the officer could finish issuing a traffic citation to her, having told the officer she was "smothering" and needed to get to her physician's office. The officer pursued her and used his car to block hers. He then used minor force to remove the woman from her car, whereupon she slapped him. He then handcuffed her in a manner that resulted in minor bruising and bleeding on her wrists. As her breathing became more labored, she was transported to a hospital where she subsequently died of a heart attack. Her family sued, claiming that her verbal protestations about her breathing coupled with the fact that she had disabled license tags on her car should have been sufficient to put the officer on notice that even the minor force he used would have been excessive for someone in her condition. The court rejected this assertion and held that the officer's actions were objectively reasonable under the Fourth Amendment. *See also Estate of Smith v. Marasco*, 430 F.3d 140 (3d Cir. 2005).

In contrast, law enforcement officers must be careful about the level of force they use against a suspect who has visible signs of an injury or special medical condition that might establish the reasonable likelihood of a suspect's vulnerable condition and thereby counsel against the use of a level of force that might otherwise have been lawfully employed. For example, in *Guite v. Wright*, 147 F.3d 747 (8th Cir. 1998), police went to a suspect's home to arrest him. The suspect was at home recovering from surgery on his left shoulder. In spite of the fact that he was wearing a sling on his left arm, officers grabbed his wrist, pushed him backward, and held him up against the open door inside the house. The court ruled that the suspect had a valid claim for excessive force under the circumstances.

Conducted Energy Devices Starting approximately in 2001, a number of law enforcement organizations began to use conducted energy devices (CEDs), more commonly referred to as *stun guns* or by the brand-name Tasers. CEDs deliver a shock to the recipient, thereby incapacitating him or her and obviating the need for deadly force. But CEDs have been linked to approximately 540 deaths between 2001 and 2013; in at least 60 of these cases, medical examiners cited CEDs as a contributing cause of death (see Amnesty International 2011, 2013).

One court described CEDs as follows:

> [T]he Taser is designed to deliver a 50,000-volt shock; the shock overrides the body's central nervous system, causing total incapacitation of the muscles and instant collapse; on the use-of-force continuum, the Taser falls in the highest category of force, just one step down from the use of deadly force; the Taser can cause severe muscle contractions that may result in injuries to muscles, tendons, ligaments, backs and joints, and stress fractures; and in a number of cases, individuals have died in custody after being tased. *Parker v. City of South Portland*, 2007 WL 1468658 (D. Me. 2007).

Given its characteristics, courts consider the use of CEDs "a significantly violent level of force." *DeSalvo v. City of Collinsville*, 2005 WL 2487829, at *4 (S.D. Ill. 2005). Thus, just as officers "may use guns only against suspects posing a threat of serious physical harm, . . . the use of tasers requires sufficient justification for their use to be reasonable." *McKenney v. Harrison*, 635 F.3d 354 (8th Cir. 2011). Accordingly, courts generally hold that the use of a CED can constitute excessive force under certain circumstances, such as when used against an unarmed arrestee who is suspected of having committed a minor crime; not actively resisting arrest; not trying to flee; and not posing an imminent threat of harm to officers or others. For example, in *Cavanaugh v. Woods Cross City*, 625 F.3d 661 (10th Cir. 2010), an officer used a CED on a woman suspected of committing a minor, noninjurious assault against her husband as she attempted to leave their apartment. She posed no danger to anyone, she was not resisting arrest, and the officer did not warn her first. The court determined this to be a constitutionally unreasonable use of excessive force. Moreover, the court concluded that a prohibition on the use of a stun gun on a nonviolent misdemeanant under such circumstances violated clearly established law such that the officer was not entitled to qualified immunity for his actions. Indeed, courts have held that misuse of CEDs can give rise to liability not only for the individual officers who use them but also to the municipalities that employ them for failing to properly train officers in the use of such devices. *E.g., Lee v. Metropolitan Government of Nashville and Davidson County*, 596 F. Supp. 2d 1101 (M.D. Tenn. 2009); *Lieberman v. Marino*, 2007 WL 789436 (E.D. Pa. 2007).

In the wake of calls for a moratorium on the use of CEDs by Amnesty International, the U.S. Department of Justice and the Police Executive Research Forum (PERF) conducted a study of the use of these devices. These two organizations jointly issued formal guidelines for the use of CEDs in November of 2006, including these recommendations:

■ *CEDs should only be used against persons who are actively resisting or exhibiting active aggression, or to prevent individuals from harming themselves or others. CEDs should not be used against a passive suspect.*

■ No more than one officer at a time should activate a CED against a person.

■ When activating a CED, law enforcement officers should use it for one standard cycle and stop to evaluate the situation (a standard cycle is five seconds).

■ Training protocols should emphasize that multiple activations and continuous cycling of a CED appear to increase the risk of death or serious injury and should be avoided where practical.

■ That a subject is fleeing should not be the sole justification for police use of a CED. Severity of offense and other circumstances should be considered before officers' use of a CED on the fleeing subject.

■ *CEDs should not generally be used against pregnant women, elderly persons, young children, and visibly frail persons unless exigent circumstances exist.*

■ CEDs should not be used on handcuffed persons unless they are actively resisting or exhibiting active aggression [or] to prevent individuals from harming themselves or others.

■ All persons who have been exposed to a CED activation should receive a medical evaluation. Agencies shall consult with local medical personnel to develop appropriate police-medical protocols.

■ A warning should be given to a person prior to activating the CED unless to do so would place any other person at risk (Cronin and Ederheimer 2006: 23–26; emphasis added).

Another study conducted by PERF did find some benefit, however, to the use of CEDs during incidents involving the use of force by police. The study compared seven law enforcement agencies that use CEDs with six agencies that do not. The researchers found:

■ "A 70-percent decrease in officer injuries associated with the use of CEDs. During the two years before CEDs were used, 13 percent of the officers involved in use-of-force incidents required medical attention. When CEDs were deployed, the percentage requiring medical attention declined to 8 percent.

■ A 40-percent decrease in suspect injuries associated with the use of conducted-energy devices. During the two years before the agencies began using CEDs, 55 percent of the suspects required medical attention, while 40 percent required medical attention after the agencies started using the devices." (Taylor et al. 2009: 4)

Finally, a recent National Institute of Justice study sheds additional light on the use of CEDs by officers. This study, entitled "Study of Death Following Electro-Muscular Disruption," found that

- the literature suggests a significant safety margin regarding the use of CEDs when they are applied pursuant to manufacturer's instructions (though the devices are not "risk free");
- all evidence suggests that the application of CEDs entails a risk as low as or lower than most alternative use-of-force mechanisms;
- CED use is associated with a substantially decreased threat of injury to officers and suspects compared to physical force;
- there is no medical evidence showing that CEDs pose a substantial risk for cardiac rhythm issues (i.e., induced cardiac dysrhythmia) in individuals when used reasonably;
- moreover, current research fails to support a significantly higher risk of cardiac arrhythmia in field applications of CEDs, even when the CED darts hit the front of the chest.
- The application of CEDs by officers to the area of the chest in front of the heart is not completely risk-free; however, present research does not support a significantly higher risk of cardiac dysrhythmia in field applications of CED darts hitting this area of the chest. (Alpert et al. 2011: vii, 9, 12, 24, 30).

Police Dogs Police have used trained canines as part of law enforcement for quite some time. The manner in which officers use police dogs as instrumentalities of force is governed by the Fourth Amendment's reasonableness requirement. One of the leading cases in this area is *Robinette v. Barnes*, 854 F.2d 909 (6th Cir. 1988). In that case, police had probable cause to believe that a man suspected of burglary was hiding inside a darkened building. After police commands for the suspect to exit the building were disregarded, they warned that they had a police dog that they would turn loose if the suspect did not come out of the building. After the initial warning produced no suspect, the police repeated their warning. When the second warning went unheeded, they released the canine. The dog subsequently apprehended the suspect by biting him on the neck, and the suspect died shortly thereafter. His estate filed a civil suit, arguing that the use of the police dog constituted the impermissible use of deadly force in violation of *Tennessee v. Garner*. The court rejected that claim:

> [W]e find that the use of a properly trained police dog to apprehend a felony suspect does not carry with it a substantial risk of causing death or serious bodily harm. Although we cannot ignore the fact that, in this case, the use of a police dog did result in a person's death, we also cannot ignore the evidence in the record which indicates that this tragic event was an extreme aberration from the outcome intended or expected. [The evidence] was unequivocal on the fact that the dogs are trained to seize suspects by the arm and then wait for an officer to secure the arrestee. 854 F.2d at 912.

Many police dogs are specially trained to attack using a technique known as the "bite and hold." Most courts that have considered this technique are in accord with the decision in *Robinette v. Barnes* and have held that the technique does not, in and of itself, constitute deadly force. *See, e.g., Jarrett v. Town of Yarmouth*, 331 F.3d 140 (1st Cir. 2003). However, the use of canines as weapons can nonetheless constitute excessive force under the facts of a particular case. For example, *Watkins v. City of Oakland*, 145 F.3d 1087, 1093 (9th Cir. 1998), held that when police improperly encouraged the continuation of an attack by a police dog, the use of force was unreasonable and therefore violated the Fourth Amendment. *See also Priester v. City of Riviera Beach*, 208 F.3d 919,

928 (11th Cir. 2000) (court declines to find qualified immunity for two police officers for excessive force and failure to intervene when the officers allowed a cooperating suspect to be bit on both of his legs by a police dog, leaving the suspect with fourteen puncture wounds overall).

Police *vehicle* searches using canines are discussed in Chapter 11 under the section "Other Issues Related to Vehicle Searches." Police use of canines to *search* in the area around a home is discussed in Chapter 3 in the context of the *Jardines* case, in the Discussion Point entitled "*Florida v. Jardines*—Dog Sniffs at Your Home: Are They Fourth Amendment Searches by Police?"

Car Chases Police vehicles, if negligently or recklessly operated, can be deadly weapons that can inflict injuries upon suspects, innocent third parties, and the officers themselves. As a rule, law enforcement officers have a duty "to avoid driving in reckless disregard for the safety of others and to exercise due care for the safety of others once pursuit is undertaken." 57 Am. Jur. 2d *Municipal, County, School, and State Tort Liability* § 439 (Supp. 2007) (citing *Lee v. City of Omaha*, 307 N.W.2d 800 (Neb. 1981)). As discussed earlier in the Discussion Point on *Scott v. Harris and Plumhoff v. Richard*, many police departments have developed policies that prohibit high-speed chases under a number of circumstances. In addition to the personal injury, or "tort," liability such chases may engender against officers, there is also potential civil liability for offices under Section 1983 that a seizure that occurs as part of such a chase violates the Fourth Amendment. The concurring justices in *Scott v. Harris* wrote to specially note that the case did not create a per se rule authorizing high-speed chases under the Fourth Amendment. "The inquiry . . . is situation specific. Among relevant considerations: Were the lives and well-being of others (motorists, pedestrians, police officers) at risk? Was there a safer way, given the time, place, and circumstances, to stop the fleeing vehicle?" 550 U.S. at 386 (Ginsburg, J., concurring). As a result, law enforcement officers are well advised to consider alternatives to bringing to an end high-speed chases that pose a risk of danger to others whose "seizure" would not be so easily deemed "reasonable" under the facts of another case.

After Making an Arrest

An arrest initiates a series of administrative and judicial procedures dealing with the arrested person and his or her property. These procedures vary among jurisdictions, but all basically deal with the same issues: the protection of the person and property of the arrestee, notification of and opportunity to exercise certain rights, safety and security of law enforcement officials and places of confinement, identification, further investigation, record keeping, and avoidance of civil liability. Booking is usually the first of these procedures to take place after arrest.

Booking

Booking is a police administrative procedure officially recording an arrest in a police register. At a minimum, booking involves recording the name of the person arrested, the name of the officer making the arrest, and the time of, place of, circumstances of, and reason for the arrest. The meaning of booking, however, is sometimes expanded to include other procedures that take place in the stationhouse after an arrest. Booking may include a search of the arrested person (including in some cases a search of his body and body cavities), fingerprinting, photographing, a lineup, or other identification procedures, such as the collection of a DNA sample under certain circumstances. The arrested person may be temporarily detained in a jail or lockup until release on bail can be arranged. For less serious offenses, the arrested person may be released on personal recognizance, under which the person agrees to appear in court when required but is not required to pay or promise to pay any money or property as security.

Booking is usually completed before the arrested person's initial appearance before the magistrate, but not necessarily. Booking procedures vary among different jurisdictions and among different law enforcement agencies within a particular jurisdiction.

Initial Appearance

After arresting a person, with or without a warrant, a law enforcement officer must take the person before a magistrate or deliver the person according to the mandate of the warrant. Recall from Chapter 2 that this initial appearance, or *Gerstein* hearing, must usually occur within forty-eight hours of the actual arrest. *County of Riverside v. McLaughlin*, 500 U.S. 44 (1991). The initial appearance is discussed in more detail in Chapter 2 as part of the section on "Preliminary Pretrial Criminal Proceedings."

Safety Considerations

Just because a suspect has been subdued does not necessarily mean that police officers or others are free from danger. The Supreme Court has therefore given law enforcement officers some latitude in protecting themselves, the arrestee, third parties, and the crime scene, if applicable.

> [I]t is not "unreasonable" under the Fourth Amendment for a police officer, as a matter of course, to monitor the movements of an arrested person, as his judgment dictates, following the arrest. The officer's need to ensure his own safety—as well as the integrity of the arrest—is compelling. Such surveillance is not an impermissible invasion of the privacy or personal liberty of an individual who has been arrested. *Washington v. Chrisman*, 455 U.S. 1, 7 (1982).

Protection and Welfare of Arrested Person and Arresting Officer When delay in taking an arrested person before a magistrate is unavoidable, the officer must keep the arrested person safely in custody for the period of the delay. The officer may reasonably restrain the person to prevent escape and may even confine the person in a jail or other suitable place. Handcuffs may be used at the officer's discretion, depending on the person's reputation or record for violence, the time of day, the number of other persons in custody, and the duration of the detention.

The officer is responsible for the health and safety of the arrested person, including providing adequate medical assistance, if necessary. Any unnecessary use of force or negligent failure to prevent the use of force by others against the arrested person may subject the officer to criminal or civil liability.

Inventory Search When a person is arrested and taken into custody, police may search the person and any container or item in his or her possession as part of the routine administrative procedure incident to booking and jailing the person. *Illinois v. Lafayette*, 462 U.S. 640 (1983), held that stationhouse inventory searches are an incidental step following arrest and preceding incarceration and are reasonable under the Fourth Amendment without any further justification. The Court said that the governmental interests justifying a stationhouse inventory search are different from, and may in some circumstances be even greater than, those supporting a search incident to arrest (see later sections of this chapter). Among those interests are prevention of theft of the arrested person's property; deterrence of false claims regarding that property; prevention of injury from belts, drugs, or dangerous instruments such as razor blades, knives, or bombs; and determination or verification of the person's identity. Furthermore, stationhouse searches are valid even though less intrusive means of satisfying those governmental interests might be possible.

If special circumstances exist, a stationhouse inventory search does not need to be conducted immediately on the arrested person's arrival at the stationhouse but may be conducted at a subsequent time. *See United States v. Edwards,* 415 U.S. 800 (1974), discussed in detail later in this chapter.

Sometimes, especially when a vehicle is involved, officers must take positive action to protect an arrested person's property or risk civil liability for damages for failure to do so. Many law enforcement agencies have adopted standard procedures for impounding arrested persons' vehicles and making an inventory of their contents. (For a discussion of impoundment and inventory of vehicles, see Chapter 12.)

Identification and Examination of an Arrested Person at Booking

Law enforcement officers may take fingerprints, footprints, and photographs of an arrested person for purposes of identification or evidence. Officers may also obtain voice exemplars or have a dentist examine a defendant's mouth for a missing tooth for identification purposes. *United States v. Holland*, 378 F. Supp. 144 (E.D. Pa. 1974). Arrestees may also be physically examined for measurements, scars, bruises, tattoos, lice, wounds, and so on. *Commonwealth v. Aljoe*, 216 A.2d 50 (Pa. 1966); *Florence v. Burlington*, 132 S. Ct. 1510 (2012) (described later in this section).

In addition, individuals arrested for certain offenses may have their DNA collected at booking via a cheek, or "buccal," swab. This DNA may be subsequently analyzed by officials to help establish the arrestee's identity.

> DNA identification of arrestees is a reasonable search that can be considered part of the routine booking procedure. When officers make an arrest supported by probable cause to hold for a more serious offense and they bring the suspect to the station to be detained in custody, taking and analyzing a cheek swab of the arrestee's DNA is, like fingerprinting and photographing, a legitimate police booking procedure that is reasonable under the Fourth Amendment. *Maryland v. King*, 133 S. Ct. 1958, 1980 (2013).

The Court in *King* found that buccal swab procedure to obtain an arrestee's DNA represented a minimal intrusion on the arrestee's privacy. In particular, the Court explained that "a buccal swab involves [a] brief and minimal intrusion. A gentle rub along the inside of the cheek does not break the skin, and it involves virtually no risk, trauma, or pain. [N]othing suggests that a buccal swab poses any physical danger whatsoever. [A] swab of this nature does not increase the indignity already attendant to normal incidents of arrest." *Maryland v. King,* 133 S. Ct. at 1979 (2013) (internal citations omitted). In addition, the Court found that the state's interest in obtaining the arrestee's DNA was substantial because (1) it helps identify the arrestee, including providing information about his criminal history; (2) it assists law enforcement with their duty to ensure that the arrestee's custody and detention does not cause unnecessary risks to detention staff, existing detainees and new detainees; (3) it facilitates the appearance of an arrestee who is charged with the crime of arrest at trial, by reducing the likelihood that the arrestee will flee; (4) it assists a court in determining whether to grant bail to an arrestee, since DNA evidence may reveal an arrestee's prior criminal record and hence danger he represents to the community; and (5) by linking the arrestee to a commission of a previous offense, the DNA evidence may "free . . . a person wrongfully imprisoned for the same offense." *King*, 133 S. Ct. at 1970–74.

King, however, involved the arrest of a suspect on felony assault charges. Thus, several times in the *King* opinion, the Court qualified its rationale by emphasizing that the defendant had been arrested for a serious offense. It is unclear, however, whether *King* also permits the collection of DNA from suspects arrested for less serious crimes, notably misdemeanors. Because the Court compared a buccal swab for DNA to fingerprinting and photographing as part of legitimate booking procedures, and because the Court deemed the nature of the invasion to be minimal, King might permit buccal swabs of arrestees taken into lawful custody on less serious charges. For example, *Haskell v. Harris*, 745 F.3d 1269 (9th Cir. 2014), upheld the constitutionality of California's DNA and Forensic Identification Data Base and Data Bank Act even though it permits DNA samples to be taken from all felony arrestees, even for so-called wobbler offenses that can be charged as either misdemeanors or felonies. And *People v. Morales*, 2013 WL 6711601 (Cal. App. 2013), upheld the DNA collection from a misdemeanor arrestee because he had a prior felony conviction.

> The difference between *King* and this case is that Morales was not arrested for a serious offense but instead for a misdemeanor offense—driving without a license. But, Morales' DNA was not collected simply based on his misdemeanor arrest. Instead, it was collected because he was on misdemeanor probation and had previous felony convictions. Given his prior criminal history, it is not a quantum leap to find Morales presented the same concerns as the person arrested for a serious felony in *King*. The point of collection in Morales's DNA sample did not violate his constitutional rights. 2013 WL 6711601, at *4.

Future case law will undoubtedly need to determine the full scope of *King*'s holding. For now, it remains an open question whether it is constitutionally permissible to collect a DNA sample from someone lawfully arrested on a misdemeanor charge.

Officials may also examine an arrestee's person, or body, at booking. In particular, following the recent Supreme Court decision in *Florence v. Burlington*, an individual who has been arrested, including someone arrested for a minor crime arrestee, may be strip searched and subjected to a visual body cavity search during the booking, or "intake," process into the general population of a jail or prison. These searches at intake may proceed regardless of whether there is reasonable suspicion that the arrestee/detainee harbors contraband on her person and regardless of the underlying crime of arrest (i.e., misdemeanor or felony arrests qualify under *Florence*). However, if the arrested individual will be detained in a holding cell separate and apart from the general population of the jail or prison, officials should only conduct a strip or visual body cavity search of the detainee at intake if they have reasonable suspicion that the detainee possesses contraband or a weapon on his body or within his body cavities. *Florence v. Burlington*, 132 S. Ct. 1510, 1518 (2012). (See the Discussion Point at the end of this section for a more detailed discussion of *Florence*.)

Beyond these basic forms of identification, police must make sure that other pretrial identification techniques, especially those in which victims or witnesses attempt to identify the arrestee as the perpetrator of a crime, comply with all applicable constitutional requirements. Chapter 14 explores these requirements in detail.

KEY POINTS

LO7

- A state must provide a fair and reliable judicial determination of probable cause as a condition for any significant pretrial restraint on liberty either before arrest or as soon as is reasonably feasible after arrest. Normally, this determination occurs during an initial appearance and should be accomplished within forty-eight hours of the suspect's arrest. A law enforcement officer may monitor the movements of an arrested person, as judgment dictates, to ensure the officer's safety and the arrest's integrity.

- Once a person is lawfully arrested and in custody, police may, as part of the routine administrative procedure incident to booking and jailing the person, conduct an inventory search of the person and any containers or items in his or her possession.

- An arrested person may be subjected to various identification and examination procedures at booking, including the obtaining of fingerprints, so long as the reasonableness requirement of the Fourth Amendment is satisfied.

- Under certain circumstances, individuals arrested may have their DNA collected at booking via an oral, or buccal, swab of the cheek, and this DNA may be later analyzed for indentification purposes.

- Arrestees, including minor crime arrestees, may be subject to a strip and visual body cavity search at booking, or intake, into the general population of a detention facility.

Effect of an Illegal Arrest

Jurisdiction to try a person for a crime is not affected by an illegal arrest:

> [T]he power of a court to try a person for crime is not impaired by the fact that he had been brought within the court's jurisdiction by reason of a "forcible abduction." . . . [D]ue process of law is satisfied when one present in court is convicted of crime after having been fairly apprised of the charges against him and after a fair trial in accordance with constitutional procedural safeguards. There is nothing in the Constitution that requires a court to permit a guilty person rightfully convicted to escape justice because he was brought to trial against his will. *Frisbie v. Collins*, 342 U.S. 519, 522 (1952).

The exclusionary rule, however, may affect the trial adversely.

The exclusionary rule, as applied to arrest, states that any evidence obtained by exploitation of an unlawful arrest is inadmissible in court in a prosecution against the person arrested (the exclusionary rule is discussed in detail in Chapter 2). If the only evidence the government has against an armed robbery suspect is a gun, a mask, and a roll of bills taken during a search incident to an unlawful arrest, the offender will very likely go free because these items will be inadmissible in court. (For more details about the exclusionary rule's applicability to searches incident to arrest, see subsequent parts of this chapter.)

A confession obtained by exploitation of an illegal arrest is also inadmissible in court. In *Brown v. Illinois*, 422 U.S. 590 (1975), the defendant was illegally arrested in a manner calculated to cause surprise, fright, and confusion and then taken to a police station. He was given *Miranda* warnings, waived his rights, and made incriminating statements, all within two hours of the illegal arrest. The Court held that *Miranda* warnings alone could not avoid the effect of the illegal arrest:

> The *Miranda* warnings are an important factor, to be sure, in determining whether the confession is obtained by exploitation of illegal arrest. But they are not the only factor to be considered. The temporal proximity of the arrest and the confession, the presence of intervening circumstances, . . . and, particularly, the purpose and flagrancy of the official misconduct are all relevant. . . . And the burden of showing admissibility rests, of course, on the prosecution. 422 U.S. at 603–04.

If evidence is not the product of illegal arrest, however, the exclusionary rule does not apply. Indirect fruits of an illegal arrest should be suppressed only when they bear a sufficiently close relationship to the underlying illegality. In *New York v. Harris*, 495 U.S. 14 (1990), police officers, who had probable cause to believe that the defendant committed murder, entered his home without first obtaining an arrest warrant in violation of *Payton v. New York* (discussed earlier in this chapter). The officers administered *Miranda* warnings and obtained an admission of guilt. After the defendant was arrested, taken to the police station, and again given *Miranda* warnings, he signed a written incriminating statement. The first statement was ruled inadmissible because it was obtained in the defendant's home by exploitation of the *Payton* violation. The statement taken at the police station, however, was ruled admissible. That statement was not the product of being in unlawful custody;

nor was it the fruit of having been arrested in the home rather than someplace else.

The police had justification to question the defendant prior to his arrest. Therefore, his subsequent statement was not an exploitation of the illegal entry into his home. Moreover, suppressing a stationhouse statement obtained after a *Payton* violation would have minimal deterrent value, because police would not be motivated to violate *Payton* just to obtain a statement from a person they have probable cause to arrest. The Court therefore held that "where the police have probable cause to arrest a suspect, the exclusionary rule does not bar the State's use of a statement made by the defendant outside of his home, even though the statement is taken after an arrest made in the home in violation of *Payton*." 495 U.S. at 21. (For more details about the exclusionary rule's applicability to confession evidence, see Chapter 13.)

Finally, law enforcement officers may be subject to civil or criminal liability for making illegal arrests or for using excessive or unreasonable force.

Searches Incident to Arrest

For more than forty years, the law governing search incident to arrest has been controlled by the U.S. Supreme Court case of *Chimel v. California*, 395 U.S. 752 (1969). In *Chimel*, law enforcement officers arrived at the defendant's home with a warrant for his arrest for the burglary of a coin shop. The defendant was not at home, but his wife let the officers in to wait for him. When the defendant arrived, the officers arrested him under the warrant and asked whether they could look around. Over his objections, the officers searched the entire house on the basis of the lawful arrest. The officers found coins and other items that were later admitted into evidence against the defendant. The U.S. Supreme Court found the search of the entire house unreasonable:

> When an arrest is made, it is reasonable for the arresting officer to search the person arrested in order to remove any weapons that the latter might seek to use in order to resist arrest or effect his escape. Otherwise, the officer's safety might well be endangered, and the arrest itself frustrated. In addition, it is entirely reasonable for the arresting officer to search for and seize any evidence on the arrestee's person in order to prevent its concealment or destruction. And the area into which an arrestee might reach in order to grab a weapon or evidentiary items must, of course, be governed by a like rule. A gun on a table or in a drawer in front of one who is arrested can be as dangerous to the arresting officer as one concealed in the clothing of the person arrested. There is ample justification, therefore, for a search of the arrestee's person and the area "within his immediate control"—construing that phrase to mean the area from within which he might gain possession of a weapon or destructible evidence. There is no comparable justification, however, for routinely searching any room other than that in which an arrest occurs—or, for that matter, for searching through all the desk drawers or other closed or concealed areas in that room itself. Such searches, in the absence of well-recognized exceptions, may be made only under the authority of a search warrant. 395 U.S. at 762–63.

276

Requirements for a Valid Search Incident to Arrest

This section explores the two major requirements for a valid search incident to arrest: (1) a lawful, custodial arrest and (2) contemporaneousness.

Lawful, Custodial Arrest

To justify a full search incident to arrest, there first must be a lawful custodial arrest.

The word *custodial* is important here. In some states, the term *arrest* applies when an officer stops a person and issues a ticket, citation, or notice to appear in court, instead of taking the person into custody and transporting the person to a police station or other place to be dealt with according to the law. A full search is not authorized unless the officer takes the arrestee into custody and transports the arrestee to a police station or other place to be dealt with according to the law. *See United States v. Robinson*, 414 U.S. 218 (1973).

Moreover, the custodial arrest must be a lawful one to justify a search incident to arrest. Courts routinely disallow searches incident to arrest and exclude evidence uncovered by police during these searches when the underlying arrest was unlawful. For example, *United States v. Brown*, 401 F.3d 588, 598–99 (4th Cir. 2005), invalidated a search incident to arrest which revealed a gun in the defendant's back pocket because his arrest for public intoxication was unlawful because he "showed no signs of physical impairment caused by alcohol consumption," and therefore police lacked probable cause to arrest him for that crime. Because the arrest was illegal, the fruits of that unlawful arrest—namely, the gun found during the search of the defendant incident to the arrest—were suppressed from evidence.

Traffic Citation Stops Are Insufficient

In *Knowles v. Iowa*, 525 U.S. 113 (1998), a police officer with probable cause to believe the defendant was speeding stopped the defendant and issued a citation. The officer could have arrested the defendant because Iowa law permitted police to arrest traffic violators and take them before a magistrate. Iowa law also permitted officers to issue a citation in lieu of arrest if it "does not affect the officer's authority to conduct an otherwise lawful search." 525 U.S. at 115. After issuing the citation, the officer searched the defendant's car, without probable cause or the defendant's consent, but based solely on Iowa's so-called search-incident-to-citation exception to the warrant requirement. The officer found marijuana.

The *Knowles* Court held that Iowa's search-incident-to-citation exception to the Fourth Amendment was unconstitutional. The search-incident-to-arrest exception is a "bright-line rule," justified only by a lawful full custodial arrest. The issuance of a citation alone is not sufficient to justify a search. Basing its decision on the two historic rationales for a search incident to arrest (e.g., officer safety and evidence destruction), the Court first discussed officer safety:

> The threat to officer safety from issuing a traffic citation, however, is a good deal less than in the case of a custodial arrest. In Robinson, we stated that a custodial arrest involves "danger to an officer" because of "the extended exposure which follows the taking of a suspect into custody and transporting him to the police station." . . . A routine traffic stop [resulting in the issuance of a citation], on the other hand, is a relatively brief encounter and "is more analogous to a so-called 'Terry stop' . . . than to a formal arrest." . . . This is not to say that the concern for safety is

absent in the case of a routine traffic stop. It plainly is not. . . . But while the concern for officer safety in this context may justify the "minimal" additional intrusion of ordering a driver and passengers out of the car, it does not by itself justify the often considerably greater intrusion attending a full field-type search. 525 U.S. at 117.

With respect to the second rationale, the need to discover and preserve evidence, the Court said, "Once Knowles was stopped for speeding and issued a citation, all the evidence necessary to prosecute that offense had been obtained. No further evidence of excessive speed was going to be found either on the person of the offender or in the passenger compartment of the car." 525 U.S. at 118.

Thus, after *Knowles*, when an officer merely issues a driver a traffic citation for failure to obey a traffic law, the officer may not, incident to issuing that citation, conduct a full search of the driver, other occupants within the vehicle, or the vehicle itself. However, if the officer instead lawfully arrests the occupants of the vehicle, then the officer (incident to those arrests) can search the occupants and the passenger compartment of their vehicle. This is discussed in more detail in the section "Motor Vehicle Searches Incident to Arrest," later in this chapter.

Custodial Arrests for Minor Crimes Justify Search Incident to Arrest

If an officer makes such a custodial arrest, even if it is for minor crimes unlikely to involve the use of weapons or destructible evidence, officers are permitted to conduct a full search incident to the arrest. For example, in *United States v. Robinson*, 414 U.S. 218 (1973), the police officer stopped the defendant for driving his vehicle without a valid operator's permit. The officer then told the defendant he was under arrest for driving without the required permit. At this point, the officer conducted a full search of the defendant's person that uncovered a cigarette package containing capsules of heroin. The Court in *Robinson* upheld the search incident to the defendant's arrest and allowed the heroin into evidence. The Court found unimportant the fact that the search incident to the defendant's arrest for failure to possess a valid operator's permit was unlikely to involve weapons or destructible evidence because the search incident to arrest is not necessarily targeted at a search for evidence but also designed to protect the arresting officer in case the suspect is armed.

A Valid Search Incident to Arrest Allows for Seizure of Items Found

A lawful custodial arrest is all that is needed to validate the seizure of an item in conjunction with a search incident to arrest. "For an item to be validly seized during a search incident to arrest, the police need not have probable cause to seize the item, nor do they need to recognize immediately the item's evidentiary nature." *United States v. Holzman*, 871 F.2d 1496, 1505 (9th Cir. 1989). Also, from the preceding discussion of the Supreme Court opinion in *Robinson*, once the officer developed the probable cause to arrest the defendant for driving without a valid permit, the officer could search the defendant and seize any contraband on the defendant (in this case, heroin) without probable cause or even reasonable suspicion.

Contemporaneousness

A search "can be incident to an arrest only if it is substantially contemporaneous with the arrest." *James v. Louisiana*, 382 U.S. 36, 37 (1965). The reason for this rule is that officers may search incident to arrest only (1) to protect themselves and (2) to prevent the destruction or concealment of evidence. A delayed search may indicate that the officers conducted the search for some other impermissible purpose.

The Meaning of _Contemporaneous_ Generally speaking, _a search is said to be contemporaneous with an arrest if the search is at the same time probable cause to arrest develops or is conducted shortly thereafter._ Though searches incident to arrest should ideally be conducted immediately following the suspect's arrest, allowing a short time to pass between the arrest and the subsequent search will usually not result in the search being invalidated for failure to satisfy the contemporaneous requirement.

- _United States v. McLaughlin_, 170 F. 3d 889, 891 (9th Cir. 1999), approved a search of the passenger compartment of a vehicle that occurred five minutes after the arrest of the driver. The search was essentially contemporaneous with the arrest in that "the arrest, the filling out of the impound paperwork before searching the car, and the initial search were all one continuous series of events closely connected in time." _See also United States v. Kila_, 2008 WL 2001241, *5 (D. Haw. 2008) (finding search of vehicle to be incident to arrest when it occurred fifteen to twenty-five minutes after arrest).

- _Curd v. City Court of Judsonia, Ark._, 141 F.3d 839, 843–44 (8th Cir. 1998), upheld a search of the defendant's purse at the stationhouse even though it occurred fifteen minutes after the defendant's arrest in her home: "The search of [the defendant's] purse at the stationhouse fifteen minutes after her arrest fell well within the constitutionally acceptable time zone for searches of persons and objects 'immediately associated' with them incident to arrest."

- Searches that occurred thirty to forty-five minutes after suspects were taken into custody were invalidated in both _United States v. Chaves_, 169 F.3d 687 (11th Cir. 1999), and _United States v. Vasey_, 834 F.2d 782 (9th Cir. 1987).

The _Edwards_ "Good Reason" Exception to the Contemporaneous Rule
Longer delays may be permitted between arrests and searches if it is not practically feasible to search an arrested person at, or near, the time of arrest. The U.S. Supreme Court made such an exception to the contemporaneousness rule in _United States v. Edwards_, 415 U.S. 800 (1974). In that case, the defendant was arrested shortly after 11:00 P.M. for attempting to break into a building and was taken to jail. Law enforcement officials had probable cause to believe that the defendant's clothing contained paint chips from the crime scene. Because the police had no substitute clothing for the defendant, they waited until the next morning to seize his clothing, on which they found paint chips matching those at the crime scene.

The Court in _Edwards_ held that, despite the delay, the clothing was lawfully seized incident to the defendant's arrest. The administrative process and the mechanics of arrest had not yet come to a halt the next morning. The police had custody of the defendant and the clothing. They could have seized the clothing at the time of arrest, but it was reasonable to delay the seizure until substitute clothing was available.

Edwards does not allow law enforcement officers to delay a search incident to arrest for as long as they wish. Nor does it sanction all delays in searching and seizing evidence incident to arrest. Officers must be able to provide _good reasons_ for

KEY POINTS

- The lawful custodial arrest that justifies a search incident to arrest is an arrest that involves taking the person into custody and transporting him or her to a police station or other place to be dealt with according to the law.

- The issuance of a traffic citation alone is not a lawful custodial arrest sufficient to justify a search incident to arrest.

- A lawful custodial arrest for minor crimes not likely to involve weapons or destructible evidence still allows police officers to conduct a search incident to the arrest.

delaying a search incident to arrest, and the duration of a delay must be reasonable under the circumstances; otherwise, the search and seizure may be declared illegal. For example:

- Practical considerations usually mandate that body cavity searches and searches of persons of the opposite sex be delayed. In these situations, the officer should remove the arrested person from the scene and conduct the search as soon as favorable circumstances prevail.

- In *United States v. Miles*, 413 F.2d 34 (3d Cir. 1969), an arrest for an armed bank robbery took place in a crowded hotel lobby, which was lit only by candles because of a power failure. Under these circumstances, the court held that it was proper for officers to make a cursory search of the arrestee for weapons at the hotel and to make a more thorough search later at the station.

- In *United States v. Willis*, 37 F.3d 313 (7th Cir. 1994), the fact that the officer, after arresting the defendant but before searching his car, needed to walk back to his patrol car to retrieve a camera in order to photograph evidence, did not invalidate the search.

- In *United States v. Gwinn*, 219 F.3d 326, 333–35 (4th Cir. 2000), the officer could not conduct an immediate search of the arrestee's shoes because he was barefoot at the time of arrest, and therefore the search of the shoes a short time later after the officer retrieved the shoes from the arrestee's residence out of a concern for the arrestee's safety, was justified. The safety concerns in *Gwinn* stemmed from the fact that if the arrestee was left barefoot, he would potentially be exposed to sharp objects capable of cutting his feet as well as cold temperatures.

Contemporaneous Does Not Include Searches Preceding Arrest As a general rule, "an incident search may not precede an arrest and serve as part of its justification." *Sibron v. New York*, 392 U.S. 40, 63 (1968). The Court elaborated on this point in *Smith v. Ohio*, 494 U.S. 541 (1990). In *Smith*, the defendant threw a bag he was carrying onto the hood of his car in response to the officer's command to approach him. When the defendant did not respond to the officer's question as to what was in the bag, the officer retrieved the bag by pushing away the defendant's hand and opened it. The officer found drug paraphernalia inside the bag and arrested the defendant. The U.S. Supreme Court ruled the drug paraphernalia evidence should have been excluded from trial because the search incident to arrest doctrine could not precede the defendant's arrest and then serve to justify it. The Court held that the exception for searches incident to arrest "does not permit the police to search any citizen without a warrant or probable cause so long as an arrest immediately follows." 494 U.S. at 543.

There is a narrow exception to *Sibron*, however, that allows a search to precede an arrest and still be a valid search incident to arrest. In *Rawlings v. Kentucky*, 448 U.S. 98, 111 (1980), the Supreme Court held that an arrest need not always precede a search if

- probable cause to *arrest* existed at the time of the search and did not depend on the fruits of the search, and
- the "formal arrest followed quickly on the heels of the challenged search."

The defendant in *Rawlings* placed drugs into Cox's purse for safekeeping. When police arrived at the home where the defendant was present, they made Cox remove the contents of her purse, including the drugs Rawlings had placed there. At this point, Rawlings claimed ownership of the drugs. Once

KEY POINTS

L012
- In general, a search incident to arrest must be contemporaneous with the arrest. A search is contemporaneous with the arrest if the search occurs at the same time probable cause to arrest develops or is conducted shortly thereafter. Short delays between a formal arrest and an incident search are generally permitted; but if the delay becomes prolonged, officers must be prepared to provide good reasons for the delay.

- A search incident to arrest may not both precede an arrest and serve as part of the arrest's justification. However, when probable cause to arrest exists before a search is conducted, a search can precede the formal arrest as long as the arrest follows immediately after the search.

he admitted ownership, police searched Rawlings's person and discovered $4,500 in cash and a knife. He was then placed under arrest. Even though the search of Rawlings's person preceded his formal arrest, the Court upheld the search as incident to his arrest because probable cause to arrest developed before the search, and the formal arrest followed immediately after the search.

Permissible Scope of a Search Incident to a Lawful Arrest

Generally, the allowable scope of a search incident to arrest depends on its purpose. *Chimel* allows a law enforcement officer to search a person incident to arrest for only two purposes:

- to search for and remove weapons that the arrestee might use to resist arrest or effect an escape; or
- to search for and seize evidence to prevent its concealment or destruction.

Thus, for searches of persons incident to their arrest, officers may search anywhere on the person that weapons or evidence may be found. The following are examples of types of property that may be seized:

- evidence of a crime;
- contraband, fruits of crime, or other items illegally possessed; and
- property designed for use, intended for use, or used in committing a crime.

See FED. R. CRIM. P. 41(c).

In addition, an officer may seize evidence of crimes other than the crime for which the arrest was made. For example, in *United States v. Jackson*, 377 F.3d 715 (7th Cir. 2004), an officer pulled over a driver of an automobile when he changed lanes without signaling. When the driver failed to produce a license and therefore could not properly be identified, the officer handcuffed the driver and placed him in the patrol car. The court characterized this action as a lawful custodial arrest. In the process of placing the driver in the patrol car, the officer searched the driver and found a large amount of crack cocaine in his crotch area. Even though the officer arrested the driver for failure to possess a valid license, the search and seizure of the cocaine was still valid:

> It would have been foolhardy to trundle [the driver] into the squad car without ensuring that he was unarmed. [The officer] was entitled to reduce danger to himself before securing [the driver] in the back seat for however long it took to find out who he really was. Likewise [the officer] was entitled to preserve any evidence that [the driver] may have been carrying. That the search turned up drugs rather than a gun (or bogus identification) does not make it less valid. 377 F.3d at 717–18.

Full Search of the Arrestee's Body

United States v. Robinson, 414 U.S. 218 (1973), and *Gustafson v. Florida*, 414 U.S. 260 (1973), held that a law enforcement officer may conduct a full search of a person's body incident to the custodial arrest of the person. These cases upheld inspections of the contents of cigarette packages seized incident to the arrests of the defendants for traffic violations. Illegal drugs were found in both cases. The Court emphasized that "in the case of lawful custodial arrest, a full search of the person is not only an exception to the warrant requirement of the Fourth Amendment, but is also a 'reasonable' search under that Amendment." 414 U.S. at 235.

In 1998, Albert Florence was arrested in New Jersey for escaping police officers there. Florence pled guilty to minor charges and was sentenced to pay a monthly fine. Florence, however, failed to consistently pay the fine as well as attend a hearing. As a result, in 2003, a warrant issued for Florence's arrest. Although Florence paid the full fine amount within one

week of the issuance of the warrant, the warrant still appeared in the New Jersey warrant database. A few years later, in 2005, Florence and his wife were stopped while driving in their vehicle by New Jersey state police. The trooper arrested Florence pursuant to the warrant in the state database. Florence was transported to a Burlington County jail and, after six days, Florence was moved to the Essex County Correctional Facility. *Florence*, 132 S. Ct. at 1514.

The Burlington County jail mandates that all arrestees shower with a "delousing agent" while undergoing a close visual inspection by officers of their naked bodies for "scars, marks, gang tattoos, and contraband." Florence was also required "to open his mouth, lift his tongue, hold out his arms, turn around, and lift his genitals." *Florence*, 132 S. Ct. at 1514.

The Essex Correctional Facility demands that arrestees be subject to a close visual search by officers for possible markings, wounds, and contraband on the entire arrestee's body. Though there is no physical contact made by the officer on the arrestee's body, officers did examine the arrestees' "ears, nose, mouth, hair, scalp, fingers, hands, arms, armpits, and other body openings." In addition, Florence claims that he was required by the officials "to lift his genitals, turn-around, and cough in a squatting position as part of the process." *Florence*, 132 S. Ct. at 1514. Florence was also asked to take a shower while his clothes were searched. These intake procedures were used by officials without consideration of the facts pertaining to the arrest, the nature of the offense underlying the arrest, or the behavior of the arrestee. Following his shower, Florence was admitted to the correctional facility. But he was released the following day because the charges against him were dropped. *Florence*, 132 S. Ct. at 1514.

The U.S. Supreme Court first noted in *Florence* the deferential test used to evaluate regulations applied by correctional officials in prisons and jails that implicate detainees' constitutional rights:

> Maintaining safety and order at these institutions requires the expertise of correctional officials, who must have substantial discretion to devise reasonable solutions to the problems they face. The Court has confirmed the importance of deference to correctional officials and explained that a regulation impinging on an inmate's constitutional rights must be upheld "if it is reasonably related to legitimate penological interests." Florence, 132 S. Ct. at 1515–16 (internal citations omitted).

In addition, the Court in *Florence* explained that deference must be accorded correctional officials in operating prisons and jails "unless there is 'substantial evidence' demonstrating their response to the situation is exaggerated." *Florence*, 132 S. Ct. at 1518 (internal citations omitted).

Under this test, the Court in *Florence* found that the visual examination by correctional officials of an arrestee's exposed body, including body cavities, upon the arrestee's admission into the general population of a correctional facility, is constitutional. The Court held that this examination may proceed regardless of whether these officials have reasonable suspicion of a weapon or other contraband concealed on the arrestee. Accordingly, though Florence was arrested for a minor crime and though officials did not have reasonable suspicion that Florence possessed a weapon or had other contraband on his person at the time he was admitted to the general population of the two correctional facilities, the Court upheld the visual inspection by officials of Florence's body and body cavities. *Florence*, 132 S. Ct. at 1518.

In reaching its holding, the Court noted that in its previous precedent in this area, substantial deference has been given to correctional officials in

Continued on next page

designing and implementing procedures to detect and prevent contraband in jails and prisons. These procedures may not necessarily contain exceptions for individual inmate situations or require individualized suspicion of inmate misconduct. In addition, the Court in *Florence* mentions that there are numerous instances of correctional facilities in the United States that permit different kinds of strip searches of all inmates. *Florence*, 132 S. Ct. at 1517.

Moreover, the Court reasoned in *Florence* that the strip searches and visual body cavity inspections of arrestees are necessary for correctional officials to be able to handle various threats posed by these "soon-to-be" newly admitted inmates. For example, the Court notes that new inmates may harbor lice, contagious infections, and open wounds that can only be discovered and treated through a close visual examination of the inmate's body. Also, such searches and inspections are necessary to find tattoos and other markings on the inmate's body indicating gang membership. Lastly, officials must perform a close visual examination of an inmate's body at intake in order to uncover contraband, including drugs, weapons, money and even pens. These items carry a risk of significant danger to correctional facility employees and other inmates. *Florence*, 132 S. Ct. at 1518–19.

In addition, according to the Court, strip and visual body cavity searches of all arrestees/detainees at intake into a jail or prison is required because gang members and other incarcerated felons may force individuals admitted to prisons for minor crimes to smuggle contraband into prisons. Placing any more restrictions on searches at intake would be hard for correctional officials to implement because they may not have access to accurate criminal records for new inmates, and newly admitted inmates may try to hide their true identity. In addition, officials work under stressful conditions at intake and have insufficient time to evaluate a particular arrestee's/detainee's circumstances before searching him or her. *Florence*, 132 S. Ct. at 1519–22.

In conclusion, according to the Court, any search restrictions at intake would "limit the intrusion on the privacy of some detainees but at the risk of increased danger to everyone in the facility, including the less serious offenders themselves." Rather, according to the Court, permitting officials to strip and visual cavity search all arrestees upon admission into the general population of a jail or prison results in "a [more] reasonable balance between inmate privacy and the needs of [correctional] institutions." *Florence*, 132 S. Ct. at 1522.

■ Do you agree or disagree with the Court's core holding in *Florence* (i.e., that minor crime arrestees may be strip searched and have their body cavities visually examined by officials at intake into the general population of a jail or prison)? Should someone arrested for a traffic violation (e.g., unpaid speeding tickets, driving on a suspended license, etc.) or a public order crime (graffiti-writing, minor gambling infraction, etc.) be subject to a full strip and visual body cavity search upon being admitted into a jail's general population? Explain fully your answer.

■ Do you agree with the Court's core rationale in *Florence*? For example, do you believe that the Court's principal reasons for allowing strip and visual body cavity searches of minor crime arrestees—discovering lice, wounds, infections, tattoos, and contraband—justify such searches when these arrestees are admitted into the general population of a jail or prison? Are there other ways to detect these "threats" with a reasonable degree of assurance other than conducting a strip search and a visual search of the oral and anal cavities of minor crime arrestees?

■ What do you think about the other reasons provided by the Court in *Florence* for permitting strip and visual body cavity searches of minor crime arrestees at intake? For example, do you agree with the Court that it would be difficult for jail personnel to assess whether an individual minor crime arrestee may have contraband or other evidence of a crime on him or her at the time of intake into the jail's general population (say, under "a reasonable suspicion of contraband" standard)? Why do you agree or disagree? What factors could jail personnel use to make this assessment (in addition to the arrestee's prior criminal record)? What about the Court's observation that gangs and incarcerated felons may force individuals admitted to prisons for minor crimes to smuggle contraband into prisons (and therefore these individuals must be subject to a strip and visual body cavity search at intake)? How likely or feasible is this scenario to occur in real life?

But what constitutes a *full search of the arrestee's body*? The following principles can be derived from court decisions dealing with this issue.

Searches on or in the Body

Searches on or in the body include the following.

Nonintrusive Searches of the Body A full search of an arrestee's body usually allows for the search and seizure of evidence on the body. For example, relatively nonintrusive seizures, such as obtaining hair samples and fingernail clippings, are usually upheld if reasonable and painless procedures are employed. *Commonwealth v. Tarver*, 345 N.E.2d 671 (Mass. 1975), upheld a seizure of hair samples from the head, chest, and pubic area of a person incident to his arrest for murder and sexual abuse of a child. More intrusive searches and seizures, such as obtaining blood samples or comparable intrusions into the body, require stricter limitations as discussed next.

Strip Searches and Body Cavity Searches The "full search" that may be effectuated as a valid search incident to arrest does not automatically extend to a strip search or any search that involves bodily intrusion. Strip searches are visual inspections of a naked human body without any intrusion into a person's body cavities. If body cavities are penetrated, then a body cavity search has occurred. Both types of searches are "intrusive and degrading and, therefore, should not be unreservedly available to law enforcement officers." *Wood v. Hancock County Sheriff's Dept.*, 354 F.3d 57 (1st Cir. 2003). Accordingly, courts have established strict limitations to when these types of searches may be conducted incident to an arrest, and, if authorized under the particular circumstances, how they are to be carried out. The guiding principle is always the "reasonableness" of the search at issue.

In *Bell v. Wolfish*, 441 U.S. 520, 559 (1979), the U.S. Supreme Court held that strip searches and visual body cavity searches may be conducted on people in custody with less than probable cause. However, there must be a need for such an intrusion of privacy. To determine if any such search was "reasonable" within the meaning of the Fourth Amendment: "the scope of the particular intrusion, the manner in which it is conducted, the justification for initiating it, and the place in which it is conducted" all need to be balanced.

As discussed earlier in the chapter, following the recent Supreme Court decision in *Florence v. Burlington*, an arrestee, including a minor crime arrestee, may be strip searched and subjected to a visual body cavity search during the booking process into the general population of a jail or prison. These searches at intake may proceed *without* reasonable suspicion of contraband on the arrestee's body or body cavities. However, under *Florence*, if the arrested individual will be detained in a holding cell apart from the general population of the jail or prison, officials should only conduct a strip or visual body cavity search of the detainee if they have reasonable suspicion that the detainee possesses contraband or a weapon on his body or within his body cavities. *Florence v. Burlington*, 132 S. Ct. 1510, 1518 (2012).

Lower courts interpreting *Florence* have approved strip and visual cavity searches of detainees and inmates in the correctional setting in a number of contexts. For example, these searches have been approved before and after court hearing visits, after trips to the prison yard, and following inmate work assignments. *See Barber v. Jones*, 2013 WL 211251 (D.N.J. 2013) (prison yard); *Myers v. City of New York*, 2012 WL 3776707 (S.D.N.Y. 2012) (court visit); *Tennell v. Rupert*, 2012 WL 1899320 (E.D. Tex. 2012) (work assignments).

Lower courts, however, have declined to apply *Florence* to strip searches of juveniles at intake into a juvenile detention facility. *See Mashburn v. Yamhill County*, 2012 WL 5879444 (D. Or. 2012), at *8 ("However, it is important to note that *Florence* . . . [is] binding precedent only as to strip searches conducted of adult arrestees, and thus, [is] clearly distinguishable from the facts of this case which concerns search policies in juvenile detention facilities. It is well-established that strip searches of juveniles pose different concerns"). Ultimately, in *Mashburn*, the court found that an official must have reasonable suspicion of contraband on the juvenile's body or within his body cavities before conducting a strip search of the juvenile at intake into a juvenile detention facility. *Mashburn*, 2012 WL at 5879444, *39.

Even when there are reasonable grounds to conduct an invasive search, the manner in which the search is executed must still be reasonable. In this regard, it is important to point out that the strip and visual body cavity searches that were approved in *Florence* occurred at intake into correctional facilities where the arrestee would be detained with others in the general population of a jail or prison. As the Supreme Court stated in *Illinois v. Lafayette*, 462 U.S. 640, 645 (1983), "the interests supporting a search incident to arrest would hardly justify disrobing an arrestee on the street." Courts consider the following factors when judging the reasonableness, and therefore constitutionality, of the way a strip search or body cavity search was performed:

- the amount of force used,
- whether sanitary conditions were employed,
- the use of threatening or abusive language,
- the degree of respect shown for the privacy of the person searched,
- whether there is actual physical penetration of cavities or orifices, and
- the presence of exigent circumstances.

In *Evans v. Stephens*, 407 F.3d 1272 (11th Cir. 2005), the court invalidated a strip and cavity search in light of the excessive force used during the search.

> The physical aspects of the searches are also disturbing. Unnecessary force was used. Evans was thrown into Jordan, causing both men to collapse. As Jordan tried to stand back up, Officer Stephens hit him with a baton-like object. It matters that a body cavity search was undertaken. In addition, while conducting the search, Stephens inserted the same baton or club—without intervening sanitation—in each Plaintiff's anus and used the same baton or club to lift each man's testicles. Apart from other issues, this last practice is highly unsanitary. 407 F.3d at 1281.

The officer in *Evans*, a white male, also used "threatening and racist" language toward the arrestees, who were both African American males, as he conducted the search.

> [I]n this case, the totality of the circumstances—for example, the physical force, anal penetration, unsanitariness of the process, terrifying language, and lack of privacy—collectively establish a constitutional violation, especially when the search was being made in the absence of exigent circumstances requiring the kind of immediate action that might make otherwise questionable police conduct, at least arguably, reasonable. 407 F.3d at 1282.

Intrusive Searches Within the Body A full search of an arrestee's body may also, under limited circumstances, allow for the search and seizure of items within, or inside, the arrestee's body. *Schmerber v. California*, 384 U.S. 757 (1966), held that a more intrusive search and seizure to obtain items within the suspect's body (i.e., blood), will be upheld only if

1. the process was a reasonable one performed in a reasonable manner (in *Schmerber*, blood was taken from a person arrested for drunk driving by a physician in a hospital environment according to accepted medical practices);
2. there was a clear indication in advance that the evidence sought would be found (in *Schmerber*, the arrestee had glassy, bloodshot eyes and the smell of alcohol emanated from his breath); and
3. there were exigent circumstances and hence insufficient time to obtain a warrant (in *Schmerber*, the blood test had to be taken before the percentage of alcohol in the blood diminished).

Note that with regard to prong 3 of *Schmerber* (i.e., the "emergency" prong), the natural diminishment of alcohol in the bloodstream does not by itself automatically create exigent circumstances. Rather, whether or not an emergency exists to justify a warrantless, nonconsensual blood test of a drunk-driving arrestee in a medical facility will be determined on a case-by-case basis using a totality of circumstances approach. *See Missouri v. McNeely*, 133 S. Ct. at 1552, 1556 (2013) ("In short, while the natural dissipation of alcohol in the blood may support a finding of exigency in a specific case, as it did in Schmerber, it does not do so categorically. Whether a warrantless blood test of a drunk-driving suspect is reasonable must be determined case by case based on the totality of the circumstances."). *McNeely*, 133 S. Ct. at 1563. Some of the circumstances, or factors, that police should consider in deciding whether there is an emergency such that they have insufficient time to obtain a warrant for a nonconsensual blood test of a drunk-driving arrestee in a medical facility, are (1) the need for the arresting officer to also respond to a vehicular accident; (2) the procedures and mechanisms available for obtaining warrants in the jurisdiction, including procedures designed to expedite obtaining warrants (e.g., the standard form warrant applications, telephonic, and/or electronic warrants); (3) the availability of a judge to issue a warrant; (4) the natural diminishment of alcohol in the arrestee's bloodstream and the accompanying loss of evidence; (5) the availability of another officer to transport the arrestee to a medical facility for a blood test while the arresting officer obtains a warrant; (6) previous difficulties, problems, or delays experienced by the arresting officer in obtaining warrants for blood tests (i.e., the officer "anticipates" based on prior experience that a delay will lead to the "destruction" of the alcohol evidence); and (7) the amount of time it typically takes in the jurisdiction to obtain a warrant in a drunk-driving case. *McNeely*, 133 S. Ct. at 1561–63, 1567–68.

Recall also that at the time of booking an arrestee into the stationhouse for a serious offense, his DNA may be collected via a buccal swab of his cheek and the DNA subsequently analyzed for identification purposes. *See Maryland v. King*, 133 S. Ct. 1958, 1980 (2013) (discussed in more detail in the earlier "After Making an Arrest" section). Though the U.S. Supreme Court upheld the more routine blood test in *Schmerber*, as well as the buccal swab procedure to obtain DNA in *King*, other, more invasive procedures may be constitutionally unreasonable.

- In *Rochin v. California*, 342 U.S. 165, 172 (1952), the Supreme Court, under particular circumstances, refused to sanction the act of pumping an arrestee's stomach in a hospital environment as part of a search for pills believed to be drugs. ("This is conduct that shocks the conscience. Illegally breaking into the privacy of the petitioner [e.g., his residence], the struggle to open his mouth and remove what was there, the forcible extraction of his stomach's contents—this course of proceeding by agents of government to obtain evidence is bound to offend even hardened sensibilities.")

- In *Winston v. Lee*, 470 U.S. 753 (1985), the Court prohibited the surgical removal under general anesthesia of a bullet from the suspect's chest area, finding the process too invasive and too risky to be reasonable under the Fourth Amendment.

Searches Immediately Associated with the Arrestee's Body A full search of the arrestee's body allows the seizure and search of items of evidence or weapons immediately associated with the arrestee's body, such as clothing, billfolds, jewelry, wristwatches, and weapons strapped or carried on the person. In this context, "immediately associated" means attached in a permanent or semipermanent way to the arrestee's body or clothing. A search of items seized in this category might include going through the pockets of clothing; examining clothing for bloodstains, hair, or dirt; examining weapons for bloodstains, fingerprints, or serial numbers; and looking in containers or other property that the arrestee is carrying (e.g., wallets, purses, backpacks). However, one item of evidence immediately associated with the suspect's body that generally may *not* be searched by police following an arrest is a cell phone (*see Riley v. California,* 134 S. Ct. 2473 (2014), described later in this chapter).

- In *Michigan v. DeFillippo*, 443 U.S. 31 (1979), the U.S. Supreme Court upheld a search incident to an arrest when the police officer inspected the suspect's shirt pockets following his lawful arrest. Drugs found in two of the suspect's shirt pockets were allowed into evidence.

- *United States v. Molinaro*, 877 F.2d 1341 (7th Cir. 1989), held that a person's wallet may be validly seized and its contents immediately searched incident to the person's arrest to prevent the destruction or concealment of evidence.

- In *Riley v. California,* the U.S. Supreme Court held that unless police have reason to believe an emergency exists (e.g., the imminent destruction of evidence, police pursuit of a fleeing suspect, or imminent, serious injury to a person), police must generally obtain a warrant prior to searching the data stored on a cell phone found on the arrestee. *See Riley*, 134 S. Ct. at 2485, 2493 ("Our holding, of course, is not that the information on a cell phone is immune from search; it is instead that a warrant is generally required before such a search, even when a cell phone is seized incident to arrest. Moreover, even though the search incident to arrest exception does not apply to cell phones, other case-specific exceptions may still justify a warrantless search of a particular phone. One well-recognized exception applies when the exigencies of the situation make the needs of law enforcement so compelling that a warrantless search is objectively reasonable under the Fourth Amendment.") *Riley*, 134 S. Ct. at 2493 (internal quotations omitted). Regarding the limited, emergency exception in the context of a search by police of data stored on a cell phone, the Court commented:

> In light of the availability of the exigent circumstances exception, there is no reason to believe that law enforcement officers will not be able to address some of the more extreme hypotheticals that have been suggested: a suspect texting an accomplice who, it is feared, is preparing to detonate a bomb, or a child abductor who may have information about the child's location on his cell phone. The defendants here recognize—indeed, they stress—that such fact-specific threats may justify a warrantless search of cell phone data. The critical point is that, unlike the search incident to arrest exception, the exigent circumstances exception requires a court to examine whether an emergency justified a warrantless search in each particular case. *Riley*, 134 S. Ct. at 2494 (internal quotations omitted).

The Court did note that though police must generally obtain a warrant prior to searching the digital data stored on an arrestee's cell phone, they "remain free to examine the physical aspects of a phone to ensure that it will not be used as a weapon—say, to determine whether there is a razor blade hidden between the phone and its case." Finally, police may seize and secure an arrestee's cell phone while they obtain a warrant to search the digital information stored on the phone. ("Both [defendant's] concede that officers could have seized and secured their cell phones to prevent destruction of evidence while seeking a warrant. That is a sensible concession"). *Riley*, 134 S. Ct. at 2485–86.

Containers Proximate to Arrestee A full search of the arrestee's body may allow the seizure and search of other personal property and containers that are not immediately associated with the arrestee's body but are in the immediate control of the arrestee (i.e., "proximate" to the arrestee) because they are within the area an arrestee could reach to grab a weapon or destroy evidence. These areas into which an arrestee might reach are commonly referred to as being within the arrestee's "**armspan**," "**wing-span**," "lunge area," "wingspread," or "grabbing distance." Examples of property that might be seized and searched in this context include

- purses;
- briefcases, attaché cases, backpacks, and luggage; and
- bundles, packages, or other containers that are near the arrestee and that he is no longer carrying.

Chimel explained this rule exists primarily to prevent an arrestee from grabbing a weapon or destroying evidence. 395 U.S. at 763. If, however, such containers are not in the immediate control of the arrestee because the arrestee could not access them for some reason (e.g., the arrestee was handcuffed, or the container was secured with locks or by some other means that made it inaccessible to the arrestee), then they generally may not be searched or seized incident to arrest.

As the following cases illustrate, the determination of the permissible area of search depends on several factors, such as the size and shape of the room, the size and agility of the arrestee, whether the arrestee was handcuffed or otherwise subdued, the size and type of evidence being sought, the number of people arrested, and the number of officers present.

- In *James v. Louisiana*, 382 U.S. 36 (1965), officers lawfully arrested the defendant for narcotics possession on a downtown street corner and took him to his home two blocks some distance away where an intensive search yielded narcotics. The Court invalidated the search because it was neither "contemporaneous" with the arrest nor confined to the immediate vicinity in which the arrest occurred.

- *United States v. Tarazon*, 989 F.2d 1045 (9th Cir. 1993), however, held that the drawers of the desk at which the defendant was sitting when he was arrested were clearly within the defendant's control and could be searched incident to the arrest moments after the arrest.

- In *People v. Spencer*, 99 Cal. Rptr. 681 (Cal. App. 1972), officers went to the defendant's trailer home to arrest him for armed robbery and found him lying in bed. One officer immediately searched under the blankets for a gun as other officers attempted to subdue the defendant, who was resisting. Two revolvers were found in a box at the foot of the bed. The court held that this box was within the area of the defendant's reach and that the revolvers were admissible in evidence.

- In *United States v. Helmstetter*, 56 F.3d 21 (5th Cir. 1995), the suspect was arrested, handcuffed, and placed in a chair. Although he was restrained, the court allowed the search and seizure of a gun under the chair incident to the suspect's arrest because of the possibility that he could still gain access to it. *See also United States v. Yanez*, 490 F. Supp. 2d 765, 777 (S.D. Tex. 2007). ("Because the sawed-off shotgun was at the foot of the bed near the edge of the mattress, and the defendant was 4 to 5 feet away from that spot at the time of the arrest, the weapon was in Yanez's 'immediate control' despite [Yanez being handcuffed]. The weapon was indeed not as readily accessible as the gun in *Helmstetter*, beneath the defendant's chair. However, the court finds that the shotgun was within the area under the defendant's immediate control or his lunge reach, and thus the search did not violate the defendant's Fourth Amendment protections.")

- Some courts permit a search incident to arrest to encompass the areas that would be within the defendant's reach if a suspect were not restrained, even if he or she was actually restrained. Although the defendant was handcuffed next to his bicycle at the time of his arrest in *United State v. Currence*, 446 F.3d 554 (4th Cir. 2006), for instance, a search incident to arrest of the inside of the bicycle's handlebars, which yielded crack cocaine, was deemed permissible. *See also United States v. Poole*, 407 F.3d 767 (6th Cir. 2005).

- If it is necessary for an arrested person to go into a different area of the premises from the area where he or she was arrested, the officer may, for protective purposes, accompany the person and search and seize evidence within the person's armspan. The following quotation from *Washington v. Chrisman*, 455 U.S. 1, 7 (1982), reflects this notion:

> [I]t is not "unreasonable" under the Fourth Amendment for a police officer, as a matter of course, to monitor the movements of an arrested person, as his judgment dictates, following the arrest. The officer's need to ensure his own safety—as well as the integrity of the arrest—is compelling. Such surveillance is not an impermissible invasion of the privacy or personal liberty of an individual who has been arrested.

- In *Chrisman*, the officer arrested the suspect on suspicion of underage drinking and then asked the suspect for his identification. When the suspect, accompanied by the officer, went to retrieve identification from his dorm room, the area within the immediate control of the arrested suspect "moved" with him. Therefore, when the officer observed marijuana seeds and a pipe on a desk in the suspect's dorm room, the officer could search and seize this evidence incident to the suspect's arrest. (Note: This evidence could also be searched and seized under the plain view doctrine, discussed in Chapter 10.)

- *Giacalone v. Lucas*, 445 F.2d 1238 (6th Cir. 1971), sheds additional light on the flexibility of the armspan rule when the arrested suspect travels from the initial place of arrest. In *Giacalone*, the court held that "if immediately after a lawful arrest, the arrestee reads the arrest warrant and without coercion consents to go to his bedroom to change into more appropriate clothing, the arresting officers—incident to that arrest—may search the areas upon which the arrestee focuses his attention and are within his reach to gain access to a weapon or to destroy evidence." 445 F.2d at 1247. Officers may not, however, deliberately move an arrested person near an object or place they want to search in order to activate the search incident to arrest exception. *United States v. Perea*, 986 F.2d 633 (2d Cir. 1993).

Container Searches Remote in Time or Place   *United States v. Chadwick*, 433 U.S. 1 (1977), held that the search of seized containers not immediately associated with an arrestee's body is not allowed if the search is remote in time and place from the arrest, or if there is no exigency.

In *Chadwick*, the defendants arrived in Boston from San Diego by train. They loaded a large, double-locked footlocker, which they had transported with them, into the trunk of their waiting car. Federal narcotics agents, who had probable cause to arrest and to search the footlocker, but who possessed no warrants, arrested the defendants. The agents took exclusive control of the footlocker and transported it and the defendants to the federal building in Boston. An hour and a half later, without the defendants' consent and without a

- The allowable purposes of a search incident to arrest are (1) to search for and remove weapons that the arrestee might use to resist arrest or effectuate an escape and (2) to search for and seize evidence to prevent its concealment or destruction.

- A law enforcement officer may conduct a full search of a person's body incident to the arrest of the person.

- A full search of the arrestee's body allows the seizure and search of weapons or other items immediately associated with the body. It also usually allows for the search and seizure of evidence on the body. In addition, a full search of the arrestee's body may, under certain circumstances, allow for searches and seizures inside, or within, the body. These latter searches and seizures may, in certain situations, include blood tests of arrestees conducted in medical facilities for evidence of alcohol in their bloodstream.

- A full search of the arrestee's body allows the seizure and search of other personal property such as luggage or other proximate containers not immediately associated with the arrestee's body but under the immediate control of the arrestee. This property may not be searched, however, if the search is remote in time and place from the arrest or no exigency exists (e.g., the suspect cannot gain access to the luggage or other proximate container to obtain a weapon or destroy evidence).

- If police conduct is justified by probable cause to believe that a violation of law has occurred, subjective intent or pretext is irrelevant for Fourth Amendment purposes.

search warrant, the agents opened the footlocker and found large amounts of marijuana. The U.S. Supreme Court held that the search of the footlocker was illegal:

> The potential dangers lurking in all custodial arrests make warrantless searches of items within the "immediate control" area reasonable without requiring the arresting officer to calculate the probability that weapons or destructible evidence may be involved. . . . However, warrantless searches of luggage or other property seized at the time of an arrest cannot be justified as incident to that arrest either if the "search is remote in time and place from the arrest," . . . or no exigency exists. Once law enforcement officers have reduced luggage or other personal property not immediately associated with the person of the arrestee to their exclusive control, and there is no longer any danger that the arrestee might gain access to the property to seize a weapon or destroy evidence, a search of that property is no longer an incident of the arrest. 433 U.S. at 14–16.

The search of the footlocker by police officers had occurred more than an hour after they gained exclusive control of it. Therefore, the search of the footlocker was remote and not a valid search incident to the defendants' arrest. Moreover, the defendants were securely in custody at the time of the search and therefore could not gain access to the footlocker to destroy evidence or retrieve a weapon. As a result, no exigency existed.

Similarly, in *United States v. $639,558 in U.S. Currency*, 955 F.2d 712 (D.C. Cir. 1992), the search of a suspect's luggage incident to his arrest was held to be invalid not only because he was handcuffed to a chair at the time of the search and therefore could not gain access to the luggage but also because the search occurred at least thirty minutes after his arrest. As a result of this delay, the search of the luggage incident to the suspect's arrest was "remote" in time from the actual arrest.

To summarize, law enforcement officers may seize and search containers not immediately associated with an arrestee's body if that property is within the arrestee's immediate control and if the search is not remote in time and place from the arrest. Once officers have the property under their exclusive control, however, and there is no further danger that the arrestee might gain access to the property to seize a weapon or destroy evidence, officers may not search the property without a warrant or consent.

Container Searches Based on Exigent Circumstances Other exigency factors need to be considered when determining whether police can make a warrantless search of a suspect's luggage or other containers as part of a valid search incident to arrest. The Supreme Court in *Chadwick* commented that "if officers have reason to believe that luggage contains some immediately dangerous instrumentality, such as explosives, it would be foolhardy to transport it to the stationhouse without opening the luggage and disarming the weapon." 433 U.S. at 15 n.9.

In *United States v. Johnson*, 467 F.2d 630 (2d Cir. 1972), police officers were notified by a reliable informant that a recent arrestee's suitcase containing a shotgun could be found near the rear door of an apartment building. The officers knew that the building was located in a transient and high-crime area and that the suitcase was probably visible to passersby. The officers rushed to the apartment building, opened the suitcase, and found the shotgun. The court upheld both the seizure and search of the suitcase:

> [I]n opening the suitcases, the police were not acting in violation of the Fourth Amendment. The "exigencies of the situation made that course imperative." . . . The officers were holding a suitcase which they had probable cause to believe contained a contraband sawed-off shotgun. There was a substantial possibility the gun was loaded. As they stood in that transient and high-crime area, their own safety and the safety of others required that they know whether they were holding a dangerous weapon over which they had no control. . . . Under these circumstances, we cannot hold that the police were required to carry the suitcase, unopened, to the police station to obtain a warrant or that an officer should have stood near or held the unopened suitcase as a warrant was obtained. The police were entitled to know what they were holding in their possession. 467 F.2d at 639.

State Departures from the Full Search Incident to Arrest Rule

Full searches incident to a lawful, custodial arrest have been criticized on the ground that they facilitate "pretext" or "subterfuge" arrests for minor offenses and searches incident to those arrests for evidence of more serious crimes for which probable cause to arrest or search is lacking. In *Whren v. United States*, 517 U.S. 806 (1996), the U.S. Supreme Court clearly stated that an officer's ulterior motives do not invalidate the officer's conduct that is justifiable on the basis of probable cause to believe that a violation of law has occurred. In short, if police conduct is justified by probable cause, subjective intent or pretext is irrelevant for Fourth Amendment purposes. The Court went on to say:

> [O]f course . . . the Constitution prohibits selective enforcement of the law based on considerations such as race. But the constitutional basis for objecting to intentionally discriminatory application of laws is the Equal Protection Clause [of the Fourteenth Amendment], not the Fourth Amendment. Subjective intentions play no role in ordinary, probable-cause Fourth Amendment analysis. 517 U.S. at 813.

Nevertheless, based on interpretations of their state constitutions, some state courts have refused to allow a full-body search incident to a lawful custodial arrest.

- The Supreme Court of Hawaii limited the warrantless search of an arrestee's person incident to a lawful, custodial arrest to
  1. disarming the arrested person when there is reason to believe from the facts and circumstances that the person may be armed; and
  2. discovering evidence related to the crime for which the person was arrested. *State v. Kaluna*, 520 P.2d 51, 60 (Haw. 1974).

  Under this more restrictive approach, officers may not search for evidence incident to an arrest when arresting a suspect for an offense that would not produce evidence (e.g., loitering and minor traffic offenses), and officers may not search for weapons unless they can point to specific facts and circumstances indicating the likelihood that the arrested person is armed and dangerous.

- Generally, when a suspect in New York is arrested for an ordinary traffic violation, such as speeding, the suspect may not be searched incident to his arrest unless there are reasonable grounds for suspecting that the officer is in danger or there is probable cause for believing that the offender is guilty of a crime rather than a traffic infraction. *See People v. Marsh*, 228 N.E.2d 783 (N.Y. 1967).

■ In *Zehrung v. State*, 569 P.2d 189, 199–200 (Alaska 1979), the Supreme Court of Alaska held that "absent specific articulable facts justifying the intrusion, . . . a warrantless search incident to an arrest, other than for weapons, is unreasonable and therefore violative of the Alaska Constitution if the charge on which the arrest is made is not one, evidence of which could be concealed on the person."

California, Colorado, and other states have adopted similar restrictions on searches incident to arrest. It is important, therefore, for law enforcement officers to familiarize themselves with the specific limitations that may have been adopted in their particular jurisdictions rather than assuming that the minimum thresholds of federal constitutional law are all that govern searches incident to arrests in their states.

Motor Vehicle Searches Incident to Arrest

For almost three decades, searches of vehicles incident to the arrest of its driver or passengers or both was governed by *New York v. Belton*, 453 U.S. 454 (1981). *Arizona v. Gant*, 129 S. Ct. 1710 (2009), however, significantly changed the law in this area.

In *Belton*, a police officer stopped a vehicle for speeding. In the process of inspecting the vehicle's registration and other documentation, the officer discovered that none of the four male occupants of the vehicle owned the vehicle nor were they related to its owner. The officer also smelled burnt marijuana and noticed on the floor of the vehicle an envelope marked "Supergold" that he associated with marijuana. The officer directed the occupants to get out of the vehicle and placed them under arrest for the unlawful possession of marijuana. After patting down each of the four men, he then picked up the envelope from the floor of the vehicle marked "Supergold" and found that it contained marijuana. At that point, the officer gave *Miranda* warnings to the men and searched them. He then searched the vehicle's passenger compartment. On the backseat he found a black leather jacket belonging to one of the vehicle's former occupants. After unzipping one of the jacket's pockets, the officer found cocaine. He then seized the jacket.

At his trial, Belton moved to suppress the cocaine the trooper seized from his jacket pocket. The Court held:

> [W]hen a policeman has made a lawful custodial arrest of the occupant of an automobile, he may, as a contemporaneous incident of that arrest, search the passenger compartment of that automobile. It follows from this conclusion that the police may also examine the contents of any containers found within the passenger compartment, for if the passenger compartment is within the reach of the arrestee, so also will containers in it be within his reach. . . . Such a container may, of course, be searched whether it is open or closed. 453 U.S. at 460–61.

Thus, under the long-standing *Belton* rule, once a police officer had arrested an occupant of a vehicle, the officer could search the passenger compartment of that vehicle and its containers, regardless of whether the occupant had been removed from the vehicle and secured with handcuffs or in some other way. The *Belton* rule had even been extended to motor vehicle occupants who were arrested after having recently departed their vehicle in *Thornton v. United States*, 541 U.S. 615 (2004). Importantly, a footnote in *Belton* defined a "container" for the purposes of motor vehicle searches incident to arrest. This definition is still instructive today. According to *Belton*, a container is any object capable of holding another object. A container thus includes "closed or open glove compartments, consoles or other receptacles located anywhere within the passenger compartment, as well as luggage, boxes, bags, clothing, and the like." 453 U.S. at 460–61 n.4. Finally, the Court in *Belton* also pointed out that only the interior of the passenger compartment of an automobile, and not the trunk, may be searched incident to arrest. But *Gant* altered this legal landscape by significantly narrowing *Belton*'s reach.

In *Arizona v. Gant*, two police officers knocked on the door of a home and requested to speak to its owner. Gant, who answered the door, explained that the owner was not at home at the time but would return later. After departing from the home, the officers learned through a records check that Gant had an outstanding warrant for his arrest for driving with a suspended license. Upon returning to the residence where they had conversed with Gant earlier in the day, the officers observed a man in the rear of the residence and a woman in a vehicle parked in the front of the residence. When a third officer arrived to the residence, the man was arrested for providing police with a false name and the woman was arrested for possession of drug paraphernalia. The two arrestees were handcuffed and placed in different patrol cars.

Subsequently, Gant arrived at the same residence in his vehicle. He parked the car on the driveway, exited the vehicle, and shut the door. One of the officers, who at the time was located approximately thirty feet from Gant, called to him. Gant and this officer began walking toward each other, and, when they were about ten to twelve feet from Gant's car, the officer arrested and handcuffed Gant.

With no other police vehicles available in which to place Gant, the arresting officer called for backup. When two additional officers arrived, Gant was put in handcuffs in the backseat of their locked patrol car. The officers then began searching through Gant's car; they found a gun and bag of cocaine in the backseat within a jacket pocket. Gant was later charged for drug possession. He moved to suppress the drug evidence by claiming that police violated the Fourth Amendment in his searching his vehicle.

Ultimately, the Court found that the search by police of Gant's vehicle was unconstitutional under the Fourth Amendment. Specifically, the Court essentially overruled *Belton* and applied rules more in line with usual search incident to arrest doctrine by holding that police may search the passenger compartment of a vehicle incident to the lawful arrest of a vehicle occupant or recent occupant when

- the arrested occupant is unsecured and within reaching distance of the passenger compartment of the vehicle at the time of the police search of that vehicle (the "safety" prong); or
- it is reasonable for the officer to believe that evidence relevant to the crime of arrest may be found in the vehicle of the arrested occupant (the "evidentiary" prong).

Applying the preceding rule to the facts in the case, the Court ruled the search of Gant's vehicle unconstitutional. First, Gant could not have reached into the passenger compartment of his vehicle at the time of the search because he and the other arrestees were outnumbered by the officers and already "handcuffed and secured in separate patrol cars." 129 S. Ct. at 1719. In addition, because defendant was arrested for driving with a suspended license, the Court concluded that no search of his car would produce any evidence of that crime.

As *Gant* illustrates, in most cases involving arrests for traffic violations, the law enforcement officer would not have any reasonable basis to believe the vehicle contains evidence relevant to the crime of arrest. In contrast, *Gant* indicated that when the underlying arrest of the vehicle occupant is for a drug crime, it would be reasonable for the officer to believe that evidence relevant to the crime of arrest may be found in the vehicle, and therefore police are generally able to search the passenger compartment of vehicles incident to

KEY POINTS

LO13

■ Police may search the passenger compartment of a vehicle incident to the lawful arrest of a vehicle occupant or recent occupant when (1) the arrested occupant is unsecured and within reaching distance of the passenger compartment of her vehicle at the time of the police search or (2) it is reasonable for the officer to believe that evidence relevant to the crime of arrest may be found in the vehicle of the arrested occupant.

drug-related arrest. At least one appellate court has extended this logic to arrests for driving under the influence of alcohol (DUI) because bottles, cans, or other containers of alcohol might be found during such a search. *United States v. Tinsley*, 365 Fed. Appx. 709, 711 (8th Cir. 2010).

Gant Applies Only to Searches Incident to the Arrest of a Vehicle Occupant

Gant has nothing to do with the so-called automobile exception to the warrant requirement under the *Carroll* doctrine (see Chapter 11 for the requirements of this exception). Indeed, various lower courts are finding that even though *Gant* does not allow a suspect's vehicle to be searched by police incident to that suspect's arrest (e.g., because the suspect is "secured" by police away from her vehicle), the police are nonetheless permitted to search the vehicle because the automobile exception is satisfied (Totten 2010).

However, if the *Gant* rule is satisfied either because the arrested occupant is within reaching distance of his vehicle at the time of the police search of that vehicle, or because the officer has reason to believe that evidence relevant to the crime of arrest may be found in the arrested occupant's vehicle, then the officer may, contemporaneously with the arrest, search the passenger compartment of the vehicle and any articles or containers, closed or open, in the passenger compartment.

If, however, a container is seized and then searched some time later after it is in the exclusive control of the police, *Chadwick* requires that a warrant be obtained. This is both because the later container search is remote in time from the car occupant's arrest and the arrested occupant would not be able to obtain a weapon or destroy evidence from the container once it is in the exclusive control of police.

In vehicles that do not have a traditional "trunk," such as vans, hatchbacks, station wagons, and sport utility vehicles (SUVs), courts have consistently defined "a 'passenger compartment' . . . 'as including all space reachable without exiting the vehicle,' excluding areas that would require dismantling the vehicle." *United States v. Pino*, 855 F.2d 357, 364 (6th Cir. 1988). The only relevant question for determining what constitutes the passenger compartment of a vehicle is whether "the area to be searched is generally 'reachable without exiting the vehicle, without regard to the likelihood in the particular case that such a reaching was possible.'" *United States v. Doward*, 41 F.3d 789, 794 (1st Cir. 1994). The passenger compartment of a vehicle may include compartments hidden by a trap door if these compartments are themselves within the passenger compartment of a vehicle. *See United States v. Poggemiller*, 375 F.3d 686, 688 (8th Cir. 2004).

CRIMINAL PROCEDURE IN ACTION

Applying Gant's Evidentiary Prong *United States v. Vinton*, 594 F.3d 14 (D.C. Cir. 2010).

On September 9, 2006, around 9:00 P.M., U.S. Park Police Officer William Alton, driving a marked cruiser in Southeast D.C., saw a green Nissan Maxima speeding, and also observed that its windows were excessively tinted. As Alton followed the car, he noticed "a thin blue line sticker on the back of [the] car," which Alton assumed

referred to the driver's probable affiliation with law enforcement, most likely the Metropolitan Police Department (MPD).

The driver promptly obeyed Alton's signal to pull over and, as Alton approached the car, the driver, Vinton, lowered all his windows. Alton asked

Continued on next page

if Vinton was in law enforcement and Vinton said he worked in "personal security." Alton immediately saw a knife with a five-and-a-half inch sheath on Vinton's backseat, in "close proximity" to Vinton, easily within reaching distance. Vinton explained the knife was used when fishing with his grandfather, but Alton saw no other fishing equipment in the car. He retrieved the knife and placed it on the roof of the car, "out of arm's reach of the driver." Alton asked if there were "any other weapons in the vehicle," and Vinton responded "no," explaining that he kept "that part of his trade at home." Alton then measured the car's windows with a tint meter and determined they exceeded D.C.'s 70 percent tint limit. He returned to his cruiser to prepare a citation.

Alton was working alone and had not called for backup. However, when an MPD officer appeared, Alton "asked him to stop" because he had found a large knife and desired assistance in conducting a protective search of the car. (Note, this type of cursory search, or vehicle "frisk," of a passenger compartment for weapons only is allowed if the officer has reasonable suspicion that the vehicle occupant is armed and dangerous; these searches are discussed in more detail in Chapter 8.) The officer told Alton there had been a double-stabbing homicide in the same vicinity approximately twenty hours earlier. Alton told Vinton he was going to conduct a search for weapons and asked twice more whether there were any weapons in the car; Vinton first responded "no" but then responded, "Not that I know of." Alton removed Vinton from the car and handcuffed him but informed him he was not under arrest. A search of the passenger compartment of the car revealed two cans of mace in the front armrest, a "butterfly knife" under the front passenger-side floor mat, a bag of Styrofoam earplugs, and a locked briefcase on the backseat. Vinton claimed he used the earplugs as sleeping aids and said the briefcase did not belong to him and he was unaware of its contents. Officer Alton phoned headquarters to request guidance on how to proceed, and U.S. Park

Police Investigator Hodge arrived shortly thereafter. Alton briefed him on the stop and Hodge conferred with a Park Police supervisor to assess whether Alton had probable cause to make an arrest. They determined that he did.

After placing Vinton under arrest for "possession of a prohibited weapon," Alton pried open the locked briefcase. Inside, he found three bags of ecstasy, three pistol magazines, a "fighting knife . . . like brass knuckles," and a .45-caliber semiautomatic pistol, cocked and loaded. Vinton was charged in a two-count indictment with unlawful possession with intent to distribute ecstasy, and using, carrying and possessing a firearm during a drug trafficking offense. He moved to suppress all of the tangible evidence recovered, and all of his statements made, during the traffic stop.

- Applying *Gant's* first or "safety prong," explain whether you think the search of the briefcase was constitutionally permissible.

- Applying *Gant's* second or "evidentiary prong," explain whether you think the search of the briefcase was constitutionally permissible. In other words, did Alton have reasonable suspicion to believe that evidence relevant to the crime of arrest—here, a weapons charge—would be found in Vinton's vehicle? Explain your reasoning.

- More generally, do you agree that the standard for police officer searches under *Gant's* second, "evidentiary" prong should be reasonable suspicion, or should it be the higher standard of probable cause because other searches for evidence in the vehicle context, such as those under the Carroll doctrine's automobile exception (see Chapter 11), must be based on a probable cause belief by officers that the vehicle contains contraband? Is there any practical or policy reason why searches for evidence incident to arrest in the vehicle context should be set at a lower standard than searches for evidence under the automobile exception? Fully explain your answer.

Searches of the Arrestee's Companions

When police make an arrest, other people are often in the vicinity in addition to the arrestee. Some courts allow an immediate frisk for weapons of the arrestee's companions without any further justification. This is sometimes called the automatic companion rule. (Frisks are discussed in greater detail in Chapter 8.) These courts believe that the protection of arresting officers from hidden weapons that could be carried by companions of an arrestee outweighs the minimal intrusion imposed on the companion during a brief pat down for weapons:

> It is inconceivable that a peace officer effecting a lawful arrest . . . must expose himself to a shot in the back from a defendant's associate because he cannot, on the spot, make the nice distinction between whether the other is a companion in crime or a social acquaintance. All companions of an arrestee within the immediate vicinity, capable of accomplishing a harmful assault on the officer, are constitutionally subjected to the cursory "pat-down" reasonably necessary to give assurance that they are unarmed. *United States v. Berryhill*, 445 F.2d 1189, 1193 (9th Cir. 1971); *see also Perry v. State*, 927 P.2d 1158 (Wyo. 1996).

Other courts reject the automatic companion rule, requiring instead that arresting officers have reasonable suspicion to believe the companion of the arrestee is armed and dangerous, based on the totality of the circumstances, before allowing the companion to be frisked for weapons. Under this approach, companionship is one factor among many to consider in deciding whether to frisk. For example, *United States v. Flett*, 806 F.2d 823 (8th Cir. 1986), upheld a pat-down search of an arrestee's companion, even though the companion made no threatening moves toward the officer and the officer noticed no bulge in the companion's clothing. The court found that "the officer reasonably perceived the subject of the frisk as potentially dangerous," justifying a frisk of the companion in the following circumstances:

- The arrestee was the subject of an arrest warrant for narcotics violations.
- The arrestee was a known member of a national motorcycle gang with violent propensities.
- The arrestee was the "enforcer" of the local chapter of the motorcycle gang and had been previously charged with a firearms violation.
- The companion was in the arrestee's house, was dressed in attire similar to that of gang members, and physically resembled known gang members.
- The officer had fifteen years of experience in law enforcement.

See also United States v. Garcia, 459 F.3d 1059 (10th Cir. 2006) (upholding frisk of another occupant of the apartment in light of drug and gang-related activity on the property).

KEY POINTS

L014
- Courts have adopted two approaches to the issue of whether police may search a suspect's companions located in the immediate area of the arrest: (1) officers may automatically conduct a frisk of the arrestee's companions for weapons, or (2) officers may conduct a frisk of the arrestee's companions for weapons if they have reasonable suspicion that these companions are armed and dangerous.

Other Issues Related to Searches Incident to Arrest

This section deals with several issues related to the search incident to arrest doctrine, including (1) who may conduct a search incident to arrest, (2) the use of force during a search incident to arrest, and (3) the limited, emergency search incident to detention doctrine.

Who May Conduct Searches Incident to Arrest?

If possible, the law enforcement officer making the arrest should conduct the search incident to the arrest. An officer who does not immediately search an arrestee, but allows another officer to do so later, risks having the later search invalidated. It would not meet the requirement of contemporaneousness, nor would it indicate a concern for the arresting officer's protection or the prevention of the destruction or concealment of evidence.

Nevertheless, if the arresting officer transfers an arrested person to the custody of another officer, the second officer may again search the arrested person. This second search is allowed because the second officer is entitled to take personal safety measures and need not rely on the assumption that the arrestee has been thoroughly searched for weapons by the arresting officer. *United States v. Dyson*, 277 A.2d 658 (D.C. App. 1971). This principle was reaffirmed in *State v. Cooney*, 149 P.3d 554 (Mont. 2006).

In *Cooney*, two officers conducted a search of the defendant outside a residence after he was arrested. Another officer then was assigned to transport the defendant. The court found that the officer responsible for transporting the defendant was allowed to conduct an additional search:

> Officer Brodie's and Officer Lewis's testimony indicates that their initial search of [defendant] outside the residence was sufficient only to ensure safety in what was a relatively secure situation. . . . Officer Kelly did not act on his own initiative [in re-searching defendant prior to transporting him]. Officer Brodie advised Officer Kelly that he should perform a more thorough search before placing [defendant] in the backseat of his police cruiser. Officer Brodie and Officer Lewis testified that they did not believe that their initial search of [defendant] outside the residence was thorough enough to ensure that [defendant] would be secured in the backseat of a police cruiser. Officer Kelly would be alone with [defendant] in this less controlled environment where [defendant] might have a greater opportunity to retrieve a hidden weapon. We agree with the District Court that under these circumstances Officer Kelly's search was commensurate with preventing Cooney from retrieving any hidden weapons that he may have had on his person. We do not read [the applicable state statute] to require a police officer to trust his personal safety to a perfunctory search performed by other officers when those same officers have advised him that their initial search was insufficient to ensure the safe transport of a prisoner. 149 P.3d at 556–57.

Use of Force During Searches Incident to Arrest

Law enforcement officers searching a person incident to arrest may use the degree of force reasonably necessary to protect themselves, prevent escape, and prevent the destruction or concealment of evidence. Courts review the use of force strictly and require officers to use as little force as necessary to accomplish their legitimate purpose. Compare, for example, *Evans v. Stephens*, 407 F.3d 1272 (11th Cir. 2005), with *Salas v. State*, 246 So.2d 621 (Fla. Dist. Ct. App. 1971).

Recall that *Evans v. Stephens* invalidated a postarrest strip search of body cavities for drugs, in part because of the excessive force used during the search. Specifically, the officer in *Evans* threw one of the arrestees, hit one of them with a baton, inserted the same baton in each arrestee's anus, and used this same baton to lift each arrestee's testicles. In contrast, *Salas* upheld a seizure of drugs incident to arrest even though the arresting officer put a choke hold on the arrestee and forced him to spit out drugs he was attempting to swallow.

Limited, Emergency Search Incident to Detention

In *Cupp v. Murphy*, 412 U.S. 291 (1973), the U.S. Supreme Court held that a law enforcement officer may conduct a limited, warrantless search of a person merely detained for investigation, which is often referred to as a limited search incident to detention. In that case, the defendant, after being notified of his wife's strangulation, voluntarily came to police headquarters and met his attorney there. Police noticed a dark spot on the defendant's finger and asked permission to take a scraping from his fingernails. The defendant refused. Under protest and without a warrant, police proceeded to take the samples, which included particles of the wife's skin and blood and fabric from her clothing. The defendant was not formally arrested until approximately one month after the samples were taken.

The Court held that the momentary detention of the defendant to get the fingernail scrapings constituted a seizure governed by the Fourth Amendment. Citing *Chimel*, the Court also recognized that under prescribed conditions, warrantless searches incident to a detention are constitutionally valid. Without an arrest or search warrant, however, a full *Chimel* search of the defendant's body and the area within his immediate control was not permissible. Nevertheless, the Court validated the search under a limited application of the *Chimel* rule based on the unique facts of the case:

- The defendant was not arrested but was detained only long enough to take the fingernail scrapings.

- The search was very limited in extent, involving only the scraping of fingernails. (A full *Chimel* search of the defendant's body and the area within his immediate control would not have been justified without an arrest.)

- The evidence—blood and skin on the fingernails—was readily destructible.

- The defendant made attempts to destroy the evidence, creating exigent circumstances.

- The officers had probable cause to arrest the defendant, even though he was not actually arrested.

Protective Sweeps

Under *Chimel*, when officers make an arrest in a home or other location, they may not conduct a full search of any areas of the premises other than searching the arrestee's person and the limited area within the arrestee's immediate control, generally referred to as the suspect's "arm span" or "wingspan" (e.g., the area from within which the arrestee may gain access to a weapon or destructible evidence). However, the protective sweep doctrine provides a limited exception to the *Chimel* rule.

Under the protective sweep doctrine, officers may

- need to pass through various rooms when entering or leaving premises to make an arrest,

- conduct a quick and limited search of premises incident to an arrest on those premises to protect both their own safety and the safety of others from potential accomplices linked to the arrestee, and

- conduct a limited search of the premises if they believe evidence is about to be destroyed or removed as they make an arrest.

These movements into other areas of the premises are not considered full-blown searches, because the officer's purpose is not to search for incriminating evidence, but rather to make an arrest as safely as possible. If one of these exceptions applies, an officer who observes a weapon or other seizable item lying open to view may seize it.

The item is admissible in court if the seizure satisfies the requirements of the plain view doctrine (see Chapter 10).

The exception to the *Chimel* rule allowing protective sweeps for accomplices during home arrests was developed in *Maryland v. Buie*, 494 U.S. 325 (1990). In *Buie*, two men, one of whom was wearing a red running suit, committed an armed robbery. The same day, police obtained an arrest warrant for the defendant and his suspected accomplice and executed the warrant for the defendant at his home. After the defendant was arrested as he emerged from the basement, one of the officers entered the basement "in case there was someone else" there and seized a red running suit lying in plain view.

In determining the reasonableness of the search of the basement leading to the plain view seizure, the U.S. Supreme Court balanced the officer's need to search against the invasion of privacy caused by the search. Possessing an arrest warrant and probable cause to believe the defendant was in his home, the officers were entitled to enter and search anywhere in the house in which the defendant might be found. Once he was found, however, the search for him was over, and the officers no longer had that particular justification for entering any rooms that had not yet been searched. Those rooms, however, were not immune from entry simply because of the defendant's expectation of privacy with respect to them. That privacy interest must be balanced against the

> interest of the officers in taking steps to assure themselves that the house in which a suspect is being or has just been arrested is not harboring other persons [e.g., accomplices] who are dangerous and who could unexpectedly launch an attack. The risk of danger in the context of an arrest in the home is as great as, if not greater than, it is in an on-the-street or roadside investigatory encounter. 494 U.S. at 333.

Thus, police officers have a limited right to conduct a protective sweep

> as a precautionary matter and without probable cause or reasonable suspicion, look in closets and other spaces immediately adjoining the place of arrest from which an attack could be immediately launched. Beyond that, however, . . . there must be articulable facts which, taken together with the rational inferences from those facts, would warrant a reasonably prudent officer in believing that the area to be swept harbors an individual posing a danger to those on the arrest scene. 494 U.S. at 334.

Protective Sweeps for Accomplices

Protective sweeps of rooms and other spaces in a home that are immediately adjacent to the room where the officer makes the arrest, looking for possible accomplices (as an attack could be "immediately launched" from these areas) may be conducted without probable cause or reasonable suspicion. For example, in *Peals v. Terre Haute Police Department*, 535 F.3d 621, 628 (7th Cir. 2008), the court upheld a protective sweep by officers after the defendant was arrested in his garage because officers confined their sweep to the garage and areas of the home immediately adjacent to the garage in which an accomplice could hide.

In contrast, to sweep places in a home that are *not* adjacent to the area in which an officer makes an arrest, police need reasonable suspicion based on specific and articulable facts that these nonadjacent rooms harbor a dangerous person who may harm the police or innocent third parties. For example, the reasonable suspicion standard for a protective sweep was satisfied when police entered the basement of a residence because it was "a confined space; [the area] was not well lit; the area contained a partial wall dividing the space into at least two areas; there were reports that other individuals were in the residence; and there were reports that [defendant] stored weapons in the basement." *United States v. Pruneda*, 518 F.3d 597, 603 (8th Cir. 2008).

Buie emphasized that protective sweeps must be limited to cursory inspections of spaces where a person may be found, such as closets and crawl spaces. *United States v. Stover*, 474 F.3d 904 (6th Cir. 2007). In contrast, searches of small spaces incapable of containing a person, such as the space between a mattress and box spring, are not permitted under the doctrine. *United States v. Blue*, 78 F.3d 56 (2nd Cir. 1996).

The sweep may last no longer than is necessary to dispel the reasonable suspicion of danger and in any event no longer than it takes to complete the arrest and depart from the premises. *See, e.g., United States v. Pruneda,* 518 F.3d 597, 603 (8th Cir. 2008). For example, in *United States v. Paradis*, 351 F.3d 21 (1st Cir. 2003), at the time police searched a bedroom of an apartment and found a gun, the defendant had already been arrested in that bedroom, a protective sweep of that room for accomplices had already happened, and the defendant had been removed from the apartment after they found him. Police had no reasonable suspicion that accomplices remained in other areas of the apartment because they had seen all of the other occupants leave the apartment prior to defendant's arrest and because they had also searched the other rooms in their efforts to find the defendant, whom they ultimately found in the bedroom. As a result, the court in *Paradis* declined to uphold the extended sweep of the bedroom and therefore excluded the gun.

Various courts have also addressed the issue of whether a protective sweep of the premises is permitted when a person is arrested outside those premises. *United States v. Soria*, 959 F.2d 855 (10th Cir. 1992), approved a protective sweep of the defendant's auto shop after the defendant was arrested during a drug transaction near the shop. The officers reasonably believed that drug-dealing activities had taken place in the shop and that others may have been hiding inside. In contrast, *United States v. Hogan*, 38 F.3d 1148 (10th Cir. 1994), invalidated a protective sweep of the defendant's residence after the defendant was arrested outside the residence. He was not home when the police first arrived, and the only possible danger to the police was the hypothetical possibility that the defendant's accomplice to the murder committed a month earlier might be in the residence.

Protective Sweeps to Prevent the Destruction of Evidence

In *Vale v. Louisiana*, 399 U.S. 30 (1970), officers arrested a defendant on an arrest warrant outside his home. Because police had observed conduct prior to the arrest that made them believe the defendant was engaging in a drug transaction, they entered the home after arresting the defendant, conducted a search without a warrant, and found narcotics. The U.S. Supreme Court invalidated the sweep of the home because, "the arresting officers satisfied themselves that no one else was in the house when they first entered the premises." 399 U.S. at 34. Without anyone inside to destroy the potential drug evidence, there were no exigent circumstances that could justify the warrantless search of a home. Police should have obtained a search warrant before entering the house to search for the drugs.

In contrast to the facts in *Vale*, if law enforcement officers "have probable cause to believe contraband is present and, in addition, based on the surrounding circumstances or the information at hand, they reasonably conclude that the evidence will be destroyed or removed before they can secure a search warrant, a warrantless search is justified." *United States v. Rubin*, 474 F.2d 262, 269 (3rd Cir. 1973). The court outlined the following considerations police may weigh in deciding whether a search incident to an arrest on the premises is justified because of a threat of evidence destruction or removal:

- the degree of urgency involved and the amount of time necessary to obtain a warrant,

- reasonable belief that the contraband is about to be removed or destroyed,

- the possibility of danger to police officers guarding the site of the contraband while a search warrant is sought,

- information indicating the possessors of the contraband are aware that the police are on their trail, and

- the ready destructibility of the contraband and the knowledge that efforts to dispose of narcotics and to escape are characteristic behaviors of persons engaged in the narcotics traffic. 474 F.2d at 268–69.

Some courts have even permitted a warrantless search after a home arrest if police have only reasonable suspicion that evidence is about to be destroyed or removed from the home. *See United States v. Hoyos*, 868 F.2d 1131 (9th Cir. 1989). Law enforcement officers should take care to learn whether reasonable suspicion or probable cause is required in their specific jurisdictions to justify warrantless entry to prevent the imminent destruction of evidence.

SUMMARY

A formal arrest is the taking of a person into custody for the commission of an offense as the prelude to prosecuting him or her for it. The basic elements constituting a formal arrest are

- a law enforcement officer's purpose or intention to take a person into the custody of the law,

- the officer's exercise of real or pretended authority,

- detention or restraint of the person to be arrested whether by physical force or by submission to assertion of authority, and

- understanding by the person to be arrested of the officer's intention to arrest.

Even when these basic elements are not all present, courts may find that an encounter between a law enforcement officer and a person entails such a significant intrusion on the person's freedom of action that it is in important respects indistinguishable from a formal arrest. Such an encounter, sometimes called a *seizure tantamount to arrest* or a *de facto arrest*, must be supported by probable cause or it is illegal. The test to determine whether a seizure is tantamount to arrest is whether, in view of all the circumstances surrounding the encounter, a reasonable person would have believed that he or she was not free to leave.

Although warrantless arrests on probable cause are permitted, courts always prefer arrests made under the authority of an arrest warrant. An arrest warrant is a written judicial order directing a law enforcement officer to arrest a particular person. An arrest warrant is issued by a magistrate on the basis of a complaint stating the essential facts constituting the offense charged, if the magistrate has probable cause to believe that the offense was committed and that the person to be arrested committed it. The magistrate may also issue a summons that merely directs the defendant to appear rather than ordering an arrest.

Law enforcement officers may make a warrantless public arrest for a felony if they have probable cause to believe that a felony has been or is being committed and that the person to be arrested has committed or is committing the felony. Officers may make a warrantless public arrest for a misdemeanor, however, only if

- officers have probable cause to believe that an offense committed in their presence was a misdemeanor, or
- a state statute or constitution allows warrantless arrests on probable cause for certain misdemeanors not committed in the officer's presence.

A warrantless misdemeanor arrest for offenses committed in the officer's presence must be made immediately; but a warrantless felony arrest may be delayed for various reasons, as long as the defendant's rights are not prejudiced by the delay.

When law enforcement officers make arrests, they should notify the arrested person that he or she is under arrest and notify the person of the officers' authority and the cause of the arrest. If the arrest is made under authority of a warrant, officers should examine the warrant to make sure it is valid on its face before carrying out its commands. When an arrest warrant is executed, officers should return the warrant as directed and explain what they have done in carrying out its commands.

Officers have no official authority to arrest without a warrant outside their jurisdiction—the geographical area for which they were elected or appointed. Nevertheless, outside their jurisdiction they have the same authority as any private citizen to arrest for misdemeanors committed in their presence and for felonies on probable cause. They may also arrest outside their jurisdiction in fresh pursuit of a criminal who has fled their jurisdiction, if the pursuit is begun promptly inside the jurisdiction and maintained continuously.

Officers may use only the amount of force reasonably necessary under the circumstances to make an arrest. Deadly force may be used only as a last resort and then only in specifically limited circumstances. Deadly force may never be used to accomplish an arrest for a misdemeanor. Officers may, however, use deadly force in self-defense to protect themselves or other innocent persons from death or serious bodily injury and need not abandon an attempt to arrest in the face of physical resistance to the arrest. Officers may also use deadly force to stop the escape of a fleeing suspect if there is probable cause to believe that the suspect has committed a crime involving the infliction or threatened infliction of serious physical harm.

Officers may not enter a dwelling to arrest a person without a warrant unless there is consent or exigent circumstances exist. An arrest warrant is required to enter a suspect's home to arrest the suspect. A search warrant is required to enter a third person's home to arrest a suspect. Exigent circumstances that would justify a warrantless entry of a dwelling to arrest are

- hot pursuit of a fleeing felon,
- imminent destruction of evidence,
- the need to prevent a suspect's escape, and
- the risk of danger to police or other persons.

In assessing the risk of danger, the gravity of the crime and the likelihood that the suspect is armed should be considered. If an arrest is begun in a public place, officers in hot pursuit may enter a dwelling without a warrant to complete the arrest.

Before officers may lawfully enter a dwelling forcibly to arrest a person, they must be refused admittance after knocking, announcing their authority and purpose, and demanding admittance. Failure to knock and announce is excused if an officer's purpose is already known, or if the officer has reasonable suspicion that knocking and announcing would cause danger to the officer or other persons, permit the escape of the suspect, or result in the loss or destruction of evidence.

An officer's duties after an arrest is made include the following: booking; bringing the arrested person before a magistrate without unnecessary delay; ensuring the health and safety of the arrested person while in the officer's custody; conducting a stationhouse inventory search of the prisoner, which may include searching and seizing any container or object in the prisoner's possession; and conducting identification procedures, which may include fingerprinting, photographing, certain physical examinations, lineups, and collecting DNA evidence for serious offenses and under certain other circumstances when an arrest is made for less serious crimes. A physical examination of the arrestee at booking, or intake, may, under certain circumstances, include a strip and visual body cavity search.

Although an illegal arrest does not affect the jurisdiction of the court to try a person, any evidence obtained as the product of the exploitation of an illegal arrest is inadmissible in a criminal proceeding against the defendant. In addition, a law enforcement officer may be civilly or criminally liable for making an illegal arrest or using unreasonable or excessive force.

Search incident to arrest is a recognized exception to the warrant requirement of the Fourth Amendment. The U.S. Supreme Court case of *Chimel v. California* permits the search of a person who has been subjected to a lawful custodial arrest for the purposes of removing weapons and preventing the concealment or destruction of evidence. A full search for weapons and seizable evidence is permitted, whether or not there is any likelihood of danger from weapons or any reason to believe evidence will be found.

Full searches of areas of premises beyond the area within the immediate control of the arrestee are prohibited. Nevertheless, an officer may look in closets and other spaces immediately adjacent to the place of arrest from which an attack could be immediately launched. Also, an officer may conduct a properly limited protective sweep of the area beyond the spaces adjacent to the place of arrest when the officer has reasonable articulable suspicion that this nonadjacent area to be swept harbors a person posing a danger to those on the arrest scene. Also, if police have reasonable suspicion or probable cause that evidence is about to be destroyed or removed from a home, they may (incident to a home arrest) conduct a limited search of the home to prevent this destruction or removal.

There must be a lawful custodial arrest before police can conduct a search incident to an arrest. A lawful custodial arrest is an arrest that involves taking the person into custody and transporting him or her to a police station or other place to be dealt with according to the law. The issuance of a citation alone is not a lawful custodial arrest; however, if there is a lawful custodial arrest, a search incident to that arrest can occur even if the crime for which the person was arrested is a minor one unless state law provides otherwise.

Also, a search incident to arrest must be substantially contemporaneous with the arrest. Generally speaking, a search is said to be contemporaneous with an arrest if the search is at the same time probable cause to arrest develops or is conducted shortly thereafter. Short delays between an arrest and an incident search are generally permitted but if the delay becomes prolonged, officers must be prepared to provide good reasons for the delay. Generally, an incident search may not precede an arrest and serve to justify it. However, if probable cause to arrest develops before the challenged search and the arrest follows quickly after the search, then a search preceding a formal arrest may be permissible.

The scope of a search incident to a lawful arrest may extend to the arrestee's body and to items and evidence immediately associated with the body. In addition, police may search incident to a suspect's lawful arrest the area within his or her immediate control—the area from which the arrestee might gain possession of a weapon or destructible evidence. Any weapon or other item of evidence found within this area, including containers, may be searched and seized. If, however, police seize these proximate containers such as luggage or other items of evidence not immediately associated with the person of the arrestee but within the arrestee's immediate control, they may not conduct a delayed search of these containers and other items after they have come within their exclusive control without a warrant or exigent circumstances.

Police may search the passenger compartment of a vehicle incident to the lawful arrest of a vehicle occupant or recent occupant when

- the arrested occupant is unsecured and within reaching distance of the passenger compartment of her vehicle at the time of the police search, or
- it is reasonable for the officer to believe that evidence relevant to the crime of arrest may be found in the vehicle of the arrested occupant.

Officers may conduct frisks of companions of the arrested person located within the immediate area of the arrest if the officers have reasonable articulable suspicion that the companions are armed and dangerous. Alternatively, some courts permit officers to conduct automatic frisks of companions of the arrestee located within the immediate area of the arrest.

Generally, the officer making the arrest should conduct the search incident to the arrest. Officers should use as little force as necessary to reasonably protect themselves, prevent escape, and prevent the destruction or concealment of evidence. The U.S. Supreme Court has approved a limited warrantless frisk of a person merely detained for investigation. Law enforcement officers may conduct such a search, however, only if they have probable cause to arrest the suspect and there is an imminent danger that crucial evidence will be destroyed if the search is not made immediately.

KEY TERMS

affidavit 245
armspan (wingspan) 288
arrest 240
arrest warrant 246
automatic companion rule 295
body cavity search 284
buccal (oral) DNA swab 273
booking 271
citizen's arrest 249
common law 248
complaint 245
container 293

contemporaneous 278
excessive force 267
exigent circumstances 254
extradition 259
felony 246
fresh pursuit 258
frisk 242
full search of the arrestee's body 284
hot pursuit 256
immediate control 287
initial appearance 272
inventory search 272

lawful custodial arrest 277
limited search incident to
   detention 297
magistrate 245
misdemeanor 245
protective sweep 298
resisting arrest 260
search incident to arrest 276
show of authority 241
stop 241
strip search 284
summons 245

REVIEW AND DISCUSSION QUESTIONS

1. Is it possible to formally arrest a mentally ill or mentally retarded person? Explain.

2. Name several ways in which a law enforcement officer or officers can prevent a routine encounter with a person on the street from being considered a seizure tantamount to arrest.

3. Give three practical reasons why a law enforcement officer should obtain an arrest warrant if possible.

4. How is a law enforcement officer's authority to arrest affected by time?

5. Is it valid to say that if an officer has strong probable cause to arrest someone, the officer may arrest the person anywhere in the country? Explain.

6. What are the major differences between an officer's felony arrest powers and an officer's misdemeanor arrest powers?

7. What is meant by a "citizen's arrest"? Explain the legal limitations on making a citizen's arrest.

8. Under what circumstances may a law enforcement officer use deadly force, and what are the potential consequences of an illegal use of deadly force? Name several circumstances under which little or no force should be used to make an arrest.

9. Do law enforcement officers have a broader right to self-defense when they are assaulted while making an arrest than when they are assaulted while simply walking or cruising their beats?

10. Assume that a law enforcement officer has probable cause to arrest a defendant for armed assault and probable cause to believe that the person is hiding in a third person's garage, which is attached to the house. What warrants, if any, does the officer need to enter the garage to arrest the defendant? What if the officer is in hot pursuit of the defendant? What if the defendant is known to be injured and unarmed?

11. Give reasons to support an argument that a law enforcement officer should never have to knock and announce before entering a dwelling to arrest a dangerous felon or a drug offender.

12. If a law enforcement officer has probable cause to arrest, does the officer have to make an arrest? If not, what alternatives to arrest are available, and under what circumstances should they be used?

13. Discuss in detail four different things a law enforcement officer must do after he or she has arrested a person.

14. Assume that while riding in the first-class section of an airplane, a person is legally arrested for transporting illegal drugs. Can the arresting officers immediately conduct searches of the following items and places incident to the arrest?

   a. The person's clothing
   b. The person's suitcase
   c. The entire first-class section of the airplane
   d. The person's body cavities

   If you approved any of the preceding searches, consider whether each search should be made. What are the possible alternatives?

15. If a defendant is arrested in an automobile for stealing the automobile, may the arresting officer search other passengers in the automobile incident to the defendant's arrest?

16. In a typical search incident to arrest situation, the arrest is followed by a search and then by a seizure. Is a search followed by a seizure and then by an arrest valid? Is a seizure followed by an arrest and then by an additional search valid?

17. What problems relative to search incident to arrest arise when the individual arrested is a person of the opposite sex?

18. Does the nature of the offense arrested for have any effect on the scope of a search incident to arrest?

19. Assume that a defendant is arrested in his kitchen for the armed robbery of a bank earlier that day. The arresting officers have an arrest warrant but no search warrant. The defendant is one of three persons wanted in the robbery. The defendant's automobile, the suspected getaway car, is parked in his driveway (and has been parked there for some time). Indicate the full extent of the arresting officers' authority to search the defendant, his premises, and his automobile under the search incident to a lawful arrest doctrine.

20. Assume the same facts as in question 19, except that the defendant is arrested while running from his house to his automobile. Indicate the full extent of the arresting officers' authority to search the defendant, his premises, and his automobile. What if the officers have only a search warrant for the defendant's house and no arrest warrant? What if it is raining heavily?

21. Is the scope of a search incident to arrest affected by any of the following circumstances?

   a. The defendant is handcuffed and chained to a pole.
   b. The defendant is unconscious.
   c. The defendant is surrounded by a group of friends.
   d. The defendant is arrested on a dark street.

22. Under *United States v. Gant*, the search of containers and other items in the passenger compartment of a vehicle is allowed incident to a custodial arrest of a vehicle occupant or recent occupant who is within reaching distance of her vehicle at the time of the police search. In light of this rule, should law enforcement officers wait until a defendant is in or very close to her vehicle before making an arrest, when possible? Moreover, under *Gant*, should officers refrain from handcuffing or otherwise restraining the arrestee until after they have conducted a search of the passenger compartment of the vehicle?

23. Under *Gant*, the search of containers and other items in the passenger compartment of a vehicle is also allowed incident to a custodial arrest of a vehicle occupant or recent occupant when it is reasonable for the officer to believe that evidence relevant to the crime of arrest may be found in the vehicle of the arrested occupant. In light of this rule, should officers make custodial arrests for offenses for which they would ordinarily not make custodial arrests (i.e., minor traffic infractions, etc.)? In general, what are examples of underlying offenses when it would be reasonable for the officer to believe that evidence relevant to the crime of arrest may be found in the vehicle of the arrested occupant? Would drug offenses qualify? A DUI or DWI arrest? An arrest for speeding or driving with a suspended license?

24. Discuss the meaning of this statement: "It is not at all clear that the 'grabbing distance' authorized in the *Chimel* case is conditioned upon the arrested person's continued capacity 'to grab.'" *People v. Fitzpatrick*, 300 N.E.2d 139, 143 (N.Y. 1973).

25. Under what circumstances might a strip search or a body cavity search be justified as a search incident to arrest or as part of a routine booking procedure for an arrestee? What about blood tests, DNA collection and analysis, stomach pumping, or surgery (i.e., to remove a bullet)?

8 Stops and Frisks

LO1 ANALYZE the distinctions among a stop, a formal arrest, a seizure tantamount to an arrest, and minimal nonintrusive contact between a citizen and a law enforcement officer.

LO2 EXPLAIN the distinctions between a frisk and a full search.

LO3 EVALUATE how to balance competing interests when determining the reasonableness of a stop and frisk.

LO4 EXPLAIN what justifies a law enforcement officer in stopping a person and what interference with the person's freedom of action the law permits.

LO5 DESCRIBE what justifies a law enforcement officer in frisking a person and the scope of the search the law permits.

LO6 APPLY the legal principles governing stops and frisks to analogous situations, such as detentions and examinations of luggage, mail, and other property.

In Chapter 7, a formal **arrest** was defined as "the taking of a person into custody for the commission of an offense as the prelude to prosecuting him for it." *State v. Murphy*, 465 P.2d 900, 902 (Or. App. 1970). Also discussed were **seizures tantamount to arrest**—encounters between a law enforcement officer and a person that intrude on the person's freedom of action to the degree that it is indistinguishable from an arrest in important respects. A stop, the focus of this chapter, involves an even less intrusive **seizure** of a person; and a frisk, also addressed in this chapter, involves a limited search of that person.

A **stop** is a police practice involving the temporary detention and questioning of a person initiated on a **reasonable suspicion** (less than **probable cause**) of criminal activity for the purposes of crime prevention and investigation. A **frisk** is a limited search, for the protection of the law enforcement officer carrying out the investigation, of a stopped person who is reasonably believed to be armed and dangerous.

Stops and frisks are not contacts in which a law enforcement officer approaches a person in a public place and asks if the person is willing to answer questions. These contacts should involve a legitimate law enforcement purpose, but they do not require the reasonable suspicion associated with a stop and frisk. The officer may not detain the person, even momentarily, whether or not the person chooses to cooperate. If, however, an initially friendly and neutral encounter somehow provides the officer with reason to suspect criminal activity or danger, the officer may be justified in making the more significant intrusions of a stop and a frisk.

The Foundations for Stops and Frisks

Law enforcement has employed stops and frisks for centuries. This section looks briefly at that history and then explores the legal foundations for this practice.

History

A law enforcement officer's power to detain and question suspicious persons dates back to the common law of England, where constables had the power to detain suspicious persons overnight to investigate their suspicious activities. In the United States, until the mid-1960s, police-initiated contacts with citizens that did not amount to arrests were generally left to the discretion of individual officers and were not subject to constitutional protections or judicial oversight. In the mid-1960s—a period of expanding constitutional rights for citizens—reform-minded individuals called for the extension of constitutional protections to all police–citizen encounters and a review of these encounters by the courts. Some in law enforcement argued that, because of their experience and professionalism, street encounters should be subject to their discretion rather than formal rules.

The reformers maintained that a free society requires that constitutional safeguards protect every citizen, especially minorities and dissidents, at all times and places. In response, the U.S. Supreme Court adopted formal guidelines governing street encounters amounting to less than arrests or full searches in three cases decided in 1968. In those three foundational cases—*Terry v. Ohio*, *Sibron v. New York*, and *Peters v. New York*—the Court attempted to resolve the conflicting interests by applying a balancing test under the **reasonableness** requirement of the Fourth Amendment.

The Foundational Cases

Terry v. Ohio The facts of *Terry v. Ohio* were stated by the U.S. Supreme Court as follows:

> At the hearing on the motion to suppress this evidence, Officer McFadden testified that while he was patrolling in plain clothes in downtown Cleveland at approximately 2:30 in the afternoon of October 31, 1963, his attention was attracted by two men, Chilton and Terry, standing on the corner of Huron Road and Euclid Avenue. He had never seen the two men before, and he was unable to say precisely what first drew his eye to them. However, he testified that he had been a policeman for 39 years and a detective for 35 and that he had been assigned to patrol this vicinity of downtown Cleveland for shoplifters and pickpockets for 30 years. He added: "Now, in this case when I looked over they didn't look right to me at the time."
>
> His interest aroused, Officer McFadden took up a post of observation in the entrance to a store 300 to 400 feet away from the two men. "I get more purpose to watch them when I seen their movements," he testified. He saw one of the men leave the other one and walk southwest on Huron Road, past some stores. The man paused for a moment and looked in a store window, then walked on a short distance, turned around and walked back toward the corner, pausing once again to look in the same store window. He rejoined his companion at the corner, and the two conferred briefly. Then the second man went through the same series of motions, strolling down Huron Road, looking in the same window, walking on a short distance, turning back, peering in the store window again, and returning to confer with the first man at the

corner. The two men repeated this ritual alternately between five and six times apiece—in all, roughly a dozen trips. At one point, while the two were standing together on the corner, a third man approached them and engaged them briefly in conversation. This man then left the two others and walked west on Euclid Avenue. Chilton and Terry resumed their measured pacing, peering and conferring. After this had gone on for 10 to 12 minutes, the two men walked off together, heading west on Euclid Avenue, following the path taken earlier by the third man.

[His suspicions aroused and fearing Terry and Chilton had a gun which they intended to use to rob the store, Officer McFadden followed them. Observing that the two men stopped in front of another store called "Zucker's," Officer McFadden intervened. He] identified himself as a police officer and asked for their names. At this point his knowledge was confined to what he had observed. . . . When the men "mumbled something" in response to his inquiries, Officer McFadden grabbed petitioner Terry, spun him around so that they were facing the other two, with Terry between McFadden and the others, and patted down the outside of his clothing. In the left breast pocket of Terry's overcoat Officer McFadden felt a pistol. He reached inside the overcoat pocket, but was unable to remove the gun. At this point, keeping Terry between himself and the others, the officer ordered all three men to enter Zucker's store. As they went in, he removed Terry's overcoat completely, removed a .38-caliber revolver from the pocket and ordered all three men to face the wall with their hands raised. Officer McFadden proceeded to pat down the outer clothing of Chilton and the third man, Katz. He discovered another revolver in the outer pocket of Chilton's overcoat, but no weapons were found on Katz. The officer testified that he only patted the men down to see whether they had weapons, and that he did not put his hands beneath the outer garments of either Terry or Chilton until he felt their guns. So far as appears from the record, he never placed his hands beneath Katz' outer garments. Officer McFadden seized Chilton's gun, asked the proprietor of the store to call a police wagon, and took all three men to the station. 392 U.S. at 5–7.

Terry and Chilton were formally charged and convicted of carrying concealed weapons. They appealed, claiming that the weapons were obtained by means of an unreasonable search and should not have been admitted into evidence at their trial. The U.S. Supreme Court affirmed the convictions holding that, even though stops and frisks represent a lesser restraint than traditional arrests and searches, the procedures are still governed by the Fourth Amendment. However, stops and frisks are not subject to as stringent a limitation as are traditional full arrests and searches. Instead of applying the probable cause standard to stops and frisks, the Court applied the fundamental test of the Fourth Amendment: the reasonableness under all the circumstances of the particular governmental invasion of a citizen's personal security.

In discussing the reasonableness of Officer McFadden's actions, the Court recognized that law enforcement officers need to protect themselves when suspicious circumstances indicate possible criminal activity by potentially dangerous persons, even though probable cause for an arrest is lacking. It would be unreasonable to deny an officer the authority to take steps to determine whether a suspected person is armed and to neutralize the threat of harm. The Court concluded:

[W]here a police officer observes unusual conduct which leads him reasonably to conclude in light of his experience that criminal activity may be afoot and that the persons with whom he is dealing may be armed and presently dangerous, where in the course of investigating this behavior he identifies himself as a policeman and makes reasonable inquiries, and where nothing in the initial stages of the encounter serves to dispel his reasonable fear for his own or other's safety, he is entitled for the protection of himself and others in the area to conduct a carefully limited search of the outer clothing of such persons in an attempt to discover weapons which might be used to assault him. 392 U.S. at 30.

Sibron v. New York and Peters v. New York Unlike in *Terry*, the U.S. Supreme Court in *Sibron* found that the officer lacked reasonable suspicion that the defendant, Sibron, was armed and dangerous. As a result, the officer's frisk of Sibron was unlawful and the drugs discovered in his pocket were inadmissible in court. At the time of the frisk, the officer had only seen Sibron conversing with other individuals he knew to be drug addicts. In addition, the officer exceeded the scope of a permissible frisk by going beyond Sibron's outer clothing and entering his pocket (see "Scope of a Frisk" later in this chapter for further discussion of this topic). The Court in *Sibron* also addressed the case of defendant Peters, whose case was consolidated with that of defendant Sibron. The Court ultimately found that the search of Peters was constitutional as a valid search incident to arrest for attempted burglary, and the burglar's tools found in his clothing were thus admissible at his trial. At the time of the officer's encounter with Peters, the officer had probable cause to arrest him for attempted burglary based on both his furtive movements and flight, and thus the search incident of Peters was justified. *Sibron v. New York*, 392 U.S. 40, 62–68 (1968). (For further discussion of searches incident to arrest, see Chapter 7.)

The Reasonableness Standard

Stop-and-frisk procedures are serious intrusions on a person's privacy. They are governed by the Fourth Amendment, which prohibits unreasonable searches and seizures.

It is quite plain that the Fourth Amendment governs "seizures" of the person which do not eventuate in a trip to the station house and prosecution for crime—"arrests" in traditional terminology. It must be recognized that whenever a police officer accosts an individual and restrains his freedom to walk away, he has "seized" that person. And it is nothing less than sheer torture of the English language to suggest that a careful exploration of the outer surfaces of a person's clothing all over his or her body in an attempt to find weapons is not a "search." Moreover, it is simply fantastic to urge that such a procedure performed in public by a policeman while the citizen stands helpless, perhaps facing a wall with his hands raised, is a "petty indignity." It is a serious intrusion upon the sanctity of the person, which may inflict great indignity and arouse strong resentment, and it is not to be undertaken lightly. *Terry*, 392 U.S. at 16–17.

Nevertheless, because a stop is more limited in scope than an arrest and a frisk is more limited in scope than a full search, stops and frisks are judged by a less rigid standard than the probable cause standard applicable to an arrest and search. *Terry* made clear that stops and frisks are governed not by the warrant clause of the Fourth Amendment but by the reasonableness clause:

We deal here with an entire rubric of police conduct—necessarily swift action based upon the on-the-spot observations of the officer on the beat—which historically has not been, and as a practical matter could not be, subjected to the warrant procedure. Instead, the conduct involved in this case must be tested by the Fourth Amendment's general proscription against unreasonable searches and seizures. *Terry*, 392 U.S. at 20.

The question for the law enforcement officer is whether it is reasonable, in a particular set of circumstances, for the officer to seize a person (e.g., make a "stop") and subject the person to a limited search (e.g., a "frisk") when there is no probable cause to arrest.

The determination of reasonableness involves a balancing of the competing interests involved in a stop-and-frisk situation. These competing interests are

1. citizen's right to privacy and right to be free from unreasonable searches and seizures versus
2. governmental interests in effective crime prevention and detection, and protection of law enforcement and others from armed and dangerous persons.

Balancing these competing interests of individual privacy and effective law enforcement in a particular situation requires an evaluation of

- whether *any* police interference at all is justified by the circumstances and,
- if so, *how extensive* an interference those circumstances justify.

In this regard, the Supreme Court has also said that the reasonableness determination for a stop-and-frisk involves a "weighing of the gravity of the public concerns served by the seizure, the degree to which the seizure advances the public interest, and the severity of the interference with individual liberty." *Brown v. Texas*, 443 U.S. 47, 51 (1979).

Stops

The U.S. Supreme Court recognized that stopping persons for the purpose of investigating possible criminal activity can be, at times, necessary to the government's interest in effective crime prevention and detection. "[I]t is this interest which underlies the recognition that a police officer may in appropriate circumstances and in an appropriate manner approach a person for purposes of investigating possibly criminal behavior even though there is no probable cause to make an arrest." *Terry v. Ohio*, 392 U.S. 1, 22 (1968).

Differentiating Stops as Seizures from Nonseizures

A stop is the least intrusive type of seizure of the person governed by the Fourth Amendment. However, not every approach of a person by a law enforcement officer for purposes of investigating possible criminal activity is considered a seizure under the Fourth Amendment. In *Terry*, the Court noted, "Obviously not all personal intercourse between policemen and citizens involves 'seizures' of persons. Only when the officer, by means of physical force or show of authority, has in some way restrained the liberty of a citizen may we conclude that a 'seizure' has occurred." 392 U.S. at 19 n.16. Chapter 7 explored in detail the tests courts employ to determine when someone is under arrest or its functional equivalent. This chapter explores the criteria courts use to determine when a stop has occurred and therefore whether a seizure of a person has taken place for Fourth Amendment purposes.

Criterion 1 for Seizures and Stops: The "Free-to-Leave" Test In *United States v. Mendenhall*, 446 U.S. 544 (1980), the U.S. Supreme Court found no seizure (and therefore no stop) on the following facts:

The events took place in the public concourse [of an airport]. The agents wore no uniforms and displayed no weapons. They did not summon the

311

respondent to their presence, but instead approached her and identified themselves as federal agents. They requested, but did not demand to see the respondent's identification and ticket. In short, nothing in the record suggests that the respondent had any objective reason to believe that she was not free to end the conversation in the concourse and proceed on her own way, and for that reason we conclude that the agents' initial approach to her [and asking her basic investigatory questions] was not a seizure. 446 U.S. at 555.

Mendenhall established a test for determining whether a person has been seized within the meaning of the Fourth Amendment. The Court used a totality-of-circumstances approach in formulating its test for seizures:

> [A] person has been "seized" within the meaning of the Fourth Amendment only if, in view of all of the circumstances surrounding the incident, a reasonable person would have believed that he was not free to leave. Examples of circumstances that might indicate a seizure, even where the person did not attempt to leave, would be [:]
>
> 1. the threatening presence of several officers[;]
> 2. the display of a weapon by an officer[;]
> 3. some physical touching of the person of the citizen[;] or
> 4. the use of language or tone of voice indicating that compliance with the officer's request might be compelled . . . in the absence of some such evidence, otherwise inoffensive contact between a member of the public and the police cannot, as a matter of law, amount to a seizure of that person. 446 U.S. at 554–55 (emphasis and numbering added).

Under this test, certain "shows of authority" by officers, such as a display of a weapon or the use of a certain language, would lead a reasonable person to believe he or she is not free to leave (therefore satisfying the *Mendenhall* definition for a seizure). It is important to note that the test in *Mendenhall* is objective: it is "not whether the [particular] citizen perceived that he was being ordered to restrict his movement, but whether the officer's words and actions would have conveyed that to a reasonable person." *See California v. Hodari D.*, 499 U.S. 621, 628 (1991).

In 2004, the Supreme Court reaffirmed its rule that asking basic investigatory questions, including a request for identification and a request to search, do not implicate the Fourth Amendment (and hence are not stops): "Asking questions is an essential part of police investigations. In the ordinary course a police officer is free to ask a person for identification without implicating the Fourth Amendment." *See Hiibel v. Sixth Judicial Dist. Ct. of Nev., Humboldt County*, 542 U.S. 177, 185 (2004).

However, in *Florida v. Royer*, 460 U.S. 491 (1983), another case occurring in an airport, the Court did find a seizure for Fourth Amendment purposes because of the intrusiveness of the conduct on the part of the officers. In particular, the officers made a show of authority; as a result, a reasonable person in the defendant's position would not feel free to leave. In *Royer*, the defendant purchased a one-way airline ticket under an assumed name and checked luggage under this assumed name. As the defendant walked toward the boarding area within the concourse, two detectives approached him because his characteristics and actions fit a "drug courier profile." Upon request, he showed the detectives his airline ticket and driver's license, which carried his correct name. The defendant explained the discrepancy in names by pointing out that a friend had placed the ticket reservation in the assumed name. The detectives, who identified themselves as narcotics investigators, told the defendant that they suspected him of transporting narcotics. The detectives did not return the defendant's ticket or his license, but they asked him to accompany them to a small room near the concourse. The Court concluded that on these facts, there was a seizure (and hence a stop) for Fourth Amendment purposes:

> Asking for and examining Royer's ticket and his driver's license were no doubt permissible in themselves, but when the officers identified themselves as narcotics agents, told Royer that he was suspected of transporting narcotics, and asked him to accompany them to the police room, while retaining his ticket and driver's license and without indicating in any way that he was free to depart, Royer was effectively seized for the purposes of the Fourth Amendment. These circumstances surely amount to a show of official authority such that "a reasonable person would have believed he was not free to leave." 460 U.S. at 501–02.

The Court distinguished *Mendenhall* (the other airport case previously discussed where no seizure occurred) in the following way:

> Here, Royer's ticket and identification remained in the possession of the officers throughout the encounter; the officers also seized and had possession of his luggage. As a practical matter, Royer could not leave the airport without them. In Mendenhall, no luggage was involved, the ticket and identification were immediately returned, and the officers were careful to advise that the suspect could decline to be searched. Here, the officers had seized Royer's luggage and made no effort to advise him that he need not consent to the search. 460 U.S. at 503.

The Supreme Court has also decided cases in the seizure context in other environments outside airports. For example, when immigration authorities enter a factory to determine if any employees are undocumented aliens and question individuals regarding their citizenship status, no Fourth Amendment seizure occurs. *I.N.S. v. Delgado*, 466 U.S. 210 (1984). In *Delgado*, the Court described the "factory surveys" by immigration authorities in the following way:

> At the beginning of the surveys several agents positioned themselves near the buildings' exits, while other agents dispersed throughout the factory to question most, but not all, employees at their work stations. The agents displayed badges, carried walkie-talkies, and were armed, although at no point during any of the surveys was a weapon ever drawn. Moving systematically through the factory, the agents approached employees and, after identifying themselves, asked them from one to three questions relating to their citizenship. If the employee gave a credible reply that he was a United States citizen, the questioning ended, and the agent moved on to another employee. If the employee gave an unsatisfactory response or admitted that he was an alien, the employee was asked to produce his immigration papers. During the survey, employees continued with their work and were free to walk around within the factory. 466 U.S. at 212–13.

In response to the defendants' argument that the entire workforce of the factory was seized during the survey because immigration officers were stationed at the exits, the Court said:

> But it was obvious from the beginning of the surveys that the INS agents were only questioning people. Persons such as [defendants] who simply

went about their business in the workplace were not detained in any way; nothing more occurred than that a question was put to them. While persons who attempted to flee or evade the agents may eventually have been detained for questioning, [defendants] did not do so and were not in fact detained. The manner in which defendants were questioned, given its obvious purpose, could hardly result in a reasonable fear that [defendants] were not free to continue working or to move about the factory. [Defendants] may only litigate what happened to them, and our review of their description of the encounters with the INS agents satisfies us that the encounters were classic consensual encounters rather than Fourth Amendment seizures. 466 U.S. at 220–21.

Application of this objective free-to-leave test was also the basis for the Supreme Court's decision in *Michigan v. Chesternut*, 486 U.S. 567 (1988). In that case, officers in a patrol car chased the defendant after they observed him run when he saw the patrol car. The chase consisted of a brief acceleration to catch up with the defendant, followed by a short drive alongside him. The Court in *Chesternut* found no stop because the defendant could not have reasonably believed that he was not free to disregard the police presence and go about his business. The Court noted that the police *did not*

- activate a siren or flasher,
- command the defendant to halt,
- display any weapons, or
- operate the patrol car in an aggressive manner to block the defendant's course or otherwise control the direction or speed of the defendant's movement.

The Court recognized that "[w]hile the very presence of a police car driving parallel to a running pedestrian could be somewhat intimidating, this kind of police presence does not, standing alone, constitute a seizure." 486 U.S. at 575.

Criterion 2 for Seizures and Stops: The "Free to Decline Requests or Terminate Encounter" Test Cases decided since *Mendenhall* have attempted to refine its test for *seizure* (e.g., whether a reasonable person feels free to leave). For example, the Court in *Florida v. Bostick*, 501 U.S. 429, 435 (1991), established that *law enforcement officers may ask a person basic investigatory questions, including requests to examine identification or search luggage, and there is no seizure for Fourth Amendment purposes* "as long as the police do not convey the message that compliance with their requests is required." In particular, *Bostick* suggested that there is no seizure when two law enforcement officers walk up to a person, who is seated on a bus, ask him a few questions, and ask whether they can search his bags. The Court said that, although the defendant in this case may not have felt free to leave, his freedom of movement was restricted by a factor independent of police conduct:

[T]he mere fact that Bostick did not feel free to leave the bus does not mean that the police seized him. Bostick was a passenger on a bus that was scheduled to depart. He would not have felt free to leave the bus even if the police had not been present. Bostick's movements were "confined" in a sense, but this was the natural result of his decision to take the bus; it says nothing about whether or not the police conduct at issue was coercive. 501 U.S. at 436.

The Court in *Bostick* went on to refine the test for seizure it had first set forth in *Mendenhall*:

[I]n order to determine whether a particular encounter constitutes a seizure, a court must consider all the circumstances surrounding the encounter to determine whether the police conduct would have communicated to a reasonable person that the person was not free to decline the officers' requests or otherwise terminate the encounter. That rule applies to encounters that take place on a city street or in an airport lobby, and it applies equally to encounters on a bus. 501 U.S. at 439–40.

In another case involving a request by law enforcement officials to search a bus passenger, the Supreme Court examined the totality of the circumstances and determined that the passenger was not seized:

There was no application of force, no intimidating movement, no overwhelming show of force, no brandishing of weapons, no blocking of exits, no threat, no command, not even an authoritative tone of voice. It is beyond question that had this encounter occurred on the street, it would be constitutional. The fact that an encounter takes place on a bus does not on its own transform standard police questioning of citizens into an illegal seizure. . . . Indeed, because many fellow passengers are present to witness officers' conduct, a reasonable person may feel even more secure in his or her decision not to cooperate with police on a bus than in other circumstances. *United States v. Drayton*, 536 U.S. 194, 204 (2002).

Drayton also held that the officer's display of a badge did not convert an otherwise non-coercive encounter into a seizure. Note that on these same facts, the Court found that the defendant bus passengers' consent to a search of their luggage and their persons was voluntary. (See Chapter 9, "Consent Searches.")

However, in *Brendlin v. California*, 551 U.S. 249 (2007), the Supreme Court found that not only the driver but also passengers are seized for Fourth Amendment purposes when an officer makes a routine *traffic stop of a private vehicle*:

A traffic stop necessarily curtails the travel a passenger has chosen just as much as it halts the driver, diverting both from the stream of traffic to the side of the road, and the police activity that normally amounts to intrusion on "privacy and personal security" does not normally (and did not here) distinguish between passenger and driver. An officer who orders one particular car to pull over acts with an implicit claim of right based on fault of some sort, and a sensible person would not expect a police officer to allow people to come and go freely from the physical focal point of an investigation into faulty behavior or wrongdoing. If the likely wrongdoing is not the driving, the passenger will reasonably feel subject to suspicion owing to close association; but even when the wrongdoing is only bad driving, the passenger will expect to be subject to some scrutiny, and his attempt to leave the scene would be so obviously likely to prompt an objection from the officer that no passenger would feel free to leave in the first place. It is also reasonable for passengers to expect that a police officer at the scene of a crime, arrest, or investigation will not let people move around in ways that could jeopardize his safety. 551 U.S. at 250; *see also Arizona v. Johnson*, 551 U.S. 323 (2009) (holding passengers are seized under the Fourth Amendment during a traffic stop).

Acknowledging that passengers of nonprivate vehicles (i.e., taxicabs and buses) may be treated differently under Fourth Amendment seizure law than passengers of private vehicles, the Court said that the "the crucial question would be whether a reasonable person in the passenger's position would feel free to take steps to terminate the encounter" and go about his business: "[T]he issue is whether a reasonable passenger would have perceived that the show of authority [by the officer] was at least partly directed at him, and that he was thus not free to ignore the police presence and go about his business." 551 U.S. at 261. Thus, with this caveat, the Court's statements in *Bostick* and *Drayton* that bus passengers were not seized under the facts of those cases, remain valid.

Criterion 3 for Seizures and Stops: "Means Intentionally Applied" Requirement

For purposes of the Fourth Amendment, a seizure requires an intentional acquisition of physical control. For example, if a parked and unoccupied police car slips its brake and pins an innocent passerby against a wall, it is likely that a tort has occurred but not a violation of the Fourth Amendment. And the situation would not change if the passerby happened, by lucky chance, to be a serial murderer for whom there was an outstanding felony arrest warrant—even if, at the time he was pinned by the unoccupied car, he was in the process of running away from two pursuing police officers. In this regard, *Brower v. County of Inyo*, 489 U.S. 593, 596–97 (1989), held that

> a Fourth Amendment seizure does not occur whenever there is a governmentally caused termination of an individual's freedom of movement (the innocent passerby), nor even whenever there is a governmentally caused and governmentally *desired* termination of an individual's freedom of movement (the fleeing felon), but only when there is a governmental termination of freedom of movement *through means intentionally applied.* (italics in original)

Accordingly, the Court has held that "no Fourth Amendment seizure would take place where a 'pursuing police car sought to stop the suspect only by the show of authority represented by flashing lights and continuing pursuit,' but accidentally stopped the suspect by crashing into him." *Sacramento v. Lewis*, 523 U.S. 833, 844 (1998).

Criterion 4 for Seizures and Stops: "Halting or Submission" Requirement

As discussed in Chapter 7, the Supreme Court has established a related principle regarding seizures: If a show of authority by a law enforcement officer does not result in a halting or submission by the person being confronted, there is no seizure under the Fourth Amendment. For example, in *California v. Hodari D.*, 499 U.S. 621 (1991), the defendant was fleeing the approach of an unmarked police car and was surprised when he confronted an officer on foot pursuing him from another direction. The defendant immediately tossed away a small rock and was soon tackled by the officer. The rock was recovered and proved to be crack cocaine. The Court held that, in the absence of any physical contact or submission to the officer's show of authority, the defendant was not seized until he was tackled. The cocaine abandoned while he was running could not, therefore, be the fruit of a seizure and subject to exclusion.

Summary of Criteria Used to Determine Whether a Stop or Seizure Occurred

To summarize, three basic questions must all be answered to determine whether a seizure or stop has occurred for Fourth Amendment purposes.

1. Did the law enforcement officer, by means of physical force or a show of authority, restrain a person's liberty? In other words, under the totality of the circumstances, would a reasonable person believe that he or she was not free to leave as a result of the officer's actions?

KEY POINT

L01

- A stop is the least intrusive type of seizure of a person under the Fourth Amendment. If, in view of all of the circumstances surrounding the incident, a reasonable person would have believed that he or she was not free to leave, decline the officer's requests or otherwise terminate the encounter, the person has been seized within the meaning of the Fourth Amendment. Only when an officer intentionally, by means of physical force or show of authority, has restrained a person's liberty has a seizure occurred. Also, for a seizure to occur, the person being confronted by the officer must have submitted to the officer's authority or force.

Alternatively, did the police conduct communicate to a reasonable person that the person was not free to decline the officers' requests or otherwise terminate the encounter and go about his business?

2. Did the police force or show of authority resulting in the termination or restriction of the person's movement, come about through governmental means intentionally applied?

3. Did the physical force or show of authority result in an actual halting or submission by the person being confronted?

If all three of the preceding inquiries are answered in the affirmative, there has been a seizure for Fourth Amendment purposes.

Note that a seizure of a suspect can, at some point, evolve beyond a stop and become an arrest requiring probable cause. Arrests and seizures tantamount to arrest were discussed in Chapter 7.

Authority to Stop

It is important for law enforcement officers to know when they have authority to stop. The details of the reasonable suspicion standard are discussed in this section.

The Reasonable Suspicion Standard A law enforcement officer may stop and briefly detain a person for investigative purposes if the officer has a reasonable suspicion *supported by articulable facts that criminal activity "may be afoot,"* even if the officer lacks probable cause. Reasonable suspicion is "considerably less than proof of wrongdoing by a preponderance of the evidence" and "is obviously less demanding than that for probable cause." *United States v. Sokolow*, 490 U.S. 1, 7 (1989). The concept of reasonable suspicion, like probable cause, is not "readily, or even usefully, reduced to a neat set of legal rules." *Illinois v. Gates*, 462 U.S. 213, 232 (1983). In evaluating the validity of a stop, courts consider the totality of the circumstances:

> The totality of the circumstances—the whole picture—must be taken into account. Based upon that whole picture the detaining officers must have a particularized and objective basis for suspecting the particular person stopped of criminal activity. . . . The analysis proceeds with various objective observations, information from police reports, if such are available, and consideration of the modes or patterns of operation of certain kinds of lawbreakers. From these data, a trained officer draws inferences and makes deductions—inferences and deductions that might well elude an untrained person.
>
> The process does not deal with hard certainties, but with probabilities. Long before the law of probabilities was articulated as such, practical people formulated certain common-sense conclusions about human behavior; jurors as fact-finders are permitted to do the same—and so are law enforcement officers. *United States v. Cortez,* 449 U.S. 411, 417–18 (1981).

The U.S. Supreme Court has also said that "officers [can] draw on their own experience and specialized training to make inferences from and deductions about the cumulative information available to them that 'might well elude an untrained person.'" *United States v. Arvizu*, 534 U.S. 266, 273 (2002).

Hunches Versus Articulable Suspicions Though an officer may certainly make logical deductions from human activity based on his experience and training, the officer must still be able to give valid reasons to justify a stop. As the Supreme Court said in *Terry*, "[I]n justifying the particular intrusion the police officer must be able to point to specific and articulable facts which, taken together with rational inferences from those facts, reasonably warrant that intrusion." 392 U.S. at 21. A court will not accept an officer's mere statement or conclusion that criminal activity was suspected. The officer must be able to back up the conclusion by reciting the specific facts that led to that conclusion. *United States v. Pavelski*, 789 F.2d 485 (7th Cir. 1986), held that an officer who testified to a "gut feeling that things were really wrong" failed to articulate any objective facts indicative of criminal activity.

In *United States v. Arvizu*, 534 U.S. 266 (2002), the U.S. Supreme Court found a law enforcement officer had reasonable suspicion to stop a vehicle under the totality of the circumstances. The officer made logical deductions based on his knowledge, training, and experience and provided valid reasons for the stop. In *Arvizu*, Agent Clinton Stoddard was working at a border patrol checkpoint designed to detect illegal immigration and smuggling across the international border. Border patrol agents also used roving patrols as well as electronic sensors to detect illegal immigration in rural areas around the checkpoint. Agent Stoddard received two reports that an electronic sensor had been triggered. The reports happened at a time of day when the area where the sensor was located experienced less human surveillance because agents routinely made a shift change at that time.

DISCUSSION POINT

What Differentiates a Hunch from Reasonable Suspicion?
United States v. Bell, 555 F.3d 535, 540 (6th Cir. 2009)

Early one afternoon, two Ohio state troopers clocked Bell's speed at 80 mph in a 65-mph zone and pulled him over accordingly. The troopers asked Bell for his license, proof of insurance, and vehicle registration. Bell informed them that he was driving a rental car and handed over his driver's license and the rental agreement. One trooper later testified that

while he was looking for the rental agreement, Bell "was moving very fast towards the glove box, and then he reached up towards the visor."

One trooper informed Bell of the reason for the stop and asked him where he was going. Bell stated that he was traveling from Detroit to Cleveland to pick up his aunt to bring her back to Detroit for a funeral. One trooper thought Bell's story "sounded rehearsed" because "he repeated that story several times" and "he said it the exact same way each time, or very similar to the way he said it before." He also noted that Bell "had a cell phone laying in his lap as if he was waiting to call someone, or he had his hands on the cell phone when he wasn't moving," and that Bell "didn't make any specific eye contact with" the trooper while Bell was speaking. The trooper also found Bell to be "overly cooperative," which he thought was not only "abnormal" but also "deceptive."

While the troopers waited for the results of a computer check of Bell's license, they discussed their interactions with Bell, again remarking that Bell did not seem nervous but sounded rehearsed instead. At

that point, they decided to call another trooper to the scene who was a canine handler.

The officers also discovered that the rental agreement was not in Bell's name but rented to a Laticia Kelley. They noticed that the rental agreement did not allow additional drivers without prior written approval. One of the troopers asked Bell if he had written permission from Avis, the rental company, to operate the vehicle. Bell replied that his girlfriend, whose name was on the rental agreement, had called Avis and obtained permission over the phone for Bell to operate the vehicle, but that he did not have written permission. Trooper Roberts then returned to the patrol car, at which time he completed the computer check on Bell's license, which had returned no warrants. The canine unit then arrived. One trooper then approached Bell's vehicle for a third time and told Bell that he was going to give Bell a warning for speeding, rather than a citation, but that Bell should exit his vehicle so the dog could sniff around his car. While they talked outside the vehicle, the dog alerted the officers to the potential presence of drugs. This led the troopers to search the trunk of the vehicle and find bags of crack

Continued on next page

cocaine. Bell conceded that the initial stop of the rent car for speeding was legal. But he argued that the troopers unlawfully exceeded the purpose of the initial stop without reasonable suspicion of further criminal activity. The government countered that officers had reasonable suspicion that Bell was engaged in other criminal activity justifying a longer stop based on several factors. Specifically, Bell (1) repeated the same story and his communications sounded rehearsed, (2) moved quickly for the rental agreement, (3) was holding a cell phone, (4) did not make eye contact with one of the troopers, (5) was overly respectful and cooperative, and (6) did not have written permission to operate the rental car.

On these facts, the court determined that reasonable suspicion was lacking in this case. It emphasized that "the mere fact that Bell was holding a cell phone on his lap is innocuous in this case and certainly not strong enough to overcome the lack of other strong factors." The court also found that either seeming nervous or being overly cooperative are not factors deserving of much weight. Finally, the court determined that although Bell "sounding rehearsed" might be given some weight, that factor was weakened because Bell repeated his story only in response to the trooper's repeated questioning, and the story lacked any indications of criminal conduct.

Yet the court nonetheless held that the dog sniff was not unlawful because Bell's detention was not unreasonably delayed beyond the purposes of the initial stop in order to conduct the dog sniff. In fact, the whole encounter lasted no longer than an average traffic stop.

> [W]e simply cannot conclude that an officer violates the Fourth Amendment merely by asking a driver to exit a vehicle to effect a dog sniff when doing so does not extend the duration of the stop and does not cause the officer unreasonably to deviate from the purpose of the initial stop. Because the measures taken to enable the dog sniff did not improperly extend Bell's detention or cause [the troopers] unreasonably to deviate from investigation of the speeding offense, we conclude that the dog sniff was not improper. 555 F.3d at 543.

- Do you agree or disagree with the court that the troopers lacked reasonable suspicion to suspect drug activity in the case? Why?

- What additional factor(s) do you think would have changed the court's view that the troopers had not been operating on a hunch but rather on reasonable suspicion?

- The troopers did not detain Bell any longer than necessary to issue a traffic warning in this case only because the canine unit was so close by. If it had taken an extra fifteen minutes for the canine unit to arrive, do you think that would have changed the outcome in the case? What about at thirty minutes? Explain your reasoning.

While driving toward the sensors to investigate, Agent Stoddard spotted a vehicle. Based on the timing of the reports he had previously received from the sensors, the location of the vehicle, and the fact that he had not seen any other vehicles in the area, Stoddard believed that this was the vehicle originally detected by the sensors. He pulled to the side of the road for the purpose of observing the vehicle as it passed by. He saw a minivan, a type of automobile that Stoddard knew, from his training, smugglers used. As the minivan approached, it decreased its speed significantly. Officer Stoddard saw five individuals inside the vehicle. Two adults, one of whom was driving, were in the front and three children were in the back. The driver appeared "stiff" and his posture "very rigid." He did not look at Office Stoddard. Based on his experience, Stoddard thought this particular fact was suspicious—most drivers acknowledge border patrol agents in that area by waving. He also noticed that the knees of the two children sitting in the back seat were "unusually high," which indicated to him that their feet may be resting on a container below.

The officer decided to follow the vehicle. As he did so, the children in the back, while facing forward, simultaneously began to wave at Stoddard in an unusual fashion. They waved for about five minutes. Stoddard thought the children had been instructed by someone to do so. As the vehicle approached an intersection near the fixed checkpoint, it put its signal light on, then turned it off and then signaled again. The vehicle then turned quickly. Stoddard thought this turn was significant because it was the last place that would have allowed the minivan to avoid the checkpoint. Also, the van turned onto a road that, because of its poor condition, Stoddard knew was mostly used by four-wheeled vehicles as opposed to minivans. Also, as an agent who patrolled this area frequently, Stoddard did not recognize this particular minivan. He also did not think this was a family headed for a picnic because he was unaware of picnic grounds in the direction the vehicle was headed.

Stoddard radioed headquarters to check the vehicle's registration and discovered that the minivan was registered to an address in an area known for illegal immigration and drug smuggling. After receiving the information, Stoddard stopped the vehicle. The defendant, the driver of the vehicle, gave Agent Stoddard permission to inspect the vehicle. Stoddard found marijuana in a bag under the children's feet in the backseat. Another bag containing marijuana was also found behind the rear seat.

Characterizing Stoddard's confrontation with the vehicle and its occupants as "a brief investigative stop," the Supreme Court found that Officer Stoddard had reasonable suspicion to justify the stop:

> Having considered the totality of the circumstances and given due weight to the factual inferences drawn by the law enforcement officer and District Court Judge, we hold that Stoddard had reasonable suspicion to believe that respondent was engaged in illegal activity. It was reasonable for Stoddard to infer from his observations, his registration check, and his experience as a border patrol agent that respondent had set out from [the nearby town where the vehicle was registered] along a little-traveled route used by smugglers to avoid the [fixed] checkpoint. Stoddard's knowledge further supported a commonsense inference that respondent intended to pass through the area at a time when officers would be leaving their backroads patrols to change shifts. The likelihood that respondent and his family were on a picnic outing was diminished by the fact that the minivan had turned away from the known recreational areas. . . . Corroborating this inference was the fact that recreational areas farther to the north would have been easier to reach by taking [a different road], as opposed to the 40-to-50-mile trip on unpaved and primitive roads. The children's elevated knees suggested the existence of concealed cargo in the passenger compartment. Finally, for the reasons we have given, Stoddard's assessment of respondent's reactions upon seeing him and the children's mechanical-like waving, which continued for a full four to five minutes, were entitled to some weight. 534 U.S. at 277.

Reasonable, Articulable Suspicion Is an Objective Standard *Arvizu* illustrates that an officer's decision to initiate a stop is judged against the following objective standard: "[W]ould the facts available to the officer at the moment of the seizure or the search 'warrant a man of reasonable caution in the belief' that the action taken was appropriate?" *Terry*, 392 U.S. at 21–22; *see also Arvizu*, 534 U.S. at 273. ("When discussing how reviewing courts should make reasonable-suspicion determinations, we have said repeatedly that they must look at the 'totality of the circumstances' of each case to see whether the detaining officer has a 'particularized and objective basis' for suspecting legal wrongdoing.")

For example, the officer must have specific facts sufficient to support a reasonable suspicion of ongoing, impending, or past criminal activity to justify the initial intrusion. In particular, for an investigative stop, the officer need only show facts indicating the possibility that criminal behavior is afoot (e.g., a "reasonable suspicion" that criminal activity is afoot).

Applies to Reasonable Suspicion of Previous Criminal Activity An officer's authority to stop is not limited to crimes about to be committed or crimes in the process of being committed. The U.S. Supreme Court authorized the stop of a person whom officers suspected of being involved in a *completed felony*:

[W]here police have been unable to locate a person suspected of involvement in a past crime, the ability to briefly stop that person, ask questions, or check identification in the absence of probable cause promotes the strong government interest in solving crimes and bringing offenders to justice. The law enforcement interests at stake in these circumstances [of past crimes] outweigh the individual's interest to be free of a stop and detention that is no more extensive than permissible in the investigation of imminent or ongoing crimes. *United States v. Hensley*, 469 U.S. 221, 229 (1985).

Discontinuation of Reasonable Suspicion An officer has a duty to discontinue an investigation and not make a stop of a person if, at the time of the intended stop, justification for the initial suspicion has disappeared. "An officer cannot continue to press his investigation when he discovers new evidence demonstrating that his original interpretation of his suspect's actions was mistaken." *State v. Garland*, 482 A.2d 139, 144 (Me. 1984); *see also State v. Hill*, 606 A.2d 793 (Me. 1992) ("In *Garland* we acknowledged an affirmative duty on the part of a police officer 'to discontinue the investigation and forego a *Terry*-type stop of [an] individual when *by the time of the intended stop* justification for the initial suspicion has evaporated.' This is simply recognition of the fact that an officer's conduct is not justified at its inception if the articulable suspicion vanishes *before* the seizure [i.e., stop] occurs.") In a similar vein, most courts hold that once the purpose of a valid stop ends (i.e., a driver is issued a warning or citation following a valid stop for a traffic infraction), any further continuation of the stop must be justified by reasonable suspicion. *See United States v. Beck*, 140 F.3d 1129, 1136 (8th Cir. 1998) ("Because the purposes of Officer Taylor's initial traffic stop of [defendant] had been completed by this point, Officer Taylor could not subsequently detain [defendant] unless events that transpired during the traffic stop gave rise to reasonable suspicion to justify Officer Taylor's renewed detention of [defendant]."); *see also State v. Baker*, 229 P.3d 650 (Utah 2010) ("In this case, Officer Robertson was justified at the inception of the stop to detain the vehicle to investigate the broken taillight. However, the reasonableness of Mr. Baker's [the passenger's] detention fails under the second prong [i.e., the scope of detention prong]. We first hold that the purpose of the stop concluded when the officers finished processing the [driver's] arrest [for driving on a suspended license]. We then hold that the drug dog sniff that occurred after the purposes of the stop had been completed violated Mr. Baker's Fourth Amendment rights.").

Bases for Forming Reasonable Suspicion

Information from Known Informants In *Adams v. Williams*, 407 U.S. 143 (1972), a law enforcement officer on patrol in his cruiser was approached by a person known to him and was told that a man seated in a nearby vehicle had a gun at his waist and was carrying narcotics. The officer approached the vehicle, tapped on the window, and asked the occupant (the defendant) to open the door. When the defendant rolled down the window instead, the officer reached in, removed a pistol from the defendant's waistband, and then arrested the defendant.

The U.S. Supreme Court held that the officer acted justifiably in responding to the informant's tip:

The informant was known to him personally and had provided him with information in the past. This is a stronger case than obtains in the case of an anonymous telephone tip. The informant here came forward personally to give information that was immediately verifiable at the scene. Indeed, under Connecticut law, the informant herself might have been subject to immediate arrest for making a false complaint had Sgt. Connolly's investigation proven the tip incorrect. Thus, while the Court's decisions indicate that this informant's unverified tip may have been insufficient for a narcotics arrest or search warrant, the information carried enough indicia of reliability to justify the officer's forcible stop of Williams.

Some tips, completely lacking in indicia of reliability, would either warrant no police response or require further investigation before a forcible stop of a suspect would be authorized. But in some situations— for example, when the victim of a street crime seeks immediate police aid and gives a description of his assailant, or when a credible informant warns of a specific impending crime—the subtleties of the hearsay rule should not thwart an appropriate police response. 407 U.S. at 146–47.

Under *Adams v. Williams*, an officer may stop a person based on an informant's tip if the tip carries "enough indicia of reliability" to provide reasonable suspicion of criminal activity. This requires an officer to have specific reasons why he or she believes a tip to be reliable. As the quoted material indicates, an anonymous telephone tip might not be sufficiently reliable without corroboration.

As the Supreme Court suggested in *Adams*, when an informant personally communicates the tip to police, and the tip contains recent information that is then corroborated by police, courts will be more willing to find reasonable suspicion to stop based on the tip. This is because the officer is able to better assess the informant's demeanor and the informant herself may risk retaliation from third parties or prosecution for providing false information to police. *See United States v. Valentine*, 232 F.3d 350 (3rd Cir. 2000). In particular, in *Valentine*, the Court held that police officers had reasonable suspicion to stop the defendant after an informant made a face-to-face report to police that he had seen a man fitting the description of the defendant moments before with a gun at 1:00 A.M. in a high-crime area known for shootings. Based on the report, two police officers stopped the defendant by force and found a gun, which the Court admitted into evidence against defendant. 232 F.3d at 354.

Information from Anonymous Informants *Alabama v. White*, 496 U.S. 325 (1990), illustrates the minimum level of corroboration needed to support an anonymous tip and provide reasonable suspicion to justify an investigatory stop. In that case, police received an anonymous telephone tip that the defendant would be leaving a particular apartment at a particular time in a particular vehicle, that she would be going to a particular motel, and that she would be in possession of cocaine. Police went immediately to the apartment building and saw a vehicle matching the caller's description. They observed the defendant leave the building and enter the vehicle, followed her along the most direct route to the motel, and stopped her vehicle just short of the motel. A consensual search of the vehicle revealed marijuana and, after the defendant was arrested, cocaine was found in her purse.

The U.S. Supreme Court held that the anonymous tip, as corroborated by independent police work, exhibited sufficient *indicia* of reliability to provide reasonable suspicion to make the stop. The Court applied the totality-of-the-circumstances approach of *Illinois v. Gates* (see Chapter 3) in determining whether the informant's tip established reasonable suspicion:

Gates made clear . . . that those factors that had been considered critical under Aguilar and Spinelli—an informant's "veracity," "reliability," and "basis of knowledge"—remain "highly relevant in determining the value of his report." . . . These factors are also relevant in the reasonable suspicion context, although allowance must be made in applying them for the lesser showing required to meet that standard. 496 U.S. at 328–29.

Like the tip in *Gates*, the anonymous tip in *White* provided virtually nothing indicating that the caller either was honest or had reliable information, nor did the tip give any indication of the basis for the caller's predictions regarding the defendant's activities. As in *Gates*, however, there was more than the tip itself. And although the tip was not as detailed and the police corroboration of the tip not as complete as in *Gates*, the required degree of suspicion was not as high:

> Reasonable suspicion is a less demanding standard than probable cause not only in the sense that reasonable suspicion can be established with information that is different in quantity or content than that required to establish probable cause, but also in the sense that reasonable suspicion can arise from information that is less reliable than that required to show probable cause. . . . Reasonable suspicion, like probable cause, is dependent upon both the content of information possessed by police and its degree of reliability. Both factors—quantity and quality—are considered in the "totality of the circumstances—the whole picture," . . . that must be taken into account when evaluating whether there is reasonable suspicion. 496 U.S. at 330–31.

After explaining the totality-of-the-circumstances approach to determine if an informant's tip can serve as a basis for reasonable suspicion, the Court in *White* held that in that case, the tip could serve as a reliable basis for reasonable suspicion: "Contrary to the court below, we conclude that when the officers stopped the respondent, the anonymous tip had been sufficiently corroborated [by police] to furnish reasonable suspicion that respondent was engaged in criminal activity and that the investigative stop therefore did not violate the Fourth Amendment." 496 U.S. at 331.

The Court's analysis of corroboration illustrates how corroboration works to supplement an anonymous tip in providing reasonable suspicion. First, although not every detail mentioned by the tipster was verified—such as the name of the woman leaving the building or the precise apartment from which she left—the officers did corroborate that a woman left the building and got into the specifically described vehicle. Because the officers proceeded to the building immediately after the call and the defendant emerged not too long thereafter, the defendant's departure was within the time frame predicted by the caller. Furthermore, because her four-mile route was the most direct way to the motel but nevertheless involved several turns, the caller's prediction of the defendant's destination was significantly corroborated even though she was stopped before she reached the motel. Moreover, the caller's ability to predict the defendant's future behavior demonstrated inside information—a special familiarity with her affairs. When significant aspects of the caller's predictions were verified, the officers had reason to believe not only that the caller was honest but also that he was well informed. Under the totality of the circumstances, the anonymous tip, as corroborated, exhibited sufficient *indicia* of reliability to justify the stop of the defendant's car.

Florida v. J. L., 529 U.S. 266 (2000), held that an anonymous tip that a person is carrying a gun is, without more, insufficient to justify a police officer's stop and frisk of that person. In *J. L.*, an anonymous caller reported to the police that a young black male standing at a particular bus stop and wearing a plaid shirt was carrying a gun. Soon thereafter, two officers arrived at the bus stop and saw three black males, one of whom was wearing a plaid shirt. Apart from the tip, the officers had no reason to suspect any of the three of illegal conduct. The officers did not see a firearm and J. L. made no threatening or otherwise unusual movements. One of the officers approached J. L., told him to put his hands up, frisked him, and seized a gun from his pocket.

The U.S. Supreme Court found that the contention that the tip was reliable because its description of the suspect proved accurate misapprehended the reliability needed for a tip to justify a *Terry* stop:

> An accurate description of a subject's readily observable location and appearance is of course reliable in this limited sense: It will help the police correctly identify the person whom the tipster means to accuse. Such a tip, however, does not show that the tipster has knowledge of concealed criminal activity. The reasonable suspicion here at issue requires that a tip be reliable in its assertion of illegality, not just in its tendency to identify a determinate person. 529 U.S. at 272.

Comparing the anonymous tip in *J. L.* to that in *White*, the Court said:

> Although the Court held that the suspicion in White became reasonable after police surveillance, we regarded the case as borderline. Knowledge about a person's future movements indicates some familiarity with that person's affairs, but having such knowledge does not necessarily imply that the informant knows, in particular, whether that person is carrying hidden contraband. We accordingly classified White as a "close case." . . . The tip in the instant case lacked the moderate indicia of reliability present in White and essential to the Court's decision in that case. 529 U.S. at 271.

Although the Court in J. L. rejected a so-called firearm exception under which a tip alleging an illegal gun would automatically justify a stop and frisk by police (even if the tip failed standard reliability testing), the Court did point out

> that a report of a person carrying a bomb need [not necessarily] bear the indicia of reliability we demand for a report of a person carrying a firearm before the police can constitutionally conduct a frisk. Nor do we hold that public safety officials in quarters where the reasonable expectation of Fourth Amendment privacy is diminished, such as airports . . . and schools . . . cannot conduct protective searches on the basis of information insufficient to justify searches elsewhere. 529 U.S. at 273–74.

Note that nothing in the *J. L.* decision limits the right of a law enforcement officer, upon receiving an anonymous tip alleging criminal behavior, to investigate the situation further. For example, the officer may observe the suspect or ask the suspect basic questions related to identifying the suspect or obtaining the suspect's consent for a search of her person and belongings. These observations or the suspect's responses to questions may, in turn, provide the reasonable suspicion to justify a stop.

Recently, the U.S. Supreme Court in *Navarette v. California* held that an anonymous 911 caller's report that she had been run off the road by another vehicle, supported a police stop of the vehicle the caller had identified because police had reasonable suspicion under the totality of the circumstances that the vehicle's driver was intoxicated. 134 S. Ct. 1683, 1686 (2014) ("After a 911 caller reported that a vehicle had run her off the road, a police officer located the vehicle she identified during the call and executed a traffic stop. We hold that the stop complied with the Fourth Amendment because, under the totality of the circumstances, the officer had reasonable suspicion that the driver was intoxicated."). Please see the Discussion Point that follows for a full description of this recent Supreme Court case, including its rationale.

DISCUSSION POINT

When Can an Anonymous 911 Call Serve as a Basis for a Traffic Stop?
Navarette v. California, 134 S. Ct. 1683 (2014)

The facts of *Navarette* are as follows:

On August 23, 2008, a Mendocino County 911 dispatch team for the California Highway Patrol (CHP) received a call from another CHP dispatcher in neighboring Humboldt County. The Humboldt County dispatcher relayed a tip from a 911 caller, which the Mendocino County team recorded as follows: "'Showing southbound Highway 1 at mile marker 88, Silver Ford 150 pickup. Plate of 8–David–94925. Ran the reporting party off the roadway and was last seen approximately five [minutes] ago." The Mendocino County team then broadcast that information to CHP officers at 3:47 p.m.

A CHP officer heading northbound toward the reported vehicle responded to the broadcast. At 4:00 p.m., the officer passed the truck near mile marker 69. At about 4:05 p.m., after making a U-turn, he pulled the truck over. A second officer, who had separately responded to the broadcast, also arrived on the scene. As the two officers approached the truck, they smelled marijuana. A search of the truck bed revealed 30 pounds of marijuana. The officers arrested the driver, petitioner Lorenzo Prado Navarette, and the passenger, petitioner José Prado Navarette. 134 S. Ct. at 1686–87.

As mentioned, the U.S. Supreme Court in *Navarette* held "that the stop complied with the Fourth Amendment because, under the totality of the circumstances, the officer had reasonable suspicion that the driver was intoxicated." 134 S. Ct. at 1686.

The Court divided the rationale for its holding into two main inquiries: (1) whether the 911 caller's report about being run off the roadway was sufficiently reliable for the officer to be able to rely upon it (i.e., in making the traffic stop) and (2) whether the 911 caller's report created reasonable suspicion to believe a crime was being committed (e.g., "drunk driving as opposed to an isolated episode of past recklessness [in driving]"). 134 S. Ct. at 1688, 1690 (internal citations omitted).

Regarding the first inquiry, the Court found the anonymous 911 tipster's report reliable because it reflected firsthand, detailed knowledge of the event reported: "By reporting [to the 911 call center] that she had been run off the road by a specific vehicle—a silver Ford F-150 pickup, license plate 8D94925—the caller necessarily claimed eyewitness knowledge of the alleged dangerous driving. That basis of knowledge lends significant support to the tip's reliability." 134 S. Ct. at 1689. The Court compared the 911 caller's knowledge in *Navarette* about the alleged wrongdoing with the knowledge reflected by the anonymous informants' reports in the two other U.S. Supreme Court cases involving anonymous tipsters discussed earlier in this chapter, *Florida v. J. L.* and *Alabama v. White*:

This [knowledge reflected by the tip in *Navarette*] is in contrast to *J. L.*, where the tip provided no basis for concluding that the tipster had actually seen the gun. Even in *White*, where we upheld the stop, there was scant evidence that the tipster had actually observed cocaine in the station wagon. A driver's claim that another vehicle ran her off the road, however, necessarily implies that the informant knows the other car was driven dangerously. 134 S. Ct. at 1689.

In addition, according to the Court, the anonymous 911 caller's tip was reliable because it was provided close in time to the event described therein (i.e., the alleged dangerous driving), and it reported a "startling event":

Police confirmed the truck's location near mile marker 69 (roughly 19 highway miles south of the location reported in the 911 call) at 4:00 p.m.

Continued on next page

(roughly 18 minutes after the 911 call). That timeline of events suggests that the caller reported the incident soon after she was run off the road. That sort of contemporaneous report has long been treated as especially reliable. In evidence law, we generally credit the proposition that statements about an event and made soon after perceiving that event are especially trustworthy because "substantial contemporaneity of event and statement negate the likelihood of deliberate or conscious misrepresentation." A similar rationale applies to a "statement relating to a startling event"—such as getting run off the road—"made while the declarant was under the stress of excitement that it caused." There was no indication that the tip in *J. L.* (or even in *White*) was contemporaneous with the observation of criminal activity or made under the stress of excitement caused by a startling event, but those considerations weigh in favor of the caller's veracity here. 134 S. Ct. at 1689 (internal citations omitted).

Finally, according to the Court in *Navarette*, the caller's tip was reliable because it was reported using the 911 emergency system. Because these calls are generally recorded, and the caller's phone number and location are generally known, it is less likely that someone could provide a "false report[] with immunity." In other words, "a reasonable officer could conclude that a false tipster would think twice before using such a system." 134 S. Ct. at 1689–90.

Regarding the second line of inquiry addressed in the Court's rationale in *Navarette*—whether the 911 caller's report created reasonable suspicion to believe a crime was being committed—the Court found that the content of the caller's report did indeed establish reasonable suspicion of drunk driving. This finding was supported by practical, everyday knowledge of how drunk drivers typically behave while driving as well as the experience of officers responding to incidents of drunk driving:

> The 911 caller in this case reported more than a minor traffic infraction and more than a conclusory allegation of drunk or reckless driving. Instead, she alleged a specific and dangerous result of the driver's conduct: running another car off the highway. That conduct bears too great a resemblance to paradigmatic [typical] manifestations of drunk driving to be dismissed as an isolated example of recklessness. Running another vehicle off the road suggests lane-positioning problems, decreased vigilance, impaired judgment, or some combination of those recognized drunk driving cues. And the experience of many officers suggests that a driver who almost strikes a vehicle or another object—the exact scenario that ordinarily causes "running [another vehicle] off the roadway"—is likely intoxicated. As a result, we cannot say that the officer acted unreasonably under these circumstances in stopping a driver whose alleged conduct was a significant indicator of drunk driving. 134 S. Ct. at 1691 (internal citations omitted).

■ Do you agree with the Court's finding in *Navarette* that the anonymous 911 caller's tip was reliable? How do we know that the caller was not someone who knew the driver or owner of the vehicle, and reported the alleged dangerous driving to the 911 call center because she had some personal grudge against the driver or owner? More broadly, how do we really know someone is reliable (i.e., truthful) when we do not know his or her identity?

■ Do you agree with the Court that the report of dangerous driving by the 911 caller created reasonable suspicion of drunk driving? Could the report just as easily support a finding that the driver may have been distracted by an "unruly child," the receipt or sending of a text message, or sleeplessness/daydreaming? *See* 134 S. Ct. at 1691.

■ Do you think the officer should have been required to verify, or corroborate, the report of dangerous driving provided by the 911 caller, prior to stopping the vehicle? What would be the advantages to requiring this type of corroboration, in terms of both the law of stops discussed in this chapter and practically speaking? The disadvantages? *See* 134 S. Ct. at 1691–92.

Information from Police Flyers, Bulletins, or Radio Dispatches Officers may stop a person or vehicle on the basis of a police flyer, bulletin, or radio dispatch. Because criminal suspects are increasingly mobile and more likely to flee across jurisdictional boundaries, police in one jurisdiction need to be able to act promptly on the basis of information contained in a bulletin or flyer from another jurisdiction. The leading Supreme Court case in this area that supports this notion is *United States v. Hensley*, 469 U.S. 221 (1985).

In *Hensley*, two armed men robbed a tavern. Later, an informant provided information to the St. Bernard police department that defendant Hensley had driven the getaway car. As a result, Officer Davis of the St. Bernard police department issued a "wanted flyer" for Hensley to other local police departments. It stated that Hensley was wanted for investigation of an aggravated robbery, provided a description of Hensley, the date and location of the robbery, and requested that other police departments retrieve and hold Hensley on behalf of St. Bernard. The flyer also warned that Hensley may be armed and dangerous.

Another police department, Covington, located about five miles from St. Bernard, received the flyer. Some officers in Covington knew Hensley, and began to monitor places he frequented. Officer Cope from Covington, who had seen or heard about the flyer, found Hensley driving in his vehicle, and stopped him. Cope recalled that the flyer sought a stop for investigation only and that in his experience the issuance of such a flyer was usually followed by the issuance of an arrest warrant. A police dispatcher was contacted to verify if there was an outstanding arrest warrant for Hensley. The dispatcher was unable to verify this information before Officer Cope's stop of Hensley's vehicle. As Cope approached Hensley's vehicle with his gun drawn, Officer Cope requested that Hensley and another passenger exit the car. A search of the car uncovered three weapons. Hensley was arrested. 469 U.S. at 223–25.

The Court found that officers may rely on a bulletin from another police department to stop a suspect *as long as* the bulletin itself is based on facts providing reasonable suspicion (for a stop):

> Neither [Hensley] nor the Court of Appeals suggests any reason why . . . a police department should not be able to act on the basis of a flyer indicating that another department has a reasonable suspicion of involvement with a crime. The law enforcement interests promoted by allowing one department to make investigatory stops based upon another department's bulletins or flyers are considerable, while the intrusion on personal security is minimal. *We conclude that, if a flyer or bulletin has been issued on the basis of articulable facts supporting a reasonable suspicion that the wanted person has committed an offense, then reliance on that flyer or bulletin justifies a stop to check identification, to pose questions to the person, or to detain the person briefly while attempting to obtain further information.* . . . Assuming the police make a *Terry* stop in objective reliance on a flyer or bulletin, we hold that the evidence uncovered in the course of the stop is admissible if the police who issued the flyer or bulletin possessed a reasonable suspicion justifying a stop, and if the stop that in fact occurred was not significantly more intrusive than would have been permitted the issuing department. 469 U.S. at 681–82 (italics added).

After articulating the relevant test, the Court in *Hensley* first found that the St. Bernard police had the required reasonable suspicion to issue the bulletin for Hensley's stop:

> We agree with the District Court that the St. Bernard police possessed a reasonable suspicion, based on specific and articulable facts, that Hensley was involved in an armed robbery. The District Judge heard testimony from the St. Bernard officer who interviewed the informant. On the strength of the evidence, the District Court concluded that the wealth of detail concerning the robbery revealed by the informant,

KEY POINTS

LO4

- A law enforcement officer may stop and briefly detain a person for investigative purposes if the officer has a reasonable suspicion supported by articulable facts of ongoing, impending, or past criminal activity. In determining reasonable suspicion, an officer may make logical deductions from human activity based on his or her observations, knowledge, experience, and training. The officer must be able to provide valid reasons for determining reasonable suspicion and may not base the suspicion on a mere hunch.

- Reasonable suspicion is a less demanding standard than probable cause, not only in the sense that it can be established with information that is different in quantity or content than that for probable cause, but also in the sense that reasonable suspicion can arise from information less reliable than that required to show probable cause.

- A law enforcement officer's decision to initiate a stop based on reasonable suspicion is judged against the objective standard: would the facts available to the officer at the moment of the seizure or the search warrant a person of reasonable caution in believing that the action taken was appropriate?

- A law enforcement officer may stop a person based on an informant's tip if, under the totality of the circumstances, the tip, plus any corroboration of the tip by independent police investigation, carries carries enough indicia of reliability to provide reasonable suspicion of criminal activity.

- An anonymous tip that a particular person at a particular location is carrying a gun is not, without

Continued on next page

more information, sufficient to justify law enforcement officers in stopping and frisking that person.

■ A law enforcement officer may stop a person on the basis of a flyer, bulletin, or radio dispatch issued by another law enforcement agency as long as the issuing law enforcement agency has a reasonable suspicion that the person named in the flyer, bulletin, or dispatch is or was involved in criminal activity.

■ An anonymous 911 caller's report that the caller has been run off the road by another vehicle supports a police stop of the vehicle that the caller has identified because such a report provides police with reasonable suspicion under the totality of the circumstances that the vehicle's driver is intoxicated.

coupled with her admission of tangential participation in the robbery, established that the informant was sufficiently reliable and credible "to arouse a reasonable suspicion of criminal activity by [Hensley] and to constitute the specific and articulable facts needed to underlie a stop." Under the circumstances, "the information carried enough indicia of reliability," to justify an investigatory stop of Hensley. 469 U.S. at 233–34 (internal citations omitted).

The Court then held that officers in the Covington police department could objectively rely on the flyer issued by the other police department:

Turning to the flyer issued by the St. Bernard police, we believe it satisfies the objective test announced today. An objective reading of the entire flyer would lead an experienced officer to conclude that Thomas Hensley was at least wanted for questioning and investigation in St. Bernard. Since the flyer was issued on the basis of articulable facts supporting a reasonable suspicion, this objective reading would justify a brief stop to check Hensley's identification, pose questions, and inform the suspect that the St. Bernard police wished to question him. As an experienced officer could well assume that a warrant might have been obtained in the period after the flyer was issued, we think the flyer would further justify a brief detention at the scene of the stop while officers checked whether a warrant had in fact been issued. 469 U.S. at 234.

Thus, because police who issued the flyer had reasonable suspicion to stop Hensley, and the officers from the other department validly relied on the flyer, Hensley's stop was constitutional under the Fourth Amendment, and the weapons found during the stop were admissible. 469 U.S. at 236.

Officers may also rely on a police radio dispatch, or bulletin, to stop a person or vehicle. Officers may rely on such a dispatch to stop a person or vehicle when the dispatch itself originates from a fellow officer who has knowledge of facts supporting reasonable suspicion for a stop. *See United States v. Nelson*, 284 F.3d 472 (3rd Cir. 2002).

If, however, it is later determined the dispatcher had no facts supporting reasonable suspicion, a stop made by officers in the field relying on the dispatcher's information may be ruled illegal. This was the holding of *Feathers v. Aey*, 319 F.3d 843 (6th Cir. 2003), where the dispatcher received a tip from an anonymous informant that was determined to be both unreliable and without a proper basis and later communicated the information in the tip to officers in the field.

Thus, the court in *Feathers* held that the stop by the officers in the field violated the Fourth Amendment because "the authorities' collective information," including the information provided by the dispatcher, "did not amount to reasonable suspicion." 319 F.3d at 851.

Note, however, that if officers in the field rely in good faith on unreliable, insufficient, or incorrect information provided by a dispatcher to justify a stop, some courts may find the stop by officers valid, at least where these officers possess other valid information that justifies the stop. *See United States v. DeLeon Reyna*, 930 F.2d 396 (5th Cir. 1991).

Permissible Scope of a Stop

Once an officer determines that a stop is justified, to what extent may the officer interfere? In other words, how long may the person be detained, how much force may be used, and how much questioning may be employed? The U.S. Supreme Court in *Florida v. Royer*, 460 U.S. 491, 500 (1983), addressed the issue:

> The predicate permitting seizures on suspicion short of probable cause is that law enforcement interests warrant a limited intrusion on the personal security of the suspect. The scope of the intrusion permitted will vary to some extent with the particular facts and circumstances of each case. This much, however, is clear: an investigative detention must be temporary and last no longer than is necessary to effectuate the purpose of the stop. Similarly, the investigative methods employed should be the least intrusive means reasonably available to verify or dispel the officer's suspicion in a short period of time. . . . It is the State's burden to demonstrate that the seizure it seeks to justify on the basis of a reasonable suspicion was sufficiently limited in scope and duration to satisfy the conditions of an investigative seizure.

Twenty years later in *Hiibel v. Sixth Judicial Dist. Ct. of Nev.*, 542 U.S. 177, 185–86 (2004), the Court described the scope of a stop in this way:

> Beginning with *Terry v. Ohio*, the Court has recognized that a law enforcement officer's reasonable suspicion that a person may be involved in criminal activity permits the officer to stop the person for a brief time and take additional steps to investigate further. To ensure that the resulting seizure is constitutionally reasonable, a *Terry* stop must be limited. The officer's action must be "justified at its inception, and reasonably related in scope to the circumstances which justified the interference in the first place." For example, the seizure cannot continue for an excessive period of time, or resemble a traditional arrest.

Ordering Driver and Passengers Out of a Vehicle During a Stop Recall from the previous discussion of Fourth Amendment seizures that when an officer makes a traffic stop of a private vehicle, both the driver and passengers are seized within the meaning of that amendment. Therefore, for the officer to make a lawful traffic stop of a vehicle and its occupants, the officer needs to possess at least reasonable suspicion that the vehicle and its occupants have committed a traffic infraction.

An officer who has lawfully stopped a motor vehicle may, for personal safety reasons, order the driver out of the vehicle, even though the officer has no reason to suspect foul play from the driver at the time of the stop. The U.S. Supreme Court said:

> We think this additional intrusion can only be described as de *minimis*. The driver is being asked to expose to view very little more of his person than is already exposed. The police have already lawfully decided that the driver shall be briefly detained; the only question is whether he shall spend that period sitting in the driver's seat of his car or standing alongside it. Not only is the insistence of the police on the latter choice not a "serious intrusion upon the sanctity of the person," but it hardly rises to the level of a "'petty indignity.'" . . . What is at most a mere inconvenience cannot prevail when balanced against legitimate concerns for the officer's safety.
> *Pennsylvania v. Mimms*, 434 U.S. 106, 111 (1977).

Maryland v. Wilson, 519 U.S. 408, 415 (1997), extended the *Mimms* rule, holding that **"an officer making a traffic stop may order passengers to get out of the car pending completion of the stop."** The Court found that the danger to an officer from a traffic stop is likely to be greater when there are passengers in addition to the driver in the stopped car. Although the justification for ordering passengers out of the car is different than that for the driver, the additional intrusion on passengers is minimal:

> [A]s a practical matter, the passengers are already stopped by virtue of the stop of the vehicle. The only change in their circumstances which will result from ordering them out of the car is that they will be outside of, rather than inside of, the stopped car. Outside the car, the passengers will be denied access to any possible weapon that might be concealed in the interior of the passenger compartment. It would seem that the possibility of a violent encounter stems not from the ordinary reaction of a motorist stopped for a speeding violation, but from the fact that evidence of a more serious crime might be uncovered during the stop. And the motivation of a passenger to employ violence to prevent apprehension of such a crime is every bit as great as that of the driver. 519 U.S. at 413–14

By implication, an officer may also order a driver or passengers to remain in a vehicle or to get back into a vehicle. An officer working alone may find it safer for the driver and passengers to remain in a vehicle where the officer can more easily control them for safety purposes.

Reasonable Investigative Methods During a Stop The permissible scope of an officer's interaction with a person is, in part, determined by the person's answers to investigative questions posed by the officer. An officer's initial questioning of a suspect may assure the officer that no further investigation is necessary.

On the other hand, evasive or implausible answers to routine investigative questions may give an officer reasonable suspicion that criminal activity is afoot and justify stopping the person for further investigation. In *United States v. Sterling*, 909 F.3d 1078 (7th Cir. 1990), the court held that narcotics investigators at the airport had reasonable suspicion to stop a woman and detain her luggage, in part, because she gave implausible answers to their questions.

> The issue now becomes whether the agents had reasonable suspicion of criminal activity by this time. We hold that they did. Once the officers had asked [the woman] a few questions, they gleaned more facts that led them to suspect criminal activity. First, they learned that [the woman] purported to have no identification on her person and that she had gone to Miami to see her cousin . . . without knowing his address or telephone number. She then told them that after she arrived in Miami, she learned that [her cousin] was driving to Chicago to visit her. Moreover, the officers learned that [the woman] met her cousin's sister in Miami, but was uncertain at first whether [her cousin's] sister was also her own cousin. Finally, the agents learned that [the woman] could not tell them the name of her hotel in Miami. The officers were entitled to interpret these answers in light of their experience. Here [the woman] had an improbable story. 909 F.2d at 1083–84.

Note that if an officer has reasonable suspicion to justify a stop of a person (i.e., based on a person giving implausible answers, information from informants, etc.) and then that person refuses in violation of state law to identify herself, the officer may be permitted to expand the scope of the detention by arresting the person. For example, in *Hiibel v. Sixth Judicial Dist. Ct. of Nev.*, 542 U.S. 177 (2004), police received a call reporting an assault of a woman by a man in a particular truck on a particular road. Sheriff Dove was sent to investigate. Upon his arrival at the scene, Dove saw a man was standing by a truck parked on the side of the road and a young woman sitting inside the truck. Dove saw skid marks behind the vehicle, leading him to believe it stopped suddenly. When Dove approached the man and informed him of his investigation into a possible fight, Dove noticed that the man appeared to be intoxicated.

The Court described the exchange between Officer Dove and the man in this way:

> The officer asked him if he had "any identification on [him]," which we understand as a request to produce a driver's license or some other form of written identification. The man refused and asked why the officer wanted to see identification. The officer responded that he was conducting an investigation and needed to see some identification. The unidentified man became agitated and insisted he had done nothing wrong. The officer explained that he wanted to find out who the man was and what he was doing there. After continued refusals to comply with the officer's request for identification, the man began to taunt the officer by placing his hands behind his back and telling the officer to arrest him and take him to jail. This routine kept up for several minutes: The officer asked for identification 11 times and was refused each time. After warning the man that he would be arrested if he continued to refuse to comply, the officer placed him under arrest. [The man was ultimately convicted under the state of Nevada's stop and identify statute for failing to identify himself by providing his name.] *Hiibel*, 542 U.S. at 177–81.

The U.S. Supreme Court began its analysis in *Hiibel* by explaining the importance to an officer of obtaining a suspect's identification during a stop:

> Obtaining a suspect's name in the course of a *Terry* stop serves important government interests. Knowledge of identity may inform an officer that a suspect is wanted for another offense, or has a record of violence or mental disorder. On the other hand, knowing identity may help clear a suspect and allow the police to concentrate their efforts elsewhere. Identity may prove particularly important in cases such as this, where the police are investigating what appears to be a domestic assault. Officers called to investigate domestic disputes need to know whom they are dealing with in order to assess the situation, the threat to their own safety, and possible danger to the potential victim. 542 U.S. at 186.

Next, the Court determined that a state may require a suspect who has been lawfully stopped to identify oneself:

> The principles of *Terry* permit a State to require a suspect to disclose his name in the course of a *Terry* stop. The reasonableness of a seizure under the Fourth Amendment is determined "by balancing its intrusion on the individual's Fourth Amendment interests against its promotion of legitimate government interests." The Nevada statute satisfies that standard. A state law requiring a suspect to disclose his name in the course of a valid *Terry* stop is consistent with Fourth Amendment prohibitions against unreasonable searches and seizures. 542 U.S. at 187–88.

In response to the defendant's argument that the state law impermissibly sanctioned his arrest on a simple refusal to identify himself, the Court said:

> These are familiar concerns. [Defendant's] concerns are met by the requirement that a *Terry* stop must be justified at its inception and

"reasonably related in scope to the circumstances which justified" the initial stop. Under these principles, an officer may not arrest a suspect for failure to identify himself if the request for identification is not reasonably related to the circumstances justifying the stop. [An officer may require identification if there is] "a reasonable basis for believing that [providing the identification] will establish or negate the suspect's connection with that crime." It is clear in this case that the request for identification was "reasonably related in scope to the circumstances which justified" the stop. The officer's request was a common-sense inquiry, not an effort to obtain an arrest for failure to identify after a *Terry* stop yielded insufficient evidence. 542 U.S. at 188–89.

Thus, an officer may request identification during a stop if it will help the officer connect the suspect to a crime he or she is investigating and the request is reasonably related to the circumstances justifying the stop. An officer must not ask for identification if the officer's only purpose for doing so is to arrest the suspect for possible failure to identify.

During a traffic stop, "reasonable investigation includes asking for the driver's license and registration, requesting that the driver sit in the patrol car, and asking the driver about his destination and purpose." *United States v. Bloomfield*, 40 F.3d 910, 915 (8th Cir. 1994); *see also United States v. Sanchez*, 417 F.3d 971, 974–75 (8th Cir. 2005). Likewise, an officer may engage in similar routine questioning of the vehicle's passengers to verify information provided by the driver. Moreover, "if the responses of the detainee and the circumstances give rise to suspicions unrelated to the traffic offense, an officer may broaden his inquiry and satisfy those suspicions." *United States v. Barahona*, 990 F.2d 412, 416 (8th Cir. 1993); *see also United States v. Johnson*, 2005 WL 2704892 (N.D. Iowa 2005), at *9 ("Because the responses of the [vehicle's] occupants and the circumstances gave rise to suspicions unrelated to the traffic offense, the officers were permitted to broaden their inquiry in order to satisfy those suspicions. Thus, the court concludes . . . that because of Trooper Noelck's reasonable suspicions unrelated to the traffic offense, Trooper Noelck was entitled to broaden his inquiry to satisfy those suspicions."). Once the purposes of an initial traffic stop are completed, however, the officer may not further detain the vehicle or its occupants unless something that occurs during the traffic stop generates reasonable suspicion to justify further detention. *United States v. Mesa*, 62 F.3d 159 (6th Cir. 1995); *see also State v. Baker*, 229 P.3d 650 (Utah 2010).

Time Issues During a Stop "[T]he brevity of the invasion of the individual's Fourth Amendment interests is an important factor in determining whether the seizure is so minimally intrusive as to be justifiable on reasonable suspicion." *United States v. Place*, 462 U.S. 696, 709 (1983). An investigative stop is not subject to any rigid time limitation, but at some point an extended stop that has not developed probable cause for an arrest can no longer be justified as reasonable. For example, the Court in *Place*, although acknowledging that there was no precise time limitation for a valid stop, refused to sanction a ninety-minute detention of a suspect's luggage. (For further discussion of this case, see "Detentions of Containers and Other Property" on page 349).

Factors Considered in Reasonableness of Length of Stop In determining the reasonableness of the duration of a stop, courts consider

■ the law enforcement purposes to be served by the stop and
■ the time reasonably needed to effectuate those purposes.

For example, in *Sharpe*, the U.S. Supreme Court commented:

In assessing whether a detention is too long in duration to be justified as
an investigative stop, we consider it appropriate to examine whether the
police diligently pursued a means of investigation that was likely to confirm
or dispel their suspicions quickly, during which time it was necessary to
detain the defendant. . . . A court making this assessment should take care to
consider whether the police are acting in a swiftly developing situation and
in such cases the court should not indulge in unrealistic second-guessing. . . .
The question is not simply whether some other alternative was available, but
whether the police acted unreasonably in failing to recognize or to pursue it.
United States v. Sharpe, 470 U.S. 675, 686–87 (1985).

In *Sharpe* itself, the Court approved a twenty-minute detention of a driver made necessary by the driver's own evasion of a drug agent and the decision of a state police officer, who had been called to assist in making the stop, to hold the driver until the agent
could arrive on the scene. The Court found that it was reasonable for the state police officer to hold the driver for the brief period pending the drug agent's arrival because

- the state police officer could not be certain that he was aware of all of the facts
  that had aroused the drug agent's suspicions; and
- as a highway patrolman, he lacked the agent's training and experience in dealing
  with narcotics investigations.

Other reasons that might justify an officer's prolonging a suspect's detention include the following:

- attempting to obtain further information in the context of a complex and rapidly
  developing situation,
- summoning assistance,
- traveling to the scene of suspected criminal activity,
- caring for injured persons or responding to other emergency circumstances, and
- dealing with evasive tactics or other delays caused by the suspect.

United States v. Quinn, 815 F.2d 153 (1st Cir. 1987), held that a defendant's detention
for investigation for twenty to twenty-five minutes did not transform the initial lawful stop
into a seizure tantamount to arrest. Although several police officers were present, they
made no threats, displayed no weapons, and exerted no physical restraint on the defendant.
Moreover, the officers had a strong suspicion of criminal activity, and there was no way they
could have significantly shortened the inquiry. *See also Commonwealth v. Feyenord*, 833
N.E.2d 590, 599–600 & n. 6 (Mass. 2005) (finding that a stop with a duration of approximately 25 minutes "was not overly prolonged or onerous in duration").

In most cases, twenty to twenty-five minutes is probably the outside time limit,
beyond which a stop becomes a seizure tantamount to arrest, requiring a justification
of probable cause. However, a few courts have permitted slightly longer stops if there is
adequate cause for the delay. For example, *United States v. Mayo*, 394 F.3d 1271 (9th Cir.
2005), permitted a forty-minute stop because reasonable suspicion gradually developed
over time, and the officers acted as diligently as they could in the context of complex
and rapidly unfolding circumstances:

The period of detention was permissibly extended because new grounds for suspicion
of criminal activity continued to unfold. The officers pursued their multiple inquiries
promptly as they arose: they questioned [defendant] regarding their suspicion of
narcotics activity; investigated the vehicle code violation; investigated [defendant's]
attempted use of another's credit card; investigated the connection between
[defendant] and [another individual], who returned to the scene while officers were

questioning [defendant]; searched [this other individual's] Dodge Caravan; and questioned [defendant] about the chemical odor associated with methamphetamine. A maximum of forty minutes to pursue all of these inquiries was not unreasonable. Therefore, the *Terry* detention did not exceed constitutional limits. 394 F.3d at 1276.

Delays in Making a Stop Under ordinary circumstances, an officer who has a reasonable suspicion that a person may be engaged in criminal activity should initiate a stop of the person immediately. Nevertheless, a short delay in making the stop may be justified in certain situations. However, as the delay between the development of reasonable suspicion on the part of the officer and the actual stop grows longer, courts may find that the suspicion has "evaporated."

For example, in *State v. Cyr*, 501 A.2d 1303 (Me. 1985), an officer had grounds to stop a truck parked in an area of recent burglaries after observing the person in the driver's seat duck down to avoid detection. However, because the officer was transporting an arrested person, he continued driving slowly past the truck. In his rearview mirror, the officer observed the truck leave its parking place and follow his cruiser. After being informed that no other police unit was available to intercept the truck, the officer stopped the truck some two to three minutes after the first observation. The court held that the suspicion had not evaporated because of the delay, as the truck remained within the officer's sight at all times and the delay was caused by an arrested person's presence in the officer's vehicle.

A longer delay, however, may cause a stop to be held illegal. For example, *United States v. Posey*, 663 F.2d 37 (7th Cir. 1981), held that suspicion had evaporated when the defendant was stopped fifteen minutes after suspicion arose and fifteen miles away from the place where the defendant was originally seen.

And though *United States v. Feliciano*, 45 F.3d 1070 (7th Cir. 1995), cast some doubt on the scope of the evaporation doctrine first adopted in *Posey*, it appears to have retained the concept of evaporation by positing that in some cases, reasonable suspicion that a person will commit a crime in the future may not suffice to justify a stop—at least where the future is a distant one:

> Our more recent cases cast considerable doubt on the existence, or at least scope, of an "evaporation" doctrine; for they do not cite *Posey*, or refer to such a doctrine, even though they involve intervals of hours. *Terry* itself involved an open time frame. The suspects [in *Terry*] had cased one store, and were in front of another when they were stopped. It was unclear whether they meant to rob the second store forthwith or to return at nightfall and hit both. It did not matter; the stop was lawful. The metaphor of evaporation is not a happy one. Water evaporates at a more or less constant rate (holding temperature constant); suspicion does not. The metaphor may not even help defendants. . . . Yet in defense of *Posey*—not of its formula or metaphor, but of its animating idea—it can be argued that an articulable suspicion of a crime to be committed in the distant future would not justify a stop. The long incubation period of the crime would both attenuate the probability that the crime would actually be committed and give the police ample time by further investigation to obtain a better "fix" on that probability. The difficult question is what is "distant" for these purposes. We need not try to answer it here. The probability that [defendant and his companion] would mug someone before they went home, which is to say within minutes or at most a few hours, was sufficient under *Terry* to justify the stop. 45 F.3d at 1074.

Use of Force During a Stop Law enforcement officers making stops may take steps "reasonably necessary to protect their personal safety and to maintain the status quo during the course of the stop." *United States v. Hensley*, 469 U.S. 221, 235 (1985). Use of force in making a stop is governed by the Fourth Amendment standard of reasonableness, judged from the perspective of a reasonable officer on the scene rather than from hindsight. The nature and quality of the intrusion on the suspect's Fourth Amendment interests must be balanced against the countervailing governmental interests. The reasonableness inquiry is an objective one—"whether the officers' actions are 'objectively reasonable' in light of the facts and circumstances confronting them, without regard to their underlying intent or motivation." *Graham v. Connor*, 490 U.S. 386, 397 (1989). Furthermore, "[t]he calculus of reasonableness must embody allowance for the fact that police officers are often forced to make split-second judgments—in circumstances that are tense, uncertain, and rapidly evolving—about the amount of force that is necessary in a particular situation." 490 U.S. at 396–97.

United States v. Seelye, 815 F.2d 48, 50 (8th Cir. 1987), listed six facts and circumstances to be considered in determining the amount and kind of force that is reasonable and consistent with an investigative stop:

1. the number of officers and police cars involved;
2. the nature of the crime and whether there is reason to believe the suspect is armed;
3. the strength of the officer's articulable, objective suspicions;
4. the need for immediate action by the officer;
5. the presence or lack of suspicious behavior or movement by the person under observation; and
6. whether there was an opportunity for the officer to have made the stop in less threatening circumstances.

United States v. Bullock, 71 F.3d 171 (5th Cir. 1995), held that law enforcement officers were justified in drawing their weapons on the defendant after stopping his vehicle for speeding. The officers had been informed over the radio that the defendant was a suspect in a bank robbery committed just hours before, and the officers were familiar with the defendant from previous encounters and knew him to be a dangerous man, who had previously resisted arrest and threatened police. *United States v. Melendez-Garcia*, 28 F.3d 1046, 1053 (10th Cir. 1994), however, held that it was unreasonable, after stopping drug suspects' vehicles, for officers to aim their guns at the suspects and handcuff them "when they outnumbered the defendants, executed the stop on an open highway during the day, had no tips or observations that the suspects were armed or violent, and the defendants had pulled their cars to a stop off the road and stepped out of their cars in full compliance with police orders." *United States v. Romain*, 393 F.3d 63 (1st Cir. 2004), held that officers were justified in temporarily placing a man against a wall because there was reasonable suspicion he was armed, and he acted belligerently and charged toward the officers upon seeing them, thereby putting others in danger. ("We conclude, without serious question, that the temporary detention—placing the [defendant] up against the wall—was justified at its inception because the officers had a reasonable suspicion that the [defendant] was armed and had acted in such a way as to threaten the person who placed the 911 call.") Also, in *United States v. Fisher*, 364 F.3d 970, 973–74 (8th Cir. 2004), the court held that officers could approach a man with guns drawn because they had information that he committed an armed assault minutes before, and the location where they stopped the man was known for gun violence.

See Table 8.1 for a comparison of a stop and a formal arrest.

Frisks

A *frisk* is a limited search of a person's body consisting of a careful exploration or pat-down of the outer surfaces of the person's clothing in an attempt to discover weapons. The law enforcement officer's determination of whether to frisk a suspect is a separate

TABLE 8.1 | Comparison of a Stop with an Arrest

	Stop	Arrest
Purpose	Brief, limited investigatory detention	To bring a suspect into custody for the commission of an offense as the prelude to criminal prosecution
Justification	Reasonable suspicion supported by articulable facts that criminal activity may be afoot	Probable cause to believe that the person to be arrested has committed or is committing a crime
Warrant	Not needed	Preferred but not needed for arrests in public places. Required to enter a suspect's home. Search warrant also needed to enter a third party's home to arrest a suspect therein.
Notice	None required	Officer usually must give notice that the person is under arrest and that the officer has the authority to arrest.
Force	Officer may use a reasonable degree of force judged from the perspective of the reasonable officer on the scene. Officer may never use deadly force to make a stop, but may use deadly force if, during the stop, it becomes necessary to act in self-defense or defense of others. Officer must use the least intrusive methods reasonably available to confirm or dispel the officer's suspicions of criminal activity.	Officer may use any reasonably necessary nondeadly force to arrest for a misdemeanor or a felony. Officer may use deadly force if, during the process of arrest, it becomes necessary to act in self-defense or defense of others. Office may also use deadly force to stop a fleeing felon from escaping if the officer has probable cause to believe that the suspect poses a threat of serious bodily harm either to the officer or to others. Deadly force may not be used to stop a fleeing misdemeanant or a fleeing felon who poses no risk of danger.
Time limit	Must be temporary and last no longer than is necessary to effectuate the purpose of the stop	Whatever time is reasonably necessary to make the arrest and bring the suspect into custody for booking and further processing
Judicial review	Someone stopped by police does not have an automatic right to prompt judicial review of the legality of the stop. If a citation is issued, it may be challenged in subsequent court proceedings.	Someone who is arrested has the right to prompt judicial review of the legality of the arrest by a neutral judicial officer, usually within forty-eight hours of the time of arrest.
Search allowed	Protective pat-down frisk of outer clothing for weapons may be conducted if, and only if, the officer has reason to believe that the person stopped is armed and dangerous.	A full body search of the arrestee for weapons and evidence may be conducted as a search incident to any valid, custodial arrest. Officers may also search the areas into which the arrestee might reach to grab weapons, contraband, or other evidentiary items.

© Cengage Learning®

issue from determination of whether to stop. A frisk serves a different governmental interest and is justified by a different set of factors. The governmental interest served is the protection of the officer and others from possible violence by persons being investigated for crime. "[W]e cannot blind ourselves to the need for law enforcement officers to protect themselves and other prospective victims of violence in situations where they may lack probable cause for an arrest." *Terry v. Ohio*, 392 U.S. 1, 24 (1968).

Balanced against this interest is the citizen's right to privacy, which is necessarily invaded by giving police the right to frisk suspects. "We must still consider, however, the nature and quality of the intrusion on individual rights which must be accepted if police officers are to be conceded the right to search for weapons in situations where probable cause to arrest for crime is lacking." 392 U.S. at 24. As noted earlier, the Court considers the frisk procedure to be a serious intrusion on a person's rights, possibly inflicting great indignity and arousing strong resentment.

Balancing these competing interests, the Supreme Court in *Terry* gave law enforcement officers the following limited frisk authority:

> Our evaluation of the proper balance that has to be struck in this type of case leads us to conclude that there must be a narrowly drawn authority to permit a reasonable search for weapons for the protection of the police officer, where he has reason to believe that he is dealing with an armed and dangerous individual, regardless of whether he has probable cause to arrest the individual for a crime. 392 U.S. at 27.

Limited Authority to Frisk

A law enforcement officer's authority to frisk is limited and narrowly drawn. An officer may not frisk everyone that he or she stops to investigate possible criminal activity. Before conducting a frisk, an officer must have "reason to believe that he is dealing with an armed and dangerous individual." An officer need not be absolutely certain that the individual is armed. Rather, the issue is "whether a reasonably prudent man in the circumstances would be warranted in the belief that his safety or that of others was in danger." 392 U.S. at 27. *An officer must be able to justify a frisk of a person by pointing to specific facts and* "specific reasonable inferences which he is entitled to draw from the facts in light of his experience." 392 U.S. at 27. Thus, frisks are governed by the same objective reasonable suspicion standard as stops.

The Supreme Court has held that this standard is not met when officers, armed with a warrant authorizing a search of a bar and bartender for narcotics, frisk the customers in that bar. An officer cannot frisk a customer, or any individual for that matter, unless the officer has reasonable suspicion that the individual is armed and dangerous:

> The "narrow scope" of the *Terry* exception does not permit a frisk for weapons on less than reasonable belief or suspicion directed at the person to be frisked [i.e., a bar customer], even though that person happens to be on premises where an authorized narcotics search is taking place. *Ybarra v. Illinois*, 444 U.S. 85 (1979).

Justification to frisk usually requires a combination of one or more factors, evaluated in the light of an officer's experience and knowledge. The more factors present, the more likely a reviewing court will find that the officer had reasonable suspicion to frisk. The following is a partial list of factors that may be considered in deciding to frisk a person:

- The suspected crime involves the use of weapons.
- The suspect is nervous or edgy about being stopped.
- There is a bulge in the suspect's clothing.
- The suspect's hand is concealed in his or her clothing.
- The suspect does not present satisfactory identification or an adequate explanation for suspicious behavior.
- The suspect behaves in a secretive, or furtive, fashion.
- The area in which the officer is operating is known to contain armed persons.
- The suspect exhibits belligerent behavior upon being stopped.
- The officer believes that the suspect may have been armed on a previous occasion.

(Many of these factors will be discussed in more detail in the section entitled "Specific Circumstances Justifying Stops and Frisks.")

Note that special considerations may apply when frisking someone of the opposite sex. If an officer of the same gender as the suspect to be frisked can be summoned to the scene in a reasonable amount of time without jeopardizing the safety of the officers present, this alternative should be explored. Alternatively, officers at the scene may request stopped persons to remove outer clothing.

Scope of a Frisk

This section will explore the permissible scope of a frisk under *Terry* and other cases. In particular, it will address the scope of a frisk in the context of both persons and vehicles.

Pat-Down of the Person's Outer Clothing The U.S. Supreme Court in *Terry* emphasized that a frisk is "a reasonable search for weapons for the protection of the police officer." 392 U.S. at 27. Because the only justifiable purpose of a frisk is the protection of the officer and others, the search must be strictly "limited to that which is necessary for the discovery of weapons which might be used to harm the officer or others nearby." 392 U.S. at 26. If the protective search goes beyond what is necessary to determine if the suspect is armed, it is no longer valid under *Terry*, and its results are inadmissible.

Therefore, a frisk must initially be limited to a pat-down of the *outer* clothing. An officer has no authority to reach inside clothing or into pockets in the *initial* stages of a frisk. During the pat-down, if the officer detects an object that feels like a weapon, the officer may then reach inside the clothing or pocket and seize it. If the object is not a weapon but is some other implement of crime (e.g., a burglar's tool), that implement is admissible in evidence for the crime to which it relates (e.g., attempted burglary).

If an officer feels no weapon-like object during the course of the pat-down, the officer can no longer have a reasonable fear that the person is armed. Any further search without probable cause would exceed the purpose of the frisk—the protection of the officer and others—and would be unreasonable under the Fourth Amendment. Evidence obtained from an unlawful frisk is inadmissible. For example, the Court in *United States v. Miles*, 247 F.3d 1009 (9th Cir. 2001), found that the officer exceeded the permissible scope of a frisk when he manipulated a small box in the defendant's pocket that did not initially feel like a weapon or weapon-like object. By manipulating the box, the officer believed that it contained bullets. He removed the box from the defendant's pocket and, after opening it, found bullets.

Because the small box did not initially feel like a weapon or weapon-like object, the officer could not further manipulate the box or remove the box from the defendant's pocket and open it. As a result, the court excluded from trial the bullets found in the box. 247 F.3d at 1014–15.

However, in *United States v. Majors*, 328 F.3d 791 (5th Cir. 2003), the court found that the officer's more intrusive frisk of the defendant's pocket was permissible because the officer could not initially discern whether or not the bulge he felt in the defendant's pocket was a weapon. The court described the officer's actions in this way:

> [Officer] Rush felt a large bulge in the left pocket of baggy shorts. Unable to identify the bulge, Rush pulled up the outside of [defendant's] pocket to see what was inside. He testified that there was no other reasonable way to verify that the bulge was not a weapon. Inside the pocket, Rush saw a plastic bag filled with smaller plastic bags containing white powder. [The powder was cocaine.] 328 F.3d at 794.

The court found the frisk permissible because the bulge may have been a weapon; as a result, the cocaine was admissible into evidence against the defendant:

> Rush did not rule out the possibility that the bulge in [defendant's] pocket was a weapon [nor had he ruled out that the softball size item in [defendant's] pocket might conceal a weapon.] The bulge in [defendant's] pocket was 'bigger than a

softball' and 'in between hard and soft.' Although Rush could not feel a knife in [defendant's] pocket, he could not tell if there was another weapon in the bulge, [such as a grenade]. Consequently, he could continue the search beyond the initial "plain feel." 328 F.3d at 795.

See also United States v. Muhammad, 644 F.3d 1022, 1027 (8th Cir. 2010) ("Muhammad concedes that Agent McCrary was permitted to perform a pat-down search to determine whether Muhammad was carrying a concealed weapon. Agent McCrary then reasonably determined that the four-inch long and three-inch wide "hard object" in Muhammad's back pocket could be a weapon or could conceal a weapon that presented a threat to officer safety, such as a knife, box cutter or razor blade. [T]his pat-down search stayed within the bounds of *Terry,* and the Fourth Amendment permitted Agent McCrary to remove the object from Muhammad's pocket [which turned out to be a wallet].")

Protective Search for Weapons Within Reach of Person Being Frisked *Michigan v. Long,* 463 U.S. 1032 (1983), approved an extension of the permissible scope of a protective search for weapons beyond the person of a suspect to include the passenger compartment of an automobile. In *Long,* two police officers patrolling at night observed a car traveling erratically and at excessive speed. When the car swerved into a ditch, the officers stopped to investigate. The driver, the only occupant of the car, met the officers at the rear of the car. He did not respond to initial requests to produce his license and registration, but after the request was repeated, he began walking toward the car to obtain the papers. Note that at this point, even though the officers had sufficient grounds for a stop, they did not have sufficient grounds to conduct a frisk for weapons. However, as the officers approached the car, they saw a hunting knife on the floorboard of the driver's side of the car. The Supreme Court held that the officers then had sufficient grounds to conduct a pat-down search of the driver and a limited search of the passenger compartment of the car for weapons:

> [T]he search of the passenger compartment of an automobile, limited to those areas in which a weapon may be placed or hidden, is permissible if the police officer possesses a reasonable belief based on "specific and articulable facts which, taken together with the rational inferences from those facts, reasonably warrant" the officers in believing that the suspect is dangerous and the suspect may gain immediate control of weapons. 463 U.S. at 1049.

Thus, if officers lawfully stop a vehicle and then develop in the course of that stop reasonable suspicion that the occupants or recent occupants are armed and dangerous, they may not only frisk the occupants but also conduct a limited search of the passenger compartment of the vehicle for weapons. As part of this search, officers can look anywhere a weapon could be hidden in the vehicle. This search is permitted to protect police from any weapons in the vicinity of the suspect.

The Court in *Long* also pointed out that "[i]f, while conducting a legitimate *Terry* search of the interior of the automobile, the officer should . . . discover contraband other than weapons, he clearly cannot be required to ignore the contraband, and the Fourth Amendment does not require its suppression in such circumstances." *Long,* 463 U.S. at 1050. In *Long,* one of the officers shined a flashlight into the car and saw a pouch protruding from under the armrest of the front seat. Because the pouch could have contained a weapon, the officer was justified in lifting

L05

KEY POINTS

- A law enforcement officer may conduct a reasonable limited protective search (frisk) for weapons when the officer has reasonable suspicion that he or she is dealing with an armed and dangerous person, whether or not the officer has probable cause to arrest.

- A frisk must initially be limited to a pat-down of a person's outer clothing. If a weapon or weapon-like object is detected, or if a nonthreatening object's identity as contraband is immediately apparent to an officer's sense of touch, the officer may reach inside clothing or a pocket and seize the object. For an object's identity as nonthreatening contraband (i.e., drugs) to be immediately apparent to an officer's sense of touch, the officer must have probable cause, upon feeling the object, that the object is this kind of contraband.

- If a law enforcement officer has a reasonable, articulable suspicion that a motor vehicle's occupant is armed and dangerous, the officer may frisk the occupant and conduct a limited search of the passenger compartment of the vehicle for weapons. The officer may look in any location in the passenger compartment that a weapon could be found or hidden. The officer may also seize items of evidence other than weapons, if discovered in plain view during the course of such a search.

the armrest, revealing an open pouch containing marijuana. Having discovered the marijuana pursuant to a legitimate frisk, the officer was justified in seizing the marijuana under the plain view doctrine. Under that doctrine, "if police are lawfully in a position from which they view an object, if its incriminating character is apparent, and if the officers have a lawful right of access to the object, they may seize it without a warrant." *Minnesota v. Dickerson*, 508 U.S. 366, 375 (1993). If, however, the police lack probable cause to believe that an object in plain view is an item subject to seizure without conducting some further search of the object (e.g., manipulating the object to look for a serial number or some other identifying characteristic), the plain view doctrine does not justify its seizure. The plain view doctrine is discussed in detail in Chapter 10.

Relying on the plain view doctrine, the Supreme Court in *Dickerson* further expanded the scope of a permissible frisk by approving a so-called plain touch (or plain feel) exception to the rule allowing only the seizure of weapons or weapon-like objects discovered in the course of a frisk. That exception allows the seizure of nonthreatening contraband, such as drugs, if its identity as contraband is immediately apparent to the sense of touch as the result of the pat-down search (e.g., the officer, upon immediately feeling the object, has probable cause based on his or her sense of touch that the object is nonthreatening contraband).

In *Dickerson* itself, the Court did not approve of the seizure of the crack cocaine found in the defendant's pocket because the officer did not have probable cause, upon feeling the object, that it was cocaine. Thus, the officer went beyond the permissible scope of a frisk when he manipulated the object to determine if it was, indeed, an illegal drug:

> Although the officer was lawfully in a position to feel the lump in respondent's pocket, because *Terry* entitled him to place his hands upon respondent's jacket [as part of a valid pat-down], the court below determined that the incriminating character of the object was not immediately apparent to him. Rather, the officer determined that the item was contraband only after conducting a further search [involving manipulation of the object], one not authorized by *Terry* or by any other exception to the warrant requirement. Because this further search of respondent's pocket was constitutionally invalid, the seizure of the cocaine that followed is likewise unconstitutional. 508 U.S. at 379.

Specific Circumstances Justifying Stops and Frisks

This section presents actual cases involving stops and frisks to show how courts evaluate the reasonableness of the actions of law enforcement officers. The cases are grouped under various headings indicating *major factors* that have influenced courts in finding the required reasonable suspicion to authorize a stop and or frisk by police, including

- behavioral cues by the suspect (i.e., flight and furtive gestures),
- suspect's association with known criminals or a prior criminal record,
- "innocent" conduct,
- admissions of guilt,

- evidentiary cues (i.e., a bulge in the suspect's pocket),
- presence in a high crime area, or
- suspect matches description in report of a violent crime.

Behavioral Cues

A law enforcement officer should evaluate reasonable suspicion of criminal activity under the totality of circumstances; that is, the officer should consider all of the behaviors exhibited by the suspect when judging whether reasonable suspicion to stop and frisk exists.

Flight and Other Forms of Evasive Behavior   In *Illinois v. Wardlow*, 528 U.S. 119, 124 (2000), the U.S. Supreme Court recognized that "nervous, evasive behavior is a pertinent factor in determining reasonable suspicion." The Court said, "Headlong flight—wherever it occurs—is the consummate act of evasion: it is not necessarily indicative of wrongdoing, but it is certainly suggestive of such." In *Wardlow*, the defendant fled when he saw a caravan of police vehicles converge on his street, which was known for heavy narcotics trafficking. Officers in one of the vehicles pursued the defendant and eventually cornered him. An officer exited the vehicle, stopped the defendant, and immediately conducted a pat-down search for weapons. The officer discovered a handgun and arrested the defendant.

The U.S. Supreme Court held that the stop was lawful because the suspect's presence in a high-crime area, coupled with his sudden flight, constituted reasonable suspicion to detain and investigate further:

> [U]nprovoked flight is simply not a mere refusal to cooperate. Flight, by its very nature, is not "going about one's business"; in fact, it is just the opposite. Allowing officers confronted with such flight to stop the fugitive and investigate further is quite consistent with the individual's right to go about his business or to stay put and remain silent in the face of police questioning. 528 U.S. at 125.

Note that unprovoked flight, alone, does not automatically provide reasonable suspicion to stop a suspect. Relying on *Wardlow*, *United States v. Jordan*, 232 F.3d 447 (5th Cir. 2000), held that the totality of the circumstances—including the defendant's "running at full sprint" from the direction of a nearby grocery store, his "looking back over his shoulder, left and right," the time (6:45 P.M. on a January evening), and place (a high-crime area)—justified the officer's decision to stop the defendant. The court said:

> *Wardlow* did not establish a bright-line test in cases where a defendant is seen to be running. Instead, citing *Terry*, *Wardlow* examined the totality of circumstances to determine whether the officer had a "reasonable, articulable suspicion that criminal activity is afoot." . . . *Wardlow* noted that an individual's presence in a "high-crime area" is a relevant consideration, as is "nervous, evasive behavior." 232 F.3d at 449.

Furtive Gestures   Evasive behavior may include other actions besides flight that are collectively referred to as furtive gestures. For example, before reaching a police roadblock in the middle of the night, if a vehicle brakes abruptly, turns into a private driveway, and hesitates in coming to a stop some distance from both the public road and the residence, these actions may constitute evasive behavior capable of contributing to an officer's determination of reasonable suspicion to stop. *See United States v. Smith*, 396 F.3d 579, 585–87 (4th Cir. 2005).

Indeed, officers may consider many types of furtive gestures as part of the totality-of-circumstances analysis for reasonable suspicion. Some examples that courts have considered as evidence of evasive behavior include

- multiple suspects providing conflicting answers to questions posed by police officers, *see, e.g., United States v. Edwards*, 424 F.3d 1106 (D.C. Cir. 2005);

- avoiding eye contact with officers, *see, e.g., United States v. Owens*, 167 F.3d 739 (1st Cir. 1999); *Hoover v. Walsh*, 682 F.3d 481, 496–97 (6th Cir. 2012);

- attempting to hide something out of an officer's line of vision, *see, e.g., People v. Carvey*, 680 N.E.2d 150 (N.Y. 1997); *United States v. Dunning*, 666 F.3d 1158, 1164 (8th Cir. 2012);

- attempting to swallow something so an officer cannot find it, *see, e.g., State v. Thomas*, 483 N.W.2d 527 (Neb. 1992);

- continually looking over one's shoulder or into a rearview mirror of a vehicle in a manner that suggests someone is trying to make sure that no one is watching, *see, e.g., United States v. Jordan*, 232 F.3d 447 (5th Cir. 2000) (shoulder case) and *United States v. Rodriguez*, 564 F.3d 735, 744 (5th Cir. 2009) (vehicle case);

- placing one's hands in pockets or pushing one's hand down into a pocket when approached by police officers in a high-crime area, *see, e.g., United States v. Mayo*, 361 F.3d 802 (4th Cir. 2004); *United States v. Simmons*, 560 F.3d 98, 108 (2nd Cir. 2009).

Association with Known Criminals or Prior Criminal Record

United States v. Cruz, 909 F.2d 422 (11th Cir. 1989), found adequate grounds, based partially on the suspect's association with known drug dealers, for both a stop and frisk under the following circumstances:

> First, the appellant was seen walking together with a known drug dealer who had negotiated with one of the agents for the delivery of fifteen grams of cocaine. Second, the agents certainly understood that the crime of drug trafficking has a particularly violent nature. Finally, the appellant's male companion was seen speaking to one of the dealers whom the agents knew was present to exchange a kilogram of cocaine. Thus under all the circumstances known to the officers at the time of the stop, we hold that the officers had reasonable suspicion to stop the appellant who had walked away from the scene of the original arrests.
>
> [The detective] also had the right to make a limited protective search for concealed weapons in order to secure the safety of herself and the safety of those around her. The factors articulated above indicated that the appellant was likely involved in narcotics trafficking and, as is judicially recognized, such individuals are often armed. 909 F.2d at 424.

In *United States v. Sprinkle*, 106 F.3d 613, 618–19 (4th Cir. 1997), the court found that defendant's presence with a companion who was a known drug criminal did not provide reasonable suspicion for officers to stop the defendant. This is because the officers did not observe the defendant engage in any illegal activity with his companion; rather, the officers only saw the defendant and his companion depart in a "normal, unhurried fashion" in a vehicle after the companion attempted to hide his face.

In addition, the court found that a person's criminal record alone cannot support reasonable suspicion to stop:

> [Defendant's companion] first got [the officer's] attention because the officer knew [the companion] had a criminal record and that he had recently finished a

sentence for a drug conviction. [The officer], however, had no information that [the companion] had returned to crime since his release. A prior criminal record 'is not, standing alone, sufficient to create reasonable suspicion.' Nevertheless, an officer can couple knowledge of prior criminal involvement with more concrete factors in reaching a reasonable suspicion of current criminal activity. 106 F.3d at 617.

See also United States v. Foster, 634 F.3d 243, 246, 248 (4th Cir. 2011) ("As in *Sprinkle*, we are convinced that—without some stronger indication of criminal activity—the articulated facts, collectively, could not have supplied an officer with the appropriate amount of suspicion necessary for a *Terry* stop. The detective was surprised to see Foster rise from [a crouched position in] the passenger seat [of a car], and, based on his knowledge of Foster's past criminal record, he found Foster's sudden arm movements [down towards the floor of the car] peculiar. Nevertheless, . . . the totality of the circumstances were not enough to validate the stop.")

"Innocent" Conduct

A series of individual lawful acts may provide reasonable suspicion of criminal activity sufficient to justify a stop, if the overall pattern of those acts is indicative of criminal activity. Officers should evaluate all circumstances in their totality rather than evaluate each act or circumstance in isolation, and officers may use their specialized training and experience to determine reasonable suspicion for a stop. *See United States v. Arvizu*, 534 U.S. 266 (2002).

Recall from the previous discussion of *Arvizu* ("The Reasonable Suspicion Standard" earlier in this chapter) that the U.S. Supreme Court in that case found the officer had reasonable suspicion to stop a vehicle under the totality of the circumstances, all of which were innocent when considered individually:

> [Defendant] argues that we must rule in his favor because the facts suggested a family in a minivan on a holiday outing. A determination that reasonable suspicion exists, however, need not rule out the possibility of innocent conduct. Undoubtedly, each of these factors alone is susceptible of innocent explanation, and some factors are more probative than others. Taken together, we believe they sufficed to form a particularized and objective basis for [the officer] stopping the vehicle, making the stop reasonable within the meaning of the Fourth Amendment. 534 U.S. at 277–78.

However, in *Reid v. Georgia*, 448 U.S. 438 (1980), the U.S. Supreme Court found an officer could not infer reasonable suspicion to stop a person from the following facts, many of which were innocent in nature:

- the defendant had arrived from Fort Lauderdale, which a Drug Enforcement Administration (DEA) agent testified is a principal place of origin of cocaine sold elsewhere in the country;
- the defendant arrived in the early morning, when law enforcement activity is diminished;
- he and his companion appeared to the agent to be trying to conceal the fact that they were traveling together; and
- they apparently had no luggage other than their shoulder bags.

Based on these facts, the Court pointed out that

> only the fact that the petitioner preceded another person and occasionally looked backward at him as they proceeded through the concourse relates

to their particular conduct. The other circumstances describe a very large category of presumably innocent travelers, who would be subject to virtually random seizures were the Court to conclude that as little foundation as there was in this case could justify a seizure. The agent's belief that the petitioner and his companion were attempting to conceal the fact that they were traveling together, a belief that was more an "inchoate and unparticularized suspicion or 'hunch,'" . . . than a fair inference in the light of his experience, is simply too slender a reed to support the seizure in this case. 448 U.S. at 441.

In contrast, *United States v. Sokolow*, 490 U.S. 1 (1989), found an overall pattern indicating criminal activity from a similar but more specific and detailed set of facts. In that case, DEA agents stopped the defendant on his arrival at Honolulu International Airport. The agents found 1,063 grams of cocaine in his carry-on luggage. When the defendant was stopped, the agents knew that

- he had paid $2,100 for two airplane tickets from a roll of $20 bills;
- he traveled under a name that did not match the name under which his telephone number was listed;
- his original destination was Miami, a source city for illicit drugs;
- he stayed in Miami for only forty-eight hours, even though a round-trip flight from Honolulu to Miami takes twenty hours;
- he appeared nervous during his trip; and
- he had checked none of his luggage.

The Court found reasonable suspicion to justify the stop, even though there was no evidence of ongoing criminal activity. Applying a totality-of-the-circumstances test, the Court said that "[a]ny of these factors is not by itself proof of any illegal conduct and is quite consistent with innocent travel. But we think taken together they amount to reasonable suspicion." 490 U.S. at 9. For further discussion of this topic, see the "Criminal Procedure in Action" on page 347.

Admissions by Defendant

Admissions of criminal conduct by a suspect may provide reasonable suspicion for a stop or frisk by police. In *United States v. Chhien*, 266 F.3d 1 (1st Cir. 2001), after the officer made a lawful traffic stop, the defendant consented to being frisked. Upon feeling a large bulge in the defendant's pocket, the officer asked what it was. The defendant responded that the bulge was a wad of cash totaling $2,000. The court held that the defendant's response provided reasonable suspicion for the officer to detain him for additional questioning. 266 F.3d at 10.

Possible Evidentiary Cues

Certain types of evidentiary cues associated with a suspect may provide a law enforcement officer with the necessary reasonable suspicion of criminal activity to stop or frisk the suspect.

Observation of Bulge or Heavy Object Recall that in *Pennsylvania v. Mimms*, 434 U.S. 106 (1977), the U.S. Supreme Court held that an officer may order a driver to exit a vehicle if the officer makes a lawful traffic stop of the driver's vehicle. Once the driver in *Mimms* did exit his vehicle, the officer saw a large bulge under the defendant's jacket. Based on this observation, the Court concluded that the officer had reasonable suspicion to frisk the driver: "The bulge in the jacket permitted the officer to conclude that [the driver] was armed and thus posed a serious and present danger to the safety of the officer. In these circumstances, any man of 'reasonable caution' would likely have conducted the pat-down." 434 U.S. at 112.

United States v. Barnes, 909 F.2d 1059 (7th Cir. 1990), upheld the seizure of a pistol discovered as the result of a pat-down of a person lawfully stopped for having altered temporary license plates. The frisk was justified because the officer observed a "heavy object" protruding from the person's jacket and the person attempted to reach for his pocket before the initial pat-down. *See also United States v. Jordan*, 635 F.3d 1181 (11th Cir. 2011) ("[O]fficers knew going into the encounter that [defendant] Jordan was present in an area known for crime. [M]ore significantly, Jordan became suspiciously defensive when confronted about walking in the middle of the street, belligerently yelling that he had not done anything wrong. *[M]ost importantly, Officer Paige saw a gun-shaped bulge in Jordan's pocket*. Once the officers became aware of these facts, they had the requisite reasonable suspicion to conduct a *Terry* stop concerning a potential firearms offense.") 635 F.3d at 1188 (italics added).

Presence in a High-Crime Area

In *Brown v. Texas*, 443 U.S. 47 (1979), police on patrol in an area with a high incidence of drug traffic stopped the defendant in an alley while he was walking away from another person. The officer later testified that the situation "looked suspicious and we had never seen that subject in that area before." The U.S. Supreme Court invalidated the stop: "The fact that appellant was in a neighborhood frequented by drug users, standing alone, is not a basis for concluding that appellant himself was engaged in criminal conduct. In short, the appellant's activity was no different from the activity of other pedestrians in that neighborhood." 443 U.S. at 52.

Illinois v. Wardlow, 528 U.S. 119 (2000) reiterated the holding in *Brown* but added that presence in a high-crime area combined with other specific suspicious information, such as unprovoked flight, may justify a stop:

> An individual's presence in an area of expected criminal activity, standing alone, is not enough to support a reasonable, particularized suspicion that the person is committing a crime [citing *Brown v. Texas*]. But officers are not required to ignore the relevant characteristics of a location in determining whether the circumstances are sufficiently suspicious to warrant further investigation. Accordingly, we have previously noted the fact that the stop occurred in a "high-crime area" among the relevant contextual considerations in a *Terry* analysis. 528 U.S. at 124 (italics supplied).

Suspect Matches Description in a Recent, "In-Person" Report of Violent Crime

In *United States v. Fisher*, 364 F.3d 970 (8th Cir. 2004), when police officers learned from a victim that he had been assaulted by a particular man with a gun, the officers were justified in stopping a man minutes later, with their guns drawn, who fit the description provided by the victim:

> The [victim] approached the officers, telling them he had been assaulted in that area by someone matching [defendant's] distinctive description moments earlier.

Although the officers did not know the [victim's] name or why he was at the location, they were nonetheless confronted with an in-person report of a serious street crime and a description of the perpetrator that matched [defendant]. The [victim's] report was corroborated by the fact that [defendant] was in close proximity to the scene of the alleged assault at or around the time it was alleged to have occurred. Based on this information, the officers had reasonable suspicion that [defendant] committed a crime, and that he was armed and dangerous.

The decision to approach [defendant] with guns drawn was reasonably necessary to the investigative stop. [T]he officers received specific information that an assailant matching [defendant's] description had used a gun in connection with an assault only minutes earlier. Moreover, the officers were approaching [defendant] in a neighborhood known for gun violence. 364 F.3d at 973.

After the officers stopped the defendant, he blurted out, without being questioned by the officers, that he had a gun. The court also upheld the subsequent frisk of the defendant to find the gun, which was in the defendant's pocket.

Detentions of Containers and Other Property

Normally, containers and other property may be seized and detained briefly for investigation based on reasonable suspicion by officers that the property contains illegal items; however, this property may not be searched absent a warrant or other valid exception to the warrant requirement (i.e., search incident to arrest exception). *Smith v. Ohio*, 494 U.S. 541 (1990), stated the general rule regarding the investigatory detention of property:

> Although the Fourth Amendment may permit the detention for a brief period of property on the basis of only "reasonable, articulable suspicion" that it contains contraband or evidence of criminal activity . . . it proscribes—except in certain well-defined circumstances—the search of that property unless accomplished pursuant to judicial warrant issued upon probable cause. 494 U.S. at 542.

United States v. Place, 462 U.S. 696 (1983), held that *Terry v. Ohio* applied to the warrantless seizure and limited investigation of personal luggage. In *Place,* based on information from law enforcement officers in Miami, DEA agents at a New York airport suspected that the defendant was carrying narcotics. When the defendant arrived at the airport, the agents approached him, informed him of their suspicion, and requested and received identification from him. When the defendant refused to consent to a search of his luggage, an agent told him that they were going to take the luggage to a federal judge to try to obtain a search warrant.

Instead, the agents took the luggage to another airport, where they subjected it to a sniffing by a trained narcotics detection dog, a procedure commonly referred to as a canine sniff or a dog sniff. The dog reacted positively to one of the bags. At this point, approximately ninety minutes had elapsed since the seizure of the luggage. The agents later obtained a search warrant for the luggage and found cocaine.

Regarding the detention of a suspect's luggage, the Court in *Place* held that "when an officer's observations lead him reasonably to believe that a traveler is carrying luggage that contains narcotics, the principles of *Terry* and its progeny would permit the officer to detain the luggage briefly to investigate the circumstances that aroused his suspicion, provided that the investigative detention is properly limited in scope." 462 U.S. at 706. In addition, the Court specifically found that the brief investigation of the luggage could include a "canine sniff" by a well-trained narcotics detection dog. This procedure was found to be uniquely limited in nature because it does not require opening the luggage, it does not expose noncontraband items to view, and it discloses only the presence or absence of narcotics. *See also Illinois v. Caballes*, 543 U.S. 405, 410 (2005). ("A dog sniff conducted during a concededly lawful traffic stop that reveals no information other than the location of a substance that no individual has any right to possess [i.e., drugs] does not violate the Fourth Amendment.")

CRIMINAL PROCEDURE **IN ACTION**

Interpreting *Arvizu*: When Does "Innocent" Conduct Support Reasonable Suspicion to Stop? *United States v. Johnson*, 581 F.3d 994 (9th Cir. 2009)

"Alaska State Trooper Vic Aye and Deputy Troy Meeks of the United States Marshals Service were serving federal warrants on the east side of Anchorage. The officers were wearing plain clothes and driving an unmarked sports utility vehicle. While the officers were stopped at a traffic light across from the First National Bank, Deputy Meeks noticed three suspicious

individuals standing in the bank's parking lot next to a tan Buick sedan. The car was parked about 20 feet from the bank's front entrance and its hood was raised. The three men—later identified as Johnson, David Brookins, and Alvin Nelson—were not looking under the hood but instead appeared to be surveying the bank and the surrounding area. As the officers drove away, Deputy Meeks observed Johnson and Nelson head toward the bank's front door. Johnson, who was wearing a hooded sweatshirt under a jacket, flipped up his hood partially obscuring his face.

"His suspicions aroused, Deputy Meeks described to Trooper Aye what he had just witnessed. The officers decided to double back for another look. By the time they circled back to the bank, the sedan's hood had been closed, and Brookins was alone in the vehicle sitting in the driver's seat. The other two men were nowhere to be seen. Trooper Aye decided to enter the bank while Deputy Meeks stayed outside to surveil Brookins.

"Once inside the bank, Trooper Aye immediately noticed a teller nervously watching Johnson and Nelson, who were standing in line. The men were whispering to each other, and Johnson appeared to be surveying the bank lobby. Trooper Aye approached another bank employee who also appeared to be eyeing the men. He surreptitiously identified himself as a state trooper and asked the employee if everything was alright. She responded 'no,' and also appeared nervous.

"Although not in uniform, Trooper Aye could still be recognized as a law enforcement officer. He was carrying several pieces of police equipment

including a sidearm, taser, and two-way radio and he was wearing a bulletproof vest underneath his outer clothing. At some point, Johnson looked directly at Trooper Aye, said something to Nelson, and immediately walked out of the bank. Deputy Meeks observed Johnson exit the bank and stand at the driver's side of the sedan. Johnson appeared to gesture to Brookins before getting into the back seat. Trooper Aye and Deputy Meeks communicated by cellular phone as to what each had just witnessed. Trooper Aye then left the bank and rejoined Deputy Meeks in the police vehicle. The officers decided to stop and question the men. They pulled behind the sedan and activated their emergency lights.

"The officers approached the car and displayed their badges. They verbally identified themselves as law enforcement officers and asked for identification. Trooper Aye told Johnson and Brookins that the whole incident "might be a misunderstanding" and that they "just want[ed] to talk with [them]." The men cooperated with the officers' request that they step out of the car. Deputy Meeks patted down Brookins and discovered a loaded .25 caliber handgun in his front pocket and a spare magazine in his back pocket. Deputy Meeks informed Trooper Aye, who was talking to Johnson, that he had found a gun. The officers then conducted a pat-down search of Johnson and located another semi-automatic pistol in his coat pocket. The officers handcuffed Johnson and Brookins and seated them on the curb. Nelson then emerged from the bank and walked toward the sedan with his hands in his pockets.

Continued on next page

"Having already discovered that his associates were armed, the officers drew their own weapons and demanded that Nelson place his hands in plain view. After conducting a pat-down frisk, which uncovered no additional firearms, the officers secured Nelson.

"The officers explained to the three suspects that the matter still could be a misunderstanding, but they needed to run their identifications to determine whether they had any active warrants or other criminal history. At that point, Johnson volunteered that he had a previous drug conviction in Florida. Johnson was convicted in Broward County, Florida, of delivery of cocaine, a second degree felony. The record before us is unclear, however, whether Johnson disclosed to the officers that the prior conviction was a felony conviction.

"Johnson was indicted in the District of Alaska on a single count of being a felon in possession of a firearm. . . . He was arrested soon thereafter in Miami, Florida, and transported to Anchorage where he was arraigned. Johnson initially pled not guilty. He filed a motion to suppress all evidence obtained as a result of the detention, including the pistol officers had found in his coat pocket." *Johnson*, 581 F.3d at 997–98.

▪ Based on the U.S. Supreme Court case of *Arvizu* described earlier regarding how seemingly "innocent" conduct under certain circumstances can support reasonable suspicion for a police stop and/or frisk, do you believe that under the totality of the circumstances here the officers had reasonable suspicion to stop and frisk defendant Johnson? Please recall as you formulate your answer *both* the factors, or circumstances, used by the Supreme Court in *Arvizu* to determine reasonable suspicion for the police stop as well as other factors discussed in this chapter that may serve as grounds for a police stop and/or frisk. In particular, do you think Johnson and his companions could have been experiencing car trouble and were seeking assistance on this matter from individuals in or near the bank? Or was there sufficient reasonable suspicion to believe they were casing a bank for the purpose of robbing it?

▪ Should officers be required to conduct some investigation aimed at eliminating most or at least some of the truly innocent explanations for an individual's suspicious behavior, before stopping or frisking that individual? Does the reasonable suspicion standard for a stop and frisk account for an officer's duty, if any, to eliminate at least some of these innocent explanations? Fully explain your answer.

▪ Do you believe the pistol found on Johnson during the police pat-down, or frisk, is admissible into evidence to prove his guilt on the charge of being a felon in possession of a firearm? Explain your answer.

Nevertheless, the Court in *Place* found that the scope of the investigative detention of the luggage exceeded the limits established in *Terry*, primarily because of the length of the detention:

> Although the 90-minute detention of respondent's luggage is sufficient to render the seizure unreasonable, the violation was exacerbated by the failure of the agents to accurately inform respondent of the place to which they were transporting his luggage, of the length of time he might be dispossessed, and of what arrangements would be made for return of the luggage if the investigation dispelled the suspicion. In short, we hold that the detention of respondent's luggage in this case went beyond the narrow authority possessed by police to briefly detain luggage reasonably suspected to contain narcotics. 462 U.S. at 710.

Although the Court did not establish any rigid time limitation on an investigative detention, it clearly indicated that efforts of officers to minimize the intrusion on Fourth Amendment rights would be considered in determining the reasonableness of the detention. For example, the court in *United States v. Avery*, 137 F.3d 343 (6th Cir. 1997), found reasonable under the totality of the circumstances the detention of the suspect's luggage for twenty-five minutes at the airport while officers conducted, in a diligent, efficient, and transparent manner, a canine sniff. The court found that reasonable suspicion existed to detain the suspect's bag for this length of time to conduct the canine sniff based on the following facts:

1. only a brief moment after he boarded the plane, [the suspect] Avery stated he had thrown his ticket away;

2. Avery lied about the origin of his trip, stating it was Orlando, when in fact it was San Juan;

3. Avery misrepresented the nature of his business in Orlando, stating that he was visiting friends on vacation, when in fact Orlando was a stopover on his way to Washington, D.C.;

4. Avery stated he could not remember the name of his hotel and had no receipts;

5. Avery's ticket was issued in a name different than his own;

6. Avery did not have any identification, although he was traveling from San Juan to Washington, D.C.;

7. Avery consented to a search of his person, but not his carry-on bag; and

8. Avery was traveling on a cash one-way ticket purchased only thirty-five minutes before departure; and

9. the officers' belief that Avery was acting suspiciously. 137 F.3d at 343, 350.

The court in *Avery* distinguished the Supreme Court's decision in *Place*, previously discussed:

> In *Place*, a luggage detention case, the court found the detention was unreasonable because there was a ninety-minute gap from seizure to sniff, the officers failed to obtain a canine sniffer expeditiously, and the officers did not inform the defendant what they were doing with his luggage. Here, the officers informed Avery what they intended to do with his bag; they quickly obtained a canine to sniff the luggage and did so within twenty-five minutes. 137 F.3d at 351.

See also United States v. Parker, 2013 WL 5707243 (E.D. Ky. 2013), at *5 ("[The officer's] detention of [the suspects] and [one suspect's] Lincoln Town Car for the purposes of the drug-dog sniff was relatively brief. There was, at most, a twenty-five minute wait for [another officer] to bring his narcotics canine, Chuck, to the scene to perform a canine sniff on the outside of the vehicle. Based on Sixth Circuit precedent, the length of this detention was reasonable.")

Note that the *Place* and *Avery* cases discussed earlier involved the detention of containers (i.e., luggage) at airports. The detention and search of carry-on luggage at airline security checkpoints are a special case because of the severe danger presented by the possibility of allowing weapons or explosives on a plane. For more details about detentions of containers at airports, see the discussion of the special needs doctrine in the section "Airport and Courthouse Searches" in Chapter 6. Searches of vehicles using canines are discussed in Chapter 11 in the section "Vehicle Searches by Dogs."

Frisks of Containers and Other Property

In a case involving the equivalent of a frisk of luggage on a bus as opposed to at an airline security checkpoint, the U.S. Supreme Court held that a law enforcement officer's physical manipulation of a bus passenger's carry-on luggage violated the Fourth Amendment's proscription against unreasonable searches. In *Bond v. United States*, 529 U.S. 334 (2000), a border patrol agent in Texas boarded a bus to check the immigration status of its passengers. As the agent walked from the rear to the front of the bus, he squeezed the soft luggage in the overhead storage space above the seats. He noticed that a canvas bag above the defendant's seat contained a "bricklike" substance. After the defendant admitted ownership of the bag and consented to its search, the agent discovered a "brick" of methamphetamine.

The Court likened the level of intrusion of squeezing the defendant's luggage to that of a frisk of his person. "Although Agent Cantu did not 'frisk' petitioner's person, he did conduct a probing tactile examination of petitioner's carry-on luggage. Obviously, petitioner's bag was not part of his person. But travelers are particularly concerned about their carry-on luggage; they generally use it to transport personal items that, for whatever reason, they prefer to keep close at hand." 529 U.S. at 337–38. The Court found the frisk of the luggage unreasonable:

> Our Fourth Amendment analysis embraces two questions. First, we ask whether the individual, by his conduct, has exhibited an actual expectation of privacy; that is, whether he has shown that "he [sought] to preserve [something] as private." *Smith v. Maryland*, 442 U.S. 735, 740 (1979). . . . Here, petitioner sought to preserve privacy by using an opaque bag and placing that bag directly above his seat. Second, we inquire whether the individual's expectation of privacy is "one that society is prepared to recognize as reasonable." . . . When a bus passenger places a bag in an overhead bin, he expects that other passengers or bus employees may move it for one reason or another. Thus, a bus passenger clearly expects that his bag may be handled. He does not expect that other passengers or bus employees will, as a matter of course, feel the bag in an exploratory manner. But this is exactly what the agent did here. We therefore hold that the agent's physical manipulation of petitioner's bag violated the Fourth Amendment. 529 U.S. at 338–39.

Note that *Bond* does not prevent law enforcement officers from boarding buses or other means of public transportation and talking to passengers. Nor does it prevent officers from asking passengers for consent to search their belongings. *Bond* merely holds that it is illegal for a law enforcement officer to squeeze a passenger's belongings absent at least reasonable suspicion to believe a container has criminal evidence within it. Normally, if an officer possessing this reasonable suspicion feels a closed, opaque, nonabandoned container and detects something in the container that he or she has probable cause to believe is contraband, the officer should, absent consent to search or an emergency such as the threat of an exploding bomb, obtain a judicial warrant before opening and searching the container. This is especially the case in a stop-and-frisk situation because the suspect has not yet been arrested, and therefore the search incident to arrest doctrine has not yet been triggered. See Chapter 7 for further discussion of this doctrine.

Traffic Stops

An ordinary traffic stop is governed by the same standards as any other stop. "[A] traffic stop is valid under the Fourth Amendment . . . if the police officer has reasonable articulable suspicion that a traffic or equipment violation has occurred or is occurring." *United States v. Botero-Ospina*, 71 F.3d 783, 787 (10th Cir. 1995); *see also United States v. Arvizu*, 534 U.S. 266, 273 (2002) (evaluating ordinary traffic stop under reasonable suspicion standard). Minor traffic or equipment violations are so common that law enforcement officers are often tempted to use them to justify an investigation based on vague suspicion that the motorist may be engaging in more serious illegal activity. For example, an officer who observes a burned-out taillight, cracked windshield, or failure to signal when changing lanes may stop a vehicle even if a hypothetical "reasonable officer" would not have been motivated by a desire to enforce the traffic laws. This particular officer may actually be interested in investigating a crime more serious than the minor traffic or equipment violation. A stop made under such pretenses is often called a pretextual stop.

In *Whren v. United States*, 517 U.S. 806 (1996), plainclothes police officers patrolling a high-drug crime area in an unmarked vehicle observed a truck driven by the defendant waiting at a stop sign for an unusually long time. Suddenly, the truck turned without signaling and drove off at an unreasonable speed. One of the officers stopped the vehicle, supposedly to warn the driver about traffic violations, and on approaching the truck the officer observed plastic bags of crack cocaine in the defendant's hands. The defendant argued that the traffic stop was pretextual and that the evidence seized should be suppressed. The U.S. Supreme Court held that police officers with probable cause to believe that a traffic violation has occurred may stop a vehicle even though the stop is a pretext to search for drugs or some other, more serious crime. "Subjective intentions play no role in ordinary, probable-cause Fourth Amendment analysis." 517 U.S. at 813. The Court emphasized, however, the distinction between its holding in *Whren* and cases involving police intrusion without probable cause. The Court indicated its pretext analysis would not apply to such cases, which lack the "'quantum of individualized suspicion' necessary to ensure that police discretion is sufficiently contained." 517 U.S. at 817–18. Therefore, pretext (the subjective motive for stopping a vehicle) is irrelevant when probable cause exists to support a stop, but pretextual stops made without probable cause are not justified.

The *Whren* decision adopted the so-called *could* test and overrode previous law in some jurisdictions that subscribed to the narrower *would* test. In other words, the question for the officer is "Could I stop the vehicle?" (because there is probable cause to believe a traffic violation has occurred), not "Would I stop the vehicle?" (because, under normal circumstances, a stop would not be made for a minor violation). The *Whren* decision essentially legitimizes pretextual stops and disregards the subjective intent of the officer in favor of judging the constitutionality of a vehicle stop on the basis of objective data: Was there probable cause to believe a violation of law occurred?

Note, however, that random stops of vehicles, based on whim, hunch, or rumor, to check licenses, registrations, or equipment are not allowed. In *Delaware v. Prouse*, 440 U.S. 648, 663 (1979), the Supreme Court held:

> [E]xcept in those situations in which there is at least articulable and reasonable suspicion that a motorist is unlicensed or that an automobile is not registered, or that either the vehicle or an occupant is otherwise subject to seizure for violation of law, stopping an automobile and detaining the driver in order to check his driver's license and the registration of the automobile are unreasonable under the Fourth Amendment.

This prohibition on random vehicle stops based on hunches by officers helps to address the concern that these stops present a potential danger of arbitrary or discriminatory enforcement of the law. *See also United States v. Brignoni-Ponce*, 422 U.S. 873 (1975) (officers conducting roving patrol near border need at least reasonable suspicion that vehicle contains undocumented persons before stopping it).

Nevertheless, the Court in *Prouse* specifically held open the possibility for states to develop methods for spot checks that involve less intrusion or that do not involve the unconstrained exercise of discretion. The Court suggested as one possible alternative the questioning of *all* oncoming traffic at roadblock-type stops.

Roadblocks and Checkpoints

Michigan Department of State Police v. Sitz, 496 U.S. 444 (1990), approved a highway sobriety checkpoint program with guidelines governing checkpoint operations, site selection, and publicity. During the only operation of the checkpoint at the time of the Court decision, 126 vehicles had passed through the checkpoint, the average delay per vehicle was twenty-five seconds, and two drivers were arrested for driving under the influence. Applying the special needs doctrine, the Court found that although a Fourth Amendment seizure occurs when a vehicle is stopped at a checkpoint, police may stop a vehicle at a valid checkpoint without reasonable suspicion that the occupants are engaging in criminal activity.

However, *Indianapolis v. Edmond*, 531 U.S. 32 (2000), held that a highway checkpoint program—the primary purpose of which was the discovery and interdiction of illegal narcotics—violated the Fourth Amendment. What distinguished this checkpoint program from those previously approved by the Court in *Sitz* is that its primary purpose was to detect evidence of criminal wrongdoing (e.g., crime control), as opposed to the public safety goals at issue in *Sitz* that made the sobriety checkpoint constitutional under the special needs doctrine (see Chapter 6).

Illinois v. Lidster, 540 U.S. 419 (2004) involved an information-seeking roadblock set up by police to locate witnesses to a hit-and-run accident that had killed a bicyclist a week earlier. The roadblock was located on the same portion of highway, in the same direction, and at about the same time of day as the accident. The Court described the roadblock as follows:

> Police cars with flashing lights partially blocked the eastbound lanes of the highway. The blockage forced traffic to slow down, leading to lines of up to 15 cars in each lane. As each vehicle drew up to the checkpoint, an officer would stop it for 10 to 15 seconds, ask the occupants whether they had seen anything happen there the previous weekend, and hand each driver a flyer. 540 U.S. at 422.

The defendant approached the checkpoint in a minivan, swerved, and nearly hit one of the officers. Officers determined that he was driving under the influence, and arrested him.

The Court noted that even though a crime control roadblock is essentially a stop, which must be justified by reasonable articulable suspicion that a driver or occupant is involved in criminal activity, an information-seeking roadblock falls into the category of legitimate special needs detentions. Such detentions are evaluated by the same standard as the highway sobriety checkpoint in *Sitz*. Balancing the need for the roadblock against its intrusiveness, the Court found:

- The relevant public concern was grave—a serious crime resulting in death. Also, the need for information was great, because the investigation had apparently stalled.

- The police advanced this grave public concern by tailoring the stops to fit important investigatory needs. "The stops took place about one week after the hit-and-run accident, on the same highway near the location of the accident, and at about the same time of night. And police used the stops to obtain information from drivers, some of whom might well have been in the vicinity of the crime at the time it occurred." 540 U.S. at 427.

- The stops interfered only minimally with motorists' Fourth Amendment liberties. "Viewed objectively, each stop required only a brief wait

KEY POINTS

L01

- A law enforcement officer may not stop a motor vehicle and detain the driver to check license and registration unless the officer has reasonable, articulable suspicion of criminal activity or unless the stop is conducted in accordance with a properly conducted highway checkpoint program.

- The test to determine the reasonableness of stopping a vehicle at a highway checkpoint involves balancing the gravity of the public concerns served by the seizure, the degree to which the seizure advances the public interest, and the severity of the interference with individual liberty.

- Police may not conduct a checkpoint for general law enforcement purposes (i.e., to detect the presence of narcotics or weapons). However, sobriety and border checkpoints have been upheld by the Supreme Court. The Court has also upheld a checkpoint designed to find witnesses to a crime involving a fatality.

in line—a very few minutes at most. Contact with the police lasted only a few seconds. . . . Police contact consisted simply of a request for information and the distribution of a flyer. . . . Viewed subjectively, the contact provided little reason for anxiety or alarm. The police stopped all vehicles systematically. . . . And there is no allegation here that the police acted in a discriminatory or otherwise unlawful manner while questioning motorists during stops." 540 U.S. at 427.

Consequently, the Court held that the roadblock in *Lidster* was lawful.

Racial Profiling and Related Practices

An issue causing great controversy and concern in recent years is the law enforcement practice of racial profiling. Although definitions of racial profiling vary greatly, the following broad definition taken from a racial profiling study design guide produced for the U.S. Department of Justice is useful for a general discussion. Racial profiling is "any police-initiated action that relies upon: the race, ethnicity, or national origin of an individual rather than [1] the behavior of that individual, or [2] information that leads the police to a particular individual who has been identified as being engaged in or having been engaged in criminal activity" (Ramirez et al. 2000: 3).

CRIMINAL PROCEDURE IN ACTION

Police Roadblocks—Are "Safety Checkpoints" Permissible? *Ex parte Jackson*, 886 So.2d 155 (Ala. 2004).

The Mobile (Alabama) Housing Authority entered into a contract with the Mobile County Sheriff's Department that permitted the Sheriff's Department to enter housing areas governed by the Housing Authority at the request of the Housing Authority and perform such policing activities as rolling patrols, foot patrols, community policing, and safety checkpoints to

establish some sort of "police presence." Pursuant to that contract, the Mobile County Sheriff's Department entered the R. V. Taylor housing project in Mobile on the evening of May 10, 2001, to set up what they called a "safety checkpoint" at a major intersection in the housing community. The Housing Authority had made no particular request for a roadblock-type stop in this instance; instead, a captain in the Sheriff's Department made the decision to set up the roadblock. The officers checked driver's licenses, automobile insurance documentation, and vehicle safety devices (e.g., seat belts, child restraints, etc.) at the roadblock. They put in place seven marked Sheriff's Department vehicles at the intersection and stopped every vehicle that came through the intersection. Most vehicles were stopped for one minute. Officers followed guidelines established by the Sheriff's Department while conducting the roadblock; those guidelines required that they perform no random searches and that the officers' activities be supervised by superior officers in the Sheriff's Department.

One officer stopped Jackson's vehicle at the roadblock. He discovered marijuana and two rolls of cash on Jackson's person and a larger quantity of marijuana in the console between the driver's seat and the passenger's seat. Hidden under the tire cover in the trunk of Jackson's vehicle was a shopping bag that contained more marijuana, scales, and numerous plastic sandwich bags. At trial, Jackson filed a motion to suppress the marijuana found on his person and in his vehicle, on the basis that the roadblock was an unreasonable seizure that violated the Fourth Amendment to the United States Constitution. 886 So.2d at 155, 163–65.

- Based on what you learned in the preceding section concerning permissible police roadblocks, do you think the court in *Jackson* found the roadblock constitutional? Explain your answer.

- In your opinion, what should constitute a permissible purpose, if any, for a police roadblock?

- How should courts go about distinguishing between a valid police roadblock and an invalid one? Should they base their decision on what the police pronounce as the roadblock's purpose? On defendant's descriptions of what actually happened at the roadblock (or other witness descriptions)? On a combination of these factors? Explain your answer.

Profiling and Pretextual Stops One of the reasons racial profiling has become a volatile issue is *Whren v. United States*, 517 U.S. 806 (1996), already discussed, which gives police wide discretion in enforcing traffic laws if they have probable cause to believe that a traffic violation is occurring or has occurred. Recall that *Whren* authorizes an officer who observes a minor traffic violation—a burned-out taillight, a cracked windshield, or failure to signal when changing lanes—to legally stop the driver even if the officer's actual intent is to look for evidence of drug offenses or other more serious offenses. Because minor traffic violations are so common, some commentators have suggested that *Whren* gives police virtually unlimited authority to stop any vehicle they wish to stop.

The basic premise of *Whren* was reaffirmed by the Supreme Court in *Arkansas v. Sullivan*, 532 U.S. 769 (2001):

> The Arkansas Supreme Court's holding to that effect [e.g., the officer's pretextual stop and arrest violated the Fourth Amendment] cannot be squared with our decision in *Whren*, in which we noted our "unwilling[ness] to entertain Fourth Amendment challenges based on the actual motivations of individual officers," and held unanimously that "[s]ubjective intentions play no role in ordinary, probable-cause Fourth Amendment analysis." That *Whren* involved a traffic stop, rather than a custodial arrest, is of no particular moment; indeed, *Whren* itself relied on *United States v. Robinson*, for the proposition that "a traffic-violation arrest . . . [will] not be rendered invalid by the fact that it was 'a mere pretext for a narcotics search.'" 532 U.S. at 771–72 (italics supplied).

Note that though *Whren* and *Sullivan* allow pretextual stops when an officer has probable cause that a traffic violation is being or has been committed, the Court in *Whren* did emphasize that racial profiling is unconstitutional:

> We of course agree with petitioners that the Constitution prohibits selective enforcement of the law based on considerations such as race. But the constitutional basis for objecting to intentionally discriminatory application of laws is the Equal Protection Clause, not the Fourth Amendment. Subjective intentions play no role in ordinary, probable-cause Fourth Amendment analysis. 517 U.S. at 813.

Profiling at Borders Regarding the use of race, or ethnicity, and traffic stops by police near the U.S. border, the Supreme Court in *United States v. Brignoni-Ponce*, 422 U.S. 873 (1975) refused to allow the apparent observation by the officer that the occupants of a car were of Mexican ancestry, by itself, justify a stop of that car near the U.S.–Mexican border. The Court did say, however, that Mexican ancestry could be one factor considered by an officer in deciding whether there is reasonable suspicion to stop a car near the U.S.–Mexican border to question occupants about their citizenship status:

> In this case the officers relied on a single factor to justify stopping respondent's car: the apparent Mexican ancestry of the occupants. We cannot conclude that this furnished reasonable grounds to believe that the three occupants were aliens. At best the officers had only a fleeting glimpse of the persons in the moving car, illuminated by headlights. Even if they saw enough to think that the occupants were of Mexican descent, this factor alone would justify neither a reasonable belief that they were aliens, nor a reasonable belief that the car concealed other aliens who were illegally in the country. Large numbers of native-born and naturalized

citizens have the physical characteristics identified with Mexican ancestry, and even in the border area a relatively small proportion of them are aliens. The likelihood that any given person of Mexican ancestry is an alien is high enough to make Mexican appearance a relevant factor, but standing alone it does not justify stopping all Mexican-Americans to ask if they are aliens. 422 U.S. at 886–87.

Disparate Enforcement of Traffic Laws Many members of racial and ethnic groups and organizations that represent their interests claim that police are abusing their broad discretion by targeting members of these groups in the unequal enforcement of traffic laws. A rash of articles, speeches, and other commentary condemn the practice of racial profiling and what have sarcastically been described as the "new" crimes of driving while black or brown (DWB) and, by extension, walking, idling, standing, shopping, and breathing while black or brown (e.g., Harris 1997; Kowalski and Lundman 2007). The issue of racial profiling has engendered much anger, fear, resentment, and mistrust on the part of minorities and has contributed to disintegrating police–community relations in many areas of the country.

The extent of the racial profiling problem is in dispute. Recent polls indicate that the majority of Americans, black and white, believe the problem is real and widespread. Also, some studies support the notion that racial profiling exists. For example, an investigation of racial profiling by the attorney general of New Jersey resulted in the conclusion that "minority motorists have been treated differently [by New Jersey State Troopers] than nonminority motorists during the course of traffic stops on the New Jersey Turnpike." (Verniero and Zoubek 1999). Also, a 2006 study in Missouri showed that African American and Hispanic drivers were stopped more frequently than their white counterparts, given their representation in the overall state population:

> For example, the likelihood that an African-American motorist was stopped is 1.57 times that of a white motorist. . . . In other words, African-Americans were 57 percent more likely than Whites to be stopped in [Missouri] in 2006. (Koster 2006)

However, in many of the reports entitled "Contacts Between Police and the Public," which themselves are based on extensive survey data, the Bureau of Justice Statistics (BJS) within the U.S. Department of Justice found that white, African American, and Hispanic drivers were stopped at similar rates, though African American and Hispanic drivers were more frequently *searched* after being stopped:

> In both 2002 and 2005 police searched about 5 percent of stopped drivers. In 2005 police searched 9.5 percent of stopped Blacks and 8.8 percent of stopped Hispanics, compared to 3.6 percent of White motorists. While the survey found that Black and Hispanic drivers were more likely than Whites to be searched, such racial disparities do not necessarily demonstrate that police treat people differently based on race or other demographic characteristics. This study did not take into account other factors that might explain these disparities. (U.S. Department of Justice 2007)

In addition, in a similar, more recent report, the BJS found that "White (8.4%), Black (8.8%) and Hispanic (9.1%) drivers were stopped by police at similar rates in 2008." However, "Black drivers were about three times as likely as White drivers and about two times as likely as Hispanic drivers to be *searched* during a traffic stop" (Eith and Durose 2011: 1). Finally, and significantly, in its most recent report on the issue of differences in the rate of vehicle stops and searches among racial or ethnic groups, the BJS discovered that "[r]elatively more black drivers (13%) than white (10%) and Hispanic (10%) drivers were pulled over in a traffic stop during their most recent contact with police." Moreover, the report noted that during the course of these stops, "White drivers were both *ticketed* and *searched* at lower rates than black and Hispanic drivers" (Durose and Langton 2013) (italics added).

To more accurately determine the extent of the problem, many state legislatures have enacted statutes providing for the collection of statistical data on racial profiling. These laws require law enforcement agencies to collect information on vehicle stops, including number of persons stopped, race and ethnicity of persons stopped, reasons for the stops, and actions taken by officers as a result of the stops. For example, the Missouri report on racial profiling previously discussed was issued in response to a state statute requiring the collection of statistical data on racial profiling. If a law enforcement agency in Missouri fails to collect and report the required data, the governor can withhold state funds from the agency. In addition, law enforcement agencies throughout the country are establishing official policies against racial profiling and are integrating discussion about racial profiling into diversity and refresher training for their officers.

At the federal level, the U.S. Department of Justice issued guidelines in 2003 which prohibit federal law enforcement agents from using race or ethnicity in making routine traffic stops.

> In making routine or spontaneous law enforcement decisions, such as ordinary traffic stops, Federal law enforcement officers may not use race or ethnicity to any degree, except that officers may rely on race and ethnicity in a specific suspect description [that is trustworthy]. This prohibition applies even where the use of race or ethnicity might otherwise be lawful (U.S. Department of Justice 2003).

Some groups have recently called for these guidelines to be reformed. For example, these groups support the expansion of the guidelines to include protection against profiling for religious minorities, the targets of national security investigations by the United States government, and for those at the country's borders (see Murphy and Shamsi 2014).

In July 2013, a member of the U.S. Congress, Representative John Conyers, introduced legislation called the End Racial Profiling Act of 2013 directed toward ending racial bias in law enforcement. This legislation has not yet become law, but it could be reintroduced during a subsequent session of Congress (as has happened in the past with this particular legislation). It seeks to ban racial profiling at all levels of law enforcement and conditions the receipt of federal money by law enforcement agencies on their making efforts to eliminate the practice. The legislation provides grants to police departments to improve their internal practices and policies related to racial profiling. It also requires departments to collect data on racial profiling and offer racial profiling prevention training. Moreover, it provides victims of racial profiling with legal tools to hold law enforcement agencies accountable. Finally, the attorney general is required by the legislation to report regularly to Congress on the data collection results. *See* 113th Congress, H.R. 2851, End Racial Profiling Act of 2013 (ERPA).

Discrimination Lawsuits for Profiling   Increasingly, citizens who claim to be the subjects of racial profiling are bringing lawsuits against the police, alleging violations of their constitutional rights as guaranteed by the Fourth, Fifth, and Fourteenth Amendments. One example is *Stewart v. City and County of Denver,* 2000 WL 130703 (10th Cir. 2000). Although the circuit court upheld the trial court's grant of summary judgment for the defendants—namely, the municipality that employed the police officers involved in the traffic stop—the case suggested what may be necessary to establish a claim of racial profiling by a city's police force. In order to bring a constitutional claim against a police force, the court in *Stewart* indicated that the plaintiff must make a specific showing of a police custom or practice in the municipality to treat a minority group such as African Americans differently than others. The plaintiff must present sufficient evidence regarding the existence of a continuing, persistent, and widespread practice of unconstitutional conduct by the city's employees.

And though the plaintiff in this case was not successful in proving a discriminatory practice or custom by the city, the circuit court, in a related action, upheld the denial of qualified immunity for two individual officers involved in the traffic stop, thereby paving the way for these officers to be subject to a civil lawsuit by the plaintiff for violation of his equal protection rights.

Police officers may also bring racial discrimination suits against their employers, such as the police department or municipality (city, county, etc.) that employs them. *See Carney v. Denver*, 534 F.3d 1269 (10th Cir. 2008) ("In racial discrimination suits [such as this one by an African American female police officer, Ms. Carney, against the City of Denver, arising out of alleged discriminatory conduct by the city's police department], the elements of a plaintiff's case are the same whether that case is brought under [any one of various federal statutes]. To make out a prima facie case of discrimination, [Ms. Carney] must demonstrate (1) membership in a protected class, (2) adverse employment action, and (3) disparate treatment among similarly situated employees. Additionally, in order for municipal liability to arise [against the City/municipality], Ms. Carney must demonstrate that the City's officials acted pursuant to a custom or policy of discriminatory employment practices.") 534 F.3d at 1273 (internal quotations and citations omitted).

In addition to individuals filing race-related suits, organizations such as the American Civil Liberties Union (ACLU) and the National Association for the Advancement of Colored People (NAACP) have filed class-action suits seeking significant monetary damages for violations of constitutional rights in the racial profiling context. These organizations may also ask a court to issue a declaration or injunction to stop racial profiling and other discriminatory practices by police. *See, e.g., Maryland State Conference of NAACP Branches v. Md. Dept. State Police*, 72 F. Supp. 2d 560 (D. Md. 1999); *Rodriguez v. Cal. Highway Patrol*, 89 F. Supp. 2d 1131 (N.D. Cal. 2000); *Melendez v. Maricopa County*, 2009 WL 2707241 (D. Ariz. 2009), at *1–*2 ("Plaintiffs are Somos America [We Are America], an immigrant advocacy group, and five Latino individuals, all of whom are either United States citizens or are lawfully present in the United States. Each of the individual Plaintiffs has been stopped, detained, questioned, and/or searched by [Maricopa County, Arizona Sheriff's Office, or MSCO] officers, allegedly in violation of their constitutional and statutory rights. According to the allegations in Plaintiffs' Complaint, in each of these instances the MCSO officers were acting pursuant to an officially-sanctioned policy, pattern, and practice of racially profiling, targeting, or otherwise discriminating against Latinos. Plaintiffs . . . seek . . . a declaration that Defendants have engaged in racial profiling and discriminatory treatment of Latino persons through illegal stops, detentions, questioning, searches, and arrests. Plaintiffs also seek to enjoin Defendants from continuing to engage in discriminatory practices.").

"Show Me Your Papers" Laws   Class-action lawsuits have also been instituted recently to challenge an increasing number of state laws allowing police, under certain circumstances, to check the immigration status of persons who have been lawfully detained (informally known as "show me your papers" laws). These lawsuits allege that these new state laws essentially encourage racial profiling by police. For example, one Arizona law *requires* an officer who has made a

> "lawful stop, detention or arrest . . . in the enforcement of any other law
> or ordinance of a county, city or town or [the State of Arizona]" to make a
> "reasonable attempt" to determine the immigration status of the person who has
> been stopped, detained or arrested, whenever "reasonable suspicion exists that
> the person is an alien and is unlawfully present." Ariz. Rev. Stat. § 11-1051(B)
> [HB 2162, 2(B) of SB 1070].

Most of this law was declared unconstitutional in *United States v. Arizona*, 703 F. Supp. 2d 890 (D. Ariz. 2010), *aff'd*, 2011 WL 1346945 (9th Cir. 2011). In June 2012, the U.S. Supreme Court issued its own opinion regarding this law, which was titled

LO6

KEY POINTS

■ Many states and the federal government have rules prohibiting racial profiling by law enforcement officers. Many states require law enforcement agencies to collect statistical data on racial profiling. Courts are increasingly receptive to arguments by plaintiffs that they have been targets of racial profiling or similar forms of discrimination and may exclude evidence, order police to stop profiling, or subject offending officers to civil rights lawsuits.

Arizona v. United States, 132 S. Ct. 2492 (2012). Although the Court blocked the majority of the provisions of SB 1070 from going into effect, Section 2(B) of SB 1070 was generally upheld by the Court:

> The Supreme Court allowed [Section 2(B)] to go forward at this early stage of the litigation, but set limits. The Court said that state and local law enforcement officers DO have some authority to question people they stop about their immigration status. However, the Court also said that there would be constitutional concerns if the police prolong detention of a person just to verify their immigration status. The Court also left the door open for future constitutional challenges based on racial profiling or other arguments that the Court did not look at in *Arizona v. United States*. (National Immigration Law Center 2012b)

As a result of Section (2)(B) going into effect in Arizona, the ACLU and other advocacy groups have challenged how the law was being enforced. In one major settlement, the South Tucson Police Department agreed to a host of policy restrictions limiting its officers' activities under the controversial law. Similar lawsuits were filed in Alabama and Georgia challenging laws modeled after the one adopted in Arizona. Settlements of some portions of these lawsuits blocked significant portions of the laws from taking effect. And although the "show me your papers" provisions of these laws remain viable for now, settlement provisions limit officers from not stopping or detaining any person in those states for the sole purpose of determining his or her immigration status (Chishti & Hipsman 2013).

Finally, law enforcement officers should be aware that targeting a person solely on the basis of race or ethnicity could result in suppression of evidence or civil liability. *See United States v. Jones*, 242 F.3d 215 (4th Cir. 2001) (suppressing drug evidence because officer stopped a car based on an uncorroborated tip, and his observation that the car had four African American occupants).

Detentions, the USA PATRIOT Act, and the War on Terror

The USA PATRIOT Act, the Authorization for Use of Military Force (AUMF) Act, and the National Defense Authorization Act (NDAA), all of which were enacted by the U.S. Congress, have broadened the government's power to detain individuals suspected of terrorism within and outside the United States for long periods of time.

Enemy Combatants, the AUMF, and the NDAA

In response to the terrorist attacks on the United States on September 11, 2001, both the legislative and executive branches of the U.S. government took actions to prevent future attacks on the country. Congress enacted the "Authorization for Use of Military Force" (AUMF) in which Congress authorized the president:

> [T]o use all necessary and appropriate force against those nations, organizations, or persons he determines planned, authorized, committed, or aided the terrorist attacks that occurred on September 11, 2001, or harbored such organizations or persons, in order to prevent any future acts of international terrorism against the United States by such nations, organizations, or persons." Pub. L. 107–40, 115 Stat. 224 (2001).

Pursuant to this grant of war authority, former president George W. Bush signed an executive order authorizing the indefinite detention and military trial of people who are suspected terrorists at "an appropriate location" outside of the United States as determined by the U.S. secretary of defense. *See* Detention, Treatment, and Trial of Certain Non-Citizens in the War Against Terrorism, 3 C.F.R. § 918 (2002). The people detained under this executive order came to be known as enemy combatants, although the technical definition of that term has evolved since then to include "an individual who was part of or supporting Taliban or al Qaeda forces, or associated forces that are engaged in hostilities against the United States or its coalition partners" (Wolfowitz Memorandum, 2004: ¶ a). U.S. courts have continued to uphold the legality of the detention of enemy combatants at Guantanamo Bay, Cuba and elsewhere under the AUMF to this day. *See, e.g.,* Gov't Filing, *In re: Guantanamo Bay Detainee Litigation*, Misc. No. 08-442 (D.D.C. March 13, 2009); *Al-Bihani v. Obama*, 2010 WL 10411 at *3 (D.C. Cir. Jan. 5, 2010); *Janko v. Gates*, 741 F.3d 136, 138 (D.C. Cir. 2014).

In addition, this authority to detain enemy combatants under the AUMF has been explicitly recognized in recent legislation passed by the U.S. Congress, which is known as the 2014 National Defense Authorization Act, or "NDAA." The NDAA gives the Armed Forces of the United States power to detain enemy combatants "without trial until the end of the hostilities authorized by the AUMF." The NDAA also gives the U.S. military the authority to try enemy combatants before military commissions, or transfer them to the "custody and control" of other countries. *See* 2014 NDAA §§1021 (a)–(c), (e) & 1022. Some groups both in the United States and elsewhere have been concerned that the broad detention authority provided by the NDAA can be used by the U.S. government and military to justify not only the potential, indefinite detention of foreign enemy combatants but also U.S. citizens, including those arrested or captured on U.S. soil. For example, regarding the original detention provision that was in the NDAA law passed by Congress and signed by the President (this provision is substantially similar to the current one), one concerned organization commented in the following way:

> President Obama signed the National Defense Authorization Act (NDAA) into law today. The statute contains a sweeping worldwide indefinite detention provision. While President Obama issued a signing statement saying he had "serious reservations" about the provisions, the statement only applies to how his administration would use the authorities granted by the NDAA, and would not affect how the law is interpreted by subsequent administrations. The statute . . . has no temporal or geographic limitations, and can be used by this and future presidents to militarily detain people captured far from any battlefield. (ACLU 2011; see also Lennard 2013).

And though President Obama did initially express reservations regarding the detention provisions contained within the NDAA law, his administration has recently succeeded in court in challenging an attempt by certain individuals to have the provisions overturned. Notably, however, the U.S. Court of Appeals for the Second Circuit held that the NDAA detention provisions do not apply to U.S. citizens or individuals detained on U.S. soil. *Hedges v. Obama*, 724 F.3d 170, 192 (2d Cir. 2013) (finding that though individual plaintiffs lacked legal grounds, or "standing," to challenge the detention provisions within the NDAA, the provisions as written do not apply to "citizens, lawful resident aliens, or individuals captured or arrested in the United States"). Final determination of this issue ultimately awaits a future U.S. Supreme Court decision.

The Geneva Conventions

A body of international law collectively referred to as the Geneva Conventions has developed over the centuries to set rules for the treatment of civilians, the sick, and prisoners of war (POWs) captured on the battlefield in war time (Schindler and Toman 2004).

The designation of an individual as a POW is highly relevant because POWs are afforded significant protection. Upon receiving POW status, one can no longer be considered a target and receives full combat immunity. Moreover, POWs must "at all times be humanely treated" and cannot be denied medical treatment (Article 13). Significantly, Article 17 also states: "no physical or mental torture, nor any other form of coercion, may be inflicted on prisoners of war to secure from them information of any kind whatever." They cannot be held in danger in a combat zone (Article 19), cannot be used as human shields (Article 23), and must be quartered under the same, or as favourable, conditions as forces of the detaining power who are in the same area (Article 25).

Common Article 3 [of the Geneva Conventions] demands minimal humanitarian guarantees for those detained or placed hors de combat, and thus specifically prohibits all kinds of murder, cruel treatment, and torture. Finally, although the wording does not expressly require fair hearings, the [prohibition against the] "passing of sentences and the carrying out of executions without previous judgment pronounced by a regularly constituted court affording all the judicial guarantees which are recognized as indispensable by civilized peoples," suggests a high-level of procedural fairness (Falk 2007: 33–34).

Enemy Combatants and the Guantanamo Detention Facility

At first, most enemy combatants were held as prisoners at the U.S. military base in Guantanamo Bay, Cuba. During this time, the United States maintained that the Geneva Convention norms did not apply to enemy combatants being held at Guantanamo, and that the combatants had no right to have their detentions reviewed by the courts of the United States. However, in *Hamdi v. Rumsfeld*, 542 U.S. 507 (2004), the U.S. Supreme Court ruled that enemy combatants who are U.S. citizens have the right to have their detentions reviewed by an impartial judge as part of the guarantees of both due process and *habeas corpus*. *Rasul v. Bush*, 542 U.S. 466 (2004), decided by the U.S. Supreme Court the same day as *Hamdi*, held that non-U.S. citizens held at Guantanamo also had the right to use *habeas corpus* to have federal courts review the legality of their detentions as enemy combatants.

In response to *Hamdi* and *Rasul*, the Department of Defense created Combatant Status Review Tribunals (CSRTs) to review the legality of enemy combatant detentions at Guantanamo (Parry 2007). These *ex parte* proceedings (meaning they took place without the accused or his or her counsel present), were declared unconstitutional by the U.S. Supreme Court in *Hamdan v. Rumsfeld*, 548 U.S. 557 (2006). In response to that ruling, Congress enacted the Detainee Treatment Act (DTA) of 2005, which legislatively authorized the use of CSRTs with the addition of certain procedural safeguards that were not originally included by the Department of Defense when it initially created the tribunals. The DTA specifically provided that the decisions of CSRTs are not reviewable by means of *habeas corpus*, but that the D.C. Circuit Court of Appeals has the limited power to judicially review "whether the decision of the CSRT was consistent with standards and procedures developed by the Secretary of Defense, and whether those standards and procedures are themselves consistent with federal law" (Parry 2006: 772, citing Pub. L. No. 109–48, § 1005(e)(2), 119 Stat. 2680, 2742 (2006)).

In addition to the detention of enemy combatants at Guantanamo Bay, Cuba, the United States has also been detaining enemy combatants at numerous covert detention centers around the world, some of which are run as secret prisons by the CIA (Hafetz 2006). The people being held outside the United States are now subject to the same procedures applicable to enemy combatants at Guantanamo Bay because Congress enacted the Military Commissions Act in 2006. This law extended the procedures of CSRTs to all non-U.S. citizens being held as enemy combatants anywhere in the world (Parry 2006: 772, citing Pub. L. No. 109–366, §§ 7(a), 10, 120 Stat. 2600, 2635–36 (2006)).

In *Boumediene v. Bush*, 553 U.S. 723 (2008), the U.S. Supreme Court held that the part of the Military Commissions Act of 2006 suspending *habeas corpus* for enemy combatants, including the Guantanamo Bay detainees, was unconstitutional. In response to this ruling, Congress passed the Military Commissions Act of 2009, which provides increased due process rights for the Guantanamo detainees, including the important *habeas corpus* right.

After President Obama took office on January 20, 2009, he suspended the military commission tribunals pending a comprehensive review of the status of each individual detained at Guantanamo. A year later, the Guantanamo Review Task Force issued its final report, indicating that its members had reached decisions on the appropriate disposition of the 240 detainees in Guantanamo at the time: 126 were approved for transfer to other countries; 36 were referred for prosecution; 48 were approved for continued detention under the AUMF; and 30 detainees from Yemen were approved for "conditional" detention based on present security conditions in Yemen.

Of the 36 Guantanamo detainees referred for prosecution, the task force determined that

- 1 detainee (Ahmed Ghailani) has been transferred to the United States District Court for the Southern District of New York and will be tried for his alleged role in the 1998 bombings of the U.S. embassies in Kenya and Tanzania. [Note: In 2011, this detainee was convicted by the District Court for his role in these bombings and received a sentence of life imprisonment without the possibility of parole. This conviction and sentence were upheld on appeal.]

- 5 detainees will be tried in the Southern District of New York, for their alleged roles in the September 11 attacks, as announced by the Attorney General.

- 6 detainees will be tried for offenses under the laws of war in a reformed military commission system [with enhanced due process rights], as announced by the Attorney General.

- 24 detainees remain under review pursuant to the joint Department of Justice–Department of Defense protocol. No final determination has yet been made as to whether or in what forum these 24 detainees will be charged.

  (U.S. Department of Justice et al. 2010). *Final Report of Guantanamo Review Task Force*, at 11–12 [hereinafter "Final Report"]. *See also New York Times,* January 26, 2011, A18; *New York Times*, October 25, 2013, A21.

Though the final report revealed the president's preference for the trial of Guantanamo detainees in U.S. federal courts as well as a legal presumption that trials would actually occur in that forum, it also reflected a formal process by which the Departments of Defense and Justice would decide whether, in individual detainee cases, prosecution of the detainee would be better suited before a military commission (or a federal court). The ultimate determination on the exact forum in which the detainee will be prosecuted resides with the U.S. attorney general in consultation with the secretary of defense.

Despite the rather comprehensive and aggressive set of goals of both the president and the task force for the Guantanamo detainees, practical realities have thus far impeded their full realization. As of the spring of 2014, Congress continues to block any additional transfers into the United States of Guantanamo Bay detainees, whether for trial in federal courts, continued detention or for any other purpose. This prohibition against allowing detainees into the United States, presumably over security concerns, has, in part, prevented the ultimate closure of the Guantanamo detention facility (along with other reasons such as the difficulty in transferring detainees to other countries). However, Congress did recently provide the president with increased flexibility to transfer detainees abroad to other countries in the reauthorization of the NDAA.

In response to Congress's ongoing, continued refusal to allow Guantanamo detainees to be tried in federal courts in the United States, President Obama in a March 2011 executive order lifted the ban on charging detainees before military commissions. New military trials, with increased due process protections for the detainees selected for these trials, were ordered to resume at Guantanamo Bay. In addition, the president mandated that periodic reviews occur for those individuals who remain detained at Guantanamo and, significantly, that these detainees be protected under the norms previously described in the Geneva Conventions. Specifically, their status must be periodically reviewed for a determination whether they remain a threat to U.S. security, should be scheduled for trial by military tribunal, or should be released. *See* Executive Order—*Periodic Review of Individuals Detained at Guantanamo Bay Naval Station Pursuant to the "AUMF"* (March 7, 2011).

Though as of late spring 2014 more than 140 individuals remain detained at Guantanamo, recent, limited progress has been made in transferring certain detainees from the detention facility to other countries, and in trying and convicting before military commissions other detainees under the Military Commissions Act of 2009:

> In [a] May 2013 speech, President Obama had restated his commitment to closing the Guantánamo detention facility [by transferring certain detainees out of the facility to other countries]. [He appointed] a new senior envoy at the State Department and Defense Department whose sole responsibility [is] to achieve the transfer of detainees, and that he was lifting the moratorium on detainee transfers to Yemen [which will now be reviewed on a case-by-case basis].
>
> While the two envoys were subsequently appointed, and there have been 12 detainees transferred from Guantánamo to other countries in the 12 months since President Obama's speech, as of May [21,] 2014 more than 140 detainees remained held at the base without charge or trial, and not a single live Yemeni national had been repatriated or transferred elsewhere since the President's speech (or indeed since July 2010)
>
> Since the speech, charges under the Military Commissions Act of 2009 have been referred against one more detainee, Ahmed Mohammed Ahmed Haza al Darbi. This Saudi Arabian man pled guilty to those charges at a hearing before a military commission judge at Guantánamo in February 2014, while agreeing not to sue the USA in relation to his prior treatment in custody after his rendition from Azerbaijan in 2002. His conviction brought to eight the number of detainees convicted by military commission since detentions began at Guantánamo in January 2002. Six of these eight men were convicted under pretrial plea bargains. Six of the seven detainees currently charged for military commission trials (all but Ahmed al Darbi) are facing a government intending to seek the death penalty. (Amnesty International 2014).

Detention of Aliens Located in the U.S. by Certification upon "Reasonable Grounds to Believe . . ." Noncitizens who are located inside the United States and suspected of terrorism are subject to the USA PATRIOT Act. Pursuant to Section 412 of the act, someone who is not a citizen of the United States, including permanent resident aliens living in the United States, can be detained for a potentially indefinite period of time if the United States attorney general certifies that he has "reasonable grounds to believe" that the noncitizen has engaged in terrorist activity. *See* 8 U.S.C. § 1226a (a)(3) (current through June 2014). Within seven days of the alien's/noncitizen's detention, the attorney general must either (1) ensure that formal proceedings have commenced to remove the alien from the United States or (2) charge the alien with a crime. If the attorney general does not proceed with either of these two options within the allotted timeframe, the noncitizen must be released. Notably, however, the law provides that an alien who has not been formally removed from the United States in a legal proceeding and "whose removal is unlikely in the reasonably foreseeable future, may be detained for additional periods of up to six months . . . if the release of the alien will threaten the national security of the United States or the safety of the community or any person." *See* 8 U.S.C. § 1226a (a)(5) and (6). This rather broad language would appear to give the attorney general considerable authority to detain for a potentially indefinite period certain noncitizen individuals whom the attorney general deems to be a "threat."

The alien who is detained under this law does maintain a limited right to have his or her detention reviewed. For example, "[t]he alien may request each 6 months in writing that the Attorney General reconsider the certification [that the alien is a terrorist] and may submit documents or other evidence in support of that request." In addition, the alien may file a habeas corpus petition to have his detention reviewed by a particular court or judge. An appeal of a final detention order is available to the United States Court of Appeals for the District of Columbia Circuit. *See* 8 U.S.C. § 1226a (b)(1) & (2) & (3).

Some commentators have raised concerns about the constitutionality of this detention provision:

> Section 412 of the USA PATRIOT Act also raises serious due process concerns. It gives the Attorney General new power to detain aliens without a hearing and without a showing that they pose a danger or a flight risk. He need only certify that he has "reasonable grounds to believe" that the alien is "described in" various anti-terrorism provisions of the [Immigration and Nationality Act], and the alien is then subject to potentially indefinite detention. (Cole 2002: 1026)

KEY POINTS

L06

■ The USA PATRIOT Act permits the potential, indefinite detention of enemy combatants who are non-U.S. citizens, including permanent resident aliens, if the United States attorney general certifies that he has "reasonable grounds to believe" that the noncitizen has engaged in terrorist activity. These foreign citizens have a limited right to challenge their detention in court in a *habeas corpus* proceeding.

SUMMARY

A law enforcement officer may stop a person for purposes of investigating possible criminal behavior even though the officer does not have probable cause to arrest the person, so long as the officer has reasonable suspicion to believe that the person is involved in criminal activity. A *stop* is the least intrusive type of seizure of a person under the Fourth Amendment. Only when an officer intentionally, by means of physical force or show of authority, has restrained a person's liberty has a seizure occurred. Also, for a seizure to occur, the person confronted by the officer must submit to the officer's force or show of authority. If, in view of all of the circumstances surrounding the incident, a reasonable person would have believed that he or she was not free to leave, decline an officer's requests, or otherwise terminate the encounter, the person has been seized within the meaning of the Fourth Amendment.

The officer making a stop must be able to justify the stop with specific facts and circumstances indicating possibly criminal behavior. This is sometimes called "reasonable, articulable suspicion of criminal activity." Reasonable suspicion is measured objectively in light of the totality of circumstances. For a valid stop, reasonable suspicion must exist as to a present, past, or impending crime. The investigative detention, or stop, must be reasonable at its inception and last no longer than necessary to achieve its purpose. The investigative methods used must be the least intrusive means reasonably available to verify or dispel the officer's suspicion. The officer, in making a stop, should use no more force than is necessary to carry out the stop, and in all cases the force used should be reasonable.

If an officer has reasonable suspicion to justify a stop of a person and that person subsequently refuses in violation of state law to identify herself, the officer may be permitted to expand the scope of the detention by arresting the person. An officer who has lawfully stopped a motor vehicle may order both the driver and passengers out of the vehicle pending completion of the stop.

A law enforcement officer may stop a person based on an informant's tip if, under the totality of the circumstances, the tip, plus any corroboration of the tip by independent police investigation, carries enough indicia of reliability to provide reasonable suspicion of criminal activity. An anonymous tip that a particular person at a particular location is carrying a gun is not, without more information, sufficient to justify law enforcement officers in stopping and frisking that person. A law enforcement officer may stop a person on the basis of a flyer, bulletin, or radio dispatch issued by another law enforcement agency as long as the issuing law enforcement agency has reasonable suspicion that the person named in the flyer, bulletin, or dispatch is or was involved in criminal activity. Furthermore, an anonymous 911 caller's report that the caller has been run off the road by another vehicle supports a police stop of the vehicle the caller has identified because such a report provides police with reasonable suspicion under the totality of the circumstances that the vehicle's driver is intoxicated.

A law enforcement officer may conduct a protective search for weapons, also called a *frisk*, if the officer has reasonable suspicion that a person is armed and dangerous. A frisk is not automatically authorized whenever there is a stop. The officer must be able to demonstrate, by specific facts and circumstances, a reasonable suspicion that the person is armed and dangerous. Because a frisk may only be performed for protective purposes, it must be limited initially to a pat-down of outer clothing. If a weapon or weapon-like object is detected, or if a nonthreatening object's identity as contraband is immediately apparent to the officer's sense of touch, the officer may reach inside the clothing or pocket and seize the object. For an object's identity as nonthreatening contraband (i.e., drugs) to be immediately apparent to the officer's sense of touch, the officer, upon immediately feeling the object, must have probable cause to believe the object is this type of contraband.

If a law enforcement officer has a reasonable, articulable suspicion that a motor vehicle's occupant is armed and dangerous, the officer may frisk the occupant and search the passenger compartment of the vehicle for weapons. The officer may look in any location in the passenger compartment that a weapon could be found or hidden. The officer may also seize items of evidence other than weapons, if discovered in plain view during the course of such a search (see Chapter 10 for further discussion of plain view doctrine). Evidence of crime seized as the result of a properly conducted frisk is admissible in court.

The test to determine the reasonableness of stopping a vehicle at a highway checkpoint involves balancing the gravity of the public concerns served by the seizure, the degree to which the seizure advances the public interest, and the severity of the interference with individual liberty. Police may not conduct a checkpoint for general law enforcement purposes (i.e., to detect the presence of narcotics or weapons). However, properly conducted checkpoints to detect drunk driving, illegal aliens at the border, and drivers without a valid license (e.g., safety checkpoints) have been upheld by courts. The Supreme Court has also upheld a checkpoint designed to find witnesses to a crime involving a fatality.

A law enforcement officer may detain property for a brief time if the officer has a reasonable, articulable suspicion that the property contains items subject to seizure. The officer may not search the property without a search warrant but may subject the property to a properly conducted canine sniff. A law enforcement officer's physical manipulation of a person's belongings absent at least reasonable suspicion that a container has criminal evidence within it is an unreasonable search under the Fourth Amendment. If an officer with reasonable suspicion to manipulate a container does detect something in the container that he or she has probable cause to believe is contraband, the officer should obtain a judicial warrant before opening and searching the container, absent an emergency.

Many states and the federal government have rules prohibiting racial profiling by law enforcement officers. Many states require law enforcement agencies to collect statistical data on racial profiling. Courts are increasingly receptive to arguments by plaintiffs that they have been targets of racial profiling and may exclude evidence, order police to stop profiling, or subject offending officers to civil rights lawsuits.

The USA PATRIOT Act permits under certain circumstances the indefinite detention of enemy combatants who are non-U.S. citizens, including permanent resident aliens, if the United States attorney general certifies that he or she has "reasonable grounds to believe" that the noncitizen has engaged in terrorist activity.

KEY TERMS

arrest 307
canine sniff (dog sniff) 346
enemy combatants 359
flight 341
frisk 307
furtive gestures 341

Geneva Conventions 359
pretextual stop 351
probable cause 307
racial profiling 353
reasonableness 308
reasonable suspicion 307

seizure 307
seizures tantamount to arrest 307
show of authority 316
"show me your papers" law 357
sobriety checkpoint 352
stop 307

REVIEW AND DISCUSSION QUESTIONS

1. Name some of the factors or circumstances that might distinguish a *Terry*-type investigative stop from police action that would not amount to a seizure under the Fourth Amendment. From your reading of Chapter 7 on arrests and this chapter, what factors or circumstances might distinguish a *Terry* stop from a seizure tantamount to arrest and a full-blown arrest?

2. In determining whether an officer has a reasonable suspicion that criminal activity is afoot, must the officer have a particular crime in mind?

3. Is less evidence required to support an investigative stop for a suspected violent crime than for a minor misdemeanor?

4. Can a lawfully stopped suspect be transported by the police to a crime scene for identification by victims or witnesses? Or would this action convert the stop into a seizure tantamount to arrest?

5. How does the test for evaluating an informant's tip in the stop-and-frisk situation differ from the test in the arrest context established in the *Gates* case discussed in Chapter 3? Why should there be different tests?

6. Must there be an immediate possibility of criminal activity to justify a stop, or would a possibility of criminal activity at some time in the future suffice? What about when an officer has reasonable suspicion of criminal activity as to a past crime?

7. Assuming that a frisk of a person is warranted, how extensive a search is permitted? Can the officer look for razor blades, nails, vials of acid, or Mace containers? Can the officer look into briefcases, shopping bags, purses, hatbands, and other containers?

8. Should an officer conducting a roadblock-type stop to check licenses and registrations be allowed to order every driver stopped out of his or her vehicle? What factors might provide justification to frisk a driver or passengers in this situation?

9. Assuming that a law enforcement officer reasonably believes that a suspect is dangerous and may gain immediate control of weapons from an automobile, how extensive a protective search of the automobile may be made? May the officer look into suitcases and other containers in the passenger compartment? In the trunk?

10. Assume that police receive an anonymous telephone tip that a Middle Eastern woman in her thirties is carrying anthrax and is about to board a train to New York City. Can potential passengers fitting the description be detained? To what extent? Can they be frisked? Can the train be prevented from leaving the station?

11. Would it be reasonable under the Fourth Amendment to subject to a canine sniff every piece of luggage to be carried on a flight to Miami, Florida? Does it matter if the dog is trained as a drug-sniffing dog or a bomb-sniffing dog?

12. If an officer reasonably suspects that an object he feels in a suspect's pocket during a valid frisk is cocaine, may he reach into the pocket and seize it?

13. May police set up a valid roadblock to check for illegal drugs? To find persons without valid documentation to be in the country? To locate eyewitnesses to any crime?

14. What are the consequences for law enforcement officers if they are determined by a court to have engaged in racial profiling or a similar practice?

15. Describe at least one additional legal power, or tool, the U.S. government or military has acquired to detain individuals since the terrorist events of September 11, 2001. What is the source of this power? Who may be detained and under what circumstances (where, for how long, etc.)? May the detained individual(s) challenge his or her detention?

9 Consent Searches

LEARNING OBJECTIVES

LO1 EXPLAIN the benefits of consent search to the law enforcement officer and the person being searched.

LO2 EVALUATE the circumstances that are considered in determining whether a consent search is voluntary.

LO3 DIFFERENTIATE between consent to enter premises and consent to search premises.

LO4 ANALYZE how the scope of a consent search is limited by the person giving consent, the area to which consent to search is given, time, and the expressed object of the search.

LO5 EVALUATE the circumstances under which a third person may be authorized to consent to a search of a person's property and how third-party consent is affected by the person's reasonable expectation of privacy.

Another well-established exception to the search warrant requirement is the **consent search**. A consent search occurs when a person *voluntarily* waives his or her Fourth Amendment rights and allows a law enforcement officer to search his or her body, premises, or belongings:

Police officers act in full accord with the law when they ask citizens for consent. It reinforces the rule of law for the citizen to advise the police of his or her wishes and for the police to act in reliance on that understanding. *United States v. Drayton*, 536 U.S. 194, 207 (2002); *see also Kentucky v. King*, 131 S. Ct. 1849, 1858 (2011) ("Officers may seek consent-based encounters [from citizens] if they are lawfully present in the place where the consensual encounter occurs. If consent is freely [voluntarily] given, it makes no difference that an officer may have approached the person with the hope or expectation of obtaining consent.") (internal quotations omitted).

Voluntary consent prohibits the consenting person from later protesting the search on constitutional grounds. Also, evidence seized as a result of a search for which valid consent is obtained becomes admissible in court, even though there was no warrant and no probable cause to search.

A consent search can benefit a consenting party who is innocent of any wrongdoing. For example, such a search may convince police that it is unnecessary to subject a citizen to the inconvenience and embarrassment of an arrest or more extensive search. *See Schneckloth v. Bustamonte*, 412 U.S. 218 (1973).

Similarly, consent searches can be an effective way for law enforcement authorities to investigate potential misconduct. Officers frequently use consent searches because they are faster than warrant procedures and do not require often difficult determinations of whether there is probable cause, either to search or to arrest. Consent searches, however, also present opportunities for abuse of Fourth Amendment rights by law enforcement officers.

A quotation from a recent U.S. Supreme Court case summarizes nicely both the law enforcement and citizen interests underlying a consent search:

> And certain categories of permissible warrantless searches have long been recognized. Consent searches occupy one of these categories. Consent searches are part of the standard investigatory techniques of law enforcement agencies and are a constitutionally permissible and wholly legitimate aspect of effective police activity. It would be unreasonable—indeed, absurd—to require police officers to obtain a warrant when the sole owner or occupant of a house or apartment voluntarily consents to a search.
>
> The owner of a home has a right to allow others to enter and examine the premises, and there is no reason why the owner should not be permitted to extend this same privilege to police officers if that is the owner's choice. Where the owner believes that he or she is under suspicion, the owner may want the police to search the premises so that their suspicions are dispelled. This may be particularly important where the owner has a strong interest in the apprehension of the perpetrator of a crime and believes that the suspicions of the police are deflecting the course of their investigation. An owner may want the police to search even where they lack probable cause, and if a warrant were always required, this could not be done. And even where the police could establish probable cause, requiring a warrant despite the owner's consent would needlessly inconvenience everyone involved—not only the officers and the magistrate but also the occupant of the premises, who would generally either be compelled or would feel a need to stay until the search was completed.

Fernandez v. California, 134 S. Ct. 1126, 1132 (2014) (internal quotations omitted).

Voluntariness of Consent: The Schneckloth Case

The U.S. Supreme Court has stated that "the Fourth and Fourteenth Amendments require that consent not be coerced, by explicit or implicit means, by implied threat or covert force." *Schneckloth*, 412 U.S. at 228. To date, the Supreme Court has resolved the tension between the effectiveness of consent searches for law enforcement and the potential for governmental abuse and coercion inherent in these searches by requiring that all consent searches be conducted voluntarily:

> Just as was true with confessions the requirement of "voluntary" consent reflects a fair accommodation of the constitutional requirements involved. In examining all the surrounding circumstances to determine if in fact the consent to search was coerced, account must be taken of subtly coercive police questions, as well as the possibly vulnerable subjective state of the person who consents. Those searches that are the product of police coercion can thus be filtered out. *Schneckloth*, 412 U.S. at 228–29.

In *Schneckloth*, Officer Rand stopped a vehicle when he noticed one of its headlights and license plate light were burnt out. Joe Alcala and defendant Robert Bustamonte were in the front seat along with Joe Gonzales, the driver. Three other passengers were in the rear. Only one of the passengers, Joe Alcala, produced identification upon the officer's request. Alcala explained that the car belonged to his brother. After all of the passengers exited the vehicle, Officer Rand asked Alcala for permission to search the car. Alcala responded, "Sure, go ahead." 412 U.S. at 220. Alcala proceeded to assist Officer Rand and two other officers in the search of the car, by opening the trunk and glove compartment. In their search, police officers discovered three stolen checks under the left rear seat.

The U.S. Supreme Court agreed with the California state appellate court that Alcala consented voluntarily to the search of the car. Therefore, the stolen checks found by police could be admitted into evidence, and the defendant, Bustamonte, was convicted of check fraud. The Court explained its holding as follows:

> We hold only that when the subject of a search is not in custody and the State attempts to justify a search on the basis of his consent, the Fourth and Fourteenth Amendments require that it demonstrate that the consent was in fact voluntarily given, and not the result of duress or coercion, express or implied. Voluntariness is a question of fact to be determined from all the circumstances. 412 U.S. at 221, 248–49.

Thus, a prosecuting attorney who attempts to introduce into court evidence obtained as a result of a consent search must prove by a preponderance of the evidence that the consent was voluntary and not the result of duress or coercion, express or implied. *Lego v. Twomey*, 404 U.S. 477, 489 (1972); *United States v. Matlock*, 415 U.S. 164, 177–78 (1974). The remainder of this chapter is devoted to explaining in detail the meaning of the *voluntariness* requirement.

Voluntariness of Consent: Examination of the Totality of the Circumstances

To determine whether consent is voluntary, courts examine the totality of the circumstances, including the following circumstances:

- force, threats of force, and other threats by police;
- submission to a fraudulent or mistaken claim of authority;

- misrepresentation or deception by police;
- arrest or detention of the suspect;
- suspect's knowledge of the right to refuse consent;
- informing suspects that they are free to go;
- clearness and explicitness of the suspect's consent;
- notification by police to the suspect's counsel; and
- advising a suspect about his or her *Miranda* rights.

Force, Threats of Force, and Other Threats

Courts find consent involuntary if law enforcement officers use force, threats of force, or other types of threats to obtain the consent. In *United States v. Al-Azzawy*, 784 F.2d 890 (9th Cir. 1985), the defendant, while kneeling outside his trailer with his hands on his head, gave permission to search the trailer as numerous police officers approached him with guns drawn. The court found that these coercive conditions rendered the consent to search involuntary. Likewise, when police officers ordered suspects to open a door to a warehouse, entered with guns drawn, and demanded that all of the occupants lie on the floor, the court found that the subsequent consent to search the warehouse was involuntary. *See United States v. Morales*, 171 F.3d 978, 983 (5th Cir. 1999); *see also United States v. Poe*, 462 F.3d 997, 1000 (8th Cir. 2006) ("To the extent the government argues that Poe's actions constituted implied consent to [Officer] Graham's entry [into the residence], we disagree. We examine the totality of the circumstances to determine whether consent was voluntary or coerced. Poe [only] opened the door following over ten minutes of persistent knocks and requests by Graham, officers were stationed at both doors of the duplex and [Officer] Northcutt had commanded Poe to open the door. A reasonable person in Poe's situation would have concluded that he had no choice but to acquiesce and open the door. Therefore, Poe's actions did not constitute . . . consent [to police entry].").

Also, in *United States v. Hatley*, 15 F.3d 856, 858 (9th Cir. 1994), the Court found involuntary the defendant's consent given after an officer threatened to take the defendant's child into custody. Lastly, involuntary consent resulted when law enforcement officials threatened defendants with jail time, monetary fines, foreclosure, property damage, or suspension of a driver's license. *See United States v. Waupekenay*, 973 F.2d 1533 (10th Cir. 1992); *Jones v. Unknown Agents of the Fed. Elec. Comm'n*, 613 F.2d 864 (D.C. Cir. 1979); *Lightford v. State*, 520 P.2d 955 (Nev. 1974); *Herzog v. Winnetka*, 309 F.3d 1041, 1044 (7th Cir. 2002).

However, a mere statement by police that they will attempt to obtain a warrant if consent is withheld is usually not considered threatening or coercive behavior. On the other hand, if the police officer indicates that a search warrant can actually be obtained, then the officer's claim should be well founded. For example, the officer should know that probable cause to obtain a search warrant exists. *See United States v. Kaplan*, 895 F.2d 618 (9th Cir. 1990); *see also United States v. Alexander*, 573 F.3d 465, 476–78 (7th Cir. 2009) ("[Officers] advised [defendant] that if she refused consent . . . they would obtain a search warrant [for the apartment]. [A]n officer's factually accurate statement that the police will take lawful investigative action in the absence of cooperation [e.g., consent] is not coercive conduct. There is no reason to doubt that the officers [here] would have obtained a search warrant [based on their probable cause to search] had they applied for one.").

Sometimes the initial encounter between a law enforcement officer and a suspect requires the officer to use force or threat of force for personal or public safety. Despite the coercive nature of the initial confrontation, an officer may still obtain a valid consent to search if the consent itself is obtained without coercion. For example, in *United States v. Alfonso*, 759 F.2d 728 (9th Cir. 1985), police with guns drawn arrested the defendant in his motel room. After determining that no weapons or other persons were in the room, the officers holstered their guns. The officers informed the defendant of the purpose of their investigation and requested consent to search his luggage. The defendant, who was not handcuffed or otherwise restrained, responded that he had "nothing to hide." The court held that the defendant's consent was voluntary, despite the initial armed confrontation. *See also United States v. Wilson*, 605 F.3d 985, 1026–28 (D.C. Cir. 2010). ("Although the raid [by the FBI apparently consisting of bursting into Harris' upstairs bedroom at night, ordering her onto the floor and handcuffing her] itself must have been startling, the agents [who were lawfully present in the residence] did not seek [Harris's] consent to search until she was out of the handcuffs, had dressed, and was seated on the couch. [FBI team leader] Ashby read the consent form to her and made sure she understood that she could choose whether to sign it or not. Moreover, she apparently weighed that decision for several minutes before signing. There was no evidence of any physical coercion, verbal threats, or other conduct that would have impinged on Harris's ability to make a voluntary decision. [T]here was valid consent.").

Submission to a Fraudulent or Mistaken Claim of Authority

A person's submission to a false assertion of authority by a police officer does not constitute a voluntary consent. Allowing a search under these circumstances does not reflect free will on the part of the consenter, but rather a mistaken demonstration of respect for the law. The consent to search is invalid, whether the officer's assertion of authority was mistaken or was deliberately designed to deceive the person.

In *Bumper v. North Carolina*, 391 U.S. 543 (1968), officers went to the home of a rape suspect to look for evidence. The home was owned and occupied by the suspect's grandmother, who let the officers in after they told her that they had a search warrant. The officers found a rifle. At the hearing on the motion to suppress the rifle, the prosecutor relied on the grandmother's consent rather than on the warrant to support the legality of the search. (In fact, no warrant was ever returned, nor was there any information about the conditions under which it was issued). On these facts, the U.S. Supreme Court held that a search cannot be justified on the basis of consent when that consent is obtained only after an untruthful announcement by the officers conducting the search that they have a valid search warrant:

> This burden [to prove voluntary consent] cannot be discharged by showing no more than acquiescence to a claim of lawful authority. A search conducted in reliance upon a warrant cannot later be justified on the basis of consent if it turns out that the warrant was invalid [or nonexistent]. When a law enforcement officer claims authority to search a home under a warrant, he announces in effect that the occupant has no right to resist the search. The situation is instinct with coercion—albeit colorably lawful coercion. Where there is coercion there cannot be consent. 391 U.S. at 548–50.

Similarly, when police merely announce themselves and their intention to search, any subsequent consent they obtain will be deemed involuntary in the absence of a warrant or other valid authorization to search. In *Johnson v. United States*, 333 U.S. 10, 13 (1948), police officers began their search by merely identifying themselves. They later announced their intention to arrest the defendant and search her hotel room. As part of its finding that the defendant did not give a valid consent under these circumstances, the Court said that "[e]ntry to defendant's living quarters, which was the beginning of the search, was demanded under color of office. It was granted in submission to authority rather than as an understanding and intentional waiver of a constitutional right." 333 U.S. at 13.

However, not all "shows of authority" by police officers will result in a finding of involuntary consent. For example, when an individual who is shown to be educated and intelligent clearly indicates to officers his willingness to allow them to view a videotape, then voluntary consent may be found despite an officer's "claim of authority." This was the holding of *United States v. Raibley*, 243 F.3d 1069, 1077 (7th Cir. 2001), where the officer told an incarcerated suspect "we are going to be viewing that tape." Though the Court characterized this language on the part of the officer as a "show of authority," the Court found the suspect's consent to view the tape voluntary because the suspect called the officer to his prison cell to watch the tape. The Court also noted that the officer did not harass the suspect in any way, and that the suspect was an educated and intelligent man who had even published several scholarly articles.

Misrepresentation or Deception

Coercion may also take the form of misrepresentation or deception on matters other than the officer's authority. A person's consent to search based on false impressions created by a law enforcement officer is not voluntary. In *Commonwealth v. Wright*, 190 A.2d 709 (Pa. 1963), officers arrested the defendant for robbery and murder and questioned him at police headquarters, but they obtained no incriminating statements. The next day officers, without a search warrant, went to the defendant's apartment to conduct a search. They falsely told the defendant's wife that the defendant had admitted the crime and had sent the police for the "stuff." The frightened and upset wife admitted the officers to the apartment and led them to money taken in the robbery. The court held that the consent given by the wife for this search by police was not voluntary: "it is well established that the consent may not be gained through stealth, deceit, or misrepresentation, and that if such exists this is tantamount to implied coercion." 190 A.2d at 711. And in *United States v. Escobar*, defendants consented to a search of their travel bags after police officers falsely claimed that a police dog had detected drugs in defendants' bags. The court found that defendants' consent to search the bags following the false claim was involuntary and hence invalid. 389 F.3d 781, 786 (8th Cir. 2004). *C.f. United States v. Khanalizadeh*, 493 F.3d 479, 484 (5th Cir. 2007) (finding the defendant's consent voluntary, in part, because the officer did not deceive the defendant).

If, however, the deceit is carried out by an undercover officer and concerns only the officer's identity as a governmental agent, a person's misplaced confidence in the agent does not make the person's consent involuntary:

> Entry of an undercover agent is not illegal if he enters a home for the "very purposes contemplated by the occupant." . . . If the occupant reveals private information to the visitor under such circumstances, he or she assumes the risk the visitor will reveal it. *United States v. Goldstein*, 611 F. Supp. 624, 626 (N.D. Ill. 1985).

In this regard, lower courts have held that "[a] government agent may obtain an invitation onto property by misrepresenting his identity, and if invited, does not need probable cause nor warrant to enter so long as he does not exceed the scope of his invitation." *United States v. Scherer*, 673 F.2d 176, 182 (7th Cir. 1982). This is primarily because the U.S. Supreme Court has held that entries onto premises by undercover agents do not generally implicate Fourth Amendment privacy interests at all, so long as the owner of the premises permits the entry. *See On Lee v. United States*, 343 U.S. 747 (1952); *Hoffa v. United States*, 385 U.S. 293 (1966).

Arrest or Detention

Even if the consenting party is in custody or is detained, the voluntariness of the consent is still determined by the totality of the circumstances. In *United States v. Watson*, 423 U.S. 411 (1976), the Supreme Court held that a consent to search is not involuntary solely because the person giving the consent is under arrest or otherwise in custody. In addition, in *United States v. Mendenhall*, 446 U.S. 544 (1980), the Supreme Court held that a person subjected to a legal *Terry*-type stop was capable of giving a valid consent to search.

Nevertheless, courts examine very carefully any consent given under circumstances of custody or detention. An arrested or detained person is believed to be "more susceptible to duress or coercion from the custodial officers." *United States v. Richardson*, 388 F.2d 842, 845 (6th Cir. 1968). As a result, it is generally more difficult to prove voluntary consent when the person giving the consent is in custody. For example, if the law enforcement officer subjects the person in custody to additional coercive action—such as handcuffing, display of weapons, or incarceration—or if the officer interrogates the person without giving *Miranda* warnings, a subsequent consent to search is very likely to be ruled involuntary. *United States v. Chan-Jimenez*, 125 F.3d 1324 (9th Cir. 1997) found involuntary a consent by a detained defendant to search a truck on an unpopulated desert highway that was obtained by an officer who requested permission to search with one hand resting on his gun. *See also Liberal v. Estrada*, 632 F.3d 1064, 1082–83 (9th Cir. 2011) (consent to search the vehicle by the defendant in police custody was not voluntary because the defendant was not provided complete *Miranda* warnings or informed he could refuse consent, and he was surrounded at the time by seven officers who were searching the area around his vehicle).

Another issue arising in this area is that if an arrest or detention is *illegal*, courts generally hold that consent to search obtained by exploitation of the illegal conduct is "fruit of the poisonous tree," unless the causal chain between the illegal arrest and the obtaining of consent has been attenuated, or weakened. Courts determine whether the causal chain has been attenuated by considering

- the time elapsed between the illegal arrest and the giving of consent;
- the presence of intervening circumstances between the arrest and the consent, including voluntary actions by the suspect;
- the purpose and flagrancy of the police misconduct surrounding the arrest; and
- whether *Miranda* warnings are given prior to any questioning surrounding the giving of consent. *See, e.g., Brown v. Illinois*, 422 U.S. 590, 603–4 (1975).

In *Florida v. Royer*, 460 U.S. 491 (1983), the defendant purchased a one-way airline ticket under an assumed name and then checked his luggage under this assumed name. As the defendant walked toward the boarding area within the concourse, two detectives approached him because his characteristics and actions fit a "drug courier profile." Upon request, the defendant showed the detectives his airline ticket and driver's license, which carried his correct name. The defendant explained the discrepancy in names by pointing out that a friend had placed the ticket reservation in the assumed name. The detectives, who identified themselves as narcotics investigators, told the defendant that they suspected him of transporting narcotics. Still holding his ticket and license, the detectives asked the defendant to accompany them to a small room near the concourse. Without the defendant's consent, one of the detectives brought the defendant's checked luggage to the room. The defendant did not respond to a request by detectives to consent to a search of the luggage, but he did use a key to unlock one of the suitcases (thereby indicating his consent). Marijuana was found in this suitcase. After the defendant claimed he did not know the combination to a lock on a second suitcase belonging to him, the officers pried it open. The defendant did not object to this action by the detectives. More marijuana was found in the second suitcase. The detectives informed the defendant he was under arrest.

The U.S. Supreme Court in *Royer* found that the defendant was illegally arrested at the time he consented to the search of his luggage because the detectives lacked probable cause for the arrest. They also held that the consent itself was tainted by this illegality and therefore was involuntary:

> Because . . . [the defendant] was being illegally detained when he consented to the search of his luggage, we agree that the consent was tainted by the illegality and was ineffective to justify the search. *Royer*, 460 U.S. at 507–8.

Also, in *United States v. Robles-Ortega*, 348 F.3d 679 (7th Cir. 2003), the Court found that an illegal entry into an apartment without a warrant "tainted" the subsequent written consent to search provided by an individual within that apartment. The Court determined that the consent must be excluded as a result of the illegal entry because

- insufficient time had passed between the illegal entry and consent;
- the police had entered the apartment in a flagrant manner by forcibly breaking down the door, drawing their guns, and ordering all occupants to the floor; and
- the written consent provided was not an intervening circumstance weakening the taint because it had been provided within minutes of the sudden and forceful illegal entry.

However, in *United States v. Wellins*, 654 F.2d 550 (9th Cir. 1981), despite an illegal arrest of the defendant, the court held that a consent to search obtained one and one-quarter hours after the illegal arrest, was valid. The court found that the causal chain between the illegal arrest and consent was weakened by giving the defendant *Miranda* warnings and allowing him to consult with his attorney and codefendant before signing a form granting consent to search.

Similarly, in *United States v. Pineda-Buenaventura*, 622 F.3d 761, 776–77 (7th Cir. 2010), the court found that two co-tenants provided valid consent because any taint from the officers' illegal entry into their apartment had been sufficiently attenuated (weakened) because of both the passage of time and the absence of coercion or flagrant conduct by police:

> Nor do we think that the initial illegal entry tainted the co-tenants' consent in any way. Considering the *Brown* factors, we find that the temporal proximity of the illegal entry and consent, taken together with the intervening circumstances, support the district court's finding that there was no taint. Forty-five minutes transpired between the time of the illegal entry and the co-tenants' verbal consents, and an hour and forty minutes passed between the entry and the written consent. There is no evidence of any coercion taking place during that time [e.g., the defendants were not handcuffed and were allowed to remain surrounded by acquaintances]; conversely, both [co-tenants] were told they did not have to consent if they did not want to. Finally, consideration of the "purpose and flagrancy of the official misconduct" weighs heavily in favor of finding that any taint was purged. The initial entry into [the cotenants'] Apartment B was a mistake on the part of the searching officers, none of whom were aware of the limitation on the warrant. Once the mistake was discovered, officers immediately withdrew from the upstairs unit to determine what should be done next. The initial entry does not appear to have been at all flagrant or purposeful, and it did not taint the co-tenants' subsequent consent.

Knowledge of the Right to Refuse Consent

This section will discuss the landmark case of *Schneckloth v. Bustamonte*, which puts forth the current legal test in the consent to search context.

The Schneckloth Rule Before the U.S. Supreme Court decision in *Schneckloth v. Bustamonte* (discussed earlier), some courts held that, to prove voluntary consent to search, the prosecution had to show that the person giving consent knew of the right to refuse consent. Other courts ruled that knowledge of the right to refuse consent was only one factor to be considered in determining voluntariness. In *Schneckloth*, the U.S. Supreme Court adopted the latter view, in which knowledge of the right to refuse consent constitutes one factor among others in the overall determination of voluntary consent. In particular, the Court commented, "Voluntariness is a question of fact to be determined from all the circumstances, and while the subject's knowledge of a right to refuse is a factor to be taken into consideration, the prosecution is not required to demonstrate such knowledge as a prerequisite to establishing a voluntary consent." 412 U.S. at 248–49.

Strictly speaking, a law enforcement officer seeking to obtain a valid consent to search from a person does not need to warn that person of his or her right to refuse consent. Nevertheless, even though formal warnings are not required for consent searches, the U.S. Supreme Court still considers a person's knowledge of the right to refuse consent as very persuasive evidence of voluntariness. For example, in *United States v. Mendenhall*, 446 U.S. 544 (1980), the Court placed special emphasis on the officers warning the defendant of her right to refuse consent in reaching its holding that defendant voluntarily consented to a search of her person and handbag. In particular, the Court commented that

> it is especially significant that the respondent was twice expressly told that she was free to decline to consent to the search, and only thereafter explicitly consented to it. Although the Constitution does not require [knowledge of the right to refuse consent], such knowledge was highly relevant to the determination that there had been consent. And, perhaps more important for present purposes, the fact that the officers themselves informed the respondent that she was free to withhold her consent substantially lessened the probability that their conduct could reasonably have appeared to her to be coercive. 446 U.S. at 558, 559.

Lower courts have also noted the importance of warning defendants of their right to refuse consent. In the case of *In re Joe R.*, 612 P.2d 927 (Cal. 1980), the court found voluntary consent to search despite the presence of several officers with drawn guns, because the officers explained the right to refuse consent. *See also United States v. Wilson,* 605 F.3d 985, 1026–28 (D.C. Cir. 2010) (despite "startling" entry into a home by FBI agents apparently consisting of bursting into the upstairs bedroom of a female homeowner at night, ordering the homeowner onto the floor and handcuffing her, the homeowner's consent to search her home was voluntary because, among other factors, she was informed of her right to refuse consent to search).

In contrast, *United States v. Jones*, 846 F.2d 358, 360–61 (6th Cir. 1988), found the consent involuntary in coercive circumstances, because the police failed to apprise the defendant, who had no formal education, of his *Miranda* rights or his right to refuse consent. The coercive environment in *Jones* consisted of police obtaining defendant's consent to search for a gun in his vehicle and home while three police patrol cars blocked defendant's vehicle, and officers ordered defendant to return to his home in their presence.

Applying *Schneckloth* to People in Police Custody   A person who is in police custody can voluntarily consent to a search without being warned of the right to refuse consent, though the warning remains a factor in the overall voluntariness inquiry. In *United States v. Watson*, 423 U.S. 411 (1976), the U.S. Supreme Court found a consent to search given by a defendant arrested in public valid, even though the defendant received no formal warnings of his right to refuse consent. In particular, the Court in *Watson* commented that "the absence of proof that [the arrested defendant] knew he could withhold his consent, though it may be a factor in the overall judgment, is not to be given controlling significance." 423 U.S. at 424. For the *Watson* Court, the lack of any explicit or implicit threats by police against defendant, the public nature of the arrest, and defendant's personal characteristics and background, all contributed to its finding of voluntary consent.

Although nearly all states follow the *Schneckloth* totality-of-the-circumstances test (and therefore conform to the "federal approach" previously discussed), a handful of states require that consenting persons be aware of their right to refuse consent in addition to requiring that the consent be voluntary. *See State v. Johnson*, 346 A.2d 66, 68 (N.J. 1975); *Penick v. State*, 440 So.2d 23 (Miss. 1991).

In particular, the New Jersey Supreme Court expanded its holding in *Johnson* in 2002 in the context of traffic stops, when it set a requirement that officers must have reasonable, articulable suspicion to believe criminal evidence exists within a vehicle before requesting consent to search a vehicle. *State v. Carty*, 790 A.2d 903, 905 (N.J. 2002); *see also State v. Elders*, 927 A.2d 1250, 1266 (N.J. 2007) (adopting same standard in New Jersey for consent to search a disabled vehicle). Still other states take a different approach. Oklahoma, for example, requires that individuals be given *Miranda* warnings before their consent to search can be obtained. Yet, Oklahoma does not require that persons in custody be specifically told that they have the right to refuse consent to search. *Case v. State*, 519 P.2d 523 (Okla. Crim. App. 1974). Arkansas also strongly favors officers informing residential occupants of their right to refuse consent prior to requesting consent to search the residence. *State v. Brown*, 156 S.W.3d 722, 732 (Ark. 2004) ("While we do not hold that the Arkansas Constitution requires execution of a written consent form which contains a statement that the home dweller has the right to refuse consent, this undoubtedly would be the better practice for law enforcement to follow.") Finally, the State of Washington has also departed from the *Schneckloth* rule by requiring that home occupants be informed of their right to refuse consent prior to police attempts to obtain consent from these occupants to search the home:

> [W]hen police officers conduct a knock and talk for the purpose of obtaining consent to search a home, and thereby avoid the necessity of obtaining a warrant, they must, prior to entering the home, inform the person from whom consent is sought that he or she may lawfully refuse to consent to the search and that they can revoke, at any time, the consent that they give, and can limit the scope of the consent to certain areas of the home. The failure to provide these warnings, prior to entering the home, vitiates any consent given thereafter. *State v. Ferrier*, 960 P.2d 927, 934 (Wash. 1998).

For a discussion of the impact state departures from the *Schneckloth* rule have had on law enforcement (e.g., when a state requires police to warn suspects of their right to refuse consent to search), see Phillips (2008, p. 1186) ("Several states' courts have interpreted their Constitutions to require law enforcement to warn subjects of their right to refuse consent before a subsequent search may be deemed valid. A review of the experience of these states indicates that a warning requirement is practical, even when accompanied by stringent administrative requirements of data tracking, supervision, and oversight—effective law enforcement is not impeded, and the informality of the encounter is not disrupted. This refutation of the Court's impracticality argument [in *Schneckloth*] explains why there is no [practical] impediment to requiring an effective warning.").

Informing Suspects That They Are Free to Go

In *Ohio v. Robinette*, 519 U.S. 33 (1996), the defendant was legally stopped for speeding and the officer asked for and was handed the defendant's license. The officer ran a computer check, which indicated that the defendant had no previous violations. The officer then asked the defendant to step out of his car, turned on his mounted video camera, issued a verbal warning, and returned his license. After receiving a negative response to questions about the defendant's possession of drugs or weapons, the officer requested and obtained consent to search his car. The officer found drugs in the car. The defendant contended that a lawfully seized person must be advised that he is free to go before his consent to search will be recognized as voluntary. The U.S. Supreme Court disagreed with the defendant:

> [J]ust as it "would be thoroughly impractical to impose on the normal consent search the detailed requirements of an effective warning," . . . so too would it be unrealistic to require police officers to always inform detainees that they are free to go before a consent to search may be deemed voluntary. 519 U.S. at 39–40.

Thus, whether police inform suspects that they are free to go is just one factor that can be considered by courts in the overall determination of whether a suspect voluntarily consented to a search. After *Ohio v. Robinette*, courts can still find voluntary consent in the absence of police informing suspects that they are free to go.

Clearness and Explicitness of Consent

Another issue in determining the voluntariness of consent is whether the expression of consent is clear, explicit, and unequivocal. Hesitation or ambiguity in giving consent could indicate that the consent is not voluntary. On the other hand, when a suspect clearly cooperates with law enforcement in their efforts to search a particular place, courts will be more inclined to find voluntary consent. *See United States v. Farrior*, 535 F.3d 210, 219 (4th Cir. 2008) (finding voluntary consent to search defendant's car, in part, because defendant cooperated with patrol officer during traffic stop).

Both written and oral consent to search are equally effective in waiving a person's right to later object to the search on constitutional grounds. A signed and witnessed writing or an electronically recorded oral statement provides the best proof of a clear, voluntary waiver of a known right. A written or recorded consent is also the best way to refute challenges later raised by the defendant.

CRIMINAL PROCEDURE IN ACTION

How Should One Interpret Robinette's Free-to-Leave Test?
United States v. Guerrero, 472 F.3d 784 (10th Cir. 2007)

"On Jan. 8, 2005, at 12:30 p.m., Mr. Guerrero and Mr. Torres stopped [in their vehicle] at a Phillips 66 station in Topeka, Kansas. Two Kansas police officers, Brian Rhodd and Tom Bronaugh, were eating lunch at a nearby Quizno's sandwich shop. Deputy Rhodd's suspicion was aroused by the difference in the two men's dress—one was in jeans and one in dress clothes—and ages, and the fact that their license plate was from California, which he considered to be a drug source state. Deputy Rhodd approached Mr. Torres and Mr. Guerrero [in their parked vehicle] and questioned them separately about their travel plans.

"Deputy Rhodd found the two defendants' stories suspicious: Mr. Torres said they were both headed to Kansas City to work construction for two weeks; Mr. Guerrero said he was going to Kansas City for a day to drop off Mr. Torres, his uncle, and then would return immediately to Los Angeles. When Deputy Rhodd asked Mr. Guerrero how his uncle had traveled to California, Mr. Guerrero did not know. Deputy Rhodd observed that Mr. Guerrero's demeanor shifted at this point from being defensive to overly polite and overly cooperative, which made me believe that something wasn't right

Continued on next page

with him. Deputy Rhodd also noticed that the car key was alone on a single key ring and that there was unspecified religious paraphernalia on the gear shift of the car, both of which he considered characteristic of drug runners. He looked through the window and saw that clothes were simply thrown across the back seat; none of them seemed to be intended for construction work, and he did not observe any construction tools.

"Deputy Rhodd then asked to see the two men's identifying documents and the car's registration. Mr. Guerrero provided a California driver's license and the car's registration, and Mr. Torres provided a Mexican identification card, which the officer thought might not be authentic. When Deputy Rhodd asked to whom the car was registered, he thought Mr. Guerrero attempted to read the name off the registration. Mr. Guerrero said that the car belonged to his girlfriend, Goudimas; the registration indicated that the owner was Elizabeth Goudima.

"Deputy Rhodd took the documents back to his patrol car, and he asked the two men no questions for ten to twelve minutes while he ran Mr. Guerrero's license and the car's registration. He discovered that the license and registration were valid, and that there were no outstanding warrants for Mr. Guerrero's arrest. Deputy Rhodd also learned that the car had traveled back and forth to Mexico a number of times over the preceding months. He called the El Paso Intelligence Center, which told him—wrongly, as it turned out—that Mr. Guerrero was not legally permitted to be in the country.

"The officer returned the paperwork and thanked the men for their time. He walked away, then stopped after a few seconds, turned back around, and asked Mr. Guerrero several new questions, including, eventually, for consent to search the car. Mr. Guerrero replied that the car belonged to his girlfriend, so he could not consent.

"At this point, testimony diverges. Deputy Rhodd testified that he explained to Mr. Guerrero that he had the capacity to consent, but did not have to; Mr. Guerrero remembers no such explanation. Deputy Rhodd testified that Mr. Guerrero verbally consented when asked a second time; Mr. Guerrero testified that he refused consent, and that Deputy Rhodd then asked a third time. Both agree that Mr. Guerrero eventually extended both hands, palms up, in response to a request for consent. Deputy Rhodd proceeded to search the car. He found 4.5 kilograms of methamphetamine near the gas tank." 472 F.3d at 785–86 (internal quotations omitted).

▪ Do you believe the court found that Deputy Rhodd's actions during the traffic stop/detention consisting of returning the identification documents and registration to Mr. Guerrero and Mr. Torres, thanking them for their time, and then walking away for a few seconds before stopping and turning around to initiate contact again with the two men, reasonably indicated that the traffic stop/detention had ended and that Mr. Guerrero, the defendant, was free to leave? Why or why not? Fully explain your answer.

▪ Was the consent to search provided by Mr. Guerrero to search the car voluntary under the totality of circumstances? In addition to the free-to-leave factor, please consider the other relevant voluntariness factors, or circumstances, you learned about in this chapter. Fully explain your answer.

Consent need not be expressed in words but may be implied from a person's gestures or conduct, including conduct that is cooperative in nature. For example, in *United States v. Benitez*, 899 F.2d 995 (10th Cir. 1990), the defendant never verbally consented to a search of his vehicle. Nevertheless, the court found valid consent because the defendant exited his vehicle, opened the trunk, and opened a suitcase contained in the trunk. In addition, in *United States v. Solis*, 299 F.3d 420, 436–37 (5th Cir. 2002), the court found voluntary consent, in part, because defendant's wife cooperated with police in searching defendant's home and showed police the exact location of the contraband.

Moreover, in *United States v. Acosta*, 363 F.3d 1141 (11th Cir. 2004), the court found that verbal permission to search combined with particular actions on the part of the defendant, was sufficient to indicate voluntary consent to search defendant's duffle bag. In *Acosta*, when the police officer asked the defendant for the key to the duffle bag and consent to search it, the defendant replied, "Yes, of course," and provided the officer with the keys. This nonverbal action contributed to the court's finding of voluntary consent.

Verbal consent to search was found insufficiently clear or explicit, however, when defendant's fiancée simply said "okay" after a police officer announced he was going to search a laundry room. *See United States v. Weidul*, 325 F.3d 50 (1st Cir. 2003). The court in *Weidul* pointed out that police had already entered the fiancée's home and conducted a search without permission. Also, at the point when defendant's fiancée said "okay," an officer had already begun walking toward the laundry room. According to the court, this statement was "not a consent to search—it was a simple acquiescence to what any reasonable person would have perceived . . . as police conduct tantamount to a claim of lawful authority to search for weapons." 325 F.3d at 54.

Notification of Counsel and Provision of *Miranda* Warnings

A defendant has no Sixth Amendment right to counsel until the initiation of adversarial judicial criminal proceedings. *Kirby v. Illinois*, 406 U.S. 682 (1972). Thus, before the filing of formal charges, police are not required to notify counsel or seek a valid waiver of counsel before soliciting a person's consent to search, even if the person is under arrest. Police refusal to allow a person to consult with counsel after that person has requested counsel, however, may be indicative of involuntariness of consent. Finally, after the filing of formal charges, police should notify appointed or retained counsel or seek a valid waiver of counsel before attempting to obtain a person's consent to search.

Moreover, though neither the Fifth Amendment nor *Miranda* require counsel to be notified before consent to search is obtained, a person in custody who is asked to provide consent should first be given *Miranda* warnings. In fact, some states require *Miranda* warnings before a person in custody can grant valid consent to conduct a search. *See Case v. State*, 519 P.2d 523 (Okla. Crim. App. 1974). Indeed, if police administer the *Miranda* warnings prior to seeking a suspect's consent, courts are more inclined to find that the suspect's consent was voluntary. *United States v. Jones*, 523 F.3d 31 (1st Cir. 2008). If the arrested person invokes *Miranda* rights by asking for an attorney or deciding to remain silent, police attempts to obtain consent should cease.

Conversely, consent given after consultation with counsel is more likely to be found voluntary. *Cody v. Solem*, 755 F.2d 1323 (8th Cir. 1985). *See also United States v. James*, 571 F.3d 707, 715 (7th Cir. 2009). Furthermore, if police have agreed with a suspect's counsel (whenever retained) not to communicate with the suspect, a breach of that agreement may invalidate any consent police do obtain from that suspect. *Hall v. Iowa*, 705 F.2d 283 (8th Cir. 1983).

Individual Factors and Personal Characteristics

Voluntariness of consent may be affected by the physical, mental, or emotional condition of the person giving consent. The following individual factors and personal characteristics will be explored in greater detail in this section:

- intoxication,
- intelligence and educational level, and
- language barriers.

In examining whether consent is voluntary, courts balance these personal characteristics against certain aspects of the police contact with the suspect resulting in his consent, such as

- police pressures and tactics used to induce cooperation;
- the length of the police contact;
- the general conditions under which the contact occurs;
- excessive physical or psychological pressure; and
- inducements, threats, or other methods used to compel a response.

For example, if a person is sick, injured, mentally ill, under the influence of alcohol or drugs, or otherwise impaired, his or her vulnerability to subtle forms of coercion may affect the voluntariness of consent. Likewise, if a person is immature, inexperienced, mentally challenged, illiterate, or emotionally upset, the impairment of perception and understanding may render any consent to search a mere submission to authority and hence involuntary. *See United States v. Gallego-Zapata*, 630 F. Supp. 665 (D. Mass. 1986).

Note, however, that any one of these individual factors or personal characteristics alone usually does not invalidate an otherwise voluntary consent obtained by police without any impermissible pressure or coercion. In other words, "the mere fact that one has taken drugs, or is intoxicated, or mentally agitated, does not render consent involuntary." *United States v. Rambo*, 789 F.2d 1289, 1297 (8th Cir. 1986). The U.S. Supreme Court also appears to support this notion that personal characteristics alone, such as being young or less educated, will not generally render a consent involuntary. Instead, police must exploit in some way these characteristics and other individual factors before consent will be deemed involuntary. *See United States v. Mendenhall*, 446 U.S. 544 (1980); *United States v. Hall*, 969 F.2d 1102, 1107–9 (D.C. Cir. 1992) (discussed in more detail later under "Intelligence and Educational Level").

Intoxication

In *United States v. Gay*, 774 F.2d 368 (10th Cir. 1985), the court examined a defendant's ability to consent while intoxicated. The court said that the issue was whether the defendant was so intoxicated that his consent to search was not the product of a rational intellect and a free will. "The question is one of mental awareness so that the act of consent was that of one who knew what he was doing. It is elementary that one must know he is giving consent for the consent to be efficacious." 774 F.2d at 377. In *Gay*, the court found voluntary consent to search the defendant's automobile glove compartment despite his intoxication, based on evidence that the defendant was able to answer questions addressed to him; produced his driver's license on request; responded when asked if he had been drinking; emptied his pockets on request; and denied access to the automobile's trunk, which was found to contain cocaine in a later search. *See also United States v. Watters*, 572 F.3d 479, 483–84 (8th Cir. 2009) ("Watters's intoxication is undisputed, but it does not invalidate his consent to search the van. The district court found that Watters was a man of mature years, whose criminal history would have familiarized him with the procedural safeguards available to him under the law. The incident occurred in a public place and lasted less than an hour. Watters was coherent and able to answer the officers' questions. Although Watters was under arrest, the officers did not threaten him, intimidate him, or make promises to him. [W]atters voluntarily consented to the search of his vehicle.").

Intelligence and Educational Level

Courts also consider a person's intelligence and educational level in determining the voluntariness of consent. In *United States v. Bates*, 840 F.2d 858, 861 (11th Cir. 1988), the court found a valid consent when "[t]he defendant, an educated man, had 'been informed of [his] right to refuse to consent to such a search.'" And in *United States v. Kaplan*, 895 F.2d 618, 622 (9th Cir. 1990), one of the court's reasons for finding voluntary consent was that the defendant, a doctor, "was not a person lacking in education and understanding." *See also United States v. Price*, 558 F.3d 270, 279–80 (3rd Cir. 2009) (finding voluntary consent by defendant's wife to search house, in part, because her "age, intelligence and education were at least average").

In addition, even if a person has a low IQ, minimal education, and certain psychological problems, these characteristics do not necessarily

---

KEY POINTS

L02
- Consent to search given in submission to force, threat of force, or other show of authority is not voluntary.

- Consent to search obtained by misrepresentation or deception is not voluntary, except that a person's misplaced trust in an undercover police agent will not alone invalidate an otherwise voluntary consent.

Continued on next page

result in a finding of involuntariness. For example, in *United States v. Hall*, 969 F.2d 1102 (D.C. Cir. 1992), a defendant with these characteristics was held to have voluntarily consented to a search of her person and tote bag because the police officer did not threaten or apply pressure to the defendant, the officer confronted defendant for a short time, and the defendant herself exhibited behavior indicating she could make decisions on her own. In addition, in *United States v. Vinton*, 631 F.3d 476, 482–83 (8th Cir. 2011), a defendant with a borderline IQ was found to have provided police with voluntary consent to search his home because

> officers did not raise their voices, draw their guns, or otherwise threaten or coerce [defendant] Vinton. The court determined that Vinton was unrestrained and rational when he consented to the searches, that he had a history of interaction with law enforcement, and that his consent to the search of the house for contraband was obtained after a five-minute conversation with a single officer in Vinton's own home.

Language Barriers

Language barriers make determining voluntariness more difficult. In *State v. Xiong*, 504 N.W.2d 428, 432 (Wis. App. 1993), the court said:

> It is incumbent upon the police to effectively communicate their objectives when seeking consent to search. Merely providing an interpreter is not enough. The interpretation must convey what is intended to be communicated. Communication is effective only if it clearly and accurately relates all pertinent information to the listener. If effective communication is not provided, then that is a form of coercion.

For example, in *United States v. Lee*, 317 F.3d 26 (1st Cir. 2003), the court found that though English was the defendant's second language, he could voluntarily consent to a search of his vehicle because he had lived in the United States for many years and had prior experience with the U.S. judicial system. However, in *United States v. Guerrero*, 374 F.3d 584 (8th Cir. 2004), though the officer provided the defendant with a consent to search form in Spanish, his first language, the court found the consent involuntary because defendant may not have read Spanish and had tremendous difficulty communicating in English with the officer. Though the officer did attempt to obtain defendant's verbal consent, the court concluded that defendant's statement merely reflected his inability to understand the officer—the defendant was simply repeating what the officer said.

Voluntary Production of Evidence

Some people confuse the voluntariness test for consent with a purely voluntary production of evidence. If a person voluntarily produces incriminating evidence, without any attempt by police to obtain consent and without coercion, deception, or other illegal police conduct, there is no search and seizure, and the evidence is admissible in court. In *Coolidge v. New Hampshire*, 403 U.S. 443 (1971), two officers went to the defendant's home, while the defendant was at the police station under investigation for murder, to check out the defendant's story with his wife. The officers asked the wife whether the defendant owned any guns, and she replied, "Yes, I will get them in the bedroom." She then took four guns out of a closet and gave them to the officers.

The officers then asked her what her husband had been wearing on the night in question, and she produced several pairs of trousers and a hunting jacket. The police seized the evidence, and it was used against the defendant in court.

The Court found no objection to the introduction of the evidence in court. In fact, the Court found that the actions of the police did not even amount to a search and seizure. Because the Court discussed in detail the significance of the actions of the police and because of the importance of the issue, the Court's opinion is quoted here at length:

> [I]t cannot be said that the police should have obtained a warrant for the guns and clothing before they set out to visit Mrs. Coolidge, since they had no intention of rummaging around among Coolidge's effects or of dispossessing him of any of his property. Nor can it be said that they should have obtained Coolidge's permission for a seizure they did not intend to make. There was nothing to compel them to announce to the suspect that they intended to question his wife about his movements on the night of the disappearance or about the theft from his employer.
>
> Once Mrs. Coolidge had admitted them, the policemen were surely acting normally and properly when they asked her, as they asked those questioned earlier in the investigation, including Coolidge himself, about any guns there might be in the house. The question concerning the clothes Coolidge had been wearing on the night of the disappearance was logical and in no way coercive. . . . And surely when Mrs. Coolidge of her own accord produced the guns and clothes for inspection, rather than simply describing them, it was not incumbent on the police to stop her or avert their eyes. . . .
>
> In assessing the claim that this course of conduct amounted to a search and seizure, it is well to keep in mind that Mrs. Coolidge described her own motive as that of clearing her husband, and that she believed that she had nothing to hide. . . . There is not the slightest implication of an attempt [by the two officers] to coerce or dominate her, or for that matter, to direct her actions by the more subtle techniques of suggestion that are available to officials in circumstances like these. To hold that the conduct of the police here was a search and seizure would be to hold, in effect, that a criminal suspect has constitutional protection against the adverse consequences of a spontaneous, good-faith effort by his wife to clear him of suspicion. 403 U.S. at 488–90.

Scope of Consent

Determination of the allowable scope of a consent search involves an examination of several issues:

■ whether permission to actually search a residence, rather than merely enter it, has been given by the suspect;

■ whether an initial consent by the suspect to enter and search a residence grants police consent to enter and search that residence on subsequent occasions;

■ the allowable area of the search;

■ the proper time for the search; and

■ the permissible object of the search.

Consent Merely to Enter

A person's consent to an officer's request to enter his or her residence does not automatically give the officer a right to search. There is a vital distinction between granting admission to one's home for the purposes of conversation and granting permission to thoroughly search the home.

In *Duncan v. State*, 176 So.2d 840 (Ala. 1965), officers investigating a murder knocked on the defendant's hotel room door and the defendant invited them in. They did not advise the defendant that they were police officers, nor did they make any request to search the defendant's room. Nevertheless, the officers conducted a search and found incriminating evidence. The court held that the defendant's invitation to enter his room to the person who knocked on the door did not constitute consent to search his room. The court said:

> To justify the introduction of evidence seized by a police officer within a private residence on the ground that the officer's entry was made by invitation, permission, or consent, there must be evidence of a statement or some overt act by the occupant of such residence sufficient to indicate his intent to waive his rights to the security and privacy of his home and freedom from unwarranted intrusions therein. An open door is not a waiver of such rights. 176 So.2d at 853.

Initial Consent Versus Subsequent Consent

Even if police are granted consent to conduct a search after being granted consent to enter a residence, such consent is limited to search on that particular occasion. Consent to enter and search on one occasion does not automatically translate into consent to enter and search premises on a subsequent occasion. For example, in *Shamaeizadeh v. Cunigan*, 338 F.3d 535, 548 (6th Cir. 2003), the court found that defendant's initial, valid consent to police officers to search his home for a possible burglar did not authorize these officers to conduct two additional warrantless searches of his home for drugs. The court separated the initial search from the other searches because with the subsequent searches, officers were summoned with particular experience in detecting drugs.

Area of Search

Assuming that an officer obtains on the proper occasion a valid consent not only to enter premises but also to search the premises, "the standard for measuring the scope of a suspect's consent under the Fourth Amendment is that of 'objective reasonableness'—what would the typical reasonable person have understood by the exchange between the officer and the suspect?" *Florida v. Jimeno*, 500 U.S. 248, 251 (1991). As a general rule, if an officer asks for and obtains consent to search a specific area, whether in a place or on a person, the officer is limited to that specific area. If the search goes beyond that area, evidence seized is inadmissible in court.

Grants of General Consent to Search Places In *Jimeno*, the Supreme Court found a police officer acted reasonably in searching a particular container within the defendant's automobile for drugs after the defendant had consented generally to a search of his automobile. The Court noted that the officer in *Jimeno* had explained to the defendant that he wanted to search for drugs prior to obtaining his consent to search the car. Moreover, the defendant did not place any restriction on the officer's search. Under these circumstances, the Court concluded that "it was objectively reasonable for the police to conclude that the general consent to search [defendant's] car included consent to search containers within that car which might bear drugs. A reasonable person may be expected to know that narcotics are generally carried in some form of container." 500 U.S. at 251.

Similarly, in *United States v. Jones*, 356 F.3d 529 (4th Cir. 2004), the court found that the officer acted reasonably when he searched a locked container within defendant's duffle bag after the defendant had told the officer he could search the bag. The court reasoned that the defendant did not qualify his consent in any way that would indicate to the officer that the locked container was "off-limits." For example, the defendant did not state that the officer could not use keys located in the bag to open the locked container. Also, the defendant failed to make any objection when the officer opened the locked box in his presence. Finally, because the officer stated that he was looking for drugs and the defendant communicated to the officer that drugs were present in the bag, "it was reasonable to conclude that Jones was referring [and consenting] to [a search of] the contents of the [locked container]." 356 F.3d at 534–35.

Restricted Grants of Consent to Search Places When a defendant restricts his or her consent in some way, courts may reach a different result. For example, in *United States v. Neely*, 564 F.3d 346, 349–51, 353 (4th Cir. 2009), consent was given to officers to search the trunk of a car. The court held that this consent did not extend to search of the passenger area of the car and that evidence found in the passenger area was inadmissible in court. Likewise, in *United States v. Wald*, 216 F.3d 1222, 1228 (10th Cir. 2000), when the police officer received permission from the defendant during a routine traffic stop to "take a quick look" inside his vehicle, the court concluded that the scope of this consent did not extend to the trunk of defendant's car. As a result, the court excluded from trial the drugs found within defendant's trunk.

Restrictions on grants of consent need not be explicit; restrictions may be implied. For example, in *People v. Cruz*, 395 P.2d 889 (Cal. 1964), an officer obtained permission to "look around" an apartment but was informed that certain property at that apartment belonged to individuals not present at the time of the search. The court held that this type of verbal consent did not authorize the officer to open and search boxes and suitcases that he had been told were the property of someone other than the person giving consent. In other words, an officer can search only the parts of premises over which the person giving consent has some possessory right or control and not personal property that the officer knows belongs to some other person.

In addition, if a residential occupant opens his door to walk outside his residence to meet with visitors who turn out to be police officers and then walks back through the open door followed by the officers, these actions do not constitute consent for the officers to enter the residence. *See United States v. Shaibu*, 920 F.2d 1423 (9th Cir. 1990) ("[Defendant] opened the door not to let the police enter, but only for himself to step out of the apartment to meet visitors outside rather than inside. There is no contention that the police expressly or impliedly asked consent to enter nor that [Defendant] expressly granted or refused entry. It is one thing to infer consent from actions responding to a police request. It is quite another to sanction the police walking in to a person's home without stopping at the door to ask permission. To infer consent in this case is only a conjecture and would exceed the scope of any recognized exception to the Fourth Amendment's bar to warrantless entry of the home.")

General Versus Restricted Grants to Search People The limitation on the area of search allowed by consent applies equally to searches of people as to searches of premises or vehicles. In a case involving both a nonverbal consent and a limitation on the area of a person to be searched by consent, a police officer asked the defendant whether he was still using or carrying narcotics. When the defendant replied that he was not, the officer asked permission to check him for needle marks. The defendant said nothing but put his arms out sideways. Instead of checking the defendant's arms, the officer patted down his coat and found marijuana cigarettes. The court held that the search went beyond the area of search to which the defendant had consented:

> Bowens' putting out his arms sideways in response to a query whether he minded allowing the officer to check 'if he had any marks on him' could hardly be said to be naturally indicative or persuasive of the giving of an intended consent to have the officer switch instead to a general search of his [coat] pockets—in which he had two marijuana cigarettes. *Oliver v. Bowens*, 386 F.2d 688, 691 (9th Cir. 1967).

In addition, in *Reedy v. Evanson*, 615 F.3d 197. 225–28 (3rd Cir. 2010), a woman named Reedy, who was a victim of a rape, consented to having a sexual assault examination performed on her by medical personnel in a hospital. As part of the examination, Reedy signed a written consent form giving hospital personnel permission to examine her blood for purposes related to investigating the assault. The Court in *Reedy* found that when police ordered hospital personnel to search Reedy's blood for drugs in order to prosecute her for illegal drug use, the police exceeded the scope of the consent Reedy had provided for a search of her person:

> Having examined the language of the consent forms from the perspective of an objectively reasonable person in Reedy's circumstances we conclude that someone who had not been accused of committing any crime and who had arrived at the hospital to be examined for the purpose of evaluating the extent of her injuries and risk of disease from a sexual assault, and for the purpose of gathering physical evidence to prosecute her assailant, would not understand that she was also consenting to having her blood tested a second time [for drugs], at the direction of a law enforcement agent, for the purpose of collecting evidence to prosecute her.

Time of Search

A consent to search may also be limited with respect to time. For example, in *United States v. Alcantar*, 271 F.3d 731 (2001), the court found an hour-long search of defendant's vehicle for drugs and weapons permissible because (1) the defendant did not object to a search of this length, and (2) one hour was reasonable in light of the fact that drugs and weapons can easily be concealed inside a vehicle. In addition, in *United States v. Carbajal-Irarte*, 586 F.3d 795, 802 (10th Cir. 2009), the Court found that police searches of the defendant's vehicle in two locations, the second of which involved a canine search, and that in total lasted approximately two hours did not exceed the scope of the defendant's consent to search. The Court reached this conclusion because the defendant had provided police with consent on multiple occasions, did not limit his consent to search to a specific time period, and police acted as diligently as they could in conducting the searches:

> [T]he search here did not exceed the duration of [defendant] Carbajal-Iriarte's consent. Carbajal-Iriarte characterizes the search as occurring in two different locations over a span of two hours. This description ignores the multiple consents to search given by Carbajal-Iriarte. That Carbajal-Iriarte repeatedly consented to these searches favors the conclusion that the duration of the search was reasonable. The first search at the truck stop lasted approximately half an hour, after which Carbajal-Iriarte agreed to go with Agent Small and Detective Tate to meet Officer Ramos for a second search. After arriving at Officer Ramos's location along Interstate 40, Carbajal-Iriarte reaffirmed his consent for the search. From the time of Carbajal-Iriarte's last consent, the search lasted just over an hour. . . . Once Officer Ruiloba arrived with the drug dog, the dog alerted to the presence of methamphetamine within a matter of minutes.
>
> Carbajal-Iriarte's consent contained no limitation on the duration of the search and can only be described as giving the officers general permission to search the vehicle. At no time did Carbajal-Iriarte seek to limit the duration of the search,

nor did the officers create the understanding that the search would be brief. It is also noteworthy that Carbajal-Iriarte's last consent was provided after voluntarily traveling to meet another officer for the express purpose of a search. . . . Finally, there is no indication . . . that the officers failed to act with due diligence in conducting the search.

In light of all of these circumstances, . . . the search was of a duration permitted by Carbajal-Iriarte's consent.

United States v. Carbajal-Irarte suggests that if police are planning to conduct multiple consent searches pertaining to the same defendant at multiple locations over the span of a few hours, they should attempt to obtain consent to search from defendant on more than one occasion (e.g., before each search and/or at each new search location).

In *State v. Brochu*, 237 A.2d 418 (Me. 1967), officers investigating the death of the defendant's wife obtained a valid consent from the defendant to search his home. The officers conducted a search and found nothing. At that time, the defendant had not been accused of anything. Later in the day, however, police received information giving them probable cause to arrest the defendant for his wife's murder and to obtain a search warrant for his premises. They arrested the defendant that evening and executed the search warrant the next day. The defendant successfully challenged the validity of this warrant by asserting that certain items seized by police were not mentioned in the warrant, and the prosecution at that point attempted to justify the second search on the basis that the defendant's earlier consent continued in effect after his arrest to the next day. The court rejected this contention because the defendant's status had changed between the two searches from that of a concerned husband to that of the accused in his wife's murder:

> The consent [from the first search] in our view should be measured on the morning of the [following day] by the status of the defendant as the accused. There is no evidence whatsoever that the consent [for the first search] was ever discussed with the defendant at or after his arrest, or that he was informed of the State's intent to enter and search his home [a second time] on the strength of a continuing consent. We conclude, therefore, that consent of the defendant had ended by [the time of the second search], and accordingly the officers were not protected thereby on the successful [second] search. 237 A.2d 421.

Therefore, if a significant period of time passes after consent to search is given, a new consent should be obtained before continuing to search, especially if intervening events suggest that a second consent might not be given so readily as the original consent. If the suspect does not renew his or her consent, a valid search warrant should be obtained.

Object of Search

If the consenting person places no limit on the scope of a search, the scope is "generally defined by its expressed object." *Florida v. Jimeno*, 500 U.S. 248, 251 (1991). Therefore, a search may be as broad as the officer's previously acquired knowledge about the crimes likely to have been committed and the items of evidence likely to be discovered. *United States v. Sealey*, 630 F. Supp. 801 (E.D. Cal. 1986).

The U.S. Supreme Court's opinion in *Jimeno*, discussed earlier, provides an example of how the stated object, or purpose, of a search can determine that search's scope. In *Jimeno*, a police officer was following the defendant's car after overhearing the defendant arranging what appeared to be a drug transaction. The officer stopped the defendant's car for a traffic infraction and declared that he had reason to believe that the defendant was carrying narcotics in the car. The officer asked permission to search the car for drugs and received the defendant's consent. During the search, the officer found cocaine inside a folded paper bag on the car's floorboard.

The Court held that a criminal suspect's Fourth Amendment right to be free from un-reasonable searches is not violated when, after the suspect gives a police officer consent to search his or her automobile, the officer opens a closed container found within the car that might reasonably hold the object of the search. In other words, the Court believed that in light of the stated object of the consent search—a search for drugs—the officer was per-mitted to look for drugs in a paper bag because this bag could contain drugs. On the other hand, if the stated object of the automobile search had been a person or another object of equal size, the Court would likely have held that the search of the bag was unconstitutional.

United States v. Rodney, 956 F.2d 295 (D.C. Cir. 1992), held that a request to con-duct a body search for drugs reasonably includes a request to conduct some search of the crotch area. Thus, if police obtain voluntary consent from a suspect to search his or her body for drugs, they may conduct a reasonable search of the suspect's crotch area because drug dealers frequently hide drugs near their genitals.

Note that the "objective reasonableness" standard depends on the facts of each case. A general consent to search a particular area of a vehicle does not necessarily allow the search of all containers in that area of the vehicle. For example, consent to search the trunk of a car may not include authorization to pry open a locked briefcase found inside the trunk. As the Court noted in *Jimeno*, "[i]t is very likely unreasonable to think that a suspect, by consenting to the search of his trunk, has agreed to the breaking open of a locked briefcase within the trunk, but it is otherwise with respect to a closed paper bag." 500 U.S. at 251–52.

Lower courts, however, have permitted searches of locked containers as well as hidden compartments and containers within vehicles when the defendant provides consent to both a complete search of his vehicle and to the seizure of any property contained within it. For example, in *United States v. Reeves*, 6 F.3d 660, 662 (9th Cir. 1993), the defendant signed a consent form allowing police to "'conduct a complete search' of the car," and seize pa-pers and other items contained within it. On these facts, the court found that a search of a locked briefcase in the hatchback area of the car and the removal of contraband from that briefcase was within the scope of defendant's consent. *See also United States v. Garcia*, 604 F.3d 186, 189–91 (5th Cir. 2010) ("Garcia did not qualify his consent to the officers, who therefore had general consent to search the truck. When the officers requested permission to search the truck after asking Garcia whether he was carrying 'anything illegal,' it was natural to conclude that they might look for hidden compartments or containers [includ-ing the area within a stereo speaker in the cab of the truck]. In sum, the search of Garcia's truck cab was reasonable. The district court did not clearly err in denying the motion to suppress [the cocaine police found within the speaker in the cab].").

And when an individual provides police with valid consent to search an entire con-tainer in his or her possession, the police may permissibly search additional containers found *within* that container. For example, in *United States v. Jackson*, 598 F.3d 340, 343, 348–49 (7th Cir. 2010), when an officer received valid consent from defendant's mother to search a case for a computer and its serial number, the court held that the scope of the officer's search could extend to a zipped exterior pocket on the case:

> The district court properly concluded that Officer Dexheimer did not exceed the scope of [defendant's mother's] Eaton's consent. Where someone [validly] consents to a general search, law enforcement may search anywhere within the general area where the sought-after item could be concealed. Eaton consented to the officer's request to search the bag, and she placed no limit on the extent of the search. Furthermore, to the extent Defendant argues that the objective of the search limited the scope of Eaton's consent, Officer Dexheimer was searching not only for a computer, but also for evidence of the computer's serial number. That serial number, together with a power cord and other computer equipment, could have been located anywhere in the computer case [including in the exterior pocket]. As such, Officer Dexheimer did not exceed the scope of Eaton's consent.

Of course, the consenting person may specifically limit the scope of a consent search to a search for a particular object. In *People v. Superior Court (Arketa)*, 89 Cal. Rptr. 316 (Cal. App. 1970), a person gave officers consent to search his house for a crime suspect. The officers instead conducted a thorough search of the house and its closets for a crowbar without advising the person that they wanted to look for a crowbar. The court invalidated the search because it went beyond the scope of the consent granted. Also, in *United States v. Turner*, 169 F.3d 84 (1999), the police, prior to obtaining defendant's consent, explained that they wanted to search places in his home that might contain physical evidence left by an intruder who had committed a recent assault. Under these circumstances, the court found that the police officers' search of the defendant's computer files fell outside the scope of his consent. The court explained that "it obviously would have been impossible to abandon physical evidence [such as a knife or clothing] in a personal computer hard drive, and bizarre to suppose . . . that the suspected intruder stopped to enter incriminating evidence into the Turner computer." 169 F.3d at 88.

In sum, law enforcement officers should confine their search to only those areas where the object for which they have consent to search could possibly be located, taking into consideration the object's size, shape, and character.

Revocation of Consent

The person giving consent to search may revoke or withdraw that consent at any time after the search has begun. In *State v. Lewis*, 611 A.2d 69 (Me. 1992), after arresting the defendant for drunk driving and releasing him on personal recognizance, a state trooper offered to drive the defendant to a nearby motel. When the defendant retrieved a carry-on bag from his car, the trooper asked for and received permission to check the bag for guns. The trooper immediately observed two large brown bags inside the carry-on bag, smelled marijuana, and asked permission to examine the bags. The defendant refused and attempted to return the carry-on bag to his car. The trooper intervened and searched the brown bags, finding marijuana. The court found that the defendant had revoked his consent to search the carry-on bag before the trooper opened the brown bags.

> Even though defendant consented to the trooper's looking inside his carry-on bag, he at no time consented to the trooper's looking into the brown bags contained therein. Rather, by expressly terminating his consent when the trooper requested to open the brown bags and by seeking to return them to his car, defendant most certainly manifested a subjective expectation of privacy with respect to those inside bags. Because those bags were always closed and their contents shielded from the trooper's view, society would regard defendant's expectation of privacy in them to be reasonable. 611 A.2d at 70.

In addition, in *United States v. Ho*, 94 F.3d 932, 933–36 (5th Cir. 1996), when the defendant first gave permission for an officer to search a portfolio in his possession and then attempted to pull away the portfolio when the officer found a blank, white card that did not appear to be contraband, the court found that the defendant had successfully withdrawn his consent for the officer to search the portfolio. Likewise, *United States v. Ibarra*, 731 F. Supp. 1037 (D. Wyo. 1990), held that a motorist's closing and locking the trunk of his car after a police officer's prior consensual search of the trunk constituted a revocation of that consent and barred any further search. However, if a motorist, after revoking her consent by closing the trunk, voluntarily reopens it, a court may find that this motorist has voluntarily renewed her consent. *See United States v. Flores*, 48 F.3d 467, 468–69 (10th Cir. 1995).

For a revocation of consent to be valid, the suspect must clearly communicate that he or she is revoking consent. Ambiguous revocations may be held to be insufficient to have accomplished the intended revocation. For example, if a suspect merely complains about the length of the search, this fact alone may not constitute revocation of that suspect's consent. *See United States v. Brown*, 345 F.3d 574 (8th Cir. 2003). Similarly, in *United States v. West*, 321 F.3d 649 (7th Cir. 2003), after the driver of an automobile provided a blanket consent to officers to search a car, the defendant, a passenger in the car, claimed ownership of a particular duffel bag located within the car. The police subsequently found cocaine in the bag. The court held that defendant's claim of ownership, without more, did not revoke the driver's consent to search the car, including the duffel bag.

United States v. West stands for the principle that revocation of consent will not be inferred from mere silence:

> [T]he question on which the lawfulness of the seizure of the cocaine turns . . . is whether [the passenger] revoked the driver's consent to search the entire car, necessarily including the bag. By [the passenger's] silence in the face of [the driver's] consent [the passenger] forfeited any right to claim that [the] consent was ineffective to authorize the search because the bag was his [e.g., the passenger's]. His silence was confirmation or ratification of [the driver's] authority to consent. 321 F.3d at 651–52.

Who May Give Consent?

In general, the only person able to give a valid consent to a search is the person whose constitutional, privacy protection against unreasonable searches and seizures would be invaded by the search if it were conducted without consent. This means, for example, that when the search of a person's body or clothing is contemplated, only that person can consent to the search. The same rule applies to searches of property, except that when several people have varying degrees of interest in the same property, more than one person may be qualified to give consent to search.

Third-Party Consent Under Actual or Apparent Authority

In certain situations, the law recognizes the authority of third persons to consent to a search of property even though they are not the persons against whose interests the search is being conducted. *United States v. Matlock*, 415 U.S. 164 (1974), stated the test for determining whether a third person can consent to a search of premises or effects:

> [W]hen the prosecution seeks to justify a warrantless search by proof of voluntary consent, it is not limited to proof that consent was given by the defendant, but may show that permission to search was obtained from a third party who possessed *common authority over or other sufficient relationship to the premises or effects sought to be inspected.* 415 U.S. at 171 (emphasis added).

Actual Common Authority In a footnote of the *Matlock* decision, the Supreme Court defined what it meant when it used the term common authority:

> Common authority is, of course, not to be implied from the mere interest a third party has in the property. The authority which justifies the third-party consent does not rest upon the law of property, with its attendant historical and legal refinements, . . . but rests rather on mutual use of the property by persons generally having joint access or control for most purposes, so that it is reasonable to recognize that any of the co-inhabitants has the right to permit the inspection in his own right and that the others have assumed the risk that one of their number might permit the common area to be searched. 415 U.S. at 171 n.7.

From this, we discern that someone with actual authority over property has the legal capacity to grant consent to search the property over which he or she has access or control.

Apparent Common Authority In addition to a third party having actual authority to consent to a search of another person's property or effects, a third party may also have apparent authority to do so. For example, a warrantless entry and search is valid when based on the consent of a third party whom the police, at the time of the entry, reasonably believe to possess common authority over the premises but who in fact does not have such authority. This does not suggest that law enforcement officers may always accept a person's invitation to enter premises:

> Even when the invitation is accompanied by an explicit assertion that the person lives there, the surrounding circumstances could conceivably be such that a reasonable person would doubt its truth and not act upon it without further inquiry. As with other factual determinations bearing upon search and seizure, determination of consent to enter must "be judged against an objective standard: would the facts available to the officer at the moment . . . 'warrant a man of reasonable caution in the belief'" that the consenting party had authority over the premises? . . . If not, then warrantless entry without further inquiry is unlawful unless authority actually exists. But if so, the search is valid. *Illinois v. Rodriguez*, 497 U.S. 177, 188–89 (1990).

Rodriguez has been construed as "appli[cable] to situations in which an officer would have had valid consent to search if the facts were as he reasonably believed them to be." *United States v. Whitfield*, 939 F.2d 1071, 1074 (D.C. Cir. 1991). *Rodriguez* would not validate, however, a search based on an erroneous view of the law. For example, an officer's erroneous belief that landlords are generally authorized to consent to a search of a tenant's premises could not provide the authorization necessary for a warrantless search.

Proving Actual or Apparent Common Authority The prosecution has the burden of showing that someone consented and that the person had actual or apparent authority to do so. Therefore, law enforcement officers must provide sufficient evidence of both consent and authority to the prosecuting attorney for presentation in court. Mutual, or common, authority involving third parties generally comes from spouses and persons involved in similar partnerships, but also occurs in roommate, parent–child, employee–employer, and other relationships. The law enforcement officer should ask reasonable questions designed to show a relationship of such common authority that either party has the right to consent to the shared real or personal property. And, of course, the answers received must reasonably show such a relationship. Reasonableness, not perfection, is the standard on which the officer's behavior is measured. Officers are not required to be correct in their deductions concerning one's authority to consent, but they must act in good faith and reasonably, based on training and experience.

Specific Types of Third-Party Consent

The remainder of this chapter examines examples of consent search situations in which the person giving the consent is not the person against whose interests the search is being conducted. Therefore, in each of these examples, the central question is whether the person providing consent has common authority, whether actual or apparent, over the searched premises or effects such that the person is capable of providing valid consent. The following examples will be explored:

- persons having equal rights or interests in property,
- landlords and tenants,
- hotel management and guests,
- hosts and guests,
- employers and employees,
- school officials and students,
- principals and agents,
- spouses,
- parents and children,
- drivers and passengers, and
- bailors and bailees.

Persons Having Equal Rights or Interests in Property (e.g., Co-Owners, Co-Tenants, Co-Renters, or Co-Lessees) It is well settled that, when two or more persons have substantially equal rights of ownership, occupancy, or other possessory interest in property to be searched or seized, any one of the persons may legally authorize a search, and any evidence found may be used against any of the other persons. In determining whether a person is a joint occupant of premises (i.e., co-tenant, co-lessee, etc.) with the capacity to give valid consent, courts consider a number of factors:

- whether the person paid rent,
- how long the person stayed,
- whether the person left belongings on the premises,
- whether the person possessed a key, and
- whether there was any written or oral agreement among other parties as to the person's right to use and occupy the premises.

For example, the court in *United States v. Kelley*, 953 F.2d 562 (9th Cir. 1992), found authority to consent to a search of the defendant's bedroom and closet under the following circumstances:

- the person giving consent had rented the apartment together with the defendant and had signed the lease,
- she described herself as the defendant's roommate, and
- she had joint access not only to the common areas of the apartment but also to the defendant's separate bedroom, where the apartment telephone was located.

Moreover, in *United States v. Matlock*, 415 U.S. 164 (1975), previously discussed, when the person providing consent to search a room slept there regularly with defendant and stored her clothing there, the Court found that this person had actual authority to consent to a search of that room, including containers within that room.

However, in *Illinois v. Rodriguez*, 497 U.S. 177 (1990), the U.S. Supreme Court held that the defendant's former co-tenant did not have actual authority to grant police consent to enter the defendant's premises without a warrant, even though she had some furniture and household effects in the premises and sometimes spent the night at the premises after moving out a month before the search at issue. The Court found that the former co-tenant lacked actual authority because

- her name was not on the lease,
- she did not contribute to the rent,
- she was not allowed to invite others to the apartment on her own,
- she never went to the premises when the defendant was not at home,
- she had moved her clothing and that of her children from the premises, and
- she had taken a key to the premises without the defendant's knowledge.

These facts convinced the Court that the former co-tenant did not possess *actual* authority to consent to the search of defendant's apartment, though the Court did remand the case to the lower court to determine if the co-tenant had *apparent* authority to consent (e.g., whether the officers could have reasonably believed the former co-tenant had authority to consent).

However, even when valid consent is obtained by police from one co-occupant (i.e., a co-owner or co-tenant) to search a residence on a particular occasion, when another co-occupant of that residence is physically present on this occasion and refuses to consent, police may not enter the residence without a warrant or the presence of some other exception to the warrant requirement (i.e., exigent circumstances such as probable cause to believe someone is being or soon will be harmed). If police nonetheless enter and search the residence based on the one co-occupant's consent, the physically present and objecting co-occupant has the right to have the search declared unreasonable and any evidence seized against him excluded in court. *Georgia v. Randolph*, 547 U.S. 103 (2006) (for further discussion of this case and its implications, see the subsequent Discussion Point and the Criminal Procedure in Action box later in this section).

In addition, the U.S. Supreme Court recently considered whether *"Randolph* applies if the objecting occupant is absent when another occupant consents." *Fernandez v. California*, 134 S. Ct. 1126, 1129–30 (2014). The Court in *Fernandez* answered this question in the negative, finding that police may search residential premises when one co-occupant consents in the *absence* of the objecting occupant:

> Our opinion in *Randolph* took great pains to emphasize that its holding was limited to situations in which the objecting occupant is physically present. We therefore refuse to extend *Randolph* to the very different situation in this case, where consent was provided by an abused woman well after [the objecting occupant] had been removed from the apartment they shared. 134 S. Ct. at 1130.

Note that in *Fernandez*, the objecting occupant, who was the male partner of the abused woman, was not present at the time the female co-occupant consented to a search by police of her apartment because he had been lawfully detained and then arrested by police for inflicting the abuse as well as an earlier robbery:

> [The male partner] does not contest the fact that the police had reasonable grounds for removing him from the apartment so that they could speak with [the abused woman], an apparent victim of domestic violence, outside of petitioner's potentially intimidating presence. In fact, he does not even contest the existence of probable cause to place him under arrest [for the abuse and robbery]. *We therefore hold that an occupant who is absent due to a lawful detention or arrest stands in the same shoes as an occupant who is absent for any other reason.* 134 S. Ct. at 1134 (italics added).

Thus, after *Fernandez*, if police *lawfully* detain or arrest a residential occupant who objects to a search of the residence, and police remove this occupant from the premises, they may subsequently obtain consent to search the residence from a co-occupant who is present at the residence. This consent, if voluntarily given, is sufficient for police to search the residence. The one caveat, or exception, to this rule is if "the police have removed the potentially objecting tenant from the entrance for the sake of avoiding a possible objection." *Randolph*, 547 U.S. at 121. This exception means that if police have no lawful reason or justification to remove the objecting occupant from the premises but still do so, his objection prevents police from searching the premises (i.e., despite another co-occupant who is present providing police with consent to search). *Fernandez*, 134 S. Ct. at 1134–35.

In *Frazier v. Cupp*, 394 U.S. 731 (1969), involving equal rights to *personal effects*, the defendant, at his murder trial, objected to the introduction into evidence of clothing seized from his duffel bag. At the time of the seizure, the duffel bag was being used jointly by the defendant and his cousin and had been left in the cousin's home. When police arrested the cousin, they asked him whether they could have his clothing. The cousin directed them to the duffel bag, and both the cousin and his mother consented to its search. During the search, the officers came upon the defendant's clothing in the bag and seized it as well. The Court upheld the legality of the search over the defendant's objections:

> Since Rawls (the cousin) was a joint user of the bag, he clearly had authority to consent to its search. The officers therefore found evidence against [defendant] while in the course of an otherwise lawful search. . . . [Defendant] argues that Rawls only had actual permission to use one compartment of the bag and that he had no authority to consent to a search of the other compartments. We will not, however, engage in such metaphysical subtleties in judging the efficacy of Rawls' consent. [Defendant], in allowing Rawls to use the bag and in leaving it in his house, must be taken to have assumed the risk that Rawls would allow someone else to look inside. We find no valid search and seizure claim in this case. 394 U.S. at 740.

DISCUSSION POINT

What Happens When One Occupant of a Residence Consents to a Police Search but Another Physically Present Occupant Refuses Consent?
Georgia v. Randolph, 547 U.S. 103 (2006)

Scott Randolph and his wife, Janet, separated in late May 2001, when she left the marital residence in Americus, Georgia, and went to stay with her parents in Canada, taking their son and some belongings. In July, she returned to the Americus house with the child. On the morning of July 6, she complained to the police that after a domestic dispute her husband

had taken their son away; and when officers reached the house, she told them that her husband was a cocaine user whose habit had caused financial troubles. She mentioned the marital problems and said that she and their son had only recently returned. Shortly after the police arrived, Scott Randolph returned and explained that he had removed the child to a neighbor's house out of concern that his wife might take the boy out of the country again; he denied cocaine use and countered that it was in fact his wife who abused drugs and alcohol.

One of the officers, Sergeant Murray, went with Janet Randolph to reclaim the child, and when they returned she not only renewed her complaints about her husband's drug use but also volunteered that there were "items of drug evidence" in the house. Sergeant Murray asked Scott Randolph for permission to search the house, which he unequivocally refused.

The sergeant turned to Janet Randolph for consent to search, which she readily gave. She led the officer upstairs to a bedroom that she identified as Scott's, where the sergeant noticed a section of a drinking straw with a powdery residue he suspected was cocaine. He then left the house to get an evidence bag from his car and to call the district attorney's office, which instructed him to stop the search and apply for a warrant. When Sergeant Murray returned to the house, Janet Randolph withdrew her consent. The police took the straw to the police station, along with the Randolphs. After getting a search warrant, they returned to the house and seized further evidence of drug use, on the basis of which Scott Randolph was indicted for possession of cocaine. He moved to suppress the evidence, as products of a warrantless search of his house unauthorized by his wife's consent over his express refusal.

The U.S. Supreme Court held "that a warrantless search of a shared dwelling for evidence over the express refusal of consent by a physically present resident cannot be justified as reasonable as to him on the basis of consent given to the police by another resident." 547 U.S. at 120. Moreover,

in applying the facts of the case to its holding, the Court commented "that in the circumstances here at issue, a physically present co-occupant's [such as Mr. Scott Randolph's] stated refusal to permit entry prevails, rendering the warrantless search unreasonable and invalid as to him." The Court continued its rule-to-fact application in this way:

> This case invites a straightforward application of the rule that a physically present [occupant such as Mr. Randolph's] express refusal of consent to a police search is dispositive as to him, regardless of the consent of a fellow occupant [e.g., Ms. Janet Randolph's consent]. Scott Randolph's refusal is clear, and nothing in the record justifies the search. 547 U.S. at 106, 122–23.

The Court did note, however, that if the encounter or exchange between the consenting co-occupant and the police provided police with another valid justification under the Fourth Amendment to enter the residence, police could reasonably enter despite the physically present co-occupant's objection. "Sometimes, of course, the very exchange of information like this in front of the objecting inhabitant may render consent irrelevant by creating an exigency that justifies immediate action on the police's part[.]" The Court gave the following examples of exigency:

- imminent threat of evidence destruction (during the time necessary to obtain a search warrant);
- hot pursuit;
- protecting against imminent threats to officer's physical safety;
- imminent destruction of a building;
- imminent flight by a suspect; and
- protecting a co-occupant or resident from imminent harm, including harm from domestic violence.

Continued on next page

Of course, if the police have probable cause to believe one of the exigencies previously listed actually exists, then they may enter the residence without a warrant or consent, and any evidence they find in plain view may be seized. (See Chapter 10 for further discussion of the plain view doctrine.) In addition, police may use information obtained from an encounter with the cooperating and consenting co-occupant to obtain a valid search warrant.

Despite noting this emergency exception to the Fourth Amendment warrant requirement, the Court held that no such emergency was present in this case:

> [N]othing in the record justifies the search on grounds independent of Janet Randolph's consent. The State does not argue that she gave any indication to the police of a need for protection inside the house that might have justified entry into the portion of the premises where the police found the powdery straw (which, if lawfully seized, could have been used when attempting to establish probable cause for the warrant issued later). Nor does the State claim that the entry and search should be upheld under the rubric of exigent circumstances, owing to some apprehension by the police officers that Scott Randolph would destroy evidence of drug use before any warrant could be obtained. 547 U.S. at 123.

- Do you agree or disagree with the Court's holding in *Randolph*? Fully explain your answer.

- Do you believe the Court's holding in *Randolph* means that victims or potential victims of violence will be less likely to receive police assistance in preventing or stopping such violence? Fully explain your answer.

- The Court in *Randolph* said that if "a potential defendant with self-interest in objecting is in fact at the door [of the residence] and objects, the co-tenant's permission does not suffice for a reasonable search, whereas [if] the potential objector [is] nearby but not invited to take part in the threshold colloquy [or exchange at the door], [the objector] loses out [e.g., the objector can neither have the search deemed unlawful, nor any evidence seized during the search excluded]." Do you agree that the physical presence requirement is a sound requirement? For example, why shouldn't the police have to make a reasonable effort to find and seek the consent of co-occupants who are not physically present at the time consent to search is requested? Might these co-occupants, once found, object to the search?

- Should the holding, or rule, of *Randolph* apply only to residences or should it apply to other objects and locations, such as business offices, vehicles, storage units and/or duffel bags? In this regard, consider what the court said in dicta in *United States v. Murphy*, 516 F.3d 1117, 1124 (9th Cir. 2008) (abrogated on other grounds by *Fernandez*, 134 S. Ct. at 1126) ("Moreover, even if the storage units could not be considered a residence, there is no reason that the rule in *Randolph* should be limited to residences. *Randolph* is rooted in the idea of common authority and the Supreme Court has extended the principle of common authority well beyond residences. In *Frazier v. Cupp*, 394 U.S. 731, 740 (1969), the Court held that the shared use of a duffel bag was enough to give rise to common authority between users such that either user could give lawful consent to a search. Id. at 740, 89 S. Ct. 1420. Certainly, business offices are also subject to the protection of the Fourth Amendment." *See Mancusi v. DeForte*, 392 U.S. 364, 369 (1968).").

Landlords and Tenants A landlord has *no implied actual or apparent authority* to consent to a search of a tenant's premises or a seizure of the tenant's property during the period of the tenancy, even though the landlord has the authority to enter the tenant's premises for the limited purposes of inspection, performance of repairs, or housekeeping services. *Chapman v. United States*, 365 U.S. 610 (1961). Once the tenant has abandoned the premises or the tenancy has otherwise terminated, however, and the landlord has regained the primary right to occupation and control, the landlord may consent to a search of the premises, even though the former tenant left personal belongings on the premises. *United States v. Sledge*, 650 F.2d 1075 (9th Cir. 1981); *see also United States v. Law*, 528 F.3d 888, 904–05 (D.C. Cir. 2008). Furthermore, because a landlord clearly has joint authority over and access to common areas of an apartment building, a landlord may give valid consent to search those areas. *United States v. Kelly*, 551 F.2d 760 (8th Cir. 1977); *see also United States v. Elliott*, 50 F.3d 180, 187 (1995).

Finally, landlords who maintain joint or common authority with tenants over a specific area of premises may give consent to a search of that area even if not actually using it at the time of the search. In *United States v. Cook*, 530 F.2d 145 (7th Cir. 1976), the defendant's landlady consented to a search of a poultry house on her property. The poultry house consisted of a large room in which the landlady had segregated an area with wire fence for her exclusive use. She gave the defendant permission to use the remaining space, but she retained the right to use that space if necessary. The defendant claimed that because neither the landlady nor her family had *actually* used the defendant's area, there was no common authority. The court upheld the search, however, ruling that the defendant had assumed the risk that the landlady would permit others to inspect the premises, including his shared area of the room.

Hotel Management and Guests The U.S. Supreme Court held that the principles governing a landlord's consent to a search of tenant's premises apply to consent searches of hotel rooms allowed by hotel managers. In *Stoner v. California*, 376 U.S. 483 (1964), police investigating a robbery went to the defendant's hotel and, in his absence, obtained permission from the hotel clerk to search his room. The police found items of evidence in the room incriminating the defendant in the robbery. The Court held that the search was illegal and that the items seized were inadmissible. The defendant's constitutional right was at stake here—not the clerk's or the hotel's right. Therefore, only the defendant, either directly or through an agent, could waive that right. The police had no basis whatsoever to believe that the defendant authorized the night clerk to permit the police to search his room:

> It is true . . . that when a person engages a hotel room he undoubtedly gives "implied or express permission" to "such persons as maids, janitors, or repairmen" to enter his room "in the performance of their duties." . . . But the conduct of the night clerk and the police in the present case was of an entirely different order. . . . No less than a tenant of a house, or the occupant of a room in a boarding house . . . a guest in a hotel room is entitled to constitutional protection against unreasonable searches and seizures. . . . That protection would disappear if it were left to depend upon the unfettered discretion of an employee of the hotel. 376 U.S. at 489–90.

Moreover, the concept of "hotel guest" has been given a broad interpretation by courts. For example, in *United States v. Kimoana*, 383 F.3d 1215 (10th Cir. 2004), the court found that although the defendant had not registered or paid for the hotel room, he could still validly consent to a search of that room because "he had stayed there overnight, left his possessions there, and carried a key to the room." According to the court, these facts "support a finding that Defendant had joint access or control over the room, and thus had actual authority to consent." 383 F.3d at 1222; *see also United States v. Rodriguez*, 414 F.3d 837, 844 (8th Cir. 2005) (person who had neither paid for nor registered for motel room could validly consent to search of room because she "was the only person who lived there").

When the term of a hotel guest's occupancy of a room expires, however, the guest loses the exclusive right to privacy in the room, whether or not the guest remains in the room. The hotel manager then has the right to enter the room and may consent to a search of the room and a seizure of items found in the room. *United States v. Larson*, 760 F.2d 852 (8th Cir. 1985); *see also United States v. Lanier*, 636 F.3d 228, 232–33 (6th Cir. 2011).

Hosts and Guests The host's authority to consent to a search of the guest's area of the premises depends on

- the length of time of the guest's stay,
- the exclusiveness of the guest's control of a particular area of the premises, and
- the guest's reasonable expectation of privacy in that area of the premises.

In general, the owner or primary occupant of the premises (the host) may validly consent to a search of the premises, and any evidence found is admissible against a guest on the premises. For example, in *United States v. Hall*, 979 F.2d 77 (6th Cir. 1992), the owner of a residence gave consent to search the room of the defendant, whom he had allowed to stay at his residence in exchange for farm work. The court held that the owner had authority to consent to the search when he owned all the furniture in the room, he had personal items stored in an adjacent room accessed through the defendant's room, the room was never locked, and there was no agreement between him and the defendant that he was not to go in the room.

If, however, the person against whom a search is directed is a long-term guest and has a section of the premises set aside for exclusive personal use, the host may not consent to a search of that area of the premises. *Reeves v. Warden*, 346 F.2d 915 (4th Cir. 1965). In addition, a host may not consent to a search of an item over which she lacks common authority, such as items that are obviously the exclusive personal property of the guest. *State v. Edwards*, 570 A.2d 193 (Conn. 1990), held that although a host/lessee of an apartment could consent to a search of her apartment, she could not consent to a search of a guest's backpack. Likewise, *United States v. Gilley*, 608 F. Supp. 1065 (S.D. Ga. 1985), held that a consent to search a home given by the home's occupant did not authorize a search of a guest's travel bag found in the living room. The guest had done nothing to diminish his natural expectation of privacy in the contents of the bag. The host lacked common authority over the bag, as she had not been authorized to open or use the bag and had not in fact opened the bag. *See also United States v. Taylor*, 600 F.3d 678, 681–85 (6th Cir. 2010) (host/sole female tenant of apartment lacked apparent authority to consent to police search of a male guest's closed shoebox when it was found by police in the corner of a closet in a little-used, spare bedroom underneath male clothing, and when the host did not have permission from the guest to open the shoebox).

Employers and Employees This section will first discuss an employer's ability to consent to a search of certain parts of the employer's premises. Next, it will explore an employee's ability to consent to a search of his or her employer's premises.

Employer's Ability to Consent In general, an employer may consent to a search of any part of the employer's premises over which the employer has exclusive or joint authority and control. *State v. Robinson*, 206 A.2d 779 (N.J. Super. 1965), held that an employer could validly consent to the search of an employee's locker in the employer's plant. The employer owned the premises; furthermore, under the terms of a contract between the employer and the employee's union, the employer retained a master key to all employee lockers. Likewise, in *United States v. Ziegler*, 474 F.3d 1184 (9th Cir. 2007), the court found that the employer could consent to a search of an employee's workplace computer, which the company owned and had informed employees was subject to periodic monitoring and inspection.

An employer may not, however, validly consent to search an area set aside for use by an employee and within the employee's exclusive control. *United States v. Blok*, 188 F.2d 1019 (D.C. Cir. 1951), held that an employee's boss could not validly consent to a search of a desk assigned for the employee's exclusive use:

> In the absence of a valid regulation to the contrary, [the employee] was entitled to, and did keep private property of a personal sort in her desk. Her superiors could not reasonably search the desk for her purse, her personal letters, or anything else that did not belong to the [employer] and had no connection with the work of the office. Their consent did not make such a search by the police reasonable. 188 F.2d at 1021.

See also United States v. Gonzalez, 328 F.3d 543, 548 (9th Cir. 2003) ("Of course, one may have an objectively reasonable expectation of privacy in private work areas given over to an employee's exclusive use.") (internal quotations omitted).

Employee's Ability to Consent An employee's ability to consent validly to a search of the employer's premises depends on the scope of the employee's authority. The average employee, such as a clerk, janitor, maintenance person, driver, or other person temporarily in charge, may not give such consent. *United States v. Block*, 202 F. Supp. 705 (S.D.N.Y. 1962).

If, however, the employee is a manager or other person of considerable authority who is left in complete charge of important duties for a substantial period of time, the employee may validly consent to a search of the employer's premises. *See United States v. Antonelli Fireworks Co.*, 155 F.2d 631 (2d Cir. 1946); *see also Burt v. State*, 2011 WL 3211249 (Tex. App. 2011), *8 (reversed on other grounds by *Burt v. State*, 396 S.W.3d 574 (Tex. Crim. App. 2013)) ("And based on what [Director of Public Safety] Shackelford knew at the time [i.e., that the office manager was an authorized signer on her employer's business bank accounts], [Shackelford] could have reasonably believed that the office manager, by reason of the nature of her employment, had 'common authority' or apparent authority to consent to the search [of her employer's office locations]").

Under this employee standard for consent searches, typical babysitters who are assigned to watch children for short periods of time have insufficient authority over the premises of their employers to give a valid consent to search the premises. *People v. Litwin*, 355 N.Y.S.2d 646 (N.Y. App. Div. 1974). And though live-in babysitters who typically reside for longer periods of time in the home to care for children may be able to validly consent to a search of areas of the home to which they have access, they generally cannot consent to a search of the homeowner's bedroom. This was the holding of *United States v. Dearing*, 9 F.3d 1428 (9th Cir. 1993), where the babysitter had a room in the home and lived there for approximately six months to care for the homeowner's special needs children. The court in *Dearing* found that the live-in babysitter could not consent to a search for a machine gun in the homeowner's bedroom because the babysitter did not have "mutual use and joint access or control for most purposes" over the bedroom. 9 F.3d at 1430. A reasonable officer should have known that the babysitter lacked this kind of use and access or control over the bedroom.

School Officials and Students

Elementary and High School Students A police search of a high school student's locker, based on consent given by a school official, is valid because of the relationship between school authorities and students. The school authorities have an obligation to maintain discipline over students, and usually they retain partial access to the students' lockers so that neither has an exclusive right to the possession and use of the lockers. In a case in which police opened the locker of a student suspected of burglary with the consent of school authorities and found incriminating evidence, the court said:

> Although a student may have control of his school locker as against fellow students, his possession is not exclusive against the school and its officials. A school does not supply its students with lockers for illicit use in harboring pilfered property or harmful substances. We deem it a proper function of school authorities to inspect the lockers under their control and to prevent their use in illicit ways or for illegal purposes. *State v. Stein*, 456 P.2d 1, 3 (Kan. 1969).

Though not squarely a consent to search case, *Zamora v. Pomeroy*, 639 F.2d 662, 670 (1981), held that high school officials have a right to inspect student lockers and relied explicitly on language from the consent to search context when it said that "[i]nasmuch as the school had assumed joint control of the locker[,] it cannot be successfully maintained that the school did not have a right to inspect it." *Zamora* found no Fourth Amendment violation when school officials permitted police to enter a school to conduct searches of lockers using drug-sniffing dogs. The court in *Zamora* acknowledged in dicta that high school officials may consent to an inspection by law enforcement officers of student lockers. 639 F.2d at 670. Furthermore, in *Commonwealth v. Carey*, 554 N.E.2d 1199, 1202 (Mass. 1990), the court noted that "the student shares joint custody of the locker with school administrators, who retain either combinations or master keys, and thus a right of access when there is reason to believe the locker is being used for illegitimate purposes." But the court in *Carey* did note that in order for school administrators to ensure that they have a right to access student lockers, they should publicize this fact in advance to the student body. 554 N.E.2d at 1202.

College Students However, consent searches of college dormitory rooms are treated similarly to searches of hotel rooms. Thus, in general, the college student must voluntarily consent to a search of his dorm room by police for a search under the consent doctrine to be valid. For example, in *Commonwealth v. McCloskey,* 272 A.2d 271 (Pa. Super. 1970), police, with the consent of the dean but not the student, searched the defendant's room at a university and found marijuana. The evidence was held inadmissible in court:

> A dormitory room is analogous to an apartment or a hotel room. It certainly offers its occupant a more reasonable expectation of freedom from governmental intrusion than does a public telephone booth. The defendant rented the dormitory room for a certain period of time, agreeing to abide by the rules established by his lessor, the University. As in most rental situations, the lessor, Bucknell University, reserved the right to check the room for damages, wear, and unauthorized appliances. Such right of the lessor does not mean [defendant] was not entitled to have a "reasonable expectation of freedom from governmental intrusion," or that he gave consent to the police search, or gave the University authority to consent to such search. 272 A.2d at 273.

For further discussion of searches of college and high school students, see the section on special needs searches in Chapter 6.

Principals and Agents A person clearly may give someone else authority to consent to a search of the person's property. The person giving the authority is called the *principal*; the person acting for the principal is called an *agent*. For example, an attorney may consent to a search of a client's premises if the attorney has been specifically authorized to do so by the client. *Brown v. State*, 404 P.2d 428 (Nev. 1965), upheld a search of the defendant's premises and a seizure of his farm animals because consent to search had been given by the defendant's attorney after consultation with the defendant. Without a specific authorization to consent to search, however, the mere existence of an attorney–client relationship gives an attorney no authority to waive a client's personal rights.

Other cases involving principal–agent relationships occur in the context of homeowners who arrange for other individuals to monitor or perform maintenance work on their homes. For example, in *State v. Kellam*, 269 S.E.2d 197 (N.C. App. 1980), homeowners gave their next-door neighbor the key to their house with instructions to "look after their house" while the owners were away. The court held that the neighbor's consent to police to search the house was valid. And in *United States v. Baswell*, 792 F.2d 755, 756–57, 759 (8th Cir. 1986), the homeowner of a vacation house, a man named Bowie, gave Williams a key to the house in order to perform basic maintenance work on the house. The court in *Baswell* found that Williams was therefore an "agent" capable of providing valid consent to police to enter and search the home:

> The district court found an implied agency relationship existed between Williams and Bowie. The district court further found that Williams, as a person who was expected to kind of look out for the property, had the right to enter the house to investigate suspicious circumstances, and that he had implied authority from Mr. Bowie to authorize the entry of investigating officers if he thought someone was doing something unlawful without Bowie's knowledge. Upon reviewing the

evidence before the district court, we cannot say that the district court clearly erred in finding that Williams had implied authority to consent to the entry and search of the vacation house [by the investigating officers]. 792 F.2d at 759 (internal quotations omitted)

In addition, in *United States v. Novello*, 519 F.2d 1078 (5th Cir. 1975), the defendant (the "principal") rented an enclosed storage area that was accessible only to the rental agent and to those working with the agent. The defendant stored his truck containing marijuana in the area. Acting on an informant's tip, law enforcement officers obtained consent to enter the enclosed area from one of the agents having access and discovered marijuana in the truck. The court held that the defendant had no reasonable expectation of privacy in the storage area and upheld the search. "One who knows that others have of right general and untrammeled access to an area, a right as extensive as his own, can scarcely have much expectation of secrecy in it or confidence about whom they may let inspect it." 519 F.2d at 1080.

A principal has the power to limit the authority of his or her agent with respect to the principal's property; for example, an employer could limit an employee's authority to show business records to certain persons and not to others. A principal may not, however, limit an agent's authority for the purpose of obstructing justice. Therefore, in a case in which a doctor told his employee to take business records and hide them from the authorities, the court said that "when an employer gives an employee access to documents intentionally and knowingly in order to obstruct justice, that employee is a custodian of those records for the purposes of a valid subpoena or seizure." *United States v. Miller*, 800 F.2d 129, 135 (7th Cir. 1986).

Spouses, Partners, and Live-In Girlfriends/Boyfriends "Where two persons, such as a husband and wife, have equal rights to the use and occupation of certain premises, either may give consent to a search, and the evidence thus disclosed can be used against either." *United States v. Ocampo*, 492 F. Supp. 1211, 1236 (E.D.N.Y. 1980). In *Roberts v. United States*, 332 F.2d 892 (8th Cir. 1964), officers questioned the defendant's wife as part of a murder investigation. The wife volunteered information that the defendant had fired a pistol into the ceiling of their home some time ago. She later validly consented to a search for and seizure of the bullet in the ceiling. The court sustained the search on the basis that

- the consent was voluntary,
- the place of the search was the home of the defendant's wife, and
- the premises were under the wife's immediate and complete control at the time of the search.

Furthermore, the bullet could not be considered a personal effect of the husband, for which the wife would have no authority to consent to search. "It is not a question of agency, for a wife should not be held to have authority to waive her husband's constitutional rights. This is a question of the wife's own rights to authorize entry into premises where she lives and of which she had control." 332 F.2d at 896–97. *See also United States v. McGee*, 564 F.3d 136, 137–41 (2d Cir. 2009) (finding that a live-in girlfriend had actual, common authority to consent to a police search of her home because even though her boyfriend had locked her out with her luggage and personal belongings inside the home, his purpose was to prevent her from leaving and not to prevent her from living in the home with him).

However, following *Georgia v. Randolph*, 547 U.S. 103, 106 (2006), discussed earlier, even when valid consent to search is obtained by police from one spouse who is a co-occupant of the residence, when another spouse who is also a co-occupant of that residence is physically present at the time of the search request and refuses to consent, police may not enter the residence without a warrant or the presence of some other exception to the warrant requirement (i.e., exigent circumstances such as probable cause to believe someone is being or will soon be harmed). If police nonetheless enter and search the residence based on the one spouse's and co-occupant's consent, the physically present and objecting spouse who is a co-occupant has the right to have the search declared unreasonable, and any evidence seized against him excluded in court.

In addition, in *Fernandez v. California*, 134 S. Ct. 1126, 1129–30 (2014), discussed earlier in more detail, the U.S. Supreme Court recently held that *Randolph* does not apply if the objecting residential co-occupant, who in *Fernandez* was the male partner, is absent when another co-occupant validly consents (in *Fernandez*, the abused female partner/co-occupant). Thus, police may search residential premises when one residential co-occupant validly consents in the *absence* of another, objecting co-occupant. If police find and seize contraband during such a search, it is admissible in court.

Note that some courts have held that estranged spouses have the authority to consent to the search of marital premises they have vacated. In particular, *United States v. Long*, 524 F.2d 660 (9th Cir. 1975), held that an estranged wife, as a joint owner of a house she had vacated, could give consent to search the house even though her husband (the temporarily absent current occupant) had changed the locks on the doors. And in another estranged husband and wife case, the court found that the wife had common authority to consent to the search of the marital home even though the wife had moved out one week prior to the search. *See United States v. Shelton*, 337 F.3d 529 (5th Cir. 2003). In *Shelton*, the court determined that the estranged wife maintained common authority over the home because

- the couple had been married for six years;
- they had lived in the marital home for at least these six years;
- neither husband nor wife had attempted to file for divorce;
- the wife had kept a key to the house; and
- after moving out of the home, the wife had visited frequently without the husband present.

In sum, the court explained its holding that the wife had common authority to consent in this way:

> [The husband's] decision to solicit [the wife's] assistance in the [illegal] bingo operation, and at the same time to perpetuate her essentially unrestricted access to the house, on par with the access that she had enjoyed while residing there as his spouse, is what vested [the wife] with common authority to consent to a search. 337 F.3d at 534.

Also, and quite appropriately, a wife does not lose the ability to consent to the search of the marital home even though an abusive husband has forced her away from the home. This was the holding of *United States v. Backus*, 349 F.3d 1298 (11th Cir. 2003), where the wife had lived in the marital house she owned jointly with her husband for five years before leaving as a result of the abuse. Though the wife remained away from the house continuously for six months and the husband changed the locks in her absence, the Court held that the wife could validly consent to the search of the home for contraband:

> Where a wife is driven by an abusive husband from the home she jointly owns and jointly occupied, the duration of her absence is likely to be influenced by the nature and extent of her fear. The greater the fear, the longer the absence. We are not willing to extend to violently abusive husbands something akin to a rule of repose against the authority of their wives to consent to a search of jointly owned property. To do so would reward unlawful behavior in direct proportion to the amount of terror it inflicts. 349 F.3d at 1305.

Parents and Children This section will first discuss a parent's ability to consent to a search of premises owned by the parent. Following this discussion, the section will explore a child's ability to consent to a search of family premises.

Parental Consent to Search A parent's consent to search premises owned by the parent will usually be effective against a child who lives on those premises:

> Hardy's father gave his permission to the officers to enter and search the house and the premises which he owned and in which his son lived with him. Under the circumstances presented here the voluntary consent of Hardy's father to search his own premises is binding on Hardy and precludes his claim of violation of constitutional rights. *Commonwealth v. Hardy,* 223 A.2d 719, 723 (Pa. 1966).

Likewise, in *United States v. Rith,* 164 F.3d 1323, 1331 (10th Cir. 1999), the consent given by parents to police to search their son's bedroom for weapons, was considered valid because the parents maintained control over the home, including the bedroom, as owners. According to the court, this control over the bedroom existed because

- there was no lock on [the son's] bedroom door,
- no agreement with [the] parents that they not enter [the son's] room without his consent, and
- no payment of rent.

As the court suggested in *Rith,* however, the following factors may indicate that a parent lacks the ability to consent to a search of an area of the parent's home occupied by the child:

- the child pays rent,
- the child uses the room or other area exclusively,
- the child has sectioned the room or other area off by using locks or in some other permanent way, or
- the child has furnished the room or other area with his or her own furniture or otherwise establishes an expectation of privacy in the room. *State v. Peterson,* 525 S.W.2d 599 (Mo. App. 1975).

Applying some of the above-mentioned factors, the Court in *United States v. James,* 571 F.3d 707, 714 (7th Cir. 2009) found that a male defendant's mother had authority to consent to a police seizure of a safe defendant had left at her house because defendant, who lived with his mother during the relevant time period, had left the safe there for a long time and did not restrict his mother from controlling the safe in any way (e.g., by placing limitations on her use of the safe).

Furthermore, parents may not consent to a search of a child's room in their home if the child has already refused to grant such consent. "Constitutional rights may not be defeated by the expedient of soliciting several persons successively until the sought-after consent is obtained." *People v. Mortimer,* 361 N.Y.S.2d 955, 958 (N.Y. 1974).

Child's Consent to Search The Supreme Court of Georgia identified certain factors to be considered in determining whether a minor's consent to search family premises is valid:

- whether the minor lived on the premises,
- whether the minor had a right of access to the premises and the right to invite others thereto,
- whether the minor was of an age at which he or she could be expected to exercise at least minimal discretion, and
- whether officers acted reasonably in believing that the minor had sufficient control over the premises to give a valid consent to search. *Davis v. State,* 422 S.E.2d 546 (Ga. 1992).

United States v. Clutter, 914 F.2d 775, 778 (6th Cir. 1990), helps to illustrate how these factors are applied in practice. In *Clutter*, two children, one twelve years of age and the other fourteen years of age, consented to the search of their parents' home. The court found this consent valid given the amount of access and control the children exercised over the premises:

> Under the circumstances of this case, where children twelve and fourteen years of age routinely were left in exclusive control of the house, and defendants' possession of large quantities of marijuana was so open and patently non-exclusive that its odor pervaded the house, the government satisfied its burden of demonstrating the initial warrantless search of the bedroom was by consent, since the boys enjoyed that degree of access and control over the house that afforded them the right to permit inspection of any room in the house, and defendants assumed that risk. 914 F.2d at 778.

And in *United States v. Sanchez*, 608 F.3d 685, 687–89 (10th Cir. 2010), the Court found that A.L., the defendant's fifteen-year-old daughter, had authority to consent to a search by police of the family home, which revealed marijuana in the garage:

> A.L. had joint access, and we agree that ample evidence supports this view. First, A.L. lived full time in the house and had unrestricted access to it, particularly to the common living areas such as the downstairs and garage. A.L. . . . . was in charge of the premises when the officers visited and . . . had no restrictions on her behavior in the home at all. Second, at the time the officers arrived at the house, A.L. was home babysitting her younger brother, a task she regularly performed alone. Based on her testimony, the district court concluded A.L. had authority to access the entire house—including the garage—at the time of the home visit. And nothing in the record suggests any restrictions or limitations whatsoever on her access to or use of any part of the home. In short, the district court did not clearly err in finding actual authority for [A.L. to consent to] the search. 608 F.3d at 689 (internal quotations omitted).

Drivers and Passengers Drivers who lack common authority over items in the vehicle in which they are driving may not validly consent to a search of those items. In *United States v. Jaras*, 86 F.3d 383, 389 (5th Cir. 1996), the court found that the driver of an automobile lacked authority to consent to a search of a passenger's suitcases located in the trunk. The court noted that there was no evidence that the driver had joint access or control over the suitcases to support a claim of actual authority. Also, the court explained that the officer could not have a reasonable belief that the suitcases belonged to the driver because the driver clearly explained to the officer that they were not his suitcases but rather belonged to the passenger. As a result, the driver also lacked apparent authority over the suitcases. But in *United States v. Harris*, 526 F.3d 1334, 1336–37, 1339–40 (11th Cir. 2008), the court found that a taxi cab driver could consent to a search of the general passenger compartment area of the taxi because the driver had joint access and control over this area, and the passenger in the taxi at the time did not object to the police search. Accordingly, a pistol found by police under a floor mat in the passenger compartment area was admissible in evidence against the passenger.

Bailors and Bailees A bailee is a person in possession of someone else's personal property with the lawful permission of the rightful owner, also referred to as a bailor. Depending on the level of control a bailee has over the personal property of another person, the bailee may be able to give legal consent for a search of that property.

Bailee in Full Possession and Control of Personal Property A bailee of personal property may consent to a search of the property if the bailee has full possession and control. For example, in *United States v. Beshore*, 961 F.2d 1380, 1382–83 (8th Cir. 1992), the court found that defendant's girlfriend could provide valid consent to police to search the defendant's car because the defendant had given his girlfriend permission to use the car and she had placed her own license plates on the car. The court reasoned that the defendant had "thus assumed the risk that [his girlfriend] would permit the vehicle to be searched." And in *United States v. Jackson*, 598 F.3d 340, 342–43, 347–48 (7th Cir. 2010), the court determined that defendant's mother could provide valid consent to a police officer to search the defendant's computer and computer case because defendant had allowed his mother to borrow and use the computer:

> Because [defendant's mother] Eaton had the apparent authority to consent to a search of the computer case, the district court properly denied Defendant's suppression motion [to suppress a gun found in a pocket of the case]. First, there is no evidence that Officer Dexheimer was aware of anything that would have alerted him that Eaton did not have authority to consent to the search. Second, Eaton told Officer Dexheimer during the traffic stop that Defendant had authorized her to take the computer and computer case, and [another officer] had previously observed Defendant freely provide the computer case to Eaton. Officer Dexheimer therefore had a reasonable basis for believing that Eaton had the authority to consent to the search.

Bailee with Mere Custody of Personal Property If a bailor gives a bailee only limited control over the bailor's property, such as for shipment, storage, or repair purposes, evidence found by law enforcement officers would not be admissible in court against the owner of the property. For example, in *United States v. Jacobsen*, 466 U.S. 109 (1984), the Court found that delivery package employees cannot consent to a search of packages they were merely moving within the company's warehouse. Also, an airline cannot validly consent to the search of a package that a person has wrapped, tied, and delivered to the airline solely for transportation purposes. *Corngold v. United States*, 367 F.2d 1 (9th Cir. 1966). Nor can the owner of a boat who agrees to store another person's property on his boat give a valid consent to police to search and seize the stored property. *Commonwealth v. Storck*, 275 A.2d 362 (Pa. 1971). In addition, *State v. Farrell*, 443 A.2d 438, 442 (R.I. 1982), held that "one who entrusts his automobile to another for the purposes of repair, or periodic inspection as required by law, does not confer the kind of mutual use or control which would empower that person to consent to a warrantless search and seizure."

CRIMINAL PROCEDURE IN ACTION

Interpreting *Georgia v. Randolph*: When Does Consent by a Co-Occupant of a Residence Give Police the Authority to Search That Residence?

United States v. Stabile, 633 F.3d 219, 224–26 (3rd Cir. 2011), provides a recent example of how courts are interpreting Georgia v. *Randolph*, discussed earlier in this section and in the preceding Discussion Point.

The facts of *Stabile* are as follows:

At 1:00 P.M. on July 24, 2006, Secret Service Special Agents Christopher Albanese and John Croes, and Detective Joseph Nieciecki of the Bergen County Sheriff's Department, arrived at Stabile's house to question Stabile about counterfeiting checks. Stabile was not at home, but [co-occupant] Deetz answered the door, invited the agents inside, asked the officers to sit at a table near the living room, and offered them something to drink. The officers informed Deetz of the purpose of their visit and explained that they

Continued on next page

suspected that Stabile had engaged in financial crimes. Albanese then asked Deetz for consent to search the house. Albanese provided Deetz with a consent form and informed Deetz that she could refuse consent. Deetz reviewed the consent form for approximately thirty minutes and then signed it. Deetz testified that one of the reasons she voluntarily signed the form was so she herself could find out about Stabile's deceptive financial practices.

Without a search warrant but with Deetz's consent, the agents began a search of the house. During the course of the search, Deetz led the agents around the house, provided the agents with documents related to Stabile's finances, and showed the agents the locations of several computers. Next to one computer, the agents found check stock, check writing software, photocopies of checks, copies of previously passed fraudulent checks, two printers, and checks with an alias. Deetz also showed the agents two computers and several hard drives in the basement of the house. At the suppression hearing, Deetz testified:

Q. And who pointed out those hard drives to the law enforcement officers?

A. I [Deetz] did.

Q. Did you provide consent for the officers to search those computers?

A. Yes, I did.

The Secret Service agents then called to the home the Bergen County Prosecutor's Office, which sent two members from its Computer Crimes Unit to disconnect the hard drives. Deetz showed the recently arrived Bergen County officers the locations of the computers and the hard drives. Deetz watched the officers remove the hard drives. When one officer had difficulty removing a hard drive, Deetz asked the officer if he needed a screwdriver. The officer replied that he did, so Deetz got a screwdriver from Stabile's toolbox and gave it to the officer. At approximately 6:00 P.M., the Bergen County officers [departed] the house, taking with them six hard drives. Stabile was not present in his house at any point during this search.

In fact, the search had been completed when Stabile arrived home, at approximately 7:15 P.M.

When Stabile finally arrived home, Deetz waited outside the house while the agents interviewed Stabile. Although the agents attempted to question Stabile, Stabile refused to answer questions without an attorney present. When informed that Deetz had already consented to the search, Stabile attempted to revoke Deetz's consent by stating "I take it back." The agents then departed.

- In light of *Georgia v. Randolph* discussed earlier in this section and in the preceding Discussion Point box, do you think the consent provided by Deetz to search the home is valid against Stabile? In other words, did the law enforcement officers have the authority to search the home based on the co-occupant Deetz's consent? To answer this question, be sure to think about the location of Stabile at the time of the initial police request for consent to search. Fully explain your answer.

- Does it matter that Stabile attempted to revoke Deetz's consent when he finally arrived at the home? Would such a revocation render the police search invalid and lead to the exclusion of any items found (i.e., documents revealing financial crimes by Stabile)?

- Does it matter that Deetz wanted to find out about Stabile's financial activities or that Deetz assisted the law enforcement officials as she did (i.e., providing them with Stabile's financial documents and even helping them to remove one of Stabile's hard drives by giving them a screwdriver)?

- Following *Fernandez v. California*, 134 S .Ct. 1126 (2014), discussed earlier in this chapter and decided after *Stabile*, does it matter why Stabile was absent from the residence at the time of the consent search by police? What if she was absent because she was at work? Because police were conducting a valid traffic stop of Stabile for speeding? Because police were conducting an invalid stop or arrest of Stabile in order to prevent her from returning to the home at the time of the search to object (to the search)?

Finally, *United States v. Most*, 876 F.2d 191 (D.C. Cir. 1989), held that a store clerk who was asked by the defendant to watch a package could not give valid consent to search the package. The court said, "We see no basis for holding that delivery people who move packages may not consent to a search, but that store clerks who watch packages may." 876 F.2d at 200 n.18.

SUMMARY

A consent search occurs when a person allows a law enforcement officer to search his or her body, premises, or belongings. Consent searches are convenient for law enforcement officers, requiring no justification, such as probable cause or a warrant; but consent searches also present many opportunities for abuse. For this reason, courts exercise a strong presumption against consent searches and place a heavy burden on prosecutors to prove that they are voluntary.

Voluntariness depends on the totality of circumstances surrounding the giving of consent. Among the circumstances considered are

- force or threat of force by police,
- fraudulent or mistaken claim of police authority,
- misrepresentation or deception by police,
- arrest or detention of consenting person,
- consenting person's awareness of the right to refuse consent to search,
- police informing consenting person that she is free to go/leave,
- clearness and explicitness of consent,
- notification of counsel and the provision of the *Miranda* warnings, and
- the physical, mental, emotional, and educational characteristics of consenting person.

The Fourth Amendment does not strictly require that a lawfully seized person be advised that he or she is free to go before the person's consent to search will be recognized as voluntary. In addition, personal characteristics alone, such as being less educated or having a low intelligence quotient (IQ), will not generally render a consent involuntary. Instead, police must exploit in some way these characteristics before consent will be deemed involuntary.

Consent to enter premises is not the equivalent of consent to search the premises. Also, a person found to have provided valid consent to one search has not necessarily provided valid consent for additional searches. The standard for measuring the scope of a suspect's consent is that of "objective reasonableness": What would the typical reasonable person have understood by the exchange between the officer and the suspect? The scope of a consent search may be limited by area, by time, and by the object for which the search is allowed. As a general rule, if an officer asks for and obtains consent from a person to search a specific area, whether in a place or on a person, the officer is limited to that specific area. However, if the consenting person places no limit on the scope of a search, the scope is generally defined by its expressed object. The person giving consent to search may revoke it at any time.

The constitutional right to consent to a search or refuse such consent is a personal right of the individual against whom the search is directed. A person other than the person against whose interests the search is being conducted cannot effectively consent to a search of property unless (1) the person has been specifically authorized to do so; (2) the person possesses common authority over, or has other sufficient relationship to, the premises or effects sought to be inspected; or (3) police reasonably believe the person has sufficient authority to consent, even though the person in fact does not have such authority.

When voluntary consent is obtained by police from one co-occupant to search a residence on a particular occasion and another co-occupant of that residence is physically present on this occasion and refuses to consent, police may not enter the residence without a warrant or the presence of some other exception to the warrant requirement (the *Randolph* rule). If police nonetheless enter and search the residence based on the one co-occupant's consent, the physically present and objecting co-occupant has the right to have the search declared unreasonable, and any evidence seized against him excluded in court. The *Randolph* rule does not apply if the objecting residential co-occupant is absent when another co-occupant validly consents. Thus, police may search residential premises when one residential co-occupant validly consents in the *absence* of another, objecting co-occupant. If police find and seize contraband during such a search, it is admissible in court.

KEY TERMS

REVIEW AND DISCUSSION QUESTIONS

1. If a person is deprived of freedom of action in a significant way by a law enforcement officer, is it necessary for that person to be given warnings of the right to refuse consent before being asked for consent to search? Explain.

2. If a law enforcement officer asks a person for consent to search his or her home for stolen jewelry when the officer's real purpose is to look for marked money, is the consent voluntary?

3. Assume that law enforcement officers have obtained a valid consent to search an arrested defendant's automobile for drugs and an initial search proves fruitless. Can the officers search the automobile again two hours later without obtaining a new consent to search? What about two days later? What about two weeks later? What changes in the defendant's status might render the initial consent no longer valid?

4. If, after giving consent to search, a person becomes nervous and revokes or limits the scope of the search, can this reaction be used by the officers as an indication of probable cause to obtain a search warrant? Can a person validly revoke or limit the scope of their initial consent to search?

5. Are third-party consents to search the defendant's premises valid in the following circumstances?

   a. A husband, out of anger at his wife, the defendant, invites the police into the marital home when the wife is away on a business trip and points out evidence incriminating the wife.

   b. The defendant's girlfriend, who lives with him part-time and who does not have a key to defendant's apartment or keep most of her belongings there, consents to a search of the defendant's apartment while the defendant is at work.

   c. A wife disobeys the instructions of her husband, the defendant, not to allow a search of their home. Does it matter whether the police know of the instructions? Does it matter whether the husband is present at the time of the search and objects to the search?

6. Is it proper for a law enforcement officer to deliberately *avoid* attempting to obtain consent to search from the defendant and instead attempt to obtain consent from someone with equal authority over the defendant's premises? Does it matter whether the law enforcement officer

had an opportunity to attempt to obtain consent from the defendant and deliberately failed to take it? What if the officer had deliberately *prevented* defendant from being physically present so as to be able to object to the search? In other words, is there a difference between deliberate avoidance and deliberate prevention in this context? Does it matter whether the officer had a *lawful* reason to prevent defendant from being physically present to object (say, lawful grounds to arrest or detain defendant)? What if the defendant was deliberately avoiding the police?

7. The dissenting opinion in *Florida v. Jimeno* stated, "Because an individual's expectation of privacy in a container is distinct from, and far greater than, his expectation of privacy in the interior of his car, it follows that an individual's consent to a search of the interior of his car cannot necessarily be understood as extending to containers in the car." 500 U.S. at 254. Discuss.

8. Should a person be able to limit the number of officers conducting a consent search? Should a person be able to choose which officer or officers conduct the consent search? Should a person be allowed to follow the officer conducting the search?

9. Can the following persons give a valid consent to search?

   a. A highly intoxicated person

   b. A five-year-old, a seven-year-old, or a ten-year-old child

   c. A senile person or a person with mental disabilities

   d. An emotionally upset person

   e. An uneducated person

10. Can the driver of a motor vehicle consent to a search of the vehicle even though a passenger objects? Does it matter if the item police wish to search belongs to the driver (and not the passenger)? Can the owner of a store consent to a search of the store even though an employee objects? Can a parent consent to a search of his or her home even though a child objects?

11. Assume that consent to obtain a blood sample from a rape suspect is obtained by telling him that the sample will be tested to determine the percentage of alcohol in his blood. Is his consent voluntary if the blood sample is actually used to match his blood with fluids found at the rape scene? *See Graves v. Beto*, 424 F.2d 524 (5th Cir. 1970).

10

The Plain View Doctrine

LO1 EXPLAIN the rationale for the plain view doctrine.

LO2 EVALUATE the requirements of the plain view doctrine.

LO3 DESCRIBE examples of prior valid intrusions into zones of privacy.

LO4 ANALYZE the various ways officers are permitted to develop probable cause for plain view searches and seizures.

LO5 EVALUATE the distinction between a plain view observation and a search, especially with respect to closer examinations of items and examinations of containers.

LO6 DISCUSS why plain view seizures need not be inadvertent.

LO7 ANALYZE the so-called plain touch or plain feel doctrine.

The U.S. Supreme Court stated the basic **plain view doctrine** in *Harris v. United States*: "It has been settled that objects falling in the plain view of an officer who has a right to be in a position to have that view may be introduced in evidence." 390 U.S. 234, 236 (1968). This doctrine was further elaborated in *Minnesota v. Dickerson*: "[I]f police are lawfully in a position from which they view an object, if its incriminating character is apparent, and if the officers have a lawful right of access to the object, they may seize it without a warrant." 508 U.S. 366, 375 (1993).

The Plain View Doctrine

The plain view doctrine permits law enforcement officers to seize evidence without a warrant. It is a recognized exception to the warrant requirement of the Fourth Amendment, even though a plain view observation technically does not constitute a search. A search occurs only if a person's property interests or reasonable expectations of privacy are infringed. If a law enforcement officer merely observes an item of evidence from a position in which the officer has a right to be, this is ordinarily not considered an infringement of a person's property or privacy rights. *See, e.g., Texas v. Brown*, 460 U.S. 730, 739 (1983): "It is important to distinguish 'plain view' . . . to justify seizure of an object, from an officer's mere observation of an item left in plain view. Whereas the latter (e.g., mere observation) generally involves no Fourth Amendment search, the former (e.g., seizure of an item) generally does implicate the Amendment's limitations upon seizures of personal property."

But the Fourth Amendment prohibits unreasonable seizures as well as unreasonable searches. The plain view doctrine, although applicable to Fourth Amendment searches, is primarily concerned with *seizures* under that Amendment:

> The right to security in person and property protected by the Fourth Amendment may be invaded in quite different ways by searches and seizures. A search compromises the individual interest in privacy; a seizure deprives the individual of dominion over his or her person or property. . . . The "plain view" doctrine is often considered an exception to the general rule that warrantless searches are presumptively unreasonable, but this characterization overlooks the important difference between searches and seizures. If an article is already in plain view, neither its observation nor its seizure would involve any invasion of privacy. . . . A seizure of the article, however, would obviously invade the owner's possessory interest. . . . If "plain view" justifies an exception from an otherwise applicable warrant requirement, therefore, it must be an exception that is addressed to the concerns that are implicated by seizures rather than by searches.

Horton v. California, 496 U.S. 128, 133–34 (1990).

Thus, if the plain view doctrine is found to apply, it will justify a warrantless seizure of an item belonging to an individual despite the apparent intrusion into that individual's possessory interest.

The plain view doctrine is justified on police convenience and safety; that is, police avoid having to risk harm to themselves and destruction to evidence in the time it would take to obtain a warrant. At the same time, the doctrine consists of "built-in" safeguards that work to prevent any potential abuse by law enforcement:

> The reason so light and transient a justification as police convenience is deemed reasonable is because of the absolutely minimal risk posed by the Plain View Doctrine to either of the two traditional Fourth Amendment values or concerns. . . . In terms of the initial intrusion or breach into the zone of privacy, the Plain View Doctrine, by definition, poses no threat whatsoever. It does not authorize the crossing of a threshold or other initiation of an intrusion. It does not even come into play until the intrusion is already a valid fait accompli. . . .
>
> In terms of the other traditional Fourth Amendment concern, preventing even a validly initiated search from degenerating into an exploratory fishing expedition or general rummaging about, the Plain View Doctrine, again by definition, poses no threat . . . , for it [generally] authorizes not even the most

minimal of further searching. It [generally] authorizes only the warrantless seizure by the police of probable evidence already revealed to them, with no further examination or searching being involved. *State v. Jones*, 653 A.2d 1040, 1045 (Md. Ct. Spec. App. 1995); *but see Arizona v. Hicks*, 480 U.S. 321, 327 (1987), discussed later in this chapter (authorizing plain view searches under limited circumstances).

Requirements of the Plain View Doctrine

The plain view doctrine does not give law enforcement officers a license to look around anywhere, at any time, and under any circumstances, and to seize anything they wish. The doctrine has two carefully prescribed requirements:

1. In viewing and accessing an object, the officer must not unreasonably intrude on any person's property or reasonable expectation of privacy. If a person's property or reasonable expectation of privacy was invaded, then to satisfy the Fourth Amendment's mandate of reasonableness, the officer must have had a valid justification for having intruded on or into a zone of privacy or area of property. (Note: This first requirement listed for the plain view doctrine—a prior, valid justification for police intrusion into a zone of privacy or area of property—encompasses the twin, related concepts under the doctrine that police must view an object from a lawful vantage point and have a lawful right of access to the object. Because most courts combine their analysis for these concepts or combine the concepts themselves, this chapter treats both concepts under the one rubric, or heading, of "valid justification for prior police intrusion into an area of property or a zone of privacy.")

2. The incriminating character of the object to be seized must be immediately apparent to the officer. In particular, the officer must have probable cause to believe that the item he or she is observing, and intends to seize, is incriminating in nature.

Requirement 1: Valid Justification for Prior Police Intrusion into an Area of Property or a Zone of Privacy

The U.S. Supreme Court has provided several examples of valid justifications for prior intrusions by police on property or into a zone of privacy that is protected by the Fourth Amendment:

> What the "plain view" cases have in common is that the police officer in each of them had a prior justification for an intrusion in the course of which he came . . . across a piece of evidence incriminating the accused. The doctrine serves to supplement the prior justification—whether it be a warrant for another object, hot pursuit, search incident to lawful arrest, or some other legitimate reason for being present unconnected with a search directed against the accused—and permits the warrantless seizure.
> *Coolidge v. New Hampshire*, 403 U.S. 443, 466 (1971).

For purposes of this chapter, a valid justification for a prior intrusion simply means that a law enforcement officer has made a legal encroachment into a constitutionally protected area or has otherwise legally invaded a person's property or reasonable expectation of privacy. Stated otherwise: "It is . . . an essential predicate to any valid warrantless seizure of incriminating evidence that the officer did not violate the Fourth Amendment in arriving at the place from which the evidence could be plainly viewed." *Horton v. California*, 496 U.S. 128, 136 (1990).

Effecting a Lawful Arrest, Search Incident to Arrest, or Protective Sweep

A law enforcement officer may lawfully seize an object that comes into view during a *lawfully executed arrest, search incident to arrest, or protective sweep.* The law of search incident to arrest and the plain view doctrine must be clearly distinguished. Under *Chimel v. California* (see Chapter 7), a law enforcement officer may search a person incident to arrest only for weapons or to prevent the destruction or concealment of evidence. The extent of the search is limited to the arrestee's body and the area within the arrestee's immediate control, "construing that phrase to mean the area from within which he might gain possession of a weapon or destructible evidence." 395 U.S. 752, 763.

The plain view doctrine does not extend the permissible area of search incident to arrest. In *Chimel*, the Supreme Court specifically said:

> There is no comparable justification, however, for routinely searching any room other than that in which an arrest occurs—or for that matter, for searching through all the desk drawers or other closed or concealed areas in that room itself. Such searches, in the absence of well-recognized exceptions, may be made only under the authority of a search warrant. 395 U.S. at 763.

Nevertheless, the law of search incident to arrest does not require law enforcement officers to ignore or avert their eyes from objects readily visible in the room where the arrest occurs. If the arresting officer observes an item of incriminating evidence open to view but outside the area under the immediate control of the arrestee, the officer may seize it—so long as the observation was made in the course of a lawful arrest or an appropriately limited search incident to arrest. For example, in *Washington v. Chrisman*, 455 U.S. 1 (1982) (also discussed in Chapter 7), the officer arrested the suspect for underage drinking and then asked the suspect for his identification. When the suspect went to retrieve identification from his dorm room, the officer accompanied him to the room. From the doorway of the suspect's room, the officer observed marijuana seeds and a pipe on a desk. The Court in *Chrisman* concluded that the officer was lawfully in the doorway to the dorm room because he had previously arrested the suspect and was therefore permitted to accompany the arrestee to the room. Because the officer possessed a valid justification for being in the arrestee's doorway, the officer was permitted, under the plain view doctrine, to seize the marijuana seeds and pipe he saw on the arrestee's desk:

> This is a classic instance of incriminating evidence found in plain view when a police officer, for unrelated but entirely legitimate reasons, obtains lawful access to an individual's area of privacy. The Fourth Amendment does not prohibit seizure of evidence of criminal conduct found in these circumstances. 455 U.S. at 9.

This same rule applies to items of evidence observed during the course of a properly limited protective sweep (see Chapter 7). Accordingly, if officers are conducting a valid protective sweep of premises, the plain view doctrine does not extend the permissible scope of the sweep, but rather it allows officers to seize incriminating evidence that comes naturally into their view from a location they are permitted to be. *United States v. Ford*, 53 F.3d 265 (D.C. Cir. 1995), nicely illustrates this point. The court in *Ford* described the following facts:

> [L]aw enforcement officers . . . arrived at the home of [defendant's] mother with an arrest warrant for [the defendant]. Upon entering the apartment, [one] agent observed [the defendant] in the apartment hallway and arrested him. The agent then conducted what the Government characterizes as a "protective sweep." He walked into the bedroom immediately adjoining the hallway in which appellant was arrested, purportedly to check for individuals who might pose a danger to those on the arrest scene. Once in the bedroom, the agent spotted a gun clip in plain view on the floor, and, although he realized that there were no people in the bedroom, the agent nevertheless continued to search. He lifted a mattress under which he found live ammunition, money, and crack cocaine, and he lifted the window shades and found a gun on the windowsill. 53 F.3d at 266.

The court allowed the gun clip into evidence under the plain view doctrine, but it excluded the evidence found under the mattress and behind the window shades:

> [T]he agent was justified in looking in the bedroom [under the protective sweep doctrine], which was a space immediately adjoining the place of arrest. And once in the bedroom, the agent could legitimately seize the gun clip which was in plain view. The agent could not, however, lawfully search beyond that—neither under the mattress nor behind the window shades—because these were not spaces from which an attack could be immediately launched. . . . We hold that the evidence taken from under the mattress and from behind the window shades was seized in violation of the Fourth Amendment and therefore was inadmissible at trial. 53 F.3d at 266.

Thus, the court in *Ford* excluded the evidence found under the mattress and behind the window shades because this evidence was discovered in places where the officer did not have a valid justification to be under the protective sweep doctrine. Recall that under that doctrine discussed in Chapter 7, the officer may only look in places where a person could be (e.g., spaces from where an attack could be immediately launched). However, the court admitted into evidence the gun clip found in plain view on the floor of the adjacent bedroom because it was located in an area within the valid scope of the protective sweep doctrine. *See also United States v. Green*, 599 F.3d 360, 376 (4th Cir. 2010) ("A protective sweep—where the circumstances justify it—does not entitle officers to conduct a full search of the premises, but rather extends only to a limited inspection of spaces where a person may actually be found. We have expressly indicated that searching under beds is within the ambit of a protective sweep. Accordingly, here, the officers' protective sweep, which encompassed a look under Boyd's bed, was appropriate. . . . Furthermore, the evidence in the record fully justified the . . . finding that the officer who discovered the cash hoard did not need to move or jostle the items under the bed to see it. He observed [the cash] in plain view. Here, the officer was lawfully in a place from which the money could be plainly viewed, and he had a lawful right to access the money. [T]he money's incriminating character, as probable proceeds from narcotics transactions and thus the fruit of illegal activity, could be immediately inferred. Accordingly, the district court did not err in denying Boyd's motion to suppress the cash seized from under his bed.") (internal citations omitted).

Conducting a Valid Stop and Frisk An officer may seize without a warrant items of evidence observed while conducting a lawful stop and frisk. (See Chapter 8 for a discussion of stops and frisks.) Again, the plain view doctrine does not extend the area of search permissible under stop-and-frisk law, but it does give the officer authority to seize readily visible objects conducted during a valid stop and frisk.

In *United States v. Ridge*, 329 F.3d 535 (6th Cir. 2003), the court permitted a plain view seizure of a gun during a valid investigative stop of a vehicle. The court described the facts in *Ridge* as follows:

> Officers stopped a van driven by [defendants] as it approached the site of a known methamphetamine laboratory where the officers were [already] conducting a [valid] search. One officer had intercepted a phone call twenty minutes earlier, and was told, "[One of the defendants is] on the way with the money." After [a codefendant] was removed from the van, officers seized a firearm that was sitting on [that defendant's] seat. 329 F.3d at 537.

On these facts, the court held "[t]he officers had a reasonable, articulable suspicion sufficient to justify a stop, which led naturally to the discovery of the weapon in plain view when [defendant] exited the van." 329 F.3d at 542.

The U.S. Supreme Court case of *Texas v. Brown*, 460 U.S. 730 (1983), involved a plain view seizure during a stop at a valid police roadblock, or checkpoint. In *Brown*, police officer Harold Maples assisted in setting up a routine driver's license checkpoint. Around midnight, Maples stopped an automobile driven by defendant Brown. While Maples asked Brown for his driver's license, Maples shined his flashlight into the car and saw Brown remove his right hand from his right pants pocket. Maples noticed that an opaque, green party balloon, knotted about one half inch from the tip, was caught between the two middle fingers of Brown's hand. Maples's experience as a police officer frequently involved in drug arrests made him aware that these types of balloons are typically used in transporting narcotics. Brown let the balloon fall to the seat near his leg and then reached to open the glove compartment. Upon seeing the balloon, Maples shifted his position to obtain a better view of the glove compartment. Maples then noticed several small plastic vials, quantities of loose white powder, and an open bag of party balloons in the glove compartment. After Brown could not find his license, Maples instructed him to get out of the car, which Brown did. Officer Maples reached into the car and picked up the green balloon. Maples noticed what appeared to be a powdery substance within the tied-off portion of the balloon (lab tests later determined this powder to be heroin). Brown was placed under arrest.

The Supreme Court in *Brown* found that Officer Maples's actions leading to the plain view seizure of the balloon were lawful: "Applying these principles, we conclude that Officer Maples properly seized the green balloon from Brown's automobile. The Court of Criminal Appeals stated that it did not 'question . . . the validity of the officer's initial stop of appellant's vehicle as a part of a license check,' and we agree." 460 U.S. at 739–40.

Recall that under stop-and-frisk law, the passenger compartment of an automobile may be lawfully searched for weapons if the officer has developed reasonable suspicion that the automobile's driver or one of its passengers is armed and dangerous. Any illegal objects found in plain view during this lawful search for weapons may also be seized:

> If while conducting a legitimate *Terry* search of the interior of the automobile [e.g., a search with the necessary reasonable suspicion], the officer should . . . discover contraband other than weapons, he clearly cannot be required to ignore the contraband, and the Fourth Amendment does not require its suppression in such circumstances. *Michigan v. Long*, 463 U.S. 1032, 1050 (1983) (italics supplied).

Executing a Valid Search Warrant In *Coolidge v. New Hampshire*, 403 U.S. 443, 465 (1971), the U.S. Supreme Court said that an "example of the applicability of the 'plain view' doctrine is the situation in which the police have a warrant to search a given area for specified objects, and in the course of the search come across some other article of incriminating character." And in *Cady v. Dombrowski*, 413 U.S. 433, 449 (1973), the U.S. Supreme Court held that an officer executing a *valid search warrant* of an automobile could legally seize items of evidence lying in plain view (e.g., a sock and a floor mat) even though they were not particularly described in the warrant:

> The seizures of the sock and the floor mat occurred while a valid warrant was outstanding, and thus could not be considered unconstitutional under the theory advanced below. As these items were constitutionally seized, we do not deem it constitutionally significant that they were not listed in the return of the warrant.

In addition, in *United States v. Gamble*, 388 F.3d 74, 76–77 (2d Cir. 2004), the court held that a valid warrant authorizing seizure of cocaine and drug paraphernalia at defendant's apartment permitted police to seize an ammunition clip found in plain view in a dresser drawer since "they had a warrant authorizing them to search for and seize cocaine and drug paraphernalia—items that could plausibly be found in a dresser drawer." *See also Walczyk v. Rio*, 496 F.3d 139, 160, n.21 (2nd Cir. 2007) (search warrant for "firearms" in home allowed for police seizure of ammunition, gun clips, and related firearms paraphernalia found in plain view).

Once officers have discharged their duties under a warrant, however, the warrant no longer provides valid justification for their presence on premises. Officers may not seize items of evidence observed in plain view after a warrant is fully executed. See, e.g., *United States v. Limatoc*, 807 F.2d 792 (9th Cir. 1987). In a similar vein, if a warrant is later found to be invalid for failing to meet the particularity requirement (or for any other reason), items seized in plain view while police executed the warrant will be excluded from evidence unless a valid exception to the warrant requirement applies.

> [T]he government's argument that the seizure of the additional items was proper under the 'plain view' doctrine, fails. The "plain-view" doctrine does not apply unless the initial entry is lawful, either pursuant to a valid warrant or under one of the recognized exceptions to the warrant requirement. Neither of these circumstances was present in this case. *United States v. Hotal*, 143 F.3d 1223, 1228 (9th Cir. 1998).

"Controlled Deliveries" The plain view doctrine is also implicated during a controlled delivery. After a brief discussion of controlled deliveries, the leading Supreme Court case in this area, *Illinois v. Andreas*, 463 U.S. 765 (1983), will be addressed.

The U.S. government has the right to inspect all incoming goods from foreign countries at the port of entry. In addition, common carriers have a common-law right to inspect packages they accept for shipment, based on their duty to refrain from carrying contraband. Although the sheer volume of goods in transit prevents systematic inspection of all or even a large percentage of these goods, common carriers and customs officials inevitably discover contraband in transit in a variety of circumstances. When such a discovery is made, it is routine procedure to notify law enforcement authorities, so that they may identify and prosecute the person or persons responsible for the contraband's movement. The arrival of law enforcement authorities on the scene to confirm the presence of contraband and to determine what to do with it does not convert the otherwise legal search by the common carrier or customs official into a government search subject to the Fourth Amendment. *United States v. Edwards*, 602 F.2d 458 (1st Cir. 1979); *see also United States v. Jacobsen*, 466 U.S. 109 (1984) (discussed later in this chapter).

Law enforcement authorities, rather than simply seizing the contraband, often make a so-called controlled delivery of the container, monitoring the container on its journey to the intended destination. Then they can identify the person dealing in the contraband when the person takes possession of and asserts control over the container. The typical pattern of a controlled delivery has been described as follows:

> They most ordinarily occur when a carrier, usually an airline, unexpectedly discovers what seems to be contraband [e.g., in luggage]. Frequently, after such a discovery, law enforcement agents restore the contraband to its container, then close or reseal the container, and authorize the carrier to deliver the container to its owner. When the owner appears to take delivery he is arrested and the container with the contraband is seized and then searched a second time for the contraband known to be there. *United States v. Bulgier*, 618 F.2d 472, 476 (7th Cir. 1980).

In *Illinois v. Andreas*, 463 U.S. 765 (1983), the leading Supreme Court case involving a controlled delivery, a large, locked metal container was shipped by air from a foreign location to the defendant in the United States. When the container arrived at a Chicago airport, a Customs inspector opened it and found a wooden table. Upon further inspection, marijuana was discovered hidden inside this table. The inspector informed federal drug enforcement authorities, and a federal agent arrived at the airport to chemically test the substance. The agent confirmed the substance as marijuana. The table with the marijuana was then resealed inside its container.

The following day, the federal agent drove to the defendant's apartment with the container. Posing as delivery men, the agent and another officer attempted to deliver the package to the defendant. In response to the agent's remark about the weight of the package, the defendant answered that it "wasn't that heavy; that he had packaged it himself, that it only contained a table." After leaving the container in a hallway at the defendant's request, the agent remained outside in the hallway and subsequently observed the defendant pull the package into his apartment. When the other officer left to get a warrant for the defendant's apartment, the agent, still in the hallway, observed the defendant leave his apartment with the container. The agent arrested the defendant. At the stationhouse, the officers reopened the container and seized the marijuana. No search warrant was obtained prior to reopening the container.

Relying on the plain view doctrine, the Supreme Court held that the controlled delivery of the container to the defendant did not violate the Fourth Amendment. According to the Court, no protected privacy interest remains in contraband in a container once government officers have lawfully opened that container and observed in plain view its illegal contents. Simply put, at this point the plain view doctrine would allow the seizure of the contraband in the container.

Furthermore, the simple act of resealing the container to enable the police to make a controlled delivery does not operate to revive or restore the lawfully invaded privacy rights. As a result, reopening the container after the controlled delivery is not a Fourth Amendment search and therefore does not require a warrant. The Court said:

> [O]nce a container has been found to a certainty to contain illicit drugs, the contraband becomes like objects physically within the plain view of the police, and the claim to privacy is lost. Consequently, the subsequent reopening of the container [after it has been resealed by police] is not a "search" within the intendment of the Fourth Amendment. 463 U.S. at 771–72.

However, if there is a substantial likelihood that the contents of the container have been changed during any gap in police surveillance related to the controlled delivery (i.e., the defendant has put the container to other uses), police should obtain a warrant before searching the container again.

Hot Pursuit of a Fleeing Suspect Law enforcement officers who are lawfully on premises in hot pursuit of a fleeing suspect may seize items of evidence observed open to their view. For example, the U.S. Supreme Court in *Coolidge v. New Hampshire*, said:

> Where the initial intrusion that brings the police within plain view of such an article is supported, not by a warrant, but by one of the recognized exceptions to the warrant requirement, the seizure is also legitimate. Thus the police may . . . come across evidence while in "hot pursuit" of a fleeing suspect. 403 U.S. 443, 465 (1971).

In addition, *Warden v. Hayden*, 387 U.S. 294 (1967), although not relying directly on plain view doctrine, provides an example of how that doctrine may be implicated when police are in hot pursuit of a suspect. In *Hayden*, the police were informed that an armed robbery had taken place and that a suspect wearing a light cap and dark jacket had entered a certain house less than five minutes before the officers arrived. Several officers entered the house and began to search for the described suspect and weapons that he had used in the robbery and might be used against them. One officer, while searching the cellar, found in a washing machine clothing of the type that the fleeing man was said to have worn.

The Court in *Hayden* first held that the entry into the house and subsequent search for the suspect and any weapons he may use was justified without a warrant because police were in "hot pursuit":

> We agree with the Court of Appeals that neither the entry without warrant to search for the robber, nor the search for him without warrant was invalid. [Police] acted reasonably when they entered the house and began to search for a man of the description they had been given and for weapons which he had used in the robbery or might use against them. Speed here was essential, and only a thorough search of the house for persons and weapons could have insured that [the suspect] was the only man present and that the police had control of all weapons which could be used against them or to effect an escape. 387 U.S. at 299.

The Court next held that the seizure of the clothing observed by the officer in the washing machine was lawful because a police officer, while in hot pursuit of a suspect, is permitted to look in places where he or she may find a weapon:

> [T]he seizure occurred . . . as part of an effort to find a suspected felon, armed, within the house into which he had run only minutes before the police arrived. The permissible scope of search must, therefore, at the least, be as broad as may reasonably be necessary to prevent the dangers that the suspect at large in the house may resist or escape. . . . [The officer] knew that the robber was armed and he did not know that some weapons had been found at the time he opened the [washing] machine. In these circumstances the inference that he was in fact also looking for weapons is fully justified. 387 U.S. at 299–300.

Because the officer found the clothing in a place he was permitted to be (e.g., inside the washing machine), the plain view doctrine would support its seizure. *See also United States v. Preston*, 2009 U.S. Dist. LEXIS 8518 (W.D.N.Y. Jan. 29, 2009), at *36 (finding seizure of items in plain view in defendant's home justified, in part, because officer had entered the home in lawful pursuit of defendant).

Responding to Certain Emergencies Related to the hot pursuit situation is an officer's observation of items open to view when responding to an emergency. In *United States v. Gillenwaters*, 890 F.2d 679 (4th Cir. 1989), a police officer responded to a report of a stabbing at the defendant's home. The victim was a visiting friend, and the officer arrived while paramedics were still tending her wounds. The officer briefly questioned the victim and also observed several incriminating items open to view in the room where the victim lay. Based on these observations, the officer obtained a warrant to search the premises. The court held that the observations were not an improper warrantless search:

> Hager [the officer] was responding to an emergency call; he arrived while the victim was still receiving emergency medical treatment on the scene; he attempted to obtain evidence from her concerning her assailant. His presence was unquestionably justified by exigent circumstances, and his observations—made in the room where the victim lay bleeding—fall within the scope of the plain view doctrine. 890 F.2d at 682.

Law enforcement officers may be tempted to justify otherwise illegal searches by resorting to this combination of the plain view doctrine and response to an emergency. Courts carefully examine these situations and invalidate searches or seizures of items of evidence if a genuine emergency did not exist, or if the officer's actions go beyond what is necessary to respond to the emergency. For example, in *Arizona v. Hicks*, 480 U.S. 321 (1987) (discussed more later in this chapter), the officer's search of suspected stolen stereo equipment went beyond what was necessary to respond to a shooting incident. Therefore, in the absence of probable cause to justify the additional search or to seize the object, the plain view doctrine did not apply.

Mincey v. Arizona, 437 U.S. 385, 393 (1978), also discussed the limited nature of warrantless searches conducted in response to emergencies and hence the limited applicability of the plain view doctrine in this context. It stated that "a warrantless search must be 'strictly circumscribed by the exigencies which justify its initiation.'" In *Mincey*, the prosecution attempted to justify an extensive four-day warrantless search of a murder suspect's apartment on the basis of a "murder scene exception" to the warrant requirement. The search occurred when there was no emergency threatening life or limb and after all persons in the apartment had been located.

The Court in *Mincey* first explained the parameters of entries and searches in response to emergencies such as a homicide. The Court said that police may make warrantless entries into premises when they reasonably believe that a person within needs immediate aid. In addition, police may also make a prompt warrantless protective search of the area to see whether other victims and potentially dangerous persons are still on the premises (e.g., police may "secure" the premises as part of a limited "victim" or "suspect" search). Any items of evidence observed in plain view during the course of these legitimate emergency activities that police have probable cause to believe are illegal may be seized. These items, in turn, are admissible in court and may also be used to obtain a warrant to more fully search the premises.

However, once the emergency justifying the initial warrantless entry has ended and the premises have been secured, police may not continue to search and seize evidence under the plain view doctrine or any other doctrine without a warrant. Any evidence seized in this context would be excluded from court. In this regard, the Court in *Mincey* refused to recognize a "murder scene exception" to the Fourth Amendment warrant requirement. The Court held that the "'murder scene exception' . . . is inconsistent with the Fourth and Fourteenth Amendments—that the warrantless search of Mincey's apartment was not constitutionally permissible simply because a homicide had recently occurred there." 437 U.S. at 395. *See also Thompson v. Louisiana*, 469 U.S. 17, 18, 22 (1984) ("Petitioner's attempt to get [emergency] medical assistance does not evidence a diminished expectation of privacy on her part. To be sure, this action would have justified the authorities in seizing evidence under the plain-view doctrine while they were in petitioner's house [without a warrant] to offer her [medical] assistance. In addition, the same doctrine may justify seizure of evidence obtained in the limited 'victim-or-suspect' search discussed in *Mincey*. However, the evidence at issue here [a pistol and incriminating letters] was not discovered in plain view while the police were assisting petitioner to the hospital, nor was it discovered during the 'victim-or-suspect' search that had been completed by the time the homicide investigators arrived. [The] warrantless 'murder scene' search of petitioner's home [is invalid].").

Another type of emergency that may support a valid, warrantless entry onto premises is a fire. Evidence of arson found in plain view as firefighters battle a fire may be seized. In *Michigan v. Tyler*, 436 U.S. 499 (1978) the Court said:

> A burning building clearly presents an exigency of sufficient proportions to render a warrantless entry "reasonable." Indeed, it would defy reason to suppose that firemen must secure a warrant or consent before entering a burning structure to put out the blaze. And once in a building for this purpose, firefighters may seize evidence of arson that is in plain view. Thus, the Fourth and Fourteenth Amendments were not violated by the entry of the firemen to extinguish the fire . . . , nor by [the] removal of the two plastic containers of flammable liquid found on the floor of one of the showrooms. 436 U.S. at 509.

United States v. Thomas, 372 F.3d 1173 (10th Cir. 2004), involved yet one more type of emergency. In *Thomas*, the emergency justifying a warrantless entry was a threat of guns in an apartment that could be used against police or other potential victims by unknown suspects. Once inside the apartment as part of this valid emergency, police were justified in seizing a gun in plain view that they had probable cause to believe had been illegally used.

Finally, police must be careful not to create or cause the underlying emergency. In *Kentucky v. King*, 131 S. Ct. 1849 (2011), in which the underlying emergency justifying police entry into defendant's apartment was the imminent threat of evidence destruction by individuals inside the apartment, the U.S. Supreme Court held that police do not create an emergency so long as they do not participate in any conduct that violates or threatens to violate the Fourth Amendment: "Where, as here, the police did not create the exigency by engaging or threatening to engage in conduct that violates the Fourth Amendment Fourth, warrantless entry to prevent the destruction of evidence is reasonable and thus allowed." 131 S. Ct. at 1858. The Court explained its reasoning as to why police in *King* did not create the emergency:

> We see no evidence that the officers either violated the Fourth Amendment or threatened to do so prior to the point when they entered the apartment. Officer Cobb testified without contradiction that the officers "banged on the door as loud as [they] could" and announced either "'Police, police, police'" or "'This is the police.'" This conduct was entirely consistent with the Fourth Amendment [knock and announce rule], and we are aware of no other evidence that might show that the officers either violated the Fourth Amendment or threatened to do so (for example, by announcing that they would break down the door if the occupants did not open the door voluntarily).
> Respondent argues that the officers "demanded" entry to the apartment, but he has not pointed to any evidence in the record that supports

this assertion. There is no evidence of a "demand" of any sort, much less a demand that amounts to a threat to violate the Fourth Amendment.

Finally, respondent claims that the officers "explained to [the occupants that the officers] were going to make entry inside the apartment," but the record is clear that the officers did not make this statement until after the exigency [of the evidence destruction] arose. As Officer Cobb testified, the officers "knew that there was possibly something that was going to be destroyed inside the apartment," and "[a]t that point, . . . [they] explained . . . [that they] were going to make entry." Given that this announcement was made after the exigency arose, it could not have created the exigency. 131 S. Ct. at 1862, 63.

CRIMINAL PROCEDURE IN ACTION

Domestic Disturbances, Protective Searches/Sweeps, and Plain View Seizures *United States v. Rodriguez*, 601 F.3d 402, 404–05 (5th Cir. 2010)

In response to a domestic disturbance call, may police conduct a protective search/sweep of a residence and seize a firearm they find in plain view?

Pastor Rodriguez appeals his conviction for possessing an unregistered sawed-off shotgun with an obliterated serial number. . . . He contends that the district court erred in denying

his motion to suppress the shotgun. Austin police officers responded to a domestic disturbance 911 call made by Rodriguez's wife, Domitila Perez Cruz. Cruz told the 911 dispatcher that Rodriguez was threatening her and had "whipped" her with a belt, causing injury. The 911 dispatcher asked whether Rodriguez had any weapons, and Cruz stated that there was a gun in the house. Cruz did not tell the operator that anyone was in the trailer other than Rodriguez and herself.

Within ten minutes of dispatch, three officers arrived at the trailer park where Rodriguez and Cruz resided. One of the officers knocked at the door, and Cruz gave them permission to enter the trailer. The officers noticed several children were present, as well as Rodriguez. They decided to separate Rodriguez and Cruz to investigate the 911 call.

Two more officers arrived shortly thereafter and immediately inquired whether the firearm had been recovered. When they determined that it had not, one of the officers asked Rodriguez if there were any weapons present. He replied in Spanish that a firearm was "in the back . . . behind him" and pointed toward a bedroom at the end of a long hallway. Two of the officers then went to the bedroom that Rodriguez had indicated and saw the butt of a shotgun on the floor between the bed and the wall. One of the officers removed the gun and took it outside where he determined that it was unloaded. While examining the gun, the officer discovered that it was [illegally] sawed-off and that the serial number had been [illegally] obliterated. The officer secured the gun in the locked trunk of his patrol

car and returned inside to assist in the completion of the investigation.

Rodriguez was arrested and charged with various firearm offenses because the shotgun was illegal. He filed a motion to suppress, claiming the police . . . had [(1)] no basis to perform the protective sweep [of his residence and (2) should not have seized the firearm located in the bedroom under the plain view doctrine].

■ Based on what you learned earlier in the chapter on permissible protective searches/sweeps by police in response to emergencies, do you believe that the domestic disturbance call in this case justified such a search/sweep? Why or why not?

■ Assume for purposes of this question that police were allowed to conduct the protective sweep of Rodriguez's residence. Was it permissible for police to enter the bedroom as part of the sweep? Why or why not?

■ Finally, was the seizure by police of the firearm located in the bedroom permissible under the plain view doctrine? In answering this question, consider not only whether police were in the bedroom validly but also whether police, upon observing the firearm, had probable cause to believe it was an illegal firearm. Even if you conclude that the requirements of the plain view doctrine were not satisfied at the time of the police seizure of the firearm, might there be any other justification for such a seizure under the circumstances presented in this case? Fully explain your answer.

Consent Searches When police obtain valid consent from a person to enter or search premises, they may seize any evidence in plain view that they have probable cause to believe is illegal in nature.

For example, in *United States v. Santiago*, 410 F.3d 193 (5th Cir. 2005), officers obtained valid consent to enter and search a residence; as a result, the court found that the officers' seizure of illegal weapons in plain view was also valid. The court first explained the facts related to defendant's consent:

> When the deputies arrived at his residence, [the defendant] opened the door allowing them to enter. Upon entering the residence, the deputies observed a firearm in plain view on a mantle in an adjacent room. [The defendant] acquiesced to the deputies' request to search his home for items that [the defendant] may have received from [a suspected burglar]. 410 F.3d at 196.

After finding that the defendant validly consented to the entry and search of his residence by police, the court determined that the firearm police observed on the mantle was admissible under the plain view doctrine:

> [I]t is also clear . . . that the firearm was seen in plain view [on the mantle]. Though we do not get the sense from the record that deputies entered into the home operating under the belief that they would discover a cache of weapons, we have never asked law enforcement "to ignore the significance of items [observed] in plain view. . . ." [T]he incriminating character of the firearm was readily apparent, as we have often recognized the interrelatedness between the possession of firearms and criminality. [F]inally, we conclude that the deputies had a lawful right of access to the firearm. [T]he gun was located in a place where the deputies had a lawful right to be. Therefore, . . . we find that the discovery of the first firearm, the .38 Taurus, fell within the ambit of the plain view doctrine. 410 F.3d at 201.

In addition, in *United States v. Beasley*, 688 F.3d 523, 528, 530–31 (8th Cir. 2012), the court found that the plain view seizure by police of defendant's personal property was lawful because the defendant's mother consented to police entering her home and retrieving the property from a back bedroom:

> [T]he items [of personal property] were validly seized under the plain view exception to the warrant requirement. [Defendant's mother] Moss invited Lieutenant Guinn into the house and escorted him to the back room where the items were located. [Defendant] did not live in Moss's home and had no expectation of privacy in the home or its back room. Nothing in the record suggests Moss lacked authority to give Lieutenant Guinn access to the room. Lieutenant Guinn testified Moss "took me to a back room in the residence" where the items were located and Moss "identified several items." Thus, Lieutenant Guinn was properly in a position to view what was in plain sight and therefore seize the suspicious items.

Vehicle Inventories/Impoundments and VIN Investigations Evidence may be seized that is observed by police in plain view during a valid inventory of a vehicle. In *South Dakota v. Opperman*, 428 U.S. 364 (1976), police conducting a routine inventory of an impounded vehicle seized both valuables belonging to the owner as well as drugs in plain view in the vehicle's glove compartment:

> The inventory was not unreasonable in scope. Respondent's motion to suppress in state court challenged the inventory only as to items inside the car not in plain view. But once the policeman was lawfully inside the car to secure the personal property in plain view, it was not unreasonable to open the unlocked glove compartment, to which vandals would have had ready and unobstructed access once inside the car. 428 U.S. at 376, n.10.

KEY POINTS

- The first requirement of the plain view doctrine allowing the warrantless seizure of items of evidence observed open to view is that police must possess a prior valid justification for an intrusion onto property or into a zone of privacy, whether that justification is a warrant for another object, hot pursuit, an arrest, a search incident to arrest, a protective sweep, a particular emergency, a consent search, a stop and frisk, vehicular inventories and VIN investigations, a controlled delivery, or some other legitimate reason.

- Once police are lawfully in a position to observe and access an item firsthand, its owner's property or

Continued on next page

The police were lawfully in the vehicle as part of an inventory, so their seizure of valuables in the passenger compartment and marijuana in the glove compartment was justified under the plain view doctrine.

One other, rather narrow instance in which the plain view doctrine applies is when police investigate a vehicle's identification number (VIN). The one case decided by the Supreme Court in this area is *New York v. Class*, 475 U.S. 106 (1986). In *Class*, a law enforcement officer stopped an automobile for a traffic infraction. After the driver voluntarily got out of the vehicle, the officer entered the vehicle and removed some papers from the dashboard in order to ascertain the VIN. (Federal law requires the VIN to be placed in the plain view of someone outside the automobile to facilitate the VIN's usefulness for various governmental purposes such as research, insurance, safety, theft prevention, and vehicle recall.) The Court held that there was no reasonable expectation of privacy in the VIN because of the important role played by the VIN in the pervasive governmental regulation of the automobile and because of the efforts of the federal government to ensure that the VIN is placed in plain view. Furthermore, the placement of papers on top of the VIN was insufficient to create a privacy interest in the VIN, because efforts to restrict access to an area do not generate a reasonable expectation of privacy where none would otherwise exist. The mere viewing of the formerly obscured VIN was not, therefore, a violation of the Fourth Amendment. Moreover, because the officer's entry into the vehicle to uncover the VIN did not violate the Fourth Amendment, the officer had a prior valid justification to be where he was when he saw a gun under the seat. The gun was thus in plain view; and, because the officer had probable cause to believe that the gun was evidence of a crime, he could seize it under the plain view doctrine.

Note that *New York v. Class* also supports this principle: If police are not conducting a search or seizure for Fourth Amendment purposes because an individual lacks a privacy expectation in a particular area or object (e.g., a VIN), then police may intrude on that area or object without implicating the Fourth Amendment. If police have probable cause to believe that an item observed from their lawful vantage point is incriminating in nature, they may search or seize the object under the plain view doctrine without a warrant. (See the later discussion in this chapter of the probable cause requirement for plain view searches and seizures.)

Finally, in *United States v. Sanchez*, 612 F.3d 1, 4–7 (1st Cir. 2010), the court found that the impoundment of defendant's motorcycle for various licensing violations was valid under the plain view doctrine, in part, because police were initially in a lawful vantage point to observe the motorcycle and its license plate:

> The only pertinent question is whether, on an objective view of the record, the impoundment (a form of seizure) was premised on evidence lawfully discovered and seized while in plain view. It is beyond serious question that the first element of this test is satisfied here [i.e., that the officer had a lawful vantage point to see the motorcycle]. The officers were in a parking lot where they had a right to be, and both the motorcycle and its license plate were easily visible to the naked eye. Thus, the officers had lawfully reached the position from which they saw the objects that they subsequently seized. For aught that appears, the officers in this case had a lawful right to seize the motorcycle where it stood.

Requirement 2: Probable Cause to Believe That the Observed Object Is Incriminating in Character

The second requirement of the plain view doctrine means that before an item may be seized, the police must have probable cause that the item is incriminating in character and hence subject to seizure, *without conducting some further search of the item*. *See Arizona v. Hicks*, 480 U.S. 321 (1987). "If . . . the police lack probable cause to believe that an object in plain view is contraband without conducting some further search of the object—i.e., if 'its incriminating character [is not] immediately apparent,' . . . the plain-view doctrine cannot justify its seizure." *Minnesota v. Dickerson*, 508 U.S. 366, 375 (1993).

For example, in *United States v. Santiago*, 410 F.3d 193 (5th Cir. 2005), previously discussed, police officers were justified in entering and searching defendant's residence because defendant consented to both the entry and search. Upon entering the residence, the officers observed a firearm in plain view on a mantle. The court found the plain view seizure of the firearm valid not only because the police were justified in entering the apartment, but also because police had *probable cause* to believe that the firearm was illegal contraband (i.e., the firearm's incriminating nature was immediately apparent):

> [T]he incriminating character of the firearm was readily apparent, as we have often recognized the interrelatedness between the possession of firearms and criminality. Given that the deputies went to [defendant's] home because they believed that he had information related to . . . recent burglaries—as [the defendant] had acted as a "fence" [to store stolen goods] for [a suspected burglar]—and because the deputies were also aware that [the defendant] had prior criminal convictions, the incriminating character of the firearm was immediately apparent. 410 F.3d at 201.

In addition, in *United States v. Gamble*, 388 F.3d 74 (2d Cir. 2004), previously discussed, police officers were justified in entering and searching the defendant's apartment because they had a valid warrant authorizing the seizure of cocaine and drug paraphernalia. Police seized an ammunition clip found in plain view during the search of a dresser drawer. The court in *Gamble* authorized the plain view seizure of the ammunition clip not only because police were justified in searching the drawer as a result of the warrant but also because they had probable cause to believe the clip was illegal contraband: "[T]he officers had probable cause to believe that the ammunition clip was connected with criminal activity because ammunition is a recognized tool of the drug-dealing trade." 388 F.3d at 77.

Courts will not always find that the incriminating character of an object observed by police in plain view is immediately apparent; that is, courts may find that an officer lacks the probable cause necessary to seize or search an object under the plain view doctrine. For example, in *United States v. Wilson*, 36 F.3d 1298, 1306 (5th Cir. 1994), because police had to make a telephone call before learning of the incriminating character of particular bank checks, the court found that the plain view seizure of these checks was unlawful: "[T]he incriminating character of the checks did not become apparent until their stolen nature was verified by the telephone call. The incriminating character of the evidence was not immediately apparent. The checkbook was not admissible under the plain view doctrine."

Similarly, in *United States v. McLevain*, 310 F.3d 434 (6th Cir. 2002), officers executing a search warrant for a residence authorizing the seizure of two individuals, one of whom did not live at the residence, found the following items in plain view: a twist tie and a cut cigarette filter under the bed in the master bedroom; a spoon with residue on a tackle box in a sink in the garage (an officer seized this residue at the scene and conducted a test to determine if it was an illegal drug); and a prescription bottle, with no label, filled with a clear liquid that looked like water (the bottle was found on a mantle in the home). The court found that none of the cited objects was immediately apparent as illegal contraband; hence, the officers could not rely on the plain view doctrine to seize or search these items:

> [T]he items found in [defendant's] home might be found under beds, in sinks, and on mantels in many homes, and not exclusively those where methamphetamine is being used. While the cut cigarette filter and the prescription bottle with fluid in it might be out of the ordinary, the police are not authorized to seize odd items. We do not care what the explanation is for the items, but we care that there may be some other explanation for the items. Defense counsel pointed out at oral argument that sometimes smokers who do not want filters in their cigarettes remove them. The "plain view" exception authorizes seizure of only those items that "immediately app[ear]" to be contraband. 310 F.3d at 442.

Furthermore, the court in this case did not agree with the officer that, based on his experience, he had probable cause to believe that the four items were illegal in nature:

> [The officer] also testified that from his experiences as a narcotics officer he suspected that the twist tie, cigarette filter, spoon, and prescription bottle with liquid were being used with methamphetamine. The connection between these items and illegal activities, however, is not enough to render these items intrinsically incriminating. The connection is not enough to make their intrinsic nature such that their mere appearance gives rise to an association with criminal activity. 310 F.3d at 442.

See also Gentry v. Sevier, 597 F.3d 838, 843, 849–50 (7th Cir. 2010) ("The facts do not indicate that the officers had . . . probable cause to search the wheelbarrow based on the items in plain view. [T]he record . . . indicates that the visible items were not such that they provided the officers with a reasonable basis to conclude that Gentry had engaged in wrongdoing. [A]lthough some of the items on the top of the pile in the wheelbarrow were visible to the officers, the items [which the officers described as 'some old beat-up stuff'] did not indicate any wrongdoing on the part of Gentry. There was no justification for a further warrantless search beneath the surface of the pile of items in the wheelbarrow. The officer who initially approached Gentry testified that Gentry was unable to give a consistent explanation for where he found the wheelbarrow. However, that alone would not justify a search of the wheelbarrow without a warrant. Gentry did not flee upon discovery and in fact turned and approached the officers. The officers thus could not perform a search of the wheelbarrow . . . in this case without first obtaining a warrant and the record does not reflect any applicable exceptions to the warrant requirement.").

Though an officer's experience may not always support a finding of probable cause to believe an object is incriminating in character, officers may certainly use their background and experience to evaluate the facts and circumstances in determining probable cause. For example, in *Texas v. Brown*, 460 U.S. 730 (1983) (discussed previously in the context of the prior valid justification requirement for plain view seizures), an officer stopped the defendant's automobile at night at a routine driver's license checkpoint, asked the defendant for his license, and shined a flashlight into the car. The officer observed an opaque green party balloon, knotted about one-half inch from the tip. After shifting his position, the officer also observed several small vials, quantities of loose white powder, and an open bag of party balloons in the open glove compartment. Based, in part, on the officer's prior experience, the Court in *Brown* held that the officer had probable cause to believe that the opaque green balloon contained an illicit substance:

> [The officer] testified that he was aware, both from his participation in previous narcotics arrests and from discussions with other officers, that

balloons tied in the manner of the one possessed by [the defendant] were frequently used to carry narcotics. This testimony was corroborated by that of a police department chemist who noted that it was "common" for balloons to be used in packaging narcotics. In addition, [the officer] was able to observe the contents of the glove compartment of [the defendant's] car, which revealed further suggestions that [the defendant] was engaged in activities that might involve possession of illicit substances. The fact that [the officer] could not see through the opaque fabric of the balloon is all but irrelevant: the distinctive character of the balloon itself spoke volumes as to its contents—particularly to the trained eye of the officer. 460 U.S. at 742–43.

Therefore, because the officer (1) was justified in stopping the car at the routine checkpoint and (2) had probable cause to believe the balloon was illegal contraband, he could validly seize the balloon under the plain view doctrine.

Another case that supports the idea that officers may use their knowledge, previous experience, and training to make a probable cause determination is *United States v. Ashley*, 37 F.3d 678, 680–81 (D.C. Cir. 1994). The court in *Ashley* found that the officer, based on his knowledge, training, and experience, had probable cause to believe the object he was feeling in "plain touch" was contraband (note: the plain touch doctrine is discussed in more detail later in this chapter):

> The district court found that probable cause did exist because [Detective] Hairston, based on his extensive knowledge concerning the packaging and transportation of drugs, could tell from the feel of the hard object located during the initial [*Terry*] pat-down that it was crack cocaine. [The court] found that based solely on the sweeping, patting, probing motion, Hairston, with his training and experience, knew immediately that the object was crack cocaine. [T]hat finding is not clearly erroneous. The officer felt the object not in Ashley's pocket, but in his groin area, between his upper thigh and his pocket. The officer testified that he had previously found narcotics in that location on suspects 10–15 times. Most important, Hairston stated—and the district court found—not merely that the object corresponded to a package of crack, but that he recognized it immediately as crack. Given these facts and findings, . . . a conclusion of probable cause in this case [is justified]." 37 F.3d at 680–81 (internal quotations omitted).

Courts interpret the term *immediately apparent* broadly to give officers a reasonable time within which to make the *probable cause* determination. For example, *United States v. Wells*, 98 F.3d 808 (4th Cir. 1996), held that an item's incriminating nature need not be determined by the first officer who observes the item, but may be based on the collective knowledge of all officers lawfully on the premises after all have observed the item.

In *Wells*, officers executed a warrant for a residence authorizing a search for evidence related to bank fraud. In the course of the search, one of the officers discovered a loaded firearm on the headboard of the defendant's bed. Following established procedures, the agent unloaded the weapon and then replaced it on the headboard. He informed fellow officers on the scene that he had found the weapon. Upon learning about the weapon, the supervising officer ordered the firearm seized as evidence. Another officer then seized the weapon. Although the warrant did not list weapons among the objects to be seized, a "criminal records review by the supervising agent prior to the search indicated that [defendant] had a prior felony conviction; the weapon, therefore, was evidence of a violation of [federal law]." 98 F.3d at 809.

Although the officer who seized the weapon in plain view lacked specific knowledge regarding the defendant's prior conviction (and therefore individually lacked probable cause to believe the weapon was illegal contraband), the court found that the plain view doctrine nonetheless justified the seizure of the weapon because the officers lawfully on the scene collectively had probable cause:

> [A]lthough the agent who actually seized the weapon pursuant to the supervising agent's instructions had no personal knowledge that [defendant] was a convicted felon, it is sufficient that the agents collectively had probable cause to believe the weapon was evidence of a crime at the time of the seizure. As a result, the incriminating nature of the firearm was immediately apparent. Thus, the seizure of the firearm was proper under the plain view doctrine. 98 F.3d at 810 (internal quotations omitted).

See also United States v. Banks, 514 F.3d 769, 775–76 (8th Cir. 2008) ("[W]e consider whether police had probable cause [under the plain view doctrine] to seize the gun case [which had a reasonable likelihood of containing a gun]. Banks argues that Officer Mathis did not know he was a felon at the time of the search [and hence he was not permitted to carry the gun]. Rather, the district court imputed the knowledge of another officer, Officer Stueckrath, to Mathis . . . , under the collective knowledge doctrine. *Applying the [collective knowledge] doctrine requires some degree of communication between the officer who possesses the incriminating knowledge and the officer who does not. When officers function as a search team [as opposed to independent actors], it is appropriate to judge probable cause upon the basis of their combined knowledge.* . . . The record shows that Officer Stueckrath was investigating Banks's fugitive [felon] status, while [Officer] . . . Mathis investigated Banks's possible involvement in narcotics. The record is clear that the officers were exchanging information and communicating with each other regarding their respective investigations. In fact, Officer Stueckrath was present either just before or just as the gun case was being opened. Even if his investigation was independent from Mathis's . . . , [Stueckrath's] presence at the seizure is enough to justify application of the collective knowledge doctrine. The district court did not err in [finding probable cause for police to seize the gun case and] allowing the firearm into evidence.") (italics added).

In certain instances, an officer wants to search rather than seize items found in plain view. As is the case for a plain view seizure, an officer, before searching an item in plain view, must have probable cause to believe that the item being observed is incriminating in nature. For example, in *Arizona v. Hicks*, 480 U.S. 321 (1987) (discussed in further detail later), an officer conducting an emergency search of an apartment after a shooting incident observed stereo equipment that he suspected was stolen. He searched the equipment by moving it for closer examination and obtained the serial numbers. Based on these serial numbers, he determined that the equipment was stolen and seized some equipment immediately and some later under the authority of a warrant. The Supreme Court held that the same probable cause standard applies to plain view searches as applies to plain view seizures. Because the officer had only a suspicion and not probable cause that the stereo equipment was stolen before searching it, the search was unreasonable under the Fourth Amendment.

Mechanical or Electrical Aids to Determine Probable Cause for Plain View Searches and Seizures

Although the plain view doctrine does not allow a law enforcement officer to conduct a further search of an object to determine its incriminating nature, it is well settled that an officer may use mechanical or electrical aids to assist in observing items of evidence and to determine probable cause for a plain view search or seizure. Of course, the officer using such an aid or device must have a valid justification for a prior intrusion onto property or into a zone of privacy, and the officer must not act unreasonably.

This section will explore the following devices in the context of plain view searches and seizures:

- flashlights,
- night vision devices,
- binoculars, and
- uncommon devices (i.e., thermal imagers, aerial mapping cameras, etc.).

Flashlights In *Texas v. Brown*, 460 U.S. 730 (1983), discussed previously, the U.S. Supreme Court found that the officer validly seized an opaque green balloon under the plain view doctrine after stopping defendant's vehicle at a lawful police checkpoint. The Court also found that shining a flashlight into the passenger compartment of the vehicle to enable the officer to see objects in plain view did not violate the Fourth Amendment:

> It is likewise beyond dispute that [Officer] Maples' action in shining his flashlight to illuminate the interior of Brown's car trenched upon no right secured to the latter by the Fourth Amendment. . . . Numerous other courts have agreed that the use of artificial means to illuminate a darkened area simply does not constitute a search, and thus triggers no Fourth Amendment protection. 460 U.S. at 739–40.

See also United States v. Desir, 257 F.3d 1233 (11th Cir. 2001). ("[T]he crack cocaine was in plain view when [the officer] shined his flashlight through the windshield of [the defendant's] car. Under the plain view doctrine, this was a sufficient alternative basis [to admit the drugs].")

Night Vision Devices Courts have approved the use of night vision goggles to make plain view observations. Similar to the use of a flashlight, these devices do not implicate the Fourth Amendment:

> The night vision goggles used in this case are not infrared or heat-sensing; instead, they merely amplify light. The goggles are commonly used by the military, police, and border patrol, and they are available to the public via Internet. More economical night vision goggles are available at sporting goods stores. Therefore, night vision goggles which merely amplify light are available for general public use. District courts addressing the use of night vision goggles . . . have determined that there are significant technological differences between the thermal imaging device . . . and night vision goggles such as those used herein. Night vision goggles do not penetrate walls, detect something that would otherwise be invisible, or provide information that would otherwise require physical intrusion. The goggles merely amplify ambient light to see something that is already exposed to public view. This type of technology is no more "intrusive" than binoculars or flashlights, and federal courts have routinely approved the use of binoculars and flashlights by law enforcement officials. . . . For these reasons, the Court finds that . . . the use of night vision goggles by [the officer] to observe the inside of Defendant's vehicle did not constitute a "search" in violation of the Fourth Amendment. *United States v. Vela*, 486 F. Supp. 2d 587, 590 (W.D. Tex. 2005).

See also People v. Lieng, 119 Cal. Rptr. 3d 200, 211 (Cal. App. 2010) ("Night goggles are commonly used by the military, police and border patrol, and they are available to the general public via Internet sales. More economical night vision goggles are available at sporting goods stores. Therefore . . . night vision goggles are available for general public use. Night vision goggles do not penetrate walls, detect something that would otherwise be invisible, or provide information that would otherwise require physical intrusion.

The goggles merely amplify ambient light to enable one to see something that is already exposed to public view. This type of technology is no more 'intrusive' than binoculars or flashlights, and courts have routinely approved the use of flashlights and binoculars by law enforcement officials. For these reasons, we find that . . . the use of night vision goggles by Sergeant Smith . . . on the Lieng property did not constitute a 'search' in violation of the Fourth Amendment.") (internal citations omitted).

Binoculars Although an argument can be made that binoculars should be treated like flashlights for Fourth Amendment purposes because they amplify the ability to see what is already in plain view, they are somewhat different. Unlike flashlights, binoculars allow areas to be viewed that may not otherwise have been viewable without an impermissible intrusion onto property or into a protected zone of privacy. Thus, courts judge the constitutional permissibility of using binoculars by scrutinizing the strength of the binoculars and the distance from which they are used in relation to whether their use infringed on the defendant's property or privacy interests. For example, in *United States v. Grimes*, 426 F.2d 706 (5th Cir. 1970), the court held that viewing the defendant's actions using common binoculars from fifty yards away did not constitute an illegal search. *See also People v. Lieng*, 119 Cal. Rptr.3d 200, 211 (Cal. App. 2010) ("courts have routinely approved the use of . . . [common] binoculars by law enforcement officials") (citations omitted). In contrast, police observations into an eighth-floor window from a vantage point 200 to 300 yards away using high-powered binoculars was held to unreasonably intrude on the defendant's reasonable expectation of privacy in *People v. Arno*, 153 Cal. Rptr. 624 (Cal. App. 1979). Key to the court's rationale was that it would have been impossible for police to see into this area without using high-powered binoculars:

> We . . . view the test of validity of the surveillance as turning upon whether that which is perceived or heard is that which is conducted with a reasonable expectation of privacy and not upon the means used to view it or hear it. So long as that which is viewed or heard is perceptible to the naked eye or unaided ear, the person seen or heard has no reasonable expectation of privacy in what occurs. Because he has no reasonable expectation of privacy, governmental authority may use technological aids to visual or aural enhancement of whatever type available. However, the reasonable expectation of privacy extends to that which cannot be seen by the naked eye or heard by the unaided ear. While governmental authority may use a technological device to avoid detection of its own law enforcement activity, it may not use the same device to invade the protected right. 153 Cal. Rptr. at 627.

Uncommon Devices Whether a device is commonly available to the general public (as opposed to not being generally available) clearly plays a role in the determination of the constitutionality of using that device to obtain probable cause based on the plain view doctrine. However, that criterion is clearly not determinative. The nature of the device's ability to intrude into protected zones of privacy (e.g., the device's ability to "penetrate" walls) lies at the heart of the constitutional analysis, as illustrated by the following cases involving a number of devices that are not commonly available:

■ In *Kyllo v. United States*, 533 U.S. 27 (2001), the U.S. Supreme Court found the use of thermal imagers to detect invisible infrared radiation emanating from a home to be unconstitutional. The Court said that the use of thermal imagers constituted a search for Fourth Amendment purposes because these devices—which are "not in general public use"—impermissibly allow law enforcement "to explore details of the home that would previously have been unknowable without physical intrusion for this purpose." 533 U.S. at 40.

It would be foolish to contend that the degree of privacy secured to citizens by the Fourth Amendment has been entirely unaffected by the advance of technology. For example, . . . the technology enabling human flight has exposed to public view (and hence, we have said, to official observation) uncovered portions of the house and its curtilage that once were private. . . . The question we confront today is what limits there are upon this power of technology to shrink the realm of guaranteed privacy. . . . While it may be difficult to refine Katz when the search of areas such as telephone booths, automobiles, or even the curtilage and uncovered portions of residences is at issue, in the case of the search of the interior of homes—the prototypical and hence most commonly litigated area of protected privacy—there is a ready criterion, with roots deep in the common law, of the minimal expectation of privacy that exists, and that is acknowledged to be reasonable. To withdraw protection of this minimum expectation would be to permit police technology to erode the privacy guaranteed by the Fourth Amendment. We think that obtaining by sense-enhancing technology any information regarding the interior of the home that could not otherwise have been obtained without physical "intrusion into a constitutionally protected area" constitutes a search—at least where (as here) the technology in question is not in general public use. This assures preservation of that degree of privacy against government that existed when the Fourth Amendment was adopted. On the basis of this criterion, the information obtained by the thermal imager in this case was the product of a search. 533 U.S. at 33–35 (internal citations omitted).

Having determined that the use of a thermal imaging device to see inside a private residence constituted a search under the Fourth Amendment, the Court concluded its opinion by holding that the use of such devices "is presumptively unreasonable without a warrant." 533 U.S. at 40.

▪ *Dow Chemical Company v. United States*, 476 U.S. 227 (1986), upheld the use of a standard precision aerial mapping camera to photograph an industrial plant complex from an aircraft flying in navigable airspace. Key to the Court's rationale was that the photographs that had been taken had not been accomplished by a physical trespass onto the company's private property, but rather had been taken using a camera to see an area that was "more comparable to an open field" because, from the sky, "it is open to the view and observation of persons in aircraft lawfully in the public airspace immediately above or sufficiently near the area for the reach of cameras." 476 U.S. at 239.

▪ *United States v. Ciraolo*, 476 U.S. 207 (1986), held that the "naked-eye observation of the curtilage [or area immediately surrounding defendant's home] by police from an aircraft lawfully operating at an altitude of 1,000 feet [does not] violate an expectation of privacy that is reasonable." The Court in *Ciraolo* found that there was no privacy violation and hence no search under the Fourth Amendment because members of the public could make similar observations of defendant's curtilage, which consisted of a fenced-in backyard, by using their own aircraft. Moreover, the police were not overly intrusive in conducting their aerial surveillance. Thus, police did not need a warrant to conduct such surveillance, which revealed marijuana plants in defendant's backyard. 476 U.S. at 213–15.

▪ In *United States. v. Riley*, 488 U.S. 445 (1989), the U.S. Supreme Court held in a plurality opinion that police observations of marijuana from a helicopter flying at a distance of four hundred feet above the defendant's greenhouse located in the curtilage of his home did not violate defendant's reasonable expectation of privacy. As a result, this surveillance did not constitute a search under the Fourth Amendment, and no warrant was required. In his rationale, Justice White explained that this type of police surveillance using a helicopter did not violate any federal aviation laws, and that a member of the public could make similar observations. In addition, helicopter flights at this height and in this area were not sufficiently rare and the particular police surveillance in this case did not interfere with defendant's use of the greenhouse, or "reveal intimate details" about defendant's property. 488 U.S. at 450–52. In her rationale, Justice O'Conner, while agreeing on the basic holding reached by the Court, chose to focus less on the fact that the police surveillance did not violate any federal aviation laws but rather on the fact that public use of airspace at a distance of four hundred feet was frequent: "[B]ecause there is reason to believe that there is considerable public use of airspace at altitudes of 400 feet and above, . . . I conclude that Riley's expectation that his curtilage was protected from naked-eye aerial observation from that altitude was not a reasonable one. However, public use of altitudes lower than that—particularly public observations from helicopters circling over the curtilage of a home—may be sufficiently rare that police surveillance from such altitudes would violate reasonable expectations of privacy, despite compliance with [Federal Aviation Administration] air safety regulations." 488 U.S. at 455.

CRIMINAL PROCEDURE **IN ACTION**

Police Helicopter Surveillance *United States v. Warford*, 439 F.3d 836 (8th Cir. 2006).

Do police need a search warrant before conducting aerial surveillance for drugs near a residence using a police helicopter, or does such surveillance not constitute a search under the Fourth Amendment (e.g., is such surveillance more akin to a plain view observation)?

The facts of *Warford* are as follows:

On August 18, 2004, Special Agents Ken Willock and Lori Lawson of the Arkansas State Police applied for and obtained a search warrant for property located at Route 5, Box 321, on Madison County Road 8030, where [defendants] Warford and Whatley resided.

The warrant authorized the police to search for marijuana, other illegal drugs, any items used in the manufacture and consumption of marijuana and other illegal drugs, [and] . . . any firearms, or money, which is being possessed illegally. The warrant was based on information provided by Millicent Morgan, who is a daughter of Warford and Whatley, and Millicent's husband, Jessie Morgan.

According to the affidavit, Millicent Morgan called Agent Willock on July 29, 2004, and stated that her father, Phillip Whatley, was involved in manufacturing and delivering marijuana and was a convicted felon in possession of firearms. Millicent stated that her father transported a large bag of marijuana to his son in Mississippi in 2003 and

that, as a child, she helped her father sprout, plant, and water seeds at his home. On August 9, 2004, Agent Lawson met with Millicent, who also disclosed a history of alleged sexual abuse by her father. Agent Lawson investigated the account by researching Department of Human Services ("DHS") records, which substantiated the reported neglect and abuse, and by speaking to Millicent's maternal grandfather, who verified her story.

On August 10, 2004, Agent Willock met with Millicent and Jessie near Rogers, Arkansas. Jessie told Willock that on March 15, 2004, while he and Whatley were meeting at a motel in Springdale, Arkansas, Whatley showed him a black metal Smith and Wesson 9 millimeter semiautomatic handgun. Whatley then asked if Jessie had a weapon that he carried with him for protection. When Jessie replied in the negative, Whatley gave him a Smith and Wesson .40 caliber semiautomatic handgun, which Jessie showed the officer. Both Jessie and Millicent said that Whatley and Warford carried the 9 millimeter handgun in their two-year-old son's diaper bag, and

Continued on next page

Millicent stated that her father always has a gun with or near him.

According to the affidavit, on August 11, Jessie and Whatley were meeting in another motel room near Rogers, Arkansas, and Whatley told Jessie that he had an SKS assault rifle at his home. Jessie then asked to clean the [nine] millimeter handgun. Whatley agreed, retrieved the gun from a diaper bag, allowed Jessie to clean it, and returned it to the bag. Agent Lawson met with Millicent and Jessie on August 12, and Millicent stated that her parents have a long history of scamming stores out of money and that her father "never goes anywhere without a gun." While acknowledging that she had not visited Whatley's property for seven years, Millicent told the agent that she believed Whatley was growing marijuana on the property, because she and Jessie had asked to visit, but her parents continually said the property is "not ready for company." She also said that her father had plenty of money, despite never holding a regular job.

On August 14, the affidavit states, Millicent told Agent Lawson that she had checked the diaper bag and the gun was still there. She also expressed concern that her younger sisters, who still lived with Warford and Whatley, were in danger of being sexually abused. Agent Lawson also discovered an outstanding warrant for Warford for a misdemeanor shoplifting charge and noted that her criminal history included several prior arrests for theft. Whatley is a convicted felon with prior convictions for a violation of the Arkansas Hot Check Law, marijuana manufacturing, and possession of firearms.

Prior to obtaining the warrant, Agent Willock learned from Sergeant Robert York of the Arkansas State Police that on August 19, the marijuana eradication program, operated jointly with the Drug Enforcement Agency ("DEA"), would be doing a helicopter flyover of the county in which Whatley's property is located. Agent Willock obtained the warrant on August 18, and Sergeant York agreed to support Agent Willock's execution of the warrant with one aircraft and ground crew.

Agents executed the search warrant on the morning of August 19, 2004. The helicopter was making its way towards the Whatley property as the officers approached the residence. As the officers began a protective sweep of the residence, Agent Willock received word from Sergeant York in the helicopter that the eradication team had observed marijuana growing on the property. Agent Willock went outside to take photographs of plots around the property, while Sergeant York directed the officers on the ground to the marijuana plants. Assisted by

Sergeant York's observation from the helicopter, the officers were able to locate and seize 482 marijuana plants growing in two heavily wooded areas approximately 100 to 150 yards from the house and in a ditch beside the driveway approximately 30 yards from the residence.

Inside the residence, the officers discovered processed marijuana, marijuana seeds, and drug paraphernalia throughout the house. They also found an M-48A high caliber rifle, a .22 caliber rifle loaded with three rounds, and part of a non-working rifle behind the front door.

Based on this evidence, a grand jury charged Warford and Whatley with conspiring to manufacture marijuana and manufacturing more than 100 marijuana plants. Whatley also was charged with three counts of unlawful possession of a firearm as a convicted felon. The defendants moved to suppress the evidence seized during the search. 439 F.3d at 839, 840. In particular, defendant Warford argued, that the marijuana plants seized outside the house should have been suppressed. He contends that they were seized as a result of the aerial observation by Sergeant York, and that because the helicopter was operating below normal cruising altitude in a manner not permissible for the general public, York's observations constituted a search for which a warrant was required. York testified that the helicopter's typical cruising altitude for spotting marijuana is 500 feet, but that investigators sometimes fly lower—in this case, down to 200 or 300 feet—to confirm a marijuana sighting. The parties dispute whether the plants observed were within the curtilage of the home or on land akin to "open fields."

[Finally,] "Federal Aviation Administration regulations permit fixed-wing-aircraft to be operated at an altitude of 500 feet above the surface in areas that are not congested, while helicopters may be operated at less than 500 feet "if the operation is conducted without hazard to persons or property on the surface." 439 F.3d at 843.

■ Based on your review of the U.S. Supreme Court cases from the preceding section, including *Dow Chemical Company, Ciraolo*, and *Riley*, should the marijuana seized by police outside but near defendants' residence be excluded in court?

■ In particular, does the aerial surveillance by police of the area near defendants' residence using a helicopter require a search warrant? Or does this surveillance revealing the presence of marijuana not qualify as a search requiring a warrant under the Fourth Amendment (e.g., is the surveillance more akin to a plain view observation)? Fully explain your answer.

Other Issues Related to Plain View Searches and Seizures

Shifting Position to Determine Probable Cause for Plain View Searches and Seizures The U.S. Supreme Court in *Texas v. Brown*, 460 U.S. 730 (1983), held that a police officer's changing of position to get a better vantage point to look inside a vehicle did not invalidate an otherwise lawful plain view observation:

> [T]he fact that [Officer] Maples "changed [his] position" and "bent down at an angle so [he] could see what was inside" Brown's car . . . is irrelevant to Fourth Amendment analysis. The general public could peer into the interior of Brown's automobile from any number of angles; there is no reason Maples should be precluded from observing as an officer what would be entirely visible to him as a private citizen. There is no legitimate expectation of privacy . . . shielding that portion of the interior of an automobile which may be viewed from outside the vehicle by either inquisitive passersby or diligent police officers. In short, the conduct that enabled Maples to observe the interior of Brown's car and of his open glove compartment was not a search within the meaning of the Fourth Amendment. 460 U.S. at 740.

Closer Examination of Items to Determine Probable Cause for Plain View Searches and Seizures How far may an officer go in examining an item more closely before the examination constitutes a plain view search rather than a mere plain view observation? (Recall that a plain view search requires probable cause; mere observation of an object in plain view from a place the officer has a lawful right to be, would not ordinarily implicate the Fourth Amendment—it is not a search.) The U.S. Supreme Court provided some guidelines in a case in which police, investigating a shooting, entered the defendant's apartment to search for the shooter, other victims, and weapons. One officer noticed stereo components and, suspecting they were stolen, read and recorded their serial numbers, moving some of the equipment in the process. After checking with headquarters and learning that the components were stolen, the officer seized some of the components and obtained warrants for others. The Court said:

> [T]he mere recording of the serial numbers did not constitute a seizure. . . . [I]t did not "meaningfully interfere" with respondent's possessory interest in either the serial numbers or the equipment, and therefore did not amount to a seizure. . . . Officer Nelson's moving of the equipment, however, did constitute a "search" separate and apart from the search for the shooter, victims, and weapons that was the lawful objective of his entry into the apartment. Merely inspecting those parts of the turntable that came into view during the latter search would not have constituted an independent search because it would have produced no additional invasion of respondent's privacy interest. . . . But taking action, unrelated to the objectives of the authorized intrusion, which exposed to view concealed portions of the apartment or its contents, did produce a new invasion of respondent's privacy unjustified by the exigent circumstance that validated the entry. *Arizona v. Hicks*, 480 U.S. 321, 324–25 (1987).

Thus, the Court excluded from evidence the stolen stereo equipment because Officer Nelson lacked probable cause to search the equipment before he moved it to record certain serial numbers. At the time of the search, the officer only suspected that the stereo equipment was stolen; he did not have probable cause to believe the equipment was stolen before he moved it.

The lesson of *Hicks* is that an officer's examination of an item of property is a *plain view search* requiring probable cause rather than a *plain view observation* if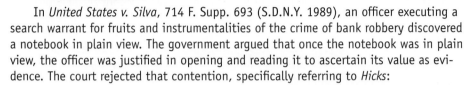

- the officer produces a new invasion of the person's property by taking action that exposes to view concealed portions of the premises or its contents, and
- the officer's action is unrelated to and unjustified by the objectives of his or her valid intrusion.

In *United States v. Silva*, 714 F. Supp. 693 (S.D.N.Y. 1989), an officer executing a search warrant for fruits and instrumentalities of the crime of bank robbery discovered a notebook in plain view. The government argued that once the notebook was in plain view, the officer was justified in opening and reading it to ascertain its value as evidence. The court rejected that contention, specifically referring to *Hicks*:

> This court can hardly imagine a less intrusive action than moving a stereo turntable to view its serial number. By comparison, the opening of a notebook or document is, if anything, a more significant intrusion since it is bound to reveal something of much greater personal value than the bottom of a turntable. Accordingly, the court is constrained to conclude that, after *Hicks*, even the minor investigation of a notebook beyond inspecting what is visible must constitute a search. 714 F. Supp. at 696.

The court further elaborated in a footnote:

> The court does not hold that an officer cannot read a document or book if it is plainly visible without opening or disturbing it in any way. The holding is limited to finding that if the incriminating nature of the document cannot be readily ascertained without moving or disturbing it, an officer may not, absent probable cause move or further search the book or document. 714 F. Supp. at 696 n.6.

However, if the officer has particular information that provides him or her with a probable cause belief that a notebook contains evidence of crime, then the officer can seize the notebook under the plain view doctrine. For example, in *United States v. Pindell*, 336 F.3d 1049 (D.C. Cir. 2003), officers had knowledge from victims of a string of robberies that the suspect recorded information while committing the robberies in a particular kind of notebook. The court held that under the plain view doctrine, the officers could seize similar notebooks they found during searches they conducted with a warrant of defendant's car and home:

> At the time he conducted the search [under warrant] of [defendant's] car, Detective Paci had already interviewed [one robbery victim], who had told him that [defendant] had been dressed as a police officer and had recorded personal information in a notebook. When [Detective] Paci found a notebook lying next to a police uniform in [defendant's] car, he had probable cause to believe that it was the same notebook that [the defendant] had used to record that information just two weeks before. At a minimum, he had probable cause to believe that the notebook could have evidentiary value because it might contain a chronology of [defendant's] daily whereabouts.
>
> Moreover, because it was by then clear to Detective Paci that [the defendant] had committed at least one other similar robbery, it was also reasonable for him to believe that the notebook might include information regarding other crimes that could be relevant in proving the offenses already under investigation. [Such] evidence of other robberies would likewise have been admissible at a trial for the robbery of [other victims].
>
> For the same reason, we conclude that Detectives Griffin and Williams had probable cause to seize the notebooks . . . that they discovered in defendant's house [while executing another warrant]. The detectives had been briefed by Detective Paci regarding the particulars of the [other victims'] robberies, including the fact that [the defendant] had used a notebook to record personal information during the former crime. When Detective Williams flipped through the notebooks to see whether they contained the currency and identification cards specified in the warrant, she discovered

names, dates, addresses, and other personal details. At that point, she had probable cause to believe that the information contained therein might constitute evidence of crimes similar to those she was investigating. We therefore conclude that the district court properly denied the motion to suppress because the seizures [of the notebooks] were lawful under the plain view doctrine. 336 F.3d at 1055–56.

Containers and Probable Cause for Plain View Searches and Seizures Ordinarily, the opening and examining of closed containers even in public by government agents are considered searches requiring a warrant because they are serious invasions of privacy. See generally *United States v. Chadwick*, 433 U.S. 1 (1977) (discussed further in Chapter 11). Nevertheless, courts have held that these actions are either not searches under the Fourth Amendment, or are justified under the plain view doctrine, under one of the following two circumstances:

- the contents of a container can be inferred from its outward appearance, distinctive configuration, transparency, or other characteristics. See *Arkansas v. Sanders*, 442 U.S. 753, 765, n.13 (1979): "Not all containers . . . deserve the full protection of the Fourth Amendment. [S]ome containers (for example a kit of burglar tools or a gun case) by their very nature cannot support any reasonable expectation of privacy because their contents can be inferred from their outward appearance. Similarly, in some cases the contents of a package will be open to 'plain view,' thereby obviating the need for a warrant," *rev'd on other grounds by California v. Acevedo*, 500 U.S. 565 (1991). *See also Robbins v. California*, 453 U.S. 420, 427 (1981) (no Fourth Amendment protection for a container "if the distinctive configuration of a container proclaims its contents, . . . if the container were transparent, or otherwise clearly revealed its contents"), *rev'd on other grounds by United States v. Ross*, 456 U.S. 798 (1982); *United States v. Banks*, 514 F.3d 769, 772–76 (8th Cir. 2008) (seizure and opening of a gun case was valid under the plain view doctrine because case's distinctive shape, configuration and markings revealed its probable contents).

- a container has already been opened and its contents examined by a private party. *See United States v. Jacobsen*, 466 U.S. 109 (1984), discussed in detail later.

The remainder of this section explores these two criteria governing the applicability of the plain view doctrine to container searches in greater detail.

Contents Can Be Inferred from Appearance, Configuration, Transparency, or Other Characteristics If the contents of a container can be inferred from its outward appearance, distinctive configuration, transparency, or other characteristic, a law enforcement officer may open and search the container. If the officer has probable cause to believe items in the container constitute illegal contraband, the officer may seize the container along with these items. For example, in *United States v. Blair*, 214 F.3d 690 (6th Cir. 2000), an officer observed a hard, off-white substance in a clear plastic bag, which itself was contained within a pill vile. The court held that the officer could, without a warrant, validly seize and conduct a field test on the substance in the bag he believed to be drugs: "Because the drugs legitimately fell into the plain view exception, their warrantless seizure was permissible." 214 F.3d at 698.

Also, in *United States v. Eschweiler*, 745 F.2d 435 (7th Cir. 1984), the court held that the removal of a key from an envelope that said "safe-deposit box key" and had the name of a bank on it was not an additional search of the envelope, which was found in plain view:

> [A] container that proclaims its contents on the outside is not a private place. This point would be obvious if the envelope had been transparent; then its contents would have been literally in plain view. The inscription and other characteristics that unequivocally revealed its contents made it transparent in the contemplation of the law. 745 F.2d at 440.

Thus, because the contents of the envelope were essentially in plain view as a result of the inscription on the outside of the envelope, the envelope could be seized and its contents searched without violating the Fourth Amendment. Moreover, because it was reasonable for the officers to conclude that the objects of the search conducted under warrant—drugs and money—could be found within the safety deposit box, the key could also be seized.

However, closed containers that do not reveal their contents generally may not be searched without a warrant. In *United States v. Donnes*, 947 F.2d 1430 (10th Cir. 1991), the court found that the defendant had a reasonable expectation of privacy in a closed, opaque camera lens case made of black leather. Because the illicit drugs contained in this "innocuously shaped" container were not "immediately apparent" until it was opened, the court held the plain view doctrine did not apply and, hence, excluded the drugs found by the officer during the warrantless opening and search of the lens case.

Containers Already Opened and Examined by a Private Party

United States v. Jacobsen, 466 U.S. 109 (1984), allowed a warrantless examination of a partially closed container by government agents after the container had been opened and its contents examined by a private party. Employees of a freight carrier examined a damaged cardboard box wrapped in brown paper and found a white powdery substance in the innermost of four plastic bags that had been concealed in a tube inside the package. The employees notified the Drug Enforcement Administration (DEA), replaced the plastic bags in the tube, and placed the tube back in the box. A DEA agent arrived and removed the tube from the box and the plastic bags from the tube. When he saw the white powder, he opened the bags and removed a small amount of the powder and subjected it to a field chemical test. The test indicated that the powder was cocaine.

The U.S. Supreme Court found that the initial invasion of the package by the freight carrier employees did not violate the Fourth Amendment, because it was a private rather than a governmental action. The Court then analyzed the additional invasions of privacy by the DEA agent in terms of the degree to which they exceeded the scope of the private search. The Court found that even if the white powder was not itself in plain view because it was enclosed in so many containers and covered with papers, the DEA agent could be virtually certain that nothing else of significance was in the package and that a manual inspection of the tube and its contents would not tell him anything more than the freight carrier employees had already told him. The agent's reexamination of the contents of the package merely avoided the risk of a flaw in the employees' recollection, rather than further infringing on someone's privacy. Had the DEA agent's conduct significantly exceeded that of the freight carrier's employees, then he would have conducted a new and different search that would have been subject to Fourth Amendment protections. The Court said:

> Respondents could have no privacy interest in the contents of the package, since it remained unsealed and since the Federal Express employees had just examined the package and had, of their own accord, invited the federal agent to their offices for the express purpose of viewing its contents. The agent's viewing of what a private party had freely made available for his inspection did not violate the Fourth Amendment. . . . Similarly, the removal of the plastic bags from the tube and the agent's visual inspection of their contents enabled the agent to learn nothing that had not previously been learned during the private search. It infringed no legitimate expectation of privacy and hence was not a "search" within the meaning of the Fourth Amendment. 466 U.S. at 119–20.

The Court further held that the agent's assertion of dominion and control over the package and its contents was a seizure; but the seizure was reasonable because the agent had probable cause to believe that the tube and plastic bags contained contraband and little else. The Court said, "[I]t is well-settled law that it is constitutionally reasonable for law enforcement officials to seize 'effects' that cannot support a justifiable expectation of privacy without a warrant, based on probable cause to believe they contain contraband." 466 U.S. at 121–22.

The Court then addressed the question of whether the additional intrusion occasioned by the field test, which had not been conducted by the freight carrier employees and therefore exceeded the scope of the private search, was an unlawful search or seizure within the meaning of the Fourth Amendment. The Court held that a chemical test that merely discloses whether a particular substance is cocaine and no other arguably private fact compromises no legitimate privacy interest. Furthermore, even though the test destroyed a quantity of the powder and thereby permanently deprived its owner of a protected possessory interest, the infringement was constitutionally reasonable. The Court reasoned that the law enforcement interests justifying the procedure were substantial and, because only a trace amount of material was involved, the seizure could have, at most, only a minimal effect on any protected property interest.

In addition, in *United States v. Oliver*, 630 F.3d 397, 407 (5th Cir. 2011), the court found that the defendant's girlfriend's previous search of a cardboard box, which she turned over to police and whose contents were later used to charge the defendant with an unemployment benefits scheme, meant that the police could search the same box without a warrant:

> In the present case, it is undisputed that Armstrong and [defendant Lonnie] Oliver had a personal relationship and had been dating for several weeks, although Armstrong testified that she did not know Oliver's last name until she was informed of it by federal authorities. Oliver sometimes stayed as an overnight guest in her home and left personal belongings, including the [cardboard] box, in her apartment. As part of her investigation, [Agent] McReynolds visited Armstrong at her apartment to inquire about Oliver and the items he had left in her home. While the agents were there, Armstrong telephoned [the co-defendant's] Henson's girlfriend, Bree, who, according to Armstrong, advised her to "get rid of anything that Lonnie left at [her] house." During this visit, Armstrong readily and willingly gave [Agent] McReynolds the box, which she had already searched, as it was not locked or otherwise safeguarded and was left in her dining room. Oliver's decision to leave his unsecured cardboard box in an easily accessible and common area of the apartment for several days without notifying or otherwise communicating his whereabouts to Armstrong made it reasonably foreseeable that she would examine his belongings, including the box, to look for a way to contact him. Given these circumstances, the court finds that the initial private search, which was reasonably foreseeable, and the searcher's act, later that day, of voluntarily giving authorities the box, in which no reasonable expectation of privacy remained, rendered the subsequent police search [without a warrant of the box] permissible under the Fourth Amendment.

To summarize, a law enforcement officer may examine, without a warrant, a container whose contents are not open to view if (1) a private

---

KEY POINTS

LO2 ■ Under the second requirement of the plain view doctrine, before a law enforcement officer may seize or search an item of property that is observed open to view, the officer must have probable cause to believe that the property is incriminating in character (i.e., illegal contraband). An officer is allowed a reasonable time within which to make the probable cause determination and the determination may be based on the collective knowledge of all officers lawfully on the scene after all have observed the item. An officer, however, may not conduct a further search of the object to make the probable cause determination.

LO3 ■ Law enforcement officers may use mechanical or electrical devices, such as binoculars and flashlights, to assist in observing items of evidence, so long as they do not unreasonably intrude on someone's property or reasonable expectation of privacy.

LO4 ■ An officer may change position to get a better vantage point without invalidating an otherwise valid plain view observation. An officer's closer examination of an item of property will be a search rather than a plain view observation if (1) the officer produces a new invasion of the property by taking action that exposes to view concealed portions of the premises or its contents and (2) the officer's action is unrelated to and unjustified by the objectives of his or her valid intrusion. Before searching an item in plain view, an officer must possess probable cause to believe that the item is incriminating in nature. A mere plain view observation does not require probable cause.

Continued on next page

party has already compromised any property privacy interest in the contents of the container and (2) the private party has informed the officer about the contents. In addition, the officer may seize the container if the officer has probable cause to believe the contents are contraband and, if relevant, the officer may conduct a chemical field test as long as only a trace amount of the substance is destroyed by the test.

Note, however, if the subsequent search by police of a container exceeds the scope of the earlier private search, the evidence discovered during the police search will be suppressed in the absence of a warrant. For example, in *United States v. Donnes*, 947 F.2d 1430 (10th Cir. 1991), discussed previously, the officer's opening and examination of the camera lens case exceeded the earlier actions by a private individual named Bertrand:

> In *United States v. Jacobsen*, the Supreme Court recognized a standard for evaluating the actions of law enforcement officials when presented with evidence uncovered during a private search. The Court stated that "[t]he additional invasions of [defendant's] privacy by the Government agent must be tested by the degree to which they exceeded the scope of the private search." The district court found that Bertrand gave the glove and its contents to the officer immediately after seeing the syringe inside the glove. Bertrand did not himself open the camera lens case which was also inside the glove. Here, . . . Bertrand never opened the camera lens case or viewed its contents prior to turning it over to the officer. This is not the case in which the conduct of the law enforcement official enabled him "to learn nothing that had not previously been learned during the private search." The officer's warrantless search of the camera lens case exceeded the scope of the private search. 947 F.2d at 1435.

L05

Inadvertence Not Required

Recall from Chapter 5 that some courts apply an inadvertence requirement to the discovery of evidence in plain view on a hard drive or similar electronic storage media if such evidence falls outside the scope of warrant issued to search for electronically stored information (ESI). Other than in that limited circumstance, the discovery of the item of evidence by an officer does not need to be inadvertent. In *Horton v. California*, 496 U.S. 128 (1990), a police officer investigating an armed robbery determined that there was probable cause to search the defendant's home for stolen property and weapons used in the robbery. His affidavit for a search warrant referred to police reports that described both the weapons and the stolen property, but the warrant issued by the magistrate only authorized a search for the stolen property. In executing the warrant, the officer did not find the stolen property but did find the weapons in plain view and seized them. The officer testified that, while he was searching for the named stolen property, he was also interested in finding other evidence connecting the defendant to the robbery. Thus, the seized evidence was not discovered "inadvertently."

In holding that inadvertence was not a necessary condition of a legitimate plain view seizure, the Court discussed *Coolidge v. New Hampshire*, 403 U.S. 443 (1971). Justice Stewart's opinion in *Coolidge* stated that "the discovery of evidence in plain view must be inadvertent." 403 U.S. at 469. Nevertheless, Justice Stewart's analysis of the plain view doctrine did not command a majority, and a plurality of the Court has since made clear that this analysis is not a binding precedent. *See Texas v. Brown*, 460 U.S. 730, 737 (1983). Justice Stewart concluded that the inadvertence requirement was necessary to avoid a violation of the express constitutional requirement that a valid warrant must particularly describe the things to be seized. *Horton* found two flaws in this reasoning:

> First, evenhanded law enforcement is best achieved by the application of objective standards of conduct, rather than standards that depend upon the subjective state of mind of the officer. The fact that an officer is interested in an item of evidence and fully expects to find it in the course of a search should not invalidate its seizure if the search is confined in area and duration by the terms of a warrant or a valid exception to the warrant requirement. If the officer has knowledge approaching certainty that the item will be found, we see no reason why he or she would deliberately omit a particular description of the item to be seized from the application for a search warrant. Specification of the additional item could only permit the officer to expand the scope of the search. On the other hand, if he or she has a valid warrant to search for one item and merely a suspicion concerning the second, whether or not it amounts to probable cause, we fail to see why that suspicion should immunize the second item from seizure if it is found during a lawful search for the first. . . .
>
> Second, the suggestion that the inadvertence requirement is necessary to prevent the police from conducting general searches, or from converting specific warrants into general warrants, is not persuasive because that interest is already served by the requirements that no warrant issue unless it "particularly describ[es] the place to be searched and the persons or things to be seized," . . . and that a warrantless search be circumscribed by the exigencies which justify its initiation. . . . Scrupulous adherence to these requirements serves the interests in limiting the area and duration of the search that the inadvertence requirement inadequately protects. Once those commands have been satisfied and the officer has a lawful right of access, however, no additional Fourth Amendment interest is furthered by requiring that the discovery of evidence be inadvertent. If the scope of the search exceeds that permitted by the terms of a validly issued warrant or the character of the relevant exception from the warrant requirement, the subsequent seizure is unconstitutional without more. 496 U.S. at 138–40.

In *Horton*, the omission of any reference to the weapons in the warrant did not enlarge the scope of the search in the slightest. In fact, if the stolen property named in the warrant had been found or surrendered at the outset, no search for weapons could have taken place:

> [T]he seizure of an object in plain view does not involve an intrusion on privacy. If the interest in privacy has been invaded, the violation must have occurred before the object came into plain view and there is no need for an inadvertence limitation on seizures to condemn it. The prohibition against general searches and general warrants serves primarily as a protection against unjustified intrusions on privacy. But reliance on privacy concerns that support that prohibition is misplaced when the inquiry concerns the scope of an exception that merely authorizes an officer with a lawful right of access to an item to seize it without a warrant. 496 U.S. at 141–42.

Following the *Horton* rule, *United States v. Ribeiro*, 397 F.3d 43 (1st Cir. 2005), found the fact that a search warrant authorized a search for cash, drug-related documents, and drug paraphernalia did not preclude the seizure of actual drugs in plain view in the defendant's apartment by police who had hoped to find drugs there:

> First, in a familiar note, [the defendant] dismisses the documentary search warrant as a mere pretense because the police intended to search for drugs from the outset. [The defendant] emphasizes that the police asked him where his drugs were immediately upon arrest, and the officers in the apartment asked his girlfriend the same question. As the district court correctly noted, however, this argument is a dead-end. As long as the search was within the scope of the warrant, it is no matter that the officers may have hoped to find drugs. The fact that an officer is interested in an item of evidence and fully expects to find it in the course of a search should not invalidate its seizure if the search is confined in area and duration by the terms of a warrant or a valid exception to the warrant requirement. 397 F.3d at 52–53 (internal quotations omitted).

Although federal courts would appear to be bound by *Horton*'s abandonment of the inadvertence requirement, at least two circuit courts apparently do not follow *Horton*. Instead, they continue to require that the discovery of evidence be inadvertent (e.g., not intentional or deliberate). *See, e.g., United States v. Murphy*, 261 F.3d 741 (8th Cir. 2001). ("A law enforcement officer is permitted to seize evidence without a warrant when the initial intrusion is lawful, the discovery of the evidence is inadvertent, and the incriminating nature of the evidence is immediately apparent. Because [the defendant] voluntarily showed his wallet to [the officer], he cannot, and does not, argue that [the officer's] discovery of his driver's license was the result of an unlawful intrusion or that the discovery was deliberate.") (internal quotations omitted); *United States v. Blair*, 214 F.3d 690, 698 (6th Cir. 2000).

In addition, several state courts retain the inadvertence requirement based on interpretations of their state constitutions. *See, e.g., Commonwealth v. Balicki*, 762 N.E. 2d 290, 298 (Mass. 2002) ("We decline to eliminate the inadvertence requirement from our [constitutional] jurisprudence."); *State v. Meyer*, 893 P.2d 159, 165 n.6 (Haw. 1995). ("[B]ecause we continue to believe that the factor of inadvertence is necessary for the protection of our citizens in order to foster the objective of preventing pretextual . . . activity, we decline to follow *Horton* to the extent it eliminated inadvertence as a requirement of a plain view sighting.").

> **KEY POINTS**
>
> L06
>
> - Plain view seizures need not be inadvertent. Even though a law enforcement officer is interested in an item of evidence and fully expects to find it in the course of a search, a plain view seizure of the item is not invalidated if the search is confined in its scope by the terms of a warrant or a valid exception to the warrant requirement.

Extension of Plain View to Other Senses

The plain view doctrine has been expanded to include other senses. The U.S. Supreme Court extended the plain view doctrine to include the sense of touch, while lower courts have extended the doctrine to cover smell, taste, and hearing. An analysis of each of these extensions of the plain view doctrine follows.

Plain Touch or Plain Feel

Minnesota v. Dickerson, 508 U.S. 366 (1993), applied the principles of the plain view doctrine to a situation in which a law enforcement officer discovered contraband through the sense of touch during an otherwise lawful search. This is sometimes called the **plain touch** or **plain feel** doctrine. In *Dickerson*, officers on patrol observed the defendant leaving a building known for cocaine traffic. When the defendant attempted to evade the officers, they stopped him and ordered him to submit to a pat-down search.

The search revealed no weapons, but the officer conducting the search felt a small lump in the defendant's jacket. The officer examined the lump with his fingers, it slid, and the officer believed it to be a lump of crack cocaine in cellophane. The officer then reached into the pocket and retrieved a small plastic bag of crack cocaine. The Court said:

> We think that this [plain view] doctrine has an obvious application by analogy to cases in which an officer discovers contraband through the sense of touch during an otherwise lawful search. The rationale of the plain view doctrine is that if contraband is left in open view and is observed by a police officer from a lawful vantage point, there has been no invasion of a legitimate expectation of privacy and thus no "search" within the meaning of the Fourth Amendment—or at least no search independent of the initial intrusion that gave the officers their vantage point. . . . The warrantless seizure of contraband that presents itself in this manner is deemed justified by the realization that to resort to a neutral magistrate under such circumstances would often be impracticable and would do little to promote the objectives of the Fourth Amendment. . . . The same can be said of tactile discoveries of contraband. *If a police officer lawfully pats down a suspect's outer clothing and feels an object whose contour or mass makes its identity immediately apparent, there has been no invasion of the suspect's privacy beyond that already authorized by the officer's search for weapons; if the object is contraband, its warrantless seizure would be justified by the same practical considerations that inhere in the plain view context.* 508 U.S. at 375–76 (italics added).

Dickerson, however, held the seizure of the package of cocaine illegal because the contraband contents of the defendant's pocket were not immediately apparent to the officer. Only after the officer squeezed, slid, and otherwise manipulated the pocket's contents did he determine that it was cocaine.

> Although the officer was lawfully in a position to feel the lump in respondent's pocket, because *Terry* entitled him to place his hands upon respondent's jacket [e.g., as part of a valid frisk], the court below determined that the incriminating character of the object was not immediately apparent to him. Rather, the officer determined that the item was contraband only after conducting a further search [by manipulating the object], one not authorized by *Terry* or by any other exception to the warrant requirement. Because this further search of respondent's pocket was constitutionally invalid, the seizure of the cocaine that followed is likewise unconstitutional. 508 U.S. at 379.

United States v. Bustos-Torres, 396 F.3d 935 (8th Cir. 2005), however, permitted a seizure of cash found in "plain touch" during a valid stop and frisk following a drug transaction:

> We have established the officers in this case lawfully stopped the Lumina and conducted the pat-down search of its occupants. In the course of frisking Mr. Alfaro for weapons, Sergeant Pavlak came across two wads of bills in Mr. Alfaro's pockets. There is no evidence, nor do the defendants argue, that Sergeant Pavlak rummaged through Mr. Alfaro's pockets or otherwise expanded the circumscribed protective search beyond the scope authorized by *Terry*. Rather, in the course of properly frisking Mr. Alfaro for weapons, the Sergeant came across the objects which turned out to be the stash. The only question remaining, therefore, is whether he was justified in seizing these objects as they came into "plain touch."

Dickerson requires the officer conducting a pat-down search have probable cause to believe the item in plain touch is incriminating evidence. To give rise to probable cause, the incriminating character of the object must be immediately identifiable. That is to say, the object must be one "whose contour or mass makes its identity immediately apparent."

We have now distilled the question to its very essence: Were the bills, by their mass and contour, immediately identifiable to the Sergeant's touch as incriminating evidence? Pondering the question with a dose of common sense, we believe they were. Sergeant Pavlak testified he found $6,000 in one of Mr. Alfaro's pockets and $4,000 in another. Officers also testified the cash consisted of twenty, fifty, and one-hundred dollar bills. Supposing Sergeant Pavlak first discovered the $4,000 wad and the money consisted entirely of one-hundred dollar bills, he would have come across a collection of forty bills, all in one pocket. We now recall the circumstances which justified the *Terry* stop in the first instance: The officers saw the defendants leave the scene of a suspected drug buy in an area known for drug traffic. Under these circumstances, Sergeant Pavlak had probable cause to believe the wad of papers he came across with his hand was indeed cash, and was likely evidence of the drug trade. As a result, we affirm the district court's denial of the defendants' motion to suppress the evidence. 396 F.3d at 945–46 (internal quotations omitted).

See also United States v. Yamba, 506 F.3d 251, 260 (3rd Cir. 2007) ("The record demonstrates that probable cause indeed existed before [Officer] Livingstone's [tactile] search [under the plain touch doctrine] went beyond the bounds of *Terry*. Livingstone testified that, when he felt Yamba's pocket, he could feel a plastic bag containing a 'soft[,] spongy-like substance.' Though it is true, as Yamba's counsel noted in cross-examination, 'grass [i.e., lawn] or oregano' might feel similarly soft or spongy, people do not normally go around with those substances in their pockets. Moreover, Officer Livingstone also felt 'small buds and seeds' along with the contents of the plastic bag. This detail is more consistent with marijuana than lawn grass or oregano. Based on Livingstone's experience, he reasonably suspected that Yamba had marijuana in his pocket. His belief was reached quickly and upon minimal manipulation of Yamba's pocket from the outside, consistent with a routine frisk allowed by *Terry*. And though Livingstone admitted to manipulating the object even after forming the belief that it was not a weapon, he only did so to 'mak[e] sure it was what [he] knew it to be.' In other words, by that point Officer Livingstone *already* had probable cause to conduct a more intrusive [tactile] search [under the plain touch doctrine] than that authorized by *Terry* alone.")

Plain Smell

In *United States v. Barry*, 394 F.3d 1070 (8th Cir. 2005), the court found probable cause for the warrantless search of defendant's vehicle based, in part, on the officer's smell of drugs emanating from the vehicle's interior:

As events unfolded, Sergeant Brothers gained the authority to make a warrantless search of [defendant] Barry's vehicle based on probable cause because, 'given the totality of the circumstances, a reasonable person could believe there [was] a fair probability that contraband or evidence of a crime would be found in' Barry's vehicle. After Barry and his companion exited the vehicle and answered a few questions, the evidence became overwhelmingly supportive of probable cause to search the vehicle. Sergeant Brothers (1) had observed a mist inside the parked vehicle; (2) had smelled marijuana and air freshener emanating from the vehicle; (3) observed Barry's and his companion's eyes were glassy and bloodshot, and both men were swaying and slowly responding to questions; (4) heard Barry and his companion give different stories for being in the alley behind closed stores at 11:18 [P.M.]; and (5) knew Verus, the drug dog, had alerted to the driver-side door handle. This conclusion is undoubtedly consistent with our court's long-standing precedent. *See, e.g., United States v. Winters*, 221 F.3d 1039, 1042 (8th Cir. 2000) (finding probable cause supported the search of a vehicle in which a state trooper smelled raw marijuana); *United States v. Peltier*, 217 F.3d 608, 610 (8th Cir. 2000) (concluding "the smell of marijuana gave the deputy probable cause to search [the defendant]'s truck for drugs").

See also United States v. Kellam, 568 F.3d 125, 135–36, n.15 (4th Cir. 2009) ("the localized smell of marijuana in [Kellam's] vehicle provided ample probable cause for the actions of the officers [in searching a purse within the vehicle].").

The application of the plain smell doctrine is not limited to vehicles. *United v. Humphries*, 372 F.3d 653 (4th Cir. 2004), found that "plain smell" by an officer near a residence may justify the search of a residence. The court said that "when the odor of marijuana emanates from an apartment, we have found that there is 'almost certainly' probable cause to search the apartment." 372 F.3d at 658; *see also United States v. Cephas*, 254 F.3d 488, 495 (4th Cir. 2001) ("Sergeant Shapiro smelled 'a strong smell of marijuana coming from the apartment.' Therefore, when [defendant] Cephas began to close the apartment door, this odor alone would almost certainly have given Sergeant Shapiro probable cause to believe that contraband—marijuana—was present in the apartment.").

The court in *Humphries* also confronted the issue of whether a plain smell could provide an officer with probable cause to arrest defendant in public without a warrant. The court found that the officer's plain smell of marijuana on defendant's person, along with other factors such as defendant's evasive conduct and presence in an area known for drug trafficking, provided the officer with probable cause to make the arrest:

> [I]f an officer smells the odor of marijuana in circumstances where the officer can localize its source to a person, the officer has probable cause to believe that the person has committed or is committing the crime of possession of marijuana. In this case, Officers Venable and Carr smelled a strong odor of marijuana immediately upon exiting their patrol car about 20 feet from Humphries. Humphries was not alone on the street, however, so the odor could not initially be tied to Humphries alone. But when Officer Venable followed Humphries as Humphries quickly walked away, getting to within 5 to 10 feet of Humphries, he continued to smell "the same strong odor of marijuana . . . coming off his person."
>
> [T]he odor of marijuana emanating from Humphries was sufficient to provide Officer Venable with probable cause to believe that marijuana was present on Humphries' person. And because Officer Venable had probable cause to believe Humphries was presently possessing marijuana, he had probable cause to arrest him for the crime of possession.

It should be noted that warrantless plain smell providing probable cause for a search may be accomplished by both humans and animals. For example, if a properly trained canine alerts to the presence of drugs in a vehicle, this action does not implicate the Fourth Amendment and thus may be accomplished without a warrant:

> [T]he use of a well-trained narcotics-detection dog—one that does not expose non-contraband items that otherwise would remain hidden from public view—during a lawful traffic stop, generally does not implicate legitimate privacy interests. . . . A dog sniff conducted during a concededly lawful traffic stop that reveals no information other than the location of a substance that no individual has any right to possess does not violate the Fourth Amendment. *Illinois v. Caballes*, 543 U.S. 405, 409–10 (2005) (internal quotations omitted).

See also United States v. Riley, 684 F.3d 758, 766 (8th Cir. 2012) ("Riley's argument is misplaced. The dog's identification of drugs in Riley's car provided probable cause that drugs were present, which entitled the officers to search the vehicle forthwith [without a warrant].") (internal quotations omitted).

Of course, the dog must be properly trained.

> [E]vidence of a dog's satisfactory performance in a certification or training program can itself provide sufficient reason to trust his alert. If a bona fide organization has certified a dog after testing his reliability in a controlled setting, a court can presume (subject to any conflicting evidence offered) that the dog's alert provides probable cause to search. The same is true, even in the absence of formal certification, if the dog has recently and successfully completed a training program that evaluated his proficiency in locating drugs.
>
> A defendant, however, must have an opportunity to challenge such evidence of a dog's reliability, whether by cross-examining the testifying officer or by introducing his own fact or expert witnesses. The defendant, for example, may contest the adequacy of a certification or training program, perhaps asserting that its standards are too lax or its methods faulty. So too, the defendant may examine how the dog (or handler) performed in the assessments made in those settings. Indeed, evidence of the dog's (or handler's) history in the field, although susceptible to . . . misinterpretation . . . , may sometimes be relevant. . . . And even assuming a dog is generally reliable, circumstances surrounding a particular alert may undermine the case for probable cause—if, say, the officer cued the dog (consciously or not), or if the team was working under unfamiliar conditions. *Florida v. Harris,* 133 S. Ct. 1050, 1057–58 (2013). (*Florida v. Harris* is discussed in more detail in Chapter 11 in the section entitled "Vehicle Searches by Dogs.")

In contrast to the use of trained canines on public roadways, their use on private property raises different Fourth Amendment concerns, given the physical intrusion onto property. If an officer brings a trained canine to investigate a residence and its immediate surroundings, such as a front porch, in an attempt to have the canine produce a positive smell, or "alert," to drugs within or near the residence, this conduct on the part of the officer constitutes a "search" under the Fourth Amendment for which the officer must generally obtain a warrant. *See Florida v. Jardines*, 133 S. Ct. 1409 (2013). For further discussion of *Jardines*, see the Discussion Point in Chapter 3 entitled "*Florida v. Jardines*—Dog Sniffs at Your Home: Are They Fourth Amendment Searches by Police?"

Plain Hearing

United States v. Ceballos, 385 F.3d 1120 (7th Cir. 2004), relying on the plain hearing doctrine, permitted the comparison of defendants' voices recorded during a valid wiretap, to their spoken voices during an arrest-booking interview:

> [T]he comparison of the defendants' [spoken] voices with those on the tapes [from the wiretap] falls within the "plain hearing" exception to the search warrant requirement. The plain view exception to the search requirement applies where an officer is: (1) lawfully present, (2) sees something in plain view not named in the warrant, and (3) whose incriminating nature is immediately present. We have recognized that the plain view doctrine applied in the context of overheard speech, creating a "plain hearing" doctrine. Because the defendants did not have a reasonable expectation of privacy in their voices during their booking interviews, their voices fall within the exception of the plain hearing exception to the search warrant requirement; the district court did not err in finding their Fourth Amendment claim [as to the comparison of voices] invalid. 385 F.3d at 1124; *see also United States v. Moncivais*, 401 F.3d 751 (6th Cir. 2005).

KEY POINTS

L07

■ If a law enforcement officer is lawfully in a position from which he or she feels an object, if the object's incriminating character is immediately apparent, and if the officer has a lawful right of access to the object, the officer may seize without a warrant under a doctrine analogous to plain view commonly referred to as the plain touch or plain feel doctrine.

■ Lower courts have permitted seizures based on plain smell and plain hearing analogies to the plain view doctrine.

SUMMARY

Under the plain view doctrine, a law enforcement officer may seize or search evidence without a warrant provided the requirements of the doctrine are satisfied. The doctrine has two requirements, all of which must be satisfied before seizure of an item of evidence can be legally justified.

First, the officer must have a valid justification for a prior intrusion onto property or into a zone of privacy. Examples of valid justifications include effecting an arrest, a search incident to an arrest, a protective sweep, a stop and frisk, executing a search warrant, a controlled delivery, hot pursuit, consent searches, vehicle inventories and VIN investigations, and responding to certain emergencies.

Second, the incriminating character of the item to be seized or searched must be immediately apparent to the officer. This simply means that before an item may be seized or searched, the officer must have *probable cause* that the item is incriminating in character without conducting some further search of the object. An officer is allowed a reasonable time within which to make the probable cause determination and the determination may be based on the collective knowledge of all officers lawfully on the scene after all have observed the item. An officer is not allowed to conduct a further search of the object to make the probable cause determination.

Officers, however, may use their experience and background in determining whether a particular item is seizable. Officers may use mechanical or electrical aids, such as a flashlight or binoculars, to assist in observing an item, so long as this does not unreasonably intrude onto property or upon someone's reasonable expectation of privacy. The officer may also shift position to get a better vantage point in relation to the object. In addition, the officer may examine items more closely, unless

- the officer produces a new invasion of the person's property by taking action that exposes to view concealed portions of the premises or its contents, and
- the officer's action is unrelated to and unjustified by the objectives of his or her valid intrusion.

If the officer's examination of an item produces a new invasion and is unrelated to and unjustified by the objectives of his valid intrusion, the officer has conducted a plain view search. Such a search must be based upon probable cause (as is the case for plain view seizures).

Furthermore, opening and examining a closed container to determine whether incriminating evidence is inside is prohibited without a warrant, unless

- the contents of the container can be inferred from its outward appearance, distinctive configuration, transparency, or other characteristics, or
- a private party has already compromised any privacy interest in the contents of the container, and the private party has informed the officer about the contents.

If, after opening and examining a container under the circumstances previously described, an officer has probable cause to believe that the items within the container are incriminating in nature, the officer may seize the container along with the items.

Under the plain view doctrine, the discovery of the item of evidence by the officer need not be inadvertent. Even though a law enforcement officer is interested in an item of evidence and fully expects or hopes to find it in the course of a search, a plain view seizure of the item is not invalidated if the search is confined in its scope by the terms of a warrant or a valid exception to the warrant requirement. Nevertheless, even though the officer is interested in finding a particular item of evidence, the officer may not expand the scope of the search beyond the original justification for the search, whether that justification is a search warrant for other items of evidence, an exception to the search warrant requirement, or some other justification.

Analogizing to the plain view doctrine, the U.S. Supreme Court allows the seizure of an object discovered through plain touch rather than plain view. Therefore, if police are lawfully in a position from which they feel an object, if its incriminating character is immediately apparent, and if the officers have a lawful right of access to the object, they may seize it without a warrant. If, however, the police lack probable cause to believe that the object felt is incriminating in character without conducting some further search of the object (e.g., its incriminating character is not "immediately apparent"), its seizure is not justified.

Lower courts have established plain smell and plain hearing analogies to the plain view doctrine.

KEY TERMS

controlled delivery 415
emergency 418
hot pursuit 417

plain feel 439
plain touch 439
plain view doctrine 409

probable cause 423
search 410
seizure 410

REVIEW AND DISCUSSION QUESTIONS

1. If law enforcement officers have a valid justification for a prior intrusion into a zone of privacy and they observe bottles that appear to contain illegal drugs, may they open the bottles and examine the contents further? May law enforcement officers use their senses of smell, taste, or touch to determine whether items are subject to seizure when they are not sure?

2. Assume that law enforcement officers have a warrant to arrest the defendant for stealing guns four months ago. The officers suspect that the guns are at the defendant's home, but that suspicion is based on stale information insufficient to obtain a search warrant. May the officers seize guns found in plain view when they arrest the defendant? Would it make any difference if the officers could have easily found out whether the guns were still at the defendant's home by contacting a reliable informant?

3. May law enforcement officers take an item off the shelf in an antique store and examine it to determine whether it is stolen? May officers do the same thing in a private home into which they have been invited by a person who does not know they are law enforcement officers?

4. Discuss the meaning of the following statement of the U.S. Supreme Court: "'Plain view' is perhaps better understood . . . not as an independent 'exception' to the warrant clause, but simply as an extension of whatever the prior justification for an officer's 'access to an object' may be." *Texas v. Brown*, 460 U.S. 730, 738–39 (1983).

5. An officer executing a search warrant for specified obscene materials seizes some magazines that are in plain view but were not specified in the warrant. What problems are presented by this scenario?

6. What are the limits on protective searches following an emergency (e.g., a homicide)? May officers routinely look throughout a house for other suspects or victims whenever they are called to a scene to respond to an emergency? May officers go into other buildings on the premises? May officers go into neighboring homes?

7. Does the plain view doctrine authorize a warrantless entry into a dwelling to seize contraband visible from outside the dwelling? Why or why not? What if an officer observes contraband from the hallway of a motel through the open door to one of the rooms? What if an officer observes contraband lying on the desk in someone's office?

8. Would it be proper for officers executing a search warrant for stolen property to bring along victims of the theft to aid the officers in seizing other stolen items not named in the warrant that might be in plain view? Why?

9. If law enforcement officers are legitimately on premises, may they record the serial numbers of any objects that they suspect are stolen property? May they take photographs of these objects?

10. Discuss the following statement from *Texas v. Brown*, 460 U.S. 730, 741 (1983): Decisions by this Court since *Coolidge* indicate that the use of the phrase "immediately apparent" was very likely an unhappy choice of words, since it can be taken to imply that an unduly high degree of certainty as to the incriminatory character of evidence is necessary for an application of the "plain view" doctrine.

11. Make an argument for and against the proposition that a package emitting a strong odor of marijuana should be immediately seizable by police under a plain smell extension of the plain view doctrine. Be sure to consider as you make your arguments both the location of the hypothetical package and whether the odor is being detected by an officer or a police canine.

11

Search and Seizure of Vehicles and Containers

LO1 EVALUATE the rationale for and the scope of searches allowed under the *Carroll* doctrine (automobile exception to the search warrant requirement).

LO2 DESCRIBE the requirements that must be met for the automobile exception to apply.

LO3 ANALYZE how the differences between a motor vehicle and a movable container with respect to expectation of privacy affect a law enforcement officer's warrantless search authority.

LO4 EVALUATE the differences between the automobile exception and the search-incident-to-arrest exception in the vehicle context.

LO5 EXPLAIN the circumstances under which a motor vehicle may be impounded.

LO6 DESCRIBE the requirements that must be met before law enforcement officers may conduct an inventory of the vehicle's contents.

LO7 ANALYZE a search and seizure situation involving a motor vehicle in terms of the reasonable expectation of privacy of the vehicle's occupants (e.g., these occupants' "standing" to challenge a search of the vehicle).

It is well settled that an automobile is a personal effect, a place, or a thing within the meaning of the Fourth Amendment, and is therefore protected against unreasonable searches and seizures. Accordingly, law enforcement officers should obtain a warrant whenever they want to search a motor vehicle unless a recognized exception to the warrant requirement applies. In particular, the courts have created an exception to the warrant requirement for motor vehicles that applies under certain circumstances. The first part of this chapter is devoted to exploring the *Carroll* doctrine, which is also referred to as the *automobile exception*. Following a discussion of the *Carroll* doctrine, this chapter will turn its attention to the concepts of vehicle impoundment and inventory. (Note that although a vehicle inventory by police is sometimes referred to as an *inventory search*, this chapter will largely rely on the term *inventory* because an inventory is really a certain type of police procedure and not a search, at least in the traditional sense of police officers looking for evidence of a crime.) In particular, an inventory is a routine administrative procedure made for the purpose of securing and creating a record of a vehicle's contents. Finally, the chapter will conclude with a discussion of standing in the vehicle context and other issues related to vehicle searches by police, such as the use of canines to search vehicles.

The *Carroll* Doctrine

The *Carroll* doctrine holds that a warrantless search of a readily mobile motor vehicle by a law enforcement officer who has probable cause to believe that the vehicle contains incriminating items subject to seizure is not unreasonable under the Fourth Amendment. The *Carroll* doctrine originated in *Carroll v. United States*, 267 U.S. 132 (1925), and is sometimes referred to as the automobile exception to the search warrant requirement.

In *Carroll*, federal prohibition agents had convincing evidence that the defendants were bootleggers who plied their trade on a certain road in a certain automobile. The agents later unexpectedly encountered the two men in the automobile on that road. They pursued the automobile, stopped it, and thoroughly searched it—without a warrant—finding several bottles of illegal liquor concealed in its upholstery. The U.S. Supreme Court held, "On reason and authority the true rule is that if the search and seizure without a warrant are made upon probable cause, that is upon a belief, reasonably arising out of circumstances known to the seizing officer, that an automobile or other vehicle contains that which by law is subject to seizure and destruction, the search and seizure are valid." 267 U.S. at 149.

Rationale for the Automobile Exception

Courts have created numerous exceptions to the warrant requirement for motor vehicles. Some of these exceptions were discussed in other chapters (e.g., Chapter 7, discussing searches of vehicles incident to a suspect's arrest; and Chapter 8, discussing *Terry* searches of lawfully stopped vehicles). The automobile exception to the warrant requirement is yet another exception justifying the search of a vehicle without a warrant.

In general, courts have allowed warrantless searches of vehicles under doctrines such as the automobile exception because they are mobile and may be quickly moved out of a particular jurisdiction. The Court in *Carroll* said:

> We have made a somewhat extended reference . . . to show that the guaranty of freedom from unreasonable searches and seizures by the Fourth Amendment has been construed, practically since the beginning of the government, as recognizing a necessary difference between a search of a store, dwelling house, or other structure in respect of which a proper official warrant readily may be obtained and a search of a ship, motor boat, wagon, or automobile for contraband goods, where it is not practicable to secure a warrant, because the vehicle can be quickly moved out of the locality or jurisdiction in which the warrant must be sought. 267 U.S. at 153.

In addition, courts allow the warrantless searches of automobiles because a person has a *lessened expectation of privacy* in a motor vehicle for the following reasons:

- an automobile travels public thoroughfares where its occupants and contents are open to view;
- it seldom serves as a residence or permanent place for personal effects;
- it is required to be registered and its occupant is required to be licensed;
- it is extensively regulated with respect to the condition and manner in which it is operated on public streets and highways (i.e., speeding limits, safety requirements such as working headlights, etc.);
- it periodically undergoes an official inspection; and
- it is often taken into police custody in the interests of public safety.

In *United States v. Chadwick*, 433 U.S. 1 (1977), the U.S. Supreme Court summarized the privacy rationale for the automobile exception in the following passage:

> One has a lesser expectation of privacy in a motor vehicle because its function is transportation and it seldom serves as one's residence or as the repository of personal effects. It travels public thoroughfares where both its occupants and its contents are in plain view.
>
> Other factors reduce automobile privacy. All States require vehicles to be registered and operators to be licensed. States and localities have enacted extensive and detailed codes regulating the condition and manner in which motor vehicles may be operated on public streets and highways. Automobiles periodically undergo official inspection, and they are often taken into police custody in the interests of public safety. 433 U.S. at 12–13 (internal quotations omitted).

Nevertheless, even though the reasonable expectation of privacy in a vehicle is less than that in a home or office, law enforcement officers must not violate that expectation when conducting searches or inventories of vehicles. Police must at all times conduct vehicle searches in a reasonable manner. In particular, the U.S. Supreme Court stated that "a search, even of an automobile, is a substantial invasion of privacy. To protect that privacy from official arbitrariness, the Court always has regarded probable cause as the minimum requirement for a lawful search." *United States v. Ortiz*, 422 U.S. 891, 896 (1975).

Requirements of the Automobile Exception

For the automobile exception to the warrant requirement to apply, two criteria must be met:

1. An officer must have probable cause to believe the motor vehicle contains items that are incriminating in character (e.g., illegal contraband).

2. The vehicle must be readily mobile such that it is capable of being moved outside the jurisdiction. (Note: No other emergency or exigent circumstance is required.)

If these two requirements for the automobile exception are satisfied, then an officer may search the vehicle without a warrant. This chapter will first turn its attention to both requirements just listed before addressing the permissible scope of a vehicle search under the automobile exception.

Probable Cause The controlling consideration in a warrantless search of a motor vehicle is probable cause. Therefore, if a law enforcement officer has a fair probability that a readily mobile motor vehicle contains items that are incriminating in character, the officer may search the vehicle. *See, e.g., United States v. Ross*, 456 U.S. 798, 809 (1982) ("In short, the exception to the warrant requirement established in *Carroll* . . . applies only to searches of vehicles that are supported by probable cause.")

In the *Carroll* decision itself, discussed at the beginning of the chapter, the Supreme Court examined whether the officers in that case had probable cause to search defendants' vehicle. The Court discussed the following facts in finding that probable cause existed to search the defendants' vehicle for evidence related to the crime of bootlegging:

> We know in this way that Grand Rapids is about 152 miles from Detroit, and that Detroit and its neighborhood along the Detroit River, which is the international boundary, is one of the most active centers for introducing illegally into this country spirituous liquors for distribution into the interior.

It is obvious from the evidence that the prohibition agents were engaged in a regular patrol along the important highways from Detroit to Grand Rapids to stop and seize liquor carried in automobiles. They knew or had convincing evidence to make them believe that the *Carroll* boys, as they called them, were so-called "bootleggers" in Grand Rapids; i.e., that they were engaged in plying the unlawful trade of selling such liquor in that city. The officers had soon after noted their going from Grand Rapids halfway to Detroit, and attempted to follow them to that city to see where they went, but they escaped observation. Two months later these officers suddenly met the same men on their way westward presumably from Detroit. The partners in the original combination to sell liquor in Grand Rapids were together in the same automobile they had been in the night when they tried to furnish the whisky to the officers, which was thus identified as part of the firm equipment. They were coming from the direction of the great source of supply for their stock to Grand Rapids, where they plied their trade. That the officers, when they saw the defendants, believed that they were carrying liquor, we can have no doubt, and we think it is equally clear that they had reasonable cause for thinking so. 267 U.S. at 160.

In *United States v. Swanson*, 341 F.3d 524 (6th Cir. 2003), the court also found probable cause sufficient to justify a warrantless search of defendant's vehicle under the automobile exception:

We conclude that the agents had both probable cause and justification for . . . searching [defendant's] automobile without a warrant. First, the agents had probable cause to . . . search the vehicle. [Defendant's companion] had used the Grand Am to deliver an automatic weapon thirty days earlier to a confidential informant; thus the vehicle was used as an instrumentality of the crime. The agents also had ample facts at their disposal to support their belief that there was further evidence of a crime inside the car. Only two days earlier, [defendant's companion] had received a Federal Express package from the confidential informant containing money as payment for automatic weapons and silencers that [defendant's companion] was to deliver by United Parcel Service. The agents had seen [defendant's companion] arrive for work at the tattoo parlor in the Grand Am that day. When they searched the tattoo parlor, the empty Federal Express package was found in the trash. They also found three handguns, but not any automatic weapons that might be the ones that were to be delivered to the confidential informant. Moreover, the agents had just spoken with [defendant]. [Defendant] had given evasive answers only to questions about guns. When asked if there was anything in the car that could get him into trouble, he replied yes. There was "a fair probability that contraband or evidence of a crime" would be found inside the automobile. 341 F.3d at 532 (internal citations omitted).

In addition, in *United States v. Benard*, 680 F.3d 1206, 1210 (10th Cir. 2012), the court found probable cause based on the totality of circumstances for police to search defendant's car for contraband (e.g., drugs) under the automobile exception:

The fact the surveillance team observed Defendant purchasing tires at the store on one occasion did not diminish the likelihood that he was [the drug buyer known as Tommy], especially since Tommy's phone calls with [store manager] Mr. Sanchez [which were wiretapped by police] included discussions of tire purchases as well as drugs. On [a specific date], Tommy and Mr. Sanchez arranged a cocaine purchase, and Defendant showed up at the tire store during the expected buy time. The totality of the circumstances established a fair probability that Defendant's car contained contraband when he drove away from the tire store after this visit, and we therefore hold that the stop and search of Defendant's vehicle was permitted under the automobile exception.

However, in *Mack v. City of Abilene*, 461 F.3d 547 (5th Cir. 2006), police officers lacked probable cause to believe a Cadillac had contraband within it:

> The Cadillac was not subject to a valid warrantless search under the automobile exception since [police officers] had no probable cause to believe that marijuana would be found in the Cadillac. Here, the informant reported to [the officers] only that Appellant sometimes kept marijuana in his Suburban, not the Cadillac. Furthermore, upon looking into the [Cadillac], [the officers] do not claim they saw or smelled something that might lead to probable cause. Therefore, no search of the Cadillac was allowed under the automobile exception.

Although the *Carroll* doctrine allows the warrantless *search* of a motor vehicle on the basis of probable cause to believe it contains items of an incriminating character, a warrantless seizure of the *vehicle itself* is allowed when police have probable cause to believe that the vehicle itself is contraband. In *Florida v. White*, 526 U.S. 559 (1999), police officers on several occasions observed the defendant using his car to deliver cocaine. Therefore, they had probable cause to believe that his car was subject to forfeiture under the Florida Contraband Forfeiture Act, which provided that any vehicle used in violation of the act "may be seized and shall be forfeited." When the defendant was later arrested at his workplace on unrelated charges, the arresting officers seized his car in accordance with the provisions of the act. During a subsequent inventory search, the police found crack cocaine in the car.

The Supreme Court held that the warrantless seizure of the automobile did not violate the Fourth Amendment:

> Although . . . the police lacked probable cause to believe that respondent's car contained contraband . . . they certainly had probable cause to believe that the vehicle itself was contraband under Florida law. Recognition of the need to seize readily movable contraband before it is spirited away undoubtedly underlies the early federal laws relied upon in *Carroll*. . . . This need is equally weighty when the automobile, as opposed to its contents, is the contraband that the police seek to secure. 526 U.S. at 564–65.

The Court noted that because the police seized the car from a public place—the defendant's employer's parking lot—the warrantless seizure did not invade the defendant's privacy. "[O]ur Fourth Amendment jurisprudence has consistently accorded law enforcement officials greater latitude in exercising their duties in public places." 526 U.S. at 565.

Readily Mobile Vehicle For a number of years, the automobile exception as set forth in *Carroll* was interpreted by the courts as requiring some exigent circumstance to conduct a search of a vehicle once it was stopped (i.e., no longer mobile). In other words, after lawfully stopping a vehicle, police were expected to apply for a warrant to search the vehicle unless some emergency situation justified the warrantless search and seizure of an automobile. For example, *Cardwell v. Lewis*, 417 U.S. 583 (1974), upheld the warrantless search and seizure of a car after determining that evidence could have been removed from the vehicle by family members of the defendant if the police had delayed in seizing the car. *See also Chambers v. Maroney*, 399 U.S. 42 (1970) ("Only in exigent circumstances will the judgment of the police as to probable cause serve as a sufficient authorization for a search.")

But a showing of exigent circumstances is no longer required. Probable cause is all that is necessary today to search or seize a readily mobile motor vehicle stopped on the road. In *Michigan v. Thomas*, 458 U.S. 259, 261 (1982), the U.S. Supreme Court said:

> It is . . . clear that the justification to conduct such a warrantless search [of an automobile] does not vanish once the car has been immobilized; nor does it depend upon a reviewing court's assessment of the likelihood in each particular case that the car would have been driven away, or that its contents would have been tampered with, during the period required for the police to obtain a warrant.

In short, any requirement that exigent circumstances must exist before the police's judgment as to probable cause will justify a warrantless search is automatically satisfied in the case of a motor vehicle that is readily mobile. "If a car is readily mobile and probable cause exists to believe it contains contraband, the Fourth Amendment . . . permits police to search the vehicle without more." *Pennsylvania v. Labron*, 518 U.S. 938, 940 (1996); *see also Maryland v. Dyson*, 527 U.S. 465, 467 (1999) (reaffirming *Labron*'s holding that the automobile exception does not require "a separate finding of exigency in addition to a finding of probable cause").

In *California v. Carney*, 471 U.S. 386 (1985), the U.S. Supreme Court provided some guidance as to what constitutes a "readily mobile vehicle." In *Carney*, Drug Enforcement Agency (DEA) agents had probable cause to search a mobile motor home parked in a lot in a large city's downtown area. The Court applied the standard that a search of a vehicle is justified under the automobile exception if the vehicle "is being used on the highways, or if it is readily capable of such use and is found stationary in a place not regularly used for residential purposes—temporary or otherwise." 471 U.S. at 392. In *Carney*, the Court found that the warrantless search of the mobile home was valid because the vehicle was readily mobile by the turn of the ignition key, and was so situated that an objective observer would conclude that it was being used not as a residence but as a vehicle.

In a footnote, the Court in *Carney* listed some factors that would indicate whether a mobile home was being used as a residence as opposed to a readily mobile vehicle:

- the vehicle's location;
- whether the vehicle is readily mobile or instead, for instance, elevated "on blocks";
- whether the vehicle is licensed;
- whether it is connected to utilities; and
- whether it has convenient access to a public road. 471 U.S. at 394 n.3.

See also United States v. Navas, 597 F.3d 492 (2d Cir. 2010) ("[T] he trailer [located] in [a warehouse resting on its legs] . . . was: (1) affixed with at least one axle and a set of wheels; and (2) capable of being attached to a cab and driven away. Therefore, we conclude that the trailer was inherently mobile at the time of the search, notwithstanding the fact that it was unhitched from the cab that initially transported it to the warehouse, [the defendants had been detained, and the warehouse itself was surrounded by police agents]. Agents had observed the trailer being used for transportation. [The trailer's] legs served only as a temporary stabilization mechanism. They could be retracted and a cab could be attached to the trailer. [T]*he trailer bore no objective indicia of residential use that might give rise to elevated privacy expectations in its contents.* [We conclude] that the warrantless search of this inherently mobile trailer was reasonable under the Fourth Amendment.") 597 F.3d at 499–501 (italics added).

In contrast to *Carney* and *Navas*, the court in *United States v. Levesque*, 625 F. Supp. 428 (D.N.H. 1985), found that the motor home/trailer in that case was not readily mobile, and therefore police should have obtained a warrant prior to searching it:

> The trailer at issue . . . was situated in a trailer park and on a lot, objectively indicating that it was being used as a residence. Although the truck which tows the trailer was only a few feet from the trailer, the trailer was not readily mobile in light of the fact that one end of the trailer was elevated on blocks and that the trailer was connected to utilities at the campground, and also because of the three quarters of an hour lead time to connect the trailer and truck. The mobile home exception to the warrant requirement thus would appear to have no application herein. 625 F. Supp. at 450–51.

In determining whether a vehicle is readily mobile, courts look to whether the vehicle is inherently capable of movement and not to whether the vehicle is actually mobile at a particular moment in time. For example, in *United States v. Mercado*, 307 F.3d 1226 (10th Cir. 2002), the court found that a vehicle that is temporarily immobile due to mechanical problems is still readily mobile for purposes of the automobile exception to the warrant requirement:

> The present case presents a unique circumstance because the car was not immobile as the result of a justifiable police stop but simply because it was having mechanical problems. Regardless, Appellant's car had not lost its inherent mobility. Additionally, the repair shop was open all night and the mechanic had indicated that the van would be operable again before morning. We are of the view that mere temporary immobility due to a readily repairable problem while at an open public repair shop does not remove the vehicle from the category of "readily-mobile." 307 F.3d at 1229.
>
> Finally, a vehicle is still considered operational and hence "readily mobile" for purposes of the automobile exception even though the defendants associated with the vehicle are detained with handcuffs in a police patrol car and multiple officers are present at the scene and possess a key to the vehicle. *United States v. Kelly*, 592 F.3d 586, 590–91 (4th Cir. 2010).

As the cases just discussed show, unless it has become clear to police that a vehicle is no longer being used for the purpose of movement or mobility (i.e., it has been elevated on blocks, many or all of its essential parts have been permanently removed, etc.), modern courts will not hesitate to find the readily mobile requirement of the automobile exception satisfied.

Apart from courts addressing whether automobiles and mobile homes qualify as "readily mobile vehicles," some courts have examined whether other vessels fit this category. For example, in *United States v. Tartaglia*, 864 F.2d 837 (D.C. Cir. 1989), police had probable cause to search a train roomette for drugs. The court found a warrantless search of the roomette justified under the circumstances:

> Because the police did not have sufficient time to procure a warrant before train 98 left Union Station and because there was more than a reasonable likelihood that the train, and therefore the roomette and its contents, would be moved before a warrant could be obtained, the warrantless search of defendant's roomette was justified. 864 F.2d at 843.

See also United States v. Denny, 441 F.3d 1220, 1225–26 (10th Cir. 2006) (the officer was permitted to enter a train sleeper to effect a seizure, in part, because this area has a reduced privacy expectation as a result of it being readily mobile and quickly able to leave the jurisdiction).

In addition, courts have upheld the searches of boats and airplanes under the automobile exception.

- In *United States v. Lauchli*, 724 F.2d 1279, 1282 (7th Cir. 1984), the court reasoned that "[t]he deputy, although without a warrant, had probable cause to promptly search the boat before it could be moved. . . . A boat on water is as elusive as a car on a highway, with ample opportunity to dispose of evidence or contraband over the side." *See also United States v. Albers*, 136 F.3d 670, 673 (9th Cir. 1998) (finding that search of houseboat valid under automobile exception, in part, because boat was found in open, public waters of a large lake and hence readily mobile, and boat had a reduced expectation of privacy as a result of being subject to entry by government authorities for compliance with safety regulations).

- Similarly, in *United States v. Nigro*, 727 F.2d 100, 107 (6th Cir. 1984), the court reasoned that "[a]n airplane is even more mobile [than an automobile] in terms of its ability to cover great distances in a short time and its capacity to move without being restricted to discrete roadways. In terms of mobility, then, airplanes are logically encompassed within the [automobile] doctrine."

Coolidge v. New Hampshire, 403 U.S. 443 (1971), is one plurality decision by the U.S. Supreme Court that has seemingly survived the previously mentioned *Labron* and *Dyson* decisions. *Coolidge* appears to stand for the principle that even though a vehicle is readily mobile and police have the necessary probable cause, it may not be searched absent a warrant if it is located on private property and there is sufficient time to get a warrant. In *Coolidge*, the Court pointed out that there was no real possibility that someone would move the car located on the defendant's property or conceal or destroy evidence within it. Also, the police had known for some time of the probable role of the defendant's automobile in a crime. They went to his home, arrested him, and escorted his wife and children to another town to spend the night. No other adults resided in the house, and the automobile was unoccupied and parked in defendant's driveway. Police towed it to the station house and searched it there without a warrant. The Court invalidated the search under the automobile exception because there was sufficient time to obtain a warrant: "In short, by no possible stretch of the legal imagination can this be made into a case where 'it is not practicable to secure a warrant,' and the 'automobile exception,' despite its label, is simply irrelevant." 403 U.S. at 462.

At least one federal circuit and one state court decision, however, cast doubt on the continuing viability of *Coolidge*. In *United States v. Brookins*, 345 F.3d 231 (4th Cir. 2003), the court upheld the warrantless search of a vehicle parked in the driveway of a private residence. The court rejected defendant's argument that the vehicle could not be searched under the automobile exception because of its location on private property:

Based upon the facts of *Coolidge*, [defendant] would posit a bright-line rule, whereby the automobile exception may never apply when a vehicle is stationed on private, residential property. We decline to adopt this construction of *Coolidge*. Nor do we find it necessary to determine the contours of the expectation of privacy in and around one's private property. Although heightened privacy interests may be triggered when a vehicle is encountered on private property, the *Coolidge* plurality opinion cannot be fairly read to create a bright-line rule precluding warrantless searches on private property under all circumstances. 345 F.3d at 237 n.8.

See also State v. Alarcon-Chavez, 821 N.W.2d 359, 367–68 (Neb. 2012) (finding vehicle could be searched by police under the automobile exception when it was parked in a private parking lot of an apartment complex, because vehicle was readily mobile and police had probable cause to believe vehicle contained contraband).

DISCUSSION POINT

How Should We Interpret *Dyson* and *Labron*?
State v. Pederson-Maxwell, 619 N.W.2d 777 (Minn. App. 2000).

On July 10, 1998, at approximately 8:00 P.M., a confidential informant met with Crookston Police Department Detective Gerardo Moreno and other law enforcement officers. The informant stated that he or she had met with individuals the previous day at the Polk County Fair in Fertile, Minnesota, who stated they could supply the informant with controlled substances.

The informant was supplied with $450 of "buy money" and an electronic transmitter to record the purchase. This informant met with Brian Christopher Johnson at the fair, and Johnson introduced the informant to Raymond Richard Krebs. Johnson and Krebs agreed to sell the informant two ounces of marijuana for $300 later in the evening.

The informant subsequently met with Krebs and Johnson. The three proceeded to a white four-door Dodge Spirit, which was registered to the appellant, Tamara Gay Pederson-Maxwell. Krebs entered the vehicle and told a female sleeping in the front seat (later identified as appellant) to open the trunk so he could get the "weed." Krebs instead grabbed a pair of boots from the back seat of the vehicle and took approximately two ounces of marijuana out of one of the boots. The informant, Krebs, and Johnson then entered a different vehicle and drove around for a short time.

The informant, after being dropped off, met with Deputy Helget. The informant told Deputy Helget that Krebs and Johnson smoked a marijuana joint while they were in the car, and that Krebs provided the informant with approximately two ounces of marijuana in exchange for $300. A short time later, the informant identified Krebs to Detective Moreno as the man who sold him the marijuana. The informant also identified appellant as the woman who was sleeping in the Dodge Spirit when Krebs obtained the marijuana. Krebs and appellant were placed under arrest. Johnson was also subsequently arrested.

The officers searched Krebs and found $517 in cash, $290 of which was marked money that the informant stated was paid in exchange for the marijuana. The appellant's purse was found to contain approximately two ounces of marijuana and $2,675 in cash. At trial, the evidence established that the actual amount of marijuana in appellant's purse totaled 39.9 grams.

Detective Moreno asked the appellant for permission to search the Dodge Spirit, but she refused. She agreed to allow Detective Moreno to drive the vehicle from the fairgrounds to the Fertile Police Department. Once at the police department, a trained drug-detection dog reacted to the presence of controlled substances in the vehicle and in the trunk. The vehicle was impounded and transported to the Northwest Regional Corrections Center in Crookston.

On July 13, 1998, officers searched the Dodge Spirit without a warrant. Three Tupperware containers filled with marijuana, a weight scale, a cellular phone, a pager, a .380-caliber semiautomatic handgun and an ammunition clip, a .38-caliber semiautomatic handgun with one loaded and one unloaded ammunition clip, an interchangeable. 45-caliber barrel, ammunition, and other items were found in the trunk of the vehicle. The appellant was charged with, and convicted of, two counts of fifth-degree controlled substance crime and one count of failing to affix a controlled substance tax stamp.

The court in *Pedersen-Maxwell* began its discussion by finding that there was probable cause to search the appellants' automobile: "In the present case, the dog's reaction did establish probable cause that there was contraband in the trunk of the car." 619 N.W.2d at 781.

In response to appellant's argument that the warrantless search of her automobile required both probable cause and an emergency, the court said:

> Appellant points to language in *Pennsylvania v. Labron* for the proposition that something more than probable cause is required to search a vehicle without a warrant[.] Appellant would have us interpret "readily mobile" as equivalent to exigent circumstances above and beyond mere probable cause. [But] *Labron* validated automobile searches based on probable cause, without requiring separate exigency requirements.
>
> The second case, *Maryland v. Dyson*, is equally unhelpful to appellant. [T]he Supreme Court in *Dyson* noted: "In this case, [the lower court] found that there was 'abundant probable cause' that the car contained contraband. This finding alone satisfies the automobile exception to the Fourth Amendment's warrant requirement." Based on the language of these two cases, the automobile exception to the Fourth Amendment's warrant requirement "does not have a separate exigency requirement." 619 N.W.2d at 781, 782.

Continued on next page

Until the U.S. Supreme Court decides a case that more clearly articulates the parameters of the readily mobile requirement to the automobile exception, officers should obtain a warrant before searching a vehicle they have probable cause to search when

- the vehicle is clearly not being used for movement (e.g., it is elevated on blocks), or
- the vehicle is located on private property and there is time to obtain a warrant.

Delay in Search If possible, warrantless searches under the *Carroll* doctrine should be conducted immediately at the scene where the vehicle is stopped. If, however, surrounding circumstances make an immediate search on the highway unsafe or impractical, the vehicle may be removed to a more convenient location. If a search is conducted without unreasonable delay after the vehicle's arrival at the new location, the probable cause factor existing on the highway remains in force, and the warrantless search is constitutionally permissible. This was the holding of *Chambers v. Maroney*, 399 U.S. 42 (1970). In *Chambers*, the police had information that armed robbers had fled the robbery scene in a light blue compact station wagon. Four men were said to be in the vehicle, one wearing a green sweater and another wearing a trench coat. The police stopped a vehicle fitting the description, arrested the four occupants, and drove the vehicle to the police station. There, police thoroughly searched the vehicle and seized evidence leading to the defendant's conviction. The U.S. Supreme Court upheld the search:

Carroll . . . holds a search warrant unnecessary where there is probable cause to search an automobile stopped on the highway; the car is movable, the occupants are alerted, and the car's contents may never be found again if a warrant must be obtained. Hence an immediate search is constitutionally permissible. Arguably, because of the preference for a magistrate's judgment, only the immobilization of the car should be permitted until a search warrant is obtained; arguably, only the "lesser" intrusion is permissible until the magistrate authorizes the "greater." But which is the "greater" and which the "lesser" intrusion is itself a debatable question and the answer may depend on a variety of circumstances. *For constitutional purposes, we see no difference between on the one hand seizing and holding a car before presenting the probable cause issue to a magistrate and on the other hand carrying out an immediate search without a warrant. Given probable cause to search, either course is reasonable under the Fourth Amendment.* On the facts before us, the blue station wagon could have been searched on the spot when it was stopped since there was probable cause to search and it was a fleeting target for a search. The probable cause factor still obtained at the station house and so did the mobility of the car unless the Fourth Amendment permits a warrantless seizure of the car and the denial of its use to anyone until a warrant is secured. In that event there is little to choose in terms of practical consequences between an immediate search without a warrant and the car's immobilization until a warrant is obtained. 399 U.S. at 51–52 (emphasis added).

Florida v. Meyers, 466 U.S. 380 (1984), upheld a warrantless search of an impounded automobile eight hours after it had been impounded and despite the fact that the automobile had already been subject to an initial, valid search on the highway. *Meyers* relied on *Michigan v. Thomas*, 458 U.S. 259 (1982), which upheld a warrantless search of an automobile after it had been stopped on the road, taken into police custody (e.g., impounded), and subjected to a valid inventory. (Impoundment and inventory are discussed later in this chapter.)

And *United States v. Johns*, 469 U.S. 478 (1985), upheld a warrantless search of containers in an impounded vehicle three days after it had been impounded. In particular, *United States v. Johns*, 469 U.S. 478 (1985), held that, when officers have probable cause to search a vehicle for a specific object, the search of a container in the vehicle that could contain that object need not be conducted at the same time as the initial seizure or search of the vehicle. Customs agents in *Johns* had seized and impounded a vehicle under the *Carroll* doctrine on the basis of probable cause to believe it contained marijuana. The Court approved a warrantless search conducted three days later of plastic bags found in the vehicle.

In the aftermath of *Johns*, officers should obtain a warrant for searches to be made more than three days after impounding a vehicle. Note again that courts have a strong preference for warrants. Law enforcement officers should consider applying for a warrant to search an automobile once it has been taken into police custody, especially when the facts and circumstances supporting probable cause may be weak or questionable. Note also that officers may validly detain a vehicle they have probable cause to search while they seek a warrant. *See United States v. Kimberlin*, 805 F.2d 210, 229 (7th Cir. 1986). ("[An] agent was sent to secure [the vehicle] until the search warrant could be obtained and the search conducted. Defendant's lawyer arranged to have the car towed, but the agent did not permit the removal. We think it clear that when an officer has probable cause to search a vehicle, it is reasonable under the Fourth Amendment to prevent removal while obtaining a warrant.")

Scope of a Vehicle Search Under the Automobile Exception

The discussion related to the scope of a search of a vehicle under the *Carroll* doctrine is divided into two sections:

- when an officer has probable cause to search the entire vehicle or a particular area of that vehicle (i.e., the trunk), and
- when an officer has probable cause to search a container located within a vehicle.

At times, of course, officers may have probable cause to search both a vehicle and containers within it; in those cases, the relevant principles discussed in both sections would apply.

Search of an Entire Vehicle or of a Particular Area in a Vehicle *United States v. Ross*, 456 U.S. 798 (1982), established the permissible scope of a warrantless search of a motor vehicle under the *Carroll* doctrine. In that case, police stopped and searched an automobile they had probable cause to believe contained narcotics.

KEY POINTS

LO1
- Under the *Carroll* doctrine, if a car is readily mobile and probable cause exists to believe it contains contraband, the Fourth Amendment permits police to search the vehicle without a warrant or other justification. The *Carroll* doctrine, also known as the automobile exception to the warrant requirement, stems from the inherent mobility of motor vehicles as well as the diminished expectation of privacy possessed by occupants of motor vehicles.

LO2
- To satisfy the readily mobile requirement of the automobile exception, the vehicle must be inherently capable of movement. No separate showing of exigency is generally needed for the automobile exception to apply.

- Officers should obtain a warrant before searching a vehicle they have probable cause to search in the following circumstances: (1) The vehicle is clearly not being used for movement (i.e., it is elevated on blocks), or (2) the vehicle is located on private property and there is time to obtain a warrant.

- If circumstances make an immediate search of a vehicle on the highway unsafe or impractical, the vehicle may be removed to a more convenient location. If a search is conducted without unreasonable delay after the vehicle's arrival at the new location, the probable cause factor existing on the highway remains in force, and the warrantless search is constitutionally permissible.

During the search, an officer found and opened a closed brown paper bag and a zippered leather pouch in the automobile's trunk, revealing heroin and a large amount of money. The Court held the search was legal:

> [T]he scope of the warrantless search authorized by [the *Carroll*] exception is no broader and no narrower than a magistrate could legitimately authorize by warrant. If probable cause justifies the search of a lawfully stopped vehicle, it justifies the search of every part of the vehicle and its contents that may conceal the object of the search. 456 U.S. at 825.

In other words, the scope of the search depends on the object of the search and the places, or locations, where there is probable cause to believe the object may be found:

> The scope of a warrantless search of an automobile thus is not defined by the nature of the container in which the contraband is secreted. Rather, it is defined by the object of the search and the places in which there is probable cause to believe that it may be found. Just as probable cause to believe that a stolen lawnmower may be found in a garage will not support a warrant to search an upstairs bedroom, probable cause to believe that undocumented aliens are being transported in a van will not justify a warrantless search of a suitcase. Probable cause to believe that a container placed in the trunk of a taxi contains contraband or evidence does not justify a search of the entire cab. 456 U.S. at 824.

Because the scope of a search depends, in part, on the object of that search, an officer with probable cause to believe an illegal alien is present within a vehicle could not search in that vehicle's glove compartment or in a similar area that is too small to conceal a person.

In addition, as the Court indicated in *Ross*, the scope of a search depends on the location in which there is probable cause to believe items of an incriminating character will be found. For example, if an officer has probable cause to believe the trunk of the vehicle contains incriminating items, the officer may only search that particular area of the vehicle. Likewise, if an officer has probable cause to believe the passenger compartment of a vehicle contains incriminating items, he or she could only search that particular area of the vehicle. But if the officer validly possessed probable cause that the entire vehicle contained items of an incriminating character, the officer could search anywhere in the vehicle those items could fit, including the passenger compartment, trunk and glove compartment. For example, in *United States v. White*, 549 F.3d 946 (4th Cir. 2008), the Court said:

> [W]hen police have probable cause to search a vehicle, "nice distinctions" among different parts of the car such as the glove compartment and trunk "give way to the interest in the prompt and efficient completion of the task at hand." In other words, officers may conduct a thorough search of the vehicle once probable cause is established. 549 F.3d at 949.

However, in *United States v. Wald*, 216 F.3d 1222, 1228 (10th Cir. 2000), the court found that the officer had developed probable cause to search the passenger compartment of a vehicle for contraband but not the trunk:

> Had [the officer] testified that he detected the odor of raw methamphetamine, such evidence, if based upon proper foundation, would have sufficed to provide probable cause for the trunk search. In the instant case, however, [the officer] testified that

he smelled only burnt methamphetamine, not raw methamphetamine, and that burnt methamphetamine has a distinctively pungent odor. Following [precedent case law], the strong odor of burnt methamphetamine, whether or not it can permeate trunks, does not provide probable cause to search a trunk, because it is unreasonable to think someone smoked drugs in the trunk of a car.

The court in *Wald* essentially held that because the officer smelled burned methamphetamine, which supported a belief that individuals had recently used the drug, the officer lacked probable cause to search the trunk of the car given the improbability of current or recent use of the drug in that area of the car. Thus, the court excluded drugs the officer found during his search of the trunk.

In contrast to odors detected by humans, sniffs by police dogs supporting probable cause to search a vehicle are not subjected to as much precision. For example, in *United States v. Rosborough*, 366 F.3d 1145 (10th Cir. 2004), when a dog trained in drug detection alerted police to the presence of drugs in the passenger area of a vehicle, the court permitted police to search the trunk of that vehicle without a warrant. According to the court, the canine sniff provided the necessary probable cause to search the trunk:

> Our holdings with regard to drug-dog alerts do not lend themselves to that level of exactness. A dog alert creates general probable cause to search a vehicle; it does not implicate the precision of a surgeon working with scalpel in hand. Thus, we hold that a canine alert toward the passenger area of a vehicle gives rise to probable cause to search the trunk as well; the search [of defendant's] vehicle subsequent to the canine alert was therefore supported by probable cause. 366 F.3d at 1153.

See also United States v. Pierce, 622 F.3d 209 (3rd Cir. 2010) ("The District Court found that [the police canine] Cole alerted to the outside of the car, which provides probable cause for a police officer to search the interior of the car. We affirm the reasoning adopted by the District Court."). (For further discussion of canine sniffs in the context of motor vehicles, see the section "Vehicle Searches by Dogs" at the end of this chapter.)

The scope of a *Carroll* doctrine search may even extend to dismantling part of the vehicle, or looking into hidden compartments within the vehicle. In *United States v. Zucco*, 71 F.3d 188 (5th Cir. 1995), police had probable cause to search an entire recreational vehicle because cocaine had been found in a cabinet during a valid consent search. When a drug-sniffing dog alerted to another part of the vehicle, police were authorized to remove a wall panel, where they discovered a large cache of cocaine.

See also United States v. Goncalves, 642 F.3d 245, 249–50 (1st Cir. 2011) ("Goncalves argues that even if the car's interior were searchable, no probable cause justified searching the engine compartment and gas cap, where the handgun and cocaine were found. But if probable cause justifies the search of a lawfully stopped vehicle, it justifies the search of *every part of the vehicle and its contents* that may conceal the object of the search. [Detective] Sullivan testified as to the use of such hiding places by drug dealers, and common sense would suggest this possibility anyway.") (internal quotations and citations omitted).

Search of a Container Found in a Vehicle When officers have probable cause to search only a particular container placed in a vehicle, they may search that container without a warrant but not the entire vehicle. In *California v. Acevedo*, 500 U.S. 565 (1991), police observed the defendant leave an apartment known to contain marijuana with a brown paper package the same size as marijuana packages they had seen earlier. He placed the bag in the trunk of his car and started to drive away. Fearing the loss of evidence, officers in an unmarked car stopped him, opened his trunk and the bag, and found marijuana.

The Court in *Acevedo* held that the Fourth Amendment does not compel separate treatment for an automobile search that extends only to a container within the vehicle. The Court said:

> The interpretation of the *Carroll* doctrine set forth in Ross now applies to all searches of containers found in an automobile. In other words, the police may search without a warrant if their search is supported by probable cause. The Court in *Ross* put it this way: "The scope of a warrantless search of an automobile . . . is not defined by the nature of the container in which the contraband is secreted. Rather, it is defined by the object of the search and the places in which there is probable cause to believe that it may be found." [The Court in *Ross*] went on to note: "Probable cause to believe that a container placed in the trunk of a taxi contains contraband or evidence does not justify a search of the entire cab." We affirm that principle. In the case before us, the police had probable cause to believe that the paper bag in the automobile's trunk contained marijuana. That probable cause now allows a warrantless search of the paper bag. The facts in the record reveal that the police did not have probable cause to believe that contraband was hidden in any other part of the automobile and a search of the entire vehicle would have been without probable cause and unreasonable under the Fourth Amendment. 500 U.S. at 579–80 (italics supplied).

Thus, if police have probable cause to believe a particular container contains items of an incriminating character, they may search that container. But they may not search other areas of the vehicle unless they have probable cause that those areas contain incriminating items.

Note that if police have probable cause to search an entire vehicle, they may conduct a warrantless search of the vehicle and any containers in the vehicle capable of holding the object of their search. For example, in *United States v. Pinela-Hernandez*, 262 F.3d 974 (9th Cir. 2001), police developed probable cause to search a vehicle for drugs by corroborating an informant's tip and as a result of certain actions by defendant. They did not obtain a warrant to search the vehicle, including certain packages in the trunk. The court in *Pinela-Hernandez* approved the search:

> The Supreme Court [in *Ross*] has held that if "probable cause justifies the search of a lawfully stopped vehicle, it justifies the search of every part of the vehicle and its contents that may conceal the object of the search." Because there was probable cause to search the car [for drugs], there was probable cause to open the trunk and to search the packages that turned out to contain marijuana. 262 F.3d at 979 (quoting *Ross*, 456 U.S. at 825). *See also United States v. Stubblefield*, 682 F.3d 502, 507 (6th Cir. 2012) ("If the police have probable cause to search a lawfully stopped vehicle for contraband, then the police have probable cause to search every part of the vehicle and all containers found therein in which the object of the search could be hidden").

In addition, in *Ross* itself, discussed earlier for its relevance to the overall scope inquiry for automobile searches, the Supreme Court found that "police officers had probable cause to search [the defendant's] entire vehicle" for drugs. 456 U.S. at 817. The Court in *Ross* overturned the lower court's holding, thereby sanctioning police actions in opening and searching without a warrant a closed paper bag and leather pouch located in the trunk of the vehicle.

Furthermore, *Wyoming v. Houghton*, 526 U.S. 295, 307 (1999), extended warrantless automobile container searches to a passenger's belongings. The Court in *Houghton* held that "police officers with probable cause to search a car may inspect passengers' belongings found in the car that are capable of concealing the object of the search." The Court found that passengers, like drivers, have a reduced expectation of privacy with regard to property that they transport in motor vehicles. Police examination of an item of a passenger's personal property is unlikely to produce the annoyance, fear, and humiliation that a search of one's body is likely to produce. In contrast, the Court found the government's interests in inspecting passengers' belongings substantial:

> As in all car-search cases, the "ready mobility" of an automobile creates a risk that the evidence or contraband will be permanently lost while a warrant is obtained. . . . In addition, a car passenger . . . will often be engaged in a common enterprise with the driver, and have the same interest in concealing the fruits or the evidence of their wrongdoing. . . . A criminal might be able to hide contraband in a passenger's belongings as readily as in other containers in the car . . . perhaps even surreptitiously, without the passenger's knowledge or permission.
> 526 U.S. at 304–05.

A few other considerations apply to the scope of searches under the automobile exception. For example, if an officer obtains probable cause to search a container after the container has been removed from a vehicle, the *Carroll* doctrine does not apply—even if the container is in the process of being returned to the vehicle. The officer must have probable cause to believe that containers subject to seizure are contained *somewhere inside the vehicle*. In *State v. Lewis*, 611 A.2d 69 (Me. 1992), after the defendant was arrested for operating a vehicle under the influence of drugs or alcohol, the officer released him on personal recognizance and offered him a ride to a motel. The defendant voluntarily retrieved from his car a carry-on bag containing two smaller bags; the officer, smelling the odor of marijuana, asked to see inside the smaller bags. When the defendant attempted to return the carry-on bag to his car, the officer opened the smaller bags and found marijuana. The court invalidated the search, holding that "the fact that the bags came from the car and were in the process of being returned to the car does not trigger the automobile exception." 611 A.2d at 71. (Searches of containers not associated with vehicles will be discussed further later.)

In addition, searches under the automobile exception do not extend to the body of an occupant of the vehicle. The U.S. Supreme Court in *Houghton* cited *United States v. Di Re*, 332 U.S. 581 (1948), for the principle that officers may not conduct searches of a car occupant's person under the automobile exception:

> *United States v. Di Re* held that probable cause to search a car did not justify a body search of a passenger. [This] case turned on the unique, significantly heightened protection afforded against searches of one's person. Even a limited search of the outer clothing . . . constitutes a severe, though brief, intrusion upon cherished personal security, and it must surely be an annoying, frightening, and perhaps humiliating experience. Such traumatic consequences are not to be expected when the police examine an item of personal property found in a car. 526 U.S. at 303 (internal quotations omitted).

Of course, as discussed in more detail in Chapter 7 addressing searches incident to arrest, if an officer has probable cause to arrest one or more occupants of a motor vehicle, the officer may conduct a search of the occupants incident to their arrest. The officer may also search the passenger compartment of a motor vehicle incident to the arrest of a vehicle occupant or recent occupant when

- the arrestee or occupant is unsecured and within reaching distance of the passenger compartment of the vehicle at the time of the police search of that vehicle, or
- it is reasonable for the officer to believe that evidence relevant to the crime of arrest may be found in the vehicle of the arrested occupant.

See Arizona v. Gant, 556 U.S. 332 (2009) (discussed in more detail in Chapter 7 in the section entitled "Motor Vehicle Searches Incident to Arrest").

As part of a valid search incident to a vehicle occupant's arrest, the officer may search for weapons and destructible evidence on the arrested person and in the passenger compartment.

Thus, the search-incident-to-arrest exception in the motor vehicle context and the *Carroll* doctrine (e.g., the automobile exception) are different in these fundamental ways:

- the search-incident-to-arrest exception allows a police search of arrested motor vehicle occupants, whereas the automobile exception does not generally permit a bodily search of these occupants;
- the permissible scope of the search-incident-to-arrest exception does not extend to a police search of the trunk, whereas the scope of the automobile exception may include a police search of this area of the vehicle (provided the requirements of this exception are satisfied); and
- the requirements of the automobile exception allowing police searches of motor vehicles include probable cause to believe incriminating evidence is located within a readily motor vehicle, whereas the requirements of the search-incident-to-arrest exception allowing police searches of motor vehicles include (1) the arrested motor vehicle occupant must be unsecured and within reaching distance of the passenger compartment of the vehicle at the time of the police search of that vehicle, or (2) it is reasonable for the officer to believe that evidence relevant to the crime for which the motor vehicle occupant is arrested, may be found in the vehicle.

Finally, if an officer has reasonable suspicion that an occupant of a vehicle is armed and dangerous, the officer may conduct a limited frisk of the occupant for weapons as well as a limited search of the passenger compartment of the vehicle for weapons. (See Chapter 8 on stops and frisks.)

Search of a Container Not Found in a Vehicle The rationale justifying a warrantless search of a container in an automobile believed to be harboring items of an incriminating nature arguably applies with equal force to any movable container believed to be carrying such an item. *United States v. Chadwick*, 433 U.S. 1 (1977), however, squarely rejected that argument. In *Chadwick*, federal railroad officials became suspicious when they noticed that a large, unusually heavy footlocker loaded onto a train was leaking talcum powder, a substance often used to mask the odor of marijuana. Narcotics agents met the train at its destination, and a trained police dog signaled the presence of a controlled substance inside the footlocker. Instead of seizing the footlocker at that time, the agents waited until the defendant arrived and placed the footlocker in the trunk of his automobile. Before he started the engine, the officers arrested him and his two companions. The agents then removed the footlocker from the trunk, moved it to a secure place in a government building, and opened it there without a warrant. They discovered a large quantity of marijuana inside the footlocker.

KEY POINTS

LO3
- When an officer has probable cause to search a readily mobile vehicle for an object that is contraband under the *Carroll* doctrine, the officer may look anywhere in the vehicle where the object could be hidden, including the trunk as well as containers that could hold the object.

- If an officer has probable cause to search only a particular container placed in a vehicle or a particular area of the vehicle, the officer may search that container

Continued on next page

On appeal, the prosecution did not argue that the locker's brief contact with the automobile's trunk made the *Carroll* doctrine applicable. Rather, the prosecution argued that the warrantless search was "reasonable" because a container such as a footlocker has some of the mobile characteristics that support warrantless searches of automobiles. The Supreme Court rejected the argument:

> The factors which diminish the privacy aspects of an automobile do not apply to respondents' footlocker. Luggage contents are not open to public view, except as a condition to a border entry or common carrier travel; nor is luggage subject to regular inspections and official scrutiny on a continuing basis. Unlike an automobile, whose primary function is transportation, luggage is intended as a repository of personal effects. In sum, a person's expectations of privacy in personal luggage are substantially greater than in an automobile. 433 U.S. at 13.

The *Chadwick* Court noted that the practical problems associated with the temporary detention of a piece of luggage during the period of time necessary to obtain a warrant are significantly less than those associated with the detention of an automobile. By invalidating the warrantless search of the footlocker, the Court reaffirmed the general principle that closed packages and containers may not be searched without a warrant. Thus, the Court declined to extend the rationale of the automobile exception to permit a warrantless search of any movable container found in a public place. *See generally California v. Acevedo*, 500 U.S. 565 (1991).

Other Container Searches Seizures and searches of containers incident to arrest are discussed in Chapter 7. Investigatory detentions of containers are discussed in Chapter 8 on stops and frisks. Plain view container searches and seizures are discussed in Chapter 10. Searches and seizures of abandoned containers are discussed in Chapter 12. Inventory searches of containers are discussed in the next section of this chapter.

CRIMINAL PROCEDURE IN ACTION

Can a Police Search Under the Automobile Exception Extend to Passenger Belongings? *State v. Mercier*, 2007 WL 1225858 (Ohio App. 1st Dist. 2007).

Madeira Police Lieutenant Chris Zumbiel testified that he had been investigating Charles Hagedorn for drug trafficking. On July 17, 2005, at about 6:40 P.M., Mercier was a passenger in Hagedorn's car. Hagedorn exited from his car, approached the vehicle of a confidential [police] informant, and sold the informant about a half pound of marijuana.

Mercier stayed in Hagedorn's car while the sale took place. Hagedorn returned to his car and drove away with Mercier still in the front passenger's seat.

Police stopped Hagedorn's car approximately one to two minutes after the sale. Lieutenant Zumbiel questioned Hagedorn, who admitted that there was marijuana in his car. Hagedorn opened a middle console and handed Zumbiel marijuana. Police removed Hagedorn from the car and patted him down,

recovering the buy money and some rolling papers. Hagedorn was then placed in a police cruiser.

Zumbiel then approached Mercier and removed her from Hagedorn's car. Zumbiel testified that "at that point [Mercier's] purse was left in the front seat. [Mercier] was placed in another cruiser." Zumbiel searched Mercier's purse. He found an Advil bottle, which he opened. The bottle contained four Adderall pills, a form of amphetamine. Zumbiel

Continued on next page

arrested Mercier. He read Mercier her Miranda rights, which she waived. Mercier told Zumbiel that a friend had given her the drugs, which she used to help her stay awake.

On cross-examination, Zumbiel testified that Mercier was not a suspect when police stopped Hagedorn's car. He also testified that when he approached Hagedorn's car, Mercier had her purse "on her person" [i.e., lap] and that Mercier left her purse on the front seat only because Zumbiel had asked her to exit from the car and leave the purse behind. *Mercier*, 2007 WL 1225858, at *1–*2.

■ Do you believe that Lieutenant Chris Zumbiel should have searched Mercier's purse? Why or why not? In answering this question, consider (1) whether the basic requirements of a police search under the automobile exception were satisfied and (2) whether the proper reach, or scope, of a search under the exception was maintained. For this second aspect, please be sure to include in your answer whether Lieutenant Zumbiel should have opened the pill ("Advil") bottle he found within Mercier's purse.

■ Assume for purposes of this question only that Lieutenant Zumbiel had been investigating the driver/owner of the car in which Mercier was a passenger *not* for drug trafficking, but rather in connection with a string of recent thefts of large-screen televisions from a local electronics store. Could Zumbiel search Mercier's purse under this changed scenario? Fully explain your answer.

Impoundment and Inventory

The police may impound motor vehicles for a variety of reasons. Accompanying a vehicle's impoundment, police routinely inventory the vehicle's contents for reasons of safety, liability, and convenience. This section explores the legal issues involved in impounding and inventorying motor vehicles.

Impoundment

Impoundment usually involves the police taking possession of a vehicle that would otherwise be left unattended and moving it to a garage or police lot for safekeeping. The main justifications for impoundment are to protect threats to public safety posed by the vehicle and to ensure the efficient movement of traffic:

> In the interests of public safety and as part of what the Court has called "community caretaking functions," . . . automobiles are frequently taken into police custody. Vehicle accidents present one such occasion. To permit the uninterrupted flow of traffic and in some instances to preserve evidence, disabled or damaged vehicles will often be removed from the highways or streets in caretaking and traffic control activities. Police will also frequently remove and impound automobiles which violate parking ordinances and which thereby jeopardize both the public safety and the efficient movement of vehicular traffic. The authority of police to seize and remove from the streets vehicles impeding traffic or threatening public safety and convenience is beyond challenge. *South Dakota v. Opperman*, 428 U.S. 364, 368–69 (1976).

Other reasons to impound vehicles include the following:

■ The driver has been arrested and taken into custody. *United States v. Lyles*, 946 F.2d 78 (8th Cir. 1991); *Colorado v. Bertine*, 479 U.S. 367 (1987) (discussed later in the section titled "Permissible Scope of Inventory Searches"); *Hodge v. Southhampton*, 838 F. Supp. 2d 67 (E.D.N.Y. 2012).

■ The driver is incapacitated by intoxication, injury, illness, or some other condition. *United States v. Ford*, 872 F.2d 1231 (6th Cir. 1989) (injury); *United States v. Lopez*, 547 F.3d 364, 372 (2d Cir. 2008) (intoxication).

- The vehicle is seized as evidence of or an instrument of a crime. *United States v. Cooper*, 949 F.2d 737 (5th Cir. 1991); *United States v. Mitchell*, 2013 WL 3808152 (M.D. Fla. 2013), at *22–*23.

- The vehicle is forfeited pursuant to a state or federal forfeiture law. *United States v. Bizzell*, 19 F.3d 1524 (4th Cir. 1994); *United States v. Nelson*, 530 F. Supp. 2d 719, 730 (D. Md. 2008).

- The vehicle and/or its parts have been reported stolen. *United States v. Mitchell*, 2013 WL 3808152 (M.D. Fla. 2013), at *22–*23 (stolen tires).

- The driver lacks a valid driver's license or valid proof of insurance. See *United States v. Penn*, 233 F.3d 1111 (9th Cir. 2000); *United States v. Cherry*, 436 F.3d 769 (7th Cir. 2006).

In many jurisdictions, the right of police to impound vehicles is defined by statute or departmental policy or both. If an officer impounds a vehicle in violation of statute or policy, or for an illegitimate reason such as harassment of the driver or searching for evidence, the impoundment may be held illegal under the Fourth Amendment. For example, in *United States v. Ibarra*, 955 F.2d 1405 (10th Cir. 1992), the court found that the officer impounded a vehicle unlawfully in violation of a state statute and the Fourth Amendment:

> Specifically, the district court found that defendant's vehicle did not obstruct the normal flow of traffic [or otherwise pose a threat to public safety]. . . . This finding is supported by the undisputed fact that the police officers at the scene did not request defendant to move his car [to the side of the road] while the officers waited forty-five minutes for the wrecker to arrive [e.g., to tow the defendant's vehicle]. The district court also found that defendant's situation did not justify removal of the vehicle under [the relevant statute] for the following reasons:
>
> **1.** there was no report that the vehicle had been stolen,
>
> **2.** the person in charge of the vehicle was able to provide for the custody of the vehicle but was never given the opportunity to do so by [the officer], and
>
> **3.** defendant was not under arrest at the time [the officer] elected to have the vehicle removed.
>
> We hold that the district court's factual findings regarding the lack of justification for the impoundment pursuant to [statute] are not clearly erroneous. Therefore [the officer's] decision [to impound the vehicle] was not reasonable and in conformance with the Fourth Amendment. 955 F.2d at 1409.

See also Miranda v. City of Cornelius, 429 F.3d 858, 865–66 (9th Cir. 2005) (unreasonable to impound vehicle parked in the driveway of defendant's home where defendant had a valid driver's license and the vehicle was "not creating any impediment to traffic or threatening public safety.")

Law enforcement officers are not *constitutionally* required to offer a person an opportunity to make other arrangements for the safekeeping of his or her vehicle, nor must they always choose methods of dealing with vehicles that are less intrusive than impoundment. As the U.S. Supreme Court stated, "[t]he reasonableness of any particular governmental activity does not necessarily or invariably turn on the existence of alternative 'less intrusive' means." *Illinois v. Lafayette*, 462 U.S. 640, 647 (1983). Therefore, nothing prohibits the exercise of police discretion to impound a vehicle rather than to lock and park it in a safe place, "so long as that discretion is exercised according to standard criteria and on the basis of something other than suspicion of evidence of criminal activity." *Colorado v. Bertine*, 479 U.S. 367, 375 (1987).

For example, in *United States v. Mayfield*, 161 F.3d 1143 (8th Cir. 1998), the court concluded that the officer's decision to impound a car rather than allow a passenger to drive it away was reasonable under the Fourth Amendment:

> Here, the arrestee was Mayfield, who did not own the car. The logical person to take custody of the car, its owner, was Mayfield's passenger. She informed the officers she could not drive because of her medication, and she lacked a driver's license. Rather than objecting to impoundment, she asked for a ride to a doctor's appointment and received one. Under these circumstances, we conclude the decision to impound the vehicle "did not so exceed the [state patrol] policy as to warrant suppression." It appears the troopers applied the impoundment policy in good faith. The troopers were not constitutionally required to choose a less intrusive way of securing the car. We conclude the decision to impound the car was reasonable, and thus did not violate the Fourth Amendment. 161 F.3d at 1144.

See also United States v. Coccia, 446 F.3d 233 (1st Cir. 2006) ("Coccia contends that the seizure (e.g., impoundment) of his car was improper because the officers did not provide him with an opportunity to arrange for someone else to pick-up the car. There is no such requirement.").

Some states, however, require officers to consider reasonable alternatives to impoundment. "Although an officer is not required to exhaust all possibilities, the officer must at least consider alternatives; attempt, if feasible, to obtain a name from the driver of someone in the vicinity who could move the vehicle; and then reasonably conclude from this deliberation that impoundment is proper." *State v. Coss*, 943 P.2d 1126, 1130 (Wash. App. 1997). *Coss* held that the impoundment of a stopped vehicle was unreasonable when the driver had a suspended license but a properly licensed passenger could have driven the vehicle away.

See also United States v. Proctor, 489 F.3d 1348, 1354–55 (D.C. Cir. 2007) ("We believe that if a standard impoundment procedure exists, a police officer's failure to adhere thereto is unreasonable and violates the Fourth Amendment. [Washington, D.C., Metropolitan Police Department's governing rule] provides that a vehicle 'classified as prisoner's property shall be disposed of in any lawful manner *in which the person arrested directs.*' General Order ("GO") 602.1 (1972). Thus, before impounding the vehicle, an officer should provide the arrestee with the opportunity to arrange for its removal. [The defendant/arrestee] Proctor, however, was afforded no such opportunity. On the contrary, [Officer] Shegan testified that the officers were required to impound Proctor's vehicle because no one was present to remove it, Proctor was not the owner and they 'weren't going to wait' for the owner to remove it. [The officer said] 'I don't believe I had a choice.' Accordingly, the officers' impoundment (seizure) decision violated GO 602.1.").

Police Inventory

Assuming a lawful impoundment, may the vehicle then be searched for incriminating evidence without a warrant? Unless the situation satisfies the requirements of the automobile exception discussed earlier in this chapter, police have no authority to conduct a warrantless investigatory search of a lawfully impounded motor vehicle. In other words, police must obtain a search warrant to search an impounded vehicle unless they have probable cause to search the vehicle and the vehicle is readily mobile.

Nevertheless, *South Dakota v. Opperman*, 428 U.S. 364, 372 (1976), approved a more limited procedure police may conduct on a lawfully impounded motor vehicle: the routine practice of local police departments of securing and inventorying the vehicle's contents, including what is in the glove compartment "since it is a customary place for documents of ownership and registration, as well as a place for the temporary storage of valuables." This limited type of warrantless procedure is allowed:

- to protect the owner's property while it remains in police custody,
- to protect the police against claims or disputes over lost, stolen, or vandalized property, and
- to protect the police from potential danger.

See Colorado v. Bertine, 479 U.S. 367, 372 (1987). ("We found [in *Opperman*] that inventory procedures serve to protect an owner's property while it is in the custody of the police, to insure against claims of lost, stolen, or vandalized property, and to guard the police from danger.") Apart from collecting and securing valuables left in the vehicle, officers should record, as part of an inventory search, the vehicle identification number, the serial number, and the make, model, and license plate number of the car so that it may be easily identified later. *Cotton v. United States*, 371 F.2d 385 (9th Cir. 1967), overruled on other grounds by *United States v. Cunag*, 386 F.3d 888 (9th Cir. 2004); *United States v. DeBardeleben*, 740 F.2d 440, 445 (6th Cir.) ("[T]he mere checking of the serial number of an automobile by opening the door does not constitute a search within the prohibitions of the Fourth Amendment."), *cert. denied*, 469 U.S. 1028 (1984).

No Warrant or Probable Cause Required for Inventory The inventory procedure is not considered a search for Fourth Amendment purposes because its object is not to find incriminating evidence as part of a criminal investigation. Rather, it is considered a routine administrative, custodial procedure made for the purpose of creating an inventory of a vehicle's contents. Inventorying the contents of a vehicle neither requires a warrant nor probable cause:

> The policies behind the warrant requirement are not implicated in an inventory search, nor is the related concept of probable cause: The standard of probable cause is peculiarly related to criminal investigations, not routine, non-criminal procedures. . . . The probable-cause approach is unhelpful when analysis centers upon the reasonableness of routine administrative caretaking functions. *Bertine*, 479 U.S. at 371 (internal quotations omitted).

However, inventories "must not be a ruse for a general rummaging in order to discover incriminating evidence." *Florida v. Wells,* 495 U.S. 1, 4 (1990). For example, in *United States v. Edwards*, 242 F.3d 928 (10th Cir. 2001), police impounded a car rented by the defendant's girlfriend after finding incriminating evidence in the car related to an alleged armed robbery committed by the defendant and his girlfriend. The court determined that the warrantless search of the vehicle that revealed the incriminating evidence could not be considered a valid inventory in light of the investigatory motives of the police:

> In this case, it is clear that the search of the rental vehicle was conducted for investigatory, rather than administrative, purposes. The officer testified that he "was assigned to the suspects' vehicle to search for any additional evidence or anything that would indicate this is their vehicle and indicate anything that would suffice that a crime occurred." He also admitted on cross-examination that he was "searching for evidence of the crime." In addition, the decision to impound the car was not made until after the search revealed incriminating evidence against [the defendant], which makes it exceedingly difficult to believe that this was an inventory search conducted to protect the police from liability after the decision was made to impound the car. Based upon the foregoing facts, we have no trouble determining that this search was conducted for investigative rather than administrative purposes and cannot be justified as a mere inventory search. 242 F.3d at 938–39.

See also United States v. Taylor, 636 F.3d 461, 464–66 (8th Cir. 2011) (invalidating "inventory" of a truck revealing narcotics because officer's own testimony at the suppression hearing indicated an investigatory pretext, or motive, to find drugs in the truck, and officer did not comply with inventory procedures).

Nevertheless, an investigatory motive will not invalidate an inventory if there is also a genuine administrative motive, and the inventory is conducted according to standard departmental procedures. For example, in *United States v. Lumpkin*, 159 F.3d 983 (6th Cir. 1998), the court found that an officer's suspicion that a particular area of the vehicle had illegal contraband did not invalidate an otherwise valid police inventory:

> An inventory search may not be conducted for purposes of investigation and must be conducted according to standard police procedures. However, the fact that an officer suspects that contraband may be found does not defeat an otherwise proper inventory search. Therefore, the fact that [the officers] may have suspected that the truck contained evidence of drug trafficking does not render their inventory search invalid if otherwise found to be lawful. 159 F.3d at 987.

In addition, in *United States v. Lopez*, 547 F.3d 364, 368, 372 (2d Cir. 2008), the court found that an expectation, or hope, on the part of the officers that drugs would be found in the vehicle did not invalidate an otherwise proper inventory:

> [I]f a search of an impounded car for inventory purposes is conducted under standardized procedures, that search falls under the inventory exception to the warrant requirement of the Fourth Amendment, notwithstanding a police expectation that the search will reveal criminal evidence. In the present case, while the officers may well have had an investigative motivation to search Lopez's car [for contraband], the circumstances called for the impoundment of his car, as Lopez was arrested for driving it while intoxicated, and the impoundment required the conduct of an inventory search. We find no reason to doubt that the . . . standards for the conduct of a warrantless inventory search were fully satisfied. We therefore affirm the district court's denial of the motion to suppress the evidence [consisting of drugs and a gun] found in the impounded car.

The "Standard Procedures" Requirement for Inventory Searches

Each law enforcement agency must have standard procedures for inventorying impounded vehicles, or the inventories will be declared illegal. In upholding the validity of an inventory of an impounded car, *South Dakota v. Opperman* emphasized that the police were using a standard inventory form pursuant to standard police procedures. The Court said, "The decisions of this Court point unmistakably to the conclusion reached by both federal and state courts that inventories pursuant to standard police procedures are reasonable." 428 U.S. at 372.

In *Florida v. Wells*, 495 U.S. 1 (1990), a state trooper stopped defendant for speeding. After the officer smelled alcohol on defendant's breath, he arrested defendant. After the car was impounded, an inventory of a locked suitcase in the car's trunk revealed marijuana. The Court found that in the absence of a policy or procedure by police to regulate this particular inventory search, it was invalid:

> In the present case, the Supreme Court of Florida found that the Florida Highway Patrol had no policy whatever with respect to the opening of closed containers encountered during an inventory search. We hold that absent such a policy, the instant search was not sufficiently regulated to satisfy the Fourth Amendment and that the marijuana which was found in the suitcase, therefore, was properly suppressed by the Supreme Court of Florida. 495 U.S. at 4–5.

The Court, however, did posit examples of valid police procedures for inventories of closed containers: "Thus, while policies of opening all containers or of opening no containers are unquestionably permissible, it would be equally permissible, for example, to allow the opening of closed containers whose contents officers determine they are unable to ascertain from examining the containers' exteriors." 495 U.S. at 4. Indeed, individual police departments may develop their own procedures for inventories and as long as they are reasonable and administered in good faith (i.e., not for the purpose of criminal investigation), the fact that a reviewing court might conceive of an alternative procedure is not controlling:

469

CHAPTER 11
SEARCH AND SEIZURE
OF VEHICLES AND
CONTAINERS

> The Supreme Court of Colorado also expressed the view that the search in this case was unreasonable . . . because [defendant] himself could have been offered the opportunity to make other arrangements for the safekeeping of his property. We conclude that here . . . reasonable police regulations relating to inventory procedures administered in good faith satisfy the Fourth Amendment, even though courts might as a matter of hindsight be able to devise equally reasonable rules requiring a different procedure. *Bertine*, 479 U.S. at 373–74.

For example, in *United States v. Wimbush*, 337 F.3d 947, 951 (7th Cir. 2003), the court sanctioned an inventory of an automobile revealing an illegal weapon because it was conducted pursuant to established police policy:

> [T]he warrantless search was valid as a routine post-arrest inventory search, which authorizes police to search vehicles in lawful custody in order to secure or protect the car and its contents. Here, police lawfully arrested [defendant] for driving without a license and for driving with an open container of alcohol, and it was undisputed that the car was searched in a manner consistent with the police department's inventory policy. [T]he district court did not clearly err by denying [defendant's] motion to suppress [the weapon] based on the search of his vehicle.

Also, in *United States v. Richardson*, 515 F.3d 74 (1st Cir. 2008), the court approved an inventory by police revealing drugs underneath a floor mat in a vehicle because the inventory was conducted pursuant to existing police procedures:

> [Defendant] Richardson contends that police impermissibly searched under the floor mats during their vehicle inventory search. The Fourth Amendment permits a warrantless inventory search if the search is carried out pursuant to a standardized policy. Troopers Maher and Nims testified that the ... State Police written inventory policy requires a search of all interior areas of a vehicle, including floor areas and all unlocked containers; that the floor area includes the area under floor mats; and that officers usually look under floor mats during an inventory search. Richardson offered no evidence to rebut Nims's and Maher's testimony. We conclude, therefore, that the district court did not commit clear error in finding that the relevant inventory search policy permitted the troopers to search under the floor mats. 515 F.3d at 77, 85 (internal citations omitted).

However, courts will invalidate an inventory search in violation of existing procedures. For example, in *United States v. Johnson*, 936 F.2d 1082, 1084 (9th Cir. 1991), because police violated an established inventory procedure under state law in opening the locked trunk of defendant's car, the court suppressed an illegal weapon found in the trunk:

> Under [state] law, "an officer may not examine the locked trunk of an impounded vehicle in the course of an inventory search absent a manifest necessity for conducting such a search." The government has made absolutely no showing of manifest necessity in this case. That failure to comply with governing state procedures renders the search of the trunk of [defendant's] car unconstitutional. . . .

We vacate [defendant's] conviction and remand with instructions to suppress evidence obtained from the inventory search of the car's trunk. 936 F.2d at 1084.

See also United States v. Taylor, 636 F.3d 461, 464–65 (8th Cir. 2011) (invalidating inventory, in part, because officer failed to comply with policy requiring police to create detailed, itemized listing of items in vehicle).

As long as a police department has established reasonable procedures for inventory searches and administers them in good faith (i.e., not for the purpose of investigating crime), minor variations from police procedures may not invalidate an otherwise lawful impoundment and inventory search. In *United States v. Kimes*, 246 F.3d 800 (6th Cir. 2001), the officer's failure to call the defendant's relatives or friends to retrieve the defendant's vehicle before impounding it did not invalidate the police's subsequent inventory of the vehicle, which revealed illegal weapons:

> In this connection [the defendant] points out that on some occasions the [police department] permitted family members or friends to remove a vehicle if its owner or operator was unable to do so. The defendant's arguments are not persuasive. Discretion as to impoundment [and inventorying] is permissible "so long as that discretion is exercised according to standard criteria and on the basis of something other than suspicion of evidence of criminal activity." Here, as we gather, [departmental] police sometimes permitted vehicles to be picked up by a driver's friends and relations if they were already present or if the driver could contact them and get them to come to the facility promptly. [The defendant] suggests that rather than towing his truck, the officers should have taken it upon themselves to call his wife and ask her to get the vehicle. He cites no authority compelling such a conclusion, and we are aware of none. 246 F.3d at 804–05.

See also United States v. Pappas, 452 F.3d 767 (8th Cir. 2006) (upholding the police inventory search in compliance with departmental procedures notwithstanding defendant's allegation that the officer's failed to complete a proper inventory search form).

Finally, standard inventory procedures need not be written. For example, in *United States v. Hawkins*, 279 F.3d 83, 86 (1st Cir. 2002), the court said:

> A warrantless search is permitted under the Fourth Amendment if it is carried out pursuant to a standardized inventory policy. Such a standardized inventory policy may be unwritten. Because the district court found that there was a standardized, albeit unwritten, inventory policy compelling officers to open containers to determine their contents during an inventory, the drug evidence was properly obtained.

See also State v. Eagle, 2012 WL 2470000 (Ariz. App. Div. 1 2012), at *3–*4.

Permissible Scope of Inventory Searches

Officers should follow standard departmental procedures regarding the allowable scope of a vehicle inventory. So long as the officer follows these procedures in good faith, and does not conduct an inventory solely for investigatory purposes, the officer has some discretion regarding the administration of an inventory. *See, e.g., Bertine*, 479 U.S. at 375. ("Nothing in [our precedent cases] prohibits the exercise of police discretion so long as that discretion is exercised according to standard criteria and on the basis of something other than suspicion of evidence of criminal activity.") In *Bertine* itself, the Court permitted an inventory of the passenger compartment of defendant's van. Furthermore, when the search revealed drugs and drug paraphernalia in a closed backpack, the Court permitted the government to rely on this evidence in defendant's trial on drug charges. 479 U.S. at 368–69.

Also, a lawful inventory may extend to a vehicle's glove compartment:

> The inventory was not unreasonable in scope. [Defendant's] motion to suppress in state court challenged the inventory only as to items inside the car not in plain view. But once the policeman was lawfully inside the car to secure the personal property in plain view, it was not unreasonable to open the unlocked glove compartment, to which vandals would have had ready and unobstructed access once inside the car. *Opperman*, 428 U.S. at 375 n.10.

In addition, courts permit an inventory of a vehicle's trunk if it is conducted pursuant to police procedures. For example, in *United States v. Rankin*, 261 F.3d 735 (8th Cir. 2001), an inventory of defendant's trunk revealed drugs. The court found the procedure valid because it was conducted "pursuant to department guidelines," and was not "a subterfuge for a 'general rummaging' for incriminating evidence." 261 F.3d at 740.

Indeed, most courts allow the opening of a *locked* trunk by police during a valid inventory conducted pursuant to existing police procedures:

> To protect themselves against spurious claims of lost or stolen property, the authorities must know the contents of any vehicle which they impound. The inventory form which the sheriff's deputy was required to complete prior to releasing the vehicle for impoundment asked him to determine if the vehicle had a spare tire. To obtain that information, it was necessary to open the trunk of the car. The Court is persuaded that under the circumstances of this case, opening the locked trunk with the keys obtained from defendant was reasonable under the Fourth Amendment as an inventory search conducted pursuant to the standard policy and practice of the sheriff's department. *United States v. Duncan*, 763 F.2d 220, 223 (6th Cir. 1985).

See also United States v. Mundy, 621 F.3d 283, 291–92 (3d Cir. 2010) ("By specifically authorizing the search of the trunk 'if accessible,' and by forbidding any 'locked areas, including the trunk area,' from being 'forced open,' the Policy ... authorized Officer Chabot to inventory 'any personal property of value' left in the trunk *once [defendant] provided the keys to it*" (italics added). *But see United States v. Tueller*, 349 F.3d 1239, 1244–46 (10th Cir. 2003) (allowing an inventory of a locked trunk under established, standardized police procedures, including the use of reasonable force to open a locked trunk).

Moreover, various courts have permitted a police inventory of the engine compartment of a vehicle. *See United States v. Lumpkin*, 159 F.3d 983, 988 (6th Cir. 1998). ("We . . . hold that a valid inventory search conducted by law enforcement officers according to standard procedure may include the engine compartment of a vehicle."); *See also United States v. Pappas*, 452 F.3d 767, 772 (8th Cir. 2006) ("[T]he inventory search, including the search of the engine compartment [for a gun], was a reasonable search under the Fourth Amendment."). Note, however, that because officers may not conduct an inventory for the purpose of investigating and finding evidence of crime, officers would generally not have reason to dismantle the vehicle, including ripping apart its upholstery. Such actions exceed the scope of a valid inventory to protect and secure the vehicle's contents.

Colorado v. Bertine, 479 U.S. 367 (1987), expanded the allowable scope of an inventory search to include the opening of closed containers found in the impounded vehicle and the examination of their contents. Recall that in *Bertine*, discussed earlier, the Court permitted an inventory search of a closed backpack in the defendant's van. The search revealed drugs in the backpack, which were admissible at the defendant's trial. Of course, police departments must have standardized criteria regulating the opening of containers found during inventory searches, both to narrow the latitude of individual police officers and to prevent the inventory search from becoming a general rummaging to discover incriminating evidence:

> But in forbidding uncanalized discretion to police officers conducting inventory searches, there is no reason to insist that they be conducted in a totally mechanical "all or nothing" fashion. . . . A police officer may be allowed sufficient latitude to determine whether a particular container should or should not be opened in light of the nature of the search and characteristics of the container itself. Thus, while policies of opening all containers or of opening no containers are unquestionably permissible, it would be equally permissible, for example, to allow the opening of closed containers whose contents officers determine they are unable to ascertain from examining the containers' exteriors. The allowance of the exercise of judgment based on concerns related to the purposes of an inventory search does not violate the Fourth Amendment. *Florida v. Wells*, 495 U.S. 1, 4 (1990).

United States v. Lozano, 171 F.3d 1129 (7th Cir. 1999), applied *Bertine* in upholding an inventory of closed duffel bags that revealed marijuana in the bed of a defendant's truck:

> In the present case, the district court judge found that the inventory search was conducted pursuant to the Peoria Police Department's standard routine of opening all closed containers [i.e., the five closed duffel bags] that might contain valuables and, therefore, was a valid inventory search. Because we believe that the district court did not commit clear error in determining that the Peoria Police Department followed standard procedure while conducting an inventory search of Lozano's automobile, we affirm the district court's denial of Lozano's motion to suppress the evidence found within five duffel bags located in the bed of his truck. 171 F.3d at 1132.

See also United States v. Murphy, 552 F.3d 405, 412–13 (4th Cir. 2009) (allowing the opening of closed containers as part of a vehicle inventory conducted pursuant to established police policies and procedures).

The importance of following established department guidelines or procedures addressing the scope of an inventory cannot be overstressed. For example, if department procedures prohibit looking inside of containers, any evidence obtained in that manner is inadmissible in court. *United States v. Ramos-Oseguera*, 120 F.3d 1028 (9th Cir. 1997), overruled on other grounds by *United States v. Nordby*, 225 F.3d 1053 (9th Cir. 2000), suppressed heroin found in the pockets of a pair of jeans discovered during an inventory of an automobile. The court said:

> Inventory searches have been held constitutional if they are conducted in accordance with the standard procedures of the agency conducting the search or come under another exception to the Fourth Amendment warrant requirement. . . . These regulations specifically provide for cataloging and/or safekeeping visible property. They do not permit searching the inside of containers. The government argues that the jeans were visible and they might have contained something valuable. The regulations, however, do not provide authority to look inside of things to find valuable items. 120 F.3d at 1036.

Moreover, *United States v. Khoury*, 901 F.2d 948 (11th Cir. 1990), held that a second examination of a diary found in a briefcase during an inventory of the defendant's impounded car exceeded the permissible scope of a lawful inventory search. As a result, the court excluded the diary as evidence from defendant's trial on drug charges. In *Khoury*, the officer's initial examination consisted of flipping through a notebook to look for items of value. He determined that the notebook was a diary but not that it had evidentiary

KEY POINTS

L05 ■ Police may impound motor vehicles when they impede traffic or threaten public safety and convenience, or when their drivers or owners are taken into custody or are incapacitated. Police may also impound vehicles after seizing them as evidence of a crime, after the vehicle has been forfeited pursuant to state law, after a vehicle or its parts have been reported stolen, or if the driver lacks a valid driver's license or valid proof of insurance.

Continued on next page

value. He later examined the notebook again and decided that it had evidentiary value. The court said:

> [Agent] Simpkins' initial inspection of the notebook was necessary and proper to ensure that there was nothing of value hidden between the pages of the notebook. Having satisfied himself that the notebook contained no discrete items of value and having decided that the diary entries themselves would have intrinsic value to [the defendant], Simpkins had satisfied the requisites of the inventory search and had no purpose other than investigation in further inspecting the notebook. Such a warrantless investigatory search may not be conducted under the guise of an inventory. 901 F.2d at 959.

Time Limitations for Inventory Searches

A vehicle inventory should be conducted as soon as possible after the impoundment, taking into consideration the police agency's personnel resources, facilities, workload, and other circumstances. An unreasonably delayed inventory indicates that police were not really concerned about safeguarding the owner's property or protecting themselves against fraudulent claims or from danger but rather were primarily interested in looking for evidence:

> [T]he Fourth Amendment requires that, without a demonstrable justification based upon exigent circumstances other than the mere nature of automobiles, the inventory be conducted either contemporaneously with the impoundment or as soon thereafter as would be safe, practical, *and* satisfactory in light of the objectives for which this exception to the Fourth Amendment warrant requirement was created. In other words, to be valid, there must be a sufficient temporal proximity between the impoundment and the inventory. When the inventory must be postponed, each passing moment detracts from the full effectuation of the objectives of the inventory, *and* indeed, disserves those objectives; at some point, the passage of time requires, to uphold the validity of the inventory, proof of some immediate and exigent circumstances (other than the mere nature of automobiles) the attention to which is more important than protecting the arrestee's property and protecting the police from false claims or danger associated with that property. *Ex Parte Boyd*, 542 So.2d 1276, 1279 (Ala. 1989).

Thus, *Ex Parte Boyd* stands for the principle that, unless emergency circumstances exist, an inventory of a vehicle must generally be conducted at the time of impoundment or shortly thereafter. In *Ex Parte Boyd*, the court invalidated an inventory conducted by police four days after they had impounded the vehicle: "We hold that the warrantless search in this case cannot be upheld as an inventory search because of the insufficient temporal proximity between the impoundment and the search, with a lack of demonstrable justification based on exigent circumstances." 542 So.2d at 1281.

Young v. Commonwealth, 2001 WL 1356395 (Va. App. 2001) (unpublished decision), citing the rule from *Ex Parte Boyd* regarding the timing of an inventory, found that a police officer's failure to conduct an inventory immediately at the scene did not render the inventory invalid under the Fourth Amendment:

> The fact that [the officer] used a private towing company to transport [the defendant's] car to the sheriff's department and conducted the inventory search only after the vehicle had been transported did not render the search unreasonable under the Fourth Amendment. A business near the scene of the stop had recently been vandalized, and [the officer] testified he believed conducting the search at the sheriff's department would

be safer. [The officer] also testified that he would have had better lighting at the sheriff's department, permitting the inference that conducting the search at that location was more likely to result in an accurate inventory. 2001 WL 1356395 at *2.

Thus, because conditions at the scene where the vehicle was impounded were not conducive to an accurate inventory, the court permitted the officer in *Young* to conduct the search upon arriving at the sheriff's department.

In sum, police should conduct an inventory as soon as possible after impounding a vehicle. Unless there is a genuine emergency, long delays between an impoundment and an inventory will result in a court invalidating the inventory, and excluding any relevant evidence found by police in the course of inventorying the vehicle.

Vehicle Inventories and the Plain View Doctrine

Although officers may not look for evidence of crime while conducting legitimate inventories, they may seize contraband or other items subject to seizure that they observe open to view. Under the *plain view doctrine*, an officer lawfully conducting an inventory of a vehicle has valid justification for a prior intrusion into a zone of privacy. If an officer then observes in the course of a valid inventory items that the officer has probable cause to believe are incriminating in character, the officer may seize these items under the plain view doctrine. In both *Opperman* and *Bertine*, officers discovered drugs in plain view while lawfully conducting inventories of impounded vehicles. Thus, the officers were permitted to seize these drugs. (For further discussion of valid plain view seizures of evidence during a lawful inventory, see Chapter 10.)

Table 11.1 shows a comparison of a *Carroll* doctrine search and an inventory.

TABLE 11.1 | Comparison of a *Carroll* Doctrine Search and an Inventory

	Search Under *Carroll* Doctrine	Inventory Search
Justification	Probable cause to search a readily mobile vehicle	Impoundment of vehicle by police
Purpose	To obtain evidence of crime	To protect the owner's property while it remains in police custody; to protect the police against fraudulent claims or disputes over lost, stolen, or vandalized property; and to protect the police from potential danger
Scope of search of entire vehicle	If there is probable cause to search the entire vehicle, the search may extend to every part of the vehicle and its contents that may conceal the object of the search, including the opening of containers. If there is probable cause to search only a container in the vehicle, then only the container and not the entire vehicle may be searched.	If standard departmental procedures are followed, inventory may extend to all areas of the vehicle in which the owner's or occupant's personal belongings might be vulnerable to theft or damage.
Scope of search of containers found in vehicle	If there is probable cause to search the entire vehicle, a container that may contain the object of the search may be searched. If there is probable cause to search only a container in a vehicle, then only the container may be searched.	If standard departmental procedures are followed, the inventory may include the opening of closed containers found within the vehicle and the examination of their contents.

Continued on next page

	Search Under *Carroll* Doctrine	Inventory Search
Time	Search should be conducted without unreasonable delay, but vehicle may be removed to another location for the search, and searches up to three days later have been upheld.	Inventory should be conducted as soon as possible after the impoundment of the vehicle, taking into consideration the police agency's human resources, facilities, workload, and other circumstances, such as an emergency requiring the inventory to be delayed.
Plain view doctrine	If items subject to seizure other than the object of the search are observed open to view during a search under the *Carroll* doctrine, the items may be lawfully seized and are admissible in evidence. (The requirements of the plain view doctrine must be satisfied.)	If items subject to seizure are observed open to view during a bona fide inventory, the items may be lawfully seized and are admissible in evidence. (The requirements of the plain view doctrine must be satisfied.)

© Cengage Learning®

Standing for Objecting to Vehicle Searches

Whether a driver or passenger can challenge a particular search by police of a vehicle under the automobile exception (for lack of probable cause, or for any other reason) depends on whether that driver or passenger has a reasonable expectation of privacy in the vehicle. Not all drivers and passengers have such an expectation of privacy, and hence under the Fourth Amendment these vehicle occupants would be said to lack standing to challenge a particular vehicle search by police.

For example, in *United States v. Haywood*, 324 F.3d 514 (7th Cir. 2003), the court found that an unauthorized, unlicensed driver of a vehicle did not have a reasonable expectation of privacy in the vehicle under the Fourth Amendment. As a result, the driver lacked standing to challenge the search of that vehicle by police.

In addition, *United States v. Riazco*, 91 F.3d 752 (5th Cir. 1996), held that a driver lacked standing to challenge a search by police because he was not authorized to drive the car under the rental agreement *and* did not have the authorized renter's permission to drive.

> Riazco, the driver of the car, did not assert a property or possessory interest in the vehicle. He neither owned nor rented it. The rental agreement specifically stated that the car was to be driven only by persons authorized by the car rental company, and Riazco was not so authorized. In fact, he admitted at the suppression hearing that he did not even have the renter's permission to drive it. 91 F.3d at 754.

See also United States v. Thomas, 447 F.3d 1191, 1194–95, 1199 (9th Cir. 2006) ("Thomas, an unauthorized driver [not listed on the car rental agreement or contract], only has standing to challenge the search [by police] of a rental automobile if he received permission to use the rental car from the authorized renter, McGuffey. Here, it is undisputed that Thomas failed to show that he received McGuffey's permission to use the car. Therefore, the district court properly concluded that Thomas lacks standing to challenge the search [uncovering drugs and cash].").

From the courts' discussion in *Riazco* and *Thomas* of the standing issue, it should be apparent that drivers who either legitimately own or rent a vehicle would have standing under the Fourth Amendment to challenge a search by police of that vehicle. Also, a driver of a rental vehicle who has been authorized by the rental company to drive the vehicle may have a reasonable expectation of privacy in the vehicle even if the rental agreement has expired. *See United States v. Cooper*, 133 F.3d 1394, 1402 (11th Cir. 1998) ("[W]e hold that society is prepared to accept as reasonable [the driver's] expectation of privacy in the overdue rental car and, therefore, he has standing to challenge law enforcement's search of the glove compartment, the trunk, and the items therein.").

Unlike drivers who validly own or rent a vehicle, passengers in a vehicle generally have no reasonable expectation of privacy in the vehicle's interior area. Therefore, passengers may not challenge warrantless searches by police of areas such as the glove compartment, the spaces under the seats, and the trunk. Such a search invades no Fourth Amendment interest of the passengers, even if it turns up evidence implicating the passengers. In this regard, the U.S. Supreme Court in *Rakas v. Illinois*, 439 U.S. 128 (1978), stated:

> We have on numerous occasions pointed out that cars are not to be treated identically with houses or apartments for Fourth Amendment purposes. But here [the defendants'] claim is one which would fail . . . , since they made no showing that they had any legitimate expectation of privacy in the glove compartment or area under the seat of the car in which they were merely passengers. Like the trunk of an automobile, these are areas in which a passenger qua passenger simply would not normally have a legitimate expectation of privacy. 439 U.S. at 148–49.

In *Rakas*, the Court commented that it was immaterial to the standing issue that the defendants who were passengers in the vehicle were present with the owner's consent. "The fact that [the defendants] were 'legitimately on [the] premises' in the sense that they were in the car with the permission of its owner is not determinative of whether they had a legitimate expectation of privacy in the particular areas of the automobile searched." 439 U.S. at 148; *see also United States v. Symonevich*, 688 F.3d 12, 21 (1st Cir. 2012) (holding, relying on *Rakas*, that a passenger who did not have a property or possessory interest in the car—i.e., was not its owner or renter—lacked standing under the Fourth Amendment to challenge a search by police that revealed drugs in a can under the passenger seat).

Note that though passengers in a vehicle generally lack standing to challenge a warrantless search of that vehicle by police, they are "seized" for Fourth Amendment purposes when a police officer stops a vehicle in which they are passengers. *See Brendlin v. California*, 551 U.S. 249 (2007); *Arizona v. Johnson*, 551 U.S. 323 (2009). As a result, passengers may challenge in court a stop of a vehicle in which they are traveling (e.g., they have "standing" to challenge such a stop). The ability to challenge a vehicular stop may also affect the ability of a passenger to successfully suppress evidence found by police during a subsequent search of the stopped vehicle in which the passenger is traveling. This is because any potentially incriminating items obtained during the search may be considered poisonous fruit of any illegal stop. (See Chapter 2 for further discussion of the fruit of the poisonous tree doctrine.)

KEY POINTS

L07

- To challenge an illegal search by police under the automobile exception, a vehicle occupant must have a reasonable expectation of privacy in the areas of the vehicle that are searched. If this expectation of privacy exists, the vehicle occupant is said to have "standing" under the Fourth Amendment to challenge the search. Drivers who either legitimately own or rent a vehicle have standing under the Fourth Amendment to challenge a search by police of that vehicle. Mere passengers in a vehicle, however, generally have no reasonable expectation of privacy in the vehicle's interior area; hence, these passengers would lack standing to challenge a vehicle search.

CRIMINAL PROCEDURE **IN ACTION**

Applying *Brendlin v. California*: Can Passengers Successfully Argue That Evidence Discovered by Police During Vehicle Searches Be Excluded in Court? *United States v. McCall*, 2007 U.S. Dist. LEXIS 46375 (W.D.N.Y. June 21, 2007)

The facts of *McCall* are as follows:

Defendant [Jamar McCall] was indicted on a two-count indictment on January 10, 2006, for unlawful possession of five grams or more of cocaine base and possession of the same with the intent to distribute it. Defendant plead not guilty.

Continued on next page

On March 6, 2003, at approximately 7:10 P.M., federal Career Criminal Task Force members Daniel Granville and Dennis Gilbert (then-officers of the [Buffalo Municipal Housing Authority or] BMHA police department) observed a gray 1997 Jeep parked in front of a house on Theodore Street, in Buffalo, New York. These officers were conducting surveillance of that house and the vehicle. They observed two unknown persons in the vehicle, when the passenger left the vehicle, went into the house, and returned to the Jeep a few minutes later. The Jeep then left the Theodore Street property and the officers lost sight of it. Around 7:35 P.M., the vehicle was spotted in a driveway on 2088 Bailey Avenue, Buffalo (some three blocks away from The-odore Street). The Jeep, with a driver and a passen-ger, left the Bailey Avenue address and traveled to a driveway on Burgard Place. The Jeep then drove to Langfield Drive, within a BMHA development.

Defendant notes that the officers did not ob-serve any drug dealing, traffic offenses, or 911 calls, and the officers lacked a warrant. Yet the of-ficers pulled the vehicle over on Langfield just east of Suffolk. There, the officers allegedly observed an unspecified traffic infraction. That infraction, however, was not identified in the Government's papers, either in response to Defendant's motion or in the supporting affidavit attached to the original Complaint from Officer Gilbert. Once the vehicle was stopped, the officers saw a small bag of mari-juana in its ashtray. The driver was identified (as Kevin Lovelady) and the passenger was identified as defendant [e.g., Jamar McCall]. Both men were required to step out of the Jeep and both were pat-ted down and frisked. Officer Gilbert alleged in the criminal Complaint that this pat down was done for officer safety. In patting down defendant, Officer Granville felt a large bulge on defendant's buttocks. Defendant was arrested and transported to a police station, where the officers recovered a knotted off sandwich bag from defendant containing 83 bags of crack cocaine.

2007 U.S. Dist. LEXIS 46375, at *4–*6.

- Based on the U.S. Supreme Court decision in *Brendlin* discussed in the previous section, does the defendant in *McCall* have standing to challenge the stop of the vehicle in which he was found by police?

- Assuming the defendant does have standing to chal-lenge the stop, is there an argument he can make to have the drugs found in the vehicle and on his person excluded in court? For example, was the initial traffic stop illegal? If so, what argument can the defendant rely on to argue that the drugs found on his person (or in the car) should be excluded? (Hint: Consult Chapter 2 on the exclusionary rule to refresh your memory re-garding the details of this concept.)

Other Issues Related to Vehicle Searches

This section will discuss the constitutionality under the Fourth Amendment of the use of tracking devices by police to monitor the movement of vehicles. Following this discussion, the section will explore the application of the Fourth Amendment to vehicle searches by dogs. (Please note that the issue of racial profiling during police traffic stops is discussed in detail in Chapter 8, in the section entitled "Racial Profiling and Related Practices").

Tracking Vehicles Using Electronic Devices

Recall from Chapter 5 that *United States v. Knotts*, 460 U.S. 276 (1983), held that the war-rantless monitoring of a vehicle traveling on the public roads using a tracking beeper did not violate the Fourth Amendment when it revealed no information that could not have been obtained through ordinary visual surveillance. Furthermore, *United States v. Jones*, 31 F.3d 1304, 1311 (4th Cir. 1994), held that "the Fourth Amendment does not prohibit the placing of beepers in contraband and stolen goods because the possessors of such articles have no legitimate expectation of privacy in substances which they have no right to possess at all." In contrast, if the monitoring of a beeper allows law enforcement to "see" a vehicle where they could not without the device (e.g., inside a private residence), then the Fourth Amend-ment prohibits the use of such a device without probable cause and a warrant. *United States v. Karo*, 468 U.S. (1984). In addition, law enforcement's installation of a GPS device on a vehicle to track the vehicle's movements, is a "search" under the Fourth Amendment. *See United States v. Jones,* 132 S. Ct. 945, 949 (2012). In general, it is advisable that police ob-tain a warrant prior to installing a GPS device on a vehicle. For more information on the U.S.

Supreme Court decision in *Jones*, see Chapter 3. For more information on tracking vehicles using electronic devices, see Chapter 5.

Vehicle Searches by Dogs

The U.S. Supreme Court has generally not considered canine sniffs of vehicles by police to be "searches" under the Fourth Amendment.

For example, in *Illinois v. Caballes*, 543 U.S. 405 (2005), an officer stopped the defendant's car for speeding. A second officer then arrived on the scene. While the first officer completed a warning ticket for the defendant's speeding violation, the second officer escorted a dog trained in drug detection around the perimeter of the vehicle. When the dog signaled, or "alerted," to the presence of possible drugs in the trunk of the defendant's vehicle, the officer searched the trunk. He discovered marijuana, and arrested the defendant.

The U.S. Supreme Court in *Caballes* found that the canine sniff of the defendant's vehicle did not constitute a search for Fourth Amendment purposes; therefore, the marijuana found in the trunk of the defendant's vehicle was admissible at the defendant's subsequent trial on drug charges:

> In this case, the dog sniff was performed on the exterior of [the defendant's] car while he was lawfully seized for a traffic violation. Any intrusion on [the defendant's] privacy expectations does not rise to the level of a constitutionally cognizable infringement. A dog sniff conducted during a concededly lawful traffic stop that reveals no information other than the location of a substance [e.g., marijuana] that no individual has any right to possess does not violate the Fourth Amendment. 543 U.S. at 409–10.

Thus, if police lawfully stop a vehicle for a traffic violation such as speeding, they may conduct a canine sniff of that vehicle. Though police should use discretion in deciding whether to conduct a canine sniff on any particular vehicle, they do not need additional suspicion or probable cause to conduct this type of law enforcement activity (apart from the reasonable suspicion or probable cause of a traffic violation that is necessary to stop the vehicle in the first place). If the canine sniff by a dog trained in drug detection alerts to the presence of drugs in a vehicle, the officers may search without a warrant the part of the vehicle to which the dog alerted. This is because such a canine sniff provides the probable cause necessary to search a readily mobile vehicle under the automobile exception. *See Caballes*, 543 U.S. at 409 (agreeing with the "the trial judge['s] [finding] that the dog sniff was sufficiently reliable to establish probable cause to conduct a full-blown search of the trunk"). Moreover, if officers discover drugs during such a search, they may seize them without a warrant.

Recently, the U.S. Supreme Court in *Florida v. Harris*, 133 S. Ct. 1050 (2013), described the process, or approach, a court should use to determine whether probable cause exists to support a police search of a vehicle based on an "alert" by a canine (i.e., to drugs). Rather than using fixed, rigid evaluation criteria, the Court put forth a totality-of-circumstances approach to determine whether a canine "alert" provides police with probable cause to search a vehicle. In particular, a court may consider circumstances such as the nature or quality of a canine's training (e.g., drug detection classes and exercises), certifications, and performance in controlled settings as well as in the field, among other factors:

> [E]vidence of a dog's satisfactory performance in a certification or training program can itself provide sufficient reason to trust his alert. If a bona fide organization has certified a dog after testing his reliability in a controlled setting, a court can

presume (subject to any conflicting evidence offered) that the dog's alert provides probable cause to search. The same is true, even in the absence of formal certification, if the dog has recently and successfully completed a training program that evaluated his proficiency in locating drugs.

A defendant, however, must have an opportunity to challenge such evidence of a dog's reliability, whether by cross-examining the testifying officer or by introducing his own fact or expert witnesses. The defendant, for example, may contest the adequacy of a certification or training program, perhaps asserting that its standards are too lax or its methods faulty. So too, the defendant may examine how the dog (or handler) performed in the assessments made in those settings. [Moreover], evidence of the dog's (or handler's) history in the field, although susceptible to the kind of misinterpretation we have discussed, may sometimes be relevant. . . . And even assuming a dog is generally reliable, circumstances surrounding a particular alert may undermine the case for probable cause—if, say, the officer cued the dog (consciously or not), or if the team was working under unfamiliar conditions.

If the State has produced proof from controlled settings that a dog performs reliably in detecting drugs, and the defendant has not contested that showing, then the court should find probable cause. If, in contrast, the defendant has challenged the State's case (by disputing the reliability of the dog overall or of a particular alert), then the court should weigh the competing evidence. In all events, the court should not prescribe, as the [lower court] did, an inflexible set of evidentiary requirements. The question—similar to every inquiry into probable cause—is whether all the facts surrounding a dog's alert, viewed through the lens of common sense, would make a reasonably prudent person think that a search would reveal contraband or evidence of a crime. A sniff is up to snuff when it meets that test. *Harris*, 133 S. Ct. at 1057–58.

It should be noted, however, that in contrast to vehicles and other objects such as luggage, the sniffing of *persons* by dogs constitutes a search protected by the Fourth Amendment.

> [S]ociety recognizes the interest in the integrity of one's person, and the Fourth Amendment applies with its fullest vigor against any intrusion on the human body. . . . [W]e hold that sniffing by dogs on the students' persons . . . [i.e., sniffing around each child, putting his nose on the child and scratching and manifesting other signs of excitement in the case of an alert] . . . is a search within the purview of the Fourth Amendment. *Horton v. Goose Creek Indep. School Dist.*, 690 F.2d 470, 478–79 (5th Cir. 1982).

See also B.C. v. Plumas Unified School Dist., 192 F.3d 1260, 1266 (9th Cir. 1999). ("We agree with the Fifth Circuit in [*Horton*] that 'close proximity sniffing of the person is offensive whether the sniffer be canine or human.' Because we believe that the dog sniff [of students] in this case infringed [plaintiff's] reasonable expectation of privacy, we hold that it constitutes a search.").

KEY POINTS

L07

- The warrantless monitoring of a beeper in a motor vehicle to trace the movement of the vehicle over public thoroughfares does not violate the reasonable expectation of privacy of the occupant of the vehicle. However, monitoring the beeper in a motor vehicle after it enters a private home or business would generally be prohibited under the Fourth Amendment absent a warrant or emergency circumstances. Moreover, if police install a GPS device on a vehicle to track the vehicle's movements, this is a "search" under the Fourth Amendment for which a warrant would generally be required.

- The use of specially trained or certified dogs to detect the smell of drugs in a vehicle does not violate the reasonable expectation of privacy of the vehicle's owner; as a result, the use of dogs in this way by a police officer is not a "search" under the Fourth Amendment. If the specially trained or certified dog alerts to the presence of contraband in the vehicle, this may provide the officer with the probable cause necessary to search a readily mobile vehicle under the automobile exception.

SUMMARY

Although the search and seizure of motor vehicles are generally governed by the warrant requirement of the Fourth Amendment, courts have created certain exceptions to the warrant requirement for motor vehicles, based on the differences between motor vehicles and fixed premises such as a residence. A motor vehicle is mobile and is used to transport criminals, weapons, and fruits and instrumentalities of crime. It seldom serves as a residence or a permanent repository of personal effects. Furthermore, a person has a reduced expectation of privacy in a motor vehicle because the vehicle travels public thoroughfares where its occupants and contents are open to view, and because the vehicle is subject to extensive governmental regulation, including periodic inspection and licensing.

One of the principal exceptions to the warrant requirement is the automobile exception as embodied in the *Carroll* doctrine. Under the *Carroll* doctrine, law enforcement officers may conduct a warrantless search of a motor vehicle if they have probable cause to believe that a readily mobile vehicle contains incriminating items subject to seizure. A search under the *Carroll* doctrine need not be conducted immediately, but may be delayed for a reasonable time and may be performed even after the vehicle has been impounded and is in police custody.

The scope of a search under the automobile exception is defined by the object of the search and the places in which there is probable cause to believe the object may be found. If officers have probable cause to believe that a particular seizable item is located somewhere in a vehicle that is readily mobile, they may conduct a full search of the vehicle as if they had a search warrant for the item. This means they may search the trunk as well as closed, opaque containers and passengers' belongings located inside the vehicle capable of holding the seizable item. If, however, police do not have probable cause to search the entire vehicle, but only probable cause to search a particular container or area inside the vehicle, they may search only that container or area but not the entire vehicle.

Warrantless searches of movable, closed, opaque containers *unassociated with a vehicle* are not allowed under the rationale of the *Carroll* doctrine, even if there is probable cause to believe they contain items subject to seizure. These types of containers found outside a vehicle and in public may only be searched under authority of a warrant or some other exception to the warrant requirement.

Motor vehicles may be removed from the highways and streets and impounded in the interests of public safety and as part of a law enforcement agency's community caretaking function. An inventory of an impounded vehicle may be conducted without a warrant. This procedure is not considered to be a search for Fourth Amendment purposes, but merely an administrative procedure. The officer making the inventory may not have the purpose of looking for incriminating evidence, but may be concerned only with protecting the owner's property, protecting the police against fraudulent claims or disputes over lost or stolen property, and protecting the police from potential danger. The inventory of a vehicle must be limited in scope and intensity by the purposes for which it is allowed and must conform to standard police procedures. Nevertheless, incriminating items found in plain view during a valid police inventory may be seized and are admissible in court (i.e., provided the requirements of the plain view doctrine are satisfied; this doctrine is discussed in Chapter 10).

Not every vehicle occupant has constitutional standing to challenge a search by police under the automobile exception. This is because some vehicle occupants, such as mere passengers in a vehicle, lack a reasonable expectation of privacy in areas within the interior of the vehicle, and hence lack standing to challenge a police search of the vehicle. In general, however, drivers who validly own or rent a vehicle have standing to challenge such a search. Finally, passengers now have standing to challenge a vehicle *stop*.

Courts generally approve tracing the location of motor vehicles on public thoroughfares by means of electronic devices (i.e., a "beeper"), and detection of drugs in motor vehicles by means of sniffing by specially trained or certified dogs. Both of these limited types of intrusion are allowed without a warrant because of the reduced expectation of privacy associated with

- motor vehicles traveling on public roadways and
- possessing contraband.

However, if police install a GPS device on a vehicle to track the vehicle's movements, this is a "search" under the Fourth Amendment for which a warrant would generally be required.

KEY TERMS

automobile exception 448
beeper 477
Carroll doctrine 448
exigent circumstances 451

impound 464
inventory 467
probable cause 449
readily mobile 452

search 448
seizure 451
standing 475

REVIEW AND DISCUSSION QUESTIONS

1. Are there any situations in which a warrant is required to search a motor vehicle? In reality, isn't the warrant requirement the exception rather than the rule in automobile cases? Fully explain your answer.

2. Do the legal principles in this chapter apply to vehicles such as bicycles, rowboats, motor homes, trains, or airplanes?

3. If a law enforcement officer has probable cause to believe a readily mobile vehicle contains small concealable items, such as drugs, jewels, or rare coins, to what extent can he or she search the vehicle without a warrant under the *Carroll* doctrine? Can the upholstery be ripped open? Can the vehicle be dismantled? Can the tires or gas cap be taken off to look inside them? Can the engine compartment be searched? Can pillows, radios, clothing, and other potential containers be examined, dismantled, or ripped apart?

4. An officer with probable cause to search a motor vehicle has the option to either conduct the search immediately or impound the vehicle and search it later at the station house. Are both options permissible under the *Carroll* doctrine? What factors should the officer consider in making this choice?

5. Describe three situations in which there would be probable cause to search a vehicle that is readily mobile.

6. Assume that a person is arrested for drunk driving late at night while driving alone on a city street. He tells the police that he does not want his car impounded and that a friend will pick up the car some time the next day. He says he will sign a statement absolving the police from any liability for any loss of or damage to the car or its contents. Can the police still impound the car? Should they?

7. Under the *Carroll* doctrine, must the police have probable cause to search a vehicle at the time it is stopped on the highway in order to search it later at the station after it is impounded? Suppose a person is arrested on the highway for drunk driving and is told to accompany officers to the station to post bond. A routine check at the station reveals that the vehicle is stolen. May the officers then search the vehicle without a warrant at the station after it has been impounded? (For purposes of this question, assume officers did not have probable cause to search the vehicle when it was on the highway.)

8. If officers have probable cause to search a vehicle stopped on the highway but no probable cause to arrest the passengers of the vehicle, can they search the passengers also? Are the passengers "containers" under the ruling of the *Ross* case? Does the answer depend on the nature of the evidence for which the officers are looking?

9. Is a warrantless installation of a beeper or GPS device proper in any of the following circumstances?

   a. Attaching a beeper or GPS device to the outside of an automobile parked on a public street

   b. Placing a beeper or GPS device somewhere inside an automobile parked on a public street

   c. Opening a closed package or luggage located in a public place to install a beeper or GPS device

   d. Attaching a beeper or GPS device to the outside of a package or luggage located in a home

   e. Placing a beeper or GPS device with money taken in a bank robbery and currently hidden in the suspected bank robber's home

10. If a person's only home is a motor home and the person travels all year long, should the *Carroll* doctrine apply to a search of the motor home? What are the relevant factors from the *Carney* case that should be considered in answering this question? Assuming the *Carroll* doctrine does apply, should there be any limits on the scope of the search allowed?

11. What if police develop probable cause to believe a readily mobile vehicle parked on private property contains incriminating items subject to seizure? Should police obtain a warrant before searching such a vehicle? What if police knew the owner of the vehicle was about to leave on a cross-country journey to visit family? What if police knew the owner was planning to begin the journey in about a week?

12. Who has standing to challenge the search of a motor vehicle by police? The stop of a motor vehicle? Would passengers ever have the ability to have evidence excluded that is found by police during a vehicle search? Explain.

13. Describe the key differences between a vehicle search under the *Carroll* doctrine and a vehicle search under the search-incident-to-arrest exception as established in *Arizona v. Gant*.

12

Open Fields and Abandoned Property

LO1 EXPLAIN how the concepts of open fields, curtilage, and reasonable expectation of privacy interrelate and their importance to the law of search and seizure.

LO2 ANALYZE a fact situation involving a description of a place, and determine whether the place is located in the open fields or is within the curtilage.

LO3 EVALUATE the differences between the open fields doctrine, the plain view doctrine, and observations into the curtilage from a vantage point in the open fields or a public place.

LO4 DESCRIBE the factors considered by courts in determining whether premises, objects, or vehicles have been abandoned, and evaluate the significance of abandonment in the law of search and seizure.

As you know by now, the Fourth Amendment to the U.S. Constitution guarantees "the right of the people to be secure in their persons, *houses*, papers, and effects, against unreasonable *searches* and seizures" (emphasis added). The words *houses* and *searches* are italicized because the meaning of open fields depends on court interpretation of the word *houses*, and the meaning of abandoned property depends on court interpretation of the word *searches*. *Hester v. United States*, 265 U.S. 57 (1924), established the concepts of open fields and abandoned property in the law of search and seizure.

As described in *Hester v. United States*, as revenue officers investigating suspected bootlegging went to Hester's father's house, they saw Henderson drive up to the house. They concealed themselves and observed Hester come out of the house and hand Henderson a quart bottle. An alarm was given. Hester went to a nearby car and removed a gallon jug, and he and Henderson fled across an open field. One of the officers pursued, firing his pistol. Henderson threw away his bottle, and Hester dropped his jug, which broke, retaining about one quart of its contents. A broken jar, still containing some of its contents, was found outside the house. The officers examined the jug, the jar, and the bottle and determined that they contained illicitly distilled whiskey. The officers had neither a search warrant nor an arrest warrant.

The defendant contended on appeal that the testimony of the two officers was inadmissible because their actions constituted an illegal search and seizure. The U.S. Supreme Court said:

> It is obvious that even if there had been a trespass, the above testimony was not obtained by an illegal search or seizure. The defendant's own acts, and those of his associates, disclosed the jug, the jar, and the bottle—and there was no seizure in the sense of the law when the officers examined the contents of each after it had been *abandoned*. . . . The only shadow of a ground for bringing up the case is drawn from the hypothesis that the examination of the vessels took place upon Hester's father's land. As to that, it is enough to say that, apart from the justification, the special protection accorded by the Fourth Amendment to the people in their "persons, houses, papers, and effects," is not extended to the *open fields*. The distinction between the latter and the house is as old as the common law. 265 U.S. at 58–59 (emphasis added).

The remainder of this chapter is devoted to a discussion of the law of search and seizure applied to open fields and abandoned property.

Open Fields

Hester stated the basic open fields doctrine: "[T]he special protection accorded by the Fourth Amendment to the people in their 'persons, houses, papers and effects' is not extended to the open fields." 265 U.S. at 59. The open fields doctrine allows law enforcement officers to search for and seize evidence in open fields without a warrant, probable cause, or any other legal justification. Even if officers trespass while searching the open fields, the trespass does not render the evidence inadmissible. *Oliver v. United States*, 466 U.S. 170 (1984).

The key issue under the open fields doctrine is the determination of the demarcation line between the area protected by the Fourth Amendment and the open fields. This depends on court interpretations of the word *houses* in the Fourth Amendment, which is an area protected by the Fourth Amendment. *Houses* has been given a very broad meaning by the courts. The term *houses* includes homes (whether owned, rented, or leased), and any other place in which a person is staying or living, permanently or temporarily. Examples of protected living quarters are hotel and motel rooms, apartments, rooming and boarding house rooms, and even hospital rooms. The term *houses* extends to places of business. *See v. City of Seattle*, 387 U.S. 541 (1967). This protection is limited, however, to areas or sections that are *not* open to the public:

> [A] private business whose doors are open to the general public is also to be considered open to entry by the police for any proper purpose not violative of the owner's constitutional rights—e.g., patronizing the place or surveying it to promote law and order or to suppress a breach of the peace. *State v. LaDuca*, 214 A.2d 423, 426 (N.J. Super. App. Div. 1965); *see also Maryland v. Macon*, 472 U.S. 463, 469 (1985) ("The officer's action in entering the bookstore and examining the wares that were intentionally exposed to all who frequent the place of business did not infringe a legitimate expectation of privacy and hence did not constitute a search within the meaning of the Fourth Amendment.").

For convenience, the remainder of this chapter uses the word *house* to refer to either residential or commercial premises covered by the Fourth Amendment. Courts have further extended the meaning of *houses* to include curtilage—the "ground and buildings immediately surrounding a dwelling house." *State v. Sindak*, 774 P.2d 895, 898 (Idaho 1989), *overruled on other grounds by State v. Clark*, 16 P.3d 931, 934 (Idaho 2000); *see also United States v. Cousins*, 455 F.3d 1116, 1121–22 (10th Cir. 2006) ("The curtilage concept originated at common law to extend to the area immediately surrounding a dwelling house the same protection under the law . . . as was afforded the house itself."). The concept of curtilage is vital to the open fields doctrine because the open fields are considered to be all the space not contained within the house or its curtilage. The following discussion focuses on the facts and circumstances that courts use in determining the extent of the curtilage.

Determining Curtilage

To determine whether property falls within a house's curtilage and hence is protected by the Fourth Amendment, the law enforcement officer must consider "the factors that determine whether an individual reasonably may expect that an area immediately adjacent to the home will remain private." *Oliver v. United States*, 466 U.S. 170, 180 (1984). *United States v. Dunn*, 480 U.S. 294, 301 (1987), described those factors:

> [W]e believe that curtilage questions should be resolved with particular reference to four factors:
> 1. *the proximity of the area claimed to be curtilage to the home,*
> 2. *whether the area is included within an enclosure surrounding the home,*
> 3. *the nature of the uses to which the area is put, and*
> 4. *the steps taken by the resident to protect the area from observation by people passing by.* (emphasis and numbering added)

These factors are not a rigid formula. Rather, they are useful analytical tools to help determine whether the area in question should be placed under the same Fourth Amendment protection as the home. For example, if the area is determined to be "curtilage," it will be provided full Fourth Amendment protection similar to a home (e.g., a warrant supported by probable cause would generally be required for police to search the "curtilage"); in contrast, an open field would not be afforded such protection. The Court emphasized that "the primary focus is whether the area in question harbors those intimate activities associated with domestic life and the privacies of the home." 480 U.S. at 301 n.4. The four factors from *Dunn* are discussed next in the following contexts:

- residential yards and porches
- fences,
- distance from the dwelling,
- multiple-occupant dwellings,
- garages,
- other outbuildings,
- unoccupied tracts, and
- driveways and other means of access to dwellings.

Residential Yards and Porches The backyard of a house is ordinarily within the curtilage of a house and is thereby protected from a warrantless search under the Fourth Amendment. *United States v. Van Dyke*, 643 F.2d 992 (4th Cir. 1980); *see also Feller v.*

West Bloomfield, 767 F. Supp. 2d 769, 775–78 (E.D. Mich. 2011). For example, in *United States v. Boger*, 755 F. Supp. 333, 338 (E.D. Wash. 1990), the court said:

> [I]t is clear that the area of Mr. Boger's backyard . . . is within the curtilage of the home. The area was enclosed with sight-obscuring fences on the east and west, and by the house on the south. An unoccupied field was to the north. The area in question was obviously used by the resident as part of the home. An outside patio was located on the rear of the home and the backyard was in grass and landscaping. Clearly the resident had taken appropriate steps to protect the area from observation on three sides and an unoccupied open field was on the fourth side.

In addition, a porch would ordinarily be considered within the curtilage of a home. *See Florida v. Jardines*, 133 S. Ct. 1409 (2013) ("While the boundaries of the curtilage are generally 'clearly marked,' the 'conception defining the curtilage' is at any rate familiar enough that it is 'easily understood from our daily experience.' Here there is no doubt that the officers entered it: The front porch is the classic exemplar of an area adjacent to the home and 'to which the activity of home life extends.'" *Jardines*, 133 S. Ct. at 1415 (citing *Oliver*, 466 U.S. 170, 182, n.12 (1984))). If a police officer enters the porch surrounding a home to gather physical evidence of a crime, such as by using trained police canines to detect the smell of drugs inside the home, this would constitute a search under the Fourth Amendment. *See Jardines*, 133 S. Ct at 1416–18. Police should obtain a warrant prior to conducting such a search on a residential porch.

However, if an officer approaches and enters the porch area of a home in the same way that any member of the public could enter in order to speak with the home's occupant, and in the course of speaking with the occupant, the officer discovers information relevant to a criminal investigation, this conduct would not be considered a Fourth Amendment search for which a warrant would ordinarily be required. ("[I]t is not a Fourth Amendment search [for police] to approach the home in order to speak with the occupant, *because all are invited to do that.* The mere 'purpose of discovering information,' in the course of engaging in that permitted conduct does not cause it to violate the Fourth Amendment.") *Jardines*, 133 S. Ct at 1416, n.4. (For a more detailed discussion of *Florida v. Jardines*, see the Discussion Point in Chapter 3 entitled "*Florida v. Jardines*—Dog Sniffs at Your Home: Are They Fourth Amendment Searches by Police?")

As reflected in *Jardines*, if a residential yard, including a porch, is accessible to the public, and the owner takes no steps to protect it from entry or observation, it may not qualify for Fourth Amendment protection (i.e., as curtilage). An officer may approach this area without a warrant to speak with the occupant. For example, in *United States v. Titemore*, 335 F. Supp. 2d 502 (D. Vt. 2004), the court found that a police officer could approach the porch area of defendant's house through a path on a portion of his yard used as a garden. The officer wished to speak with defendant about his possible involvement in an act of vandalism. The court described the officer's approach to defendant's house, from Patten Shore Road, in the following way:

> The porch area is clearly visible from the road. There is a rail fence along Patten Shore Road that partially restricts access to the porch. The rail fence is essentially decorative. There is also a garden in the area of the path from Patten Shore Road to the porch, although due to that time of year little vegetation would restrict access. There was a dysfunctional doorbell and a lamp converted to a plant holder on opposite sides of the sliding door. The [porch] was used as an outside sitting area by the defendant. Although some views from the porch were restricted by trees, there were unrestricted views of a neighbor's house and the lake. Some neighbors had approached the residence by invitation in the past by following the same path taken by [the officer]. There were no signs restricting access to the porch in any way. 335 F. Supp. 2d at 504–05.

Thus, because this area of defendant's yard containing the path to the porch was accessible to the public, and defendant had not restricted access to this area, the officer could make a warrantless entry into this area without violating the Fourth Amendment:

> In this case, it was reasonable for [the officer] to approach the residence at the sliding door [on the porch for a knock and talk visit with defendant]. Many factors support this conclusion. The sliding door at the porch is clearly visible from two public streets. In fact, the sliding door is more open to public view than the door on the west side of the house. Moreover, there is no barrier between the porch and [another road adjacent to defendant's home]. 335 F. Supp. 2d at 506 (quotations omitted).

The court in *Titemore* distinguished other cases where police were prohibited from entering backyards enclosed with fences, to gain access to a home:

> This case presents very different facts. [The officer] did not approach a back door in an enclosed yard. He was confronted by a house with no front door and simply chose one of the side doors. Moreover, unlike the back doors at issue in the cases cited by [the defendant], the sliding door in this case was not enclosed or blocked from public view. 335 F. Supp. 2d at 506.

In sum, law enforcement officers should consider the residential yard and porch of a house as curtilage, unless there are clear indications that the person residing in the house allowed members of the public access to the yard and porch and thus had no reasonable expectation of privacy in these areas. (Recall from Chapter 3 the discussion of the U.S. Supreme Court's decision in *Katz* that the Fourth Amendment "search" question is, in part, determined by whether or not an individual's reasonable expectation of privacy is violated. If no such privacy expectation has been violated or none exists, then police may not have conducted a "search" under the Fourth Amendment requiring a warrant [i.e., unless police physically intruded, or "trespassed," upon one's yard or porch without a justification such as an emergency or explicit or implied consent]. If police entry into a yard or porch would constitute a trespass or a violation of an individual's reasonable expectation of privacy, police should obtain a warrant prior to entering the yard or porch. The notion of a police search via a physical trespass is discussed more in Chapter 3 in the context of *United States v. Jones*, 132 S. Ct. 945, 953 [2012].) It should be noted that *Jones* specifically stated that its trespass-related holding did not extend to open fields: "Quite simply, an open field, unlike the curtilage of a home, . . . is not one of those protected areas enumerated in the Fourth Amendment."

Fences If the area immediately surrounding a house is enclosed by a fence, the area within the fence is usually defined as the curtilage. *United States v. Swepston*, 987 F.2d 1510 (10th Cir. 1993), found that a chicken shed located a hundred feet from the defendant's house was within the curtilage of the house. A barbed wire fence enclosed the shed and the house and *no fence separated the two structures*. In addition, the defendant

- maintained a path between the house and the shed and visited the shed regularly,
- neither the house nor the shed could be seen from a public road or adjoining property, and
- there was no evidence that the shed was not being used for intimate activities of the home.

In contrast, marijuana gardens located about three hundred feet from the co-defendant's house in *Swepston* were found to be outside the curtilage:

> [A]lthough the gardens were encircled by a barbed wire fence, *they were outside the fence that encircled [the codefendant's] house, and they were separated from [his] house by the chainlink fence.* . . . [T]he area within the barbed wire fence contained

numerous chickens and chicken huts and was used primarily for the raising of game chickens. These huts were visible to the . . . officers as they overflew the area, and indicated to them that the area was not being used for intimate activities of the home. Finally, [the codefendant] did little to protect the marijuana gardens from observation by those standing in the open fields surrounding [his] property. 987 F.2d at 1515 (emphasis added).

Because the marijuana gardens were located outside the curtilage in the "open fields," police would not need a warrant to search this area. (Note that a later case by the same court that decided *Swepston—United States v. Cousins*, 455 F.3d 1116 (10th Cir. 2006)—overruled *Swepston* in part, but continued to apply the *Swepston* facts related to the curtilage concept. The overruling dealt only with the technical legal standard by which appellate courts review lower court decisions on issues related to curtilage. *See Cousins*, 455 F.3d at 1121 ("In the past, we have reviewed district courts' curtilage determinations for clear error. However, based on the [U.S] Supreme Court decision in *Ornelas v. United States*, 517 U.S. 690 [1996], we now conclude that ultimate curtilage conclusions are to be reviewed under a *de novo* standard although we continue to review findings of historical facts for clear error.")

In addition, in *United States v. Struckman*, 603 F.3d 731 (9th Cir. 2010), the court concluded that defendant's backyard was curtilage, in part, because it was entirely enclosed by a fence: "Struckman's backyard—a small, enclosed yard [surrounded on all sides by a six-foot-high fence] adjacent to a home in a residential neighborhood—is unquestionably such a clearly marked area to which the activity of home life extends, and so is curtilage subject to Fourth Amendment protection." 603 F.3d at 739 (internal quotations omitted).

If a piece of land is already outside the curtilage, erecting fences around it or taking other steps to protect its privacy does not establish that the expectation of privacy in the land is legitimate and bring the land within the curtilage. In *Oliver v. United States*, 466 U.S. 170 (1984), to conceal their criminal activities, the defendants planted marijuana on secluded land and erected fences and "No Trespassing" signs around the property. The Court said:

> [I]t may be that because of such precautions, few members of the public stumbled upon the marijuana crops seized by the police. Neither of these suppositions demonstrates, however, that the expectation of privacy was legitimate in the sense required by the Fourth Amendment. The test of legitimacy is not whether the individual chooses to conceal asserted "private" activity. Rather, the correct inquiry is whether the government's intrusion infringes upon the personal and societal values protected by the Fourth Amendment. . . . [W]e find no basis for concluding that a police inspection of open fields accomplishes such an infringement. 466 U.S. at 182–83.

Finally, whether a fence defines the curtilage of a home may depend on the nature of the fence. *United States v. Brady*, 734 F. Supp. 923 (E.D. Wash. 1990), found that the fence was not sufficient to define the curtilage:

> There was no "no trespassing" sign posted on or near the gate. The fence was not a sight-obstructing fence. The fence did not completely enclose the property in that there was a wide gap on either side of the gate which could reasonably be construed to be a pedestrian path. The fence was not of a type which evidenced an intent to exclude strangers. 734 F. Supp. at 928.

Also, recall from the previously discussed *United States v. Titemore*, 335 F. Supp. 2d 502, 504–05 (D. Vt. 2004), that even though the defendant had erected a decorative "rail" fence between the public road and the yard area surrounding his porch, the court found that the officer could make a warrantless entry into this area without violating the Fourth Amendment. The fence only "partially restrict[ed]" access to the porch.

Distance from the Dwelling The definitive trend among lower courts after the U.S. Supreme Court's decision in *Dunn*, discussed previously, is to use a totality-of-circumstance approach in determining the extent of the curtilage, with the distance from an individual's dwelling as one of many factors to be weighed in making the determination:

> It is of course true, as the Government argues, that a bright-line rule would be easier to administer than the fact-specific rule announced by *Dunn*. The Seventh Circuit, writing in 1976, before *Dunn*, did try to establish the "clear rule" that any outbuilding or area within 75 feet of the house is within the curtilage and any outbuilding or area further than 75 feet is outside the curtilage. But this decision cannot be reconciled with the Supreme Court's warning in *Dunn* against mechanistic application of any one factor, and has not been accepted by other Circuits. Thus the Ninth Circuit has stated: There is not . . . any fixed distance at which curtilage ends. And the Fourth Circuit, even before *Dunn*, explicitly criticized the [clear] rule [approach], and pointed out that distance is just one of many factors to be weighed when determining the reach of the curtilage. The Seventh Circuit itself has not mentioned [the "clear rule" approach] in the past twelve years, and its last discussion of the case implicitly challenged [that approach]. *United States v. Reilly*, 76 F.3d 1271, 1277 (2d Cir. 1996).

In *Reilly*, the court found that defendant's cottage located 375 feet away from defendant's main dwelling, and a wooded area located 125 feet from the cottage, was still within defendant's curtilage, and hence protected from a warrantless search by police under the Fourth Amendment. During a warrantless search of the wooded area near the cottage, police discovered marijuana. In particular, using the *Dunn* factors, the court found that the cottage and woods were within the curtilage of defendant's main dwelling because

- these areas were secluded;
- private activities occurred in these areas; and
- defendant had taken steps to enclose the property, such as erecting fences and planting hedgerows.

Because the cottage and woods were within the curtilage, and the police had no warrant when initially searching these areas, the marijuana discovered there was inadmissible at defendant's trial. *See also State v. Mell*, 182 P.3d 1, 6 (Kan. App. 2008) ("Turning to the first factor [of distance, or proximity to a dwelling], we note that the State concedes that the proximity of the area in question to the Mells' home supports a finding of curtilage. *There is no fixed distance at which curtilage ends*. Indeed, a photo of the scene demonstrated that the area in question was located not far from the back door of the Mells' residence. Thus, the first factor—the proximity of the area in question to the Mells' home—favors [a finding of curtilage].") (emphasis added).

Multiple-Occupant Dwellings Multiple-occupancy dwellings are treated differently than single-occupancy dwellings for purposes of determining the extent of the curtilage. Generally speaking, the shared areas of large, multiple-occupancy buildings (e.g., common corridors, passageways, driveways, parking lots, porches, patios, and yards) are not entitled to the protection of the Fourth Amendment because individual tenants do not have a reasonable expectation of privacy with respect to those areas. *United States v. Nohara*, 3 F.3d 1239 (9th Cir. 1993); *see also State v. Floyd*, 2006 WL 2059285 (N.J. Super. A.D. 2006), at *3 ("Here, defendant was but one tenant in a multi-occupancy building. As such, he had no reasonable expectation of privacy in the backyard, front porch or hallways shared by all of the tenants.") (internal citation omitted).

Nevertheless, multiple-occupancy dwellings are all different and courts examine the particular facts and circumstances of each case in determining the curtilage. For example, in *Fixel v. Wainwright*, 492 F.2d 480 (5th Cir. 1974), two law enforcement officers who had been informed that narcotics were being sold on the defendant's premises observed the defendant's residence in a four-unit apartment building. Over a forty-five-minute period, several people entered the defendant's apartment. Each time, the defendant went into his backyard and removed a shaving kit from beneath some rubbish under a tree. One officer went into the backyard and seized the shaving kit, while the other officer arrested the defendant. Chemical analysis revealed that the shaving kit contained heroin. The court held that the backyard was a protected area and that the seizure and search of the shaving kit were illegal:

> The backyard of Fixel's home was not a common passageway normally used by the building's tenants for gaining access to the apartments. . . . Nor is the backyard an area open as a corridor to salesmen or other businessmen who might approach the tenants in the course of their trade. . . . This apartment was Fixel's home, he lived there, and the backyard of the building was completely removed from the street and surrounded by a chainlink fence. . . . While the enjoyment of his backyard is not as exclusive as the backyard of a purely private residence, this area is not as public or shared as the corridors, yards, or other common areas of a large apartment complex or motel. Contemporary concepts of living such as multi-unit dwellings must not dilute Fixel's right to privacy any more than is absolutely required. We believe that the backyard area of Fixel's home is sufficiently removed and private in character that he could reasonably expect privacy. 492 F.2d at 484. *See also State v. Wilson*, 140 P.3d 452 (Kan. App. 2006), at *7 (finding that the yard area behind a duplex was curtilage within the protection of the Fourth Amendment because a wood fence separated the yard from a neighbor's property, the yard contained mostly recreational items indicating its use for leisure activities for duplex residences, and the yard was made as "secluded" as possible by the residents).

In contrast, *United States v. Soliz*, 129 F.3d 499, 502–03 (9th Cir. 1997), held that a parking area adjacent to an apartment complex was not within the curtilage for the following reasons:

- the public could see through the chain-link fence surrounding the entire complex;
- the parking area was not used for intimate, or private, activities;
- no measures had been made to shield the parking lot from outside observation (i.e., "the gate [to the parking area] was strewn on the ground, and the property [including the parking area] could be viewed from both the street and the alley"); and
- the defendant took no steps to ensure his privacy (i.e., "there were no 'No Trespassing' signs posted").

Likewise, in *Sanchez v. City of Los Angeles*, 2010 WL 2569049 (C.D. Cal. 2010), the court found that plaintiff did not have any Fourth Amendment protection in an area consisting of the backyard of a multiple-unit property:

> [E]ven if Inspector Tolentino did enter the backyard to inspect the exterior of Unit 1423 without permission, based on the facts as alleged, it appears to the Court that plaintiff did not have a reasonable expectation of privacy in the open and accessible common backyard of the multi-unit property. While Fourth Amendment protection may [at times] extend to common areas of multi-unit residences, in this case, based on the facts as alleged by plaintiff, the area in question was not included in any type of enclosure that prevented or restricted observation of the yard by others. The facts as alleged raise the inference that multiple units overlook the common area in which [property manager]

Perez was repairing a cabinet when Tolentino walked up the driveway. Plaintiff could not reasonably expect privacy in the backyard of a multi-unit residence that was connected to an easily accessible driveway where the facts raise the inference that the yard was not enclosed in any way nor shielded from the view of anyone passing by, or from the occupants of the other units on the property. 2010 WL 2569049, at *13.

Porches, patios, and fire escapes outside an apartment or unit in a multiple-occupancy dwelling generally fall within the curtilage of the apartment or unit. *See, e.g., State v. Johnson*, 793 A.2d 619 (N.J. 2002). Note that although the court in *Johnson* found that the porch was part of the curtilage, it also found that a police officer, who observed the defendant place an object in a hole by a post on the porch, could enter the porch to view the object more closely. The officer was permitted to enter the porch without a warrant because this area was accessible to members of the public visiting the dwelling, and was an area shared by all tenants of the dwelling:

> Here, [the officer] and his partner went to 695 Martin Luther King Boulevard to investigate a report of drug activity. They were there for a legitimate investigative purpose. [The officer] did not go beyond the porch, thus restricting his movements to the places that any other visitor could be expected to go. Defendant's diminished expectation of privacy on the porch was further indicated by the fact that when he placed the package in a hole beside the post on the porch of the multiple-family row house, a portion of the home which all residents and visitors must use to enter, there were four other people on the porch that evening. In short, the conduct that enabled [the officer] to observe the object in the hole was not a search within the meaning of the Fourth Amendment. Any object in the hole could have been observed by inquisitive passersby or any other member of the public. 793 A.2d at 629–30 (internal citations omitted).

Because the officer was permitted to be on the porch, he could seize the object in plain view, which he believed to be cocaine:

> We conclude, therefore, that all three elements of the plain view doctrine were met in this case. [The officer] was lawfully on the porch. . . . [T]he incriminating nature of this "light-colored" object [which defendant had placed in a hole beside a post on the porch] was immediately apparent based on probable cause after the object was visualized in the hole by Officer Wilson. Thus, we hold that the conduct of the police in seizing the clear plastic bag [containing cocaine] from the hole was reasonable under the plain view doctrine and violated neither the federal nor the New Jersey Constitution. 793 A.2d at 636.

If a porch, patio, or similar area of a particular apartment in a multi-occupancy dwelling was *not* readily accessible to most tenants or members of the visiting public, police would, in such a case, need a warrant to enter and search and seize items from this area of the curtilage. For example, in *State v. Neanover*, 812 N.E.2d 127 (Ind. App. 2004), the court found that police violated defendant's Fourth Amendment rights when they searched and seized garbage on defendant's landing area/patio, which itself was attached to a multiple-unit apartment building:

> Neanover had a subjective expectation of privacy insofar as she treated the landing area outside her apartment door [on the third floor of an apartment building] as a combination [recreational] patio/storage space, a zone of privacy akin to curtilage. Although the third-floor landing was open and accessible to the general public, the landing was not *readily* accessible. Thus, although the garbage was seized [by officers] from an open landing that was accessible to virtually anyone who cared to climb the three flights of stairs to gain access to it, it is unlikely that many people would feel so motivated unless they were visiting one of the [only] two apartments located on that level. Given these facts, we cannot

say that Neanover's expectation of privacy was unreasonable. We conclude that the warrantless search and seizure of Neanover's garbage violated her Fourth Amendment rights. 812 N.E.2d at 130–31.

Fire escapes outside an apartment or unit in a multiple-occupancy dwelling are generally considered part of the curtilage. A fire escape in a nonfireproofed building is required outside each apartment as a secondary means of exit for the occupants of that particular apartment. Although it is true that, in the event of fire, people might have occasion to lawfully pass over the fire escape of an apartment other than their own, this would be the only time that one might be lawfully on the fire escape of another. *People v. Terrell*, 277 N.Y.S.2d 926 (N.Y. 1967). Therefore, fire escapes are generally considered part of the curtilage of a multi-occupancy dwelling, and police must generally obtain a warrant before entering these areas. The court in *Terrell* said:

> [T]he observations [of drugs and drug paraphernalia] surreptitiously made by the police from the fire escape which created the probable cause were made in the course of a trespass and were consequently illegal. The entrance into the residential apartment [including the fire escape] without a warrant was illegal and violative of the Fourth Amendment and all evidence and admissions obtained as a result thereof must be suppressed. 277 N.Y.S. at 938.

See also People v. Toodle, 400 N.W.2d 670, 675 (Mich. App. 1986) (citing with approval *Terrell*'s holding that fire escapes are part of the curtilage).

Garages A garage, and the area immediately surrounding it, is ordinarily considered part of the curtilage, especially if the garage is near or attached to the dwelling house and used in connection with it. In *State v. Ross*, 959 P.2d 1188, 1192 (Wash. App. 1998), where the garage was located within twenty-five to forty yards from a street abutting defendant's home, the court prohibited the warrantless entry by police into the area immediately surrounding the garage:

> We hold that the unannounced, plain-clothed, after-dark, warrantless, side-entries onto the curtilage of [the defendant's] garage to investigate a marijuana grow were unreasonable under the Fourth Amendment; the search warrant based thereon was invalid; and the evidence seized with the warrant [e.g., the marijuana] should have been suppressed. 959 P.2d at 1192.

The court found the particular warrantless entry unconstitutional because of the manner in which police accessed the area by the garage where they detected marijuana:

> The discovery here was not accidental; rather the officers entered [the defendant's] property specifically to investigate an informant's tip about a marijuana grow operation. They acted secretly by going on the property at night, in an unmarked car, in plain clothes, and without identifying themselves to [the defendant]. They did not use the most direct access to the front door, from Woodbourne [Street], the locus of [the defendant's] address and front gate. Rather they accessed the driveway and garage from Luzader [Street], abutting the side of the house. According to [the defendant], to reach the spot where they smelled the marijuana, the officers had to deviate nearly ten feet from a direct route between their patrol car and the gate to the side path to the front door. Moreover, they made no attempt to talk to [the defendant], but instead clearly tried to avoid him. 959 P.2d at 1190–91.

Also, in *Commonwealth v. Murphy*, 233 N.E.2d 5 (Mass. 1968), where a garage and a house were surrounded on three sides by a fence and the garage was close to the house (e.g., fifty to seventy-five feet from the street), the court found that the garage was within the curtilage. *See also Commonwealth v. Diaz*, 751 N.E.2d 935 (Mass. App. Ct. 2001), at *2–*3. ("[T]he defendant's garage was in close proximity to his home and located within a chain-link fence enclosing the property. Under these circumstances courts have held that the garage is 'within the curtilage' of the defendant's house. We conclude, therefore, that the defendant had a reasonable expectation of privacy in his garage and that the circumstances were not sufficiently exigent to permit a warrantless search.") (internal citations omitted).

A garage not used by its owner in connection with the residence, however, was held to be outside the curtilage. *People v. Swanberg*, 255 N.Y.S.2d 267 (N.Y. 1964). Furthermore, a garage used in connection with a multiple-unit dwelling was held to be outside the curtilage because it was used in common by many tenants of the dwelling. *People v. Terry*, 454 P.2d 36 (Cal. 1969); *see also People v. Bermudez*, 2006 WL 6091793 (Cal. App. 1st Dist. 2006) (warrantless search by police permitted of a garage accessible to both other tenants and outside visitors).

Other Outbuildings In determining whether an outbuilding is part of the curtilage, courts consider factors such as

- distance from the dwelling house,
- presence and location of fences or other enclosures,
- use of the building, and
- attempts to protect the area from observation.

In the previously discussed *United States v. Dunn*, 480 U.S. 294 (1987), a barn located fifty yards from a fence surrounding a house and sixty yards from the house itself was held to be outside the curtilage. The Court found that the owner had done little to protect the barn area from observation by those standing in the open fields. The Court also found it especially significant that law enforcement officials possessed objective data indicating that the barn was not being used for intimate activities of the home. Rather, they knew that a truck carrying a container of phenylacetic acid was backed up to the barn, a strong odor of the acid emanated from the barn, and the sound of a pumplike motor could be heard from within the barn. These activities suggested the barn was being used for the manufacture of drugs.

United States v. Calabrese, 825 F.2d 1342 (9th Cir. 1987), found that a structure located about fifty feet from a main residence and its two *attached* garages were not within the curtilage. Significant to the court's determination was law enforcement officials' knowledge, obtained during a previous legal search, that the detached structure was being used to manufacture methamphetamine and not for domestic activities.

In contrast, the court in *United States v. Johnson*, 256 F.3d 895 (9th Cir. 2001) indicated that a shed located forty to fifty yards from defendant's main residence could fall within the curtilage of defendant's home:

> Based on the combination of the (1) the rural setting, (2) the fence around the home and shed, (3) the lack of objective data pointing to illegal activity [in the shed] prior to entry, and (4) the inability to see the shed from the "open fields," one could find that the shed was so intimately tied to the home itself that it should be placed under the home's "umbrella" of Fourth Amendment protection. 256 F.3d at 904 (internal quotations omitted).

In addition, in *United States v. Romero-Bustamente*, 337 F.3d 1104 (9th Cir. 2003), the court concluded that defendant's shed was within the curtilage of his home. The court first described the shed's location in relationship to defendant's home and backyard in this way:

> [Defendant] Romero lives in a house at 10 Escalada Street in Nogales, Arizona; the property is approximately 10–15 feet north of the border with Mexico. The property is surrounded by, in parts, a brick wall and, in other parts, a wire link fence. There is a space in front of the house, facing the street, and an enclosed backyard behind the house. At the back of the backyard is a shed, and there is a space of about two

and half feet between the shed and the fence. The distance from the back door of the house to the shed is approximately twenty feet, and the backyard itself is no more than thirty feet deep. 337 F.3d at 1106.

The court concluded under these circumstances that the home's backyard containing the shed fell within the curtilage because "Romero's yard was small, enclosed, adjacent to his house, and located behind his house; . . . as a matter of law, the backyard falls within the curtilage." 337 F.3d at 1108.

Unoccupied Tracts An unoccupied, uncultivated, remote tract of land is generally held to be outside the curtilage and in the open fields:

> [T]he term "open fields" may include any unoccupied or undeveloped area outside of the curtilage. An open field need be neither "open" nor a "field" as those terms are used in common speech. For example . . . a thickly wooded area nonetheless may be an open field as that term is used in construing the Fourth Amendment. *Oliver v. United States*, 466 U.S. 170, 180 n.11 (1984).

In *Oliver*, involving a warrantless police seizure of marijuana from a secluded, unoccupied plot of land surrounded by fences and "No Trespassing" signs, the Court stated that "an individual may not legitimately demand privacy for activities conducted out of doors in fields, except in the area immediately surrounding the home." 466 U.S. at 178. The Court in *Oliver* upheld the warrantless police search and seizure of marijuana on the defendant's unoccupied, remote tract of land because it was located in the "open fields," an area where individuals lack any reasonable expectation of privacy. The Court said:

> [O]pen fields do not provide the setting for those intimate activities that the [Fourth] Amendment is intended to shelter from government interference or surveillance. There is no societal interest in protecting the privacy of those activities such as the cultivation of crops, that occur in open fields. Moreover, as a practical matter these lands usually are accessible to the public and the police in ways that a home, an office, or commercial structure would not be. It is not generally true that fences or "No Trespassing" signs effectively bar the public from viewing open fields in rural areas. And . . . the public and police lawfully may survey lands from the air. For these reasons, the asserted expectation of privacy in open fields is not an expectation that "society recognizes as reasonable." 466 U.S. at 179.

In *Maine v. Thornton* (decided in the same opinion as *Oliver v. United States*), police officers received a tip that marijuana was being grown in the woods behind the defendant's residence and entered the woods by a path between the residence and a neighboring house. They followed the path until they reached two marijuana patches that were fenced with chicken wire and displayed "No Trespassing" signs. When the officers determined that the patches were on the defendant's property, they obtained a search warrant and seized the marijuana. The Court held that the officers' initial actions were not an unreasonable search and seizure, because the area was an open field. And *Conrad v. State*, 218 N.W.2d 252, 257 (Wis. 1974), held that the Fourth Amendment did not apply to a local sheriff's warrantless digging in a field about 450 feet from the defendant's house to find the body of the defendant's wife, who had disappeared:

> Under the "open fields" doctrine, the fact that evidence is concealed or hidden is immaterial. The area [the open field] is simply not within the protection of the Fourth Amendment. If the field where the body was found does not have

constitutional protection, the fact that the sheriff, rather than observing the evidence that might have been in plain view, dug into the earth to find the body and committed a trespass in so doing does not confer protection.

In addition, in *United States v. Mathis*, 738 F.3d 719 (6th Cir. 2013), the court determined that a particular unoccupied and undeveloped commercial site was outside the curtilage and within the "open fields":

> The site qualifies as an open field. Though typically found in more rural areas, an open field need not be a "field." On the date of the search, the site was unoccupied and undeveloped (as one might reasonably understand "undeveloped" in an urban setting), consisting of a partially demolished building and debris strewn throughout a paved lot. [T]he property here is not sufficiently private to enjoy protection analogous to a dwelling's curtilage. Rather, it is easily accessible to the public. [T]he property's commercial status has no bearing on whether the property is an open field. . . . The lower court did not err in finding the site an open field. The property here was undeserving of Fourth Amendment protection; [the] objection to the warrantless searches therefore fails. 738 F.3d at 731 (internal citations omitted).

Driveways and Other Means of Access to Dwellings In *Robinson v. Commonwealth*, 612 S.E.2d 751 (Va. App. 2005), a police officer entered defendants' driveway without a warrant to investigate an alleged underage drinking party at defendants' home. The court determined that the area of the driveway from where the officer made his observations of minors consuming alcohol was "curtilage" under the Fourth Amendment:

> Applying the factors [from the U.S. Supreme Court's decision in *Dunn*] to this case, we conclude that the portion of the driveway from which [the officer] observed the juveniles drinking beer—the area next to the bush—falls within the curtilage of the [defendants'] home. First, the area next to the bush is within a few feet of the home itself. Second, the [defendants] testified that they used the area for washing cars and unloading groceries, home-related activities that evidence the nature of the uses to which the area is put. Third, although the area next to the bush is not included within an enclosure surrounding the home, the area is protected from public observation. Specifically, although the [defendants] did not erect a fence or post any no-trespassing signs, the trees and layout of the driveway obscure the area from public view. It is evident, therefore, that the area next to the bush is protected from observation by people passing by. Given that three out of the four *Dunn* factors are satisfied, we are compelled to conclude that the area next to the bush is intimately tied to the home itself and, thus, falls within the curtilage of the [the defendants'] home. 612 S.E. 2d at 758.

Interestingly, even though the police officer in *Robinson* was found to be on the curtilage, which is an area generally protected from warrantless entry by police, the court admitted the officer's observations of underage drinking as evidence at trial because defendants had opened their house (and driveway) to members of the public on the particular night when the underage drinking party occurred. Therefore, on that particular night, defendants lacked a reasonable expectation of privacy in the driveway:

> [W]e therefore conclude that the [defendants] extended an implied invitation to the public to enter their driveway on the night of the party. We further conclude that, when [the officer] entered the curtilage with the purpose of "investigating" the allegations of underage drinking, he did not exceed the scope of this implied invitation because, at the point in time when he viewed the illicit activity, he had gone no further than an ordinary member of the public would have gone in an attempt to contact the occupants of the property. Accordingly, . . . the [defendants] had no reasonable expectation of privacy in the area of the driveway by the bush [on the night of the party], and [the officer's] actions neither implicated nor violated the Fourth Amendment. 612 S.E. 2d at 419–20.

In addition, the court in *Commonwealth v. Ousley*, 393 S.W.3d 15, 26–29, 33 (Ky. 2013), ruled that a particular location on a driveway was part of the curtilage of a home because of that location's close distance, or proximity, to the home. In *Ousley*, closed trashcans were located just a few feet from a home on the driveway. The police officer's warrantless search of the cans violated the Fourth Amendment, and the drug evidence discovered inside the cans was excluded from evidence in court.

In general, if an officer gathers information while situated in a public place or a place where an ordinary citizen with legitimate business might be expected to be, the officer does not invade an individual's Fourth Amendment interests, including his or her reasonable expectation of privacy. Therefore, an observation by a police officer from an ordinary means of access to a dwelling, such as a driveway, walkway, front porch or side door, may not violate a person's reasonable expectation of privacy if a member of the public could have also made a similar observation. For example, in *Robinson v. Commonwealth*, 612 S.E. 2d 751 (Va. App. 2005), discussed earlier, the court found that the officer was permitted to make observations from the defendants' driveway. Though the court determined that the driveway was part of the curtilage of the defendants' dwelling, an area that is normally considered "constitutionally protected," the observations of underage drinking made by the officer on the particular occasion in question were admissible as evidence because any member of the public could have also made them:

> [B]ecause the [defendants] had extended an implied invitation to the public to use the driveway to access the front door of their home, they had no reasonable expectation of privacy in that area. And, because the [defendants] had no reasonable expectation of privacy in the illicit activities that were clearly visible from their driveway, the Fourth Amendment does not apply to any observations made by a police officer who was present in the driveway and complying with the terms of that implied invitation. Because the Fourth Amendment does not apply, no warrant is required and, therefore, no exception to the warrant requirement is needed. Because [the officer's] observations do not implicate the Fourth Amendment, those observations are admissible in their entirety. 612 S.E. 2d at 621.

Regardless of which sense an officer uses to detect criminal activity from a vantage point in public or in a place where an ordinary citizen with legitimate business might be expected to be (i.e., observations from a private sidewalk or driveway that leads to a home's entry point), the officer does not have authority to enter into a constitutionally protected area such as the inside of a home to make a *search or seizure* without a warrant. Only a search warrant gives this authority, unless there is an emergency or another recognized exception to the search warrant requirement applies:

> An officer is not entitled to conduct a warrantless entry and seizure of incriminating evidence [inside premises] simply because he has seen the evidence from outside the premises. "Incontrovertible testimony of the senses that an incriminating object is on premises belonging to a criminal suspect may establish the fullest possible measure of probable cause. But even where the object is contraband, this Court has repeatedly stated and enforced the basic rule that the police may not enter [premises] and make a warrantless seizure," absent exigent circumstances. *United States v. Wilson*, 36 F.3d 205, 209 n.4 (1st Cir. 1994).

See also DeMayo v. Nugent, 475 F. Supp. 2d 110, 115, 120 (D.Mass. 2007) ("The protection of privacy in one's home or residence stands at the core

KEY POINTS

LO1

- Law enforcement officers may search for items of evidence in the open fields without a warrant or probable cause, and may seize items if they have probable cause to believe that they are items of an incriminating character (i.e., contraband).

- *Open fields* generally refers to unoccupied, undeveloped areas of land that are not contained within the curtilage of the home; they need be neither open nor fields. The curtilage is the area around the home that harbors intimate activities associated with domestic life and the privacies of the home.

- The area within the curtilage is determined by considering four factors: (1) the proximity of the area claimed to be curtilage to the home, (2) whether the area is included within an enclosure surrounding the home, (3) the nature of the uses to which the area is put, and (4) the steps taken by the resident to protect the area from observation by people passing by.

Continued on next page

of this constitutional prohibition against [unreasonable searches and seizures under the Fourth Amendment]. Such a warrantless entry into one's home will pass constitutional muster only if the government can prove that it satisfies an exception to this general rule. The lack of exigent circumstances [in this case] thus bars the application of an exception to the general and presumptively unconstitutional conclusion that must attach to [state police officers'] warrantless entry into [plaintiff's] home.").

In *United States v. Taylor*, 90 F.3d 903 (4th Cir. 1996), in which *both* probable cause and exigent circumstances were found, an officer approached the defendant's front door, looked through his picture window adjacent to the door, and observed a large amount of money and what appeared to be illegal drugs on the dining room table. When someone inside the house quickly closed the blinds, the officer "had a reasonable basis for concluding that there was probable cause to believe that criminal activity was in progress in the house and that there was an imminent danger that evidence would be destroyed unless the officers immediately entered the house and took possession of it." 90 F.3d at 909–10. Therefore, in cases like *Taylor* where there is both probable cause to believe a crime is occurring in the home and that exigent circumstances exist, police would be justified in entering the home and seizing evidence related to the crime. *See also United States v. Carrico*, 2007 WL 1160412 (W.D. Va. 2007), at *4 ("Furthermore, exigent circumstances permit a warrantless search when probable cause to search exists and officers reasonably believe that contraband or other evidence may be destroyed or removed before a search warrant can be obtained.") (internal citations omitted).

Plain View, Open Fields, and Observations into Constitutionally Protected Areas

Law enforcement officers often confuse the open fields and plain view doctrines. The *plain view doctrine* (discussed in Chapter 10) states that a law enforcement officer with a valid justification for a prior intrusion into a zone of privacy may seize items of evidence observed open to view, if their incriminating character is immediately apparent (i.e., the officer has probable cause to seize the items). On the other hand, under the open fields doctrine, an officer need not be concerned with the validity of the justification for the prior intrusion into a zone of privacy or a person's reasonable expectation of privacy. Open fields are not a zone of privacy; therefore, they do not support any reasonable expectation of privacy. Accordingly, the officer not only may seize items that are open to view in the open fields but also may search for items hidden from view and seize them. Of course, all seizures must be based on probable cause that the items are subject to seizure.

In addition, from a vantage point in the open fields or a public place, officers may, without a warrant, make observations into constitutionally protected areas, such as a home or its curtilage. "[A] law enforcement 'officer's observations from a public vantage point where he has a right to be' and from which the activities or objects he observes are 'clearly visible' do not constitute a search within the meaning of the Fourth Amendment." *United States v. Taylor*, 90 F.3d 903, 908 (4th Cir. 1996); *see also Smith v. Ray*, 409 Fed. Appx. 641, 648, n.5 (4th Cir. 2011). These warrantless plain view observations may be enhanced by electrical or mechanical means such as flashlights or binoculars as well as certain other technological devices. (For a detailed discussion of the use of technology and the plain view doctrine, see Chapter 10.) These plain view observations, in turn, may provide the probable cause necessary to obtain a warrant from a judge to search a home and its curtilage. Note that absent an emergency or valid consent, these observations would not justify the immediate entry by officers into a constitutionally protected area.

Aerial Observations In two major cases, the U.S Supreme Court has found that warrantless police surveillance from the air of curtilage does not violate the Fourth Amendment. First, in *California v. Ciraolo*, 476 U.S. 207 (1986), the Court held that the Fourth Amendment was not violated by a warrantless aerial observation from an altitude of 1,000 feet of a fenced-in backyard within the curtilage of a home. Because the police observations took place from public navigable airspace using an airplane, from which any member of the public flying in that airspace could have observed everything the officers observed, the defendant's privacy expectation that his backyard was protected from such observation was not an expectation that society was prepared to recognize as reasonable.

CRIMINAL PROCEDURE IN ACTION

When Are Plain View Observations Made from Areas Within the Curtilage? *United States v. Conrad*, 578 F. Supp. 2d 1016, 1023–24 (N.D. III. 2008)

[A] team of law enforcement officials attempted to make contact with the occupants of Roger Conrad's family home in Geneva, Illinois (hereinafter "the Geneva Residence"). The evidence revealed that the agents called the telephone line in the Geneva Residence and knocked on the door multiple times, but no one answered. Specifically, commencing

at approximately 7:00 AM [one day], law enforcement agents knocked on the door and rang the doorbell five separate times at 30 minute intervals. At approximately 9:00 AM, Special Agent McDonough talked to Roger Conrad on the telephone. Special Agent McDonough informed Roger Conrad that FBI agents were at his Geneva Residence looking for his son, David Conrad. When Agent McDonough inquired about David Conrad being at the Geneva Residence, it is undisputed that Roger Conrad asked the agents to look in the driveway and see what cars were present. In response, the agents looked in the driveway and Agent McDonough communicated to Roger Conrad that a black Porsche was in the driveway. Roger Conrad then informed the agents that the black Porsche belonged to David Conrad and that he was at the Geneva Residence because his vehicle was there. At some point, Roger Conrad gave the agents David Conrad's cell phone number and the phone number to the Geneva Residence and told them to call. The agents were never able to reach David Conrad on the telephone. It is also undisputed that Roger Conrad did not give any law enforcement agents permission to go to the back of his Geneva residence or to enter the back deck at the Geneva Residence.

After receiving this information, the law enforcement agents . . . proceeded to the back of Roger Conrad's Geneva Residence. The home did not have a fence around it or any other obstruction around its perimeter. Further, there was no specific

path or pathway leading from the front of the home to the back of the home. Sergeant Zaglifa testified that he walked to the back of the Geneva Residence where he found sliding glass doors that entered into the lower level of the home. He knocked on these doors and looked into them, but no one answered and he did not see anyone. Law enforcement officers then proceeded up a set of back stairs that led to a deck attached to the back of the Geneva Residence. The rear deck abutted the main living level of the home and was accessible from the stairs. The stairs had a railing about 39 to 40 inches high. The same railing enclosed the back deck. At the top of the back stairs, a gate separated the stairs from the deck. The gate contained a latch, but not a lock. The latch secured the gate.

The officers walked up the stairs, opened the gate, and entered the back deck. . . . They walked onto the deck and up to glass doors. The back glass doors opened directly onto the deck. The officers looked through the doors and the windows, but initially did not observe anyone. They looked directly into the main living area of the Geneva Residence, including the kitchen.

While on the back deck, it is undisputed that the officers subsequently observed David Conrad on the couch in the family room of the residence. They could not observe him from the back sliding glass doors. Instead, the evidence revealed that the officers saw him through a bay window of the Geneva Residence off to [the] left of the sliding

Continued on next page

glass doors. The bay window is not directly over the deck—instead, the officers had to stand or lean on the railing of the deck to see into the window. The agents also observed an open pill bottle. The precise location of the pill bottle, however, is not relevant to this analysis because it is clear that the agents saw an open pill bottle somewhere in the general vicinity of where David Conrad was lying on the couch.

Agent McDonough then called Roger Conrad in Florida to relay what law enforcement had seen related to David Conrad. Although Roger Conrad and Agent McDonough tell very different versions of what was relayed during that conversation, the Court need not resolve this factual dispute. Agent McDonough admits that he mistakenly informed Roger that the pills were on the coffee table next to David Conrad. He also informed Roger Conrad that his son was on the couch, not moving, and they were concerned about him. Based on Agent McDonough's representations of what the agents had observed from looking into a window off the back deck of the Geneva Residence, Roger Conrad ultimately informed Agent McDonough where the family hid the spare key and granted agents permission to enter the residence to check on his son. The FBI obtained the hidden key and entered the Geneva Residence. Shortly after entering, the agents confirmed that David Conrad was in good health and simply sleeping on the couch.

Agent Keegan testified that the law enforcement officers immediately identified themselves to Defendant, and waited a couple of minutes for him to be fully alert. She [Agent Keegan] credibly testified that David Conrad was fully alert and responsive when they questioned him. Once he was alert, Agent Keegan questioned Defendant about child pornography, and Defendant made inculpatory statements in response to the questioning. According to Agent Keegan's testimony, David Conrad made "a spontaneous statement—he says I think I have some child pornography on my laptop in the Porsche." When Agent Keegan told David Conrad that they would want to have that child pornography as well, David Conrad willingly went out to his Porsche and got it for her. Both Agent Keegan and Sergeant Zaglifa testified that Defendant then retrieved the laptop from his vehicle and willingly turned it over to law enforcement. Sergeant Zaglifa credibly testified—corroborated by Agent Keegan's testimony—that Defendant took Sergeant Zaglifa out to his Porsche, retrieved the laptop, and gave it to Sergeant Zaglifa.

■ Were the law enforcement officers and agents inside the curtilage of defendant's residence when they observed David Conrad and the pill bottle? Or were they outside the curtilage (i.e., in the "open fields") and hence permitted to make the warrantless observations into the Geneva residence? Be sure to consider the key circumstances or factors discussed previously in this chapter to decide whether the area (e.g., the back deck of the Geneva residence) is located within the curtilage of the residence.

■ Based on your answer to question 1, do you think that defendant's motion to suppress the statements regarding the child pornography and any related evidence obtained from his laptop should be granted? In particular, were the officers' warrantless observations obtained in violation of defendant's Fourth Amendment rights?

Second, and applying the same reasoning as in *Ciraolo*, the Court in *Florida v. Riley*, 488 U.S. 445, 451–52 (1989), held that police observation of the defendant's greenhouse within the curtilage from a helicopter flying at four hundred feet did not violate the defendant's reasonable expectation of privacy and was therefore not a search requiring a warrant.

And in *Dow Chemical Co. v. United States*, 476 U.S. 227 (1986), the U.S. Supreme Court held that a government agency's aerial photography of a chemical company's two-thousand-acre outdoor industrial plant complex from navigable airspace was not a search prohibited by the Fourth Amendment. The Court analogized this particular complex to an "open field":

> [T]he open areas of an industrial plant complex with numerous plant structures spread over an area of 2,000 acres are not analogous to the "curtilage" of a dwelling for purposes of aerial surveillance; such an industrial complex is more comparable to an open field and as such it is open to the view and observation of persons in aircraft lawfully in the public airspace immediately above or sufficiently near the area for the reach of cameras. 476 U.S. at 239.

For further discussion of the cases in this section, including *Ciraolo*, *Riley*, and *Dow Chemical Co.*, see Chapter 10.

Abandoned Property

The meaning of abandoned property depends on court interpretations of the word *searches* in the Fourth Amendment. As defined earlier, a search occurs "when an expectation of privacy that society is prepared to consider reasonable is infringed." *United States v. Jacobsen*, 466 U.S. 109, 113 (1984). It follows that no search occurs when a law enforcement officer observes, examines, or inspects property whose owner has "voluntarily discarded, left behind, or otherwise relinquished his interest in the property in question so that he could no longer retain a reasonable expectation of privacy with regard to it." *United States v. Colbert*, 474 F.2d 174, 176 (5th Cir. 1973); *see also Blanchard v. Lonero*, 452 Fed. Appx. 577, 583 (5th Cir. 2011). Because there is no search under the Fourth Amendment, officers may lawfully seize abandoned property without a warrant or probable cause, and it is admissible in court.

The main difference between the abandonment doctrine and the plain view doctrine turns on the nature of the place from which the officer seizes an object. Under the plain view doctrine, which is discussed in detail in Chapter 10, a law enforcement officer with a valid justification for a prior intrusion into a zone of privacy may seize items of evidence observed open to view if their incriminating character is immediately apparent (e.g., the officer must have probable cause to believe that the observed items are incriminating in character). The plain view doctrine applies only after a law enforcement officer has made a valid prior intrusion into a zone of privacy. On the other hand, if a law enforcement officer, acting lawfully, seizes objects that have been voluntarily discarded on the street, in a public park, or in some other *location not protected by the Fourth Amendment* (e.g., "open fields"), the seizure is legal under the abandonment doctrine. Note that the abandonment doctrine, unlike the plain view doctrine, involves no prior intrusion into a zone of privacy. Law enforcement officers must learn this distinction because, in order to lawfully seize items abandoned within a zone of privacy, all elements of the plain view doctrine must be satisfied for the evidence to be admissible.

In particular, when law enforcement officers attempt to justify a seizure of property on the ground that it was abandoned, they must be prepared to prove

- an individual's intent to abandon property under the totality of the circumstances, and
- lawfulness of the police behavior (e.g., the abandonment must be voluntary and not the product of unlawful police behavior).

Intent to Abandon Property

The main determinant of whether property is abandoned is the intent of the person vacating or discarding the property to relinquish all title, possession, or claim to that property. "[I]ntent may be inferred from words spoken, acts done, and other objective facts." *United States v. Colbert*, 474 F.2d 174, 176 (5th Cir. 1973); *see also Blanchard v. Lonero*, 452 Fed. Appx. 577, 583 (5th Cir. 2011). In addition, *United States v. Caballero-Chavez*, 260 F.3d 863 (8th Cir. 2001), explained how courts use a totality of circumstances approach in order to determine whether a suspect intended to abandon property:

> Whether property has been abandoned is a question of fact we review for clear error. In conducting that review, we look to the totality of the circumstances, noting in particular two factors: whether the suspect denied ownership of the property and whether he physically relinquished the property. Abandonment is determined on the basis of the objective facts available to the investigating officers, not on the basis of [the defendant's] subjective intent. 260 F.3d at 866–67 (internal quotations omitted).

As the court stated in *Caballero-Chavez*, two important and overarching circumstances, or factors, for the determination of intent to abandon are

- denials, or disclaimers, of ownership of property by the suspect; and

- physical relinquishment of property by the suspect.

See also United States v. Le, 402 F. Supp. 2d 1068 (D.N.D. 2005) (adopting totality of circumstances approach and the aforementioned two overarching factors from *Caballero-Chavez*, to determine a suspect's intent to abandon property).

The cases that follow in this section will address these factors and others that courts have evaluated in order to determine whether a suspect abandoned his or her property. For organizational purposes, the factors bearing on the intent to abandon property will be addressed in the following contexts:

- premises,

- objects,

- garbage, and

- motor vehicles.

Premises *Abel v. United States*, 362 U.S. 217 (1960), is the foundational U.S. Supreme Court case addressing abandoned property. In *Abel*, officers of the former Immigration and Naturalization Service arrested the defendant in his hotel room and charged him with being in the United States illegally. Before he was escorted out of his room, he was permitted to pack his personal belongings. He packed nearly everything in the room except for a few things that he left on a windowsill and in a wastebasket. Then he checked out, turned in his keys, and paid his bill. Shortly thereafter, an FBI agent, with the permission of the hotel management, searched the defendant's room without a warrant. In the wastebasket, the FBI agent found a hollow pencil containing microfilm and a block of wood containing a "cipher pad." The Court held that the search for and seizure of the pencil and block of wood were legal because the defendant had abandoned the room and its contents:

> No pretense is made that this search by the F.B.I. was for any purpose other than to gather evidence of crime, that is, evidence of petitioner's espionage. As such, however, it was entirely lawful, although undertaken without a warrant. This is so for the reason that at the time of the search petitioner had vacated the room. The hotel then had the exclusive right to its possession, and the hotel management freely gave its consent that the search be made. Nor was it unlawful to seize the entire contents of the wastepaper basket, even though some of its contents had no connection with crime. So far as the record shows, petitioner had abandoned these articles. He had thrown them away. There can be nothing unlawful in the Government's appropriation of such abandoned property. . . . The two items which were eventually introduced in evidence were assertedly means for the commission of espionage, and were themselves seizable as such. These two items having been lawfully seized by the Government in connection with an investigation of crime, we encounter no basis for discussing further their admissibility as evidence. 362 U.S. at 241.

In addition, in *United States v. Caballero-Chavez*, 260 F.3d 863 (8th Cir. 2001), the court held that defendants abandoned their motel room by repeatedly disclaiming any interest in the room and its contents; as a result, defendants could not challenge a search by police of that room uncovering a bag containing cocaine:

> In this case, when questioned in the [hotel's] restaurant, the defendants denied staying at the hotel. After voluntarily accompanying the officers to Room 222, the

defendants denied the room was theirs and denied ever being in the room. When taken into Room 222, they denied that the luggage bags on the floor and a bed were theirs and then denied that the duffel bag [containing the cocaine] under the bathroom sink was theirs. The officers did not find a key card to Room 222 when the defendants voluntarily emptied their pockets, and the bags in the room and under the sink bore no identifying tags. Given the defendants' repeated disclaimers, the district court's finding that they abandoned any interest in Room 222 and its contents is not clearly erroneous. That the abandonment occurred in response to an investigation of illegal drug activity does not render it involuntary. 260 F.3d at 867.

Moreover, in *United States v. Stevenson*, 396 F.3d 538, 544–45 (4th Cir. 2005), the court found that the defendant intended to abandon his apartment based on

- a letter the defendant wrote to his girlfriend in which he gave away his property in the apartment to her and referred to himself as "a former renter,"
- the fact the defendant was in jail and facing sentencing on a felony charge, and
- the fact the defendant was approximately five weeks behind in rent and had made no effort to contact the landlord to arrange an agreement.

Therefore, because the defendant was found to have abandoned his apartment and thus no longer had any reasonable expectation of privacy in the property, he could not challenge in court the warrantless search and seizure by police of illegal weapons from the apartment.

Other factors courts have evaluated in the context of intent to abandon residential premises include defendants

- telling landlords they are leaving the premises,
- holding a moving sale,
- being observed leaving the premises,
- leaving the premises in state of disarray,
- leaving no personal belongings on the premises, and
- neglecting to lock doors.

Applying these factors, courts have determined that defendants abandoned residential premises even though they had time remaining on their lease, rental agreement, or room reservation. *See United States v. Hoey*, 983 F.2d 890, 893 (8th Cir. 1993) ("In this case, Hoey's acts and intent indicate that she abandoned the apartment. She personally told her landlord that she was leaving. She was six weeks behind on her rent. She held a moving sale, and her neighbor saw her leaving the apartment. . . . Courts have found abandonment even in cases in which the abandoning party had time left on the rental period."); *see also United States v. James,* 2007 WL 14338 (D.Minn. 2007), at *2–*3 (abandonment of hotel room found despite one day remaining on room reservation).

In making a determination that a defendant intended to abandon residential premises, courts rely on the totality of the circumstances; indeed, the presence of one factor alone will not generally lead to a finding of abandonment. For example, a person's mere absence from premises does not establish abandonment unless other factors show that the person intended to abandon the premises. *See United States v. Robinson*, 430 F.2d 1141 (6th Cir. 1970) (no intent to abandon premises merely because defendant was in police custody and incarcerated); *United States v. Stevenson*, 396 F.3d 538 (4th Cir. 2005) ("[The evidence of incarceration] certainly would not have compelled the finding that [defendant] had no intention of returning to the apartment. After all, one could be in jail for a substantial amount of time, maintain an empty apartment on the outside, and intend to return to the apartment upon release.").

The nonpublic areas of a business office are normally protected by the Fourth Amendment against unreasonable searches and seizures. However, similar to a residence, if a private office is abandoned by its occupant, it does not have this protection. The indications of intent to abandon for an office are also similar to those for a room or house. For example, in *Mullins v. United States*, 487 F.2d 581 (8th Cir. 1973), U.S. Postal Service inspectors, without a warrant, searched for and seized business records from an office that had previously been rented by the defendant. This search and seizure was made on June 12, 1972. Over the defendant's objection that he did not intend to abandon the office and its records, the court found the following facts indicative of intent to abandon:

- the defendant rented the office from May 1, 1971, through October 31, 1971;

- the defendant left that state in August 1971;

- he paid no rent on the office beginning November 1, 1971;

- neither the defendant nor his wife, business associates, or employees visited the office after November 1, 1971; and

- the office had been padlocked by the U.S. district attorney during February 1972.

Objects Intent to abandon objects involves similar considerations to intent to abandon premises. For example, a strong indication of a person's intent to abandon an object is leaving the object unattended and unclaimed for a long period of time. In *United States v. Robinson*, 390 F.3d 853 (6th Cir. 2004), the court held that a package had been abandoned because defendant had failed to claim it for more than thirty days, which was the established time period for making arrangements for the handling of such a package:

> [T]he Fed Ex package could properly be characterized as abandoned, so that [defendant] cannot challenge its seizure by federal agents. The Mailboxes, Etc. store manager testified that the rental agreement on [the] mailbox had lapsed at the time the subject package was delivered. The record also includes a standard Mailboxes, Etc. service agreement providing that packages sent to an expired mailbox "may be discarded or destroyed" after 30 days if the customer fails to make arrangements for forwarding, and there is no dispute that the subject package had been delivered to the . . . store more than 30 days before the agents seized it.

Thus, because the defendant had abandoned the package, the agents could lawfully seize the package and search its contents. Moreover, the marijuana found inside the package was admissible against the defendant at his trial on drug charges.

Law enforcement officers may pick up items immediately after a person drops, throws away, or otherwise discards them. In these cases, courts cannot rely on the length of time the item has been left unattended to determine whether the object has been abandoned. Courts must look to other circumstances, such as the defendant's conduct and the manner of disposal. In *Smith v. Ohio*, 494 U.S. 541 (1990), officers in an unmarked police vehicle observed the defendant carrying a brown paper grocery bag. One of the officers asked the defendant to "come here a minute" and identified himself as a police officer. The defendant threw the bag he was carrying onto the hood of his car and turned to face the approaching officer. The officer rebuffed the defendant's attempt to protect the bag, opened it, and discovered drug paraphernalia. The U.S. Supreme Court said: "[A] citizen who attempts to protect his private property from inspection, after throwing it on a car to respond to a police officer's inquiry, clearly has not abandoned that property." 494 U.S. at 543–44.

Also, in *United States v. Most*, 876 F.2d 191 (D.C. Cir. 1989), when a defendant, pursuant to store policy, left a bag with a clerk for safekeeping while shopping, the court refused to find that this act constituted abandonment:

> In our view, it is clear that the defendant did not abandon his bag simply by entrusting it to the care of the store clerks. Unlike the defendant in [a precedent case], [defendant here] never denied ownership of the bag. To the contrary, one of the cashiers testified that defendant "continuously asked me [to hold the bag] before he left the store." [The defendant] . . . did not place his bag within the

reach of the world generally. Although [defendant] had departed the store when the search occurred, his brief absence—preceded by a renewed request that the clerks continue to watch his bag—hardly constituted an act of abandonment.

It should also be noted that the other individuals involved in this episode did not appear to regard the defendant's bag as abandoned. One of the cashiers testified adamantly (to the evident chagrin of the government's attorney) that none of the customers could have picked up the bag because the cash register was supervised and the cashier "was watching the bag" at all times. More significantly, the police officer who executed the search did not treat the bag as abandoned. He did not simply open it immediately and examine its contents, as he would have been entitled to do if the bag had been abandoned. Rather, he examined the exterior of the bag in a gingerly fashion, opening it only when the feel of hard, rocklike objects aroused his suspicions. The officer testified that, if this initial inspection had revealed nothing unusual, he would not have continued with the search. [T]his testimony undermines the government's abandonment theory: it suggests that the officer himself believed that the defendant retained an expectation of privacy in his belongings. 876 F.2d at 197.

Regarding the defendant's reasonable expectation of privacy in the bag, the court commented that defendant maintained such an expectation because the store required all customers to surrender personal bags in their possession to the store cashier prior to shopping and thus customers such as the defendant expected the store's supervision of these bags to be both "conscientious and professional." 876 F.2d at 199. Because the defendant did not abandon the bag, and maintained a reasonable expectation of privacy in it, the court excluded the cocaine found by the officer after seizing and searching the defendant's bag.

In contrast, however, when the manner of disposal indicates that a defendant intended to relinquish possession or control of property because of consciousness of guilt or fear of potential apprehension, the courts usually find abandonment. For example, in *United States v. Morgan*, 936 F.2d 1561 (10th Cir. 1991), the court found that the defendant voluntarily abandoned a gym bag based on the following facts:

- When he saw police, he threw the bag off a porch.

- He made no attempt to retrieve the bag or to ask officers or anyone else to retrieve it for him.

- He made no attempt to protect the bag or its contents from inspection.

- He made no manifestations, verbal or otherwise, to indicate that he retained a reasonable privacy interest in the bag.

The court noted that "[w]hile an abandonment must be voluntary, '[t]he existence of police pursuit or investigation at the time of abandonment does not of itself render the abandonment involuntary.'" 936 F.2d at 1570; *see also United States v. Soto-Beniquez*, 356 F.3d 1, 36 (1st Cir. 2004) ("The district court's Fourth Amendment conclusion was correct. Once [defendant] Fernández-Malavé abandoned the weapon and drugs by throwing them out of the window, he had no reasonable expectation of privacy in those items and their seizure [by police] did not itself violate his Fourth Amendment rights. It is well settled that if a defendant abandons property while he is being pursued by police officers, he forfeits any reasonable expectation of privacy he may have had in that property.").

Another indication of intent to abandon an object is the defendant's own words of disclaimer of ownership or possession. "'Whether an abandonment has occurred is determined on the basis of objective facts available to the investigating officers, not on the basis of the owner's subjective intent.' . . . When considering whether the circumstances support a finding of abandonment, 'two important factors are denial of ownership and physical relinquishment of the property.'" *United States v. Landry*, 154 F.3d 897, 899 (8th Cir. 1998). For example, in *United States v. Lee*, 916 F.2d 814 (2d Cir. 1990), the defendant on three separate occasions told officers he was traveling without luggage. When informed that a maroon suitcase was sitting unclaimed in the baggage area, he adamantly denied that it was his. The court held that the defendant intended to abandon his suitcase and thereby forfeited any legitimate expectation of privacy in it. *See also United States v. Fulani*, 368 F.3d 351, 354–55 (3d Cir. 2004) ("We are satisfied that viewing the facts in their totality, [the defendant's] explicit denial of ownership of the bag (when he spoke to [the first officer]), coupled with his two implicit denials (when he remained silent in response to [the second officer's] bus-wide questioning [regarding ownership of the bag]), show [the defendant's] clear and unequivocal abandonment of his privacy interest in the overhead bag." Because the defendant was found to have abandoned the bag in the overhead rack of the bus, the heroin found inside by the police officer was admissible against the defendant at his trial on drug charges).

Also, in *United States v. Lipscomb*, 539 F.3d 32, 36 (1st Cir. 2008), the court determined that the defendant lacked a privacy interest in a certain firearm and drugs because he denied that they were his.

> During the hearing on the motion to suppress, [the defendant] Lipscomb repeatedly asserted that neither the crack cocaine nor the gun was his. He claimed no interest in the items and denied that the government seized them from him. In cases involving defendants who fail to establish or claim ownership of an item, we have concluded that they lack a sufficient privacy interest to assert a Fourth Amendment violation. In the instant case, Lipscomb actively disowned any interest in any of the seized items; thus, according to his own testimony, he lacks the expectation of privacy required to challenge the seizure of the crack cocaine and gun. We therefore affirm the district court's denial of the motion to suppress on this basis, and we need not reach any of the alternate grounds identified by the court.

Some courts have found that disclaimer of ownership *alone* may not provide sufficient indication of intent to abandon. For these courts, other facts must also be present, such as suspects leaving a scene without taking certain objects with them (e.g., the "physical relinquishment" or discarding of objects):

> [The defendant's] statement that the duffel bag did not belong to him was a truthful statement of fact that cannot alone provide a basis for inferring an intent on his part to abandon the bag. While he may have also intended to disassociate himself from the incriminating contents of the bag, Professor LaFave has cautioned that a mere disclaimer of ownership in an effort to avoid making an incriminating statement in response to police questioning should not alone be deemed to constitute abandonment. . . . The question is whether the owner has voluntarily discarded, left behind, or otherwise relinquished his interest in the property in question so that he could no longer retain a reasonable expectation of privacy with regard to it at the time of the search. Thus, if a person lawfully arrested disclaims any interest in the container and declines to take it with him, his readiness to depart the scene and leave an object such as a suitcase or briefcase in the control of no one may fairly be characterized as abandonment. *United States v. Perea*, 848 F. Supp. 1101, 1103 (E.D.N.Y. 1994) (internal quotations omitted); *see also People v. Jackson*, 2007 WL 778163 (Mich. App. 2007), at *2.

Garbage Courts treat abandoned garbage differently for Fourth Amendment purposes depending on whether it is located inside or outside the curtilage of a particular residence. When the trash searched or seized by police is located within the curtilage of a residence, courts generally afford it normal Fourth Amendment protections (e.g., police need a warrant before seizing and searching garbage located in this area). For example, in *United States v. Certain Real Property*, 719 F. Supp. 1396 (E.D. Mich. 1989), a police officer, disguised as a trash collector, walked up the defendant's driveway and invaded his curtilage to retrieve trash bags placed by the doorway for collection. In holding the warrantless seizure illegal, the court said that "the government decided to do directly what it already could do indirectly, and that trip up the side driveway makes all the difference for Fourth Amendment purposes." 719 F. Supp. at 1407. In a footnote, the court said that the police could have had the regular garbage collector deliver the garbage bags to them after they had been removed by the collector from the curtilage of the home. *See also Commonwealth v. Ousley*, 393 S.W.3d 15, 29, 33 (Ky. 2013) ("The police in this case walked onto the Appellee's property and into an area near his home late at night to search trash in closed trash containers which ended up containing evidence of drug trafficking. The containers had not been put out on the street for trash collection. Because the police invaded the curtilage without a search warrant, the search was illegal. Thus, this Court affirms the decision of the Court of Appeals, which found that the trial court erred in not suppressing the evidence.").

The Fourth Amendment does not prohibit the warrantless search and seizure by police of garbage left *outside* the curtilage of the home, however. In *California v. Greenwood*, 486 U.S. 35 (1988), police suspected the defendant of narcotics trafficking, but did not have probable cause to search his house. Police obtained from the regular trash collector garbage bags left at the curb in front of the defendant's house. The U.S. Supreme Court held that even if the defendants had an expectation of privacy in garbage left on the curb, it was not one that society was prepared to accept as reasonable:

> [R]espondents exposed their garbage to the public sufficiently to defeat their claim to Fourth Amendment protection. *It is common knowledge that plastic garbage bags left on or at the side of a public street are readily accessible to animals, children, scavengers, snoops, and other members of the public.* . . . *Moreover, respondents placed their refuse at the curb for the express purpose of conveying it to a third party, the trash collector, who might himself have sorted through respondent's trash or permitted others, such as the police, to do so. Accordingly, having deposited their garbage in an area particularly suited for public inspection and, in a manner of speaking, public consumption, for the express purpose of having strangers take it,* . . . *respondents could have had no reasonable expectation of privacy in the inculpatory items that they discarded.* . . . *[T]he police cannot reasonably be expected to avert their eyes from evidence of criminal activity that could have been observed by any member of the public.* 486 U.S. at 40–41 (emphasis added).

Thus, because law enforcement officials and other individuals can search and seize items without a warrant that are left at the curb of a home, police were permitted to use the items found in the garbage bags to obtain a search warrant for defendant's home, where they discovered controlled substances.

The court in *United States v. Williams*, 669 F.3d 903, 904–05 (8th Cir. 2012) also found that police could search garbage left curbside without a warrant:

> [T]he only evidence in the record as to the location from which the trash was pulled [without a warrant] is Detective Miller's statement in the affidavit that he "retrieved three bags of trash that had been *left at the curb for pick-up by a trash company*" (emphasis added). It is well settled that there is no reasonable expectation of privacy in trash left at the curb in an area accessible to the public for pick-up by a trash company. Therefore, the district court did not err in denying the motion to suppress [a handgun and ammunition found on the basis of a search warrant which was obtained, in part, from evidence consisting of cocaine residue discovered in the trash pull.]

Also, *United States v. Dunkel*, 900 F.2d 105 (7th Cir. 1990), *vacated on other grounds*, *Dunkel v. United States*, 498 U.S. 1043 (1991), held that the defendant, a dentist, had no reasonable expectation of privacy in a trash bin located off the parking lot of a building that he owned and that housed several other businesses. All businesses used the same trash bin, and the parking lot and trash bin were accessible to patients, employees, and the general public. No warrant was needed to search for and seize financial records discarded in the trash bin. And in *United States v. Walker*, 624 F. Supp. 99 (D. Md. 1985), law enforcement officers found a paper shopping bag out in the open alongside a road in a sparsely populated rural setting. No attempt had been made to protect the bag from damage from the elements, from removal by a passerby, or from disturbance by an animal. The court held that these facts indicated that the defendant had no reasonable expectation of privacy in the contents of the bag.

Thus, after the U.S. Supreme Court's decision in *Greenwood*, the only time police need a warrant to search and seize garbage is when it is located inside a residence or in the area immediately surrounding a residence (e.g., the "curtilage"). Police generally do not need a warrant to search and seize garbage left on a public street curb outside a residence or on the street itself. Some states, however, have provided their citizens with more protections under the Fourth Amendment than those provided by the U.S. Supreme Court in *Greenwood*. For example, New Jersey requires its officers to obtain a warrant prior to searching garbage left at the curb of a home. *State v. Hempele*, 576 A.2d 793 (N.J. 1990); *see also State v. Crane*, 254 P.3d. 117 (N.M. App. 2011) ("The Court [of Appeals of New Mexico] in *State v. Granville* adopted the approach taken by [New Jersey in] *State v. Hempele*, the seminal case recognizing a reasonable expectation of privacy in residential garbage left for collection under a state constitution").

DISCUSSION POINT

When Do Defendants Have a Reasonable Expectation of Privacy in Their Garbage? *United States v. Segura-Baltazar*, 448 F.3d 1281 (11th Cir. 2006).

The facts of *Baltazar* are as follows:

In the course of a drug investigation involving a suspect known only as "Alejandro," police identified numerous incoming calls from a phone number registered to Bernabe Perez, an alias of the defendant, at 480 Sheringham Court in Roswell, Georgia. Based on that

information, police began surveillance at 480 Sheringham Court. Officer Ronald Gooden of the City of Roswell Police Department determined that it would be helpful to inspect the trash discarded from the house at 480 Sheringham Court, and he contacted the Roswell sanitation department for assistance.

Gooden learned that trash was normally collected from the suspect's home on Wednesdays. Accordingly, he met with Jerry Kimbral, the sanitation truck driver for that route, on Wednesday, January 14, 2004, the normal collection day. Officer Gooden and Kimbral drove to 480 Sheringham Court in an empty garbage truck. They found garbage left for collection in front of the house to the left of a mailbox, in an area that was not enclosed by a fence and that was approximately fifty-five to sixty-five feet from the residence and three to six feet from the curb. The garbage was contained in bags which, in turn, were found inside large garbage cans that were covered with lids. Kimbral emptied the bags into the garbage truck and drove to the Roswell police department, where Officer Gooden retrieved the trash and processed it for evidence. The same procedure was repeated on other normal collection Wednesday[s]—January 21, 2004, February 4, 18, and 25, 2004, and March 3 and 10, 2004.

On two other occasions, the trash-pull procedures were slightly different. The magistrate judge described the events of January 28, 2004, in these terms:

Gooden was with Kimbral and another sanitation department employee, Luiz Gordado, whom Gooden understood spoke Spanish. On that morning, part of the garbage was located in the garbage cans at the curb. Gooden also observed garbage cans, containing what appeared to be bags of garbage, sitting to the left side of the residence near the garage. Kimbral informed Gooden that it was customary for him to collect the garbage from the location next to the garage when it was left there and not at the curb. He asked if Gooden wanted him to collect that garbage. Gooden instructed Kimbral and Gordado to verify with the resident that the garbage was to be collected. Kimbral and Gordado walked up and knocked on the door of the residence. After conferring with a female at the door, they collected the garbage located next to the garage. That garbage, along with the garbage located next to the curb, was placed in the truck, and Gooden retrieved the garbage at the police department where he examined it for evidence.

Similarly, on Wednesday February 11, 2004, Gooden and Kimbral retrieved trash from cans that

Continued on next page

were sitting to the left of the residence near the garage. They followed the same procedures they employed on January 28; the only difference was that there was no trash at the curb on February 11.

The police recovered many inculpatory items from the trash pulls indicating that the residents of 480 Sheringham Court were involved in illegal drug activity. Specifically, they found 42 grams of methamphetamine, 41 grams of marijuana, plastic wrappings that field-tested positive for cocaine, and numerous bags containing residue that field-tested positive for cocaine, marijuana, and methamphetamine. Additionally, the police found papers depicting names with numerical amounts listed next to each name (which they believed were drug ledgers); financial documents indicating the presence of large amounts of currency, including evidence of wire transfers exceeding $10,000; and boxes that had contained wireless surveillance cameras and monitors that would enable a user to see in low light conditions. Officer Gooden testified that, based on his experience, devices such as these are often used by drug dealers as countersurveillance tools. Finally, the police recovered two types of magazines for semiautomatic handguns, an empty box of 12-gauge shotgun shells, and one live round of .45-caliber ammunition.

Based on the evidence obtained through the trash pulls and information provided by a confidential informant, Gooden obtained a federal search warrant for the house located at 480 Sheringham Court. The search warrant was executed on March 25, 2004. During the ensuing search police recovered approximately 1200 grams of methamphetamine, 130 grams of cocaine, two semiautomatic handguns, two .22-caliber rifles, one shotgun, $19,631 in U.S. currency, and numerous forms of identification bearing several different names matched with the defendant's picture.

Defendant Segura-Baltazar argued that the district court . . . erred by . . . refusing to suppress the evidence recovered from the trash pulls.

448 F.3d at 1284–85.

The Court in *Segura-Baltazar,* however, ultimately agreed with the district court that the evidence found in the garbage bags left by the defendant's mailbox near the street curb and in front of the defendant's home need not be excluded from court:

> We readily affirm the district court's denial of the motion to suppress the evidence recovered from trash left at the curb in front of Segura-Baltazar's house. Indeed, the facts of this case are strikingly similar to those considered in [the U.S. Supreme Court case of] *Greenwood* [discussed in the preceding section]. The only apparent distinctions—that the garbage in

> *Greenwood* was placed on the curb (as opposed to three to six feet from the curb) and was in only an opaque garbage bag (as opposed to a garbage bag that was placed inside a garbage can)—are insufficient to warrant any different outcome. Having placed the garbage near the curb for the purpose of conveying it to third parties, the trash collector, or other members of the public, we cannot find that appellant had a reasonable expectation of privacy in the inculpatory items discarded [(i.e., the drugs, drug paraphernalia, and ammunition)]. 448 F.3d at 1286.

Thus, because defendant lacked a reasonable expectation of privacy in the garbage left near the street curb and in front of his home, police were permitted to seize the garbage and search it without a warrant.

Concerning the garbage left near his home, the Court also found that the defendant lacked a reasonable expectation of privacy in this garbage:

> Taken together, the facts of this case lead us to the conclusion that [defendant] Segura-Baltazar did not have a reasonable expectation of privacy in the trash that he left in the usual course of events for collection outside but near his home. The trash was placed in a location where it was customarily retrieved by sanitation employees, it was left there at the designated time for trash collection, and it was clearly visible and accessible from the street. 448 F.3d at 1289.

Thus, because defendant lacked a reasonable expectation of privacy in this garbage near his home, it could be seized and searched by police without a warrant. The incriminating evidence found during this search (i.e., the drugs, drug paraphernalia, and ammunition) was also admissible in court against the defendant.

In sum, all of the evidence found by police in defendant's garbage could be used to obtain a search warrant to search defendant's home. This evidence as well as the evidence found by police during the execution of the search warrant was admissible in court, and resulted in defendant's conviction on both drugs and weapons charges. 448 F.3d at 1294.

■ Do you agree with the Court's holding that the evidence found in the garbage bags left by the defendant's mailbox near the street curb and in front of the defendant's home need not be excluded from court (e.g., defendant's Fourth Amendment rights were not violated by the warrantless seizure and search of defendant's garbage left in this location)? Recall that the garbage was located three to six feet from the curb and found inside large cans that were covered with lids. Do these facts matter in your opinion for whether the defendant has a

Continued on next page

reasonable expectation of privacy in this garbage? For whether the garbage was abandoned? For the open fields and curtilage distinction?

■ Do you agree with the court's holding that the evidence found in the garbage bags sitting next to the defendant's residence need not be excluded from court (i.e., the defendant's Fourth Amendment rights were not violated by the warrantless seizure and search of the garbage left in this location)? In formulating your answer, be sure to consider who retrieved the garbage bags and the circumstances surrounding their retrieval. For example, would the court have been more likely to have reached a different holding had the police retrieved the garbage by themselves from the area near the defendant's residence (e.g., without the assistance of the sanitation employees)? Why or why not? Also, do you think the court would have held differently if the garbage were not visible from the street or not ordinarily retrieved by the sanitation employees from this location near the home? Finally, what if the sanitation employees did not normally pick up the garbage from the defendant's residence on the day police requested their assistance in retrieving the garbage (or, alternatively, the defendant did not normally leave it out for pickup on this day)?

Motor Vehicles In *United States v. Ramirez*, 145 F.3d 345 (5th Cir 1998), the court found that defendant abandoned his vehicle based on testimony provided by relatives and others that defendant had fled the country and left his car behind. As a result, the defendant could not challenge the warrantless search and seizure of the vehicle by police uncovering drugs:

> On several occasions, law enforcement officers contacted relatives of [the defendant] in an attempt to locate him and determine ownership of the car. His wife and mother-in-law indicated that [the defendant] had fled to Mexico. [C]ooperating individuals informed law enforcement agents that [the defendant] had fled, leaving his car behind. Because he abandoned the property, [the defendant] cannot successfully challenge the search of the car. The evidence from the car [e.g., drugs] was properly admitted into evidence. 145 F.3d at 353.

In addition, *United States v. Hastamorir*, 881 F.2d 1551 (11th Cir. 1989), held that the defendant's repeated disclaimers of knowledge of, or interest in, a vehicle and its contents extinguished any reasonable expectation of privacy the defendant had in the vehicle and its contents, and was an abandonment of the vehicle for Fourth Amendment purposes. As a result, the defendant could not challenge in court the warrantless search and seizure by police of the vehicle that revealed cocaine (e.g., he lacked "standing"). *See also United States v. Alexander*, 573 F.3d 465, 473 (7th Cir. 2009) ("The officers knew that the Buick [Riviera] was titled in Feljstad's name and that *Alexander had disclaimed that the vehicle was his*. That is enough to establish abandonment. . . . [T]he officers had no knowledge at the time of [their] search that Alexander claimed to be the true owner of the Buick by virtue of making the payments on it, as Alexander later claimed in an affidavit filed with the district court. A reasonable person in the searching officers' position would believe that Alexander relinquished his property interests in the Riviera. Therefore, Alexander abandoned the vehicle and his Fourth Amendment rights were not violated by the [warrantless] vehicle search.") (italics added).

Moreover, *United States v. Tate*, 821 F.2d 1328 (8th Cir. 1987), held that the defendant, who fled on foot from a stolen truck after shooting two troopers who had legally stopped the truck, abandoned the truck and its contents and any expectation of privacy he had in either.

Note that an officer with probable cause to search a readily mobile motor vehicle may also be able to justify a warrantless search of the vehicle under the *Carroll* doctrine, also referred to as the *automobile exception* to the warrant requirement. (See Chapter 11 for further discussion of this particular exception to the warrant requirement.)

509

Lawfulness of Police Behavior

An abandonment must be voluntary and not the product of coercive, illegal police behavior:

> In order to be effective, abandonment must be voluntary. It is considered involuntary if it results from a [police] violation of the Fourth Amendment. [P]roperty is considered to have been involuntarily abandoned if the defendant discards it as a consequence of illegal police conduct. *United States v. Flynn*, 309 F.3d 736, 738 (10th Cir. 2002) (internal quotations omitted).

See also United States v. Ojeda-Ramos, 455 F.3d 1178, 1187 (10th Cir. 2006); *United States v. Miller*, 974 F.2d 953, 958 (8th Cir. 1992) ("An abandonment that occurs in response to proper police activity has not been coerced in violation of the Fourth Amendment.").

The following cases found abandonment as a result of a person voluntarily discarding or disclaiming ownership of an object in response to lawful police activities:

- An officer asked the defendant, a bus passenger, whether she owned a tote bag on a rack above her seat, and she denied ownership. *United States v. Lewis*, 921 F.2d 1294 (D.C. Cir. 1990); *see also United States v. Ojeda-Ramos*, 455 F.3d 1178, 1180, 1187 (10th Cir. 2006) ("[Defendant] Ojeda-Ramos's abandonment of the suitcase [by disclaiming any interest in it] was voluntary. [O]jeda-Ramos was not seized by [Officer] Dunlap's order to leave the bus and claim luggage [in the cargo bay area]. Moreover, . . . Dunlap's seizure of Ojeda-Ramos when he asked Ojeda-Ramos to follow him to the parcel storage room [of the bus station] was reasonable. Thus, his abandonment of the suitcase was not the result of a Fourth Amendment violation. [Also,] Ojeda-Ramos's claim that any abandonment of the suitcase was rendered involuntary due to the fact he could not speak English, which in turn placed him at the mercy of the officers and unable to assert his rights, is unavailing because it is contradicted by the evidence.")

- The defendant discarded his wallet on the floor of the stationhouse following a valid arrest by police. *See United States v. Kelly*, 329 F.3d 624, 629 (8th Cir. 2003) ("The arrest was not infirm. Further, when [the defendant] Kelly discarded the wallet to avoid its discovery he also discarded any privacy interest he may have had in the wallet or its contents").

- In response to a fictitious sign placed by police on a highway indicating an approaching checkpoint, or roadblock, the defendant's passenger threw a sack containing drugs out of a vehicle. *United States v. Flynn*, 309 F.3d 736 (10th Cir. 2002).

In particular, the court in *Flynn* found that the defendant had voluntarily abandoned the sack, despite the fact that the police "created a ruse" by placing a fictitious sign on the highway:

> [The defendant] maintains he only discarded the property on the ramp as a result of . . . law enforcement's illegal conduct in operating a [fictitious] narcotics checkpoint. This reliance is misplaced. [The defendant] never reached a drug checkpoint. He discarded the property prior to being stopped by the police. Up to that moment, he acted voluntarily in response to a ruse established by the police (i.e., the signs warning of a fictitious checkpoint on I-40). The posting of signs to create a ruse does not constitute illegal police activity. In fact, had [the defendant] continued driving eastbound on I-40, he would never have been stopped because the checkpoint warned of by the signs did not exist. Even the police car ahead on I-40 was unoccupied. The creation of a ruse to cause the defendant to abandon an item is not illegal. Here, the defendant abandoned the property before being stopped by the police. He retained no reasonable expectation of privacy in the object. The abandonment in this situation was voluntary.

KEY POINTS

L04
- Property is abandoned, for purposes of the Fourth Amendment, if its owner has voluntarily discarded, left behind, otherwise relinquished, and/or denied his or her interest in the property so as to no longer retain a reasonable expectation of privacy with regard to it. To determine abandonment, courts examine (1) the defendant's intent to abandon the property under the totality of the circumstances, and (2) the lawfulness of the police behavior.

Continued on next page

Because the defendant voluntarily abandoned the sack by throwing it from his vehicle, police could lawfully seize and search it. Moreover, the drugs found inside the sack by police were admissible at the defendant's trial.

In *California v. Hodari D.*, 499 U.S. 621 (1991), involving only *attempted* unlawful police activity, a law enforcement officer, without probable cause or reasonable articulable suspicion, pursued the defendant on mere suspicion of involvement in a drug transaction. As the officer approached the defendant, the defendant tossed away a small rock. A moment later, the officer tackled the defendant. The rock he threw away was later determined to be crack cocaine. The court held that, although the seizure of the defendant was illegal, the defendant tossed away the crack cocaine *before* he was seized. Therefore, the abandonment of the cocaine did not occur as a result of any *unlawful, completed police activity*, and the cocaine was admissible in court:

> [A]ssuming that [Officer] Pertoso's pursuit in the present case constituted a "show of authority" enjoining Hodari to halt, since Hodari did not comply with that injunction he was not seized [by the officer] until he was tackled. The cocaine abandoned while he was running was in this case not the fruit of [this] [illegal] seizure, and his motion to exclude evidence of it was properly denied. 499 U.S. at 629.

However, "[w]hen an individual abandons an object in response to an officer's violation of his constitutional rights, the violation taints the abandonment, making it involuntary." *United States v. Mendez*, 827 F. Supp. 1280, 1284 (S.D. Tex. 1993). For example, in *United States v. Stephens*, 206 F.3d 914 (9th Cir 2000), the court first found that defendant abandoned the bag he had brought with him onto a passenger bus: "[T]he district court found that [defendant] denied ownership of the bag three times. The district court concluded that these repeated denials objectively demonstrated an intent to abandon the property. This factual finding is not clearly erroneous." 206 F.3d at 917.

Next, the court found that this abandonment was the result of an illegal seizure by police:

> [T]he next question is whether [the defendant] abandoned the bag as a result of an unlawful seizure. An abandonment must be voluntary, and an abandonment that results from Fourth Amendment violation cannot be voluntary. Abandonment will not be recognized when it is the result of prior illegal police conduct. [The defendant] argues that he involuntarily abandoned the bag as a result of an unlawful seizure. We agree. 206 F.3d at 917.

Because the defendant in *Stephens* abandoned the bag after he had been illegally seized, the court suppressed the cocaine found by police within the bag. Note that this case differs from *Hodari D.*, discussed earlier, because in *Hodari D.* the defendant abandoned the cocaine *before* being illegally seized by police. *See also United States v. Nicholson*, 144 F.3d 632, 640 (10th Cir. 1998) ("[W]e may not justify the detectives' subsequent opening of Defendant's luggage on the basis that Defendant . . . abandoned his luggage by failing to claim ownership. Abandonment must be voluntary. Because any abandonment was a direct consequence of the detectives' Fourth Amendment violation in initially handling [and searching] Defendant's luggage without a warrant, we deem such abandonment involuntary as a matter of law [and suppress the fruits of the search, which consisted of cocaine and marijuana inside the luggage].").

KEY POINTS

- Property that is found to be abandoned may be searched and seized without a warrant or other justification and without violating the Fourth Amendment.

- Courts consider a variety of circumstances in determining intent to abandon property, including the defendant (1) disclaiming or denying interest or ownership in the property, (2) departing the scene, (3) making no attempt to retrieve or protect the property, (4) leaving the property in the care of no one, (5) leaving the property unattended for a long time, and (6) discarding or otherwise relinquishing the property.

- Discarding property as a direct result of the unlawful activity of a law enforcement officer is not voluntary abandonment but a forced response to the unlawful police behavior. Such property will be excluded from evidence at trial.

- A person who establishes a reasonable expectation of privacy or ownership/possessory interest in property has not abandoned that property, and the property may not be searched or seized without a warrant or other legal justification.

- Absent state law to the contrary, when a person leaves garbage outside the curtilage of a home (e.g., on the curb of a public street), the person no longer has a reasonable expectation of privacy in the garbage and the Fourth Amendment does not prohibit the warrantless search and seizure of the garbage. However, garbage left inside a home or on the home's curtilage would ordinarily receive full Fourth Amendment protection; hence, police would ordinarily need a warrant to search garbage left in these locations.

511

SUMMARY

Open fields generally refers to unoccupied, undeveloped areas of land that are not contained within the curtilage of the home. The curtilage is the area around the home that harbors intimate activities associated with the privacies of the home.

A law enforcement officer may search for items of evidence lying in the open fields without a search warrant or probable cause, and may seize items in the open fields that he or she has probable cause to believe are incriminating in character (i.e., contraband). An officer may also legally make observations from a vantage point in the open fields into constitutionally protected areas such as a home to detect criminal activity or evidence as long as the reasonable expectations of privacy and property interests of the individuals being observed are not violated. Absent an emergency or valid consent, however, an officer should not enter into these constitutionally protected areas without a warrant. Nonetheless, an officer may use his or her observations from a vantage point in the open fields to obtain such a warrant.

Whether a piece of land or a building falls within the curtilage is determined by considering the following four factors: (1) the proximity to the home of the area claimed to be curtilage, (2) the inclusion of the area within an enclosure surrounding the home, (3) the nature of how the area is put to use, and (4) the steps the resident has taken to protect the area from observation by passersby.

When examining whether a particular area falls within the curtilage or open fields, courts have tended to analyze the defendant's reasonable expectation of privacy related to that area. Law enforcement officers, therefore, must be careful to avoid warrantless intrusions not only into the curtilage, or area immediately surrounding a person's house, but also into any other area that the person reasonably seeks to preserve as private.

A law enforcement officer, without a warrant or probable cause, may retrieve items of evidence that have been abandoned by their owners without violating Fourth Amendment rights. Property has been abandoned when its owner has voluntarily discarded, left behind, otherwise relinquished and/or disclaimed his or her interest in the property so as to no longer retain a reasonable expectation of privacy with regard to it. To determine abandonment, courts examine (1) the defendant's intent to abandon the property and (2) the lawfulness of the police behavior.

Courts use a totality-of-circumstances approach when evaluating whether an individual intended to abandon property. Courts rely on two general circumstances, or factors, in determining whether an individual intended to abandon property: (1) disclaimers, or denials, of ownership in the property and (2) physical relinquishment of the property.

In the particular case of *premises*, the following are examples of factors that courts may examine in their totality in order to determine whether a suspect intended to abandon premises: (1) removing personal belongings; (2) failing to lock doors; (3) being observed vacating the premises or telling others about vacating the premises; (4) not paying rent for a long time; (5) being away from the premises for an extended time; (6) not communicating with anyone regarding the premises; (7) not attending to or caring for the premises; and (8) holding a moving sale, turning in keys, or paying final rent and other bills.

In the particular case of determining intent to abandon *objects*, a court may examine the following factors: (1) leaving the object unattended for an unreasonable period of time; (2) discarding the object out of consciousness of guilt or fear of apprehension; (3) disclaiming or denying interest in the object and leaving it unprotected in the care of no one; and (4) allowing the object to be taken away in the ordinary course of events, without objection, or leaving the object behind (i.e., "physical relinquishment" of the object).

Intent to abandon *vehicles* is determined by the same considerations as those for premises and objects.

In general, *garbage* left on the curb of a public street for removal by trash collectors has been abandoned, and police may search and seize it without a warrant or probable cause. Police, however, need a warrant to search and seize garbage located within a residence or on the curtilage of the residence.

To have a valid abandonment, property must be abandoned voluntarily and not as a result of unlawful activity by a law enforcement officer. Property abandoned as a result of illegal police conduct will be excluded from evidence.

KEY TERMS

abandoned property 500
curtilage 485

houses 484
open fields 484

physical trespass 487
reasonable expectation of privacy 487

REVIEW AND DISCUSSION QUESTIONS

1. Does the term *open fields* include any place that is public or private outside the curtilage, including forests, lakes, woods, city streets and sidewalks, and stadiums?

2. Which of the following, if any, would be considered a house for purposes of the Fourth Amendment? Why is this an important consideration when evaluating the issue of curtilage and open fields?

    a. Tent

    b. Motor home

    c. Sailboat

    d. Cave

3. The dissent in *California v. Hodari D.* said that "a police officer may now fire his weapon at an innocent citizen and not implicate the Fourth Amendment—as long as he misses his target." Do you agree with this interpretation of *Hodari*? To help answer this question, consider the following: If a person throws away an item of criminal evidence after being illegally shot at by a police officer, is the item abandoned? What if the person throws the item away before being illegally shot by the officer but after the officer has begun pursuing the suspect? Is the item abandoned in this situation?

4. Would a person's Fourth Amendment rights be violated by law enforcement officers who, after illegally arresting the person, entered the person's fenced and posted rural property to observe a marijuana field surrounded by a forest?

5. Compare the plain view doctrine, the open fields doctrine, and the abandonment doctrine (in formulating your comparisons, be sure to include the concept of reasonable expectation of privacy).

6. If a person abandons property inside the curtilage of someone else's property, may a law enforcement officer seize the abandoned property? What about inside someone else's house?

7. Is observing activities inside a house in the country by looking into a window with binoculars from a nearby field or forest any different from observing activities in a tenth-story apartment from a window in an adjacent apartment building? What about from a window in an apartment building three blocks away?

8. Does an object's value have any bearing on the question of whether a person abandoned it? Can a person who runs away from his or her automobile to avoid apprehension by the police be said to give up all reasonable expectations of privacy in the vehicle? What if the person locks the vehicle before fleeing? In a related vein, does the size or other physical characteristics of an object have any bearing on the question of whether a person abandoned it?

9. For each place listed in question 2, what indications of intent to abandon would give a law enforcement officer authority to search for and seize items left at that place?

10. If a person undergoes emergency surgery after being shot by police while driving a stolen automobile, which of the following, if any, has the person abandoned?

    a. Clothing worn at the time of the shooting

    b. Wallets and other items in the pockets of the clothing

    c. Bullets surgically removed

    d. The automobile

11. Are there any limits on a search conducted outside the curtilage of a home or business (e.g., in the "open fields")? Can police use a backhoe or bulldozer? Can they search at any time of the day and for as long as they want? Can they use as many personnel and make as much noise as they want?

13 Interrogations, Admissions, and Confessions

©istock.com/Rich Legg

The Self-Incrimination Clause of the Fifth Amendment guarantees that no person "shall be compelled in any criminal case to be a witness against himself." This so-called negative right gained international prominence as a result of the U.S. Supreme Court's landmark decision in *Miranda v. Arizona*, 384 U.S. 436 (1966), a case that radically changed the course of law enforcement in the area of admissions, confessions, and interrogations.

The Self-Incrimination Clause also applies in settings other than those covered by *Miranda*. For example, barring grants of immunity, witnesses and targets alike may invoke the privilege during grand jury proceedings. Similarly, those called to testify before congressional or other governmental hearings may also refuse to answer questions if their responses would tend to incriminate themselves unless they, too, have been granted immunity. This chapter, though, focuses the law governing statements that criminal justice professional commonly take from criminal suspects or defendants.

The terms *statement, admission, interrogation,* and *confession* are used throughout this chapter.

- **Statement** is a broad term meaning simply any oral or written declaration or assertion.
- **Admission** means a person's statement or acknowledgment of facts tending to incriminate that person, but not sufficient of itself to establish guilt of a crime. An admission,

LO1 DESCRIBE how the test for the admissibility of a defendant's admission or confession evolved from exclusively focusing on due process voluntariness to also including the Fifth Amendment Self-Incrimination Clause and the Sixth Amendment Right to Counsel.

LO2 ANALYZE whether the *Miranda* requirements apply to a particular fact situation—that is, whether the suspect was subject to custodial interrogation.

LO3 EXPLAIN under what circumstances further attempts at interrogation may be made after a suspect has exercised his or her right to remain silent, has requested the assistance of an attorney, or has waived the *Miranda* rights and submitted to interrogation.

LO4 EVALUATE whether the *Miranda* requirements have been satisfied in a case in which they apply—that is, whether the warnings were adequate, whether the rights were clearly waived, and whether the suspect was competent to waive the rights.

LO5 DISCUSS the effect of *Miranda* in court.

LO6 DIFFERENTIATE the right to counsel under the Fifth and Sixth Amendments, and understand the distinct limitations placed on obtaining statements from suspect under each approach.

alone or in connection with other facts, tends to show the existence of one or more, but not all, elements of a crime. For example, suspects often admit that they were present at the scene of a crime but deny that they committed the crime.

- An **interrogation** is the process through which law enforcement officials pose questions or engage in other activities that are the functional equivalent of asking direct questions to someone whom they suspect is involved in criminal activity.

- A **confession** means a person's statement or acknowledgment of facts establishing that person's guilt of all elements of a crime.

There are three approaches taken to safeguarding constitutional rights in the interrogation context:

1. The Due Process Clauses of the Fifth and Fourteenth Amendments guarantee that any and all statements, admissions, and confessions to be introduced against a criminal defendant at trial be voluntary.

2. The Self-Incrimination Clause of the Fifth Amendment guarantees that any and all statements, admissions, and confessions that are a product of custodial interrogation cannot be introduced against a criminal defendant at trial unless certain procedural warnings (known as *Miranda* rights) were given to the person prior to the onset of custodial interrogation.

3. The Right to Counsel Clause of the Sixth Amendment protects criminal defendants from making statements, admissions, or confessions without the presence and effective assistance of counsel after the initiation of formal criminal proceedings.

The Due Process Voluntariness Approach

Early English common law recognized out-of-court confessions to be weak evidence. Sir William Blackstone, the English legal commentator and scholar, wrote that such confessions were "the weakest and most suspicious of all testimony; even liable to be obtained by artifice, false hopes, promises of favor, or menaces; seldom remembered accurately, or reported with due precision; and incapable in their nature of being disproved by other negative evidence" (Blackstone 1769: 357). Since that time, the law has always been concerned with the due process implications about confessions.

Suspicion of confessions obtained as a result of police interrogations waned for a period of time in U.S. history, but it resurfaced in the 1930s as courts began to take note of the often brutal police tactics that were used against criminal suspects (Penney 1998). In fact, the Wickersham Commission, a federal commission set up to investigate police conduct in the early 1930s, used the term *the third degree* to describe police tactics at the time (Penney 1998: 336–37). They defined the term as "the inflicting of pain, physical or mental, to extract confessions or statements" (Wickersham Commission 1931: 19).

> The Commission documented the use of a litany of sadistic practices, including beating with fists, blackjacks, rubber hoses, and telephone books; the use of hot lights; confinement in airless and fetid rooms; and hanging from windows. The Commission was also concerned with psychologically abusive tactics, such as incommunicado detention, prolonged relay questioning, stripping the suspect of clothing, and the deprivation of sleep and food (Penney 1998: 336).

The Wickersham Commission's report facilitated widespread change in policing in the United States. The report not only set in motion many efforts to stop police corruption and brutality (see Skolnick and Fyfe 1993) but also affected the decision making of the U.S. Supreme Court. The Court began citing the Wickersham Commission's report on police brutality in obtaining confessions as evidence that confessions were often involuntary or unreliable.

The landmark case excluding confessions on constitutional grounds was *Bram v. United States*, 168 U.S. 532 (1897). *Bram* marked the first time the Supreme Court relied on the Fifth Amendment privilege against self-incrimination as a basis for holding that confessions had to be made voluntarily. In the years following *Bram*, however, the Court turned to the Due Process Clauses of the Fifth and Fourteenth Amendments as a justification for excluding confessions that were not voluntarily given. Under this approach, exemplified in *Brown v. Mississippi*, 297 U.S. 278 (1936), the "totality of the circumstances" of each confession had to be examined to determine both the *voluntariness* of a confession and its overall reliability.

Brown v. Mississippi concerned a case in which "several African-American defendants confessed to murder charges only after having been beaten and tortured by the local sheriff acting in conjunction with an angry white mob. The confessions were the sole evidence used against the *Brown* defendants to secure their convictions" (Godsey 2005: 488). In reversing the defendants' convictions, the Supreme Court reaffirmed that confessions beaten out of suspects were clearly inadmissible because they were involuntary, just as they had been under *Bram*; but the Court reached this conclusion under a different constitutional rationale. Under *Brown*'s due process approach, involuntary statements are unconstitutional for the following reasons:

1. An involuntary statement is considered to be inherently untrustworthy or unreliable, and convictions based on unreliable evidence violate due process.

2. Coercive police practices are a violation of "fundamental fairness," an essential element of due process. Therefore, a confession coerced by the police violates due process, even if that confession is otherwise reliable.

3. Free choice is an essential aspect of due process, and an involuntary confession cannot be the product of a person's free and rational choice.

4. Our system of justice is an accusatorial, not an inquisitorial, system—"a system in which the State must establish guilt by evidence independently and freely secured and may not by coercion prove its charge against an accused out of his own mouth." *Rogers v. Richmond*, 365 U.S. 534, 540–41 (1961).

The "Focus of the Investigation Test" of *Escobedo v. Illinois*

In 1964, the Supreme Court decided *Escobedo v. Illinois*, 378 U.S. 478 (1964). The suspect in *Escobedo* had been arrested, but not indicted or arraigned. He asked to see his lawyer, but the police denied that request and continued to interrogate him.

518

PART IV
INTERROGATIONS,
IDENTIFICATIONS, TRIALS,
AND POST-CONVICTION
REMEDIES

Contrary to popular belief, the case did not alter the voluntariness test that had already existed to help achieve the Fifth and Fourteenth Amendment's guarantees of due process. Rather, *Escobedo* added another constitutional dimension to the law of interrogations by holding that the Sixth Amendment right to counsel offered protection during preindictment interrogations because the "right to use counsel at the formal trial would be a very hollow thing if, for all practical purposes, the conviction is already assured by pretrial examination." 378 U.S. at 487.

Unlike the voluntariness test, *Escobedo* did not employ a totality-of-the-circumstances approach. Instead, it took a single circumstance and made it the single determinative factor in all cases in which it occurred. The Court said that "when the process shifts from investigatory to accusatory—when its focus is on the accused and its purpose is to elicit a confession . . . the accused must be permitted to consult with his lawyer." 378 U.S. at 492. This came to be known as the *Escobedo* "focus of investigation test."

Escobedo is more interesting for its rationale than it is for any precedential value. It embraced the notion that the Sixth Amendment's right to counsel had relevance in stages of criminal prosecutions before trial. Notably, *Escobedo* was decided on the heels of the Supreme Court's decision in *Gideon v. Wainwright*, 372 U.S. 335 (1963), in which it held that the Fourteenth Amendment's Due Process Clause incorporated the Sixth Amendment right to counsel, thereby making it applicable to the states. *Escobedo*'s "focus of the investigation test" became largely irrelevant in the wake of *Miranda v. Arizona*'s ruling regarding custodial interrogations, which focused on the Fifth Amendment's Self-Incrimination Clause in the wake of that clause being held to apply to the states through the Fourteenth Amendment in *Malloy v. Hogan*, 378 U.S. 1 (1964). Still, *Escobedo* established the notion that the Sixth Amendment also has a role in "shield[ing] the individual, after formal accusation, from the more knowledgeable and skilled forces of the prosecution" (Ruebner 1994: 545).

Miranda v. Arizona

Two years after *Escobedo* was decided, the U.S. Supreme Court shifted its approach to confessions yet again, this time focusing on the Fifth Amendment's privilege against self-incrimination.

> In the landmark decision of *Miranda v. Arizona*, 384 U.S. 436, 467–68 (1966), the Court recognized that custodial interrogations, by their very nature, generate "compelling pressures which work to undermine the individual's will to resist and to compel him to speak where he would not otherwise do so freely." To combat the inherent pressures of the interrogation room and thereby protect the privilege against self-incrimination, the *Miranda* Court mandated that law enforcement officers follow certain procedural safeguards. These safeguards require that prior to custodial interrogation, law enforcement officers advise the suspect of his rights to remain silent and to have an attorney present during questioning. Unless the prosecution can demonstrate compliance with these safeguards, it is prohibited from using statements elicited from a suspect during custodial interrogation. *Miranda*'s requirement that suspects be warned of their right to have counsel present during questioning, in effect, has created a Fifth Amendment right to counsel during pre-indictment custodial interrogation that is distinct from the right to counsel assured by the Sixth Amendment. (Kuller 1986: 259–60).

The U.S. Supreme Court's opinion in *Miranda v. Arizona* encompassed three other cases, all of which dealt with the admissibility of statements obtained from a person subjected to custodial police interrogation. All four cases shared the features of incommunicado interrogation—questioning of a person cut off from the rest of the world in a police-dominated atmosphere—resulting in self-incriminating statements without ever having been warned of constitutional rights.

In the *Miranda* opinion, the Court reviewed the facts in each of the four cases and condemned specific police interrogation techniques as prescribed in police manuals:

> It is obvious that such an interrogation environment is created for no purpose other than to subjugate the individual to the will of his examiner. This atmosphere carries its own badge of intimidation. To be sure, this is not physical intimidation, but it is equally destructive of human dignity. The current practice of incommunicado interrogation is at odds with one of our Nation's most cherished principles—that the individual may not be compelled to incriminate himself. Unless adequate protective devices are employed to dispel the compulsion inherent in custodial surroundings, no statement obtained from the defendant can truly be the product of his free choice. 384 U.S. at 457–58.

The Court then established procedural safeguards to protect the privilege against self-incrimination—the familiar *Miranda* warnings:

> [W]hen an individual is taken into custody or otherwise deprived of his freedom by the authorities in any significant way and is subjected to questioning, the privilege against self-incrimination is jeopardized. Procedural safeguards must be employed to protect the privilege and unless other fully effective means are adopted to notify the person of his right of silence and to assure that the exercise of the right will be scrupulously honored, the following measures are required. *He must be warned prior to any question that he has the right to remain silent, that anything he says can be used against him in a court of law, that he has the right to the presence of an attorney, and that if he cannot afford an attorney one will be appointed for him prior to any questioning if he so desires.* Opportunity to exercise these rights must be afforded to him throughout the interrogation. After such warnings have been given, and such opportunity afforded him, the individual may knowingly and intelligently waive these rights and agree to answer questions or make a statement. But unless and until such warnings and waiver are demonstrated by the prosecution at trial no evidence obtained as a result of interrogation can be used against him.
> 384 U.S. at 478–79 (emphasis added).

No additional warnings are required. Hence, the suspect has no right to be informed of the charges against him or her at the time of arrest or during any custodial interrogation. *United States v. Clenney*, 631 F.3d 658 (4th Cir. 2011).

Shortly after the *Miranda* decision, in 1968, Congress enacted 18 U.S.C. Section 3501, which conditioned the admissibility of a suspect's statement made during custodial interrogation only on its voluntariness. Its intent was to legislatively overrule *Miranda* by statutorily returning to the due process voluntariness test. But "the government rarely invoked Section 3501 or challenged *Miranda* in court during this period" (Clymer 2002: 455). In 1999, though, a federal court of appeals relied on Section 3501 when upholding the admissibility of statements that had been voluntarily given by a suspect who had not been given *Miranda* warnings. The U.S. Supreme Court reversed, reasoning that because *Miranda* presented a constitutional rule, it could not be legislatively overruled by an act of Congress. Thus, the Court reaffirmed that *Miranda* and cases in its progeny "govern the admissibility of statements made during custodial interrogation in both state and federal courts." *Dickerson v. United States*, 530 U.S. 428, 432 (2000).

KEY POINTS

LO1

- Involuntary statements violate the constitutional guarantee of due process because they are inherently untrustworthy, unreliable, fundamentally unfair, and fail to respect a person's autonomy rights to make free and rational choices.

- The Sixth Amendment's Right to Counsel Clause has relevance in stages of criminal prosecutions before trial, including during custodial interrogations.

- To protect against the inherently coercive environment attendant to custodial interrogations, all suspects in custody must be given *Miranda* warnings before being subjected to any questioning or other forms of interrogation.

- *Miranda* warnings are constitutionally required to protect suspects' Fifth Amendment privilege against self-incrimination.

- The privilege against self-incrimination does not protect suspects from being compelled by the state to produce real or physical evidence, but only protects them from being compelled to provide testimonial evidence—that is, a communication that explicitly or implicitly relates a factual assertion or discloses information.

Continued on next page

- *Miranda* has helped professionalize the conduct of police officers and improve their interrogation techniques.

- Coercive police activity is necessary for an admission or confession to be found involuntary. If no police coercion occurred, any statement is considered voluntary, regardless of the suspect's mental or physical condition. If police coercion occurred, the voluntariness of the statement is evaluated on the basis of the totality of the circumstances surrounding the giving of the statement. Except for the use of physical violence by the police, no single fact or circumstance is solely determinative of whether the coercion overcame the defendant's will.

- Satisfaction of *Miranda* requirements is a relevant consideration in determining the voluntariness of an admission or confession, but it is not conclusive.

- Only voluntary admissions or confessions that were obtained in compliance with *Miranda* requirements are admissible in court.

Miranda's **Limitation to Testimonial Evidence** The U.S. Supreme Court has long held that the privilege against self-incrimination does not protect suspects from being compelled to produce real or physical evidence. Rather, the privilege "protects an accused only from being compelled to testify against himself, or otherwise provide the State with evidence of a testimonial or communicative nature." *Schmerber v. California*, 384 U.S. 757, 761 (1966).

"[I]n order to be testimonial, an accused's communication must itself, explicitly or implicitly, relate a factual assertion or disclose information. Only then is a person compelled to be a 'witness' against himself." *Doe v. United States*, 487 U.S. 201, 210 (1988). Accordingly, although other constitutional concerns may exist when law enforcement seeks to have a suspect produce identification or otherwise provide one's name and address, participate in a lineup, provide fingerprints, or give a voice, handwriting, breath, or blood sample, because these acts are not testimonial in nature, they raise no Fifth Amendment concerns.

In *Pennsylvania v. Muniz*, 496 U.S. 582 (1990), police arrested the defendant for driving under the influence and asked him a series of questions without giving him *Miranda* warnings. While responding, his confusion and failure to speak clearly indicated a state of drunkenness. The Court held that *Miranda* did not require suppression of the defendant's responses merely because the slurred nature of his speech was incriminating:

> Under *Schmerber* and its progeny . . . any slurring of speech and other evidence of lack of muscular coordination revealed by Muniz's responses to [the officer's] direct questions constitute nontestimonial components of those responses. Requiring a suspect to reveal the physical manner in which he articulates words, like requiring him to reveal the physical properties of the sound produced by his voice [see *United States v. Dionisio*, 410 U.S. 1 (1973)] does not, without more, compel him to provide a "testimonial" response for purposes of the privilege. 496 U.S. at 592.

The Impact of *Miranda* *Miranda* has had some palpable benefits that were not foreseen at the time the decision was rendered. For example, it has made ordinary citizens much more aware of their constitutional rights, and it has notably improved psychological interrogation methods by police (Meares and Harcourt 2001). But perhaps more important, *Miranda* helped to professionalize law enforcement.

> *Miranda* . . . effectively eradicated the last vestiges of third-degree police interrogation practices in America. The Warren Court in *Miranda* sent an unmistakable message—to police, to prosecutors, and to trial courts—that strong-arm tactics would no longer be tolerated. In the . . . decades since *Miranda* became law, American police interrogation methods have become entirely psychological in nature. To be sure, coercive practices sometimes still occur, but they appear to be exceptional. Not surprisingly, however, only rarely are confessions found to be involuntary or suppressed from evidence in trial proceedings due to police improprieties. . . . [P]olice have fashioned increasingly subtle and sophisticated interrogation techniques—such as the Behavioral Analysis Interview and the Nine-Step Method Fred Inbau and his co-authors introduced in the most recent edition of their well-known interrogation training manual—and seek to manipulate suspects

into confessing without the appearance of manipulation. . . . [T]hese techniques are more psychologically sophisticated than earlier methods. Although the Warren Court may have placed greater restraints on their behavior during custodial questioning, police have met the challenges of *Miranda* by devising increasingly clever and ingenious interrogation strategies with which to persuade suspects to confess. (Leo 1996: 669–74).

Voluntariness and Due Process After *Miranda*

Miranda works in conjunction with the due process voluntariness test. The *Miranda* decision dictates that statements obtained in violation of *Miranda* rights are not admissible even if they were otherwise made voluntarily. And, as *Miranda* recognized, "the failure to provide *Miranda* warnings in and of itself does not render a confession involuntary." *New York v. Quarles*, 467 U.S. 649, 655 n.5 (1984). However, although satisfaction of *Miranda*'s requirements is a relevant consideration in determining the voluntariness of a confession, it is not conclusive. Statements given after *Miranda* warnings may nonetheless be inadmissible if they were not given voluntarily but, rather, were coerced. *Berkemer v. McCarty*, 468 U.S. 420, 433 n.20 (1984). The following sections explore the various ways in which the due process voluntariness standard might be violated even if the technical requirements of *Miranda* are fully satisfied.

Physical Force *Brown v. Mississippi*, 297 U.S. 278 (1936), made it clear that police may not use physical force to extract a confession. That is still the law today. But law enforcement officers are authorized to use a reasonable amount of force to make an arrest, defend themselves or others, or stop a fleeing felon. What happens when police lawfully use force, Mirandize someone, and then question the suspect? Consider *United States v. Marrero*, 651 F.3d 453 (6th Cir. 2011), in which the suspect resisted arrest by punching and kicking state troopers and then attempted to flee. Troopers used Tasers to disable the defendant (see Chapter 6). Once secured, the defendant was examined by medical personnel and declined to be taken to the hospital. About thirty minutes later, officers read the defendant *Miranda* warnings. He waived his rights and ultimately confessed. Thereafter, he challenged the waiver as having being involuntarily obtained because "police questioned him when he was unable to fully and knowingly participate in any conversation due to the fact that he had been stunned with a taster multiple times during his struggle with police officers." 651 F.3d at 470. Under totality of circumstances, the court concluded that the defendant's statements were voluntary because, even though he had been stunned a dozen times, he had been given water, been offered an opportunity to rest, and been examined by medical personnel, and declined to go to the hospital. Key to the court's rationale was that the officers did not question the defendant under any coercive circumstances. The court did not, however, evaluate the continuing neuropsychological effects of having been tazed a dozen times. Consider that recent experimental research has demonstrated that being tazed even once significantly reduces a person's performance on several measures of cognitive functioning (see White, Ready, Kane, and Dario 2014). It remains to be seen how courts evaluate such studies when determining the voluntariness of statements made to police in the hours following an incident in which a suspect has been tazed.

Psychological Coercion by Police and Its Effect on Voluntariness Tactics falling shy of physical brutality have proven to be much more difficult to analyze under a due process framework. Coercive conduct by police, including some subtle forms of psychological pressures, might render a resulting confession involuntary and thus violate

522

PART IV
INTERROGATIONS,
IDENTIFICATIONS, TRIALS,
AND POST-CONVICTION
REMEDIES

of due process. The test for voluntariness of a statement was stated in *Townsend v. Sain*, 372 U.S. 293, 307–08 (1963):

> If an individual's "will was overborne" or if his confession was not "the product of a rational intellect and a free will," his confession is inadmissible because coerced. These standards are applicable whether a confession is the product of physical intimidation or psychological pressure. . . . Any questioning by police officers which, in fact, produces a confession which is not the product of a free intellect renders that confession inadmissible.

Table 13.1 summaries the kinds of police conduct that have been held to violate due process.

TABLE 13.1	Psychological Tactics That Violate Due Process	
Conduct	**Example(s)**
Threats of violence	■ In *Lam v. Kelchner*, 304 F.3d 256 (3d Cir. 2002), a statement was held to be involuntary because undercover police threatened the defendant with gang violence.
	■ A confession was excluded in *Griffin v. Strong*, 983 F.2d 1540, 1543 (10th Cir. 1993), in which a police officer told the suspect that if he did not confess, he would be placed back in the general jail population where jail inmates would "'come down and smash [his] guts all over the floor."
Other threats	■ In *People v. Phelps*, 456 N.W.2d 290 (Neb. 1990), a confession was held to be involuntary where the police officers indicated that a lack of cooperation from a sexual assault suspect would lead to a painful penile swab procedure to obtain evidence.
	■ *State v. Chavarria*, 33 P.3d 922, 927 (N.M. Ct. App. 2001), invalidated statements as involuntary when they were made after a public employee was threatened with job termination if a statement was not given to police.
	■ Threats to extend period of incarceration—including through revocation of bail bond, probation, or parole—render a statement involuntary. *E.g., United States v. Mashburn*, 406 F.3d 303, 305 (4th Cir. 2005); *State v. Tuttle*, 650 N.W.2d 20, 28–29 (S.D. 2002).
Confinement under shockingly inhumane conditions	■ *Brooks v. Florida*, 389 U.S. 413 (1967), a confession was invalidated when a suspect had been confined naked for thirty-five days in a "windowless sweatbox" that had no furnishings or facilities except for a hole in the floor. During his confinement, he was fed only small amounts of soup and water each day.
	■ In *United States v. Koch*, 552 F.2d 1216 (7th Cir. 1977), a confession was deemed involuntary when the suspect had been confined in a "boxcar" cell for six hours, during which time he had no visibility outside the cell, no hygiene, and no ability to speak with others.
Interrogation after lengthy, unnecessary delays	■ Under 18 U.S.C. Section 3501(c), a federal court may exclude a confession when the confession is made after six hours following arrest, but prior to an initial appearance or arraignment if the delay between arrest and arraignment is unreasonable in light of the means of transportation and the distance traveled to the nearest available magistrate. Several states have adopted similar provisions. *E.g., Williams v. State*, 825 A.2d 1078 (Md. 2003).
Denial of necessary medical care	■ Threats not to provide needed medical treatment unless a suspect confesses render the statements involuntary. *State v. Wright*, 587 N.E.2d 906, 910 (Ohio Ct. App. 1990).

Continued on next page

Conduct	Example(s)
	■ Continued interrogation of an injured, depressed, and medicated suspect in extreme pain while being treated in a hospital intensive care unit renders statements involuntary. *Mincey v. Arizona*, 437 U.S. 385 (1978).
Deprivations of food or sleep	■ Deprivations of food or sleep can result in a confession being found involuntary. *Greenwald v. Wisconsin,* 390 U.S. 519 (1968); *Watts v. Indiana,* 338 U.S. 49 (1949).
Relay questioning over extended periods of interrogation	■ In *Ashcraft v. Tennessee,* 322 U.S. 143 (1944), the suspect was interrogated for thirty-six hours with virtually no break, thereby depriving the suspect of any rest. The Court invalidated the confession as involuntary. *See also Davis v. North Carolina,* 384 U.S. 737 (1966).

© Cengage Learning®

Practices That Do Not Violate Due Process Courts have found the following practices insufficiently coercive to violate due process: promises of leniency, encouragement to cooperate, promises of psychological treatment, and appeal to religious beliefs.

Promises of Leniency "[A] confession is not involuntary merely because the suspect was promised leniency if he cooperated with law enforcement officials." *United States v. Guarno,* 819 F.2d 28, 31 (2d Cir. 1987); *see also United States v. Brave Heart,* 397 F.3d 1035, 1041 (8th Cir. 2005). However, an outright lie promising that someone will not be prosecuted if they confess will render a confession involuntary. *See United States v. Rogers,* 906 F.2d 189, 191 (5th Cir. 1990); *Albritton v. State,* 769 So. 2d 438, 442 (Fla. Dist. Ct. App. 2000).

Encouragement to Cooperate Encouraging a suspect's cooperation in a noncoercive manner, including telling the probable penalties, does not violate due process. *United States v. Ballard,* 586 F.2d 1060 (5th Cir. 1978).

Promises of Psychological Treatment *United States v. McClinton,* 982 F.2d 278, 283 (8th Cir. 1992), found the defendant's confession voluntary even though police "told him that he was not a bad person and that he would receive help for his drug and alcohol problems if he talked to them." *See also United States v. Barbour,* 70 F.3d 580 (11th Cir. 1995).

Appeal to Religious Beliefs In *Welch v. Butler,* 835 F.2d 92 (5th Cir. 1988), a born-again Christian police officer orchestrated and led a nearly three-hour prayer session with the suspect, during which he used his religious beliefs with respect to divine forgiveness and salvation to convince the suspect to confess. In upholding the voluntariness of the defendant's confession, the court stated that orchestrating the prayer session "set up a situation that allowed Welch to focus for some time on those concerns with a fellow Christian in the hope that his desire to be saved would lead him to confess." *See also Berghuis v. Thompkins,* 560 U.S. 370 (2010).

Trickery and Deception by Police and Their Effect on Voluntariness Police are permitted to lie to suspects during the interrogation.

"[D]eceit and subterfuge are within the 'bag of tricks' that police may use in interrogating suspects." *State v. Schumacher,* 37 P.3d 6, 13–14 (Idaho Ct. App. 2001). "[M]ere trickery alone will not necessarily invalidate a confession." *United States v. Bell,* 367 F.3d 452, 461 (5th Cir. 2004). Deception is "not alone sufficient to render a confession inadmissible." *People v. McNeil,* 711 N.Y.S.2d 518, 520 (N.Y. App. Div. 2000). The United States Supreme Court has upheld this proposition, and virtually every state has supported the Supreme Court's holding. *Frazier v. Cupp,* 394

KEY POINTS

L02 ■ The determination of whether a suspect is in custody for purposes of receiving *Miranda* protection depends on whether there is a formal arrest or restraint on freedom of movement of the degree associated with a formal arrest. The degree of force used to restrain the suspect is important to this determination.

Continued on next page

- A suspect questioned in a police station or in a correctional facility is not necessarily in custody for *Miranda* purposes if his or her freedom to depart the interview or interrogation is not restricted in any way.

- Interrogation of a person at his or her home or place of business, or in a public place, is usually held to be noncustodial so long as other indicia of arrest (e.g., handcuffs or restrictions on the person's movement) are not present.

- *Miranda* warnings are not required before general on-the-scene questioning about the facts surrounding a crime, or other general questioning of citizens in the fact-finding process.

- *Miranda* warnings are not required in connection with the ordinary *Terry*-type investigative stop and the ordinary traffic stop, because these stops are noncustodial.

- Police interrogation of a person after the person has summoned the police or otherwise initiated the conversation is usually found to be noncustodial.

U.S. 731 (1969). Indeed, it is rather stunning to see the enormous number of cases in which confessions were held to be valid. Yet, judges found that government officials lied to defendants about significant matters resulting in incriminating statements. Police have lied about matters such as the following: witnesses against the defendant, earlier statements by a now-deceased victim, an accomplice's willingness to testify, whether the victim had survived an assault, "scientific" evidence available, including DNA and fingerprint evidence, and the degree to which the investigating officer identified and sympathized with the defendant. For the Supreme Court Justices and judges throughout the nation, no matter the nature of the deception, with one major exception, the issue relates entirely to whether the lies "tend to produce inherently unreliable statements." *Sheriff v. Bessey*, 914 P.2d 618, 622 (Nev. 1996). Or, as another court stated, whether the "police misrepresentations . . . [are] sufficiently egregious to overcome a defendant's will so as to render a confession involuntary." *State v. Buntin*, 51 P.3d 37, 42 (Utah Ct. App. 2002). (Marcus 2006: 612–13).

In spite of the general proposition that police may use trickery or deceit during interviews and interrogations, some ruses can go too far.

- Verbal misrepresentations appear to be fair game, but the manufacture of false evidence is viewed by courts as having crossed an impermissible line for due process purposes. *State v. Patton*, 826 A.2d 783 (N.J. Super. App. Div. 2003), for example, ruled a confession involuntary when the suspect was presented with an audiotape of an alleged eyewitness when the voice was actually that of a police officer. *State v. Cayward*, 552 So. 2d 971 (Fla. Dist. Ct. App. 1989), invalidated a confession made after police presented the suspect with a fake lab report matching the suspect's DNA to crime scene evidence.

- Lies about law and its processes, especially those that falsely promise suspects that they will be released if they confess, violate due process. Similarly, lies about the severity of the crime can render a confession involuntary, especially when police imply someone will not be charged with a homicide because a victim lives when, in fact, the victim is actually deceased. *State v. Ritter*, 485 S.E.2d 492 (Ga. 1997).

The Effect of Particular Personal Characteristics of Suspects on Voluntariness Courts also examine the personal characteristics of defendants in determining the voluntariness of an admission or confession. Some of the characteristics considered important are age; mental capacity; education level; physical or mental impairment from illness, injury, or intoxication; and experience in dealing with the police. However, the U.S. Supreme Court said that these personal characteristics are "relevant only in establishing a setting in which actual coercion might have been exerted to overcome the will of the suspect." *Procunier v. Atchley*, 400 U.S. 446, 453–54 (1971). This principle was elaborated upon in *Colorado v. Connelly*, 479 U.S. 157 (1986).

[W]hile mental condition is surely relevant to an individual's susceptibility to police coercion, mere examination of the confessant's state of mind can never conclude the due process inquiry. . . . [C]oercive police activity is a necessary predicate to the finding that a confession is not "voluntary" within the meaning of the Due Process Clause of the Fourteenth Amendment. 479 U.S. at 165–67 (emphasis added).

State courts may provide greater protection than the U.S. Constitution with respect to determining the voluntariness of a confession. For example, *State v. Rees*, 748 A.2d 976

(Me. 2000), found that because the defendant suffered from dementia, his statements to police officers were not the product of the free exercise of his will and rational intellect. The court stressed that there was no finding of improper or incorrect conduct on the part of the police. The decision pointed out that the determination that the defendant's dementia rendered him incapable of making a voluntary statement under the circumstances was based not on the Fifth or Fourteenth Amendment, but the Maine Constitution.

The Fifth Amendment Self-Incrimination Approach: Applying *Miranda*

Miranda requires that specific warnings be given to suspects subject to custodial interrogation, regardless of whether the police are investigating a felony or a misdemeanor. The Supreme Court defined the term *custodial interrogation* as "questioning initiated by law enforcement officers after a person has been taken into custody or otherwise deprived of his freedom of action in any significant way." *Miranda*, 384 U.S. at 444. Although the rule seems straightforward enough, a number of issues arise in cases regarding the application of *Miranda* that typically hinge on the meaning of four terms: *custody, interrogation, warning*, and *waiver*. Before exploring the meanings of each of these terms, it should be emphasized that *Miranda* warnings technically do not need to be given until custodial interrogation begins. Police are well advised, however, to provide all suspects their *Miranda* warnings upon taking them into custody, even if they do not intend to question a suspect right away. This may help to ensure that any custodial statement will be admissible in court.

Custody

The definition of custody is commonly stated as a question: would a reasonable person in the suspect's position have felt free "to terminate the interrogation and leave"? *Thompson v. Keohane*, 516 U.S. 99, 112 (1995). But the "free to leave" test has been called into question by other Supreme Court decisions that focus instead on the indicia of arrest. Regardless of the somewhat inconsistent ways in which the question is phrased, courts attempt to answer the question of custody by considering the totality of the circumstances surrounding the questioning of a suspect from the viewpoint of a reasonable person who is "neither guilty of criminal conduct and thus overly apprehensive nor insensitive to the seriousness of the circumstances." *United States v. Bengivenga*, 845 F.2d 593, 596 (5th Cir. 1988).

The circumstances that are typically evaluated when trying to determine whether a suspect has been in "custody" include the following criteria:

- the degree of restraint or force used to physically detain the suspect;
- the location of the encounter and whether it was familiar to the suspect or at least neutral or public;
- the number of officers questioning the suspect;
- the duration and character of the interrogation, including the degree of psychological coercion used to detain the individual;
- the language used to summon the suspect;
- the extent to which the suspect is confronted with evidence of guilt; and
- whether the suspect initiated contact with the police.

Other factors may be relevant in any particular case, and no one factor is determinative of the issue. Some factors, however, that may be relevant for determining the voluntariness of a confession may not be relevant to determinations of whether someone is in custody for

526

PART IV
INTERROGATIONS,
IDENTIFICATIONS, TRIALS,
AND POST-CONVICTION
REMEDIES

Miranda purposes. For example, in *Yarborough v. Alvarado*, 541 U.S. 652 (2004), the Supreme Court held that courts should not consider a person's experience with the police when examining the question of custody. The lower court in the case had suppressed a confession given by a seventeen-year-old defendant. It reasoned that a juvenile is more likely to feel he is not free to leave a police station during questioning than an adult would be. But in reversing the lower court, the Supreme Court determined that requiring police to consider the individual characteristics of a suspect when determining the issue of custody would transform what is supposed to be an objective test into a subjective one that would be more difficult for officers to understand and apply to the facts of any given case. Accordingly, law enforcement personnel, and courts reviewing their actions, are required only to balance the objective indicia of custody against those that indicate that there was no custody.

Prior to *Alvarado*, nearly all jurisdictions that had addressed the issue of whether juvenile status may be relevant to the *Miranda* custody determination held that juvenile status was a proper consideration. *E.g.*, *A.M. v. Butler*, 360 F.3d 787 (7th Cir. 2004); *People v. Braggs*, 810 N.E.2d 472 (Ill. 2004). After *Alvarado*, some state and federal courts continued to consider age, either as a factor in the "totality of the circumstances" review or by analyzing whether a "reasonable juvenile" would have felt free to terminate the interview. *See Murray v. Earle*, 405 F.3d 278 (5th Cir. 2005); *In re C.H.*, 763 N.W.2d 708 (Neb. 2009). Other courts concluded that *Alvarado* prohibited consideration of a juvenile suspect's age in a *Miranda* custody analysis. *E.g.*, *In re J.F.* 987 A.2d 1168 (D.C. 2010); *In re C.S.C.*, 118 P.3d 970 (Wyo. 2005). This disagreement prompted the U.S. Supreme Court to decide *J.D.B. v. North Carolina*, 131 S. Ct. 2394 (2011).

On the afternoon of September 29, 2005, a uniformed police officer removed J.D.B., a thirteen-year-old, special education student, from his seventh-grade social studies class. He was escorted to a conference room in his middle school where three adults—two school officials and another police officer—were waiting. The door to the conference room was then closed, and police questioned J.D.B. about some neighborhood break-ins in which he was a suspect.

North Carolina law requires that juveniles under the age of fourteen be informed of their *Miranda* rights and also that they have the right to have a parent or guardian present during questioning. Yet the officers who interrogated J.D.B. never told him that he had the right to remain silent, that he was free to leave at any time, or that he could have a family member present during questioning. At one point, the assistant principal told J.D.B. that he should "do the right thing because the truth always comes out in the end." J.D.B. then incriminated himself when he asked whether he would "still be in trouble" if he returned the stolen items. One of the police officers replied that "it would be helpful," but that "this thing is going to court . . . what's done is done." The officer then told J.D.B. that if he was going to continue breaking into people's houses, he "would have to look at getting a secure custody order" that would result in J.D.B. being "sent to juvenile detention before court." Only at that point did the officer tell J.D.B. that he did not have to talk to him and that he could leave if he wanted to, but he hoped J.D.B. "would listen to what [the officer] had to say." J.D.B. then confessed to the breaking and enterings and larcenies and wrote a written statement. Afterward, J.D.B. was permitted to ride the school bus home. Another officer was waiting for J.D.B. when he got off the school bus. When another officer then arrived with a search warrant based on J.D.B.'s confession, he took the officers into his residence and gave them the stolen items. No one attempted to contact J.D.B.'s guardian before the search of the home and seizure of the stolen items.

The U.S. Supreme Court ruled that a minor's age properly informs *Miranda*'s custody analysis under the totality of the circumstances because children's ability to withstand coercion markedly differs from those of adults. The Court explained:

> [S]o long as the child's age was known to the officer at the time of the interview, or would have been objectively apparent to a reasonable officer, including age as part of the custody analysis requires officers neither to consider circumstances

"unknowable" to them, . . . nor to "anticipat[e] the frailties or idiosyncrasies" of the particular suspect being questioned." . . . [Moreover, this] does not mean that a child's age will be a determinative, or even a significant, factor in every case, but it is a reality that courts cannot ignore. 131 S. Ct. at 2406.

The following sections explore in more detail the other objective criteria that courts use to make this determination under the totality of the circumstances.

The Degree of Physical Restraint or Force Used to Physically Detain a Suspect An absence of physical restraint and the lack of any use of force are indicative of a noncustodial interrogation. *United States v. Plumman*, 409 F.3d 919 (8th Cir. 2005). Conversely, curtailing a person's freedom of movement in a manner or to a degree that it is the functional equivalent of arrest indicates custody. *Stansbury v. California*, 511 U.S. 318 (1994). The clearest example of such a functional equivalent of arrest is physical restraint of the suspect, such as handcuffing. Of course, a person can be restrained without being in handcuffs. If, for example, an officer holds a gun on a suspect, the officer clearly creates a custodial situation. *United States v. Shareef*, 100 F.3d 1491 (10th Cir. 1996).

Not all physical restraints of a suspect, however, will give rise to a finding of custody. If someone other than a law enforcement officer restrains a person, the restraint does not constitute custody for *Miranda* purposes. For example, in *Wilson v. Coon*, 808 F.2d 688 (8th Cir. 1987), a brief restraint of the defendant by a medical technician for medical purposes was held not to constitute custody.

The Location of the Encounter The place of interrogation is an important but not necessarily conclusive factor in determining custody for *Miranda* purposes. As a rule, interrogation in public places such as stores, restaurants, bars, streets, and sidewalks is usually considered noncustodial because people are in such locations by personal choice, are not isolated from the outside world, and rarely present a police-dominated atmosphere. Table 13.2 summarizes the indicia of custody at common nonpublic locations.

TABLE 13.2	The Role of Location in Determining Custody	
Location	**Indicia of Custodial Finding**	**Indicia of Noncustodial Finding**
Police stations	Stationhouse questioning of suspects is the most police-dominated of environments and thus is one of the most inherently intimidating atmospheres in which someone may be questioned by police.	Whether the suspect voluntarily agreed to go to the police station to be questioned. Even if the police transport a suspect to a stationhouse, if the suspect volunteered to go with police after being told they were not under arrest, then the questioning is likely to be considered noncustodial. *E.g., Mason v. Mitchell,* 320 F.3d 604 (6th Cir. 2003).
Prisons and jails	Incarceration alone is insufficient to constitute custody for *Miranda* purposes. *Howes v. Fields,* 132 S. Ct. 1181 (2012). Custody in this context depends on a change in the surroundings of a prisoner, which results in an added imposition on his freedom of movement such as being handcuffed, shackled, or put in an interview room from which the inmate is not permitted to leave. *E.g., United States v. Chamberlain,* 163 F.3d 499 (8th Cir. 1998).	An inmate was not "in custody" for *Miranda* purposes when he voluntarily agreed to questioning conducted in an unlocked room of a correctional facility, and was told he could leave the room at any time. *United States v. Menzer,* 29 F.3d 1223 (7th Cir. 1994). A lack of *Miranda* custody was also found in *Howes v. Fields,* 132 S. Ct. 1181 (2012), in which the defendant was escorted from his cell and interviewed in a well-lit prison conference room for more than five hours by armed deputies who sometimes used a very sharp tone and profanity. The fact that he was never physically restrained, was offered food and water, and was told he could leave and return to his cell at any time was key to the Court's decision.

Continued on next page

Location	Indicia of Custodial Finding	Indicia of Noncustodial Finding
Homes	When someone's freedom of movement in their home has been significantly restrained, then questioning a suspect in his or her home may become custodial. For example, *United States v. Madoch*, 149 F.3d 596 (7th Cir. 1998), determined a suspect was in custody because agents rushed into the home, ordered the suspect into the kitchen and told her not to leave the room, answer the phone, or attend to her six-month-old baby without being escorted by an agent.	Ordinarily, interrogation of a person in his or her home is noncustodial because the person is in familiar surroundings and there is no police-dominated atmosphere. However, if police turn a home into a police-dominated environment, an interrogation might be deemed custodial. For example, *Orozco v. Texas*, 394 U.S. 324 (1969), upheld a custody finding when a suspect was questioned at 4:00 A.M. in his bedroom by four officers.
Places of business	When a suspect's freedom of movement at work has been significantly restrained, such as when placed in a closely confined area and confronted by police, then questioning a suspect at work home may become custodial. *United States v. Steele*, 648 F. Supp. 1375 (N.D. Ind. 1986).	Interrogation at a suspect's place of business is usually noncustodial because it represents familiar surroundings. *United States v. Venerable*, 807 F.2d 745 (8th Cir. 1986).
Hospitals	When a suspect is brought to the hospital by police and is not "free to leave" because the suspect is handcuffed, then such a hospital-based detention is likely to be held to be custodial for *Miranda* purposes. *State v. Lescard*, 517 A.2d 1158 (N.H. 1986)	Custody is not established because a suspect is unable to leave the hospital due to his or her medical condition because a hospital setting lacks a compelling atmosphere, questioning is routine, and the suspect, although confined, is not confined by the police. *E.g.*, *State v. Pontbriand*, 878 A.2d 227 (Vt. 2005).
Crime scenes	*Miranda* specifically stated that "general on-the-scene questioning as to facts surrounding a crime or other general questioning of citizens in the fact-finding process" is not an indicator of custody. 384 U.S. at 477.	When someone is restrained at a crime scene to a degree associated with formal arrest—such as when a suspect is handcuffed—such restraint indicates custody for *Miranda* purposes. *United States v. Horton*, 490 F. Supp. 2d 1161 (D. Kan. 2007).

© Cengage Learning®

The Number of Officers Questioning the Suspect The more police officers present at the scene of questioning, the more complete the police control is over the interrogation environment, a factor indicating that a suspect was in custody. *Sprosty v. Buchler*, 79 F.3d 635, 643 (7th Cir.), *cert. denied*, 519 U.S. 854 (1996), for example, determined a suspect was in custody for *Miranda* purposes because five officers dominated the scene in which he was questioned. The entire encounter lasted for nearly three hours, during which four officers searched the defendant's mobile home and a fifth "armed officer was exclusively occupied with guarding" the defendant. The same number of officers questioning a suspect in *United States v. Quinn*, 815 F.2d 153, 154–56 (1st Cir. 1987), however, was determined to be noncustodial when the questioning lasted for only twenty-five minutes while outside on the suspect's driveway. Thus, the number of officers present is clearly only one of many factors to be considered when applying the totality-of-the-circumstances test for custody.

The Duration and Character of the Interrogation

Focus of the Investigation *Miranda* is generally understood to have abandoned the "focus of investigation" test of *Escobedo* to determine when an interrogated suspect is entitled to warnings. *Beckwith v. United States,* 425 U.S. 341 (1976), specifically held that even though a suspect is clearly the focus of a criminal investigation, the suspect need not be given *Miranda* warnings if he or she is not otherwise in custody or deprived of freedom of action in any significant way. The focus concept may still have some vitality, however, as one of the circumstances to be considered in determining the custody issue, but only if an officer's views or beliefs are somehow manifested to the person under interrogation and affect how a reasonable person in that position perceives his or her freedom to leave:

> An officer's knowledge or beliefs may bear upon the custody issue if they are conveyed, by word or deed, to the individual being questioned. . . . Those beliefs are relevant only to the extent they would affect how a reasonable person in the position of the individual being questioned would gauge the breadth of his or her "freedom of action." . . . Even a clear statement from an officer that the person under interrogation is a prime suspect is not, in itself, dispositive of the custody issue, for some suspects are free to come and go until the police decide to make an arrest. The weight and pertinence of any communications regarding the officer's degree of suspicion will depend upon the facts and circumstances of the particular case. *Stansbury v. California*, 511 U.S. 318, 325 (1994).

Investigative and Traffic Stops The ordinary *Terry*-type investigative stop and the ordinary traffic stop are noncustodial for purposes of *Miranda* and do not require the administration of *Miranda* warnings due to their brief and public nature. *Berkemer v. McCarty*, 468 U.S. 420 (1984). This is true even in traffic stops involving the investigation of driving under the influence. *Pennsylvania v. Bruder*, 488 U.S. 9 (1988).

Time of Interrogation The hour at which an interrogation takes place may also be an important factor to determining if someone is in custody for *Miranda* purposes. Questioning conducted during business hours is less likely to be considered custodial than is an interrogation conducted in the late evening or early morning. For example, the fact that questioning took place at 4:00 A.M., even though it occurred at the suspect's home, was a significant reason for the Supreme Court decision that the interrogation was determined to be custodial in the *Orozco* case (see earlier discussion under "Homes").

Duration of Interrogation "Relay" interrogations that last for hours are likely to indicate that the suspect was in custody, especially if the suspect was denied food, water, bathroom breaks, or rest during a so-called marathon questioning session. Such tactics, as discussed earlier, may also violate due process. *Davis v. North Carolina*, 384 U.S. 737 (1966); *Ashcraft v. Tennessee*, 322 U.S. 143 (1944).

Presence of Other Persons *Miranda* expressly indicated a concern for the suspect who is "cut off from the outside world." 384 U.S. at 445. Therefore, an interrogation of a suspect conducted in the presence of family, friends, or neutral persons is likely to be considered noncustodial. *People v. Butterfield*, 65 Cal. Rptr. 765 (Cal. App. 1968). Likewise, deliberately removing a suspect from the presence of family, friends, and others is indicative of custody. *United States v. Griffin*, 922 F.2d 1343 (8th Cir. 1990) held that a suspect was in custody in his home when police sent his parents away and did not allow the suspect to leave the room in which he was being questioned unescorted by police.

Probation Interviews A probationer, although subject to a number of restrictive conditions governing various aspects of life, is not in custody for purposes of *Miranda* simply by reason of the probationer status. A probation interview, unlike a custodial arrest, is arranged by appointment at a mutually convenient time and is conducted in familiar, nonintimidating surroundings. It does not become custodial for *Miranda* purposes because the probation officer could compel attendance and truthful answers at the interview. *Minnesota v. Murphy*, 465 U.S. 420 (1984).

LO2
LO3

- Interrogation, for purposes of *Miranda*, refers not only to express questioning but also to any words or actions on the part of police (other than those normally attendant to arrest and custody) that the police should know are reasonably likely to elicit an incriminating response from the suspect.

- An incriminating response is any response, whether inculpatory or exculpatory, that the prosecution may seek to introduce at trial.

- Routine questions regarding a suspect's name, address, height, weight, eye color, date of birth, and age (to complete booking or other pretrial procedures) are not considered interrogation for purposes of *Miranda*; incriminating statements made in response to such questions are admissible.

- Questions asked by law enforcement officers in an emergency situation that poses a threat to public safety do not have to be preceded by *Miranda* warnings.

- *Miranda* warning requirements apply only to custodial interrogations conducted by law enforcement officers and not to questioning by private citizens.

LO4

- If, after receiving *Miranda* warnings, a person clearly and unambiguously invokes the right to remain silent, the interrogation must cease. Similarly, if the person clearly and unambiguously requests an attorney, the interrogation must cease until an attorney is present or, alternatively, until there is at least a fourteen-day break in *Miranda* custody.

- Generally, a second custodial interrogation of a person who has exercised the *Miranda* right of silence is permissible after a lapse

Continued on next page

Execution of Search Warrants In the absence of other factors indicating custody such as physical restraint, a person who is detained "during the execution of a search warrant is normally not in custody for *Miranda* purposes." *United States v. Saadeh*, 61 F.3d 510, 520 (7th Cir. 1995); *see also Michigan v. Summers*, 452 U.S. 692 (1981). In *United States v. Bennett*, 329 F.3d 769 (10th Cir. 2003), police initially used firearms to subdue and then handcuff a defendant who was home at the time of the execution of a search warrant. But once they searched him for weapons and found none, the police removed the handcuffs and told the suspect he was not under arrest. He then voluntarily agreed to go with police to a stationhouse for questioning, even though he had been told that he did not need to go with police. In ruling on the admissibility of statements the suspect made during the interrogation, the court discounted the initial use of firearms and handcuffs because, at the time he was questioned, his "freedom of action was not 'curtailed to a degree associated with formal arrest.'" 329 F.3d 775.

In contrast, *United States v. Kim*, 292 F.3d 969 (9th Cir. 2002), found that the defendant was in custody when she was questioned during the search of a store given other indicia of the functional equivalent of arrest. Not only did the police control over the store during the search create a police-dominated environment, but also the police treatment of the defendant would have led any reasonable person to feel as if he or she were under arrest. For one thing, the defendant was locked in the store and, therefore, was not free to leave. Also, the defendant's husband and another relative tried to join her in the store, but police kept them apart, thereby physically isolating her "from two family members who could have provided both moral support and, given her limited English, a more complete understanding of the overall situation." 292 F.3d at 977.

The Language Used to Summon the Suspect The language used by police to summon a suspect can be an ambiguous factor. Language is generally relevant to custody determinations only to the extent that language communicates custody or coercion. For example, when police tell a suspect, "You're under arrest," or "Stay here and don't move," such language unambiguously indicates that the suspect is in custody. But what if an officer were to say, "You should not leave. If you know what's good for you, you will stay and tell me everything I want to know"? (Swift 2006: 1093). The same is true for language that communicates coercion.

The language used to summon someone for questioning is particularly important in cases in which the person being questioned was an inmate in a jail or prison. For example, in *Arthur v. State*, 575 So. 2d 1165, 1189 (Ala. Ct. Crim. App. 1990), the court found that a detainee at a correctional work release center was in custody for *Miranda* purposes when he had been summoned by his shift supervisor and questioned by him concerning a discrepancy in the inmate's reported work hours and the earnings he reported to correctional authorities. However, when inmates are told that they do not need to speak with the officials seeking to question them, or that they are "free" to leave the interrogation and return to their normal routine within the correctional facility, courts usually find that any statements made during such questioning were noncustodial. *State v. Owen*, 510 N.W.2d 503 (Neb. Ct. App. 1993).

The Extent to Which the Suspect Is Confronted with Evidence of Guilt Police coercion in a law enforcement–dominated environment can give rise to a finding that a suspect was in custody. Psychological pressure can be so intense that it creates an atmosphere of coercion constituting custody for *Miranda* purposes. In *United States v. Beraun-Panez*, 812

F.2d 578 (9th Cir. 1987), the police separated the defendant from his co-worker in a remote rural location. During this time they repeatedly accused him of lying, confronted him with false or misleading witness statements, and employed good cop–bad cop interrogation tactics. They also put the defendant in fear of deportation, consistently "insisting on the 'truth' until he told them what they sought," thereby establishing "a setting from which a reasonable person would believe that he or she was not free to leave." 812 F.2d at 580.

A similar finding of custody was made in the following case:

> [T]he agents appeared at Hanson's door eight months after the arson attempt, awakened him, and asked him to accompany them to the field station in their vehicle to look at photos. Hanson did not initiate contact with the agents. . . . He traveled to the field station in the locked back seat of the government truck. Once in the isolated office in the field station, Hanson was told that he was a suspect in the arson attempt, that he was not under arrest, and that he was free to leave. Hanson [however] was dependent upon the agents to find his way out of the building and back to his home. Hanson was with the agents for three hours. . . . The agents wanted a confession from Hanson, and it appears that they deliberately waited until they had the suspect in an intimidating environment before they advised him of their true purpose for bringing him to the station. . . . A reasonable person in Hanson's position would not have believed that he was free to the leave the field office unhindered by the agents. Upon consideration of the totality of the circumstances, we find that substantial evidence and law support the finding that Hanson was in custody when the agents questioned him, and that he should have received the *Miranda* warnings. *United States v. Hanson*, 237 F.3d 961, 965 (8th Cir. 2001).

Whether the Suspect Initiated Contact with the Police If a suspect summons the police or initiates the interview, or both, a court is likely to hold a subsequent interrogation noncustodial. In *United States v. Jonas*, 786 F.2d 1019 (11th Cir. 1986), for instance, the defendant learned indirectly that an FBI agent wanted to contact him. He called the agent, agreed to talk with the FBI, and appeared voluntarily at FBI offices. The interview was held to be noncustodial.

Interrogation

The *Miranda* requirements apply only if a person in custody is subjected to interrogation. In the *Miranda* context, *interrogation* is a broad term that encompasses more than express questioning. It includes any statements that are reasonably likely to elicit an incriminating response from the viewpoint of the reasonable perceptions of a suspect. The Supreme Court has defined an "incriminating response" as "any response—whether inculpatory or exculpatory—that the prosecution may seek to introduce at trial." *Rhode Island v. Innis*, 446 U.S. 291, 302 n.5 (1980).

Rhode Island v. Innis involved a murder suspect who had been taken into custody by the police. After he was given *Miranda* warnings, he invoked his right to counsel. While transporting the defendant, the police asked him no direct questions. However, they did talk among themselves about how unfortunate it was that they did not find the murder weapon in the case, because the crime scene was near a school for children with disabilities. One officer said to another, "[T]here's a lot of handicapped children running around in this area, and God forbid one of them might find a weapon with shells and they might hurt themselves." Another officer responded: "[I]t would be too bad if a little girl would pick up the gun, maybe kill herself." 446 U.S. 294–95. At that point, the suspect interrupted the police officers' conversation and told them that he would show them where he had hidden the gun.

of a significant time period, if the person's right to terminate questioning at the first interrogation was scrupulously honored, fresh *Miranda* warnings are given, and no pressure to cooperate or other illegal tactics are used.

■ When the Fifth Amendment right to counsel under *Miranda* is invoked during custodial interrogation, police may not interrogate the defendant further without counsel present unless the defendant initiates further communication with the police. If the defendant initiates further communication, interrogation may proceed if the defendant makes a voluntary, knowing, and intelligent waiver of the right to counsel and the right to silence.

■ If an initial statement was obtained in violation of *Miranda*, but without coercion or other illegal means to break the defendant's will, a subsequent statement obtained after the administration of a valid set of warnings followed by a knowing, intelligent, voluntary waiver of *Miranda* rights is admissible.

532

PART IV
INTERROGATIONS,
IDENTIFICATIONS, TRIALS,
AND POST-CONVICTION
REMEDIES

A unanimous Supreme Court held that *Miranda* was implicated even though the police did not directly question the suspect.

> We conclude that the *Miranda* safeguards come into play *whenever a person in custody is subjected to either express questioning or its functional equivalent.* That is to say, the term "interrogation" under *Miranda* refers not only to express questioning, but also to any words or actions on the part of the police (other than those normally attendant to arrest and custody) that the police should know are reasonably likely to elicit an incriminating response from the suspect. The latter portion of this definition focuses primarily upon the perceptions of the suspect, rather than the intent of the police. This focus reflects the fact that the *Miranda* safeguards were designed to vest a suspect in custody with an added measure of protection against coercive police practices, without regard to objective proof of the underlying intent of the police. 446 U.S. at 300–01 (italics added).

However, a divided court decided that the officers' conversation in *Innis* was not the functional equivalent of interrogation and, therefore, that his incriminating statements as to where he had hidden the gun were admissible.

The "Functional Equivalent" of Interrogation The following cases illustrate situations in which courts have found the actions of police to constitute the functional equivalent of interrogation: coached lineups, reverse lineups, and psychiatric examinations.

Coached Lineups In *Innis*, the Supreme Court said that "the use of lineups in which a coached witness would pick the defendant as the perpetrator" would constitute the functional equivalent of interrogation. 446 U.S. at 299. It so reasoned because the practice was "designed to establish that the defendant was in fact guilty as a predicate for further interrogation." 446 U.S. at 299.

Reverse Lineups The *Innis* Court also said that the use of reverse lineups was the functional equivalent of interrogation. A reverse lineup is a practice "in which a defendant would be identified by coached witnesses as the perpetrator of a fictitious crime, with the object of inducing him to confess to the actual crime of which he was suspected in order to escape the false prosecution." 446 U.S. at 299. A variation on reverse lineups was also held to be the functional equivalent of interrogation in *In re Durand*, 293 N.W.2d 383 (Neb. 1980), a case in which the police showed the suspect police reports of other crimes to which they did not believe the suspect to be connected. The court stated that the officers "should have known that showing the defendant the police reports was likely to elicit an incriminating response from the defendant." 293 N.W.2d at 420.

Psychiatric Examinations In *Estelle v. Smith*, 451 U.S. 454 (1981), the Supreme Court held that psychiatric examinations constitute interrogations for *Miranda* purposes because the responses to the questions asked of the defendant during such an examination could be introduced at trial against the defendant. *Miranda* warnings, however, are not required before compulsory psychiatric examinations if the testimony is intended for use in the determination of whether a juvenile is competent to stand trial as an adult. *See United States v. Juvenile Male*, 554 F.3d 456 (4th Cir. 2009).

Certain Psychological Ploys May or May Not Be "Functional" Interrogation The *Innis* Court also mentioned the use of certain psychological ploys "such as to 'posi[t] the guilt of the subject,' to 'minimize the moral seriousness of the offense,' and 'to cast blame on the victim or on society'" as being "techniques of persuasion, no less than express questioning," that are the functional equivalent of interrogation in a custodial setting. 446 U.S. at 299. But determining which psychological ploys that posit the guilt of the suspect are the functional equivalents of interrogation and which ones are not has proven to be a tricky venture.

These psychological ploys are considered to be the *functional equivalent of interrogation*: seeking a suspect's "cooperation," making pleas or directives to conscience, implying blame, confronting a suspect with evidence, and confronting a suspect with an accomplice.

Seeking a Suspect's "Cooperation" Asking a suspect to cooperate in the investigation and implying that such cooperation would be beneficial to the suspect is the functional equivalent of interrogation because it is likely to elicit an incriminating response. This is especially true in cases in which police suggest that it is the "last chance" or "only chance" for a suspect to cooperate or to tell the suspect's side of the story. *E.g., United States v. Padilla*, 387 F.3d 1087 (9th Cir. 2004).

Making Pleas or Directives to the Conscience Pleading with a suspect to "tell the truth" or "come clean" (or commanding the suspect to do so) is the functional equivalent of interrogation. *E.g., United States v. Tyler,* 164 F.3d 150 (3d Cir. 1998).

Implying Blame In *United States v. Rambo,* 365 F.3d 906 (10th Cir. 2004), policing began a discussion with the suspect by telling him "that much of the blame will fall on [his] shoulders." The court ruled this was the very type of ploy that posits the guilt of the suspect that *Innis* specified would constitute the functional equivalent of interrogation.

Confronting Suspect with Evidence Following *Innis*, most courts consider confronting a suspect with evidence of guilt to be the functional equivalent of interrogation. For example, in *Drury v. State*, 793 A.2d 567, *cert. denied*, 537 U.S. 942 (2002), an officer was investigating a burglary at a local convenience store in which some adult magazines, cigarettes, liquor, and lottery tickets were stolen. A tire iron that was used to pry open the door to the store was recovered from the inside of the store. A tip led the officer to call the defendant in for questioning. Once the suspect was in the stationhouse, and without having administered any *Miranda* warnings, the officer put the tire iron and a trash bag containing the stolen magazines on a table in front of the suspect. The officer then told the suspect that the evidence would be tested for fingerprints. In response, the suspect offered reasons why his fingerprint would be on both the tire iron and the magazines, making incriminating statements in the process. The court ruled that the officer had engaged in the functional equivalent of interrogation because the officer must have known that his conduct would be likely to elicit an incriminating response from the suspect.

It should be noted, however, that courts differentiate "confronting" a suspect with evidence against him or her from merely "informing" the person of such evidence. For example, in *State v. Bragg*, 48 A.3d 769 (Me. 2012), the Supreme Judicial Court of Maine ruled that an officer's statement to defendant that her breath test result was 0.13% blood alcohol content, and that presumptive level of intoxication in Maine was 0.08%, were merely matter-of-fact communications about evidence that did not rise to level of "interrogation," for *Miranda* purposes.

The line between "confronting" a suspect with evidence and merely "informing" the suspect about evidence is not always clear. Consider *United States v. Thomas*, 11

534

PART IV
INTERROGATIONS,
IDENTIFICATIONS, TRIALS,
AND POST-CONVICTION
REMEDIES

F.3d 1392 (7th Cir. 1993), in which the defendant asked an agent a question about the evidence against her. He responded to the question by explaining the evidence they had obtained which contradicted her alibi. She then made incriminating statements. She sought to have those statements suppressed, arguing that the agent knew his recitation of the evidence was likely to elicit an incriminating response and, therefore, was the functional equivalent of interrogation. The Seventh Circuit acknowledged that providing unsolicited information to a suspect concerning the evidence against him or her may constitute interrogation, but responding to a request for such information is qualitatively different from police initiating a confrontation with the suspect using such evidence.

Confronting a Suspect with an Accomplice *Nelson v. Fulcomer*, 911 F.2d 928 (3d Cir. 1990), held that "confronting a suspect with his alleged partner in crime and the fact that the partner has confessed is precisely the kind of psychological ploy that *Innis*'s definition of interrogation was designed to prohibit." However, when a suspect asks for the source of information against him or her and is then presented with the inculpatory statements of victims, witnesses, or accomplices, courts generally hold that such suspects were not subjected to interrogation or its functional equivalent. *Roth v. State*, 788 A.2d 101 (Del. 2001).

The following psychological ploys are not the functional equivalent of interrogation: directly responding to questions, allowing a suspect to talk with friends or family, and placing suspects in the same location with other suspects.

Directly Responding to Questions In *United States v. Taylor,* 985 F.2d 3 (1st Cir. 1993), the defendant was being arrested on drug possession charges. She asked the police, "Why is this happening to me?" An officer replied, "You can't be growing dope on your property like that." In response, the woman made a series of incriminating statements. The court ruled that the officer's comment in response to her initial question was not a psychological ploy designed to get the defendant to make an incriminating statement, but rather was a direct response to her question. *See also United States v. Briggs*, 273 F.3d 737 (7th Cir. 2001).

Allowing a Suspect to Talk with Friends or Family *Whitehead v. Cowan*, 263 F.3d 708 (7th Cir. 2001), involved a situation in which police left an arrested suspect alone with a female acquaintance. Outside police presence and with no encouragement from the police, the woman convinced the defendant to confess to her. Even if the police had hoped that the defendant might make incriminating statements to the woman, their mere "hope" that he might do so was not deemed to be a sufficient psychological ploy to render their actions the functional equivalent of interrogation. *See also Arizona v. Mauro*, 481 U.S. 520 (1987).

Placing Suspects in the Same Location with Other Suspects For *Miranda* purposes, "simply placing two individuals or suspects in the same area does not focus the police attention on a suspect in such a way that the suspect necessarily would feel added pressure . . . to say something" and therefore is not considered to be the functional equivalent of interrogation. *United States v. Vazquez*, 857 F.2d 857 (1st Cir. 1988). Thus, if two suspects find themselves being detained in the same cell or waiting area and make incriminating statements that are overheard by police, police may benefit from what they overhear because *Innis*'s functional equivalent of interrogation test is not satisfied merely by placing two suspects together in the same location.

Some psychological ploys—such as "invitations" to talk and confronting a suspect with a witness or witness statements—fall into gray areas. Courts are divided about whether these psychological ploys constitute interrogation.

"Invitations" to Talk Courts are divided on whether invitations to discuss a case constitute the functional equivalent of interrogation. *United States v. Rambo*, 365 F.3d 906, 909–10 (10th Cir. 2004), held that a police officer's repeatedly saying, "If you want to talk to me about this stuff, that's fine" was the functional equivalent of interrogation. *Commonwealth v. D'Entremont*, 632 N.E.2d 1239 (Mass. 1994), however, ruled that a police officer's having told a suspect in custody that she would be willing to speak with him about the case was not the functional equivalent of interrogation. The court reasoned that even though the officer's invitation "struck a responsive chord," it merely constituted "an expression of her availability if [the defendant] wanted to talk." 632 N.E.2d at 1244.

Confrontation of Suspect with a Witness or Witness Statements In *Commonwealth v. DeJesus*, 787 A.2d 394 (Pa. 2001), an officer's having told the defendant that he had been implicated in shootings by two witnesses was held to be the functional equivalent of interrogation. The same finding of interrogation was reached in *State v. Uganiza,* 702 P.2d 1352 (Haw. 1985), in which police showed the defendant written statements of witnesses implicating the defendant in the crime. Yet in *Shedelbower v. Estelle*, 885 F.2d 570 (9th Cir. 1989), telling a defendant that a rape victim had identified his picture was held not to be interrogation under *Innis*. Similarly in *People v. Easley,* 592 N.E.2d 1036 (Ill. 1992), telling the defendant that other inmates had reported that he was one of the perpetrators of a murder was also held not to constitute interrogation.

Statements That Are Beyond the Reach of *Miranda* Although the definition of interrogation is broad, many situations fall outside the definition or fall within well-recognized exceptions to rules regarding interrogation.

Volunteered Statements The most obvious situation not constituting interrogation is a volunteered statement—a statement made of a person's own volition and not in response to questioning by a law enforcement officer. Volunteered statements sometimes occur when a person, intentionally or unintentionally, makes an incriminating statement in the presence of a law enforcement officer. *United States v. Wright*, 991 F.2d 1180 (4th Cir. 1993), found no interrogation when the defendant, standing in the doorway to his bedroom while it was being legally searched and without any provocation by police, admitted that he had purchased a rifle. Volunteered statements occur more frequently, however, when a person is in custody. For example, during a homicide arrest in *People v. Jenkins*, 268 N.E.2d 198 (Ill. App. 1971), the arresting officer told the suspect that he was being arrested for killing a woman. Unprompted, the suspect responded, "The bitch needed killing." The statement was held to be admissible as a volunteered, spontaneously made statement.

Law enforcement officers need not interrupt a volunteered statement to warn a suspect of *Miranda* rights. The *Miranda* opinion specifically said that "[t]here is no requirement that police stop a person who enters a police station and states that he wishes to confess to a crime, or a person who calls the police to offer a confession or any other statement he desires to make." 384 U.S. at 478.

Clarifying Questions Because many volunteered statements are ambiguous, an officer may try to clarify what is being said. A voluntary statement will not be judged to have evolved into an interrogation "simply because an officer, in the course of [the suspect's] narration, asks [him] to explain or clarify something he has already said voluntarily." *State v. Porter*, 281 S.E.2d 377, 385 (N.C. 1981). Thus, a statement will continued to be viewed as one that was purely volunteered even if police asked some clarifying questions. But to qualify as truly clarifying questions, the questions cannot

536

PART IV
INTERROGATIONS,
IDENTIFICATIONS, TRIALS,
AND POST-CONVICTION
REMEDIES

be directed toward expanding on the person's original statement in an attempt to enhance the suspect's guilt. Rather, the question must merely be aimed at clearing up or explaining the statement. For example, in *People v. Savage*, 242 N.E.2d 446 (Ill. App. 1968), a man walked into a police station and said: "I done it; I done it; arrest me; arrest me." An officer asked him what he had done, and he said he killed his wife. Then the officer asked him how, and he replied, "With an axe, that's all I had." The court held that the officer's clarifying questions were not interrogation and, therefore, no *Miranda* warnings were required.

Routine Booking Questions   As part of routine booking procedures, police gather and record various identifying information about the suspect. These data normally include the suspect's name, address, age, weight, and physical description. Collectively, this is referred to as "routine booking information." Although seemingly innocuous, routine booking information can constitute incriminating evidence in some cases. For example, if a teenager is arrested for public intoxication, she will make an incriminating statement if she answers the question "How old are you?"

In *Pennsylvania v. Muniz*, 496 U.S. 582 (1990), a police officer noticed the defendant-driver had stopped his vehicle on the side of the road. When the officer asked him if he needed help, the officer noticed the scent of alcohol on Muniz's breath. After the officer told him "to stay put" until his condition improved, Muniz sped off when the officer got back to his patrol car. The officer then pulled Muniz over and asked him to complete three field sobriety tests, all of which Muniz failed. Muniz was then arrested and taken to a police station. At the station, Muniz was told he would be videotaped during the booking procedures, but he was not Mirandized. During booking, the officer asked Muniz for his name, address, weight, eye color, date of birth, and age. The officer also asked, "[D]o you know what the date was of your sixth birthday?" Muniz replied that he did not know. Over defense counsel's objections, the video and audio portions of the booking proceedings were entered into evidence at Muniz's trial for driving under the influence and Muniz was convicted. He appealed on the grounds that the evidence should have been excluded because the tests were incriminating and completed prior to Muniz being Mirandized.

The Court had previously decided that asking a suspect to participate in field sobriety tests or to take a blood alcohol test was "not an interrogation within the meaning of *Miranda*." *South Dakota v. Neville*, 459 U.S. 553, 565 n.15 (1983). The *Muniz* Court held that routine questions asked to a suspect to determine whether he or she understands instructions on how to perform physical sobriety tests or breathalyzer tests, as well as routine booking questions regarding the suspect's name, address, eye color, weight, date of birth, and age are not interrogation, and therefore fall outside *Miranda*. Moreover, because evidence of slurred speech in response to such questions is not testimonial, it is also admissible even if *Miranda* warnings were not given. A plurality of the *Muniz* Court, however, decided that the "sixth birthday" question constituted interrogation for *Miranda* purposes because it was designed to elicit an incriminating response.

The routine questioning exception to *Miranda* does not apply when a police officer has reason to believe that a suspect's answer to a routine question may be self-incriminating. Thus, although asking a person his or her place of birth is usually not interrogation, the same question assumes a completely different character when an Immigration and Custom Enforcement (ICE) agent asks a suspected illegal alien. *United States v. Gonzalez-Sandoval*, 894 F.2d 1043 (9th Cir. 1990), held that such a question was interrogation for *Miranda* purposes. Likewise, *United States v. Disla*, 805 F.2d 1340 (9th Cir. 1986), held that asking a defendant his place of residence subjected him to interrogation in a case where the officer knew that a large quantity of cocaine and cash had been found at a particular apartment and the residents of the apartment had not been identified.

Spontaneous Questions When law enforcement officers ask questions spontaneously, impulsively, or in response to an emergency, the questions are usually held not to be interrogation. In *People v. Morse*, 452 P.2d 607 (Cal. 1969), a jailer and a guard were called to a cell area, where they found a prisoner near death from strangling. While tending to the injured prisoner, they asked another prisoner about the incident and received incriminating replies. The court held that the questioning was done in a context of "stupefied wonderment," not one of incisive inquiry, and that it was not interrogation for purposes of *Miranda*.

Questions Related to Public Safety Questions that a law enforcement officer asks out of a concern for public safety are closely related to spontaneous questions. In *New York v. Quarles*, 467 U.S. 649 (1984), two police officers were approached by a woman who said she had just been raped and that her assailant had entered a nearby supermarket carrying a gun. One of the officers entered the store and spotted the defendant, who matched the description given by the woman. The officer pursued him with a drawn gun and ordered him to stop and put his hands over his head. The officer then frisked him and discovered that he was wearing an empty shoulder holster. After handcuffing the defendant, the officer asked him where the gun was. He nodded toward some empty cartons and responded, "The gun is over there." Although the defendant was in police custody when he made his statements, and the facts fell within the coverage of *Miranda*, the Supreme Court held that there was a public safety exception to the *Miranda* warning requirement:

> The police in this case, in the very act of apprehending a suspect, were confronted with the immediate necessity of ascertaining the whereabouts of a gun which they had every reason to believe the suspect had just removed from his empty holster and discarded in the supermarket. So long as the gun was concealed somewhere in the supermarket, with its actual whereabouts unknown, it obviously posed more than one danger to the public safety: An accomplice might make use of it or a customer or employee might later come upon it.

The Court concluded that the need for answers to questions in situations posing a threat to the public safety outweighed the need to protect the Fifth Amendment's privilege against self-incrimination. Furthermore, the Court held that the availability of the public safety exception does not depend on the motivation of the individual officers involved. The Court recognized that in a spontaneous, emergency situation like the one in *Quarles*, most police officers act out of different, instinctive motives: a concern for their own safety and that of others, and, perhaps, the desire to obtain incriminating evidence from the suspect. A rigid adherence to the *Miranda* rules is not required when police officers ask questions reasonably prompted by a concern for the public safety. Finally, the Court acknowledged that the public safety exception lessens the clarity of the *Miranda* rule, but expressed confidence that the police would instinctively respond appropriately in situations threatening the public safety.

Courts construe the public safety exception narrowly, applying it only where there is "an objectively reasonable need to protect the police or the public from any immediate danger associated with [a] weapon." *United States v. Mobley*, 40 F.3d 688, 693 (4th Cir. 1994). In *United States v. Basher*, 629 F.3d 1161 (9th Cir. 2011), for instance, the defendant's unwarned statement in response an officer's question about the location of gun was held admissible under the public safety exception because the officer knew there was at least one gun at a campsite and did not know whether the suspect was unarmed.

Interrogation by Private Citizens As a rule, the *Miranda* warning requirements apply only to custodial interrogations conducted by state actors—governmental

538

PART IV
INTERROGATIONS,
IDENTIFICATIONS, TRIALS,
AND POST-CONVICTION
REMEDIES

officials who act on behalf of the state. Certainly, law enforcement officers are state actors, but so are those people who act under their direction. Therefore, so long as a private citizen is not acting in concert with law enforcement officials, incriminating statements made by a person in response to custodial interrogation by a private citizen are admissible in court despite a lack of prior warnings. *See United States v. Romero*, 897 F.2d 47 (2d Cir. 1990).

Interrogation by Undercover Agents For Fifth Amendment purposes, conversations between suspects and undercover agents do not implicate *Miranda* because suspects cannot reasonably claim police compulsion from those they assume are not police agents. *Illinois v. Perkins*, 496 U.S. 292 (1990), was a case in which police placed an undercover agent in a jail cell with a defendant who was incarcerated on charges unrelated to the murder that the agent was investigating. When the undercover agent asked the defendant whether he had ever killed anyone, the defendant made statements implicating himself in the murder. Because *Miranda*'s premise is that the danger of coercion results from the interaction of custody and official interrogation, the *Perkins* Court rejected the argument that *Miranda* warnings were required whenever a suspect is technically in custody and converses with someone who happens to be a government agent. The Court reasoned that *Miranda* forbids coercion, not mere strategic deception by taking advantage of suspects' misplaced trust in those they believe to be fellow prisoners.

Assertion of *Miranda* Rights Must Be Clear and Unambiguous Unlike due process rights, which apply all the time, the rights guaranteed under the Self-Incrimination Clause of the Fifth Amendment must be invoked. Once in custody, suspects may invoke *Miranda* rights at any time prior to or during an interrogation, so long as they do so clearly and unambiguously so that a reasonable police officer under the circumstances would understand the suspect's intentions. *Davis v. United States*, 512 U.S. 452 (1994).

No Particular Words Are Necessary No particular words are required to invoke the Fifth Amendment right to remain silent. A suspect, therefore, does not need to use formal language like "I invoke my right to remain silent." Colloquialisms such as "I don't want to talk to you" would be sufficient. For example, in *Tice v. Johnson*, 647 F.3d 87(4th Cir. 2011), the court found that a suspect's statement that he "decided not to say any more" was sufficient to invoke his Fifth Amendment rights.

Silence Insufficient to Invoke Right In a fractured, plurality opinion, the U.S. Supreme Court held in *Salinas v. Texas*, 133 S. Ct. 2174 (2013), that one must not merely be silent in order to invoke one's Fifth Amendment privilege against self-incrimination, at least in the context of *noncustodial* police interrogation. In other words, to invoke the right to remain silent in this context, one must ironically not be silent but, rather, speak to communicate the intention of subsequently standing mute.

The Court summarized the facts of *Salinas* as follows:

> [T]wo brothers were shot and killed in their Houston home. There were no witnesses to the murders, but a neighbor who heard gunshots saw someone run out of the house and speed away in a dark-colored car. Police recovered six shotgun shell casings at the scene. The investigation led police to [Salinas], who had been a guest at a party the victims hosted the night before they were killed. Police visited [Salinas] at his home, where they saw a dark blue car in the driveway. He agreed to hand over his shotgun for ballistics testing and to accompany police to the station for questioning.

[Salinas's] interview with the police lasted approximately one hour. All agree that the interview was noncustodial, and the parties litigated this case on the assumption that he was not read *Miranda* warnings. For most of the interview, petitioner answered the officer's questions. But when asked whether his shotgun "would match the shells recovered at the scene of the murder," [Salinas] declined to answer. Instead, [he] "looked down at the floor, shuffled his feet, bit his bottom lip, clenched his hands in his lap, and began to tighten up." After a few moments of silence, the officer asked additional questions, which petitioner answered.

Salinas was subsequently charged with murder. He did not testify at his trial. But prosecutors argued that his silence in response to the officer's question concerning the shell casings suggested that he was guilty. Salinas was convicted and appealed. He argued that the prosecution's introduction of his silence violated this Fifth Amendment privilege against self-incrimination. The Supreme Court rejected this argument. The plurality opinion reasoned that Salinas's Fifth Amendment claim to protect his precustodial silence failed because Salinas did not *assert* his right to remain silent; rather, he *was* silent.

[Salinas's] Fifth Amendment claim fails because he did not expressly invoke the privilege against self-incrimination in response to the officer's question. It has long been settled that the privilege "generally is not self-executing" and that a witness who desires its protection "must claim it." Although "no ritualistic formula is necessary in order to invoke the privilege," a witness does not do so by simply standing mute. 133 S. Ct. at 2178 (internal citations omitted).

The four dissenting justices criticized the logic of the majority opinion for "undermining the basic protection that the Fifth Amendment provides" since, prior to the *Salinas* decision, the privilege against self-incrimination usually operated

to allow a citizen to remain silent when asked a question requiring an incriminatory answer. To permit a prosecutor to comment on a defendant's constitutionally protected silence would put that defendant in an impossible predicament. He must either answer the question or remain silent. If he answers the question, he may well reveal, for example, prejudicial facts, disreputable associates, or suspicious circumstances—even if he is innocent. If he remains silent, the prosecutor may well use that silence to suggest a consciousness of guilt. And if the defendant then takes the witness stand in order to explain either his speech or his silence, the prosecution may introduce, say for impeachment purposes, a prior conviction that the law would otherwise make inadmissible. Thus, where the Fifth Amendment is at issue, to allow comment on silence directly or indirectly can compel an individual to act as "a witness against himself"—very much what the Fifth Amendment forbids. And that is similarly so whether the questioned individual, as part of his decision to remain silent, invokes the Fifth Amendment explicitly or implicitly, through words, through deeds, or through reference to surrounding circumstances. 133 S. Ct. at 2185–86 (Breyer, J., dissenting).

Time will tell if *Salinas*'s "use it or lose it" approach to the privilege against self-incrimination proves workable. For now, it appears that the safest course of action for noncustodial suspects subject to policing questioning who do not wish their silence to be used against them—and who do not wish to waive their Fifth Amendment rights—should state, "I wish to remain silent" or similar words to that effect. It is also important to keep in mind that *Salinas* involved silence in the face of questioning that

540

PART IV
INTERROGATIONS,
IDENTIFICATIONS, TRIALS,
AND POST-CONVICTION
REMEDIES

occurred before any arrest and before *Miranda* warnings were given. Warnings were unnecessary since Salinas was not subject to custodial interrogation at the time (see the section on "Effect of Silence Pre- and Postwarnings" later in this chapter).

Ambiguous Words If a statement by a suspect is ambiguous or equivocal, most courts hold that the police have no duty to clarify the suspect's intent; they may proceed with the interrogation, although a few courts require police to clarify the defendant's wishes with respect to the request for counsel. *See, e.g., United States v. Fouche*, 833 F.2d 1284 (9th Cir. 1987), *cert denied*, 486 U.S. 1017 (1988). *Davis*, the leading Supreme Court precedent on this point, involved a suspect who said, "Maybe I should talk to a lawyer." 512 U.S. at 455. The Court held that statement was too ambiguous to qualify as a clear assertion of the right to counsel. The following statements have also been held to be too ambiguous to qualify as an unequivocal assertion of the right to counsel:

- "So if I requested a lawyer, there would be one that would come right now?" *United States v. Bezanson-Perkins*, 390 F.3d 34, 36, 40 (1st Cir. 2004).
- "Do you think I need a lawyer?" *Diaz v. Senkowski*, 76 F.3d 61, 63 (2d Cir. 1996).
- "I think I need a lawyer." *Burket v. Angelone*, 208 F.3d 172, 197–98 (4th Cir. 2000).
- "I can have a lawyer present through all this, right?" *United States v. Younger*, 398 F.3d 1179, 1187–88 (9th Cir. 2005).
- "When can I talk to a lawyer?" and "If I do this [meaning talk to the investigator], can I also talk to a lawyer after?" *People v. Lynn*, 278 P.3d 365, 366 (Colo. 2012).

Courts also require clear and unambiguous assertions of the right to remain silent. Thus, a suspect's statements that "I just don't think that I should say anything" and "I need somebody that I can talk to" were held to be too ambiguous to constitute valid invocations of *Miranda* rights. *Burket v. Angelone*, 208 F.3d 172, 199 (4th Cir. 2000). Similarly, "I am not sure if I should be talking to you" is *not* an unambiguous invocation of the right to remain silent. *United States v. Plugh*, 648 F.3d 118, 128 (2d Cir. 2011).

No Creation of Ambiguity Where None Exists Of course, when a suspect makes an ambiguous or equivocal statement, police may attempt to clarify whether he or she actually wants an attorney even though they are under no obligation to do so. However, if a suspect clearly and unambiguously invokes *Miranda* rights, courts will not allow an accused's responses to further interrogation to be used to cast retrospective doubt on the clarity of the initial request itself. In *Smith v. Illinois*, 469 U.S. 91, 99 (1984), the Court said, "No authority, and no logic, permits the interrogator to proceed . . . on his own terms and as if the defendant had requested nothing, in the hope that the defendant might be induced to say something casting retrospective doubt on his initial statement that he wished to speak through an attorney or not at all."

Behavior Must Be Consistent with Assertion If a suspect clearly and unambiguously invokes *Miranda* rights, but then acts in a manner inconsistent with the assertion of the rights, courts almost always hold that the suspect's assertion of *Miranda* rights was equivocal and, therefore, invalid. For example, in *United States v. Drapeau*, 414 F.3d 869, 874 (8th Cir. 2005), the suspect clearly stated that he "did not want to talk to agents" after he was advised of his *Miranda* rights. Yet he then made an unprompted offer to cooperate with the police, rendering his assertion of the right to remain silent ambiguous. Thus, police could continue the interrogation without violating *Miranda*.

Multiple Attempts at Interrogation After Assertion of *Miranda* Rights After *Miranda* rights have been clearly and unambiguously invoked, interrogation must stop. Nevertheless, under certain circumstances, courts have admitted statements obtained after multiple attempts to question suspects.

Attempts After Right to Silence Is Invoked Once a suspect clearly and unambiguously invokes the right to remain silent, police must "scrupulously honor" the defendant's assertion of the right. However, under limited conditions, subsequent interrogation of a suspect who exercised the *Miranda* right of silence after being given warnings may be permissible.

In *Michigan v. Mosley*, 423 U.S. 96 (1975), the defendant was arrested early in the afternoon in connection with certain robberies and was given *Miranda* warnings by a police detective. After indicating that he understood the warnings, the defendant declined to discuss the robberies, and the detective ceased the interrogation. Shortly after 6:00 P.M. the same day, after giving another set of *Miranda* warnings, a different police detective questioned the defendant about a murder that was unrelated to the robberies. The defendant made an incriminating statement that was used against him at his trial. The Court held that admitting the defendant's statement into evidence did not violate *Miranda*. Even though *Miranda* states that the interrogation must cease when the person in custody indicates a desire to remain silent, *Mosley* held that "neither this passage nor any other passage in the Miranda opinion can sensibly be read to create a per se proscription of indefinite duration upon any further questioning by any police officer on any subject, once the person in custody has indicated a desire to remain silent." 423 U.S. at 102–03. The Court then gave several reasons for allowing a second interrogation in *Mosley*:

- The defendant's right to cut off questioning had been "scrupulously honored" by the first detective.
- The first detective ceased the interrogation when the defendant refused to answer and did not try to wear down his resistance by repeated efforts to make him change his mind.
- The second interrogation was directed toward a different crime with a different time and place of occurrence.
- The second interrogation began after a significant time lapse and after the defendant had been given a fresh set of warnings.

Cases with fact patterns similar to *Mosley*'s routinely uphold the admissibility of incriminating statements made by a suspect after the passage of time. These cases suggest the following guidelines for conducting a second custodial interrogation of a person who has exercised the *Miranda* right to remain silent:

- Scrupulously honor the person's right to terminate questioning at the initial interrogation.
- Allow a significant amount of time to intervene between the first and second interrogation attempts.
- Give the person complete *Miranda* warnings again.
- Do not employ any pressure to cooperate or other psychological ploys or tactics.

Attempts After Right to Counsel Is Invoked *Miranda* created a rigid rule that a suspect's request for an attorney is per se an invocation of Fifth Amendment rights, requiring that all interrogation cease. This rigid rule is based on an attorney's unique ability to protect the Fifth Amendment rights of a client undergoing custodial interrogation. Once an accused person indicates that he or she is not competent to deal with the authorities without legal advice, courts closely examine any later choice to make a decision without counsel's presence. Therefore, although an accused may waive *Miranda* rights and submit to interrogation, the Supreme Court has recognized that additional safeguards are necessary after an accused has clearly asserted the right to counsel.

542

PART IV
INTERROGATIONS,
IDENTIFICATIONS, TRIALS,
AND POST-CONVICTION
REMEDIES

The leading case in this area is *Edwards v. Arizona*, 451 U.S. 477 (1981). The defendant in *Edwards* voluntarily submitted to questioning but later stated that he wanted an attorney before the discussions continued. The following day, detectives accosted the defendant in the county jail, and when he refused to speak with them, they told him that he "had" to talk. The Court held that incriminating statements made without his attorney present violated the defendant's rights under the Fifth and Fourteenth Amendments:

> [W]hen an accused has invoked his right to have counsel present during custodial interrogation, a valid waiver of that right cannot be established by showing only that he responded to further police-initiated custodial interrogation even if he has been advised of his rights. We further hold that an accused, such as [the defendant], having expressed his desire to deal with the police only through counsel, is not subject to further interrogation by the authorities until counsel has been made available to him, unless the accused himself initiates further communication, exchanges, or conversations with the police. 451 U.S. at 484–85.

Edwards's requirement that counsel be "made available" refers to more than an opportunity to consult with an attorney outside the interrogation room. Rather, the Supreme Court has held that *Edwards* prohibits "all police-initiated interrogation unless the accused has counsel with him at the time of questioning." *Minnick v. Mississippi*, 498 U.S. 146, 153 (1990). Thus, once a suspect clearly invokes the right to counsel, "interrogation must cease, and officials may not reinitiate interrogation without counsel present, whether or not the accused has consulted with his attorney." 498 U.S. at 153. The *Minnick* rule has no time limitation and is effective as long as the suspect remains in *Miranda* custody. Therefore, once a defendant invokes the right to counsel, the police are forever barred from initiating further custodial interrogation of the defendant unless defense counsel is present at the interview. If, however, there is a break in *Miranda* custody, *Edwards* may not apply.

In *Maryland v. Shatzer*, 559 U.S. 98 (2010), while the defendant was incarcerated on unrelated charges, a detective attempted to question him about allegations Shatzer had sexually molested his son. The defendant invoked his right to have counsel present during questioning and the detective scrupulously honored that request by terminating the encounter. He was released back into the general prison population and the investigation was closed. Roughly three years later, a different detective reopened the investigation and attempted to question Shatzer, who was still incarcerated. This time, the defendant waived his *Miranda* rights and made inculpatory statements. The Supreme Court upheld the admissibility of those statements with the following reasoning:

1. *Edwards* prevents police from coercing or badgering a suspect into waiving his previously asserted *Miranda* rights while held in uninterrupted *Miranda* custody since the first refusal to waive.

2. But when a suspect is released from *Miranda* custody and returned to his normal life for some time before a subsequently attempted interrogation, there is little reason to think that his change of heart has been coerced.

3. Fourteen days is an appropriate period of time after release from *Miranda* custody to provide a suspect to become reacclimated to his normal life, consult with friends and counsel, and shake off any residual coercive effects of prior custody.

4. Because the defendant in *Shatzer* was released from custodial interrogation within the prison setting and returned back to his normal inmate routine for more than fourteen days, there was a sufficient break in *Miranda* custody such that the logic of *Edwards* was held to be inapplicable.

Without at least a fourteen-day break in *Miranda* custody as explained in *Shatzer*, *Minnick* even bars further police-initiated interrogation about *unrelated charges* unless counsel is present. "[T]he presumption raised by a suspect's request for counsel—that he considers himself unable to deal with the pressures of custodial interrogation without legal assistance—does not disappear simply because the police have approached the suspect, still in custody, still without counsel, about a separate investigation." *Arizona v. Roberson*, 486 U.S. 675, 683 (1988). In summary, unless counsel is present, or unless the accused initiates further conversations, a waiver of *Miranda* rights after invocation of the right to counsel is presumed involuntary. Incriminating statements obtained after such an involuntary waiver, regardless of their merit, will be suppressed.

Of course, if police action after the suspect has invoked his or her right to counsel does not constitute interrogation or its functional equivalent, then *Miranda*, *Edwards*, and *Minnick* do not apply. For example, the defendant in *Arizona v. Mauro*, 481 U.S. 520 (1987), was in custody on suspicion of murdering his son. He indicated that he did not wish to be questioned further without a lawyer present, and the questioning ceased. The defendant's wife, who was being questioned in another room, asked to speak to her husband. They were allowed to speak, but an officer was present in the room, and the conversation was tape-recorded with the couple's knowledge. The recording was used against the defendant at his trial. The U.S. Supreme Court held that the actions of the police were not the functional equivalent of police interrogation. No evidence indicated that the officers sent the wife in to see her husband for the purpose of eliciting incriminating statements. Nor was the officer's presence in the room improper, because there were legitimate reasons for his presence, including the wife's safety and various security considerations. Furthermore, it is improbable that the defendant would have felt he was being coerced to incriminate himself simply because he was told his wife would be allowed to speak to him. Even though the police knew there was a possibility that the defendant would incriminate himself, "[o]fficers do not interrogate a suspect simply by hoping that he will incriminate himself." 481 U.S. at 529. The Court held that the officers acted reasonably and that the defendant's tape-recorded statements could be used against him at trial.

Finally, the suspect may change his or her mind and re-initiate conversation with the police. But since there are reasons to be skeptical of such changes of heart while someone is in custody, law enforcement officers are well advised to follow the example of the officer in *McKinney v. Ludwick*, 649 F.3d 484 (6th Cir. 2011), in which the court upheld an interrogation following the defendant's initial invocation of the right to counsel because the defendant had waved down the officer to ask about future proceedings of the case and then signed a written statement that he had asked to discuss the case.

Attempts After an Unwarned Admission In *Oregon v. Elstad*, 470 U.S. 298 (1985), a law enforcement officer investigating a burglary obtained an admission from the defendant in a custodial setting without first giving him the *Miranda* warnings. Shortly thereafter, at the stationhouse, the defendant received complete *Miranda* warnings, waived his rights, and gave a written confession. The Court held that, although the initial unwarned admission was inadmissible in court, the written confession was admissible. The Court reasoned that, despite the *Miranda* violation before the officer obtained the first admission, no coercion or other illegal means were used to break the defendant's will; in other words, the first admission was voluntary. In admitting the written confession, the Court said:

> We must conclude that, absent deliberately coercive or improper tactics in obtaining the initial statement, the mere fact that a suspect has made an unwarned admission does not warrant a presumption of compulsion. A subsequent administration of *Miranda* warnings to a suspect who has given a voluntary but unwarned

KEY POINTS

L05

- *Miranda* requirements apply regardless of the nature or severity of the offense being investigated.

- *Miranda* is inapplicable to civil proceedings such as customs procedures, civil commitments, extradition proceedings, and license revocation proceedings.

- Before custodial interrogation of a person, a law enforcement officer must warn the person (1) of the right to remain silent;

Continued on next page

(2) that anything said can be used against the person in a court of law; (3) of the right to the presence of an attorney; and (4) that if the person cannot afford an attorney, one will be appointed prior to any questioning.

- *Miranda* warnings need not be given in the exact form described in the *Miranda* decision, so long as the warnings reasonably convey to a suspect his or her *Miranda* rights.

- Law enforcement officers should give complete *Miranda* warnings before conducting custodial interrogations, even if they believe that the suspect knows his or her rights or that the suspect is not indigent.

- *Miranda* warnings do not need to be given to suspects repeatedly if a short time has passed from the time of initial warnings to the time of interrogation. However, if warnings have "gone stale," then they need to be administered again. To avoid staleness problems, law enforcement officials should always rewarn suspects of the *Miranda* rights whenever there has been a break in the continuity of interrogation.

statement ordinarily should suffice to remove the conditions that precluded admission of the earlier statement. In such circumstances, the finder of fact may reasonably conclude that the suspect made a rational and intelligent choice whether to waive or invoke his rights. 470 U.S. at 314.

In effect, *Elstad* significantly limited the application of the "fruit of the poisonous tree" doctrine to *Miranda* violations. The doctrine applies only if the previous *Miranda* violation is accompanied by deliberately coercive or improper tactics in obtaining the initial statement (i.e., there was a due process violation during the initial interrogation). Otherwise, the initial *Miranda* violation is deemed sufficiently attenuated by a voluntary waiver of a subsequent administration of *Miranda* rights. Thus, the practical lesson of *Elstad* is that, after an admission is obtained as a result of interrogating a suspect who did not receive *Miranda* warnings, the officer should carefully comply with all *Miranda* procedures in all subsequent interrogations before obtaining further statements, no matter how much time has elapsed between interrogations. This will ensure that later statements will have a better chance of being admitted, even if an earlier statement is ruled inadmissible because of a *Miranda* violation. Furthermore, even if an officer believes that a statement has been obtained in violation of *Miranda*, the officer need not warn that the statement cannot be used against the suspect. "Police officers are ill equipped to pinch-hit for counsel, construing the murky and difficult questions of when 'custody' begins or whether a given unwarned statement will ultimately be held inadmissible." 470 U.S. at 316.

In the wake of the *Elstad* decision, some unscrupulous law enforcement officers developed a protocol to manipulate their way around *Miranda*. They would deliberately withhold *Miranda* warnings to obtain unwarned confessions; stop the interrogation for a break; return to the suspect; provide *Miranda* warnings; and then obtain a second confession they thought would be admissible under *Elstad*. In *Missouri v. Seibert*, 542 U.S. 600 (2004), the U.S. Supreme Court ruled that *Elstad* did not cover such situations. Thus, such intentional attempts to circumvent *Miranda* would result in suppression of both prewarning and postwarning statements. In other words, law enforcement officers' intent matters. Honest mistakes are the realm of *Elstad*; but calculated decisions to circumvent *Miranda* will result in suppression under *Seibert*.

Sufficiency of *Miranda* Warnings

Law enforcement officers must provide *Miranda* warnings to all suspects before conducting custodial interrogations, regardless of whether the offense is a major felony or a minor misdemeanor. Law enforcement officers should not assume that suspects know their rights just because suspects have prior experience with the criminal justice system. Nor should police assume that a suspect has the financial means to be able to afford an attorney, and therefore think that they need not advise the suspect of the right to appointed counsel for a suspect who cannot afford an attorney for him- or herself. In fact, most courts require the full *Miranda* warnings to be provided to all suspects regardless of how knowledgeable the suspects may be about their rights—even to suspects who are police officers or practicing attorneys. *United States v. Street*, 472 F.3d 1298 (11th Cir. 2006); *United States v. Farinacci-Garcia*, 551 F. Supp. 465 (D.P.R. 1982). *Miranda* does not apply, though, to any civil proceedings such as customs procedures, civil commitments, extradition proceedings, and license revocation proceedings.

The warnings need not be given in the exact form used in the *Miranda* decision. *California v. Prysock*, 453 U.S. 355 (1981), held that no "talismanic incantation" of *Miranda* warnings are required; rather, all that is necessary is that the words used reasonably convey to a suspect his or her *Miranda* rights. *Florida v. Powell*, 559 U.S. 50 (2010), for example, upheld a warning in which police told the defendant he had "the right to talk to a lawyer before answering any of [their] questions" and "the right to use any of these rights at any time . . . during th[e] interview." The Court concluded this warning satisfied *Miranda*'s requirement to notify suspects of the right to have an attorney present during questioning.

Warnings will be deemed invalid, however, if one or more of the essential *Miranda* rights are omitted. For example, in *Watson v. Detella*, 122 F.3d 450, (7th Cir. 1997), the warnings given were held to be inadequate because they merely informed the suspect of a right to counsel without explaining a lawyer would be appointed to assist the suspect during interrogation if the suspect could not afford one for himself. Similarly in *United States v. Tillman*, 963 F.2d 137 (6th Cir. 1992), warnings were also determined to be inadequate because the suspect was not told that if he gave up his right to silence, whatever he said could be used against him. To avoid such problems, most law enforcement agencies distribute *Miranda* warning cards for their officers to use when informing persons subjected to custodial interrogation of their rights.

Although it is clearly not required by *Miranda* or the U.S. Constitution, some jurisdictions have added another right that must be communicated to suspects prior to commencing custodial interrogation: Suspects are advised that if they answer some questions without a lawyer, they have the right to stop the questioning at any time and to ask to speak with an attorney (Kahn, Zapf, and Cooper 2006).

Manner of Giving Warnings

Miranda warnings must be stated clearly in a language understood by the suspect. Moreover, the warnings must be delivered in an unhurried manner so that the person being warned understands his or her rights and feels free to claim them without fear. The warnings should not be given in a careless, indifferent, or superficial manner. When warnings are given to an immature, illiterate, or impaired person, the warnings must be given in language that the person can comprehend and on which the person can act intelligently. If necessary, the officer should explain and interpret the warnings. The test is whether the words used by the officer, in view of the age, intelligence, and demeanor of the person being interrogated, convey a clear understanding of all *Miranda* rights. *North Carolina v. Butler*, 441 U.S. 369, 374–75 (1979); *United States v. Rodriguez-Preciado*, 399 F.3d 1118, 1127 (9th Cir. 2005).

Timing of Warnings It is clear that *Miranda* warnings must be given prior to beginning custodial interrogation. But the passage of time can complicate matters.

Initial Interrogation To comply with the mandate to give suspects their *Miranda* rights *before* they are subjected to custodial interrogation, police sometimes read *Miranda* rights upon taking the suspect into custody even though not required until someone is subjected to custodial interrogation. When this occurs, a significant amount of time might pass before custodial interrogation takes place. Although it is always a good idea to rewarn a suspect before starting any custodial interrogation, the passage of time usually does not compromise a *Miranda* warning.

Courts have consistently upheld the integrity of *Miranda* warnings even when several hours have elapsed between the reading of the warning and the interrogation. In *United States v. Frankson*, 83 F.3d 79, 83 (4th Cir. 1996), the court held that the defendant's "initial *Miranda* warning was in no way compromised by the passage of two and one-half hours between the issuance of his warning and the point at which he began to confess his crimes and cooperate with the police."

KEY POINTS

LO3
LO4

- After warnings of *Miranda* rights have been given to a person subjected to custodial interrogation and the person has been given an opportunity to exercise the rights, the person may voluntarily, knowingly, and intelligently waive the rights, either explicitly or impliedly, and then agree to answer questions or make a statement. But unless and until such warnings and waiver are demonstrated

Continued on next page

by the prosecution at trial, no evidence obtained as a result of interrogation can be used against the person.

■ To constitute a full and effective waiver of *Miranda* rights, (1) the relinquishment of the right must have been voluntary in the sense that it was the product of a free and deliberate choice rather than police intimidation, coercion, or deception; and (2) the waiver must have been made with a full awareness both of the nature of the right being abandoned and the consequences of the decision to abandon it. This second requirement is satisfied by careful administration of the *Miranda* warnings to a competent suspect.

■ Before formal criminal proceedings are instituted against a particular suspect (such as an indictment, preliminary hearing, or arraignment), undercover agents do not need to administer *Miranda* warnings to suspects before obtaining statements. This applies even if they are in custody, as questioning by someone undercover is not inherently coercive in the way that routine custodial interrogations by known police officers can be.

■ A request to see someone other than a lawyer is not an assertion of *Miranda* rights, although a denial of such a request may have some bearing on the voluntariness of the statements.

■ Police are not required to inform uncharged suspects of attorneys' attempts to reach them or otherwise keep them abreast of the status of their legal representation or of other information that may be useful to their defense before giving *Miranda* warnings and obtaining a waiver of *Miranda* rights.

Subsequent Interrogations Sometimes a suspect waives *Miranda* rights and submits to interrogation; then, after an interval of time, police want to interrogate the suspect again. The general rule is that *Miranda* rights do not need to be repeated "so long as the circumstances attending any interruption or adjournment of the process [are] such that the suspect has not been deprived of the opportunity to make an informed and intelligent assessment of his interest involved in the interrogation, including his right to cut off questioning." *Bivins v. State*, 642 N.E.2d 928, 939 (Ind. 1994). In other words, so long as the initial warnings have not "gone stale," they do not need repeating. *United States v. Ferrer-Montoya*, 483 F.3d 565, 569 (8th Cir. 2007). Determining when warnings have "gone stale," however, is not always easy.

In *Commonwealth v. Wideman*, 334 A.2d 594, 598 (Pa. 1975), the court listed five factors relevant to determining whether an accused must be reinformed of his or her *Miranda* rights:

■ the time lapse between the last *Miranda* warnings and the accused's statement,

■ interruptions in the continuity of the interrogation,

■ whether there was a change of location between the place where the last *Miranda* warnings were given and the place where the accused's statement was made,

■ whether the same officer who gave the warnings also conducted the interrogation resulting in the accused's statement, and

■ whether the statement elicited during the complained-of interrogation differed significantly from other statements that had been preceded by *Miranda* warnings.

Applying these factors, the *Wideman* court held that the *Miranda* warnings had "gone stale" because twelve hours had passed between the warnings and the time of interrogation, the defendant had been moved to another location, and a different set of police officers conducted the interrogation. But more recent cases have upheld statements made much longer than twelve hours after *Miranda* warnings were given under circumstances when other factors may have also contributed to the staleness of warnings.

Jones v. State, 119 S.W.3d 766, 800–01 (Tex. Ct. Crim. App. 2003), for example, upheld statements made two days after the warnings, even though "the interrogation was conducted by a different person (belonging to a different law enforcement agency)" in a different location and the statement "involved different events than earlier statements made immediately after *Miranda* warnings." Key to the court's rationale was that there was "no reason to believe appellant suffered from any emotional state that would have impaired his understanding of the earlier-given warnings." 119 S.W.3d at 801. But *Ex Parte J.D.H.*, 797 So.2d 1130 (Ala. 2001), invalidated a confession made sixteen days after *Miranda* warnings were given. And in *State v. DeWeese*, 582 S.E.2d 786 (W. Va. 2003), the court invalidated a confession made seven days after the administration of warnings. The *DeWeese* court used the same criteria listed nearly thirty years earlier by the *Wideman* court, but added an additional component: the "apparent intellectual and emotional state of the suspect." 582 S.E.2d at 799.

To avoid staleness problems, law enforcement officials should always readminister *Miranda* warnings whenever there has been a break in the continuity of interrogation.

Waiver of *Miranda* Rights

After *Miranda* warnings have been given to a person about to be subjected to custodial interrogation, and the person has had an opportunity to exercise the rights, "the individual may knowingly and intelligently waive these rights and agree to answer questions or make a statement. But unless and until such warnings and waiver are demonstrated by the prosecution at trial no evidence obtained as a result of interrogation can be used against him." *Miranda*, 384 U.S. at 478–79. In the *Miranda* context, a waiver is a voluntary and intentional relinquishment of a known right. A valid waiver of *Miranda* rights means that a suspect has voluntarily given up the right to silence or the right to counsel.

The dissenting justices in *Miranda* worried that requiring law enforcement officers to give warnings to suspects prior to interrogation would severely impact the ability of police to investigate and solve crimes because if suspects were aware of these rights, they would not voluntarily choose to waive them. Many commentators, including police, prosecutors, politicians, scholars, and the media, echoed these concerns (see Leo 1996: 622). But these fears were not well founded. *Miranda* has had "only a negligible effect on the ability of police to elicit confessions, solve crimes, and secure convictions" (645; see also Thomas and Leo 2002). In fact, more than three-quarters of all suspects waive their *Miranda* right to remain silent and agree to talk to the police (Leo 1996: 659). Some studies report even higher numbers; Cassell and Hayman (1996) found that 84 percent of suspects waived their *Miranda* rights at the initial stages of an interrogation. And Domanico, Cicchini, and White (2012) reported that a whopping 93 percent of suspects in their study waived their *Miranda* rights. Once interrogation begins, few suspects who originally waive their *Miranda* rights subsequently assert them, with studies placing the percentage of suspects who do so between 1.1 percent (Leo 1996) and 4 percent (Cassell and Hayman 1996). And when suspects confess, "Confessions are very rarely excluded from evidence in court as a result of *Miranda*," as research suggests this occurs in less than 1 percent of all cases (Leo 1996: 677).

Express Versus Implied Waivers Suspects can validly waive their *Miranda* rights expressly or impliedly.

Express Waivers Express waivers occur when a suspect says, writes, or otherwise acknowledges that he or she is aware of his or her *Miranda* rights and voluntarily elects to give up those rights with knowledge of the consequences of doing so. To obtain an express waiver, after *Miranda* warnings have been administered, a law enforcement officer should ask the suspect whether he or she understands the rights that have been explained. The officer should then ask the suspect whether he or she wishes to talk without first consulting a lawyer or having a lawyer present during questioning. If the officer receives an affirmative answer to both questions, the officer should carefully record the exact language in which the answer was given, preserving it for possible future use in court. The officer may then proceed with the interrogation.

If possible, the officer should always try to obtain a written waiver of rights from the suspect before questioning. A written waiver is almost always ruled by courts to be sufficient if the suspect is literate and there is no evidence of police coercion. Figure 13.1 is a suggested form for obtaining a written waiver of *Miranda* rights. If a suspect refuses to sign a waiver form, but agrees to talk with police, such an oral waiver is valid, albeit harder to prove in the absence of other evidence, such as an audio or video recording of the oral waiver. *United States v. Oliver*, 630 F.3d 397, 410 (5th Cir. 2011).

Implied Waivers Law enforcement officers may not always be able to obtain express written or oral waivers of *Miranda* rights. *North Carolina v. Butler*, 441 U.S. 369 (1979), held that express waivers are not required. Implied waivers are valid if, under

STATEMENT OF RIGHTS

Case File _____ Police Dept. _____

Date _____ Time _____ Place _____

THE FOLLOWING SEVEN STATEMENTS MUST BE FULLY UNDER-STOOD BY YOU BEFORE WE CAN CONTINUE. IF YOU DO NOT UNDERSTAND A STATEMENT, ASK THAT IT BE EXPLAINED:

1. You have the right to remain silent.
2. Anything you say can and will be used against you in a court of law.
3. You have the right to talk to a lawyer and have the lawyer present with you while you are being questioned.
4. If you cannot afford to hire a lawyer, one will be appointed to represent you before any questioning, if you wish.
5. You can decide at any time to exercise these rights and not answer any questions or make any statements.
6. Do you understand each of these rights I have explained to you?
7. Having these rights in mind, do you wish to talk to us now without a lawyer present?

ACKNOWLEDGEMENT AND WAIVER OF RIGHTS

THE ABOVE STATEMENT OF MY RIGHTS HAS BEEN READ AND EX-PLAINED TO ME AND I FULLY UNDERSTAND WHAT MY RIGHTS ARE. KNOWING THIS I AM WILLING TO ANSWER QUESTIONS OR TO MAKE A STATEMENT WITHOUT A LAWYER PRESENT.

Witness _____ Signed _____
(Advising Officer or Witness)   (Individual Advised of Rights)

Witness _____ Education _____
(Officer or Witness)   (Name of school and last grade completed)

STATEMENT

Page No. _____ of _____ Page Statement

I have read the above statement, have signed each page of the statement, and acknowledge receipt of a true copy of the statement.

I give this statement without threat, coercion or promise of any kind.

Witness _____

Witness _____ Signed _____

Page No. _____ of _____ Page Statement   Date _____

Page No. _____ of _____ Page Statement

I have read the above statement, have signed each page of the statement, and acknowledge receipt of a true copy of the statement.

I give this statement without threat, coercion or promise of any kind.

Witness _____

Witness _____ Signed _____

FIGURE 13.1 | Suggested Form for Waiver of *Miranda* Rights

the totality of the circumstances, evidence shows that a suspect knew of his or her *Miranda* rights and then voluntarily waived them. Factors to be considered include

- whether the defendant understood his rights,
- the defendant's willingness to speak,
- whether the defendant expressed any desire to remain silent,
- whether the defendant's answers were in a narrative form rather than monosyllabic responses,
- whether there are any facts that cast doubt on the voluntariness of the waiver, and
- whether the defendant subsequently exercises his *Miranda* rights.

State v. Stephenson, 915 A.2d 327 (Conn. Ct. App. 2007).

The following is a summary of some of the guiding principles courts utilize in examining whether a valid implied waiver of *Miranda* rights occurred.

Silence Is Not a Waiver The *Miranda* opinion made it clear that "a valid waiver will not be presumed simply from the silence of the accused after warnings are given[;] . . . there must be an allegation and evidence which show that an accused was offered counsel but intelligently and understandably rejected the offer. Anything less is not a waiver." 384 U.S. at 475.

In *Berghuis v. Thompkins*, 560 U.S. 370 (2010), the defendant was properly Mirandized and then interrogated about a shooting in which one victim died. At no point did he say that he wanted to remain silent, that he did not want to talk with the police, or that he wanted an attorney. He was largely silent during the three-hour interrogation, but near the end, he answered "yes" when asked if he prayed to God to forgive him for the shooting. He moved to suppress that statement, claiming that he had invoked his Fifth Amendment right to remain silent, that he had not waived that right, and that his inculpatory statements were involuntary. In a five-to-four decision, the Court held that the suspect's silence during the interrogation did not unambiguously invoke his right to remain silent. Rather, he impliedly waived the privilege against self-incrimination when he knowingly and voluntarily made a statement to the police. Finally, the officer's appeal to the suspect's religious beliefs did not render his statement involuntary.

Justice Sotomayor dissented in *Berghuis*, saying that the majority decision meant that "a suspect who wishes to guard his right to remain silent against such a finding of 'waiver' must, counterintuitively, speak—and must do so with sufficient precision to satisfy a clear-statement rule that construes ambiguity in favor of the police." 560 U.S. at 391. She went on to say, "What in the world must an individual do to exercise his constitutional right to remain silent beyond actually, in fact, remaining silent?" 560 U.S. at 409. Her critique of *Berghuis* majority's logic led some commentators to conclude that the words used in *Miranda* warnings are fatally outdated since "telling a suspect that he has the right to remain silent is no longer accurate" (Cicchini 2012: 918).

Words Indicating a Waiver Any comprehensible oral statements of understanding and willingness to speak are usually acceptable as a waiver of *Miranda* rights. Examples of valid waivers are a suspect making these statements:

- "I might as well tell you about it." *United States v. Boykin*, 398 F.2d 483, 484 (3d Cir. 1968).
- "I want to say some things." *United States v. Castro-Higuero*, 473 F.3d 880, 886 (8th Cir. 2007).
- "That means I ain't got to say nothing right now, 'til I talk to my lawyer [but] . . . I can talk to you if I want to." *State v. Murphy*, 747 N.E.2d 765, 778 (Ohio 2001).

Moreover, if the suspect indicates his or her desire to invoke *Miranda* rights in the future, rather than the present, such an invocation will not be valid. Thus, in *Thompson v. State*, 235 So.2d 354 (Fla. App. 1970), the court ruled that a suspect impliedly waived his right to counsel under *Miranda* when he indicated his desire to talk to a lawyer at some time in the future, but agreed to answer questions by police first without a lawyer being present.

Gestures Indicating a Waiver Courts have approved nonverbal waivers, including nods, *Ragland v. Commonwealth*, 191 S.W.3d 569 (Ky. 2006); *United States v. Chapa-Garza*, 62 F.3d 118 (5th Cir. 1995), and shrugs *State v. Brammeier*, 464 P.2d 717 (Or. App. 1970).

Actions Indicating a Waiver Sometimes a suspect will indicate an understanding of *Miranda* rights and then simply begin to make a statement without any other verbal or nonverbal indication of waiver. Most courts hold that, once the suspect has been informed of *Miranda* rights and indicates an understanding of those rights, choosing to speak without a lawyer present is sufficient evidence of a knowing and voluntary waiver of the rights. *United States v. Cardwell*, 433 F.3d 378, 389–90 (4th Cir. 2005).

Defendants have argued that a number of other actions or behaviors constitute either an invocation of *Miranda* rights, or evidence that an implied waiver was not knowing, intelligent, and voluntary. In spite of the fact that courts are supposed to presume

550

PART IV
INTERROGATIONS,
IDENTIFICATIONS, TRIALS,
AND POST-CONVICTION
REMEDIES

a lack of waiver in the *Miranda* context, it is clear that courts often construe the actions of suspects as implied waivers. Consider the following cases:

- A request to see or talk with someone other than an attorney is not an assertion of *Miranda* rights, although a denial of such a request may have some bearing on the voluntariness of the statements. *Watkins v. Callahan*, 724 F.2d 1038 (1st Cir. 1984), found a valid waiver of *Miranda* rights when the defendant indicated he was ready to make a statement after calling his family instead of calling an attorney. *Fare v. Michael C.*, 442 U.S. 707 (1979), held that a juvenile waived his *Miranda* rights even though he had been denied a request to speak to his probation officer. The Court found that the request, made by an experienced older juvenile with an extensive prior record, did not constitute an invocation of the right to remain silent, nor was it tantamount to a request for an attorney. However, some states (e.g., Colorado, Connecticut, Illinois, Indiana, and North Dakota) require a parent, guardian, or other interested adult, such as an attorney, to be notified before a juvenile may be found to have waived *Miranda* rights. *E.g.*, Colo. Rev. Stat. § 19-2-511.

- A request for counsel made by a suspect to a friend or relative is not the same as a request to the police. Thus, in a case in which a suspect told his brother to post bond for him and to get him a lawyer, the suspect's request to his brother did not operate as an exercise of his *Miranda* rights even though the police were aware of the request. Moreover, the suspect's subsequent statements to the police indicated that he had impliedly waived his *Miranda* rights. *People v. Smith*, 246 N.E.2d 689 (Ill. App. 1969).

Implied Waivers Through "Initiating" Further Communication *Oregon v. Bradshaw*, 462 U.S. 1039 (1983), attempted to explain what would constitute the initiation of further communication with the police by a suspect after the suspect had invoked his or her *Miranda* rights:

> [T]here are undoubtedly situations where a bare inquiry by either a defendant or by a police officer should not be held to "initiate" any conversation or dialogue. There are some inquiries, such as a request for a drink of water or a request to use a telephone that are so routine that they cannot be fairly said to represent a desire on the part of an accused to open up a more generalized discussion relating directly or indirectly to the investigation. Such inquiries or statements, by either an accused or a police officer, relating to routine incidents of the custodial relationship, will not generally "initiate" a conversation in the sense in which that word was used in *Edwards*. 462 U.S. at 1045.

In contrast, when a suspect "initiates" conversation with regard to substantive or procedural matters concerning the crime, *Bradshaw* considers such initiation to constitute a waiver of *Miranda* rights. *Bradshaw* involved a suspect who was in custody and had invoked the right to counsel. The suspect subsequently asked a police officer, "Well, what is going to happen to me now?" The Supreme Court ruled that the suspect's question "evinced a willingness and a desire for a generalized discussion about the investigation; it was not merely a necessary inquiry arising out of the incidents of the custodial relationship." 462 U.S. at 412. Accordingly, the incriminating statements that the suspect made over the course of the discussion he had with the police officer were deemed admissible.

Selective Waivers Sometimes, suspects specifically invoke their *Miranda* rights in a narrow way while acting in a manner that suggests they impliedly waive their *Miranda* rights with regard to other aspects of a case. These are referred to as selective waivers or qualified waivers. Most courts give little weight to selective waivers. They find that so long as a suspect understands that they do not have to talk to law enforcement authorities without the assistance of counsel, a suspect's attempt to carve out a partial exception to an otherwise knowing and voluntary waiver will usually be ineffective. *United States v. Frazier*, 476 F.2d 891 (D.C. Cir. 1973) is a typical example of this. In *Frazier*, the defendant agreed to talk with police without an attorney being present, but he refused to allow police to take notes during the interrogation. Although this indicated that he may have misunderstood that his oral statements could, in fact, be used as evidence against him in court, the court upheld his waiver and allowed his oral statements to be used against him at trial.

Similarly, once a suspect has been given *Miranda* warnings, the suspect's refusal to give a written statement outside the presence of his or her attorney does not render ineffective the suspect's clear waiver of rights for the purpose of giving an oral statement. In *Connecticut v. Barrett*, 479 U.S. 523 (1987), the suspect, who was in custody on a sexual assault charge, was given the *Miranda* warnings and indicated to the police that he would not make a written statement outside the presence of his attorney. He then clearly expressed his willingness to speak with the police without an attorney, and he made an oral statement admitting his involvement in the sexual assault. The Court held that the defendant's exercise of his right to counsel was limited by its terms to the making of written statements and did not prohibit further police questioning leading to the oral confession. The same result has occurred when suspects agreed to talk, but refused to have sessions recorded. *E.g.*, *State v. Bell*, 745 S.W.2d 858 (Tenn. 1988).

There are, however, cases in which defendants can make selective waivers of their rights for some purposes while preserving their rights to silence and counsel for other purposes as illustrated by *State v. Jones*, 607 S.E.2d 498 (W. Va. 2004). The defendant, a juvenile, and his attorney agreed to allow police to administer a polygraph test to the defendant. After the test was concluded, however, police interrogated the defendant without his lawyer being present with regard to the answers he provided during the polygraph examination even though the defendant requested consultation with his attorney. The court ruled that *Miranda* was violated because the selective waiver as to the polygraph examination did not extend to being an implied waiver for any subsequent interrogation.

The Requirements for Valid Waivers of *Miranda* Rights Regardless of whether express or implied, *Miranda* made clear that any waiver must be "made voluntarily, knowingly and intelligently." 384 U.S. at 475. Courts begin their evaluation of purported waivers by presuming that a defendant did not waive his or her rights. Courts will not presume that suspects waived their *Miranda* rights just because they ultimately confessed. 384 U.S. at 475. Rather, courts examine the totality of the circumstances surrounding the alleged waiver by examining two distinct lines of inquiry as set forth by the U.S. Supreme Court in *Moran v. Burbine*, 475 U.S. 412, 421 (1986).

First the relinquishment of the right must have been voluntary in the sense that it was the product of a free and deliberate choice rather than intimidation, coercion or deception. Second, the waiver must have been made with a full awareness both of the nature of the right being abandoned and the consequences of the decision to abandon it. Only if "the totality of the circumstances surrounding the interrogation" reveals both an uncoerced choice and the requisite level of comprehension may a court properly conclude that the *Miranda* rights have been waived.

The prosecution then must prove, by a preponderance of the evidence, that the words and actions of the suspect evidenced a knowing, intelligent, and voluntary waiver of his or her *Miranda* rights. *Colorado v. Connelly*, 479 U.S. 157 (1986). Therefore, when no written waiver or unambiguous oral waiver can be obtained, law enforcement officers should record all circumstances surrounding the attempt to obtain an implied waiver so that the prosecution will have evidence to prove that the waiver was voluntary, knowing, and intelligent.

552

PART IV
INTERROGATIONS,
IDENTIFICATIONS, TRIALS,
AND POST-CONVICTION
REMEDIES

Burbine's *Voluntariness Prong* This prong is exclusively concerned with the absence of police coercion as illustrated by *Colorado v. Connelly*, 479 U.S. 157 (1986). Connelly, of his own accord and without any prompting, approached a police officer and said that he had murdered someone and wanted to talk to the police about it. The officer immediately advised Connelly of his *Miranda* rights. Connelly responded by saying that he understood his rights, but he wanted to talk about the murder anyway "because his conscience had been bothering him." 479 U.S. at 160. It turned out that Connelly was mentally ill, suffering from schizophrenia. During an actively psychotic phase, he went to the police to confess because auditory hallucinations that he believed to be "the voice of God" commanded him to do so. 479 U.S. at 161. Even though his severe mental illness made him feel compelled to confess, Connelly's waiver of *Miranda* rights was held to be voluntary because it was free of any governmental coercion.

When governmental coercion is at issue, most courts examine the voluntariness of a *Miranda* waiver by inquiring if the suspect's capacity for self-determination was critically impaired. *United States v. Pelton*, 835 F.2d 1067, 1073 (4th Cir. 1987), said, "Agents may properly initiate discussions on cooperation, and may indicate that they will make this cooperation known. . . . General encouragement to cooperate is far different from specific promises of leniency." With respect to the use of psychological tactics, *Miller v. Fenton*, 796 F.2d 598, 605 (3d Cir. 1986), *cert. denied sub nom*, 479 U.S. 989, said:

> These ploys may play a part in the suspect's decision to confess, but so long as that decision is a product of the suspect's own balancing of competing considerations the confession is voluntary. The question . . . is whether . . . statements were so manipulative or coercive that they deprived [the defendant] of his ability to make an unconstrained, autonomous decision to confess.

Applying this principle, *Miller v. Fenton* upheld a confession as voluntary even though the police officer feigned extreme sympathy toward the defendant, encouraged the defendant to "unburden" himself by confessing to murder, promised to get the defendant psychological help, and lied to the defendant that the victim was still alive at the time the interrogation began and then, during the interview, told the suspect that the victim had died.

Burbine's Understanding Prong *Burbine's* second requirement is that a waiver must be made with full awareness of both the right being abandoned and the consequences of the decision to abandon that right. Normally, this prong is satisfied by careful administration of the *Miranda* warnings to a suspect.

> The Constitution does not require that a criminal suspect know and understand every possible consequence of a waiver of the Fifth Amendment privilege. . . . The Fifth Amendment's guarantee is both simpler and more fundamental: A defendant may not be compelled to be a witness against himself in any respect. The *Miranda* warnings protect this privilege by insuring that a suspect knows that he may choose not to talk to law enforcement officers, to talk only with counsel present, or to discontinue talking at any time. The *Miranda* warnings ensure that a waiver of these rights is knowing and intelligent by requiring that the suspect be fully advised of this constitutional privilege, including the critical advice that whatever he chooses to say may be used as evidence against him. *Colorado v. Spring*, 479 U.S. 564, 574 (1987).

Specific Factors Considered When Applying the *Burbine* Test for Waivers Courts commonly consider the factors in this section when examining the validity of *Miranda* waiver. The list is not exhaustive because courts must consider the totality of the circumstances surrounding an interrogation to determine if a waiver was knowing, intelligent, and voluntary.

Competency of the Suspect The inquiry as to whether a suspect has the requisite level of comprehension to validly waive *Miranda* rights is directed at the **competency** of the suspect. In determining competency to waive *Miranda* rights, courts examine the totality of the circumstances surrounding the waiver, with no single factor controlling.

Intelligence No specific level of intelligence constitutes a minimum threshold for suspects to be considered competent to waive their *Miranda* rights. Thus, suspects with below-average IQs may be competent to waive their rights. *Smith v. Mullin*, 379 F.3d 919, 933 (10th Cir. 2004), for example, upheld a waiver by a defendant with the cognitive abilities of a twelve-year-old because he had prior experience with the criminal justice system and understood *Miranda* warnings. But when law enforcement personnel are dealing with an impaired suspect whose cognitive abilities are low, they must take special care to insure that the language they use is understood by the suspect.

Education No specific level of education constitutes a minimum threshold for suspects to be considered competent to waive their *Miranda* rights. *United States v. Bautista-Avila*, 6 F.3d 1360 (9th Cir. 1993), upheld a waiver by a defendant with a sixth-grade Mexican education because the officer read him his rights in Spanish and the defendant said that he understood his rights.

Age Suspects who may be too young to understand *Miranda* warnings pose special problems for the criminal justice system. Developmental psychology has demonstrated that reasoning and decision-making skills continue to develop throughout childhood and early adolescence (Larson 2003: 649). In fact, research has consistently shown that most teenagers under the age of sixteen do not understand either the language of *Miranda* rights or some of the concepts underlying those rights, such as the role of defense counsel in criminal prosecutions (Beyer 2000; Feld 2006; Grisso et al. 1997). For example, Grisso and colleagues (1981: 129) found that one-third of children "with few or no prior felony referrals believed that defense attorneys defend the interests of the innocent but not the guilty." In spite of these facts, courts routinely uphold waivers by teenagers between the ages of fourteen and eighteen. Courts, however, often find that juveniles who are preteens or younger lack the intellectual development to make a knowing, intelligent, and voluntary waiver of *Miranda* rights. *E.g., Murray v. Earle*, 405 F.3d 278 (5th Cir. 2005). Recall, however, that several states have laws that require a parent, guardian, or other interested adult, such as an attorney, to be notified before a juvenile may waived *Miranda* rights.

Familiarity with the Justice System A complete lack of familiarity with the justice system certainly does not call into question a suspect's competency to invoke or waive *Miranda* rights. Nonetheless, courts usually find that suspects who have some prior experience in the justice system are less likely to be susceptible to mild forms of psychological tactics used by police to get suspects to confess. Thus, in a close case, prior criminal justice experience weighs toward the validity of a waiver of *Miranda* rights. For example, *United States v. Palmer*, 203 F.3d 55 (1st Cir. 2000), held a waiver to be valid—even though the defendant was going through heroin withdrawal at the time of the interrogation—because the defendant had sixteen prior arrests. *Hardaway v. Young*, 302 F.3d 757 (7th Cir. 2002), upheld a waiver by a fourteen-year-old defendant because he had been arrested at least nineteen times in the past and appeared to understand his *Miranda* rights as a result of his prior experience with the justice system, in spite of his relative youth. And *United States v. Plugh*, 648 F.3d 118 (2d Cir. 2011), upheld a waiver, in part, because defendant was familiar with *Miranda* rights due to his experience as a state corrections officer.

554

PART IV
INTERROGATIONS,
IDENTIFICATIONS, TRIALS,
AND POST-CONVICTION
REMEDIES

Physical and Mental Condition *Mincey v. Arizona*, 437 U.S. 385, 399 (1978), ruled that *Miranda* was violated when a police officer interrogated a hospitalized patient after having been seriously wounded.

It is hard to imagine a situation less conducive to the exercise of "a rational intellect and a free will" than Mincey's. He had been seriously wounded just a few hours earlier, and had arrived at the hospital "depressed almost to the point of coma," according to his attending physician. Although he had received some treatment, his condition at the time of Hust's interrogation was still sufficiently serious that he was in the intensive care unit. He complained to Hust that the pain in his leg was "unbearable." He was evidently confused and unable to think clearly about either the events of that afternoon or the circumstances of his interrogation, since some of his written answers were on their face not entirely coherent. Finally, while Mincey was being questioned he was lying on his back on a hospital bed, encumbered by tubes, needles, and breathing apparatus. He was, in short, "at the complete mercy" of Detective Hust, unable to escape or resist the thrust of Hust's interrogation. 437 U.S. at 398–99.

Yet, courts have upheld waivers under many circumstances in which suspects were injured or in pain, so long as they were alert and responsive during questioning. *Reinert v. Larkins*, 379 F.3d 76 (3d Cir. 2004), for example, upheld the defendant's implied waiver even though the interrogation was taking place in an ambulance as the defendant was being taken to a hospital because he was "alert and coherent" during questioning. *United States v. Cristobal*, 293 F.3d 134, 142 (4th Cir. 2002), upheld a waiver by a defendant suffering from postsurgical pain in spite of being on a narcotic painkiller because the medication apparently did not affect his thinking.

Drug or Alcohol Use Although drugs or alcohol certainly impair cognitive functioning, suspects under the influence of drugs or alcohol may nonetheless validly waive their *Miranda* rights. The critical question in such cases is the degree of impairment. If the suspect is functioning reasonably well, then courts usually uphold their waivers. For example, although the defendant was intoxicated in *Clagett v. Angelone*, 209 F.3d 370 (4th Cir. 2000), because he did not slur his speech or have trouble walking, the court upheld his waiver. A *Miranda* waiver was similarly upheld in *United States v. Walker*, 272 F.3d 407, 412–13 (7th Cir. 2001), in spite of the fact that the defendant was vomiting during the interrogation due to heroin withdrawal, because a doctor said the defendant was alert and "with the program."

KEY POINTS

L05 ■ Statements taken in violation of *Miranda–Edwards* requirements are inadmissible in court as substantive evidence in the prosecution's case-in-chief to prove the defendant's guilt of crime, but they may be used to impeach the defendant's testimony at trial or to discover witnesses, so long as the statements were voluntarily given.

Continued on next page

Explicitness of the Waiver The more explicit a waiver, the more likely it is to be ruled valid. For example, *Wilcher v. Hargett*, 978 F.2d 872, 877 (5th Cir. 1992), upheld a waiver even though the interrogation involved repeated questioning of the suspect over a six-day period because the defendant received *Miranda* warnings and signed written waivers before each questioning period. However, even a meticulously obtained written waiver cannot overcome other misconduct that calls into question the legitimacy of a waiver. *Hart v. Att'y Gen. of Fla.*, 323 F.3d 884, 893–94 (11th Cir. 2003), for example, invalidated a written waiver obtained after careful explanation of *Miranda* because the interrogating officer contradicted the written warnings by saying that signing the waiver form "honesty will not hurt you" in response to the defendant's questions regarding the benefits of having counsel present during the interrogation.

Language Barriers *Miranda* warnings must be given in a language understood by the suspect. Thus, providing warnings in English to non-English-speaking suspects, or to suspects whose knowledge of the English language is minimal, will not suffice. But if *Miranda* rights are translated into a language that a suspect can understand, even if the translation is imperfect due to misspellings or grammar errors, then a waiver of those rights is usually upheld. *E.g.*, *Thai v. Mapes*, 412 F.3d 970 (8th Cir. 2005).

Failures to Disclose Information About the Interrogation In *Colorado v. Spring*, 479 U.S. 564 (1987), the defendant contended that police failure to inform him of the potential subjects of interrogation constituted police trickery and deception as condemned in *Miranda*, and rendered his waiver of *Miranda* rights invalid. Citing *Burbine*, the Court disagreed, saying that a valid waiver does not require that police supply a suspect with all useful information to help calibrate his or her self-interest in deciding whether to speak. Similarly, *United States v. Tapp*, 812 F.2d 177 (5th Cir. 1987), held that the interrogating officer's failure to inform the defendant that he was the target of the investigation did not render his waiver of *Miranda* rights involuntary.

Failures to Disclose Outside Information and Events Recall that in *Burbine*, police failed to let Moran know that his public defender had been trying to contact him. Although Moran otherwise made a voluntary waiver and confessed, he later challenged the validity of his waiver on the grounds that it was not "knowing" because he did not know that his lawyer had been trying to contact him. The U.S. Supreme Court rejected this claim, reasoning that "[e]vents occurring outside of the presence of the suspect and entirely unknown to him surely can have no bearing on the capacity to comprehend and knowingly relinquish a constitutional right. . . . We have never read the Constitution to require that the police supply a suspect with a flow of information to help him calibrate his self-interest in deciding whether to speak or stand by his rights." 475 U.S. at 422.

In spite of upholding the actions of the police, the *Burbine* Court warned that a more flagrant violation by the police might rise to the level of a due process violation. Therefore, police should not interpret *Burbine* as generally approving dishonest or shady dealings with defense attorneys in interrogation situations occurring before the initiation of formal charges. In fact, some states have explicitly rejected *Burbine* on the basis of state constitutional law.

A Suggested Dialogue Social scientific literature on *Miranda* rights is replete with data demonstrating the shortcomings of *Miranda* warnings in protecting Fifth Amendment rights (e.g., Rogers 2008). Recall that between 80 and 93 percent of suspects waive their *Miranda* rights and submit to questioning (Cassel and Hayman 1996; Domanico et al. 2012; Leo 1996).

> According to some researchers, the police obtain these extraordinarily high waiver rates because they employ techniques specifically designed to overcome the invocation of rights. These include, for example, minimizing the *Miranda* procedure as a mere formality, as well as other techniques . . . .
>
> [Moreover], most suspects do not fully understand their *Miranda* rights, in part because the warnings are sometimes difficult to comprehend, and in part because many suspects are poorly educated and do not read well. Comprehension problems are further exacerbated when a suspect is a juvenile, mentally impaired, or mentally disordered. In one well-known study, only 21% of juveniles and 42% of adults fully understood the *Miranda* warning that was presented to them. (Domanico et al. 2012: 8–9)

KEY POINTS

- Involuntary statements obtained from a defendant cannot be used for any purpose in a criminal trial.

- A defendant's silence after receiving the *Miranda* warnings may not be used against the defendant at trial for any purpose. In contrast, silence in response to questions asked prior to *Miranda* warnings (i.e., silence in response to questions that were not the product of custodial interrogations) may be used at trial, particularly if the defendant does not expressly invoke his or her Fifth Amendment right to silence.

- The fruit of the poisonous tree doctrine does not apply to physical evidence derived from statements made in violation of *Miranda*, nor does it bar the use of a second statement that was voluntarily given after a valid waiver of *Miranda* was obtained following an initial *Miranda* violation.

- If suspects are interrogated without having been given *Miranda* warnings, the only remedy is that their unwarned statements may not be admitted at trial as substantive evidence against them. They have no viable Section 1983 claim against the officers who failed to honor their *Miranda* rights.

556

PART IV
INTERROGATIONS,
IDENTIFICATIONS, TRIALS,
AND POST-CONVICTION
REMEDIES

Psychologist Thomas Grisso (2003) developed three psychological tests that are considered to be the "gold standard" for assessing comprehension of *Miranda* rights and, therefore, determining the validity of any waiver of these rights. When combined, these three assessments get at the three functional components necessary for a valid waiver:

> (1) "understanding of the *Miranda* warnings" (i.e., the words and phrases used to convey to them the rights to silence and legal counsel); (2) "perceptions of the intended functions of the rights" (i.e., establishing an accurate perception about the adversarial nature of the interrogation, the attorney-client relationship, and the right against self-incrimination); and (3) "expectancies and reasoning concerning probable outcomes of waiver or non-waiver of the rights" (i.e., the capacity to reason about the probable consequence of waiver or non-waiver decisions). (Ferguson 2012: 1470)

The scientifically validated Grisso tests are designed for trained experts in forensic psychology, not justice professionals. However, the essence of the Grisso tests can be incorporated into a dialogue that law enforcement officers can have with any suspect to help ensure that a waiver of Fifth Amendment rights will be upheld as both knowing and intelligent—something that is particularly important when interrogating a suspect who is a juvenile, intellectually impaired, or mentally disordered. A suggested dialogue from an actual case is presented in the following Criminal Procedure in Action.

CRIMINAL PROCEDURE **IN ACTION**

A Dialogue Approach to *Miranda* Waivers

In an influential article, Gregory DeClue (2007) provided an example of how investigators can talk with a suspect whose waiver is potentially vulnerable to attack on the grounds that the suspect did not really understand his or her Fifth Amendment rights and, therefore, could not knowingly and intelligent waive them. DeClue recommended a dialogue approach to obtaining

Miranda waivers from vulnerable suspects, including juveniles and people whose behavior suggests either intellectual disability or active mental illness (see also Ferguson 2012).

The following is a transcript from a videotaped interrogation of a seventeen-year-old female suspected of committing a murder. She was described as being of average intelligence and having no significant psychiatric conditions other than behavioral problems. Note how the officer took special care to make sure the suspect understood her rights by asking the suspect to explain, in her own words, each right the detective read to her. He was careful to clarify any misconceptions that her own explanations revealed.

> Detective G: There's a couple things that we want you to know. I understand that since you've been here you've been great. You've been talking to everybody and trying to tell your side of the story. Our job is to gather all of the facts, okay, and try to put this whole picture together. It's kind of like

a big jigsaw puzzle. We try to put it together. We had to talk to a bunch of people and get a whole bunch of information and you're kind of the last person on the list to talk to, so we can get your side. But there's some things I want to go over first before we talk about any of that stuff. How old are you?

- L: Seventeen.

- Detective G: Okay, um, do you go to school?

- L: No.

- Detective G: . . . How far did you go in school? . . . Do you think you understand the court system a little bit? . . . I'm sure you've watched television and seen different things. When somebody gets arrested for a crime there's certain rights that they have. I'm gonna go over those rights with you because I want to make sure that you understand them. The first right that they talk about is: *I understand that I have a right to remain silent.* Do you understand that?

Continued on next page

- L: Mm-hm [yes].

- Detective G: What does that mean?

- L: I'm not s'pose to say anything.

- Detective G: Is it you're not supposed to say anything or you don't have to say anything?

- L: I don't have to say anything.

- Detective G: Okay. So if you want to say something you could, but if you didn't want to, you also have that right.

- L: Okay.

- Detective G: *I understand that anything I say can be used against me in a court of law.* Do you understand that?

- L: Mm-hm [yes].

- Detective G: What does that mean?

- L: That mean anything I say, that could be brought up again in court.

- Detective G: Correct. *I understand that I have a right to talk to an attorney and have him or her present with me while I'm being questioned.* Do you understand that?

- L: Mm-hm [yes].

- Detective G: What does that mean to you?

- L: That I could hire a lawyer and that, um, discussing it, he be right there.

- Detective G: He could be with you, or she could be with you, when you're talking.

- L: Mm-hm [yes].

- Detective G: Okay. *I understand that if I want an attorney and cannot afford one that an attorney will be appointed to represent me free of charge before any questioning.* Do you understand that?

- L: Mm-hm [yes].

- Detective G: What does that mean?

- L: Like a public defender.

- Detective G: Okay, um, if you came in here today and you had no money to afford, to pay for an attorney, would you still have the right to have one before we talked?

- L: Mm. I don't know. Yeah. I don't know.

- Detective G: Okay. Let's go over that. It says [pointing to the page] if I want an attorney and cannot afford one that an attorney will be appointed to represent me free of charge before any questioning.

- L: Okay.

- Detective G: Okay. So in other words if you came in here and you didn't have the money for an attorney but you wanted one, you could get one before you talked. Is that right or wrong?

- L: Right.

- Detective G: Okay. And feel free to correct me if I say something that's not correct. Okay. *I understand that at any time I can decide to exercise these rights and not answer any questions or make any statements.* Do you understand that?

- L: Yeah.

- Detective G: What does that mean?

- L: If you ask me a question, that I don't have to answer it.

- Detective G: Correct. If we talked for however long we talked and all of a sudden you decided, you know what, I don't want to talk anymore, do you have that right?

- L: Mm-hm [yes].

- Detective G: Yes you do. Okay. *Understanding these rights explained to me I wish to make a statement at this time.* Would you like to talk about what happened today? (DeClue 2007: 433–35) (italics added).

■ Assuming that L then talked with the detective, do you think a court would find that L made a knowing, intelligent, and voluntary waiver of her rights? Explain your reasoning.

■ What, if any, do you see as the potential drawbacks to police following the example set forth above? Do you think that some suspects who engage in such a dialogue might stand on their rights and refuse to talk to investigators? Why or why not? Be sure to take into account that L originally thought that her Miranda rights meant that she was "not s'pose to say anything." Only after the dialogue with the detective did she come to understand that although she had the right not to talk, she was actually allowed to do so.

■ Do you think the dialogue approach to *Miranda* rights and waivers should be used with all suspects or only those who are vulnerable suspects? Why? Do you think police identification of vulnerability poses a challenge to selective use of this approach? Explain your reasoning.

558

PART IV
INTERROGATIONS,
IDENTIFICATIONS, TRIALS,
AND POST-CONVICTION
REMEDIES

Effect of *Miranda–Edwards* in Court

In spite of *Dickerson v. United States*, 530 U.S. 428 (2000), holding that *Miranda* warnings are constitutionally required, violations of *Miranda* rights produce few consequences compared to those that are normally triggered by other violations of constitutional criminal procedure rights.

Miranda Violations Are Barred Only in Prosecution's Case-in-Chief Statements taken in violation of *Miranda* are inadmissible in court as substantive evidence to prove the defendant's guilt. Such statements are permitted to be used at trial for impeachment purposes. *Harris v. New York*, 401 U.S. 222 (1971); *Oregon v. Hass*, 420 U.S. 714 (1975). Similarly, a statement taken in violation of *Edwards v. Arizona* may be used to impeach a defendant's false or inconsistent testimony at trial, even though the same statement may not be used as substantive evidence. *Michigan v. Harvey*, 494 U.S. 344 (1990). And *Michigan v. Tucker*, 417 U.S. 433 (1974), held that a *Miranda* violation that resulted in the discovery of a witness did not preclude the government from later calling that witness to testify at trial. Criminal justice professionals should not interpret these cases as opportunities to evade the requirements of *Miranda–Edwards*. An admission or confession obtained in compliance with those cases is much more valuable to the prosecution than an illegally obtained voluntary statement to be used only for impeachment or discovery of witnesses. In addition, involuntary statements obtained from a defendant cannot be used for any purpose in a criminal trial without violating due process, *Mincey v. Arizona*, 437 U.S. 385 (1978), unless the admission of an involuntary statement is found to be harmless error. *Arizona v. Fulminante*, 499 U.S. 279 (1991).

Effect of Silence Pre- and Postwarnings It has been long settled that a defendant's silence after receiving *Miranda* warnings cannot be used against a defendant at trial either in the prosecution's case-in-chief or for the purpose of impeachment.

> [W]hen a person under arrest is informed as *Miranda* requires, . . . it does not comport with due process to permit the prosecution during the trial to call attention to his silence at the time of arrest and to insist that because he did not speak about the facts of the case at that time, as he was told he need not do, an unfavorable inference might be drawn as to the truth of his trial testimony. *Doyle v. Ohio*, 426 U.S. 610, 619 (1976).

Presumably, *Salinas v. Texas*, 133 S. Ct. 2174 (2013), discussed previously in the chapter, has not altered this approach to postwarning silence. It is clear from *Salinas*, though, that the bar on discussing postwarning silence does not apply to a defendant's silence before *Miranda* warnings are given because "such silence is probative and does not rest on any implied assurance by law enforcement authorities that it will carry no penalty." *Brecht v. Abrahamson*, 507 U.S. 619, 628 (1993); *see also Jenkins v. Anderson*, 447 U.S. 231, 239–44 (1980) (holding that when a defendant takes stand at trial, his or her silence may be used by the prosecution for impeachment purposes if that silence occurred before the defendant's arrest and the administration of *Miranda* warnings); *Fletcher v. Weir*, 455 U.S. 603, 607 (1982) (permitting silence after a defendant's arrest, but before *Miranda* warnings were administered, to be used for impeachment purposes by the prosecution if the defendant takes the stand at trial).

Fruit of the Poisonous Tree Doctrine Inapplicable The fruit of the poisonous tree doctrine (see Chapter 2) is usually applied to prevent the "fruits" of a constitutional violation from being used

KEY POINTS

LO6

- The Sixth Amendment right to counsel is triggered ("attaches") when formal criminal proceedings have begun. As a result, a person is entitled to the help of a lawyer at or after the time that judicial proceedings have been initiated against him, whether by way of formal charge, preliminary hearing, indictment, information, or arraignment.

- Once the Sixth Amendment right to counsel has attached, providing a defendant with *Miranda* warnings,

Continued on next page

in court. However, the Supreme Court has limited this doctrine in two important ways in the Fifth Amendment context.

- As previously discussed, *Oregon v. Elstad*, 470 U.S. 298 (1985), held that when a suspect being subjected to custodial interrogation makes incriminating statements without having been given his or her *Miranda* rights, but subsequently repeats those incriminating statements after having been read his or her *Miranda* rights, the latter statements are admissible so long as the initial un-Mirandized statements were not obtained involuntarily (i.e., a due process violation occurs because deliberately coercive or improper tactics were used to obtain the initial statement).

- The fruit of the poisonous tree doctrine does not apply to physical evidence derived from statements made in violation of *Miranda*. In *United States v. Patane*, 304 F.3d 1013 (10th Cir. 2002), *rev'd*, 542 U.S. 630 (2004), statements made by a suspect in response to police questions that were designed to elicit an incriminating response were suppressed because the defendant had not been read his *Miranda* rights. In response to being asked if he had any firearms, the defendant told police he had a handgun in his bedroom. The gun was suppressed as fruit of the poisonous tree because it was discovered as a result of the defendant's unwarned statements. On appeal, the U.S. Supreme Court reversed, holding that the failure to properly advise a suspect of *Miranda* rights does not trigger the fruit of the poisonous tree doctrine so long as the suspect's unwarned statements were voluntary. Some states, however, have declined to follow *Patane* on state law grounds. *E.g.*, *Commonwealth v. Martin*, 827 N.E.2d 198 (Mass. 2005); *State v. Knapp*, 700 N.W.2d 899 (Wis. 2005).

Section 1983 Claims Barred for *Miranda* Violations In *Chavez v. Martinez*, 538 U.S. 760 (2003), a suspect was interrogated by police while he was in the hospital being treated for gunshot wounds he sustained during an altercation with the police. In spite of the fact that the interrogation interrupted the suspect's medical care, the officer refused to stop the questioning of the suspect (over the objections of medical personnel) until the suspect admitted that he had pointed a gun at an officer. He eventually made such an admission. However, at no time during the interrogation had the suspect been given his *Miranda* rights. The suspect was never charged with a crime, but he subsequently sued the police under 42 U.S.C. Section 1983 for a number of claims. The district court ruled in his favor that the police had violated his Fifth Amendment rights. The U.S. Court of Appeals for the Ninth Circuit affirmed, but the Supreme Court reversed in a highly fractured plurality opinion. As a result, the only remedy for suspects who are interrogated without being Mirandized first is that their unwarned statements may not be admitted at trial as substantive evidence against them. There is no civil enforcement mechanism against officers who failed to honor *Miranda* rights.

Interrogation and the Sixth Amendment

The Sixth Amendment to the U.S. Constitution provides that "[i]n all criminal prosecutions, the accused shall enjoy the right . . . to have the Assistance of Counsel for his defense." Recall that *Escobedo v. Illinois*, 378 U.S. 478 (1964), tied the Sixth Amendment

560

PART IV
INTERROGATIONS,
IDENTIFICATIONS, TRIALS,
AND POST-CONVICTION
REMEDIES

right to counsel to pretrial criminal proceedings once the suspect had become the focus of the investigation. Although *Escobedo* was short-lived, its core holding—that the Sixth Amendment right to counsel has application at pretrial stages of criminal prosecutions—remains a vital principle in constitutional criminal procedure.

Attachment of Sixth Amendment Right to Counsel

The right to counsel under the Sixth Amendment differs from the right to counsel under *Miranda* that flows from the Fifth Amendment. The sole purpose of the right under *Miranda* is to ensure that a suspect's will is not overborne by coercive police interrogation tactics while the suspect is in custody. Thus, it exists to prevent compulsory self-incrimination only when a suspect is subject to custodial interrogation. In contrast, the Sixth Amendment is not concerned with compulsion in the self-incrimination context; rather, it protects those facing criminal adversarial proceedings in court. Thus, the Sixth Amendment right to counsel is triggered ("attaches") when formal criminal proceedings "have been initiated against him whether by way of formal charge, preliminary hearing, indictment, information, or arraignment." *Fellers v. United States*, 540 U.S. 519, 523 (2004).

Once the Sixth Amendment right to counsel attaches and is invoked or asserted, authorities may not engage in any conduct that is designed to elicit an incriminating response from the defendant without the presence or waiver of counsel. *Brewer v. Williams*, 430 U.S. 387 (1977). This means that a defendant may not be questioned without his or her lawyer being present unless a valid waiver of the Sixth Amendment right to counsel is first obtained. Recall that in *Moran v. Burbine*, no Fifth Amendment violation was found when the police failed to disclose to the suspect that his family had retained a lawyer for him and that lawyer had been trying to reach the defendant. Had formal criminal proceedings begun, and thus the right to counsel under the Sixth Amendment attached, a constitutional violation would have occurred. *Patterson v. Illinois*, 487 U.S. 285, 296 n.9 (1988).

Fifth Amendment "Interrogation" Versus Sixth Amendment "Deliberate Elicitation" The Sixth Amendment right to counsel attaches under circumstances that are qualitatively different from those giving rise to a Fifth Amendment right to counsel. Thus, *Miranda*'s focus on custodial interrogation is inapplicable when examining Sixth Amendment rights. Rather, the Sixth Amendment bars the use of any statements made by a defendant in response to the actions of law enforcement that might *deliberately elicit an incriminating response*. Deliberate elicitation occurs when state officials create "a situation likely to induce . . . incriminating statements without the assistance of counsel." *United States v. Henry*, 447 U.S. 264, 274–75 (1980).

The deliberate elicitation standard is broader than the protections afforded suspects under the Fifth Amendment because it prohibits authorities from engaging in conduct that would not be considered "interrogation" or its functional equivalent under *Miranda*. Perhaps one of the most notable differences between the two amendments' approaches is that the Sixth Amendment bars the use of any secret investigatory techniques, whereas the Fifth Amendment does not. Consider the following leading cases.

Deliberate Elicitation Violates Right to Counsel Once the Sixth Amendment right to counsel attaches, the state must not do anything that deliberately or knowingly interferes with that right.

■ In *Massiah v. United States*, 377 U.S. 201 (1964), after the defendant was indicted, federal agents obtained incriminating statements from him in the absence of his counsel. While the defendant was free on bail, his co-defendant, in cooperation with the federal agents, engaged the defendant in conversation in the presence of a hidden radio transmitter located in the co-defendant's car. Because the defendant was not in custody, no Fifth Amendment rights under *Miranda* were applicable; however, because he had already been indicted, the defendant's Sixth Amendment right to counsel had attached. The Supreme Court determined that the statements were inadmissible because the government violated the defendant's Sixth Amendment rights by using "his own incriminating words, which federal agents had deliberately elicited from him after he had been indicted and in the absence of his counsel." 377 U.S. at 206.

■ The Supreme Court affirmed the continuing validity of *Massiah* in *Brewer v. Williams*, 430 U.S. 387 (1977), a case often referred to as the "Christian Burial Speech" case. The defendant, Williams, had been arrested, arraigned, and jailed in Davenport, Iowa, for abducting a ten-year-old girl in Des Moines, Iowa. He needed to be transported by police from where he was captured in Davenport to Des Moines where his trial would take place. His lawyer in Davenport was denied permission to ride in the back seat of the police car with Williams during the 160-mile drive. Accordingly, both that lawyer and the one who was representing Williams in Des Moines advised him not to make any statements during the trip. Pursuant to their instructions, "[a]t no time during the trip did Williams express a willingness to be interrogated in the absence of an attorney." 430 U.S. at 392. The police officers transporting Williams agreed not to question him during the trip. However, soon after the police began their trip with the defendant from Davenport to Des Moines, one officer engaged the defendant in "a wide-ranging conversation covering a variety of topics, including the subject of religion." 430 U.S. at 392. One of the officers then said the following to Williams, whom he addressed as "Reverend":

"I want to give you something to think about while we're traveling down the road. . . . Number one, I want you to observe the weather conditions, it's raining, it's sleeting, it's freezing, driving is very treacherous, visibility is poor, it's going to be dark early this evening. They are predicting several inches of snow for tonight, and I feel that you yourself are the only person that knows where this little girl's body is, that you yourself have only been there once, and if you get snow on top of it you yourself may be unable to find it. And, since we will be going right past the area on the way into Des Moines, I feel that we could stop and locate the body, that the parents of this little girl should be entitled to a Christian burial for the little girl who was snatched away from them on Christmas Eve and murdered. And I feel we should stop and locate it on the way in rather than waiting until morning and trying to come back out after a snow storm and possibly not being able to find it at all." Williams asked [the officer] why he thought their route to Des Moines would be taking them past the girl's body, and [he] responded that he knew the body was in the area of Mitchellville, a town they would be passing on the way to Des Moines. [The officer] then stated: "I do not want you to answer me. I don't want to discuss it any further. Just think about it as we're riding down the road."

As the car approached Grinnell, a town approximately 100 miles west of Davenport, Williams asked whether the police had found the victim's shoes. When [an officer] replied that he was unsure, Williams directed the officers to a service station where he said he had left the shoes; a search for them proved unsuccessful. As they continued towards Des Moines, Williams asked whether the police had found the blanket, and directed the officers to a rest area where he said he had disposed of the blanket. Nothing was found. The car continued towards Des Moines, and as it approached Mitchellville, Williams said that he would show the officers where the body was. He then directed the police to the body of [the victim]. 430 U.S. at 392–93.

562

PART IV
INTERROGATIONS,
IDENTIFICATIONS, TRIALS,
AND POST-CONVICTION
REMEDIES

Because Williams had already been arraigned, formal adversarial proceedings had commenced against him; he therefore had a Sixth Amendment right to have legal representation during the time in which he made incriminating statements in response to the officer's "Christian Burial Speech." The Court said that there could be no doubt that the officer "deliberately and designedly set out to elicit information from Williams just as surely as and perhaps more effectively than if he had formally interrogated him." 430 U.S. at 399. Thus, relying on *Massiah*, the Court ruled that Williams's statements were inadmissible because they had been obtained by police in violation of his Sixth Amendment right to counsel.

- *United States v. Henry*, 447 U.S. 264 (1980), upheld the suppression of statements made by an indicted and imprisoned defendant to a paid, undisclosed government informant who was in the same cell block. Although the informant did not question the defendant, the informant "stimulated" conversations with him and developed a relationship of trust and confidence with him. As a result, the defendant made incriminating statements without the assistance of counsel. This indirect and surreptitious type of interrogation was an impermissible interference with the Sixth Amendment in violation of *Massiah* because the government "intentionally created a situation likely to induce [the defendant] to make incriminating statements without the assistance of counsel." 447 U.S. at 274 (1980). Key to the Court's rationale was the fact that the government had "singled out" the defendant as the informant's target, used an informant whose "apparent status [was that of] a person sharing a common plight" with the defendant, and agreed to pay the informant only if he provided useful information. *See also Randolph v. California*, 380 F.3d 1133 (9th Cir. 2004); *Manning v. Bowersox*, 310 F.3d 571 (8th Cir. 2002).

- *Maine v. Moulton*, 474 U.S. 159 (1985), held that even when a confrontation between an accused and a police agent is initiated by the accused, the government may not deliberately attempt to elicit information without counsel present. In *Moulton*, two co-defendants had been indicted on several theft-related offenses. During a meeting in which the two defendants met to discuss strategy for their upcoming trial, Moulton suggested that the two kill one of the state's witnesses against them. The co-defendant and his lawyer subsequently met with police and confessed to his participation in a series of thefts that included the charges for which he and Moulton had already been indicted, as well as other thefts. In exchange for a promise that no further charges would be brought against him, the defendant agreed to testify against Moulton and otherwise cooperate in the ongoing police investigation. As part of that agreement, the co-defendant allowed a recording device to be placed on his telephone line so that police could record conversation that he had with Moulton. During several telephone conversations, the co-defendant got Moulton to make several incriminating statements. He also got Moulton to make incriminating statements during meetings between the two defendants while the co-defendant was wired with a recording device.

The state attempted to distinguish the actions of the police in this case from those in *Massiah* and *Henry* on the grounds that in those cases, "the police set up the confrontation between the accused and a police agent at which incriminating statements were elicited." 474 U.S. at 175. In contrast, Moulton had initiated the recorded telephone conversations and had requested the in-person meeting in which another conversation was recorded. The Supreme Court rejected this distinction and held that the guarantee of the Sixth Amendment includes the government's affirmative obligation not to circumvent the protections afforded the accused who invokes his or her right to rely on counsel as a "medium" between the accused and the government. The Court continued:

[T]he Sixth Amendment is not violated whenever—by luck or happenstance—the State obtains incriminating statements from the accused after the right to counsel has attached. . . . However, knowing exploitation by the State of an opportunity to confront the accused without counsel being present is as much a breach of the State's obligation not to circumvent the right to assistance of counsel as is the intentional creation of such an opportunity. Accordingly, the Sixth Amendment is violated when the State obtains incriminating statements by knowingly circumventing the accused's right to have counsel present in a confrontation between the accused and a state agent. 474 U.S. at 176.

- *Powell v. Texas*, 492 U.S. 680 (1989), held that the Sixth Amendment is violated when a psychiatric or psychological examination of the defendant is performed, but defense counsel is not given adequate notice of the examination, its scope, and nature. However, there is no Sixth Amendment violation when defense is notified of a psychiatric or psychological exam and chooses not to attend. *Re v. Snyder*, 293 F.3d 678 (3d Cir. 2002).

- In *Fellers v. United States*, 540 U.S. 519 (2004), the defendant had been indicted by a grand jury on charges related to the distribution of methamphetamine. When police subsequently arrested him in his home, they told him he had been charged with distributing methamphetamine. In response, the defendant made incriminating statements. In holding that the police violated his Sixth Amendment right to counsel, the Court stated:

> [T]here is no question that the officers in this case "deliberately elicited" information from petitioner. Indeed, the officers, upon arriving at petitioner's house, informed him that their purpose in coming was to discuss his involvement in the distribution of methamphetamine and his association with certain charged co-conspirators. Because the ensuing discussion took place after petitioner had been indicted, outside the presence of counsel, and in the absence of any waiver of petitioner's Sixth Amendment rights, the Court of Appeals erred in holding that the officers' actions did not violate the Sixth Amendment standards established in *Massiah* . . . and its progeny. 540 U.S. at 524–25.

Passive Receipt of Information Does Not Violate the Right to Counsel

A defendant's Sixth Amendment rights are not violated when an informant, either through prior arrangement or voluntarily, reports the defendant's incriminating statements to the police. "[T]he defendant must demonstrate that the police and their informant took some action, beyond merely listening, that was designed deliberately to elicit incriminating remarks." *Kuhlmann v. Wilson*, 477 U.S. 436, 459 (1986). For example, in *United States v. LaBare*, 191 F.3d 60, 65–66 (1st Cir. 1999), the court ruled that a defendant's incriminating statements to a cellmate were admissible when the cellmate simply reported the statements to federal authorities under a general agreement to report what he might hear from other prisoners about violations of law, but was instructed not to directly question anyone. "Where a jail-mate simply agrees to report whatever he learns about crimes from other inmates in general, . . . there is not enough to trigger *Massiah*."

Offense-Specific Nature of the Sixth Amendment Right to Counsel

The Sixth Amendment right to counsel, unlike the right to counsel under *Miranda* flowing from the Fifth Amendment's privilege against self-incrimination, is *offense specific*. Thus, invocation of the Sixth Amendment right to counsel bars police from

564

PART IV
INTERROGATIONS,
IDENTIFICATIONS, TRIALS,
AND POST-CONVICTION
REMEDIES

deliberately eliciting incriminating information regarding only the offense at issue; it does not bar police-initiated interrogation or other activities designed to elicit an incriminating response on unrelated charges:

> The purpose of the Sixth Amendment counsel guarantee—and hence the purpose of invoking it—is to "protec[t] the unaided layman at critical confrontations" with his "expert adversary," the government, after "the adverse positions of government and defendant have solidified" with respect to a particular alleged crime. . . . The purpose of the *Miranda–Edwards* guarantee, on the other hand—and hence the purpose of invoking it—is to protect a quite different interest: the suspect's "desire to deal with the police only through counsel." . . . This is in one respect narrower than the interest protected by the Sixth Amendment guarantee (because it relates only to custodial interrogation) and in another respect broader (because it relates to interrogation regarding any suspected crime and attaches whether or not the "adversarial relationship" produced by a pending prosecution has yet arisen). *McNeil v. Wisconsin*, 501 U.S. 171, 177–78 (1991).

The prohibition against deliberate attempts to elicit information in the absence of counsel is not intended to hamper police investigation of crimes other than the crime for which adversary proceedings have already commenced. The police need to investigate crimes for which formal charges have already been filed as well as new or additional crimes. Either type of investigation may require surveillance of persons already indicted. Moreover, police who are investigating a person suspected of committing one crime and formally charged with having committed another crime may seek to discover evidence of either crime. In seeking evidence relating to pending charges, however, police investigators are limited by the Sixth Amendment rights of the accused. Therefore, incriminating statements relating to pending charges will be inadmissible at the trial of those charges—even though police were also investigating other crimes—if, in obtaining the evidence, the government violated the Sixth Amendment by knowingly circumventing the accused's right to the assistance of counsel. On the other hand, evidence relating to charges to which the Sixth Amendment right to counsel had not attached at the time the evidence was obtained will not be inadmissible merely because other charges were pending at the time. *Maine v. Moulton*, 474 U.S. 159 (1985).

In *Texas v. Cobb*, 532 U.S. 162 (2001), the defendant confessed to a home burglary but denied knowledge of a woman and child's disappearance from the home. He was indicted for the burglary, and counsel was appointed to represent him on that charge. He later confessed to his father that he had killed the woman and child in the course of the burglary, and his father contacted the police. After police arrested him and administered *Miranda* warnings, he waived his *Miranda* rights and confessed to the murders. On appeal of his capital murder conviction, he argued that his confession should have been suppressed because it was obtained in violation of his Sixth Amendment right to counsel. He claimed that the right attached when counsel was appointed in the burglary case, which was "factually related" to the capital murder charge. The Court rejected the claim and held that, because burglary and capital murder are not the *same offense* under Texas law, and because the Sixth Amendment right to counsel is "offense specific," the failure to obtain the defendant's counsel's permission did not bar the police from interrogating him regarding the murders. His confession was therefore admissible.

Waiver of Sixth Amendment Right to Counsel

As with the Fifth Amendment right to counsel under *Miranda*, a defendant may waive his or her right to counsel under the Sixth Amendment. Also, as it is with the Fifth Amendment, there is a strong presumption against implied waivers of counsel in the Sixth Amendment context, given the essential function that defense counsel plays in the administration of justice.

[It is] incumbent upon the State to prove "an intentional relinquishment or abandonment of a known right or privilege." That standard has been reiterated in many cases. We have said that the right to counsel does not depend upon a request by the defendant, . . . and that courts indulge in every reasonable presumption against waiver. This strict standard applies equally to an alleged waiver of the right to counsel whether at trial or at a critical stage of pretrial proceedings. *Brewer v. Williams*, 430 U.S. 387, 404 (1977) (internal citations omitted).

Thus, to show that a valid waiver of counsel for Sixth Amendment purposes exists, the prosecution must prove that

1. the defendant was aware of the right to counsel, and
2. the defendant knowingly, intelligently, and voluntarily relinquished the right.

This is qualitatively no different from waivers in the Fifth Amendment context under *Miranda*. *Patterson v. Illinois*, 487 U.S. 285 (1988).

Miranda Warnings Sufficient to Provide Knowledge of Right to Counsel

The Supreme Court created *Miranda* warnings to safeguard the Fifth Amendment privilege against self-incrimination. In spite of this, *Patterson v. Illinois*, 487 U.S. 285 (1988), held that the *Miranda* warnings are also sufficient to inform a defendant of the right to have counsel present during questioning once the Sixth Amendment right to counsel has attached, as well as the consequences of a decision to waive the Sixth Amendment right during such questioning:

[W]hatever warnings suffice for *Miranda's* purposes will also be sufficient in the context of post-indictment questioning. The State's decision to take an additional step and commence formal adversarial proceedings against the accused does not substantially increase the value of counsel to the accused at questioning, or expand the limited purpose that an attorney serves when the accused is questioned by authorities. With respect to this inquiry, we do not discern a substantial difference between the usefulness of a lawyer to a suspect during custodial interrogation, and his value to an accused at post-indictment questioning. 487 U.S. at 298–99.

Waiver After *Miranda* Warnings

Once a defendant suspect has been informed of his right to counsel under the Sixth Amendment by having been "admonished with the warnings prescribed by [the Supreme] Court in Miranda" and has been sufficiently apprised of the nature and consequences of abandoning his or her Sixth Amendment rights, the defendant's "waiver on this basis will be considered a knowing and intelligent one." *Patterson*, 487 U.S. at 296.

Subsequent Waiver After Initial Invocation of the Sixth Amendment Rights

Recall that under *Edwards v. Arizona*, 451 U.S. 477 (1981), after a knowing and voluntary waiver of *Miranda* rights, law enforcement officers may continue questioning until and unless the suspect clearly requests an attorney. Similar to the rule in *Edwards* for Fifth Amendment purposes, the Supreme Court has held that once a defendant has unambiguously invoked his or her right to counsel under the Sixth Amendment at or after the initiation of adversary judicial proceedings, any further interrogation of the defendant without counsel actually being present is not permitted if the police initiate the discussion. *Patterson v. Illinois*, 487 U.S. 285 (1988). But, as the following Discussion Point illustrates, invoking the right is important.

DISCUSSION POINT

Should It Matter If a Defendant Stays Silent When Formal Criminal Proceedings Commence? *Montejo v. Louisiana*, 556 U.S. 778 (2009).

At a preliminary hearing required by Louisiana law, Montejo was charged with first-degree murder. Although he remained silent at the hearing, the court declared Montejo indigent and automatically appointed counsel to represent him. Later that day, the police approached Montejo and read him *Miranda* rights, after which he agreed to go along on a trip to locate the murder weapon. During the excursion, he wrote an inculpatory letter of apology to the victim's widow. Upon returning, Montejo finally met his court-appointed attorney. At trial, his letter was admitted over defense objection, and he was convicted and sentenced to death.

The state high court rejected Montego's claim that the letter should have been suppressed under the rule of *Michigan v. Jackson*, 475 U.S. 625 (1986). In *Jackson*, several defendants requested counsel at their arraignments on murder charges. Before counsel had been provided to them, police officers questioned the defendants after advising them of their *Miranda* rights. The defendants waived their *Miranda* rights and agreed to talk with police who, in turn, were able to obtain confessions from the defendants. The U.S. Supreme Court held that the confessions were obtained in violation of the Sixth Amendment right to counsel because police initiated contact with the defendants after they had invoked their right to counsel and, in so doing, sought a waiver of that right before counsel had actually been provided to the defendants. The Louisiana Supreme Court reasoned *Jackson* did not apply because Montejo stood mute at his hearing while the judge ordered the appointment of counsel. Thus, he never actually asserted his Sixth Amendment right to counsel.

The U.S. Supreme Court upheld Montejo's conviction but disagreed with the state court's rationale, believing its interpretation of *Jackson* would lead to practical problems because in roughly half the states counsel is appointed without a request from the defendant upon a finding of indigency. The Court also rejected Montejo's proposal that defendants should not have invoked their Sixth Amendment rights because such an approach would depart fundamentally from the rationale of *Jackson*, whose presumption was created by analogy to *Edwards's* approach to protecting *Miranda* rights. The Court reasoned that both *Edwards* and *Jackson* were meant to prevent police from badgering defendants into changing their minds about the right to counsel once they invoked it, but a defendant who never asked for counsel had not yet made up his mind in the first instance.

Ultimately, the Court overruled *Jackson* and declared a new rule to protect criminal defendants' Sixth Amendment rights to counsel that mirrors *Edwards's* antibadgering approach in the Fifth Amendment context—namely, that a defendant in custody cannot be interrogated once he has asserted his Sixth Amendment right to counsel unless the defendant initiates further communications with police.

The Court remanded the case to give Montejo an opportunity to argue that his letter of apology should still have been suppressed under the rule of *Edwards*. Thus, if Montejo clearly asserted the right to counsel when the officers approached him about accompanying them on the excursion for the murder weapon, then no interrogation should have taken place unless Montejo initiated it. Even if Montejo subsequently agreed to waive his rights, that waiver would have been invalid had it followed an "unequivocal election of the right."

- Applying the logic of *Edwards* in the Sixth Amendment context as *Montejo* instructs, do you think his letter should have been suppressed from evidence? Why or why not?

- On remand, Montejo's claims were dismissed because his motion to suppress had been based on the Fifth Amendment. His Sixth Amendment concerns were not evident until trial when, under state law, the testimony came too late to affect the propriety of the admission of the evidence (because, as explained in Chapter 15, new bases for an objection cannot be raised for the first time on appeal). Moreover, assuming, for the sake of argument, that the letter was improperly admitted into evidence, it was deemed harmless error (see Chapter 15). Do you agree or disagree with the outcome in this case? Explain your reasoning.

In light of *Montejo*, if a defendant reinitiates contact with police after requesting that counsel be provided under the Sixth Amendment (i.e., after asserting the right once formal criminal proceedings have been commenced against the suspect), and the defendant is readvised of his or her *Miranda* rights and then knowingly and voluntarily waives them, following the parallel *Edwards* rule for the Fifth Amendment, such a waiver of the Sixth Amendment right to counsel will likely be upheld as valid.

Remedies for Violations of the Sixth Amendment Right to Counsel Violations of the Sixth Amendment right to counsel in the interrogation context are treated in much the same way *Miranda* violations are treated. Thus, any incriminating statements made by a defendant that are obtained in violation of the Sixth Amendment are inadmissible at trial in the prosecution's case-in-chief. *Michigan v. Harvey*, 494 U.S. 344 (1990). But so long as statements obtained in violation of the Sixth Amendment were voluntary (i.e., due process was not also violated), then statements are admissible under one of two circumstances: (1) if necessary to show inconsistencies in a defendant's statement for impeach or perjury purposes; and (2) if one of the exceptions to the exclusionary rule discussed in Chapter 2 applies (e.g., good faith, attenuation, etc.). *Kansas v. Ventris*, 556 U.S. 586 (2009).

Subsequent Waiver After Initial Violation of the Sixth Amendment Recall that, under *Oregon v. Elstad*, 470 U.S. 298 (1985), if a suspect being subjected to custodial interrogation makes incriminating statements without having been given his or her *Miranda* rights, subsequent reiterations of those incriminating statements after having been properly Mirandized can purge the taint of the initial constitutional violation so long as the initial statements were knowingly and voluntarily given. Thus, *Elstad* held that the fruit of the poisonous tree doctrine applies only if the initial *Miranda* violation was accompanied by deliberately coercive or improper tactics in obtaining the initial statement. Although the Supreme Court has not yet ruled on whether the *Elstad* would similarly disallow the fruit of the poisonous tree doctrine to Sixth Amendment violations, at least one U.S. Circuit Court of Appeals has extended *Elstad* to the Sixth Amendment realm.

In *Fellers v. United States*, 540 U.S. 519 (2004), the Supreme Court determined that postindictment statements made by a defendant in response to police statements while being arrested on methamphetamine charges violated the defendant's Sixth Amendment right to counsel. There was no indication, however, that the defendant's statements were anything other than purely voluntary. The Court ended its decision in *Fellers* by remanding the case for consideration of the question of whether the Sixth Amendment required suppression of Feller's "jailhouse statements on the ground that they were the fruits of previous questioning conducted in violation of the Sixth Amendment deliberate-elicitation standard." On remand, the Eighth Circuit answered that question in the negative.

> In contrast with the statements made at Fellers's home, Fellers's jailhouse statements were given after a proper administration of *Miranda* warnings and a proper oral and written waiver of his *Miranda* rights. The *Miranda* warnings fully informed Fellers of "the sum and substance" of his Sixth Amendment rights, and his waiver of his *Miranda* rights operated as a knowing, intelligent, and voluntary waiver of his right to counsel [under *Patterson*, 487 U.S. at 293–94]. He was thus given all of the information he needed to decide whether to invoke his Sixth Amendment rights. Furthermore, no evidence indicates that either Fellers's initial statements or his subsequent jailhouse statements were coerced, compelled, or otherwise involuntary. As a result, the condition that made his prior statements inadmissible—the inability to have counsel present or to waive the right to counsel—was removed. *United States v. Fellers*, 397 F.3d 1090 (8th Cir.), *cert denied*, 546 U.S. 933 (2005).

LO6

KEY POINTS

- After a defendant has been formally charged and has requested counsel, law enforcement authorities may not deliberately elicit incriminating statements either directly or by surreptitious methods concerning the crimes for which the defendant has been charged. The Sixth Amendment, however, does not bar police-initiated interrogation or other activities designed to elicit an incriminating response on unrelated crimes for which the defendant has not been charged or has not invoked the right to counsel.

- Any incriminating statements made by a defendant that are obtained in violation of the Sixth Amendment are inadmissible at trial in the prosecution's case in chief, but such statements are admissible for impeachment purposes if they were obtained voluntarily.

568

PART IV
INTERROGATIONS,
IDENTIFICATIONS, TRIALS,
AND POST-CONVICTION
REMEDIES

SUMMARY

An admission or confession obtained by a law enforcement officer is inadmissible in court unless (1) it is voluntary and (2) the requirements of *Miranda v. Arizona* are satisfied. A statement is involuntary if it is a product of police coercion, whether by force or by subtler forms of coercion, and if, in the totality of the circumstances, the statement is not the result of a person's free and rational choice. In determining voluntariness, courts consider the personal characteristics of the defendant, such as age, mental capacity, physical or mental impairment, and experience with the police, in establishing the setting in which coercion might operate to overcome the defendant's will.

Miranda held that a statement obtained by police during a custodial interrogation of a defendant is inadmissible unless the police used certain procedural safeguards to secure the defendant's privilege against self-incrimination. Those procedural safeguards are (1) giving warnings of rights and (2) obtaining a valid waiver of those rights, before an interrogation is begun. Therefore, the major issues of *Miranda* fall into four categories: custody, interrogation, warnings, and waiver.

A person is in custody if there is a formal arrest or restraint on freedom of movement of the degree associated with a formal arrest. Custody is determined by examining, from a reasonable person's point of view, the totality of facts and circumstances surrounding an encounter between a person and law enforcement authorities. These include the place; the time; the presence of family, friends, or other persons; physical restraint; and coercion or domination by the police.

Interrogation refers not only to express questioning but also to any words or actions on the part of police that the police should know are reasonably likely to elicit an incriminating response. Nevertheless, clarifying questions, spontaneous questions, and routine questions are not considered to be interrogation for *Miranda* purposes. In addition, volunteered statements are not the product of interrogation and are not subject to the *Miranda* requirements. Multiple attempts at interrogation are permitted after a defendant's invocation of the right to silence, but the defendant's right to cut off questioning must be scrupulously honored, fresh warnings must be given, and no coercion or other pressures may be employed. If the defendant has exercised the right to counsel, further interrogation without counsel may be conducted only upon the initiation of the defendant and the waiver of *Miranda* rights.

Miranda warnings must be recited clearly and unhurriedly in a language understood by the suspect. Special care must be taken to carefully explain the meaning of the warnings to immature, illiterate, or impaired persons. *Miranda* requirements apply regardless of the nature or severity of the offense being investigated. *Miranda* does not apply to civil proceedings such as customs procedures, civil commitments, extradition proceedings, and license revocation proceedings.

A person who waives the *Miranda* rights to remain silent and to have an attorney may be questioned. To be effective, a waiver of *Miranda* rights must be voluntary and made with a full awareness of both the nature of the right being abandoned and the consequences of the decision to abandon it. Waiver will not be inferred from mere silence but may be expressed by a great variety of words and gestures. If possible, an officer should obtain a written waiver of rights, because a written waiver provides the best evidence of a voluntary and intentional relinquishment of a known right.

After a defendant has been formally charged and has requested counsel, law enforcement authorities are prohibited under the Sixth Amendment from using any methods, however surreptitious or indirect, to elicit incriminating evidence from the defendant in the absence of counsel.

REVIEW AND DISCUSSION QUESTIONS

1. Would any of the following actions cause a statement of a suspect to be involuntary?

   a. Making an appeal to the suspect's moral or religious beliefs

   b. Confronting the suspect with the deceased or seriously injured victim of the crime in question

   c. Starting an argument with, challenging, or baiting the suspect

2. Does a person need a lawyer to help decide whether to waive *Miranda* rights? Is the compelling atmosphere of a custodial setting just as likely to influence a person's decision to waive rights as it is to influence the decision to confess?

3. Is a person's giving of consent to search an inculpatory or exculpatory statement? Should a person in custody be given *Miranda* warnings before being asked for consent to search? Why must police give elaborate warnings before custodial interrogation but no warnings before obtaining consent to search?

4. Assume that a person has been formally arrested for one crime, and police want to question that person about another, unrelated crime. Are *Miranda* warnings required to be given before the questioning? If the answer is no, what additional circumstances might cause *Miranda* warnings to be required?

5. It is reasonable to assume that a person under investigation for a crime might think that complete silence in the face of an accusation might not look good to a judge or a jury. Should the *Miranda* warnings include a statement that a person's silence may not be used against the person in any way?

6. Should suspects be told the nature and seriousness of the offense for which they are being interrogated? What if a person believes that he or she is being investigated for an accident caused by driving while intoxicated but does not know that a person in the other vehicle has died?

7. What would be the advantages and disadvantages of requiring law enforcement officers to tape-record the entire process of administration of *Miranda* warnings and the suspect's invocation or waiver of rights?

8. Is it proper for a law enforcement officer to inform a suspect who has just invoked the *Miranda* right to counsel that the case against the suspect is strong and that immediate cooperation with the authorities would be beneficial in the long run? If the suspect says, "What do you mean?" would this be considered an initiation of further communication by the suspect and a waiver of the right to counsel?

9. Considering the confusion and pressures associated with being arrested and transported to a police station, should arrested persons be advised, in addition to the *Miranda* warnings, of where they are being taken, what is going to happen to them, how long they will be held, and with whom they may communicate?

10. Would the *Massiah* rule be violated if conversations of an indicted and imprisoned person were obtained by means of a listening device installed in that person's cell?

11. In *New York v. Quarles*, the Court said, "We think police officers can and will distinguish almost instinctively between questions necessary to secure their own safety or the safety of the public and questions designed solely to elicit testimonial evidence from a suspect." Do you agree or disagree with this statement? Describe three situations in which the distinction might not be so easy for a police officer to make.

LO1 DEFINE the terms *confrontation*, *showup*, *lineup*, and *photo array*.

LO2 DESCRIBE how perception is a selective and interpretive process that can contribute to mistakes in identification procedures that can, in turn, lead to wrongful convictions.

LO3 EXPLAIN the three phases of memory.

LO4 DISCUSS both of the estimator variables (including event factors and individual witness factors) that influence our ability to remember events accurately, and understand how these factors can contribute to mistakes in identification procedures that can in turn lead to wrongful convictions.

LO5 EXPLAIN why the presence of counsel is required at a pretrial confrontation with witnesses conducted after the initiation of adversary judicial proceedings.

LO6 ANALYZE when a law enforcement officer may use a one-person showup and the ways in which the inherent suggestiveness of the showup may be reduced.

LO7 EVALUATE the factors that indicate accuracy or reliability of an identification even if the identification procedure was unnecessarily suggestive.

LO8 EXPLAIN the proper procedures for conducting a lineup and a photographic identification procedure.

You have undoubtedly heard the expression "seeing is believing." Juries accept this adage as a truism when they consider the testimony of an eyewitness. But there are serious problems with the accuracy of pretrial confrontation techniques that lead to most eyewitness identifications.

A **confrontation** is any presentation of a suspect to a victim of or witness to a crime for the purpose of identifying the perpetrator of the crime. Pretrial confrontation of a suspected criminal with witnesses or victims has long been an accepted law enforcement technique to identify perpetrators of crime and also to clear innocent suspects. Most eyewitness identifications occur as a result of one of two pretrial confrontation techniques: showups or lineups.

A **showup** is the presentation of a single suspect to a victim of or witness to a crime for the purpose of identifying the perpetrator of the crime. A **lineup** is the presentation of several persons at one time to a victim of or witness to a crime for the purpose of identifying the perpetrator of the crime. A lineup gives the victim or witness several choices (a suspect may or may not be included). Both procedures can also be conducted using photographs. A **photographic showup** is a presentation of a single photograph of a suspect to a victim of or witness to a crime, and a **photographic lineup** (also called a **photo array**) is a presentation at one time of several photographs, including that of a suspect, to a victim of or witness to a crime.

Decades of research have demonstrated that eyewitness identifications, regardless of the technique used, are remarkably unreliable. This chapter explores the factors that contribute to the unreliability of eyewitness identifications and the ways in which criminal justice professionals can conduct pretrial confrontations to minimize identification errors.

Mistaken Identifications: The Role of Perception and Memory

Unreliability of eyewitness identification testimony may have many causes.[1] First, it is possible that an eyewitness is lying. Concerns about truthful witnesses can be traced back millennia. Juries are expected to assess the veracity of all witnesses, and cross-examination is presumed to reveal when eyewitnesses have motivation to lie, just as it would with any other witness. More troubling, however, is the eyewitness who honestly believes his or her testimony is the truth, but is incorrect.

Although there is no truly accurate way to know how often mistaken identifications result in wrongful convictions, decades of research on the topic point to it as the leading cause (Goss 1999; Huff et al. 2003; Sporer 1966). In fact, the Innocence Project (2014)—a national organization devoted to helping wrongfully convicted prisoners prove their innocence using DNA evidence—reports that 72 percent of the convictions overturned by DNA evidence involved a mistaken eyewitness. Moreover, as Figure 14.1 illustrates, multiple eyewitnesses misidentified the same innocent person in 38 percent of the cases.

"[D]espite its inherent unreliability, much eyewitness identification evidence has a powerful impact on juries. . . . All evidence points rather strikingly to the conclusion that there is almost nothing more convincing than a live human being who takes the stand, points a finger at the defendant, and says, 'That's the one!'" *Watkins v. Sowders*, 449 U.S. 341, 352 (1981). Yet, as Figure 14.2 illustrates, mistaken identification is the leading cause of wrongful convictions.

The data in Figure 14.1 are based on DNA exonerations conducted by the Innocence Project. However, as Wells and Quinlivan (2009: 2) explain:

> There are several reasons why the true numbers would have to be dramatically higher.
> . . . First, in a large percentage of the old cases (in which convicted persons claim to have been misidentified) the biological evidence for DNA testing has deteriorated, has been lost, or has been destroyed. Moreover, virtually all DNA exoneration cases involved sexual assault because those are the cases for which definitive biological evidence (contained in semen) is available to trump the mistaken identification. Such biological evidence is almost never available for murders, robberies, drive-by shootings, and other common crimes that have relied on eyewitness identification evidence. A recent study of lineups in Illinois indicates that only 5 percent of lineups conducted in Chicago, Evanston, and Joliet were sexual assault cases (Mecklenburg 2006). Most lineup identifications were for non-sexual assaults, robberies, and murders for which there is almost no chance

---

[1] Fradella, H. F. (2006). "Why Judges Should Admit Expert Testimony on the Unreliability of Eyewitness Testimony." *Federal Courts Law Review*, 2006(3), 1–29. Reprinted with the gracious permission of the *Federal Courts Law Review*.

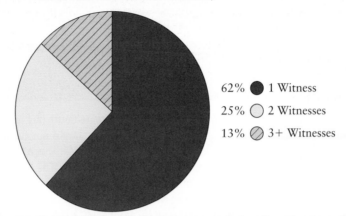

**Number of Witnesses Misidentifying
the Same Innocent Defendant**
(based on 175 eyewitness misidentification cases
in the first 239 DNA exonerations)

62% ● 1 Witness
25% ○ 2 Witnesses
13% ◐ 3+ Witnesses

From the Innocence Project, available at http://www.innocenceproject.org/docs/Eyewitness_ID_Report.pdf.
Reproduced with permission.

FIGURE 14.1 | Number of Witnesses Identifying the Same Innocent Defendant

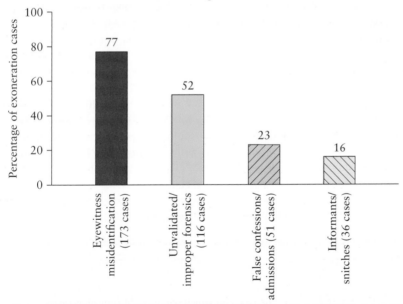

Contributing Causes of Wrongful Convictions (first 225 DNA exonerations)
Total is more than 100% because wrongful convictions can have more than one cause.

From The Innocence Project, available at http://www.innocenceproject.org/understand/. Reproduced by permission.

FIGURE 14.2 | Factors Leading to Wrongful Convictions

that DNA would be available to trump a mistaken identification. In addition, we would normally expect sexual assault victims to be among the most reliable of eyewitnesses because sexual assault victims usually have a longer and closer look at the culprit than other crime witnesses (compared to robberies, for instance). For these reasons, the DNA exoneration cases can only represent a fraction, probably a very small fraction, of the people who have been convicted based on mistaken eyewitness identification.

(See also Gross et al. 2004.)

574

PART IV
INTERROGATIONS,
IDENTIFICATIONS, TRIALS,
AND POST-CONVICTION
REMEDIES

Flowe, Mehta, and Ebbesen (2011) empirically confirmed Wells and Quinlivan's intuitive logic. They examined a random sample of 725 felony cases from the archives of a district attorney's office in a large, southwestern U.S. city. They found that one out of every three suspects had positive ID evidence in their case. Moreover, eyewitness identifications by both strangers and acquaintances were associated with increased odds of prosecution.

In the following sections, we explore the scientific reasons why eyewitness identifications are so unreliable.

Perception

Given the many causes of misidentification, the U.S. Supreme Court has held that identifications that occur under questionable circumstances should not be admitted at trial. "[R]eliability is the linchpin in determining the admissibility of identification testimony." *Manson v. Brathwaite*, 432 U.S. 98, 114 (1977). The Supreme Court's demand for reliability in identification procedures is a result of its conclusion that "the vagaries of eyewitness identification are well known; the annals of criminal law are rife with instances of mistaken identification." 432 U.S. at 119 (quoting *United States v. Wade*, 388 U.S. 218, 228 [1967]). To prevent such misidentifications, the Court in *Manson v. Brathwaite* reiterated its belief in the criteria for examining the reliability of identifications set down in *Neil v. Biggers*, 409 U.S. 188 (1972). The criteria include "the opportunity of the witness to view the criminal at the time of the crime, the witness's degree of attention, the accuracy of the witness's prior description of the criminal, the level of certainty demonstrated by the witness at the confrontation, and the length of time between the crime and the confrontation." 409 U.S. at 199–200. All of these legal factors seem straightforward, but they depend on complex psychological issues pertaining to perception and memory.

Unintentional inaccuracy of eyewitness testimony stems from the fact that memories are not exact recordings of events. First and foremost, memory is dependent on perception. We tend to think of perception as the recognition and interpretation of stimuli received through our basic senses—sight, hearing, touch, taste, and smell. But perception is really a complicated neurological process: "the total amalgam of sensory signals received and then processed by an individual at any one time" (Friedland 1990: 181). This process is highly selective. It is as dependent upon psychological factors as it is on physical senses because it is an "interpretive process" (Buckhout 1976: 76). In fact, the "actual" sensory data we perceive is "processed in light of experience, learning, preferences, biases, and expectations" (Chemay 1985: 724).

One of the most important factors that affects our ability to perceive is the sheer volume of sensory stimulation that bombards us. "Perception is highly selective because the number of signals or amount of information impinging upon the senses is so great that the mind can process only a small fraction of the incoming data" (Friedland 1990: 181). We focus on certain stimuli while filtering out others (Cowan 2000). This results not only in incomplete acquisition of sensory data but also in differential processing (i.e., interpretation) of events. Even when lighting and distance conditions are good for observation, a person experiencing sensory overload—"overwhelmed with too much information in too short a period of time" (Chemay 1985: 726)—may still experience incomplete acquisition.

Another important factor that affects perception is incomplete sensory acquisition, and the human mind's ability to fill these gaps to make a logical story. Unfortunately, the details often fit logically, but inaccurately (Roberts 2004).

Finally, the type of stimuli involved also affects perception. In particular, people are poor perceivers of duration (we tend to overestimate how long something takes), time (it "flies by" or "drags on"), speed, distance, height, and weight

(Friedland 1990: 181–82). It is important to keep in mind that people are not aware of their individual variations in the process of perception. How we perceive and synthesize sensory data are unconscious processes.

Memory

Memory is another unconscious process that concerns the acquisition, retention, and recall of past experience. All three component phases of the process of memory are affected by a number of physical and psychological factors that can taint the accuracy of memories. Even someone's mood can taint the accuracy of a memory (Forgas et al. 2005). Yet juries often fail to comprehend the complexities of memory when assessing the testimony of an eyewitness, which can, in turn, lead to conviction of an innocent person.

Acquisition Phase The first phase in the development of memory is the acquisition phase (also called the encoding phase). During this phase, sensory data, as perceived by the individual, are encoded in the appropriate areas of the cerebral cortex (Haber and Haber 2000). Accordingly, the acquisition of memories depends on perception. Perception, however, depends on a number of individualized factors, and this phase in the process of developing memories is affected by those same factors. Sensory overload is particularly important. It can lead to so many gaps in memory that confabulation—"the creation or substitution of false memories through later suggestion"—can occur (Chemay 1985: 726; see also Mazzoni 1999).

Perceptual variability aside, one more important factor affects memory acquisition. A person's expectations influence the way in which details about an event are encoded. An observer tends to seek out some information and avoid other information, an effect called the confirmation bias (Risinger 2002)—we see what we're expecting to see.

Retention Phase The next part of the memory process is the retention phase (also called the storage phase). During this phase, the brain stores the memory until it is called upon for retrieval. Clearly, the amount of data being encoded and retained affects this phase. The greater the amount of data presented, especially in shorter periods of time, the less that will be retained. The other important factor is the retention interval—how much time passes between storage of the memory and retrieval of it. But a third, far less obvious factor than the amount of data or the retention interval has the most potentially negative effect on memory retention: the postevent misinformation effect. Exposure to subsequent information affects the way in which earlier memories are retained (Patterson 2006). This means that an eyewitness exposed to postevent misinformation can accept misinformation as if it were an accurate account (Brigham et al. 1999).

> For example, a witness to a traffic accident may later read a newspaper article which stated that the driver had been drinking before the accident. "Post-event information can not only enhance existing memories but also change a witness's memory and even cause nonexistent details to become incorporated into a previously acquired memory." When witnesses later learn new information which conflicts with the original input, many will compromise between what they saw and what they were told later on. (Cohen 1996: 246–47)

Retrieval Phase Finally, during the retrieval phase, "the brain searches for the pertinent information, retrieves it, and communicates it" (Chemay 1985: 725; see also Haber and Haber 2000). This process occurs when eyewitnesses describe what they observed to police, when they participate in lineup or photo-array identifications, and when they testify in court. Several factors affect retrieval.

576

PART IV
INTERROGATIONS,
IDENTIFICATIONS, TRIALS,
AND POST-CONVICTION
REMEDIES

Time is a very important factor in memory retrieval. As a rule, the longer the time period between acquisition, retention, and retrieval, the more difficulty we have retrieving the memory (Bartol and Bartol 2004).

It has also been repeatedly demonstrated that retrieval of memories can be affected by unconscious transference. In this phenomenon, different memory images may become combined or confused with one another (Bingham 1999; Geiselman et al. 1996). For example, this effect can manifest itself when an eyewitness accurately recalls an innocent bystander at the scene of a crime but incorrectly identifies him as the perpetrator (Perfect and Harris 2003).

Estimator Variables Impacting Perception and Memory

Memory is also affected by a number of phenomena that collectively are referred to as estimator variables—factors over which the criminal justice system has no control. Estimator variables can be broken down into two categories: event factors and witness factors.

Event factors include time, "lighting conditions, changes in visual adaptation to light and dark, duration of the event, speed and distance involved, and the presence or absence of violence" (Cohen 1996: 242; see also Haber and Haber 2000). Witness factors include stress, fear, physical limitation on sensory perception (e.g., poor eyesight, hearing impairment, alcohol or drug intoxication), expectations, age (the very young and very old have unique problems), and gender (Cohen 1996: 242; see also Haber and Haber 2000).

Time as an Event Factor   Both common sense and our own experience inform us about how time affects memory. First and foremost, the longer one has to examine something, the better the memory formation will be and the more accurate recall will be. Conversely, the less time someone has to witness an event, the less complete—and less accurate—both perception and memory will be (Memon 2003). The rate at which events happen is a related factor. Given the limitations of human perception, when things happen very quickly, memory can be negatively affected. This is true even when an eyewitness has a reasonable period of time to observe an event: Attention is focused on processing a fast-moving series of events, rather than on a particular aspect of the occurrence (Haber and Haber 2000).

We all know that memories tend to fade over time. Research has confirmed that time delay impacts the accuracy of identification, but to a much smaller degree than might be expected. This may be due to the fact that memory does not disappear in increments over time. Instead, it fades fairly rapidly immediately following the event—a phenomenon referred to as the forgetting curve (Sikstrom 2002). After the initial fade, confabulation is more likely. Such filling or alteration of memory by postevent discussions has a much more powerful negative impact on the accuracy of recall than does the passage of time alone (Haber and Haber 2000).

Event Significance and Violence as Event Factors   Overall event significance plays an important role in the accuracy of memory recall. When people fail to perceive that a significant event is transpiring, their attention is not focused on the event. This lack of attention leads to poorer perception and memory of the event. Conversely, when people are aware that a significant event is taking place, their attention is better focused. Correspondingly, perception and memory of the event is improved (Leippe et al. 1975).

In terms of eyewitness accuracy, this phenomenon often translates into high levels of inaccuracy in identifications for the perpetrator of a petty theft, and higher rates of accuracy for a more significant nonviolent crime (Chemay 1985: 728). The use of the limiting phrase "nonviolent crime" here is important: The seriousness of the crime is not a determinative factor of event significance and the corresponding attention being paid

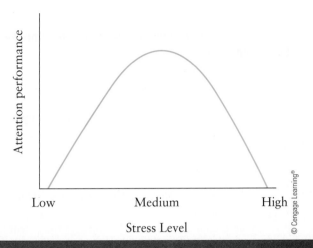

FIGURE 14.3 | The Yerkes–Dodson Curve

to the event. The *violence* level of the crime is also important. Even when witnesses understand that they are watching a significant event, "the more violent the act, the lower will be the accuracy and completeness of perception and memory" (Chemay 1985: 728). This is a function of the negative impact high levels of arousal and stress can produce.

Arousal and Stress as Event Factors Many people believe that stress heightens perception and memory. In fact, research suggests that perception and memory acquisition function most accurately when the subject is exposed to a moderate amount of stress (Loftus 1986; Clifford 1979). This is often referred to as the *Yerkes–Dodson law* and is illustrated in Figure 14.3. This law holds that when stress levels are too low, people do not pay sufficient attention; and when stress levels are too high, the ability to concentrate and perceive are negatively impacted (Loftus 1986).

The Yerkes–Dodson law (see Figure 14.3) has a strong effect on people's ability to perceive and remember certain details of an event. *Detail significance* refers to the minutiae of a crime scene as opposed to its overall significance. When people are concerned about personal safety, they tend to focus their attention on the details that most directly affect their safety, such as "blood, masks, weapons, and aggressive actions" (Bartol and Bartol 1994: 221). While focusing on these details, they pay less attention to the other details of the crime scene, such as characteristics of the perpetrator (e.g., facial features, hair color and style, clothing, height, weight), the crime scene, and other important details (Deffenbacher et al. 2004; Morgan et al. 2004). This phenomenon manifests itself particularly when a weapon is present. The so-called **weapons effect** describes crime situations in which a weapon is used, and witnesses spend more time and psychic energy focusing on the weapon rather than on other aspects of the event. The weapons effect results in incomplete or inaccurate information about the crime scene and the perpetrator. This effect is magnified when the use of a weapon comes as a surprise to a witness (Pickel 1999; Steblay 1992).

Expectancies and Stereotypes as Witness Factors "A person's expectations and stereotypes can also affect both perception and memory: what he perceives and encodes is, to a large extent, determined by cultural biases, personal prejudices, effects of training, prior information, and expectations induced by motivational states, among others" (Chemay 1985: 726–27). Whether the hunter is looking for deer, or one is searching for Bigfoot or the Loch Ness Monster, what we expect to see clearly influences what we think we have seen (Bartol and Bartol 1994: 227). Unfortunately, stereotypes affect expectations in terms of who looks like a criminal. For example:

[I]n one experiment a "semi-dramatic" photograph was shown to a wide variety of subjects, including whites and blacks of varying backgrounds. The photograph showed several people sitting in a subway car, with a black man standing and conversing with a white man, who was also standing, but holding a razor. Over half of the subjects reported that the black man had been holding the razor, and several described the black man as "brandishing it wildly." Effectively, expectations and stereotypes cause people to see and remember what they want or expect to see or to remember. This phenomenon should be of concern to the criminal justice system as "[t]here is evidence that some people may in fact incorporate their stereotype of 'criminal' in their identification of suspects." (Chemay 1985: 727)

Age and Gender as Witness Factors   Age is an important factor affecting witnesses' memories. Children usually fail to retain as many details as adults, but the percentage of "correct" information that children are able to recall is proportionally similar to that of adults (Bingham et al. 1999). In terms of making accurate identifications, preschoolers are much less likely than adults to make a correct identification. But after the age of five or six, children do not differ significantly from adults in their ability to make an accurate identification (Pozzulo and Lindsay 1998). However, children up to the age of thirteen are more likely than adults to correctly reject a target-absent lineup (i.e., a lineup that does not contain an actual suspect, but rather contains all foils; see Pozzulo and Lindsay 1998). In contrast, elderly witnesses are much less reliable than younger ones (Yarmey 1996). The elderly frequently believe events they imagined were actually perceived, a mistake known as a reifying error (Memon and Gabbert 2003). And both children and the elderly are particularly "susceptible to the effects of suggestive questioning or post-event misinformation" (Pozzulo and Lindsay 1998: 16).

Gender has much less significance on memory accuracy than age. Some studies suggest that women might have slightly higher accuracy rates in facial recognition, and other studies suggest that recall is consistent with gender stereotypes (Lindholm and Christianson 1998; cf. Herrmann et al. 1992). For example, a woman might pay more attention to clothing, while a man might take notice of the make of a car (Loftus et al. 1987). These gender differences, however, are generally considered to have little significance on the overall accuracy of eyewitness identifications (Vrij 1998).

Race of the Offender as a Witness Factor   An eyewitness is much more likely to identify accurately someone of his or her own race than someone of a different race (Golby et al. 2001; Kleider and Goldinger 2001). The same is true, although arguably to a lesser extent, for cross-ethnic identifications (Sporer 2001). Because of cross-racial identification bias, people apply more lenient criteria in identifying someone of a different race or ethnicity and use more stringent requirements when identifying someone of the same racial or ethnic group (Doyle 2001). The result of cross-racial bias is a higher rate of false positive identifications, especially when a Caucasian eyewitness identifies an African American suspect

(Doyle 2001; Golby et al. 2001). Combinations of event factors (e.g., duration and conditions of viewing) interact with cross-racial bias to further inhibit the reliability of cross-racial identifications (MacLin 2001). Courts have begun to take notice of this significant limitation on identification accuracy. The Supreme Court of New Jersey, for example, has mandated that juries be instructed on the risks of inaccuracies in cross-racial identifications when an "identification is a critical issue in the case, and an eyewitness's cross-racial identification is not corroborated by other evidence giving it independent reliability." *New Jersey v. Cromedy*, 727 A.2d 457, 467 (N.J. 1999).

DISCUSSION POINT

How Can We Reduce Mistaken Identifications? The Innocence Project: The Case of Antonio Beaver

Since it was founded in 1992, the Innocence Project has helped to exonerate more than 270 people, including 17 who were on death row. Antonio Beaver is one of those people.

On August 15, 1996, a twenty-six-year-old white woman drove into a St. Louis parking lot planning to park her car and return to work. After parking, she approached a man in the lot, thinking he was the parking attendant. The man told her that she had to move her car immediately or it would be towed, and he followed her back to the car. As she got in the car to leave, the man told her she could stay. As she got back out, the man attacked her with a screwdriver and told her to give him the keys and her purse. She struggled with him and then decided to flee; she threw her purse on the seat and jumped out of the car. As she was exiting the car, she noticed that the man was bleeding and that there was blood inside the driver's side door. She ran into a nearby parking garage and called the police.

The victim described her attacker to police as a clean-shaven African American man wearing a baseball cap. She said the man was 5'10" tall, with a "David-Letterman–like" gap between his teeth. The next day, the victim helped police draw a composite sketch of the attacker and police recovered the victim's car in East St. Louis. Latent fingerprints and swabs of the blood stain inside the driver's side door were collected.

Six days later, a detective arrested Antonio Beaver because he thought Beaver resembled the composite sketch in this case. However, Beaver had a full mustache, was 6'2" tall, and had chipped teeth.

The same detective then prepared a live lineup, including Beaver and three other men—two of them police officers. Beaver and the other nonofficer were the only two to wear baseball caps, and Beaver was the only one with noticeable defects to his teeth. The victim identified Beaver.

Beaver was charged with first-degree robbery and tried in April 1997. The victim testified that Beaver was the man who attacked her; the prosecution argued that the victim's clear memory of the crime meant that she was better able to identify the perpetrator. The defense presented evidence showing that fingerprints collected from the victim's car—including prints from the driver's side and the rearview mirror—did not match the victim or Beaver. They argued that prints left on the rearview mirror indicated that the person who left them must have driven the car.

After several hours of deliberations over two days, the jury convicted Beaver of first-degree robbery. He was sentenced to eighteen years in prison. In 2001, Beaver filed a motion on his own behalf requesting DNA testing. The state opposed the motion, but the court granted a hearing on the issue in 2005. The Innocence Project accepted Beaver's case and filed another brief on his behalf in 2006. The state agreed to testing in October 2006, and the results proved that Beaver could not have committed this crime. He was exonerated on March 29, 2007. He was forty-one years old at the time of his exoneration and had served more than a decade in prison.

From The Innocence Project, www.innocenceproject.org/Content/Antonio_Beaver.php. Reproduced by permission.

■ What factors described in this chapter do you think contributed to the wrongful conviction of Antonio Beaver?

■ How could the police have improved the reliability of the identification in this case?

580

PART IV
INTERROGATIONS,
IDENTIFICATIONS, TRIALS,
AND POST-CONVICTION
REMEDIES

Physical Appearance of the Offender as a Witness Factor   Another variable that affects the accuracy of an eyewitness's identification of a suspect is the facial distinctiveness of the suspect. Suspects with faces that an eyewitness perceives as either highly attractive or highly unattractive are much more likely to be remembered accurately than faces that lack distinctiveness (Sarno and Alley 1997). A complicating matter, however, is that some characteristics of facial distinctiveness are easily changed. For example, a suspect can disguise himself or herself during the perpetration of a crime, or change his or her appearance after it by altering hairstyle, hair color, the presence or absence of facial hair, the wearing of glasses, and so on (Vrij 1998). These easily changed facial features are called malleable characteristics. Although some distinctive facial features might increase subsequent recognition of a person, to be accurate, the two comparisons must use nonmalleable characteristics—such as the shape of someone's nose, the distinctiveness of eyes, dimples, scars, and so on. That, however, is often easier said than done.

In 1999, the U.S. Department of Justice (1999) recommended that eyewitnesses be given an "appearance-change instruction" (ACI) before participating in a lineup or photo array in which a suspect appeared with some malleable characteristic change. Subsequent research, however, cautions against doing so. It is unwise to give an ACI instruction because it "increases false identifications without increasing correct identifications" (Molinaro, Arndorfer, and Charman 2013: 9).

Systemic Variables Impacting Perception and Memory

In addition to the various witness and situational factors affecting the accuracy of identifications, a number of factors under the control of the criminal justice system impact the reliability of eyewitness identifications. These variables primarily concern the ways in which pretrial confrontations between suspects and victims or witnesses occur, including the conduct of law enforcement officers during the administration of a showup, lineup, or photo array. We will return to these systemic factors in more detail later in this chapter. First, however, we will review the requirements that the law imposes on justice system professionals when conducting pretrial identification procedures.

Sixth Amendment Requirements for Pretrial Identifications

Recall that the Sixth Amendment guarantees defendants the right to the effective assistance of counsel at "critical stages" in all criminal prosecutions. *Kirby v. Illinois*, 406 U.S. 682, 689 (1972). In 1967, the Supreme Court decided several important cases dealing with pretrial identifications.

The *Wade–Gilbert* Rule

United States v. Wade, 388 U.S. 218 (1967), and *Gilbert v. California*, 388 U.S. 263, 272 (1967), both held that a postindictment, pretrial lineup is a "critical stage" of a criminal prosecution that triggers the right to counsel. The Court reached this conclusion in light of its determination that counsel is needed to prevent suggestive techniques that could lead to wrongful convictions. *Wade*, 388 U.S. at 228–29. The *Wade* court listed a number of such suggestive procedures that had been documented in numerous published judicial opinions:

[T]hat all in the lineup but the suspect were known to the identifying witness, that the other participants in a lineup were grossly dissimilar in appearance to the suspect, that only the suspect was required to wear distinctive clothing which the culprit allegedly wore, that the witness is told by the police that they have caught the culprit after which the defendant is brought before the witness alone or is viewed in jail, that the suspect is pointed out before or during a lineup, and that the participants in the lineup are asked to try on an article of clothing which fits only the suspect. 388 U.S. at 233 (internal citation omitted).

To combat such suggestive practices, the Court held that *conducting a postindictment lineup* "without notice to and in the absence of his counsel denies the accused his Sixth Amendment right to counsel and calls in question the admissibility at trial of the in-court identifications of the accused by witnesses who attended the lineup." *Gilbert*, 388 U.S. at 272. As with other critical stages of criminal prosecutions, if a suspect is unable to afford a lawyer, he or she is entitled to have one appointed by the court to assist at the confrontation. Additionally, if a suspect requests the advice and presence of his or her own lawyer and that lawyer is not immediately available, a substitute lawyer may be called for the purpose of the confrontation. *Wade*, 388 U.S. at 237 n.9; *Zamora v. Guam*, 394 F.2d 815 (9th Cir. 1968).

The Rationale Underlying the Court's Decision in *Wade–Gilbert* The Supreme Court's reasoning in *Wade* and *Gilbert* was based on (1) the inherent unreliability of eyewitness identifications and (2) the possibility of improper suggestions being made to witnesses during the confrontation procedure:

[T]he confrontation compelled by the State between the accused and the victim or witnesses to a crime to elicit identification evidence is peculiarly riddled with innumerable dangers and variable factors which might seriously, even crucially, derogate from a fair trial. The vagaries of eyewitness identification are well-known; the annals of criminal law are rife with instances of mistaken identification. . . . The identification of strangers is proverbially untrustworthy. . . . A major factor contributing to the high incidence of miscarriage of justice from mistaken identification has been the degree of suggestion inherent in the manner in which the prosecution presents the suspect to witnesses for pretrial identification. A commentator has observed that "[t]he influence of improper suggestion upon identifying witnesses probably accounts for more miscarriages of justice than any other single factor—perhaps it is responsible for more such errors than all other factors combined." . . . Suggestion can be created intentionally or unintentionally in many subtle ways. And the dangers for the suspect are particularly grave when the witness's opportunity for observation was insubstantial, and thus his susceptibility to suggestion the greatest.

Moreover, "[i]t is a matter of common experience that, once a witness has picked out the accused at the lineup, he is not likely to go back on his word later on, so that in practice the issue of identity may (in the absence of other relevant evidence) for all practical purposes be determined there and then, before the trial." 388 U.S. at 228–29.

582

PART IV
INTERROGATIONS,
IDENTIFICATIONS, TRIALS,
AND POST-CONVICTION
REMEDIES

The Court was concerned that it would be difficult to determine what happened at a lineup or other identification confrontation conducted in secret:

> [T]he defense can seldom reconstruct the manner and mode of lineup identification for judge or jury at trial. Those participating in a lineup with the accused may often be police officers; in any event, the participants' names are rarely recorded or divulged at trial. The impediments to an objective observation are increased when the victim is the witness. Lineups are prevalent in rape and robbery prosecutions and present a particular hazard that a victim's understandable outrage may excite vengeful or spiteful motives. In any event, neither witnesses nor lineup participants are apt to be alert for conditions prejudicial to the suspect. And if they were, it would likely be of scant benefit to the suspect since neither witnesses nor lineup participants are likely to be schooled in the detection of suggestive influences. Improper influences may go undetected by a suspect, guilty or not, who experiences the emotional tension which we might expect in one being confronted with potential accusers. Even when he does observe abuse, if he has a criminal record he may be reluctant to take the stand and open up the admission of prior convictions. Moreover any protestations by the suspect of the fairness of the lineup made at trial are likely to be in vain; the jury's choice is between the accused's unsupported version and that of the police officers present. In short, the accused's inability effectively to reconstruct at trial any unfairness that occurred at the lineup may deprive him of his only opportunity meaningfully to attack the credibility of the witness's courtroom identification. 388 U.S. at 230–32.

The Court believed that the presence of counsel at the pretrial confrontation with witnesses would prevent misconduct by those conducting the confrontation. In addition, counsel would have firsthand knowledge of what occurred at the confrontation and could cross-examine witnesses later at a suppression hearing or trial and point out improprieties that might have occurred:

> Since it appears that there is grave potential for prejudice, intentional or not, in the pretrial lineup, which may not be capable of reconstruction at trial, and since presence of counsel itself can often avert prejudice and assure a meaningful confrontation at trial, there can be little doubt that for Wade the post-indictment lineup was a critical stage of the prosecution at which he was "as much entitled to such aid [of counsel] . . . as at the trial itself." . . . Thus both Wade and his counsel should have been notified of the impending lineup, and counsel's presence should have been a requisite to conduct of the lineup, absent an "intelligent waiver." 388 U.S. at 236–37.

The Court's ruling recognizes the defendant's need for assistance at critical stages of the prosecution, when the absence of counsel might result in an unfair trial.

When the *Wade–Gilbert* Right to Counsel Attaches The right to counsel guaranteed under *Wade–Gilbert* does not apply at the outset of criminal case. Rather, the right must "attach" upon a triggering event.

Applies to Live Showups and Lineups at or After Initiation of Adversarial Criminal Proceedings Although the language of *Wade* and *Gilbert* concerned postindictment pretrial identifications, an indictment per se is not necessary to trigger the right to counsel under *Wade–Gilbert*. *Kirby v. Illinois*, 406 U.S. 682, 689 (1972), held that the right to counsel attaches to pretrial identification procedures that are conducted "at or after the initiation of adversary judicial criminal proceedings— whether by way of formal charge, preliminary hearing, indictment, information or arraignment."

> The initiation of judicial criminal proceedings is far from a mere formalism. It is the starting point of our whole system of adversary criminal justice. For it is only then that the government has committed itself to prosecute, and only then that the adverse positions of government and defendant have solidified. It is then that a defendant finds himself faced with the prosecutorial forces of organized society, and immersed in the intricacies of substantive and procedural criminal law. It is this point, therefore, that marks the commencement of the "criminal prosecutions" to which alone the explicit guarantees of the Sixth Amendment are applicable. 406 U.S. at 689–90.

Applying this reasoning, the U.S. Supreme Court held in *Moore v. Illinois*, 434 U.S. 220 (1977), that a defendant has a right to counsel during any identification procedure, including one-on-one identifications, once adversarial proceedings have begun, even if no indictment has been handed down yet in a case. *Moore* ruled that the *Wade–Gilbert* rule for counsel attached during a preliminary hearing since that process began adversarial proceedings under the applicable Illinois statute.

In contrast, there is no Sixth Amendment right to counsel at any pretrial confrontation *before* adversary judicial criminal proceedings begin. *Kirby*, 406 U.S. at 689. So, when someone is merely a suspect and has not been formally charged with any crime, *Wade–Gilbert* does not apply—and, therefore, suspects need not be advised of any right to counsel at pretrial identification. However, because state laws differ regarding what process begins formal adversarial judicial proceedings, law enforcement officers conducting pretrial identification procedures must determine at what point in the criminal justice process the right to counsel attaches in their jurisdiction.

For example, police filing a complaint that seeks an arrest warrant is not a critical state of criminal proceeding that triggers the right to counsel under *Kirby*. *Anderson v. Alameida*, 397 F.3d 1175 (9th Cir. 2005). As in the federal system, the law of many states reflects the notion that when police make an arrest pursuant to an arrest warrant issued upon the filing of a complaint, they need not advise suspects of their right to counsel because arrest has never been held by the U.S. Supreme Court to qualify as a "critical stage" giving rise to any Sixth Amendment right to counsel. *See United States v. Gouveia*, 467 U.S. 180, 190 (1984); *Beck v. Bowersox*, 362 F.3d 1095, 1101–02 (8th Cir. 2004); *State v. Pierre*, 890 A.2d 474 (Conn. 2006). Some states, however, do consider the issuance of an arrest warrant as instituting formal adversarial judicial proceedings. *E.g.*, *Cannaday v. State*, 455 So.2d 713 (Miss. 1984), *cert. denied*, 469 U.S. 122 (1985); *People v. Bustamante*, 634 P.2d 927 (Cal. 1981); *People v. Jackson*, 217 N.W.2d 22 (Mich. 1974); *Commonwealth v. Richman*, 320 A.2d 351 (Pa. 1974); *People v. Blake*, 320 N.E.2d 625 (N.Y. 1974).

Does Not Apply for Preparatory Steps *Wade* stated that there is no right to counsel at preparatory steps in the gathering of the prosecution's evidence, such as "systematized or scientific analyzing of the accused's fingerprints, blood sample, clothing, hair, and the like."

Does Not Apply to Photo Arrays In *United States v. Ash*, 413 U.S. 300 (1973), the Court held that there is no right under the Sixth Amendment to have counsel present to observe a photographic array, even after indictment. The Court reasoned that "since the accused is not present at the time of the photographic array, there is no possibility that he might be misled by his lack of familiarity with the law or overpowered by his professional adversary." 413 U.S. at 317. The same logic applies to the showing of videotaped lineups, *State v. Jones*, 849 So.2d 438 (Fla. Ct. App. 2003); *United States v. Amrine*, 724 F.2d 84 (8th Cir. 1983), and the playing of tape-recorded voice arrays. *United States v. Dupree*, 553 F.2d 1189 (8th Cir. 1977).

Waiver of the *Wade–Gilbert* Right to Counsel

Postindictment pretrial identifications that are conducted in violation of the *Wade–Gilbert* mandates pertaining to counsel are inadmissible unless a valid waiver of Sixth Amendment rights was obtained before the confrontation. *Gilbert*, 388 U.S. at 272; *Moore v. Illinois*, 434 U.S. 220, 231 (1977). As with most other waivers of constitutional rights, waivers of the right to the presence of counsel at pretrial identification procedures must be knowing, intelligent, and voluntary. Whether this standard is met is determined under the totality of the circumstances of each case "including the background, experience, and conduct of the accused." *Johnson v. Zerbst*, 304 U.S. 458, 464 (1938). This standard is identical to the one used to determine the validity of waivers of the Sixth Amendment right to the presence of counsel at interrogations (see Chapter 13). However, given the rights involved, a form with the warning contained in Figure 14.4 is suggested for the purpose of obtaining a waiver of the *Wade–Gilbert* right to counsel at confrontations because providing *Miranda* warnings in their standard form would not adequately advise defendants of their rights at pretrial identification procedures.

The information contained in the form shown in Figure 14.4 should be more than sufficient to establish a valid waiver. *Dallio v. Spitzer*, 343 F.3d 553 (2d Cir. 2003), for example, upheld a waiver of Sixth Amendment rights under *Wade–Gilbert* even though the warning provided to the suspect did not explicitly warn him of the dangers and disadvantages of consenting to participation in a lineup. All that is necessary is that the defendant be warned that the results of the confrontation can and will be used against the defendant in court, that the defendant has the right to the presence and assistance of counsel at the confrontation, and that if the defendant cannot afford an attorney to be present at the confrontation, one will be provided at no cost before any confrontation is conducted.

Although having the suspect sign an explicit waiver is the best evidence of the validity of a waiver, the form need not be signed. *Paulino v. Castro*, 371 F.3d 1083 (9th Cir. 2004), for example, upheld a waiver even though the defendant refused to sign a waiver. The defendant had been informed of his rights and never

Pretrial Identification Warning and Waiver

Name: _____ Address: _____

Age: _____ Place: _____

Date: _____ Time: _____

Warning

Before appearing at any confrontation with any witnesses being conducted by (Name of Police Department) in relation to (Description of Offense), you are entitled to be informed of your legal rights.

The results of the confrontation can and will be used against you in court.

You have the right to the presence and advice of an attorney of your choice at any such confrontation.

If you cannot afford an attorney and you want one, an attorney will be appointed for you at no expense, before any confrontation is held.

Waiver

I have been advised of my right to the advice of an attorney and to have an attorney present at any confrontation with witnesses, and that if I cannot afford an attorney, one will be appointed for me before any such confrontation occurs. I understand these rights.

I do not want an attorney and I understand and know what I am doing.

No promises have been made to me and no pressures of any kind have been used against me.

_____
Signature of Suspect

Certification

I, (Name of Officer), hereby certify that I read the above warning to (Name of Suspect) on (Date), that this person indicated an understanding of the rights, and that this person signed the WAIVER form in my presence.

_____
Signature of Officer

_____
Witness

© Cengage Learning®

FIGURE 14.4 | Pretrial Identification Warning and Waiver

unambiguously requested counsel. Yet, because he agreed to participate in the lineup after having been informed of his rights, his refusal to sign the waiver form was irrelevant to his having knowingly, intelligently, and voluntarily waived his rights under *Wade–Gilbert*.

Due Process and Pretrial Identifications

The Due Process Clauses of the Fifth and Fourteenth Amendments guarantee all suspects the right to have all identification procedures conducted in a fair and impartial manner. These due process rights during confrontations apply regardless of whether the pretrial procedures occur before or after the attachment of the Sixth Amendment right to counsel under *Wade–Gilbert*.

The *Stovall v. Denno* Rule

Even before *Kirby* was decided, the Supreme Court held in *Stovall v. Denno*, 388 U.S. 293 (1967), that due process forbids any pretrial identification procedure that is unnecessarily suggestive and conducive to irreparable mistaken identification.

> As the Court pointed out in *Wade* itself, it is always necessary to "scrutinize any pretrial confrontation. . . ." The Due Process Clause of the Fifth and Fourteenth Amendments forbids a lineup that is unnecessarily suggestive and conducive to irreparable mistaken identification. When a person has not been formally charged with a criminal offense, *Stovall* strikes the appropriate constitutional balance between the right of a suspect to be protected from prejudicial procedures and the interest of society in the prompt and purposeful investigation of an unsolved crime. *Kirby*, 406 U.S. at 690–91.

Whether a confrontation violates due process because it is unnecessarily suggestive is evaluated by courts under the totality of the circumstances surrounding the pretrial identification. *Stovall*, 388 U.S. at 302.

Showups Under *Stovall* Showups are highly suggestive and, accordingly, produce high levels of false identifications (Yarmey 1998). Moreover, showups have a biasing effect on any subsequent identification at a lineup or in court (Behrman and Vayder 1994). Showups should, therefore, not be used unless there is some extenuating circumstance that prevents a photo array or lineup from being used. In fact, some courts have ruled that showups that occur without some showing as to the necessity of having conducted the showup will be inadmissible. *E.g.*, *State v. Dubose*, 699 N.W.2d 582 (Wis. 2005). The impending death or blindness of an eyewitness, for example, is an emergency situation that would justify a showup. Another exigent circumstance is when police lack probable cause to arrest someone, but have temporarily detained a suspect who matches a general eyewitness description under *Terry v. Ohio*. A showup under such a situation would allow police to conduct an identification procedure rather than simply releasing a potentially guilty perpetrator.

When a showup does occur, either because it is unplanned (i.e., not prearranged) or due to some exigent circumstance, law enforcement officers must exercise great care to ensure that the identification procedures are not unnecessarily suggestive and conducive to irreparable mistaken identification. When officers do so, the following types of showups have been held to be admissible.

Spontaneous Showups Unarranged, spontaneous showups are not considered impermissibly suggestive for constitutional law purposes. For example, in *United States v. Boykins*, 966 F.2d 1240 (8th Cir. 1992), an unaccompanied witness, while walking toward the courtroom on the day of trial, recognized the defendant as one of the armed intruders who had previously broken into her home. She told the prosecuting attorney, who accompanied her down the hall to confirm the identification. She later identified the defendant in court. The court allowed the in-court identification, finding that the witness recognized the defendant without any suggestion from the government. "While a lineup is certainly the preferred method of identification, a witness who spontaneously recognized a defendant should be allowed to testify to that fact." 966 F.2d at 1243.

Cruising Crime Area Showups resulting from a crime victim or witness cruising the area of the crime in a police car also rarely present constitutional problems of suggestiveness. Cruising the area is an accepted investigative technique when police have no suspect for a crime that has just occurred. Witness memories are still fresh, and perpetrators are still likely to be in the area with their clothes or appearance unaltered. Of course, police should not coach witnesses by suggesting that certain persons look suspicious or have bad reputations.

Certain Arranged, "On-the-Scene" Showups A more common type of showup is the arranged on-the-scene showup, in which a suspect is arrested or apprehended at or near the scene of a crime and is immediately brought before victims or witnesses by a law enforcement officer for identification purposes. If adversary judicial criminal proceedings have not been initiated, the suspect has no right to counsel at this type of confrontation. But does an on-the-scene showup satisfy the *Stovall* requirements regarding suggestiveness? Although courts differ, the prevailing view is that practical considerations may justify a prompt on-the-scene showup under the *Stovall* test. For example, in *Johnson v. Dugger*, 817 F.2d 726, 729 (11th Cir. 1987), the court said:

> Although show-ups are widely condemned . . . immediate confrontations allow identification before the suspect has altered his appearance and while the witness's memory is fresh, and permit the quick release of innocent persons. . . . Therefore, showups are not unnecessarily suggestive unless the police aggravate the suggestiveness of the confrontation.

CRIMINAL PROCEDURE IN ACTION

Is This Showup Unnecessarily Suggestive? *United States v. Watson*, 76 F.3d 4 (1st Cir. 1996).

As Alexander Milette was bicycling home to the Cathedral Project, a Porsche drove past him and stopped in front of his house. Trevor Watson got out of the car, carrying a loaded pistol of the type favored by the Boston police, a Glock 9-mm semiautomatic. After accusing Milette of liking "hitting on" women, Watson aimed the gun at Milette's stomach. Someone said "Don't shoot him." Instead, Watson pistol-whipped Milette's head, causing the gun to fire into a building and then to jam. Milette, bleeding, ran while Watson unjammed the gun and fired again, hitting the building Milette ran behind. Milette sought sanctuary at a friend's house and was helped with his bleeding head.

Watson had jumped back into the Porsche, only to have it stall out in a deep puddle. A nearby off-duty Boston Police officer, Officer Christopher Shoulla, heard the shots, drove to the project, and put out a call on his police radio. Officer Shoulla saw Watson and asked him to stop. Watson instead fled, clutching his right pocket, and, ironically, ran right past Milette and past another youth.

Two other Boston officers arrived and gave chase. Watson threw the gun, as he ran, into a small garden.

Officer Shoulla stopped Watson at gunpoint. When the officers patted down Watson and determined he had no gun, they retraced Watson's steps and found it within forty seconds.

One officer saw Milette, still holding a bloody towel to his head, and had the others bring Watson over. Watson was brought over by patrol car and Milette was asked by the police, "What's the story?" Milette looked, and identified Watson as his assailant. He later testified he was 100 percent sure of that identification. Watson was also identified by the other youth past whom he had run.

- Evaluate whether you think this showup is constitutionally permissible or defective.

- Explain the factors you use to support your due process analysis.

588

PART IV
INTERROGATIONS,
IDENTIFICATIONS, TRIALS,
AND POST-CONVICTION
REMEDIES

Law enforcement officers should use on-the-scene showups only when a suspect can be shown to a witness minutes after the crime has occurred. Furthermore, officers should not add in any way to the already inherent suggestiveness of the on-the-scene identification. For example, the officer should not say or do anything to lead the witness to believe that the suspect is believed to be the perpetrator or that the suspect has been formally arrested, has confessed, or has been found with incriminating items. If there is a significant delay between the commission of the crime and the confrontation, officers should take the suspect to the station and conduct a lineup.

Photographic Evidence from a Crime Scene Photographs of suspects in the act of committing the crime (e.g., bank robbery surveillance photographs) do not present any problems of suggestiveness and mistaken identification. Presenting such photographs to witnesses shows the actual perpetrator of the crime in the act rather than suggesting a number of possible perpetrators. The photographs refresh the witness's memory of the actual crime and thereby strengthen the reliability of a witness's subsequent in-court identification. *United States v. Browne*, 829 F.2d 760 (9th Cir. 1987).

Lineups and Photo Arrays Under *Stovall* Lineups and photo arrays must be conducted in ways that are not unnecessarily suggestive or otherwise conducive to irreparable mistaken identification. Nothing should be done, therefore, that makes the suspect (or the suspect's photo) "stand out" from the other people used in a lineup or from the other pictures used in a photo array. Following the procedures set forth later in this chapter under the heading "Guidelines for Lineups and Photo-Array Identification Procedures" should not only help to ensure that the due process mandates of *Stovall* are met but also help increase the reliability of any identification made as a result of these confrontation procedures.

Reliability Trumps *Stovall*

If a pretrial confrontation is not unnecessarily suggestive, then the identification is admissible. If, however, the confrontation is deemed to have been impermissibly suggestive, that fact alone does not necessarily mean that the identification will be inadmissible. Under federal law and the law applicable in many states, such an identification may still be able to be used in court if it were reliably made in spite of the suggestive nature of the confrontation. Thus, an evaluation of the reliability of an identification will become necessary if a court rules that a confrontation was tainted by impermissible suggestion. The goal of this reliability evaluation is to ensure that valuable evidence is not discarded unless using an identification would violate a defendant's due process rights.

The Reliability Factors of *Neil v. Biggers* and *Manson v. Brathwaite* In 1972, the U.S. Supreme Court decided *Neil v. Biggers*, 409 U.S. 188, which focused on whether the identification was accurate or reliable despite the suggestiveness of the identification procedure. The Court said:

> It is the likelihood of misidentification that violates a defendant's right to due process. . . . Suggestive confrontations are disapproved because they increase the likelihood of misidentification, and unnecessarily suggestive ones are condemned for the further reason that the increased chance of misidentification is gratuitous. 409 U.S. at 198.

Biggers involved a defendant who had been convicted of rape on evidence consisting, in part, of a victim's visual and voice identification of the defendant at a station-house showup seven months after the crime. At the time of the crime, the victim was in her assailant's presence for nearly a half hour, and the victim directly observed her assailant indoors and under a full moon outdoors. The victim testified at trial that she had no doubt that the defendant was her assailant. Immediately after the crime, she gave the police a thorough description of the assailant that matched the description of the defendant. The victim had also made no identification of others presented at previous showups or lineups or through photographs.

Despite its concern about the seven-month delay between the crime and the confrontation, the Supreme Court held that the central question was "whether under 'the totality of the circumstances' the identification was reliable even though the confrontation procedure was suggestive." 409 U.S. at 199. The Court listed the following five factors to be considered in evaluating the likelihood of misidentification:

- witness's opportunity to view the criminal at the time of the crime,
- witness's degree of attention,
- accuracy of the witness's prior description of the criminal,
- level of certainty demonstrated by the witness at the confrontation, and
- length of time between the crime and the confrontation.

Applying these factors, the Court found no substantial likelihood of misidentification and held the evidence of the identification admissible in court.

Five years after the decision in *Biggers*, the Supreme Court decided *Manson v. Brathwaite*, 432 U.S. 98, 114 (1977), in which the Court said, "[R]eliability is the linchpin in determining the admissibility of identification testimony." In *Manson*, the Court reiterated the five reliability factors of *Biggers* and emphasized that they should be balanced against the corrupting effect of the suggestive identification itself. In *Manson*, two days after a drug sale, an undercover drug officer viewed a single photograph of a suspect that had been left in his office by a fellow officer. After finding that the single photographic display was unnecessarily suggestive, the Court considered the five *Biggers* factors affecting reliability and found that the undercover officer made an accurate identification. The Court noted that the officer was no casual observer but a trained police officer, that he had sufficient opportunity to view the suspect for two or three minutes in natural light, that he accurately described the suspect in detail within minutes of the crime, that he positively identified the photograph in court as that of the drug seller, and that he made the photographic identification only two days after the crime.

Then the Court analyzed the corrupting effect of the suggestive identification and weighed it against the factors indicating reliability:

> These indicators of Glover's ability to make an accurate identification are hardly outweighed by the corrupting effect of the challenged identification itself. Although identifications arising from single-photograph displays may be viewed in general with suspicion, . . . we find in the instant case little pressure on the witness to acquiesce in the suggestion that such a display entails. D'Onofrio had left the photograph at Glover's office and was not present when Glover first viewed it two days after the event. There thus was little urgency and Glover could view the photograph at his leisure. And since Glover examined the photograph alone, there was no coercive pressure to make an identification arising from the presence of another. The identification was made in circumstances allowing care and reflection. 432 U.S. at 116.

Therefore, under the totality of the circumstances, the Court held the identification reliable and the evidence admissible.

The lesson of the *Biggers* and *Manson* cases is that, even though a pretrial confrontation may have been unnecessarily suggestive, the evidence may still be admissible in

590

PART IV
INTERROGATIONS,
IDENTIFICATIONS, TRIALS,
AND POST-CONVICTION
REMEDIES

court if the identification was otherwise reliable. These cases, however, should not be interpreted as evidencing a lack of concern about conducting fair and impartial identification procedures. As the Court stated in *Manson*:

> [I]t would have been better had D'Onofrio presented Glover with a photographic array including "so far as practicable . . . a reasonable number of persons similar to any person then suspected whose likeness is included in the array." . . . The use of that procedure would have enhanced the force of the identification at trial and would have avoided the risk that the evidence would be excluded as unreliable. 432 U.S. at 117.

Applying the Reliability Factors For nearly three decades, scholars have urged that the *Biggers–Manson* reliability test is not "a satisfactory method of measuring reliability" (Rosenberg 1991: 292). The framework of these cases

> lacks the architecture to serve two functions intended by the Court, namely the safeguard against wrongful convictions function and the incentive to avoid suggestive procedures function. Both biological science (via DNA) and social science (via eyewitness identification experiments) have shed new light on the eyewitness identification errors and have revealed these errors to be much more prevalent than the 1977 Court could have surmised (Wells and Quinlivan 2009: 21).

Despite heavy criticism, the Supreme Court "has yet to confront the need to overhaul" the test (O'Toole and Shay 2006: 116). Thus, the five factors set forth in *Biggers–Manson* remain the test for determining the admissibility of identifications that were initially tainted by some level of being impermissibly suggestive, at least in the federal court system. As discussed in more detail later, however, several jurisdictions have taken it upon themselves to address the shortcomings of the *Biggers–Manson* approach.

Cases Upholding Identifications as Reliable As the following cases illustrate, courts are loathe to exclude eyewitness identifications as unreliable even when they were made under highly suggestive circumstances.

■ *United States v. Thody*, 978 F.2d 625, 629 (10th Cir. 1992), applied the *Biggers–Manson* factors to find an identification of a bank robber reliable despite an impermissibly suggestive lineup.

> Each witness had an adequate opportunity to observe Thody closely during the two robberies. All three witnesses testified at the suppression hearing that at least once they were within a few feet of Thody, and that they were able to observe McIntosh and him for several minutes. Woods and Harshfield were within arm's reach of Thody while complying with his instructions. The light was good, and there is no question that the attention of these three employees was riveted on Thody and his companion. Dillard testified that she had been trained to remember the descriptions of robbers. When the second robbery took place Harshfield immediately recognized Thody from the July 12 robbery, exclaiming to Woods, "It's him!" The descriptions of the robbers given by Harshfield, Woods, and Dillard after the robberies also corroborated one another to the degree that descriptions of subtleties in nose size, presence or lack of facial hair, and hair color corresponded significantly. The witnesses were unequivocal in their testimony, both at trial and at the suppression hearing. Despite attempts by defense counsel to unearth inconsistencies, no significant inconsistencies materialized. Also, only one week separated the confrontation from the robbery.

■ *United States v. Wong*, 40 F.3d 1347 (2d Cir. 1994), also found an identification to be reliable in spite of suggestive techniques. A witness to a restaurant shooting was shown three photo arrays from which she selected the defendant's photo because it "looked like the shooter." The police then held a lineup that featured the defendant along with five or six other "Asian males of similar general appearance." 40 F.3d 1359. The witness identified the defendant as someone who "looked like" the shooter, but added that she could not be sure because he appeared to be "taller than she remembered the gunman to be" by six to eight inches. Police then dimmed the lights to re-create the lighting conditions in the restaurant at the time of the shooting and told the witness that they could not accept "a possibly." She then identified the defendant even though "he was taller than she remembered the gunman to be [because he] had 'the same facial features, fair skin, [and] rather big, huge eyes.'" 40 F.3d 1358. The court found that although the police statements to the witness at the time of the lineup "involved some element of suggestiveness," the conduct of law enforcement was not unduly suggestive because although "the detective's comment created the risk of prompting an identification on something less than total certainty, it did not suggest that [the witness] choose any particular participant, nor did it confirm the correctness of her choice after it had been made." 40 F.3d at 1358–59. Moreover, to the extent that the lineup was unnecessarily suggestive, the court ruled the identification was reliable in spite of the height difference between the witness's initial description of the shooter and the height of the defendant. The court reasoned:

> The circumstances of this case seem to indicate that [the witness] chose Wong *despite* his height, not because of it. In any event, [her] testimony was that Wong was in a crouched position, shooting, when she observed him in the restaurant, rendering a misestimate of his height understandable without significantly undercutting the reliability of her identification. 40 F.3d at 1359.

Because the witness observed the shooter "after she ducked under the table at the restaurant, staring him in the face for two to three seconds before he turned away, thereby allowing her to accurately identify the defendant's facial features," the court concluded the identification was reliable enough to be admissible.

■ In *Clark v. Caspari*, 274 F.3d 507 (8th Cir. 2001), the court ruled that a showup following the robbery of a liquor store was unnecessarily suggestive for the following reasons:

> The circumstances surrounding [witnesses'] identifications indicate that the procedures used were improperly suggestive. The record reveals that prior to the identifications, [the witnesses] were asked to identify several suspects that had been apprehended by the police. When they arrived on the scene, [they] saw only [the two African American defendants]. Both individuals were handcuffed, and were surrounded by white police officers, one of whom was holding a shotgun. Under these circumstances, [the witnesses] may have felt obligated to positively identify [the defendants], so as not to disagree with the police, whose actions exhibited their belief that they had apprehended the correct suspects. Essentially, [the witnesses] were given a choice: identify the apprehended suspects, or nobody at all. This coercive scenario increased the possibility of misidentification. 274 F.3d at 511.

The court, however, ruled that the witnesses' identifications were reliable and therefore admissible even though neither of the two witnesses had been able to provide a description of the robbers. Key to the court's rationale was that both witnesses "had the opportunity to clearly view the perpetrators at the time of

592

PART IV
INTERROGATIONS,
IDENTIFICATIONS, TRIALS,
AND POST-CONVICTION
REMEDIES

the robbery" and the fact that only thirty minutes had passed from the time of the robbery to the time of the showup. 274 F.3d at 512.

■ *Howard v. Bouchard*, 405 F.3d 459 (6th Cir. 2005), upheld an identification of a shooting suspect even though the identifying witness had seen the defendant in court, sitting with his lawyer at the defense table, just an hour before a lineup was conducted. In addition, the defendant stood out in the lineup due to his height (he was at least three inches taller than the foils) and his hairstyle—a "high-fade haircut that the witnesses later said was so distinctive." 405 F.3d at 471. The court found that these factors were only minimally suggestive. Moreover, the court found that the suggestiveness was outweighed by the reliability of the identification. This conclusion, however, is somewhat remarkable because the eyewitness initially only "got a glance" at the shooter while passing by the scene in a moving truck at a distance of three to six feet, and then viewed the shooter for "a split-second again" when he heard the sound of shots being fired at a distance of approximately fifteen feet. The witness then viewed the shooter a third time as he was picking up shells from sixty to ninety seconds at a distance of thirty to forty feet. All three opportunities to view the shooter from the truck occurred in the early morning hours while the area was lit by street lamps. The court was nonetheless persuaded that the opportunity for the witness to have viewed the shooter was sufficient because the witness was "participating in a repossession, which by its stressful nature generally demands heightened attention" and because the witness expressed certainty as to the identification. 405 F.3d at 473.

■ In *State v. Thompson*, 839 A.2d 622 (Conn. App. Ct. 2004), during the time that police transported to a showup a witness to a shooting, one officer told the witness that the person they were holding was "probably the shooter," that they believed they "have the person," and that police "need[ed the witness] to identify him." 839 A.2d at 271. Although the court found the confrontation to be "highly and unnecessarily suggestive," the court ruled the identification was reliable because the witness had a "good, hard look" at the shooter in daylight, the identification occurred less than two hours after the shooting, and the witness was sure of his identification. 839 A.2d at 272.

■ In *State v. Johnson*, 836 N.E.2d 1243 (Ohio Ct. App. 2005), the wife of a murder victim had been unable to identify the defendant from a photo array conducted approximately one month following the homicide. Seven months later, however, she identified the defendant in court at a preliminary hearing. During that proceeding, the defendant "was dressed in clothing from the Department of Youth Services and may have been handcuffed and . . . he was the only young African-American male seated at the defense table." 836 N.E.2d 1258. The court nonetheless ruled that the identification was reliable because the witness had observed the gunman for more than a minute at the time of the shooting from a distance of only a few feet, and because she had an opportunity to stare into his eyes. When she identified the defendant in court, she testified: "Those eyes, those eyes. I will never forget those eyes." 836 N.E.2d at 1250. Given her level of certainty, the court dismissed her initial inability to identify the defendant at the photo array and admitted her subsequent in-court identification.

■ *United States v. DeCologero*, 530 F.3d 36 (1st Cir. 2008), declared a photo array impermissibly suggestive because four of the six photos used by police in an array did not resemble defendant. Yet the court upheld the identification as reliable because the two victims both had the opportunity to view their assailants for a substantial period of time.

Cases Excluding Identifications as Unreliable As the following cases illustrate, courts usually only exclude an impermissibly suggestive identification under highly limited circumstances. To warrant exclusion, either none of the *Biggers–Manson* factors provide a basis for the reliability of the identification, or the factors that do provide such indicia of reliability have to be significantly outweighed by a glaring inconsistency in one of the important *Biggers–Manson* factors.

■ *United States v. De Jesus-Rios*, 990 F.2d 672 (1st Cir. 1993), found that a boat captain's identification of a woman who had contracted for cargo transport was not otherwise reliable after an impermissibly suggestive one-person showup. The court had no problem with the first, second, and fifth *Biggers-Manson* factors but was troubled by application of the third and fourth factors (the accuracy of the witness's prior description of the criminal and the level of certainty the witness demonstrated at the confrontation):

> Agent Marti testified that, on the date the cocaine was discovered, February 8, 1991, Rivera [the boat captain] described the suspect as "white" and approximately five feet, two inches tall. Rivera's testimony at the suppression hearing and Agent Dania's trial testimony revealed that during his February 11, 1991, interview with Agent Dania, Rivera again described her as "white." It was not until after the February 16, 1991, showup that Rivera described the suspect as having "light brown" skin. Moreover, Rivera also failed to provide an accurate description of her height (five feet, six inches) at either of his pre-showup descriptions.
>
> The record also contains uncontroverted evidence that, despite having been asked at the February 16, 1991, showup to signal the agents when he positively identified Eva Rios, Rivera waited until after she approached the agents and began speaking with them (as scheduled) to signal. We hardly think that this constitutes a high degree of certainty on Rivera's part, particularly in light of the showup procedure at issue here. Prior to that showup, Rivera was informed that the agents were meeting the suspect in front of the customs building at a specific time. Although a few other women also may have walked by the customs building that morning, only Eva Rios stopped to speak with the agents. 990 F.2d at 678.

■ *Raheem v. Kelly*, 257 F.3d 122 (2d Cir. 2001), two witnesses to a shooting gave police a description of the perpetrator that included mention of a distinctive article of clothing: a three-quarter-length black leather coat. The defendant was placed in a lineup in which he was the only person in a black leather coat. The court ruled the lineup was unduly suggestive. But the court also excluded the identification as unreliable because almost all of the *Biggers–Manson* criteria weighed in favor of the unreliability of the identification. Specifically, the witnesses had an opportunity to see a variety of people in a dimly lit bar prior to the shooting, during which time their degree of attention was low, as they were watching football, drinking, and talking with others. Moreover, after a shot had been fired, the witnesses admitted that they focused their attention on the gun, not at the person holding it. Other than the witnesses' description of the shooter's coat, they had been able to provide only "general information as to the shooter's age, height, and weight" while being unable to provide any details about the shooter's face. 257 F.3d at 138. And, the witnesses were not confident in their identifications. Given the lack of indicia of reliability under so many of the *Biggers–Manson* factors, added to "the fact that both witnesses repeatedly cited the coat worn by [the shooter] as influential in their selection of [the defendant]," the court stated that it could not conclude that the identifications "had reliability independent of the black leather coat" and therefore excluded the identification on due process grounds. 257 F.3d at 140.

KEY POINTS

LO7

- Due process requires that the totality of the circumstances surrounding any identification must not be so overly suggestive as to cause a substantial likelihood of irreparable misidentification. All lineups and showups must be conducted in a fair and impartial manner.

- The central question surrounding any identification is whether under the totality of the circumstances it was reliable, even though the confrontation procedure was suggestive. Factors to be considered in evaluating the reliability of an identification are (1) the witness's opportunity to view the criminal at the time of the crime, (2) the witness's degree of attention, (3) the accuracy of the witness's prior description of the criminal, (4) the level of certainty demonstrated by the witness at the confrontation, (5) the length of time between crime and the confrontation, and (6) the corrupting effect of the suggestive identification.

In *United States v. Rogers*, 387 F.3d 925 (7th Cir. 2004), police inadvertently placed one drug offender in the same jail cell as a suspect that he had earlier been unable to identify in a photo array. The court not only found this to have been unnecessarily suggestive but also held the subsequent identification to be unreliable because eleven months had passed from the date of the alleged drug transaction and the date of the photo array, and because the eyewitness did not have a good opportunity to observe the defendant, had not been paying significant attention as an acquaintance allegedly purchased drugs from the defendant, and admitted he could not pick the defendant out of the earlier photo array because "most black guys look alike" to him.

Law enforcement officers have control over the conduct of the identification procedures, but they have little or no control over the five factors determining the reliability of the identification. Therefore, officers should conduct all identification procedures fairly and impartially. To avoid the risk that identification evidence will be excluded as unreliable, officers should follow the guidelines for lineups or photo-array identifications that appear later in this chapter.

Exigent Circumstances Exception

In an emergency, courts are more likely to condone highly suggestive identification procedures such as one-person showups, or excuse violations of the *Wade–Gilbert* right-to-counsel rule, because an immediate identification by a witness may be the only identification possible. For identification purposes, an emergency can be defined as a witness in danger of death or blindness or a suspect in danger of death.

The leading case on emergency identifications is *Stovall v. Denno*, 388 U.S. 293 (1967), in which the defendant was arrested for stabbing a doctor to death and seriously wounding his wife, who was hospitalized for major surgery. Without affording the defendant time to retain counsel, police arranged with the wife's surgeon to bring the defendant to her hospital room, where she identified the defendant as her assailant. The Court held:

> A claimed violation of due process of law in the conduct of a confrontation depends on the totality of the circumstances surrounding it, and the record in the present case reveals that the showing of the defendant to the wife in an immediate hospital confrontation was imperative. . . . Here was the only person in the world who could possibly exonerate Stovall. Her words, and only her words, "He is not the man" could have resulted in freedom for Stovall. The hospital was not far distant from the courthouse and jail. No one knew how long Mrs. Behrendt might live. Faced with the responsibility of identifying the attacker, with the need for immediate action, and with the knowledge that Mrs. Behrendt could not visit the jail, the police followed the only feasible procedure and took Stovall to the hospital room. Under these circumstances, the usual police station lineup, which Stovall now argues he should have had, was out of the question. 388 U.S. at 302.

Note that identification procedures involving critically injured persons should only be conducted with the approval of medical authorities. The importance of obtaining an identification is secondary in importance to the treatment and care of an injured person.

DISCUSSION POINT

Was the Lineup in Antonio Beaver's Case Unnecessarily Suggestive?

Recall the case of Antonio Beaver from the first Discussion Point in this chapter.

- Applying the law of *Stovall v. Denno*, do you think the lineup in Beaver's case was unnecessarily suggestive? Why or why not?

- Assume for the sake of argument that a court were to rule that the lineup in Beaver's case had been unnecessarily suggestive. Applying the *Biggers–Manson* factors, do you think the pretrial identification should be admitted into evidence anyway on reliability grounds? Explain your answer.

Problems with the *Biggers–Manson* Approach to Reliability

In spite of the shortcoming of perception and memory, jurors cling to misperceptions about the unreliable nature of eyewitness identifications. In 2004, psychologist Elizabeth Loftus and colleagues surveyed one thousand potential jurors in the District of Columbia.

- Forty-six percent of respondents erroneously believed "that the witness on the stand is effectively narrating a video recording of events that she can see in her 'mind's eye' for jurors" (p. 6).

- "Almost two-thirds of the respondents (66%) thought the statement 'I never forget a face' applied 'very well' or 'fairly well' to them" (p. 6).

- "Thirty-seven percent . . . thought the presence of a weapon would make a witness' memory for event details *more* reliable, while 33% believed that the presence of a weapon either would have no effect or were not sure of what effect a weapon would have. Only three out of ten potential jurors correctly understood that the presence of a weapon tends to make an eyewitness' memory for details less reliable" (p. 8).

- "Thirty-nine percent of the respondents actually thought that event violence would make a witness' memory for event details *more* reliable, while 33% . . . thought that event violence either would have no effect or were not sure of what effect event violence would have. Only three out of ten potential jurors correctly understood that event violence tends to make an eyewitness' memory for details less reliable" (p. 9).

- "Over 40% of the survey respondents thought that witness time estimates were accurate or were not sure whether such estimates were accurate. . . . [Almost 25 percent] believed that witnesses *underestimate* the actual time. In all, 63% of the survey respondents do not understand what scientific research has demonstrated about a witness' ability to gauge the duration of an event—the jurors either believed witness's subjective time estimates or thought that witnesses tended to actually see a face for longer than claimed—while only 37% of the total respondents correctly understood events unfold faster than witnesses think they do" (p. 11).

- "Nearly 40% of survey respondents agreed that 'an eyewitness' level of confidence in his or her identification is an excellent indicator of that eyewitness' reliability.' Thus, four out of ten jurors, absent education on this subject by a qualified expert, would assess witness testimony under the mistaken impression that there is a very strong correlation between witness confidence and witness accuracy" (p. 13).

- "A large plurality of the survey respondents (48%) thought cross-race and same-race identifications are of equal reliability and many of the other respondents either did not know or thought a cross-racial identification would be more reliable.

595

596

PART IV
INTERROGATIONS,
IDENTIFICATIONS, TRIALS,
AND POST-CONVICTION
REMEDIES

Only 36% of the survey respondents would actually treat a cross-racial identification as less reliable" (p. 15).

■ More than "a quarter of potential jurors believed that a show-up is either *more* reliable than a line-up procedure or that the two procedures are equally reliable" even though showups are inherently suggestive (p. 16).

Notably, justice professionals labor under similar misperceptions. Wise, Safer, and Maro (2011) found that police officers had limited knowledge of eyewitness factors—even those who worked in departments that had implemented the Department of Justice (1999) guidelines for identification procedures.

Given these common misperceptions about perception and memory, the reliability factors set forth in *Biggers–Manson* are significantly underinclusive insofar as they ignore scientific data. Because this shortcoming can lead to the admissibility of an unreliable identification under the *Biggers–Manson* approach to reliability, some states have rejected *Biggers–Manson* on state constitutional law grounds.

States Rejecting *Biggers–Manson* Massachusetts and New York, for example, apply a bright-line, categorical rule that any out-of-court identifications that were unnecessarily or impermissibly suggestive are inadmissible. *Commonwealth v. Martin*, 850 N.E.2d 555 (Mass. 2006); *People v. Duuvon*, 77 N.Y.2d 541 (N.Y. 1991). Wisconsin similarly excludes all showup identifications unless some exigent circumstances necessitated a showup because, under the facts of the case, a lineup or photo array could not have been conducted. *State v. Dubose*, 699 N.W.2d 582 (Wis. 2005).

"Utah and Kansas have adopted a refined version of the [*Biggers–Manson*] test on state law grounds, using reliability factors that have a firmer grounding in the social science" (O'Toole and Shay 2006: 115). New Jersey and Oregon went even further by abandoning a due process approach to the reliability of suggestive identifications. Instead, these two states shifted the focus in identification cases to a scientific evaluation of reliability under their state rules of evidence. Under this approach, judges do not apply the *Biggers–Manson* reliability factors, but rather analyze the estimator and systems variables described earlier in this chapter, often with the assistance of expert witnesses. *State v. Henderson*, 27 A.3d 872 (N.J. 2011); *State v. Lawson*, 352 Or. 724 (Or. 2012).

The Supreme Court's Refusal to Abandon *Biggers–Manson* In 2012, the U.S. Supreme Court decided *Perry v. New Hampshire*, 132 S. Ct. 716 (2012), its first case in thirty-five years concerning the admissibility of eyewitnesses identifications. Unlike the high courts of New Jersey and Oregon, the U.S. Supreme Court seemingly ignored all of the evidence of the factors that actually affect the reliability of eyewitness identifications and instead clung to the *Biggers–Manson* approach to reliability.

The Court described the facts of the *Perry* case as follows:

> Around 3 A.M. on August 15, 2008, the Nashua, New Hampshire Police Department received a call reporting that an African-American male was trying to break into cars parked in the lot of the caller's apartment building. When an officer responding to the call asked [an] eyewitness . . . to describe the man, [she] pointed to her kitchen window and said the man she saw breaking into the car was standing in the parking lot, next to a police officer. . . . Perry's arrest followed this identification. 132 S. Ct. 717–18.

Perry conceded that even though the police had not done anything impermissible to render the identification unnecessarily suggestive, the circumstances—independent of police conduct—rendered the eyewitness, Nubia Blandon's, identification of Perry unreliable for several reasons, including these:

(1) the significant distance between Blandon's window and the parking lot (2) the lateness of the hour; (3) [a] van that partly obstructed Blandon's view; (4) Blandon's concession that she was "so scared [she] really didn't pay attention" to what Perry was wearing; (5) Blandon's inability to describe Perry's facial features or other identifying marks; (6) Blandon's failure to pick Perry out of a photo array; and (7) Perry's position next to a uniformed, gun-bearing police officer at the moment Blandon made her identification. 132 S. Ct. at 729.

The Court granted certiorari to resolve a split among federal circuit courts of appeal regarding whether "the Due Process Clause requires the trial judge to conduct a preliminary assessment of the reliability of an eyewitness identification made under suggestive circumstances not arranged by the police." 132 S. Ct. at 723. In rejecting Perry's arguments, the Court explained that "the potential unreliability of a type of evidence does not alone render its introduction at the defendant's trial fundamentally unfair." 132 S. Ct. at 728. Rather, law enforcement must do something to render an identification unnecessarily suggestive before the Due Process Clause requires judicial inquiry into the reliability of an eyewitness identification.

Guidelines for Lineups and Photo-Array Identification Procedures

The police and the prosecution have discretion to conduct lineups. Although the police, the prosecution, or the court may grant a suspect's request for a lineup, a suspect has no right to a lineup. *Sims v. Sullivan*, 867 F.2d 142 (2d Cir. 1989). The following are guidelines for the law enforcement officer in conducting lineup identification procedures.

Special Considerations Before the Administration of a Lineup

Law enforcement officers should consider the following before conducting a lineup:

- A law enforcement officer should not conduct a lineup without first discussing with a prosecuting attorney the legal advisability of a lineup.
- A lineup should be conducted as soon after the arrest of a suspect as practicable. Promptly conducted lineups enable innocent arrestees to be released, guarantee that witnesses' memories are fresh, and ensure that crucial identification evidence is obtained before the suspect is released on bail or for other reasons. When possible, lineup arrangements (e.g., contacting witnesses and locating innocent participants) should be completed before the arrest of the suspect.
- A person in custody may be compelled to participate in a lineup without violating Fourth or Fifth Amendment rights.
  - Most courts hold that once a person is in custody, his or her liberty is not further infringed under the Fourth Amendment by being presented in a lineup for witnesses to view. *State v. Wilks*, 358 N.W.2d 273 (Wis. 1984); *People v. Hodge*, 526 P.2d 309 (Colo. 1974).

598

PART IV
INTERROGATIONS,
IDENTIFICATIONS, TRIALS,
AND POST-CONVICTION
REMEDIES

■ The Fifth Amendment is not violated by "compelling the accused merely to exhibit his person for observation by a prosecution witness prior to trial [which] involves no compulsion of the accused to give evidence having testimonial significance. It is compulsion of the accused to exhibit his physical characteristics, not compulsion to disclose any knowledge he might have." *United States v. Wade*, 388 U.S. 218, 222 (1967).

■ Compelling people who are not in custody to appear in a lineup involves a much greater intrusion on liberty, and therefore implicates the Fourth Amendment. Forcing someone who is not in custody to appear for a lineup is usually accomplished by order of a court or grand jury, although some states have enacted statutes that create special procedures for doing so. Regardless of the procedure used, U.S. jurisdictions are split on whether such orders to appear require reasonable suspicion, probable cause, or some other standard.

> [A] number of states have . . . adopt[ed] "temporary detention orders" which may be issued for the detention of persons to obtain fingerprints, photographs, blood samples, and other physical evidence when reasonable grounds exist. The "reasonable grounds" standard generally requires that reasonable suspicion exist that the person from whom the evidence is sought is connected to the commission of an offense. Some states, however, require only that there be reasonable cause to believe a crime has been committed and that the ordered identification procedure "may contribute to the identification of the individual who committed such offense." One court has held that appearance similar to that of the alleged perpetrator or similarity in modus operandi between a previously committed offense and the one under investigation is insufficient, standing alone, to meet the latter standard (Ringel 2007: §18:4).

> Some courts have upheld the ordering of a person not in custody to appear in a lineup in serious cases, in which the public interest in law enforcement outweighed the privacy interests of the person. *State v. Hall*, 461 A.2d 1155 (N.J. 1983); *Wise v. Murphy*, 275 A.2d 205 (D.C. App. 1971). Other courts have held that a person not in custody cannot be ordered to participate in a lineup unless there is probable cause to arrest. *In re Armed Robbery, Albertson's, on August 31, 1981*, 659 P.2d 1092 (Wash. 1983); *Alphonso C. v. Morgenthau*, 376 N.Y.S.2d 126 (N.Y. 1975).

■ If the suspect has a right to counsel at a lineup, the suspect should be informed of that right. If the suspect chooses to waive the right to counsel, a careful record should be made of the suspect's waiver and agreement to voluntarily participate in the lineup. (See Figure 14.4.)

■ If the suspect chooses to have an attorney present at the lineup, the lineup should be delayed a reasonable time to allow the attorney to appear. The attorney must be allowed to be present from the beginning of the lineup, or "the moment [the suspect] and the other lineup members were within the sight of witnesses." *United States v. LaPierre*, 998 F.2d 1460, 1464 (9th Cir. 1993). The attorney should be allowed to consult with the suspect before the lineup and to observe all the proceedings, take notes, and tape-record the identification process in whole or in part. If the attorney has suggestions that might improve the fairness of the proceedings, the officer in charge may follow them if they are reasonable and practicable. The suspect's attorney should not be allowed to control the proceedings, however.

■ Even when the suspect's counsel is not required at a lineup because formal criminal proceedings have not yet been instituted or the suspect has knowingly, intelligently, and voluntarily waived the right to counsel, the officer conducting the lineup should consider allowing counsel to be present to minimize subsequent challenges to the fairness of the lineup. *State v. Taylor*, 210 N.W.2d 873 (Wis. 1973).

■ The names of all persons participating in the lineup, the names of the officers conducting the lineup, and the name of the suspect's attorney, if any, should be recorded and preserved.

■ Witnesses should not be allowed to view photographs of the suspect before the lineup. If a witness has viewed such photographs before the lineup, the officer conducting the lineup should inform the suspect's counsel and the court of any identification of the suspect's photograph, any failure to identify the suspect's photograph, and any identification of a photograph of someone other than the suspect.

■ Before viewing the lineup, each witness should be required to give to the officer in charge of the lineup a written description of the perpetrator of the crime. A copy should be made available to the suspect's counsel.

Guidelines for Administering Lineups and Photo Arrays

In light of the empirical research demonstrating systemic problems with eyewitness identification, the American Psychology and Law Society (Wells et al. 1998) and the U.S. Department of Justice (1999) both published guides for reforming the way the criminal justice system approaches eyewitness evidence. Following the issuance of those reports, the American Bar Association (ABA) issued the following "Statement of Best Practices for Promoting the Accuracy of Eyewitness Identification Procedures" (2004). The procedures they recommend apply to both the live administration of lineups and to photo arrays.

One Suspect per Lineup or Array Only one suspect should appear in the lineup. If there are two or more suspects, no two should appear together in the same lineup or photo array.

Double-Blind Administration Whenever practicable, the person who conducts a lineup or photo array and all others present (except for defense counsel, when his or her presence is constitutionally required) should be unaware of which of the participants is the suspect.

■ The person who administers a lineup or photo array affects the reliability of any identification. The procedure should be double-blind—that is, neither the witness nor the person administering the lineup or photo array should know who the suspect is and who the foils are (Wells and Seelau 1995). That procedure greatly reduces, if not eliminates, suggestive questioning by the administrator and other possibilities of the administrator unduly influencing the witness, either consciously or unconsciously (Steblay 1997). To enhance the reliability of the double-blind procedure, eyewitnesses should be instructed that they should not assume that the person administering the lineup knows who the suspect is. Doing so helps to decrease the likelihood of witnesses looking for cues from the administrator of the identification procedure.

■ If a double-blind procedure is not used, the administrator of the lineup should not engage in unnecessary conversation with witnesses. Most important, the administrator should not indicate by word, gesture, or other means of communication any opinion as to the identity or guilt of the suspect. The administrator especially should not coax, coach, or tell witnesses that they have chosen the person suspected of the crime or have made the "correct" decision.

600

PART IV
INTERROGATIONS,
IDENTIFICATIONS, TRIALS,
AND POST-CONVICTION
REMEDIES

If more than one witness is called to view a lineup, those who have already viewed the lineup should not be allowed to converse with persons who have not yet viewed the lineup. Witnesses who have viewed the lineup should be kept in a room separate from witnesses who have not yet viewed the lineup. Furthermore, only one witness at a time should be present in the room where the lineup is being conducted.

Witness Instructions Upon entering the room in which the lineup is being conducted, each witness should be handed a form for use in the identification. The form should be signed by the witness and the law enforcement officer conducting the lineup. Many police departments use lineup forms like the one in Figure 14.5. A copy of the witness identification form should be given to the suspect's attorney at the time each witness completes viewing the lineup. It should be noted, however, that many lineup forms are missing two key instructions that the ABA recommends be provided to all witnesses before the lineup is conducted. If the form does not contain the following two instructions, they should be orally told to witnesses:

■ Eyewitnesses should be instructed that the perpetrator may or may not be in the lineup. Explicitly informing a witness that the suspect may not be in the lineup or array reduces the pressure on the witness to make an identification. This, in turn, decreases the risk that the witness will make a questionable identification by selecting "the person who best resembles the culprit relative to the others in the lineup" or array (Wells and Seelau 1995: 778–79).

■ Eyewitnesses should be instructed that they need not identify anyone, but, if they do so, they will be expected to state in their own words how certain they are of any identification they make or the lack thereof. This procedure reduces a witness's use of relative decision making by encouraging a witness to use an absolute threshold (Levi and Lindsay 2001; Steblay 1997).

Specific Guidelines for Foil Selection, Number, and Presentation Methods

The American Psychology and Law Society (Wells et al. 1998) and the U.S. Department of Justice (1999) also recommended specific guidelines regarding the selection and presentation of foils.

Appearance of Foils The people who appear in a lineup or photo array other than the suspect are called foils or fillers. Foils should be chosen for their similarity to the witness's description of the perpetrator. For a lineup or photo array to be fair, the actual suspect should not stand out from the other participants in a lineup or photo array (Wells and Seelau 1995). Fitzgerald and colleagues (2013) conducted a meta-analysis of 17 independent studies that provided data from 6,650 participants. They found that

> [c]ompared with lineups with moderate or high similarity fillers, lineups with low similarity fillers were far more likely to elicit suspect identifications. This was true regardless of whether the suspect was guilty or innocent, underscoring the importance of ensuring the suspect does not stand out from the fillers. (p. 151)

But constructing a truly fair lineup or photo array can be difficult. Although the participants should not be clones of each other, they should generally be of the same race, should be similarly dressed (although preferably not in clothing matching witnesses' descriptions of clothing worn by the culprit), should not be of substantially differing height and weight, and should not have visible distinctive features (e.g., all should have similar or absent facial hair; either all or none should have tattoos, etc.; see Judges 2000; Wells and Seelau 1995).

Lineup Identification Form for Witnesses

Your Name: _____ Date of Birth: _____

Address: _____

Telephone Number: _____ Case Number: _____

Place Viewed: _____ Officer: _____

Agency: _____

TO THE WITNESS: You have been asked to look at a lineup. This is either a presentation in person of several individuals or a presentation of several photographs. You may or may not be able to identify a person in the lineup. Please look at all the persons before making any choice. If you do not identify a person in the lineup, please indicate below. If you do identify a person, please indicate the number of the person on this form.

You must look at this display and make an independent identification *without assistance*. Do not ask any questions about the people being shown. You may, however, ask the officer to have persons in the lineup say certain words, do certain things, or wear certain clothing, if you think it will aid you. Do not ask anyone for help or discuss this with anyone except the officer. There is no "right" answer, so do not ask whether you have made the "right" choice.

Please mark your choice with an "X":

I do not identify anyone

I identify   1   2   3   4   5   6   7   8

COMMENTS: _____

_____

_____

_____

Thank you for your cooperation.

_____ Date and Time _____
Viewer's Signature

_____ Date and Time _____
Officer's Signature/Badge Number

© Cengage Learning®

FIGURE 14.5 | Lineup Identification Form for Witnesses

Number of Foils Lineups and photo arrays should use a sufficient number of foils to reasonably reduce the risk of an eyewitness selecting a suspect by guessing rather than by recognition. The witness should not know how many individuals will be shown to them in a lineup or photo array.

The number of foils presented along with the suspect is also important to lineup or photo-array fairness. The more people who participate in a lineup, the less likely a suspect will be identified merely by chance. The same is true of photo arrays: The more photographs presented to the witness, the less likely it is the suspect will be identified by chance.

602

PART IV
INTERROGATIONS,
IDENTIFICATIONS, TRIALS,
AND POST-CONVICTION
REMEDIES

Accordingly, most experts recommend that at least six people be in a lineup or photo array (Levi 1998; Wells et al. 1998). To decrease chance identifications, England routinely uses nine or ten people, and Canada uses twelve (Levi and Lindsay 2001).

Sequential Versus Simultaneous Presentation of Foils   Historically, all of the participants in a photo array or lineup were presented to the witness at the same time—a practice that continues to this day. But research has demonstrated that sequential viewing of photographs or lineup participants one after another, rather than simultaneous presentation of foils (viewing of all participants at once), is preferable. As with the previous precaution, this procedure reduces a witness's use of relative decision making by encouraging a witness to use an absolute threshold (Levi and Lindsay 2001; Steblay 1997). "Critical tests of this hypothesis have consistently shown that a sequential procedure produces fewer false identifications than does a simultaneous procedure with little or no decrease in rates of accurate identification" (Wells and Seelau 1995: 772; see also Klobuchar et al. 2006).

Foil Behavior at Lineups   Suspects should be allowed to choose their position in the lineup and to change that position after each viewing. This promotes fairness and eliminates any claim that the positioning of the suspect in the lineup was unduly suggestive.

Lineup participants may be compelled to speak for purposes of voice identification. As stated in the *Wade* opinion, "[C]ompelling Wade to speak within hearing distance of the witnesses, even to utter words purportedly uttered by the robber, was not compulsion to utter statements of a 'testimonial' nature; he was required to use his voice as an identifying physical characteristic, not to speak his guilt." 388 U.S. at 222–23. Hence, there is no Fifth Amendment violation when a lineup participant is compelled to speak in this way. Each person in the lineup, however, should be asked to speak the same words in roughly the same tone of voice (e.g., all should whisper, all should shout, or all should talk "normally"). Moreover, police must take care to make sure that one voice does not stand out among the others. For example, *United States v. Garcia-Alvarez*, 541 F.3d 8 (1st Cir. 2008), held that a voice identification was impermissibly suggestive because the suspect had a Dominican accent, but the other lineup participants did not.

If any body movements or gestures are necessary, they should be made one time only by each person in the lineup and repeated only at the express request of the observing witness or victim. Again, the officer conducting the lineup should keep a careful record of any person's failure to cooperate.

Additional Considerations for Photographic Arrays

Photo arrays bring their own set of cautions concerning suggestibility. Law enforcement officers should pay attention to the following concerns when assembling a photo array.

■ "In the absence of exigent circumstances, presentation of a single photograph to the victim of a crime amounts to an unnecessarily suggestive photographic identification procedure." *United States v. Jones*, 652 F. Supp.

KEY POINTS

L08

■ Only one suspect should appear in any lineup or photo array.

■ Whenever possible, lineups and photo arrays should be administered using a double-blind procedure; that is, neither the witness nor the person administering the lineup or photo array should know who the suspect is and who the foils are.

■ Eyewitnesses should be instructed that the perpetrator may or may not be in the lineup; that they need not identify anyone; and, if they do make an identification, then they will be expected to state in their own words how certain they are of any identification they make.

■ Foils should be chosen for their similarity to the witness's description of the perpetrator, without the suspect standing out in any way from the foils and without other factors drawing undue attention to the suspect. Although the participants should not be clones of each other, they should generally be of the same race, should be similarly dressed (although preferably not in clothing matching witnesses' descriptions of clothing worn by the culprit), should not be of substantially differing height and weight, and should not have visible distinctive features (e.g., all should have similar or absent facial hair; either all or none should have tattoos, etc.).

■ A minimum of six people should appear in any lineup or photo array; seven to nine people is preferable.

Continued on next page

1561, 1570 (S.D.N.Y. 1986); *see also Simmons v. United States*, 390 U.S. 377 (1968); *United States v. Smith*, 429 F. Supp.2d 440, 450 (D. Mass. 2006) ("It is axiomatic that identifications achieved through the use of a single photo are highly problematic. A single photo shown to an eyewitness [the proverbial "Is this the man you saw?" question] plainly suggests the guilt of the person pictured."). Thus, photos should be sequentially presented in arrays of at least six pictures.

- Photos should either all be color pictures or all black and white. Arrays that mix color and black-and-white photos might be held to be unnecessarily suggestive. *E.g., O'Brien v. Wainwright*, 738 F.2d 1139 (11th Cir. 1984).

- If possible, mug shot photos should not be used. Mug shots may prejudice the suspect by implying that he or she has a criminal record. If the use of mug shots is unavoidable, only frontal views should be used and their identity as mug shots should be disguised such that arrest information, height markings, and the like are not visible. *E.g., Cikora v. Dugger*, 840 F.2d 893, 894 (11th Cir. 1988). If mug shot photos are used, they should not be displayed in a photographic array alongside ordinary photographs. *Perry v. Lockhart*, 871 F.2d 1384, 1391 (8th Cir.), *cert. denied*, 493 U.S. 959 (1989).

- If police have no suspect, the display of a mug book to a witness or victim presents no problems of being suggestive so long as a reasonable number of photographs are shown and careful records kept of all pictures shown and pictures identified.

- A photograph in a photographic display may be altered (to show what the person would look like with a beard or a hat, for example) so long as all other photographs in the display are altered in the same way. *United States v. Dunbar*, 767 F.2d 72 (3d Cir. 1985).

Recording Procedures Whenever practicable, the police should videotape or digitally video-record identification procedures, including the witness's confidence statements and any statements made to the witness by the police.

- Absent videotaping or digital video recording, a photograph should be taken of each lineup or photo array, and a detailed record made describing with specificity how the entire procedure (from start to finish) was administered, also noting the appearance of the foils and of the suspect and the identities of all persons present. Some courts hold that a failure to properly photograph or record an identification procedure allows courts to presume that the procedure was unduly suggestive. *Smith v. Campbell*, 781 F. Supp. 521 (M.D. Tenn. 1991).

- Regardless of the way in which a lineup is memorialized, and for all other identification procedures, including photo arrays, the police shall, immediately after completing the identification procedure and in a nonsuggestive manner, request witnesses to indicate their level of confidence in any identification and ensure that the response is accurately documented.

- Obtaining a statement of confidence level before other information can prevent contamination of a witness's judgment increases the reliability of an identification (Wells and Seelau 1995). Because confidence level at the time of initial identification is a powerful force in determining both the admissibility of an out-of-court identification and the weight accorded to it by the trier of fact, it should be self-evident why an uncontaminated statement of

KEY POINTS

- Sequential viewing of photographs or lineup participants one after another, rather than simultaneous viewing of all participants, is preferable.

- Immediately after completing an identification procedure, police must, in a nonsuggestive manner, request witnesses to indicate their level of confidence in any identification, and ensure that the response is accurately documented and record their responses.

- Whenever practicable, the police should videotape or digitally video-record identification procedures, including the witness's confidence statements and any statements made to the witness by the police.

- Lineups and photo arrays must be properly documented in a detailed record that describes with specificity how the entire procedure (from start to finish) was administered, also noting the appearance of the foils and of the suspect and the identities of all persons present.

- Before, during, and after an identification procedure, police and prosecutors should avoid giving witnesses any feedback on whether they feel they have made a "good" or "correct" identification.

- Multiple lineups or photo arrays involving the same suspect and witnesses are inherently suggestive and strongly discouraged.

- Place the people in a lineup or photos in a photo array in different positions each time a lineup or array is administered to multiple witnesses for the same case.

- When showing a new suspect to a witness in a second or subsequent lineup or photo array, avoid reusing the same people as foils.

603

604

PART IV
INTERROGATIONS,
IDENTIFICATIONS, TRIALS,
AND POST-CONVICTION
REMEDIES

high confidence should be obtained at the time of an initial identification (Smith, Lindsay, and Pryke 2000; Weber and Brewer 2006). But the importance of initial confidence goes beyond the obvious in light of a phenomenon called confidence malleability: "the tendency for an eyewitness to become more or less confident in his or her identification as a function of events that occur after the identification" (Wells and Seelau 1995: 774; see also Penrod and Cutler 1995).

Immediate Postlineup or Post-Photo-Array Procedures The American Psychology and Law Society (Wells et al. 1998) and the U.S. Department of Justice (1999) recommend that the following procedures be followed after a lineup or photo array is conducted.

- Police and prosecutors should avoid at any time giving the witness feedback on whether he or she selected the "right" person—the person believed by law enforcement to be the culprit. This procedure not only helps to reduce confidence malleability but also helps to avoid both confabulation and the postevent misinformation effect.

- The officer conducting the lineup should take complete notes of everything that takes place at the lineup and should prepare an official report of all the proceedings, to be filed in the law enforcement agency's permanent records. The report should include the time, location, identity of persons present, statements made, photographs or videotapes of the lineup, and the lineup identification form (see Figure 14.5) for each witness viewing the lineup. A copy of the report should be sent to the prosecuting attorney and made available to the suspect's attorney.

- A defendant has no right to have counsel present at a postlineup police interview with an identifying witness. *Sams v. Walker*, 18 F.3d 167 (2d Cir. 1994).

Multiple Lineups or Photo Arrays Special procedures are recommended by the American Psychology and Law Society (Wells et al. 1998) and the U.S. Department of Justice (1999) when multiple identification procedures are used.

Avoid Multiple Identification Procedures Using the Same Witness and Suspect Multiple lineups or photo arrays involving the same suspect and witness are inherently suggestive and strongly discouraged. In *Foster v. California*, 394 U.S. 440 (1969), the eyewitness was unable to make a positive identification at the first lineup, in which Foster was placed with considerably shorter men. After meeting Foster one-on-one, the witness made a tentative, uncertain identification. At a second lineup, the eyewitness was finally convinced that Foster committed the crime and positively identified him. Foster was the only person who appeared in both lineups. The U.S. Supreme Court reversed the conviction:

> The suggestive elements in this identification procedure made it all but inevitable that [the witness] would identify petitioner whether or not he was in fact "the man." In effect, the police repeatedly said to the witness, "This is the man." . . . This procedure so undermined the reliability of the eyewitness identification as to violate due process. 394 U.S. at 443.

Vary Position of Participants When Multiple Lineups Are Used for Multiple Witnesses Place the people in a lineup or photos in a photo array in different positions each time a lineup or array is administered to multiple witnesses for the same case. In theory, witnesses should have no contact with each other. Nonetheless, in case one witness manages to communicate to another the position of the person whom they believe to be the suspect, varying the positions of the suspect and the foils will help to eliminate the possibility of such a contamination of the identification procedures.

DISCUSSION POINT

Can Identifications Be Improved Using Double-Blind Administration? The Innocence Project: The Case of Anthony Michael Green

In June 1998, a Caucasian woman was attacked in her room at the Cleveland Clinic Inn, where she was staying following cancer treatment at the Cleveland Clinic Hospital. On the night of the crime, she had responded to a knock at her door.

When she opened the door, a hand reached inside and grabbed her by the throat. The assailant held a knife near her face, pushed her into the room, and demanded money from her. After the victim gave him some money, the perpetrator ordered her to sit on the bed and to undress. The assailant then told her to put her clothing back on and went toward the door. After he arrived at the door, however, the assailant walked back over to the victim and ordered her to undress again. He pushed the victim onto the bed and raped her. The victim testified at trial that the perpetrator said his name was Tony during the attack. . . .

Approximately an hour and a half after the perpetrator left her room, the victim called the Cleveland Clinic security, who notified the Cleveland Police Department, and both agencies responded to the scene. The victim's initial description of the assailant was an African American male, around twenty-three years old, 5'8", 165 pounds, medium build, brown eyes, black short afro, pockmarked face with pimples, wearing a black ski-cap type of hat and a "doo rag," a black T-shirt with cutoff sleeves, and gray pleated pants. . . .

A few days after the attack, the victim was shown a photo array that depicted young African American males and included Green's former work identification photograph. After viewing this first array, the victim stated that she saw one person "that resembled [her] attacker, but just not enough." The following day, she was shown a photo array comprised of booking photographs. Green's photograph was the only photograph repeated in both arrays. The booking photographs contained biographical placards on them, including the subject's height, weight, and age. The card on Green's photograph gave a height, weight, and age description that matched the description given by the victim to the police. She identified Green as her assailant from this second photo array.

Mr. Green's subsequent conviction was based almost exclusively on the eyewitness identification made by the victim. He served thirteen years in prison for a crime that DNA evidence later proved he did not commit. Since his release, the real perpetrator of this crime confessed and was convicted.

From The Innocence Project, www.innocenceproject.org/Content /Anthony_Michael_Green.php. Reproduced by permission.

■ What factors do you think contributed to the wrongful conviction of Anthony Michael Green?

■ The Innocence Project asserts, "It is unlikely that a 'blind' administrator would have decided to perform two lineups and include pedigree information in the second. Because the victim lacked confidence in her first identification, it is improbable that Mr. Green would have been identified through a double-blind sequential procedure had it been employed." Do you agree with this statement? Why or why not?

Use Different Foils for Different Suspects for the Same Witness When showing a new suspect to a witness in a second or subsequent lineup or photo array, avoid reusing the same people as foils. That way, the witness should not have seen any of the people previously used in subsequent lineups or photo arrays.

Effect of Improper Identification Procedures

To enforce the standards set out by the U.S. Supreme Court with respect to pretrial identifications, rules have been established for the admission of identification evidence in court. Rule 12 of the Federal Rules of Criminal Procedure requires a defendant to file a

606

PART IV
INTERROGATIONS,
IDENTIFICATIONS, TRIALS,
AND POST-CONVICTION
REMEDIES

pretrial motion to suppress identification evidence before a trial begins. If the motion is granted either because a confrontation was made in violation of the defendant's right to counsel, or because an identification is unreliable and thereby violates a defendant's right to due process of law, the court must exclude at trial

- any evidence of the pretrial identification presented as a part of the prosecutor's case in chief, and
- any identification made by a witness in court who participated in the tainted pretrial identification.

Like most other constitutional violations, if an unnecessarily suggestive and unreliable identification was improperly admitted into evidence at trial, appellate courts will apply the harmless error rule (see Chapter 15). Thus, if there is other sufficient evidence of guilt, a conviction will be sustained on appeal in spite of the erroneous admission of the unreliable identification. For example, *United States v. Brown*, 441 F.3d 1330 (11th Cir. 2006), upheld a conviction obtained using evidence from an unreliable lineup because both DNA evidence and a confession provided overwhelming evidence of the defendant's guilt.

Independent Source Doctrine

If a pretrial identification is ruled to be inadmissible on either Sixth Amendment or due process grounds, an eyewitness may still be allowed to make an in-court identification. *Coleman v. Alabama*, 399 U.S. 1 (1970).

In *Gilbert v. California*, 388 U.S. 263 (1967), the Supreme Court held that such an in-court identification would be constitutionally permissible if the identification were based on a source independent of the illegally tainted pretrial identification procedure. Courts will rule that an in-court identification has an **independent source** when the identifying witness, by drawing on personal memory of the crime and observations of the defendant during the crime, has such a clear and definite image of the defendant that the witness can make an identification unaffected by the illegal confrontation. The prosecution bears the burden of persuasion to prove, by clear and convincing evidence, that a witness has a source independent from the illegal confrontation for identifying the perpetrator of the crime. *Tomlin v. Myers*, 30 F.3d 1235 (9th Cir. 1994). Factors to be considered by judges in determining an independent source are set out in *Wade*:

> Application of [the independent source test] requires consideration of various factors; for example, the prior opportunity to observe the alleged criminal act, the existence of any discrepancy between any pre-lineup description and the defendant's actual description, any identification prior to the lineup of another person, the identification by picture of the defendant prior to lineup, failure to identify the defendant on a prior occasion, and the lapse of time between the alleged act and the lineup identification. It is also relevant to consider those facts which, despite the absence of counsel, are disclosed concerning the conduct of the lineup. 388 U.S. at 241.

For example, *McKinon v. Wainwright*, 705 F.2d 419 (11th Cir. 1983), found an independent source for the identification of an accused at trial when the witness had known the accused long before the crime was committed and had spent several hours with the accused on the day of the crime.

Law enforcement officers should gather and record information on these factors from witnesses. Officers should obtain as much detail as possible because strong evidence of an independent source for identification of a criminal can salvage an improperly conducted identification procedure. Of course, if the defendant does not meet the threshold requirement of showing that the in-court identification was tainted by impermissible suggestiveness, then "independent reliability [of the in-court identification] is not a constitutionally required condition of admissibility . . . and the reliability of the identification is simply a question for the jury." *Jarrett v. Headley*, 802 F.2d 34, 42 (2d Cir. 1986).

Courts use the same independent-source factors to determine the admissibility of in-court identifications that are based on pretrial identification procedures administered in violation of a defendant's Fourth Amendment rights. *United States v. Crews*, 445 U.S. 463 (1980); *United States v. Meyer*, 359 F.3d 820 (6th Cir. 2004). For example, in *United States v. Slater*, 692 F.2d 107 (10th Cir. 1982), the photograph used for an out-of-court identification had been obtained through an illegal arrest. The court held that the in-court identification of the defendant was admissible, however, because "the witnesses . . . had each actually seen the crime committed at close hand, there was little discrepancy between the pretrial descriptions and the defendant's actual description, there was no identification of another person or failure to identify the defendant, and the person who committed the crime made no attempt to conceal his face." 692 F.2d at 108. *See also United States v. Foppe*, 993 F.2d 1444 (9th Cir. 1993) (admitting an in-court identification even though an out-of-court photo identification was the inadmissible fruit of illegal arrest because the eyewitness had a chance to observe the defendant indoors at close range under good lighting conditions).

SUMMARY

Both human perception and memory are complicated, highly selective, unconscious processes that can be negatively affected by a number of factors. Perception depends both on the acuity of the physical senses and a number of psychological factors that affect how sensory data is processed in light of experience, learning, preferences, biases, and expectations. Memory has three critical stages: acquisition or encoding, retention, and recall or retrieval. All three stages are affected by physical and psychological factors that can taint the accuracy of a memory. These factors include time, lighting conditions, changes in visual adaptation to light and dark, duration of the event, speed and distance involved, the presence or absence of violence, stress, fear, physical limitation on sensory perception (e.g., poor eyesight, hearing impairment, alcohol or drug intoxication), expectations, age (the very young and very old have unique problems), and gender.

A criminal suspect has a right to counsel at all lineups and showups conducted at or after the initiation of adversary judicial criminal proceedings against the suspect. The emergency showup is the only exception to this rule. In every other case, the suspect should be warned of the right to counsel in accordance with the form appearing in Figure 14.4.

If a lineup or showup is conducted before adversary judicial criminal proceedings are initiated against a suspect, the suspect is not entitled to the presence or advice of counsel. Nevertheless, all pretrial identification procedures, whether lineups or showups, must be conducted in accordance with due process, which forbids any pretrial identification procedure that is unnecessarily suggestive and conducive to irreparable mistaken identification. As further interpreted by the U.S. Supreme Court, due process simply requires that all pretrial identifications be reliable in the totality of the circumstances; otherwise, evidence of the identification is inadmissible in court.

The following factors should be considered in determining reliability: the witness's opportunity to view the criminal at the time of the crime, the witness's degree of attention, the accuracy of the witness's prior description of the criminal, the level of

608

PART IV
INTERROGATIONS,
IDENTIFICATIONS, TRIALS,
AND POST-CONVICTION
REMEDIES

certainty demonstrated by the witness at the confrontation, and the length of time between the crime and the confrontation. These factors are weighed against the corrupting effect of a suggestive identification.

Officers conducting lineups or photo arrays are advised to follow the guidelines for these identification procedures presented in this chapter.

A criminal suspect is not entitled to the presence or advice of counsel at photographic identification procedures no matter when those procedures are held. Nevertheless, such procedures must be conducted as fairly and impartially as possible, and identifications are evaluated by the reliability test described in the preceding paragraph. Officers are advised to follow the guidelines for photographic identifications provided in this chapter.

If a pretrial identification is excluded on either Sixth Amendment or due process grounds, a subsequent in-court identification may be permissible under the following circumstances: If the prosecution proves, by clear and convincing evidence, that the in-court identification is not the product of the tainted pretrial confrontation, but rather stems from an independent source, such as the witness's personal observations and memory of the defendant at the scene of the crime.

KEY TERMS

acquisition phase (encoding phase) 575
confabulation 575
confidence malleability 604
confirmation bias 575
confrontation 581
cross-racial identification bias 578
double-blind (administration of lineup or photo array) 599
estimator variables 576
event factors 576
foils (fillers) 600
forgetting curve 576

incomplete sensory acquisition 574
independent source 606
lineup 571
malleable characteristics 579
memory 575
perception 574
photographic lineup (photo array) 571
photographic showup 571
postevent misinformation effect 575
reifying error 578
retention phase (storage phase) 575

retrieval phase 575
sensory overload 574
sequential presentation of foils 602
showup 571
simultaneous presentation of foils 602
unconscious transference 576
unnecessarily suggestive identification 586
weapons effect 577
witness factors 576
Yerkes–Dodson law 577

REVIEW AND DISCUSSION QUESTIONS

1. What are some of the factors that affect perception in the "normal" human adult who is free from any physical perceptual impairments? How might these factors affecting perception interfere with the accuracy of an eyewitness identification?

2. Describe the three phases of memory and at least one psychological factor that might impair the accuracy of memory in each phase.

3. Estimator variables—those variables concerning the accuracy of an eyewitness identification over which the criminal justice system has no control—include both "event factors" and "witness factors." Describe the significance of at least three event factors and three witness factors, explaining how each estimator variable might negatively affect the accuracy of an eyewitness identification.

4. Why should a person not have a right to demand an immediate lineup to clear him- or herself and avoid the many inconveniences associated with being arrested?

5. State three ways in which a law enforcement officer conducting a lineup can decrease the suggestibility of the lineup. State three ways in which a law enforcement officer can decrease the suggestibility of a one-person showup.

6. Assume that a suspect is about to be placed in a lineup and is told by a law enforcement officer that she has a right to counsel at the lineup. If the suspect asks, "Why do I need a lawyer?" what should the officer say?

7. Why should photographic identification procedures not be used first when a subsequent physical lineup is contemplated?

8. What arguments would a defense attorney make at a suppression hearing under each of the following circumstances?

    a. The witness identified the defendant's photograph at a pretrial photographic display but failed to identify the defendant at a later physical lineup.

    b. The witness failed to identify the defendant's photograph at a pretrial photographic display but identified the defendant at a later physical lineup.

    c. The witness identified the defendant's photograph at a pretrial photographic display and also identified the defendant at a later physical lineup.

9. Is it possible to conduct a fair lineup when the suspect is unusually tall or short or has very distinctive features or deformities?

10. Would an emergency one-person showup be justified if the suspect and not the victim were seriously injured? In what ways could the suggestibility of the showup be decreased?

11. Would certain suggestive pretrial identification procedures be excusable in a small rural police department as opposed to a large urban police department? What procedures might be excusable, and why?

12. Discuss the following quotation from Justice William J. Brennan's dissenting opinion in *United States v.*

Ash, 413 U.S. 300, 344 (1973), in which the U.S. Supreme Court held that there is no right to counsel at any photographic identification procedure: "There is something ironic about the Court's conclusion today that a pretrial lineup identification is a 'critical stage' of the prosecution because counsel's presence can help to compensate for the accused's deficiencies as an observer, but that a pretrial photographic identification is not a 'critical stage' of the prosecution because the accused is not able to observe at all."

13. Would there be any need for counsel at a lineup if the entire lineup procedure were recorded on both audiotape and videotape?

14. A person subject to interrogation who is under "formal arrest or restraint on freedom of movement of the degree associated with a formal arrest" is entitled to an attorney. Why isn't a person subject to a pretrial identification procedure entitled to an attorney when he or she is under the same type of restraint?

15. Assume that a victim of a rape or other sexual assault recalled that her assailant had a distinctive smell. What legal issues are presented by conducting a lineup for the purposes of smell identification? Are the issues different if a showup between the victim and a suspect is conducted shortly after the crime?

15 Criminal Trials, Appeals, and Postconviction Remedies

Chapter 2 presented an overview of the dual-court systems of the United States and the pretrial processes used in them. This chapter covers the judicial processes used during criminal trials, appeals, and postconviction proceedings.

At first blush, criminal trial and posttrial judicial processes may appear to be the exclusive concern of prosecutors, defense attorneys, and judges. But trials and appeals are heavily dependent on the work law enforcement professionals do when investigating crimes. After all, if the constitutional and statutory mandates of criminal procedure covered throughout this book are not met, evidence may be declared inadmissible. Indeed, if key evidence is suppressed through the application of the exclusionary rule, prosecutors may not be able to meet their burden of persuasion of proving a case beyond a reasonable doubt.

In addition, criminal justice professionals play important roles during judicial proceedings. Police officers, civilian investigators, and forensic scientific professionals are often key witnesses in criminal cases for both the prosecution and defense. And correctional officials, most especially probation officers, provide important information that judges use when imposing criminal sentences. Thus, it is essential that justice professionals understand not only the judicial processes used at trial but also those that occur after a verdict is delivered. This chapter is designed to provide an overview of these important processes.

LO1 EVALUATE the constitutionality of lengthy delays in criminal cases from the perspectives of constitutional and statutory speedy trial act guarantees.

LO2 EXPLAIN how the Confrontation Clause serves to protect the rights of the criminally accused.

LO3 DISCUSS the limitations of the Compulsory Process Clause in complex criminal prosecutions involving overseas actors or witnesses.

LO4 EXPLAIN the scope of the right to a trial by jury.

LO5 ANALYZE the ways in which the jury selection process helps to increase the likelihood that a defendant will receive a trial by a fair and impartial jury.

LO6 EXPLAIN the rights, duties, and functions of the judge, the jury, the prosecuting attorney, and the defendant in a criminal trial.

LO7 DESCRIBE the different types of evidence.

LO8 EVALUATE the powers of and limitations on judges in determining the sentence.

LO9 DESCRIBE the steps in a criminal appeal.

LO10 ANALYZE the impact that appellate standards of review have on the outcome of criminal appeals.

LO11 CONTRAST the major differences between appeal and *habeas corpus*.

Criminal Trials

Once all pretrial processes have occurred and all pretrial motions have been ruled upon, a case will proceed to trial if the defendant has not pled guilty. At the outset, it should be noted that criminal trials are relatively rare. As Figure 15.1 illustrates, of the felony cases that are prosecuted to a verdict, 94 percent are resolved by plea bargain. If, however, a case is one of the roughly 5 percent of felony cases to go to trial, then the rights outlined in this chapter will apply.

The Right to a Speedy and Public Trial

Preaccusation Speedy Trial Rights Recall from Chapter 1 that the Sixth Amendment guarantees the right to a speedy and public trial. But the Sixth Amendment's speedy trial guarantee does not apply until after an arrest is made, an indictment is issued, or the defendant is otherwise formally charged. *United States v. Marion*, 404 U.S. 307 (1971). Statutory law and the Fourteenth Amendment provide procedural safeguards against *preaccusation* delay in bringing a criminal case to trial.

A *statute of limitations* requires that prosecution commence within a specified period of time from the date of the alleged commission of the offense. Doing so prevents persons from having to defend themselves against charges when the facts have become obscured by the passage of time. For example, many states require that misdemeanor prosecutions commence within six months or one year from the date of the alleged crime, whereas most felonies typically have longer limitations periods, such as three, five, or ten years. Select felonies, such as murder, are usually not subject to any statutory limitations period. But because statutes of limitations are not a constitutional mandate, not all states have them. As of the writing of this book, neither South Carolina nor Wyoming has a statute of limitations for any criminal offense.

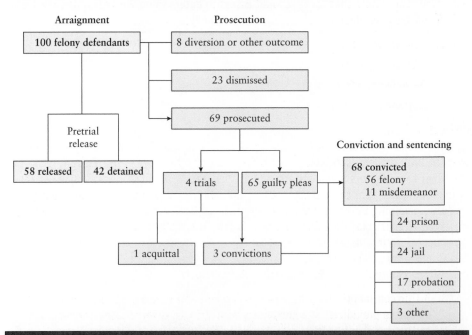

FIGURE 15.1 | Typical Outcomes in Felony Cases in 75 of the Largest Counties in the United States

Source: Bureau of Justice Statistics. 2010. *Felony Defendants in Large Urban Counties*, 2006. Washington, D.C.: U.S. Department of Justice.

Due process principles also protect defendants from unreasonable preaccusation delays. In fact, due process may be violated even if an indictment is brought within the prescribed statute of limitations if the government unreasonably delayed prosecution either to harass a defendant or to gain a tactical advantage for itself in a manner which causes actual prejudice to the defendant. *United States v. Lovasco*, 431 U.S. 783 (1977). For example, in *Howell v. Barker*, 904 F.2d 889 (4th Cir. 1990), the court held that a twenty-seven-month delay in serving an arrest warrant violated due process because the defendant's alibi witness could not be located at the time of trial. Courts rarely find such due process violations, though; in fact, unsubstantiated claims that memories have faded or that either evidence or witnesses could not be located are routinely rejected. *E.g., Jones v. Angelone*, 94 F.3d 900 (4th Cir. 1996).

Postaccusation Speedy Trial Rights In *Klopfer v. North Carolina*, 386 U.S. 213 (1967), the Supreme Court held that the right to a speedy trial was so fundamental to the American scheme of justice that the Sixth Amendment's guarantee was applicable to the states via the operation of the Fourteenth Amendment's Due Process Clause. In doing so, the Court explained that a speedy trial serves to

- prevent unnecessary incarceration prior to trial,
- minimize "anxiety and concern accompanying public accusation," and
- limit the possibility that delays will interfere with the defendant's ability to present an effective defense due to faded memories, unavailable witnesses, and the loss of exculpatory evidence.

In *Barker v. Wingo*, 407 U.S. 514 (1972), the U.S. Supreme Court held that intentional or negligent delay by the prosecution that prejudices a defendant's right to defend himself or herself is grounds for dismissal of the charges. In *Barker*, the Court identified four factors that courts should assess in determining whether a particular defendant has been deprived of the right to a speedy trial:

1. "length of delay,
2. the reason for the delay,
3. the defendant's assertion of his right, and
4. prejudice to the defendant."

407 U.S. at 530.

The *Barker* Court said that the length of the delay was to some extent a "triggering mechanism." If there is no delay that is prejudicial on its face, judicial inquiry into the other three factors is not necessary. Courts generally consider delays approaching or exceeding one year to be presumptively prejudicial, thereby triggering an inquiry into the remaining *Barker* factors. *See Doggett v. United States*, 505 U.S. 647 (1992). However, no particular time limit is prescribed by law. Rather, courts must examine "the peculiar circumstances of the case" because "the delay that can be tolerated for an ordinary street crime is considerably less than [that] for a serious, complex conspiracy charge." 407 U.S. at 530–31. For example:

- A thirteen-month delay between indictment and trial was determined to be presumptive prejudicial in a conspiracy to distribute cocaine case. However, due to the complexity of the case, the court found no speedy trial violation. *United States v. Bass*, 460 F.3d 830 (6th Cir. 2003).
- A delay of twenty-five months was held not to be presumptively prejudicial because the defendant was involved in multiple criminal proceedings in different geographic areas. *United States v. Jones*, 91 F.3d 5 (2d Cir. 1996).

614

PART IV
INTERROGATIONS,
IDENTIFICATIONS, TRIALS,
AND POST-CONVICTION
REMEDIES

■ A twenty-nine-month delay on charges of being a felon in possession of a firearm was held not to violate defendant's speedy trial rights. Notably, thirteen months of the delay were attributable to the government. The court nonetheless rejected the defense argument that it was lengthy enough to give rise to presumption of prejudice primarily for two reasons. First, the defendant did not assert his right to speedy trial until he filed motion to dismiss less than one month before the trial was scheduled to begin. Second, the court found he was not actually prejudiced because police officers' inability to remember particular facts did not undermine his defense, but rather weakened the prosecution's case. *United States v. Schreane*, 331 F.3d 548 (6th Cir. 2003).

Separate from any Sixth Amendment speedy trial rights are those created under speedy trial statutes. Congress enacted the federal Speedy Trial Act of 1974, establishing specific time periods for different stages of federal prosecutions. 18 U.S.C. §§ 3161–74.

■ An information or indictment must be filed within thirty days of the arrest or the service of a summons on the defendant (sixty days if the grand jury is not in session).

■ A trial must usually begin within seventy days of the filing of the information, filing of an indictment, or the date of the defendant's initial appearance, whichever is later.

■ A trial must generally begin within ninety days of the government's detaining a defendant who is solely awaiting trial.

The Speedy Trial Act works independently from the guarantee of the Sixth Amendment; thus, violation of its statutory requirements does not trigger a *Barker* analysis.

Certain types of delay are not counted toward the time periods specified in the Speedy Trial Act. Such *excludable time* includes

■ delays caused by the absence or unavailability of a defendant or an essential witness, such as when their whereabouts are unknown due to their avoiding apprehension;

■ delays while a defendant is involved in other judicial proceedings such as
  ■ examinations to determine the defendant's competency or other relevant mental or physical capacity,
  ■ hearings on pretrial motions,
  ■ bail revocation hearings following bond violation,
  ■ trials involving other charges against defendant,
  ■ judicial consideration of proposed plea agreements,
  ■ *interlocutory appeals*—rare provisional appeals from a ruling on a matter of law (e.g., on an important pretrial motion) which is in doubt and needs to be answered by an appellate court in order for trial to proceed without causing irreparable harm to the case or a party;

■ reasonable delays to align the speedy trial clock of multiple defendants; and

■ reasonable delays which serve "ends of justice."

All fifty U.S. states have enacted speedy trial laws as well, although the time limits vary dramatically from state to state.

If speedy trial rights are violated, the court must dismiss the case against the defendant. Dismissal, however, can be without or with prejudice. A *dismissal without prejudice* allows for a case to be refiled, whereas a *dismissal with prejudice* bars future prosecution on the charge(s) dismissed. Courts generally weigh three factors when deciding whether to dismiss a case with or without prejudice:

1. the seriousness of the offense;
2. the circumstances leading to dismissal, most especially
   a. whether the government was merely negligent or if it acted in bad faith, and
   b. the degree of prejudice caused by the delay; and
3. the effect reprosecution would have on the administration of justice in light of the Speedy Trial Act's intent. 18 U.S.C. § 3162(a)(1)–(2).

Public Trial Although the Sixth Amendment guarantees a criminal defendant the right to a public trial, the First Amendment implicitly gives the press and the general public the right to attend criminal trials. Therefore, the "right to an open public trial is a shared right of the accused and the public, the common concern being the assurance of fairness." *Press-Enterprise Co. v. Superior Court*, 478 U.S. 1, 7 (1986). In addition to ensuring fairness, the constitutional commitment to public trials helps to maintain confidence in the criminal justice system, promote informed discussion of governmental affairs, ensure that judges and prosecutors perform their duties responsibly, encourage witnesses to come forward, and discourage perjury. *Waller v. Georgia*, 467 U.S. 39 (1984). Although a defendant may waive the Sixth Amendment right to a public trial and request a closed proceeding, such a request must be balanced against the First Amendment rights of the press and the public to have access to criminal trials.

Confrontation of Witnesses

The **Confrontation Clause** of the Sixth Amendment guarantees accused persons the right to confront hostile witnesses at their criminal trial. This right is designed to promote the truth-finding function of a trial by "ensur[ing] the reliability of the evidence against a criminal defendant by subjecting it to rigorous testing in the context of an adversary proceeding before the trier of fact." *Maryland v. Craig*, 497 U.S. 836 (1990). This rigorous testing is accomplished both through the defendant's face-to-face confrontation during the witness's testimony and through the opportunity for **cross-examination**. To accomplish the former goal, the defendant is entitled to be present at all important stages of the criminal trial, unless the right to be present is waived (1) by voluntarily being absent from the courtroom, *Taylor v. United States*, 414 U.S. 17 (1973), or (2) by continually disrupting the proceedings after being warned by the court. *Illinois v. Allen*, 397 U.S. 337, 343–44 (1970).

The defendant's right to the opportunity for cross-examination permits the defendant to test both the witness's credibility and the witness's knowledge of relevant facts of the case:

> The opportunity for cross-examination . . . is critical for ensuring the integrity of the fact-finding process. Cross-examination is "the principal means by which the believability of a witness and the truth of his testimony are tested." Indeed the Court has recognized that cross-examination is the "greatest legal engine ever invented for the discovery of the truth."
> *Kentucky v. Stincer*, 482 U.S. 730, 736 (1987).

Cross-examination is discussed in more detail later.

615

616

PART IV
INTERROGATIONS,
IDENTIFICATIONS, TRIALS,
AND POST-CONVICTION
REMEDIES

The Confrontation Clause has never been interpreted as an absolute bar to the admission of out-of-court testimony. Rather, the Supreme Court interpreted the Confrontation Clause within the context of the centuries-old rules on the admissibility of *hearsay evidence*. Hearsay evidence is defined by Rule 801(c) of the Federal Rules of Evidence as "a statement, other than one made by the declarant while testifying at the trial or hearing, offered in evidence to prove the truth of the matter asserted." This is a fancy way of saying that people may not testify in a judicial proceeding about what they heard someone else say out of court if the substance of the other person's out-of-court statement is concerned with what the parties are trying to prove or disprove in court. In general, the Confrontation Clause prohibits the admission of hearsay evidence because the defendant cannot confront an absent declarant.

In *Ohio v. Roberts*, 448 U.S. 56, 66 (1980), the Supreme Court specifically ruled that hearsay evidence posed no Confrontation Clause problem so long as (1) the out-of-court declarant was "unavailable" to testify at trial, and (2) the statement bore some "indicia of reliability." The case went on to explain that hearsay statements that were covered by any of the more than twenty "firmly rooted" exceptions to the hearsay rule were presumptively admissible. Moreover, even those hearsay statements not covered by an applicable hearsay exception could still be admitted into evidence without running afoul of the Confrontation Clause if the statement were somehow demonstrated to have "particularized guarantees of trustworthiness." 448 U.S. at 66. In 2004, however, the Supreme Court reversed itself when *Crawford v. Washington*, 541 U.S. 36 (2004), overruled *Ohio v. Roberts*. The *Crawford* decision interpreted the Confrontation Clause more literally and more in line with what history suggests the Framers had in mind when they wrote the Sixth Amendment. *Crawford* held that any out-of-court statement that was "testimonial" in nature—no matter how reliable it might be—was inadmissible unless the defendant had the opportunity to cross-examine the declarant. 448 U.S. at 68. *Crawford*, therefore, did not implicate nontestimonial out-of-court statements, the admissibility of which continues to be governed by the law of evidence and its rules on hearsay.

> [The Confrontation Clause] applies to "witnesses" against the accused—in other words, those who "bear testimony." "Testimony," in turn, is typically "[a] solemn declaration or affirmation made for the purpose of establishing or proving some fact." An accuser who makes a formal statement to government officers bears testimony in a sense that a person who makes a casual remark to an acquaintance does not. The constitutional text, like the history underlying the common-law right of confrontation, thus reflects an especially acute concern with a specific type of out-of-court statement.

Although the *Crawford* Court made it clear that the Confrontation Clause bars the admission of statements that are testimonial in nature, it did not fully define what it meant by "testimonial." Instead, the Court recognized there were competing notions of what might be considered testimonial, and it left the precise meaning of the term open for future consideration. It did specify that "prior testimony at a preliminary hearing, before a grand jury, or at a former trial" were clearly "testimonial" statements, as were statements made during police interrogations. 44 U.S. at 68. This language created an ambiguity in the law. The Court clarified this ambiguity somewhat in *Davis v. Washington*, 547 U.S. 813 (2006), when it provided the following definition of testimonial evidence for Confrontation Clause purposes:

Statements are nontestimonial when made in the course of police interrogation under circumstances objectively indicating that the primary purpose of the interrogation is to enable police assistance to meet an ongoing emergency. They are testimonial when the circumstances objectively indicate that [the] primary purpose of the interrogation is to establish or prove past events potentially relevant to later criminal prosecution. 547 U.S. at 822.

Thus, under *Crawford* and *Davis*, "initial inquiries" by police at a crime scene are not likely to produce responses that are "testimonial" because police "need to know whom they are dealing with in order to assess the situation, the threat to their own safety, and possible danger to the potential victim." 547 U.S. at 832. Accordingly, the *Davis* Court upheld the admissibility of 911 phone calls because the caller was speaking about events as they were actually happening, rather than describing past events. Similarly, in *Michigan v. Bryant*, 131 S. Ct. 1143 (2011), police had been dispatched to a gas station parking lot where a shooting victim identified his killer and described the shooting before he died. Reasoning that the victim's identification and description were not testimonial statements because they had a "primary purpose . . . to enable police assistance to meet an ongoing emergency," 131 S. Ct. at 1150, they were properly admitted at the trial without violating the Confrontation Clause. In contrast, however, when police question people to investigate a crime with the intent of gathering evidence to be used during a criminal prosecution, responses to such police questions will be deemed "testimonial." As such, the Confrontation Clause will bar the admissibility of such statements at trial.

The Confrontation Clause does not just apply to testimonial statements made to police. In *Melendez-Diaz v. Massachusetts*, 557 U.S. 305 (2009), the U.S. Supreme Court ruled that crime lab reports are "testimonial" and, therefore, are inadmissible at trial unless the forensic professional who conducted the analysis on the evidence and prepared such a report is subject to cross-examination. This, in turn, means that a surrogate, such as an analyst's supervisor, may not go to court and testify at trial as to the contents of the original analyst's report since only the original analyst knows "the particular test and testing process he [or she] employed" and the lab report generated from that testing is a testimonial document "created solely for an evidentiary purpose." *Bullcoming v. New Mexico*, 131 S. Ct. 2705, 2715, 2717 (2011). However, in a highly fractured opinion (with no majority of justices concurring in any part of the decision), the Court ruled that the Confrontation Clause does not bar an expert witness from discussing a lab report prepared by someone else (provided the report is not admitted into evidence) if that report formed the basis of the expert's independent opinion in case (see Table 15.2 later in the chapter for more information about expert testimony). *Williams v. Illinois*, 132 S. Ct. 2221 (2012). Some scholars have questioned whether the result in *Williams* created "a substantial loophole in *Crawford's* confrontation right. Prosecutors [may] be able to introduce any forensic analysis without triggering the Confrontation Clause [and defendants may] lose the opportunity to cross-examine forensic analysts and expose bias, lack of qualifications, and manipulation of testing, even where those analysts could be produced to testify at trial." (Keenan 2012: 23).

KEY POINTS

LO2

■ The Confrontation Clause of the Sixth Amendment guarantees accused persons the right to confront hostile witnesses at their criminal trial. Specifically, the Confrontation Clause bars the admission of any out-of-court statement that is testimonial in nature—no matter how reliable it might be—unless the defendant has the opportunity to cross-examine the declarant.

■ Out-of-course statements are nontestimonial—and, therefore, not subject to the Confrontation Clause—when made in the course of police interrogation under circumstances objectively indicating that the primary purpose of the interrogation is to enable police assistance to meet an ongoing emergency. Conversely, out-of-court statements are testimonial when the circumstances objectively indicate that the primary purpose of the interrogation is to establish or prove past events potentially relevant to later criminal prosecution. Such testimonial statements are not admissible at trial unless the defense has the opportunity to cross-examine the declarant.

Guarantee of Compulsory Process

The Compulsory Process Clause guarantees the defendant's right to compel the attendance of favorable witnesses at trial, usually by means of a court-issued *subpoena*. To obtain compulsory process, the defendant must show that a witness's testimony would be relevant, material, favorable to the defendant, and not cumulative. *United States v. Valenzuela-Bernal*, 458 U.S. 858 (1982). Cumulative evidence is evidence tending to prove the same point as evidence already offered, and is generally disallowed because it does little more than contribute to inefficiency. Cumulative evidence should not be confused with corroborating evidence, which supplements or strengthens evidence already presented as proof of a factual matter.

The guarantee of compulsory process is generally limited to witnesses within the jurisdiction of a court. Thus, no constitutional violation occurs just because a defense witness is located in an area outside a court's subpoena power. *See United States v. Greco*, 298 F.2d 247 (2d Cir. 1962). This poses some unique challenges for crimes involving activity beyond the borders of the United States.

KEY POINTS

L03

- The Compulsory Process Clause guarantees the defendant's right to compel the attendance of favorable witnesses at trial, usually by means of a court-issued subpoena, so long as the person to be summoned is within the geographical area subject to a court's subpoena power.

DISCUSSION POINT

Should the Compulsory Process Clause Apply to People Outside the United States? *United States v. Moussaoui*, 382 F.3d 453 (4th Cir. 2004).

On September 11, 2001, terrorists hijacked three planes and crashed them into the Pentagon and the World Trade Center towers in New York. A fourth plane, apparently destined for the United States Capitol, crashed in Pennsylvania after passengers wrested control from the hijackers. Zacarias Moussaoui, the so-called twentieth hijacker, was in custody on the

date of the attacks on immigration violations. However, he was alleged to have trained at an Al Qaeda camp, entered the U.S. illegally, and took flying lessons in Oklahoma—the same *modus operandi* as the other hijackers. He was subsequently charged under a series of terrorism laws for which the U.S. government sought the death penalty.

Moussaoui contended that the testimony of several enemy combatants in U.S. military custody were necessary for him to mount his defense. Agreeing with legal scholars and editorials in the *New York Times*, the district court agreed that Moussaoui's compulsory process rights required that the government produce enemy combatants for deposition by Moussaoui's legal team. The government appealed, contending that "because the enemy combatant witnesses are foreign nationals outside the boundaries of the United States, they are beyond the process power of the district court and, hence, unavailable to Moussaoui." 382 F.3d at 463.

On appeal, the Fourth Circuit stated that it would have sided with the government if the witnesses Moussaoui sought had not been in U.S. custody because "United States courts lack power to subpoena witnesses, (other than American citizens) from foreign countries."

382 F.3d at 464. However, because the witnesses Moussaoui sought were in U.S. custody, the Fourth Circuit sided with Moussaoui and allowed the district court to issue a court order directing the secretary of defense to produce the witnesses so they could testify.

- Moussaoui ultimately pled guilty to six counts of criminal conspiracy arising out of the September 11th attacks. But the key facts in his case were that the witnesses whose testimony he sought to compel were in U.S. custody, even if outside the physical borders of the country. What are the implications of *Greco* and *Moussaoui* for foreign nationals who are not in U.S. custody? How does this affect the rights of people charged under a number of laws the United States prosecutes for actions occurring abroad, including cases targeting narcotics, terrorism, piracy, human trafficking and other human rights–related crimes?

- Since 1977, Congress has ratified treaties with almost fifty foreign countries that require these nations to assist U.S. law enforcement in obtaining witnesses and evidence for trial. But these treaties do not allow private persons or defense attorneys to obtain such assistance. Critique this state of affairs under the Fifth, Sixth, and Fourteenth Amendments.

Right to a Trial by Impartial Jury

The Sixth Amendment to the U.S. Constitution guarantees a defendant in a criminal prosecution the right to trial by an impartial jury. The right to a trial by jury was made applicable to the states through the due process clause of the Fourteenth Amendment in *Duncan v. Louisiana*:

> Because we believe that trial by jury in criminal cases is fundamental to the American scheme of justice, we hold that the Fourteenth Amendment guarantees a right of jury trial in all criminal cases which—were they to be tried in federal court—would come within the Sixth Amendment guarantee. 391 U.S. 145, 149 (1968).

There is, however, no right to a jury trial in juvenile court proceedings because, technically, they are not criminal proceedings. *McKeiver v. Pennsylvania*, 403 U.S. 528 (1971).

The right to a trial by jury means that the government must provide a defendant with a jury trial in all criminal prosecutions except those for petty offenses. *Baldwin v. New York*, 399 U.S. 66, 69 (1970), held that "no offense can be deemed 'petty' for purposes of the right to trial by jury where imprisonment for more than six months is authorized." A defendant who is prosecuted in a single proceeding for multiple counts of a petty offense, however, does not have a constitutional right to a jury trial, even if the aggregate of sentences authorized for the offense exceeds six months. *Lewis v. United States*, 518 U.S. 322 (1996). For an offense punishable by a sentence of six months or less, a defendant has a constitutional right to a jury trial only if the additional statutory penalties "are so severe that they clearly reflect a legislative determination that the offense in question is a 'serious' one." *Blanton v. City of North Las Vegas*, 489 U.S. 538, 543 (1989). In *Blanton*, the Supreme Court upheld the denial of a jury trial to a drunk-driving defendant who faced up to six months incarceration, finding that the other statutory penalties—which included community service, a fine of up to $1,000, special conditions of probation including an educational course on alcohol abuse, and loss of a driver's license for ninety days—were not severe enough to reflect that the state legislature believed the offense to be a "serious one." Note, however, that a number of states provide a statutory right to a trial by jury for driving under the influence cases and other misdemeanor crimes for which a period of incarceration may be imposed, even if less than six months.

Defendants who do not wish to be tried by a jury may, with the approval of the court, waive their right to a jury trial and, instead, opt for a *nonjury trial* known as a bench trial. Although a defendant has no absolute constitutional right to a bench trial, a criminal defendant may want such a trial in lieu of a jury trial for a number of reasons, most frequently because the defendant believes that a jury might be biased or prejudiced against him or her and therefore would not provide a fair and impartial trial. When a defendant seeks to waive the constitutional right to a trial by jury, such a waiver, like those of other constitutional rights, must be voluntary, knowing, and intelligent. If waived, the judge must evaluate the evidence at trial to reach a verdict in addition to performing the judge's other regular duties, which are essentially the same in either a jury or nonjury trial. Therefore, the remainder of this section focuses on jury trials.

Once it has been determined that the trial will be by jury, the next step in the criminal proceeding is the selection of the jurors. Jurors perform the crucial tasks of weighing the evidence, determining the credibility of witnesses, finding the facts, and ultimately rendering a verdict of guilty or not guilty. Because of the importance of the jury's functions, detailed rules govern the selection of jurors to protect the prosecution or the defendant from having a person prejudiced against its cause sitting as a member of the jury during the trial.

620

PART IV
INTERROGATIONS,
IDENTIFICATIONS, TRIALS,
AND POST-CONVICTION
REMEDIES

Summoning the Venire To assemble a jury, potential jurors receive a *summons* in the mail ordering them to appear in court at a specified time and date. The people who are so summoned comprise the **venire**—the prospective jurors for cases. The summons is usually accompanied by a juror questionnaire (like the one in Figure 15.2) that is used to make sure the recipient is qualified to serve as a member of the venire panel. In a run-of-the mill case, forty or fifty people might be summoned in order to select a twelve-person jury. In a high-profile case, hundreds might be called for jury service.

Of course, just because a person is summoned to jury service does not mean he or she will respond to the summons. Any number of factors might prevent someone

FIGURE 15.2 | Sample Juror Qualification Questionnaire

summoned from responding. Some people simply never receive a summons because they are transient. And upward of 45 percent of people in some jurisdictions simply ignore jury summonses even though a warrant can be issued for the arrest of anyone who disregards a court order like a jury summons.

The venire is supposed to be representative of society as a whole. Federal law and the law of most states require that no citizen be excluded from service as a juror on account of race, color, religion, gender, national origin, or economic status. But this does not mean that the venire must be "a perfect mirror of the community or accurately [reflect] the proportionate strength of every identifiable group." *Swain v. Alabama*, 380 U.S. 202, 208 (1965). It does mean that the venire is supposed to be drawn from a fair cross-section of the community. *Taylor v. Louisiana*, 419 U.S. 522 (1975). Unfortunately, this foundation of constitutional law has proven to be more aspirational than effective in reality.

Historically, venire panels have not been representative of a community. Middle-aged to older white men were overrepresented for decades, mainly because the venire used to be drawn exclusively from the voter-registration rolls. As we began to recognize that homogeneity in the venire led to both blatant and subtle forms of discrimination, jury administrators began to use telephone lists, motor vehicle or driver's license rolls, and welfare and unemployment lists in assembling the venire, thereby increasing the cross-section of the community from which venire panels are drawn.

The jury questionnaire used to screen the venire is another factor contributing to the exclusion of people from jury service who might comprise a more diverse venire, thereby increasing the representativeness of the jury pool. For example, the visually or hearing impaired were prohibited from serving on juries, as were those who did not speak English, those convicted of felonies, and those who were not U.S. citizens. Although those who are deaf or do not speak English have begun to serve on juries, their ability to do so depends on the services of translators who may or may not be available in any given jurisdiction. Felons are permanently excluded from jury service in more than half the states and in the federal justice system; the remaining states place various restrictions on jury service for convicts, including restrictions for those people on probation or parole.

Another impediment to a representative jury is the way in which jurors are compensated for their time. Jurors are often paid only a nominal amount for their service. Because minorities are overrepresented in low-paying jobs, they are disproportionately excluded from jury service on the grounds that serving would cause them an economic hardship.

Finally, the remaining exclusions or exemptions from jury service also work to prevent a truly diverse jury from being assembled. Public officials, including police and fire department employees, are excluded by federal law 28 U.S.C. Section 1863(b)(5) in light of the essential roles they perform each day. Full-time students, teachers, clergy members, and lawyers were historically exempted from service or, alternatively, were given the opportunity to exempt themselves from jury service; that is no longer the case in most states. Because full-time students age eighteen or older cannot make up lost time in school, most states permit them to defer their jury service until a time when school is not in session.

The *Voir Dire* Process Once otherwise qualified venirepersons are then assembled in a courtroom, the actual process of selecting a jury from the venire panel begins. That process is known as ***voir dire***, a Latin term meaning "to speak the truth." Its main purpose is to weed out venire members who would not be fair and impartial jurors. Typical questions relate to whether prospective jurors know the defendant, the attorneys, or any of the witnesses; whether they have read about the case in the newspapers; whether they have racial, nationality, or gender biases; and whether they have formed any opinions on the case.

622

PART IV
INTERROGATIONS,
IDENTIFICATIONS, TRIALS,
AND POST-CONVICTION
REMEDIES

Either attorney may seek to **strike for cause** a member of the venire either because the prospective juror has some relationship to one of the participants in the case, or because the case presents issues on which the potential juror is biased, prejudiced, or predisposed to a particular outcome because of their belief system, experiences, or media exposure to the case. Both sides in a criminal case have an unlimited number of strikes for cause.

Both sides also are able strike a limited number of venire members when there is no good cause to do so using a **peremptory challenge**. Federal Rule of Criminal Procedure 24(b) gives both sides twenty peremptory strikes in capital cases; the prosecution gets six and the defendant ten in noncapital felony cases; and each side gets three in misdemeanor cases. Most states have similar rules. Regardless of the number of peremptory strikes each side has, the purpose of these strikes is usually the same. Originally, they were designed and used for a curative purpose: to correct the mistake of a judge for failing to strike a juror for cause. And they are still used in that manner today. But they are also used by lawyers to exclude from the jury those people whom they believe to be hostile to their side of the case, even if not so hostile that the venireperson in question would be struck for cause. In other words, attorneys use peremptory strikes to eliminate the jurors they feel might not vote for their side during the jury deliberations process. Counsel must be careful, however, not to run afoul of the federal Constitution when they are exercising their peremptory challenges.

In 1986, the U.S. Supreme Court decided *Batson v. Kentucky*, 476 U.S. 79 (1986). The case involved an African-American male who was convicted of burglary by a jury comprised of all Whites. The prosecution used four of its six peremptory challenges to strike African Americans from the venire. The Supreme Court held that the prosecution's actions violated the equal protection guarantee of the Constitution when it used its peremptory strikes to eliminate people on the basis of race.

> [T]he State's privilege to strike individual jurors through peremptory challenges is subject to the command of the Equal Protection Clause. Although a prosecutor ordinarily is entitled to exercise peremptory challenges "for any reason at all, as long as that reason is related to his view concerning the outcome" of the case to be tried . . . the Equal Protection Clause forbids the prosecutor to challenge potential jurors solely on account of their race or on the assumption that black jurors as a group will be unable impartially to consider the State's case against a black defendant. 476 U.S. at 89.

The Supreme Court extended its holding in *Batson* to cover strikes based on gender in *J.E.B. v. Alabama ex rel. T.B.*, 511 U.S. 127 (1994). The principle of nondiscrimination at the core of *Batson* and *J.E.B.* has not been extended by the Supreme Court to other categories, such as ethnicity, religion, or sexual orientation, although some lower courts have done so on their own.

A *Batson* challenge to a peremptory strike occurs in three phases. First, the party suspecting that a peremptory strike has been exercised by opposing counsel in violation of *Batson* must object and make a showing

KEY POINTS

L04
- The Sixth Amendment guarantees the right to a trial by jury in all criminal prosecutions except those for petty offenses.

- A petty offense is normally considered any crime for which the maximum penalty is imprisonment for less than six months. Some states provide a right to a trial by jury even for some misdemeanors that might otherwise qualify as petty offenses, such as driving under the influence.

- When the Sixth Amendment right to a trial by jury does not apply, or, alternatively, if a defendant waives his or her right be tried by a jury, a bench trial will take place in which the judge acts as both the trier of law and the trier of fact.

L05
- In order to assemble a jury, potential jurors receive a summons in the mail ordering them to appear in court at a specified time and date. The people who are summoned comprise the venire—the prospective jurors for cases. The venire must be drawn from a fair cross-section of the community, although that does not guarantee that the venire will accurately reflect the proportionate strength of every identifiable group in the community.

- During *voir dire*, the venire is screened through a series of questions designed to exclude those who would not be fair and impartial jurors. Venirepersons who exhibit a bias may be stricken for cause; others may be excused for no reason at all through the exercise of peremptory challenges, so long as these strikes are not exercised in a discriminatory manner.

Continued on next page

that the juror in question is "a member of a racial group capable of being singled out for differential treatment." 476 U.S. at 94. The objecting party bears the burden of persuasion in establishing a prima facie case of impermissible discrimination. Once that is done, the side seeking to exercise the peremptory strike must respond to the objection by offering a nondiscriminatory reason for wanting to strike the particular juror.

Impaneling the Petit Jury Once all the challenges available to both the prosecution and the defense are exercised, the judge selects the members of the venire who will be the **petit jury** in the case. The petit jury is normally comprised of twelve people who will serve as the trier of fact at trial. In some cases, additional jurors are selected as alternates; they hear the evidence just as the other jurors do, but they do not enter deliberations unless one of the regular twelve jurors becomes ill, dies, or is unable to serve for some other reason. After administering an oath to the jurors, the judge admonishes the jurors not to discuss the case with anyone until they go into deliberations to decide the case after hearing all the evidence. Once the jury is impaneled, the constitutional safeguard of double jeopardy attaches. (See the discussion of the Fifth Amendment in Chapter 1.)

Historically, juries have been composed of twelve members. In *Williams v. Florida*, 399 U.S. 78, 100–02 (1970), however, the U.S. Supreme Court held that a six-member jury satisfied the Sixth Amendment:

> The purpose of the jury trial . . . is to prevent oppression by the Government. . . . Given this purpose, the essential feature of a jury obviously lies in the interposition between the accused and his accuser of the common-sense judgment of a group of laymen, and in the community participation and shared responsibility which results from this group's determination of guilt or innocence. The performance of this role is not a function of the particular number of the body which makes up the jury. To be sure, the number should probably be large enough to promote group deliberation, free from outside attempts at intimidation, and to provide a fair possibility for obtaining a representative cross-section of the community. But we find little reason to think that these goals are in any meaningful sense less likely to be achieved when the jury numbers six, than when it numbers 12—particularly if the requirement of unanimity is retained. And, certainly the reliability of the jury as a fact-finder hardly seems likely to be a function of its size. . . .
>
> Similarly, while in theory the number of viewpoints represented on a randomly selected jury ought to increase as the size of the jury increases, in practice the difference between the 12-man and the six-man jury in terms of the cross-section of the community represented seems likely to be negligible.

Juries of fewer than six people, however, have been held to violate the Sixth Amendment. *Ballew v. Georgia*, 435 U.S. 223 (1978).

Order of Presentation at Trial

Once the jury has been impaneled and instructed regarding the presumptions of innocence (and sanity, if relevant to a particular case), the trial begins. Recall from Chapter 2 that it is the prosecution's burden to introduce sufficient evidence to rebut or overcome the presumption of innocence such that the jury finds the defendant guilty beyond a reasonable doubt. In contrast, the defense need not present any evidence at

624

PART IV
INTERROGATIONS,
IDENTIFICATIONS, TRIALS,
AND POST-CONVICTION
REMEDIES

all in most criminal cases, although the defense usually does present evidence to establish reasonable doubt. (The only time the defense bears any burden of persuasion at a criminal trial is in cases in which the defense raises an *affirmative defense*, like insanity or entrapment, which serves to exonerate a defendant on the grounds of justification or excuse even though the prosecution has met its burden of persuasion of proving every element of the charged offense.) Table 15.1 summarizes the order in which evidence is typically presented in a criminal trial.

TABLE 15.1 | Order of Presentation at Trial

Procedure	What Happens
Opening statements	The parties present an overview of their case. This normally includes their "theory" of the case and an outline or roadmap of the evidence they plan to present over the course of trial. The prosecution usually goes first because it bears the burden of persuasion at trial. The defendant may then, but is not required to, make an opening statement at that time. Defense counsel might elect to wait until the prosecutor has presented the government's evidence before giving an opening statement, thereby concealing the defense strategy until the government has disclosed its case.
Prosecution's case-in-chief	The prosecution calls witnesses and presents other evidence in an attempt to prove the defendant's guilt. When a prosecutor calls a witness, a *direct examination* is conducted. *Direct examinations* are comprised of a series of open-ended questions (e.g., who, what, when, where, how, why). When the prosecutor finishes the direct examination of any witness, the defendant is guaranteed the right to conduct a cross-examination. Questions on cross-examination tend to be closed ended in that they typically ask for a yes or no answer. Cross-examination questions usually focus on undermining the credibility of the witness by exploring inconsistencies, inaccuracies, biases, or inadequacies of observation. Following cross-examination, the prosecutor is permitted to clarify questions raised in cross-examination and to attempt to rehabilitate the witness in the eyes of the jury. This second round of questioning is called *redirect examination*. It is usually strictly limited to matters raised on cross-examination. On rare occasions, a judge may permit *re-cross-examination* as well.
Motion for judgment of acquittal	Although not required, the defense may move for a *judgment of acquittal* at the end of the prosecution's case in chief. This motion basically asks the judge to dismiss the case because no reasonable jury could find the defendant guilty beyond a reasonable doubt in light of the insufficient evidence presented by the prosecution. As you might imagine, such motions are rarely granted.
Defense's case-in-chief	The defense conducts direct examination of its witnesses and presents other evidence in an attempt to create reasonable doubt about the defendant's guilt. The prosecution then gets to cross-examine witnesses called by the defense. In most criminal cases, the defendant exercises his or her Fifth Amendment right to remain silent by electing not to testify, thereby avoiding cross-examination. The prosecution may not comment to the jury about the defendant not testifying because it is his or her constitutional right not do so. *Griffin v. California*, 380 U.S. 609 (1965).

Continued on next page

Continued from previous page

Procedure	What Happens
Renewed motion for judgment of acquittal	The defense may (but is not required to) renew its motion for acquittal after presenting its case in chief. Again, these motions are rarely granted.
Rebuttal case by prosecution	Although not routine, the prosecution may be permitted to introduce additional evidence after the defense has closed its case-in-chief. Such evidence is usually limited to rebutting evidence presented by the defense.
Closing arguments	Both sides of the case are permitted to summarize their respective cases to the jury and present arguments why the verdict should be in their favor. Usually the prosecution gets to make its *closing argument* first; then the defense makes its closing argument, and finally, the prosecution gets the "last word" during a short rebuttal.
Jury instructions	In some jurisdictions, the jury may be instructed by the judge as to the applicable law at the start of the trial or before closing arguments. But in most trials, the judge instructs the jury after the closing arguments have been made. The judge may summarize the evidence for the jury members, help them recall details, and attempt to reduce complicated evidence into its simplest elements. However, the judge may not express an opinion on any issue of fact in the case or favor either side in summarizing the evidence. Furthermore, when a jury has no sentencing function, it should be instructed to "reach its verdict without regard to what sentence might be imposed." *Rogers v. United States*, 422 U.S. 35, 40 (1975).
Jury *deliberations*	After being instructed by the judge about the governing law, the jury leaves the courtroom to conduct its *deliberations* in private.
Verdict	In all federal and most state criminal criminals, the jury deliberates until all members of the jury vote unanimously to either convict or acquit the defendant. In state jury trials, a verdict of fewer than twelve members of a twelve-member jury satisfies the Sixth Amendment. *Apodaca v. Oregon*, 406 U.S. 404 (1972), for example, upheld a conviction by ten votes of a twelve-member jury. And *Johnson v. Louisiana*, 406 U.S. 356 (1972), held that conviction by nine votes of a twelve-member jury in a state court did not violate the due process guarantee of the Fourteenth Amendment. If, however, a state uses six-member juries, the verdict must be unanimous. *Burch v. Louisiana*, 441 U.S. 130 (1979). If the jury cannot reach a verdict by the required number of votes, a judge may declare a hung jury, which results in the jury being discharged and the case being retried or dismissed.

Adapted from Owen, Stephen S., Henry F. Fradella, Tod W. Burke, and Jerry Joplin. 2015. *The Foundations of Criminal Justice* (2nd ed.). New York: Oxford University Press.

Four types of evidence are commonly presented at trial. *Testimonial evidence* is oral testimony given under oath. *Real evidence* (also referred to as "physical evidence") consists of tangible objects such as documents, drug paraphernalia, clothing, and weapons. The scientific examination of real evidence, in a laboratory, for example, yields *scientific evidence*—the formal results of forensic investigatory and scientific techniques. Finally, *demonstrative evidence* has no evidential value by itself. Rather, it serves as a visual or auditory aid to assist the fact finder in understanding the evidence. Charts, maps, videos, and courtroom demonstrations are forms of demonstrative evidence.

A complex series of rules govern the admissibility of evidence at trial. Table 15.2 summarizes some of the more common rules of evidence.

Limitations of Scientific Evidence Subject to the limitations of either the *Frye* or *Daubert* tests explained in Table 15.2, scientific evidence analyzing materials such as blood, firearms, and fingerprints has been routinely admitted into evidence for years. But separating science from pseudoscience has never been an easy task. Even under *Daubert*, just when a scientific principle or discovery crosses the line between the experimental and reliably demonstrable stages is difficult to define.

TABLE 15.2 | Summary of Major Rules of Evidence

Best evidence rule	The *best evidence rule* means that to prove the content of a writing, recording, or photograph, the original is generally required because copies are too easily altered.
Competency to testify	A witness must have personal knowledge of the matter about which he or she is testifying; must be capable of understanding the duty to tell the truth—something he or she is required to do by an oath or affirmation; must be capable of expressing him- or herself so as to be understood by the jury either directly or through an interpreter. People who cannot differentiate between truth and nontruth, such as young children and those who are affected by certain types of serious mental illnesses, generally are not competent to be witnesses in court.
Hearsay	*Hearsay* is secondhand evidence. It is testimony that is not based on personal knowledge, but rather is a repetition of what another person has said: "My brother Bob told me he saw Jones enter the store that evening." The general rule is that hearsay evidence is not admissible because it is impossible to test its truthfulness; there is no way to cross-examine as to the truth of the matter. There are numerous exceptions to this rule, however, ranging from dying declarations and ancient writings to statements showing the speaker's state of mind.
Relevancy	Evidence is *relevant* if it shows the existence of any fact that is of consequence to the determination of the action by making that fact more probable or less probable than it would be without the evidence. Evidence that does not tend to prove or disprove any material fact in dispute is irrelevant and inadmissible. Evidence regarding the accused's motive, intent, ability, and opportunity to commit a crime would all be relevant. In contrast, information about the defendant's character, prior convictions, or a reputation would not normally be relevant and is, therefore, inadmissible.
Cumulative or unduly prejudicial evidence	Even relevant evidence may be inadmissible if its use would be a waste of time because it is cumulative (duplicative of other evidence), or if it could unfairly prejudice, confuse, or mislead the jury.
Privilege	Privileged communications protect confidential discussions in certain relationships in which we want to foster open, honest communications. The law usually recognizes privileges that include communications between attorney and client, clergy member and penitent, physician and patient, psychotherapist and patient, and lawfully married husbands and wives.

Continued on next page

Lay opinions	Because opinions are subjective beliefs, most witnesses are not permitted to give their opinions other than general opinions that are rationally based on their own common perceptions, such whether someone acted drunk, smelled like alcohol, appeared upset, or looked tired.
Expert opinions	For much of the twentieth century, the *Frye* test governed the admissibility of scientific testimony. *Frye v. United States*, 293 F. 1013 (D.C. Cir. 1923), refused to allow an expert to testify about the results of a lie detector test because the instrument had not gained general acceptance in the scientific community. The purpose behind the *Frye* test was to prevent unfounded scientific principles or conclusions based on such principles from being used at trial. Shortcomings of the *Frye* test, however, caused the drafters of the federal rules of evidence to replace *Frye* with rules that the U.S. Supreme Court fleshed out in *Daubert v. Merrill-Dow Pharmaceuticals, Inc.*, 509 U.S. 579 (1993).

Daubert established that trial court judges are supposed to act as gatekeepers who have a special obligation to ensure the reliability of scientific evidence. *Daubert* suggested several factors (that are neither exhaustive nor applicable to every case) that might be used in evaluating whether a particular scientific theory, study, or test is both valid and reliable, including whether it

- is empirically testable and capable of replication;
- has been published or subjected to peer review;
- has a known or potential rate of error that is acceptably low;
- is logical, avoids bias, and has construct validity (how well data fits into preexisting theory);
- adheres to recognized research methods and, if applicable, to proper sampling and statistical procedures for data analysis; and
- is generally accepted in the relevant scientific community (making *Frye* a part of *Daubert*'s test, but no longer the dispositive factor).

In *United States v. Scheffer*, 523 U.S. 303 (1998), the U.S. Supreme Court applied *Daubert* to the very technology at issue in *Frye*. The Court ruled that because polygraph techniques are not sufficiently reliable to pass muster under *Daubert*, the exclusion of polygraph evidence proffered by a defendant does not violate the defendant's Sixth Amendment right to present a defense.

Initially, *Daubert* applied only to scientific evidence. But in *Kumho Tire Co. v. Carmichael*, 526 U.S. 137 (1999), the Supreme Court held that all expert testimony that involves scientific, technical, or other specialized knowledge must meet the *Daubert* test for admissibility.

Adopted from Neubauer, David W., and Henry F. Fradella. 2014. *America's Courts and the Criminal Justice System* (11th ed.). Belmont, CA: Wadsworth.

628

PART IV
INTERROGATIONS,
IDENTIFICATIONS, TRIALS,
AND POST-CONVICTION
REMEDIES

Daubert has been reasonably effective at keeping "junk science" (unreliable findings, often by persons with questionable credentials) out of evidence, especially in civil cases seeking monetary compensation based on scientifically questionable claims (Buchman 2004). *Daubert*'s impact on forensic science in criminal cases, however, has been surprisingly less dramatic (Fisher 2008; Neufeld 2005). Indeed, unreliable forensic scientific evidence or false or misleading testimony by forensic experts either caused or contributed to wrongful convictions in approximately 50 percent of the first 317 postconviction DNA exoneration cases by the Innocence Project (2014).

Many forensic techniques, such as hair and fiber analysis, toolmark comparisons, and fingerprint analysis, rely upon a simple "match game," whereby a forensic analyst compares a known sample to a questioned sample and makes the highly subjective determination that the two samples originated from the same source. Although lacking a true scientific foundation, such evidence often plays a prominent role in many criminal cases because of the availability of trace evidence, which is easy to leave at a crime scene. Other forensic fields, including comparative bullet lead analysis and arson investigation, rely on assumptions that are "under-researched and oversold." (Gabel and Wilkinson 2008: 1002). Table 15.3 summarizes some of the problems with forensic scientific evidence that has been routinely used in criminal trials in the United States.

TABLE 15.3	Problems with Forensic Scientific Evidence Under *Daubert*
Hair microscopy	Used since the nineteenth century, this technique uses a microscope to compare hair samples using characteristics like color, pigment distributions, and texture. The technique has rarely been subjected to rigorous peer review or proficiency testing. Moreover, the few tests that have been performed revealed that error rates are quite high. In an FBI scientific paper entitled "Correlation of Microscopic and Mitochondrial DNA Hair Comparisons," the authors found that even the most competent hair examiners make significant errors. In 11 percent of the cases in which the hair examiners declared two hairs to be "similar," DNA testing revealed that the hairs did not match. In some jurisdictions, hair microscopy is being phased out and replaced by the more sensitive and discriminating mitochondrial DNA typing test. Yet, many local prosecutors continue to rely on hair microscopy because mitochondrial DNA typing remains relatively expensive and is offered in only a few laboratories. A study of Innocence Project prisoners found nearly 22 percent of prisoners exonerated by DNA evidence had been wrongly convicted based, in large part, on hair comparisons. Yet, results of this technique are routinely used in court even though Saks and Koehler (2005) reported error rates as high as 12 percent error rate for microscopic hair comparisons.
Serology	Serology is a branch of biochemistry that tests serums found in the human body (in blood, semen, and other bodily fluids). It can be reliable, yet in 40 percent of the DNA exoneration cases, conventional serology had been used by the prosecutor to secure a conviction. The case transcripts reveal that in the vast majority of these cases, the crime lab serologist misrepresented the data to the advantage of the prosecution.

Continued on next page

Fingerprinting	This process compares the impressions of prints from fingers or palms left at a crime scene to known impressions. Empirical studies are just starting to reveal that thousands of misidentification errors are made each year, especially because "non-mate prints can sometimes appear more similar than mate print pairs" to the FBI's automated fingerprint identification system (Cole, Welling, Dioso-Villa, and Carpenter 2008). Wrongful convictions have also resulted from the misapplication of fingerprint identification. For example, Stephen Cowans was convicted and served six years in prison for shooting a Boston police officer. Two fingerprint experts told a jury during the trial that a thumbprint left by the perpetrator was "unique and identical" to Cowans's print because it matched at 16 points. Postconviction DNA testing excluded Cowans as the perpetrator.
Compositional analysis of bullet lead	This technique compares the quantity of various elements that comprise a lead slug recovered from a crime scene with the composition of the lead found in unused bullets seized from a suspect. In criminal cases, to say that two samples are similar can be very misleading. In fact, the National Research Council of the National Academies of Sciences (2004) concluded that variations in the manufacturing process rendered this technique "unreliable and potentially misleading." As a result, the FBI has discontinued the use of this technique, but hundreds, if not thousands, of criminal defendants may have been convicted based, in part, on this faulty pseudo-science.
Firearm, toolmark, bite mark, shoeprint, and forensic document comparisons	Like examinations of hair samples, these types of forensic analyses rely on an examiner to make comparisons between a crime scene sample and a known exemplar. Thus, they are subject to the same human errors based on subjective judgments as these other techniques. The reliability of these techniques is questionable in light of either unestablished or unacceptably high error rates. For example, a classic study (Risinger, Denbeaux, and Saks 1989) reported that forensic-document examiners were correct between 36 and 45 percent of the time, that they erred partially or completely 36 to 42 percent of the time, and that they were unable to draw a conclusion in 19 to 22 percent of cases. Experts have recently noted that there is little empirical evidence to support the uniqueness of teeth marks, shoeprints, or weapon markings (Moriarty 2007). Saks and Koehler (2005) reported error rates as high as 64 percent for bite-mark comparison and 40 percent for handwriting comparisons.

Source: Neubauer, David W., and Henry F. Fradella. (2014). *America's Courts and the Criminal Justice System* (11th ed.). Belmont, CA: Wadsworth/Cengage Learning.

Due, in large part, to many of the shortcomings listed in Table 15.3, the National Academies of Sciences (NAS) issued a scathing report on forensic science in the United States in 2009. The report concluded that, among all existing forensic methods, "only nuclear DNA analysis has been rigorously shown to have the capacity to consistently, and with a high degree of certainty, demonstrate a connection between an evidentiary sample and a specific individual or source" (p. 100). In contrast, most other types of forensic analyses lack sufficient systematic research to even "validate the discipline's basic premises and techniques" (p. 22). Accordingly, the NAS called for the creation of an independent federal agency to oversee forensic science

KEY POINTS

LO6
LO7

■ Once the petit jury has been sworn and instructed regarding the presumptions of innocence (and sanity, if relevant to a particular case), the trial begins.

■ A complex series of rules govern the admissibility of evidence at trial.

Continued on next page

KEY POINTS

LO6
LO7

- Trials begin with opening statements. The prosecution then introduces evidence in its case in chief. The defense then has a change to present its case. After rebuttal evidence, if any, attorneys make closing arguments. The jury is then instructed as to the governing law and then deliberates until reaching a verdict.

- In most criminal criminals, juries deliberate until all members of the jury vote unanimously to either convict or acquit the defendant; unanimous verdicts are required if a petit jury is comprised of only six people. If a twelve-person jury is used, some states permit verdicts by a nine- or ten-person majority vote.

- At trial, parties use testimony, real/phsycial evidence, scientific evidence, and demonstrative evidence.

in the United States. As of the writing of this book, no such action has been taken.

As the NAS report makes clear, DNA (deoxyribonucleic acid) is the gold standard of forensic science. As a result, prisoners and their representatives are demanding that old cases be reopened so that DNA tests (not available at the time of the original trial) be performed. However, in *District Attorney's Office v. Osborne* (2009), the U.S. Supreme Court ruled that prisoners have no constitutional right to postconviction DNA testing that might prove their innocence.

Two limitations to DNA evidence should be highlighted. First, biological evidence that can be subjected to DNA testing is available in only about 10 percent of criminal cases (Garrett 2008). Second, even when evidence is available, that evidence may have been contaminated or otherwise rendered unreliable because of mistakes by police or crime lab personnel, including mix-up of samples, deficiencies in lab proficiency testing, and problems with or miscalculations of matching criteria—something that jurors often do not understand (Lieberman, Miethe, Carrell, and Krauss 2008).

Sentencing

If a criminal trial ends in an acquittal, the defendant is set free. If, however, the defendant is convicted, then the defendant is sentenced. Rule 32 of the Federal Rules of Criminal Procedure and similar state provisions require judges to impose sentence without unnecessary delay. This protects the defendant from a prolonged period of uncertainty about the future. Thus, sentencing usually occurs within a few weeks of conviction.

Sentencing is technically a part of the judicial process. As a rule, the imposition of a criminal sentence is the responsibility of a trial court judge, although a handful of jurisdictions allow a jury to fix a defendant's sentence. A judge's determination of the sentence is perhaps the most sensitive and difficult decision a judge has to make due to its effect on the defendant's life. The responsibility for sentencing, however, is shared by the judiciary with both the legislative and executive branches of government. Legislatures set the parameters for criminal sentences when they designate crimes at a particular level of offense, and designate the permissible punishments for those offenses. The executive branch controls the imposition of sentence through two mechanisms, parole and executive clemency. The most important and frequently used of the two is the parole system (discussed later). The chief executive (i.e., the governor of a state or the president of the United States) may instead choose to grant executive clemency—a *pardon*—in which an inmate is "forgiven" for his or her crime and the sentence commuted accordingly.

Sentencing Schemes The level of judicial sentencing discretion today is quite different than it was some years ago. From the 1940s through the 1950s, the rehabilitative model was the dominant philosophical justification behind criminal sentencing (Allen 1981). Accordingly, judges were supposed to tailor sentences to each offender, with the goal of changing the offender's behavior for the better. This approach involved what is called indeterminate sentencing. Legislatures prescribed a range of permissible sentences, usually setting a minimum but leaving the maximum up to the discretion of the judge. In other jurisdictions, legislatures set a minimum and maximum range but left the judge free to impose sentence as he or she saw fit using any criteria. Corrections officials—usually parole boards—were free to release inmates at any time if they believed them to be rehabilitated.

This system sometimes led to great disparities in sentences for similar or even identical crimes. Some of the differences in sentences were due to the philosophy of the sentencing judge, some were due to strategic lawyering, and some were due to discrimination on the basis of race, ethnicity, class, gender, and sexual orientation (Wang 1999; Reiman 1995).

In response to the concerns over disparate sentencing, Congress passed the Sentencing Reform Act of 1984. 18 U.S.C. §§ 3551 et seq. That act created the United States Sentencing Commission and empowered it to create a uniform set of federal sentencing guidelines. These guidelines were intended to reduce sentencing disparities and to realistically project the needs of the federal correctional system. The Sentencing Commission promulgated the Federal Sentencing Guidelines, which went into effect on November 1, 1987. This officially moved the federal sentencing schema to a determinate sentencing structure: The sentence is fixed or predetermined for a given offense, with only minor adjustments, if any, being permissible based on the specific facts of a case.

As Table 15.4 illustrates, *The Federal Sentencing Guidelines* consist of a grid of forty-three offense levels, roughly measuring the seriousness of crime for which sentence is to be imposed, and six criminal history categories based on the defendant's prior convictions of felonies and misdemeanors.

TABLE 15.4 | *The Federal Sentencing Guidelines*: Table (in Months of Imprisonment)

	Offense Level	I (0 or 1)	II (2 or 3)	III (4, 5, 6)	IV (7, 8, 9)	V (10, 11, 12)	VI (13 or more)
Zone A	1	0–6	0–6	0–6	0–6	0–6	0–6
	2	0–6	0–6	0–6	0–6	0–6	1–7
	3	0–6	0–6	0–6	0–6	2–8	3–9
	4	0–6	0–6	0–6	2–8	4–10	6–12
	5	0–6	0–6	1–7	2–8	6–12	9–15
	6	0–6	1–7	2–8	6–12	9–15	12–18
	7	0–6	2–8	4–10	8–14	12–18	15–21
	8	0–6	4–10	6–12	10–16	15–21	18–24
Zone B	9	4–10	6–12	8–14	12–18	18–24	21–27
	10	6–12	8–14	10–16	15–21	21–27	24–30
Zone C	11	8–14	10–16	12–18	18–24	24–30	27–33
	12	10–16	12–18	15–21	21–27	27–33	30–37
Zone D	13	12–18	15–21	18–24	24–30	30–37	33–41
	14	15–21	18–24	21–27	27–33	33–41	37–46
	15	18–24	21–27	24–30	30–37	37–46	41–51
	16	21–27	24–30	27–33	33–41	41–51	46–57
	17	24–30	27–33	30–37	37–46	46–57	51–63
	18	27–33	30–37	33–41	41–51	51–63	57–71
	19	30–37	33–41	37–46	46–57	57–71	63–78
	20	33–41	37–46	41–51	51–63	63–78	70–87
	21	37–46	41–51	46–57	57–71	70–87	77–96

Continued on next page

Offense Level	I (0 or 1)	II (2 or 3)	III (4, 5, 6)	IV (7, 8, 9)	V (10, 11, 12)	VI (13 or more)
22	41–51	46–57	51–63	63–78	77–96	84–105
23	46–57	51–63	57–71	70–87	84–105	92–115
24	51–63	57–71	63–78	77–96	92–115	100–125
25	57–71	63–78	70–87	84–105	100–125	110–137
26	63–78	70–87	78–97	92–115	110–137	120–150
27	70–87	78–97	87–108	100–125	120–150	130–162
28	78–97	87–108	97–121	110–137	130–162	140–175
29	87–108	97–121	108–135	121–151	140–175	151–188
30	97–121	108–135	121–151	135–168	151–188	168–210
31	108–135	121–151	135–168	151–188	168–210	188–235
32	121–151	135–168	151–188	168–210	188–235	210–262
33	135–168	151–188	168–210	188–235	210–262	235–293
34	151–188	168–210	188–235	210–262	235–293	262–327
35	168–210	188–235	210–262	235–293	262–327	292–365
36	188–235	210–262	235–293	262–327	292–365	324–405
37	210–262	235–293	262–327	292–365	324–405	360–life
38	235–293	262–327	292–365	324–405	360–life	360–life
39	262–327	292–365	324–405	360–life	360–life	360–life
40	292–365	324–405	360–life	360–life	360–life	360–life
41	324–405	360–life	360–life	360–life	360–life	360–life
42	360–life	360–life	360–life	360–life	360–life	360–life
43	life	life	life	life	life	life

The Sentencing Reform Act of 1984 also created a sentencing method in which the sentence imposed by a judge generally determined the actual time that a convicted person would serve in prison. The act also made restitution a mandatory sentence for conviction of certain crimes.

One of the more controversial aspects of determinate sentencing is the notion of *minimum mandatory sentences*. Such sentences are set by legislatures and require a defendant to serve a statutorily set minimum period of incarceration if convicted of a particular offense. Judges dislike these sentences because they do not have the ability to fashion a sentence appropriate to the facts of a particular case; all offenders are sentenced the same way without regard to individual circumstances. These types of sentences have been adopted in many states and in the federal system for drug offenses, the commission of crimes using a firearm, and repeat felony offenders (e.g., "three strikes and you're out" laws). Some states have even designed minimum mandatory sentences for first-time misdemeanor offenders of driving under the influence laws.

Although the federal sentencing guidelines greatly curtailed discretionary sentencing, they did not completely eliminate discretion. In practice, the guidelines really just shifted power from the judge to the prosecutor. "[A]lmost without exception, the United States Department of Justice predetermined the outcome by the way in which it charged a defendant" (Jordan 2006: 624). That being said, judges did retain some power to affect the sentence imposed on a particular defendant through the use of *sentencing departures*. Unless the defendant was convicted of a crime carrying a mandatory minimum sentence, judges were permitted to make limited adjustments to the sentencing range called *upward departures* or *downward departures*, depending on whether the range is being increased or decreased. Judges were authorized to grant downward departures from the sentencing guidelines when a defendant provided substantial assistance in the investigation or prosecution of another person, and when the judge felt it necessary to correct unjust effects of the guidelines in extraordinary cases. Mustard (2001: 311) found that judicial use of sentencing departures perpetuated "differences in the length of sentence . . . on the basis of race, gender, education, income, and citizenship. These disparities occur in spite of explicit statements in the guidelines that these characteristics should not affect the sentence length." In fact, these impermissible factors accounted for more than half of the sentencing disparities found in Mustard's study (see also Schanzenbach 2005). At the time the guidelines went into effect through 2005, the Federal Sentencing Guidelines were mandatory. Some states, like California, adopted mandatory guidelines similar to the Federal Sentencing Guidelines. But most of the states that adopted sentencing guidelines opted for a voluntary guideline system wherein judges may sentence a defendant outside the guideline range as the facts of a case may warrant in their discretion. Federal judges gained the same prerogative in January 2005 when the U.S. Supreme Court invalidated the Federal Sentencing Guidelines in the companion cases of *United States v. Booker* and *United States v. Fanfan*, 543 U.S. 220 (2005).

Booker declared that the Federal Sentencing Guidelines were unconstitutional "because they permitted a sentencing judge to impose a sentence based on facts found by a judge, not a jury," and therefore violated the Sixth Amendment's guarantee to have a jury decide factual issues under the proof beyond a reasonable doubt standard (Jordan 2006: 628). The Court, however, did not invalidate the Guidelines in their entirety. Rather, the Court's remedy was to excise the portions of federal law mandating the use of the Guidelines, thereby rendering them advisory. Federal courts now use the sentencing guidelines to help establish presumptively reasonable sentences from which sentencing judges and appellate courts can vary if they are unreasonable in light of the facts of a particular case. *Rita v. United States*, 551 U.S. 338 (2007). Thus, a judge can depart downward from the recommended sentence based on his or her personal disagreement with the Guidelines without making individualized determinations about the defendant or mitigation. For example, *Kimbrough v. United States*, 552 U.S. 85 (2007), upheld a judge's ability to narrow the sentencing gap between crack cocaine and powder cocaine that existed in the Guidelines. And, as explored in the next Criminal Procedure in Action box, subsequent cases have increased judicial discretion in this area even more.

Studies assessing the impact of *Booker* and *Fanfan* report inconsistent findings. The U.S. Sentencing Commission (2010) asserted that the increase in judicial discretion in the wake of the Guidelines becoming merely advisory has increased racial disparities in sentencing outcomes. In contrast, when analyzing the same data using a different methodology, Ulmer, Light, and Kramer (2011) found no significant changes in sentencing disparities. And Fischman and Schanzenbach (2012) reported a decrease in racial disparities after *Booker* once certain other factors, such as statutory mandatory minimum sentences (discussed in more detail later), were statistically controlled for. It is important to recognize, however, that methodological limitations prevent such studies from operationalizing all of the variables that might account for sentencing outcomes.

CRIMINAL PROCEDURE **IN ACTION**

What Is the Appropriate Sentence?

In *Spears v. United States*, 555 U.S. 261 (2009), the defendant was convicted of conspiracy to distribute at least 50 grams of cocaine base and at least 500 grams of powder cocaine. At sentencing, the court determined that the drug quantities involved yielded an offense level of 38, that his criminal history justified placing him in the guidelines' criminal history Category IV.

As illustrated in Table 15.3, the resulting advisory sentencing guidelines range was imprisonment for 324 to 405 months.

Under the mandatory minimum laws in effect at the time, someone convicted of possessing five grams of crack cocaine (the approximate weight of two pennies) received at least five years in prison and someone convicted of possessing fifty grams of crack cocaine receive a mandatory minimum sentence of ten years. In contrast, the weight required to trigger the same sentences with powder cocaine was one hundred times greater. The sentencing judge believed this 100:1 ratio between quantities of powder and crack cocaine to be excessive. Accordingly, the judge recalculated the offense level using a 20:1 ratio, resulting in an offense level of 34 with a sentencing range of 210 to 262 months' imprisonment. The judge imposed a 240-month sentence, the statutory minimum.

- Do you think it was right for the judge to recalculate the offense level using his own 20:1 ratio rather than apply the 100:1 ratio contained in the Guidelines? Why or why not?

- Since the time *Spears* upheld the sentencing judge's actions as having acted properly within his discretion, the U.S. Sentencing Commission reduced the sentencing ratio amount of powder cocaine versus crack cocaine that triggers the same penalty to approximately 18:1. Thus, today, 28 grams of crack cocaine now triggers a five-year mandatory minimum prison sentence and 280 grams of crack triggers a mandatory minimum 10-year sentence. Yet, an 18:1 ratio in sentencing disparity still exists between crack and powered cocaine sentences. Critique this sentencing scheme for two forms of the same drug. Does your opinion change when you consider that about two-thirds of

the crack cocaine users in the United States are White or Hispanic, but more than 80 percent of the defendants sentenced under federal crack cocaine laws are African American? Explain your reasoning.

- If you had been the sentencing judge in *Spears*, what sentence would you have imposed? Why?

In *People v. Binkerd*, 155 Cal. App. 4th 1143 (2007), the defendant was driving home from a party when she collided into oncoming traffic, killing the friend and co-worker who had been her passenger. Her blood alcohol concentration was more than twice the legal limit. At her sentencing for vehicular homicide, the probation officer had recommended a jail sentence of less than one year, a sentence the deceased victim's family supported. Yet, the judge sentenced the defendant to 64 months in state prison after seeing pictures of the defendant posted on her MySpace page wearing a T-shirt reading "I ♥ Patrón" (a brand of tequila) while drinking with friends after the fatal accident. The judge thought that the photos indicated the defendant lacked remorse and therefore deserved a tough sentence.

- Do you think it is appropriate for a judge to consider information posted on social networking sites into account when imposing a criminal sentence? Explain.

- If you were the sentencing judge, what weight, if any, would you have given the facts that the driver had recently graduated from college and the victim's family begged the judge to be lenient? Why?

- The defendant's sentence was overruled on appeal (on grounds unrelated to the judge's consideration of the MySpace photos) and she was resentenced to three years in jail. What do you think would have been a fair sentence in this case? Why?

Presentence Investigation and Report To tailor a sentence that is appropriate for a particular offender, a judge needs information about the defendant that would not be garnered during the course of trial or during a Rule 11 allocution hearing. The gathering of this information is referred to as a presentence investigation (PSI). Probation officers generally conduct PSIs, investigating the convicted defendant's prior criminal background; financial condition; educational, military, employment, and social history; relationships with family and friends; use of alcohol or controlled substances;

and circumstances affecting the defendant's behavior, such as their mental status, that may assist the court in imposing sentence. After a PSI is completed, the investigating probation officer prepares a presentence investigation report (PSIR) for the sentencing judge containing all of the relevant information gathered during the PSI. The PSIR may also include information on the effects of the offense on the victims, as well as available alternatives to imprisonment. The report usually concludes with a sentencing recommendation, including any "special conditions of probation" that are designed to rehabilitate the offender, like alcohol or drug rehabilitation, anger management, psychotherapy, and so forth.

Statutes or rules usually require a court to consider a PSIR before imposing sentence. And judges live up to this obligation, rarely acting without due deference to the PSIR. Therefore, PSIRs are quite important. Judges overwhelmingly tend to impose sentences in accordance with the recommendations contained in a PSIR even though they are not bound to do so (Campbell et al. 1990; Rush and Robertson 1987).

Sentencing Options When we speak of the *correctional system*, we are actually referring to a variety of agencies, institutions, and programs that seek to punish or rehabilitate (or both) someone convicted of a crime. In addition to court-ordered fines and the revocation or suspension of state-granted licenses, the most typical sentences involve

- probation;
- intermediate sanctions, such as halfway houses, boot camps, work furlough camps, and the like; and
- incarceration in jails (for most misdemeanor offenses) or prisons (for most felonies), which may or may not be followed by a period of supervised release commonly referred to as parole.

Sentencing Hearing Sentence is imposed at a sentencing hearing. The sentencing hearing is quick compared to the other phases in the criminal process. It generally takes less than thirty minutes, and often lasts only ten or fifteen minutes.

At the sentencing hearing and before any sentence is imposed, Rule 32 of the Federal Rules of Criminal Procedure requires that the judge

- provide the defendant's attorney an opportunity to speak on the defendant's behalf and
- address the defendant personally in order to permit the defendant to speak or present any information to mitigate the sentence.

These provisions enable the defendant and defense counsel to present any information that may assist the court in determining punishment. The prosecution has an equivalent opportunity to speak to the court. In addition, in most jurisdictions, the victim of the crime (or their next of kin if the victim is dead or unable to speak on his or her own behalf) may participate at sentencing either by making an oral statement in open court or by submitting a written statement to the court. This is called a victim impact statement. The court, in its discretion, may allow others, such as the victim's family and friends and members of the victim's community, to participate at sentencing.

The U.S. Constitution places several substantive limitations on the information that a judge may consider when determining a criminal sentence at or before the actual sentencing hearing. Due process prohibits a judge from relying on materially untrue assumptions. *Townsend v. Burke*, 334 U.S. 736 (1948). Due process also prohibits a judge from vindictively imposing a harsher punishment on a defendant for exercising constitutional rights. *North Carolina v. Pearce*, 395 U.S. 711 (1969). And, as made clear when the Supreme Court invalidated the once-mandatory nature of the Federal Sentencing Guidelines, the Sixth Amendment restricts a judge to impose a sentence that is based solely on the "facts reflected in the jury verdict or admitted by the defendant," not other facts that have not been proven beyond a reasonable doubt. *Booker*, 543 U.S. at 228.

The First Amendment prohibits a judge from considering the defendant's religious or political beliefs. *United States v. Lemon*, 723 F.2d 922 (D.C. Cir. 1983). *Wisconsin v. Mitchell*, 508 U.S. 476 (1993), however, held that, although the First Amendment protects the defendant's "abstract beliefs" from being considered at sentencing, a sentence may be enhanced because the defendant intentionally selected the victim on account of the victim's race. The Court explained that the "Constitution does not erect a per se barrier to the admission of evidence concerning one's beliefs and associations at sentencing simply because those beliefs and associations are protected by the First Amendment." 508 U.S. at 486.

Finally, the Eighth Amendment prohibits the imposition of excessive fines and the infliction of cruel and unusual punishments on persons convicted of a crime. (See Chapter 1 for a discussion of the Eighth Amendment.)

After imposing sentence, but before adjourning the sentencing hearing, the court must notify the defendant of the defendant's right to appeal, including any right to appeal the sentence.

Judgment

A **judgment** is the written evidence of the final disposition of the case. It is signed by a judge or the clerk of a court. A judgment of conviction sets forth the plea or verdict and the sentence. If the defendant is found not guilty or is entitled to be discharged for some other reason, judgment is entered accordingly, and the defendant is guaranteed by the Double Jeopardy Clause to be free forever from any further prosecution for the crime charged. (See Chapter 1 for a discussion of double jeopardy.) If the defendant is found guilty, the judge must pass sentence on the defendant before entering judgment.

The formal entry of judgment is important for the appeals process (discussed later) because appeals may be taken only from cases that have come to a final judgment. This means that an appellate court will not decide any legal issues, nor will it review the denial of any motions, until the trial court has finally disposed of the case. The reason for this rule is to prevent unnecessary delays in the conduct of trials that would result if parties could appeal issues during the course of a trial. (There are minor exceptions to this final judgment rule, such as for interlocutory appeals, but these exceptions are beyond the scope of this text.)

Posttrial Motions

Motion for Judgment of Acquittal After judgment has been entered, the defendant still has several motions available to challenge the court's decision. One of these is the **motion for judgment of acquittal,** sometimes mistakenly called by its civil law counterpart as a *motion for judgment notwithstanding the verdict.* This is the same motion that the defense can make at the close of the prosecution's case-in-chief during trial, and again at the close of the defense case-in-chief during trial.

Continued on next page

Statutes and rules usually provide that this motion can be renewed even after the jury has been discharged, if it is made within a specified time after the discharge. Courts do not usually grant these motions unless

- the prosecution's evidence was insufficient or nonexistent on a vital element of the offense charged, or
- the indictment or information did not state a criminal offense under the law of the jurisdiction.

Motion for New Trial Another motion available to a defendant is a motion for a new trial. This motion may be made in addition to a motion for acquittal. When made alone, a motion for a new trial is sometimes deemed to include a motion for acquittal. In the latter case, if the defendant moves for a new trial, the court granting it may either enter a final judgment of acquittal or grant a new trial. The court may grant a new trial if it is required in the interest of justice. The usual ground for granting a new trial is insufficient evidence to support the verdict. Some courts also consider errors of law and improper conduct of trial participants during the trial under the motion.

Another ground for granting a motion for a new trial is the discovery of new evidence, which carries with it an extended time period for making the motion. The time period varies among jurisdictions, but is usually longer than the period for other motions to allow a reasonable time to discover new evidence. To justify granting a motion for a new trial on the grounds of newly discovered evidence, the defendant must show several things: that the new evidence was discovered after the trial, that it will probably change the result of the trial, that it could not have been discovered before the trial by the exercise of due diligence, that it is material to the issues involved, and that it is not merely cumulative or impeaching.

Motion for Revision or Correction of Sentence In some jurisdictions, by motion of either the defendant or the court, the defendant may obtain a revision or correction of sentence. The power to revise a sentence enables a trial court to change a sentence that is inappropriate in a particular case, even though the sentence may be legal and was imposed in a legal manner. The power to revise a sentence includes a limited power to increase as well as to reduce the sentence. In contrast to the power to revise, the power to correct a sentence enables a court to change a sentence because the sentence was either illegal or imposed in an illegal manner. An example of an illegal sentence is one that was in excess of the statutory maximum. An example of an illegally imposed sentence is one in which the judge did not personally address the defendant and give the defendant an opportunity to be heard before sentencing, when required by statute. The power to revise or correct a sentence must be exercised within specific time periods, or the power is lost.

- A defendant may file posttrial motions seeking to have a judge set aside a conviction, order a new trial, or modify a sentence.

- A defendant may challenge a criminal conviction by filing an appeal from a judgment of conviction alleging that legal errors or arbitrary or capricious rulings by the judge prejudiced the defendant from having received a fair trial. Alternatively, a defendant may allege that factual determinations made at trial were clearly erroneous.

- Alleged errors of law are reviewed on appeal *de novo*. Alleged errors of factual determinations are reviewed for clear error, a highly deferential standard. Abuses of judicial discretion are also reviewed with great deference.

- Appellate determinations of either plain error or prejudicial error normally result in a conviction being overturned. Appellate determinations of harmless error, however, result in convictions being upheld.

- Prisoners in state custody who allege that certain errors of a constitutional magnitude were not corrected on appeal may file a petition for a writ of *habeas corpus* in federal district court or a similar civil petition for postconviction relief in state courts. Generally, this type of relief is granted only for select constitutional errors during a criminal trial that "had substantial and injurious effect or influence in determining the jury's verdict." Federal prisoners may file similar petitions under 28 U.S.C. Section 2255.

Remedies After Conviction

A defendant has two major avenues of relief after being convicted of a crime: appeal and *habeas corpus*. Both of these postconviction remedies will be addressed in turn.

638

PART IV
INTERROGATIONS,
IDENTIFICATIONS, TRIALS,
AND POST-CONVICTION
REMEDIES

Appeals

A defendant has a right to **appeal** after being convicted of a crime and after the trial judge has decided all posttrial motions and entered final judgment in the case. The appeal procedure varies among different jurisdictions and is not described in detail in this book. It involves, among other things, the filing of a notice of appeal, the designation of the parts of the trial record to be considered on appeal, the filing of a statement of points on appeal, the filing of briefs, and the arguing of the briefs before an appellate court. If a defendant is unable to afford a lawyer to handle an appeal, statutes and court rules provide for court appointment of a lawyer free of charge.

In some jurisdictions, the prosecution may also appeal adverse trial court decisions, but the right is usually more limited than the defendant's right. Typical statutes allow appeal by the prosecution of adverse rulings made before the jury hears the case or in cases in which the defendant has appealed. The procedure for appeal by the prosecution is essentially the same as appeal by the defendant.

Standards of Appellate Review Appellate courts generally do not disturb the factual findings of the lower courts. This practice is due to the **standard of review**. When reviewing factual determinations, the standard of review is generally referred to as the **clearly erroneous** standard. Under this standard, the factual determinations of the trial level court are left undisturbed unless it is patently clear from a review of the record that a factual error was made. Evidence is presented and witnesses testify at trial level, so the trial court alone has the opportunity to observe a witness's facial expressions, body language, and vocal intonations. Accordingly, appellate courts are highly deferential to the factual findings of trial courts, and appellate reversals under the clearly erroneous standard are quite rare.

Most appellate inquiries concern review of questions of law. Because appellate judges are just as qualified to review questions of law as trial court judges, their review is *de novo* or plenary. In other words, they review the law without any deference to the legal decisions of the trial court. The following example illustrates this point.

Suppose a law enforcement officer obtained a confession from a defendant but failed to give *Miranda* warnings before a custodial interrogation. During the trial, the judge erroneously permitted the officer who obtained the confession to read it to the jury over the objection of the defense. The jury convicted the defendant. On appeal, the defendant argues that the trial judge committed an error of law in allowing the jury to hear the confession. The appellate court would very likely reverse the conviction because of the trial judge's error. Along with reversal, the usual procedure is to remand the case (send it back to the trial court for a new trial) with instructions to exclude the confession from the jury in the new trial. A different jury would then hear the evidence, without the illegally obtained confession, and render another verdict. Therefore, even though a conviction is reversed on appeal, the defendant is not necessarily acquitted and freed. The defendant has simply won the right to be tried again.

The other standard of review that appellate courts apply is called the **abuse of discretion** standard. This highly deferential standard is applied by appellate courts reviewing the discretionary decision making of a trial court judge. Many rulings are left to the discretion of a trial court, such as whether to allow expert testimony, what the scope of permissible examination will be, and whether to sanction a party. If one wishes to challenge such a ruling on appeal, it must be shown that the trial court made decisions in an arbitrary, capricious, or unreasonable manner.

Reversible Versus Harmless Error Generally, to obtain appellate court review of an issue, the appealing party (called the *appellant*) must preserve its claim by making a specific timely objection at or before trial. This is called the *contemporaneous objection rule*. If the appellant fails to make a timely objection, an appellate court will consider the claim only if it constitutes plain error. Plain errors are defects seriously affecting substantial rights that are so prejudicial to a jury's deliberations "as to undermine the fundamental fairness of the trial and bring about a miscarriage of justice." *United States v. Polowichak*, 783 F.2d 410, 416 (4th Cir. 1986).

On the other hand, even when an appellant preserves a claim by timely objection and the appellate court finds that the trial court erred, the appellate court may still affirm the conviction if it finds that the error was "harmless." This so-called harmless error rule avoids "setting aside of convictions for small errors or defects that have little, if any, likelihood of having changed the result of the trial." *Chapman v. California*, 386 U.S. 18, 22 (1967). If the error was of constitutional dimensions, the appellate court must determine "beyond a reasonable doubt that the error complained of did not contribute to the verdict obtained." 386 U.S. at 23. If the error was not of constitutional dimensions, the appellate court must determine with "fair assurance after pondering all that happened without stripping the erroneous action from the whole that the judgment was not substantially swayed by the error." *Kotteakos v. United States*, 328 U.S. 750, 765 (1946).

Most types of error are subject to harmless error analysis, including classic trial errors involving the erroneous admission of evidence. *Arizona v. Fulminante*, 499 U.S. 279 (1991). Some types of error, however, involve rights so basic to a fair trial that they can never be considered harmless. Here are some examples:

- Conflict of interest in representation throughout the entire proceeding. *Holloway v. Arkansas*, 435 U.S. 475 (1978).

- Denial of the right to an impartial judge. *Chapman v. California*, 386 U.S. 18 (1967).

- Racial, ethnic, or sex discrimination in grand jury or petit jury selection. *Vasquez v. Hillery*, 474 U.S. 254 (1986); *Batson v. Kentucky*, 476 U.S. 79 (1986); *J.E.B. v. Alabama ex rel. T.B.*, 511 U.S. 127 (1994).

- Failure to inquire whether a defendant's guilty plea is voluntary. *United States v. Gonzalez*, 820 F.2d 575 (2d Cir. 1987).

If an appellate court finds that a trial court committed no errors of law or only harmless errors, it affirms the defendant's conviction. If the appeal was heard in an intermediate appellate court, however, the defendant may still have an additional, discretionary appeal to the highest appellate court in the jurisdiction. And even if the appeal was heard in the highest appellate court in a state, the defendant may still file a petition for a writ of certiorari with the U.S. Supreme Court.

When an appellate court decides a case, it delivers a written opinion to explain and justify its decision. In this way the higher court explains the trial judge's errors and also informs the losing party that it has lost and why. The decisions of appellate courts are compiled and published in books of reported court decisions, which can be found in law libraries. Attorneys and judges use these reported decisions as authorities for arguing and deciding future cases that raise issues similar to those already decided.

Habeas Corpus

Federal *Habeas Corpus* for State Prisoners State prisoners who challenge the fact or duration of their confinement on constitutional grounds and seek immediate or speedier release may petition for a writ of habeas corpus (also known as the "Great Writ") in federal district court. The federal statute governing the *habeas corpus* remedy is 28 U.S.C. Section 2254. A state prisoner who challenges the conditions of confinement or attempts to obtain damages for violations of constitutional rights should seek relief by means of a civil action under 42 U.S.C. Section 1983, not by filing a petition for a writ of *habeas corpus*.

640

PART IV
INTERROGATIONS,
IDENTIFICATIONS, TRIALS,
AND POST-CONVICTION
REMEDIES

Since the Judiciary Act of 1867, *habeas corpus* has been available to state prisoners "in all cases where any person may be restrained of his or her liberty in violation of the Constitution or of any treaty or law of the United States." Initially, the constitutional grounds for which *habeas corpus* relief could be granted were limited to those relating to the jurisdiction of the state court, but the U.S. Supreme Court extended the scope of the writ to all constitutional challenges by its decision in *Fay v. Noia*, 372 U.S. 391 (1963):

> Although in form the Great Writ is simply a mode of procedure, its history is inextricably intertwined with the growth of fundamental rights of personal liberty. For its function has been to provide a prompt and efficacious remedy for whatever society deems to be intolerable restraints. Its root principle is that in a civilized society, government must always be accountable to the judiciary for a man's imprisonment: if the imprisonment cannot be shown to conform with the fundamental requirements of law, the individual is entitled to his immediate release. Thus there is nothing novel in the fact that today *habeas corpus* in the federal courts provides a mode for the redress of denials of due process of law. Vindication of due process is precisely its historic office. 372 U.S. at 401–02.

Brecht v. Abrahamson, 507 U.S. 619, 623 (1993), held that the standard for determining whether *habeas corpus* relief must be granted for a constitutional trial error is whether the error "had substantial and injurious effect or influence in determining the jury's verdict."

Violations of state law are not valid grounds for a *habeas* action unless such violations are of constitutional magnitude. For example, *Brown v. Sanders*, 546 U.S. 212 (2006), held Section 2254 relief was unavailable when a jury had considered a state sentencing guideline that was later invalidated by state high court of last resort because the claim did not present any violation of a constitutional right.

In 1976, the U.S. Supreme Court limited all federal *habeas corpus* review of state prisoners' claims of violations of federal constitutional rights, holding that "where the State has provided an opportunity for full and fair litigation of a Fourth Amendment claim, a state prisoner may not be granted federal *habeas corpus* relief on the ground that evidence obtained in an unconstitutional search or seizure was introduced at his trial." *Stone v. Powell*, 428 U.S. 465, 494 (1976). However, *Stone* does not bar an ineffective assistance of counsel *habeas* claim based on mishandling or failing to raise a valid Fourth Amendment issue. *Kimmelman v. Morrison*, 477 U.S. 365 (1986).

Given *Stone*'s limitation on habeas relief for alleged Fourth Amendment violations, most *habeas* claims involve

- Fifth Amendment claims concerning statements obtained in violation of *Miranda*,

- Sixth Amendment claims concerning the failure to provide appointed counsel,

- Sixth Amendment ineffective assistance of counsel claims,

- due process or equal protection claims based on significant judicial error (e.g., refusal to give a warranted jury instruction or prejudicial errors on evidence rulings),

- due process or equal protection claims based on prosecutorial misconduct (e.g., *Brady* violations for withholding exculpatory evidence), or

- insufficiency of evidence claims.

Prisoners must exhaust available state remedies before a federal court will consider their constitutional claim on *habeas corpus*. This rule means that, if an appeal or other procedure to hear a claim is still available by right in the state court system, the prisoner must pursue that procedure before a federal *habeas corpus* application will be considered. Federal *habeas corpus* review may likewise be barred if a defendant is unable to show cause for noncompliance with a state procedural rule and to show some actual prejudice resulting from the alleged constitutional violation. *Wainwright v. Sykes*, 433 U.S. 72 (1977); *Dretke v. Haley*, 541 U.S. 386 (2004).

The remedies available to courts deciding *habeas corpus* petitions include reclassifying a petitioner's conviction or ordering the state to retry or resentence a petitioner. Release of a prisoner is granted only if the state fails to comply with the court's order of relief. *Burkett v. Cunningham*, 826 F.2d 1208 (3rd Cir. 1987).

In response to the bombing of the federal building in Oklahoma City, Congress passed the Antiterrorism and Effective Death Penalty Act of 1996 (AEDPA). The *habeas corpus* provisions of that act established a one-year limitation on filing *habeas corpus* petitions from the date

- of the final judgment on direct appellate review;

- of the removal of any state-imposed impediment that unconstitutionally prevented the filing of a petition;

- of the Supreme Court's announcement of a new, retroactively applicable constitutional right (which is rare); or

- on which the facts supporting the claims presented could have been discovered through the exercise of due diligence.

The AEDPA also provided new procedures governing the disposition of second or successive petitions. Before a federal district court will hear a second or successive petition, the petitioner must obtain an authorization order from a three-judge panel in the appropriate court of appeals. *Burton v. Stewart*, 549 U.S. 147 (2007). The grant or denial of an authorization order cannot be appealed to the U.S. Supreme Court and is not subject to rehearing. In *Felker v. Turpin*, 518 U.S. 651 (1996), the Supreme Court held that the "gatekeeping" requirements were constitutional, but found nothing in the law to limit or remove its authority to hear original petitions for *habeas corpus*, thereby preserving its own power to review.

In *Herrera v. Collins*, 506 U.S. 390 (1993), the U.S. Supreme Court held that claims of actual innocence are not valid *habeas* actions unless there is an independent constitutional violation in the underlying criminal proceedings that led to the state prisoner's wrongful conviction. Yet, *Herrera* left open the possibility that an actual innocence claim in a death penalty case might present a valid due process claim if there was no state avenue of postconviction relief: "A truly persuasive demonstration of 'actual innocence' made after trial would render the execution of a defendant unconstitutional." 506 U.S. at 417. Twenty years later, in *McQuiggin v. Perkins*, 133 S. Ct. 1924, 1930 (2013), the Court ruled that a plea of actual innocence can overcome AEDPA's statute of limitations for *habeas* filings to prevent a "fundamental miscarriage of justice."

Today, many claims of actual innocence concern DNA evidence that was not available at the time of trial and conviction, but that subsequently becomes available and casts doubt on the validity of a conviction. Under such circumstances, a prisoner is entitled to have such evidence considered in *habeas* proceedings. *House v. Bell*, 547 U.S. 518 (2006). However, as previously mentioned, a prisoner does not have any constitutional right to access evidence for postconviction DNA testing to support a claim of actual innocence. *District Attorney's Office for Third Judicial Dist. v. Osborne*, 557 U.S. 52 (2009).

642

PART IV
INTERROGATIONS,
IDENTIFICATIONS, TRIALS,
AND POST-CONVICTION
REMEDIES

Habeas Corpus Relief for Federal Prisoners In 1948, Congress enacted a statute that was designed to serve as a substitute for *habeas corpus* for federal prisoners. The primary purpose of the statute was to shift the jurisdictions of the courts hearing *habeas corpus* applications. The statute did not change the basic scope of the remedy that had been available to federal prisoners by *habeas corpus*. That statute, 28 U.S.C. Section 2255, provides, in relevant part:

> *Federal custody; remedies on motion attacking sentence.* A prisoner in custody under sentence of a court established by Act of Congress claiming the right to be released upon the ground that the sentence was imposed in violation of the Constitution or laws of the United States, or that the court was without jurisdiction to impose such sentence, or that the sentence was in excess of the maximum authorized by law, or is otherwise subject to collateral attack, may move the court which imposed the sentence to vacate, set aside, or correct the sentence.

> * * *

> An application for a writ of *habeas corpus* in behalf of a prisoner who is authorized to apply for relief by motion pursuant to this section, shall not be entertained if it appears that the applicant has failed to apply for relief, by motion, to the court which sentenced him, or that such court has denied him relief, unless it also appears that the remedy by motion is inadequate or ineffective to test the legality of his detention.

A *Section 2255 motion* is, therefore, the correct mechanism for a federal prisoner to challenge the validity of a federal criminal conviction. The statute recognizes four grounds on which an inmate in federal custody may seek relief:

- The sentence was imposed in violation of the Constitution or laws of the United States.
- The court was without jurisdiction to impose such sentence.
- The sentence was in excess of the maximum authorized by law.
- The sentence is "otherwise subject to collateral attack."

Although the final criterion may appear broad, Section 2255 relief may only be granted under it if a violation of federal law caused a *"fundamental defect which inherently results in a complete miscarriage of justice [or] an omission inconsistent with the rudimentary demands of fair procedure." Davis v. United States*, 417 U.S. 333, 346 (1974) (quoting *Hill v. United States*, 368 U.S. 424, 428 [1962]).

Section 2255 is similar in many respects to the *habeas* remedy for state prisoners, including in terms of time limitations. Section 2255 motions, for example, must be usually filed within one year of the date on which a judgment of conviction becomes final, such as the day after the deadline for filing a petition for certiorari or when such a petition is denied. There are, however, some significant distinctions between state and federal *habeas*-type relief that are beyond the scope of this text.

State Postconviction Relief Almost all states have postconviction procedures permitting prisoners to challenge constitutional violations. These procedures may derive from statutes, court rules, or the common law. Many of these state remedies are as extensive in scope as federal *habeas corpus* for state prisoners. Other states provide much narrower remedies. (The differences in postconviction remedies among the states are beyond the scope of this text and are not discussed here.)

SUMMARY

643

CHAPTER 15
CRIMINAL
TRIALS, APPEALS, AND
POSTCONVICTION REMEDIES

The Sixth Amendment and various statutory provisions provide numerous procedural protections to those accused of crimes. Statutes of limitations provide preaccusation protections by requiring that prosecutions commence within a specified period of time from the date of the alleged commission of the offense. Due process also provides preaccusation even if an indictment is brought within the prescribed statute of limitations if the government unreasonably delayed prosecution either to harass a defendant or to gain a tactical advantage for itself in a manner that causes actual prejudice to the defendant.

After a person has been arrested or formally charged with a crime, both the Sixth Amendment guarantee of a speedy trial and speedy trial statutes serve to prevent unnecessary incarceration prior to trial, minimize "anxiety and concern accompanying public accusation," and limit the possibility that delays will interfere with the defendant's ability to present an effective defense due to faded memories, unavailable witnesses, and the loss of exculpatory evidence.

Once a trial starts, the Sixth Amendment generally mandates that all adult trials be open to the public. The Amendment also guarantees that the accused can confront all witnesses providing testimonial evidence against him or her via cross-examination, as well as compel the appearance of witnesses favorable to the defense so long as those people are within the geographic subpoena power of the court.

The Sixth Amendment right to a fair and impartial jury is achieved in practice through the jury selection process. This process employs summoning prospective jurors from a fair cross-section of the community, asking them questions in *voir dire* to screen out people who may be biased in the case, and excusing a limited number of people without cause so long as doing so does not violate equal protection guarantees. Once this process is complete, a petit jury is sworn and trial begins. Attorneys start the trial by making opening statements. The prosecution then presents its case in chief by calling witnesses and conducting direct examinations. The defense may then cross-examine the witnesses. At the conclusion of the prosecution's case, the judge may dismiss a charge if the prosecution failed to prove any essential element of a crime. Otherwise, the defense presents its case in chief. The attorneys then make closing arguments, after which the jury is instructed as to the law and then deliberates until reaching a verdict. Unless any posttrial motions are granted, judgment is then entered.

After the entry of judgment, the defendant can appeal a conviction. Questions of fact and discretionary rulings are viewed on appeal with great deference to the decisions at trial. Questions of law, however, are reviewed de novo. A conviction may be overturned only in cases in which an appellate court finds plain error or prejudicial error; harmless errors do not result in reversals.

After all appeals have been exhausted, defendants in custody are usually able to attack their convictions collaterally in civil postconviction relief proceedings. State prisoners who challenge the fact or duration of their confinement on constitutional grounds and seek immediate or speedier release may petition for a writ of *habeas corpus* in federal district court. Federal prisoners may do the same via similar proceedings by filing a motion for postconviction relief under 28 U.S.C. Section 2255.

KEY TERMS

abuse of discretion 638
allocution hearing 634
appeal 638
bench trial (nonjury trial) 619
clearly erroneous 638

compulsory process 618
Confrontation Clause 615
cross-examination 615
de novo 638
determinate sentencing 630

downward departures 633
harmless error 639
hung jury 625
indeterminate sentencing 630
judgment 636

REVIEW AND DISCUSSION QUESTIONS

1. Compare and contrast the constitution and statutory protections designed to protect those suspected of having committed criminal acts from facing prejudicial delays in having their cases brought to trial.

2. Explain the difference between a testimonial and nontestimonial communication for the purposes of the Confrontation Clause.

3. What is the difference between a jury trial and a bench trial? When does a criminal defendant have the right to jury trial? Why might a defendant waive that right and opt for a bench trial?

4. How is a jury summoned, screened, and ultimately selected to sit on a criminal case?

5. What limits does the U.S. Constitution place on the exercise of peremptory challenges?

6. Describe the sequence of a criminal trial, defining all of the specialized terms needed to explain each stage in the trial process.

7. Compare and contrast *Frye* and *Daubert*'s approach to the use of scientific evidence at trial. The rules for admissibility of scientific evidence notwithstanding, what concerns have the Innocence Project and the National Academies of Science raised about a range of forensic scientific techniques?

8. Why is it important to differentiate a verdict from a judgment?

9. What are the primary differences between indeterminate sentencing schemes and determinate ones?

10. What is a presentence investigation report? What information is usually contained in one? Why are these reports important to the criminal sentencing process?

11. Compare and contrast the three major ways in which a criminal defendant can obtain relief from the courts after a verdict of guilty.

abandoned property Property whose owner has voluntarily discarded it, left it behind, or has otherwise relinquished his or her interest in it and no longer retains a reasonable expectation of privacy with regard to it. Law enforcement officers may lawfully seize abandoned property without a warrant or probable cause because the Fourth Amendment does not apply.

abuse of discretion Discretionary decisions of courts of original jurisdiction are reviewed on appeal using the *abuse of discretion* standard. This highly deferential standard of review invalidates a discretionary decision only if it can be shown to have been made in an arbitrary, capricious, or unreasonable manner. See **standard of review**.

accessible to the public exception Any person may intercept an electronic communication made through a system "that is configured so that . . . [the] communication is readily accessible to the general public." This section allows for access to public websites, but prohibits access to websites protected from public access via usernames and passwords.

acquisition phase (encoding phase) Memory recording phase in which sensory data, as perceived by the individual, are encoded in the appropriate areas of the cerebral cortex.

acquittal A judgment of a court that the defendant is not guilty of the offense for which he or she has been tried. It is based on the verdict either of a jury or of a judicial officer in a bench trial. An acquittal on all charges is a final court disposition terminating criminal jurisdiction over the defendant.

actual authority A right, gained through ownership, possession, or permission, which empowers a person to do an act or grant permission for others to act with respect to property.

administrative law The rules and regulations promulgated by a governmental agency that is empowered through statutory law to make such rules.

administrative search A routine inspection of a home or business by governmental authorities responsible for determining compliance with various statutes and regulations (e.g., fire, health, safety, and housing codes).

admission An admission or acknowledgment of a fact by a person that tends to incriminate the person; it is not sufficient of itself to establish guilt of a crime. An admission, alone or in connection with other facts, that tends to show the existence of one or more, but not all, of the elements of a crime. See **confession**.

affiant The person swearing out an affidavit.

affidavit A written statement sworn to or affirmed before an officer authorized to administer an oath or affirmation. Unlike a deposition, an affidavit requires no notice to the adverse party or opportunity for cross-examination. In the criminal law, law enforcement officers and others use affidavits to provide information to a magistrate in order to establish probable cause for the issuance of an arrest warrant or a search warrant.

affirmative defense A defense, such as insanity or entrapment, in which the defendant bears the burden of persuasion to prove the existence of all elements of the defense.

aggrieved person A person who was a party to any intercepted wire or oral communication or a person against whom the interception was directed who may move to suppress the contents of or evidence derived from oral or wire intercepts that were obtained in violation of Title III in either a state or federal proceeding.

allocute, allocution Allocution is the process of meeting the requirement under Federal Rule of Criminal Procedure 11 that requires that a criminal defendant provide a "factual basis" for a plea of guilty. To allocute, the defendant must admit in open court to the conduct central to the criminality of crimes charged. This is accomplished at an allocution hearing, sometimes referred to as a *change of plea* proceeding.

allocution hearing The judicial proceeding at which a criminal defendant *allocutes* by giving a factual basis for a plea of guilty.

anticipatory search warrant A warrant to search a particular place for a particular seizable item that has not yet arrived there. The affidavit submitted in application for the warrant must establish probable cause that evidence of a certain crime will be located at a specific place in the future. If some triggering condition (other than the mere passage of time) is necessary for probable cause to search and seize to exist, then probable cause must also presently exist to believe the triggering condition will, in fact, occur.

antiforensics Computer tools for hiding, destroying, or counterfeiting the information on which digital forensics experts rely and, by extension, undermining the evidentiary reliability of that information.

apparent authority The appearance of being either the owner, lawful occupant, or legal agent of the owner of property such that, under the facts and circumstances apparent at a given time, a reasonable person would think that the person had the legal authority to act or grant permission to act with respect to that property.

appeal An application to or proceeding in an appellate court for review or rehearing of a judgment, decision, or order of a lower court or other tribunal in order to correct alleged errors or injustices or *plain errors*. Plain errors are those defects in a trial that so seriously affect the rights of the accused that a failure to correct them—even those that were not objected to at trial—would undermine the fundamental fairness of the trial and bring about a miscarriage of justice. See **harmless error doctrine**.

appeal of right When an appellate court is required by law to hear an appeal of a certain type of case.

appellant In appellate cases, the party bringing an appeal; also known as the *petitioner*.

appellate jurisdiction Lawful authority or power of a court to review a decision made by a lower court or to hear an appeal from a judgment of a lower court.

appellee The party responding to an appeal. Also called the *respondent*.

appurtenant Property that is incident to, belonging to, or going with the principal property. This includes buildings on the land (e.g., sheds) and other things attached to or annexed to the land that may be searched during the execution of a warrant for the search of the principal property. For example, a detached garage, even if not named in a warrant, can be searched as an appurtenant building to a house.

armspan (wingspan) The area into which an arrestee could reach to grab a weapon or destroy evidence. It is the area that is deemed to be within the arrestee's immediate control for purposes of the search incident to arrest exception. See **immediate control.**

arraignment The hearing before a court having jurisdiction in a criminal case in which the identity of the defendant is established, the defendant is informed of the charge and of his or her rights, and the defendant is required to enter a plea. The defendant's entering of a plea is the crucial distinguishing element of the arraignment.

arrest A seizure of a person in which the person is taken into governmental custody for the purpose of charging the person with a criminal offense (or, for juveniles, a delinquent act or status offense). See **show of authority.**

arrest warrant A written order issued by a magistrate or other proper judicial officer, upon probable cause for a particularly described offense, that directs a law enforcement officer to arrest a particular person described in the warrant by name or other unique characteristics.

attenuation doctrine An exception to the fruit of the poisonous tree doctrine that allows the admission of tainted evidence if that evidence was obtained in a manner that is sufficiently removed or "attenuated" from unconstitutional search or seizure, thereby rendering the evidence admissible at trial.

aural transfer An electronic transfer containing the human voice at any point between and including the point of origin and the point of reception, such as over telephone lines or via cellular telephone.

automatic companion rule A rule that allows a law enforcement officer to frisk the companion of an arrestee for weapons because of a concern for officer safety without any further justification.

automobile exception See *Carroll* doctrine.

bail To obtain the release from custody of an arrested or imprisoned person by pledging money or other property as a guarantee of the person's appearance in court at a specified date and time.

bailee, bailor A *bailee* is a person in possession of someone else's personal property with the lawful permission of the rightful owner—the *bailor*. A bailee of personal property may consent to a search of the property if he or she has full possession and control. In contrast, a bailee who has only mere custody of a bailor's property could not lawfully consent to a search of that property.

beeper A radio transmitter, usually battery operated, that emits periodic signals that can be picked up by a radio receiver.

bench trial A trial in which there is no jury and in which a judicial officer determines all issues of fact and law. Also known as a *nonjury trial*.

beyond a reasonable doubt The prosecutorial burden of proof. Because the accused is presumed innocent, the prosecution must prove all the elements of the crime(s) charged in its case beyond a reasonable doubt. If the prosecution fails to meet this burden of proof on any element, the defendant must be acquitted.

bill of attainder A special act of a legislature that declares a person or group of persons has committed a crime and imposes punishment without a court trial. Under our system of separation of powers, only courts may try a person for a crime or impose punishment for violation of the law. Article I, Section 9 of the U.S. Constitution restrains Congress from passing bills of attainder; Article I, Section 10 of the U.S. Constitution restrains the states.

Bill of Rights The first ten amendments to the U.S. Constitution added to guarantee basic individual liberties, including freedom of speech, freedom of the press, freedom of religion, and freedom to assemble and petition the government. The guarantees of the Bill of Rights originally applied only to acts of the federal government. By operation of the Fourteenth Amendment's Due Process Clause (added in 1868), all fundamental rights specified in the Bill of Rights have been selectively incorporated such that they are applicable to the states as well. See **selective incorporation**.

binds over If a magistrate finds probable cause to believe that a defendant committed an offense, then the magistrate binds over the defendant to the trial court for adjudication of the felony charges.

booking A police administrative procedure that officially records an arrest in a police register. Booking involves, at the minimum, recording the names of the person arrested and the officer making the arrest, and the time, place, circumstances of, and reason for the arrest. Sometimes booking also means other procedures that take place in the stationhouse after an arrest, such as fingerprinting or photographing the arrested person.

border searches A type of special needs search that allows law enforcement personnel at U.S. borders or their functional equivalents (e.g., international airline terminals, cruise ship terminals, or some other place where someone may be stopped for the first time upon entering the country) to conduct searches without any individualized suspicion without violating the Fourth Amendment, so long such searches are conducted reasonably.

burden of persuasion The duty to establish a particular issue or proposition by the quantity of evidence required by law (e.g., probable cause, preponderance of the evidence, clear and convincing evidence, or beyond a reasonable doubt). In criminal cases, the prosecution's burden of persuasion is to prove every element of the crime charged beyond a reasonable doubt.

burden of production The duty of the party presenting an issue or fact to produce or "come forward" with sufficient evidence to support a favorable finding on that issue or fact; also referred to as the *burden of coming forward*.

burden of proof A generic term that encompasses both the burdens of production and persuasion. See **burden of production** and **burden of persuasion**.

canine sniff (dog sniff) Search procedure in which a trained narcotics detection dog sniffs for illegal materials.

Carroll **doctrine** Sometimes referred to as the *automobile exception* to the search warrant requirement, this search and seizure doctrine originated in *Carroll v. United States*, 267 U.S. 132 (1925). It states that a warrantless search of a motor vehicle under exigent circumstances by a law enforcement officer who has probable cause to believe that the vehicle contains items subject to seizure is not unreasonable under the Fourth Amendment.

case-in-chief The portion of a trial or adversarial hearing in which a party presents evidence by calling and conducting the direct examination of witnesses.

challenge for cause A formal objection to a prospective juror based on the assumption that the juror cannot reach a fair and impartial verdict on the particular case. These may be *fact-partial challenges* (based on the person's background, opinions, biases, or personal knowledge of the facts of a case) or *principal challenges* (the prospective juror has personal knowledge of the participants in the case).

circumstantial evidence Indirect evidence that requires the trier of fact to reason through the evidence and infer the existence of some fact in dispute. If circumstantial evidence is believed, it requires additional inferences, and it may require the fact finder to examine a chain of evidence in order to accept the fact at issue.

citizen's arrest Under the common law rule in force in most states, a private citizen may arrest a person if the citizen (1) has probable cause to believe that the person has committed a felony or (2) actually witnessed a suspect commit or attempt to commit a misdemeanor. Law enforcement officers outside their territorial jurisdiction generally have the same authority as private citizens to arrest without a warrant.

civil rights Generally, the constitutionally guaranteed rights of a person by virtue of the person's status as a member of civil society, except those rights involving participation in the establishment, support, or management of the government.

clear and convincing evidence A higher level of proof than the preponderance of the evidence standard, yet it falls short of proof beyond a reasonable doubt. It is the standard of proof in some civil cases. It is also the level of proof to which a defendant in some criminal cases must establish an affirmative defense. If there is clear and convincing evidence, the trier of fact should be reasonably satisfied as to the existence of the fact, yet he or she may have some doubts.

clearly erroneous The standard of review that an appellate court applies to factual determinations made by a court of original jurisdiction. Under this deferential standard, an appellate court will not overturn any factual decisions made by the lower court unless the factual determinations are *clearly erroneous*. See **standard of review**.

closing argument A statement made by each party at the end of a trial, after all the evidence has been presented and the jury has been instructed. Each side recapitulates the facts and evidence it has presented and attempts to convince the judge or jury of the correctness of its position.

collateral estoppel doctrine An issue of ultimate fact that has once been determined by a valid and final judgment cannot again be litigated between the same parties in any future lawsuit.

common authority The authority that justifies third-party consent to search based on mutual use of the property by those who have joint access or control for most purposes. It may be based on *actual common authority* (the official legal capacity to grant consent to search the property over which someone has lawful access or control) or *apparent common authority* (someone whom police reasonably believe to possess actual common authority over the premises, but who, in fact, does not have such authority).

common law The system of law that originated and developed in England based on court decisions, custom, and usage rather than on written laws created by legislative enactment; judge-made law that evolves based on the principles of precedent and *stare decisis*.

competency In criminal procedure, a judicial determination that a criminal defendant understands his or her situation and has the intellectual wherewithal to stand trial or waive certain constitutional rights.

competency to stand trial Standard that requires defendants to have (1) a rational as well as factual understanding of the proceedings against them and (2) sufficient present ability to consult an attorney with a reasonable degree of rational understanding in order to assist in their own defense.

complaint A sworn written statement presented to a proper judicial officer alleging that a specified person has committed a specified crime and requesting prosecution.

compulsory process Coercive means, such as subpoenas and arrest warrants, used by courts to procure the attendance in court of persons wanted as witnesses or otherwise; the right of a criminal defendant as set forth in the Sixth Amendment to the U.S. Constitution to compel competent, material witnesses to appear in court and testify as part of the defense's case.

computer forensics The use of scientifically derived and proven methods toward the preservation, collection, validation, identification, analysis, interpretation, documentation, and presentation of digital evidence derived from digital sources for the purpose of facilitating or furthering the reconstruction of events found to be criminal.

computer trespasser exception An exception to the requirements of Title III in which victims of computer attacks by hackers may authorize law enforcement officials to intercept wire or electronic communications of a computer trespasser, if specific statutory requirements are satisfied.

concurrent jurisdiction When both the state and federal courts (or when two courts within the same court system) have original jurisdiction over the same matter.

confabulation The creation or substitution of false memories through later suggestion that incorrectly fills in the gaps in a person's memory.

confession A statement in which a person admits facts revealing his or her guilt as to all elements of a particular crime. See **admission**.

confidence malleability The "tendency for an eyewitness to become more or less confident in his or her identification as a function of events that occur after the identification."

confirmation bias The tendency to search for or interpret new information in a way that confirms one's preconceptions, and to avoid information and interpretations that contradict prior beliefs.

confrontation (1) The right of an accused person to come face to face with an adverse witness in court, to object to the testimony of the witness, and to cross-examine the witness. The Sixth Amendment to the U.S. Constitution guarantees the right of confrontation to defendants in federal criminal prosecutions. The Due Process Clause of the Fourteenth Amendment makes this Sixth Amendment guarantee applicable to the states. (2) Any presentation of a suspect to a victim or witness of a crime for the purpose of identifying the perpetrator of the crime. The term *confrontation* includes showups, lineups, and photo arrays.

Confrontation Clause The Sixth Amendment guarantee that accused persons have the right to confront hostile witnesses at their criminal trial.

consent search A search of a person's body, premises, or belongings conducted by a law enforcement officer after the person has given voluntary permission.

consent surveillance When one party to a communication consents to the interception of the communication, neither Title III nor the Fourth Amendment prevents the use of the communication in court against another party to the communication.

constitutional law (1) The study of foundational or basic laws of nation states and other political organizations. (2) The interpretation and application of the provisions of the U.S. Constitution, the constitutions of the states, or both.

container Any object capable of holding another object. A container thus includes "closed or open glove compartments, consoles or other receptacles located anywhere within the passenger compartment of a vehicle, as well as luggage, boxes, bags, clothing, and the like."

contemporaneous At the same time.

contraband Items whose possession is prohibited by law.

controlled delivery Monitoring a container known or reasonably believed to contain contraband while on its journey to the intended destination. A controlled delivery may qualify as a triggering event for the purposes of an anticipatory search warrant.

correctional system The variety of agencies, institutions, and programs that seek to punish or rehabilitate someone convicted of a crime using such tools as fines, probation, intermediate sanctions, incarceration, and parole. Also simply called *corrections*.

corroboration Additional information that confirms or strengthens the truthfulness of a fact or assertion to support or enhance its believability.

court of general jurisdiction A criminal court that has trial jurisdiction over all criminal offenses, including all felonies, and that may or may not hear appeals. It also has original jurisdiction over all felonies, and frequently has appellate jurisdiction over the decisions of a court of limited jurisdiction.

court of limited jurisdiction A criminal court whose trial jurisdiction is limited to adjudicating particular types of offenses, such as misdemeanors, traffic cases, drunk-driving cases, and so forth.

covert entry warrant A search warrant that specifically authorizes officers to enter unoccupied premises, search for specified evidence, and then leave—without seizing the evidence they find and without leaving a trace that an entry has been made. Officers usually photograph or videotape the evidence or otherwise document exactly what they saw and its exact location. However, under the USA PATRIOT Act, items discovered during the execution of a covert entry warrant may be seized if there is a "reasonable necessity for the seizure." The practice has come to be known as a "sneak-and-steal" search.

Crime Control Model The repression of criminal conduct through prevention and the swift apprehension, conviction, and punishment of offenders. One of Herbert Packer's two competing conceptualizations of value systems that function in the U.S. system of criminal justice. Compare to **Due Process Model**.

critical stages of criminal prosecutions Proceedings during criminal prosecutions at which the accused is entitled to the assistance of counsel because his or her substantial rights may be affected by what transpires. Critical stages include preindictment preliminary hearings, bail hearings, postindictment pretrial lineups, postindictment or postarraignment interrogations, arraignments, felony trials, misdemeanor trials involving a potential jail sentence, first appeals as a matter of right, juvenile delinquency proceedings involving potential confinement, sentencing hearings, and hearings regarding psychiatric examinations.

cross-examination The questioning of one party's witness by the opposing party after direct examination. The purpose of cross-examination is to discredit the witness's information and impeach the witness's credibility as a means of testing the accuracy of his or her testimony. The scope of cross-examination is usually limited to matters covered during direct examination.

cross-racial identification bias When people apply more lenient criteria in identifying someone of a different race or ethnicity and use more stringent requirements when identifying someone of the same racial or ethnic group. The result of cross-racial bias is a higher rate of false positive identifications, especially when a Caucasian eyewitness identifies an African American suspect.

cruel and unusual punishment Punishment that is prohibited under the Cruel and Unusual Punishment Clause of the Eighth Amendment. This clause limits the punishment that may be imposed on conviction of a crime in two ways: (1) by imposing substantive limits on what can be made criminal and punished as such and (2) by prohibiting certain kinds of punishment, such as torture and divestiture of citizenship, that violate "evolving standards of decency that mark the progress of a maturing society." *Trop v. Dulles*, 356 U.S. 86, 101 (1958).

curtilage The grounds and buildings immediately surrounding a dwelling that are used for domestic purposes in connection with the dwelling. Areas within the curtilage of a home are protected against unreasonable searches and seizures by the Fourth Amendment to the U.S. Constitution.

custodial arrest An arrest in which the person arrested is taken into custody and not merely given a ticket, citation, or notice to appear.

custodial interrogation The questioning (or its functional equivalent) of a person in custody.

custody (1) Legal or physical control of a person or thing; legal, supervisory, or physical responsibility for a person or thing. (2) A person is in custody for purposes of *Miranda v. Arizona* when the person is deprived of freedom of action in any significant way.

defamation A false, public statement of fact (not opinion) that injures or damages a person's reputation. Defamation in writing is called *libel*; spoken defamation is called *slander*. Defamation is a class of speech that is not protected by the First Amendment to the U.S. Constitution.

defendant The party against whom a criminal case is filed.

deliberate elicitation A statement made by a suspect when state officials create "a situation likely to induce . . . incriminating statements without the assistance of counsel."

demonstrative evidence Material that has no evidential value by itself. Rather, it serves as a visual or auditory aid to assist the fact finder in understanding the evidence. Charts, maps, videos, and courtroom demonstrations are forms of demonstrative evidence.

de novo Anew; starting over from the beginning. In appellate review of the decisions of courts of original jurisdiction, *de novo* grants no deference to the lower court. Rather, the appellate court reviews the legal issues presented in the case anew. See **trial de novo** and **standard of review**.

deposition A witness's out-of-court testimony taken under oath prior to trial and recorded or transcribed. Depositions are usually taken orally and require notice to the adverse party so that the adverse party may attend the deposition and cross-examine the witness. Depositions are used to preserve the testimony of a prospective witness who may be unable to attend or be prevented from attending a trial or hearing. A deposition may also be used as part of the discovery process to gain information about a case. Deposition testimony may be used to contradict or impeach the testimony of the deponent when the deponent later testifies as a witness at a hearing or trial. See **discovery**.

derivative evidence Tainted evidence that is directly derived from an unconstitutional search or seizure and is, therefore, inadmissible under the fruit of the poisonous tree doctrine unless one of the exceptions to that doctrine (e.g., attenuation, inevitable discovery, good faith, etc.) is applicable. Sometimes called *secondary evidence*.

determinate sentencing See **sentence/sentencing**.

direct evidence Firsthand evidence that does not require presumptions or inferences in order to establish a proposition of fact.

direct examination The initial examination of a witness in a trial by the party on whose behalf the witness is called. The attorney asks specific questions, and the witness is expected to give testimony favorable to the party calling the witness. See **cross-examination**.

discovery A procedure by which a party obtains a legal right to compel the opposing party to permit access to information in order to promote the orderly ascertainment of the truth during trial. Discovery in criminal cases usually involves allowing the moving party to obtain, inspect, copy, or photograph items within the possession or control of the opposing party. The process can also be used to compel access to witnesses for the purpose of conducting a deposition.

dismissal with prejudice Bars future prosecution on dismissed charges.

dismissal without prejudice Case dismissal with allowance for refiling at a later time.

DNA searches The term used to collectively describe the taking of DNA samples from criminal offenders, storing a genetic profile in a searchable database, and then comparing a genetic sample against the database of known exemplars.

double-blind administration An identification procedure in which neither the witness nor the person administering a lineup or photo array should know who the suspect is and who the foils are.

Double Jeopardy Clause A legal command of the Fifth Amendment to the U.S. Constitution that prohibits the same sovereign (e.g., the federal government or a state government) from prosecuting someone for the same offense after acquittal or conviction, and from imposing multiple punishments on someone for the same offense. See **dual sovereignty doctrine**.

downward departures See **sentencing departures**.

dual sovereignty doctrine The doctrine which provides that, "[w]hen a defendant in a single act violates the 'peace and dignity' of two sovereigns [e.g., two different state governments] by breaking the laws of each, he has committed two distinct 'offences.'" *Heath v. Alabama*, 474 U.S. 82, 88 (1985). Double jeopardy does not arise when a single act exposes a defendant to prosecution by two separate sovereigns, such as the federal government and a state government, or the governments of two different states.

Due Process Model Crime prevention through due process of law vis-à-vis formal, adjudicative, adversary fact-finding processes that are concerned with legal guilt. One of Herbert Packer's two competing conceptualizations of value systems that function in the U.S. system of criminal justice. Compare to **Crime Control Model**.

due process of law The legal notion, guaranteed by the Fifth and Fourteenth Amendments to the U.S. Constitution, that laws and legal procedures will conform to the rules and principles established in our system of justice for the enforcement and protection of individual rights. Due process is traditionally associated with the principles of adequate and fair notice and the right to be heard. It also protects against the exercise of arbitrary governmental power, and guarantees equal and impartial dispensation of law according to the settled course of judicial proceedings or in accordance with fundamental principles of distributive justice.

due process revolution The U.S. Supreme Court's ideological shift during the 1960s civil rights era toward "constitutionalizing" criminal procedure with a focus on individual rights and liberties.

effective assistance of counsel The principle that merely providing the accused with an attorney is not enough; that attorney must defend the accused in a reasonably competent manner. The Sixth Amendment's guarantee of the right to counsel to assist the accused in all criminal prosecutions is meaningless if counsel's representation falls below an objective standard of reasonableness.

electronic communication Any transfer of signs, signals, writing, images, sounds, data, or intelligence of any nature transmitted in whole or in part by a wire, radio, electromagnetic, photoelectronic, or photo-optical system that affects interstate or foreign commerce but does not include (1) any wire communication or oral communication, (2) any communication made through a tone-only paging device, (3) any communication from a tracking device, or (4) electronic funds transfer information stored by a financial institution in a communications system used for the electronic storage and transfer of funds.

Electronic Communications Privacy Act of 1986 (ECPA) A statute providing for certain privacy rights with respect to electronic communications.

electronic surveillance Searches conducted using wiretaps, bugs, or other electronic or mechanical devices to overhear conversations or obtain other kinds of information.

emergency See **exigent circumstances**.

eminent domain The power of the government to take private property for "public use" so long as the owner of such property is fairly compensated for the seizure of his or her property.

en banc A special session of a court in which all the judges of the court participate, as opposed to a session presided over by a single judge or a mere quorum of judges.

enemy combatants Designation given to individuals who were captured by the United States on suspicion of being involved in terrorist activities by being a part of or supporting Taliban or al-Qaeda forces, or associated forces that are engaged in hostilities against the United States or its coalition partners. The USA PATRIOT Act apparently authorized

the indefinite detention of enemy combatants who are not citizens of the United States, including permanent resident aliens living in the United States, if the U.S. attorney general certifies that he or she has "reasonable grounds to believe" that the noncitizen has engaged in "terrorist activity." The constitutionality of the indefinite detention of enemy combatants has yet to be decided by the U.S. Supreme Court.

equal protection of the laws The Fourteenth Amendment to the U.S. Constitution provides, in part, that no state shall "deny to any person within its jurisdiction the equal protection of the laws." This constitutional guarantee prohibits states from denying any person or class of persons the same protection of the law enjoyed by other persons or other classes of persons in similar circumstances. Thus, no state may adopt laws, regulations, or policies that establish categories of people receiving unequal treatment on the basis of race, religion, or national origin. No clause in the U.S. Constitution specifically guarantees that equal protection applies to actions of the federal government, but the federal government is prohibited from denying a person equal protection of federal laws by judicial interpretations of the Due Process Clause of the Fifth Amendment.

Establishment Clause The provision in the First Amendment to the U.S. Constitution that provides that neither Congress nor a state legislature (by virtue of the Fourteenth Amendment) may "make any law respecting an establishment of religion." This means that no legislature may enact a law that establishes an official church that all Americans must accept and support, or to whose tenets all must subscribe, or that favors one church over another.

estimator variables Variables that affect the memory of a witness and over which the criminal justice system has no control. Estimator variables include *event factors* (e.g., time, lighting conditions, changes in visual adaptation to light and dark, duration of the event, speed and distance involved, and the presence or absence of violence) and *witness factors* (e.g., stress, fear, physical limitation on sensory perception—poor eyesight, hearing impairment, alcohol or drug intoxication—expectations, age, and gender).

event factors Memory and perception estimator variables such as "time, lighting conditions, changes in visual adaptation to light and dark, duration of the event, speed and distance involved, and the presence or absence of violence."

evidence Anything offered to a court or jury through the medium of witnesses, documents, exhibits, or other objects to demonstrate or ascertain the truth of facts at issue in a case; the means by which facts are proved or disproved in court. *Direct evidence* is firsthand evidence that does not require a presumption to be made or an inference to be drawn in order to establish a proposition of fact. *Circumstantial evidence* is indirect evidence of some fact in dispute that requires the trier of fact to presume or infer the existence of some fact to reach some logical conclusion. Subtypes of evidence include *testimonial evidence* (oral testimony given under oath), *real* or *physical evidence* (tangible objects that have evidentiary value), *scientific evidence* (the formal results of forensic investigatory techniques), and *demonstrative evidence* (visual or auditory aids created for use at trial to assist the trier of fact in understanding evidence). See also **judicial notice**.

excessive force The use of more force than is reasonably necessary to make an arrest, prevent an escape, stop a fleeing suspect, subdue someone in lawful custody, or to lawfully defend oneself, another person, or property. The use of excessive force gives rise to both criminal and civil liability for assault, battery, and other crimes against the person (including homicide and attempted homicide charges), as well as for civil rights lawsuits for deprivations of constitutional rights under the Fourth, Fifth, Eighth, and Fourteenth Amendments to the U.S. Constitution.

excludable time Types of delays that are not counted toward the time periods specified in the Speedy Trial Act.

exclusionary rule A rule developed by the U.S. Supreme Court that states that evidence obtained in violation of a person's constitutional rights by law enforcement officers or agents will be inadmissible in a criminal prosecution against the person whose rights were violated. Subject to several exceptions, the exclusionary rule usually also prohibits the introduction of derivative evidence, both tangible and testimonial, that is the product of the primary evidence or that is otherwise acquired as an indirect result of an unlawful search or seizure.

exclusive jurisdiction Cases that are required to be adjudicated in a particular court. For example, federal courts have exclusive jurisdiction over bankruptcy, patent, and copyright actions; thus, state courts may not hear such disputes.

exculpatory evidence Any evidence that may be favorable to the defendant at trial either by tending to cast doubt on the defendant's guilt or by tending to mitigate the defendant's culpability, thereby potentially reducing the defendant's sentence. Under *Brady v. Maryland*, 373 U.S. 83, 87 (1963), "the suppression by the prosecution of evidence favorable to an accused upon request violates due process where the evidence is material either to guilt or punishment, irrespective of the good faith or bad faith of the prosecution."

exigent circumstances Serious situations developing suddenly and unexpectedly that demand immediate action rather than conformity with the usual requirements of law.

They usually include emergency situations that have given rise to imminent danger to life, serious damage to property, imminent escape of a suspect, or the imminent destruction of evidence.

***ex parte, in camera* review** When a judge reviews relevant information on his or her own, without all of the information being disclosed to opposing counsel or being revealed in open court.

ex post facto From Latin, meaning "after the fact." An *ex post facto* law is "one which makes that criminal which was not so at the time the action was performed, or which increases the punishment, or, in short, in relation to the offense or its consequences, alters the situation of a party to his disadvantage." *Lindsey v. Washington*, 301 U.S. 397 (1937). *Ex post facto* laws are prohibited by Article I, Sections 9 and 10, of the U.S. Constitution and similar provisions of state constitutions.

express waiver A waiver from a suspect who acknowledges that he or she is aware of his or her *Miranda* rights and voluntarily elects to give up those rights with knowledge of the consequences of doing so.

extradition The surrender of an accused or convicted person by the state to which the person has fled (the asylum state), to the state with jurisdiction to try or punish the person (the demanding state), upon demand of the latter state, so that the person may be dealt with according to its laws. The governor of the demanding state issues an extradition warrant. The delivery of the person to the demanding state occurs under the executive or judicial authorization of the asylum state. The U.S. Constitution, Article IV, Section 2, requires the officials of a state to arrest and return an accused fugitive to another state for trial upon demand of the governor of the latter state. Most states have adopted the Uniform Criminal Extradition Act, which provides uniform extradition procedures among the states.

fact-partial challenge See **challenge for cause**.

federalism The constitutional division of power between the state and federal governments in which certain powers are granted the federal government concerning national matters, whereas all other governmental powers are reserved for the states.

felony In general, a crime of a more serious nature than those designated as misdemeanors. Felonies are distinguished from misdemeanors by place of punishment and possible duration of punishment, as defined by statute. The statutory definition of felony may differ between states and between the federal government and various states. Typically, a felony is a crime with a possible punishment of death or

imprisonment in a state or federal prison facility for a period of one year or more.

fighting words Words that are so highly inflammatory they are likely to provoke the average person to retaliation and thereby cause a breach of the peace. Such speech is not protected by the First Amendment to the U.S. Constitution.

flight When a suspect runs away, hides, or attempts to escape from the police.

flight risk Whether a defendant is likely to flee before trial. If flight risk is determined to be high, then a defendant may be denied bail and held in custody pending the disposition of the case.

foils, fillers The people who appear in a lineup or photo array other than the suspect.

Foreign Intelligence Surveillance Act (FISA) A statute enacted by the U.S. Congress that authorizes and regulates the electronic surveillance of foreign powers and their agents within the United States, as well as any individual or group that is not linked to a foreign government but who "engages in international terrorism or activities in preparation therefore." FISA permits federal agents to conduct electronic surveillance and physical searches for national defense purposes. Unlike normal search warrants or Title III intercept orders, FISA warrants do not require a showing of probable cause to believe that a crime has been or is being committed. Rather, FISA only requires probable cause that the surveillance is of an authorized person or group for purposes relating to the gathering of foreign intelligence or preventing terrorism. Additional findings, however, are required if the targets of the investigation are U.S. citizens or lawful resident aliens. FISA warrants are usually issued by Foreign Intelligence Surveillance Court (FISC), although the U.S. attorney general may authorize FISA surveillance for periods up to one year without FISC approval under certain circumstances. See **Title III of the Omnibus Crime Control and Safe Streets Act of 1968.**

Foreign Intelligence Surveillance Court (FISC) Special Article III court created by Congress to review FISA applications.

forgetting curve The phenomenon in which memory declines with the passage of time but not at a linear rate. Rather, memory tends to fade fairly rapidly immediately following a stressful event.

Franks hearing An adversarial judicial proceeding named after the U.S. Supreme Court's decision in *Franks v. Delaware,* 438 U.S. 154 (1978). It holds that a court must conduct an evidentiary hearing to determine the validity of a warrant after a criminal defendant has made a *prima facie* showing

that an affidavit submitted in support of the warrant contained material statements that were deliberately false or demonstrated reckless disregard for the truth. If the judge concludes such misconduct occurred, the offending material must be severed or stricken from the warrant application. If the information remaining after severance still establishes probable cause, then the warrant will be upheld. If, however, the information remaining in the affidavit after the offending data is set aside fails to establish probable cause, then "the search warrant must be voided and the fruits of the search excluded to the same extent as if probable cause was lacking on the face of the affidavit." 483 U.S. at 155–56.

Free Exercise Clause The provision in the First Amendment to the U.S. Constitution that provides that neither Congress nor a state legislature (by virtue of the Fourteenth Amendment) may enact any law that "prohibits the free exercise" of religion. This clause allows people to practice freely their religion so long as those practices do not conflict with otherwise valid laws.

fresh pursuit Immediate pursuit of a fleeing criminal with intent to apprehend him or her. Fresh pursuit generally refers to the situation in which a law enforcement officer attempts to make a valid arrest of a criminal within the officer's jurisdiction, and the criminal flees outside the jurisdiction to avoid arrest, with the officer immediately pursuing. An arrest made in fresh pursuit will be legal if the pursuit was started promptly and maintained continuously. Many states have adopted the Uniform Act on Fresh Pursuit to govern fresh pursuits that take an arresting officer into a neighboring state.

frisk A pat-down or limited search of a person's body and clothing for weapons conducted for the protection of the police officer when the officer has reasonable, articulable suspicion that he or she is dealing with an armed and dangerous individual.

fruit of the poisonous tree doctrine The doctrine that evidence is inadmissible in court if it was obtained indirectly by exploitation of some prior unconstitutional police activity (e.g., an illegal arrest or search or a coerced confession). The evidence indirectly obtained is sometimes called *derivative evidence.*

Frye test A common law test for the admissibility of scientific evidence that required the party seeking to introduce the evidence to prove that the scientific principle at issue was "generally accepted in the relevant scientific community."

full search of the arrestee's body A full search usually allows for the search and seizure of evidence on the body—for example, relatively nonintrusive seizures, such as obtaining hair samples and fingernail clippings, and seizures of hair samples from the head, chest, and pubic area of a person incident to arrest for murder or sexual assault. More intrusive searches and seizures, such as obtaining blood samples or comparable intrusions into the body, require stricter limitations.

fundamental rights Those rights that are fundamental to U.S. notions of liberty and justice, such as the freedom of speech, the freedom of religion, the freedom to travel, the right to access the courts, and the right to vote. See **selective incorporation** and **standard of review**.

furtive gestures Secretive or evasive behaviors that contribute to a law enforcement officer's determination of reasonable, articulable suspicion to conduct a stop or frisk.

general warrant A warrant that fails to meet the Fourth Amendment's particularity requirement because it is too general.

Geneva Conventions A body of international laws that has developed over the centuries to set rules for the treatment of civilians, the sick, the injured and wounded, and prisoners of war (POWs) captured on the battlefield in war time that is separate and distinct from the treatment of criminals.

good-faith exception An exception to the exclusionary rule for illegal searches conducted in good faith. Under this exception, whenever a law enforcement officer acting with objective good faith has obtained a search warrant from a detached and neutral judge or magistrate and acted within its scope, evidence seized pursuant to the warrant will not be excluded, even though the warrant is later determined to be invalid. The good-faith exception has been extended to protect police who acted in good-faith reliance upon a statute (subsequently found invalid) that authorized warrantless administrative searches.

GPS (global positioning system) A satellite-based system consisting of a network of satellites orbiting the Earth that emit precise microwave signals such that a GPS-enabled receiver can determine the location, speed, direction, and time of a vehicle or container that is equipped with a GPS tracking device.

grand jury A jury, usually composed of sixteen to twenty-three persons, selected according to law and sworn in, whose duty is to receive criminal complaints, hear the evidence put forth by the prosecution and find indictments when it is satisfied that there is probable cause that an accused person has committed a crime and should be brought to trial. Grand juries may also investigate criminal activity generally and investigate the conduct of public agencies and officials. In many states, all felony charges must be considered by a grand jury before filing in the trial court. Unlike a trial jury, which hears a case in order to render a verdict of guilty or not guilty, a grand jury decides only whether there is sufficient evidence to cause a person to be brought to trial for a crime.

habeas corpus The name of a writ issued by a court and directed to a person detaining or confining another (usually the superintendent of a confinement facility) commanding him or her to bring the body of the person detained before a judicial officer and to show cause whether the detention is legal. Article I, Section 9, Clause 2, of the U.S. Constitution provides that "[t]he privilege of the Writ of Habeas Corpus shall not be suspended, unless when in Cases of Rebellion or Invasion the public safety may require it." The right of a person to the writ depends on the legality of the detention and not on the person's guilt or innocence.

harmless error doctrine The principle that an appellate court should not overturn a criminal conviction for minor errors that had little, if any, likelihood of having contributed to the ultimate result of the trial. In contrast, harmful errors—especially plain error—are those that likely contributed to a conviction and therefore require the overturning of a conviction in order to comport with the requirements of due process and the Sixth Amendment guarantee of a fair trial. See **appeal**.

harmless errors Trial errors that likely contributed to a conviction and therefore require the overturning of a conviction in order to comport with the requirements of due process and the Sixth Amendment guarantee of a fair trial. See **harmless error doctrine**.

hearsay evidence Evidence of a statement made other than by a witness testifying at a trial or hearing offered to prove the truth of the matter asserted. The statement may be oral or written, or may be nonverbal conduct intended as a substitute for words.

hearsay rule Simply stated, the rule that hearsay evidence is inadmissible. The basis of the hearsay rule is that the credibility of the person making a statement is the most important factor in determining the truth of the statement. If a statement is made out of court, there is no opportunity to cross-examine the person making the statement or to observe the person's demeanor. Without these methods of determining the truth of the statement, the statement may not be admitted into evidence. Many exceptions to the hearsay rule allow the admission of hearsay evidence for various reasons of trustworthiness of the evidence and practical necessity.

hot pursuit The immediate pursuit by a law enforcement officer of a person into a house or other constitutionally protected area in response to an emergency. Examples of emergencies that will justify a hot pursuit are escape of a fleeing felon or other dangerous person, avoidance of arrest by a person suspected of a crime, and prevention of the destruction or concealment of evidence. Once inside the house or other constitutionally protected area, officers may search the premises if necessary to alleviate the emergency; any items of evidence observed lying open to view may be legally seized under the plain view doctrine.

houses A term that includes homes (whether owned, rented, or leased) and any other place in which a person is staying or living, permanently or temporarily. Examples of protected living quarters are hotel and motel rooms, apartments, rooming and boarding house rooms, and even hospital rooms. The term also extends to places of business. This protection is limited, however, to areas or sections that are not open to the public.

hung jury The term used to describe the situation when a petit jury is unable to reach a verdict.

immediate control Personal property and containers that are not immediately associated with an arrestee's body but are close enough that the arrestee could reach to grab a weapon or destroy evidence.

immunity Freedom or exemption from prosecution granted to a witness to compel answers to questions or the production of evidence, which the witness might otherwise refuse to do on the grounds of the Fifth Amendment privilege against self-incrimination. Two types of immunity that may be granted are transactional immunity and use immunity. Under *transactional immunity,* a witness may be compelled to testify despite the privilege against self-incrimination, but the witness is protected from any prosecution for crimes to which his or her compelled testimony relates. Under *use immunity,* a witness may be compelled to testify despite the privilege against self-incrimination, but the witness is protected from the use of the compelled testimony and any evidence derived from it. Use immunity would still permit prosecution for related offenses based upon evidence derived from independent sources. A witness's failure to answer questions or produce evidence within the subject of the investigation as ordered by the court constitutes contempt of court.

impeaching When a witness's testimony at trial is contradicted, often by testimony the witness has given during deposition.

implied waiver When a suspect knows of his or her *Miranda* rights and voluntarily waives them without doing so expressly.

impound To take a vehicle, document, or other object into the custody of the law or of a court or law enforcement agency for safekeeping or examination.

incarceration Imprisonment in a correctional facility. A *jail* is typically a county-run detention center designed to hold inmates for short periods of time, typically up to a maximum of one year. A *prison* is a correctional facility designed to hold prisoners for long periods of time, typically for periods of at least one year and up to the time that a prisoner is released, dies, or is executed. See **correctional system/ corrections**.

incommunicado interrogation The interrogation of a suspect cut off from the rest of the world in a police-dominated atmosphere. It often results in self-incriminating statements being made without full warnings of constitutional rights.

incomplete sensory acquisition When a person fails to perceive all of the relevant stimuli during a critical incident due to stress, distraction, or otherwise. This can lead to identification errors since gaps in memory may be filled-in with details that fit logically, but may be inaccurate.

independent source Evidence that is not causally linked to unconstitutional governmental activity is admissible so long as the challenged evidence is first discovered during lawful police activity or, alternatively, although initially discovered unlawfully, is later obtained lawfully in a manner independent of the original discovery.

independent source doctrine An exception to the fruit of the poisonous tree doctrine that allows the admission of tainted evidence if that evidence was also obtained through a source wholly independent of the primary constitutional violation.

indeterminate sentencing See **sentencing**.

indictment A formal written accusation submitted by a grand jury to a court, alleging that a specified person has committed a specific offense. An indictment, like an information, is usually used to initiate a felony prosecution. In some jurisdictions, all felony accusations must be by indictment; in others, felony trials will ordinarily be initiated by the filing of an information by a prosecutor.

inevitable discovery doctrine A variation of the independent source doctrine allowing the admission of tainted evidence if it would inevitably have been discovered in the normal course of events. Under this exception, the prosecution must establish by a preponderance of the evidence that, even though the evidence was actually discovered as the result of a constitutional violation, the evidence would ultimately or inevitably have been discovered by lawful means, for example, as the result of the predictable and routine behavior of a law enforcement agency, some other agency, or a private person.

inference A permissible conclusion or deduction that the trier of fact may reasonably make based on the facts that have been established by the evidence, but the trier of fact is not required to do so.

informant A person who gives information to the police regarding criminal activity.

information A formal, written accusation submitted to a court by a prosecutor, without the approval or intervention of a grand jury, alleging that a specified person has committed a specific offense. An information is similar in nature and content to an indictment and serves as an alternative to the indictment in some jurisdictions to initiate usually felony prosecutions. Some jurisdictions initiate felony prosecutions only through indictment; others allow use of the information only after the defendant has waived an indictment.

initial appearance The first appearance of an accused person in the first court having jurisdiction over his or her case. Its primary purpose is to ensure that an arrest was supported by probable cause.

instruction A direction or explanation given by a trial judge to a jury informing its members of the law applicable to the case before them. Attorneys for both sides normally furnish the judge with suggested instructions.

intercept Aural or other acquisition of the contents of any wire, electronic, or oral communication through the use of any electronic, mechanical, or other device.

interlocutory appeals Rare provisional appeals from a ruling on a matter of law (such as on an important pretrial motion) that is in doubt and needs to be answered by an appellate court in order for trial to proceed without causing irreparable harm to a case or party.

intermediate courts of appeals In the hierarchical structure of courts, a rank higher than trial courts of original jurisdiction and below the court of last resort.

intermediate sanctions A range of criminal sanctions that fall short of total incarceration but are more stringent than probation. Sanctions include house arrest, electronic monitoring, or required living in a community-based correctional facility such as a halfway house, a boot camp, a work furlough camp, and so on. See **correctional system**.

intermediate scrutiny Asks whether a governmental classification is substantially related to achieving an important governmental interest. Intermediate scrutiny is used to adjudicate Equal Protection Clause issues that involve quasi-suspect classifications. See **standard of review**.

interrogation The questioning (or its functional equivalent) of a person suspected of a crime with the intent of eliciting incriminating admissions from the person. Volunteered statements, questions directed at clarifying a suspect's statement, brief, routine questions, spontaneous questions, and questions necessary to protect the safety of the police and public are not considered interrogation for purposes of *Miranda*.

inventory A routine administrative, custodial procedure made for the purpose of creating an inventory of a vehicle's contents.

inventory search The routine practice of police departments of securing and recording the contents of a lawfully impounded vehicle. This is done to protect the vehicle owner's property while it remains in custody, and to protect the police from potential danger and from claims or disputes over lost or stolen property.

items subject to seizure Items for which a search warrant may be issued. Federal Rule of Criminal Procedure 41(c) specifies that "[a] warrant may be issued for any of the following: (1) evidence of a crime; (2) contraband, fruits of crime, or other items illegally possessed; (3) property designed for use, intended for use, or used in committing a crime; or (4) a person to be arrested or a person who is unlawfully restrained." Most states have similar rules.

judgment The final, authoritative determination or decision of a court upon a matter within its jurisdiction. Judgments include a court's decision of conviction or acquittal of a person charged with a crime, a final court order, the issuance of a writ, or the imposition of a criminal sentence.

judicial notice A process that excuses a party from having to introduce evidence in order to prove a fact because a court determines that the fact is commonly known in the community without the need for formal proof.

judicial review The power of courts to invalidate acts of the legislative or executive branches upon a judicial determination that such acts violate a provision of the U.S. Constitution.

jurisdiction (1) The territory, subject matter, or person over which lawful authority may be exercised by a court or other justice agency, as determined by statute or constitution. For example, criminal cases are not within the jurisdiction of the probate court. (2) The jurisdiction of a court, more specifically, is the lawful authority or power to hear or act on a case or question and to pass and enforce judgment on it.

jury A body of persons, selected and sworn according to law, to inquire into certain matters of fact and to render a verdict or true answer based on evidence presented before it. Also referred to as a *petit jury*. See **grand jury**.

jury nullification The power of a jury to acquit regardless of the strength of the evidence against a defendant. Nullification usually occurs when the defendant is particularly sympathetic, or when the defendant is prosecuted for violating an unpopular law.

jury panel The prospective jurors for cases. See **venire**.

jury trial A trial in which a jury is the trier of fact responsible for making factual findings such as whether a defendant is guilty of a crime.

justice of the peace See **magistrate**.

knock and announce Law enforcement officers must knock and announce their presence, authority, and purpose before entering premises to execute a search or arrest warrant, unless permission was granted to execute a no-knock warrant. This rule flows from the Fourth Amendment's requirement of reasonableness. As a result of the Supreme Court's decision in *Hudson v. Michigan*, evidence obtained following a knock-and-announce violation is no longer excluded from trial. (Note, however, that the police officer may be subject to a civil lawsuit or an internal disciplinary procedure for failure to comply with the knock-and-announce rule.)

law Body of rules enacted by public officials in a legitimate manner and backed by the force of the state.

lawful custodial arrest When law enforcement takes a suspect into custody in accordance with the law. It is one requirement before police may conduct a search incident to arrest.

limited search incident to detention When a law enforcement officer conducts a limited, warrantless search of a person merely detained for investigation.

lineup A confrontation (definition 2) involving the presentation of several persons, which may or may not include the person suspected of committing a crime, to a victim or witness of the crime for the purpose of identifying the perpetrator.

litigants The parties involved in a specific case.

magistrate A judicial officer of a court of limited jurisdiction or with limited or delegated authority. A magistrate issues arrest warrants, search warrants, and summonses; sets bail; orders release on bail; and conducts arraignments and preliminary examinations of persons charged with serious crimes. A magistrate may also have limited authority to try minor cases or to dispose of cases on a guilty plea.

malleable characteristics Facially distinctive characteristics of a suspect that are easily changed by wearing a disguise or by altering hair style, hair color, the presence or absence of facial hair, the wearing of glasses, and so on.

mandatory appellate jurisdiction When an appellate court holds the appeal of right for a case.

mandatory sentences Legislatively determined sentences that require a defendant to serve a statutorily set minimum period of incarceration if convicted of a particular offense.

memory The unconscious process of acquiring, storing, retaining, and recalling past experiences.

mere suspicion A hunch or the feeling of intuition for which there is no proof.

minimization requirements Title III of the Omnibus Crime Control and Safe Streets Act of 1968 requires authorized interceptions of electronic communication to be conducted in a manner that minimizes the interception of communications that are not specifically related to the purpose of the Title III intercept warrant. These efforts must be objectively reasonable under the circumstances.

***Miranda* warning** The warning the law enforcement officers must give to those in custody before interrogation begins regarding suspects' rights to remain silent and right to counsel under the Fifth Amendment.

misdemeanor In general, a crime of less serious nature than those designated as felonies. In jurisdictions that recognize the felony–misdemeanor distinction, a misdemeanor is any crime that is not a felony. Misdemeanors are usually punished by fine or by incarceration in a local confinement facility rather than a state prison or penitentiary. The maximum period of confinement that may be imposed for a misdemeanor is defined by statute and is usually less than one year.

mosaic theory A theory used to support the rationale that GPS surveillance requires probable cause and a warrant because such technology provides such a "detailed patchwork of information" that it reveals a mosaic of an individual's life—a profile not simply of where he goes but also of his associations—the implications of which conjure the protections of the First Amendment as well as the Fourth.

motion An oral or written request made to a court at any time before, during, or after court proceedings, asking the court to make a specified finding, decision, or order. In criminal proceedings, the prosecution, the defense, or the court itself can make a motion.

motion for judgment of acquittal A motion made by the defense in a criminal case arguing that no reasonable juror could possibly conclude that guilt was proven beyond a reasonable doubt. If the judge agrees and grants the motion, the trial ends and retrial is barred by double jeopardy.

motion to suppress A motion made by defendants who believe they are aggrieved by either an unlawful search and seizure or an unlawfully obtained admission or confession. The purpose of a motion to suppress is to enable the defendant to invoke the exclusionary rule and prevent the use of illegally obtained evidence at trial and to enable the court to resolve the issue of the legality of a search and seizure or confession without interrupting the trial.

no-knock warrant A warrant that specifically authorizes law enforcement personnel to enter premises and execute the warrant without first knocking and announcing their authority and purpose. For such a warrant to issue, reasonable, articulable suspicion must exist for believing that compliance with the knock-and-announce rule would result in the destruction of evidence or in some harm to the executing officer or others.

nolo contendere From Latin, meaning "I do not wish to contest." A defendant's plea to a criminal charge in which the defendant states that he or she does not contest the charge, but neither admits guilt nor claims innocence. A plea of *nolo contendere* subjects the defendant to the same legal consequences as a guilty plea.

nonjury trial See **bench trial**.

not guilty by reason of insanity A plea that a defendant may enter at an arraignment, which seeks to excuse the defendant's criminal acts on the grounds that severe mental illness prevented the defendant from knowing the nature and quality of his or her actions or, alternatively, prevented the defendant from appreciating the wrongfulness of his or her acts.

obscene, obscenity Indecent or profane materials that are not protected by the First Amendment to the U.S. Constitution. When examined as a whole by an average person applying contemporary community standards, they appeal to the prurient interest by depicting sexual conduct in a patently offensive way and lack serious literary, artistic, political, or scientific value.

open fields The portions of a person's premises lying outside the curtilage of his or her home or business and therefore not protected by the Fourth Amendment of the U.S. Constitution.

opening statement The part of a trial before the presentation of evidence in which the attorney for each party gives an outline of what that party intends to prove by the evidence it will present. The primary purpose of the opening statement is to acquaint the judge and jury in a general way with the nature of the case.

oral communication Any words spoken by a person, under the expectation that this communication will not be subject to interception. See **electronic communication**.

original jurisdiction Jurisdiction of a court or administrative agency to hear or act upon a case from its beginning and to pass judgment on the law and the facts.

pardon A form of executive clemency in which a person convicted of a crime is legally "forgiven" and his or her sentence is commuted.

parole The conditional release of an incarcerated prisoner before his or her sentence term expires, and which requires the parolee to be supervised by a parole officer. See **correctional system; probation**.

particularity The constitutional mandate of the Fourth Amendment that warrants (and affidavits or applications for warrants) must describe very specifically "the place to be searched and the persons or things to be seized." Failure to comply with the level of specificity required to satisfy the particularity requirement can result in judicial denial for an application for a warrant. A warrant that was erroneously granted in the absence of particularity can later be invalidated, thereby jeopardizing the search(es) or seizure(s) conducted pursuant to the warrant. See **general warrant; good-faith exception**.

pat-down See **frisk**.

perception The total mix of sensory signals received from one's basic senses and then processed by an individual at any one time.

pen register A device that records outgoing addressing information (e.g., numbers dialed from a particular, monitored telephone). Because such a device does not intercept a "communication" per se, Title III of the Omnibus Crime Control and Safe Streets Act of 1968 does not apply to the use of pen registers.

peremptory challenge A formal objection to a prospective juror for which no reason need be given. The judge will automatically dismiss a juror to whom a peremptory challenge is made so long as the peremptory challenge was not exercised in a discriminatory manner that violates the Equal Protection Clause of the Fourteenth Amendment to the U.S. Constitution. The number of peremptory challenges available to each party is limited by statute or court rule.

petitioner In appellate cases, the party bringing an appeal; also known as the *appellant*.

petition for a writ of *certiorari* When a party seeking review of a lower court's decision asks the appellate court to exercise its discretionary appellate jurisdiction. This formal brief sets forth the reasons why the court should accept jurisdiction. If the high court decides to accept discretionary appellate jurisdiction and thereby review a decision of a lower court, it grants the petition and issues a writ of *certiorari*. See **writ of** *certiorari*.

petit jury See **jury**.

photographic lineup Presentation at one time of several photographs, including that of a suspect, to a victim of or witness to a crime. Also called a *photo array*.

photographic showup Presentation of a single photograph of a suspect to a victim of or witness to a crime.

physical trespass Occurs when police physically intrude upon or occupy private property—papers, effects, houses or persons—for the purpose of obtaining information or discovering information. These actions by police constitute a search under the Fourth Amendment.

plain error See **appeal**.

plain feel doctrine Same as plain touch doctrine.

plain touch doctrine If police are lawfully in a position from which they can feel an object, and if its incriminating character is immediately apparent (e.g., police have probable cause to believe the item they are feeling is incriminating in character), and if the officers have a lawful right of access to the object, they may seize it without a warrant. If, however, the police lack probable cause to believe that the object felt is subject to seizure without conducting some further search of the object, its seizure is not justified. See **plain view doctrine**.

plain view doctrine "[I]f police are lawfully in a position from which they view an object, if its incriminating character is apparent (e.g., police have probable cause to believe the item they are viewing is incriminating in character), and if the officers have a lawful right of access to the object, they may seize it without a warrant." *Minnesota v. Dickerson*, 508 U.S. 366, 375 (1993).

plea A defendant's formal answer in court to the charge contained in a complaint, information, or indictment that he or she is guilty or not guilty of the offense charged, or does not contest the charge. The pleas in a criminal case in most U.S. jurisdictions include guilty, not guilty, *nolo contendere*, and not guilty by reason of insanity.

plea bargain The exchange of prosecutorial or judicial concessions, or both, in return for a guilty plea. Common concessions include a lesser charge, the dismissal of other pending charges, a recommendation by the prosecutor for a reduced sentence, or a combination of these. The guilty plea arrived at through the process of plea bargaining is sometimes called a *negotiated plea*.

postevent misinformation effect Subsequent exposure to incorrect information can affect the way in which memories are retained.

prejudicial error A requirement for a successful appeal; the error must have been such that it could have affected the outcome of the case.

preliminary examination Same as **preliminary hearing**.

preliminary hearing The proceeding before a judicial officer in which three matters must be decided: whether a crime was committed, whether the crime occurred within the territorial jurisdiction of the court, and whether there is probable cause to believe that the defendant committed the crime. A chief purpose of the preliminary hearing is to protect the accused from an inadequately based prosecution in felony cases by making a judicial test of the existence of probable cause early in the proceedings.

preponderance of the evidence The standard of proof in most civil cases. It is commonly understood as proof that something is more likely than not.

presentence investigation (PSI) Probation officers generally conduct *presentence investigations* into a convicted defendant's prior criminal background; financial condition; educational, military, employment, and social history; relationships with family and friends; use of alcohol or controlled substances; and circumstances affecting the defendant's behavior, such as their mental status, that may assist the court in imposing sentence.

presentence investigation report (PSIR) The written results of the PSI, typically including a sentencing recommendation.

presumption A conclusion or deduction that the law requires the trier of fact to make in the absence of evidence to the contrary. The two presumptions that apply at the start of every criminal case are the *presumption of innocence* (i.e., that a criminal defendant is presumed innocent until proven guilty beyond a reasonable doubt), and the *presumption of sanity* (that a criminal defendant is presumed sane until the defendant proves that he or she was insane by the requisite burden of persuasion). See **inference**.

pretextual stop When a law enforcement officer uses some pretext—such as observing a burned-out tail light, cracked windshield, or failure to signal when changing lanes—to stop a suspect vehicle in the interest of investigating a crime more serious than the minor traffic or equipment violation.

***prima facie* evidence/case** A case established by prima facie evidence, and which will prevail until contradicted and overcome by other sufficient evidence. Prima facie evidence is defined as evidence sufficient to establish a given fact and which, if not rebutted or contradicted, will remain sufficient.

principal challenges See **challenge for cause**.

privacy See **reasonable expectation of privacy**.

probable cause The fair probability that someone is involved in criminal activity or that contraband or evidence of a crime will be found in a particular place. Probable cause is the level of proof required to justify the issuance of an arrest warrant or search warrant, all arrests made without a warrant, and most searches made without a warrant. Probable cause exists when the facts and circumstances within a person's knowledge and of which he or she has reasonably trustworthy information are sufficient in themselves to justify a person of reasonable caution and prudence in believing that something is true. It means something less than certainty but more than mere suspicion, speculation, or possibility. It has often been referred to as meaning "more likely than not."

probation The conditional freedom without imprisonment granted by a judicial officer to an alleged or adjudicated adult or juvenile offender, as long as the person meets certain conditions of behavior. See **correctional system; parole.**

probation revocation A formal process used to revoke an offender's probation and thereby subject the offender to a harsher criminal sentence, usually one involving some form of incarceration. This process involves a hearing in which the government must prove that a probationer has violated the terms of his or her probation. The burden of persuasion is typically preponderance of the evidence. Probation revocation proceedings are not technically part of the criminal prosecution process, so a probationer facing revocation has no constitutional right to be represented by court-appointed counsel at a revocation proceeding; state law, however, may grant such a right.

procedural criminal law Law that sets forth the mechanisms through which substantive criminal laws are administered—for example, the laws that regulate how police investigate crimes, such as searching for and seizing evidence and interrogating suspects.

procedural due process Rights recognized as within the protection of the Due Process Clause: the right to timely notice of a hearing or trial that adequately informs the accused of the charges against him or her; the right to present evidence in one's own behalf before an impartial judge or jury; the right to be presumed innocent until proven guilty by legally obtained evidence; and the right to have the verdict supported by the evidence presented at trial.

property Anything that is owned by a person or a legal entity. *Real property* concerns land and real estate, such as a house, apartment, or office building; *personal property* is everything else, such as cars, clothing, and jewelry.

property bond Type of bond in which a defendant (or friends or relatives) pledges a piece of property as collateral.

proportionality The principle that limits the criminal sanction by prohibiting punishment that is grossly excessive in relation to the crime committed. The Supreme Court has equivocated on whether the Eighth Amendment's Cruel and Unusual Punishment Clause includes, as part of its guarantee, any requirement of proportional punishment.

prosecution In criminal cases, the party that files the case. May be called by several names, depending on the jurisdiction, including but not limited to, "the State," "the People," and "the Commonwealth."

prospective search warrant See **anticipatory search warrant.**

protective sweep A doctrine that permits officers to conduct a quick and limited search of premises incident to an arrest to protect their own safety and the safety of others from potential accomplices linked to the arrestee. If officers believe evidence is about to be destroyed or removed as they make a home arrest, they may conduct a limited sweep of the premises to prevent this destruction or removal.

provider exception An employee or agent of a communications service provider may intercept and disclose communications, including to law enforcement, in order to protect the rights or property of the provider as part of the ordinary course of business without violating Title III.

public safety An exception to *Miranda*'s usual warning requirements, where the need for answers to questions in situations posing a threat to public safety outweighs the need to protect the Fifth Amendment's privilege against self-incrimination.

qualified waiver See **selective waiver.**

quasi-suspect classifications Laws that implicate the constitutional guarantee of equal protection of the laws by differentiating or drawing distinctions between classes of people based on sex or gender or illegitimacy.

racial profiling Broadly defined as "any police-initiated action that relies upon: the race, ethnicity, or national origin of an individual rather than [1] the behavior of that individual, or [2] information that leads the police to a particular individual who has been identified as being engaged in or having been engaged in criminal activity."

rational basis test In constitutional adjudication, the lowest standard of review (i.e., the most deferential) is *rational basis test*. It asks if the governmental classification at issue is rationally related to a legitimate governmental interest. It is used to adjudicate all Due Process Clause and Equal Protection Clause issues that do not involve a right or classification that gives rise to a higher, more deferential standard of review. See **standard of review.**

readily mobile Inherently capable of movement; one of the two requirements that must be met before a vehicle may be searched by police under the automobile exception to the warrant requirement (the other requirement is probable cause). Courts examine several factors to determine whether a vehicle is "readily mobile," including its location, access to public roads, whether it is resting "on blocks," whether it is licensed, and/or whether it is connected to utilities.

real evidence Evidence consisting of tangible objects such as contracts, bank statements, or other documentary evidence; firearms; drug paraphernalia; clothing; and traces of objects that may be found at a crime or accident scene, such as fingerprints or trace amounts of drugs. Also referred to as *physical evidence*.

real-time, cell-site data searching The use of a cell phone's radio transmitter to triangulate the location of the cell phone using the location of cell towers relaying the signal.

reasonable, articulable suspicion The level of proof necessary to support a stop and frisk. Unlike *mere suspicion* (i.e., a hunch or intuitive feeling), it is the level of proof for which a person can articulate the reasons why he or she is suspicious, and thereby serve as the basis for suspicion being deemed objectively reasonable.

reasonable expectation of privacy An individual's honest expectation—and one that society would be willing to acknowledge as legitimate—that he or she would be entitled to be free from unreasonable governmental intrusion in a particular place or item. Violations of a person's reasonable expectation of privacy constitute a search or seizure for Fourth Amendment purposes, thereby giving rise to various constitutional and statutory rights and procedures to persons with proper standing.

reasonable doubt In criminal cases or in juvenile delinquency cases, the accused is presumed innocent until proven guilty beyond a reasonable doubt. Proof beyond a reasonable doubt requires that all of the elements of a crime have been factually established to a reasonable, but not absolute or mathematical, certainty; a possibility or probability is not sufficient.

reasonableness The general standard or measure used to evaluate police searches and seizures under the Fourth Amendment.

reasonable suspicion A suspicion for which law enforcement officers can articulate a reasonable basis.

reasonably likely to elicit an incriminating response Making a statement that, although not necessarily even in the form of a question, is likely to cause a suspect to say something incriminating.

rebuttal (1) The opportunity to reopen the case-in-chief to present evidence to counter, disprove, or contradict evidence presented by the opposing party. (2) The final portion of an oral argument in which the appellant or petitioner presents arguments to counter those made by the appellee or respondent.

recognizance When a defendant is released by a judge without any formal bail if the judge believes the defendant is unlikely to flee and poses little risk to the community.

re-cross-examination The opportunity to conduct a second round of cross-examination after the opposing party has conducted a redirect examination.

redaction In evaluating the constitutional sufficiency of a search warrant, the practice of invalidating clauses in the warrant that are constitutionally insufficient for lack of probable cause or particularity while preserving clauses that satisfy the Fourth Amendment. Also referred to as the *doctrine of severability*.

redirect examination A reexamination of a witness by a prosecuting attorney in order to rehabilitate him or her after cross-examination.

reifying error A belief that events that were imagined were actually perceived.

remand To send back a case so that a lower court may retry all or part of the case in accordance with the rulings of the appellate court.

resisting arrest Interfering with a law enforcement officer's lawful ability to take a person into custody.

respondent The party responding to an appeal. Also called the *appellee*.

retention phase (storage phase) The memory stage when the brain stores a memory until it is called on for retrieval.

retrieval phase The memory stage when the brain searches for pertinent information and then retrieves and communicates it.

roving wiretap A special type of warrant that authorizes the wiretapping of a particular suspect's communications wherever they are made, thereby dispensing with the normal requirement that interceptions be limited to a fixed location. Roving taps on either landline or cellular phones do not violate the particularity requirement of the Fourth Amendment if the surveillance is limited to communications involving an identified speaker and relates to crimes in which the speaker is a suspected participant.

Rule 41 Rule 41 of the Federal Rules of Criminal Procedure mandates that people are entitled to have notice that their premises have been searched and, if items were seized during a search, that those items have been taken. If a search warrant is executed when premises are unoccupied, Rule 41 requires that timely notice be given to the lawful occupant of the searched property not only that a search warrant was executed but also what was taken.

scientific evidence The formal results of forensic investigatory techniques (often in documentary form) such as autopsy reports, firearm matches, and DNA analyses.

scientific jury selection The use of behavioral scientists from a variety of disciplines (e.g., sociology, psychology, marketing, communications, etc.) as jury consultants who assist in jury selection by attempting to compile and implement an "ideal" juror profile.

sealing/putting under seal The process of placing records in special protective custody so that they are not accessible to anyone without a special court order.

search 1. An examination or inspection of a location, vehicle, or person by a law enforcement officer for the purpose of locating objects believed to relate to criminal activities or wanted persons. 2. Any official intrusion into matters and activities as to which a person has exhibited a reasonable expectation of privacy. The general rule is that any search conducted without a search warrant is unreasonable. Courts, however, have fashioned several well-defined exceptions to this rule. A warrant is not required, therefore, for a search incident to arrest, a consent search, an observation of evidence falling under the plain view doctrine, search of a motor vehicle under the *Carroll* doctrine, searches conducted in the open fields, observations and seizures of abandoned property, and frisks conducted as a part of brief, limited, investigative detention. See **stop and frisk**.

search incident to arrest A recognized exception to the search warrant requirement that allows a law enforcement officer who legally arrests a person to conduct a warrantless search of that person contemporaneous with the arrest.

search warrant An order in writing, issued by a proper judicial officer, directing a law enforcement officer to search a specified person or premises for specified property and to bring it before the judicial authority named in the warrant. A search warrant may be issued for weapons, contraband, fruits of crime, instrumentalities of crime, and other evidence of crime (see **items subject to seizure**). The Fourth Amendment to the U.S. Constitution states that "no warrants shall issue, but upon probable cause, supported by oath or affirmation, and particularly describing the place to be searched and the persons or things to be seized." The judicial officer, before issuing the warrant, must determine whether there is probable cause to search based on information supplied in an affidavit by a law enforcement officer or other person.

Section 2255 motion A *habeas*-type civil action in which persons in federal custody may challenge the constitutionality of their detention.

seizable items Same as **items subject to seizure**.

seizure 1. Under the Fourth Amendment prohibition against unreasonable searches and seizures, a seizure of the *person* can be defined as follows: "[A] person has been 'seized' within the meaning of the Fourth Amendment only if, in view of all of the circumstances surrounding the incident, a reasonable person would have believed that he was not free to leave, ranging from a minimally intrusive stop and frisk to

formal custodial arrests." 2. Under the Fourth Amendment's prohibition against unreasonable searches and seizures, a seizure of *property* "occurs when there is some meaningful interference with an individual's possessory interests in that property." *United States v. Jacobsen*, 466 U.S. 109, 113 (1984). Usually, a seizure involves the taking into custody by a law enforcement officer of an item of property believed to relate to criminal activity.

seizure tantamount to arrest Encounter between a law enforcement officer and a person that intrudes on the person's freedom of action to the degree that it is indistinguishable from an arrest in important respects.

selective incorporation An approach to the interpretation of the Fourteenth Amendment's Due Process Clause positing that fundamental rights—those implicit in the concept ordered liberty—apply to the states as well as to the federal government. Under this approach, many, but not all, of the provisions of the Bill of Rights have been selectively incorporated by the Fourteenth Amendment. See **fundamental rights**.

selective prosecution A violation of the Constitution's guarantee of equal protection of the law in which similarly situated offenders are not prosecuted, but the defendant was prosecuted because of some unjustifiable standard such as race, religion, or other arbitrary classification.

selective waiver When a suspect specifically invokes his or her *Miranda* rights in a narrow way while acting in a manner that suggests he or she has impliedly waived *Miranda* rights with regard to other aspects of a case. Also known as a *qualified waiver*.

sensory overload Incomplete sensory acquisition by a person overwhelmed with too much information in too short a period of time as a function of differential processing of stimuli.

sentencing The criminal penalties imposed by a court upon a person duly convicted of a crime within the relevant sentencing scheme. In *indeterminate sentencing* schemes, legislatures prescribed a range of permissible sentences, usually setting a minimum sentence, but leaving the maximum up to the discretion of the judge. In *determinate sentencing* schemes, legislatures fix or predetermine the sentence for a given offense. *Minimum mandatory sentences* are a type of determinate sentence in which judges have no discretion whatsoever to vary from the statutorily defined punishment. In contrast, many determinate sentences allow a judge to make minor adjustments only if the specific facts of a case fall into some statutorily recognized reason for enhancing the sentence (called an *upward departure*) or diminishing the sentence (called a *downward departure*). A criminal sentence is usually imposed at a sentencing hearing.

sentencing departures When a judge makes adjustments to a convicted party's mandatory minimum sentence; called *upward departures* or *downward departures*.

sentencing hearing A critical stage of a criminal prosecution in which a judge reviews: a *presentence investigation report*; mitigating arguments made by the defendant, defense counsel, and, under some circumstances, defense witnesses; arguments made by the prosecution; and, in some jurisdictions, a victim impact statement made or submitted by the victim or the victim's family. After weighing all of this information, the judge imposes a formal criminal sentence.

Sentencing Reform Act of 1984 Federal legislation that created the United States Sentencing Commission and empowered it to create a uniform set of federal sentencing guidelines to reduce sentencing disparities and realistically project the needs of the federal correctional system. The commission promulgated the Federal Sentencing Guidelines, which went into effect on November 1, 1987.

sequential presentation of foils Presentation of photographs or lineup participants one after another. Preferred to simultaneous presentation of foils.

severability See **redaction**.

severance The process of *severance* involves removing or redacting false portions of an affidavit in application for a warrant that were made either knowingly or with reckless disregard for the truth. See *Franks* **hearing**.

show of authority The combination of an officer's words and actions that would convey to a reasonable person that his or her freedom of movement is being restricted such that the person is not free to leave. If the person submits to the officer's authority, an arrest has been made. If the suspect does not submit to the officer's show of authority and attempts to flee, then no arrest occurs.

"show me your papers" laws Laws permitting police under certain circumstances to check the immigration status of individuals they detain.

showup A confrontation (definition 2) involving the presentation of a single suspect to a victim or witness of a crime for the purpose of identifying the perpetrator of the crime.

simultaneous presentation of foils Viewing all participants in a lineup or photo array at one time.

"sneak-and-peek" warrants See **covert entry warrants**.

"sneak-and-steal" search See **covert entry warrants**.

sobriety checkpoint Fixed checkpoints on highways or roads at which law enforcement officers stop all vehicles or a predetermined number of vehicles in an attempt to apprehend those who may be driving under the influence of drugs or alcohol.

special needs doctrine An exception to the warrant and probable cause requirements of the Fourth Amendment where special needs of the government "beyond the normal need for law enforcement, make the warrant and probable-cause requirement impracticable."

Speedy Trial Act of 1974 Legislation that established specific time periods for different stages of federal prosecutions. (1) An information or indictment must be filed within thirty days of the arrest or the service of a summons on the defendant (sixty days if the grand jury is not in session). (2) A trial must usually begin within seventy days of the filing of the information, filing of an indictment, or the date of the defendant's initial appearance, whichever is later. (3) A trial must generally begin within ninety days of the government's detaining a defendant who is solely awaiting trial.

staleness Information on which probable cause was initially based is no longer valid because too much time has passed since the search warrant was issued (e.g., there may no longer be good reason to believe that property is still at the same location), thus rendering the warrant void. Staleness is an important factor in determining the validity of probable cause to search.

standard of review The strictness (or level of deference) with which an appellate court will review the actions of a lower court. See **fundamental rights**; **rational basis test**; **intermediate scrutiny**; **strict scrutiny**; **clearly erroneous**; and **abuse of discretion**.

standing The legal right of a person to judicially challenge the conduct of another person or the government for an invasion of a reasonable expectation of privacy. In general, standing depends on whether the person seeking relief has a legally sufficient personal interest at stake to obtain judicial resolution of merits of the dispute.

state actor An official who acts on behalf of the state.

state court of last resort The highest court in a court system's hierarchical structure; every state and the federal system has one.

statement A broad term meaning simply any oral or written declaration or assertion.

statute of limitations A law that requires that prosecution commence within a specified period of time from the date of the alleged commission of the offense.

statutory law Those laws duly enacted by a legislative body empowered to make such laws under the provisions of a constitution.

stop The brief seizure of a person for investigation based on an officer's reasonable suspicion of criminal activity; a detention that does not involve an intention to arrest.

stop and frisk A shorthand term for the law enforcement practice involving the temporary investigative detention of a person and the pat-down search of the person's outer clothing for weapons.

Stored Communications Act (SCA) The portion of the ECPA that allows law enforcement authorities to obtain e-mail, like other forms of stored electronic communications, during the first 180 days of storage using normal search warrant procedures; after 180 days, the government may access stored communications using either a search warrant, or, after giving notice to the subscriber, a subpoena.

strict scrutiny The most stringent standard of review, *strict scrutiny* examines whether a challenged law is narrowly tailored to achieve a compelling governmental interest. Strict scrutiny is used to adjudicate Equal Protection Clause issues that involve suspect classifications, and to adjudicate both Equal Protection Clause and Due Process Clause issues that infringe upon fundamental rights. See **standard of review**.

strike for cause A formal objection to a prospective juror based on the assumption that the juror cannot reach a fair and impartial verdict on the particular case. These may be *fact-partial challenges* (based on the person's background, opinions, biases, or personal knowledge of the facts of a case) or *principal challenges* (the prospective juror has personal knowledge of the participants in the case). Also known as *challenge for cause*.

subpoena A written order issued by a judicial officer requiring a specified person to appear in a designated court at a specified time in order to testify in a case under the jurisdiction of that court, or to bring a document, piece of evidence, or other thing for use or inspection by the court. A subpoena to serve as a witness is called a *subpoena ad testificandum*.

subpoena *ad testificandum* A subpoena to serve as a witness.

subpoena *duces tecum* A subpoena to bring a document, piece of evidence, or other thing into court.

substantive criminal laws Statutes that set forth criminal acts and define their elements.

substantive due process Basic protections against the enactment by states or the federal government of arbitrary and unreasonable legislation or other measures that would violate peoples' rights.

summons A written order issued by a judicial officer requiring a person accused of a criminal offense to appear in a designated court at a specified time to answer the charge or charges.

Supremacy Clause Article VI, Section 2 of the U.S. Constitution; provides that constitutional law trumps all other forms of law, including statutory law (laws enacted by legislative bodies), common law (law as set forth by judges in published judicial decisions), and administrative law.

surety bond A type of bail bond provided by bail agent (usually acting as an agent for an insurance company) in exchange for a fee, which is usually 10 percent of the amount of the bond.

suspect classifications Laws that implicate the constitutional guarantee of equal protection of the laws by differentiating or drawing distinctions between classes of people based on race, religion, and national origin.

symbolic speech Conduct that expresses an idea or opinion, such as wearing buttons or clothing with political slogans, displaying a sign or a flag, or burning a flag, which is therefore protected by the First Amendment's guarantee of freedom of speech.

testimonial communications To be testimonial, a "communication must itself, explicitly or implicitly, relate a factual assertion or disclose information" that is "the expression of the contents of an individual's mind." *Doe v. United States*, 487 U.S. 201, 210 n.9 (1988). The Fifth Amendment protects a person against being incriminated by his or her own compelled testimonial communications. This protection is applicable to the states through the Fourteenth Amendment. The privilege against self-incrimination is not violated by compelling a person to appear in a lineup, to produce voice exemplars, to furnish handwriting samples, to be fingerprinted, to shave a beard or mustache, or to take a blood-alcohol or breathalyzer test.

testimonial evidence Oral testimony given under oath. Anyone called to give testimony in a criminal case is subject to the requirements of the Sixth Amendment's Confrontation Clause.

time, place, and manner restrictions Restrictions by a governmental entity on free speech and expression that is protected by the First Amendment in content-neutral ways for the good of society. To be valid, a time, place, or manner regulation must further an important or substantial governmental interest, be unrelated to the suppression of free expression, be narrowly tailored to serve the government's interest such that the restriction on free speech is not greater than is necessary to achieve the governmental interest, and still leave open ample, alternative means for people to communicate their message.

Title III of the Omnibus Crime Control and Safe Streets Act of 1968 A federal law governing *electronic surveillance* that applies to private searches and seizures of wire communications, oral communications, or electronic communications, as well as those involving governmental actors. The privacy protections under Title III are much greater than those provided under the Fourth Amendment. Title III has its own statutory exclusionary rule that applies only to wire or oral communications; it does not apply to illegally intercepted electronic communications, the remedies for which include criminal penalties and civil suits.

tone-only pagers Devices that send a tone to a person's pager but display no other information. The recipient of the tone-only page must then call a service to find out the number of the person who paged them.

tracking beeper An electronic tracking device used to monitor the location of the object to which the beeper is attached.

trap-and-trace device A device that records incoming addressing information to a phone line, such as caller ID information. Because such a device does not intercept a "communication" per se, Title III of the Omnibus Crime Control and Safe Streets Act of 1968 does not apply to the use of these devices.

treason Actions that attempt or conspire to overthrow a government or to help a foreign government overthrow, make war against, or seriously injure one's nation. Treason is the only crime to be defined in the U.S. Constitution (in Article III, Section 3).

trial by jury The Sixth Amendment guarantees that defendants in certain criminal prosecutions have the right to a trial in which an impartial jury serves as the *trier of fact*. The same right was made applicable to the states through the Due Process Clause of the Fourteenth Amendment in *Duncan v. Louisiana*.

trial *de novo* A new trial or retrial in which the whole case is gone into again as if no trial had been held before. In a trial *de novo*, matters of fact as well as law may be considered, witnesses may be heard, and new evidence may be presented, regardless of what happened at the first trial.

trier of fact The party responsible for making factual findings such as whether a defendant is guilty of a crime. In a *bench trial*, a trial is conducted without a jury so that the judge acts as the trier of fact in addition to ruling on matters of law.

triggering condition A condition precedent (other than the passage of time) that will establish probable cause to conduct a search or seizure at some time in the future. See **anticipatory search warrant**.

unconscious transference A phenomenon in which different memory images may become combined or confused with one another.

under seal A judicial procedure in which a court grants special permission for for a legal document to be filed without it becoming a publicly-available record because the document contains sensitive or confidential information.

unnecessarily suggestive identification Any identification procedure that unnecessarily suggested the person to be identified.

upward departures See **sentencing departures**.

venire The group of persons summoned to appear in court as potential jurors for a particular trial, or the persons selected from the group of potential jurors to sit in the jury box; from that second group those acceptable to the prosecution and the defense are finally chosen as the jury. Sometimes referred to as the *jury panel*.

venue The geographical area from which the jury is drawn and in which a court with jurisdiction may hear and determine a case—usually, the county or district in which the crime is alleged to have been committed.

verdict The decision made by a jury in a jury trial, or by a judicial officer in a nonjury trial, that a defendant is either guilty or not guilty of the offense for which he or she has been tried. In entering a judgment, a judicial officer has the power to reject a jury verdict of guilty, but must accept a jury verdict of not guilty. Thus, a jury verdict of not guilty results in a judgment of acquittal; but a verdict of guilty does not necessarily result in a judgment of conviction.

victim impact statement When the victim of a crime (or next of kin if the victim is dead or unable to speak on his or her own behalf) participates at sentencing either by making an oral statement in open court or by submitting a written statement to the court.

video surveillance The use of video cameras that record only images and not aural communications.

vindictive prosecution A due process violation that occurs when a prosecutor increases the number or severity of charges to penalize a defendant who exercises his or her constitutional or statutory rights.

voir dire French, meaning "to speak the truth." (1) An examination conducted by the court or by the attorneys of a prospective juror or witness to determine whether he or she is competent or qualified for service. (2) During a trial, a hearing conducted by the court out of the presence of the jury on some issue upon which the court must make an initial determination as a matter of law.

waiver The voluntary and intentional relinquishment or abandonment of a known right or privilege.

warrant A written order or writ issued by a judicial officer or other authorized person commanding a law enforcement officer to perform some act incident to the administration of justice.

weapons effect A psychological phenomenon that occurs in crime situations in which a weapon is used, and witnesses spend more time and psychic energy focusing on the weapon rather than on other aspects of the event. The weapons effect results in incomplete or inaccurate information about the crime scene and the perpetrator. See *Yerkes–Dodson* **law**.

wingspan The area into which an arrestee could reach to grab a weapon or destroy evidence. It is the area that is deemed to be within the arrestee's immediate control for purposes of the search incident to arrest exception.

wire communication Any aural transfer made in whole or in part through the use of facilities for the interstate transmission of communications by the aid of wire or cable connections.

witness (1) A person who directly sees or perceives an event or thing or who has expert knowledge relevant to a case. (2) A person who testifies to what he or she has seen or perceived or what he or she knows. (3) A person who signs his or her name to a document to attest to its authenticity; sometimes called an *attesting witness*.

witness factors Memory and perception estimator variables such as stress, fear, physical limitations on sensory perception (e.g., poor eyesight, hearing impairment, alcohol or drug intoxication), expectations, age (the very young and very old have unique problems), and gender.

writ of assistance A form of general warrant issued by the British Colonial courts against the American colonists in the mid-eighteenth century to enforce the Trade Acts. Writs of assistance authorized royal customs officers to search houses and ships at will in order to discover and seize smuggled goods or goods on which the required duties had not been paid. The reaction of the colonists against the writs of assistance was strong and one of the major causes of the American Revolution.

writ of *certiorari* A discretionary writ issued from an appellate court for the purpose of obtaining from a lower court the record of its proceedings in a particular case. In the U.S. Supreme Court, and in some states, this writ is the mechanism for discretionary review. A request for review is made by petitioning for a writ of *certiorari*, and granting of review is indicated by issuance of the writ.

writ of *habeas corpus* A civil order by a court directing the release of a person in state custody. Such a writ is issued if a prisoner is successful in the judicial proceedings in which the prisoner filed a petition for a writ of *habeas corpus*.

Yerkes–Dodson law The optimal functioning of perception and memory as a function of an optimally moderate amount of stress. When stress levels are too low, people do not pay sufficient attention; and when stress levels are too high, the abilities to concentrate and perceive are negatively affected. See **weapons effect**.

Select Bibliography

Chapter 1. Individual Rights Under the United States Constitution

Baker, Sir John, *Human Rights and the Rule of Law in Renaissance England,* 2 NW. U. J. INT'L HUM. RTS. 3 (2004).

Barrett Lain, Corinna, *Countermajoritarian Hero or Zero? Rethinking the Warren Court's Role in the Criminal Procedure Revolution,* 152 U. PA. L. REV. 1361 (2004).

Berman, Harold J., *The Western Legal Tradition in a Millennial Perspective: Past and Future,* 60 LA. L. REV. 739 (2000).

BRADLEY, CRAIG, THE FAILURE OF THE CRIMINAL PROCEDURE REVOLUTION (1993).

Broussard, Sylvia, et al., *Undergraduate Students' Perceptions of Child Sexual Abuse: The Impact of Victim Sex, Perpetrator Sex, Respondent Sex, and Victim Response,* 6 J. FAM. VIOLENCE 267, 269–72 (1991).

Carr John A., *Free Speech in the Military Community: Striking a Balance between Personal Rights and Military Necessity,* 45 A.F. L. REV. 303 (1998).

Dollar, Katherine, et al., *Influence of Gender Roles on Perceptions of Teacher/Adolescent Student Sexual Relations,* 50 SEX ROLES 91 (2004).

Feld, Barry C., *Race, Politics, and Juvenile Justice: The Warren Court and the Conservative "Backlash,"* 87 MINN. L. REV. 1447 (2003).

Friendly, Henry, *The Fifth Amendment Tomorrow: The Case for Constitutional Change,* 37 U. CIN. L. REV. 671 (1968).

Gaubatz, Derek L., *RLUIPA at Four: Evaluating the Success and Constitutionality of RLUIPA'S Prisoner Provisions,* 28 HARV. J.L. & PUB. POL'Y 501 (2005).

Greene, David, *The Need for Expert Testimony to Prove Lack of Serious Artistic Value in Obscenity Cases,* 10 NEXUS J. OP. 171 (2005).

Grossman, Steven, *Proportionality in Non-Capital Sentencing: The Supreme Court's Tortured Approach to Cruel and Unusual Punishment,* 84 KY. L.J. 107 (1995).

Johnson, Morgan F., *Heaven Help Us: The Religious Land Use and Institutionalized Persons Act's Prisoners Provisions in the Aftermath of the Supreme Court's Decision in* Cutter v. Wilkinson, 14 AM. U.J. GENDER SOC. POL'Y & L. 585 (2006).

Kamisar, Yale, *Equal Justice in the Gatehouses and Mansions of American Criminal Procedure,* in A CRIMINAL JUSTICE IN OUR TIME (E. Dick Howard, ed., 1965).

Levine, Kay L., *Women as Perpetrators of Crime: No Penis, No Problem,* 33 FORDHAM URB. L.J. 357 (2006).

MONKKONEN, ERIC, POLICE IN URBAN AMERICA, 1860–1920 (1981).

Neely, Richard, *The Warren Court and the Welcome Stranger Rule,* in THE WARREN COURT: A RETROSPECTIVE (Bernard Schwartz, ed., 1996).

PALMER, JOHN W., AND STEPHEN E. PALMER, CONSTITUTIONAL RIGHTS OF PRISONERS (9th ed., 2010).

Quas, Jodi A., et al., *Effects of Victim, Defendant, and Juror Gender on Decisions in Child Sexual Assault Cases,* 32 J. APPLIED SOC. PSYCHOL. 1993 (2002).

Riebli, Frank, *The Spectre of Star Chamber: The Role of an Ancient English Tribunal in the Supreme Court's Self-Incrimination Jurisprudence,* 29 HASTINGS CONST. L.Q. 807 (2002).

Shepherd, JoAnne Nelson, *Free Speech and the End of Dress Codes and Mandatory Uniforms in Mississippi Public Schools,* 24 MISS. C. L. REV. 27 (2004).

WALKER, SAMUEL, POPULAR JUSTICE (1980).

WEBER, MAX, LAW IN ECONOMY AND SOCIETY (1954).

Chapter 2. Criminal Courts, Pretrial Processes, and the Exclusionary Rule

BLACKSTONE, WILLIAM, COMMENTARIES ON THE LAWS OF ENGLAND 24 (9th ed., 1783).

Corinis, Jennifer W., Note: *A Reasoned Standard for Competency to Waive Counsel after* Godinez v. Moran, 80 B.U.L. REV. 265 (2000).

Felthous, Alan R., *The Right to Represent Oneself Incompetently: Competency to Waive Counsel and Conduct One's Own Defense Before and After* Godinez, 18 MENTAL & PHYSICAL DISABILITY L. REP. 105, 110 (1994).

FRADELLA, HENRY F. MENTAL ILLNESS AND CRIMINAL DEFENSES OF EXCUSE IN CONTEMPORARY AMERICAN LAW (2007).

HALE, MATTHEW, 1 THE HISTORY OF THE PLEAS OF THE CROWN (1736).

Katz, Charles M., and Cassia C. Spohn, *The Effect of Race and Gender on Bail Outcomes: A Test of an Interactive Model,* 19 AM. J. CRIM. JUST. 161 (1995).

Krug, Peter, *Prosecutorial Discretion and Its Limits,* 50 AM. J. COMP. L. 643 (2002).

Lynch, Timothy, *Reassessing the Exclusionary Rule,* 22-DEC CHAMPION 12 (1998).

MENNINGER, KARL, THE CRIME OF PUNISHMENT (1968).

Meyers, Alaya B., *Supreme Court Review: Rejecting the Clear and Convincing Evidence Standard for Proof of Incompetence,* 87 J. CRIM. L. & CRIMINOLOGY 1016 (1997).

Morris, Grant H., *Placed in Purgatory: Conditional Release of Insanity Acquittees,* 39 ARIZ. L. REV. 1061 (1997).

NEUBAUER, DAVID, AND HENRY F. FRADELLA, AMERICA'S COURTS AND THE CRIMINAL JUSTICE SYSTEM (2011).

Norwood, Kimberly Jade, *Shopping for a Venue: The Need for More Limits on Choice,* 50 U. Miami L. Rev. 267 (1995).

Perlin, Michael L., *"The Borderline Which Separated You from Me": The Insanity Defense, the Authoritarian Spirit, the Fear of Faking, and the Culture of Punishment,* 82 Iowa L. Rev. 1375 (1997).

Shapiro, David L., *Ethical Dilemmas for the Mental Health Professional: Issues Raised by Recent Supreme Court Decisions,* 34 Cal. W. L. Rev. 177, 182 (1997).

Spohn, Cassia C., How Do Judges Decide? (2008).

Wang, Lu-in, *The Complexities of Hate,* 60 Ohio St. L.J. 799 (1999).

Washburn, Kevin K., *Restoring the Grand Jury,* 76 Fordham L. Rev. 2333 (2008).

Whitebread, Charles H., and Christopher Slobogin, Criminal Procedure: An Analysis of Cases and Concepts (4th ed., 2000).

Winick, Bruce J., *Criminal Law: Reforming Incompetency to Stand Trial and Plead Guilty: A Restated Proposal and a Response to Professor Bonnie,* 85 J. Crim. L. & Criminology 571 (1995).

Wiseman, Samuel, *Discrimination, Coercion, and the Bail Reform Act of 1984: The Loss of the Core Constitutional Protections of the Excessive Bail Clause,* 36 Fordham Urb. L.J. 121 (2009).

Chapter 3. Basic Underlying Concepts: Privacy, Probable Cause, and Reasonableness

Federal Torts Claim Act: 28 U.S.C.A. § 1346(b); 28 U.S.C.A. § 2680(h).

Fradella, Henry F., Weston J. Morrow, Ryan G. Fischer, and Connie E. Ireland, *Quantifying Katz: Empirically Measuring "Reasonable Expectations of Privacy" in the Fourth Amendment Context,* 38 Am. J. Crim. L. 101 (2011).

Chapter 4. Criminal Investigatory Search Warrants

Adler, Andrew, *The Notice Problem, Unlawful Electronic Surveillance, and Civil Liability Under the Foreign Intelligence Surveillance Act,* 61 U. Miami L. Rev. 393 (2007).

Chan, Cecilia, *Search-Warrant Process in DUIs Faster for Phoenix Police.* Arizona Republic (Apr. 11, 2013) http://www.azcentral.com/community/phoenix/articles/20130410phoenix-police-search-warrant-process-duis-faster-brk.html.

Duncan, Jr., Robert M., *Surreptitious Search Warrants and the USA PATRIOT Act: "Thinking Outside the Box but within the Constitution," or a Violation of Fourth Amendment Protections?* 7 N.Y. City L. Rev. 1 (2004).

Gilmore, Kelly A., *Preserving the Border Search Doctrine in a Digital World: Reproducing Electronic Evidence at the Border,* 72 Brook. L. Rev. 759 (2007).

Jekot, Wayne, *Computer Forensics, Search Strategies, and the Particularity Requirement,* 12 U. Pittsburgh J. Tech. L. & Pol'y 2 (2007).

Lichtblau, Eric and David Johnston, *Court to Oversee U.S. Wiretapping in Terror Cases,* N.Y. Times, Jan. 18, 2007, at A1.

Martin, Katherine Lee, *"Sacrificing the End to the Means": The Constitutionality of Suspicionless Subway Searches,* 15 Wm. & Mary Bill Rts. J. 1285 (2007).

Owen, Stephen S., and Tod W. Burke, *DNA Databases and Familial Searching,* 43(4) Crim. Law Bull. 617 (2007).

Risen, James and Eric Lichtblau, *Bush Lets U.S. Spy on Callers Without Courts,* N.Y. Times, Dec. 16, 2005, at A1.

Swingle, H. Morley, and Lane P. Thomasson, *Beam Me Up: Upgrading Search Warrants with Technology,* 69 J. Mo. Bar 16 (2013).

U.S. Department of Justice, *Searching and Seizing Computers and Obtaining Electronic Evidence in Criminal Investigations* (3d ed., 2009) www.cybercrime.gov/ssmanual/index.html

Chapter 5. Searches for Electronically Stored Information and Electronic Surveillance

Behr, Darrin J., *Anti-Forensics: What It Is, What It Does and Why You Need to Know,* 255-DEC N.J. L. 9 (2008).

Brenner, Susan W., *Nanocrime,* 2011 U. Ill. J. L. Technol. & Pol'y 39 (2011).

Carroll, Ovie L., Stephen K. Brannon, and Thomas Song, *Computer Forensics: Digital Forensic Analysis Methodology,* 56 Computer Forensics 1 (2008).

Chesney, Robert, and Benjamin Wittes, *A Tale of Two NSA Leaks: One Is Unsurprising, and Damaging. The Other Is Worth Debating,* The New Republic (June 10, 2013) http://www.newrepublic.com/article/113427/nsa-spying-scandal-one-leak-more-damaging-other.

Donahue, Laura, J., *NSA Surveillance May Be Legal—but It's Unconstitutional.* Washington Post (June 21, 2013) http://articles.washingtonpost.com/2013-06-21/opinions/40110321_1_electronic-surveillance-fisa-nsa-surveillance.

Feldman, Noah, *The Secret Law Behind NSA's Verizon Snooping,* Bloomberg View (June 6, 2013) http://www.bloomberg.com/news/2013-06-06/the-secret-law-behind-nsa-s-verizon-snooping.html.

Gershman, Bennett L., *Privacy Revisited: GPS Tracking as Search and Seizure,* 30 Pace L. Rev. 927 (2010).

Jekot, Wayne, *Computer Forensics, Search Strategies, and the Particularity Requirement,* 7 U. Pitt. J. Tech. L. & Pol'y 2 (2007).

Kerr, Orin S., *The Mosaic Theory of the Fourth Amendment,* 111 Mich. L. Rev. 311 (2012).

Levin, Avne, and Patricia Sanchez Abril, *Two Notions of Privacy Online*, 11 Vanderbilt J. Entertainment and Tech. L. 1001 (2009).

Mohay, George, Alison Anderson, Byron Collie, Olivier de Vel, and Rod McKemmish, Computer and Intrusion Forensics (2004).

Morrison, Steven R., *What the Cops Can't Do, Internet Service Providers Can: Preserving Privacy in Email Contents*, 16 Va. J.L. & Tech. 253 (2011).

Nelson, Bill, Amelia Phillips, and Christopher Steuart, Guide to Computer Forensics and Investigations (2010).

Newell, Bryce Clayton, *Rethinking Reasonable Expectations of Privacy in Online Social Networks*, 17 Rich. J.L. & Tech. 12 (2011).

Plourde-Cole, Haley, Note, *Back to* Katz: *Reasonable Expectation of Privacy in the Facebook Age*, 38 Fordham Urb. L.J. 571 (2010).

Small, Jacob M., *Storing Documents in the Cloud: Toward an Evidentiary Privilege Protecting Papers and Effects Stored on the Internet*, 23 Geo. Mason U. Civ. Rts. L.J. 255 (2013).

Weaver, Russell L., *The Fourth Amendment, Privacy, and Advancing Technology*, 80 Miss. L. J. 131 (2011).

Weir, Bryan K., *It's (Not So) Plain to See: The Circuit Split on the Plain View Doctrine in Digital Searches*, 21 Geo. Mason U. Civ. Rts. L.J. 83 (2010).

Withers, Kenneth J., *Electronically Stored Information: The December 2006 Amendments to the Federal Rules of Civil Procedure*, 4 Nw. J. Tech. & Intell. Prop. 171 (2006).

Yeager, Eric, *Looking for Trouble: An Exploration of How to Regulate Digital Searches*, 66 Vand. L. Rev. 685 2013).

Chapter 6. Administrative and Special Needs Searches

Koloms, Alysa B., Note, *Stripping Down the Reasonableness Standard: The Problems with Using* In Loco Parentis *to Define Students' Fourth Amendment*, 39 Hofstra L. Rev. 169 (2011).

Martin, Katherine Lee, *"Sacrificing the End to the Means": The Constitutionality of Suspicionless Subway Searches*, 15 Wm. & Mary Bill Rts. J. 1285 (2007).

Primus, Eve Brensike, *Disentangling Administrative Searches*, 111 Colum. L. Rev. 254 (2011).

Regensburger, Derek, *DNA Databases and the Fourth Amendment: The Time Has Come to Reexamine the Special Needs Exception to the Warrant Requirement and the Primary Purpose Test*, 19 Alb. L.J. Sci. & Tech. 319 (2009).

Chapter 7. Arrests, Searches, Incident to Arrest, and Protective Sweeps

Alpert, Geoffrey. P., Michael R. Smith, Robert J. Kaminski, Lorie A. Fridell, John MacDonald, and Bruce Kubu, *Police Use of Force, Tasers, and Other Less-Lethal Weapons* (2011) https://www.ncjrs.gov/pdffiles1/nij/232215.pdf.

Amnesty International, *Annual Report 2013—The State of the World's Human Rights* (2013) http://www.amnesty.org /en/region/usa/report-2013#section-157-4.

Amnesty International, *US Authorities Urged to Control Tasers as Official Report on Deaths Issued* (2011) http://www .amnesty.org/en/library/asset/AMR51/048/2011 /en/8b903284-8407-4f6f-adaa-d08d922705c4 /amr510482011en.pdf.

Cronin, James M., and Joshua A. Ederheimer, *Conducted Energy Devices: Development of Standards for Consistency and Guidance* (2006) www.ojp.usdoj.gov/BJA/pdf /CED_Standards.pdf.

Dery III, George M., *A Case of Doubtful Certainty: The Court Relapses Into Search Incident to Arrest Confusion in* Arizona v. Gant, 44 Ind. L. Rev. 395 (2011).

Richardson, L. Song, *Arrest Efficiency and the Fourth Amendment*, 95 Minn. L. Rev. 2035 (2011).

Taylor, Bruce, Daniel Woods, Bruce Kubu, Chris Koper, Bill Tegeler, Jason Cheney, Mary Martinez, James Cronin, and Kristin Kappelman, *Comparing Safety Outcomes in Police Use-of-Force Cases for Law Enforcement Agencies That Have Deployed Conducted Energy Devices and a Matched Comparison Group That Have Not: A Quasi-Experimental Evaluation* (2009) https://www.ncjrs.gov/pdffiles1/nij/grants/237965.pdf.

Totten, Christopher, Arizona v. Gant *and Its Aftermath: A Doctrinal "Correction" Without the Anticipated Privacy "Gains,"* 46 Crim. L. Bull. 1293 (2010).

Chapter 8. Stops and Frisks

American Civil Liberties Union, *South Tucson Officials Agree to Important Revision of Police Practices Related to SB 1070* (n.d.) https://www.aclu.org/criminal-law-reform-racial -justice/south-tucson-officials-agree-comprehensive -revision-police.

Amnesty International, *Another Year, Same Missing Ingredient* (2014) http://www.amnestyusa.org/sites/default/files /amr510322014en_0.pdf.

Chishti, Muzaffar, and Faye Hipsman, *Alabama Settlement Marks Near End of a Chapter in State Immigration Enforcement Activism* (2013) http://www.migrationpolicy.org /article/alabama-settlement-marks-near-end-chapter -state-immigration-enforcement-activism.

Cole, David, *In Aid of Removal: Due Process Limits on Immigration Detention*, 51 Emory L.J. 1003 (2002).

Durose, Matthew, and Lynn Langton, *Police Behavior During Traffic and Street Stops, 2011* (2013) http://www.bjs .gov/index.cfm?ty=pbdetail&iid=4779.

Eith, Christine, and Matthew Durose, *Special Report: Contacts between Police and the Public, 2008* (2011) http://www .bjs.gov/content/pub/pdf/cpp08.pdf.

Falk, Barbara J., *The Global War on Terror and the Detention Debate: The Applicability of Geneva Convention III*, 3 J. Int'l L. & Int'l Relations 31 (2007).

Greenberg, Karen J., and Joshua L. Dratel, eds., The Torture Papers: The Road to Abu Ghraib (2005).

Hafetz, Jonathan, *Habeas Corpus, Judicial Review, and Limits on Secrecy and Detentions at Guantanamo*, 5 Cardozo Pub. L., Pol'y & Ethics J. 127 (2006).

Harris, David A., *The Stories, the Statistics, and the Law: Why "Driving While Black" Matters*, 84 Minn. L. Rev. 265 (1999).

Chris Koster, *Executive Summary on 2006 Missouri Vehicle Stops* (2006) https://archive.org/stream /2006VehicleStopsReport#page/n0/mode/2up.

Kowalski, Brian R., and Richard J. Lundman, *Vehicle Stops by Police for Driving While Black: Common Problems and Some Tentative Solutions*, 35 J. Crim. Just. 165 (2007).

Lennard, Natasha, *Obama Signs NDAA 2014, Indefinite Detention Remains*, Salon (Dec. 27, 2013) http://www.salon .com/2013/12/27/obama_signs_ndaa_2014_indefinite _detention_remains.

Murphy, Laura, and Hina Shamsi, *The Perversity of Profiling*, ACLU Blog of Rights (Apr. 12, 2014) https://www.aclu.org /blog/national-security-criminal-law-reform-racial-justice /perversity-profiling.

National Immigration Law Center, *Federal Court Blocks Most Provisions of Georgia and Alabama's Anti-Immigrant Laws* (2012a) http://nilc.org/nr082012.html.

National Immigration Law Center, *Supreme Court Decision on Arizona's SB 1070* (2012b) http://nilc.org /sb1070scotusqa.html.

Parry, John T., *Terrorism and the New Criminal Process*, 15 Wm. & Mary Bill Rts. J. 765 (2007).

Ramirez, Deborah, et al., A Resource Guide on Racial Profiling Data Collection Systems: Promising Practice and Lessons Learned (2000).

Schindler, Dietrich, and Jiri Toman, *The Laws of Armed Conflicts: A Collection of Conventions, Resolutions and Other Documents* (4th ed., 2004).

U.S. Department of Justice, et al., *Final Report—Guantanamo Review Task Force* (June 2010) http://www.justice.gov /ag/guantanamo-review-final-report.pdf.

U.S. Department of Justice, Civil Rights Division,, *Guidance Regarding the Use of Race by Federal Law Enforcement Agencies* (2003) www.justice.gov/crt/about/spl /documents/guidance_on_race.pdf

U.S. Dept. of Justice, Office of Justice Programs, *Police Stop White, Black and Hispanic Drivers at Similar Rates According to Department of Justice Report* (2007) http://ojp .gov/newsroom/pressreleases/2007/BJS07020.htm.

Verniero, Peter, and Paul H. Zoubek, *Interim Report of the State Police Review Team Regarding Allegations of Racial Profiling* (1999) http://www.state.nj.us/lps/intm _419.pdf.

Weiser, Benjamin, *Ex-Detainee Gets Life Sentence in Embassy Blasts*, N.Y. Times (Jan. 26, 2011), at A18.

Weiser, Benjamin, *Former Detainee's Right to Speedy Trial Wasn't Violated, U.S. Appeals Panel Rules*, N.Y. Times (Oct. 25, 2013), at A21.

White House, The, Office of the Press Secretary, *Fact Sheet: New Actions on Guantanamo and Detainee Policy* (March 2011) http://www.whitehouse.gov/the-press -office/2011/03/07/fact-sheet-new-actions-guant -namo-and-detainee-policy.

Wolfowitz, Paul, Deputy Secretary for the Navy, to the Secretary of the Navy, *Order Establishing Combatant Status Review Tribunal* (July 7, 2004) http://www.defenselink .mil/news/Jul2004/d20040707review.pdf.

Yin, Tung, *Procedural Due Process to Determine Enemy Combatant Status in the War Against Terror*, 73 Tenn. L. Rev. 351 (2006).

Chapter 9. Consent Searches

Park, Arthur J., *Automobile Consent Searches: The Driver's Options in a Lose–Lose Situation*, 14 Rich. J.L. & Pub. Int. 461 (2011).

Phillips, Matthew, *Effective Warnings Before Consent Searches: Practical, Necessary , and Desirable*, 45 Am. Criminal L. Rev. 1185 (2008).

Sekhon, Nirej, *Willing Suspects and Docile Defendants: The Contradictory Role of Consent in Criminal Procedure*, 46 Harv. C.R.-C.L. L. Rev. 103 (2011).

Chapter 10. The Plain View Doctrine

Citron, Evan B., *Say Hello and Wave Goodbye: The Legitimacy of Plain View Seizures at the Threshold of the Home*, 74 Fordham L. Rev. 2761 (2006).

Chapter 11. Search and Seizure of Vehicles and Containers

Kegl, Daniel, *The Single-Purpose Container Exception: A Logical Extension of the Plain View Doctrine Made Unworkable by Inconsistent Application*, 30 N. Ill. U. L. Rev. 237 (2009).

Whitebread, Charles, and Christopher Slobogin, Criminal Procedure: An Analysis of Cases and Concepts (6th ed., 2007).

Chapter 12. Open Fields and Abandoned Property

Leonetti, Carrie, *Open Fields in the Inner City: Application of the Curtilage Doctrine to Urban and Suburban Areas*, 15 Geo. Mason U. Civ. Rts. L.J. 297 (2005).

Chapter 13. Interrogations, Admissions, and Confessions

Agar II, James R., *The Admissibility of False Confession Expert Testimony*, 1999 Army Law. 26 (1999).

Beyer, Marty, *Immaturity, Culpability and Competency in Juveniles: A Study of 17 Cases*, 15 Crim. Just. 26 (2000).

Blackstone, William, Commentaries on the Laws of England (1765).

Cassell, Paul G., and Bret S. Hayman, *Police Interrogation in the 1990s: An Empirical Study of the Effects of Miranda*, 43 UCLA L. Rev. 839 (1996).

Cicchini, Michael D., *The New Miranda Warning*, 65 S. Methodist U. L.R., 911 (2012).

Clymer, Steven D., *Are Police Free to Disregard Miranda?* 112 Yale L.J. 447 (2002).

DeClue, Gregory, *Oral Miranda Warnings: A Checklist and a Model Presentation*, 35 J. Psychiatry & L. 421 (2007).

Domanico, Anthony J., Michael D. Cicchini, and Lawrence T. White, *Overcoming Miranda: A Content Analysis of the Miranda Portion of Police Interrogations*, 49 Idaho L. Rev. 1 (2012).

Feld, Barry C., *Juveniles' Competence to Exercise Miranda Rights: An Empirical Study of Policy and Practice,* 91 Minn. L. Rev. 26 (2006).

Ferguson, Andrew Guthrie, *The Dialogue Approach to Miranda Warnings and Waivers*, 49 Am. Crim. L. Rev. 1437 (2012).

Fulero, Solomon M., and Caroline Everington, *Assessing Competency to Waive Miranda Rights in Defendants with Mental Retardation,* 19 L. & Hum. Behav. 533 (1995).

Godsey, Mark A., *Rethinking the Involuntary Confession Rule: Toward a Workable Test for Identifying Compelled Self-Incrimination,* 93 Cal. L. Rev. 465 (2005).

Gohara, Miriam S., *A Lie for a Lie: False Confessions and the Case for Reconsidering the Legality of Deceptive Interrogation Techniques,* 33 Fordham Urb. L.J. 791 (2006).

Grisso, Thomas, Evaluating Competencies: Forensic Assessments and Instruments (2d ed., 2003).

Grisso, Thomas, et al. *Juveniles' Competence to Stand Trial: A Comparison of Adolescents' and Adults' Capacities as Trial Defendants*, 27 L. & Hum. Behav. 333 (2003).

Grisso, Thomas, Juveniles' Waiver of Rights: Legal and Psychological Competence (1981).

Grisso, Thomas, *The Competence of Adolescents as Trial Defendants,* 3 Psychol. Pub. Pol. & L. 3 (1997).

Hafetz, Jonathan, *Torture, Judicial Review, and the Regulation of Custodial Interrogations,* 62, N.Y.U. Ann. Surv. Am. L. 433 (2007).

Kahn, Rachel, Patricia A. Zapf, and Virginia G. Cooper, *Readability of Miranda Warnings and Waivers: Implications for Evaluating Miranda Comprehension,* 30 L. & Psychol. Rev. 119 (2006).

Kuller, Althea, Moran v. Burbine: *Supreme Court Tolerates Police Interference with the Attorney–Client Relationship,* 18 Loy. U. Chi. L.J. 251 (1986).

Larson, Kimberly, *Improving the "Kangaroo Courts": A Proposal for Reform in Evaluating Juveniles' Waiver of Miranda,* 48 Vill. L. Rev. 629 (2003).

Leo, Richard A., *The Impact of Miranda Revisited,* 86 J. Crim. L. & Criminology 621 (1996).

Marcus, Paul, *It's Not Just About Miranda: Determining the Voluntariness of Confessions in Criminal Prosecutions,* 40 Val. U. L. Rev. 601 (2006).

Meares, Tracey L., and Bernard E. Harcourt, *Transparent Adjudication and Social Science Research in Constitutional Criminal Procedure,* 90 J. Crim. L. & Criminology 733 (2000).

Paulsen, Monrad G., *The Fourteenth Amendment and the Third Degree,* 6 Stan. L. Rev. 411 (1954).

Penney, Steven, *Theories of Confession Admissibility: A Historical View,* 25 Am. J. Crim. L. 309 (1998).

Rogers, Richard, *A Little Knowledge Is a Dangerous Thing: Emerging Miranda Research and Professional Roles for Psychologists,* 63(8) Am. Psychologist 776 (2008).

Ruebner, Ralph, *Police Interrogation: The Privilege Against Self-Incrimination, the Right to Counsel, and the Incomplete Metamorphosis of Justice White,* 48 U. Miami L. Rev. 511 (1994).

Skolnick, Jerome H., and James J. Fyfe, Above the Law: Police and the Excessive Use of Force (1993).

Swift, Katherine M., *Drawing a Line Between Terry and Miranda: The Degree and Duration of Restraint,* 73 U. Chi. L. Rev. 1075 (2006).

Thomas III, George C., and Richard A. Leo, *The Effects of Miranda v. Arizona: "Embedded" in Our National Culture?* 29 Crime & Just. 203 (2002).

White, Michael D., Justin T. Ready, Robert J. Kane, and Lisa M. Dario, *Examining the Effects of the TASER on Cognitive Functioning: Findings from a Pilot Study with Police Recruits,* 10 J. Experimental Criminology 267 (2014).

Wickersham Commission, National Commission on Law Observance and Enforcement, Pub. No. 11, *Report on Lawlessness in Law Enforcement* (1931).

Wilson, Alexander J., *Defining Interrogation under the Confrontation Clause After Crawford v. Washington,* 39 Colum. J.L. & Soc. Probs. 257 (2005).

Chapter 14. Pretrial Visual Identification Procedures

Bartol, Curt R., and Anne M. Bartol, Psychology and Law (2d ed., 1994).

Behrman, Bruce W., and Lance T. Vayder, *The Biasing Influence of a Police Showup: Does the Observation of a Single Suspect Taint Later Identification?* 79 Perceptual & Motor Skills 1239 (1994).

Brigham, John C., Adina W. Wasserman, and Christian A. Meissner, *Disputed Eyewitness Identification Evidence: Important Legal and Scientific Issues,* 36 Ct. Rev. 12 (1999).

Buckhout, Robert, *Psychology and Eyewitness Identification,* 2 L. & Psychol. Rev. 75 (1976).

Chemay, Frederick E., *Unreliable Eyewitness Evidence: The Expert Psychologist and the Defense in Criminal Cases,* 45 LA. L. REV. 721 (1985).

Clifford, B. R., *Eyewitness Testimony: The Bridging of a Credibility Gap,* in PSYCHOLOGY, LAW AND LEGAL PROCESSES (David P. Farrington, Keith Hawkins, & Sally M. Lloyd-Bostock, eds., 1979).

Cohen, Peter J., *How Shall They Be Known? Daubert v. Merrell Dow Pharmaceuticals and Eyewitness Identification,* 16 PACE L. REV. 237 (1996).

Collins, Winn S., *Safeguards for Eyewitness Identification,* 77-Mar. WIS. LAW. 8 (2004).

Cowan, Nelson, *The Magical Number 4 in Short-Term Memory: A Reconsideration of Mental Storage Capacity,* 24 BEHAV. & BRAIN SCIENCES 87 (2000).

Deffenbacher, Kenneth A., Brian H. Bornstein, Steven D. Penrod, and E. Kiernan McGorty, *A Meta-Analytic Review of the Effects of High Stress on Eyewitness Memory,* 28 L. & HUM. BEHAV. 687 (2004).

Doyle, James M., *Discounting the Error Costs: Cross-Racial False Alarms in the Culture of Contemporary Criminal Justice,* 7 PSYCHOL., PUB. POL'Y & L. 253 (2001).

Ehlers, Scott, *Eyewitness Identification: State Law Reform,* 29 Apr. CHAMPION 34 (2005).

Farmer, Jr., John J., New Jersey Attorney General, *Letter to County Prosecutors* et al. 1-2 (Apr. 18, 2001) www.state.nj.us/lps/dcj/agguide/photoid.pdf.

Fitzgerald, Ryan J., Heather L. Price, Chris Oriet, and Steve D. Charman, *The Effect of Suspect-Filler Similarity on Eyewitness Identification Decisions: A Meta-Analysis,* 19(2) PSYCHOL., PUB. POL'Y & L. 151 (2013).

Flowe, Heather D., Amrita Mehta, and Ebbe B. Ebbesen, *The Role of Eyewitness Identification Evidence in Felony Case Dispositions,* 17 PSYCHOL., PUB. POL'Y & L. 140 (2011).

Forgas, Joseph P., Simon M. Laham, and Patrick T. Vargas, *Mood Effects on Eyewitness Memory: Affective Influences on Susceptibility to Misinformation,* 41 J. EXPERIMENTAL SOCIAL PSYCHOL. 574 (2005).

Friedland, Steven I., *On Common Sense and the Evaluation of Witness Credibility,* 40 CASE W. RES. L. REV. 165, 181 (1990).

Geiselman, R. Edward, David Haghighi, and Ronna Stown, *Unconscious Transference and Characteristics of Accurate and Inaccurate Eyewitnesses,* 2 PSYCHOL., CRIME & L. 197 (1996).

Giuliana, A. L., L. Mazzoni, Manila Vannucci, and Elizabeth F. Loftus, *Misremembering Story Material,* 4 LEGAL & CRIMINOLOGICAL PSYCHOL. 93 (1999).

Golby, Alexandra J., John D. E. Gabrieli, Joan Y. Chiao, and Jennifer L. Eberhardt, *Differential Responses in the Fusiform Region to Same-Race and Other-Race Faces,* 4 NATURE-NEUROSCIENCE 845 (2001).

Gross, Samuel R., Kristen Jacoby, Daniel J. Matheson, Nicholas Montgomery, and Sujata Patil, *Exonerations in the United States 1989 through 2003,* 95 J. CRIM. L. & CRIMINOLOGY 523 (2004).

Gross, William David, *The Unfortunate Faith: A Solution to the Unwarranted Reliance Upon Eyewitness Testimony,* 5 TEX. WESLEYAN L. REV. 307, 313 (1999).

Haber, Ralph N., and Lyn Haber, *Experiencing, Remembering and Reporting Events: The Cognitive Psychology of Eyewitness Testimony,* 6 PSYCHOL., PUB. POL'Y & L. 1057 (2000).

Herrmann, Douglas J., Mary Crawford, and Michelle Holdsworth, *Gender-Linked Differences in Everyday Memory Performance,* 83 BRITISH J. PSYCHOL. 221 (1992).

Hoffman, Jascha, *Suspect Memories,* LEGAL AFFAIRS (Feb. 2005), at 42.

HUFF, C. RONALD, ARYE RATTNER, AND EDWARD SAGARIN, CONVICTED BUT INNOCENT: WRONGFUL CONVICTION AND PUBLIC POLICY (2003).

Judges, Donald P., *Two Cheers for the Department of Justice's Eyewitness Evidence: A Guide for Law Enforcement,* 53 ARK. L. REV. 231 (2000).

Kleider, Heather M., and Stephen D. Goldinger, *Stereotyping Ricochet: Complex Effects of Racial Distinctiveness on Identification Accuracy,* 25 L. & HUM. BEHAV. 605 (2001).

Klobuchar, Amy, Nancy K. Mehrkens Steblay, and Hilary Lindell Caligiuri, *Improving Eyewitness Identifications: Hennepin County's Blind Sequential Lineup Pilot Project,* 4 CARDOZO PUB. L. POL'Y & ETHICS J. 381 (2006).

Leippe, Michael R., Gary L. Wells, and Thomas M. Ostrom, *Crime Seriousness as a Determinant of Accuracy in Eyewitness Identification,* 63 J. APPLIED PSYCHOL. 345 (1978).

Levi, Avaraham M., *Are Defendants Guilty If They Were Chosen in a Lineup?* 22 L. & HUM. BEHAV. 389 (1998).

Levi, Avraham M., and C. L. Lindsay, *Lineup and Photo Spread Procedures: Issues Concerning Policy Recommendations,* 7 PSYCH. PUB. POL., & L. 776 (2001).

Lindholm, Torun, and Sven Ake Christianson, *Gender Effects in Eyewitness Accounts of a Violent Crime,* 4 PSYCHOL., CRIME & L. 323 (1998).

Loftus, Elizabeth F., *Ten Years in the Life of an Expert Witness,* 10 L. & HUM. BEHAV. 241 (1986).

Loftus, Elizabeth F., Mahzarin R. Banaji, Jonathan W. Schooler, and Rachael A. Foster, *Who Remembers What? Gender Differences in Memory,* 26 MICH. QTRLY. REV. 64 (1987).

MacLin, Otto H., M. Kimberly MacLin, and Roy S. Malpass, *Race, Arousal, Attention, Exposure and Delay: An Examination of Factors Moderating Face Recognition,* 7 PSYCHOL., PUB. POL'Y & L. 134 (2001).

Mecklenburg, S., *Addendum to the Report to the Legislature of the State of Illinois: The Illinois Pilot Program on Sequential Double-Blind Identification Procedures* (2006) www.chicagopolice.org/Addendum%20to%20IP-Report.pdf.

Medwed, Daniel S., *Anatomy of a Wrongful Conviction: Theoretical Implications and Practical Solutions,* 51 VILL. L. REV. 337 (2006).

Memon, Amina, and Fiona Gabbert, *Improving the Identification Accuracy of Senior Witnesses: Do Prelineup Questions and Sequential Testing Help?* 88 J. APPLIED PSYCHOL. 341 (2003).

Memon, Amina, Lorraine Hope, and Ray Bull, *Exposure Duration: Effects on Eyewitness Accuracy and Confidence*, 94 British J. Psychol. 339 (2003).

Molinaro, Peter F., Andrea Arndorfer, and Steve D. Charman, *Appearance-Change Instruction Effects on Eyewitness Lineup Identification Accuracy Are Not Moderated by Amount of Appearance Change*, 37(6) L. & Hum. Behav. 432 (2013).

Morgan, Charles A., et al., *Accuracy of Eyewitness Memory for Persons Encountered During Exposure to Highly Intense Stress*, 27 Int'l J. Psychiatry & L. 265 (2004).

National District Attorneys Association, *Task Force Recommendations on Eyewitness Identification*, 39 Apr. Prosecutor 16 (2005).

O'Toole, Timothy P., and Giovanna Shay, *Manson v. Brathwaite Revisited: Towards a New Rule of Decision for Due Process Challenges to Eyewitness Identification Procedures*, 41 Val. U. L. Rev. 109 (2006).

Patterson, Helen M., and Richard I. Kemp, *Co-witnesses Talk: A Survey of Eyewitness Discussion*, 12 Psychol., Crime & L. 181 (2006).

Penrod, Steven D., and Brian L. Cutler, *Witness Confidence and Witness Accuracy: Assessing Their Forensic Relation*, 1 Psychol. Pub. Pol'y & L. 817 (1995).

Perfect, Timothy J., and Lucy J. Harris, *Adult Age Differences in Unconscious Transference: Source Confusion or Identity Blending?* 31 Memory & Cognition 570 (2003).

Pickel, Kerri L., *The Influence of Context on the "Weapon Focus" Effect*, 23 L. & Hum. Behav. 299 (1999).

Plato, Portrait of Socrates, Being the Apology, Crito, and Phaedo of Plato (R. W. Livingstone, ed., 1938).

Pozzulo, Joanna D., and R. C. L. Lindsay, *Identification Accuracy of Children Versus Adults: A Meta-Analysis*, 22 L. & Hum. Behav. 549 (1998).

Rattner, Arye, *Convicted but Innocent: Wrongful Conviction and the Criminal Justice System*, 12 L. & Hum. Behav. 283, 287–91 (1988).

Ringel, William E., Searches and Seizures, Arrests and Confessions § 18:4 (2007).

Risinger, D. Michael, Michael J. Saks, William C. Thompson, and Robert Rosenthal, *The Daubert/Kumho Implications of Observer Effects in Forensic Science: Hidden Problems of Expectation and Suggestion*, 90 Calif. L. Rev. 1, 7 (2002).

Roberts, Andrew, *The Problem of Mistaken Identification: Some Observations on Process*, 8 Int'l J. Evid. & Proof 100 (2004).

Rosenberg, Benjamin E., *Rethinking the Right to Due Process in Connection with Pretrial Identification Procedures: An Analysis and a Proposal*, 79 Ky. L.J. 259 (1991).

Sarno, Julie A., and Thomas R. Alley, *Attractiveness and the Memorability of Faces: Only a Matter of Distinctiveness?* 110 Am. J. Psychol. 81 (1997).

Scheck, Barry, Peter Neufeld, and Jim Dwyer, Actual Innocence: Five Days to Execution, and Other Dispatches from the Wrongly Convicted (2000).

Sikstrom, Sverker, *Forgetting Curves: Implications for Connectionist Models*, 45 Cognitive Psychol. 95 (2002).

Smith, Steven M., R. C. L. Lindsay, and Sean Pryke, *Postdictors of Eyewitness Errors: Can False Identifications Be Diagnosed?* 85 J. Applied Psychol. 542 (2000).

Sporer, Siegfried L., et al., Psychological Issues in Eyewitness Identification (1966).

Sporer, Siegfried Ludwig, *Recognizing Faces of Other Ethnic Groups: An Integration of Theories*, 7 Psychol., Pub. Pol'y & L. 36 (2001).

Steblay, Nancy Mehrkens, *A Meta-Analytic Review of the Weapon Focus Effect*, 16 L. & Hum. Behav. 413 (1992).

Steblay, Nancy Mehrkens, *Social Influence in Eyewitness Recall: A Meta-Analytic Review of Lineup Instruction Effects*, 21 L. & Hum. Behav. 283 (1997).

U.S. Department of Justice, *Eyewitness Evidence: A Guide for Law Enforcement* (Oct. 1999) www.ncjrs.gov/pdffiles1/nij/178240.pdf.

Vrij, Aldert, *Psychological Factors in Eyewitness Testimony*, in Psychology and Law: Truthfulness, Accuracy, and Credibility (Amina Memon, Aldert Vrij, and Ray Bull, eds., 1998).

Weber, Nathan, and Neil Brewer, *Positive Versus Negative Face Recognition Decisions: Confidence, Accuracy, and Response Latency*, 20 Applied Cognitive Psychol. 17 (2006).

Wells, Gary L., and Eric P. Seelau, *Eyewitness Identification: Psychological Research and Legal Policy on Lineups*, 1 Psychol., Pub. Pol'y & L. 765, 779 (1995).

Wells, Gary L., Mark Small, Steven D. Penrod, Roy S. Malpass, Solomon M. Fulero, and C. A. E. Brimacombe, *Eyewitness Identification Procedures: Recommendations for Lineups and Photospreads*, 22 L. & Hum. Behav. 603, 633 (1998).

Wise, Richard A., Martin A. Safer, and Christina M. Maro, *What U.S. Law Enforcement Officers Know and Believe About Eyewitness Factors, Eyewitness Interviews and Identification Procedures*, 25(3) Applied Cognitive Psychol. 488 (2011).

Yarmey, A. Daniel, *The Elderly Witness*, in Psychological Issues in Eyewitness Identification (Siegfried Ludwig Sporer, Roy S. Malpass, & Guenter Koehnken, eds., 1996).

Yarmey, A. Daniel, *Person Identification in Showups and Lineups*, in Eyewitness Memory: Theoretical and Applied Perspectives (Charles P. Thompson and Douglas J. Herrmann eds., 1998).

Chapter 15. Criminal Trials, Appeals, and Postconviction Remedies

Adler, Stephen J., The Jury: Trial and Error in the American Courtroom (1994).

Allen, Francis A., The Decline of the Rehabilitative Ideal (1981).

Barber, Jeremy W., *The Jury Is Still Out: The Role of Jury Science in the Modern American Courtroom*, 31 Am. Crim. L. Rev. 1225 (1994).

Campbell, Curtis, Candace McCoy, and Chimezie Osigweh, *The Influence of Probation Recommendations on Sentencing Decisions and Their Predictive Accuracy,* 54 FED. PROBATION 13 (1990).

CLEAR, TODD R., HARM IN AMERICAN PENOLOGY: OFFENDERS, VICTIMS, AND THEIR COMMUNITIES (1994).

DeCicco, Fred Anthony, *Waiver of Jury Trials in Federal Criminal Cases: A Reassessment of The "Prosecutorial Veto,"* 51 FORDHAM L. REV. 1091 (1983).

Fischman, Joshua B., and Max M. Schanzenbach, *Racial Disparities, Judicial Discretion, and the United States Sentencing Guidelines,* 9(4) J. EMPIRICAL LEGAL STUD. 729 (2012).

FISHER, JIM, FORENSICS UNDER FIRE: ARE BAD SCIENCE AND DUELING EXPERTS CORRUPTING CRIMINAL JUSTICE? (2008).

Fuchs, Andrew J., *The Effect of* Apprendi v. New Jersey *on the Federal Sentencing Guidelines: Blurring the Distinction Between Sentencing Factors and Elements of a Crime,* 69 FORDHAM L. REV. 1399, 1413 (2001).

Gabel, Jessica D., and Margaret D. Wilkinson, *"Good" Science Gone Bad: How the Criminal Justice System Can Redress the Impact of Flawed Forensics,* 59 HASTINGS LAW J. 1001 (2008).

Garrett, Brandon L., *Judging Innocence,* 108 COLUMBIA L. REV. 55 (2008).

Innocence Project, *Understand the Causes: Unreliable or Improper Forensic Science* (2014) http://www.innocenceproject.org/understand/Unreliable-Limited-Science.php.

Johnstone, A. C., *Peremptory Pragmatism: Religion and the Administration of the* Batson *Rule,* 1998 U. CHI. LEGAL F. 441 (1998).

Jordan, Sandra D., *Have We Come Full Circle? Judicial Sentencing Discretion Revived in* Booker *and* Fanfan, 33 PEPP. L. REV. 615 (2006).

Keenan, Dylan O. (2012). Bullcoming *and Cold Cases: Reconciling the Confrontation Clause with DNA Evidence,* 30 YALE L. & POL'Y REV. *Inter Alia,* 13 (2012).

Lieberman, Joel D., Terance D. Miethe, Courtney A. Carrell, and Daniel A. Krauss, *"Gold Versus Platinum: Do Jurors Recognize the Superiority and Limitations of DNA Evidence Compared to Other Types of Forensic Evidence?* 14 PSYCHOL., PUB. POL'Y & L. 27 (2008).

Mustard, David B., *Racial, Ethnic, and Gender Disparities in Sentencing: Evidence from the U.S. Federal Courts,* 44 J. LAW & ECON. 285 (2001).

National Academies of Sciences, *Strengthening Forensic Science in the United States: A Path Forward* (2009).

Neufeld, Peter J., *The (Near) Irrelevance of* Daubert *to Criminal Justice and Some Suggestions for Reform,* 95 AM. J. OF PUBLIC HEALTH (2005).

Olivares, Kathleen M., Velmer S. Burton, Jr., and Francis T. Cullen, *The Collateral Consequences of a Felony Conviction: A National Study of Legal Codes 10 Years Later,* 60 FED. PROBATION 10 (Sept. 1996).

REIMAN, JEFFREY, THE RICH GET RICHER AND THE POOR GET PRISON: IDEOLOGY, CLASS, AND JUSTICE (1995).

Rush, Christina, and Jeremy Robertson, *Presentence Reports: The Utility of Information to the Sentencing Decision,* 11 L. & HUM. BEHAV. 147–155 (1987).

Saunders, Kurt M., *Race and Representation in Jury Service Selection,* 36 DUQ. L. REV. 49 (1997).

Schanzenbach, Max, *Racial and Sex Disparities in Prison Sentences: The Effect of District-Level Judicial Demographics,* 24 J. LEGAL STUD. 57 (2005).

Ulmer, Jeffery T., Michael T. Light, and John H. Kramer, *Racial Disparity in the Wake of the* Booker/Fanfan *Decision: An Alternative Analysis to the USSC's 2010 Report,* 10(4) CRIMINOLOGY & PUBLIC POL'Y 1077 (2011).

U.S. Sentencing Commission, *Demographic Differences in Federal Sentencing Practices: An Update of the Booker Report's Multivariate Regression Analysis* (2010).